# Contributors

Peter Achinstein
*Johns Hopkins University*

Felicia Ackerman
*Brown University*

Laird Addis
*University of Iowa*

Linda Alcoff
*Syracuse University*

J. V. Allen
*University of Pittsburgh*

Robert F. Almeder
*Georgia State University*

William P. Alston
*Syracuse University*

C. Anthony Anderson
*University of Minnesota*

Robert Audi
*University of Nebraska–Lincoln*

Michael Ayers
*Wadham College, Oxford*

David Bakhurst
*Queen's University at Kingston, Canada*

Thomas Baldwin
*Clare College, Cambridge*

David Bell
*University of Sheffield*

Akeel Bilgrami
*Columbia University*

Graham Bird
*University of Manchester*

David Bloor
*University of Edinburgh*

David Blumenfeld
*Georgia State University*

Laurence BonJour
*University of Washington*

Clive Borst
*Keele University*

L. S. Carrier
*University of Miami*

Albert Casullo
*University of Nebraska–Lincoln*

R. M. Chisholm
*Brown University*

Lorraine Code
*York University, Ontario*

L. Jonathan Cohen
*The Queen's College, Oxford*

Stewart Cohen
*Arizona State University*

John J. Compton
*Vanderbilt University*

Earl Conee
*University of Rochester*

John Cottingham
*University of Reading*

Robert Cummins
*University of Arizona*

Edwin Curley
*University of Illinois at Chicago*

Fred D'Agostino
*University of New England, Australia*

Vrinda Dalmiya
*Montana State University*

Jonathan Dancy
*Keele University*

Fred Dretske
*Stanford University*

Catherine Z. Elgin
*Lexington, Massachusetts*

Edward Erwin
*University of Miami*

Richard Feldman
*University of Rochester*

Richard Foley
*Rutgers University*

Dagfinn Føllesdal
*University of Oslo and Stanford University*

Graeme Forbes
*Tulane University*

Richard Fumerton
*University of Iowa*

Don Garrett
*University of Utah*

Margaret Gilbert
*University of Connecticut*

Carl Ginet
*Cornell University*

Hans-Johann Glock
*University of Reading*

Alan H. Goldman
*University of Miami*

Alvin I. Goldman
*University of Arizona*

Jorge J. E. Gracia
*State University of New York at Buffalo*

Richard E. Grandy
*Rice University*

A. C. Grayling
*St. Anne's College, Oxford*

John Greco
*Fordham University*

Patrick Grim
*State University of New York at Stony Brook*

Charles Guignon
*University of Vermont*

Susan Haack
*University of Miami*

# A Companion to
# Epistemology

*Blackwell*
*Companions to*
*Philosophy*

# A Companion to
# Epistemology

*Edited by*

## JONATHAN DANCY

*and*

## ERNEST SOSA

BLACKWELL
*Reference*

Copyright © Basil Blackwell Ltd 1992, 1993
Editorial organization © Jonathan Dancy and Ernest Sosa 1992, 1993

First published 1992
First published in paperback 1993

Blackwell Publishers
108 Cowley Road, Oxford OX4 1JF, UK

238 Main Street
Cambridge, Massachusetts 02142, USA

*British Library Cataloguing in Publication Data*

A CIP catalogue record for this book is available from the British Library.

*Library of Congress Cataloging-in-Publication Data*

A Companion to epistemology / edited by Jonathan Dancy and Ernest Sosa.
    p.    cm.   — (Blackwell companions to philosophy)
Includes bibliographical references and index.
ISBN 0-631-17204-1
ISBN 0-631-19258-1 (Pbk)
1.  Knowledge, Theory of.   I. Dancy, Jonathan.
II. Sosa, Ernest.   III. Series.
BD161.C637   1992                                                      92-32205
121—dc20                                                                  CIP

Typeset in 9½ on 11pt Photina by Alden Multimedia
Printed in Great Britain by T. J. Press Ltd, Padstow, Cornwall.

This book is printed on acid-free paper

# Contents

P. M. S. Hacker
*St John's College, Oxford*

Andy Hamilton
*Keele University*

Peter H. Hare
*State University of New York at Buffalo*

Gilbert Harman
*Princeton University*

Adrian Heathcote
*Australian National University*

John Heil
*Davidson College, North Carolina*

Risto Hilpinen
*University of Miami*

Jaakko Hintikka
*Florida State University*

Christopher Hookway
*University of Birmingham*

Jim Hopkins
*King's College London*

Paul Horwich
*Massachusetts Institute of Technology*

Bruce Hunter
*University of Alberta*

Terence Irwin
*Cornell University*

Frank Jackson
*Australian National University*

Jerrold J. Katz
*City University of New York*

Jaegwon Kim
*Brown University*

Richard F. Kitchener
*Colorado State University*

Peter D. Klein
*Rutgers University*

Hilary Kornblith
*University of Vermont*

John Lachs
*Vanderbilt University*

Keith Lehrer
*University of Arizona*

Noah M. Lemos
*DePauw University*

Ernest LePore
*Rutgers University*

J. H. Lesher
*University of Maryland*

Paisley Livingston
*McGill University*

Steven Luper-Foy
*Trinity University, Texas*

Marilyn McCord Adams
*University of California, Los Angeles*

Gregory McCulloch
*University of Nottingham*

Scott MacDonald
*University of Iowa*

David McNaughton
*Keele University*

David B. Martens
*Mount Royal College, Calgary*

Jack Meiland
*University of Michigan*

Phillip Mitsis
*Cornell University*

J. N. Mohanty
*Temple University, Philadelphia*

Jame Montmarquet
*Tennessee State University*

Paul K. Moser
*Loyola University at Chicago*

Alexander Nehamas
*Princeton University*

Anthony O'Hear
*University of Bradford*

M. Okrent
*Bates College, Lewiston, Maine*

George Pappas
*Ohio State University*

Christopher Peacocke
*Magdalen College, Oxford*

David Pears
*Christ Church, Oxford*

Michael Pendlebury
*University of the Witwatersrand*

Philip Pettit
*Australian National University*

Alvin Plantinga
*University of Notre Dame*

Leon Pompa
*University of Birmingham*

Richard Popkin
*Washington University, St Louis, Missouri*

John F. Post
*Vanderbilt University*

Nicholas Rescher
*University of Pittsburgh*

G. A. J. Rogers
*Keele University*

Jay Rosenberg
*University of North Carolina*

R. M. Sainsbury
*King's College London*

Wesley C. Salmon
*University of Pittsburgh*

Donald W. Sherburne
*Vanderbilt University*

Sydney Shoemaker
*Cornell Universty*

Robert K. Shope
*University of Massachusetts at Boston*

Harvey Siegel
*University of Miami*

John Skorupski
*University of St Andrews*

Brian Skyrms
*University of California at Irvine*

R. C. Sleigh
*University of Massachusetts at Amherst*

Steve Smith
*Wolfson College, Oxford*

P. F. Snowdon
*Exeter College, Oxford*

Elliott Sober
*University of Wisconsin, Madison*

Tom Sorell
*University of Essex*

Roy A. Sorensen
*New York University*

Ernest Sosa
*Brown University*

Edward Stein
*New York University*

Mark Steiner
*Hebrew University, Jerusalem*

Matthias Steup
*St Cloud State University*

Charlotte Stough
*University of California at Santa Barbara*

Steven K. Strange
*Emory University*

Barry Stroud
*University of California, Berkeley*

Robert S. Tragesser
*Columbia University*

John Troyer
*University of Connecticut*

Thomas Tymoczko
*Smith College, Northampton, Massachusetts*

James Van Cleve
*Brown University*

Jonathan Vogel
*Amherst College, Massachusetts*

Douglas N. Walton
*University of Winnipeg*

Kenneth R. Westphal
*University of New Hampshire*

Samuel C. Wheeler III
*University of Connecticut*

Nicholas P. White
*University of Michigan, Ann Arbor*

Michael Williams
*Northwestern University*

R. S. Woolhouse
*University of York*

# Introduction

JONATHAN DANCY

The present Companion, like the majority of the other volumes in the Blackwell Companions to Philosophy series, is organized as a standard reference book, with alphabetically arranged articles of varying length (anything from 250 to 3500 words) on leading theories, thinkers, ideas, distinctions and concepts in epistemology. It aims for a broad readership, while recognizing that the nature of contemporary epistemology inevitably imposes restrictions on this. In some other areas of philosophy it remains feasible to design a book which is largely accessible to the general reader; in epistemology, however, the main readership is likely to be students from undergraduate level upwards, as well as professional philosophers, and it is to them that the Companion is primarily addressed. A minority of topics resist treatment other than at an advanced level: they have not for that reason been excluded, lest coverage of the area become incomplete. But the vast majority are accessible to all levels of the intended readership.

Not all entries will be comprehensible on their own: at least, not to the inexperienced reader. This is where the cross-referencing system comes in. I have used two interrelated methods of guiding readers from one entry to another. Within the text itself terms or names occur in small capitals; this will often occur where reference is made to DESCARTES, or to REALISM, for example. This means that there is an entry on this person or topic, and that it would be worthwhile having a look at it for present purposes. The mere fact that there is an entry on this person or topic, however, is not sufficient for me to flag it. Not all references to Descartes or to realism are significant. What is more, a person or topic may not be flagged in this way on its first occurrence in an entry; I may wait for the best moment, as it were. And sometimes one and the same person or topic is flagged more than once in the same entry, where there has been a long gap or I think it particularly appropriate for some other reason.

Most of the flagging that is done within the body of the text is of this form; a word or phrase is highlighted in the sentence, as I highlighted DESCARTES above. In doing this, I have not insisted slavishly that the word highlighted be *exactly* the same one as the headword that the reader is effectively being referred to. For instance, I may direct the reader to an entry on realism by flagging the remark that Santayana was a REALIST. Sometimes, however, I was unable to work the cross-reference into the text in this way. On these occasions it is inserted at the end of the relevant sentence or paragraph.

There are also cross-references to be found at the end of most entries. These fulfil two functions. First, they enable me to point out areas to which the present entry is related, but which have not occurred significantly in the text. Second, they enable me to insist a bit that you should consider again looking at an entry that has already been flagged in the text. So if you see a person or topic flagged both within and at the end of an entry, you can take it that I think you really should have a look at it.

The Blackwell series of Companions is conceived as related primarily to Anglo-American philosophy. The topics the editors chose to cover were selected with this in mind. But this does not mean that other traditions are completely ignored. There is an entry on Indian epistemology and, as well as a general entry on continental epistemology, there are many entries on individual thinkers in that tradition. We do not pretend, however, to give that tradition as detailed coverage as we give to the one which is our main focus.

It might be thought that the jacket illustration is symptomatic of our general approach. Here we have the solitary thinker working in private. Isn't he a wonderful example of the CARTESIAN approach to epistemology which is so characteristic of the Anglo-American analytic tradition, and which is so vehemently rejected on the Continent? There is some truth in this, which we will come to in a moment. There are two points to be made against it. First, the attempt to escape from the clutches of the Cartesian paradigm is as common within the analytic tradition as it is outside. Second, our solitary thinker is not as solitary as all that. He is reading a book, which could be taken to show that he is not relying entirely on his own resources, as the Cartesian mind is supposed to do (*see* REID, TESTIMONY). Against this, one could point out that the picture exemplifies a conception of knowledge as something to be gained by rational enquiry and perception rather than in practical life and action. This 'logocentrism' may be a more insidious feature of the Cartesian approach, and certainly the emphasis on practice and action is distinctive of Continental epistemology (*see* for example HEIDEGGER), as is an emphasis on social considerations.

One difficulty the editors faced in deciding which topics to cover derived from the interconnectedness of philosophical areas. Epistemology can be to some extent separated from adjacent areas, but only with a justified sense of artificiality. The nearest areas are metaphysics, philosophy of mind and philosophy of science. These gave us two problems, one theoretical and one practical. The practical one was that in considering whether to include an entry on a topic, we had to ask ourselves whether there would be an entry on it in one of the other Companions, and if so how our entry should be related to that one. At the limit, we have an entry on natural science, an area which will on its own occupy a large part of one Companion. But there are many other occasions where the shortness of our coverage here is caused by our sense that the major entry on this topic should not appear in a *Companion to Epistemology*. The theoretical one was that there are many occasions where views in epistemology are dependent on views in metaphysics or in the philosophy of mind, and we could not hope to cover everything equally well. Contributors were asked to concentrate on epistemology, and the entries have been written accordingly. When reading entries on individual thinkers, therefore, you should bear in mind that these entries do not pretend to be complete accounts of their subject's work in philosophy; they are concentrating on the epistemology as far as that is possible. The same applies to topics. The entry on natural science is concerned only with the epistemology of science, the entry on religious belief limits itself to epistemological considerations, and so on. The limitation to epistemology is normally implicit rather than explicit; otherwise every entry would have to be headed 'X's epistemology' or 'the epistemology of Y'.

This Companion has two editors, divided by the Atlantic (and rejoined by electronic mail). Its general shape was conceived during a very pleasant weekend which I spent in Providence, RI, in Spring 1989. Thereafter, I relied on Ernest Sosa for a constant stream of suggestions about who in the US we might approach as potential contributors – a stream that was evidence of his enviable knowledge of the profession. UK contributors were my responsibility. Beyond that, the detailed editing of contributions has been my province, though I am very grateful to my co-editor for help and advice on the occasional knotty points that arose. I am, of course, equally grateful to our contributors for being willing to undertake what in many cases was a fairly thankless and far from easy task – and for the openness with which so many of them received my suggestions for changes to suit my own idea of how things should be. I have had many occasions to express my appreciation of the professionalism of the profession.

Finally, I want to thank my wife Sarah, who helped me with various aspects of the editing process, and my son Hugh, who spent two weeks last autumn turning entries into computer-readable form. For a while this Companion was a family affair.

*Keele, February 1992*

# A

**a priori/a posteriori** The a priori/a posteriori distinction has been applied to a wide range of objects, including concepts, propositions, truths and knowledge. Our primary concern will be with the *epistemic* distinction between a priori and a posteriori knowledge. The most common way of marking the distinction is by reference to KANT's claim that a priori knowledge is absolutely independent of all experience (*see* A PRIORI KNOWLEDGE). It is generally agreed that S's knowledge that *p* is independent of experience just in case S's belief that *p* is *justified* independently of experience. Some authors (Butchvarov, 1970; Pollock, 1974), however, find this *negative* characterization of a priori knowledge unsatisfactory and have opted for providing a *positive* characterization in terms of the type of justification on which such knowledge is dependent. Finally, others (Putnam, 1983; Chisholm, 1989) have attempted to mark the distinction by introducing concepts such as necessity and rational unrevisability rather than in terms of the type of justification relevant to a priori knowledge.

One who characterizes a priori knowledge in terms of justification which is independent of experience is faced with the task of articulating the relevant sense of experience. Proponents of the a priori often cite 'intuition' or 'intuitive apprehension' as the source of a priori justification. Furthermore, they maintain that these terms refer to a distinctive type of experience that is both common and familiar to most individuals. Hence, there is a broad sense of experience in which a priori justification is *not* independent of experience. An initially attractive strategy is to suggest that a priori justification must be independent of *sense* experience. But this account is too narrow since memory, for example, is not a form of sense experience but justification based on memory is presumably not a priori. There appear to remain only two options: provide a general characterization of the relevant sense of experience or enumerate those sources which are experiential. General characterizations of experience often maintain that experience provides information specific to the actual world while non-experiential sources provide information about all possible worlds. This approach, however, reduces the concept of non-experiential justification to the concept of being justified in believing a necessary truth. Accounts by enumeration face two problems: (1) there is some controversy about which sources to include on the list; and (2) there is no guarantee that the list is complete. It is generally agreed that perception and memory should be included. INTROSPECTION, however, is problematic. Beliefs about one's conscious states and about the manner in which one is appeared to are plausibly regarded as experientially justified. Yet some, such as Pap (1958), maintain that experiments in imagination are the source of a priori justification. Even if this contention is rejected and a priori justification is characterized as justification independent of the evidence of perception, memory and introspection, it remains possible that there are other sources of justification. If it should be the case that clairvoyance, for example, is a source of justified beliefs, such beliefs would be justified a priori on the enumerative account.

The most common approach to offering a positive characterization of a priori justification is to maintain that in the case of basic a priori propositions, understanding the proposition is sufficient to justify one in believing that it is true. This approach faces two pressing issues. What is it to understand a proposition in the manner which suffices for justification? How does such understanding justify one in believing a proposition? Proponents of the approach typically distinguish understanding the words used to express a proposition from apprehending the proposition itself and maintain that it is the latter which is relevant to a priori justification. But this move simply shifts the problem to that of specifying what it is to apprehend a proposition. Without a solution to this problem, it is difficult, if not impossible, to evaluate the account since one cannot be sure that the requisite sense of apprehension does not justify paradigmatic a posteriori propositions as well. Even less is said about the manner in which apprehending a proposition justifies one in believing that it is true. Proponents are often content with the bald assertion that one who understands a basic a priori proposition can thereby 'see' that it is true. But what requires explanation is how understanding a proposition enables one to see that it is true.

Difficulties in characterizing a priori justification in terms either of independence from experience or of its source have led some to introduce the concept of necessity into their accounts, although this appeal takes various forms. Some have employed it as a necessary condition for a priori justification, others have employed it as a sufficient condition, while still others have employed it as both. In claiming that necessity is a criterion of the a priori, Kant held that necessity is a *sufficient* condition for a priori justification (*see* A PRIORI KNOWLEDGE). This claim, however, needs further clarification. There are three theses regarding the relationship between the a priori and the necessary which can be distinguished: (1) If $p$ is a necessary proposition and S is justified in believing that $p$ is necessary, then S's justification is a priori; (2) If $p$ is a necessary proposition and S is justified in believing that $p$ is necessarily true, then S's justification is a priori; and (3) If $p$ is a necessary proposition and S is justified in believing that $p$, then S's justification is a priori (*see* NECESSITY, MODAL KNOWLEDGE). (2) and (3) have the shortcoming of settling by stipulation the issue of whether a posteriori knowledge of necessary propositions is possible. (1) does not have this shortcoming since the recent examples offered in support of this claim by Kripke (1980) and others have been cases where it is alleged that knowledge of the *truth value* of necessary propositions is knowable a posteriori. (1) has the shortcoming, however, of either ruling out the possibility of being justified in believing that a proposition is necessary on the basis of testimony or else sanctioning such justification as a priori. (2) and (3), of course, suffer from an analogous problem. These problems are symptomatic of a general shortcoming of the approach: it attempts to provide a sufficient condition for a priori justification solely in terms of the modal status of the proposition believed without making reference to the manner in which it is justified. This shortcoming, however, can be avoided by incorporating necessity as a *necessary* but not sufficient condition for a priori justification as, for example, in Chisholm (1989). Here there are two theses which must be distinguished: (1) If S is justified a priori in believing that $p$, then $p$ is necessarily true; and (2) If S is justified a priori in believing that $p$, then $p$ is a necessary proposition. (1) has the shortcoming of precluding the possibility of being a priori justified in believing a *false* proposition. (2), however, allows this possibility. A further problem with both (1) and (2) is that it is not clear whether they permit a priori justified beliefs about the modal status of a proposition. For they require that in order for S to be justified a priori in believing that $p$ is a necessary proposition it must be necessary that $p$ is a necessary proposition. But the status of iterated modal propositions is controversial. Finally, (1) and (2) both preclude by stipulation the position advanced by Kripke (1980) and Kitcher (1980) that there is a priori knowledge of contingent propositions.

The concept of rational unrevisability has also been invoked to characterize a priori justification. The precise sense of rational unrevisability as well as its relationship to a priori justification have been presented in different ways. Putnam (1983) takes rational unrevisability to be both a necessary and sufficient condition for a priori justification while Kitcher (1980) takes it to be only a necessary condition. There are also two different senses of rational unrevisability that have been associated with the a priori: (1) a proposition is *weakly* unrevisable just in case it is rationally unrevisable in light of any future *experiential* evidence; and (2) a proposition is *strongly* unrevisable just in case it is rationally unrevisable in light of *any* future evidence. Let us consider the plausibility of requiring either form of rational unrevisability as a *necessary* condition for a priori justification. The view that a proposition is justified a priori only if it is *strongly* unrevisable entails that if a non-experiential source of justified beliefs is fallible but self-correcting, it is not an a priori source of justification. Casullo (1988) has argued that it is implausible to maintain that a proposition which is justified non-experientially is *not* justified a priori merely because it is revisable in light of further *non-experiential* evidence. The view that a proposition is justified a priori only if it is weakly unrevisable is not open to this objection since it excludes only revision in light of *experiential* evidence. It does, however, face a different problem. To maintain that S's justified belief that *p* is justified a priori is to make a claim about the type of evidence that *justifies* S in believing that *p*. On the other hand, to maintain that S's justified belief that *p* is rationally revisable in light of experiential evidence is to make a claim about the type of evidence that can *defeat* S's justification for believing that *p* rather than a claim about the type of evidence that *justifies* S in believing that *p*. Hence, it has been argued by Edidin (1984) and Casullo (1988) that to hold that a belief is justified a priori only if it is weakly unrevisable is either to confuse *supporting* evidence with *defeating* evidence or to endorse some implausible thesis about the relationship between the two such as that if evidence of kind A can defeat the justification conferred on S's belief that *p* by evidence of kind B then S's justification for believing that *p* is based on evidence of kind A.

See also A PRIORI KNOWLEDGE; ANALYTICITY; INTUITION AND DEDUCTION; KANT.

BIBLIOGRAPHY

BonJour, L.: *The Structure of Empirical Knowledge* (Cambridge, MA: Harvard University Press, 1985).
Butchvarov, P.: *The Concept of Knowledge* (Evanston: Northwestern University Press, 1970).
Casullo, A.: 'Revisability, reliabilism, and a priori knowledge', *Philosophy and Phenomenological Research* 49 (1988), 187–213.
Chisholm, R. M.: *Theory of Knowledge* 3rd edn (Englewood Cliffs: Prentice-Hall, 1989).
Edidin, A.: 'A priori knowledge for fallibilists', *Philosophical Studies* 46 (1984), 189–97.
Kitcher, P.: 'A priori knowledge', *Philosophical Review* 89 (1980), 3–23.
Kripke, S.: *Naming and Necessity* (Cambridge, MA: Harvard University Press, 1980).
Pap, A.: *Semantics and Necessary Truth* (New Haven: Yale University Press, 1958).
Pollock, J.: *Knowledge and Justification* (Princeton: Princeton University Press, 1974).
Putnam, H.: '"Two dogmas" revisited', in his *Philosophical Papers* 3 vols. Vol. 3, *Realism and Reason* (Cambridge: Cambridge University Press, 1983), 87–97.

ALBERT CASULLO

**a priori knowledge** The contemporary discussion of a priori knowledge has been largely shaped by KANT (1781). Central to his discussion are three distinctions. The first is an *epistemic* distinction, which divides knowledge into two broad categories: a priori and a posteriori. Kant's characterization of a priori knowledge as knowledge absolutely independent of all experience requires some clarification. For he allowed that a proposition known a priori could depend on experience in at least two ways: (1) experience is necessary to acquire the concepts involved in the proposition; and (2) experience is necessary to entertain the proposition. It is generally accepted, although Kant is not explicit on this point, that a proposition is known a priori only if it is justified independently of experiential evidence (see A PRIORI/A POSTERIORI). The second distinction is the *metaphysical* distinction between necessary and contingent propositions. A necessarily true (false) proposition is one which is true (false) and could not have been false (true). A contingently true (false) proposition is one which is true (false) but could have been false (true). An alternative way of marking the distinction characterizes a necessarily true (false) proposition as one which is true (false) in all possible worlds. A contingently true (false) proposition is one which is true (false) in only some possible worlds including the actual world (*see* NECESSARY/CONTINGENT). The final distinction is the *semantical* distinction between analytic and synthetic propositions. This is the most difficult to characterize since Kant offers several ostensibly different ways of marking the distinction. The most familiar states that a proposition of the form 'All A are B' is analytic just in case the predicate is contained in the subject; otherwise, it is synthetic (*see* ANALYTICITY).

Utilizing these three distinctions, Kant went on to defend three theses which are at the core of the contemporary debate: (1) the existence of a priori knowledge; (2) a close relationship between the a priori and the necessary; and (3) the existence of synthetic a priori knowledge. In defending the existence of a priori knowledge, Kant did not attempt to analyse the concept of justification which is independent of experience. Instead, he (1781, p. 42) offered a criterion for distinguishing a priori knowledge from a posteriori knowledge: 'if we have a proposition which in being thought is thought as *necessary*, it is an *a priori* judgment'. Since Kant took it to be evident that there are necessary propositions which are known, the existence of a priori knowledge is quickly established. This defence of the existence of a priori knowledge, however, is inextricably tied to his account of the relationship between the a priori and the necessary. The operative principle appears to be that all knowledge of necessary propositions is a priori. Kant (1781, p. 11) also endorses the converse of this principle: all a priori knowledge is of necessary propositions. The conjunction of these two principles, however, does not entail that the categories of the necessary and the a priori are coextensive, since it does not entail that all necessary

propositions are knowable. Kant's defence of the existence of synthetic a priori knowledge gives special prominence to mathematics. For it was the principles of arithmetic and geometry that provided his most enduring examples of necessary propositions which are arguably synthetic (*see* MATHEMATICAL KNOWLEDGE).

Much of the recent work on a priori knowledge can be seen as either disputing or defending one of these three Kantian positions. Recent attacks on the existence of a priori knowledge fall into three general camps. Some, such as Putnam (1979) and Kitcher (1983), begin by providing an analysis of the concept of a priori knowledge and then argue that alleged examples of a priori knowledge fail to satisfy the conditions specified in the analysis. Attacks in the second camp generally proceed independently of any particular analysis of the concept of a priori knowledge but focus, instead, on the alleged source of such knowledge. Benacerraf (1973), for example, argues that the faculty of intuition which is alleged by some proponents of the a priori to be the source of mathematical knowledge cannot fulfil that role. A third form of attack is to consider prominent examples of propositions alleged to be knowable only a priori and to show that they can be justified by experiential evidence. MILL's view that mathematical propositions can be inductively justified has received some support from Kitcher (1983) and Casullo (1988a). An alternative strategy is provided by QUINE (1963), who maintains that mathematical propositions can be justified only in so far as they are part of a larger theory which has a satisfactory match with experience.

Recent work in modal logic has renewed interest in the topic of necessary truth. Accompanying this renewed interest has been a re-examination of Kant's views on the relationship between the necessary and the a priori. It has become a common theme in recent work to reiterate that the a priori/a posteriori distinction is an epistemic one, while the necessary/contingent distinction is a metaphysical one. Hence, it cannot be assumed without further argument that they are coextensive. Furthermore, Saul Kripke (1980) has forcefully argued that there are necessary a posteriori propositions as well as contingent a priori propositions. Several recent analyses of a priori knowledge, such as Kitcher (1983), have the consequence that some contingent propositions are knowable a priori.

The Kantian position that has received most attention is the claim that some a priori knowledge is of synthetic propositions. Initially, there were two different reactions. Some did not dispute the general claim but were concerned exclusively with some of Kant's particular examples of alleged synthetic a priori knowledge. FREGE, for example, challenged only the claim that the truths of arithmetic are synthetic (see MATHEMATICAL KNOWLEDGE). Others, such as AYER (1946), disputed the general claim and tried to establish that all a priori knowledge is of analytic propositions. A third, more radical, reaction came from Quine (1963), who challenged the cogency of the analytic/synthetic distinction. Given the close relationship between the a priori and the analytic forged by Kant's critics, some view Quine's attack as calling into question the cogency of the a priori/a posteriori distinction as well.

The claim that there exists a priori knowledge is clearly the most fundamental of the three Kantian theses. Evaluating Kant's defence of the first thesis, however, requires addressing the second thesis regarding the relationship between the necessary and the a priori. The third thesis, although important, is less fundamental. For, on the one hand, if there is no a priori knowledge, the question of whether there is synthetic a priori knowledge does not arise. On the other hand, if the analytic/synthetic distinction is not a cogent one, the issue of the synthetic a priori again does not arise. It might be thought that the demise of the analytic/synthetic distinction calls into question the cogency of the a priori/ a posteriori distinction as well. But it is difficult to see how this could be defended short of identifying the a priori with the analytic or uncritically assuming some necessary connection between the two concepts. Hence,

our primary concern will be to review briefly the case for and against a priori knowledge.

Kant's defence of the claim that mathematical propositions are knowable only a priori exemplifies a general pattern frequently utilized by proponents of the a priori. They begin by maintaining that there is a class of propositions whose members all have a particular feature. They then go on to argue that no proposition having this feature can be known on the basis of experience. Hence, if there is knowledge of the propositions in question, such knowledge must be a priori. In Kant's case, the class consists of mathematical propositions and the feature is necessity. Let us grant the claim that mathematical propositions are necessary and consider the key claim that experience cannot provide knowledge of necessary propositions. The phrase 'knowledge of necessary propositions' masks a crucial distinction between knowledge of the *general modal status* of a proposition as opposed to knowledge of its *truth value* (see NECESSITY, MODAL KNOWLEDGE). The basis of Kant's (1781, p. 43) contention that knowledge of necessity is a priori is the observation that 'Experience teaches us that a thing is so and so but not that it cannot be otherwise.' This observation, however, establishes at most that *the general modal status* of necessary propositions cannot be known on the basis of experience. It does not support the conclusion that the *truth value* of a necessary proposition cannot be known on the basis of experience. For it allows that experience can provide knowledge that a thing *is* so and so. Hence, Kant's observation fails to support his key claim that knowledge of mathematical propositions, such as that $7 + 5 = 12$, is a priori. For this is a claim about knowledge of the *truth value* of such propositions rather than a claim about knowledge of their *general modal status*. A proponent of the a priori can retreat at this point and maintain that even if it has not been established that knowledge of the *truth value* of necessary propositions is a priori, nevertheless a case has been provided for maintaining that knowledge of the *general modal status* of a proposition is a priori. This contention, however, seems to rest solely on

5

the assumption that experience can provide information only about the actual world. Although this assumption derives some plausibility from the observation that one cannot 'peer' into other possible worlds, it conflicts with the fact that a good deal of our scientific knowledge goes beyond what is true of only the actual world. And yet we are not at all tempted to think that such knowledge is a priori. Consequently, if a posteriori knowledge of some non-actual worlds is possible, it remains to be shown why such knowledge of all non-actual worlds is not possible.

Another feature of mathematical propositions, as well as others, which is often cited in support of the claim that knowledge of them is a priori is their alleged immunity from empirical disconfirmation. It is argued that if experiential evidence justifies us in believing mathematical propositions then it must be possible for experiential evidence to justify us in rejecting such propositions. But, the argument continues, we would not regard any experiences as justifying us in rejecting a mathematical proposition. Ayer (1946), for example, invites us to consider a situation where we count what we had taken to be five pairs of objects and find that they amount only to nine. He contends that in such a situation we would not reject the proposition that $2 \times 5 = 10$, but would explain away the discrepancy as merely apparent by invoking whatever empirical hypothesis fits best with the facts of the situation. It should be noted, however, that it is a standard feature of scientific practice to explain away isolated cases of apparent disconfirming instances to well-established generalizations by invoking some auxiliary hypotheses. Hence, more needs to be said at this point to substantiate the claim that mathematical propositions are immune from empirical disconfirmation. If a scientific principle which has received favourable support in the past were suddenly faced with a large number of apparent disconfirming instances and attempts to explain away those instances as merely apparent fail because the empirical hypotheses invoked to explain them away were not supported by independent tests,

then it is evident that experience would have provided sufficient justification for rejecting the principle. Hence, in assessing Ayer's contention that experience cannot provide sufficient justification for rejecting a mathematical principle, one must consider a situation which incorporates the features present in the case of disconfirming the scientific principle: (1) a large number of apparent disconfirming instances to a mathematical principle; and (2) independent tests which fail to support the auxiliary hypotheses introduced to explain away the disconfirming instances as merely apparent. It has been argued (Casullo, 1988a) that in such circumstances it is unreasonable to dismiss the experiential disconfirming evidence as merely apparent since the bulk of one's evidence indicates that it is genuine.

A third feature of mathematical propositions often cited in support of the claim that they are knowable only a priori is their alleged certainty. It is argued that if a mathematical proposition were justified on the basis of experiential evidence, its justification would be inductive in character. Since no inductive justification can confer certainty on its conclusion, it is concluded that mathematical propositions are knowable only a priori. The task facing proponents of the argument, however, is to specify the sense in which mathematical propositions are certain. It might be thought that the deductive character of mathematical PROOF supplies the needed answer. But there are several problems with this answer. The most obvious is that the conclusion of a mathematical proof is known with certainty only if the premises from which the proof begins are known with certainty. But the deductive character of mathematics provides no account of the sense in which basic mathematical propositions are known with certainty. Furthermore, a priorists typically maintain that it is only basic mathematical propositions and their obvious consequences that are known with certainty. Hence, the question which must be addressed is the sense in which basic mathematical propositions are certain. It has often been maintained that epistemically basic propositions are certain in the sense that a mistake regarding them is not possible. On this account, S's belief that $p$ is certain just in case necessarily if S believes that $p$, then it is true that $p$. It is evident that this sense of certainty is trivially satisfied by any necessary truth which S believes. Consequently, it does not underwrite the claim that only propositions known a priori are certain. An alternative manner of specifying the requisite sense of certainty is to invoke the degree of support a proposition enjoys. A proposition which has the highest degree of support is one which is not open to future disconfirmation. More precisely, $p$ is certain for S just in case there is no epistemically possible situation in which S would be less justified in believing that $p$. On this account of certainty, the argument faces the same difficulty as the earlier argument based on immunity to empirical disconfirmation. For if mathematical propositions are not immune to such disconfirmation, there are epistemically possible situations in which S would be less justified in believing them (see CERTAINTY).

In closing let us consider two sceptical arguments against the a priori. Some writers, such as PUTNAM (1983), have taken QUINE's (1963) claim that 'no statement is immune to revision' as denying the existence of a priori knowledge. Clearly, there are two separate issues involved in evaluating this contention: (1) the correctness of Quine's claim; and (2) the bearing of the claim, if correct, on the existence of a priori knowledge. Since we have already argued that there is reason to doubt that mathematical propositions are immune from experiential disconfirmation, let us grant (1) and consider (2). Clearly, if Quine's claim is to bear on the a priori, it is minimally necessary that the following thesis be true: (3) If S knows a priori that $p$ then $p$ is rationally unrevisable. The plausibility of (3) rests on the idea that a priori knowledge is independent of experience. It is alleged that if a proposition is susceptible to empirical disconfirmation then it is not independent of experience in the requisite sense. It has been argued (Casullo, 1988b) that there is reason to be dubious about this line of argument. For the statement that S

knows that $p$, independently of experience appears to entail only: (1) S has justification for believing that $p$ which is sufficient for knowledge; (2) this justification is independent of experience; and (3) the other conditions for knowledge are satisfied. But (1), (2) and (3) are compatible with (4) the possibility of experiential evidence which defeats the nonexperiential justification S has for believing that $p$ (see A PRIORI/A POSTERIORI).

A recurrent concern of those who resist endorsing a priori knowledge is that the existence of such knowledge appears mysterious. If there is a priori knowledge, then, presumably, it has its source in some human cognitive processes. But proponents of the a priori say little about these processes or the manner in which they produce a priori knowledge. At best, reference is made to processes such as 'intuition' or 'intuitive apprehension' along with the claim that they are familiar to anyone who has ascertained the validity of a step in logical proof. This response has two shortcomings. From the fact that there may be a distinctive phenomenological experience which occurs when one ascertains the validity of a step in a proof, it does not follow that these experiences accompany or are constitutive of the operation of a distinctive cognitive process. Furthermore, it is questionable whether invoking such processes explains how we are justified in believing mathematical or logical principles. For example, it is sometimes claimed that the intuitive apprehension of abstract entities is in some way analogous to the perception of physical objects. Benacerraf (1973) has drawn attention to one significant problem with such claims. Perception is a process which involves causal interaction between perceivers and the objects of perception. Abstract entities, however, are incapable of standing in causal relations. Given this disanalogy, some alternative explanation of how intuitive apprehension produces a priori knowledge is necessary.

In summary, we have found that a number of traditional arguments in support of the existence of a priori knowledge as well as several sceptical arguments against it are inconclusive. Proponents of a priori know-ledge are left with the task of (1) providing an illuminating analysis of a priori knowledge which does not involve strong constraints which are easy targets of criticism; and (2) showing that there is a belief-forming process which satisfies the constraints provided in the analysis together with an account of how the process produces the knowledge in question. Opponents of the a priori, on the other hand, must provide a compelling argument which does not either (1) place implausibly strong constraints on a priori justification; or (2) presuppose an unduly restrictive account of human cognitive capacities.

*See also* ANALYTICITY; EMPIRICISM; INTUITION AND DEDUCTION; KANT; LOGICAL POSITIVISM; MATHEMATICAL KNOWLEDGE; MILL.

BIBLIOGRAPHY

Ayer, A. J.: *Language, Truth and Logic* 2nd edn (London: Gollancz, 1946).
Benacerraf, P.: 'Mathematical truth', *Journal of Philosophy* 70 (1973), 661–79.
Casullo, A.: 'Necessity, certainty, and the a priori', *Canadian Journal of Philosophy* 18 (1988[a]), 43–66.
Casullo, A.: 'Revisability, reliabilism, and a priori knowledge', *Philosophy and Phenomenological Research* 49 (1988[b]), 87–213.
Kant, I.: *Critique of Pure Reason* (1781) trans. N. Kemp Smith (London: Macmillan, 1964).
Kitcher, P.: *The Nature of Mathematical Knowledge* (Oxford: Oxford University Press, 1983).
Kripke, S.: *Naming and Necessity* (Cambridge, MA: Harvard University Press, 1980).
Putnam, H.: 'What is mathematical truth?', in his *Philosophical Papers* 3 vols. Vol. 1, *Mathematics, Matter and Method* 2nd edn (Cambridge: Cambridge University Press: 1979), 60–78.
Putnam, H.: '"Two dogmas" revisited', in his *Philosophical Papers* 3 vols. Vol. 3, *Realism and Reason* (Cambridge: Cambridge University Press, 1983), 87–97.
Quine, W. V.: 'Two dogmas of empiricism', in his *From A Logical Point of View* 2nd edn (New York: Harper & Row, 1963), 20–46.

ALBERT CASULLO

**abduction** Inductive reasoning tests hypotheses against experience: typically, we derive predictions from hypotheses and establish whether they are satisfied. An account of induction leaves unanswered two prior questions: How do we arrive at the hypotheses in the first place? And on what basis do we decide which hypotheses are worth testing? These questions concern the logic of discovery or, in Charles S. Peirce's terminology, abduction. Many empiricist philosophers have denied that there is a logic (as opposed to a psychology) of discovery. Peirce, and followers such as N. R. Hanson, insisted that there is a logic of abduction.

The logic of abduction thus investigates the norms employed in deciding whether a hypothesis is worth testing at a given stage of inquiry, and the norms influencing how we should retain the key insights of rejected theories in formulating their successors.

*See also* INDUCTION; PEIRCE.

BIBLIOGRAPHY

Hanson, N. R.: *Patterns of Discovery* (Cambridge: Cambridge University Press, 1958).
Peirce, C. S.: *Collected Papers* vol. VII, ed. A. Burks (Cambridge, MA: Harvard University Press, 1958), pp. 89–164.

CHRISTOPHER HOOKWAY

**absurdity** An absurdity is any obviously, patently, or otherwise undeniably false proposition, such as $0 = 1$ or, for some proposition $p$, the proposition $p$ & *not-p*. Absurdities play the most important role in *reductio ad absurdum* arguments conducted in classical logic. – One wants to demonstrate $p$. Assume that *not-p*. Show that *not-p* implies a false proposition $A$. Since any proposition that implies a false proposition is false, *not-p* is false, so that *not-not-p* is true, and *not-not-p* is logically equivalent to $p$. That is, from the fact that *not-p* implies *A*, one infers that *p*. Such a demonstration of *p* would be controversial if the falsehood of *A* were in doubt. Hence it would be best if *A* were patently or uncontroversially false, i.e. *absurd*.

BIBLIOGRAPHY

Kneale, W. and Kneale, M.: *The Development of Logic* (Oxford, Clarendon Press, 1962).

ROBERT S. TRAGESSER

**Academy (Plato)** PLATO (*c.*429–347 BC) founded his school, named after a district of Athens, between 387 and 367 BC. Studies centred on philosophy, mathematics and science. The conjecture that Plato's *Republic* accurately describes its curriculum, however, seems wrong. It focused on Platonic thinking through the headships of Speusippus and Xenocrates (d. 314). It was later dominated by the scepticisms of Arcesilaus (d. 241) and Carneades (d. 129). In the first century BC it was dominated by a Platonism that was assimilated to the views of ARISTOTLE and STOICISM. Its subsequent history is unclear, and its activity apparently ceased with the closing of the pagan schools by Justinian in 529 AD.

BIBLIOGRAPHY

Zeller, E.: *Die Philosophie der Griechen in ihrer geschichtlichen Entwicklung*, 6th edn. (Hildesheim, 1963), II.1.2 and III.1.1–2.

NICHOLAS P. WHITE

**act/object analysis** According to the act/object analysis of experience, every experience with content involves an object of experience to which the subject is related by an act of awareness (the event of experiencing that object). This is meant to apply not only to perceptions, which have material objects (whatever is perceived), but also to experiences like hallucinations and dream experiences, which do not. Such experiences none the less appear to represent *something*, and their objects are supposed to be whatever it is that they represent. Act/object theorists may differ on the nature of objects of experience, which have been treated as properties, Meinongian objects (which may not exist or have any form of being), and, more commonly, private mental entities with sensory qualities. (The term 'sense-data' is now usually applied to the latter, but has also been used as a general term for objects of sense experiences, as in the work of G. E. MOORE.) Act/object theorists may also differ on the relationship between objects of experience and objects of perception. In terms of REPRESENTATIVE REALISM, objects of perception (of which we are 'indirectly aware') are always distinct from objects of experience (of which we are 'directly aware'). Meinongians, however, may simply treat objects of perception as *existing* objects of experience.

*See also* ADVERBIAL THEORY; DIRECT REALISM; EXPERIENCE; REPRESENTATIVE REALISM; SENSE-DATA.

BIBLIOGRAPHY

Ayer, A. J.: *The Foundations of Empirical Knowledge* (London: Macmillan, 1940).
Jackson, F.: *Perception: a Representative Theory* (Cambridge: Cambridge University Press, 1977).
Moore, G. E.: *Philosophical Studies* (London: Kegan Paul, 1922).
Perkins, M.: *Sensing the World* (Indianapolis: Hackett, 1983).

MICHAEL PENDLEBURY

**adverbial theory** In its best-known form the adverbial theory of experience proposes that the grammatical object of a statement attributing an experience to someone be analysed as an adverb. For example,

(1) Rod is experiencing a pink square

is rewritten as

Rod is experiencing (pink square)-ly.

This is presented as an alternative to the

ACT/OBJECT ANALYSIS, according to which the truth of a statement like (1) requires the existence of an object of experience corresponding to its grammatical object. A commitment to the explicit adverbialization of statements of experience is not, however, essential to adverbialism. The core of the theory consists, rather, in the denial of objects of experience (as opposed to objects of perception) coupled with the view that the role of the grammatical object in a statement of experience is to characterize more fully the sort of experience which is being attributed to the subject. The claim, then, is that the grammatical object is functioning as a modifier, and, in particular, as a modifier of a verb. If this is so, it is perhaps appropriate to regard it as a special kind of adverb at the semantic level.

See also EXPERIENCE; REPRESENTATIVE REALISM.

BIBLIOGRAPHY

Chisholm, R. M.: *Perceiving: A Philosophical Study* (Ithaca, NY: Cornell University Press, 1957).
Clark, R.: 'Sensing, perceiving, thinking', in *Essays on the Philosophy of Roderick M. Chisholm* ed. E. Sosa, *Grazer Philosophische Studien* (1981), 273–95.
Cornman, J.: *Perception, Common Sense, and Science* (New Haven: Yale University Press, 1975).
Ducasse, C. J.: *Nature, Mind, and Death* (La Salle: Open Court, 1951).

MICHAEL PENDLEBURY

**agnosticism** There are two forms of agnosticism: weak and strong. Consider *theism*: the proposition there is such a person as God – an almighty and all knowing and wholly good creator of the world. A weak agnostic is someone who believes neither that there is such a person nor that there is not. In this respect an agnostic is to be contrasted with an atheist, who holds that there is no God, and a theist, who holds that there is. So the theist affirms theism; the atheist denies it; and the agnostic withholds it, having no view as to whether or not this proposition is true. A strong agnostic adds that it isn't *possible* to know or have a justified belief about the truth of theism, so that no one else should have a view on it either.

ALVIN PLANTINGA

**Alston, William P. (1921–)** Alston has contributed to epistemology on many topics: the analysis of justification and knowledge, the foundationalism–coherentism and internalism–externalism controversies, epistemic principles, religious epistemology, perception and numerous others. He is known both for his own positions and for incisively developing distinctions now important in the literature.

His early papers on FOUNDATIONALISM distinguished *levels* of justification and thereby showed that even if one is not directly (non-inferentially) justified in the second-order belief that one is justified in believing *p*, one may be directly justified in believing *p*. Since foundationalists as such need not require second-order justification regarding basic beliefs, this distinction undercuts much criticism previously considered decisive against foundationalism in all forms. In distinguishing many grades of privileged access, Alston also showed that neither foundationalists nor other epistemologists must regard INFALLIBILITY or some version of Cartesian certainty as the only alternatives to COHERENTISM in accounting for the varieties of justification. Regarding justification in general, Alston draws a contrast between deontological and 'strong position' notions. Roughly, the former treat justification as fulfilment of epistemic duty, the latter as a matter of being in a good position with respect to the truth of *p*, e.g. being able simply to see that *p* is true. He argues that much of the literature on justification fails to take account of this distinction, and he shows how the distinction can explain major disagreements. For instance, the former conception goes well with an internalist view, since one has introspective access to grounds of one's obligations, such as a memory of having promised to do something or a conviction that lying is wrong; the latter suggests an at least partly externalist view on justification, since one does not in general have such access to the reliability of one's position with respect to discerning the truth of p (see VIRTUE EPISTEMOLOGY; RELIGIOUS BELIEF; EXTERNALISM/INTERNALISM).

Alston's own account of justification is a distinctive blend of internalism and externalism: if I justifiedly believe p, I must both have an appropriate access to my grounds and, by virtue of them, be in a good position vis-à-vis the truth of p. This condition normally also holds for knowledge, but Alston has rigorously argued that under special conditions knowledge is possible without justification and thereby on grounds to which one lacks access. For knowledge, as for justification, perception is a paradigmatic source. In both cases, moreover, first-order success is possible without second-order success; e.g. one can know that p without knowing that one does, or even that one's source, say perception, is reliable. But can we know or justifiedly believe perception *is* reliable? In discussing epistemic circularity, Alston argues that while a kind of circularity is implicit in plausible attempts to show the reliability of perception, it does not prevent one's justifiedly believing, or even knowing, that perception *is* reliable. To this extent, at least, scepticism is answerable.

In recent work, Alston has pursued at least three major epistemological projects. He has defended the theory of appearing as an account of perception. He has developed a doxastic practice approach in metaepistemology, arguing, along lines suggested by the work of REID, that justification is rooted in a certain kind of social practice. And, using these resources and many others in and outside epistemology, he has built an account of the possibility of perception of, and thereby justified beliefs about, God.

WRITINGS

'Varieties of privileged access', *American Philosophical Quarterly* 8 (1971), 223–41.

'Two types of foundationalism', *Journal of Philosophy* 73 (1976), 165–85.
'Concepts of epistemic justification', *The Monist* 68 (1985), 57–89.
'An internalist externalism', *Synthese* 74 (1988), 265–83.
*Epistemic Justification* (Ithaca, NY: Cornell University Press, 1989). (This contains all of the above.)
*Perceiving God* (Ithaca, NY Cornell University Press, 1991).

ROBERT AUDI

**analyticity** The true story of analyticity is surprising in many ways. Contrary to received opinion, it was the empiricist Locke rather than the rationalist Kant who had the better informal account of this type of a priori proposition. Frege and Carnap, represented as analyticity's best friends in this century, did as much to undermine it as its worst enemies. Quine and Putnam, represented as having refuted the analytic/synthetic distinction, not only did no such thing, but, in fact, contributed significantly to undoing the damage done by Frege and Carnap. Finally, the epistemological significance of the distinction is nothing like what it is commonly taken to be.

LOCKE's account of analytic propositions was, for its time, everything that a succinct account of analyticity should be (Locke, 1924, pp. 306–8). He distinguishes two kinds of analytic propositions, identity propositions in which 'we affirm the said term of itself', e.g. 'Roses are roses', and predicative propositions in which 'a part of the complex idea is predicated of the name of the whole', e.g. 'Roses are flowers' (pp. 306–7). Locke calls such sentences 'trifling' because a speaker who use them 'trifles with words'. A synthetic sentence, in contrast, such as a mathematical theorem, states 'a real truth and conveys with it instructive real knowledge' (pp. 307–8). Correspondingly, Locke distinguishes two kinds of 'necessary consequences', analytic entailments where validity depends on the literal containment of the conclusion in the premiss and synthetic entailments where it does not. (Locke did not originate this concept-containment notion of analyticity. It is discussed by Arnauld and Nicole, and it is safe to say it has been around for a very long time (cf. Arnauld, 1964, pp. 59–65).)

KANT'S account of analyticity, which received opinion tells us is the consummate formulation of this notion in modern philosophy, is actually a step backwards. What is valid in his account is not novel, and what is novel is not valid. Kant repeats Locke's account of concept-containment analyticity, but introduces certain alien features, the most important being his characterization of analytic propositions as propositions whose denials are logical contradictions (Kant, 1783, p. 14). This characterization suggests that analytic propositions based on Locke's part–whole relation or Kant's explicative copula are a species of logical truth. But the containment of the predicate concept in the subject concept in sentences like 'Bachelors are unmarried' is a different relation from the containment of the consequent in the antecedent in sentences like 'If John is a bachelor, then John is a bachelor or Mary read Kant's *Critique*'. The former is *literal* containment whereas the latter is, in general, not. Talk of the 'containment' of the consequent of a logical truth in the antecedent in cases like our example is only metaphorical, a way of saying 'logically derivable'.

Kant's conflation of concept containment with logical containment caused him to overlook the issue of whether logical truths are synthetic a priori and the problem of how he can say mathematical truths are synthetic a priori when they cannot be denied without contradiction. Historically, the conflation set the stage for the disappearance of the Lockean notion. Frege, whom received opinion portrays as second only to Kant among the champions of analyticity, and Carnap, whom it portrays as just behind Frege, were jointly responsible for the disappearance of concept-containment analyticity.

FREGE was clear about the difference between concept containment and logical containment, expressing it as like the difference between the containment of 'beams in a house' and the containment of a 'plant in the

seed' (Frege, 1953, p. 101). But he found the former, as Kant formulated it, defective in three ways: it explains analyticity in psychological terms; it does not cover all cases of analytic propositions; and, perhaps most important for Frege's logicism, its notion of containment is 'unfruitful' as a definitional mechanism in logic and mathematics (Frege, 1953, pp. 100–1). In an invidious comparison between the two notions of containment, Frege observes that with logical containment 'we are not simply taking out of the box again what we have just put into it' (ibid., p. 101). To overcome these shortcomings, Frege defines analytic propositions as consequences of laws of logic plus definitions, consequences that 'cannot be inspected in advance' (ibid., pp. 4, 100–1). This definition makes logical containment the basic notion. Analyticity becomes a special case of logical truth, and, even in this special case, the definitions employ the power of definition in logic and mathematics rather than mere concept combination.

CARNAP, attempting to overcome what he saw as a shortcoming in Frege's account of analyticity, took the remaining step necessary to do away explicitly with Lockean–Kantian analyticity. As Carnap saw things, it was a shortcoming of Frege's explication that it seems to suggest that definitional relations underlying analytic propositions can be extra-logical in some sense, say, in resting on linguistic synonymy. To Carnap, this represented a failure to achieve a uniform formal treatment of analytic propositions and left us with a dubious distinction between logical and extra-logical vocabulary. Hence, he eliminated the reference to definitions in Frege's explication of analyticity by introducing 'meaning postulates', e.g. statements such as '(∀x) (x is a bachelor → x is unmarried)' (*see* Carnap, 1965, pp. 222–9). Like standard logical postulates on which they were modelled, meaning postulates express nothing more than constraints on the admissible models with respect to which sentences and deductions are evaluated for truth and validity. Thus, despite their name, meaning postulates have no more to do with meaning than any other statement expressing a necessary truth. In defining analytic propositions as consequences of (an expanded set of) logical laws, Carnap explicitly removed the one place in Frege's explication where there might be room for concept containment, and with it, the last trace of Locke's distinction between semantic and other 'necessary consequences'.

QUINE, the staunchest critic of analyticity of our time, performed an invaluable service on its behalf – albeit one that has gone almost completely unappreciated. Quine made two devastating criticisms of Carnap's meaning postulate approach which expose it as both irrelevant and vacuous. It is irrelevant because, in using particular words of a language, meaning postulates fail to explicate analyticity for sentences and languages generally, that is, they do not define it for variable 'S' and 'L' (Quine, 1953, pp. 33–4). It is vacuous because, although meaning postulates tell us what sentences are to count as analytic, they do not tell us what it is for them to be analytic (ibid., p. 33).

Received opinion has it that Quine did much more than refute the analytic/synthetic distinction as Carnap tried to draw it. Received opinion has it that Quine demonstrated there is no distinction, however anyone might try to draw it. But this, too, is incorrect. To argue for this stronger conclusion, Quine had to show that there is no way to draw the distinction outside logic, in particular, in linguistics. In the absence of a particular theory in linguistics corresponding to Carnap's, Quine's argument had to take an entirely different form. Some inherent feature of linguistics had to be exploited in showing that no theory in this science can deliver the distinction. But the feature Quine chose was a principle of operationalist methodology characteristic of the school of Bloomfieldian linguistics. Quine succeeds in showing that meaning cannot be made objective sense of in linguistics if making sense of a linguistic concept requires, as that school claims, operationally defining it in terms of substitution procedures which employ only concepts unrelated to that linguistic concept. But Chomsky's revolution in linguistics replaced the Bloomfieldian taxonomic model of grammars with the hypothetico-deductive model of generative linguistics, and, as a consequence, such operational definition was removed as the standard for concepts in linguistics. The standard of theoretical definition which replaced it was far more liberal, allowing the members of a family of linguistic concepts to be defined with respect to one another within a set of axioms which state their systematic interconnections – the entire system being judged by whether its consequences are confirmed by the linguistic facts. Quine's argument does not even address theories of meaning based on this hypothetico-deductive model (Katz, 1988b, pp. 227–52; Katz, 1990, pp. 199–202).

PUTNAM, the other staunch critic of analyticity, performed a service on behalf of analyticity fully on a par with, and complementary to, Quine's. Whereas Quine refuted Carnap's formalization of Frege's conception of analyticity, Putnam refuted this very conception itself. Putnam put an end to the entire attempt, initiated by Frege and completed by Carnap, to construe analyticity as a logical concept (Putnam, 1962, pp. 647–58; 1970, pp. 189–201; 1975a, pp. 131–93).

However, as with Quine, received opinion has it that Putnam did much more. Putnam is credited with having devised science fiction cases, from the robot cat case to the twin earth case, that are counter examples to the traditional theory of meaning. Again, received opinion is incorrect. These cases are only counter examples to Frege's version of the traditional theory of meaning. Frege's version claims *both* (1) that sense determines reference, and (2) that there are instances of analyticity, say, typified by 'cats are animals', and of synonymy, say typified by 'water' in English and 'water' in twin earth English. Given (1) and (2), what we call 'cats' could not be non-animals and what we call 'water' could not differ from what the twin earthers call 'water'. But, as Putnam's cases show, what we call 'cats' could be Martian robots and what they call 'water' could be something other than $H_2O$. Hence, the cases are counter examples to Frege's version of the theory.

Putnam himself takes these examples to refute the traditional theory of meaning *per se* because he thinks other versions must also subscribe to both (1) and (2). He was mistaken in the case of (1). Frege's theory entails (1) because it defines the sense of an expression as the mode of determination of its referent (Frege, 1952, pp. 56–78). But sense does not have to be defined this way, or in any way that entails (1). It can be defined as (D).

> (D) Sense is that aspect of the grammatical structure of expressions and sentences responsible for their having sense properties and relations like meaningfulness, ambiguity, antonymy, synonymy, redundancy, analyticity, and analytic entailment. (Katz, 1972; 1990, pp. 216–24)

(Note that this use of sense properties and relations is no more circular than the use of logical properties and relations to define logical form, for example, as that aspect of grammatical structure of sentences on which their logical implications depend.)

(D) makes senses internal to the grammar of a language and reference an external matter of language use – typically involving extra-linguistic beliefs. Therefore, (D) cuts the strong connection between sense and reference expressed in (1), so that there is no inference from the modal fact that 'cat' refers to robots to the conclusion that 'Cats are animals' is not analytic. Likewise, there is no inference from 'water' referring to different substances on earth and twin earth to the conclusion that our word and theirs are not synonymous. Putnam's science fiction cases do not apply to a version of the traditional theory of meaning based on (D).

The success of Putnam's and Quine's criticisms in application to Frege's and Carnap's theory of meaning together with their failure in application to a theory in linguistics based on (D) creates the option of overcoming the shortcomings of the Lockean–Kantian notion of analyticity without switching to a logical notion. This option was explored in the 1960s and 1970s in the course of developing a theory of meaning modelled on the hypothetico-deductive paradigm for grammars introduced in the Chomskyan revolution (Katz, 1972).

This theory automatically avoids Frege's criticism of the psychological formulation of Kant's definition because, as an explication of a grammatical notion within linguistics, it is stated as a formal account of the structure of expressions and sentences. The theory also avoids Frege's criticism that concept-containment analyticity is not 'fruitful' enough to encompass truths of logic and mathematics. The criticism rests on the dubious assumption, part of Frege's logicism, that analyticity *should* encompass them. (Benacerraf, 1981, p. 25). But in linguistics where the only concern is the scientific truth about natural languages, there is no basis for insisting that concept-containment analyticity encompass truths of logic and mathematics. Moreover, since we are seeking the scientific truth about trifling propositions in natural language, we will eschew relations from logic and mathematics that are too fruitful for the description of such propositions. This is not to deny that we want a notion of necessary truth that goes beyond the trifling, but only to deny that *that* notion is the notion of analyticity in natural language.

The remaining Fregean criticism points to a genuine incompleteness of the traditional account of analyticity. There are analytic relational sentences, for example, 'Jane walks with those with whom she herself strolls', 'Jack kills those he himself has murdered', etc., and analytic entailments with existential conclusions, for example, 'I think', therefore, 'I exist'. The containment in these sentences is just as literal as that in analytic subject–predicate sentences like 'Bachelors are unmarried'. I will now show how a theory of meaning constructed as a hypothetico-deductive systematization of sense as defined in (D) overcomes the incompleteness of the traditional account in the case of such relational sentences. (For a treatment of the existential sentences, *see* Katz, 1988a.)

Such a theory of meaning makes the principal concern of semantics the explanation of sense properties and relations like synonymy, antonymy, redundancy, analyticity, ambiguity, etc. Furthermore, it makes grammatical structure, specifically, sense structure, the basis for explaining them. This leads directly to the discovery of a new level of grammatical structure, and this, in turn, makes possible a proper definition of analyticity. To see this, consider two simple examples. It is a semantic fact that 'male bachelor' is redundant and that 'spinster' is synonymous with 'woman who never married'. In the case of the redundancy, we have to explain the fact that the sense of the modifier 'male' is already contained in the sense of its head 'bachelor'. In the case of the synonymy, we have to explain the fact that the sense of 'spinster' is identical to the sense of 'woman who never married' (compositionally formed from the senses of 'woman', 'never' and 'married'). But in so far as such facts concern relations involving the components of the senses of 'bachelor' and 'spinster' and in so far as these words are syntactic simples, there must be a level of grammatical structure at which syntactic simples are semantically complex. This, in brief, is the route by which we arrive a level of *decompositional semantic structure* that is the locus of sense structures masked by syntactically simple words.

Discovery of this new level of grammatical structure was followed by attempts to represent the structure of the senses found there. Without going into the details of sense representation, it is clear that, once we have the notion of decompositional representation, we can see how to generalize Locke's and Kant's informal, subject–predicate account of analyticity to cover relational analytic sentences. Let a simple sentence S consist of a n-place predicate P with terms $T_1, \ldots, T_n$ occupying its argument places. Then:

(A)  S is analytic in case, first, S has a term $T_i$ which consists of an m-placed predicate Q ($m > n$ or $m = n$) with terms occupying its argument places, and second, P is contained in Q and, for each term $T_j$ of $T_1, \ldots, T_{i-1}, T_{i+1}, \ldots, T_n$, $T_j$ is contained in the term of Q which occupies the argument place in Q

corresponding to the argument place occupied by $T_j$ in P. (Katz, 1972)

To see how (A) works, suppose that 'stroll' in 'Jane walks with those with whom she herself strolls' is decompositionally represented as having the same sense as 'walk idly and in a leisurely way'. The sentence is analytic by (A) because the predicate 'stroll' (the sense of 'stroll') contains the predicate 'walk' (the sense of 'walk') and the term 'Jane' (the sense of 'Jane' associated with the predicate 'walk') is contained in the term 'Jane' (the sense of 'she herself' associated with the predicate 'stroll'). The containment in the case of the other terms is automatic.

The fact that (A) itself makes no reference to logical operators or logical laws indicates that analyticity for subject–predicate sentences can be extended to simple relational sentences without treating analytic sentences as instances of logical truths. Further, the source of the incompleteness is no longer explained, as Frege explained it, as the absence of 'fruitful' logical apparatus, but is now explained as mistakenly treating what is only a special case of analyticity as if it were the general case. The inclusion of the predicate in the subject is the special case (where $n = 1$) of the general case of the inclusion of an n-place predicate (and its terms) in one of its terms. Note that the defects Quine complained of in connection with Carnap's meaning postulate explication are absent in (A). (A) contains no words from a natural language. It explicitly uses variable 'S' and variable 'L' because it is a definition in linguistic theory. Moreover, (A) tells us what the property is in virtue of which a sentence is analytic, namely, redundant predication, that is, the predicational structure of an analytic sentence is already found in the content of its term structure.

Received opinion has been anti-Lockean in holding that necessary consequences in logic and language belong to one and the same species. This seems wrong because the property of redundant predication provides a non-logical explanation of why true statements made in the literal use of analytic sentences are necessarily true. Since the property ensures that the objects of the predication in the use of an analytic sentence are chosen on the basis of the features to be predicated of them, the truth conditions of the statement are automatically satisfied once its terms take on reference. The difference between such a linguistic source of necessity and the logical and mathematical sources vindicates Locke's distinction between two kinds of 'necessary consequences'.

Received opinion concerning analyticity contains another mistake. This is the idea that analyticity is inimical to science. In part, the idea developed as a reaction to certain dubious uses of analyticity such as Frege's attempt to establish LOGICISM and Schlick's, Ayer's and other LOGICAL POSITIVISTS' attempts to deflate claims to metaphysical knowledge by showing that alleged synthetic a priori truths are merely empty analytic truths (Schlick, 1949, p. 285; Ayer, 1946, pp. 71–87). In part, it developed as also a response to a number of cases where alleged analytic, and hence, necessary, truths, e.g. the law of excluded middle, had subsequently been taken as open to revision. Such cases convinced philosophers like Quine and Putnam that the analytic/synthetic distinction is an obstacle to scientific progress.

The problem if there is one is not analyticity in the concept-containment sense, but the conflation of it with analyticity in the logical sense. This made it seem as if there is a single concept of analyticity which can serve as the grounds for a wide range of a priori truths. But, just as there are two analytic/synthetic distinctions, so there are two concepts of CONCEPT. The narrow Lockean/Kantian distinction is based on a narrow notion of concept on which concepts are senses of expressions in the language. The broad Fregean/Carnapian distinction is based on a broad notion of concept on which concepts are conceptions – often scientific ones – about the nature of the referent(s) of expressions (Katz, 1972, pp. 450–2, and curiously, Putnam, 1981, p. 207). Conflation of these two notions of concept produced the illusion of a single concept with the content of

philosophical, logical and mathematical conceptions but with the status of linguistic concepts. This encouraged philosophers to think that they were in possession of concepts with the content to express substantive philosophical claims, e.g. such as Frege's, Schlick's, Ayer's, etc., and with a status that trivializes the task of justifying them by requiring only linguistic grounds for the a priori propositions in question.

Thus, there is no need to reject the analytic/synthetic distinction in toto to prevent analyticity from being put to dubious uses. All that is necessary is to keep the original, narrow distinction from being broadened. This insures that propositions expressing the content of broad concepts cannot receive the easier justification appropriate to narrow ones. Accordingly, in so far as the wholesale rejection of the analytic/synthetic distinction was based on a concern about dubious philosophy, particularly the possibility of blocking scientific progress, it threw out the baby with the bath water.

Finally, there is an important epistemological implication of separating the broad and narrow notions of analyticity. Frege and Carnap took the broad notion of analyticity to provide foundations for necessity and a priority, and, hence, for some form of rationalism, and nearly all rationalistically inclined analytic philosophers followed them in this. Thus, when Quine dispatched the Frege–Carnap position on analyticity, it was widely believed that necessity, a priority, and rationalism had also been despatched, and, as a consequence, that Quine had ushered in an 'empiricism without dogmas' and NATURALIZED EPISTEMOLOGY. But given there is still a notion of analyticity which enables us to pose the problem of how necessary, synthetic a priori knowledge is possible (moreover, one whose narrowness makes logical and mathematical knowledge part of the problem), Quine did not undercut the foundations of rationalism. Hence, a serious reappraisal of the new empiricism and naturalized epistemology is, to say the least, very much in order (Katz, 1990).

*See also* A PRIORI KNOWLEDGE; INTUI-

TION AND DEDUCTION; KANT; LOCKE; MATHEMATICAL KNOWLEDGE; PHILOSOPHICAL KNOWLEDGE.

BIBLIOGRAPHY

Arnauld, A.: *The Art of Thinking* (Indianapolis: Bobbs-Merrill, 1964).

Ayer, A. J.: *Language, Truth, and Logic* (London: Gollancz, 1946).

Benacerraf, P.: 'Frege: The last logicist', in *Midwest Studies in Philosophy* 6 (Minneapolis: University of Minnesota Press, 1981).

Carnap, R.: 'Meaning postulates', in his *Meaning and Necessity*, 2nd edn (Chicago: University of Chicago Press, 1965).

Frege, G.: 'On sense and reference', in *Translations from the Philosophical Writings of Gottlob Frege*, trans. P. T. Geach and M. Black (Oxford: Blackwell, 1952).

Frege, G.: *Foundations of Arithmetic* (Oxford: Blackwell, 1953).

Kant, I.: *Critique of Pure Reason* (1781) trans. N. Kemp Smith (London: Macmillan, 1964).

Kant, I.: *Prolegomena to any Future Metaphysic* (1783) trans. L. W. Beck (Indianapolis: Bobbs-Merrill, 1950).

Katz, J. J.: *Semantic Theory* (New York: Harper & Row, 1972).

Katz, J. J.: *Cogitations* (New York: Oxford University Press, 1988[a]).

Katz, J. J.: 'The refutation of indeterminacy', *Journal of Philosophy* 85 (1988[b]), 227–52.

Katz, J. J.: *The Metaphysics of Meaning* (Cambridge, MA: MIT Press, 1990).

Locke, J.: *An Essay Concerning Human Understanding* (Oxford: Clarendon Press, 1924).

Putnam, H.: 'It ain't necessarily so', *Journal of Philosophy* 59 (1962), 658–71.

Putnam, H.: 'The meaning of "meaning" ', in *Language, Mind, and Knowledge*: Minnesota Studies in the Philosophy of Science (Minneapolis: University of Minnesota Press, 1975[a]).

Putnam, H.: 'Is semantics possible?' (1970); reprinted in his *Mind, Language, Reality* (Cambridge: Cambridge University Press, 1975[b]), 139–52.

Putnam, H.: *Reason, Truth, and History* (Cambridge: Cambridge University Press, 1981).

Quine, W. V.: 'Two dogmas of empiricism', in his *From a Logical Point of View* (Cambridge, MA: Harvard University Press, 1953).

Schlick, M.: 'Is there a factual a priori?', in *Readings in Philosophical Analysis* eds H. Feigl and W. Sellars (New York: Appleton-Century-Crofts, 1949).

JERROLD J. KATZ

**anamnesis** 'Recollection', or anamnesis has several roles in PLATO's epistemology. In the *Meno* (80–6) it is invoked to explain the behaviour of an uneducated boy who answers a geometrical problem that he has never heard. At the same time it is used to solve a paradox about inquiry and learning. In the *Phaedo* it is said to explain our possession of concepts, construed as knowledge of Forms, which we supposedly could not have gained from experience. Recollection also appears in the *Phaedrus*, but is notably absent from important presentations of Plato's epistemological views in the *Republic* and other works.

BIBLIOGRAPHY

Gosling, J. C. B.: *Plato* (London: Routledge, 1973), ch. 16.

Gulley, N.: *Plato's Theory of Knowledge* (London: Methuen, 1962), ch. 1.

White, N.P.: *Plato on Knowledge and Reality* (Indianapolis: Hackett, 1976), chs 2–3.

NICHOLAS P. WHITE

**antinomy** An antinomy occurs when we are able to argue for, or demonstrate, both a proposition and its contradictory (*see* PRINCIPLE OF CONTRADICTION), but where we cannot now fault either demonstration. We would eventually hope to be able 'to solve the antinomy' by managing, through careful thinking and analysis, eventually to fault either or both demonstrations.

Many paradoxes are an easy source of antinomies. For example, Zeno gave some famous let us say logical-*cum*-mathematical arguments which might be interpreted as demonstrating that motion is impossible. But our eyes as it were demonstrate motion (exhibit moving things) all the time. Where did Zeno go wrong? Where do our eyes go wrong? If we cannot readily answer at least one of these questions, then we are in antinomy. In the *Critique of Pure Reason* KANT gave demonstrations of the same kind – in the Zeno example they were obviously not the same kind – of both, e.g. that the world has a beginning in time and space, and that the world has no beginning in time or space. He argues that both demonstrations are at fault because they proceed on the basis of 'pure reason' unconditioned by sense experience.

BIBLIOGRAPHY

Beck, L. W.: 'Antinomy of pure reason', in *Dictionary of the History of Ideas* ed. P. P. Wiener (New York, Charles Scribner's Sons, 1973), vol. 1.
Kant, I.: *Critique of Pure Reason* trans. N. Kemp Smith (London: Macmillan, 1964).
Kneale, W. and Kneale, M.: *The Development of Logic* (Oxford: Clarendon Press, 1962).

ROBERT S. TRAGESSER

**apodeictic** A proposition *p* is apodeictic when it is demonstrable in a sense entailing not only that *p* is true, but also that it is not possibly false. For Aristotle, an apodeictically true proposition was one inferred by formal-logical syllogism from incontrovertibly true premises (*Posterior Analytics*, 1.71b–72c). Sometimes 'apodeictic' is used loosely to mean that a proposition is recognized to be beyond dispute; and sometimes it is taken to mean that it *must* be true (without any reference to demonstration).

ROBERT S. TRAGESSER

**aporia** Any difficult problem that arises when we are trying to extend our knowledge of a matter, and that threatens seriously to impede our further progress, is called an aporia, especially when there seem to be equally strong arguments for and against any solution. An ANTINOMY is an especially nasty aporia.

BIBLIOGRAPHY

Peters, F. E.: *Greek Philosophical Terms* (London: University of London, 1967).

ROBERT S. TRAGESSER

**apperception** This is LEIBNIZ's term for inner awareness or self-consciousness, in contrast with 'perception' or outer awareness. He held, in opposition to DESCARTES, that adult humans can have experiences of which they are unaware; experiences which may affect what they do, but which are not brought to self-consciousness. Indeed there are creatures, such as animals and babies, which completely lack the ability to reflect on their experiences, and to become aware of them as experiences of theirs. The unity of a subject's experience, which stems from his capacity to recognize all his experiences as his, was dubbed by KANT the transcendental unity of apperception. This apprehension of unity is transcendental, rather than empirical, because it is presupposed in experience and cannot be derived from it. Kant used the need for this unity as the basis of his attempted refutation of scepticism about the external world. He argued that my experiences could only be united in one self-consciousness if at least some of them were experiences of a law-governed world of objects in space. Outer experience is thus a necessary condition of inner awareness.

*See also* INTROSPECTION.

BIBLIOGRAPHY

Kant, I.: *Critique of Pure Reason* trans. N. Kemp-Smith (London: Macmillan, 1964).
Leibniz, G. W.: *New Essays on Human Understanding* (1704) trans. P. Remnant and J. Bennett (Cambridge: Cambridge University Press, 1981), esp. pp. 53–7.

DAVID MCNAUGHTON

**Aquinas, Thomas (1225–74)** Theologian and philosopher, born near Naples. Aquinas's fundamental epistemic category is that of cognition (*cognitio*). He endorses the

Aristotelian view that the soul is potentially all things and holds that cognition is its actually becoming a given thing or, as he sometimes puts it, its being assimilated to that thing in a certain way (*Summa theologiae* Ia.12.4, 17.3, 76.2.AD4, 84.2.AD2). His account of this basic notion of cognition involves both a metaphysical account of the two relata in the relation of cognitive assimilation – the human soul and the objects of human cognition – and a psychological theory identifying the sorts of powers the soul must possess and the processes it must engage in if cognitive assimilation of this sort is to be possible.

According to Aquinas's metaphysics, the reality to which human beings are assimilated in cognition is made up of basic elements (particular substances and accidents) that are joined together in various ways to form complexes (accidents inhering in particular substances). He holds that the soul must possess cognitive powers capable of rendering it isomorphic with an external reality of this sort. The intellective soul's activity of understanding (*intellectus*) allows human beings both to grasp, via sense perception, the natures of substances and accidents and to link them together into complexes (subject–predicate propositions). But cognition is not restricted to the sort of intake of information made possible by sense perception and understanding; human beings are also able, by virtue of a distinct activity of discursive thought (*ratio, ratiocinatio*), to acquire new cognition of things by drawing inferences from things already cognized. Aquinas's strictly epistemological views are to be found within this broad metaphysically- and psychologically-oriented account of cognition (*Commentary on Aristotle's Posterior Analytics* Prologue; *Summa theologiae* Ia.75–86; *Disputed Questions on Truth* I, X).

Aquinas's most detailed epistemological reflections occur in the context of his discussion of the propositional attitude *scientia*, which he conceives of as the paradigm of knowledge. To have *scientia* with respect to a given thing is to have complete and certain cognition of its truth; that is, to hold a given proposition on grounds that guarantee its truth in a certain way. Following Aristotle, Aquinas holds that grounds of this sort are provided only by demonstrative syllogisms, and so he maintains that the objects of *scientia* are propositions one holds on the basis of demonstrative syllogisms. To have *scientia* with respect to some proposition *p*, then, is to have a particular sort of inferential justification for *p* (*Commentary on Aristotle's Posterior Analytics* I.4).

Now Aquinas holds that because the sort of justification essential to *scientia* is inferential, it is also derivative: *scientia* acquires its positive epistemic status from the premises of the demonstrative syllogism and the nature of the syllogistic inference. Hence, he holds a principle of inferential justification according to which one is justified in holding the conclusion of some demonstration only if one is justified in holding the demonstration's premises. The premises that ground *scientia* are not only logically but also epistemically prior to the conclusion (*Commentary on Aristotle's Posterior Analytics* I.6).

Aquinas argues that our justification for holding the premises of demonstrative syllogisms cannot in every case be inferential: some propositions must have their positive epistemic status not by virtue of an inference (*per demonstrationem*) but non-inferentially, by virtue of themselves (*per se*) (*Commentary on Aristotle's Posterior Analytics* I.4, 7). Propositions that are known by virtue of themselves (*per se nota*) are Aquinas's epistemic first principles, the foundations of his foundationalist account of *scientia*. He offers two sorts of argument for his epistemological FOUNDATIONALISM. The first proceeds by attacking rival accounts of justification, concluding that inferential justification is possible only if there is non-inferential justification. If one holds that all justification is inferential and if a person is inferentially justified in holding some proposition only if he is justified in holding the premises of the relevant inference, then one is committed to an infinite regress of justification (*see* INFINITE REGRESS ARGUMENT). If the regress is linear, then there can be no justification since one cannot possess an infinite number of distinct inferences. But if one tries to avoid this sceptical result by maintaining that the regress of justification circles back on itself in such a way that an inferentially justified conclusion appears as part of the (proximate or remote) justification for itself, then one is committed to absurdities such as that one and the same proposition can be at once epistemically both prior and posterior to some other proposition and that some proposition can be epistemically prior to itself. Aquinas concludes that if inferential justification is to be possible, there must be non-inferential justification (*Commentary on Aristotle's Posterior Analytics* I.7–8).

His second argument for foundationalism rests on his positive characterization of the nature of non-inferential justification. He holds that certain propositions (immediate propositions) are knowable *per se* by virtue of the fact that their predicates belong to the definition (*ratio*) of their subjects (*Commentary on Aristotle's Posterior Analytics* I.5). We are non-inferentially justified in holding propositions of this sort because when we are aware that a proposition's predicate belongs to the definition of its subject, we are directly aware of the proposition's necessary truth and cannot be mistaken about it (*Commentary on Aristotle's Posterior Analytics* I.7, 19, 20, 44; *Summa theologiae* Ia.17.3.AD2). To be aware that a given proposition is of this sort we must conceive its subject and predicate, which requires us to have attained explicit grasp of the real natures referred to by the subject and predicate terms (*Commentary on Aristotle's Posterior Analytics* I.2, 4, II.8). For example, when we have grasped the real nature *human being* (the real definition of which is *rational animal*), we cannot help but be aware of the necessary truth of the proposition 'A human being is an animal'. Aquinas holds, however, that attaining explicit grasp of the real natures of things can be difficult, and so he holds that not all propositions in which the predicate belongs to the definition of the subject are actually known to be of that sort. The subjects and predicates of certain purely formal, a priori propositions (e.g. those of logic and mathematics) are more easily cognized by human beings (because of their relative independence from

matter), and so most people will recognize first principles of this sort as such and be non-inferentially justified in holding them. The subjects and predicates of a posteriori propositions (e.g. those of natural science), however, are accessible only with difficulty, and hence objective first principles of this sort may not be recognized as such. Aquinas holds that each of us has experience of being directly acquainted with the necessary truth of at least some first principles and that this provides us with sufficient reason for thinking that there is non-inferential justification (*Commentary on Aristotle's Posterior Analytics* I.4, 25, 41; *Commentary on Boethius's De Trinitate* 5).

This account of non-inferential justification requires him to give an account of our cognitive relations to universal real natures (such as *human being*), the elements out of which complex (propositional) knowledge is built. He thinks of his account as resolving an ancient epistemological puzzle. The puzzle is how human beings, whose senses provide access to a world of irreducibly particular corporeal objects, can have cognition of universals. Aquinas rejects Platonist and Neoplatonist solutions that postulate the possibility of some sort of extrasensory contact with independent, immaterial universals. He not only rejects the existence of universals of this sort, but also holds that because human beings are by nature unified corporeal substances whose natural form of access to the world is through the bodily senses, all human cognition arises from sense perception. Aquinas's solution to the epistemological puzzle is a theory of intellective abstraction: cognition of universals, like all human cognition, originates from sense perception, and so from the external world of material particulars; but human beings possess a cognitive capacity (in particular what he calls an active intellect), which acts on sensory data to produce intelligible universals. We cognize the universal real natures that constitute the subjects and predicates of epistemic first principles when we possess actually intelligible species or forms abstracted by this mechanism from the material conditions that render them merely potentially intelligible

(*Commentary on Aristotle's Posterior Analytics* II.20; *Summa theologiae* Ia.79, 84–6; *Disputed Questions on Truth* X.6).

According to Aquinas, then, we have paradigmatic knowledge when we hold a first principle by virtue of seeing that its predicate belongs to the definition of its subject (i.e. when we possess understanding – *intellectus* – of it) or hold a proposition on the basis of a demonstrative syllogism the premisses of which we hold in that way (i.e. have *scientia* with respect to it). He recognizes, however, that these conditions restrict paradigmatic knowledge to a very narrow range, and he allows that there is knowledge other than paradigmatic knowledge. First, following the ancient Greek distinction between demonstrative and dialectical reasoning, he allows that dialectical (*probabile, persuasoria*) reasoning can provide epistemic justification. Reasoning of this sort is distinguished by virtue of its producing conclusions that are not certain but merely probable. So-called probable arguments rely on premisses that are not necessary and certain but possess some positive epistemic status (propositions held by most people, on good authority, inductive grounds, etc.) and make use of broadly inductive argument forms (enumerative induction, analogy, probabilistic argument forms, etc.). Justificatory grounds of this sort give rise not to *scientia* but to opinion (*opinio*) or belief (*fides*), and Aquinas holds that one can be justified in holding propositions one holds in this way (*Commentary on Aristotle's Posterior Analytics* Prologue, I.44; *Commentary on Boethius's De Trinitate* 2.1.AD5; *Summa theologiae* IIaIIae.2.1, 2.9.AD3; *Summa contra gentiles* I.9).

Second, Aquinas extends the strict account of demonstrative reasoning to take account of the particular condition of human epistemic subjects. Because human beings' epistemic access to the world is through the bodily senses, propositions about sensible objects are in many cases epistemically prior *for us* both in the sense that we acquire them first and in the sense that we find them easiest to accept as true (*Commentary on Aristotle's Posterior Analytics* I.4, 42). Consequently, he allows that propositions about sensible

objects can function as epistemic first principles grounding what is *for us* (though not unqualifiedly) *scientia*. Demonstrations the ultimate premisses of which are not paradigmatic but only qualified first principles of this sort are not paradigmatic, explanatory demonstrations (*demonstrationes propter quid*) but non-paradigmatic, merely factual demonstrations (*demonstrationes quia*). They establish the truth of the conclusion but fail to provide for it the certain and complete justification that would be provided by a demonstration deriving from necessary truths about the universal real natures of things (*Commentary on Aristotle's Posterior Analytics* I.23; *Summa theologiae* Ia.1–2). Since Aquinas holds that it is difficult for us to grasp the real natures of corporeal objects, he claims that the sort of knowledge we can have of the natural world via natural science is for the most part non-paradigmatic *scientia* that relies on merely factual demonstrations the ultimate premisses of which are propositions about the accidental properties of sensible corporeal objects (*Commentary on Aristotle's Posterior Analytics* I.4). Similarly, since we cannot grasp God's essence, our knowledge of divine matters via natural theology is non-paradigmatic *scientia* deriving from propositions about sensible objects (*Commentary on Boethius's De Trinitate* 2; *Summa theologiae* Ia.1; *Summa contra gentiles* I.6–9).

WRITINGS

*Commentary on Aristotle's Posterior Analytics* trans. F. R. Larcher (Albany: Magi Books, 1970).
*Disputed Questions on Truth* trans. R. W. Mulligan, J. V. McGlynn and R. W. Schmidt (Chicago: Henry Regnery, 1952–54), 3 vols.
*Division and Methods of the Sciences* (Questions 5–6 of *Commentary on Boethius's De Trinitate*) trans. A. Maurer (Toronto: Pontifical Institute of Mediaeval Studies, 1986).
*Faith, Reason, and Theology* (Questions 1–4 of *Commentary on Boethius's De Trinitate*) trans. A. Maurer (Toronto: Pontifical Institute of Mediaeval Studies, 1987).
*Summa contra gentiles* trans. A. C. Pegis, J. F.

Anderson, V. J. Bourke and C. J. O'Neil (Notre Dame: University of Notre Dame Press, 1975), 5 vols.

*Summa theologiae* trans. Fathers of the English Dominican Province (Westminster: Christian Classics, 1981), 5 vols.

BIBLIOGRAPHY

Aertsen, J.: *Nature and Creature: Thomas Aquinas's Way of Thought* (Leiden: Brill, 1988).

Grabmann, M.: *Die theologische Erkenntnis- und Einleitungslehre des heiligen Thomas von Aquin* (Freiburg: Paulusverlag, 1948).

Kretzmann, N.: 'Infallibility, error, and ignorance', in *Aristotle and His Medieval Interpreters* ed. M. Tweedale (Supplementary volume to *Canadian Journal of Philosophy*, forthcoming).

Lonergan, B.: *Verbum: Word and Idea in Aquinas* (Notre Dame: University of Notre Dame Press, 1967).

MacDonald, S.: 'Aquinas's epistemology', in *Aquinas* eds N. Kretzmann and E. Stump (Cambridge: Cambridge University Press, 1992).

SCOTT MACDONALD

**argument** A group of statements, some of which purportedly provide support for another. The statements which purportedly provide the support are the *premises* while the statement purportedly supported is the *conclusion*. Arguments are typically divided into two categories depending on the *degree* of support they purportedly provide. *Deductive* arguments purportedly provide *conclusive* support for their conclusions while *inductive* arguments purportedly provide only *probable* support. Some, but not all, arguments succeed in providing support for their conclusions. Successful deductive arguments are valid while successful inductive arguments are strong. An argument is *valid* just in case if all its premises are true then its conclusion *must* be true. An argument is *strong* just in case if all its premises are true its conclusion is *only probably* true. Deductive logic provides methods for ascertaining whether or not an argument is valid whereas inductive logic provides methods for ascertaining the degree of support the premises of an argument confer on its conclusion.

*See also* INFORMAL FALLACIES; INDUCTION; PROOF.

BIBLIOGRAPHY

Haack, S.: *Philosophy of Logics* (Cambridge: Cambridge University Press, 1978).

Jeffrey, R.: *Formal Logic: Its Scope and Limits* 2nd edn (New York: McGraw-Hill, 1981).

Kahane, H.: *Logic and Philosophy* 6th edn (Belmont: Wadsworth, 1990).

Salmon, W.: *Logic* 2nd edn (Englewood Cliffs: Prentice-Hall, 1973).

Skyrms, B.: *Choice and Chance* 3rd edn (Belmont: Wadsworth, 1986).

ALBERT CASULLO

**argument from analogy** This argument is intended to establish our right to believe in the existence and nature of OTHER MINDS. It admits that it is *possible* that the objects we call persons are, other than ourselves, mindless automata, but claims that we none the less have sufficient reason for supposing this not to be the case. There is more evidence that they are not mindless automata than that they are.

The classic statement of the argument comes from J.S. Mill. He writes:

I am conscious in myself of a series of facts connected by an uniform sequence, of which the beginning is modifications of my body, the middle is feelings, the end is outward demeanour. In the case of other human beings, I have the evidence of my senses for the first and last links of the series, but not for the intermediate link. I find, however, that the sequence between the first and last is as regular and constant in those other cases as it is in mine. In my own case I know that the first link produces the last through the intermediate link, and could not produce it without. Experience, therefore, obliges me to conclude that there must be an intermediate link; which must either be the same in others as in myself, or a different one; . . . by supposing the link to be of the same nature . . . I conform to the legitimate rules of experimental enquiry. (1867, pp. 237–8)

As an inductive argument this is very weak, because it is condemned to arguing from a single case. But to this we might reply that none the less we have more evidence that there are other minds than that there are not.

The real criticism of the argument is due to WITTGENSTEIN (1953). It is that the argument assumes that we at least *understand* the claim that there are subjects of experience other than ourselves, who enjoy experiences which are like ours but not ours; it only asks what reason we have to suppose that claim true. But if the argument does indeed express the ground of our right to believe in the existence of others, it is impossible to explain how we are able to achieve that understanding. So if there is a place for the argument from analogy, the problem of other minds – the real, hard problem, which is how we acquire a conception of another mind – is insoluble. The argument is either redundant or worse.

*See also* OTHER MINDS; PRIVATE LANGUAGE ARGUMENT; SOLIPSISM; WITTGENSTEIN.

BIBLIOGRAPHY

Malcolm, N.: 'Knowledge of other minds', *Journal of Philosophy* 55 (1958), 969–78; reprinted in his *Knowledge and Certainty* (Englewood Cliffs: Prentice-Hall, 1963).
Mill, J. S.: *An Examination of Sir William Hamilton's Philosophy* 3rd edn (London: Longmans, 1867).
Wittgenstein, L.: *Philosophical Investigations* (Oxford: Blackwell, 1953).

JONATHAN DANCY

**argument from illusion** This is usually intended to establish that certain familiar facts about illusion disprove the theory of perception called naïve or DIRECT REALISM. There are, however, many dif-ferent versions of the argument which must be distinguished carefully. Some of these distinctions centre on the content of the premisses (the nature of the appeal to illusion); others centre on the interpretation of the conclusion (the kind of direct realism under attack). Let us begin by distinguishing importantly different versions of direct realism which one might take to be vulnerable to familiar facts about the possibility of perceptual illusion.

DIRECT REALISM

A crude statement of direct realism might go as follows. In perception, we sometimes directly perceive physical objects and their properties; we do not always perceive physical objects by perceiving something *else*, e.g. a sense-datum (*see* SENSE-DATA). There are, however, difficulties with this formulation of the view. For one thing a great many philosophers who are *not* direct realists would admit that it is a mistake to describe people as actually *perceiving* something other than a physical object. In particular, such philosophers might admit, we should never say that we *perceive* sense-data. To talk that way would be to suppose that we should model our understanding of our relationship to sense-data on our understanding of the ordinary use of perceptual verbs as they describe our relation to the physical world, and that is the last thing paradigm sense-datum theorists should want. At least many of the philosophers who objected to direct realism would prefer to express what they were objecting to in terms of a technical (and philosophically controversial) concept such as *acquaintance*. Using such a notion we could define direct realism this way: In *veridical* experience we are directly acquainted with parts (e.g. surfaces) or constituents of physical objects. A less cautious version of the view might drop the reference to veridical experience and claim simply that in all experience we are directly acquainted with parts or constituents of physical objects (*see* KNOWLEDGE BY ACQUAINTANCE/BY DESCRIPTION).

Because one can interpret the relation of

acquaintance or awareness as one that is not *epistemic*, i.e. not a kind of propositional knowledge, it is important to distinguish the above views read as *ontological* theses from a view one might call *epistemological direct realism*: In perception we are, on at least some occasions, non-inferentially justified in believing a proposition asserting the existence of a physical object (*see* DIRECT REALISM).

What relevance does illusion have for these two forms of direct realism?

## ILLUSION, HALLUCINATION AND DIRECT REALISM

The fundamental premiss of the argument from illusion seems to be the thesis that things can appear to be other than they are. Thus, for example, a straight stick when immersed in water looks bent; a penny when viewed from a certain perspective looks elliptical; something that is yellow when placed under red fluorescent light looks red. In all of these cases, one version of the argument goes, it is implausible to maintain that what we are directly acquainted with is the real nature of the object in question. Indeed, it is hard to see how we can be said to be aware of the real physical object at all. In the above illusions the things we were aware of actually *were* bent, elliptical and red, respectively. But, by hypothesis, the real physical objects lacked these properties. Thus we were not aware of the real physical objects.

So far, if the argument is relevant to any of the direct realisms distinguished above, it seems relevant only to the claim that in *all* sense experience we are directly acquainted with parts or constituents of physical objects. After all, even if in illusion we are not acquainted with physical objects, their surfaces, or their constituents, why should we conclude anything about the nature of our relation to the physical world in *veridical* experience?

We are supposed to discover the answer to this question by noticing the similarities between illusory experience and veridical experience and by reflecting on what makes illusion possible at all. Illusion can occur because the nature of the illusory experience is determined, not just by the nature of the object perceived, but also by other conditions, both external and internal. But all of our sensations are subject to these causal influences and it would be gratuitous and arbitrary to select from the indefinitely many and subtly different perceptual experiences some special ones as those which get us in touch with the 'real' nature of the physical world. Red fluorescent lights affect the way things look, but so does sunlight. Water reflects light, but so does air. We have no unmediated access to the external world.

Still, why should we conclude that we are aware of something other than a physical object in experience? Why should we not conclude that to be aware of a physical object just is to be appeared to by that object in a certain way? (*see* ADVERBIAL THEORY). There are indefinitely many ways in which objects appear to us but why not construe all of those ways of appearing as simply different kinds of direct appearing *relations* holding between us and the physical world? There is no need to infer that there is anything other than our yellow object under those red lights. We need only describe that yellow object as standing in the relation of appearing red to us.

At this point, it might be profitable to move from considering the possibility of illusion to considering the possibility of hallucination. Instead of comparing paradigmatic veridical perception to illusion, let us compare it to complete hallucination. For any experience or sequence of experiences we take to be veridical, we can imagine qualitatively indistinguishable experiences occurring as part of an hallucination. For those who like their philosophical arguments spiced with a touch of science, we can imagine that our brains were surreptitiously removed in the night, and unbeknown to us are being stimulated by a neurophysiologist so as to produce the very sensations that we would normally associate with a trip to the Grand Canyon. Now let us ask what we are aware of in this complete hallucination. Obviously we are not aware of physical objects, their surfaces, or their constituents. Nor can we even construe the experience as one of an object's appearing to us in a certain way. It is after all a complete hallucination and the objects we take to exist before us are simply not there. But if we compare hallucinatory experience with the qualitatively indistinguishable veridical experiences, should we not conclude that it would be *ad hoc* to suppose that in veridical experience we are aware of something radically different from what we are aware of in hallucinatory experience? Again, it might help to reflect on our belief that the *immediate* cause of hallucinatory experience and veridical experience might be the very same brain event, and it is surely implausible to suppose that the effects of this same cause are radically different – acquaintance with physical objects in the case of veridical experience; something else in the case of hallucinatory experience.

This version of the argument from hallucination would seem to address straightforwardly the ontological versions of direct realism. The argument is supposed to convince us that the ontological analysis of sensation in both veridical and hallucinatory experience should give us the same results, but in the hallucinatory case there is no plausible physical object, constituent of a physical object, or surface of a physical object with which we can identify experience. If we add one additional premiss we would also get an argument against epistemological direct realism. That premiss is that in a vivid hallucinatory experience we might have precisely the same justification for believing (falsely) what we do about the physical world as we do in the analogous, phenomenologically indistinguishable, veridical experience. But our justification for believing that there is a table before us in the course of a vivid hallucination of a table is surely not non-inferential in character. It certainly isn't if non-inferential justification is supposed to consist in some unproblematic access to the fact that makes true our belief – by hypothesis the table doesn't exist. But if the justification that hallucinatory experience gives us is the same as the justification we get from the parallel veridical experience, then we should not describe a veridical experience as giving

us non-inferential justification for believing in the existence of physical objects. In both cases we should say that we believe what we do about the physical world on the basis of what we know directly about the character of our experience.

## CRITICISMS

In this brief space, I can only sketch some of the objections that might be raised against arguments from illusion and hallucination. Let us begin with a criticism that accepts most of the presuppositions of the arguments. Even if the possibility of hallucination establishes that in some experience we are not acquainted with constituents of physical objects, it is not clear that it establishes that we are never acquainted with a constituent of physical objects. Suppose, for example, that we decide that in both veridical and hallucinatory experience we are acquainted with sense-data. At least some philosophers have tried to identify physical objects with 'bundles' of actual and possible sense-data (*see* PHENOMENALISM). Hallucinatory experience on this view is non-veridical precisely because the sense-data one is acquainted with in hallucination do not bear the appropriate relations to other actual and possible sense-data. But if such a view were plausible one could agree that one is acquainted with the same kind of thing in veridical and non-veridical experience but insist that there is still a sense in which in veridical experience one is acquainted with constituents of a physical object.

A different sort of objection to the argument from illusion or hallucination concerns its use in drawing conclusions we have not stressed in the above discussion. I mention this objection to underscore an important feature of the argument. At least some philosophers (Hume, for example) have stressed the rejection of direct realism on the road to an argument for general SCEPTICISM with respect to the physical world. Once one abandons epistemological direct realism, one has an uphill battle indicating how one can legitimately make the inference from sensation to physical objects. But a philosopher who appeals to the *existence* of illusion and hallucination to develop an argument for scepticism can be accused of having an epistemically self-defeating argument. One could justifiably infer sceptical conclusions from the existence of illusion and hallucination only if one justifiably believed that such experiences exist, but if one is justified in believing that illusion exists one must be justified in believing at least some facts about the physical world (for example, that straight sticks look bent in water). The key point to stress in replying to such arguments is that strictly speaking the philosophers in question need only appeal to the *possibility* of vivid illusion and hallucination. Although it would have been psychologically more difficult to come up with arguments from illusion and hallucination if we did not believe that we actually had such experiences, I take it that most philosophers would argue that the possibility of such experiences is enough to establish difficulties with direct realism. Indeed, if one looks carefully at the argument from hallucination discussed earlier, one sees that it nowhere makes any claims about actual cases of hallucinatory experience.

Another reply to the attack on epistemological direct realism focuses on the implausibility of claiming that there is any process of *inference* involved in our beliefs about the world around us. Even if it is possible to give a phenomenological description of the subjective character of sensation, it requires a special sort of skill that most people lack. Our perceptual beliefs about the physical world are surely direct at least in the sense that they are unmediated by any sort of conscious inference from premises describing something other than a physical object. The appropriate reply to this objection, however, is simply to acknowledge the relevant phenomenological fact and point out that from the perspective of an epistemologist it is beside the point. In attacking epistemological direct realism, the philosopher is attacking a claim about the nature of our justification for believing propositions about the physical world. Such a philosopher need make no comment at all about the causal genesis of such beliefs.

I have mentioned that proponents of the argument from illusion and hallucination have often intended it to establish the existence of sense-data, and many philosophers have attacked the so-called sense-datum inference presupposed in some statements of the argument. When the stick looked bent, the penny looked elliptical and the yellow object looked red, the sense-datum theorist wanted to infer that there was something bent, elliptical and red, respectively. But such an inference is surely suspect. In general we do not infer that because something appears to have a certain property, there is something that has that property. When I say that Jones looks like a doctor, I surely wouldn't want anyone to infer that there must actually be someone there who is a doctor. In assessing this objection it will be important to distinguish different uses of words like 'appears' and 'looks'. At least sometimes to say that something looks F is only to express a tentative belief that it is F and the sense-datum inference from an F 'appearance' in this sense to an actual F would be hopeless. However, it also seems that we use the 'appears'/'looks' terminology to describe the phenomenological character of our experience and the inference might be more plausible when the terms are used this way. Still, it does seem to me that the arguments from illusion and hallucination will not by themselves constitute strong evidence for a sense-datum theory. Even if one concludes that there is something common to both the hallucination of a red thing and a veridical visual experience of a red thing, one need not describe that common constituent as awareness of something red. The adverbial theorist would prefer to construe the common experiential state as 'being appeared to redly', a technical description intended only to convey the idea that the state in question need not be analysed as relational in character. Those who opt for an ADVERBIAL THEORY of sensation need to make good the claim that their artificial adverbs can be given a sense that is not parasitic upon an understanding of the adjectives transformed into adverbs. Still other philosophers might try to reduce the common element in veridical and non-veridical experience to some kind of intentional state, more like belief or judgement. The idea here is that the only thing common to the two experiences is the fact that in both I spontaneously take there to be present an object of a certain kind. The above objections can be stated within the general framework presupposed by proponents of the arguments from illusion and hallucination. A great many contemporary philosophers are, however, uncomfortable with the intelligibility of the concepts needed to even make sense of the theories attacked. Thus at least some who object to the argument from illusion do so not because they defend direct realism. Rather they think there is something confused about all this talk of direct awareness or acquaintance. Contemporary EXTERNALISTS, for example, usually insist that we understand epistemic concepts by appeal to nomological connections. On such a view the closest thing to *direct* knowledge would probably be something like a judgement which is not *caused* by other beliefs. If we understand direct knowledge this way, it is not clear how the phenomena of illusion and hallucination would be relevant to the claim that on at least some occasions our judgements about the physical world are reliably produced by processes that do not take as their input beliefs about something else.

*See also* DIRECT REALISM; PHENOMENALISM; PROBLEM OF THE EXTERNAL WORLD; REPRESENTATIVE REALISM.

BIBLIOGRAPHY

Austin, J. L.: *Sense and Sensibilia* (Oxford: Oxford University Press, 1968).
Ayer, A. J.: *The Problem of Knowledge* (Edinburgh: Penguin, 1956).
Barnes, W. H. F.: 'The myth of sense-data', *Proceedings of the Aristotelian Society* 45 (1944-5), 89-117.
Price, H.H.: *Perception* (London: Methuen, 1932).
Russell, B.: *The Problems of Philosophy* (Oxford: Oxford University Press, 1959).
Sellars, W.: *Science. Perception and Reality* (London: Routledge and Kegan Paul, 1963);
see especially 'Empiricism and the Philosophy of Mind'.

RICHARD FUMERTON

**Aristotle (384–322 BC)** Greek philosopher, born in Stagira in northern Greece. Aristotle is influenced by questions raised in PLATO's dialogues (especially the *Meno* and *Theaetetus*) about the definition of knowledge and the conditions for justification. Though none of his works is devoted exclusively or primarily to epistemology, he discusses many epistemological problems. Different discussions seem to rely on different, sometimes conflicting, epistemological assumptions. (We might seek to resolve this conflict by tracing a development in Aristotle's thought.) He discusses several of the issues that become explicit topics of debate among Hellenistic philosophers; indeed both sides in some Hellenistic debates can claim support from Aristotle. It is particularly useful to trace his tendencies towards acceptance of a foundationalist view of justification, and some tendencies towards accepting some form of coherence as the appropriate condition for justification.

I. THE CONCEPT OF KNOWLEDGE

The Aristotelian terms usually translated by 'know' are '*epistasthai*' (cognate abstract noun: '*epistêmê*'), '*gignôskein*' ('*gnôsis*') and '*eidenai*'. '*Gignôskein*' and '*eidenai*' are used in many contexts, and applied to knowledge of many different sorts of propositions (about general laws, particular facts, observable and non-observable states of affairs, and so on); '*epistasthai*', by contrast, sometimes refers specifically to scientific knowledge. Moreover, '*epistêmê*' may refer either (a) to a body of truths known, or (b) to the state of someone who knows them; hence in sense (a) mathematics or astronomy counts as an *epistêmê* (so that 'science' is the proper translation), and in sense (b) someone who knows such a science counts as having *epistêmê* (so that 'knowledge' is the proper translation). The primary example of an *epistêmê* (in sense (a)) is a demonstrative science (*see* 2 below), but it is not the only example. Aristotle does not confine his use of the term '*epistêmê*' to demonstrative science; crafts and disciplines that lack a rigorous demonstrative structure are also cases of *epistêmê*.

There is no reason to deny that Aristotle is discussing questions about knowledge; but the examples of knowledge that he has in mind are not always those that would seem most natural to us (though they come to seem more natural if we think of epistemology as continuous with the philosophy of science). His explicit comments are mostly about *epistêmê*; and sometimes we need to take this into account in order to see what he assumes about knowledge in general.

## 2. THE NATURE OF KNOWLEDGE

In the *Posterior Analytics* Aristotle states explicit conditions for knowledge. This is Aristotle's major work on the structure of scientific knowledge (*epistêmê*); it is not an account of how to acquire such knowledge (on which see 4 below), but an account of what we must have acquired if we are to count as possessing such knowledge.

A scientific theory that expresses genuine knowledge must be demonstrative. A demonstrative science has a rigorously deductive structure; it is arranged in demonstrative syllogisms which present the theorems of the science as deductions from first principles that are necessarily true, prior to and better known than the conclusions, and explanatory of the conclusions derived from them. Aristotle assumes (cf. Plato, *Meno* 98a) that if I know that *p*, then (1) I can justify my belief that *p*, and (2) I know the justification *q*. He insists on (2) because it does not seem satisfactory if I can simply *state q*; it seems reasonable to demand that I should also know why *q* is true and why *q* justifies *p* (*Post. An.* i 2).

To satisfy this second condition, three options are available: (a) An infinite regress; (b) A circle: my sequence of justifications avoids an infinite regress because it eventually comes back to the original belief that I sought to justify; (c) Foundationalism: some propositions are self-justifying, so that we can know them (or have some other suitable cognitive relation to them) without justifying them by appeal to any other propositions, and these are the basis for our knowledge of other propositions.

Hellenistic Sceptics, especially Agrippa, reject all three options, and so conclude that justification, and hence knowledge, is impossible. Aristotle agrees with them (in anticipation) in rejecting the first two options; he disagrees with them, however (*Post. An.* i 3), in so far as he accepts the third option; in his view, we have a self-justifying intuitive grasp (*nous: Post. An.* ii 19) of the first principles of each science.

Aristotle's argument, then, is a statement of a FOUNDATIONALIST position. His candidates for fundamental, self-justifying propositions are rather surprising; they are the basic principles of specific sciences. These are different from, say, the basic axioms recognized by Descartes as objects of intuition; Aristotelian *nous* extends to these, but not only to these. Aristotle's first principles differ even more sharply from the sensory states or propositions that count as basic for an empiricist foundationalist (though Aristotle may be a foundationalist about these too; see the next two sections). Given Aristotle's conception of a science, the first principles cannot be justified by anything more fundamental within the science of which they are principles. But it is natural to argue that the scientific theory as a whole has to be justified by reference to the empirical evidence and other considerations that lead us to construct one sort of theory rather than another. (This might be taken as an objection to Aristotle, or as an objection to the interpretation just suggested.) Aristotle certainly agrees that scientific theory has to be founded on the applicable empirical observations and other relevant considerations. But he does not explain how he reconciles this relation of theory to experience with the epistemological status that he claims for the first principles of a scientific theory.

## 3. PERCEPTION AND KNOWLEDGE

Aristotle's discussion of the epistemology of sense-perception appears in *De Anima* ii–iii, as part of his account of the nature of perception as a capacity of the soul, to be compared and contrasted with imagination, thought and desire. He offers three formulae for the understanding of perception: (F1) The perceiver becomes like the object (417a18). (F2) The perceiver that was potentially F (e.g. white) becomes actually F when it perceives the actually F object (418a3). (F3) The perceiver acquires the form, but not the matter, of the object (424a18–24). F3 is intended to capture the truth in F1–2 without the misleading suggestion that the perceiver becomes physically similar to the object. The 'form without the matter' expresses a systematic correspondence between features of the perceiver and features of the object without implying physical similarity. (The nose does not smell like an onion when we smell an onion.)

The three formulae of perception assume a realist view of perception (so that an object is white, square, etc. in its own right, whether or not we perceive it as such). Aristotle seems to intend to hold this realist view throughout his discussion of perception, but some of his remarks do not seem to be consistent with it. At one point he claims that when an object is perceived as red, it becomes actually red, and its becoming red consists in its being perceived as red. This claim seems to conflict with F1–3 for they assume the objective existence of real perceptible qualities independent of the perceiver, but the claim about when something is 'actually red' seems to imply that the existence of red etc. depends on their being perceived. (For Aristotle's attempt to resolve this apparent conflict in his view, see 426a20–6.) Aristotle seems to take this view partly because he believes that each sense is infallible about its special objects (427b8–16); and he intends this view as a defence against sceptical attacks on the senses (Met. 1010b14–26). But his claim about 'actual' redness does not show that the senses are infallible about the external (perceiver-independent) qualities of objects; and so it does not seem to meet the most serious sceptical arguments.

Aristotle attributes to a 'common sense' the perception of size, shape and number, which are all perceived by motion (425a14–20). These are related to, though not the same as, the properties that Plato calls 'common'. Plato argues that certain properties are common, in contrast to the proper objects of particular senses, because they are grasped by the rational soul itself, not by the senses (Tht. 184–6); Aristotle, however, rejects Plato's argument, suggesting instead that these properties are grasped by a unified faculty of perception. He may be influenced by the assumption that perception by itself, without interpretation or further inference, is a reliable foundation for claims to knowledge; and this assumption may rest in turn on foundationalist assumptions about justification.

4. METHOD

Aristotle discusses the proper method of inquiry in empirical science and in philosophical argument. The similarities and differences that he sees between the two forms of inquiry throw some light on his epistemological outlook.

His descriptions of empirical inquiry suggest that it proceeds from perceptual observations ('appearances', *phainomena*) through induction (*epagôgê*) until we reach experience (*empeiria*), which is the best way to reach first principles: 'Hence it is a task for experience to supply the principles about a given area. . . . For if our inquiry (*historia*) leaves out none of the facts that truly hold of things, we will be able to find and produce a demonstration of whatever admits of demonstration, and if something does not admit of demonstration, to make this evident also' (*Prior An.* 46a17–27). Aristotle's own *Historia Animalium*, for instance, is a collection of appearances introduced as preliminary to the exposition of the theory (see HA 491a7–14, PA 640a12–16). Aristotle recognizes observation and experience not only as the basis for forming theories, but also as a means of testing them; and for this purpose he advocates the collection of new observations (see GA 760b28–33). His general description of empirical inquiry is intelligible in the light of the foundationalist attitudes we have traced elsewhere.

29

His attitude to philosophical inquiry seems different from his attitude to empirical inquiry, even though he describes both forms of inquiry in rather similar terms, as beginning from 'appearances'. In describing philosophical argument, he says 'We must, as in the other cases, set out the appearances, and then first raise the puzzles [about them]. In this way we must prove, ideally, all the common beliefs, and if not all of them, at least most of them, and the most important. For if the difficulties are dissolved, and the common beliefs are left standing, that will be a sufficient proof' (*Nic. Ethics* 1145a2–7). This method is dialectical, and Aristotle thinks dialectical inquiry is the appropriate way to advance towards the first principles of the sciences (*Topics* 101a36–b4). In this case the 'appearances' are 'common beliefs' (*endoxa*), the views of 'the many and the wise' (*Topics* 104a8); they are not confined (as they characteristically are in the case of empirical inquiry) to perceptual observations. Appearances do not appear to play the foundational role in dialectical inquiry that they play in empirical inquiry. In dialectical inquiry Aristotle recognizes that it may be appropriate to reject some common beliefs if they do not fit with what seems, on other grounds, to be the best theory. In this case his arguments seem to appeal to considerations of COHERENCE that reject any appeal to an infallible foundation. The epistemology underlying Aristotle's own philosophical argument is difficult to reconcile with some of the epistemological assumptions that he sometimes seems to accept. We can illustrate this tension in Aristotle's thinking by examining some of his anti-sceptical arguments.

## 5. REPLIES TO SCEPTICISM

In *Metaphysics* iv Aristotle discusses several challenges to propositions that he regards as basic first principles. He includes a discussion (iv 5) of sceptical arguments about the senses. These arguments are derived from conflicting appearances, as follows: (1) Different people's perceptual appearances conflict (e.g. the water seems cold to me and hot to you, the tower seems square to me and round to you). (2) There is no reason to prefer one appearance over the other (they are 'equipollent'). (3) Hence we should suspend judgement about which appearance is true (*Met.* 1009a38–b12; cf. Sextus, *Pyrr. Hyp.* i 8, 10).

Aristotle denies that conflicting perceptual appearances are always equipollent. He insists that we often have a satisfactory criterion for preferring one of a pair of conflicting appearances over the other. He recognizes that the criterion itself may be challenged; but he rejects the challenges (1010b3–11). Since discrimination between appearances is not as difficult as the sceptic suggests it is, the sceptic's problem does not arise.

The sceptic assumes that (1) we are justified in believing that p only if we can prove p by appeal to some further principle q; and (2) we can prove p in this way only if we are justified in believing q independently of believing p, and we can produce the proof of all the predecessors of p (i.e. of q, of the justification of q, . . . etc.). We can stop an infinite regress only if the sceptic agrees to a principle; but he will not agree to one, because at each stage he can demand a further proof (Sextus, *Pyrr. Hyp.* ii 53). Aristotle rejects the sceptic's assumptions. He argues that his opponents have the wrong conception of the proper sort of justification; they look for demonstrations when they should not (1006a5–11, 1011a3–13). In asking why we believe the doctor, or how we can tell we are awake, the sceptics keep asking for a further principle, so that they will not have to take anything on trust without a demonstration. But this demand will never yield the right sort of justification; 'it would go on to infinity, so that there would be no demonstration that way either' (1006a8–9). Once the sceptics see that the demand for demonstration is the source of their puzzles, and is itself an unreasonable demand, they will give up their challenge (1011a11–16).

Aristotle might mean that a good reply to the sceptic will point to infallible self-justifying foundations that we can rely on to provide the sorts of criteria that are beyond sceptical doubt or question. In fact, however, his reply to the sceptic seems to undermine the assumptions that would lead us to look for that sort of foundation. For he seems to suggest that a criterion need not be, or rest on, some infallible foundation; it only needs to be one that we have good reason – in the light of the rest of our beliefs – for accepting. If this is what Aristotle means, then he appeals to coherence. But he does not pursue the issue far enough to formulate or defend the epistemological assumptions underlying his reply to scepticism.

*See also* SEXTUS EMPIRICUS.

WRITINGS

A convenient translation of Aristotle's complete works is *The Complete Works of Aristotle: The Revised Oxford Translation* 2 vols (Princeton: Princeton University Press, 1984). The Clarendon Aristotle series contains useful commentaries on individual works: J. Barnes (trans. and ed.) *Posterior Analytics* (Oxford: Clarendon, 1975); D. W. Hamlyn (trans. and ed.) *De Anima* (1968); C. A. Kirwan (trans. and ed.) *Metaphysics* iv. v, vi (1971).

BIBLIOGRAPHY

A helpful survey of Aristotle's epistemology (including discussion of his moral epistemology) is C. C. W. Taylor, 'Aristotle's epistemology', in *Epistemology*, ed. S. Everson (Cambridge: Cambridge University Press, 1990), ch. 6. For a longer treatment of the topics discussed in this entry *see* T. H. Irwin, *Aristotle's First Principles* (Oxford: Clarendon, 1988), chs 2–3, 6–9, 14. For further bibliography, see Everson (above) and *Articles on Aristotle*, eds J. Barnes, M. Schofield, and R. Sorabji (London: Duckworth, 1975–9), especially vols 1 and 4. On the connection of some issues in Aristotle with issues in more recent epistemology, *see* R. M. Chisholm, *The Foundations of Knowing* (Minneapolis: University of Minnesota Press, 1982).

TERENCE IRWIN

**Armstrong, David M. (1926–)** Born in Melbourne, Australia, Armstrong taught at the University of London and at Melbourne University, and was Challis Professor of Philosophy at Sydney University, 1964–91. Besides his work in epistemology, his main contributions to philosophy have been in philosophy of mind and metaphysics.

There are two strands to Armstrong's work in epistemology, which make it distinctive. First, Armstrong revives an idea that originated in the work of F. P. Ramsey, which he calls RELIABILISM. The central core of reliabilism (for non-inferential knowledge) is the identification of knowledge with nomically reliable true belief, i.e. belief that arises as a result of the law-like connection between ourselves and the world. If one is placed before a tree and has all of one's faculties, then the belief that is formed as a result of the perception counts as knowledge because the nomic relation between the tree and the perceptual process serves as an objective justification of the belief. This justification is OBJECTIVE rather than subjective because the individual need not, and indeed may not, be aware of the requisite nomic relation in order to be justified in having the belief.

The analogy that Armstrong favours for this model of knowledge is given by the thermometer. A thermometer is a reliable guide to the temperature because there is a nomic relation between the two. The thermometer correctly represents the amount of heat in a room in the same way that a belief about the tree correctly represents the external environment. Thus, in a sense, belief measures the environment.

For inferential knowledge Armstrong appeals to the framework of classical deductive logic and scientific INDUCTION. The use of the latter he justifies by INFERENCE TO THE BEST EXPLANATION. A sighting of many black ravens and no non-black ones serves to justify the generalization 'All ravens are black', in the sense that it is more probable given the evidence than any alternative hypothesis (*see* HEMPEL'S PARADOX). Thus the best explanation for the sighting of only black ravens is that all ravens are, in fact, black. Armstrong is thus opposed to a Humean scepticism concerning induction (*see* PROBLEMS OF INDUCTION) without feeling the need to align himself to any formal inductive logic in the manner of CARNAP.

Armstrong argues that this response to inductive scepticism follows from a belief in strong laws of nature. Armstrong conceives of laws as contingent relations between universals, and calls these strong laws. Since laws are conceived of as more than simply universal generalisations the justification of induction is able to rest upon its shoulders. The property of Blackness is tied to the property of Ravenhood, and that is why it is reasonable to assert the generalization that all ravens are black given a sample.

The second major strand to Armstrong's thought in epistemology is a belief in the Moorean certainties. Like MOORE, and unlike RUSSELL, Armstrong believes that some of our beliefs are so fundamental that philosophical doubt cannot be rationally entertained. He believes, for example, that one cannot seriously entertain a rational doubt that one has a body. Any philosophical speculation designed to produce such a doubt would require an argument with some contingent premiss that is more assertible than the doubted proposition and, in this case, such a one cannot be found.

The belief in Moorean certainties is intimately related to Armstrong's REALISM. The existence of the external world is a Moorean certainty, its character the object of scientific discovery, and the only entities a metaphysics should postulate are those required by good scientific explanations.

*See also* CAUSAL THEORIES IN EPISTE-MOLOGY; DIRECT REALISM; INTROSPEC-TION; KNOWLEDGE AND BELIEF; OTHER MINDS; SELF-KNOWLEDGE AND SELF-IDENTITY.

WRITINGS

*A Materialist Theory of Mind* (London: Routledge & Kegan Paul, 1968), esp. ch. 10.
*Belief, Truth and Knowledge* (Cambridge: Cambridge University Press, 1973).
'Epistemological foundations for a materialist theory of mind', in his *The Nature of Mind* (Brighton: Harvester Press, 1981).

'What makes induction rational?', in *Dialogue*, forthcoming.

ADRIAN HEATHCOTE

**association** A relation between two or more ideas such that the appearance of one of them in the mind naturally leads one or more of the others to appear there. Locke appealed to 'the association of ideas' to explain certain sorts of error that the mind seems naturally prone to, as when the 'wrong' idea appears instead of the associated 'right' one. For HUME the discovery of the 'principles of association' was as central to the task of a positive science of the human mind as he thought the principle of universal gravitation had been to an understanding of physical nature. No particular associations were seen as intrinsic to a given idea; they are established in each individual mind only by repeated experience. Hume thought all comings and goings of mental items, or all transitions in our thinking, are instances of one or another of only three 'principles of association': resemblance, contiguity, and cause and effect. These are '*to us* the cement of the universe'. This led to an 'associationist' movement or school of psychology which envisaged systematic explanations of all human behaviour along similar lines. Early experimental psychology studied the ways in which associations are originally established.

BIBLIOGRAPHY

Hume, D.: *A Treatise of Human Nature* (1739) ed. L. A. Selby-Bigge, revised P. H. Nidditch (Oxford: Oxford University Press, 1978).
Hume, D.: *An Enquiry Concerning Human Understanding* (1748) in *Enquiries Concerning Human Understanding and Concerning the Principles of Morals* ed. L. A. Selby-Bigge, revised P. H. Nidditch (Oxford: Oxford University Press, 1975).
Locke, J.: *An Essay Concerning Human Understanding* (London, 1690); ed. P. H. Nidditch (Oxford: Clarendon Press, 1975).

BARRY STROUD

**ataraxia** A Greek term sometimes translated by 'tranquillity', it refers to a state of mind characterized by the absence of disturbance or stress, which was cultivated by Pyrrhonian sceptics in antiquity. Sceptics equated *ataraxia* with the end (*telos*) of scepticism, that for the sake of which sceptical argumentation was undertaken, and the most desirable state of human existence. The Pyrrhonian view was that *ataraxia* resulted from suspending belief about the nature of reality. To that end sceptics argued against all dogmatic philosophical theories. Claiming Pyrrho as a model of philosophical detachment and tranquility, sceptics regarded philosophy primarily as a practical enterprise and a way of life.

*See also* PYRRHONISM; SEXTUS EMPIRICUS.

CHARLOTTE STOUGH

**Augustine, St (354–430)** Theologian, Bishop of Hippo in North Africa. Augustine builds his epistemology around an account of our certain knowledge of necessary truth. His paradigms of this sort of truth include basic mathematical and logical truths such as '7 + 3 = 10' and 'there is one world or it is not the case that there is one world' (*De libero arbitrio* II.8.83, *Contra academicos* III.10.23), but also propositions about value and morality ('what is incorruptible is better than what is corruptible', 'we should live justly'; *De libero arbitrio* II.10.110–14). Certain knowledge of truths of this sort rests on direct awareness of their necessity, immutability and eternality. He groups together with these logically necessary propositions a small group of contingent propositions that can be known with certainty ('I exist', 'I seem to see white'; *De civitate Dei* XI.26, *Contra academicos* III.11.26). He appeals to our knowledge of particular truths of these sorts to establish against the sceptic the general possibility of knowledge.

Augustine argues that it follows from the nature of the paradigm objects of knowledge that truth is perceptible only by the mind or reason (*mens, ratio*) and not by sense perception (*see* PLATO). Since all objects of the senses are contingent and mutable we cannot have knowledge through sense perception. We discern intelligible objects directly by turning within the immaterial soul and away from sense perception and the material world (*De libero arbitrio* II.8, *Confessiones* III–IV, VII.10). He develops his notion of direct acquaintance in terms of the metaphors of light and vision. Just as our seeing material objects depends on their being illuminated by the light of the sun, our intellectual vision of intelligible objects depends on their being illuminated by an intelligible light, truth itself (*De libero arbitrio* II.8.92, 9.108, 12.130, *Soliloquia* 18.15). Hence, knowledge of immutable, eternal truths requires direct acquaintance not only with certain kinds of objects but also with the fact that those objects have the property of being necessary, immutable and eternal. Augustine identifies truth itself with God, who is himself necessary, immutable, and eternal, and hence maintains that our knowledge of truth rests on divine illumination (*Confessiones* IV.15, VII.10, *Soliloquia* I.6.12).

Augustine distinguishes between beliefs grounded in this sort of intellectual vision and beliefs justified in other ways (*De utilitate credendi* 11.25). The former sort constitutes paradigm or strict knowledge (*scientia, sapientia*), and when a belief is grounded in this way we can be said to have understanding (*intellectus*). The latter constitutes mere belief or (when the justification is sufficient) knowledge only in a broad sense (*Retractationes* I.14.3). The justification associated with understanding differs from that associated with mere belief not only in degree but also in kind. Understanding of a proposition requires evidence that is internally related to the proposition, so that one possesses the reason for the truth of the proposition. Other sorts of evidence – for example, TESTIMONY – can provide justification but are only externally related to the propositions they support. One can be said to know (in a broad sense) a theorem of geometry, for example, when one believes it on the testimony of a geometer, but one can be said to understand that theorem only when one grasps its proof. Augustine holds that a vast number of our beliefs – for example, all those about events and places we have not ourselves experienced and about other people's beliefs and attitudes – rest on the testimony of others and that, despite the fact that beliefs based on testimony lack the paradigm sort of justification provided by intellectual vision, we are nevertheless epistemically justified in holding many beliefs of this sort (*De utilitate credendi* 9.22–10.23, 11.25).

Augustine's famous recommendation that, in theological matters, one ought to believe in order that one may attain understanding is based in part on his distinction between kinds of justification. The testimony of Scripture and the Church (validated both by their historical reliability and by miracles) sufficiently grounds propositions of Christian doctrine so that we are justified in accepting them (*Confessiones* VI.5, *De utilitate credendi* 14.32–16.34). Nevertheless creatures possessing reason can (and perhaps are obligated to) acquire understanding of those propositions to some degree; that is, acquire for those propositions a basis of the sort provided by intellectual vision (*Epistola* CXX). Augustine's work in philosophical theology is an attempt to provide for propositions of Christian doctrine, which are justifiably believed on testimony, the sort of internal justification necessary for understanding.

WRITINGS

*Confessions*, trans. R. S. Pine-Coffin (Harmondsworth: Penguin, 1961).

*Contra academicos*, trans. M. P. Garvey (Milwaukee: Marquette University Press, 1957).

*De civitate Dei*, trans. H. Bettenson (Harmondsworth: Penguin, 1972).

*De libero arbitrio*, trans. A. S. Benjamin and L. H. Hackstaff (New York: Macmillan, 1964).

*De utilitate credendi* and *Soliloquia*, trans. J. H. S. Burleigh, *Augustine: Earlier Writings* (Philadelphia: Westminster Press, 1953), 291–323 and 23–63.

*Epistola* CXX, trans. W. Parsons, *Saint Augustine: Letters 83–130* (New York: Fathers of the Church, 1953), 300–17.

*Retractationes*, trans. M. I. Bogan (Washington, D.C.: Catholic University of America Press, 1968).

BIBLIOGRAPHY

Gilson, E.: *The Christian Philosophy of Saint Augustine* trans. L. E. M. Lynch (New York: Random House, 1960), Part One.

Kretzmann, N.: 'Faith seeks, understanding finds: Augustine's charter for Christian philosophy', in *Christian Philosophy* ed. T. P. Flint (Notre Dame: University of Notre Dame Press, 1990), pp. 1–36.

Markus, R. A.: 'Augustine: reason and illumination' and 'Augustine: sense and imagination', in *Cambridge History of Later Greek and Early Medieval Philosophy* ed. A. H. Armstrong (Cambridge: Cambridge University Press, 1967), chs 23 and 24.

Nash, R. H.: *The Light of the Mind: Saint Augustine's Theory of Knowledge* (Lexington: The University Press of Kentucky, 1969).

SCOTT MACDONALD

**Austin, John L(angshaw) (1911–60)** British philosopher, who spent his working life at Oxford. Austin, like RYLE, adopted a revolutionary approach to philosophy. Like Ryle he saw philosophy as an attempt to map families of concepts, such as excuses in 'A plea for excuses', and, like Ryle, his primary interest was in the rich and complex terms of everyday discourse. Austin's interest in epistemology cannot therefore be regarded as a straightforward contribution to its traditional debates. He sought instead to show that traditional issues and rivalries were often spurious or confused. Two publications in particular mark Austin's attention to this project, namely his influential paper 'Other minds' and his book *Sense and Sensibilia*. In the former he examines a traditional scepticism about knowledge; in the latter he queries a traditional defence of PHENOMENALISM largely due to A. J. Ayer. In two papers, 'Truth' and 'Unfair to facts', Austin outlines his account of truth. Beyond that, his work on moral issues in 'A plea for excuses' and 'If's and can's', and on speech acts in 'Performative utterances' and *How To Do Things With Words* falls strictly outside the scope of epistemology, though it follows the same revolutionary path.

In 'Other minds' the novelty of his approach is made clear from the start, for he claims not to understand the very terms in which the traditional debate about knowledge is couched. He seeks to make headway instead by examining the ways in which we use the term 'know'. He considers a number of examples of 'statements of particular current empirical fact' (1961, p. 45) which we may claim to know in order to explore the ways in which such a claim might properly be queried and defended. If my claim 'There's a bittern' is queried by asking 'Do you know?' or 'How do you know?' I may reply by citing, *inter alia*, my past experience ('I was brought up in the Fens'), my current evidence ('I hear it') or some specific feature ('Because of its booming'). Such responses in their appeal to expertise, authority and to possible specific illusions or mistakes throw light on the commitments involved in saying appropriately 'I know' rather than merely 'I believe'.

Austin held that there was some analogy between the commitments involved in saying 'I know' and in saying 'I promise'. He thought also that mistakes had been made in theory of knowledge through what he called the 'descriptive fallacy', that is, the mistake of assuming that uses of language such as 'I know' could function only in a descriptive way. He thought that fallacy in part was responsible for the view that 'belief' and 'knowledge' described mental states in which the latter is simply a superior, and perhaps infallible, version of the former. His own view quite explicitly was that we are always liable to be mistaken and that it was futile to embark on a theory of knowledge which denied this liability.

One common criticism has been that Austin's account deals only with the conditions for *claiming to know* rather than with the conditions for *knowing*. It has also been thought that a failure to recognize this distinction led Austin into the fallacy of supposing that if it is appropriate to make a claim, then that claim must be true. But Austin explicitly marks the required distinction when he says, 'We are often right to say we know even in cases where we turn out subsequently to have been mistaken' (1961, p. 66). Austin's interest was more in exploring and classifying our uses of 'know' than in

providing a traditional definition of knowledge in terms of necessary and sufficient conditions. His own programme moved away from what he regarded as a sterile tradition towards a more progressive task. It did not require him to suppose that his own enquiry was actually a contribution to that sterile debate.

In *Sense and Sensibilia* Austin applied the same approach to traditional debates about perception. His target in this context was principally, though not exclusively, the phenomenalism outlined in AYER's *Foundations of Empirical Knowledge*. Here too Austin believed that traditional assumptions had been unclear or erroneous, and that progress was to be made not by clinging to the traditional framework but by rejecting it. Austin recognized that Ayer's theory had the advantage of a modern formulation, but he thought of Ayer's project as irredeemably traditionalist.

His main objections to Ayer are that the phenomenalists' crucial introduction of the term 'sense-datum' was based on errors and misunderstandings, and that its subsequent use led philosophical thinking about perception astray. He thought that the naive opposition between 'physical (or material) object' and 'sense-datum' presented a misleadingly simple picture of the objects of perception which in turn encouraged an impoverished choice between NAIVE REALISM and phenomenalism. Austin's procedure here parallels that of other philosophers, such as Kant, Wittgenstein and Ryle, who sought to show that opposed traditional theories were all mistaken because each of them, and the belief that one had to choose between them, rested on erroneous assumptions.

Austin claimed that the traditional ARGUMENT FROM ILLUSION failed to distinguish 'illusion' from 'delusion' and 'hallucination', failed to give an adequate account of such terms as 'looks', 'seems' and 'appears', and subverted the common use of the term 'real'. Since Austin held that these complex discriminations marked our understanding of perceptual error he thought that there was no single coherent 'argument from illusion' and that its generalized conclusion introducing the term 'sense-datum' was therefore unjustified. He points out the error of thinking that in cases of illusion, and in uses of 'appear', what is presented to us is not part of a public, physical world. He believed that in arguments such as Ayer's the opposition 'physical object/sense-datum' had been erroneously conflated with the 'real/apparent' distinction.

Ayer defended himself against Austin's attack in 'Has Austin refuted sense-data?', but he did not succeed in reviving phenomenalism. Ayer makes a number of concessions to Austin's criticism, but where he rejects that criticism he tends to assume that terms like 'sense-datum statement' or his preferred alternative 'experiential statement' are perfectly clear and legitimate. He thus tends to beg the question against Austin's central complaint. Ayer persists in the simple opposition between 'experiential statement' and 'physical object statement', though he now concedes that this distinction no longer needs the traditional argument from illusion. But Ayer's new account of this distinction remains questionable. For the claim is that physical object statements allow the possibility of mistake just because they 'go beyond' immediate presentation to the senses, while this is not true of 'experiential statements'. Despite this Ayer now holds that experiential statements are not incorrigible. His position may not be simply inconsistent; but it remains unclear how we are to identify statements which are corrigible but not susceptible of mistake.

*See also* AYER; SCEPTICISM; SENSE-DATA.

WRITINGS

*Philosophical Papers* (Oxford: Oxford University Press, 1961).
*Sense and Sensibilia* (Oxford: Oxford University Press, 1962).
*How To Do Things With Words* (Oxford: Oxford University Press, 1962).

BIBLIOGRAPHY

Ayer, A. J.: 'Has Austin refuted sense-data?' *Synthese* 17 (1967): reprinted in Fann (1969).
Fann, K. T. ed.: *A Symposium on J. L. Austin* (London: Routledge and Kegan Paul, 1969).
Stroud, B.: *The Significance of Philosophical Scepticism* (Oxford: Oxford University Press, 1985).

GRAHAM BIRD

**avowals** The verb 'to avow' has been adopted by many philosophers of mind as the translation of the German verb '*äussern*'. The usual alternative translations are 'to express' or 'to utter'.

In WITTGENSTEIN's later work avowals are the keystone of a new philosophy of mind, founded on the rejection of the CARTESIAN idea that a person discloses the contents of his mind by identifying inner objects and describing them. According to Wittgenstein, an avowal of an intention is not based on a self-examination which parallels the investigation of the world around us: it is only marginally liable to error; and in certain cases is an artificial expression of the intention replacing a natural one (e.g. a raised fist). Each of these three points makes its contribution to the new philosophy of mind, which some of Wittgenstein's followers have accepted in its entirety and which, perhaps, nobody can totally reject. But the third point may be the most important one, because it shows how language can develop directly out of behaviour which antedates it. This makes it possible to explain how we can learn, and communicate with, mentalistic language, which were things that remained mysterious when intentions, feelings, etc. were treated as private objects. So it prepares the way for a NATURALISTIC, rather than an intellectualist answer to scepticism about other minds.

*See also* OTHER MINDS; SELF-KNOWLEDGE AND SELF-IDENTITY; WITTGENSTEIN.

BIBLIOGRAPHY

Malcolm, N.: *Nothing is Hidden* (Oxford: Blackwell, 1986), esp. ch. 8.
Wittgenstein, L.: *Philosophical Investigations* trans. G. E. M. Anscombe (Oxford: Blackwell, 1953).

DAVID PEARS

**axiomatization, axiomatics** A THEORY usually emerges as a body of (supposed) truths that are not neatly organized, making the theory difficult to survey or study as a whole. The axiomatic method is an idea for organizing a theory (Hilbert, 1970): one tries to select from among the supposed truths a small number from which all the others can be seen to be deductively inferable. This makes the theory rather more tractable since, in a sense, all the truths are contained in those few. In a theory so organized, the few truths from which all others are deductively inferred are called *axioms*. David Hilbert had argued that, just as algebraic and differential equations, which were used to study mathematical and physical processes, could themselves be made mathematical objects, so axiomatic theories, like algebraic and differential equations, which are means of representing physical processes and mathematical structures, could be made objects of mathematical investigation.

In the tradition (as in Leibniz, 1704), many philosophers had the conviction that all truths, or all truths about a particular domain, followed from a few principles. These principles were taken to be either metaphysically prior or epistemologically prior or both. In the first sense, they were taken to be entities of such a nature that what exists is 'caused' by them. When the principles were taken as epistemically prior, that is, as *axioms*, either they were taken to be epistemically privileged (e.g. SELF-EVIDENT, not needing to be demonstrated) or (again, inclusive 'or') to be such that all truths do indeed follow from them (by deductive inferences). Gödel (1984) showed – in the spirit of Hilbert, treating axiomatic theories as themselves mathematical objects – that mathematics, and even a small part of mathematics, elementary number theory, could not be axiomatized, that, more precisely, any class of axioms which is such that we could effectively decide, of any proposition, whether or not it was in that class, would be too small to capture all of the truths.

*See also* GEOMETRY; SPINOZA; THEORY.

BIBLIOGRAPHY

Gödel, K.: 'On formally undecidable propositions of Principia Mathematica and related systems I', in *Kurt Gödel: Collected Works* vol. I, *Publications 1929–1936*, eds S. Feferman et al. (Oxford: Clarendon Press, 1986), 145–95.

Henkin, L., Suppes, P. and Tarski, A. eds: *The Axiomatic Method* (Amsterdam: North-Holland, 1959).

Hilbert D.: 'Axiomatic thinking', in *Hilbert: Toward a Philosophy of Modern Mathematics II* ed. J. Fang (Hauppauge: Paideia, 1970), 187–98.

Leibniz, G. W.: *New Essays on Human Understanding* (1704) trans. P. Remnant and J. Bennett (Cambridge: Cambridge University Press, 1981).

ROBERT S. TRAGESSER

**Ayer, A(lfred) J(ules) (1910–89)** British philosopher who worked in London and Oxford. Though Ayer proved to be one of the most important modern epistemologists, there is relatively little epistemology in *Language, Truth and Logic*, his first and most famous book. Indeed, to the extent that epistemology is concerned with the a priori justification of our ordinary or scientific beliefs, the early Ayer explicitly abjures the subject, since the validity of such beliefs 'is an empirical matter, which cannot be settled by a priori means' (1946, p. 33). But he does take positions which have bearings on epistemology. For example, he is a PHENOMENALIST, believing that material objects are LOGICAL CONSTRUCTIONS out of actual and possible sense-experiences, and an anti-foundationalist, at least in one sense, denying that there is a bedrock level of indubitable propositions on which empirical knowledge can be based. As regards the main specifically epistemological problem he addresses, the problem of our knowledge of other minds, he is essentially behaviouristic, since the verification principle pronounces that the hypothesis of the occurrence of intrinsically inaccessible experiences is unintelligible (1946, pp. 170–1; *see* LOGICAL POSITIVISM; THE PROBLEM OF OTHER MINDS; VERIFICATIONISM).

These themes are developed in Ayer's

second book, *The Foundations of Empirical Knowledge*. The ARGUMENT FROM ILLUSION is deployed towards the conclusion that the objects of perception are SENSE-DATA. This was famously criticized by AUSTIN in *Sense and Sensibilia*. Actually, Ayer's official position is that there are two different 'languages' for describing our experiences, sense-data language and material object language, and the question is whether there are 'grounds for preferring one method of description to another' (Ayer, 1947, p. 28). But if the relationship between sense-data language and material object language is that of reducing language to reduced, ontological consequences would seem to follow, since it is natural to say that all that 'really' exists is the ontology of the reducing language. Ayer goes on to sketch an essentially Humean account of the applicability of material object language, except that whereas Hume is an error theorist about our commonsense notion of the external world, Ayer takes those aspects of our sense-data which Hume regarded as responsible for errors like belief in the continued existence of material objects, as being instead constitutive of what such phenomena consist in. Thus, according to Ayer, there is nothing more to the continued existence of material things than (a) resemblance between individual sense-data, (b) comparative stability of the contexts in which such resemblances are manifested, (c) systematic repeatability of sense-data, and (d) dependence of the repeatability upon the movements of the observer (1946, pp. 243–59; *see also* HUME; THE PROBLEM OF THE EXTERNAL WORLD).

Ayer's main contributions to epistemology are in his book *The Problem of Knowledge*, which he himself regarded as superior to *Language, Truth and Logic* (Ayer, 1985, p. 122). The book opens with general considerations about knowledge and how it is to be distinguished from true belief, and continues with discussions of scepticism about knowledge of (1) the external world, (2) the past and future and (3) the existence of other minds. About knowledge versus true belief, Ayer is a RELIABILIST: a true belief is not knowledge if it is arrived at 'by a process

which is not generally reliable' (1956, p. 31). Ayer emphasizes the context-dependence of the reliability of a process, and is consequently in a position to accommodate 'RELEVANT ALTERNATIVE' cases, in which a normally reliable process, such as looking at an array of objects, is unreliable, even though it might, by chance, lead to the formation of a true belief. So far as Gettier cases are concerned, he could say that the reliable process in the formation of inferential beliefs is application of deductive logic to true beliefs (*see* GETTIER PROBLEM). But this seems to blur a distinction between the process – in this case deductive reasoning – and that on which it operates. The 'No False Lemmas' principle on which Gettier cases turn, that true beliefs arrived at by deductive reasoning are knowledge only if the premises of the reasoning are also true, is something which perhaps cannot be subsumed under an account of what makes for reliability in mechanisms of perceptual belief-formation. If so, there is then an interesting question of what makes the concept of knowledge univocal in its application to inferential and non-inferential cases.

Ayer then goes on to develop a FALLIBILIST type of FOUNDATIONALISM, according to which processes of justification or verification terminate in someone's having an experience, but there is no class of infallible statements based on such experiences. Consequently, in making such statements based on experience, even simple reports of observation, we 'make what appears to be a special sort of advance beyond our data' (1956, p. 78). And it is the resulting gap which the sceptic exploits. Ayer describes four possible responses to the sceptic: Naïve Realism, according to which material objects are directly given in perception, so that there is no advance beyond the data; Reductionism, according to which physical objects are logically constructed out of the contents of our sense-experiences, so that again there is no real advance beyond the data; a position according to which there is an advance, but it can be supported by the canons of valid inductive reasoning; and lastly a position called 'Descriptive Analysis', according to which 'we can give an account of the procedures that we actually follow . . . but there [cannot] be a proof that what we take to be good evidence really is so' (1956, p. 81) .

Ayer considers each style of response in turn, most noticeably rejecting the second, phenomenalist, option, on the grounds of the impossibility of giving phenomenalist translations of material object discourse. Such translations would be in the form of counterfactuals about possible experiences, and Ayer stresses the main difficulty for phenomenalism of analysing the spatio-temporal framework in which observations take place (1956, pp. 123–4). There is also, in the context of his own discussion, the problem that the more *recherché* the analyses become the more the gap between actual experience and what we claim on its basis widens, so that even a successful phenomenalism would not help against the sceptic.

Ayer finally opts for Descriptive Analysis: 'the reason why our sense-experiences afford us grounds for believing in the existence of physical objects is simply that sentences which are taken as referring to physical objects are used in such a way that our having the appropriate experiences counts in favour of their truth' (1956, p. 132). In other words, having such experiences is exactly what justification of our ordinary beliefs about the nature of the world *consists in*. The suggestion is, therefore, that the sceptic is making some kind of mistake or indulging in some sort of incoherence in supposing that our experience may not rationally justify our commonsense picture of what the world is like. Against this, however, is the familiar fact that the sceptic's undermining hypotheses seem perfectly intelligible and even epistemically possible. Ayer's response seems weak relative to the power of the sceptical puzzles.

*See also* AUSTIN; the GIVEN.

WRITINGS

*Language, Truth and Logic* (London: Gollancz, 1946).
*The Foundations of Empirical Knowledge* (London: Macmillan, 1947).
*The Problem of Knowledge* (London: Macmillan, 1956).
*More of My Life* (Oxford: Oxford University Press, 1985).

GRAEME FORBES

# B

Bacon, Francis, Lord Verulam (1561–1626) English philosopher and statesman. While Bacon's philosophy in the wide sense embraces a whole cosmology, in the narrow sense it centres primarily on the identification of a fruitful method for the investigation of nature, with consequent utilitarian benefits. Indeed, it is roughly correct to say that Bacon's identification of knowledge with power was not contingent: it was the practical success of a theory which was for him the hallmark of its truth. Bacon began from a rejection of traditional Scholastic philosophy, which he held provided no method for advancing knowledge, and the oversimple empiricism of the alchemists. He also attacked what he called the Idols: it was false that the human senses are the measure of things; we each have our predispositions which are liable to mislead; our language is itself a further source of misapprehension; and the inherited unsubstantiated theories of the philosophers are mostly wrong.

To escape these causes of error we need to follow a new 'method of induction', which could bring both knowledge and control over nature. Baconian induction has often been misinterpreted as a commitment to INDUCTION by simple enumeration, and his whole programme dismissed as 'inductive' in some pejorative sense. But Bacon explicitly rejected such a method. Rather, he should be seen as subscribing to a version of the hypothetico-deductive method: the positing of causal hypotheses (the forms), which are then brought to the test of experience. The putative identification of the forms, he held, could only follow a rigorous and systematic collection of data or 'histories' of natural phenomena.

Aspects of Bacon's method found expression in the work of early members of the Royal Society such as Boyle and Newton, but the *opera* or works to which Bacon aspired were not scholarly tomes but the practical achievements of the engineer and the chemist. And although Bacon was aware of rising sceptical challenges to knowledge claims, his work largely side-stepped the epistemological concerns that later feature in Descartes and Locke in favour of measuring theories by the pragmatic test of results. Successful theories, he held, might be regarded as certain.

*See also* NATURAL SCIENCE.

WRITINGS

*Novum Organum* (1620): in *The New Organon and Related Writings* ed. F. H. Anderson (New York: Liberal Arts Press, 1960).
*The Advancement of Learning* (1605): (London: Everyman, 1915).


BIBLIOGRAPHY

Hesse, M.: 'Francis Bacon's philosophy of science', in *A Critical History of Western Philosophy* ed. D.J. O'Connor (London: Macmillan, 1964), 141–52.
Pérez-Ramos, A.: *Francis Bacon's Idea of Science and the Maker's Knowledge Tradition* (Oxford: Oxford University Press, 1988).
Rossi, P.: *Francis Bacon. From Magic to Science* (London: Routledge and Kegan Paul, 1968).

G.A.J. ROGERS

basic beliefs *see* EMPIRICISM; EXPERIENCE; FOUNDATIONALISM; GIVEN, THE; REGRESS ARGUMENT.

Bayesianism The Bayesian approach to the

philosophical problems of scientific method, and to epistemology in general, is based on the observation that belief is not simply a yes-or-no affair. Rather, there are *gradations* of belief, and this fact is captured within the Bayesian framework by means of the following fundamental principle:

(B) The degrees of belief of an ideally rational person conform to the mathematical principles of probability theory.

For example, one principle of probability theory is

$$Prob(H) + Prob(-H) = 1$$

(The probabilities of any hypothesis and of its negation add up to one.) So it follows from (B) that your degree of belief that there is life on Mars plus your degree of belief that there is no life on Mars should, if you are rational, equal one. If (B) is correct, then the probability calculus constrains rational combinations of degrees of belief in much the same way that principles of deductive logic restrict rational combinations of full belief. The Bayesian idea is that many methodological puzzles stem from a fixation upon all-or-nothing belief and may be resolved by means of the enriched probabilistic 'logic' of partial belief.

For this purpose a particularly useful theorem of the probability calculus, named after the eighteenth-century English clergyman who pioneered the approach, is

$$Prob(H/E) = \frac{Prob(H) \times Prob(E/H)}{Prob(E)}$$

(Bayes' theorem)

(The probability of H, on the assumption that E is true, is equal to the unconditional probability of H, times the probability of E given H, divided by the unconditional probability of E.) Now suppose one could establish (B). One could then infer that the degrees of belief, b(. . .), of a rational person must satisfy the equation

$$b(H/E) = \frac{b(H) \times b(E/H)}{b(E)}$$

And this constraint turns out to have numerous methodological applications.

Suppose, for example, that H stands for a hypothesis and E for some evidence claim, and that H predicts the truth of E. Consider a rational person for whom the truth of E and H are uncertain. That is, $0 < b(H) < 1$ and $0 < b(E) < 1$. We also have

$$b(E/H) = 1$$

since it is an axiom of probability that if A entails B then $Prob(B/A) = 1$. Therefore,

$$b(E/H) > b(E)$$

Therefore, employing Bayes' theorem, we find that

$$b(H/E) > b(H)$$

In other words, rationality requires that the degree of belief in H, assuming the discovery of E, be greater than the unconditional degree of belief in H. Consider now a plausible probabilistic explication of what it is for one thing to be evidence for something else: namely, the discovery of E would be evidence in favour of H if rationality requires that b(H/E) > b(H). Given this clarification of the notion of evidence, it follows that in the above circumstances the discovery of E would tend to confirm H. Thus we have supplied a rationale for the intuitive evidential value of successful prediction.

A further item of scientific methodology that can be easily explained along these lines is that relatively surprising predictions have greater evidential value. For it is natural to take the ratio b(H/E)/b(H) as a measure of the degree of support given to H by the discovery of E, and to take b(E) as an inverse measure of the surprisingness of such a discovery. Now since $b(E/H) = 1$, we have from Bayes' theorem

$$b(H/E) = \frac{b(H) \times 1}{b(E)}$$

$$\therefore \frac{b(H/E)}{b(H)} = \frac{1}{b(E)}$$

Thus, the more surprising the prediction, the greater the ratio of b(H/E) to b(H), and so the greater the degree of confirmation.

Bayesianism deals with other issues similarly, combining the idea of confirmation as increase of rational degree of belief with the principle that rational degrees of belief must satisfy the probability calculus. Some of the further problems that can be handled is this way are:

–why a broad spectrum of facts will confirm a theory more than a narrow data set
–what is wrong with *ad hoc* hypotheses
–how it is possible for the discovery of a non-black non-raven to confirm the hypothesis that all ravens are black (HEMPEL'S PARADOX of confirmation)
–whether prediction has more evidential value than mere accommodation of data
–why we ought to base our judgements on as much data as possible
–how statistical hypotheses can be tested even though they are unfalsifiable.

If all this can really be done, we shall have an impressive body of accomplishments (Hesse, 1974; Horwich, 1982; Howson and Urbach, 1989). However, the Bayesian framework appears to embody several highly dubious assumptions, and one might well suppose, therefore, that no solutions within that framework can possibly be satisfactory. Here are some of the main objections.

In the first place, it seems far-fetched to suppose that people actually have precise, numerical, degrees of belief. Can the mind really contain the state of believing to degree .15296 that quantum mechanics is true? That there are such states is a sophisticated psychological hypothesis without much empirical support. Granted, if we had evidence to suggest that Maximization of Expected Utility were a law of decision-making (Jeffrey, 1983), then the existence of the theoretical quantities involved in this law – including numerical degrees of belief – would be supported. Or if we could justifiably suppose that people's preferences satisfied the axioms of von Neumann and Morgenstern, or Savage's axioms, then again it could be concluded that numerical degrees of belief

are real states of mind. But it is well known that experimental results cast considerable doubt on these suppositions (Slovic, 1990).

In response it could be said that the Bayesian approach need not be committed to the literal existence of precise, numerical degrees of belief. The vital assumption, which is not controversial, is that there are belief gradations of *some* sort; their representation by numbers should perhaps be seen as nothing more than a heuristic device – something done for the sake of convenience, without commitment to its truth.

A second objection focuses on the Bayesian's fundamental postulate: that any numerical degrees of belief that do exist must, if they are *rational*, satisfy the probability calculus. Although there are various lines of reasoning which purport to establish this thesis, none is compelling (Earman, 1992). The best known of them is the 'dutch book' argument (Ramsey, 1926; de Finnetti, 1937; Skyrms, 1975), and it goes roughly as follows. Defining a person's degree of belief in a proposition as a function of the odds at which he is prepared to bet on its truth, it can be proved that if his degrees of belief don't satisfy the probability calculus then he will be prepared to accept a collection of bets which is guaranteed to lead to a loss. Therefore, since it would surely be irrational for him knowingly to put himself in such a no-win situation, it would be irrational to have a system of degrees of belief that violates the probability calculus. QED. However, the definition of 'degree of belief' that is employed in this argument presupposes that people maximize their expected utility. And, as I have just mentioned, there is a lot of room for scepticism about that assumption (and about the preference axioms to which it is equivalent). So the 'dutch book' argument is far from airtight.

Worse still, there is positive reason to think that its conclusion, Principle (B), is false; for it requires logical omniscience. The probability of any tautology is 1 and of any contradiction is 0. Yet it is surely quite rational to be less than perfectly confident in the truth of *some* tautologies – those that are especially hard to prove – and quite rational to give non-zero degrees of belief to contradictions that are hard to recognize as such.

One possible Bayesian response to these difficulties is to repeat that the picture of rational degrees of belief obeying the probability calculus should be regarded as an *idealization*. It is uncontroversial that one ought to be certain of elementary logical truths, and that one ought not be confident in the truth of obviously incompatible hypotheses. The probabilistic model of belief provides a sharp, perspicuous way of capturing these trivialities, and to the extent that it goes beyond them it need not be construed realistically.

A third alleged problem for Bayesians is the difficulty of establishing the proper way to define 'the degree of confirmation of hypothesis H by evidence E', and the moral has been drawn that no probabilistic definition is entirely adequate (Glymour, 1980). Some Bayesians characterize degree of support as the *difference* between b(H/E) and b(H), some say it is the *ratio* of these degrees of belief, and a great variety of other formulas are suggested in the literature. All parties are able to point to cases where they capture our intuitions more successfully than the others, and there seems to be no way of telling which, if any, is correct.

Once again, however, the natural Bayesian response is pragmatic. We are at liberty to pick one rather than another measure of 'degree of support' solely on grounds of utility. The only fact that must be respected is that data provide support for a hypothesis to the extent that they ought to increase one's degree of belief in it. As long as this uncontroversial intuition is preserved, none of the applications of Bayesianism will depend essentially on which definition of 'degree of support' is used.

A further complaint is that many interesting epistemological questions are not answered by Bayesianism. One might wonder, for example, whether there are any constraints on rational belief *beyond* conformity with the probability calculus, and if so what they are. How should we approach GOODMAN's 'grue problem'? Should we perhaps recognize canons of reason dictating that, prior to any evidence, higher probabilities be assigned to simpler hypotheses than to more complex ones? But if so, what form do these principles take and how might they be justified? Although there are some extensions of Bayesianism – notably the work of Carnap (1950) – that try to address these questions, the attempts, despite great formal ingenuity, are crude and unpromising. Yet on its own the fundamental thesis of Bayesianism leaves us completely in the dark.

It must be said, however, that this thesis might well illuminate many problems sufficiently to help resolve them, without offering anything like a complete picture of scientific methodology. Bayesianism does not tell us how to decide whether a hypothesis is projectible. It does not specify how a person's state of belief should change under the impact of new data and the recognition of new theoretical possibilities. It doesn't solve the traditional problem of induction. But so what? The desire for a complete and perfectly correct theory of science is not what Bayesianism need be intended to satisfy.

One may think of the model, rather, as an idealization whose function is to cast our crude uncontroversial ideas into a clear form where their joint implications can be most easily discerned. This is not to deny that it can be of interest to investigate more realistic models of belief, more sensitive epistemological norms, more accurate measures of confirmation, and more extensive areas of methodology. If one is doing 'epistemology naturalized', and therefore trying to obtain a theory of science that is true and systematic, then such investigations are appropriate. But if the point is to solve the many puzzles whose origin is the oversimplification that belief is an all-or-nothing matter, then it is by no means clear that anything more realistic than the Bayesian idealization is needed. It purports to offer the ideal compromise between accuracy and simplicity – enabling us to represent the issues starkly without neglecting their essential ingredients or obscuring them with unnecessary detail.

*See also* PROBABILITY.

BIBLIOGRAPHY

Carnap, R.: *Logical Foundations of Probability* (Chicago: University of Chicago Press, 1950).

De Finetti, B.: 'Foresight: its logical laws, its subjective sources' (1937), in *Studies in Subjective Probability* eds H. E. Kyburg and H. E. Smokler (New York: John Wiley, 1964).

Earman, J.: *Bayes or Bust: A Critical Examination of Bayesian Confirmation Theory* (Cambridge, MA: MIT Press, 1992).

Glymour, C.: *Theory and Evidence* (Princeton: Princeton University Press, 1988).

Hesse, M.: *The Structure of Scientific Inference* (Berkeley: University of California Press, 1974).

Horwich, P. G.: *Probability and Evidence* (Cambridge: Cambridge University Press, 1982).

Howson, C. and Urbach, F.: *Scientific Inference: The Bayesian Approach* (La Salle: Open Court, 1989).

Jeffrey, R. C.: *The Logic of Decision* (Chicago: University of Chicago Press, 1983).

Ramsey, F. P.: 'Truth and probability' (1926), in *Foundations: Essays by F. P. Ramsey* ed. D. H. Mellor (London: Routledge and Kegan Paul, 1978)

Skyrms, B.: *Choice and Chance* 2nd edn (Belmont: Dickenson, 1975).

Slovic, P.: 'Choice', in *Thinking: An Invitation to Cognitive Science* eds D. Osherson and E. Smith, vol. 3 (Cambridge, MA: MIT Press, 1990).

PAUL HORWICH

**behaviourism** Epistemologists have discussed a variety of doctrines, which have been called 'behaviourism'. One of these, logical behaviourism, holds that sentences about the mental are equivalent in meaning to sentences about behaviour or behavioural dispositions. For example, 'Smith feels depressed' might be translated by a behaviourist as 'Smith is speaking in a flat monotone and is not exhibiting his usual animation'. A standard problem for such translations is that what is asserted by the first sentence may be true while the second assertion may be false. That might happen, for example, if the subject is depressed but is deliberately acting in a non-depressed manner. Another problem is that Smith might act so as to simulate depression, or at least be disposed to do that, even if he is not depressed. He might, for example, be disposed to act depressed so as to deceive someone into falsely believing that he really is depressed.

A second view, methodological behaviourism, holds that psychologists should, for methodological reasons, reject all mentalistic explanations. A basic problem for this view is that the question of what causes human behaviour appears to be an empirical question; if the evidence supports the postulation of mentalistic causes, it is difficult to see how all mentalistic explanations can be rejected solely on methodological grounds. This problem is avoided by a third behaviouristic doctrine, associated with the late B. F. Skinner, which might be called 'empirical behaviourism'. On this view, there are mental events but no mentalistic causes; behaviour is explainable in terms of such variables as: genetic make-up, states of deprivation, current environmental stimuli and histories of reinforcements and punishments. A particularly difficult problem for this view is to explain the acquisition and use of human language without appealing to mentalistic causes.

A fourth type of behaviourism, metaphysical behaviourism, is the thesis that there are no mental events, states or processes. In philosophy, this view is more commonly called 'eliminative materialism'. There are other types of behaviourism as well.

*See also* PSYCHOLOGY AND EPISTEMOLOGY.

BIBLIOGRAPHY

Chomsky, N.: 'Review of *Verbal Behavior*', *Language* 35 (1959), 26–58.

Erwin, E.: *Behavior Therapy: Scientific, Philosophical and Moral Foundations* (New York: Cambridge University Press, 1978), chs 2 and 3.

Skinner, B. F.: *About Behaviorism* (New York: Knopf, 1974).

Zuriff, G. E.: *Behaviorism: A Conceptual Reconstruction* (New York: Columbia University Press, 1985).

EDWARD ERWIN

**belief** The ground-level epistemological concepts of *truth*, *falsity* and *justification* apply primarily to beliefs, and only derivatively, if at all, to knowledge. Belief is thus central to epistemology.

### THE STANDARD PICTURE

PLATO, in the *Meno*, set the tone for subsequent discussion. There, and in the *Theaetetus*, he distinguishes knowledge, belief, opinion and judgement, and advances a conception of these states of mind according to which they incorporate a pair of components, one intentional or representational, one causal. In F.P. Ramsey's phrase, a belief is viewed as 'a map of neighbouring space by which we steer' (Ramsey, 1978, p. 134).

This dual-component picture of belief constitutes what has become the standard picture. It was embellished, for instance, by HUME, who regarded beliefs as 'ideas' supplemented by a particular 'sentiment or feeling' in virtue of which those ideas come to serve as guides to behaviour. This conception, like Descartes', depicts beliefs as conscious episodes. Although we are often conscious of our beliefs, however, our being conscious of them seems inessential to their psychological role.

The standard picture is nowadays reflected in the notion that beliefs are to be located among the *propositional attitudes*, states of mind comprising (1) propositional contents paired with (2) attitudes toward those contents. In addition to beliefs, these include desires, wishes, intentions, fears, doubts and hopes. The objects of belief, then, are taken to be propositions. Propositions are expressible sententially: Agathon's belief that rhubarb is poisonous is expressed by the sentence, 'Rhubarb is poisonous'. This has suggested to some that belief-states themselves possess a sentential structure, that they are maps in some literal sense. Jerry Fodor (1981), for one, supposes beliefs to be internal sentences, neurally realized inscriptions, that make up a 'language of thought'. Others, suspicious of the notion of a language of thought, nevertheless agree that beliefs possess a logical form mirroring that of sentences.

This is one way of filling out the standard picture, but not the only way. Robert Stalnaker (1987, chs 2, 3) has pointed out that the thesis that beliefs are sententially characterizable does not entail that beliefs *themselves* must have a sentential structure. Stalnaker holds that beliefs are attitudes directed, not towards sentence-like propositions, but towards the world. Belief-states are best characterized by sets of 'possible worlds', alternative 'ways the world may be'. The content of Agathon's belief that rhubarb is poisonous might be represented as a set of possible worlds, those in which rhubarb is poisonous. The constituents of possible worlds are possible objects and events, rather than concepts or descriptions of objects and events, and logical relations among propositions believed are grounded in relations among sets of possible worlds.

A conception of this sort might account for our ambivalence about beliefs ascribable to creatures lacking in linguistic abilities. Spot, we say, believes there is a squirrel in the tree. But can we be confident that we have captured the content of Spot's belief? Beliefs seem to owe their character to relations they bear to other beliefs. My believing that this is a *tree*, for instance, might be thought to require that I believe many other things: that trees are living things, that trees have leaves, that if I set fire to this tree it will burn, and so on. But how many of these background beliefs could we plausibly credit to Spot?

On Stalnaker's view, however, in ascribing a belief about trees to Spot we need suppose only that Spot has *some* mechanism for dividing alternative situations into those featuring and those lacking trees. The mechanism may be a crude one, cruder, certainly, than the mechanisms underlying the abilities of adult human beings. Nevertheless, Spot's belief concerns trees in part because the proposition believed partitions the set of possible worlds relevant to the explanation of Spot's capacities at the same place the proposition believed by an ordinary human being does.

### REALISM, ANTI-REALISM, AND ELIMINATIVISM

Both Fodor and Stalnaker defend 'realist'

versions of the standard picture. Both take beliefs to be genuine states causally implicated in behaviour. Others deflate the standard picture, imagining that beliefs (and other propositional attitudes) possess only an attenuated kind of reality. QUINE (1960, § 45), for instance, links the ascription of attitudes to the translation of utterances. Just as, for Quine, there is no translation-independent fact of the matter as to what a given sentence means, there is no non-contextual fact of the matter as to what a given agent believes. Belief, like meaning, is 'indeterminate'. Donald DAVIDSON (1984, essays 9–12) echoes this sentiment. We can concoct distinct, but equally apt, schemes of belief-ascription for any agent. These schemes will depend partly on us, the ascribers, since they hinge on correlations between an agent's utterances and sentences in our language. It makes no sense, then, to talk of beliefs or meanings independently of a particular linguistic context.

A different anti-realist tack is taken by Daniel Dennett (1987, chs 2, 3), who defends an 'instrumentalist' conception of belief. We have a practical interest in regarding certain 'systems' – people, animals, machines, even committees – as rational, as registering, on the whole, what is true and as reasoning in accord with appropriate norms. In so doing, we take up the 'intentional stance'. We are, as a result, in a position to make sense of and, within limits, to predict the behaviour of the systems in question. The practical success of this enterprise, however, does not depend on its yielding true descriptions of states and goings-on inside agents.

It is but a brief step from anti-realism to out-and-out scepticism about belief. Stephen Stich (1983), Patricia Churchland (1986) and Paul Churchland (1981) have argued that the concept of belief belongs to an outmoded 'folk psychology'. Folk psychology provides a theory of intelligent behaviour. Beliefs are among the theoretical entities postulated by this theory. Were we to abandon the theory, we would thereby 'eliminate' its postulated entities. Beliefs would go the way of caloric, phlogiston and the ether, theoretical items dropped from our inventory of constituents of the world when theories in which they figured were replaced by better theories. Eliminativists contend that recent advances in psychology and neuroscience suggest that folk psychology is, even now, being eclipsed by better theories, and that, in consequence, it is reasonable to deny the existence of beliefs.

Critics respond that this claim is self-defeating. If eliminativists were right, then, by their own lights, it would be impossible to believe what they say (though, of course, it would be equally impossible to believe it false). The criticism misses the target. A proposition may be true but pragmatically unstable. I cannot coherently claim always to lie, yet, for all that, I may always lie. As things stand, eliminativists are obliged to articulate their position using concepts that have their home in the folk theory they attack. Presumably a replacement theory would bring with it a stock of concepts that would enable the point to be made without involving reference to beliefs.

Eliminativism has not been widely embraced. It is not clear that the theoretical advances touted by eliminativists would eradicate belief. Psychology might replace the concept of belief with something finer-grained; 'belief' could turn out to designate a *range* of states. Were that to happen, however, we might regard it as a discovery about the deeper character of belief, not its elimination. And were neuroscience to abandon reference to beliefs, we should have no more reason to doubt their existence, than we have reason to doubt the reality of trees, rocks, and solid surfaces because such things are ignored by basic physics.

PROBABILITY THEORIES

Thus far, belief has been depicted as being all-or-nothing. Agathon believes that rhubarb is poisonous or he does not. But it is sometimes urged that belief admits of degrees. Agathon believes that rhubarb is poisonous, but he believes still more firmly that rhubarb is a vegetable. According to Ramsey (1978), beliefs, so regarded, may usefully be treated as probabilities. Agathon assigns a certain probability to 'rhubarb is poisonous' and a certain, presumably higher, probability to 'rhubarb is a vegetable'. One advantage of this perspective is that it allows belief to be quantified and thereby raises the prospect of a rigorous science of behaviour. If we can represent agents as harbouring certain probabilities and simultaneously assign numerical values to their wants, we may be in a position to predict their preferences for various courses of action, hence their behaviour – assuming that agents will endeavour to do what they most prefer. The perspective is nowadays associated with decision-theory (*see* BAYESIANISM).

Decision-theory provides a framework for representing rational action. It may also, as Richard Jeffrey (1983, appendix) has shown, accommodate action that is less than perfectly rational. On the whole, however, decision-theory has the flavour of a normative, rather than a descriptive theory of behaviour. This has led some to dismiss it as irrelevant to psychological explanation. Others, most notably Davidson (1984, essays 9, 10, 13), have argued that psychology includes an irreducibly normative component. In ascribing beliefs and other propositional attitudes to agents, we are obliged to exercise *charity*, obliged, that is, to assign beliefs and desires in a way that optimizes the rationality of those agents. It is, on Davidson's view, a 'synthetic a priori' truth about agents that, on the whole, they satisfy the canons of decision-theory (*see* PRINCIPLE OF CHARITY).

## VOLUNTARISM

The notion that believing is subject to norms suggests that agents are in a position to decide on their beliefs. That seems unlikely. Acquiring a belief is like catching cold. I may be able to bring it about that I hold a certain belief (as Pascal recommends in the case of the belief that God exists), just as I may bring it about that I catch cold. But *believing* appears not to be voluntary. Not everyone agrees. DESCARTES, for instance, writes as though believing depends on some prior act of will. In *Meditation IV*, he says that 'when something is proposed to us by the intellect',

we are free 'either to affirm or deny' that something.

Although what we believe is surely a function of our other states of mind, it is doubtful that belief essentially involves willing. Indeed, Bernard Williams (1978, ch. 6) has argued that believing is *necessarily* non-voluntary. In the Cartesian spirit, however, some philosophers advocate a two-tiered conception of belief. Thus Keith Lehrer (1990, ch. 2) distinguishes believing and accepting. We *believe* propositions for a variety of reasons. Agathon may believe that rhubarb is poisonous because he was hypnotized or as a result of wishful thinking. His *accepting* that rhubarb is poisonous, however, requires that he do so because he has grounds for thinking it true. Acceptance is governed by epistemic norms, is at least partly subject to voluntary control, and has functional affinities to belief. Perhaps this would satisfy Descartes. Still, the notion of acceptance, like that of degrees of belief, merely extends the standard picture, and does not replace it.

## ATTACKS ON THE STANDARD PICTURE

The standard picture is not without its critics, however. Gilbert RYLE (1949, ch. 5) regards beliefs as 'tendencies' to say and do various things. If Agathon believes that rhubarb is poisonous, he will be disposed to assent to the sentence 'rhubarb is poisonous', to refuse to eat rhubarb, and so on. In this respect beliefs resemble dispositions like fragility. If a glass is fragile, it will, under the right conditions, break when struck by a solid object. Ryle is often accused of reducing beliefs and other states of mind to behaviour, but this is misleading. A glass's being fragile is not its breaking, and Agathon's believing that rhubarb is poisonous is not his saying so. Ryle is explicit on the point: What Agathon does given that he believes rhubarb is poisonous will depend on *what else* Agathon believes, what he wants, and so on. If Agathon *wants* to be poisoned, for instance, and believes that this is rhubarb, he may well eat it. Functionalists (like Fodor) have made much of this idea.

In one important respect, however, Ryle's conception of belief clashes with the standard picture. The latter depicts the connection between belief and behaviour as causal. Ryle, in contrast, argues that mental states like belief are not causes of behaviour any more than a glass's fragility – its tendency to break – is a cause of its breaking. Beliefs are dispositional states *triggered* causally. But because these states are characterised by reference to behaviour, their connection with behaviour is conceptual, not causal. Explaining Agathon's behaviour by reference to Agathon's belief about rhubarb is like explaining a move in chess by describing it as 'taking a pawn', and not like explaining its starting to rain by reference to falling temperature.

This non-causal conception of psychological explanation sets Ryle off from his functionalist successors. As Davidson (1980) has pointed out, however, any causal relation can be described in such a way that cause and effect are conceptually linked. The falling temperature may be described as the cause of its raining. Thus: The cause of the rain is what caused it to rain. The claim is unilluminating, perhaps, but neither false nor evidence for the absence of a straightforward causal relation. Ironically, Davidson's own theory of belief has recently come under attack as being at odds with causal theories.

The standard picture of belief has proved remarkably resilient. It continues to inform our psychological and epistemological speculations. Its replacement, or out-and-out elimination, though conceivable, is not yet on the horizon.

*See also* COLLECTIVE BELIEF; QUINE; REASONS/CAUSES.

BIBLIOGRAPHY

Churchland, P.M.: 'Eliminative materialism and the propositional attitudes', *Journal of Philosophy* 78 (1981), 67–90.
Churchland, P.S.: *Neurophilosophy* (Cambridge, MA: Bradford Books/MIT Press, 1986).
Davidson, D.: 'Mental events', in his *Essays on Actions and Events* (Oxford: Clarendon Press, 1980).
Davidson, D.: *Inquiries into Truth and Interpretation* (Oxford: Clarendon Press, 1984).
Dennett, D.C.: *The Intentional Stance* (Cambridge: Bradford Books/MIT Press, 1987).
Fodor, J.A.: 'Propositional attitudes', in his *Representations* (Brighton: Harvester, 1981).
Jeffrey, R.C.: *The Logic of Decision* 2nd edn (Chicago: University of Chicago Press, 1983).
Lehrer, K.: *Theory of Knowledge* (Boulder: Westview Press, 1990).
Quine, W.V.: *Word and Object* (Cambridge, MA: MIT Press, 1960).
Ramsey, F.P.: *Foundations: Essays in Philosophy, Logic, Mathematics, and Economics* ed. D.H. Mellor (London: Routledge and Kegan Paul, 1978).
Ryle, G.: *The Concept of Mind* (London: Hutchinson, 1949).
Stalnaker, R.C.: *Inquiry* (Cambridge, MA: Bradford Books/MIT Press, 1987).
Stich, S.P.: *From Folk Psychology to Cognitive Science: The Case against Belief* (Cambridge, MA: Bradford Books/MIT Press, 1983).
Williams, B.: *Descartes: The Project of Pure Enquiry* (Harmondsworth: Pelican Books, 1978).

JOHN HEIL

**belief in and belief that**  Traditionally, belief has been of epistemological interest in its *propositional* guise: S believes that *p*, where *p* is a proposition towards which an agent, S, exhibits an attitude of acceptance. Not all belief is of this sort. If I trust what you say, I believe *you*. And someone may believe in Mrs Thatcher, or in a free-market economy, or in God. It is sometimes supposed that all belief is 'reducible' to propositional belief, belief-*that*. Thus, my believing *you* might be thought a matter of my believing, perhaps, *that* what you say is true; and your belief in free markets or in God, a matter of your believing *that* free-market economies are desirable or *that* God exists.

It is doubtful, however, that non-propositional believings can, in every case, be reduced in this way. Debate on this point has tended to focus on an apparent distinction between belief-that and belief-in, and the application of this distinction to belief in God (*see* Swinburne, 1981). Some philosophers have followed AQUINAS (*see Summa Theologiae*) in supposing that to believe in God is simply to believe that certain truths hold: that God exists, that he is benevolent, etc. Others (e.g. Hick, 1957) argue that belief-in is a distinctive attitude, one that includes essentially an element of *trust*. More commonly, belief-in has been taken to involve a combination of propositional belief together with some further attitude.

H.H. Price (1969) defends the claim that there are different sorts of belief-in, some, but not all, reducible to beliefs-that. If you believe in God, you believe that God exists, that God is good, etc. But, according to Price, your belief involves, in addition, a certain complex pro-attitude toward its object. One might attempt to analyse this further attitude in terms of additional beliefs-that: S believes in *x* just in case (1) S believes that *x* exists (and perhaps holds further factual beliefs about *x*); (2) S believes that *x* is good or valuable in some respect; and (3) S believes that *x*'s being good or valuable in this respect is itself is a good thing. An analysis of this sort, however, fails adequately to capture the further *affective* component of belief-in. Thus, according to Price, if you believe in God, your belief is not merely that certain truths hold; you possess, in addition, an attitude of commitment and trust towards God.

Notoriously, belief-in outruns the evidence for the corresponding belief-that. Does this diminish its rationality? If belief-in presupposes belief-that, it might be thought that the evidential standards for the former must be at least as high as standards for the latter. And any additional pro-attitude might be thought to require a further layer of justification not required for cases of belief-that.

Some philosophers have argued that, at least for cases in which belief-in is synonymous with *faith* (or faith-in), evidential thresholds for constituent propositional beliefs are diminished (*see* e.g. Audi, 1990). You may reasonably have faith in God or Mrs Thatcher, even though beliefs about their respective attributes, were you to harbour them, would be evidentially substandard.

Belief-in may be, in general, less suscep-tible to alteration in the face of unfavourable evidence than belief-that. A believer who encounters evidence against God's existence may remain unshaken in his belief, in part because the evidence does not bear on his pro-attitude. So long as this is united with his belief that God exists, the belief may survive epistemic buffeting – and reasonably so – in a way that an ordinary propositional belief-that would not.

*See also* RELIGIOUS BELIEF.

BIBLIOGRAPHY

Audi, R.: 'Faith, belief, and rationality', *Philosophical Perspectives* 5 (1990).
Aquinas: *Summa Theologiae* trans. Fathers of the English Dominican Province (Westminster: Christian Classics, 1981), 5 vols.
Hick, J.: *Faith and Knowledge* (London: 1957); 2nd edn (London: Macmillan, 1967).
Price, H. H.: *Belief* (London: George Allen and Unwin, 1965), ch. 2.9.
Swinburne, R.: *Faith and Reason* (Oxford: Clarendon Press, 1981).

JOHN HEIL

**Bergmann, Gustav (1906–1987)** Bergmann, the last active member of the VIENNA CIRCLE, retained his positivist heritage in denying any general problem of scepticism, but abandoned it in his commitment to the primacy of metaphysics. Thus 'epistemology is merely the ontology of the knowing situation' (1964, p. 126), and the task is to show, ontologically, *how* and *what* we know and not *that* we know.

In taking commonsense (perception and knowledge of mind-independent objects, existence of other minds, discoverable regularities in nature) and the findings of science for granted, Bergmann showed the influence of Russell, Wittgenstein and especially MOORE. His EMPIRICISM was expressed in the proposition that all undefined descriptive signs in the ideal language must refer to simple entities (particulars, universals) with which we are directly acquainted in either sense experience or introspection. The ideal language must also reflect the commonsense division of propositions into contingent and necessary, a distinction the reality and importance of which Bergmann defended in his 'Two cornerstones of empiricism' (1954, pp. 78–105), the other cornerstone being just that of reduction to phenomenological simples.

Bergmann's greatest contributions to philosophy lie in philosophy of mind. Taking cues from Brentano and Meinong, he developed an account of intentionality designed in part to exhibit his disavowal of materialist theories of mind while maintaining his commitment to deterministic psychology and, more important, to show how knowledge of mind-independent objects is possible. In so doing, he hoped, in the spirit of Moore, definitively to show the way out of the Cartesian circle of ideas and thus ontologically to secure realism.

WRITINGS

The Metaphysics of Logical Positivism (Madison: University of Wisconsin Press, 1954).
Philosophy of Science (Madison: University of Wisconsin Press, 1957).
Meaning and Existence (Madison: University of Wisconsin Press, 1959).
Logic and Reality (Madison: University of Wisconsin Press, 1964).
Realism: A Critique of Brentano and Meinong (Madison: University of Wisconsin Press, 1967).
New Foundations of Ontology ed. William Heald (Madison: University of Wisconsin Press, 1992).

LAIRD ADDIS

**Berkeley, George (1685–1753)** Berkeley was educated at Trinity College, Dublin, which elected him Junior Fellow in 1707 and with which he remained connected until appointed Dean of Derry in 1724. In 1734 he was appointed Bishop of Cloyne. His main philosophical works were An Essay towards a New Theory of Vision (1709), A Treatise concerning the Principles of Human Knowledge (1710) and Three Dialogues between Hylas and Philonous (1713), but Alciphron (1732), Siris (1744) and a number of shorter works are of philosophical interest. He was an important influence on Hume, Reid and Kant.

Berkeley's 'immaterialism' is a metaphysical system opposed to the 'modern philosophy' of Descartes, Locke and other Mechanists, whose account of matter as an independent substance Berkeley thought set up a rival to God. His arguments have sweeping implications for epistemology. Hume describes them as 'the best lessons of scepticism . . . either among the ancient or modern philosophers', but Berkeley's own claim is that they close the door to scepticism opened by 'the materialists'.

Berkeley's central aim is not, as popularly supposed, to cast doubt on the existence of physical objects. His system is structured round the principle that spirits are the only independent, active beings or, in the philosophical sense, 'substances'. Sensible things or bodies exist, but as inert beings dependent on a mind which perceives them (Principles I 7, 89, etc.). His argument radically reinterprets the traditional notion of substance. According to the logical side of the Aristotelian doctrine, independent substance and dependent accident exist on different ontological levels, indeed in categorically different senses of 'exist'. As the ultimate subjects of predication, substances are also the substrates of change: they are principles of activity, and change is understood in terms of their natures or essences. Despite a different notion of causal explanation, Mechanist theory of substance has a broadly similar shape. Berkeley's argument accordingly has two sides, corresponding to the logico-ontological independence of spirits and to their activity. The first involves a radical theory of perception, the second, an equally radical philosophy of physics.

SPIRITS AND IDEAS

Berkeleyan spirits, like Aristotelian substances, 'exist in the first place and primary sense' (Siris 263), whereas the esse of sensible things is percipi (Principles I 4). The notion of substance is stripped away from the allegedly 'groundless and unintelligible' theory of predication, and the 'in' of 'Accidents (or qualities) exist in substances' is reinterpreted as the 'in' of 'The colour I see exists in my mind' (ibid. I 49). Spirits are substances which 'support' sensible qualities or ideas by perceiving them (ibid. I 7, 135). Talk of material substance 'supporting' qualities is an empty metaphor (ibid. I 17). This identification of 'sensible qualities' with 'ideas' becomes understandable if we recognize that, although Berkeley often uses 'idea' interchangeably with 'sensation' (ibid. I 4), he does not mean by it a state or modification of the mind, but something more in accordance with Descartes' traditional account of the idea of the sun as 'the sun itself as it exists in the understanding', i.e. as it is experienced or conceived of. Since (Berkeley claims) sensible qualities are ideas in this sense, and 'for an idea to exist in an unperceiving thing is a manifest contradiction', it follows that 'there is not any other substance than spirit' (ibid. I 7).

Berkeley is denying, as self-contradictory and absurd, that behind bodies as they appear to the senses lie bodies as they are in themselves, independent 'unthinking' substances: he saw this precisely as not denying the existence of bodies, but as making them more immediately accessible to us. The crux of the argument is his rejection of the notion of a quality which is not an idea, i.e. which is not sense-relative. There cannot be 'real' and independent qualities which are *like* ideas, since 'an idea can be like nothing but another idea' (ibid. I 8). Moreover, our belief that we can conceive of bodies as they exist absolutely, independently of perception, is an illusion engendered by the possibility of imagining something without imagining someone by to perceive it: we forget that we are imagining it as we ourselves would perceive it (ibid. I 22f; *Dialogues* I 200). Yet these general arguments depend on the support of a broad attack on the doctrine according to which 'primary' mechanical qualities qualify things as they are in themselves, while 'secondary' qualities, such as colours and smells, exist (unless as 'bare powers') only 'in the mind' as a product of the primary qualities of the minute parts (cf. Locke, *Essay* 2.8.7–17).

## PRIMARY AND SECONDARY QUALITIES, SIGHT AND TOUCH, AND ABSTRACTION

One of Berkeley's arguments against the distinction between primary and secondary qualities is that it is impossible to form an idea of an extended, moving body without giving it some colour or other mind-dependent quality: what is inseparable from the mind-dependent must itself be mind-dependent (*Principles* I 10). Yet this argument seems weak in the case of qualities perceived by both sight and touch, since what is perceivable by either sense alone must be separable from the other. More fundamental, therefore, is Berkeley's denial that there are such ideas of two senses. In the *New Theory of Vision* he draws this conclusion from a brilliant discussion of a series of problems in optics, including the 'MOLYNEUX PROBLEM'. Molyneux and Locke both argued that a man born blind and made to see would be unable to tell distance and depth by sight, since 'he has not yet attained the Experience, that what affects his touch so or so, must affect his sight so or so' (Locke *Essay* 2.9.8). Berkeley argues that the only connections between objects of sight and touch are such contingent correlations. The former are signs of the latter, but in themselves numerically and qualitatively distinct (*New Theory* 47–157).

A further range of arguments is directed towards showing that determinate size, shape and motion is sense-relative. Behind these arguments lies the thought that 'external' extension, supposed the common object of (say) the naked eye and a view through a microscope, has to be conceived of as infinitely divisible and so, having an infinite number of parts, as of no determinate size or shape (*Principles* I 11,47; *Dialogues* I 184–193). Berkeley holds that, in contrast to this absurdity, any perceived extension is determinate, composed of a finite number of *minima sensibilia* (*New Theory* 80–5).

Berkeley attributes many errors to a common source: the assumption that what may be marked off by language can also be both abstracted in thought and separated in reality. The existence of sensible things is falsely supposed separable from their being perceived, primary from secondary qualities, and extension from both sight and touch. The Introduction of the *Principles* is accordingly devoted to an attack on Locke's theory of abstract ideas. Although Locke is misrepresented, Berkeley's own account of abstract thought (in fact, much like Locke's) is an important statement of the nominalist view that in reasoning we hold particulars in mind while focusing on those aspects of them marked by the language we employ.

### KNOWLEDGE OF SPIRIT, SPIRIT'S ACTIVITY AND THE LAWS OF PHYSICS

Berkeley reserves the term 'idea' for objects of 'perception', i.e. sense and imagination. Spirit is known (in one's own case) 'immediately, or intuitively', 'by reflection' (*Dialogues* III 231f). Despite the word 'reflection', his model for this immediate self-consciousness was not Locke's 'inner sense' so much as Cartesian 'pure intellect', a term he occasionally uses (ibid. I 193f; *De Motu* 53; *Siris* 303). By its means we attain a 'notion' of spirit which we can employ in our thought about God and other finite spirits (*Principles* I 135–40). No idea could represent spirit because ideas are self-evidently passive (we do not perceive power), whereas spirit is an active substance. It is to our consciousness of our own volition that we owe our notion of causal agency. It is therefore a contradiction that any sensible or unthinking thing should be a true cause (ibid. I 27f). Berkeley is here adapting the Cartesian doctrine, developed by Malebranche, that matter is the passive object of God's will.

These materials supply an argument for God's existence and a conception of physical laws as strictly contingent. Since all ideas require a cause, and ideas of sense are not caused by us, there must be some other spirit which causes them in us. Since they occur in an admirable and useful 'train or series', they are evidently the work of a wise and benevolent 'governing spirit whose will constitutes the Laws of Nature' (ibid. I 30–2). The scientist's task is not, therefore, to penetrate to the unknown essences of things, knowledge of which would make the world intelligible. There are no such essences behind our contingent generalizations. Science progresses purely through the drawing of analogies between phenomena, which it is the function of such theoretical terms as 'gravity' and 'attraction' to mark (ibid. I 101–9).

### REAL THINGS, DIVINE IDEAS AND SCEPTICISM

'The ideas imprinted on the senses by the Author of Nature are called *real things*.' With this interpretation of ordinary language Berkeley pre-empts the criticism that, together with mind-independent objects, he has done away with the distinction between reality and illusion or fiction. The involuntary, distinct and regularly connected ideas of sense are those which matter for the purposes of action (ibid. I 30–6). An objection from lively dreams is met with the principle of Berkeley's reductionism: the realist necessarily concedes all that is needed, since he too must 'distinguish *things* from *chimeras* . . . by some perceived difference' (*Dialogues* III 235). The objection that Berkeleyan 'real things' cease to exist when not perceived leads, in the Principles, to the suggestion that God may perceive them continuously (I 45). In the *Dialogues*, moreover, it is argued that the involuntariness of ideas of sense implies that they ('or their archetypes') have an existence distinct from our minds: causal independence implies ontological independence. Since they (or things like them) are ideas, they must exist in another mind, the one that exhibits them to us (II 211–16). We may conclude that 'they exist, during the intervals between the times of my perceiving them' (ibid. III 230f).

Critics have complained that with this conception of a dependable, archetypal order of nature, distanced from finite perceivers, as also in his account of our inference to OTHER MINDS, Berkeley leaves no less room than the realist for scepticism. Yet he never argues simply that 'materialism' leaves room for doubt, but that it postulates what is contradictory, indeterminate or otherwise unintelligible. It is these disadvantages of matter, none of which (he argues) attach to spirit and its ideas, which in his view encourage scepticism (ibid. III 231–4).

*See also* IDEALISM; LOCKE; PHENOMEN-ALISM; PRIMARY AND SECONDARY QUALITIES.

WRITINGS

*An Essay towards a New Theory of Vision* (1709), *A Treatise concerninq the Principles of Human Knowledge* (1710) and *Three Dialogues between Hylas and Philonous* (1713): in *Berkeley: Philosophical Works* ed. M.R. Ayers (London: Dent, 1975).
*Alciphron or the Minute Philosopher* (1732) and *Siris: a Chain of Philosophical Reflections and Enquiries concerning the Virtues of Tar-water* (1744); in his *Works* eds A.A. Luce and T.E. Jessop (London: Nelson, 1948–51).

BIBLIOGRAPHY

Dancy, J.: *Berkeley: an Introduction* (Oxford: Blackwell, 1987).
Foster, J. and Robinson, H. eds: *Essays on Berkeley* (Oxford: Clarendon Press, 1985).
Grayling, A.C.: *Berkeley: The Central Arguments* (London: Routledge, 1986).
Pitcher, G.: *Berkeley* (London: Routledge and Kegan Paul, 1977).
Sosa, E. ed.: *Essays on the Philosophy of George Berkeley* (Dordrecht: Reidel, 1987).
Tipton, I.C.: *Berkeley: the Philosophy of Immaterialism* (London: Methuen, 1974).
Turbayne, C. ed.: *Berkeley: Critical and Interpretative Essays* (Minneapolis: University of Minnesota Press, 1982).
Winkler, K.P.: *Berkeley: an Interpretation* (Oxford: Clarendon Press, 1989).

MICHAEL AYERS

**Blanshard, Brand** (1892–1987) American philosopher, who taught at the University of Michigan, Swarthmore College and Yale. Blanshard attended the University of Michigan but left at the end of his junior year upon being awarded a Rhodes Scholarship to Merton College, Oxford. His studies were interrupted by the First World War but, having taken an MA at Columbia, where he studied with Dewey, he returned to Oxford to finish his work for the graduate BSc degree. He then went to Harvard where he completed a PhD thesis under the direction of C.I. LEWIS. However, in spite of his work with DEWEY and LEWIS, it was Oxford that decisively shaped Blanshard's ideas. Blanshard thought that the PRAGMATISM of Dewey and Lewis was challenging but untenable. Later in his career, he became an uncompromising foe of positivism and linguistic philosophy. He remained a traditionalist, never deviating from the IDEALISM he learned from H.H. Joachim and, particularly, F.H. Bradley. In epistemology, he became British Idealism's last living representative.

Blanshard's most significant epistemological work is *The Nature of Thought* (1939). It contains trenchant criticisms of both EMPIRICISM and the correspondence theory of TRUTH. Blanshard is careful to distinguish between questions about the test of truth (i.e. justification) and questions about its nature but, unlike some contemporary philosophers, is certain that both must be explicated in terms of coherence. His argument, which he develops with considerable force, is that explicating justification and truth in disparate terms leads inevitably to scepticism. What is less clear is whether Blanshard himself has a satisfactory solution to this problem for he, too, seems to decouple the test of truth from its nature. As the test of truth, coherence is coherence with 'the system of present knowledge', whereas truth in its nature is coherence with 'a system complete and all-inclusive' (1939, vol. 2, p. 269). Why, then, suppose that a judgement's coherence with our current beliefs tells us anything about its relations to an ideally completed system? Blanshard replies that, indeed, no judgement in our current system is wholly true: this is the familiar idealist doctrine of degrees of truth which he argues, plausibly, follows necessarily from his holistic conceptions of meaning and justification. However, the thought that current judgements are at least partially true depends on the claim that 'thought is related to reality as the partial to the perfect fulfilment of a purpose' (ibid., p. 262). But Blanshard's only justification for this teleological postulate is that, without it, scepticism results.

Unlike that of some idealists, Blanshard's writing is admirably clear; and although his arguments and positions were going out of fashion when he first presented them, they will be found sympathetic by many contemporary philosophers, at least in their critical aspect. If Blanshard is neglected today, it is somewhat unjustly.

WRITINGS

*The Nature of Thought*, 2 vols (London: Allen and Unwin, 1939).
*Reason and Analysis* (La Salle: Open Court; London: Allen and Unwin, 1962).

MICHAEL WILLIAMS

**Brentano, Franz** (1838–1917) German psychologist and philosopher. Brentano's principal contributions to the theory of knowledge derive from the account of conscious states that he sets forth in his *Psychology from an Empirical Standpoint*, first published in 1874.

Our conscious states, according to Brentano, are all objects of 'inner perception'. Every such state is such that, for the person who is in that state, it is *evident* to that person that he or she is in that state. (Brentano does not mean that each of our conscious states is an object of an *act* of perception; hence the doctrine does not lead to an infinite regress.) The expression 'evident', for Brentano, is purely epistemic; his use of 'evident' is equivalent to the epistemic use of 'certain'.

He holds that there are two types of conscious state – those that are 'physical' and those that are 'intentional'. His use of 'physical' in this context is somewhat misleading, for he takes it to mean the the same as 'sensory'. A *'physical'*, or *sensory*, state is a sensation or sense-impression – a qualitative individual composed of parts that are spatially related to each other. *Intentional* states (e.g. believing, considering, hoping, desiring) are characterized by the facts that (1) they are 'directed upon objects', (2) objects may be 'directed upon' without existing (e.g. we may fear things that do not exist), and (3) such states are not sensory. There is no sensation, no sensory individual, that can be identified with any particular intentional attitude.

Following LEIBNIZ, Brentano distinguishes two types of CERTAINTY: the certainty we can have with respect to the existence of our conscious states; and that a priori certainty that may be directed upon necessary truths. These two types of certainty may be combined in a significant way. At a given moment I may be certain, on the basis of inner perception, that there is believing, desiring, hoping and fearing; and I may also be certain a priori that there cannot be believing, desiring, hoping and fearing unless there is a *substance* that believes, desires, hopes and fears. In such a case, it will be certain for me (Brentano says that I will 'perceive') that there is a substance that believes, desires, hopes and fears. It is also axiomatic, Brentano says, that, if one is certain that a substance of a certain sort exists, then one is identical with that substance.

Brentano makes use of only two purely epistemic concepts: that of *being certain*, or *evident*, and that of *being probable*. If a given hypothesis is *probable*, in the epistemic sense, for a particular person, then that person can be *certain* that that hypothesis is probable for him. Making use of the principles of probability, one may calculate the probability that a given hypothesis has on one's evidence base.

But if our evidence-base is composed only of necessary truths and the facts of inner perception, then it is difficult to see how it could provide justification for any contingent truths other than those that pertain to states of consciousness. How could such an evidence-base even lend *probability* to the hypothesis that there is a world of external physical things? Brentano was reluctant to concede that his theory of knowledge might have such sceptical consequences. (In his theological writings, he attempts to prove a priori the existence of a personal God and he concludes that we have 'a probability approaching certainty' that such a being exists. But, unlike Descartes, he does not attempt to base his theory of knowledge upon such a conclusion.)

Perhaps the most significant thing about Brentano's theory of knowledge is the general problem that he leaves us with. If (a) the knowledge that we have is based upon necessary truths and certain facts about our conscious states, and if (b) application of the principles of probability to this evidence base does not provide probability for our common sense beliefs, then (c) it would seem to be questionable whether we can have *any* justification for such beliefs.

One solution was suggested by Alexius Meinong, who had studied with Brentano in Vienna: those intentional attitudes that we ordinarily call 'perceiving' and 'remembering' provide 'presumptive evidence' – that is to say, *prima facie* evidence – for their intentional objects. For example, believing that one is looking at a group of people tends to justify the belief that there is a group of people that one is looking at. How, then, are we to distinguish merely '*prima facie*' justification from the real thing? This type of solution would seem to call for principles that specify, by reference to further facts of inner perception, the conditions under which merely *prima facie* justification may become real justification.

See also PRIMA FACIE REASONS.

WRITINGS

*The True and the Evident* (London: Routledge and Kegan Paul, 1966).
*Sensory and Noetic Consciousness* (London: Routledge and Kegan Paul, 1981).

BIBLIOGRAPHY

McAlister, L.L. ed.: *The Philosophy of Brentano* (London: Duckworth, 1976).

R.M. CHISHOLM

**burden of proof**   The strength or weight of argument required by one side to convince the other side. The concept of burden of proof marks a balance between the competing points of view in a critical discussion, or in other adversarial types of dialogue. As more weight is gained by the argumentation of one side, its point of view is justified more strongly, and the burden of proof passes to the other side. As one side rises, the other falls, and the burden of proof passes accordingly.

Recognition and use of burden of proof can be a powerful factor in reasoned persuasion. There are two main uses for the notion. The first is when, having gained a temporary advantage, we announce that the burden of proof now lies with the other side, and simply wait to see what, if anything, they produce; if nothing emerges we claim the victory, even though our own reasoning may have been far from conclusive. The second is where we attempt to claim that our own view enjoys some antecedent presumption in its favour, so that the burden of proof lies *initially* with our opponents. The dictates of common sense are often held to enjoy this privileged position.

See also CIRCULAR REASONING; INFORMAL FALLACIES.

BIBLIOGRAPHY

Brown, R.: 'The burden of proof', *American Philosophical Quarterly* 7 (1970), 74–82.
Sproule, J.M.: 'The psychological burden of proof', *Communication Monographs* 43 (1976), 115–29.
Walton, D.N.: Burden of proof', *Argumentation* 2 (1988), 233–54.

DOUGLAS N. WALTON

# C

---

**Carnap, Rudolf (1891–1970)** Carnap was born in Ronsdorf, Germany, and died in Los Angeles. Although he was for a time a member of the VIENNA CIRCLE of logical positivists, he later became a leader of the movement known as LOGICAL EMPIRICISM.

Carnap's doctoral dissertation, *Der Raum* (1921), exhibited a neo-Kantian orientation, but shortly after completing it he became a thoroughgoing empiricist. Impressed by the method of analysis advocated in Bertrand Russell (1914) he undertook the project that culminated in his *Der logische Aufbau der Welt* (1928), which he saw as a precise execution of the sort of LOGICAL CONSTRUCTION Russell recommended. Strongly influenced by Ernst Mach, he began using sensations as a basis; later (before publication), because of considerations of Gestalt psychology, he changed the basis to total momentary experiences. In this work he also showed how a physicalistic basis could be adopted; in fact, he subsequently adopted it himself. He held a longstanding commitment to his 'principle of tolerance' – that the choice of a language is a matter of efficiency, not a question of ontology. In *Meaning and Necessity* (1956a) this theme is elaborated, with emphasis upon the meaninglessness of such ontological issues.

In keeping with his EMPIRICIST outlook, Carnap adopted a verifiability criterion of meaning (*see* VERIFICATIONISM). In early days he demanded conclusive verifiability, but latter relaxed the requirement to testability, and then to confirmability to some degree (1936–7, 1956b). This development paralleled his realization that scientific knowledge could not be grounded in certainty.

Carnap's chief interests came to be centred, in the early 1940s, on probability and degree of confirmation, an area that occupied him for the rest of his life. He distinguished two concepts of PROBABILITY, degree of confirmation and relative frequency; his work focused almost exclusively on the former. He constructed a monumental system of inductive logic based on the notion of probability as a logical relation between evidence and hypothesis (1950), which he intended as the foundation of a formalization of confirmation in science. He refined and extended this work until his death in 1970. One of the most valuable aspects is his 'clarification of the explicandum' (1950, chs I, II, IV). The major difficulty with his system is the inescapable need for a priori probability measures on factual propositions. He concludes that the basic principles of inductive logic must be based on 'inductive intuition' (Schilpp, 1963, p. 978).

In addition to the above-mentioned work, Carnap made contributions of first importance to logic, semantics, and the foundations of mathematics. He also contributed significantly to the unity of science movement.

*See also* EXISTENCE; NATURAL SCIENCE; PROTOCOL SENTENCES; SCHLICK; SOLIPSISM.

WRITINGS

*Der Raum* (Jena: Universität Jena, 1921).
'Testability and Meaning', *Philosophy of Science* 3 (1936), 419–71, 4 (1937), 1–40.
'Empiricism, semantics, and ontology', in his *Meaning and Necessity* 2nd edn (Chicago: University of Chicago Press, 1956[a]), 205–21.
'The methodological character of theoretical concepts', *Minnesota Studies in the Philosophy of Science* vol. 1, eds H. Feigl and M. Scriven (Minneapolis: University of Minnesota Press, 1956[b]), 38–76.
*The Logical Foundations of Probability* (Chicago:

University of Chicago Press, 1950; 2nd edn, with new Preface, 1962).

*Der logische Aufbau der Welt* (Berlin: 1928) trans. R. A. George *The Logical Structure of the World* (Berkeley & Los Angeles: University of California Press, 1967).

BIBLIOGRAPHY

Goodman, N.: *The Structure of Appearance* (Cambridge, MA: Harvard University Press, 1951).
Russell, B.: *Our Knowledge of the External World* (London: Allen and Unwin, 1914).
Schilpp, P.A. ed.: *The Philosophy of Rudolf Carnap* (La Salle: Open Court, 1963).

WESLEY C. SALMON

**Cartesianism** The name given to the philosophical movement inaugurated by René DESCARTES (after 'Cartesius', the Latin version of his name). The main features of Cartesianism are (1) the use of methodical doubt as a tool for testing beliefs and reaching certainty; (2) a metaphysical system which starts from the subject's indubitable awareness of his own existence; (3) a theory of 'clear and distinct ideas' based on the innate concepts and propositions implanted in the soul by God (these include the ideas of mathematics, which Descartes takes to be the fundamental building blocks of science); (4) the theory now known as 'dualism' – that there are two fundamentally incompatible kinds of substance in the universe, mind (or thinking substance) and matter (or extended substance). A corollary of this last theory is that human beings are radically heterogeneous beings, composed of an unextended, immaterial consciousness united to a piece of purely physical machinery – the body. Another key element in Cartesian dualism is the claim that the mind has perfect and transparent awareness of its own nature or essence.

JOHN COTTINGHAM

**causal theories in epistemology** What makes a belief *justified* and what makes a true belief *knowledge*? It is natural to think that whether a belief deserves one of these appraisals depends on what caused the subject to have the belief. In recent decades a number of epistemologists have pursued this plausible idea with a variety of specific proposals. Let us look first at some proposed causal criteria for knowledge and then at one for justification.

KNOWLEDGE

Some causal theories of knowledge have it that a true belief that *p* is knowledge just in case it has the right sort of causal connection to the fact that *p*. Such a criterion can be applied only to cases where the fact that *p* is a sort that can enter into causal relations; this seems to exclude mathematical and other necessary facts and perhaps any fact expressed by a universal generalization; and proponents of this sort of criterion have usually supposed that it is limited to perceptual knowledge of particular facts about the subject's environment.

For example, ARMSTRONG (1973, ch. 12) proposed that a belief of the form 'This (perceived) object is F' is (non-inferential) knowledge if and only if the belief is a completely reliable sign that the perceived object is F; that is, the fact that the object is F contributed to causing the belief and its doing so depended on properties of the believer such that the laws of nature dictate that, for any subject *x* and perceived object *y*, if *x* has those properties and believes that *y* is F, then *y* is F. (Dretske (1981) offers a rather similar account, in terms of the belief's being caused by a signal received by the perceiver that carries the information that the object is F.)

This sort of condition fails, however, to be sufficient for non-inferential perceptual knowledge because it is compatible with the belief's being unjustified, and an unjustified belief cannot be knowledge. For example, suppose that your mechanisms for colour perception are working well, but you have been given good reason to think otherwise, to think, say, that magenta things look chartreuse to you and chartreuse things look magenta. If you fail to heed these reasons you have for thinking that your colour perception is awry and believe of a thing that looks

57

magenta to you that it is magenta, your belief will fail to be justified and will therefore fail to be knowledge, even though it is caused by the thing's being magenta in such a way as to be a completely reliable sign (or to carry the information) that the thing is magenta.

One could fend off this sort of counter-example by simply adding to the causal condition the requirement that the belief be justified. But this enriched condition would still be insufficient. Suppose, for example, that in an experiment you are given a drug that in nearly all people (but not in you, as it happens) causes the aforementioned aberration in colour perception. The experimenter tells you that you've taken such a drug but then says, 'No, wait a minute, the pill *you* took was just a placebo.' But suppose further that this last thing the experimenter tells you is false. Her telling you this gives you justification for believing of a thing that looks magenta to you that it is magenta, but a fact about this justification that is unknown to you (that the experimenter's last statement was false) makes it the case that your true belief is not knowledge even though it satisfies Armstrong's causal condition.

Goldman (1986, ch. 3) has proposed an importantly different sort of causal criterion, namely, that a true belief is knowledge if it is produced by a type of process that is 'globally' and 'locally' reliable. It is globally reliable if its propensity to cause true beliefs is sufficiently high. Local reliability has to do with whether the process would have produced a similar but false belief in certain counter-factual situations alternative to the actual situation. This way of marking off true beliefs that are knowledge does not require the fact believed to be causally related to the belief, and so it could in principle apply to knowledge of any kind of truth.

Goldman requires the global reliability of the belief-producing process for the justification of a belief; he requires it also for knowledge because justification is required for knowledge. What he requires for knowledge but does not require for justification is local reliability. His idea is that a justified true belief is knowledge if the type of process that produced it would *not* have produced it in any

relevant counterfactual situation in which it is false (*see* RELEVANT ALTERNATIVES).

What makes an alternative situation relevant? Goldman does not try to formulate a criterion of relevance, but in giving examples of what he takes to be relevant alternative situations he makes remarks that suggest one. Suppose, he says, that a parent takes a child's temperature with a thermometer that the parent selected at random from several lying in the medicine cabinet; only the particular thermometer chosen was in good working order; it correctly shows the child's temperature to be normal but if it had been abnormal then any of the other thermometers would have erroneously shown it to be normal. The parent's actual true belief is caused by a globally reliable process but, Goldman says (1986, p. 45), because it was 'just luck' that the parent happened to select a good thermometer 'we would not say that the parent knows that the child's temperature is normal'. Goldman gives another example:

> Suppose Sam spots Judy across the street and correctly believes that it is Judy. If it were Judy's twin sister, Trudy, he would mistake her for Judy. Does Sam know that it is Judy? As long as *there is a serious possibility* [emphasis added] that the person across the street might have been Trudy rather than Judy . . . , we would deny that Sam knows. (1986, p. 46)

Goldman suggests that the reason for denying knowledge in the thermometer example is that it was 'just luck' that the parent did not pick a non-working thermometer and in the twins example the reason is that there was 'a serious possibility' that it might have been the other twin Sam saw. This suggests the following criterion of relevance: an alternative situation, where the same belief is produced in the same way but is false, is relevant just in case at some point before the actual belief was caused the chance of that situation's having come about instead of the actual situation was too high: it was too much a matter of luck that it didn't come about.

This would mean that the proposed criterion of knowledge is the following: a justified true belief that $p$ is knowledge just in case there is no alternative non-$p$ situation in which the subject is similarly caused to believe that $p$ and which is such that at some point in the actual world there was a serious chance that that situation might occur instead of the actual one.

This avoids the sorts of counterexamples we gave for the causal criteria we discussed earlier, but it is vulnerable to ones of a different sort. Suppose you stand on the mainland looking over the water at an island, on which are several structures that look (from at least some point of view) as would barns. You happen to be looking at one of these that is in fact a barn and your belief to that effect is justified, given how it looks to you and the fact that you have no reason to think otherwise. But suppose that the great majority of the barn-looking structures on the island are not real barns but fakes. Finally, suppose that from any viewpoint on the mainland all of the island's fake barns are obscured by trees and that circumstances made it very unlikely that you would have got to a viewpoint not on the mainland. Here, it seems, your justified true belief that you are looking at a barn is not knowledge, despite the fact that there was not a serious chance that there would have developed an alternative situation where you are similarly caused to have a false belief that you are looking at a barn.

That example shows that the 'local reliability' of the belief-producing process, on the 'serious chance' explication of what makes an alternative relevant, is not sufficient to make a justified true belief knowledge. Another example will show that it is also not necessary. Suppose I am justified in believing the truth that Cornell defeated Brown in their basketball game last night by hearing it so reported by a radio newscaster, and there is nothing at all untoward in the way the newscaster came to say what he did. But suppose further that at the same time, unknown to me, on the other local station a newscaster reads from mistyped copy and says that Brown defeated Cornell. Since I pretty much

randomly chose which local station to listen to, the probability that I would end up with a similarly caused but false belief about the outcome of the Cornell–Brown game was about one-half, a serious chance. Yet surely I know the outcome of the game on the basis of hearing the non-defective newscast as well as I ever know such a thing on such a basis.

These examples make it seem likely that, if there is a criterion for what makes an alternative situation relevant that will save Goldman's claim about local reliability and knowledge, it will not be simple.

## JUSTIFICATION

The interesting thesis that counts as a causal theory of justification (in the meaning of 'causal theory' intended here) is the following: a belief is justified just in case it was produced by a type of process that is 'globally' reliable, that is, its propensity to produce true beliefs – which can be defined (to a good enough approximation) as the proportion of the beliefs it produces (or would produce were it used as much as opportunity allows) that are true – is sufficiently great (*see* RELIABILISM).

This proposal will be adequately specified only when we are told (1) how much of the causal history of a belief counts as part of the process that produced it, (2) which of the many types to which the process belongs is *the* type for purposes of assessing its reliability, and (3) relative to what world or worlds is the reliability of the process type to be assessed (the actual world, the closest worlds containing the case being considered, or something else?). Let us look at the answers suggested by Goldman, the leading proponent of a reliabilist account of justification.

(1) Goldman (1979, 1986) takes the relevant belief producing process to include only the proximate causes internal to the believer. So, for instance, when recently I believed that the telephone was ringing the process that produced the belief, for purposes of assessing reliability, includes just the causal chain of neural events from the stimulus in my ears inward and other concurrent brain states on which the production

of the belief depended; it does not include any events in the telephone, or the sound waves travelling between it and my ears, or any earlier decisions I made that were responsible for my being within hearing distance of the telephone at that time. It does seem intuitively plausible that the facts on which the justification of a belief depends should be restricted to internal ones proximate to the belief. Why? Goldman doesn't tell us. One answer that some philosophers might give is that it is because a belief's being justified at a given time can depend only on facts directly accessible to the believer's awareness at that time (for, if a believer ought to hold only beliefs that are justified, she can tell at any given time what beliefs would then be justified for her) (*see* EXTERNALISM/INTERNALISM). But this cannot be Goldman's answer because he wishes to include in the relevant process neural events that are not directly accessible to consciousness.

(2) Once the reliabilist has told us how to delimit the process producing a belief, he needs to tell us which of the many types to which it belongs is the relevant type. Consider, for example, the process that produces your current belief that you see a book before you. One very broad type to which that process belongs would be specified by 'coming to a belief as to something one perceives as a result of activation of the nerve endings in some of one's sense-organs'. A narrower type to which that same process belongs would be specified by 'coming to a belief as to what one sees as a result of activation of the nerve endings in one's retinas'. A still narrower type would be given by inserting in the last specification a description of a particular pattern of activation of the retina's receptor cells. Which of these or other types to which the token process belongs is the relevant type for determining whether the type of process that produced your belief is reliable?

If we select a type that is too broad, we will classify as having the same degree of justification various beliefs that intuitively seem to have different degrees of justification. Thus the broadest type we specified for your belief that you see a book before you applies also to

perceptual beliefs where the object seen is far away and seen only briefly through fog, and intuitively the latter sort of belief is less justified. On the other hand, if we are allowed to select a type that is as narrow as we please, then we make it out that an obviously unjustified but true belief is produced by a reliable type of process. For example, suppose I see a blurred shape through the fog far off in a field and unjustifiedly, but correctly, believe that it is a sheep; if we include enough details about my retinal images in specifying the type of the visual process that produced that belief, we can specify a type that is likely to have only that one instance and is therefore 100 per cent reliable. Goldman conjectures (1986, p. 50) that the relevant process type is 'the *narrowest* type that is *causally operative* in producing the belief token in question'. Presumably, a feature of the process producing a belief was causally operative in producing it just in case *some* alternative feature is such that, had the process had that feature instead, it would not have led to that belief. (We need to say 'some' here rather than 'any', because, for example, when I see an oak tree the particular 'oakish' shape of my retinal images is clearly causally operative in producing my belief that I see a tree even though there are alternative shapes, for example, 'sprucish' ones, that would have produced the same belief.) (*See* RELIABILISM.)

(3) Should the justification of a belief in a hypothetical, non-actual example turn on the reliability of the belief-producing process in the possible world of the example? That leads to the implausible result that in a world run by a Cartesian demon – a powerful being who causes the other inhabitants of the world to have rich and coherent sets of perceptual and memory impressions that are all illusory – the perceptual and memory beliefs of the other inhabitants are all unjustified, for they are produced by processes that are, in that world, quite unreliable. If we say instead that it is the reliability of the processes in the actual world that matters, we get the equally undesirable result that if the actual world is a demon world then our perceptual and memory beliefs are all unjustified.

Goldman's solution (1986, p. 107) is that

the reliability of the process types is to be gauged by their performance in 'normal' worlds, that is, worlds consistent with 'our general beliefs about the world . . . about the sorts of objects, events and changes that occur in it'. This gives the intuitively right results for the problem cases just considered, but it implies an implausible relativity regarding justification. If there are people whose general beliefs about the world are very different from mine, then there may, on this account, be beliefs that *I* can correctly regard as justified (ones produced by processes that are reliable in what I take to be normal worlds) but that *they* can correctly regard as not justified.

However these questions about the specifics are dealt with, there are reasons for questioning the basic idea that the criterion for a belief's being justified is its being produced by a reliable process.

Doubt about the *sufficiency* of the reliabilist criterion is prompted by a sort of example that Goldman himself uses for another purpose. Suppose that being in brain-state B always causes one to believe that one is in brain-state B. Here the reliability of the belief-producing process is perfect. But 'we can readily imagine circumstances in which a person goes into brain-state B and therefore has the belief in question, though this belief is by no means justified' (Goldman, 1979, p. 6). Doubt about the *necessity* of the condition arises from the possibility that one might know that one has strong justification for a certain belief and yet that knowledge is not what actually prompts one to believe. For example, I might be well aware that, having read the weather bureau's forecast that it will be much hotter tomorrow, I have ample reason to be confident that it will be hotter tomorrow, but I irrationally refuse to believe it until my Aunt Hattie tells me that she feels in her joints that it will be hotter tomorrow. Here what prompts me to believe does not justify my belief, but my belief is nevertheless justified by my knowledge of the weather bureau's prediction and of its evidential force: I can cite it to refute any suggestion that I ought not to be holding the belief. Indeed, given my justification and that there's

nothing untoward about the weather bureau's prediction, my belief, if true, can be counted knowledge. This sort of example raises doubt whether any causal condition, be it a reliable process or something else, is necessary for either justification or knowledge.

*See also* EXTERNALISM/INTERNALISM; MEMORY; NATURALIZED EPISTEMOLOGY; PERCEPTUAL KNOWLEDGE; RELIABILISM.

BIBLIOGRAPHY

Armstrong, D.M.: *Belief, Truth and Knowledge* (London: Cambridge University Press, 1973).

Dretske, F.: 'Conclusive reasons', *Australasian Journal of Philosophy* 49 (1971), 1–22.

Dretske, F.: *Knowledge and the Flow of Information* (Cambridge, MA: MIT Press, 1981).

Dretske, F. and Enc, B.: 'Causal theories of knowledge', *Midwest Studies in Philosophy* 9 (1984), 517–28.

Ginet, C.: 'Contra reliabilism', *Monist* 68 (1985), 175–88.

Ginet, C.: 'Justification: it need not cause but it must be accessible', *Journal of Philosophical Research* 15 (1990), 93–107.

Ginet, C.: 'The fourth condition', in *Philosophical Analysis* ed. D.F. Austin (Amsterdam: Kluwer, 1988), 105–17.

Goldman, A.I.: 'Discrimination and perceptual knowledge', *Journal of Philosophy*, 73 (1976), 771–91.

Goldman, A.I.: 'What is justified belief?', in *Justification and Knowledge* ed. G. Pappas (Dordrecht, Reidel, 1979), 1–23.

Goldman, A.I.: *Epistemology and Cognition* (Cambridge, MA: Harvard University Press, 1986).

CARL GINET

**certainty** Issues surrounding certainty are inextricably connected with those concerning SCEPTICISM. For many sceptics have traditionally held that knowledge requires certainty, and, of course, they claim that certain knowledge is not possible. In part, in order to avoid scepticism, the anti-sceptics have generally held that knowledge does not require certainty (*see* PRAGMATISM; Lehrer, 1974; Dewey, 1960). A few anti-sceptics have held, *with* the sceptics, that knowledge does require certainty but, *against* the sceptics, that certainty is possible (Moore, 1959; Klein, 1981, 1990). The task here is to provide a characterization of certainty which would be acceptable to both the sceptics and the anti-sceptics. For such an agreement is a pre-condition of an interesting debate between them.

It seems clear that certainty is a property that can be ascribed to either a person or a belief. We can say that a *person*, S, is certain; or we can say that a *proposition*, p, is certain. The two uses can be connected by saying that S has the right to be certain just in case p is sufficiently warranted (Ayer, 1956). I will follow the lead of most philosophers who have taken the second sense, the sense in which a *proposition* is said to be certain, as the important one to be investigated by epistemology. An exception is Unger who defends scepticism by arguing that psychological certainty is not possible (Unger, 1975).

In defining certainty, it is crucial to note that the term has both an absolute and relative sense. Very roughly, one can say that a proposition is absolutely certain just in case there is no proposition more warranted than it (Chisholm, 1977). But we also commonly say that one proposition is more certain than another, implying that the second one, though less certain, is still certain.

Now some philosophers, notably Unger (1975), have argued that the absolute sense is the only sense, and that the relative sense is only apparent. Even if those arguments are unconvincing (*see* Cargile, 1972; Klein, 1981), what remains clear is that there is an absolute sense and it is that sense which is crucial to the issues surrounding scepticism.

So let us suppose that the interesting question is this: What makes a belief or proposition absolutely certain?

There are several ways of approaching an answer to that question. Some, like Russell, will take a belief to be certain just in case there is no *logical* possibility that our belief is false (Russell, 1922). On this definition propositions about physical objects (objects occupying space) cannot be certain. However, that characterization of certainty should be rejected precisely because it makes the question of the existence of absolutely certain empirical propositions uninteresting. For it concedes to the sceptic the impossibility of certainty about physical objects too easily (Ayer, 1956; Moore, 1959). Thus, this approach would not be acceptable to the anti-sceptics.

Other philosophers have suggested that the role that a belief plays within our set of actual beliefs makes a belief certain. For example, WITTGENSTEIN has suggested that a belief is certain just in case it can be appealed to in order to justify other beliefs but stands in no need of justification itself (Wittgenstein, 1969). Thus, the question of the existence of beliefs which are certain can be answered by merely inspecting our practices to determine whether there are any beliefs which play the specified role. This approach would not be acceptable to the sceptics. For it, too, makes the question of the existence of absolutely certain beliefs uninteresting. The issue is not whether there are beliefs which play such a role, but whether there are any beliefs which should play that role. Perhaps our practices cannot be defended.

Let us return to the suggested, rough characterization of absolute certainty given above, namely that a belief, p, is certain just in case there is no belief which is more warranted than p. Although it does delineate a necessary condition of absolute certainty and it is preferable to the Wittgensteinian approach mentioned above, it does not capture the full sense of 'absolute certainty'. The sceptics would argue that it is not strong enough. For, according to this rough characterization, a belief could be absolutely certain and yet there could be good grounds for doubting it – just as long as there were equally good grounds for doubting every proposition that was equally warranted. In addition, to say that a belief is certain is to say, in part, that we have a guarantee of its truth. There is no such guarantee provided by this rough characterization.

A Cartesian characterization of the concept of absolute certainty seems more promising. Roughly, this approach is that a proposition, p, is certain for S just in case S is warranted in believing that p and there are absolutely no grounds whatsoever for doubting it. Now one could characterize those grounds in a variety of ways (Firth, 1976; Miller, 1978; Klein, 1981, 1990). For example, a ground, g, for making p doubtful for S could be such that (a) S is not warranted in denying g and:

(b1) if g is added to S's beliefs, the negation of p is warranted; or
(b2) if g is added to S's beliefs, p is no longer warranted; or
(b3) if g is added to S's beliefs, p becomes less warranted (even if only slightly so).

Although there is a guarantee of sorts of p's truth contained in (b1) and (b2), those notions of grounds for doubt do not seem to capture a basic feature of *absolute* certainty delineated in the rough account given above. For a proposition, p, could be immune to grounds for doubt, g, in those two senses and yet another proposition would be 'more certain' if there were no grounds for doubt like those specified in (b3). So, only (b3) can succeed in providing *part* of the required guarantee of p's truth.

An account like that contained in (b3) can provide only part of the guarantee because it is only a *subjective* guarantee of p's truth. S's belief system would contain adequate grounds for assuring S that p is true because S's belief system would warrant the denial of every proposition that would lower the warrant of p. But S's belief system might contain false beliefs and still be immune to doubt in this sense. Indeed, p itself could be certain and false in this subjective sense.

An *objective* guarantee is needed as well. We can capture such *objective* immunity to doubt by requiring, roughly, that there be no *true* proposition such that if it is added to S's beliefs, the result is a reduction in the warrant for p (even if only very slight). I say 'roughly' because there will be the problem of so-called 'misleading defeaters'. That is, there will be true propositions which if added to S's beliefs result in lowering the warrant of p because they render evident some false proposition which actually reduces the warrant of p. It is debatable whether mis-

leading defeaters provide genuine grounds for doubt. But this is a minor difficulty which can be overcome (Klein, 1981, esp. pp. 148–56). What is crucial to note is that given this characterization of objective immunity to doubt, it follows trivially that p is true and that there is a set of true propositions in S's belief set which warrant p and which are themselves objectively immune to doubt.

Thus, we can say that a belief that p is absolutely certain just in case it is *subjectively* and *objectively* immune to doubt. In other words a proposition, p, is absolutely certain for S if and only if (1) p is warranted for S and (2) S is warranted in denying every proposition, g, such that if g is added to S's beliefs, the warrant for p is reduced (even if only very slightly) and (3) there is no true proposition, d, such that if d is added to S's beliefs the warrant for p is reduced (even if only very slightly).

This is an account of absolute certainty which captures what is demanded by the sceptic. If a proposition is certain in this sense, it is indubitable and guaranteed both subjectively and objectively to be true. In addition, such a characterization of certainty does not automatically lead to scepticism (*see* Klein, 1981, 1990). Thus, this is an account of certainty that satisfies the task at hand, namely to find an account of certainty that provides the precondition for a debate between the sceptic and anti-sceptic.

BIBLIOGRAPHY

Ayer, A.J.: *The Problem of Knowledge* (London: Macmillan, 1956).
Cargile, J.: 'In reply to "A Defense of Scepticism"', *Philosophical Review* 81 (1972), 229–36.
Chisholm, R.: *Theory of Knowledge* 2nd edn (Englewood Cliffs: Prentice-Hall, 1977).
Dewey, J.: *The Quest for Certainty* (New York: Putnam, 1960).
Firth, R.: 'The anatomy of certainty', *Philosophical Review* 76 (1976), 3–27.
Klein, P.: *Certainty: A Refutation of Scepticism* (Minneapolis: University of Minnesota Press, 1981).

Klein, P.: 'Epistemic compatibilism and canonical beliefs', in *Doubting: Contemporary Perspectives on Scepticism* eds M.D. Roth and G. Ross (Boston: Kluwer, 1990), 99–117.

Klein, P.: 'Immune belief systems', *Philosophical Topics* 14 (1986), 259–80.

Lehrer, K.: *Knowledge* (Oxford: Oxford University Press, 1974).

Miller, R.: 'Absolute certainty', *Mind* 87 (1978), 46–65.

Moore, G.E.: *Philosophical Papers* (New York: Macmillan, 1959).

Russell, B.: *Our Knowledge of the External World* (London: Allen and Unwin, 1922).

Unger, P.: *Ignorance: A Case for Scepticism* (Oxford: Oxford University Press, 1975).

Wittgenstein, L.: *On Certainty* (Oxford: Blackwell, 1969).

PETER D. KLEIN

**Chisholm, Roderick (1916–)** Chisholm is an American philosopher who has been influential in a number of different areas of philosophy, including epistemology, metaphysics, and ethics. He was an undergraduate at Brown University and then a graduate student at Harvard in 1938–42. After finishing his studies, he served in the military as a clinical psychologist. He then returned to Brown University in 1947, where he remained on the faculty until his retirement.

In 1942 Chisholm published in *Mind* his first paper on epistemology, 'The problem of the speckled hen'. Since then, he has addressed every major problem in epistemology. The most important of his writings on epistemology are *Perceiving* (1957), *The Foundations of Knowing* (1982), and, most famously, the 1966, 1977 and 1989 editions of *Theory of Knowledge*. The result of all this work is an epistemological system whose scope and subtlety are unsurpassed in the twentieth century.

At the base of Chisholm's system is a basic notion of justification, which he uses to give definitions of various terms of epistemic appraisal. For example, in the third edition of *Theory of Knowledge* (hereafter *TK*3), he defines 'beyond reasonable doubt' as follows: $p$ is beyond reasonable doubt for an individual $S =_{df} S$ is more justified in believing $p$ than in withholding judgement on $p$. In addition, he defines when $p$ is certain (nothing is more justified for $S$ to believe), when $p$ is evident ($S$ is as justified in believing $p$ as in withholding judgement on what is counterbalanced), when $p$ is epistemically in the clear ($S$ is as justified in believing $p$ as in withholding judgement on $p$), when $p$ is probable ($S$ is more justified in believing $p$ than in disbelieving $p$), and when $p$ is counterbalanced ($S$ is as justified in believing $p$ as in disbelieving $p$, and vice versa).

Chisholm then uses these terms of epistemic appraisal to formulate a number of epistemic principles. The principles are expressed as conditionals, whose antecedents describe sufficient logical conditions for the application of these terms of appraisal. In the most straightforward case, a principle will assert that if certain non-epistemic conditions are satisfied (e.g. conditions about what $S$ is experiencing, believing, etc.), then a proposition $p$ has a certain epistemic status for $S$ (e.g. it is evident or beyond reasonable doubt for $S$).

The definitions above tell us to understand this status in terms of an undefined notion of justification. Thus, Chisholm's project in epistemology can be seen as the counterpart of a project in ethics that seeks to describe various sets of non-moral conditions that are sufficient to make an action morally right. The ethicists who try to carry out this project are at odds with utilitarians, since for utilitarians there is but one source of moral obligation – namely, utility. These non-utilitarian ethicists insist that there are other sources as well, ones that aren't directly concerned with the maximization of happiness. Equality and fairness, for example, are among the usual candidates. Analogously, Chisholm insists that there is more than one source of epistemic justification.

The principal sources of empirical justification in Chisholm's system are self-presentation (of certain kinds of psychological states – e.g. thinkings, desirings, intendings and sensings), perception, memory, belief coupled with a lack of negative coherence, and, finally, positive coherence among propositions with some antecedent positive epistemic status. Corresponding to each of these sources, Chisholm proposes an epistemic principle describing the conditions under which the source produces justification. For example, his principle for self-presenting psychological states is as follows (*TK3*, 19): 'If the property of being F is self-presenting, if S is F, and if S believes himself to be F, then it is certain that he is F.'

Chisholm has a reputation as one of leading FOUNDATIONALISTS of the twentieth century, but as the above list of sources makes plain, Chisholm is also a COHERENTIST. However, unlike a pure coherentist, he doesn't think that positive coherence relations are the only source of empirical justification. Indeed, he doesn't think that positive coherence is capable of generating justification for propositions that have nothing else to recommend them. It cannot create justification *ex nihilo*. On the other hand, it can ratchet justification up a notch for propositions that already have some other source of justification.

A key to understanding Chisholm's general approach to epistemology is to understand the metaphysical status of his principles. And for this, it is necessary to understand the status of the basic notion of justification that he uses to define his terms of epistemic appraisal. According to Chisholm, the basic notion is one that we bring to epistemology. It is only because we have a pre-philosophical idea of justification that we are able to identify instances of beliefs that are clearly justified, and it is this, he says, that allows the epistemological project to get off the ground. Thus, he is a particularist when it comes to matters of epistemological method. He begins by examining particular instances of beliefs that he takes to be justified, and then out of these instances he tries to abstract out general conditions of justification, which he expresses in the form of epistemic principles.

There is also an important presupposition that shapes how Chisholm conceives this basic notion of justification. He presupposes that we can improve and correct our beliefs by reflection, eliminating those that are unjustified and adding others that are justified (*TK3*, 1 and 5). This presupposition acts as a constraint when we try to use particular instances of justified belief to formulate general conditions of justification. It forces us to look for conditions to which we have reflective access, since otherwise there would be no reason to think that we could eliminate unjustified beliefs and add justified ones simply by being reflective. In effect, this is to say that it forces us to be internalists (*see* EXTERNALISM/INTERNALISM).

The basic notion of justification that we bring to epistemology is vague, says Chisholm, but he doesn't think it has to remain vague. On the contrary, he thinks that in the process of formulating epistemic principles, the notion becomes less and less vague, until eventually we are in a position to give a precise characterization of it. The characterization he gives is in terms of ethical requirements on our believings and withholdings. For example, to say that S is more justified in believing p than withholding on p (i.e. to say that p is beyond reasonable doubt for S) is to say that S is required to prefer the former over the latter (*TK3*, 59).

In turn, Chisholm conceives these ethical requirements as SUPERVENING on non-normative states. Specifically, they supervene on our conscious states (*TK3*, 60). As such, a proposition could not have an epistemic status different from the one it does have for us without our conscious states being different.

So, this is how Chisholm understands the metaphysical status of his principles: he thinks of them as necessary truths, and the truths they express are ultimately ones about the relationship between our conscious states at a time and ethical requirements on our believings and withholdings.

This view, when combined with his particularism, yields a position that Chisholm calls (*TK2*, 124–34) 'CRITICAL COGNITIVISM', which he sees as an alternative to scepticism, intuitionism and reductionism in epistemology (and in ethics as well). Unlike the sceptic, Chisholm begins with the presupposition that some of our beliefs are justified and indeed that some constitute knowledge. Unlike the

65

intuitionist, he denies that there is some special faculty that tells which beliefs are justified (just as he denies that there is some special faculty that tells which actions are good). And unlike the reductionist, he denies that the truths of epistemology can be reduced to empirical truths. Instead, the relationship is one of supervenience.

*See also* COMMONSENSISM AND CRITICAL COGNITIVISM; CRITERIA AND KNOWLEDGE; ETHICS AND EPISTEMOLOGY; MORAL EPISTEMOLOGY; PHENOMENALISM; PROBLEM OF THE CRITERION; REID.

WRITINGS

'The problem of the speckled hen', *Mind*, 51 (1942), 71–9.
*Perceiving: A Philosophical Study* (Ithaca, NY: Cornell University Press, 1957).
*The Foundations of Knowing* (Minneapolis: University of Minnesota Press, 1982).
*Theory of Knowledge* (Englewood Cliffs: Prentice-Hall, 1966, 1977 and 1989).

RICHARD FOLEY

**circular reasoning** Circular reasoning is very important and characteristic of all kinds of everyday argumentation where feedback is used. So it is often quite correct and useful – not fallacious, as traditionally portrayed in the logic textbooks. Studying circular reasoning, for example, is very important for artificial intelligence, e.g. in expert systems. Circular reasoning can be used fallaciously, however, in arguments which require the use of premisses that can be shown to be better established than the conclusion to be proved. The requirement here is one of evidential priority (*see* INFORMAL FALLACIES: *Arguing in a Circle*). Arguing in a circle becomes a fallacy of *petitio principii* or begging the question where an attempt is made to evade the burden of proving one of the premisses of an argument by basing it on the prior acceptance of the conclusion to be proved. (*See* Walton 1987, pp. 124–44.) So the fallacy of begging the question is a systematic tactic to evade fulfilment of a legitimate

BURDEN OF PROOF by the proponent of an argument in dialogue by using a circular structure of argument to block the further progress of dialogue and, in particular, to undermine the capability of the respondent, to whom the argument was directed, to ask legitimate critical questions in reply.

BIBLIOGRAPHY

Basu, D.K.: 'A question of begging', *Informal Logic* 8 (1986), 19–26.
Mackenzie, J.D.: 'Begging the question in dialogue', *Australasian Journal of Philosophy* 62 (1984), 174–81.
Walton, D.N.: *Informal Logic: A Handbook for Critical Argumentation* (Cambridge: Cambridge University Press, 1989).
Walton, D.N.: *Begging the Question* (New York: Greenwood Press, 1991).
Walton, D.N. and Batten, L.M.: 'Games, graphs and circular arguments', *Logique et Analyse* 106 (1984), 133–64.

DOUGLAS N. WALTON

**cogito** The name given to Descartes' famous dictum 'I am thinking, therefore I exist' (*je pense, donc je suis*; Latin *cogito ergo sum*). The French phrase appears in the *Discourse on the Method* (1637); the Latin formulation in the *Principles of Philosophy* (1644). The term 'the Cogito' is commonly used by commentators to refer not just to the dictum, but to the whole process of reasoning whereby the Cartesian meditator becomes aware of the indubitable existence of the thinking subject. The definitive account of that process occurs in the Second Meditation, where Descartes says that 'I am, I exist (*sum, existo*) is necessarily true as often as it is put forward by me or conceived in my mind'.

*See also* DESCARTES; SELF-KNOWLEDGE AND SELF-IDENTITY.

BIBLIOGRAPHY

Hintikka, J.: 'Cogito ergo sum: inference or performance?', *Philosophical Review* 72 (1964), 3–32; reprinted in *Descartes: A collection of critical essays* ed. W. Doney (London: Macmillan, 1968).

Williams, B.: 'The certainty of the Cogito', in *Descartes: A collection of critical essays* ed. W. Doney (London: Macmillan, 1968).

JOHN COTTINGHAM

**coherentism**   Coherence is a major player in the theatre of knowledge. There are coherence theories of belief, truth and justification. These combine in various ways to yield theories of knowledge. We shall proceed from belief through justification to truth. Coherence theories of belief are concerned with the content of beliefs. Consider a belief you now have, the belief that you are reading a page in a book. So what makes that belief the belief that it is? What makes it the belief that you are reading a page in a book rather than the belief that you have a centaur in the garden?

One answer is that the belief has a coherent place or role in a system of beliefs. Perception has an influence on belief. You respond to sensory stimuli by believing that you are reading a page in a book rather than believing that you have a centaur in the garden. Belief has an influence on action. You will act differently if you believe that you are reading a page than if you believe something about a centaur. Perception and action underdetermine the content of belief, however. The same stimuli may produce various beliefs and various beliefs may produce the same action. The role that gives the belief the content it has is the role it plays in a network of relations to other beliefs, the role in inference and implication, for example. I infer different things from believing that I am reading a page in a book than from any other belief, just as I infer that belief from different things than I infer other beliefs from.

The input of perception and the output of action supplement the central role of the systematic relations the belief has to other beliefs, but it is the systematic relations that give the belief the specific content it has. They are the fundamental source of the content of beliefs. That is how coherence comes in. A belief has the content that it does because of the way in which it coheres within a system

of beliefs (Rosenberg, 1988). We might distinguish weak coherence theories of the content of beliefs from strong coherence theories. Weak coherence theories affirm that coherence is one determinant of the content of belief. Strong coherence theories of the content of belief affirm that coherence is the sole determinant of the content of belief.

When we turn from belief to justification, we confront a similar group of coherence theories. What makes one belief justified and another not? The answer is the way it coheres with the background system of beliefs. Again there is a distinction between weak and strong theories of coherence. Weak theories tell us that the way in which a belief coheres with a background system of beliefs is one determinant of justification, other typical determinants being perception, memory and intuition. Strong theories, by contrast, tell us that justification is solely a matter of how a belief coheres with a system of beliefs. There is, however, another distinction that cuts across the distinction between weak and strong coherence theories of justification. It is the distinction between positive and negative coherence theories (Pollock, 1986). A positive coherence theory tells us that if a belief coheres with a background system of belief, then the belief is justified. A negative coherence theory tells us that if a belief fails to cohere with a background system of beliefs, then the belief is not justified. We might put this by saying that, according to a positive coherence theory, coherence has the power to produce justification, while according to a negative coherence theory, coherence has only the power to nullify justification.

A strong coherence theory of justification is a combination of a positive and a negative theory which tells us that a belief is justified if and only if it coheres with a background system of beliefs.

Let us illustrate the foregoing distinctions with an example. Coherence theories of justification and knowledge have most often been rejected as being unable to deal with perceptual knowledge (Audi, 1988; Pollock, 1986), and, therefore, it will be most appropriate to consider a perceptual example which will serve as a kind of crucial test. Suppose that a person, call her Trust, works with a scientific instrument that has a gauge for measuring the temperature of liquid in a container. The gauge is marked in degrees. She looks at the gauge and sees that the reading is 105 degrees. What is she justified in believing and why? Is she, for example, justified in believing that the liquid in the container is 105 degrees? Clearly, that depends on her background beliefs. A weak coherence theorist might argue that, though her belief that she sees the shape 105 is immediately justified as direct sensory evidence without appeal to a background system, the belief that the liquid in the container is 105 degrees results from coherence with a background system of beliefs affirming that the shape 105 is a reading of 105 degrees on a gauge that measures the temperature of the liquid in the container. This sort of weak coherentism combines coherence with direct perceptual evidence, the foundation of justification, to account for justification of our beliefs.

A strong coherence theory would go beyond the claim of the weak coherence theory to affirm that the justification of all beliefs, including the belief that one sees the shape 105, or even the more cautious belief that one sees a shape, results from coherence with a background system. One may argue for this strong coherence theory in a number of different ways. One line of argument would be appeal to the coherence theory of the content of belief. If the content of the perceptual belief results from the relations of the belief to other beliefs in a system of beliefs, then one may argue that the justification of the perceptual beliefs also results from the relations of the belief to other beliefs in the system. One may, however, argue for the strong coherence theory without assuming the coherence theory of the content of beliefs. It may be that some beliefs have the content that they do atomistically but that our justification for believing them is the result of coherence. Consider the very cautious belief that I see a shape. How could the justification for that belief be the result of coherence with a background system of beliefs? What might the background system tell us that would justify that belief? Our background system contains a simple and primal theory about our relationship to the world. To come to the specific point at issue, we believe that we can tell a shape when we see one, that we are trustworthy about such simple matters as whether we see a shape before us or not. We may, with experience, come to believe that sometimes we think we see a shape before us when there is nothing there at all, when we see an after-image, for example, and so we are not perfect, not beyond deception, yet we are trustworthy for the most part. Moreover, when Trust sees the shape 105, she believes that the circumstances are not those that are deceptive about whether she sees that shape. The light is good, the numeral shapes are large, readily discernible, and so forth. These are beliefs that Trust has that tell her that her belief that she sees a shape is justified. Her belief that she sees a shape is justified because of the way it is supported by her other beliefs. It coheres with those beliefs, and so she is justified.

There are various ways of understanding the nature of this support or coherence. One way is to view Trust as inferring that her belief is true from the other beliefs. The inference might be construed as an INFERENCE TO THE BEST EXPLANATION (Harman, 1973; Goldman, 1988; Lycan, 1988). Given her background beliefs, the best explanation Trust has for the existence of her belief that she sees a shape is that she does see a shape. Thus, we might think of coherence as inference to the best explanation based on a background system of beliefs. Since we are not aware of such inferences for the most part, the inferences must be interpreted as unconscious inferences, as information processing, based on or accessing the background system. One might object to such an account on the grounds that not all justifying inference is explanatory and, consequently, be led to a more general account of coherence as successful competition based on a background system (BonJour, 1985; Lehrer, 1990). The belief that one sees a shape competes with the claim that one does not, with the claim that one is deceived, and other sceptical objections. The background system of belief informs one that one is trustworthy and enables one to meet the objections. A belief coheres with a background system just in case it enables one to meet the sceptical objections and in that way justifies one in the belief. This is a standard strong coherence theory of justification (Lehrer, 1990).

It is easy to illustrate the relationship between positive and negative coherence theories in terms of the standard coherence theory. If some objection to a belief cannot be met in terms of the background system of beliefs of a person, then the person is not justified in that belief. So, to return to Trust, suppose that she has been told that a warning light has been installed on her gauge to tell her when it is not functioning properly and that when the red light is on, the gauge is malfunctioning. Suppose that when she sees the reading of 105, she also sees that the red light is on. Imagine, finally, that this is the first time the red light has been on, and, after years of working with the gauge, Trust, who has always placed her trust in the gauge, believes what the gauge tells her, that the liquid in the container is at 105 degrees. Though she believes what she reads, her belief that the liquid in the container is at 105 degrees is not a justified belief because it fails to cohere with her background belief that the gauge is malfunctioning. Thus, the negative coherence theory tells us that she is not justified in her belief about the temperature of the contents in the container. By contrast, when the red light is not illuminated and the background system of Trust tells her that under such conditions that gauge is a trustworthy indicator of the temperature of the liquid in the container, then she is justified. The positive coherence theory tells us that she is justified in her belief because her belief coheres with her background system.

The foregoing sketch and illustration of coherence theories of justification have a common feature, namely, that they are what are called internalistic theories of justification (*see* EXTERNALISM/INTERNALISM.) They are theories affirming that coherence is a matter of internal relations among beliefs and that justification is a matter of coherence. If, then, justification is solely a matter of internal relations between beliefs, we are left with the possibility that the internal relations might fail to correspond with any external reality. How, one might object, can a completely internal subjective notion of justification bridge the gap between mere true belief, which might be no more than a lucky guess, and knowledge, which must be grounded in some connection between internal subjective conditions and external objective realities?

The answer is that it cannot and that something more than justified true belief is required for knowledge. This result has, however, been established quite apart from consideration of coherence theories of justification. What is required may be put by saying that the justification one has must be undefeated by errors in the background system of belief. A justification is undefeated by errors just in case any correction of such errors in the background system of belief would sustain the justification of the belief on the basis of the corrected system. So knowledge, on this sort of positive coherence theory, is true belief that coheres with the background belief system and corrected versions of that system. In short, knowledge is true belief plus justification resulting from coherence and undefeated by error (Lehrer, 1990). The connection between internal subjective conditions of belief and external objective realities results from the required correctness of our beliefs about the relations between those conditions and realities. In the example of Trust, she believes that her internal subjective conditions of sensory experience and perceptual belief are connected with the external objective reality of the temperature of the liquid in the container in a trustworthy manner. This background belief is essential to the justification of her belief that the temperature of the liquid in the container is 105 degrees, and the correctness of that background belief is essential to the justification remaining undefeated. So our background system of beliefs contains a simple theory about our relation to the external world which justifies certain of our beliefs that cohere with that system. For such justification to convert to knowledge, that theory must be sufficiently free from error so that the coherence is sustained in corrected versions of our background system of beliefs. The correctness of the simple background theory provides the connection between the internal conditions and external realities.

The coherence theory of truth arises naturally out of a problem raised by the coherence theory of justification. The problem is that anyone seeking to determine whether she has knowledge is confined to the search for coherence among her beliefs. The sensory experiences she has are mute until they are represented in the form of some perceptual belief. Beliefs are the engine that pulls the train of justification. But what assurance do we have that our justification is based on true beliefs? What justification do we have that any of our justifications are undefeated? The fear that we might have none, that our beliefs might be the artifact of some deceptive demon or scientist, leads to the quest to reduce truth to some form, perhaps an idealized form, of justification (Rescher, 1973; Rosenberg, 1980). That would close the threatening sceptical gap between justification and truth. Suppose that a belief is true if and only if it is ideally justified for some person. For such a person there would be no gap between justification and truth or between justification and undefeated justification. Truth would be coherence with some ideal background system of beliefs, perhaps one expressing a consensus among belief systems or some convergence toward consensus. Such a view is theoretically attractive for the reduction it promises, but it appears open to profound objections. One is that there is a consensus that we can all be wrong about at least some matters, for example, about the origins of the universe. If there is a consensus that we can all be wrong about something, then the consensual belief system rejects the equation of truth with consensus. Consequently, the equation of truth with coherence with a consensual belief system is itself incoherent.

Coherence theories of the content of our beliefs and the justification of our beliefs themselves cohere with our background systems but coherence theories of truth do not. A defender of coherentism must accept the logical gap between justified belief and truth, but she may believe that her capacities suffice to close the gap to yield knowledge. That view is, at any rate, a coherent one.

*See also* CONCEPT; GETTIER PROBLEM; TRUTH.

BIBLIOGRAPHY

Audi, R.: *Belief, Justification and Knowledge* (Belmont: Wadsworth, 1988).

Bender, J. ed.: *The Current State of the Coherence Theory* (Dordrecht: Kluwer, 1989).

BonJour, L.: *The Structure of Empirical Knowledge* (Cambridge, MA: Harvard University Press, 1985).

Chisholm, R.M.: *Theory of Knowledge* 3rd edn (Englewood Cliffs: Prentice-Hall, 1989).

Goldman, A.: *Empirical Knowledge* (Berkeley: University of California Press, 1988).

Harman, G.: *Thought* (Princeton: Princeton University Press, 1973).

Lehrer, K.: *Theory of Knowledge* (Boulder: Westview, 1990).

Lycan, W.G.: *Judgement and Justification* (New York: Cambridge University Press, 1988).

Pollock, J.: *Contemporary Theories of Knowledge* (Totowa: Rowman and Littlefield, 1986).

Rescher, N.: *The Coherence Theory of Truth* (Oxford: Oxford University Press, 1973).

Rosenberg, J.: *One World and Our Knowledge of it* (Dordrecht: Reidel, 1980).

KEITH LEHRER

**collective belief** In everyday speech we often refer to the beliefs of a group of people. We say such things as 'The union believes that a strike would succeed', and 'In the opinion of the government war is inevitable'. How are such claims to be interpreted? Do they imply the existence of a 'group mind'?

Many assume that a simple summative (or aggregative) analysis is correct. That is, they assume that a group believes that $p$ if and only if all or at least most members of the group personally believe that $p$ (*see* e.g. Quinton, 1975, pp. 9, 17).

A related analysis which has been considered is this: a group believes that *p* if and only if all or most members believe that *p* and this is common knowledge in the group (Gilbert, 1987, 1989; see also Bach and Harnish, 1979, p. 270). ('Common knowledge' is a technical term from Lewis, 1969.)

Neither of these analyses copes well with cases such as the following. A committee has to reach a view on some matter, for instance, whether taxation should be increased. Only one individual believes that taxation should be increased, but he is feared by the others and they 'go along' with him, voting in favour of increasing taxes. It seems that we can now say that in the committee's view taxation should be increased. If this is so, then an analysis of group belief in terms of what most members believe cannot be correct for all cases.

An alternative analysis has been proposed according to which, roughly, a group believes something if and only if the members understand that they are jointly committed to uphold the belief in question as a body. Thus when speaking as members of a committee individuals must express the committee view rather than their personal belief. (For details, *see* Gilbert, 1987, 1989.)

In so far as group belief in this sense is a common phenomenon, empirical investigation will need special sensitivity to determine whether an individual is expressing a group or a personal belief on a particular occasion, and the epistemology of group beliefs in this sense will require special investigation.

*See also* BELIEF.

BIBLIOGRAPHY

Bach, K. and Harnish, R.M.: *Linguistic Communication and Speech Acts* (Cambridge, MA: MIT Press, 1979).
Gilbert, M.: 'Modelling collective belief', *Synthese* 73 (1987), 185–204.
Gilbert, M.: *On Social Facts* (London and New York: Routledge, 1989).
Lewis, D.K.: *Convention* (Cambridge, MA: Harvard University Press, 1969).

Quinton, A.: 'Social objects', *Proceedings of the Aristotelian Society* 75 (1975), 1–27.

MARGARET GILBERT

**commonsensism and critical cognitivism**
Commonsensism is the view that we know, most, if not all, of those things which ordinary people think they know and that any satisfactory epistemological theory must be adequate to the fact that we do know such things. Defenders of commonsense, such as Thomas REID and G.E. MOORE, maintain, for example, that we know that there are material or physical objects having shape and size in three dimensions, that there are other people who think and feel and have bodies, and that we and other things, such as the earth, have existed for many years. Commonsensism claims it is more reasonable for us to hold these particular commonsense beliefs than any epistemological theory which implies that we do not know such things. In this respect, commonsensism is incompatible with, and rejects, various forms of SCEPTICISM and certain traditional forms of EMPIRICISM, such as those represented by BERKELEY and HUME. In this spirit, Moore writes, 'There is no reason why we should not, in this respect, make our philosophical opinions agree with what we necessarily believe at other times. There is no reason why I should not confidently assert that I do really *know* some external facts, although I cannot prove this assertion except by simply assuming that I do. I am, in fact, as certain of this as anything; and as reasonably certain of it' (Moore, 1922, p. 162). While commonsensism claims we can be confident that any theory is mistaken that implies that we do not know that there are material objects or facts about other minds, philosophers such as Reid and Moore are also astute critics, carefully pointing out mistaken assumptions which generate sceptical conclusions. Reid's criticism of the empiricist theory of ideas is an especially noteworthy example.

Some philosophers claim that we know things about physical objects and other minds, but attempt to reduce, translate or analyse statements about the 'external world' and other minds into statements of a 'less problematic' variety. For example, some claim that we do know that there are tables and chairs, but the statement 'I am seated at a table' can be translated or reduced to statements about one's present sense experience or about 'permanent possibilities of sensations'. This is the approach of Berkeley and the PHENOMENALISTS. Similarly, some who concede that one can know, for example, that 'Smith believes it will rain' attempt to reduce this statement into statements about Smith's having certain dispositions to behave in various ways (*see* RYLE; BEHAVIOURISM). Commonsensism rejects these forms of 'reductionism' on the ground that they do not capture the meaning of what it is we think we know when we claim to know that there are tables or that someone believes it will rain. It may ask precisely *what* statements about our sense experiences or dispositions to behave express what we think we know about tables or someone's believing that it will rain. Moore writes, 'Some philosophers seem to . . . use such expressions as, e.g., "The earth has existed for many years past", as if they expressed something which they really believed, when in fact they believe that every proposition, which such an expression would *ordinarily* be understood to express, is, at least partially, false . . . I wish, therefore, to make it quite plain that I was not using the expressions . . . in any such subtle manner. I meant by each of them precisely what every reader, in reading them, will have understood me to mean' (1959, p. 36).

Though commonsensism holds that a satisfactory epistemological theory must be adequate to the fact that we know certain things about physical objects, other minds, and the past, it is not committed to any particular account of how we know such things or even to the view that we can formulate a satisfactory account of how we know such things. The defender of commonsense holds that he knows or is justified in believing certain things quite independently of his being able to say how he knows or his knowing some criterion of knowledge or jus-

tification. Moore expresses this view when he writes, 'We are all, I think, in this strange position that we do *know* many things, with regard to which we *know* further that we must have evidence for them, and yet we do not know *how* we know them' (1959, p. 44).

Some defenders of commonsense have tried to formulate 'marks' of commonsense beliefs. Reid, for example, suggests that a commonsense belief is one (1) which is universally held by mankind, (2) whose acceptance is reflected in the common structure of all languages, (3) whose contradictory is not merely false, but absurd, and (4) that is irresistible, so that even those who question them are compelled to believe them when engaging in the practical affairs of life. But whatever the merits of Reid's attempts to identify the range of commonsense beliefs, it would be a mistake to take him to hold that we must first identify some mark or criterion of commonsense beliefs before they are evident to us.

'Critical cognitivism' is a term coined by Roderick CHISHOLM to refer to a certain approach to the problems of epistemology. According to Chisholm (1977, 1982), we may distinguish two sorts of epistemological questions. The first sort of question may be put, '*What* do we know?' or 'What is the *extent* of our knowledge?' The second may be put, 'How are we to decide, in any particular case, *whether* we know?' or 'What are the *criteria* of knowing?' Philosophers who assume that they have an answer to the second sort of question and then try to work out an answer to the first, Chisholm calls 'methodists'. Those who assume that they have an answer to the first sort of question and then try to answer the second, he calls 'particularists'. Chisholm takes Locke and Hume to be methodists and Reid and Moore to be particularists. Critical cognitivism assumes that one can identify particular instances of knowledge, and given answers to the first sort of question develop an answer to the second, that one can formulate criteria of knowledge. (For further discussion of particularism and methodism, *see* PROBLEM OF THE CRITERION.)

Chisholm's version of critical cognitivism

exemplifies the two features of commonsensism mentioned above. He assumes that we know certain facts about the material objects around us, other minds, and the past, and that any satisfactory account of the criteria of knowledge must be adequate to this fact. Like commonsensism, it rejects certain forms of scepticism, traditional empiricism and reductionism. The critical cognitivist and defender of commonsense hold that scepticism and traditional empiricism 'rest upon some premiss which is, beyond comparison, less certain than is the proposition which it is designed to attack' (Moore, 1922, p. 228). Critical cognitivism, however, goes beyond commonsensism in (a) offering a positive account of how we know commonsense propositions, and (b) holding that there are just four sources of our knowledge: external perception, memory, self-awareness or inner consciousness, and reason. It asserts (1) that we do know facts about the external world, other minds, and the past, (2) that we have no other sources of knowledge, and, therefore, (3) our knowledge of the external world, other minds, and the past is yielded by these four sources.

Critical cognitivists such as Reid and Chisholm hold that one sort of fact can function as a 'sign' or evidence for a different sort of fact. For example, certain psychological facts about one's sensations or the way one is 'appeared to' can, under certain conditions, function as evidence for beliefs about external, physical objects. Critical cognitivism also holds that knowledge yielded by these four traditional sources can function as signs or evidence for certain 'problematic' kinds of claims, such as those about ethical values and other minds. For example, Reid tells us 'certain features of the countenance, sounds of the voice, and gestures of the body, indicate certain thoughts and dispositions of the mind' (Reid, 1785, Essay VI, ch. V). According to Reid, our knowledge of certain non-mental facts about bodies, gestures and voices can, under certain conditions, confer warrant upon our beliefs about other minds. Similarly, Chisholm writes, 'My own feeling is a sign of the evil nature of ingratitude, and so it could be said to confer evidence upon the statement that ingratitude is evil' (Chisholm, 1977, p. 126). According to Chisholm, certain non-ethical facts can, under certain conditions, confer warrant upon our ethical beliefs. These facts about our emotional experiences are known through inner consciousness and, though they are not themselves ethical facts, they can confer warrant on ethical beliefs.

The critical cognitivist claims that there are *only* four sources of knowledge. What is the status of this claim? If he assumes, *ab initio*, that there are just four sources, then it appears that, like the methodist, he is assuming some general principle about how we are to decide whether we know. 'If some putative instance of knowledge can't be accounted for in terms of just these four sources, then it isn't knowledge.' However, there are two alternatives for the critical cognitivist. First, he might simply hold that we have no particular knowledge of any other source, that we have no experience, for example, of the operation of a faculty of moral or religious intuition. Alternatively, we may take the critical cognitivist not to assume from the start that there are just four sources, but rather to hold that since we can account for everything we ordinarily think we know in terms of these four sources, we have no reason to recognize any other source. Whether this conclusion is justified depends, of course, on whether these sources can accommodate everything it is reasonable for us to think we know. This is a point with which any particularist or critical cognitivist will agree.

*See also* CHISHOLM; MOORE; THE PROBLEM OF THE CRITERION; REID.

BIBLIOGRAPHY

Chisholm, R.M.: *The Foundations of Knowing* (Minneapolis: University of Minnesota Press, 1982).
Chisholm, R.M.: *Theory of Knowledge* 2nd edn (Englewood Cliffs: Prentice-Hall, 1977).
Madden, E.H.: The metaphilosophy of commonsense', *American Philosophical Quarterly* 20 (1983), 23–36.

Moore, G.E.: *Philosophical Papers* (London: George Allen and Unwin, 1959).

Moore, G.E.: *Philosophical Studies* (London: Routledge and Kegan Paul, 1922).

Reid, T.: *Essays on the Intellectual Powers of Man* (1785) ed. B. Brody (Cambridge, MA: MIT Press, 1969).

Reid, T.: *Thomas Reid's Inquiry and Essays* eds K. Lehrer and R.E. Beanblossom (Indianapolis: Bobbs-Merrill, 1975).

Sosa, E.: 'The foundations of foundationalism', *Nous* 14 (1980), 547–64.

NOAH M. LEMOS

**concepts** Mental states have contents: a belief may have the content that I will catch the train, a hope may have the content that the prime minister will resign. A concept is something which is capable of being a constituent of such contents. More specifically, a concept is a way of thinking of something – a particular object, or property, or relation, or some other entity.

Several different concepts may each be ways of thinking of the same object. A person may think of himself in the first-person way, or think of himself as the spouse of Mary Smith, or as the person located in a certain room now. More generally, a concept $c$ is distinct from a concept $d$ if it is possible for a person rationally to believe '$c$ is such-and-such' without believing '$d$ is such-and-such'. As words can be combined to form structured sentences, concepts have also been conceived as combinable into structured complex contents. When these complex contents are expressed in English by 'that . . .' clauses, as in our opening examples, they will be capable of being true or false, depending on the way the world is.

Concepts are to be distinguished from stereotypes and from conceptions. The stereotypical spy may be a middle-level official down on his luck and in need of money. None the less we can come to learn that Anthony Blunt, art historian and Surveyor of the Queen's Pictures, is a spy; we can come to believe that something falls under a concept while positively disbelieving that the same thing falls under the stereotype associated with the concept. Similarly, a person's conception of a just arrangement for resolving disputes may involve something like contemporary Western legal systems. But whether or not it would be correct, it is quite intelligible for someone to reject this conception by arguing that it does not adequately provide for the elements of fairness and respect which are required by the concept of justice.

A theory of a particular concept must be distinguished from a theory of the object or objects it picks out. The theory of the concept is part of the theory of thought and epistemology; a theory of the object or objects is part of metaphysics and ontology. Some figures in the history of philosophy – and perhaps even some of our contemporaries – are open to the accusation of not having fully respected the distinction between the two kinds of theory. Descartes appears to have moved from facts about the indubitability of the thought 'I think', containing the first-person way of thinking, to conclusions about the non-material nature of the object he himself was. But though the goals of a theory of concepts and a theory of objects are distinct, each theory is required to have an adequate account of its relation to the other theory. A theory of concepts is unacceptable if it gives no account of how the concept is capable of picking out the objects it evidently does pick out. A theory of objects is unacceptable if it makes it impossible to understand how we could have concepts of those objects.

A fundamental question for philosophy is: what individuates a given concept – that is, what makes it the one it is, rather than any other concept? One answer, which has been developed in great detail, is that it is impossible to give a non-trivial answer to this question (Schiffer, 1987). An alternative approach, favoured by the present author, addresses the question by starting from the idea that a concept is individuated by the condition which must be satisfied if a thinker is to possess that concept and to be capable of having beliefs and other attitudes whose contents contain it as a constituent. So, to take a simple case, one could propose that the logical concept *and* is individuated by this condition: it is the unique concept $C$ to possess which a thinker has to find these forms of inference compelling, without basing them on any further inference or information: from any two premisses A and B, ACB can be inferred; and from any premiss ACB, each of A and B can be inferred. Again, a relatively observational concept such as *round* can be individuated in part by stating that the thinker finds specified contents containing it compelling when he has certain kinds of perception, and in part by relating those judgements containing the concept and which are not based on perception to those judgements that are. A statement which individuates a concept by saying what is required for a thinker to possess it can be described as giving the *possession condition* for the concept.

A possession condition for a particular concept may actually make use of that concept. The possession condition for *and* does so. We can also expect to use relatively observational concepts in specifying the kind of experiences which have to be mentioned in the possession conditions for relatively observational concepts. What we must avoid is mention of the concept in question as such within the content of the attitudes attributed to the thinker in the possession condition. Otherwise we would be presupposing possession of the concept in an account which was meant to elucidate its possession. In talking of what the thinker finds compelling, the possession conditions can also respect an insight of the later WITTGENSTEIN: that a thinker's mastery of a concept is inextricably tied to how he finds it natural to go on in new cases in applying the concept.

Sometimes a family of concepts has this property: it is not possible to master any one of the members of the family without mastering the others. Two of the families which plausibly have this status are these: the family consisting of some simple concepts $o$, $1$, $2$, . . . of the natural numbers and the corresponding concepts of numerical quantifiers *there are $o$ so-and-so's, there is $1$ so-and-so, . . .*; and the family consisting of the concepts *belief* and *desire*. Such families have come to be known as 'local holisms'. A local HOLISM does not prevent the individuation of a concept by its possession condition. Rather, it demands that all the concepts in the family be individuated simultaneously. So one would say something of this form: *belief* and *desire* form the unique pair of concepts $C1$ and $C2$ such that for a thinker to possess them is to meet such-and-such condition involving the thinker, $C1$ and $C2$. For these and other possession conditions to individuate properly, it is necessary that there be some ranking of the concepts treated. The possession conditions for concepts higher in the ranking must presuppose only possession of concepts at the same or lower levels in the ranking.

A possession condition may in various ways make a thinker's possession of a particular concept dependent upon his relations to his environment. Many possession conditions will mention the links between a concept and the thinker's perceptual experience. Perceptual experience represents the world as being a certain way. It is arguable that the only satisfactory explanation of what it is for perceptual experience to represent the world in a particular way must refer to the complex relations of the experience to the subject's environment. If this is so, then mention of such experiences in a possession condition will make possession of that concept dependent in part upon the environmental relations of the thinker. Burge (1979) has also argued from intuitions about particular examples that, even though the thinker's non-environmental properties and relations remain constant, the conceptual content of his mental state can vary if the thinker's social environment is varied. A possession condition which properly individuates such a concept must take into account the thinker's social relations, in particular his linguistic relations.

Concepts have a normative dimension, a fact strongly emphasized by Kripke. For any judgement whose content involves a given concept, there is a *correctness condition* for that judgement, a condition which is dependent in part upon the identity of the concept. The normative character of concepts also extends into the territory of a thinker's reasons for making judgements. A thinker's visual perception can give him good reason for judging 'That man is bald'; it does not by itself give him good reason for judging 'Rostropovich is bald', even if the man he sees is Rostropovich. All these normative connections must be explained by a theory of concepts. One approach to these matters is to look to the possession condition for a concept, and consider how the referent of the concept is fixed from it, together with the world. One proposal is that the referent of the concept is that object (or property, or function, . . .) which makes the practices of judgement and inference mentioned in the possession condition always lead to true judgements and truth-preserving inferences. This proposal would explain why certain reasons are necessarily good reasons for judging given contents. Provided the possession condition permits us to say what it is about a thinker's previous judgements that makes it the case that he is employing one concept rather than another, this proposal would also have another virtue. It would allow us to say how the correctness condition is determined for a judgement in which the concept is applied to a newly encountered object. The judgement is correct if the new object has the property which in fact makes the judgemental practices mentioned in the possession condition yield true judgements, or truth-preserving inferences.

*See also* COHERENTISM; LINGUISTIC UNDERSTANDING.

BIBLIOGRAPHY

Burge, T.: 'Individualism and the mental', *Midwest Studies in Philosophy* 4 (1979), 73–121.
Frege, G.: 'The thought', in *Logical Investigations* ed. P. Geach (Oxford: Blackwell, 1977).
Kripke, S.: *Wittgenstein on Rules and Private Language* (Oxford: Blackwell, 1982).
Peacocke, C.: 'What are concepts?', *Midwest Studies in Philosophy* 14 (1989), 1–28.
Schiffer, S.: *Remnants of Meaning* (Cambridge, MA: MIT Press, 1987).

CHRISTOPHER PEACOCKE

**continental epistemology** For the purposes of this entry continental epistemology will be defined as the cluster of problems concerning knowledge in French and German philosophy of the nineteenth and twentieth centuries. This time frame can be justified on the grounds that with Hegel a decidedly different orientation to knowledge began to emerge.

Problems of knowledge and truth are as central to the continental tradition as they are to the Anglo-American tradition, but because they start from a different place different sorts of questions arise. This different starting point is HEGEL's perception of the historical dimension of knowledge. Hegel was influenced by KANT's critique of the limits of reason and his recognition of the subjective input into knowledge. But Hegel drew two conclusions from these claims that Kant did not draw: the fundamental limit to reason is its embeddedness in a historical context, which further suggests that the categories of interpretation Kant identified must themselves be understood as historically situated and thus limited. It is this insight into the historical nature of reason, knowledge and even truth that might be said to begin a different trajectory of development in epistemology on the European continent.

The claim of historicity follows simply from the fact that there is a subjective component to knowledge and that subjects are historical creatures, incapable of fully transcending their historical location. For Hegel, a particular, such as a singular historical moment, cannot contain the universal, though it exemplifies a moment of the universal. This means that a belief can be both partial and true simultaneously, and that truth needs to be understood as indexed to the perspective of a history and a culture. Furthermore, on Hegel's view the locus of belief formation cannot be meaningfully understood as an isolated individual. The individual, as a particular, is also an exemplification of a universal, the spirit of an age, for example. The individual's beliefs must therefore be understood within this context. These two shifts – from the ahistorical to the historical and from the individual to the culture as a whole –

produced a turn in the way in which epistemology has been done in France and Germany since Hegel's time. Neither claim has been superseded, and the continental schools of thought all develop further and in diverse ways these fundamental insights.

Where for Descartes the problem was how to get to the Real beyond mere sensory ideas, for Hegel the problem was how to get to knowledge through historical location. And whereas Descartes posited a unified, self-knowing subject essentially separate from reality and linked to it only by potentially deceiving sensory organs, Hegel's subject is in part an effect of the Real, as a partial representative of the Absolute Spirit. So the question whether the subject can pass over an interminable gulf between its consciousness and the object world does not arise; for Hegel subject and object, particular and universal, and appearance and essence are ontologically connected at their core. The essence of a thing shines forth in its appearance, just as the universal manifests itself only in the particular. The problem of SCEPTICISM thus never arises.

The key epistemic problem for Hegel is not how can we know anything at all, but how can we move from a partial and limited historical perspective to absolute knowledge. This move is necessary because it is only from the perspective of absolute knowledge that we can judge the validity of claims to partial truth, since the criterion of truth is ultimately the universal, or the ability of a particular to be subsumed within the universal synthesis of all truths. Hegel's answer here further reveals the differences between continental and Anglo-American epistemology. His solution is not a methodology or set of procedures which a subject can utilize, since no methodology can permit one to become ahistorical or perspectiveless, but rather history itself – the dialectical movement of the rational Real in history through social revolutions, philosophical reflection, and the subsequent development of consciousness. The end-point and highest level of this consciousness is the attainment of absolute knowledge, defined as an all-inclusive synthesis of the whole.

MARXIST epistemology offers a materialist account of historical perspective, in which the spirit of an age expressed in knowledge arises fundamentally from economic practices. And where Hegel historicizes Kant's categories, Marx politicizes them, by connecting them to class interests. His concept of IDEOLOGY offers an analysis of how power relations affect belief formation as well as the constitution of identities and subjective experience. But like Hegel, Marx posits an end to history: through concrete political struggle we can exert control over the conditions of knowledge production and achieve an absolute synthesis involving political, epistemic and historical dimensions simultaneously.

In NIETZSCHE one gets Hegelian perspectivism for the first time without an absolute end and without a dialectic progression. Knowledge for Nietzsche is again material, but now based on desire and bodily needs more than social labour. Perspectives are to be judged not from their relation to the absolute but on the basis of their effects in a specific era. The possibility of any truth beyond such a local, pragmatic one becomes a problem in Nietzsche, since neither a noumenal realm nor an historical synthesis exists to provide an absolute criterion of adjudication for competing truth claims: what get called truths are simply beliefs that have been held for so long that we have forgotten their genealogy. In this Nietzsche reverses the Enlightenment dictum that truth is the way to liberation by suggesting that truth claims, in so far as they are considered absolute and transhistorical, shut down the possibilities for debate and conceptual progress and thus cause rather than alleviate backwardness and unnecessary misery. Nietzsche moves back and forth without resolution between the positing of transhistorical truth claims, such as his claim about the will to power, and a kind of epistemic nihilism that calls into question not only the possibility of truth but the need and desire for it as well. But perhaps most importantly, Nietzsche introduces the notion that truth is a kind of human practice, a move in a game whose rules are contingent rather than necessary. The evaluation of truth claims should be based on their strategic effects, not their ability to represent a reality conceived of as separate and autonomous of human influence.

In the twentieth century five major orientations to epistemology developed in different ways from this point: phenomenology, critical theory, hermeneutics, post-structuralism, and feminism. PHENOMENOLOGY in some ways returned to the Cartesian project of bracketing prejudgements to gain a direct awareness of being. But the objectivist conception of the Real found in Descartes is rejected as ontic and replaced with an ontological conception which conceives of the object in its relation to consciousness, thus rejecting a subject/object split. The object of knowledge is not a thing in itself but the thing for-me and my lived experience (*see* IN ITSELF/FOR ITSELF). Sartre offers a notion of the world as a system of objects where meanings and values are organized in light of the individual's project. Existentialist philosophy in general asserted the reality of the particular over the universal, which meant that the criterion of truth no longer required the capacity to be subsumed within a universal. The problem of SUBJECTIVISM this might seem to entail was avoided by reorienting the ontology of truth from the ontic to the ontological: from the subject-less object to lived experience and a Sartrian world. Subjectivism could further be avoided by a collective notion of the subject, as SARTRE tried to develop in his later work.

Philosophical HERMENEUTICS can be viewed as an epistemological fellow-traveller of phenomenology to the extent it continues the focus on the subjective input into knowledge and seeks to break down the subject/object separation found in both Cartesianism and positivism. GADAMER'S hermeneutics, for example, explores the way in which a knower's 'horizon', made up of their prejudgements, historical location and conceptual tradition, both limits and enables understanding. Truth, on his view, is a kind of emergent property of a dialogic interaction between reader and text, knower and object, each of which come to the interaction with a

kind of horizon. Truth occurs when the interaction produces a fusion. One primary effect of this is to reorient the notion of truth as a property of propositional content to an event with temporal specificity.

The Frankfurt School also offered a critique of the ontology of the knowing process found in Cartesian-based epistemologies, but Adorno and Horkheimer's main target was what they called instrumental reason and the Enlightenment belief in the necessary connection between knowledge and freedom. Instrumental reason allows only for means–end calculations and posits itself as politically neutral yet the best route to liberation. Adorno and Horkheimer's major insight was to see this objectivist stance as founded in the desire for mastery and implicated in the practices of domination within the West. For Horkheimer, instead of a distanced, disinterested position over the object, which simply serves to conceal the values and interests of the knower, we should see ourselves as embedded within social locations and understand reality as the product of an interaction between society and nature. For Adorno, what is needed urgently from within the dialectic of Enlightenment reason is an immanent, negative critique which will disrupt the systematically circular confirmations of instrumental reason, rearticulate and reinvigorate Enlightenment ideals, and thus advance the dialectic. Their concept of critical theory was a continuation of Kant's immanent critique of reason, but this time through revealing the artificially constrained concept of reason under commodity production and the ideological and non-rational elements at work in justification strategies in this era.

HABERMAS'S project as the heir apparent of critical theory has been to foreground questions of epistemology raised by the movement's work, in particular, the nature of the epistemic basis needed to justify the claims of the critical theorists themselves. He has rejected the possibility of an interest-free reason, but argued that interests can themselves be rationally evaluated. But his main work has been to suggest a new communication-based model for epistemic evaluation. Inquiry occurs in an intersubjective context in which the goal is better understood as mutual agreement than knowledge of an object. The pragmatic aspects of this context, such as the power relations among the participants, are salient with respect to the epistemic validity of its outcome. Unequal power relations can inhibit participants' input into the discussion, thus distorting the resulting conclusions. Habermas's analysis here effectively integrates epistemological and political considerations. This provides a new perspective on Marx's concept of ideology and a new proposal about how we can enact the Enlightenment project of achieving liberation through knowledge.

If the above three movements have in common an attempt to develop a new synthesis of subject and object, post-structuralism returns us to a Nietzschean scepticism towards the possibility of liberation through reason. The term post-structuralism refers to a cluster of writings in reaction against (but in some ways a development of) the structuralist work of Saussure and Lévi-Strauss. Where phenomenology was concerned with what occurs in experience, structuralism was interested in the conditions which make that experience possible. These conditions were theorized as existing in the structural relations between constituents of experience rather than in relations of reference between those constituents and an outside world. Post-structuralism continues this turn away from reference as the prime criterion of truth but rejects the positing of universal and ahistorical structures. Though very disparate, post-structuralists are probably united in the belief that knowledge systems are ultimately contingent and connected intrinsically to power relations and to desire. In this and in their conceptualization of truth as a kind of strategic, linguistic practice post-structuralists are influenced most importantly by Nietzsche.

For DERRIDA, Western epistemology is logocentric in the sense that it assumes the neutrality and transparency of knowledge and of language. Language works precisely because it is not transparent, because it represses those elements which make meaning possible. Derrida's main project has been to reveal the ways in which knowledge is dependent on its other. Beliefs are justified or epistemically validated not because they correspond to a transcendental signified or a reality outside or behind the text, but through the always plural and shifting, deferred play of interrelationships between textual elements. Justification is therefore inherently unstable and ultimately undecidable. FOUCAULT has similarly been concerned to reveal the 'positive (or constitutive) unconscious of knowledge', though he theorizes this primarily in terms of desire and power rather than the endless deferral of signification. Foucault emphasizes much more than Derrida the level of materiality at play in the web of elements which produce knowledge, a materiality involving bodies and pleasures and non-linguistic practices as well as linguistic ones.

For both Derrida and Foucault, the outcome of knowledge production is contingent and even arbitrary in an epistemic sense. On Derrida's view, the binary terms through which meaning operates are necessarily in a relation of hierarchy but the choice of which term is dominant is essentially arbitrary. In a similar vein, Foucault sees regimes of truth as the product of as much historical accident as identifiable causes. Given the underdetermination of epistemic causes or reasons, belief formation, strategies of justification and epistemologies themselves must be explained in significant measure by reference to non-rational forces.

It is unclear how post-structuralism understands TRUTH. One possibility is to construct a meta-level analysis, in which justification works internal to a discourse, but where the post-structuralist account of discourses themselves have a different epistemic status by operating at a different level. But this position would seem to be self-refuting to the extent that it accords a degree of transparency to post-structuralist discourses that they maintain is impossible. Another option is to see truth as only a kind of validating but redundant attribution, similar to Tarski's view. But post-structuralists tend to see truth as more substantive, as marking a kind of conceptual domination, a claiming of hegemony, and effecting a curtailment of conflicting discursive moves. This suggests that truth is a kind of strategy within a language-game, and that as a criterion of justification the true is judged in terms of its strategic effects or the configuration of possibilities a claim makes possible, rather than by its correspondence to a non-linguistic realm. This strategic account of truth is the position adopted most often by post-structuralists, in both giving an account of how truth operates in discourse and in explaining the status of their own claims.

French feminist philosophy has developed yet another approach to knowledge building from this point. Irigaray suggests that there is a relation of isomorphism between the validity conditions and a priori assumptions of Western knowledge and male subjectivity. The impulse to achieve non-fallible knowledge from a position which is itself conceived of as disinterested is a desire for a kind of mastery which is essentially phallic. And the post-structuralist critique of logocentrism has also been largely gender-blind, completely inattentive to the maleness of both the interests involved in and the linear style of knowledge production in the West. The power and desire post-structuralists take to be formative in knowledge is not sexually neutral but masculine.

Continental epistemology is thus a heterogeneous terrain, yet the following list of family resemblances within this terrain may prove useful:

1. There is a general rejection of the CAR-TESIAN framing of epistemology as concerned with scepticism and with divining an accessible criterion of justification a believer can use to improve the epistemic status of their beliefs.
2. There is a turn away from focus on propositional content and the representational and referential status of claims to their interrelationships.
3. Connected to this, the ontology of knowing shifts from a separated subject and object, where the object world is set up as transcendent of subjectivity, to a 'lived world', an intersubjective dialogic realm, or a discursively constructed world.
4. Assumptions about the power and neutrality of reason are replaced with a critique of reason as ideological, dominating and limited and an attention to the unconscious, irrational forces at work in belief formation.
5. Truth is reconceptualized as perspectival, historical, indexed to a spatio-temporal context and plural.
6. A primary concern is with the politics of truth: what is the relationship between knowledge and liberation? What are the power relations of knowledge production in our society? And how are the marks of epistemic justification and ontologies of truth connected to masculinity?

See also DEATH OF EPISTEMOLOGY; EPOCHE; FEMINIST EPISTEMOLOGY; HEGEL; HISTORICISM; HUSSERL; IN ITSELF/FOR ITSELF; NIETZSCHE.

BIBLIOGRAPHY

(Asterisked titles contain further bibliographic information on this topic)

Adorno, T. and Horkheimer, M.: *Dialectic of Enlightenment* trans. J. Cumming (New York: Continuum, 1987).

Baynes, K., Bohman, J. and McCarthy, T. eds: *After Philosophy: End or Transformation* (Cambridge, MA: MIT Press, 1987).*

Bernstein, R.: *Beyond Objectivism and Relativism* (Philadelphia: University of Pennsylvania Press, 1983).

Dreyfus, H. and Rabinow, P.: *Michel Foucault: Beyond Structuralism and Hermeneutics* 2nd edn (Chicago: University of Chicago Press, 1983).

Grosz, E.: *Sexual Subversions: Three French Feminists* (Sydney: Allen and Unwin, 1989).*

Heidegger, M.: *Being and Time* trans. J. Macquarrie (New York: Harper and Row, 1962).

Horkheimer, M.: *Critical Theory* trans. M. J. O'Connell (New York: Continuum, 1972).

Irigaray, L.: *Speculum of the Other Woman* trans. G. Gill (Ithaca, NY: Cornell University Press, 1985).

Lyotard, J.-F.: *The Postmodern Condition: A*

*Report on Knowledge* trans. G. Bennington and B. Massumi (Minneapolis: University of Minnesota Press, 1985).

Megill, A.: *Prophets of Extremity* (Berkeley: University of California Press, 1985).

Rorty, R.: *Philosophy and the Mirror of Nature* (Princeton: Princeton University Press, 1979).

Rouse, J.: *Knowledge and Power* (Ithaca, NY: Cornell University Press, 1987).

Sartre, J.-P.: *Being and Nothingness* trans. H. Barnes (New York: Simon and Schuster, 1956).

LINDA ALCOFF

**convention**  There are two principal ways in which words or signs are given meaning, 'by ostension' and 'by convention'.

In *meaning by ostension* words or signs of a language are assigned entities as their meaning, e.g. mental entities such as ideas, experiences, concepts or non-mental entities such as concrete things, classes, functions, universals. *Generally speaking*, the entities assigned are so chosen that it will make sense to ask 'Is *s* true (of the world)?' for sentences *s* in the language at issue, as when, for example, in 'Cynthia's ring is gold', 'Cynthia's ring' is assigned Cynthia's ring, and 'is gold' is assigned a function from each and every thing in the world to *True* or *False* according as that thing is gold or not. Solely for our convenience here, let us call this sort of truth *O-truth*.

In *meaning by convention* words or signs of a language have meaning by virtue of more or less explicit rules for the use of the words or signs in relation to one another. The meaning of a word in this sense will not lie in an entity assigned to it, but will lie wholly in its rule-governed use with respect to other words or signs. *Generally speaking* (but not always), it is supposed that the language has a logical or logic-like syntax and that the rules for the use of the words or signs are rules for logical or logic-like operations (e.g. those generating formal-logical 'deductions' from given sentences or formulas). Then, for given such rules for a language, meanings for words are instituted 'by convention' by specifiying a subset X of the sentences or formulas

in the language. Relative to the given rules, the meanings of the signs in the sentences or formulas in the set X are implicitly defined (*see* DEFINITION) through X and the rules.

*Example:*  Language consists of signs $x$, $y$, 0, 1, 2, = as a binary relation sign, + as a binary operation sign. The formulas will all be of the form $\_ + \_ = \_$, or $\_ + \_ = \_ + \_$, or $\_ = \_ + \_$ where we distribute x, y, 0, 1, 2 in all possible ways over the _'s. The rules are:

(1) Wherever $x$ occurs, you may substitute 0, 1, or 2.

(2) If $W = Z$ occurs, you may substitute Z for W whenever W occurs in the position $\_ =$ or $= \_$.

Here are the formulas X that, together with the rules, implicitly define the signs $x$, $y$, 0, 1, 2, +, = : $x + 0 = x$, $x + y = y + x$. So what, for example, does 0 mean? It means, among other things, that $x + 0 = x$, $0 + 0 = 0$, $1 + 0 = 1$, $2 + 0 = 2$, $0 + x = x$, $0 + 1 = 1$, . . . (*see* AXIOMATICS)

Since the subset of formulas or sentences X which are settled on do implicitly define the words or signs composing them, it is said that they are true by convention – since the X determine the meanings of the words or signs composing them, we could say that they are true by virtue of the meanings of words or signs composing them. It is also usually said that the formulas or sentences derived from the X by exercise of the given rules for the uses of signs are also true by convention. Solely for our convenience here, let us call this sort of truth *C-truth*.

We have formal-logical syntaxes rich enough to enable us to formal-logically regiment the languages of the sciences. At least for the thus regimented languages of the natural sciences, we would expect most of the words occurring in a scientific theory to have two components of meaning, one determined by ostension, the other by convention. Thus some of the sentences (statements, propositions, theorems, etc.) of such a theory may be true by convention (C-true), some may be O-true, some O-false. However, on some views, some of the words or signs composing the language of our scientific theory may not have ostensive meanings, e.g. this is sometimes held of the peculiarly logical words such as 'not', 'or', 'all', and sometimes it is also held of mathematical words, and also of 'theoretical terms' rather than 'observational terms' when it is thought that sense-experience is the only source of O-meaning and that we need expressions in scientific theory (theoretical terms) that cannot be given such an observational meaning.

Since sentences whose words have C-meaning but no O-meaning might logically imply sentences whose terms do have an O-meaning (as when only observational terms are given an O-meaning), and since, say, the implicit and explicit definitions in a theory may be variously chosen so that sentences are true by convention on one choice, but not on another, and yet the same sentences have O-truth under either choice, and since it is not inconceivable that some subject matters, such as logic and even mathematics may be only a matter of C-truth, there is much philosophical difficulty in the exact characterization of C-truth, O-truth, and the relation between them.

BIBLIOGRAPHY

Quine, W.V.: 'Truth by convention', in his *The Ways of Paradox* (Cambridge, MA: Harvard University Press, 1976), ch. 9.

Quine, W.V.: 'Two dogmas of empiricism', in his *From a Logical Point of View* (Cambridge, MA: Harvard University Press, 1953), ch. 2.

Russell, B.: *Our Knowledge of the External World* (London: Allen and Unwin, 1980), chs 4, 5.

Torretti, R.: *Philosophy of Geometry from Riemann to Poincaré* (Dordrecht: Reidel, 1978), ch. 4, esp. 4.4.

ROBERT S. TRAGESSER

**criteria and knowledge** Except for alleged cases of things that are evident for one just by being true, it has often been thought, anything that is known must satisfy certain criteria as well as being true (*see* CRITERION, CANON). These criteria are general principles specifying what sorts of considerations C will make a proposition p evident to us.

Traditional suggestions include: (a) if a proposition p, e.g. that $2 + 2 = 4$, is clearly and distinctly conceived, then p is evident (*see* DESCARTES, HUME): or simply, (b) if we can't conceive p to be false, then p is evident: or (c) whatever we are immediately conscious of in thought or experience, e.g. that we seem to see red, is evident. These might be criteria whereby putative self-evident truths, e.g. that one clearly and distinctly conceives p, 'transmit' the status as evident they already have for one without criteria to other propositions like p. Alternatively, they might be criteria whereby epistemic status, e.g. p's being evident, is 'originally created' by purely non-epistemic considerations, e.g. facts about how p is conceived which are neither self-evident nor already criterially evident.

However it is 'originally created', presumably epistemic status, including degrees of warranted acceptance or probability, can be 'transmitted' deductively from premises to conclusions. Criteria then must say when and to what degree, e.g., p and q is warranted, given the epistemic considerations that p is warranted and so is q. (Must the logical connection itself be evident?) It is usually thought warrant can also be 'transmitted' inductively, as when evidence that observed type A things have regularly been F warrants acceptance, in the absence of undermining (overriding) evidence, of an unobserved A as F. Such warrant is DEFEASIBLE. Thus, despite regular observations of black crows, thinking an unobserved crow black might not be very warranted if there recently have been radiation changes potentially affecting bird colour.

Traditional criteria do not seem to make evident propositions about anything beyond our own thoughts, experiences and necessary truths, to which deductive or inductive criteria may be applied. Moreover, arguably, inductive criteria, including criteria warranting the best explanations of data, never make things evident or warrant their acceptance enough to count as knowledge.

Contemporary philosophers, however, have defended criteria whereby, e.g., considerations concerning a person's facial expression, may (defeasibly) make her pain or anguish evident (Lycan, 1971). More often, they have argued for criteria whereby some propositions about perceived reality can be made evident by sense experience itself or by evident propositions about it. For instance, in the absence of relevant evidence that perception is currently unreliable, it is evident we actually see a pink square *if* we have the sense experience of seeming to see a pink square (Pollock, 1986): or *if* it is *evident* we have such experience: or *if* in sense experience we spontaneously think we see a pink square. The experiential consideration allegedly can be enough to make reality evident, albeit defeasibly. It can do this on its own, and doesn't need support from further considerations such as the absence of undermining evidence or inductive evidence for a general link between experience and reality. Of course, there can be undermining evidence. So we need criteria that determine when evidence undermines and ceases to undermine.

Warrant might also be *increased* rather than just 'passed on'. The COHERENCE of probable propositions with other probable propositions might (defeasibly) make them all more evident (Firth, 1964). Thus even if seeming to see a chair initially made a chair's presence only probable, its presence might eventually become evident by cohering with claims about chair perception in other cases (Chisholm, 1989). The latter may be warranted in turn by 'memory' and 'introspection' criteria, as often suggested, whereby recalling or introspecting *p* defeasibly warrants *p*'s acceptance. Some philosophers argue further that coherence doesn't just increase warrant, and defend an overall coherence criterion: excluding perhaps initial warrant for propositions concerning our beliefs and their logical interrelations, what warrants any proposition to any degree for us is its coherence with the most coherent system of belief available (BonJour, 1985).

Contemporary epistemologists thus suggest the traditional picture of criteria may need alteration in three ways. Additional evidence may subject even our most basic judgements to rational correction, though they count as evident on the basis of our

criteria. Warrant may be transmitted other than through deductive and inductive relations between propositions. Transmission criteria might not simply 'pass' evidence on linearly from a foundation of highly evident 'premisses' to 'conclusions' that are never more evident.

Criteria then standardly take the form: 'if *C*, then (in the absence of undermining evidence) *p* is evident or warranted to degree *d*'. Arguably, criteria don't play much role initially in forming our beliefs. (*But see* Pollock, 1986.) For them to be the standards of epistemic status for us, however, it's typically thought criterial considerations must be ones in the light of which we can at least check, and perhaps correct, our judgement (*see* EXTERNALISM/INTERNALISM). Traditionally, epistemologists have therefore thought criterial considerations must be at least discover*able* through reflection or introspection and thus ultimately concern internal factors about our conception, thoughts or experience. However, others think objective checks must be publicly recognizable checks (*see* PRIVATE LANGUAGE ARGUMENT; PROBLEM OF RULE FOLLOWING) and thus that criterial considerations must ultimately concern public factors, e.g. that standard conditions (daylight, eyes open, etc.) for reliable perceptual reports obtain.

What makes criteria correct? For many epistemologists, their correctness is an irreducible necessary truth, a matter of brute metaphysics or of our linguistic conventions, concerning epistemic status and the considerations that determine it. Others object that it remains mysterious why particular considerations are criterial unless notions of the evident or warranted or correct are further defined in non-epistemic terms. Criteria might be definable, for example, as principles reflecting our deepest self-critical thoughts about what considerations yield truth, or as norms of thought that practical rationality demands we adopt if we are to be effective agents. However, many will *further* object that satisfying criteria *must* yield truth or be prone to. They insist that necessarily (1) whatever is warranted has an objectively good chance of truth and (2) whatever is evident is true or – to allow for the defeasibly evident – almost invariably true. Epistemic notions allegedly lose their point unless they somehow measure a proposition's actual prospects for truth for us.

Against (1) and (2), a common objection is that no considerations relevantly guarantee truth, even for the most part, or in the long run (*but see* BonJour, 1985). This is not obvious with traditional putative criterial considerations like clear and distinct conception or immediate awareness. But, critics argue, when talk of such considerations is unambiguously construed as talk of mental activity, and is not just synonymous with talk of clearly and distinctly or immediately knowing, there's no necessary connection between being criterially evident on the basis of such considerations and being true (Sellars, 1979). The mere coincidence in some cases that the proposition we conceive is true can't be what makes the proposition evident.

None the less, (1) and (2) might be necessary, while the correctness of putative criteria is a contingent fact: given various facts about us and our world, it is no coincidence that adhering to these criteria leads to truth, almost invariably or frequently. Given our need to survive with limited intellectual resources and time, perhaps it isn't surprising that in judging issues we only demand criterial considerations that are fallible, checkable, correctible and contingently lead to truth. However, specifying the relevant truth connections is highly problematic (*see* RELIABILISM). Moreover, reliability considerations now seem to be criterial for criteria although reliability, e.g. concerning perception, is not always accessible to introspection and reflection. Perhaps traditional accessibility requirements may be rejected. Possibly, instead, what makes a putative criterion correct can differ from the criterial considerations that make its correctness evident. Thus, there might be criteria for (defeasibly) identifying criteria, e.g. whether propositions 'feel right', or are considered warranted, in 'thought experiments' where we imagine various putative considerations

present and absent. Later reflection and inquiry might reveal what makes them all correct, e.g. reliability, or being designed by God or nature for our reliable use, etc.

In any case, if criterial considerations do not guarantee truth, knowledge will require more than truth and satisfying even the most demanding criteria (*see* GETTIER PROBLEM). Whether we know we see a pink cube on a particular occasion may also require that there fortunately be no *discoverable* facts (e.g. of our presence in a hologram gallery) to undermine the experiential basis for our judgement – or perhaps instead that it's no accident our judgement is true rather than merely probably true, given the criteria we adhere to and the circumstances (e.g. our presence in a normal room). Claims that truths which satisfy the relevant criteria are known can clearly be given many interpretations.

Many contemporary philosophers address these issues about criteria with untraditional approaches to meaning and truth. Pollock (1974), for example, argues that learning ordinary concepts like 'bird' or 'red' involves learning to make judgements with them in conditions, e.g. perceptual experiences, which warrant them, albeit defeasibly since we also learn to correct the judgements despite the presence of such conditions. These conditions are not logically necessary or sufficient for the truth of judgements. None the less the identity of our ordinary concepts makes the criteria we learn for making judgements necessarily correct. Although not all warranted assertions are true, there is no idea of their truth completely divorced from what undefeated criterial considerations allow us to assert. However, satisfying criteria still seems in some way compatible with future defeat, even frequent, and with not knowing, just as it was with error and defeat in more traditional accounts.

By appealing to defeasibly warranting criteria then, it seems we can not *show* we know *p* rather than merely satisfy the criteria. Worse, critics argue, we can not even have knowledge by satisfying such criteria. Knowing *p* allegedly requires more. But what evidence, besides that entitling us to claim the currently undefeated satisfaction of criteria, could entitle us to claim more, e.g. that *p* won't be defeated? Yet knowers, at least on reflection, must be entitled to give assurances concerning these further conditions (Wright, 1984). Otherwise we wouldn't be interested in a concept of knowledge as opposed to the evident or warranted. These contentions might be disputed to save a role for defeasibly warranting criteria. But why bother? Why can't a pink cube manifest itself in visual experiences that are essentially different from those where it merely appears present (McDowell, 1982)? We thereby know objective facts through experiences that are criterial for them and make them indefeasibly evident. However, to many, this requires a seamless, quite mystifying, fusion of appearance and reality. Alternatively, perhaps knowledge requires exercising an ability to judge accurately in specific relevant circumstances, but doesn't require criterial considerations which, as a matter of general principle, make propositions evident, even if only in the absence of undermining evidence or contingently, no matter what the context. Arguably, however, our position for giving relevant assurances doesn't improve with these new conditions for knowing.

It is difficult to formulate general principles determining when criterial warrant is and isn't undermined (Pollock, 1974). So one might think that warrant in general depends just on what is presupposed as true and relevant in a potentially shifting context of thought or conversation, not on general criteria. However, defenders of criteria may protest that coherence, *at least*, remains as a criterion applicable across contexts.

It is often felt that *p* can not be evident by satisfying criteria unless it is evident that (a) criterial considerations obtain, and also evident either that (b) the criteria have certain correctness-making features e.g. leading to truth, or just that (c) the criteria are correct. Otherwise any conformity to pertinent standards is in a relevant sense only accidental (BonJour, 1985). Yet vicious regress or circularity loom, unless (a)–(c) or supporting propositions are evident without criteria. At worst, as sceptics argue, nothing

can be warranted; at best a consistent role for criteria is limited. A common reply is that being criterially warranted, by definition, just requires that adequate (checkable) criterial considerations in fact obtain, i.e. that (a)–(c) be true. There is no need to demand further cognitive achievements for which one or more of (a)–(c) must also be evident, e.g. actually checking that criterial considerations obtain, proving truth or likelihood of truth on the basis of these considerations, or proving warrant on their basis.

Even so, how *can* propositions stating which putative criteria are correct be warranted? Any proposal for criterial warrant invokes the classic sceptical charge of vicious regress or circularity (*see* PROBLEM OF THE CRITERION). Yet again, arguably, as with *p* above, correct criteria must in fact be satisfied, but this fact itself needn't be *already* warranted. So, one might argue there's no debilitating regress or circle of warrant, even when, as may happen with some criterion, its correctness is warranted ultimately only because it itself is satisfied (van Cleve, 1979). Independent, ultimately non-criterial, evidence is not needed. None the less, suppose we argue that our criteria are correct, because, e.g. they lead to truth, are confirmed by thought experiments, or are clearly and distinctly conceived as correct, etc. However we develop our arguments, they won't persuade those who, doubting the criteria we conform to, doubt our premises or their relevance. Dismissing our failure as merely conversational and irrelevant to our warrant, moreover, may strike sceptics and non-sceptics alike as question-begging or as arbitrarily altering what warrant requires. For the charge of ungrounded dogmatism to be inappropriate, more than the consistency of criterial warrant, including warrant about warrant, may be required, no matter what putative criteria we conform to.

*See also* CHISHOLM; COMMONSENSISM AND CRITICAL COGNITIVISM.

BIBLIOGRAPHY

BonJour, L.: *The Structure of Empirical Knowledge*

(Cambridge, MA: Harvard University Press, 1985).

Chisholm, R.M.: *Theory of Knowledge* 3rd edn (Englewood Cliffs: Prentice-Hall, 1989).

Firth, R.: 'Coherence, certainty, and epistemic priority', *Journal of Philosophy* 61 (1964), 545–57.

Lycan, W.G.: 'Non-inductive evidence: recent work on Wittgenstein's "criteria"', *American Philosophical Quarterly* 8 (1971), 109–25.

McDowell, J.: 'Criteria, defeasibility, and knowledge', *Proceedings of the British Academy* 68 (1983), 455–79.

Pollock, J.: *Knowledge and Justification* (Princeton: Princeton University Press, 1974).

Pollock, J.: *Contemporary Theories of Knowledge* (Totowa: Rowman and Littlefield, 1986).

Sellars, W.: 'More on givenness and explanatory coherence', *Justification and Knowledge* ed. G. Pappas (Dordrecht: D. Reidel, 1979).

van Cleve, J.: 'Foundationalism, epistemic principles, and the Cartesian circle', *Philosophical Review* 88 (1979), 55–91.

Wright, C.J.G.: 'Second thoughts about criteria', *Synthese* 58 (1984), 383–405.

BRUCE HUNTER

**criterion, canon**  Except for alleged cases of self-evident truths, it is often thought that anything that is known must satisfy certain criteria or standards (Sextus Empiricus, 1933). These criteria are general principles specifying the sorts of considerations that will make a proposition evident or just make accepting it warranted to some degree. Common suggestions for this role include: if one clearly and distinctly conceives a proposition $p$, e.g. that $2 + 2 = 4$, $p$ is evident: or, if $p$ coheres with the bulk of one's beliefs, $p$ is warranted. These might be criteria whereby putative self-evident truths, e.g. that one clearly and distinctly conceives $p$, 'transmit' the status as evident they already have without criteria to other propositions like $p$, or they might be criteria whereby purely non-epistemic considerations, e.g. facts about logical connections or about conception that need not be already evident or warranted, originally 'create' $p$'s epistemic status. If that in turn can be 'transmitted' to other propositions, e.g. by deduction or induction, there will be criteria specifying when it is.

See also CRITERIA AND KNOWLEDGE; SEXTUS EMPIRICUS.

BIBLIOGRAPHY

Chisholm, R.M.: *Theory of Knowledge* 3rd edn (Englewood Cliffs: Prentice-Hall, 1989), 6–7, 61–74.

van Cleve, J.: 'Foundationalism, epistemic principles, and the Cartesian circle', *Philosophical Review* 88 (1979), 55–91.

Lycan, W.G.: 'Non-inductive evidence: recent work on Wittgenstein's "criteria"', *American Philosophical Quarterly* 8 (1971), 109–25.

Pollock, J.: *Knowledge and Justification* (Princeton: Princeton University Press, 1974), 3–22, 33–49, 81–5, 255–64.

Sextus Empiricus: *Outlines of Empiricism* (Cambridge, MA: Harvard University Press, 1933; London: William Heinemann, 1933), 17, 125–203, 213–75.

BRUCE HUNTER

**critical cognitivism**  *see* COMMONSENSISM AND CRITICAL COGNITIVISM.

# D

---

Davidson, Donald (1930–) American philosopher. Davidson argues that if many of our beliefs cohere with many others, then many of our beliefs are true. This has, as Davidson emphasizes, striking consequences for traditional epistemological issues: if it is right, then the refutation of SCEPTICISM requires only the weak premiss of belief COHERENCE.

To understand his argument for this conclusion, we must consider the notion of radical interpretation. A 'radical interpreter' is defined to be someone who faces the problem of content attribution given only knowledge of the correlations between his informant's local circumstances and the occasion sentences that the informant holds true (together with general principles of warranted deductive and non-demonstrative inference). Now Davidson takes it to be a necessary truth that any content-bearing state can be interpreted under these epistemological conditions, and argues from this that there is no way the radical interpreter can discover the speaker to be largely wrong about the world. The argument is that the interpreter has no alternative but to interpret sentences held true according to the events and objects in the outside world that cause the sentence to be held true. In effect, Davidson holds that the radical interpreter's strategy must be first to find out what causes the informant to say what he does, and then to identify the truth conditions of the informant's utterances (more or less comprehensively) with their causes. But, Davidson concludes, if the radical interpreter does proceed this way, he cannot but accept that, in general, the informant's utterances about the world are true (by the interpreter's lights).

Suppose that, for the sake of the argument, we assume that the radical interpreter's epistemological position does have a privileged metaphysical standing. It looks like all that follows is that the sentences that the informant holds true must be true by the interpreter's lights. It is possible that what the informant says should be true by the interpreter's lights may still generally be false. It looks like the possibility of a *folie à deux* is left open by the principle of charity (which is, of course, just what the sceptic always thought).

Davidson is quite aware of this problem; he offers the following argument in reply. It cannot be the rule that what the informant says, though true by the interpreter's lights, is nevertheless false. For imagine for a moment an interpreter who is omniscient about the world and about what does and would cause a speaker to assent to any sentence in his repertoire. The omniscient interpreter, using the same method as the fallible interpreter, finds the fallible speaker largely consistent and correct. By his own standards, of course, but since these are objectively correct, the fallible speaker is seen to be largely correct by the objective standards. So the sceptic is finally refuted.

Many philosophers find that the following line of argument provides a *reductio* of the notion that radical interpretation should proceed by the exercise of charity: if an omniscient being interprets my utterances (or beliefs) so that they come out true by its lights, then it will misinterpret me whenever I say (or believe) something false.

WRITINGS

'On the very idea of a conceptual scheme', in his *Inquiries into Truth and Interpretation* (Oxford: Oxford University Press, 1984).
'Empirical content', in *Truth and Interpretation:*

*Perspectives on the Philosophy of Donald Davidson* ed. E. LePore (Oxford: Blackwell, 1986).
'A coherence theory of truth and knowledge', ibid.

ERNEST LEPORE

**death of epistemology** Rumours about the death of epistemology began to circulate widely in the 1970s. Death notices appeared in such works as *Philosophy and the Mirror of Nature* (1979) by Richard RORTY and Williams's *Groundless Belief* (1977). Of late, the rumours seem to have died down, but whether they will prove to have been exaggerated remains to be seen.

Arguments for the death of epistemology typically pass through three stages. At the first stage, the critic characterizes the task of epistemology by identifying the distinctive sorts of questions it deals with. At the second stage, he tries to isolate the theoretical ideas that make those questions possible. Finally, he tries to undermine those ideas. His conclusion is that, since the ideas in question are less than compelling, there is no pressing need to solve the problems they give rise to. Thus the death-of-epistemology theorist holds that there is no barrier in principle to epistemology's going the way of, say, demonology or judicial astrology. These disciplines too centred on questions that were once taken very seriously indeed, but as their presuppositions came to seem dubious, debating their problems came to seem pointless. Furthermore, some theorists hold that philosophy, as a distinctive, professionalized activity, revolves essentially around epistemological inquiry, so that speculation about the death of epistemology is apt to evolve into speculation about the death of philosophy generally.

Clearly, the death-of-epistemology theorist must hold that there is nothing special about philosophical problems. This is where philosophers who see little sense in talk of the death of epistemology disagree. For them, philosophical problems, including epistemological problems, are distinctive in that they are 'natural' or 'intuitive': that is to say, they can be posed and understood taking for granted little or nothing in the way of contentious, theoretical ideas. Thus, unlike problems belonging to the particular sciences, they are 'perennial' problems that could occur to more or less anyone, anytime and anywhere. But are the standard problems of epistemology really as 'intuitive' as all that? Or if they have indeed come to seem so commonsensical, is this only because commonsense is a repository for ancient theory? These are the sorts of question that underlie speculation about epistemology's possible demise.

Because it revolves round questions like this, the death-of-epistemology movement is distinguished by its interest in what we may call 'theoretical diagnosis': bringing to light the theoretical background to philosophical problems so as to argue that they cannot survive detachment from it. This explains the movement's interest in historical-explanatory accounts of the emergence of philosophical problems. If certain problems can be shown not to be perennial, but rather to have emerged at definite points in time, this is strongly suggestive of their dependence on some particular theoretical outlook; and if an account of that outlook makes intelligible the subsequent development of the discipline centred on those problems, that is evidence for its correctness. Still, the goal of theoretical diagnosis is to establish logical dependence, not just historical correlation. So although historical investigation into the roots and development of epistemology can provide valuable clues to the ideas that inform its problems, history cannot substitute for problem-analysis.

The death-of-epistemology movement has many sources: in the pragmatists, particularly JAMES and DEWEY, and in the writings of WITTGENSTEIN, QUINE, SELLARS and AUSTIN. But the project of theoretical diagnosis must be distinguished from the 'therapeutic' approach to philosophical problems that some names on this list might call to mind. The practitioner of theoretical diagnosis does not claim that the problems he analyses are 'pseudo-problems', rooted in 'conceptual confusion'. Rather, he claims that, while genuine, they are wholly internal to a particular intellectual project whose generally unacknowledged theoretical commitments he aims to isolate and criticize.

Turning to details, the task of epistemology, as these radical critics conceive it, is to determine the nature, scope and limits, indeed the very possibility of human knowledge. Since epistemology determines the extent to which knowledge is possible, it cannot itself take for granted the results of any particular forms of empirical inquiry. Thus epistemology purports to be a non-empirical discipline, the function of which is to sit in judgement on all particular discursive practices with a view to determining their cognitive status. The epistemologist (or, in the era of epistemologically-centred philosophy, we might as well say 'the philosopher') is someone professionally equipped to determine what forms of judgement are 'scientific', 'rational', 'merely expressive', and so on. Epistemology is therefore fundamentally concerned with sceptical questions. Determining the scope and limits of human knowledge is a matter of showing where and when knowledge is possible. But there is a project called 'showing that knowledge is possible' only because there are powerful arguments for the view that knowledge is impossible. Here the SCEPTICISM in question is first and foremost radical scepticism, the thesis that with respect to this or that area of putative knowledge we are never so much as justified in believing one thing rather than another. The taks of epistemology is thus to determine the extent to which it is possible to respond to the challenges posed by radically sceptical arguments by determining where we can and cannot have justifications for our beliefs. If it turns out that the prospects are more hopeful for some sorts of beliefs than for others, we shall have uncovered a difference in epistemological status. The 'scope and limits' question and problem of radical scepticism are two sides of one coin.

This emphasis on scepticism as the fundamental problem of epistemology may strike some philosophers as misguided. Much recent work on the concept of knowledge, particularly that inspired by Gettier's demonstration of the insufficiency of the standard 'justified true belief' analysis, has been carried on independently of any immediate concern with scepticism. I think it must be admitted that philosophers who envisage the death of epistemology tend to assume a somewhat dismissive attitude to work of this kind. In part, this is because they tend to be dubious about the possibility of stating precise necessary and sufficient conditions for the application of any concept. But the determining factor is their thought that only the centrality of the problem of radical scepticism can explain the importance for philosophy that, at least in the modern period, epistemology has taken on. Since radical scepticism concerns the very possibility of justification, for philosophers who put this problem first, questions about what special sorts of justification yield knowledge, or about whether knowledge might be explained in non-justificational terms, are of secondary importance. Whatever importance they have will have to derive in the end from connections, if any, with sceptical problems.

In light of this, the fundamental question for death-of-epistemology theorists becomes, 'What are the essential theoretical presuppositions of arguments for radical scepticism?' Different theorists suggest different answers. RORTY traces scepticism to the 'representationalist' conception of belief and its close ally, the correspondence theory of truth. According to Rorty, if we think of beliefs as 'representations' that aim to correspond with mind-independent 'reality' (mind as the mirror of nature), we will always face insuperable problems when we try to assure ourselves that the proper alignment has been achieved. In Rorty's view, by switching to a more 'pragmatic' or 'behaviouristic' conception of beliefs as devices for coping with particular, concrete problems, we can put scepticism, hence the philosophical discipline that revolves around it, behind us once and for all.

Other theorists stress epistemological FOUNDATIONALISM as the essential background to traditional sceptical problems. There are reasons for preferring this approach. Arguments for epistemological conclusions require at least one epistemological premiss. It is, therefore, not easy to see how metaphysical or semantic doctrines of the sort emphasized by Rorty could, by themselves, generate epistemological problems, such as radical scepticism. On the other hand the case for scepticism's essential dependence on foundationalist preconceptions is by no means easy to make. It has even been argued that this approach 'gets things almost entirely upside down'. The thought here is that foundationalism is an attempt to save knowledge from the sceptic, and is therefore a reaction to, rather than a presupposition of, the deepest and most intuitive arguments for scepticism. Challenges like this certainly need to be met by death-of-epistemology theorists, who have sometimes been too ready to take for obvious scepticism's dependence on foundationalist or other theoretical ideas. This reflects, perhaps, the dangers of taking one's cue from historical accounts of the development of sceptical problems. It may be that, in the heyday of foundationalism, sceptical arguments were typically presented within a foundationalist context. But the crucial question is not whether some sceptical arguments do take foundationalism for granted but whether there are any that do not. This issue – indeed, the general issue of whether scepticism is a truly intuitive problem – can only be resolved by detailed analysis of the possibilities and resources of sceptical argumentation.

Another question concerns why anti-foundationalism leads to the death of epistemology rather than a non-foundational, hence COHERENTIST, approach to knowledge and justification. It is true that death-of-epistemology theorists often characterize justification in terms of coherence. But their intention is to make a negative point. According to foundationalism, our beliefs fall naturally into broad epistemological categories that reflect objective, context-independent relations of epistemological priority. Thus, for example, experiential beliefs are thought to be naturally or intrinsically prior to beliefs about the external world, in the sense that any evidence we have for the latter must derive in the end from the former. This relation of epistemic priority is, so to say, just a fact. Foundationalism is therefore committed

to a strong form of REALISM about epistemological facts and relations, call it 'epistemological realism'. For some anti-foundationalists, talk of coherence is just a way of rejecting this picture in favour of the view that justification is a matter of accommodating new beliefs to relevant background beliefs in contextually appropriate ways, there being no context-independent, purely epistemological restrictions on what sorts of beliefs can confer evidence on what others. If this is all that is meant, talk of coherence does not point to a theory of justification so much as to the deflationary view that justification is not the sort of thing we should expect to have theories about. There is, however, a stronger sense of 'coherence' which does point in the direction of a genuine theory. This is the radically holistic account of justification, according to which inference depends on assessing our entire belief-system or 'total view' in the light of abstract criteria of 'coherence'. But it is questionable whether this view, which seems to demand privileged knowledge of what we believe, is an alternative to foundationalism or just a variant form. Accordingly, it is possible that a truly uncompromising anti-foundationalism will prove as hostile to traditional coherence theories as to standard foundationalist positions, reinforcing the connection between the rejection of foundationalism and the death of epistemology.

The death-of-epistemology movement has some affinities with the call for a 'naturalized' approach to knowledge. Quine argues that the time has come for us to abandon such traditional projects as refuting the sceptic by showing how empirical knowledge can be rationally reconstructed on a sensory basis, hence *justifying* empirical knowledge at large. We should concentrate instead on the more tractable problem of *explaining* how we 'project our physics from our data', i.e. how retinal stimulations cause us to respond with increasingly complex sentences about events in our environment. Epistemology should be transformed into a branch of natural science, specifically experimental psychology. But though Quine presents this as a suggestion about how to continue doing epistemology, to philosophers who think that the traditional questions still lack satisfactory answers, it looks more like abandoning epistemology in favour of another pursuit entirely. It is significant, therefore, that in subsequent writings Quine has been less dismissive of sceptical concerns. But if this is how 'naturalized' epistemology develops, then for the death-of-epistemology theorist, its claims will open up a new field for theoretical diagnosis.

See also NATURALIZED EPISTEMOLOGY; REPRESENTATION; REPRESENTATIVE REALISM; TRUTH.

BIBLIOGRAPHY

Kaplan, M.: 'Epistemology on holiday', Journal of Philosophy (1991).
Quine, W. V.: 'Epistemology naturalized,' in his Ontological Relativity and Other Essays (New York: Columbia University Press, 1969).
Quine, W.V.: 'The nature of natural knowledge', in S. Guttenplan, Mind and Nature (Oxford: Oxford University Press, 1975).
Rorty, R.: Philosophy and the Mirror of Nature (Princeton: Princeton University Press, 1979).
Rorty, R.: Consequences of Pragmatism (Minneapolis: University of Minnesota Press, 1982).
Rorty, R.: Objectivity, Relativism and Truth, (Cambridge: Cambridge University Press, 1991).
Stroud, B.: 'Skepticism and the possibility of knowledge', Journal of Philosophy (1984).
Williams, M.: Groundless Belief (Oxford: 1977).
Williams, M.: Unnatural Doubts (Oxford: Blackwell, 1992).

MICHAEL WILLIAMS

**defeasibility** The warrant a proposition $p$ has for us on the basis of evidence $e$ is *defeasible* when expanded evidence could decrease $p$'s warrant. For example, 'The next crow I see will be black' is less warranted when, despite evidence $e$ that observed crows were black, we are told on usually reliable authority that there are many albino birds nearby, and have no evidence this present testimony

is an exception. Our actual warrant depends on our total evidence. In stock cases, we don't 'lose' $e$, but its import is undercut when it and the rest of our original total evidence is combined with *additional* evidence $e'$. With *holistic* warrant the situation seems different. For instance, the warrant $p$ has through membership in the most coherent system of belief available is *defeasible* when there could be a more coherent system available which omits $p$. Much else may disappear from our original system or evidence. Various philosophically interesting senses of 'defeasible' correspond to different senses in which there 'could' be defeating evidence, e.g. because it is logically possible that there is evidence that, combined with our present evidence, makes $p$ less warranted, or because there actually are past or future events whose discovery, combined with our present evidence, would make $p$ less warranted, etc.

See also CRITERIA AND KNOWLEDGE; EVIDENCE; GETTIER PROBLEM; PRIMA FACIE REASONS.

BIBLIOGRAPHY

Chisholm, R.M.: Theory of Knowledge 3rd edn (Englewood Cliffs: Prentice-Hall, 1989), pp. 49–60.
Firth, R.: 'Coherence, certainty, and epistemic priority', Journal of Philosophy 61 (1964), 545–57.
Firth, R.: 'Anatomy of certainty', Philosophical Review 76 (1967), 3–27.
Pollock, J.: Contemporary Theories of Knowledge (Totowa: Rowman and Littlefield, 1986), pp. 36–46, 176.

BRUCE HUNTER

**definition** Complex expressions either *reporting* or *instituting* equivalences among verbal or symbolic expressions, in form, definitions are either *explicit* or *implicit*.

A definition that *institutes* explains how an expression *will be* used henceforth. A definition that *reports* explains how an expression *has been* used. An *explicit* definition explains, by means of words given *in use*, how an expression given *in mention* has been or will be used (*see* USE/MENTION). An *implicit* definition explains how an expression has been or will be used by using it, usually in conjunction with the use of other expressions.

Dictionary definitions are reportive and explicit. Symbols introduced in technical writings are usually institutive and explicit. When a word is learned in the context of its use, that context *in effect* provides a reportive, implicit definition. Formal, axiomatic systems, in which the meaning of each expression is gathered from its formal-logical relationships with the other expressions, provide institutive, implicit definitions.

BIBLIOGRAPHY

Frege, G.: *The Basic Laws of Arithmetic* trans. and ed. M. Furth (Berkeley and Los Angeles: University of California Press, 1967).
Quine, W.V.: 'Implicit definition sustained', in his *The Ways of Paradox* (Cambridge, MA: Harvard University Press, 1976), ch. 13.
Quine, W.V.: 'Vagaries of definition', in his *The Ways of Paradox* (Cambridge, MA: Harvard University Press, 1976), ch. 7.

ROBERT S. TRAGESSER

**Derrida, Jacques** (1930–) French philosopher, born in Algiers. Derrida argues against foundational and essentialist metaphysics and epistemology. As a paradigm example, *Speech and Phenomena* examines HUSSERL's attempt to ground knowledge on contents which can be present before a unitary self:

1. For Husserl, there is no consciousness of present contents as present except by reference to the just-past and the just-to-come. So 'intentional contents' cannot be entirely present before the mind. The ultimate data, by Husserl's own account, include always-non-present items, and are experienced that way.
2. Intentional contents, as repeatables, are what they are by virtue of other possible cases. But then an intentional object cannot be present to the self as such.

Derrida thus supplements SELLARS's attack on SENSE-DATA with an argument against the givenness of intentional contents generally. Meanings are essentially repeatables; what is fully present can only be particulars. So meanings cannot in principle be given as such. 'Intelligible' data have the same difficulties in functioning cognitively as sense-data have.

3. The necessary 'traces' of what cannot be given make thought and experience language-like, because their meaning is partly non-present. That is, no pure meaning can be present to consciousness as a foundation which grounds interpretation. Thus thought is language-like and itself subject to interpretation.

Derrida draws many Quinean consequences from the idea that thought is no more transparent than writing. Moreover, Derrida, emerging from a thorough grounding in Heidegger, Levinas and Hegel, is anti-essentialist about the theory-builder, the self. The attack above on presence is also part of an attack on the unitary self which can be self-present in its given nature. If the subject is not given, but is rather on a par with other 'posits', then a basis for an epistemologically significant division between 'inner' and 'outer' disappears. Thus also the notion of the subjective as a realm of representations which must somehow be matched with the objective, evaporates. Derrida thus shows that a genuine anti-essentialism is also post-Cartesian.

*See also* NECESSARY/CONTINGENT; QUINE; SELF-KNOWLEDGE AND SELF-IDENTITY.

WRITINGS

*La Voix et le Phénomène* (Paris: Presses Universitaires de France, 1967); trans. D. Allsion, *Speech and Phenomena* (Evanston: Northwestern University Press, 1973).
*De la Grammatologie* (Paris: Editions de Minuit, 1967); trans. G. Spivak, *Of Grammatology* (Baltimore: Johns Hopkins University Press, 1976).
*Marges de la Philosophie* (Paris: Editions de

Minuit, 1972); trans. A. Bass, *Margins of Philosophy* (Chicago: University of Chicago Press, 1982).

*Limited Inc.* (Evanston: Northwestern University Press, 1988).

SAMUEL C. WHEELER III

**Descartes, René (1596–1650)** French philosopher, scientist and mathematician. Descartes is often called the 'father of modern philosophy', on the grounds that he made epistemological questions the primary and central questions of the discipline. But this is misleading for several reasons. In the first place, Descartes' conception of philosophy was very different from our own. The term 'philosophy' in the seventeenth century was far more comprehensive than it is today, and embraced the whole of what we nowadays call natural science, including cosmology, and physics, as well as subjects like anatomy, optics and medicine. Descartes' reputation as a 'philosopher' in his own time was based as much as anything on his contributions in these scientific areas. In the second place, even in those Cartesian writings that are philosophical in the modern academic sense, the epistemological concerns are rather different from the conceptual and linguistic inquiries that characterize present-day 'theory of knowledge'. Descartes saw the need to base his scientific system on secure metaphysical foundations; by 'metaphysics' he meant inquiries into 'God and the soul and in general all the first things to be discovered by philosophizing' (letter to Mersenne of 11 November 1640). These foundational inquires included, to be sure, questions about knowledge and certainty; but even here, Descartes is not *primarily* concerned with the criteria for knowledge claims, or with definitions of the epistemic concepts involved; his aim, rather, is to provide a unified framework for understanding the universe. In place of the fragmented scholastic world of separate disciplines, each with its own methods and standards of precision, he aimed to construct a coherent theory of the world and man's place within it. And this project required him 'once in the course of his life' systematically to test all his former beliefs, and to subject them to radical scrutiny, in order to see whether he could 'establish anything at all in the sciences that was stable and likely to last' (AT VII 17; CSM II 12).

René Descartes was born in France on 31 March 1596, in the small town near Tours which now bears his name, and educated at the Jesuit college of La Flèche in Anjou. As a young man he was strongly influenced by the Dutchman Isaac Beeckman, who awakened his lifelong interest in mathematics – a discipline in which he discerned the precision, order and certainty which merited the title of *scientia* (Descartes' term for systematic and reliable knowledge based on indubitable foundations). In 1628, Descartes emigrated to Holland where he was to live for most of the rest of his life. In 1633, he had ready a treatise on cosmology and physics, *Le Monde*; but he cautiously withdrew the work from publication when he heard of the condemnation of Galileo by the Inquisition for rejecting (as Descartes himself did) the geocentric theory of the universe. But in 1637 Descartes decided to release for publication (in French) a sample of his scientific work, the *Optics*, *Meteorology* and *Geometry*, together with an autobiographical introduction entitled *Discourse on the Method of rightly conducting one's reason and reaching the truth in the sciences*. Criticisms of his arguments led Descartes to compose his philosophical masterpiece, the *Meditations on First Philosophy*, published in Latin in 1641. In 1644 Descartes produced, in Latin, a mammoth compendium of his metaphysical and scientific views, the *Principles of Philosophy*, which he hoped would become a university textbook to rival the standard texts based on Aristotle. In 1649 he published *The Passions of the Soul*, a lengthy treatise on ethics and psychology. The same year he accepted an invitation to go to Stockholm to give philosophical instruction to Queen Christina of Sweden. He was required to provide tutorials at the royal palace at five o'clock in the morning, and the strain of this break in his habits (he had maintained the lifelong custom of lying in bed late into the morning) led to his catching pneumonia. He died on 11 February 1650, just short of his fifty-fourth birthday.

Descartes' views on knowledge were conditioned by the time in which he lived, which had witnessed a gradual erosion of beliefs held for centuries and apparently based on straightforward observation and 'common sense'. The most notable example of this was the long-held conviction, bolstered by the authority of the Church, that an immovable earth was the centre of the universe. Galileo's discovery of the moons of Jupiter (made when Descartes was a nine-year-old schoolboy at La Flèche) was but one piece in a mounting pile of evidence suggesting that the traditional view was radically mistaken. Descartes became obsessed by the thought that no lasting progress could be made in the sciences unless a systematic method could be devised for sifting though our preconceived opinions and establishing which of them, if any, was reliable. 'Suppose we had a basket full of apples and were worried that some of them were rotten. How would be we proceed? Would we not begin by tipping the whole lot out and then pick up and put back only those we saw to be sound?' (AT VII 481; CSM II 324). Descartes' 'method of doubt' involves a determined effort to test our preconceived opinions or 'prejudices' (*praejudicia*) to the limit, by applying a series of deliberate sceptical techniques (often derived from classical arguments for doubt which had been revived in the sixteenth century). He points out first, that the senses (sight, hearing, touch, etc.) are often unreliable, and 'it is prudent never to trust entirely those who have deceived us even once' (First Meditation); later, he cited such instances as the straight stick which looks bent in water, and the square tower which looks round from a distance. This ARGUMENT FROM ILLUSION (as it is called today), has not, on the whole, impressed commentators; and some of Descartes' contemporaries pointed out that since such sensory errors come to light as a result of further sensory information, it cannot be right to cast wholesale doubt on the evidence of the senses. But Descartes himself regarded the argument from illusion as only the first stage in a softening up process which would 'lead the mind away from the senses'. He admits that there are some cases of sense-based belief about which doubt would be

insane – 'for example the belief that I am sitting here by the fire, wearing a winter dressing gown' (ibid.).

At this point, Descartes introduces a fresh reason for doubt – the celebrated 'dreaming argument'. 'How often, asleep at night, am I convinced of just such familiar events, that I am here in my dressing gown, sitting by the fire, when in fact I am lying undressed in bed.' Observing that there are 'no conclusive signs' by which being awake can be distinguished from being asleep, Descartes proceeds, in effect, to mount a general doubt about whether we are justified in asserting the real extra-mental existence of any particular object which we appear to perceive via the senses. Critics of this argument have suggested that the very concept of dreaming is parasitic on the concept of waking life, so that, again, we have not been offered a *general* reason for doubting the existence of external objects. Descartes' defenders, however, can plausibly reply that if in any particular instance the possibility that one is dreaming cannot be ruled out, the solitary doubter has no guarantee of the independent existence of any given object of perception. The conclusion which Descartes eventually draws is that any sciences which make existential assumptions (such as physics, astronomy and medicine) are potentially doubtful, and that only disciplines like arithmetic and geometry 'which deal only with the simplest and most general things, regardless of whether they exist in nature or not' enjoy cast iron certainty (AT VII 20; CSM II 14).

Yet even this last certainty is undermined in Descartes' most radical argument for doubt – the deceiving God hypothesis: if, as I have been taught, there is an omnipotent being who created me, then 'how do I know that he has not brought it about that I go wrong every time I add two and three or count the sides of a square?' (ibid.). There may, of course, be no God; but in that case, Descartes reasons, I owe my existence not to a divine creator but to some chance chain of imperfect causes. And in that case there is even less reason to suppose that my basic mathematical judgements are sound. By the end of the First Meditation, the meditator is 'tumbling around' in a vortex of doubt. There is 'not one of my former beliefs about which a doubt may not properly be raised'; and Descartes dramatizes this horror of extreme uncertainty by invoking a 'supremely powerful and malicious demon' intent on deceiving me in any way he possibly can.

Despite the commonly employed label 'Cartesian scepticism' it is important to realize that Descartes is in no sense a sceptic. The systematic doubt is merely a means to an end: the aim is to demolish in order to rebuild – to throw out the rubble and loose sand in order to reach a bedrock of certainty (AT VII 546; CSM II 373). That bedrock is reached in the Second Meditation in the famous Cogito argument: 'let the demon deceive me as much as he can, he will never bring it about that I am nothing so long as I think I am something. So... I must finally conclude that this proposition, *I am, I exist* is necessarily true whenever it is put forward by me or conceived in my mind' (AT VII 25; CSM II 17). As Descartes phrased it in the *Discourse*, 'I am thinking therefore I exist' ( *je pense donc je suis*) is 'so firm and sure that the most extravagant suppositions of the sceptics were incapable of shaking it' (AT VI 32; CSM I 127). The most interesting epistemic feature of the Cogito argument is the way in which Descartes extrudes certainty from the very process of doubting: the act of casting doubt on the proposition that one is thinking confirms its truth, and this in turn unavoidably implies that there must be an existing subject. At least one existential truth, *I exist*, survives everything the sceptic can throw at it.

Descartes' questioning of his previous beliefs is not as radical as is often supposed. In order to reach the certainty of the Cogito, he has to rely (as he later admitted) on an unquestioned underlying conceptual apparatus – for example, his grasp of what is meant by knowledge, or by doubt, and of the principle that 'in order to think one must exist' (AT VIII 8; CSM I 196). It may be seen from this that the Cartesian project is not, as is sometimes suggested, 'the validation of reason'; apart from the fleeting (and later to be retracted) suggestion in the First Meditation that even the fundamental truths of logic and mathematics might be unstable, there is never any attempt to start with a completely blank slate. If the doubt were as extreme as that, the very process of systematic meditation could never get off the ground in the first place. What Descartes aims to show, rather, is that there is an inescapable logical limit to scepticism about what exists: pushing such doubt to its limits shows that it is self-defeating. And once the existence of at least one item, the thinking self, has been arrived at, Descartes will attempt systematically to reconstruct a reliable body of knowledge. But here we come up against the most striking feature of the Cartesian system from an epistemological point of view: its radically subjective orientation. Descartes has to reconstruct knowledge 'from the inside outwards' – from awareness of self to knowledge of the external world. And given the wholesale doubts he has raised about the latter, he can only reinstate it by relying on the resources of his own subjective consciousness. One such resource is the idea he finds within him of a supremely perfect being; and (by a complex and notoriously problematic causal argument) he reasons that this can only have been placed in his mind by a really existing perfect creator – God (Third Meditation). Once God's existence is established by this route, Descartes can proceed to reinstate his former belief in an external world, reasoning that, since God has given him a powerful propensity to believe that many of his ideas have their source in real external objects, such objects must exist – otherwise the deity would be systematically deceiving him, which would be incompatible with divine perfection (Sixth Meditation).

Two important points need to be made about the general Cartesian approach to knowledge. The first is that when Descartes' reconstruction project has been completed, the resulting edifice is very different from the 'commonsense', pre-philosophical world of the man of the senses. Physical objects exist – that much is guaranteed – but 'they may not at all exist in the way that exactly corresponds to my sensory grasp of them – for in many cases the grasp of the senses is obscure and confused' (AT VII 80; CSM II 55). In order to achieve a reliable grasp of the nature of physical reality Descartes urges that we must systematically disregard the confused deliverances of the senses, and rely instead on the 'clear and distinct' concepts of pure mathematics which God has implanted in our souls. And hence the resulting structure of Cartesian science sets out (not always convincingly) to reduce all physics to 'what the geometers call *quantity*, and take as the object of their demonstrations, i.e. that to which every kind of division shape and motion is applicable' (*Principles of Philosophy*, Part II, article 64). The world of the senses, the qualitative world of smells and tastes and colours and sounds, is thus resolutely excluded from Cartesian science – an exclusion which remains to this day a problem for those who wish, as Descartes did, to achieve a systematic and unified understanding of reality.

The second point to be made about Descartes' system is that his foundational project, even when construed in the relatively modest way suggested above, cannot, it seems, entirely escape what has come to be known as the 'bootstrap' problem. God, once his existence is established, functions in Descartes' system as an epistemic guarantor: 'the certainty and truth of all knowledge depends uniquely on my awareness of the true God, to such an extent that I was incapable of perfect knowledge about anything until I became aware of him' (Fifth Meditation). But if this is the case, it is not easy to see how Descartes is in a position to establish the reliability of the knowledge needed to establish God's existence in the first place. This problem, which has come to be known as the 'Cartesian Circle' was graphically highlighted by Descartes' contemporary Antoine Arnauld: 'How do you avoid reasoning in a circle when you say that we are sure that what we clearly and distinctly perceive is true only because God exists, yet we are sure that God exists only because we clearly and distinctly perceive this?' Descartes wrestled with the challenge at length (notably in the Second and Fourth Replies to the *Objections* published with the *Meditations*); his contem-

porary critics were not satisfied by his answers, and from a present day standpoint it is probably fair to say that the consensus view of Cartesian-style 'foundational epistemology' is that it is doomed to failure by its very ambitiousness. But even here the power of Descartes' thinking is manifest; for a great part of the history of the philosophy of our own century has been, in effect, a struggle to escape from Descartes' individualistic and autocentric perspective on the problems of knowledge and certainty – a perspective which, whether we like it or not, has become part of our conceptual heritage.

*See also* SCEPTICISM, CONTEMPORARY; SELF-KNOWLEDGE AND SELF-IDENTITY.

WRITINGS

'AT' refers, by volume and page number, to the standard Franco-Latin edition of Descartes: *Oeuvres de Descartes* eds C. Adam and P. Tannery, 12 vols (Paris: 1887–1913); revised edn (Paris: Vrin/CNRS, 1964–76).

'CSM' refers by volume and page number to the standard English translation: *The Philosophical Writings of Descartes* eds J. Cottingham, R. Stoothoff and D. Murdoch, vols 1 and 2 (Cambridge: Cambridge University Press, 1975); for Descartes' philosophical correspondence, see vol. III ('CSMK') by the same translators and A. Kenny (Cambridge: Cambridge University Press, 1991).

BIBLIOGRAPHY

Beyssade, J.-M.: *La Première Philosophie de Descartes* (Paris: Flammarion, 1979).

Cottingham, J.: *Descartes* (Oxford: Blackwell, 1986).

Curley, E.M.: *Descartes against the Sceptics* (Oxford: Blackwell, 1978).

Frankfurt, H.: *Demons, Dreams and Madmen: The defense of reason in Descartes' Meditations* (New York: Bobbs-Merrill, 1970).

Kenny, A.: *Descartes* (New York: Random House, 1968).

Popkin, R.: *The History of Skepticism from Erasmus to Descartes* 4th edn (Berkeley: University of California Press, 1979).

Williams, B.: *Descartes: The Project of Pure Enquiry* (Harmondsworth: Penguin, 1978).

Wilson, M.: *Descartes* (London: Routledge, 1978).

JOHN COTTINGHAM

**Dewey, John (1859–1952)** American philosopher and educationist. After beginning his long and prolific career as a neo-Hegelian and neo-Kantian, Dewey developed a type of pragmatism ('instrumentalism') which incorporated in naturalized form many Hegelian and Kantian themes. He taught at Michigan, Chicago and finally at Columbia University.

Dewey so often expressed hostility towards epistemology that many commentators have supposed that his own philosophy lacked what could be properly called an epistemology. To be sure, Dewey did not treat epistemological issues in isolation from other problems. Such isolation, he believed, was partly responsible for the fundamental flaws in previous theories of knowledge. For Dewey, knowing can be understood only in the context of a 'theory of inquiry' (i.e. a natural history of thinking as a life process). His focus was primarily on the *process* of knowing (Dewey, 1984, p. 131). In his view, such traditional philosophical tasks as analysis of objects of knowledge and of principles of epistemic justification can be accomplished only within a general theory of the activity of inquiry.

In the context of such a theory, it becomes apparent, Dewey argued, that all previous epistemologies have been examples of 'The Spectator Theory of Knowledge' (i.e. the view that the knower is only passively related to the thing known; Dewey, 1984, p. 19). Central to Dewey's account of the active process of inquiry is the 'situation'. Influenced by both neo-Hegelianism and PEIRCE, Dewey considered inquiry a natural, dialectical process by which over time a 'indeterminate situation' is made to become a 'unified whole' (Dewey, 1986, p. 108).

Commentators have often charged that Dewey, confusing methodology with epistemology, presented an account of coming-to-know as an analysis of knowledge itself (Murphy, 1989, p. 203). However, Georges Dicker (Dicker, 1976, pp. 22–9) has persuasively argued that Dewey intended to show that there is no special act of knowing distinct from and brought about by the natural process of inquiry.

Critics of Dewey's instrumentalism have further charged that he confused an account of the application of knowledge with a genuinely epistemological account of the possession of knowledge and consequently failed to provide the latter. But, in Dewey's pragmatism, to *have* knowledge is precisely to have the ability to anticipate the consequences of manipulating things in the world (Dewey, 1910, pp. 77–111). The metaphysics of Dewey's theory of inquiry is crucial. He conceived of knowledge in terms of processes, abilities and dispositions, not in the traditional Spectator terms of mental acts and occurrents.

A third objection has frequently been made from Dewey's time to our own. Commentators complain that Dewey rejected REALISM in saying that 'the object of knowledge' is the product of inquiry. Undeniably, Dewey sometimes lapsed into the idealistic idiom of his early work. In such lapses he neglected to make distinctions crucial to steering his epistemology safely through the tortuous channel between the Spectator Theory and IDEALISM. For example, on occasion he forgot to distinguish between saying that inquiry produces *knowledge* of objects and saying that it produces the *objects* of knowledge (Dewey, 1984, p. 88). The former assertion is consistent with realism, while the latter entails idealism.

This longstanding misreading of Dewey as an idealist has recently been given added currency by philosophers who applaud the constructivism they believe is to be found in Dewey. Some philosophers, most prominently Richard RORTY (Rorty, 1979, pp. 6, 381), compound the error by claiming Dewey as an ally in their total rejection of epistemology. It is hard to say whether the understanding of Dewey's epistemology suffers more from attacks by his enemies or more from praise by his friends.

To understand Dewey's original and powerful form of realism, it is necessary to disentangle what changes in the process of inquiry from what does not change. As H.S. Thayer (1990, pp. 447–8) points out, those readers still in the grip of the Spectator view of 'knowing as an internal activity in minds' are baffled by the thesis 'that the object and situation in which inquiry is completed consists of existentially changed constituents and relations from that with which inquiry begins . . . [but] knowledge is not a modification of objects of knowledge'.

Although Dicker and Thayer have made a good start, Dewey's theory of knowledge has not yet been elaborated in a way that brings it into the mainstream of Anglo-American epistemology. Few epistemologists today appreciate what Dewey's thought can contribute to the solution of problems addressed by other theorists of knowledge.

WRITINGS

*The Quest for Certainty* in *John Dewey: The Later Works 1925–1953* vol. 4, 1929 (Carbondale: Southern Illinois University Press, 1984).
*The Influence of Darwin on Philosophy and Other Essays in Contemporary Thought* (New York: Henry Holt and Company, 1910).
*Logic: The Theory of Inquiry* in *John Dewey: The Later Works 1925–1953*, vol. 12, 1938 (Carbondale: Southern Illinois University Press, 1986).

BIBLIOGRAPHY

Dicker, G.: *Dewey's Theory of Knowing* (Philadelphia: Philosophical Monographs, 1976).
Murphy, A.E.: 'Dewey's epistemology and metaphysics', in *The Philosophy of John Dewey* eds P.A. Schilpp and L.E. Hahn 3rd edn (Carbondale: Southern Illinois University Press, 1989).
Rorty, R.: *Philosophy and the Mirror of Nature* (Princeton: Princeton University Press, 1979).
Thayer, H. S.: 'Dewey and the theory of knowledge', *Transactions of the C.S. Peirce Society* 26 (1990), 443–58.

PETER H. HARE

**dialectic (Hegel)**　Hegel uses several kinds of 'dialectic'.

*Dialectical analysis* determines the content and proper application of concepts. It begins with an elementary, general concept from a domain of inquiry, examines its content and range of application, and criticizes its failure to account for salient features of examples in its purported domain. This justifies introducing a more sophisticated concept to account for the domain, on which the analysis is repeated. The result of dialectical analysis is an integrated network of concepts which specifies the proper domain of each and which preserves the legitimate content of earlier concepts in the final, most comprehensive and adequate concept.

For example, Hegel's *Logic* analyses concepts which purport to characterize the whole of reality. The first concept treated is 'being', which is criticized for its descriptive vacuity and for connoting stasis, which ill describes a fundamental trait of reality, viz. change. These defects justify introducing the interim concept of 'nothing' and then the concept of 'becoming'. This concept is then in its turn submitted to analysis.

*Dialectical arguments* offer indirect proof. They justify controversial principles for a domain by criticizing the simplest principle from that domain. Hegel believes that inadequacies in a principle can be generated internally – between the principle and examples from its domain. These inadequacies specify more accurately the proper range of application of the principle *and* they justify the introduction of a more sophisticated principle which purports to account for the original examples and for the pitfalls of the previous principle. The dialectical examination is then repeated. Increasingly sophisticated principles are justified by showing that they are the simplest principles which can account accurately for the relevant phenomena in the domain. Such arguments often argue regressively from an obvious phenomenon to demonstrate either necessary or sufficient conditions for the possibility of that phenomenon.

For example, Hegel's *Phenomenology of Spirit* begins its defence of a non-foundational epistemology by arguing against non-conceptual knowledge (KNOWLEDGE BY ACQUAINTANCE). He purports to show that no such view can account for our obvious abilities to distinguish among different objects of knowledge or to specify the relevant spatial or temporal scope of ostensive reference without admitting that concepts are essential even in the most elementary examples of human knowledge. This failure justifies introducing a view of knowledge that admits elementary concepts for sensory qualities. This view is then submitted to analysis and used in a further indirect proof.

*Dialectical relations* hold between things, concepts or phenomena when two or more of them appear to be independent but are in fact interdependent. Typically, these dependencies would now be expressed as biconditional relations.

*Dialectical developments* occur in history or in society when an historical or social phenomenon either depends upon or generates a distinct and opposed phenomenon, where these phenomena ultimately are encompassed within a larger framework. *Dialectical explanations* explain dialectical relations or dialectical developments by emphasizing their dialectical character.

*See also* HEGEL.

BIBLIOGRAPHY

Baum, M.: *Die Entstehung der hegelschen Dialektik* (Bonn: Bouvier, 1986).
Müller, G.E.: 'The Hegel legend of "Thesis, Antithesis and Synthesis"', *Journal for the History of Ideas* 19 (1958), 411–14.
Pinkard, T.: *Hegel's Dialectic: The Explanation of Possibility* (Philadelphia: Temple University Press, 1988).
Westphal, K.R.: 'Hegel's solution to the dilemma of the criterion', *History of Philosophy Quarterly* 5 (1988), 173–88.
Wolff, M.: *Der Begriff des Widerspruchs. Eine Studie zur Dialektik Kants und Hegels* (Königstein: Hain, 1981).

KENNETH R. WESTPHAL

**dialectic (Plato)** From *dialegesthai*, to converse, dialectic is in general the pursuit of philosophical issues through conversation. Pre-Platonic philosophers like Zeno and some Sophists cultivated ways of refuting opponents in discussion, and Socrates regarded conversation as essential to philosophical activity, partly because it forced people to say what they really believed. Plato uses various methods under the general heading of 'asking and answering questions' (*Cratylus* 390c). In earlier works theses and definitions are scrutinized and usually refuted. In the *Meno* and *Phaedo* dialectic employs a method of 'hypothesis', in which propositions about Forms are examined and provisionally accepted. In the *Republic*, however, Plato seems to think that this method can ultimately attain the certainty of an 'unhypothesized' principle, seemingly concerned with the Good (510–11, 533–4). Subsequent works, like the *Phaedrus* and *Sophist*, are silent on hypothesis, and associate dialectic with 'collection and division', used for dividing and classifying kinds or Forms, and so providing definitions.

*See also* PLATO.

BIBLIOGRAPHY

Robinson, R.: *Plato's Earlier Dialectic* 2nd edn (Oxford: Oxford University Press, 1953).
Stenzel, J.: *Studien zur Entwicklung der platonischen Dialektik* (Leipzig–Berlin, 1931).
Vlastos, G.: 'The Socratic Elenchus', *Oxford Studies in Ancient Philosophy* 1 (1983), 27–58.

NICHOLAS P. WHITE

**different constructions in terms of 'knows'** The question of the nature of the different constructions in terms of 'knows' and of their interrelations can be approached either in terms of the general semantical and pragmatic nature of the concept of knowledge, or else through the facts of ordinary usage and of concepts taken from ordinary usage and from our prima facie intuitions about the alleged inferential relationships between natural language sentences. For reasons of space, the scope of this article is restricted to the logico-semantical approach. There are nevertheless reasons to believe that this is the only self-explanatory approach and that the true nature of the very concepts and generalizations of the ordinary language approach can only be understood from the semantical vantage point. (Examples of the natural language-driven approaches are found among the papers reprinted in Schwartz, 1977; and in Salmon and Soames, 1988. Cf. also Hintikka and Hintikka, 1989, ch. 9.)

What is the point of having the notion of knowledge in our conceptual repertoire in the first place? The best available answer is that we often want to restrict our attention, for instance our practical preparations, to only some of the contingencies that we might have to heed. We *know that* S iff we are entitled to restrict our attention to those scenarios in which S is true. What is meant by 'entitled to' here is a question that concerns the definition of knowledge. What is discussed in this article is not affected by it. Likewise, the precise nature of the 'contingencies' or 'scenarios' involved here does not matter to most of what is said in this article. What is crucial is their logical type, i.e. that they are to be described by sentences (propositions) rather than by names or predicates.

This characterization presupposes that a space of possible states of affairs or courses of events is given. They are usually called, and will be called here, by the misleading term 'possible worlds'. Since no comprehensiveness in space or time is intended, a less misleading term would be 'scenario' or perhaps even 'situation'.

More explicitly, what is involved in *knowing that* is a space of possible worlds on which a two-place relation is defined for each agent (knower). A world $w_1$ bears this relation to $w_0$ with respect to $b$ iff $w_1$ is compatible with whatever it is that $b$ knows in $w_0$. Such worlds are called epistemic $b$-alternatives to $w_0$.

Now *knowing that* can be characterized by the following truth-condition:

(1) $b$ knows that S in $w_0$ iff S is true in each epistemic $b$-alternative to $w_0$.

Some fine-tuning is needed here in that S might be undefined in some possible worlds. This does not affect the theme of this article, however.

The usual formal counterpart '$K_b$' for '$b$ knows that' will be used here.

Besides the *knows that* construction we have to discuss also the following constructions, among others:

(i) $b$ knows whether . . .
(ii) $b$ knows who (what, which, when, where, . . .) . . .
(iii) $b$ knows how . . .
(iv) $b$ knows why . . .
(v) $b$ knows $d$ (*knows* with a direct grammatical object)

The possible-worlds analysis opens the door for the analysis of all these different constructions. In some ways, it almost forces the right analysis on us. For instance, what is the logical form of the following sentence?

(2) Jessica knows who committed the murder.

This can be taken to be of the form

(3) j knows who [say $x$, is such that] Mx.

Here (3) can apparently be analysed as

(4) $(\exists x)\, K_J\, Mx$

(where '$x$' is taken to range over persons). This sounds quite plausible. What else can there be to *knowing who* is such-and-such than *knowing of some one* person that he or she is such-and-such? Let us accept (4) provisionally as an analysis of (2).

From the possible-worlds analysis of *knowing that* it is seen what is involved in (4). The knowledge-operator $K_J$ involves several possible worlds as a member of which the individual $x$ is being considered. This makes sense only on the assumption that criteria of identity across the boundaries are objectively given. Imaginary lines connecting the embodiments of the same individual in different worlds are called *world lines*.

The analysis of (2) as (4) reveals much of the logical behaviour of (1), e.g. when it is implied by a simpler sentence of the form

(5) $K_J$ Mc.

But can this analysis be generalized? The other wh-constructions (ii) differ from knowing who only with respect to the range of the bound variable $x$. How these ranges go together with the behaviour of quantification in natural language is an interesting subject which nevertheless does not affect this article. (These different ranges correspond in fact closely to the different Aristotelian categories; see Hintikka, 1983b.) But can the analysis be extended to more complex cases? What is needed here is an insight into the way quantifiers operate. The crucial thing about them is not the idea of existence, nor the idea of generality, but the idea of a *dependent quantifier*, exemplified by

(6) $(\forall x) (\exists y) Rxy$

To understand the logic of quantification is to understand such dependent quantifiers as '$(\exists y)$' in (6). But if you understand quantifier dependence, you *ipso facto* understand quantifier independence. What is needed is simply a notation for such independence. The independence of the quantifier $(Q_0 x)$ of certain others, say $(Q_1 y)$, $(Q_2 z)$, . . . , within the scope of which it occurs, will be indicated by writing it as

(7) $(Q_0 x/Q_1 y, Q_2 z, \ldots )$

This may need an explanation. (Cf. here Hintikka and Sandu, 1989.) In the conventional logical notation dependence is determined by the scope conventions, e.g. by the brackets that are associated with a quantifier. Unfortunately, the usual scope notation is unnecessarily restrictive, ruling out certain perfectly natural and interpretable possibilities, e.g. the possibility that the scopes of two quantifiers might overlap only partially, so that neither scope is completely within the other. What is needed is a way of temporarily excusing a quantifier from the scope of

another, and this is precisely what the slash notation accomplishes.

A full understanding of the new notation is provided by its semantics. Such semantics can be spelled out most easily in its full generality by means of game-theoretical semantics. (*See* Hintikka, 1983a.) There the independence referred to here in intuitive terms becomes but a special case of the general game-theoretical concept of informational independence. The basic idea is so intuitive, however, that the reader can be spared the technicalities. Moreover, once you grasp the basic idea, you can see how it can be extended to all other parts of our logical vocabulary.

The crucial features of the analysis of all the different wh-constructions (i)–(iv) can now be expressed by saying that these wh-words are essentially *informationally independent logical operators* of different logical types and of different categories. Indeed, the analysis of (i)–(iii) can be expressed roughly as follows:

(i) $b$ knows whether $S_1$ or $S_2$ iff

(8) $K_b (S_1 (v/K_b) S_2)$

(ii) $b$ knows who (say $x$) satisfies $S[x]$ iff

(9) $K_b (\exists x/K_b) S[x]$

(iii) $b$ knows how X is done iff

(10) $K_b (\exists m/K_b)$ (X is done by the method $m$)

A moment's reflection (or a minimal acquaintance with game-theoretical semantics) shows that (8)–(10) are logically equivalent to the following:

(11) $K_b S_1 \vee K_b S_2$

(12) $(\exists x) K_b S[x]$

(13) $(\exists m) K_b$ (X is done by the method $m$)

These do not use the idea of informational independence. Hence there is nothing intrinsically wrong about such analyses as (4).

What makes the difference is that the independence analysis, unlike the original one exemplified by (4), can be extended to more complex cases. The following are cases in point:

(14) Albert knows whom everybody admires most.

(15) Bob knows which of one's parents, one's father or one's mother, everyone loves more.

The most natural readings of (14)–(15) assign to them the following logical forms:

(16) $K_a (\forall x) (\exists y/K_a) Axy$

(17) $K_b (\forall x) (Fx (v/K_b) Mx)$

Somewhat surprisingly, (16)–(17) do not reduce to the usual independence-free notation of epistemic logic. Why not? Why are they not for instance equivalent to the following?

(18) $(\forall x)(\exists y)K_a Axy$

(19) $(\forall x)(K_a Fx \ v \ K_a Mx)$

The reasons are subtle, and cannot be given here in detail. Very roughly speaking, a closer analysis of the semantics of epistemic logic shows that quantifiers binding from the outside into the scope of '$K_a$' so to speak range over individuals known to $a$, while there is no such restriction on other quantifiers. But if so, (18)–(19) obviously cannot be the respective logical forms of (14)–(15) whereas (16)–(17) can.

Of course, (14) has an entirely different reading on which its logical form is

(20) $(\exists y) K_a(\forall x)Axy$

Since there are no subtle problems about this kind of reading, it is simply disregarded here.

The nature of (16)–(17) is illuminated further by their equivalence with the following:

(21) $(\exists f) K_a (\forall x) (Axf(x))$

(22) $(\exists f)K_a (\forall x) ((f(x) = 1 \ \& \ Fx) \ v \ (f(x) = 0 \ \& \ Mx))$

This treatment can be extended to all other wh-questions. What makes the difference between the different cases is the logical type of the entities involved. Indeed, the why-construction (iv) can be analysed along the same lines as soon as we realize that an explanans is of the logical type of proposition. Roughly speaking, the analysis of

(23) It is known why F

will be

(24) $K(\exists S/K)(S \ \& \ N(S \rightarrow F))$.

The details, including the nature of the necessity operator 'N', have not yet been analysed in the literature.

The independence notation also enables us to see the difference of knowing who someone, say $b$, is, independently of how he or she is referred to, and knowing him or her as $b$. These can be expressed respectively as:

(25) $K(\exists x/K) ((b/K) = x)$ and

(26) $K(\exists x/K) (b = x)$

There is still another sense of knowing who in which it amounts to knowing who all the people are who satisfy a certain condition, say $S[x]$. This sense is also parallel with the others. It can be expressed by

(27) $K(\exists X/K) (\forall x)(S[x] \leftrightarrow Xx)$

One special use of the wh-constructions may be worth mentioning. Knowing how is used both (a) for knowing how something is done and (b) for knowing that and being able to apply to that knowledge in practice ('know-how'). The latter sense is sometimes thought to be sui generis. In reality, the corresponding sense of applied knowledge occurs in all the wh-constructions (ii) as well, as a survey of ordinary usage easily shows.

What remains is to treat the direct-object construction. Such a treatment has been available for a long time, but epistemologists have failed – or refused – to avail themselves of it, even though it possesses a better claim to psycholinguistic reality than any other logico-epistemological theory. One source of the failure is a failure to analyse the criteria of cross-identification mentioned above. Philosophers have wishfully thought that reality might do their job for them by means of causal links between objects and their names, of supplies of ready-made temporarily persisting objects, etc.

In reality, world lines can be drawn in different ways, and are so drawn in our actual conceptual system. (*See here* Hintikka and Hintikka, 1989, essay 8; Hintikka, 1975, ch. 3.) One set of world lines is the one on which the semantics of *wh*-constructions with *knows* is based. To the extent that you understand the meaning of these constructions, you *ipso facto* master these world lines, which I shall call (like the corresponding method of identification) *public*. However, another set of world lines is drawn on the basis of some particular knower's, say *b*'s, first-hand cognitive relations to persons, objects, places, times, etc. These relations create a framework which can be used for cross-identification. In the case of visual knowledge, this framework is one's visual space. More generally, the totality of one's direct cognitive relations to other entities creates a kind of story or drama, not to say a soap opera. Persons, objects, places, etc., which play the same role in this personal soap opera can be considered identical, even if their identity is not known by the person or question and although they are therefore different public (publicly identified) persons in his or her epistemic alternatives. I shall call this method of identification (and the world lines based on it) *perspectival*. In the case of visual knowledge, it amounts to identifying persons and objects occupying the same slot in the knower's (seer's) visual space even if the perceiver does not see who or what they are.

The direct-object construction is just like the *wh*-constructions except that it relies on perspectival world lines instead of public ones. If the quantifiers relying on the former

are $(Ex)$, $(Ay)$, etc., we have the following parallelism:

$(28)$ $b$ knows who $d$ is   equals

$(29)$ $K_b$ $(\exists x/K_b)$ $(d = x)$

whereas

$(30)$ $b$ knows $d$   equals

$(31)$ $K_b$ $(Ex/K_b)$ $(d = x)$

As in the case of $(25)$ we also have a slightly different reading of $(30)$:

$(32)$ $K_b$ $(Ex/K_b)$ $((d/K_b) = x)$

This diagnosis of the direct-object construction admits of more corroborating evidence than can be rehearsed here. Suffice it to suggest that it has even historical implications. For instance, the ancient Greek predilection for the direct-object construction is clearly connected with their preference of situation-centred conceptualizations. Closer to home, the contrast between the two pairs of quantifiers and the two kinds of world lines is intimately related to Russell's distinction between knowledge by description (and its objects) and knowledge by acquaintance (and objects of acquaintance). (Cf. Russell in Salmon and Soames, 1988; *see* KNOWLEDGE BY ACQUAINTANCE/BY DESCRIPTION.)

The logical analyses outlined above help to put the ordinary language-driven approaches to a deeper perspective. For reasons of space, only a few such applications can be mentioned here. For instance, the difference between concepts informationally dependent and independent of K provides for epistemic contexts a good rational reconstruction of the *de dicto* vs. *de re* distinction, which therefore is not an irreducible and inexplicable one. Likewise, the distinction between attributive vs. referential uses of definite descriptions and other referring expressions can easily be analysed. Furthermore, the idea of a rigid designator turns out to be a mirage. First of all, it is relative to a method of drawing world lines. Russellian 'logically proper names' like *this* and *that* are supposed to be 'rigid designators' for perspectival reference in analogy to proper names, which are claimed to be rigid designators for public reference. Of course, in reality even proper names are not rigid designators in epistemic contexts, for one can very well fail to know who the reference of a proper name is.

Much more interesting than the shortcomings of the ordinary language driven approach are their deeper reasons. (For these reasons, *see also* Hintikka, 1991.) Some of the most crucial ingredients of a satisfactory semantical analysis of *wh*-constructions with *knows* are not expressed in most natural languages with any standard syntactical device. This is especially true of the phenomenon of informational independence, which occurs in so many different grammatical and logical categories that it is so to speak beyond the ingenuity of the linguistic community to express it by any uniform syntactical device.

But if a distinction is not expressed by any uniform syntactical construction or other syntactical device, an approach which starts from the syntax of natural language and relies heavily on syntactical generalizations will inevitably overlook phenomena like informational independence and therefore *inter alia* the right analysis of *wh*-constructions with knows.

Once this is realized, further peculiarities of the logical forms of more complex *wh*-constructions with *knows* can be mastered. All told, there are interesting general theoretical reasons why the foot of the letter – meaning the foot of the syntax of natural language – is not the right starting place for an analysis of the different constructions with *knows*.

The analysis outlined here is an improvement on such earlier treatments as Hintikka (1975, ch. 1 and 1976). Most of the details of earlier discussions remain unaffected by the improvements, however.

The treatment of *knows who* sketched here should be compared with Boër and Lycan (1986). For the linguistic theory of *wh*-constructions, cf. e.g. Hirschbühler (1979).

BIBLIOGRAPHY

Boër, S.E. and Lycan, W.G.: *Knowing Who* (Cambridge, MA: MIT Press, 1986).
Hintikka, J.: *The Intentions of Intentionality* (Dordrecht: Reidel, 1975), esp. chs 1 and 3.
Hintikka, J.: *The Semantics of Questions and the Questions of Semantics* (Helsinki: Societas Philosophica Fennica, 1976).
Hintikka, J.: *The Game of Language* (Dordrecht: Reidel, 1983[a]).
Hintikka, J.: 'Semantical games, the alleged ambiguity of "is", and Aristotelian categories', *Synthese* 54 (1983[b]), 443–68.
Hintikka, J.: 'Paradigms for language theory', *Acta Philosophica Fennica* (1991).
Hintikka, J. and Hintikka, M.B.: *The Logic of Epistemology and the Epistemology of Logic* (Dordrecht: Kluwer Academic, 1989), esp. essays 8 and 9.
Hintikka, J. and Sandu, G.: 'Informational independence as a semantical phenomenon', *Logic, Methodology and Philosophy of Science* VIII ed. J.E. Fenstad, I.T. Frolov and R. Hilpinen (Amsterdam: North-Holland, 1989), 571–89.
Hirschbühler, P.: *Syntax and Semantics of Wh-Constructions* (Bloomington: Indiana University Linguistics Club, 1979).
Lewis, D.: *Philosophical Papers* vol. 1 (New York: Oxford University Press, 1983).
Schwartz, S.P. ed.: *Naming, Necessity, and Natural Kinds* (Ithaca, NY: Cornell University Press, 1977).
Salmon, N. and Soames, S., eds: *Propositions and Attitudes* (Oxford: Oxford University Press, 1988).

JAAKKO HINTIKKA

**direct realism** A view about what the objects of perception are. Direct realism is a type of REALISM, since it is assumed that these objects exist independently of any mind that might perceive them; and so it thereby rules out all forms of idealism and phenomenalism, which hold that there are no such independently existing objects. Its being a 'direct' realism rules out those views defended under the rubric of 'critical realism,' or 'REPRESENTATIVE REALISM', in which there is some non-physical intermediary – usually called a 'sense-datum' or a 'sense impression' – that must first be perceived or experienced in order to perceive the object that exists independently of this perception. According to critical realists, such an intermediary need not be perceived 'first' in a temporal sense, but it is a necessary ingredient which suggests to the perceiver an external reality, or which offers the occasion on which to infer the existence of such a reality. Direct realism, on the other hand, denies the need for any recourse to mental go-betweens in order to explain our perception of the physical world.

Often the distinction between direct realism and other theories of perception is explained more fully in terms of what is 'immediately' perceived, rather than 'mediately' perceived. The terms are BERKELEY'S, who claims (1713, p. 46) that one might be said to hear a coach rattling down the street, but this is mediate perception as opposed to what is 'in truth and strictness' the immediate perception of a sound. Since the senses 'make no inferences', the perceiver is then said to infer the existence of the coach, or to have it suggested to him by means of hearing the sound. Thus, for Berkeley, the distinction between mediate and immediate perception is explained in terms of whether or not either inference or suggestion is present in the perception itself.

Berkeley went on to claim that the objects of immediate perception – sounds, colours, tastes, smells, sizes and shapes – were all 'ideas in the mind'. Yet he held that there was no further reality to be inferred from them; so that the objects of mediate perception – what we would call 'physical objects' – are reduced to being simply collections of ideas. Thus Berkeley uses the immediate–mediate distinction to defend IDEALISM. A direct realist, however, can also make use of Berkeley's distinction to define his own position. D.M. ARMSTRONG does this by claiming that the objects of immediate perception are all occurrences of sensible qualities, such as colours, shapes and sounds; and these are all physical existents, and not ideas or any sort of mental intermediary at all (Armstrong, 1961, pp. xii, 23). Physical objects, all mediately perceived, are the bearers of these properties immediately perceived.

Berkeley's and Armstrong's way of drawing the distinction between mediate and immediate perception – by reference to inference or the lack of it – houses major difficulties. We are asked to believe that some psychological element of inference or suggestion enters into our mediate perception of physical objects such as coaches and camels. But this is implausible. First, there are cases in which it is plausible to assert that someone perceived a physical object – a tree, say – even when that person was unaware of perceiving it. (We can infer from his behaviour in carefully walking around it that he did see it, even though he does not remember seeing it.) Armstrong would have to say that in such cases inference was present, because seeing a tree would be a case of mediate perception; although here it would have to be an unconscious inference. But this seems baseless; there is no empirical evidence that any sort of inference was made at all.

Second, it seems that whether a person infers the existence of something from what he perceives is more a question of talent and training than it is a question of what the nature of the objects inferred really is. For instance, if we have three different colour samples, a trained artist might not have to infer their difference; instead, he might see their difference immediately. Someone with less colour sense, however, might see patches A and B as being the same in colour, and patches B and C as being the same, but also see that A is darker than C. On this basis he might then infer that A is darker than B, and B darker than C; and so inference might be present in determining difference in colour, but colour was supposed to be an object of immediate perception. On the other hand, a park ranger might not have to infer that the animal he sees is a Florida panther; he sees it to be such straightaway. Someone unfamiliar with the Everglades, however, might have to infer this from the creature's markings. Hence, inference need not be present in cases of perceiving physical objects; yet perception of physical objects was supposed to be mediate perception.

A more straightforward way to distinguish between different objects of perception was advanced by ARISTOTLE in *De Anima* (p. 567), where he spoke of objects directly or essentially perceived as opposed to those objects incidentally perceived. The former comprise perceptual properties, either those discerned by only one sense (the 'proper sensibles'), such as colour, sound, taste, smell and tactile qualities, or else those discerned by more than one sense, such as size, shape, and motion (the 'common sensibles'). The objects incidentally perceived are the concrete individuals which possess the perceptual properties; that is, particular physical objects.

According to Aristotle's direct realism, we perceive physical objects incidentally; that is, only by means of the direct or essential perception of certain properties that belong to such objects. In other words, by perceiving the real properties of things, and only in this way, can we thereby be said to perceive the things themselves. These perceptual properties, though not existing independently of the objects that have them, are yet held to exist independently of the perceiving subject; and the perception of them is direct in that no mental messengers have to be perceived or sensed in order to perceive these real properties.

Aristotle's way of defining his position seems superior to the psychological account offered by Armstrong, since it is unencumbered with the extra baggage of inference or suggestion. Yet a common interpretation of the Aristotelian view leads to grave difficulties. This interpretation identifies the property of the perceived object with a property of the perceiving sense organ. It is based on Aristotle's saying that in perception the soul takes in the form of the object perceived without its matter (ibid., p. 580). On this interpretation, it is easy to think of direct realism as being committed to the view that 'colour as seen', or 'sound as heard' were independently existing properties of physical objects. But such a view has been rightly disparaged by its critics and labelled as 'naïve realism'; for this is a view holding that the way things look or seem is exactly the way things are, even in the absence of perceivers to whom they appear that way.

The chief difficulty of naïve realism is well presented by an argument of Bertrand RUSSELL's (Russell, 1962, p. 9). Russell claims that an ordinary table appears to be of different colours from different points of view and under different lighting conditions. Since each of the colours appearing has just as much right to be considered real, we should avoid favouritism and deny that the table has any one particular colour. Russell then went on to say the same sort of thing about its texture, shape and hardness. All of these qualities are what we might call 'appearance determined' qualities; that is, they are not real independent of how they appear to perceivers; so the real table, for Russell, was something apart from the directly perceived colours, sounds, smells and tactual qualities – all of which Russell termed 'sense-data.' It is from these sense-data that Russell believed that we inferred the existence of physical objects.

Russell's argument, however, only works against the 'naïve' version of direct realism. It should first be noted that the argument does not show that the table has no real colour, shape, or texture, but only that we might not know which of the apparent properties are the real properties of the table. So the most that Russell can prove with his argument is that we must remain sceptical about the real properties of the table; but this might be enough to show that we have no right to talk about its real properties at all. If we did have some way of determining which were the real properties, however, then Russell's argument loses its sting. A step towards making this determination this can be taken by questioning Russell's initial supposition that some perceiver-dependent properties might turn out to be real properties. To agree with this assumption is to fall into the error of naïve realism. Instead, the clear-headed direct realist would be on safer ground in denying that the directly apprehended real properties are 'colours as seen', 'sounds as heard', or 'textures as felt'; for this is to confuse real properties of things with the appearances they present to perceivers.

The direct realist should instead begin by insisting that real properties are not perceiver-dependent. This would mean that if colour is to be a real property, it must be specified in terms that do not require essential reference to the visual experience of perceivers. One way to do this would be to identify the colour of a surface with the character of the light waves emitted or reflected from that surface (Armstrong, 1968, p. 283). This would be an *empirical* identification; that is, the predicate 'is coloured' and the predicate 'reflects or emits light of a certain wave length' would refer to the one and the same property.

To say, then, that fire engines are red even at night would be to say that their surfaces, under normal conditions of illumination, would reflect light at the red end of the colour spectrum. This is still compatible with saying that they are not red in the dark, in that they are not now reflecting any such light. This gets around Russell's problem about choosing the 'real colour' of an object. Another way to make this point is to say that the 'standing colour' of fire engines remains red no matter what the conditions of illumination; whereas, their 'transient colour' changes according to changes in such lighting conditions (Armstrong, 1968, pp. 284–5).

Similar reductions could be made with regard to the other sensible properties that seemed to be perceiver-dependent: sound could be reduced to sound waves, tastes and smells to the particular shapes of the molecules that lie on the tongue or enter the nose, and tactual qualities such as roughness and smoothness to structural properties of the objects felt. All of these properties would be taken to be distinct from the perceptual experiences that these properties typically give rise to when they cause changes in the perceiver's sense organs. When critics complain that such a reduction would 'leave out the greenness of greens and the yellowness of yellows' (Campbell, 1976, p. 67), the direct realist can answer that it is by identifying different colours with distinct light waves that we can best explain how it is that perceivers in the same environment, with similar physical constitutions, can cite similar colour *experiences* of green, or of yellow.

If such a general reductive programme could be made plausible, it would show that Locke's 'secondary qualities' – colour, sound, taste and smell – were really 'primary qualities' after all, in that they could be specified apart from their typical effects on perceivers (Locke, 1690, p. 135) (*see* PRIMARY AND SECONDARY QUALITIES). A direct realist could then claim that one directly perceives what is real only when there is no difference between the property proximately impinging on the sense organ and that property of the object which gives rise to the sense organ's being affected. For colour, this would mean that the light waves reflected from the surface of the object must match those entering the eyes; and, for sound, it means that the sound waves emitted from the object must match those entering the ear. A difference in the property at the object from that at the sense organ would result in illusion, not veridical perception. Perhaps this is simply a modern version of Aristotle's idea that in genuine perception the soul (now the sense organ) takes in the form of the perceived object.

If it is protested that illusion might also result from an abnormal condition of the perceiver, this can also be accepted. If one's colour experience deviated too far from normal, even when the physical properties at the object and the sense organ were the same, then misperception or illusion would result. But such illusion could only be noted against a backdrop of veridical perception of real properties. Thus, the chance of illusion due to subjective factors need not lead to Democritus's view of colours, sounds, tastes, and smells as existing merely 'by convention'. The direct realist could insist that there must be a real basis in veridical perception for any such agreement to take place at all; and veridical perception is best explained in terms of the direct perception of the properties of physical objects. It is explained, in other words, when our perceptual experience is caused in the appropriate way.

This reply on the part of the direct realist does not, of course, serve to refute the global sceptic, who claims that, since our perceptual experience could be just as it is without there being any real properties at all, we have no knowledge of any such properties. But no view of perception alone is sufficient to refute such global scepticism (Pitcher, 1971, p. 219). For such a refutation we must go beyond a theory that claims how best to explain our perception of physical objects, and defend a theory that best explains how we obtain knowledge of the world.

*See also* ARISTOTLE; ARGUMENT FROM ILLUSION; EXPERIENCE; PERCEPTUAL KNOWLEDGE; PROBLEM OF THE EXTERNAL WORLD; REPRESENTATIVE REALISM; SARTRE; SENSATION/COGNITION.

BIBLIOGRAPHY

Aristotle: *De Anima* trans. J.A. Smith in *The Basic Works of Aristotle* ed. R. McKeon (New York: Random House, 1941).

Armstrong, D.M.: *Perception and the Physical World* (London: Routledge and Kegan Paul, 1961).

Armstrong, D.M.: *A Materialist Theory of the Mind* (London: Routledge and Kegan Paul, 1968).

Armstrong, D.M.: *The Nature of Mind and Other Essays* (Ithaca, NY: Cornell University Press, 1981).

Berkeley, G.: *Three Dialogues between Hylas and Philonous* (1713) in *Berkeley: Philosophical Works* ed. M.R. Ayers (London: Dent, 1975).

Campbell, K.: *Metaphysics: an Introduction* (Encino: Dickinson, 1976).

Carrier, L.S.: *Experience and the Objects of Perception* (Washington: University Press of America, 1981).

Locke, J.: *An Essay concerning Human Understanding* (1690); ed. P. H. Nidditch (Oxford: Oxford University Press, 1975).

Pitcher, G.: *A Theory of Perception* (Princeton: Princeton University Press, 1971).

Russell, B.: *The Problems of Philosophy* (1912); 28th impr. (Oxford: Oxford University Press, 1962).

L.S. CARRIER

**disposition** A lump of sugar is cubical, has mass, and is soluble. It is common to distinguish the third of these properties from the first two. Solubility is a *dispositional* as distin-guished from a *categorical* trait. In ascribing solubility to sugar, we ascribe to it a tendency: It would dissolve were it placed in a (suitable) liquid.

RYLE (1949) argues that certain states of mind are best regarded dispositionally. Believing, for instance, is not a matter of consciously entertaining thoughts, but of being disposed to say and do various things (including entertaining thoughts), depending on the circumstances. Ryle, however, seems to deny that dispositions are genuine features of the items possessing them: 'Dispositional statements are neither reports of observed or observable states of affairs nor yet reports of unobserved or unobservable states of affairs' (p. 125).

'Realists' about dispositions come in two flavours. Some suppose dispositions to have a 'basis' in non-dispositional features of objects (Averill, 1990; Prior, 1985). Others (e.g. Goodman, 1955; Mellor, 1974) forgo the dispositional–categorical distinction, and take physical properties to be dispositions, some of which have a basis in other dispositions.

*See also* BEHAVIOURISM.

BIBLIOGRAPHY

Averill, E.W.: 'Are physical properties dispositions?', *Philosophy of Science* 57 (1990), 118–32.

Goodman, N.: *Fact, Fiction, and Forecast* (London: 1955); 2nd edn (Indianapolis: Bobbs-Merrill, 1965).

Mellor, D.H.: 'In defense of dispositions', *Philosophical Review* 53 (1974), 157–81.

Prior, E.: *Dispositions* (Atlantic Highlands: Humanities Press, 1985).

Ryle, G.: *The Concept of Mind* (London: Hutchinson, 1949).

JOHN HEIL

**dogmatism** Like 'fanaticism', dogmatism is ordinarily a term of abuse, and a term one doesn't apply to oneself. (How often do you hear someone describe himself as a dogmatist?) The term has a variety of analogically related uses. In one use, to say of someone that she is a dogmatist is to say that she holds her views more strongly than is appropriate, more strongly than the evidence warrants, for example; alternatively, it is to say that she holds her views uncritically, without paying sufficient heed to objections and alternatives, or to the limitations of human reason (*see* KANT). 'Dogmatism' is therefore an indexical term; whether you properly apply it to a given doctrine or belief depends upon where you yourself stand.

ALVIN PLANTINGA

**Dutch book argument**   *see* BAYESIANISM; PROBABILITY.

# E

empiricism  An epistemological movement according to which (1) nothing around us can be known to be real unless its existence is revealed in or inferable from information we gain directly in sense experience or in introspection of our subjective states, or later recall, and (2) genuine, intelligible differences in our claims about this world must express these knowable differences in experience. Either the truth of rival hypotheses ('the world rests on an elephant' vs. 'it rests on a tortoise') must make a potential difference to experience or their terms (e.g. 'tortoise', 'elephant') must be differentially definable in terms of experience.

The empiricist movement found its greatest proponents in the seventeenth and eighteenth centuries (see LOCKE, BERKELEY, HUME). However since then it has continued to have many important and influential advocates and sympathizers (see MILL, JAMES, RUSSELL, LEWIS, CARNAP, AYER, QUINE).

As a result of their constraints on knowledge and meaning, empiricists tend to be sceptical of necessary truths that are independent of mind and of language, and of putative eternal abstract entities (e.g. forms or universals of justice, triangularity etc.). (See A PRIORI KNOWLEDGE, MATHEMATICAL KNOWLEDGE.) They are particularly sceptical of faculties of intellectual, non-sensuous intuition through which such things are allegedly known. Empiricism, like any philosophical movement, is often challenged to show how its claims about the structure of knowledge and meaning can themselves be intelligible and known within the constraints it accepts (see PROBLEM OF THE CRITERION). Are the empiricist claims themselves empirically based? If so, how? If not, what is their status?

Empiricists furthermore need to show (1) what is revealed directly in sense experience and how, and (2) what can be inferred from it and how. The general makeup and workings of the world (e.g. there are crows, all crows are black, crows look black in standard observation conditions, there are electrons, etc.) are thought to be inferable from more particular facts. For traditional empiricists, only what we are immediately presented with in consciousness, or are immediately aware of, is non-inferentially knowable. In current sense experience, this consists of the occurrence of particular sensible qualities (that colour, that shape, that flavour, that odour, etc.), and, from past experience, it consists of those we immediately recall, perhaps less vividly. We might describe an experience as one of 'that rotten egg smell' or of seeming to smell a rotten egg. However, it is typically thought, what is not revealed directly is whether the odour is actually that of a rotten egg or ever has been, or whether it even inheres in or is produced by anything that exists independently of our experience. Any of these claims go beyond the non-inferentially knowable sensory character of our experience.

Because they distinguish so sharply between the inferentially and the non-inferentially knowable, empiricists are always challenged to show how the former can be derived from the latter without making general assumptions about the world and how it affects our experience. If these assumptions are somehow warranted non-empirically, empiricism seems compromised. If they aren't, SCEPTICISM must be embraced. Sometimes scepticism (concerning God, universals, even matter) seems welcome, othertimes not so welcome.

HUME forcefully posed the problem.

Traditional empiricism notes that we know the nature of the odour directly but can only infer its probable cause – the egg. But any inference must work by simple induction from experienced correlations of that odour and rotten eggs, and this is only possible if we have been able to acquire information about the presence of rotten eggs directly in experience – which empiricism claims to be impossible (*see* PROBLEM OF THE EXTERNAL WORLD).

Some empiricists commonsensically expand the non-inferentially knowable to include what we automatically take ourselves to perceive in our environment on particular occasions (e.g. that we smell a rotten egg). These ordinary judgements made in sense experience are legitimate without being inferable from something more basic in experience. In particular cases, additional evidence may perhaps show them to be defective and illegitimate, but, as empiricists recognize, even our immediate recollections of past experience may be mistaken. Occasional mistakes aren't reason for denying that our senses can directly inform us of what exists outside us. Although science may challenge our commonsense claims about the nature of the objects we see and their properties, we may none the less be assured, Locke for instance argued, that we see objects outside us with properties responsible for the way we experience them. But wherever exactly we place the inferential/non-inferential distinction, Hume's problems reappear. For example, how do we know the black thing we see is an egg, that the black egg we see is the same egg as the rotten one we smell and the white one we saw yesterday, that exposure to warm air caused the egg to rot, that that was so because of such and such physical or chemical constitution of the egg, etc.?

Other empiricists expand the forms of legitimate non-deductive inference instead. After all, as Hume argued, the empiricist credentials of simple induction are suspect. It seems to rest on conceivably false assumptions for which we can't have empirical evidence, e.g. that nature tends to be uniform, that our experience isn't idiosyncratic (*see* PROBLEMS OF INDUCTION). If

induction isn't privileged, perhaps, as Russell (1912) suggested, particular hypotheses concerning persisting objects and processes distinct from but responsible for our experience are warranted because they simplify and explain the regularities and irregularities in our experience (*see* INFERENCE TO THE BEST EXPLANATION). Science, moreover, may provide explanatory hypotheses that are better than, and radically different from, those of commonsense.

Of course, empiricists might also expand both the non-inferentially knowable and the forms of non-deductive inference. In any case, the reliability of particular inductions and simplifications in commonsense and science, Russell thought, depends on the truth of very general postulates about the regularities that hold in the world, in experience, and in the relation between the two. These matters of fact couldn't in turn be established by experience without circularity. Whatever truth there was in empiricism as an account of how we reliably gain information about the world couldn't itself be established by experience, though it couldn't be refuted by experience either. Some empiricists might claim that the unrefuted reliability of such sources of information is sufficient for them to provide us with knowledge or at least warranted belief. But Russell, like most traditional epistemologists, demanded more. This left him in no better position than Hume. Sometimes he suggested these general postulates of science and commonsense might be somehow non-empirically known, sometimes instead that they might be warranted by fitting the data and rendering as coherent as possible our instinctive beliefs and particular scientific inductions and simplifications. Limitations to empiricism needed acknowledgement, however reluctantly.

Many empiricists, however, change the nature of the inference by reducing the content of our claims about reality to claims about appearance. BERKELEY suggested claims about cherries I don't experience were just claims about what experiences other persons, possibly divine, do and don't have or imagine. MILL, along with most empiricists since, instead suggested they were really just complex claims about what sense experiences one would have (e.g. experiences of red or sweetness) were one to have others (e.g. experiences of opening one's eyes or putting something to mouth) (*see* PHENOMENAL-ISM). They were merely claims about the *possibilities* of experience. They weren't claims about a material world distinct from these possibilities, yet responsible for them. Thus they could be warranted by straightforward induction (including analogy) from experienced and remembered patterns of experience. (Induction remained a problem.) The standard objection, due to CHISHOLM, is that the permanent possibility of material objects looking different in different material conditions shows that material object claims can't be equivalent in meaning to claims solely about actual and possible experience. This charge has led many to abandon empiricist epistemology altogether.

For others, e.g. QUINE, the fact that particular hypotheses explain and predict experience only in conjunction with other particular hypotheses about the circumstances of observation and with general hypotheses about how the world and observers interact shows only that empiricists can't reduce hypotheses one by one to possible experience. Hypotheses can always be saved in the face of recalcitrant experience by revising other hypotheses. Apart from observation sentences, individual claims in isolation from others don't get tested by experience and don't bear empirical significance. Only sets of hypotheses or theories do. This position is known as HOLISM.

Indeed empiricism may survive its traditional foundations. For Quine the content of non-inferentially warranted observation reports is behaviouristically determined by ranges of sensory stimulation prompting the unreserved assent of speakers, rather than by sensuous qualities presenting themselves to our immediate awareness. There may be further hope in holism. Since the empirical significance and test of our theories ultimately lies in the consequences their truth has for experience, warrant for our theories seems ultimately a matter of the warrant which experience so far provides for predicting these

consequences. Natural science appeals to natural selection to explain why induction over certain patterns of stimulation is reliable and thus why these patterns of observation and induction are warranted. Of course, natural science is itself the product of induction and simplifying hypothesizing, and warranted as a result (*see* NATURALIZED EPISTEMOLOGY).

Empiricist strictures are clearly preserved in the genesis of knowledge, but less clearly in its warrant. Does science, by allowing us to give an explanation of the reliability of our forms of observation and induction, show why particular observations and inductions are warranted and thus confirm, alter, and increase the warrant of particular observations, hypotheses, and inductions? Or does it provide all their warrant, even initially? In either case, the truth in empiricism has become a contingent matter not known a priori but revealed by empirical science, and its norms are perhaps relevant only to us and the sentient creatures from whom we have evolved. If so, we don't need to embrace the claims of poetry over empirical science to challenge empiricism's credentials. Particularly objectionable, perhaps, is the apparent vision of our cognitive and linguistic lives as consisting in learned verbal responses to stimuli, the successful prediction and control of which is the primary function of acquiring these dispositions, however much the patterns they manifest reflect inherited and uninherited environmental adaptations.

Some empiricists, inspired by Berkeley, have thought talk of material objects as things over and above actual and possible experience quite unintelligible, not simply dubiously warranted. Talk of purple triangles can make sense without experience of purple triangles because we can think of what appropriately compares and contrasts with purple squares and non-purple triangles in our experience. Perhaps (possibly *contra* Berkeley), we can even abstract from such comparisons and contrasts to form a way of thinking of purple triangles in general. However, experience cannot generate a conception of entirely unexperienced (unperceived, unimagined, unconceived) items, still less one of objects distinct from the possible experience of anyone and everyone but (partly) responsible for these possibilities. (Others think we can show the unintelligibility of talk of truth as correspondence between thought and mind independent fact.)

Inspired by Moore, Russell (1912) influentially claimed that this argument confuses our experiences or conceptions (our mental acts) with their objects or contents. The former are necessarily mental acts, but what we experience or conceive isn't. Thus we have a basis in experience for an idea of objects that aren't simply possibilities of experience. More radical empiricists may object that the act/object distinction itself isn't simply given to consciousness but requires explication in empiricist terms. Even so, Russell (1948) argued that *non*-experience must be definable with whatever definition of experience empiricists use to state their own view, logical concepts like 'not', 'some', '=', and logical ingenuity. The empiricist demand that meaningful talk be definable in experiential terms could then be compatible with intelligible talk of matter as something quite unlike immediate experience and more than just possibilities of experience.

As for logical concepts, empiricists sometimes ground our understanding of them in our experience of mental states, e.g. 'not' in our frustration. Critics often object that this absurdly turns judgements like 'This isn't blue' into judgements about our minds and confuses terms for logical operations we perform on names, predicates and propositions with names or predicates standing for experienced mental states. Other empiricists argue that logical notions are definable in logically and empirically unproblematic fashion, e.g. as truth-tables define logical operators as connectives yielding truth/falsehood from truths/falsehoods of empirically unproblematic meaning.

Similar questions arise with 'categories' like substance, causality, person. Empiricists often reduce the categories to collections of qualities, events or experiences – ordered only in space and time but otherwise without necessary connection or point of collective reference – or distinguish categorially-related qualities and events from otherwise unrelated ones only in terms of how we are disposed to think, feel, infer or act with respect to them. For instance, Hume notoriously gave two definitions of cause: an event followed by another where events like the former are regularly followed by the latter, and also an event followed by another where the appearance of the former leads one to *expect* the latter.

RATIONALISTS scorn empiricists for giving woefully inadequate analyses of crucial notions or for confusing psychology with philosophy. They conclude that categories cannot be explicated in experiential terms and their application to experience must be underwritten non-empirically by appeal to general principles not warranted by experience.

Empiricists instead often see Hume as insightfully recognizing the real, intelligible, albeit downgraded, content of the categories. Or, as insightfully recognizing the real, albeit cognitively downgraded, status of categorial judgements as mere dispositions of inference and action. In the latter case, the descriptions we are disposed to give of events, qualities, and their spatio-temporal order are true/false, warranted/unwarranted, but the dispositions themselves aren't. Recently, other empiricists have rejected the reductionism that underwrites downgrading. We learn to ascribe most concepts ('red', as much as 'cherry' or 'cause') on the basis of distinctive experiential conditions and patterns (e.g. looking red) which are neither necessary nor sufficient for their truth. Arguably, these core experiences then constitute good but defeasible reasons for these ascriptions – as a matter of logical necessity or meaning, not empirically confirmed fact.

Empiricists often argue that what makes propositions necessarily true isn't a realm of necessary facts but just the way we think or speak. Many claim that these propositions are reducible upon definition of their terms to tautologies whose denials are self-contradictory (*see* ANALYTICITY, LOGICAL POSITIVISM). Their form rather than what they say about the world makes them true. They are thus knowable a priori rather than through sense experience. However, the necessity of logical truth and the adequacy of definition still need explanation. Broader appeals can be made to our inability to conceive or combine ideas in our minds (*see* LOCKE, HUME) or to our resolutions or conventions never to assert/deny certain statements or combinations of statements (*see* HOBBES, AYER, LEWIS, CARNAP). Critics frequently argue that accounting for all and only necessary truths requires appealing to what can't be said without contradiction or to what logically follows from our resolutions/conventions of speech – precisely what needs explaining (Pap, 1958).

Moreover, consider how well we know basic general logical and mathematical principles, sometimes even after considering just a few examples. There is little obvious connection to the quantity and quality of our introspected attempts at conceiving combinations of ideas, or to our introspective knowledge of our psychological, practical, or linguistic proclivities. Nor, for that matter, to the warrant the variety and quantity of perceived instances of such principles might provide through inductive or explanatory inference. Yet suppose we allow that through consideration of particular examples, actual and hypothetical, we arrive by abstraction at a knowledge transcending them in content and the inferential warrant they yield. That seems tantamount to embracing rationalist metaphors of intellectually seeing and grasping the truth – metaphors for which empiricists typically condemn a priori intuition and its objects as hopelessly occult. Some empiricists (e.g. Locke, Russell) seem willing to embrace the metaphors up to a point. Others (e.g. Quine), perhaps more consistently empiricist, abandon the NECESSARY/CONTINGENT, non-empirical/empirical distinctions for a broader HOLISM. Empiricists sometimes instead argue that knowledge of necessities is knowledge of the rules or norms governing thinking and speaking, not knowledge of our social or psychological customs or of the contents of our minds. They need to address more clearly what these distinctions involve (*see* INTUITION/DEDUCTION).

From KANT to WITTGENSTEIN (*see* PRIVATE LANGUAGE ARGUMENT) and SELLARS, empiricists have also been challenged to show how even the most basic knowledge or understanding is possible without allegedly derivative knowledge. Sellars, for example, argues that for 'that's red' or 'that's the same in colour' to be correct and express knowledge, more than a reliable disposition to say such things before red objects is needed; governance by rules and thus general knowledge concerning when such sentences are correctly uttered and thus legitimate is required. That in turn requires more particular and general knowledge, all conforming to norms or standards of thinking whose authority we recognize as interpersonally binding. Empiricism then is deeply incoherent, whatever the ultimate explanation of this authority – whether as principles necessary for any possible empirical consciousness, principles necessary for any effective agency, or just reflections of our agreement about particular cases. Such arguments are the bane of empiricists, partly for their seductiveness, partly for their obscurity, partly for their far-reaching importance.

*See also* EPICURUS; LOGICAL POSITIVISM; RATIONALISM.

BIBLIOGRAPHY

Ayer, A.J.: *Language, Truth, and Logic* 2nd edn (London: Gollancz, 1946).
Bennett, J.: *Locke, Berkeley, Hume: Central Themes* (Oxford: Clarendon Press, 1971).
Cornman, J.: *Perception, Common Sense, and Science* (New Haven: Yale University Press, 1975).
Lewis, C.I.: *An Analysis of Knowledge and Valuation* (La Salle: Open Court, 1946).
Pap, A.: *Semantics and Necessary Truth* (New Haven: Yale University Press, 1958).
Pollock, J.: *Knowledge and Justification* (Princeton: Princeton University Press, 1974).
Quine, W.V.: *Ontological Relativity* (New York: Columbia University Press), chs 3, 5.
Russell, B.: *The Problems of Philosophy* (1912): (Oxford: Oxford University Press, 1967).
Russell, B.: *Human Knowledge: Its Scope and Limits* (London: Allen and Unwin, 1948).

Sellars, W.: *Science, Perception, and Reality* (London: Routledge and Kegan Paul, 1963).

BRUCE HUNTER

**Epicurus** (*c*.341–271 BC) Greek philosopher, founder of a school of philosophy at Athens. Epicurus is arguably the first thinker in antiquity to develop a full-fledged EMPIRICIST epistemology. Although not the first to claim that knowledge is derived from the senses or that abstract conceptions arise through the repeated imprint of sensory experience on the memory, Epicurus is the first to have combined these claims with the assertion that sensation alone, as opposed to reason, offers an indubitable foundation for knowledge and a sure defence against scepticism. It is this reliance on sensation to meet sceptical challenges about justification that sets him apart from his predecessors and gives his theory a self-consciously empiricist cast. At the same time, however, fundamental differences in perspective and method separate Epicurus from many later empiricists. He does not take as his point of departure, for instance, the familiar empiricist doctrine that agents have complete and incorrigible access to their own sense-contents; nor does he begin from the perspective of the subject's own awareness and then attempt to justify further inferences to external objects. Rather, he has in mind a wider naturalistic programme rooted in his atomist analysis of perception. He provides detailed naturalistic explanations of the causal effects of various external objects on percipients, with the consequence that the representational and informational character of the resulting sensory states is often wider than what is subjectively accessible to agents themselves.

Epicurus' most distinctive and notorious doctrine is that all sensations are true. Much of his effort on its behalf is spent attacking the following two alternatives: (1) all sensations are false, or (2) some sensations are false. He insists that the scepticism endorsed in (1) is self-refuting since it is impossible to commit oneself consistently to such a view either in theory or in practice. If (2) were true, he argues, a criterion would need to be established for distinguishing true sensations from false; but there can be no such criterion other than sensation itself. Against the objection that different senses may provide conflicting reports, not all of which can therefore be true, Epicurus argues that no sense ever actually contradicts the report of another, since the objects of the various senses are all different. Of course, when faced with incommensurable reports from different senses, it is not clear why we should not suspend judgment rather than conclude that they are all true. To meet such sceptical objections, Epicurus appeals to his general causal theory of sensation. What guarantees the truth of all sensations, he claims, are the causal processes that bring them about. The senses are reliable in their own spheres, since they merely transmit their information mechanically and passively, adding nothing to what they are recording. As in Locke, there is a strong emphasis both on the passivity of the perceiver and on the mechanisms of representation, though for the Epicurean the process of representation is underwritten not by mental impressions but by the physical images (*eidola*) continually being emitted by external objects. In isolation, such *eidola* are not infallible guides to the nature of external objects *per se*; but when properly assessed, he claims, they lead to true judgments about external reality.

Epicurus' account is vulnerable, no doubt, to many of the objections raised against imagist theories of sensation and thought. But it was instrumental in establishing an overall theoretical framework that was to have enduring influence from Gassendi and Hobbes to J.S. Mill.

*See also* SEXTUS EMPIRICUS.

WRITINGS

Many of the relevant texts are set out and lucidly discussed in A.A. Long and D.N. Sedley, *The Hellenistic Philosophers* (Cambridge: Cambridge University Press, 1987), which includes a detailed bibliography.

PHILLIP MITSIS

**epistemic virtue** Following Aristotle (1941, Bk VI, ch. 1), we may begin by distinguishing two broadly different sorts of 'intellectual virtues'. There are those qualities of wisdom and good judgement which are conducive to a happy, or moral, or successful life. And there are those qualities of character which are conducive, we think, to the discovery of *truth* (and the avoidance of error). The latter correspond to the 'epistemic virtues' in contemporary epistemology.

Such a teleological characterization of the epistemic virtues raises, however, a number of interesting problems. The progress of science, we would like to think, leads us not only closer to the truth, but to discover ever better means of accomplishing this end. But does this mean that we are becoming ever more epistemically virtuous – or is there a difference between the progress of knowledge and the improvement of epistemic *character*? Relatedly, there is this sceptical problem. Suppose that the world were so vastly different from the way it is presently conceived that the very characteristics we *take* to be truth-conducive actually are leading us deeper and deeper into error; suppose, too, that certain seemingly very simple-minded attitudes and procedures are actually more truth-conducive than these other attitudes. Would the apparent 'fool' then be the epistemically virtuous inquirer? Or must we somehow relativize what counts as an epistemic virtue roughly to the way the world appears to be? And if we do, is there any specifiable thing to which these virtues *are* conducive? Finally, even leaving aside these sceptical worries, there is the question of whether truth and the avoidance of error are a *complete* characterization of the ends of intellectual life – or must we add some reference, say, to the power and scope of our truths?

First, let us try to distinguish epistemic virtue from mere truth-conduciveness in general. Two persons can differ in the quantity and quality of their evidence – even in the quality of the means by which that evidence was acquired – without, it seems, being different in epistemic virtue. For the epistemic virtues should be *personal qualities* –

not evidentiary states, hypotheses, theories, strategies, or anything else. Aristotle's evidence and methodology may have been inferior, from the standpoint of truth-conduciveness, to those of later inquirers; but we regard him none the less as an ideal inquirer, in so far as his personal qualities suit him to this role. The progress of science, then, may make us better instruments for arriving at truth, but not better people – even from a purely epistemic standpoint.

Which personal qualities, though, comprise the epistemic virtues? First and foremost among these is what may be termed 'epistemic conscientiousness' – i.e. one's desire to attain truth and avoid falsehood. But is having, or even being thoroughly suffused with, this desire enough to make one (overall) epistemically virtuous? Some have, I think, supposed so – cf. Kornblith (1983) – but I would argue not, for two reasons. First, if one's present degree of confidence in the truth (and truth-conduciveness) of one's current beliefs is excessive, desire for the truth may lead to intellectual DOGMATISM – not virtue. Second, though, if one's confidence in one's own powers of discernment is too low, this may cause the desire for truth to lead one to avoid valuable sources of information – for fear one will be misled. Accordingly, I want to maintain that an important role for the epistemic virtues is that of *regulating* one's desire for truth. In carrying out this regulative function, two broadly complementary types of epistemic qualities come into play. First, there are qualities of *impartiality* (an openness to the ideas of others, a willingness to interact with and learn from them, a lack of jealousy and personal bias, a lively sense of one's own fallibility, and so forth). Second, though, there are qualities of intellectual *courage* (the willingness to conceive and examine alternatives to popularly held beliefs, perseverance in the face of opposition and even ridicule).

There is a related point to be made here. If we think of epistemic virtue *merely* in terms of one's desire for truth, the virtues of impartiality take on seemingly too subjective an aspect. Thus, the willingness to listen to others becomes the willingness to listen to others in so far as one thinks them likely sources of the truth – and so forth. But, of course, even the worst dogmatist may possess that sort of 'impartiality'.

As noted, the virtues of impartiality and courage are complementary, not contradictory. An ideal inquirer can, and should, have ample quantities of both. Of course, in any given situation, a relatively greater amount of one quality, or one type of quality, may be required; but which one and to what extent may be clear only in hindsight. Thus, in so far as an optimal mix of these virtues may not be knowable at any given time, I would not want to require that the epistemically virtuous must strike this correct balance.

Let us move on, then, to the problem of scepticism mentioned earlier. If the world is radically different from the way it appears, to the point that apparent epistemic vices are actually truth-conducive, presumably this should *not* make us retrospectively term such vices 'virtues' even if they are and have always been truth-conducive. The proper solution to this difficulty, I would suggest, is simply to make the epistemic virtues qualities which a truth-desiring person would *want* to have. For even if, unbeknown to us, some wild sceptical possibility is realized, this would not affect our desires (it being, again, unknown). Such a characterization, moreover, would seem to fit the virtues in our catalogue. Almost by definition, the truth-desiring person would want to be epistemically conscientious. And, given what seem to be the conditions pertaining to human life and knowledge, the truth-desiring person will also want to have the previously cited virtues of impartiality and intellectual courage.

Are, though, truth and the avoidance of error rich enough desires for the epistemically virtuous? Arguably not. For one thing, the virtuous inquirer aims not so much at having true beliefs as at *discovering* truths – a very different notion. Perpetual reading of a good encyclopaedia will expand my bank of true beliefs without markedly increasing humankind's basic stock of truths. For Aristotle, too, one notes that true belief is not, as such, even a concern; the concern, rather, is the discovery of scientific or philosophical truth. But

of course the mere expansion of our bank of truths – even of scientific and philosophic truths – is not itself the complete goal here. Rather one looks for new truths of an appropriate kind – rich, deep, explanatorily fertile, say. By this reckoning, then, the epistemically virtuous person seeks at least three related but separable ends: to discover new truths, to increase one's explanatory understanding, to have true rather than false beliefs.

Another important area of concern for epistemologists is the relation between epistemic virtue and epistemic *justification*. Obviously, an epistemically virtuous person is not thereby justified in every belief of hers, for not every belief of an epistemically virtuous person must itself, I take it, be virtuous. But is a virtuously formed belief automatically a justified one? I would hold that if a belief is virtuously formed, this fully justifies that *person* in having it; but the *belief* itself may lack adequate justification (as the evidence for it may be, through no fault of this person, still inadequate). Different philosophers on this point, however, will apparently have different intuitions. (*See* e.g. Goldman, 1980; BonJour, 1985, ch. 3; EXTERNALISM/INTERNALISM.)

Another area of concern is whether we are *responsible* for having, or not having, appropriate epistemic virtues. Here, following Aristotle, let us concede that we are only responsible for our bad (or good) epistemic habits in so far as these have resulted from our past actions. But this, notice, does not necessarily make our responsibility for exemplifying particular virtues (or vices) on particular occasions indirect – derivative from our responsibility for action. For if we become habitually careless (as Aristotle suggests) by doing careless things, it is just as true that we are responsible (culpable) for doing careless things to the extent that we can be faulted, on those occasions, for *being* careless.

*See also* FEMINIST EPISTEMOLOGY; VIRTUE EPISTEMOLOGY.

BIBLIOGRAPHY

Aquinas, T.: *Summa Theologiae* Blackfriars edn,

trans. W.D. Hughes, (New York: McGraw-Hill, 1969), 1a2ae, 57–9.

Aristotle: *Nichomachean Ethics* trans. W.D. Ross, in *The Basic Works of Aristotle* ed. R.M. McKeon (New York: Random House, 1941), Book VI.

BonJour, L.: *The Structure of Empirical Knowledge* (Cambridge, MA: Harvard University Press, 1985), Part One.

Code, L.: *Epistemic Responsibility* (Hanover: Brown University Press, 1987).

Goldman, A.: 'The internalist conception of justification', *Midwest Studies in Philosophy* 5 (1980), 27–51.

Kornblith, H.: 'Justified belief and epistemically responsible action', *Philosophical Review* 92 (1983), 33–48.

Montmarquet, J.A.: 'Epistemic virtue', *Mind* 96 (1987), 482–97.

Sosa, E.: 'Knowledge and intellectual virtue', *The Monist* 68 (1985), 226–44.

JAMES A. MONTMARQUET

**epoche** the epoche or the transcendental reduction, is for HUSSERL the basic method of PHENOMENOLOGY. Instead of focusing on the normal objects of our acts, be they physical objects, actions, persons or general features that many objects can have in common (*see* ESSENCE), one reflects on the structures of one's own consciousness, and studies the *noemata*, the features that make one's consciousness be consciousness of those objects. Although we are not normally aware of these features, they are a *sine qua non* for the appearance of a world. Husserl therefore calls them transcendental, and the reflection that leads to them, where the ordinary objects are bracketed, the transcendental reduction. Husserl got the idea of the transcendental reduction in 1906. It marks the transition from the early phenomenology of the *Logical Investigations* (1900–1) to the 'idealist' phenomenology of the *Ideas* and later works, in Husserl's very special sense of 'idealism'.

DAGFINN FØLLESDAL

**essence (Husserl)** For HUSSERL an object's essence (*eidos*) is not something peculiar to that object, but a feature that the object can share with other objects, e.g. the triangularity of a triangle or the greenness of a tree. Mathematics is the most highly developed study of essences. By performing an eidetic reduction, one passes from focusing on the individual physical object to focusing on one of its essences. By further adding a transcendental reduction (*see* EPOCHE), one reflects on the *noemata* (structures) of the former acts and thereby arrives at phenomenology, which is the study of the *noemata* of acts directed towards essences.

DAGFINN FØLLESDAL

**essence (Plato)** Definitions stating 'what X is' are central to PLATO's philosophy. He often maintains that one must know 'what' something is before one can know other facts about it (e.g. *Meno* 71, 100), and sometimes that to know 'what' something is, one must be able to give a definition of it. He usually regards a definition as describing an *eidos*, 'Form', or *ousia*, 'essence' or 'being'. He regards these as objective entities, not constituted by human usage or judgements. He suggests sometimes that a definition gives an analysis of something into constituents, and sometimes that it specifies something by features distinguishing it from all other things. Plato seemingly denies that any sensible particular is an *ousia*, and so that there is any saying 'what it is', i.e. that it is or has an essence. On one interpretation, however, Plato believes in 'abstract particulars', which do have essential connections to Forms.

BIBLIOGRAPHY

Allen, R.E.: *Plato's Euthyphro and the Earlier Theory of Forms* (London: Routledge and Kegan Paul, 1970).

Gosling, J.C.B.: *Plato* (London: Routledge, 1973), ch. 11.

Penner, T.: *The Ascent from Nominalism* (Dordrecht: Reidel, 1987).

Robinson, R.: *Plato's Earlier Dialectic* 2nd edn (Oxford: Clarendon Press, 1953).

White, N.P.: *Plato on Knowledge and Reality* (Indianapolis: Hackett, 1976).

NICHOLAS P. WHITE

**essentialism**  *see* NECESSARY/CONTINGENT.

**ethics and epistemology**  The analogies between these two areas are many and various, and increasingly explored. In general, ethics as a subject has been more exhaustively investigated, and the tendency has been for epistemologists to use for their own purposes results which they take to have been established on the other side. Since they are commonly ill-informed about the solidity of these 'results', the resulting epistemology is often unstable. A good example of this is the early debate between internalists and externalists in the theory of justification (*see* Goldman, 1980; BonJour 1980 and EXTERNALISM/INTERNALISM). Externalists noted the common suggestion that an action can be the right one to do even though the agent had no notion of this fact and did it for quite other reasons. They suggest, analogously, that a belief may be justified even though the believer has no notion of the facts that make it so. Internalists noted the equally common view that moral evaluation focuses on agents, since the nature of actions is determined at least partly by their agents' conceptions of what they are doing. This being so, facts of which agents have no idea cannot go to make what they do either right or wrong. Analogously, the facts that make believers justified or unjustified in the beliefs they adopt must be facts available to them.

What is happening here is that each side is appealing to long-established but rival moral traditions; but the matter is so contentious in ethics that there are no firm results there for epistemologists to use in this kind of way.

A second example would be the use of the idea of the Naturalistic Fallacy (*see* FACT/VALUE) to determine the chances of various forms of NATURALISM in epistemology (e.g. CAUSAL THEORIES of justification). *See* Alston (1978).

More recently, and in my view more reliably, the growth of VIRTUE EPISTEMOLOGY and the idea of distinctive EPISTEMIC VIRTUES is clearly one which is (or should be) largely informed by results in ethics. FEMINIST EPISTEMOLOGY is also likely to attempt to use approaches deemed promising in ethics. The general thrust here is the thought that we should attempt to understand the cognitive agent in ways informed by the best attempts to understand the moral agent.

*See also* CHISHOLM.

BIBLIOGRAPHY

Alston, W.P.: 'Meta-ethics and meta-epistemology', in *Values and Morals* eds A.I. Goldman and J. Kim (Reidel: Dordrecht, 1978), 275–97.
BonJour, L.: 'Externalist theories of empirical knowledge', *Midwest Studies in Philosophy* 5 (1980), 53–73.
Chisholm, R.M.: *Perceiving: a philosophical study* (Cornell University Press: New York, 1957), Part I: 'The ethics of belief'.
Dancy, J.: 'Intuitionism in meta-epistemology', *Philosophical Studies* 42 (1982), 395–408.
Goldman, A.I.: 'What is justified belief?', in *Justification and Knowledge* ed. G. Pappas (Reidel: Dordrecht, 1979), 1–23.
Goldman, A.I.: 'The internalist conception of justification', *Midwest Studies in Philosophy* 5 (1980), 27–51.

JONATHAN DANCY

**evidence**  The notion of evidence figures prominently in several epistemological issues. A good way to raise the central philosophical questions about evidence is in the context of a discussion of a theory of epistemic justification known as 'evidentialism'. Evidentialism, suggested by Chisholm (1977) and defended explicitly in Feldman and Conee (1985), holds that a belief is epistemically justified for a person if and only if the person's evidence supports that belief. Working out the details of this view requires resolving several questions about the concept of evidence, including the following: (1) What sorts of things can be evidence? (2) Under what conditions does a body of evidence support a particular proposition or belief? (3) What is it for someone to have something as evidence? Of course, these questions retain their interest whatever the merits of evidentialism.

## 1. WHAT IS EVIDENCE?

The concept of evidence appealed to in evidentialism, and in epistemology generally, differs from the related concept of evidence used in the law. In the law, or at least in informal discussions of the law, evidence includes physical objects and events. Weapons and footprints, for example, are ordinarily said to be evidence. In philosophical discussions, evidence is generally taken to be either internal states such as beliefs, or the believed propositions themselves. Thus, the belief (or proposition) that a weapon of certain type was used might be evidence for one person's guilt.

A crucial question about the nature of evidence is whether evidence is limited to other beliefs (or believed propositions) or whether it includes other mental states such as perceptual experiences. Various reasons have been advanced for thinking that only beliefs can be evidence, one being that the evidence for a belief confers justification on the belief, but only something that is itself justified can confer justification on anything else, and only beliefs (or other doxastic states) can be justified. (*See* BonJour, 1985, ch. 4.) Sosa (1974, 1980) argues that non-doxastic states, such as experiences, can also count as evidence. On this view, some beliefs are basic, in the sense that they are justified by experience rather than by other beliefs. Sosa argues that the experiences which justify basic beliefs need not be justified themselves. Van Cleve (1985), adopting a point made by Sosa (1980), contends that only states that are themselves justified could 'transmit' justification, but non-justified states might 'generate' justification. Both Sosa and van Cleve claim that since justification SUPER-VENES on non-epistemic properties, there must be some non-epistemic states that are sufficient for, and thus generate, justification. (*See* FOUNDATIONALISM, CRITERIA

AND KNOWLEDGE, INFINITE REGRESS ARGUMENT.)

## 2. EVIDENTIAL SUPPORT

Holding that experiences count as evidence adds complexity to an already difficult set of questions about the evidential support relation. The new questions are about exactly what makes it the case that an experiential state counts as evidence for one belief (or proposition) rather than another. It is easy to be fooled by superficial linguistic facts that seem to link certain experiences to certain beliefs. It may seem clear that the fact that something looks blue to S justifies S in believing that the thing is blue (absent any counterevidence). More generally, if a thing looks F to S, then S is justified in believing that it is F provided S does not have any evidence against its being F. (*See* van Cleve, 1985, pp. 96–7; Moser, 1985, ch. 5.) This may seem right, but the formulation masks complexities. To say that something 'appears blue' to a person is to say, roughly, that it induces a certain sort of internal state in the person. To say that it is blue is to say that it has certain physical properties of some sort. It appears, pending further analysis of colour words, that these propositions are only contingently related and that our inclination to think it obvious that one justifies the other results from the accident that the word 'blue' appears in the sentences used to express both propositions. This temptation would be eliminated if we described the internal appearance state in some other terminology. (Why think that the fact that an object appears in manner 1,256 justifies the belief that the object is blue?)

Furthermore, if one says that the experience of seeing a blue object normally justifies one in believing that one sees something blue, then it is hard to see how one can avoid saying that the experience of seeing a 23-sided object normally justifies one in believing that one sees something 23-sided. But this conclusion is implausible; not all experiences typically justify the corresponding proposition about the experienced object. (*See* Sosa, 1988, p. 171.)

To this, one might reply that to those of us who aren't equipped to 'pick-up' on 23-sidedness, 23-sided things don't appear 23-sided, whereas blue things typically do appear blue to us. So, the cases are disanalogous. This reply raises questions about the nature of appearances. Imagine a person who was designed to sense 23-sidedness. It seems possible that the visual image that such a person has when looking at a 23-sided object would be the same as the one a normal person would have when looking at that object. But the reply holds that the 23-sided object appears differently to these two individuals. While there is a difference in their abilities to extract information from a visual array, it is difficult to understand what makes their appearances different.

In addition to the questions about how experiential states provide evidential support, there are many traditional epistemological issues which can be framed as questions about the nature or extension of the evidential support relation. Traditional debates about our knowledge of the external world or of other minds and questions about knowledge based on induction are largely questions about the adequacy of our evidence for external world propositions, propositions about other minds, and of inductive evidence generally.

It is extraordinarily difficult to state in a general way the conditions under which a body of evidence provides evidential support for a belief. The mere existence of a logical or probabilistic connection between the evidence and the belief is not sufficient for evidential support. If it were adequate, then all the distant and unseen necessary or probabilistic consequences of one's justified beliefs would themselves be justified. Since that is clearly unacceptable, one might say instead that if evidence $e$ provides epistemic support for proposition $p$ for person S, then $e$ must entail or make probable $p$ and S must 'grasp' the connection between $e$ and $p$. This reply seems to over-intellectualize the situation, since people seem not to grasp such matters routinely, and it invites a troublesome regress if requiring this 'grasp' of the evidential connection amounts to requiring the justified

belief that $e$ supports $p$. There is no generally accepted view about what is necessary or sufficient for epistemic support.

## 3. HAVING EVIDENCE

A further question about evidence concerns exactly what it is to *have* something as evidence. Stored somewhere in one's memory are an enormous number of facts. Many of these facts may bear on some proposition, $p$, that one believes. While considering $p$, one may think of only some of these stored facts. If prompted in one way, one might recall some of these facts, and if prompted in other ways, one might recall other facts. Some of them may be accessible only with complex and detailed prompting. But which of these facts are part of the evidence one has and are relevant to the assessment of the epistemic merit of the current belief? A highly restrictive view would limit the evidence to what one actually has currently in mind. A highly liberal view would include as part of one's evidence everything stored in one's mind. This renders justified some beliefs that seem, from an intuitive viewpoint, quite unreasonable. There is no clearly acceptable way to carve out a theory positioned between these two extremes (*see* Feldman, 1988).

### RIVALS TO EVIDENTIALISM

A different set of questions about evidence concerns the connection between evidence and epistemic justification. Evidentialism holds that questions about epistemic justification turn entirely upon matters pertaining to evidence. Rival views hold that other sorts of matters play a central role in determining which beliefs are justified. For example, Kornblith (1983) argues that a belief is epistemically justified only if the believer has gone about gathering evidence for it in an epistemically responsible manner (*see* EPISTEMIC VIRTUE). Goldman (1986) defends RELIABILISM which, like some other causal theories of justification, implies that having supporting evidence is neither necessary nor sufficient for justification, since on standard understandings of reliabilism, a belief can be caused in a reliable way even though the believer does not have anything that could plausibly be regarded as good evidence for it. The debate on these matters is surely not settled, but it is instructive to notice that defenders of evidentialism's rivals, such as Goldman (1986), often go to some lengths to adjust their theories so that they share the straightforward implications of evidentialism. They do not defend the implications of the simple versions of their theories.

BIBLIOGRAPHY

BonJour, L.: *The Structure of Empirical Knowledge* (Cambridge, MA: Harvard University Press, 1985).

Chisholm, R.M.: *Theory of Knowledge* 2nd edn (Englewood Cliffs: Prentice-Hall, 1977).

van Cleve, J.: 'Epistemic supervenience and the rule of belief', *The Monist* 68 (1985), 90–104.

Feldman, R. and Conee, E.: 'Evidentialism', *Philosophical Studies* 48 (1985), 15–34.

Feldman, R.: 'Having evidence', in *Essays Presented to Edmund Gettier* ed. D. Austin (Dordrecht: Kluwer, 1988), 83–104.

Goldman, A.: *Epistemology and Cognition* (Cambridge, MA: Harvard University Press, 1986).

Kornblith, H.: 'Justified belief and epistemically responsible action', *Philosophical Review* 92 (1983), 33–48.

Moser, P.: *Empirical Justification* (Dordrecht: Reidel, 1985).

Sosa, E.: 'How do you know?', *American Philosophical Quarterly* 11 (1974), 113–22.

Sosa, E.: 'The foundations of foundations', *Nous* 14 (1980), 547–64.

Sosa, E.: 'Beyond scepticism, to the best of our knowledge', *Mind* 97 (1988), 153–88.

RICHARD FELDMAN

**evolutionary epistemology** This is an approach to the theory of knowledge that sees an important connection between the growth of knowledge and biological evolution.

An evolutionary epistemologist claims that the development of human knowledge proceeds through some natural selection process, the best example of which is Darwin's theory of biological natural selection. The three major components of the model of natural selection are variation, selection and retention. According to Darwin's theory of natural selection, variations are not pre-designed to perform certain functions. Rather, those variations that perform useful functions are selected, while those that do not are not selected; such selection is responsible for the appearance that variations intentionally occur. In the modern theory of evolution, genetic mutations provide the blind variations (blind in the sense that variations are not influenced by the effects they would have – the likelihood of a mutation is not correlated with the benefits or liabilities that mutation would confer on the organism), the environment provides the filter of selection, and reproduction provides the retention. Fit is achieved because those organisms with features that make them less adapted for survival do not survive in competition with other organisms in the environment that have features which are better adapted. Evolutionary epistemology applies this blind variation and selective retention model to the growth of scientific knowledge and to human thought processes in general.

The parallel between biological evolution and conceptual (or 'epistemic') evolution can be seen as either literal or analogical. The literal version of evolutionary epistemology sees biological evolution as the main cause of the growth of knowledge. On this view, called the 'evolution of cognitive mechanisms program' (EEM) by Bradie (1986) and the 'Darwinian approach to epistemology' by Ruse (1986), the growth of knowledge occurs through blind variation and selective retention because biological natural selection itself is the cause of epistemic variation and selection. The most plausible version of the literal view does not hold that all human beliefs are innate but rather that the mental mechanisms which guide the acquisition of non-innate beliefs are themselves innate and the result of biological natural selection. Ruse (1986, ch. 5) defends a version of literal evolutionary epistemology which he links to sociobiology. (*See* Bradie's essay in Rescher, 1990, pp. 33–8, for criticism of this view.)

On the analogical version of evolutionary

epistemology, called the 'evolution of theories program' (EET) by Bradie (1986) and the 'Spencerian approach' (after the nineteenth-century philosopher Herbert Spencer) by Ruse (1986), the development of human knowledge is governed by a process analogous to biological natural selection, rather than by an instance of the mechanism itself. This version of evolutionary epistemology, introduced and elaborated by Donald Campbell (1974a and 1974b) as well as Karl POPPER, sees the (partial) fit between theories and the world as explained by a mental process of trial and error known as epistemic natural selection.

Both versions of evolutionary epistemology are usually taken to be types of NATURALIZED EPISTEMOLOGY because both take some empirical facts as a starting point for their epistemological project (see Quine, 1969 and QUINE). The literal version of evolutionary epistemology begins by accepting evolutionary theory and a materialist approach to the mind and, from these, constructs an account of knowledge and its development. In contrast, the analogical version does not require the truth of biological evolution; it simply draws on biological evolution as a source for the model of natural selection. For this version of evolutionary epistemology to be true, the model of natural selection need only apply to the growth of knowledge, not to the origin and development of species. Crudely put, evolutionary epistemology of the analogical sort could still be true even if creationism is the correct theory of the origin of species.

Although they do not begin by assuming evolutionary theory, most analogical evolutionary epistemologists are naturalized epistemologists as well; their empirical assumptions (at least implicitly) come from psychology and cognitive science, not evolutionary theory. Sometimes, however, evolutionary epistemology is characterized in a seemingly non-naturalistic fashion. Campbell (1974b, p. 142) says that 'if one is expanding knowledge beyond what one knows, one has no choice but to explore without the benefit of wisdom' (i.e. blindly). This, Campbell admits, makes evolutionary epistemology

close to being a tautology (and so not naturalistic). Evolutionary epistemology does assert the analytic claim that when expanding one's knowledge beyond what one knows, one must proceed to something that is not already known, but, more interestingly, it also makes the synthetic claim that when expanding one's knowledge beyond what one knows, one must proceed by blind variation and selective retention. This claim is synthetic because it can be empirically falsified. The central claim of evolutionary epistemology is *synthetic*, not *analytic*. If the central claim were analytic, then all non-evolutionary epistemologies would be logically contradictory, which they are not. Campbell is right that evolutionary epistemology does have the analytic feature he mentions, but he is wrong to think that this is a *distinguishing* feature, since any plausible epistemology has the same analytic feature (see Skagestad, 1978, p. 613).

Two of the deeper issues that arise in the literature involve questions about REALISM (i.e. what sort of metaphysical commitments does an evolutionary epistemologist have to make?), and progress (i.e. according to evolutionary epistemology, does knowledge develop towards a goal?). (On realism, see Campbell, 1974a, pp. 447–50; Bradie, 1986, pp. 444–51; Skagestad, 1978, pp. 617–19; Ruse's essay in Rescher, 1990, pp. 101–10; and Stein's essay in Rescher, 1990, pp. 119–29. On progress, see Bradie, 1986, pp. 426–7; Ruse, 1990, and Stein, 1990.) With respect to realism, many evolutionary epistemologists endorse what is called hypothetical realism, a view that combines a version of epistemological SCEPTICISM and tentative acceptance of metaphysical REALISM. With respect to progress, the problem is that biological evolution is not goal-directed, but the growth of human knowledge seems to be. Campbell (1974a) worries about the potential disanalogy here but is willing to bite the bullet and admit that epistemic evolution progresses towards a goal (truth) while biological evolution does not. Some have argued that evolutionary epistemologists must give up the 'truth-tropic' sense of progress because a natural selection model is in essence non-teleological; instead, following Kuhn (1970), an operational sense of progress can be embraced along with an evolutionary epistemology.

Among the most frequent and serious criticisms levelled against evolutionary epistemology is that the analogical version of the view is false because epistemic variation is not blind (see, for example, Skagestad, 1978, 613–16; and Ruse, 1986, ch. 2). Stein and Lipton (1990) have argued, however, that this objection fails because, while epistemic variation is non random, its constraints come from heuristics which, for the most part, are the result of epistemic blind variation and selective retention. Further, Stein and Lipton argue that these heuristics are analogous to biological pre-adaptations, evolutionary precursors (such as a half-wing, a precursor to a wing) which have some function other than the function of their descendent structures; the guidedness of epistemic variation is, on this view, not the source of disanalogy, but the source of a more articulated account of the analogy.

Many evolutionary epistemologists try to combine the literal and the analogical versions (see Bradie, 1986, pp. 403–11; Stein and Lipton, 1990, pp. 42–6), saying that those beliefs and cognitive mechanisms which are innate result from natural selection of the biological sort and those which are not innate result from natural selection of the epistemic sort. This is reasonable as long as the two parts of this hybrid view are kept distinct. An analogical version of evolutionary epistemology with biological variation as its only source of blindness would be a null theory; this would be the case if all our beliefs are innate or if our non-innate beliefs are not the result of blind variation. An appeal to the blindness of biological variation is thus not a legitimate way to produce a hybrid version of evolutionary epistemology since doing so trivializes the theory. For similar reasons, such an appeal will not save an analogical version of evolutionary epistemology from arguments to the effect that epistemic variation is not blind (see Stein and Lipton, 1990, pp. 42–5).

Although it is a relatively new approach to theory of knowledge, evolutionary epistemology has attracted much attention, primarily because it represents a serious attempt to flesh out a naturalized epistemology by drawing on several disciplines. If science is relevant to understanding the nature and development of knowledge, then evolutionary theory is among the disciplines worth a look. Insofar as evolutionary epistemology looks there, it is an interesting and potentially fruitful epistemological programme.

See also GENETIC EPISTEMOLOGY; NATURALIZED EPISTEMOLOGY.

BIBLIOGRAPHY

Bradie, M.: 'Assessing evolutionary epistemology', Biology and Philosophy 1 (1986), 401–59.
Callebaut, W. and Pinxter, R. eds: Evolutionary Epistemology: A Multiparadigm Program (Dordrecht: Reidel, 1987); includes an extensive bibliography.
Campbell, D.T.: 'Evolutionary epistemology', in The Philosophy of Karl Popper, Book 1, ed. P.A. Schilpp (LaSalle: Open Court, 1974a), 413–63; reprinted in Evolution, Theory of Rationality and the Sociology of Knowledge eds G. Radnitsky and W.W. Bartley III (LaSalle: Open Court, 1987), 47–89.
Campbell, D.T.: 'Unjustified variation and selection in scientific discovery', in Studies in Philosophy of Biology, eds F.J. Ayala and T. Dobzhansky (Berkeley: University of California Press, 1974b), 139–61.
Kuhn, T.: The Structure of Scientific Revolutions 2nd edn (Chicago: University of Chicago Press, 1970).
Quine, W.V.: 'Epistemology naturalized', in his Ontological Relativity and Other Essays (New York: Columbia University Press, 1969), 69–90.
Rescher, N. ed.: Evolution, Cognition and Realism (Lanham: University Press of America, 1990).
Ruse, M.: Taking Darwin Seriously (Oxford: Blackwell, 1986).
Skagestad, P.: 'Taking evolution seriously: critical comments on D.T. Campbell's evolutionary epistemology', The Monist 61 (1978), 611–21.
Stein, E. and Lipton, P.: 'Where guesses come

from: evolutionary epistemology and the anomaly of guided variation', *Biology and Philosophy* 4 (1990), 33–56.

EDWARD STEIN

**existence** Philosophers often debate the existence of different kinds of things: nominalists question the reality of abstract objects like classes, numbers and universals; some positivists doubt the existence of theoretical entities like neutrons or genes; and there are debates over whether there are sense-data, events, and so on. Some philosophers may be happy to talk about abstract objects and theoretical entities while denying that they really exist. This requires a 'metaphysical' concept of 'real existence': we debate whether numbers, neutrons and sense-data are really existing things. But it is difficult to see what this concept involves and the rules to be employed in settling such debates are very unclear.

Questions of existence seem always to involve general kinds of things: do numbers, sense data or neutrons exist? Some philosophers conclude that existence is not a property of individual things, 'exists' is not an ordinary predicate. If I refer to something, and then predicate existence of it, my utterance seems to be tautological: the object must exist for me to be able to refer to it, so predicating existence of it adds nothing. And to say of something that it did not exist would be contradictory.

According to Rudolf CARNAP, philosophical questions of existence always concern whether to adopt a general linguistic or conceptual framework. Questions of which framework to employ do not concern whether the entities posited by the framework 'really exist'; they are rather settled by its pragmatic usefulness. Philosophical debates over existence misconstrue 'pragmatic' questions of choice of framework as substantive questions of fact. Once a framework is adopted, there are substantive 'internal' questions: are there any prime numbers between 10 and 20? 'External' questions about choice of framework have a different status.

More recent philosophers, notably QUINE, have questioned the distinction between linguistic framework and internal questions arising within it. But Quine agrees that we have no 'metaphysical' concept of existence against which different purported entities can be measured. If quantification over numbers (or over sense-data) forms part of the general theoretical framework which best explains our experience, the claim that there are such things (that they exist) is true. Scruples about admitting the existence of too many different kinds of objects depend not on a metaphysical concept of existence but rather on a desire for a simple and economical theoretical framework.

*See also* ONTOLOGICAL COMMITMENT.

BIBLIOGRAPHY

Carnap, R.: *Meaning and Necessity* 2nd edn (Chicago, Chicago University Press, 1956), 205–21.
Moore, G.E.: 'Is existence a predicate?', *Proceedings of the Aristotelian Society*. Supp. vol. 15 (1936), 175–88.
Quine, W.V.: *From a Logical Point of View* (Cambridge, MA: Harvard University Press, 1953), ch. I.
Quine, W.V.: *Ontological Relativity and Other Essays* (New York: Columbia University Press, 1969), ch. 4.

CHRISTOPHER HOOKWAY

**experience, theories of** It is not possible to define experience in an illuminating way. Readers, however, know what experiences are through acquaintance with some of their own, e.g. a visual experience of a green afterimage, a feeling of physical nausea or a tactile experience of an abrasive surface (which might be caused by an actual surface – rough or smooth – or which might be part of a dream, or the product of a vivid sensory imagination).

The essential feature of every experience is that it *feels* a certain way – that there is something that it is like to have it. We may refer to this feature of an experience as its *character*.

Another core feature of the sorts of experiences with which this article is concerned is that they have representational *content*. (Unless otherwise indicated, the term 'experience' will be reserved for these below.) The most obvious cases of experiences with content are sense experiences of the kind normally involved in perception. We may describe such experiences by mentioning their sensory modalities and their contents, e.g. *a gustatory experience* (modality) *of chocolate ice cream* (content), but do so more commonly by means of perceptual verbs combined with noun phrases specifying their contents, as in 'Macbeth saw a dagger'. This is, however, ambiguous between the perceptual claim 'There was a (material) dagger in the world which Macbeth perceived visually' and 'Macbeth had a visual experience of a dagger' (the reading with which we are concerned).

As in the case of other mental states and events with content, it is important to distinguish between the properties which an experience *represents* and the properties which it *possesses*. To talk of the representational properties of an experience is to say something about its content, not to attribute those properties to the experience itself. Like every other experience, a visual experience of a pink square is a mental event, and it is therefore not itself either pink or square, even though it represents those properties. It is, perhaps, fleeting, pleasant or unusual, even though it does not represent those properties. An experience may represent a property which it possesses, and it may even do so in virtue of possessing that property, as in the case of a rapidly changing (complex) experience representing something as changing rapidly, but this is the exception and not the rule.

Which properties can be (directly) represented in sense experience is subject to debate. Traditionalists include only properties whose presence could not be doubted by a subject having appropriate experiences, e.g., colour and shape in the case of visual experience, and (apparent) shape, surface texture, hardness, etc., in the case of tactile experience. This view is natural to anyone who has an egocentric, CARTESIAN perspective in epistemology, and who wishes for pure data in experience to serve as logically certain foundations for knowledge (*see* SENSE-DATA). Others who do not think that this wish can be satisfied, and who are more impressed with the role of experience in providing animals with ecologically significant information about the world around them, claim that sense experiences represent properties, characteristics and kinds which are much richer and much more wide-ranging than the traditional sensory qualities. We don't see only colours and shapes, they tell us, but also earth, water, men, women and fire; we don't smell only odours, but also food and filth. There is no space here to examine the factors relevant to a choice between these alternatives. In this article the more liberal view will be assumed except when it is incompatible with a position under discussion.

Given the modality and content of a sense experience, most of us will be aware of its character even though we cannot describe that character directly. This suggests that character and content are not really distinct, and there is a close tie between them. For one thing, the relative complexity of the character of a sense experience places limitations on its possible content; e.g. a tactile experience of something touching one's left ear is just too simple to carry the same amount of content as a typical everyday visual experience. Furthermore, the content of a sense experience of a given character depends on the normal causes of appropriately similar experiences, e.g. the sort of gustatory experience which we have when eating chocolate would not represent chocolate unless it were normally caused by chocolate. Granting a contingent tie between the character of an experience and its possible causal origins, it again follows that its possible content is limited by its character.

Character and content are none the less irreducibly different, for the following reasons. (1) There are experiences which completely lack content, e.g. certain bodily pleasures. (2) Not every aspect of the character of an experience with content is relevant to that content, e.g. the unpleasantness of an aural experience of chalk squeaking on a board may have no representational significance. (3) Experiences in different modalities may overlap in content without a parallel overlap in character, e.g. visual and tactile experiences of circularity feel completely different. (4) The content of an experience with a given character may vary according to the background of the subject, e.g. a certain aural experience may come to have the content 'singing bird' only after the subject has learned something about birds.

## ONTOLOGICAL THEORIES

### The act/object analysis

According to the ACT/OBJECT ANALYSIS of experience (which is a special case of the act/object analysis of consciousness), every experience involves an object of experience even if it has no material object. Two main lines of argument may be offered in support of this view, one phenomenological and the other semantic.

In outline, the phenomenological argument is as follows. Whenever we have an experience, even if nothing beyond the experience answers to it, we seem to be presented with something *through* the experience (which is itself diaphanous). The object of the experience is whatever is so presented to us – be it an individual thing, an event, or a state of affairs.

The semantic argument is that objects of experience are required in order to make sense of certain features of our talk about experience, including, in particular, the following. (1) Simple attributions of experience (e.g. 'Rod is experiencing a pink square') seem to be relational. (2) We appear to refer to objects of experience and to attribute properties to them (e.g. 'The after-image which John experienced was green'). (3) We appear to quantify over objects of experience (e.g. 'Macbeth saw something which his wife did not see').

The act/object analysis faces several problems concerning the status of objects of experience. Currently the most common view is that they are SENSE-DATA – private

mental entities which actually possess the traditional sensory qualities represented by the experiences of which they are the objects. But the very idea of an essentially private entity is suspect. Moreover, since an experience may apparently represent something as having a determinable property (e.g. redness) without representing it as having any subordinate determinate property (e.g. any specific shade of red), a sense-datum may actually *have* a determinable property without having any determinate property subordinate to it. Even more disturbing is that sense-data may have contradictory properties, since experiences can have contradictory contents. A case in point is the waterfall illusion: if you stare at a waterfall for a minute and then immediately fixate on a nearby rock, you are likely to have an experience of the rock's moving upwards while it remains in exactly the same place. The sense-datum theorist must either deny that there are such experiences or admit contradictory objects.

These problems can be avoided by treating objects of experience as *properties*. This, however, fails to do justice to the appearances, for experience seems not to present us with bare properties (however complex), but with properties embodied in individuals. The view that objects of experience are Meinongian objects accommodates this point. It is also attractive in so far as (1) it allows experiences to represent properties other than traditional sensory qualities, and (2) it allows for the identification of objects of experience and objects of perception in the case of experiences which constitute perceptions (*see* ACT/OBJECT ANALYSIS). But most philosophers will feel that the Meinongian's acceptance of impossible objects is too high a price to pay for these benefits.

A general problem for the act/object analysis is that the question of whether two subjects are experiencing one and the same thing (as opposed to having exactly similar experiences) appears to have an answer only on the assumption that the experiences concerned are perceptions with material objects. But in terms of the act/object analysis the question must have an answer even when this condition is not satisfied. (The answer is always negative on the sense-datum theory; it could be positive on other versions of the act/object analysis, depending on the facts of the case.)

In view of the above problems, the case for the act/object analysis should be reassessed. The phenomenological argument is not, on reflection, convincing, for it is easy enough to grant that any experience appears to present us with an object without accepting that it actually does. The semantic argument is more impressive, but is none the less answerable. The seemingly relational structure of attributions of experience is a challenge dealt with below in connection with the adverbial theory. Apparent reference to and quantification over objects of experience can be handled by analysing them as reference to experiences themselves and quantification over experiences tacitly typed according to content. (Thus 'The after-image which John experienced was green' becomes 'John's after-image experience was an experience of green', and 'Macbeth saw something which his wife did not see' becomes 'Macbeth had a visual experience which his wife did not have'.)

### Pure cognitivism

Pure cognitivism attempts to avoid the problems facing the act/object analysis by reducing experiences to cognitive events or associated dispositions; e.g. Suzy's experience of a rough surface beneath her hand might be identified with the event of her acquiring the belief that there is a rough surface beneath her hand, or, if she does not acquire this belief, with a disposition to acquire it which has somehow been blocked.

This position has attractions. It does full justice to the cognitive contents of experience, and to the important role of experience as a source of belief acquisition. It would also help clear the way for a naturalistic theory of mind, since there seems to be some prospect of a physicalist/functionalist account of belief and other intentional states. But pure cognitivism is completely undermined by its failure to accommodate the fact that experiences have a felt character which cannot be reduced to their content (see above).

### The adverbial theory

The ADVERBIAL THEORY is an attempt to undermine the act/object analysis by suggesting a semantic account of attributions of experience which does not require objects of experience. Unfortunately, the oddities of explicit adverbialisations of such statements have driven off potential supporters of the theory. Furthermore, the theory remains largely undeveloped, and attempted refutations have traded on this. It may, however, be founded on sound basic intuitions, and there is reason to believe that an effective development of the theory (which is merely hinted at below) is possible.

The relevant intuitions are (1) that when we say that someone is experiencing 'an $A$', or has an experience 'of an $A$', we are using this content-expression to specify the type of thing which the experience is especially apt to fit, (2) that doing this is a matter of saying something about the experience itself (and maybe also about the normal causes of like experiences), and (3) that there is no good reason to suppose that it involves the description of an object which the experience is 'of'. Thus the effective role of the content-expression in a statement of experience is to modify the verb it complements, not to introduce a special type of object.

Perhaps the most important criticism of the adverbial theory is the 'many property problem', according to which the theory does not have the resources to distinguish between e.g.

(1) Frank has an experience of a brown triangle

and

(2) Frank has an experience of brown and an experience of a triangle,

which is entailed by (1) but does not entail it. The act/object analysis can easily accommodate the difference between (1) and (2) by claiming that the truth of (1) requires a single object of experience which is both brown and triangular, while that of (2) allows for the possibility of two objects of experience, one brown and the other triangular. Note, however, that (1) is equivalent to

(1*) Frank has an experience of something's being both brown and triangular,

and (2) is equivalent to

(2*) Frank has an experience of something's being brown and an experience of something's being triangular,

and the difference between these can be explained quite simply in terms of logical scope without invoking objects of experience. The adverbialist may use this to answer the many-property problem by arguing that the phrase 'a brown triangle' in (1) does exactly the same work as the clause 'something's being both brown and triangular' in (1*). This is perfectly compatible with the view that it also has the 'adverbial' function of modifying the verb 'has an experience of', for it specifies the experience more narrowly just by giving a necessary condition for the satisfaction of the experience (the condition being that there is something both brown and triangular before Frank).

*The state theory*

A final position which should be mentioned is the state theory, according to which a sense experience of an *A* is an occurrent, non-relational state of the kind which the subject would be in when perceiving an *A*. Suitably qualified, this claim is no doubt true, but its significance is subject to debate. Here it is enough to remark that the claim is compatible with both pure cognitivism and the adverbial theory, and that state theorists are probably best advised to adopt adverbialism as a means of developing their intuitions.

*See also* ACT/OBJECT ANALYSIS; ADVERBIAL THEORY; ARGUMENT FROM ILLUSION; REPRESENTATION; REPRESENTATIVE REALISM; SENSATION/COGNITION; SENSE-DATA; DIRECT REALISM.

BIBLIOGRAPHY

Anscombe, G.E.M.: 'The intentionality of sensation: a grammatical feature', in *Analytical Philosophy: Second Series* ed. R.J. Butler (Oxford: Blackwell, 1968).
Armstrong, D.M.: *A Materialist Theory of Mind* (London: Routledge and Kegan Paul, 1968).
Castañeda, H.-N.: 'Perception, belief, and the structure of physical objects and consciousness', *Synthese* 35 (1977), 285–351.
Clark, R.: 'Sensing, perceiving, thinking', in *Essays on the Philosophy of Roderick M. Chisholm* ed. E. Sosa, *Grazer Philosophische Studien* (1981), 273–95.
Jackson, F.: 'On the adverbial theory of visual experience', *Metaphilosophy* 6 (1975), 127–35.
Jackson, F.: *Perception: A Representative Theory* (Cambridge: Cambridge University Press, 1977).
Leon, M.: 'Character, content, and the ontology of experience', *Australasian Journal of Philosophy* 65 (1987), 377–99.
Peacocke, C.: *Sense and Content: Experience, Thought, and their Relations* (Oxford: Clarendon Press, 1983).
Pendlebury, M.: 'Sense experiences and their contents: a defence of the propositional view', *Inquiry* 33 (1990), 215–30.
Sellars, W.: 'The adverbial theory of objects of sensation', *Metaphilosophy* 6 (1975), 144–60.
Swartz, R.J. ed.: *Perceiving, Sensing, and Knowing* (Berkeley: University of California Press, 1965).
Tye, M.: 'The adverbial theory: a defence of Sellars against Jackson', *Metaphilosophy* 6 (1975), 135–43.

MICHAEL PENDLEBURY

**explanation** Since at least the time of Aristotle philosophers have emphasized the importance of explanatory knowledge. In simplest terms, we want to know not only *what* is the case but also *why* it is. This consideration suggests that we define an explanation as an answer to a why-question. Such a definition would, however, be too broad, because some why-questions are requests for consolation (Why did *my* son have to die?) or moral justification (Why should women not be paid the same as men for the same work?)

It would also be too narrow because some explanations are responses to how-questions (How does radar work?) or how-possibly-questions (How is it possible for cats always to land on their feet?)

In its most general sense, 'to explain' means to make clear, to make plain, or to provide understanding. Definitions of this sort are philosophically unhelpful, for the terms used in the definiens are no less problematic than the term to be defined. Moreover, since a wide variety of things require explanation, and since many different types of explanation exist, a more complex explication is required. Our discussion will be facilitated by introducing a bit of technical terminology. The term 'explanandum' is used to refer to that which is to be explained; the term 'explanans' refers to that which does the explaining. The explanans and the explanandum taken together constitute the explanation.

One common type of explanation occurs when deliberate human actions are explained in terms of conscious purposes. 'Why did you go to the pharmacy yesterday?' 'Because I had a headache and needed to get some aspirin.' It is tacitly assumed that aspirin is an appropriate medication for headaches and that going to the pharmacy would be an efficient way of getting some. Such explanations are, of course, *teleological*, referring, as they do, to goals. The explanans is not the realization of a future goal – if the pharmacy happened to be closed for stocktaking the aspirin would not have been obtained there, but that would not invalidate the explanation. Some philosophers would say that the antecedent desire to achieve the end is what does the explaining; others might say that the explaining is done by the nature of the goal and the fact that the action promoted the chances of realizing it (e.g. Taylor, 1964). In any case it should not be automatically assumed that such explanations are causal. Philosophers differ considerably on whether these explanations are to be framed in terms of causes or reasons (*see* REASONS/CAUSES), and there are many differing analyses of such concepts as intention and agency. Expanding the domain beyond consciousness, FREUD maintained, in addition, that much human behaviour can be explained in terms of *unconscious* wishes. These Freudian explanations should probably be construed as basically causal.

Problems arise when teleological explanations are offered in other contexts. The behaviour of non-human animals is often explained in terms of purpose; e.g. the mouse ran to escape from the cat. In such cases the existence of *conscious* purpose seems dubious. The situation is still more problematic when a super-empirical purpose is invoked – e.g. the explanation of living species in terms of God's purpose, or the vitalistic explanation of biological phenomena in terms of an entelechy or vital principle. In recent years an 'anthropic principle' has received attention in cosmology (*see* Barrow and Tipler, 1986). All such explanations have been condemned by many philosophers as *anthropomorphic*.

The foregoing objection notwithstanding, philosophers and scientists often maintain that *functional explanations* play an important and legitimate role in various sciences such as evolutionary biology, anthropology and sociology. For example, in the famous case of the peppered moth in Liverpool, the change in colour from the light phase to the dark phase and back again to the light phase provided adaptation to a changing environment and fulfilled the *function* of reducing predation on the species. In the study of primitive societies anthropologists have maintained that various rituals (e.g. a rain dance), which may be inefficacious in bringing about their *manifest* goals (e.g. producing rain), actually fulfil the *latent* function of increasing social cohesion at a period of stress (e.g. during a drought). Philosophers who admit teleological and/or functional explanations in common sense and science often take pains to argue that such explanations can be analysed entirely in terms of efficient causes, thereby escaping the charge of anthropomorphism (*see* Wright, 1976); again, however, not all philosophers agree.

Mainly to avoid the incursion of unwanted theology, metaphysics, or anthropomorphism into science, many philosophers and scientists – especially during the first half of the twentieth century – held that science provides only descriptions and predictions of natural phenomena, but not explanations. Beginning in the 1930s, however, a series of influential philosophers of science – including Karl Popper (1935) Carl Hempel and Paul Oppenheim (1948), and Hempel (1965) – maintained that empirical science *can* explain natural phenomena without appealing to metaphysics or theology. It appears that this view is now accepted by the vast majority of philosophers of science, though there is sharp disagreement on the nature of scientific explanation.

The foregoing approach, developed by Hempel, Popper and others, became virtually a 'received view' in the 1960s and 1970s. According to this view, to give a scientific explanation of any natural phenomenon is to show how this phenomenon can be subsumed under a law of nature. A particular rupture in a water pipe can be explained by citing the universal law that water expands when it freezes and the fact that the temperature of the water in the pipe dropped below the freezing point. General laws, as well as particular facts, can be explained by subsumption. The law of conservation of linear momentum can be explained by derivation from Newton's second and third laws of motion. Each of these explanations is a deductive argument; the premises constitute the explanans and the conclusion is the explanandum. The explanans contains one or more statements of universal laws and, in many cases, statements describing initial conditions. This pattern of explanation is known as the *deductive–nomological* (D–N) model. Any such argument shows that the explanandum *had to occur* given the explanans.

Many, though not all, adherents of the received view allow for explanation by subsumption under statistical laws. Hempel (1965) offers as an example the case of a man who recovered quickly from a streptococcus infection as a result of treatment with penicillin. Although not all strep infections clear up quickly under this treatment, the probability of recovery in such cases is high, and this is sufficient for legitimate explanation accord-

ing to Hempel. This example conforms to the *inductive–statistical* (I–S) model. Such explanations are viewed as arguments, but they are inductive rather than deductive. In these cases the explanans confers high inductive probability on the explanandum. An explanation of a particular fact satisfying either the D–N or the I–S model is an argument to the effect that the fact in question *was to be expected* by virtue of the explanans.

The received view has been subjected to strenuous criticism by adherents of the *causal/mechanical* approach to scientific explanation (*see* Salmon, 1990). Many objections to the received view were engendered by the absence of causal constraints (due largely to worries about Hume's critique) on the D–N and I–S models. Beginning in the late 1950s, Michael Scriven advanced serious counterexamples to Hempel's models; he was followed in the 1960s by Wesley Salmon and in the 1970s by Peter Railton. In general, according to this view, one explains phenomena by identifying causes (a death is explained as resulting from a massive cerebral haemorrhage) or by exposing underlying mechanisms (the behaviour of a gas is explained in terms of the motions of constituent molecules).

A *unification* approach to explanation has been developed by Michael Friedman and Philip Kitcher (*see* Kitcher, in Kitcher and Salmon, 1989). The basic idea is that we understand our world more adequately to the extent that we can reduce the number of independent assumptions we must introduce to account for what goes on in it. Accordingly, we understand phenomena to the degree that we can fit them into a general world picture or *Weltanschauung*. In order to serve in *scientific* explanations, the world picture must be scientifically well founded.

In contrast to the foregoing views – which stress such factors as logical relations, laws of nature, and causality – a number of philosophers (e.g. Achinstein, 1983; van Fraassen, 1980, ch. 5) have urged that explanation, and *not* just scientific explanation, can be analysed entirely in pragmatic terms.

During the past half-century much

philosophical attention has been focused on explanation in science and in history. Considerable controversy has surrounded the question of whether historical explanation must be scientific, or whether history requires explanations of different types. Many diverse views have been articulated; the foregoing brief survey does not exhaust the variety. (For a more comprehensive account, *see* Salmon, 1990.)

In everyday life we encounter many types of explanation, which appear not to raise philosophical difficulties, in addition to those already discussed. Prior to take-off a flight attendant explains how to use the safety equipment on the aeroplane. In a museum the guide explains the significance of a famous painting. A mathematics teacher explains a geometrical proof to a bewildered student. A newspaper story explains how a prisoner escaped. Additional examples come easily to mind. The main point is to remember the great variety of contexts in which explanations are sought and given.

Another item of importance to epistemology is the widely held notion that nondemonstrative inference can be characterized as INFERENCE TO THE BEST EXPLANATION. Given the variety of views on the nature of explanation, this popular slogan can hardly provide a useful philosophical analysis.

*See also* HISTORICAL KNOWLEDGE; SOCIAL SCIENCE.

BIBLIOGRAPHY

Achinstein, P.: *The Nature of Explanation* (New York: Oxford University Press, 1983).
Barrow, J.D. and Tipler, F.J.: *The Anthropic Cosmological Principle* (Oxford: Clarendon Press, 1986).
Hempel, C.G.: *Aspects of Scientific Explanation* (New York: The Free Press, 1965).
Hempel, C.G. and Oppenheim, P.: 'Studies in the logic of explanation', *Philosophy of Science* XV (1948), 135–75; reprinted, with added Postscript, in Hempel (1965).
Kitcher, P. and Salmon, W.C. eds: *Scientific Explanation*, Vol. XIII, *Minnesota Studies in the Philosophy of Science* (Minneapolis: University of Minnesota Press, 1989).
Popper, K.R.: *The Logic of Scientific Discovery* (New York: Basic Books, 1959).
Railton, P.: 'Probability, explanation, and information', *Synthese* 48 (1981), 233–56.
Rubin, D.-H.: *Explaining Explanation* (London: Routledge, 1990).
Salmon, W.C.: *Four Decades of Scientific Explanation* (Minneapolis: University of Minnesota Press, 1990); reprinted from Kitcher and Salmon, 1989.
Taylor, C.: *The Explanation of Behaviour* (London: Routledge and Kegan Paul, 1964).
van Fraassen, B.C.: *The Scientific Image* (Oxford: Clarendon Press, 1980).
Wright, L.: *Teleological Explanations* (Berkeley: University of California Press, 1976).

WESLEY C. SALMON

**external world** see PROBLEM OF THE EXTERNAL WORLD.

**externalism/internalism** The most generally accepted account of this distinction is that a theory of justification is *internalist* if and only if it requires that all of the factors needed for a belief to be epistemically justified for a given person be *cognitively accessible* to that person, *internal* to his cognitive perspective; and *externalist*, if it allows that at least some of the justifying factors need not be thus accessible, so that they can be *external* to the believer's cognitive perspective, beyond his ken. However, epistemologists often use the distinction between internalist and externalist theories of epistemic justification without offering any very explicit explication.

The externalism/internalism distinction has been mainly applied (as above) to theories of epistemic justification. It has also been applied in a closely related way to accounts of knowledge and in a rather different way to accounts of belief and thought content. We will consider each of these applications, devoting most of our attention to the first.

The internalist requirement of cognitive accessibility can be interpreted in at least two ways: a strong version of internalism would require that the believer actually be aware of the justifying factors in order to be justified; while a weaker version would require only that he be capable of becoming aware of them by focusing his attention appropriately, but without the need for any change of position, new information, etc. Though the phrase 'cognitively accessible' suggests the weak interpretation, the main intuitive motivation for internalism, viz. the idea that epistemic justification requires that the believer actually have in his cognitive possession a reason for thinking that the belief is true (see further below), would require the strong interpretation.

Perhaps the clearest example of an internalist position would be a FOUNDATIONALIST view according to which foundational beliefs pertain to immediately experienced states of mind and other beliefs are justified by standing in cognitively accessible logical or inferential relations to such foundational beliefs. Such a view could count as either a strong or a weak version of internalism, depending on whether actual awareness of the justifying elements or only the capacity to become aware of them is required. Similarly, a COHERENTIST view could also be internalist, if both the beliefs or other states with which a justificandum belief is required to cohere and the coherence relations themselves are reflectively accessible.

It should be carefully noticed that when internalism is construed in this way, it is neither necessary nor sufficient by itself for internalism that the justifying factors literally be internal mental states of the person in question. Not necessary, because on at least some views, e.g. a direct realist view of perception, something other than a mental state of the believer can be cognitively accessible; not sufficient, because there are views according to which at least some mental states need not be actual (strong version) or even possible (weak version) objects of cognitive awareness. Also, on this way of drawing the distinction, a hybrid view (like the ones discussed below), according to which some of the factors required for justification must be cognitively accessible while others need not and in general will not be, would count as an externalist view. Obviously too, a view that

was externalist in relation to a strong version of internalism (by not requiring that the believer actually be aware of all justifying factors) could still be internalist in relation to a weak version (by requiring that he at least be capable of becoming aware of them).

The most prominent recent externalist views have been versions of RELIABILISM, whose main requirement for justification is roughly that the belief be produced in a way or via a process that makes it objectively likely that the belief is true. (For discussion of the variety of specific forms that a reliabilist account can take, see Goldman, 1986, pp. 43–53.) What makes such a view externalist is the absence of any requirement that the person for whom the belief is justified have any sort of cognitive access to the relation of reliability in question. Lacking such access, such a person will in general have no reason for thinking that the belief is true or likely to be true, but will, on such an account, none the less be epistemically justified in accepting it. Thus such a view arguably marks a major break from the modern epistemological tradition, stemming from DESCARTES, which identifies epistemic justification with having a reason, perhaps even a conclusive reason, for thinking that the belief is true. An epistemologist working within this tradition is likely to feel that the externalist, rather than offering a competing account of the same concept of epistemic justification with which the traditional epistemologist is concerned, has simply changed the subject.

Two general lines of argument are commonly advanced in favour of justificatory externalism. The first starts from the allegedly commonsensical premiss that knowledge can be unproblematically ascribed to relatively unsophisticated adults, to young children, and even to higher animals. It is then argued that such ascriptions would be untenable on the standard internalist accounts of epistemic justification (assuming that epistemic justification is a necessary condition for knowledge), since the beliefs and inferences involved in such accounts are too complicated and sophisticated to be plausibly ascribed to such subjects. Thus only an externalist view can make sense of such commonsense ascriptions and this, on the presumption that commonsense is correct, constitutes a strong argument in favour of externalism. An internalist may respond by challenging the initial premiss, arguing that such ascriptions of knowledge are exaggerated, while perhaps at the same time claiming that the cognitive situation of at least some of the subjects in question is less restricted than the argument claims. A quite different response would be to reject the assumption that epistemic justification is a necessary condition for knowledge, perhaps by adopting an externalist account of knowledge, rather than justification, like those discussed below.

The second general line of argument for externalism points out that internalist views have conspicuously failed to provide defensible, non-sceptical solutions to the classical problems of epistemology. In striking contrast, however, such problems are in general easily solvable on an externalist view. For example, Goldman (1986, pp. 393–94) offers a one-page solution, in a footnote, of the problem of induction. Thus if we assume both that the various relevant forms of scepticism are false and that the failure of internalist views so far is unlikely to be remedied in the future, we have good reason to think that some externalist view is true. Obviously the cogency of this argument depends on the plausibility of the two assumptions just noted. An internalist can reply, first, that it is not obvious that internalist epistemology is doomed to failure, that the explanation for the present lack of success may simply be the extreme difficulty of the problems in question. Secondly, it can be argued that most or even all of the appeal of the assumption that the various forms of scepticism are false depends essentially on the intuitive conviction that we do have reasons in our grasp for thinking that the various beliefs questioned by the sceptic are true – a conviction that the proponent of this argument must of course reject.

The main objection to externalism rests on the intuition that the basic requirement for epistemic justification is that the acceptance of the belief in question be rational or responsible in relation to the cognitive goal of truth, which seems to require in turn that the believer actually be aware of a reason for thinking that the belief is true (or at the very least, that such a reason be available to him). Since the satisfaction of an externalist condition is neither necessary nor sufficient for the existence of such a cognitively accessible reason, it is argued, externalism is mistaken as an account of epistemic justification. This general point has been elaborated by appeal to two sorts of putative intuitive counterexamples to externalism. The first of these challenges the necessity of the externalist conditions for epistemic justification by appealing to examples of belief which seem intuitively to be justified, but for which the externalist conditions are not satisfied. The standard examples of this sort are cases where beliefs are produced in some very nonstandard way, e.g. by a Cartesian demon, but none the less in such a way that the subjective experience of the believer is indistinguishable from that of someone whose beliefs are produced more normally (*see* Foley, 1985). Cases of this general sort can be constructed in which any of the standard externalist conditions, e.g. that the belief be a result of a reliable process, fail to be satisfied. The intuitive claim is that the believer in such a case is none the less epistemically justified, as much so as one whose belief is produced in a more normal way, and hence that externalist accounts of justification must be mistaken.

Perhaps the most interesting reply to this sort of counterexample, on behalf of reliabilism specifically, holds that reliability of a cognitive process is to be assessed in 'normal' possible worlds, i.e. in possible worlds that are actually the way our world is commonsensically believed to be, rather than in the world which actually contains the belief being judged. Since the cognitive processes employed in the Cartesian demon case are, we may assume, reliable when assessed in this way, the reliabilist can agree that such beliefs are justified. The obvious further issue is whether or not there is an adequate rationale for this construal of reliabilism, so that the reply is not merely *ad hoc*. (*See* Goldman, 1986, pp. 107, 113.)

The second, correlative way of elaborating the general objection to justificatory externalism challenges the sufficiency of the various externalist conditions by citing cases where those conditions are satisfied, but where the believers in question seem intuitively not to be justified. Here the most widely discussed examples have to do with possible occult cognitive capacities like clairvoyance. Considering the point in application once again to reliabilism specifically, the claim is that a reliable clairvoyant who has no reason to think that he has such a cognitive power, and perhaps even good reasons to the contrary, is not rational or responsible and hence not epistemically justified in accepting the beliefs that result from his clairvoyance, despite the fact that the reliabilist condition is satisfied.

One sort of response to this latter sort of objection is to 'bite the bullet' and insist that such believers are in fact justified, dismissing the seeming intuitions to the contrary as latent internalist prejudice. A more widely adopted response attempts to impose additional conditions, usually of a roughly internalist sort, which will rule out the offending example while still stopping far short of a full internalism (see e.g. Goldman, 1986, pp. 111–12). But while there is little doubt that such modified versions of externalism can indeed handle particular cases well enough to avoid clear intuitive implausibility, the issue is whether there will not always be equally problematic cases that they cannot handle, and also whether there is any clear motivation for the additional requirements other than the general internalist view of justification that externalists are committed to reject.

A view in this same general vein, one that might be described as a hybrid of internalism and externalism (see Swain, 1981; Alston, 1989, ch. 9), holds that epistemic justification requires that there be a justificatory factor that is cognitively accessible to the believer in question (though it need not be actually grasped), thus ruling out, e.g., a pure reliabilism. At the same time, however, though it must be objectively true that beliefs for which such a factor is available are likely to be true, this further fact need not be in any way grasped or cognitively accessible to the believer. In effect, of the two premises needed to argue that a particular belief is likely to be true, one must be accessible in a way that would satisfy at least weak internalism, while the second can be (and normally will be) purely external. Here the internalist will respond that this hybrid view is of no help at all in meeting the objection that the belief is not held in the rational, responsible way that justification intuitively seems to require, for the believer in question, lacking one crucial premise, still has no reason at all for thinking that his belief is likely to be true.

An alternative to giving an externalist account of epistemic justification, one which may be more defensible while still accommodating many of the same motivating concerns, is to give an externalist account of knowledge directly, without relying on an intermediate account of justification. Such a view will obviously have to reject the justified true belief account of knowledge, holding instead that knowledge is true belief which satisfies the chosen externalist condition, e.g. is a result of a reliable process (and perhaps further conditions as well). This makes it possible for such a view to retain an internalist account of epistemic justification, though the centrality of that concept to epistemology would obviously be seriously diminished.

Such an externalist account of knowledge can accommodate the commonsense conviction that animals, young children, and unsophisticated adults possess knowledge, though not the weaker conviction (if such a conviction even exists) that such individuals are epistemically justified in their beliefs. It is also at least less vulnerable to internalist counterexamples of the sorts discussed above, since the intuitions involved there pertain more clearly to justification than to knowledge. What is uncertain is what ultimate philosophical significance the resulting conception of knowledge is supposed to have. In particular, does it have any serious bearing on traditional epistemological problems and on the deepest and most troubling versions of scepticism, which seem in fact to be primarily concerned with justification, rather than knowledge?

A rather different use of the terms 'internalism' and 'externalism' has to do with the issue of how the content of beliefs and thoughts is determined: according to an internalist view of content, the content of such intentional states depends only on the non-relational, internal properties of the individual's mind or brain, and not at all on his physical and social environment; while according to an externalist view, content is significantly affected by such external factors. Here too a view that appeals to both internal and external elements is standardly classified as an externalist view.

As with justification and knowledge, the traditional view of content has been strongly internalist in character. The main argument for externalism derives from the philosophy of language, more specifically from the various phenomena pertaining to natural kind terms, indexicals, etc. that motivate the views that have come to be known as 'direct reference' theories. Such phenomena seem at least to show that the belief or thought content that can be properly attributed to a person is dependent on facts about his environment – e.g. whether he is on Earth or Twin Earth, what in fact he is pointing at, the classificatory criteria employed by the experts in his social group, etc. – not just on what is going on internally in his mind or brain. (*See* Putnam, 1975; Burge, 1979.)

An objection to externalist accounts of content is that they seem unable to do justice to our ability to know the contents of our beliefs or thoughts 'from the inside', simply by reflection. If content is dependent on external factors pertaining to the environment, then knowledge of content should depend on knowledge of these factors – which will not in general be available to the person whose belief or thought is in question.

The adoption of an externalist account of mental content would seem to support an externalist account of justification in the following way: if part or all of the content of a belief is inaccessible to the believer, then both the justifying status of other beliefs in relation to that content and the status of that content as justifying further beliefs will be similarly inaccessible, thus contravening the internalist requirement for justification. An internalist must insist that there are no justification relations of these sorts, that only internally accessible content can either be justified or justify anything else; but such a response appears lame unless it is coupled with an attempt to show that the externalist account of content is mistaken.

*See also* CONCEPT; EPISTEMIC VIRTUES; ETHICS AND EPISTEMOLOGY; INFINITE REGRESS ARGUMENT; SCEPTICISM, CONTEMPORARY.

BIBLIOGRAPHY

Alston, W.P.: *Epistemic Justification* (Ithaca, NY: Cornell University Press, 1989).
Armstrong, D.M.: *Belief, Truth and Knowledge* (London: Routledge and Kegan Paul, 1968).
BonJour, L.: *The Structure of Empirical Knowledge* (Cambridge, MA: Harvard University Press, 1985), ch. 3.
Burge, T.: 'Individualism and the mental', *Midwest Studies in Philosophy* 4 (1979), 73–121.
Foley, R.: 'What's wrong with reliabilism?', *The Monist* 68 (1985), 188–202.
Fumerton, R.: 'The internalism/externalism controversy', in *Philosophical Perspectives* 2 (1988), 442–59.
Goldman, A.: *Epistemology and Cognition* (Cambridge, MA: Harvard University Press, 1986).
Luper-Foy, S.: 'The reliabilist theory of rational belief', *The Monist* 68 (1985), 203–25.
Nozick, R.: *Philosophical Explanations* (Cambridge, MA: Harvard University Press, 1981), ch. 3.
Pollock, J.: *Contemporary Theories of Knowledge* (Totowa: Rowman and Littlefield, 1986), ch. 4.
Putnam, H.: 'The meaning of "meaning"', in his *Mind, Language and Reality* (Cambridge: Cambridge University Press, 1975), 215–71.
Swain, M.: *Reasons and Knowledge* (Ithaca, NY: Cornell University Press, 1981).

LAURENCE BONJOUR

# F

**fact/value** The distinction between facts and values has outgrown its name: it applies not only to matters of fact vs. matters of value, but also to statements that something *is*, vs. statements that something *ought* to be, the case. Roughly, factual statements – 'is-statements' in the relevant sense – represent some state of affairs as obtaining, whereas normative statements – evaluative and deontic ones – attribute goodness to something, or ascribe, to an agent, an obligation to act. Neither distinction is merely linguistic. Specifying a book's monetary value is making a factual statement, though it attributes a kind of value: 'That is a good book' expresses a value judgement, though the term 'value' is absent (nor would 'valuable' be synonymous here with 'good'). Similarly, 'We are morally obligated to fight' superficially expresses an *is*-statement, and 'By all indications it ought to rain' makes a kind of *ought*-claim; but the former is an *ought*-statement, the latter an (*epistemic*) *is*-statement.

Theoretical difficulties also beset the distinction. Some have absorbed values into facts, holding that all value is instrumental, roughly: to have value is to contribute – in a *factually* analysable way – to something further which is (say) deemed desirable. Others have suffused facts with values, arguing that facts (and observations) are 'theory-impregnated' and contending that values are ineliminable in theory choice. But while some philosophers doubt that fact/value distinctions can be sustained, there persists a sense of a deep difference between evaluating, or attributing an obligation and, on the other hand, saying how the world is.

Fact/value distinctions may be defended by appeal to the notion of intrinsic value: value a thing has in itself and thus independently of its consequences. Roughly, a value statement (proper) is an ascription of intrinsic value: one to the effect that a thing is to some degree good in itself. This leaves open whether ought-statements are implicitly value statements; but even if they imply that something has intrinsic value – e.g. moral value – they can be independently characterized, say by appeal to rules that provide (justifying) *reasons* for action. One might also ground the fact value distinction in the attitudinal (or even motivational) component apparently implied by the making of valuational or deontic judgements; thus, 'It is a good book, but that is no reason for a positive attitude towards it' and 'You ought to do it, but there is no reason to' seem inadmissible, whereas substituting, respectively, 'an expensive book' and 'you will do it' yields permissible judgements. One might also argue that factual judgements are the kind which are in principle appraisable scientifically, and thereby anchor the distinction on the factual side. This line is plausible, but there is controversy over whether scientific procedures are 'value-free' in the required way.

Philosophers differ regarding the sense, if any, in which epistemology is normative (roughly, valuational). But what precisely is at stake in this controversy is no clearer than the problematic fact/value distinction itself. Must epistemologists as such make judgements of value or epistemic responsibility? If epistemology is naturalizable, then even epistemic principles simply articulate under what conditions – say, appropriate perceptual stimulations – a belief is justified, or constitutes knowledge. Its standards of justification, then, would be like standards of, e.g., resilience for bridges. It is not obvious, however, that the appropriate standards can be established without independent judgements that, say, a certain kind of evidence is good enough for justified belief (or knowledge). The most plausible view may be that justification is like intrinsic goodness: though it SUPERVENES on natural properties, it cannot be analysed wholly in factual statements.

See also NATURALIZED EPISTEMOLOGY.

BIBLIOGRAPHY

Dewey, J.: *Theory of Valuation* (Chicago: University of Chicago Press, 1939).
Frankena, W.K.: *Ethics* 2nd edn (Englewood Cliffs: Prentice-Hall, 1973).
Goldman, A.I.: *Epistemology and Cognition* (Cambridge, MA: Harvard University Press, 1986).
Hempel, C.G.: *Aspects of Scientific Explanation* (New York: Free Press, 1965).
Moore, G.E.: *Principia Ethica* (Cambridge: Cambridge University Press, 1903).

ROBERT AUDI

**fallibilism**   The idea that any of our opinions about the world or about anything else might turn out false. It is associated particularly with C.S. PEIRCE and Karl POPPER, although many epistemologists would admit to being fallibilists to some degree because the underlying idea, that human beings are ever prone to error in their judgements, is clearly true. What separates fallibilists from other philosophers is the confidence each is ready to rest on what seem to be our epistemological successes. Even among fallibilists there are significant differences on this point. Both Peirce and Popper see human beings in biological terms, as organisms striving to adapt themselves to their environment. But while Peirce sees the aims of knowledge-seeking as the removal of the invitation of doubt, an aim which will in the long run be successfully achieved by a convergence of all enquirers on the truth, Popper insists that we never have positive reasons to accept any belief. His fallibilism, indeed, is hard to distinguish from SCEPTICISM.

BIBLIOGRAPHY

Hookway, C.: *Peirce* (London: Routledge and Kegan Paul, 1985)

Peirce, C.S.: *Collected Papers* 8 vols (Cambridge, MA: Belnap Press, 1931–58).
Popper, K.R.: *Conjectures and Refutations* (London: Routledge and Kegan Paul, 1963).
Popper, K.R.: *Objective Knowledge* (Oxford: Clarendon Press, 1972).

ANTHONY O'HEAR

**feminist epistemology**   Feminist epistemological projects are at once political and revisionist. Because they focus upon *practices* of knowledge construction, one of their principal effects is to move the question 'Whose knowledge are we talking about?' to a central analytical position. Posing this question challenges many of the governing ideals of the post-positivist empiricist epistemologies that occupy the standard-setting and monitoring positions in Anglo-American philosophy. Feminists have shown that behind the mask of objectivity and value-neutrality these epistemologies present to the world, there is a complex power structure of vested interest, dominance and subjugation.

Born of the consciousness-raising practices of the 1960s, feminist enquiry has revealed gaps, cognitive dissonances and lack of fit between women's diverse experiences and the theories, categories and conceptual schemes that purport to explain – to *know* – them. Hence by uncovering the exclusionary assumptions that have enabled the epistemologies of the mainstream to establish their authority, feminists are effecting shifts in the perceived tasks of epistemology. Eschewing normative aims of determining what an ideal knower ought to do, they are producing critical analyses of what historically and materially 'situated' knowers actually do (cf. Haraway, 1988).

Two principal although neither unified nor entrenched positions have coalesced out of 'second-wave' feminist enquiry: feminist empiricism and feminist standpoint theory. In some of these theories, biology and the social sciences are accorded the centrality, if not precisely the paradigmatic status, that post-positivist epistemologies accord to the physical sciences (cf. Harding, 1986; Longino, 1990). Other versions draw their analyses more specifically from mainstream epistemology rather than from its philosophy-of-science offspring (Duran 1990; Code, 1991).

Feminist empiricists argue that, far from being as neutral and objective as their self-presentation indicates, traditional empiricists are caught in the androcentricity of the positions from which they speak. Feminists contend that the goal of knowledge-production, and hence of science, is to produce knowledge cleansed of androcentric and sexist biases, and (latterly) of racist, classist and other 'distortions'. Their central claim is that an unabashedly value-laden yet rigorous empiricism, informed by feminist ideology, can produce more adequate knowledge than standard methods ignorant of their specificity, and of their complicity in a sex/gender system, can produce. In short, an informed political commitment can yield a better empiricism.

Some exponents of feminist empiricism (cf. Harding, 1986) argue that despite the theory's promise, its feminism undermines its empiricism. The fact that a feminist empiricist *qua* knowing subject cannot be an abstract, ahistorical, disembodied individual so flagrantly violates a basic empiricist tenet that the epistemology cannot even be called empiricist. Others propose ways of reconciling feminism and empiricism. Nelson (1990) maintains that Quinean empiricism demands neither the stark individualism nor the theory-neutrality of the classical theories. Hence it is a valuable resource for feminists. Duran (1990) contends that post-Quinean 'naturalized' epistemologies offer feminists the most promising option. Departing from traditional preoccupations with determining whether knowledge is possible, NATURALIZED EPISTEMOLOGIES assume that people can and do have knowledge. With the help of cognitive science, they abandon transcendence to examine how people actually know, individually and socially. None the less, because they adhere to principles of empirical objectivity, they are effective tools for producing knowledge of the physical and social world.

Longino (1990) argues for a contextual empiricism. She claims that evidential reasoning is context-dependent, and data count as evidence only in relation to background assumptions and hypotheses. Knowledge construction is a thoroughly social practice; hence incorporating values and ideology into enquiry does not require an indiscriminate tolerance of individual subjective preferences. Objectivity is ensured by social criticism, to which all products of enquiry are submitted. Such criticism can unmask androcentricity even in 'good' science and inquiry, even from an admittedly interested position, itself open to criticism. Yet it retains a rigorous commitment to the evidence. Code (1991) develops an approach that is residually empiricist in its realism. It departs from canonical EMPIRICISM in maintaining that subjectivity is socially constructed; and in proposing that knowing other people is a better model of cognitive activity than knowing medium-sized physical objects. It departs more sharply still in characterizing itself as a mitigated, yet critical, perspectival RELATIVISM.

Feminist standpoint theorists (cf. Hartsock, 1983) contend that neither orthodox nor feminist empiricists can adequately account for the varied historical and material conditions out of which people produce knowledge. The authoritative, standard-setting knowledge in Western societies is derived from and tested against the social experiences of a limited segment of the population: white, middle-class, educated men. In consequence, women (like the proletariat of Marxist theory) are oppressed in marginal, underclass epistemic positions. Science as practice has created an esoteric discourse to which few women gain ready access. It has explained their limited success with 'scientifically proven facts' about their intellectual inferiority. These facts have been established by a methodology not explicitly designed to oppress women, which has oppressed them none the less. Yet their oppression can be turned into an epistemic advantage, for it requires women to know their oppressors and the systems that legitimate them better than the oppressors know themselves, simply in order to survive. In consequence, the knowledge produced from a feminist standpoint grounded in women's historical-material circumstances has an explanatory, transformative and emancipatory potential which more modest, empiricist projects can never realize.

Critics object that because there is no single, unified feminist perspective, standpoint theory obliterates differences, and hence fails by its own feminist standards. Others challenge its claims to epistemic privilege, arguing that its 'locatedness' produces a perspective on social reality that must be as limited as any other. It remains to be seen how these problems will be solved; but the importance of standpoint theory's commitment to producing faithful, if often critical, analyses of women's experiences, together with its analyses of oppression and its legitimation by hegemonic epistemic values, cannot be gainsaid.

Feminist empiricist and standpoint theories attest to the influence of postmodern criticisms of the epistemological projects of the Enlightenment. In challenging humanistic conceptions of subjectivity, and taking the particularities of knowers into account, these epistemologies endorse the anti-essentialism of post-modernism. Like post-modernists, standpoint and empiricist feminists are (variously) critical of attempts to tell one true story, to develop a single master narrative. Yet many feminists are wary of opting for a post-modernism that would require an indifferent tolerance of multiple perspectives. Such a position could not contest the androcentrism and ingrained sexism of the epistemologies of the mainstream.

In consequence of feminist critiques, epistemologists can no longer assume that 'reason is alike in all men'. Knowers cannot be represented as mere place-holders in an infinitely replicable process, whose minds convert information into knowledge, leaving it untouched by its passage through them. The 'whose knowledge?' question contests the assumption that knowers can be self-reliant, free from dependence upon their locational peculiarities. Indeed, feminists have uncovered notable coincidences between the traits attributed to ideal knowers in science-oriented western societies, and the norms of middle-class male psychosexual development in those same societies (cf. Keller, 1985). These coincidences are the twentieth-century manifestation of a persistent historical practice of defining reason, rationality and objectivity through the exclusion of attributes and traits commonly associated with femininity (cf. Lloyd, 1984). They leave no doubt that the invisible knowing subject in mainstream epistemology and philosophy of science is implicitly male. It is not surprising that the knowledge he produces is androcentric: it derives from typically male experiences.

Moving the 'whose knowledge?' question to a central place thus demands revisions in the conceptions of subjectivity that mainstream epistemologists commonly take for granted. Most notably, the detached, disinterested knowing subject, who is a neutral spectator of the world, has to be displaced. Subjectivity is itself produced, constructed in social-political-racial-class-ethnic-cultural-religious circumstances. When epistemology becomes a project of understanding how people know, how they can best negotiate their local circumstances and the global situations in which their localities are embedded; when the abstract individualism of traditional epistemology gives way to a specifically located subjectivity, then the ideal of transcending the limitations of 'partial perspective' to achieve a view from nowhere becomes suspect.

Now because they rely on a purified, value-neutral, physical-science model of knowledge, mainstream epistemologists believe that every act of knowing is replicable by every other knower in the same observation conditions. Replicability is virtually synonymous with objectivity. Granting the methodology of the physical sciences the standard-setting and -monitoring role in knowledge-construction has significant consequences. Theorists of knowledge have, historically, judged women's traditional arts and skills 'unscientific', hence unworthy of the label 'knowledge'. Analogous exclusions are apparent in psychology, anthropology, history and sociology, which have worked with objectivist epistemologies indifferent to the partiality, and frequent imperialism, that structure even their claims to neutrality (cf. Harding, 1986; Haraway, 1988; Longino, 1990; Nelson, 1990). Co-operative projects of enquiry tend to count as no more than the sum of their parts, with every participant singly and separately accountable to the evidence. Results (= knowledge) become his individual achievement, monologically presented to an objective and disinterested public.

Contesting the epistemological individualism of the mainstream, many feminists maintain that knowledge-construction is a social, communal activity. People have to learn how to attend to 'the evidence' before they can make knowledge from it, and such learning is necessarily a social – hence socially variant – activity. Moreover, the community plays a decisive role as critic and arbiter in the justification of knowledge claims, and in determining whose projects gain recognition, whose knowledge counts.

Once knowledge-production and epistemology are relocated within social-political locations, OBJECTIVITY, too, has to be reconstructed as a socially produced and mediated value. Objectivity is achieved as much in consequence of intersubjective, communal criticism – the secular counterpart of peer review in the academy – as in consequence of scrupulous attention to 'the evidence' (cf. Longino, 1990). Evidence counts *as* evidence within contexts determined as much by social as by purely observational criteria. Hence burdens of proof are redistributed *laterally* (across communities of enquirers) and not just vertically (from a transcendent observer to the data). It becomes as important to know about the credibility of knowledge-claimants, their critics and interlocutors as it is to know how, empirically, to verify a claim 'on its own merits' (cf. Code, 1987). Knowledge-claimants are as accountable to the community as to the facts; and the idea(l) of pure enquiry can no longer be upheld. Indeed, feminists argue that only people with the resources and power to believe that they can transcend and control their circumstances would see the detachment that the ideal demands as

even a theoretical option. Enquiry comes out of, and is intricated with, human purposes, whether at commonsensical or at esoteric, scientific levels. Those purposes have to be evaluated if knowledge of the world and other people is to achieve its emancipatory potential, locally and globally (cf. Longino, 1990; Code, 1991).

Because knowledge-production is a social practice, engaged in by embodied, gendered, historically-, racially- and culturally-located knowers, its products cannot fail to bear the marks of their makers. Yet the constructivism implied in the claim that knowledge is *made*, not found, is constrained by the intransigence of a reality that has always to be negotiated. Cognitive options are further limited by the stubborn conservatism of traditions, practices, institutions and social structures that resist wishful negation or reconstruction. None the less, cognitive agents are sufficiently free and unconstrained in their projects of constructing knowledge that they remain accountable for the knowledge they produce (cf. Code, 1987).

So long as epistemology is conceived as a project of determining necessary and sufficient conditions for justifying knowledge claims and refuting scepticism, then the product of feminist enquiry will not be *a* feminist epistemology. Their emphasis on the 'Whose knowledge?' question distinguishes feminist projects from the absolutism that quests for necessary and sufficient conditions betray. Yet the importance of epistemological questions to feminism cannot be denied; for it is only by gaining access to authoritative epistemic positions that women can achieve the emancipation that feminist politics are committed to realizing. Hence feminist epistemologists are working to determine criteria for adjudicating knowledge claims when foundational appeals are no longer permissible. They are devising methods for analysing knowledge that is at once socially constructed and bears the marks of its makers; and constrained by a reality independent from those makers. They are developing epistemological analyses cognizant of the specificities of their subject matters (their intractability to reductive analysis) yet open to critical debate across a plurality of locations and methods.

*See also* CONTINENTAL EPISTEMOLOGY.

BIBLIOGRAPHY

Code, L.: *What Can She Know? Feminist Theory and the Construction of Knowledge* (Ithaca, NY: Cornell University Press, 1991).
Code, L.: *Epistemic Responsibility* (Hanover: University Press of New England, 1987).
Duran, J.: *Toward a Feminist Epistemology* (Savage, MD: Rowman and Littlefield, 1990).
Haraway, D.: 'Situated knowledges: The science question in feminism and the privilege of partial perspective', *Feminist Studies* 14 (1988), 575–99.
Harding, S.: *The Science Question in Feminism* (Ithaca, NY: Cornell University Press, 1986).
Hartsock, N.: 'The feminist standpoint: developing the ground for a specifically feminist historical materialism', in *Discovering Reality: Feminist Perspectives on Epistemology, Methodology, and Philosophy of Science* eds S. Harding and M.B. Hintikka (Dordrecht: Reidel, 1983).
Keller, E.F.: *Reflections on Gender and Science* (New Haven: Yale University Press, 1985).
Lloyd, G.: *The Man of Reason* (Minneapolis: University of Minnesota Press, 1984).
Longino, H.: *Science as Social Knowledge* (Princeton: Princeton University Press, 1990).
Nelson, L.H.: *Who Knows: From Quine to a Feminist Empiricism* (Philadelphia: Temple University Press, 1990).

LORRAINE CODE

**first philosophy** The term 'First Philosophy' was used by Aristotle for metaphysics or the study of being *qua* being. But when a modern philosopher such as QUINE describes his naturalism as 'abandonment of the goal of a first philosophy', he takes this to involve the denial that our knowledge is 'answerable to any supra-scientific tribunal' (1981, p. 72). The paradigm of what is thus repudiated is found in DESCARTES' *Meditations on First Philosophy* which undertakes to refute scepticism and explain the legitimacy of the sciences relying only on what is absolutely certain or indubitable. A first philosophy would thus be a philosophical investigation whlch was prior to, and more secure than, investigations in the special sciences.

BIBLIOGRAPHY

Descartes, R.: *Meditations on First Philosophy* (1641) in *The Philosophical Writings of Descartes* trans. J. Cottingham, R. Stoothoff and D. Murdock (Cambridge: Cambridge University Press, 1985).
Quine, W.V.: *Theories and Things* (Cambridge, MA: Harvard University Press, 1981).

CHRISTOPHER HOOKWAY

**Firth, Roderick (1917–87)** American philosopher. Firth wrote his dissertation under C.I. LEWIS, and taught at Harvard from 1953 until his death. He published an influential article on Ideal Observer theories in ethics, but the bulk of his work was in epistemology.

Firth, like LEWIS, was a staunch defender of FOUNDATIONALISM. He believed that empirical knowledge ultimately rests on self-warranted beliefs about sensory experience, and that beliefs about physical objects can be justified without appeal to any principles beyond ordinary inductive inference. His defence of PHENOMENALISM (1950) against attacks like CHISHOLM'S is subtle and cogent; it has been neglected rather than refuted. Firth contends that critics have ignored the fact that the phenomenalists' theory of meaning entails that the *sentences* available to express *statements* about the external world will inevitably be much less numerous than the statements themselves. When a phenomenalist who initially says 'Physical-object statement *p* entails sense-datum statement *s*' is led (by some version of the 'argument from perceptual relativity') to say '*s* could be false and *p* true', Firth contends that the second assertion should not be interpreted as strictly inconsistent with the first. What is actually going on, Firth claims, is that the sentence '*p*' is being used to express different (though closely related) statements in the two assertions: the statement expressed by the first occurrence of '*p*' is in fact false if '*s*' is false, but the state-of-affairs which makes the statement expressed by '*p*' false is none the less more appropriately expressed by '*p*' than by 'not-*p*'.

WRITINGS

'Radical empiricism and perceptual relativity', *Philosophical Review* 59 (1950), 164–83, 319–31.
'Coherence, certainty, and epistemic priority', *Journal of Philosophy* 61 (1964), 545–57.
'The anatomy of certainty', *Philosophical Review* 76 (1967), 3–27.
'Are epistemic concepts reducible to ethical concepts?', in *Values and Morals* eds A. Goldman and J. Kim (Dordrecht: Reidel, 1978), 215–30.
*Selected Philosophical Writings* (Harvard University Press, forthcoming).

JOHN TROYER

**Foucault, Michel (1926–84)** French philosopher, born in Poitiers. If knowledge is the product of historically-specific, contingent modes of inquiry, what effect has this had on our own knowledges? Foucault attempted to answer this question for bodies of knowledge in the human sciences, principally psychiatry, penology and sexology. Influenced by Nietzsche, Bachelard and Canguilhem, Foucault's project was to reveal the 'positive unconscious of knowledge', or those hidden but constitutive elements in the background of the process of knowing. These elements remain unexamined when the key to meaning is assumed to be the 'referent' of claims or the intentions of a believing subject. Foucault proposed that at a deeper level rules for the constitution of beliefs operate to determine whether statements have meaning and can function within specific discourses. Briefly, a discourse is the conglomeration of statements, concepts, objects and practices produced by an *episteme*, which is the total set of relations or discursive regularities that set out the possibilities of meaning and truth. These rules are immanent in that they are simple regularities between the elements of a discourse, and they are contingent in that they do not arise from transcendental facts

about language or human beings. Foucault's method of 'archaeology' attempts to identify these internal relations between discursive elements without reference to intentions or representations.

Around 1970 Foucault introduced into this analysis a new formative element, power, and developed a new 'genealogical' method to describe what he called 'power/knowledge'. He conceived of power as existing not in individuals but in social relations and as involved as much with domination and constraint as with the production of knowledges, pleasures and subjectivities. He formulated the dyad power/knowledge to indicate that each is always implicated in the other, in the sense that the negotiations and strategic movements of power create the open spaces where discourses can emerge, but that power is exercised *through* knowledge. Genealogy, an approach borrowed from Nietzsche, is the examination of the relationship between power and specific knowledges.

Foucault's project was political in that it was motivated towards dislodging our dogmatic attachments to present categories and concepts, by revealing their genesis in the mire of contingent conceptual transformations, historical conflict and political struggle. His exploration of the history of madness, for example, had as its prime directive not an illumination of the past but a liberation of the present, via a demonstration of the contingent ways madness has been conceptualized and treated and the variable ways the distinction between the mad and the sane has been drawn. Given such contingencies, the operations of power are necessary to explain the emergence of all knowledge systems.

Because he often claimed that not only theories are contingent but also the criterion of distinction between true and false, Foucault's work has been called self-defeating and incapable of sustaining the political critique he himself desired. His proponents have argued that his claims were regional or specific and too modest to be able to undermine all knowledge claims, and thus capable of sustaining his own. They also argue that his historical narratives have successfully called into question many current categories of analysis, and that herein lies his political impact. His primary influence on epistemology, if he is to have any, will most likely be in the introduction of power as a salient ingredient in all conceptualizations of knowledge and truth.

*See also* CONTINENTAL EPISTEMOLOGY; NIETZSCHE; SOCIAL SCIENCE.

WRITINGS

*Language, Counter-Memory, Practices* ed. D. Bouchard (Ithaca, NY: Cornell University Press, 1977).

*L'Archéologie du Savoir* (Paris: 1969); trans. A. Sheridan *The Archaeology of Knowledge* (New York: Pantheon, 1972).

*Les Mots et les Choses: Une Archéologie des Sciences Humaines* (Paris: 1966); trans. A. Sheridan *The Order of Things* (New York: Random House, 1970).

*Naissance de la Clinique: Une Archéologie du Regard Medical* (Paris: 1963); trans. A. Sheridan *The Birth of the Clinic: An Archaeology of Medical Perception* (New York: Vintage, 1973).

*Power/Knowledge: Selected Interviews and Other Writings, 1972–1977* ed. C. Gordon (New York: Pantheon, 1980).

*Surveiller et Punir: Naissance de la Prison* (Paris: 1975); trans. A. Sheridan *Discipline and Punish: The Birth of the Prison* (New York: Pantheon, 1977).

LINDA ALCOFF

## foundationalism

INITIAL ACCOUNT

Foundationalism is a view concerning the *structure* of the system of justified belief possessed by a given individual. Such a system is divided into 'foundation' and 'superstructure', so related that beliefs in the latter depend on the former for their justification but not vice versa. However, the view is sometimes stated in terms of the structure of *knowledge* rather than of justified belief. If knowledge is true justified belief (plus,

perhaps, some further condition), one may think of knowledge as exhibiting a foundationalist structure by virtue of the justified belief it involves. In any event, I will construe the doctrine as concerned primarily with justified belief, though I will feel free to speak of knowledge instead from time to time.

The first step towards a more explicit statement of the position is to distinguish between *mediate* (indirect) and *immediate* (direct) justification of belief. To say that a belief is *mediately* justified is to say that it is justified by some appropriate relation to other justified beliefs, e.g., by being inferred from other justified beliefs that provide adequate support for it, or, alternatively, by being *based on* adequate reasons. Thus if my reason for supposing that you are depressed is that you look listless, speak in an unaccustomedly flat tone of voice, exhibit no interest in things you are usually interested in, etc., then my belief that you are depressed is justified, if at all, by being adequately supported by my justified belief that you look listless, speak in a flat tone of voice. . . .

A belief is *immediately* justified, on the other hand, if its justification is of some other sort, e.g. if it is justified by being based on experience or if it is 'self-justified'. Thus my belief that you look listless may not be based on anything else I am justified in *believing* but just on the way you look to me. And my belief that $2 + 3 = 5$ may be justified not because I infer it from something else I justifiably believe, but simply because it seems obviously true to me.

In these terms we can put the thesis of foundationalism by saying that all mediately justified beliefs owe their justification ultimately to immediately justified beliefs. To get a more detailed idea of what this amounts to it will be useful to consider the most important argument for foundationalism, the regress argument. Consider a mediately justified belief that $p$ (we are using lower case letters as dummies for belief contents). It is, by hypothesis, justified by its relation to one or more other justified beliefs, $q$ and $r$. Now what justifies each of these, e.g. $q$? If it too is mediately justified that is because it is related appropriately to one or more further justified beliefs, e.g. *s*. By virtue of what is *s* justified? If it is mediately justified, the same problem arises at the next stage. To avoid both circularity and an infinite regress, we are forced to suppose that in tracing back this chain we arrive at one or more immediately justified beliefs that stops the regress, since their justification does not depend on any further *justified belief*. (For more details, *see* INFINITE REGRESS ARGUMENT.) More accurately, since each mediately justified belief may be supported by more than one other justified belief, the general picture is that of a multiply branching tree structure, with the original belief at its base. In those terms, foundationalism can be formulated as the view that every mediately justified belief is at the origin of such a structure, at the tip of each branch of which is an immediately justified belief. (*See* Alston, 1989, chs 1, 2.)

## ALTERNATIVE VERSIONS

I have been presenting foundationalism as a view concerning the structure *that is in fact exhibited* by the justified beliefs *of a particular person*. It has sometimes been construed in ways that deviate from each of the italicized phrases in the previous sentence. Thus it is sometimes taken to characterize the structure of 'our knowledge' or 'scientific knowledge', rather than the structure of the cognitive system of an individual subject. As for the other phrase, foundationalism is sometimes thought of as concerned with how knowledge (justified belief) is acquired or built up, rather than with the structure of what a person finds herself with at a certain point. Thus some people think of scientific inquiry as starting with the recording of observations (immediately justified observational beliefs), and then inductively inferring generalizations. Again, foundationalism is sometimes thought of not as a description of the finished product or of the mode of acquisition, but rather as a proposal for how the system could be *reconstructed*, an indication of how it *could* all be built up from immediately justified foundations. This last would seem to be the kind of foundationalism we find in DESCARTES. However foundationalism is most

usually thought of in contemporary Anglo-American epistemology as an account of the structure actually exhibited by an individual's system of justified belief.

It should also be noted that the term is used with a deplorable looseness in contemporary literary circles, and even in certain corners of the philosophical world, to refer to anything from realism – the view that reality has a definite constitution regardless of how we think of it or what we believe about it – to various kinds of 'absolutism' in ethics, politics, or wherever, and even to the truism that truth is stable (if a proposition is true, it stays true!). This essay will continue to focus on foundationalism as it was explained above.

## VIEWS CONCERNING THE FOUNDATIONS

Since foundationalism holds that all mediate justification rests on immediately justified beliefs, we may divide variations in forms of the view into those that have to do with the immediately justified beliefs, the 'foundations', and those that have to do with the modes of derivation of other beliefs from these, how the 'superstructure' is built up. The most obvious variation of the first sort has to do with what modes of immediate justification are recognized. Many treatments, both pro and con, are parochially restricted to one form of immediate justification – self-evidence, self-justification (self-warrant), justification by a direct awareness of what the belief is about, or whatever. It is then unwarrantedly assumed by critics that disposing of that one form will dispose of foundationalism generally (Alston, 1989, ch. 3). The emphasis historically has been on beliefs that simply 'record' what is directly given in experience (Lewis, 1946) and on self-evident propositions (Descartes' 'clear and distinct perceptions and Locke's 'perception of the agreement and disagreement of ideas'). But self-warrant has also recently received a great deal of attention (Alston 1989, ch. 11; Chisholm, 1977, ch. 2), and there is also a RELIABILIST version, according to which a belief can be immediately justified just by being acquired by a reliable belief-forming process that does not take other beliefs as inputs (BonJour, 1985, ch. 3).

Foundationalisms also differ as to what further constraints, if any, are put on foundations. Historically it has been common to require of the foundations of knowledge that they exhibit certain 'epistemic immunities', as we might put it, immunity from error (*see* INFALLIBILITY), refutation (*see* INCOR-RIGIBILITY), or doubt (*see* INDUBITABILITY). Thus Descartes, along with many other seventeenth- and eighteenth-century philosophers, took it that any knowledge worthy of the name would be based on cognitions the truth of which is guaranteed (infallible), that were maximally stable, immune from ever being shown to be mistaken (incorrigible), and concerning which no reasonable doubt could be raised (indubitable). Hence the search in the *Meditations* for a divine guarantee of our faculty of rational intuition. Criticisms of foundationalism have often been directed at these constraints (Lehrer, 1974; Will, 1974; both responded to in Alston, 1989, ch. 2). It is important to realize that a position that is foundationalist in a distinctive sense can be formulated without imposing any such requirements on foundations. (*See* the next section.)

As for the second dimension of variation, modes of derivation of the superstructure from the foundations, Descartes, along with Locke and many other early modern philosophers, took the hard line that deductive inference from the foundations is the only way to get mediate knowledge in a strict sense, for nothing else would *guarantee* that truth is preserved in the process. Locke was also interested in weaker forms of support, in his account of Judgment and Probability in Bk IV of the *Essay*, but not much progress was made toward a systematic account (*see* INTUITION AND DEDUCTION). In our century foundationalists have widely recognized that the Cartesian demands are too limiting, but there is little consensus on what to put in their place. There is general agreement that inductive and probabilistic inference are required, and INFERENCE TO THE BEST EXPLANATION has been popular of

late (*see* e.g. Moser, 1989), but the discussions have tended to bog down in numerous difficulties concerning these modes of inference. CHISHOLM (1977, ch. 4) is well known for attempting to cut the Gordian knot by boldly saying that we have to countenance whatever modes of derivation enable us to get from what direct knowledge we have to whatever else it is we are justified in believing.

TYPES OF FOUNDATIONALISM

There are various ways of distinguishing types of foundationalist epistemology by the use of the variations we have been enumerating. Plantinga (1983) has put forward an influential conception of 'classical foundationalism', specified in terms of limitations on the foundations. He construes this as a disjunction of 'ancient and medieval foundationalism', which takes foundations to comprise what is self-evident and 'evident to the senses', and 'modern foundationalism' that replaces 'evident to the senses' with 'incorrigible', which in practice was taken to apply only to beliefs about one's present states of consciousness. Plantinga himself developed this notion in the context of arguing that items outside this territory, in particular certain beliefs about God, could also be immediately justified. A popular recent distinction is between what is variously called 'strong' or 'extreme' foundationalism and 'moderate', 'modest' or 'minimal' foundationalism, with the distinction depending on whether various epistemic immunities are required of foundations. Finally I have distinguished 'simple' and 'iterative' foundationalism (Alston, 1989, ch. 1), depending on whether it is required of a foundation only that *it* be immediately justified, or whether it is also required that the higher level belief that *the former belief is immediately justified* is itself immediately justified. In the essay just referred to I suggest that the plausibility of the stronger requirement stems from a 'level confusion' between beliefs on different levels.

## ALTERNATIVES TO FOUNDATIONALISM

The classic opposition is between foundationalism and COHERENTISM. Coherentism denies any immediate justification. It deals with the regress argument by rejecting 'linear' chains of justification and, in effect, taking the total system of belief to be epistemically primary. A particular belief is justified to the extent that it is integrated into a coherent system of belief. More recently, PRAGMATISTS like John DEWEY have developed a position known as contextualism, which avoids ascribing any overall structure to knowledge. Questions concerning justification can only arise in particular contexts, defined in terms of assumptions that are simply taken for granted, though they can be questioned in other contexts, where other assumptions will be privileged.

## CRITICISMS OF FOUNDATIONALISM

Foundationalism can be attacked both in its commitment to immediate justification and in its claim that all mediately justified beliefs ultimately depend on the former. Though, in my opinion, it is the latter that is the position's weakest point, most of the critical fire has been directed to the former. As pointed out above, much of this criticism has been directed against some particular form of immediate justification, ignoring the possibility of other forms. Thus much anti-foundationalist artillery has been directed at the 'myth of the given', the idea that facts or things are 'given' to consciousness in a preconceptual, pre-judgemental mode, and that beliefs can be justified on that basis (Sellars, 1963). The most prominent general argument against immediate justification is a 'level ascent' argument, according to which whatever is taken to immediately justify a belief can only do so if the subject is justified in supposing that the putative justifier has what it takes to do so. Hence, since the justification of the original belief depends on the justification of the higher level belief just specified, the justification is not immediate after all (BonJour, 1985, ch. 2). In my view, we lack adequate support for any such higher level requirement for justification; and if it were imposed we would be launched on an infinite regress, for a similar requirement would hold equally for the higher level belief that the original justifier was efficacious.

*See also* INFINITE REGRESS ARGUMENT; PERCEPTUAL KNOWLEDGE; PRIVATE LANGUAGE ARGUMENT; SELLARS.

BIBLIOGRAPHY

Alston, W.P.: *Epistemic Justification* (Ithaca, NY: Cornell University Press, 1989).
Bonjour, L.: *The Structure of Empirical Knowledge* (Cambridge, MA: Harvard University Press, 1985).
Chisholm. R.M.: *Theory of Knowledge* 2nd edn (Englewood Cliffs: Prentice-Hall, 1977).
Lehrer, K.: *Knowledge* (New York: Oxford University Press, 1974).
Lewis, C.I.: *An Analysis of Knowledge and Valuation* (La Salle: Open Court, 1946).
Moser, P.: *Knowledge and Evidence* (New York: Cambridge University Press, 1989).
Plantinga, A.: 'Reason and belief in God', in *Faith and Rationality* eds A. Plantinga and N. Wolterstorff (Notre Dame: University of Notre Dame Press, 1983).
Sellars, W.: 'Empiricism and the philosophy of mind', in his *Science, Perception, and Reality* (London: Routledge and Kegan Paul, 1963).
Will, F.: *Induction and Justification* (Ithaca, NY: Cornell University Press, 1974).

WILLIAM P. ALSTON

**Frege, Gottlob (1848–1925)** German philosopher and mathematician. Frege, professor of mathematics at the University of Jena, devoted his intellectual life to a single, narrowly circumscribed project: the reduction of arithmetic to pure logic (*see* LOGICISM). In the attempt to implement this programme, however, Frege found himself increasingly forced to confront the broader philosophical problems which it raised: problems concerning the nature of logic, language, meaning and the mind. As a result he formulated theories concerning identity, truth, validity, existence, sense, reference, generality, logical form, number, objects, concepts, thoughts and judgements. His importance extends, therefore, far beyond the narrow confines of the foundations of arithmetic: his influence on Carnap, Russell and Wittgenstein was formative, for example, and his significance within contemporary Anglo-American philosophy is second to none. He is now widely viewed as the father of analytic philosophy.

Broadly speaking, Frege's significance for epistemology is twofold. On the one hand, the revolution that he inaugurated inevitably assigns a less central role to epistemological considerations than that typically assigned to them in post-Cartesian philosophy. As Dummett has emphasized, one of the hallmarks of post-Fregean, 'analytic' philosophy is that questions concerning the nature of our knowledge or the justification of our beliefs are displaced from the centre of the philosophical stage by questions concerning meaning and understanding (*see* Dummett, 1973, pp. 665–70). For Frege and those who follow him, in other words, one must first ask how it is possible even to mean, or say, or grasp the thought that *p*; and only when an adequate answer to this fundamental question has been formulated is one justified in turning to such intrinsically subsidiary questions as whether we genuinely know that *p*, whether our belief that *p* is justified, and so forth. From within this perspective, then, issues concerning the nature of thoughts – their structure, their truth-value, their expressibility in language and their intelligibility – are prior to and independent of issues in epistemology. More radically, indeed, they are also prior to and independent of issues in psychology and the philosophy of mind; for although thinking and judging are mental acts, there is, in Frege's view, nothing subjective or psychological about *what* we think and judge (*see* PSYCHOLOGISM).

On the other hand, Frege made a number of contributions within epistemology, most notably via the analysis he provided of our cognitive access to abstract objects in general, and to numbers in particular. Abstract objects are self-subsistent entities that possess no spatio-temporal properties and are devoid of causal powers. They must, it seems, be imperceptible; and if so, then the problem immediately arises as to how we can have any contact with, or knowledge of, them.

Frege's solution was this. Our knowledge of abstract objects is not concerned with 'objects which we come to know as something alien from without through the medium of the senses, but with objects given directly to our reason and, as its nearest kin, utterly transparent to it' (Frege, 1884, p. 115). The most fundamental factor in our knowledge of any object, whether abstract or concrete, is our grasp of its identity condition – our knowledge of which object it is. In the case of abstract objects, then, we must provide identity conditions which, while accessible to reason, do not depend upon any sensory awareness of those objects. Accordingly, Frege introduces a procedure of abstraction which is designed to transform an equivalence relation (i.e. one that is transitive, reflexive and symmetrical) holding between empirical entities, into a strict identity holding between abstract objects (*see* Frege, 1884, p. 74). If *R* is an equivalence relation, and if *a* and *b* are empirical objects, then we can transform the statement '*aRb*' into one of the form '*f(a)* = *f(b)*', where the terms '*f(a)*' and '*f(b)*' will refer to abstract objects. For example, if line *a* is parallel to line *b*, then we are entitled to say: the direction of *a* is identical with the direction of *b*. Or again, if there are as many red things on the table as there are blue, then we can say: the number of red things is identical with the number of blue things. These identity statements specify identity conditions for abstract objects (directions and numbers, respectively); and these statements are intelligible because they make the same claim as the statements from which they are abstracted, and which mention only perceptible objects and the empirically ascertainable relations that hold between them. In this way, according to Frege, we can begin to have knowledge of abstract objects in spite of the fact that we can have no intuitions or perceptions of them.

See also ANALYTICITY; INTUITION AND
DEDUCTION.

WRITINGS

*Die Grundlagen der Arithmetik* (Breslau: 1884);
trans. J.L. Austin, *The Foundations of Arith-
metic* (Oxford: Blackwell, 1974).
'Über Sinn und Bedeutung', *Zeitschrift für
Philosophie und philosophische Kritik* 100
(1892), 25–50; trans. P.T. Geach and M.
Black, 'On sense and reference', in *Transla-
tions from the Philosophical Writings of Gottlob
Frege* (Oxford: Blackwell, 1960), 56–78.
'Der Gedanke. Eine logische Untersuchung',
*Beiträge zur Philosophie des deutschen Idealis-
mus* I (1918), 58–77; trans. P.T. Geach and
R.H. Stoothoff, 'Thoughts', in *Logical Inves-
tigations* (Oxford: Blackwell, 1977), 1–30.

BIBLIOGRAPHY

Bell, D.: *Frege's Theory of Judgement* (Oxford:
Clarendon Press, 1979).
Dummett, M.A.E.: *Frege: Philosophy of Language*
(London: Duckworth, 1973).
Wright, C.: *Frege's Conception of Numbers as
Objects* (Aberdeen: Aberdeen University
Press, 1983).

DAVID BELL

**Freud, Sigmund (1856–1939)** Austrian
founder of psychoanalysis, who worked in
Vienna until the Nazi occupation of 1938; he
died in London. Psychoanalysis can be linked
with the Kantian tradition in epistemology,
as indicating how hypotheses about mental
representation cast light on general features
and limits of knowledge. Freud held that the
rationally connected motives of which we are
aware (including beliefs and desires) are
underlain and shaped by others, apparently
formed in infancy, which are pre-rational,
only proto-realistic, and concerned with
basic bodily processes. These motives cause
*wish-fulfilments*, that is, representations of
situations in which they are satisfied; and
their operation is traceable in terms of *unconscious phantasy* (cf. Segal, 1978, ch. 2; and for
italicized terms generally, *see* Laplanche and
Pontalis, 1973).

For example, some common epistemic
phantasies can be illustrated by the following
dream. A teacher had been greatly surprised
when a devoted pupil – who had made a
special effort to be taught by him, and was
trying hard to master his ideas – suddenly
revealed a desire to suck his penis. That night
he dreamt that *a lamb had come to suck milk
from his finger*. . . It was clear to him that the
suckling in his dream represented his
teaching, the lamb his pupil who had come to
imbibe his ideas, and his milk-giving finger
the penis this pupil had wanted to suck.

The dream can be seen as representing the
fulfilment both of a specific sexual wish, and
also of phantasies in which the dreamer
compared his teaching with bodily activities,
both sexual and nurturing, and his ideas
with semen and milk. In particular, in this
context he represented his penis as fulfilling
the role of a feeding breast. This was a
phantasy related to his rivalry with women;
and it was plainly continuous with many of
his conscious beliefs, including a conviction
he often emphasized, that women were
inferior because less creative than men.

At a personal level such phantasies are
maintained not because they correspond
with reality but because they obscure it; and
they in turn sustain a variety of other motives
which share this function. Phantasies of this
kind can implement *projection*, since they not
only wishfully satisfy, but also enable one to
represent oneself as lacking and others as
having aspects and feelings which are painful
to contemplate, envious, destructive, and so
forth. Projective phantasies seem to play a
particularly significant role in development,
and hence in the unconscious organization of
adult psychic and social life. (Thus the activities of teacher and pupil above were apparently based on phantasies about the phallic
transmission of knowledge, which could also
serve to project feelings of lack, envy, etc. into
women, as well as on their conscious beliefs.)

The role of projection thus contrasts with
the traditional idea that we construct our
representation of OTHER MINDS by
analogy with what we know of ourselves
through introspection (*see* ARGUMENT
FROM ANALOGY). Rather, a main part of

our construction consists in systematically attributing to others motives which we will *not* recognize in ourselves. Such projection, however, can both subserve social co-ordination and attain a measure of accuracy. This is sometimes fairly clearly exemplified in the attitudes of rival groups, which achieve internal cohesion on the basis of similar projective phantasies, and are hence disposed to mutual distrust. Where their projections mirror one another closely, each group may construct a very full picture of the malignancy of the other, while thereby remaining ignorant as to its own. (Hence, paradoxically, it is often only when such motives have been sufficiently disowned that they can be acted on, with the full ferocity justified by imaginary innocence and purity.)

Phantasy and belief are mutually sustaining, so that beliefs are apt to serve purposes of misrepresentation even when true, and to be maintained for this role alone when false. Hence the study of phantasy, and the avoidance of error based on it, seems a serious epistemological concern. More generally, psychoanalysis suggests that our picture of the world, like the language we speak, is in good part that which an elaborate co-ordina-tion of psychological mechanisms (including projection) requires us to construct. Hence the nature and working of our representations are best understood in light of the mechanisms underlying them; and such accuracy as they do achieve is often inexplicable, except as the result of a co-ordination of representations and objects established by evolution.

WRITINGS

*Standard Edition of the Complete Psychological Works of Sigmund Freud* (London: Hogarth, 1955).

BIBLIOGRAPHY

Laplanche, J. and Pontalis, J.-B.: *The Language of Psychoanalysis* (London: Hogarth, 1987).
Neu, J.: *The Cambridge Companion to Freud* (Cambridge: Cambridge University Press, 1991).
Segal, H.: *Introduction to the Work of Melanie Klein* (London: Hogarth, 1987).
Wollheim, R.: *Freud* (London: Fontana, 1971); a philosophically informed account of Freud's work.

JIM HOPKINS

# G

Gadamer, Hans-Georg (1900–) German philosopher. Hermeneutics traditionally was a theory of the interpretation of meaning principally concerned with biblical exegesis. Gadamer's project has been to develop a more generalized philosophical HERMENEUTICS which can give an account of the conditions of all interpretation. And to the extent that all understanding involves an act of interpretation, this account will apply to understanding in general. Gadamer takes as his point of departure a recognition of the embeddedness of all inquiry in language and in history. Knowers operate within what he calls a horizon which includes their prejudices or pre-judgements, explicit and implicit conceptual commitments, and their situated frame of reference, and is both the enabling condition for and the constraint upon knowledge. Given this, the meaning of both reason and truth must be rethought. Reason cannot be counterposed to prejudice or the authority of tradition if we are incapable of transcending tradition (in part because we are incapable of transcending linguisticality) and if we can engage in knowing only within the confines of tradition's historical trajectory (even while this trajectory is constantly being transformed). And truth cannot be the appropriation of external, timeless facts when it only emerges in dialogic encounters between specific elements, each of which has a horizon that contributes to its formation. On Gadamer's view, then, the Cartesian ontology of the knowing process presents an OBJECTIVIST picture which is most vulnerable to the arbitrariness of authority, since it assumes a degree of control and isolation on the part of the subject that simply does not obtain. An acknowledgement of our historical and linguistic embeddedness will require a new ontology of knowing and a new account of truth, but will improve our knowledge at least about the nature of knowledge itself.

See also CONTINENTAL EPISTEMOLOGY; HEGEL; SOCIAL SCIENCE.

## WRITINGS

Kleine Schriften 3 vols (Tübingen: J.C.B. Mohr, 1967); partially trans. D. Linge Philosophical Hermeneutics (Berkeley: University of California Press, 1976).
Wahrheit und Methode (Tübingen: J.C.B. Mohr, 1960); Truth and Method (New York: Seabury Press, 1975).

LINDA ALCOFF

genetic epistemology The study of the epistemic transitions from less adequate epistemic states to more advanced ones. Construed even more broadly as a theory of the development, evolution, genesis or history of knowledge, one can find important contributions to genetic epistemology by Aristotle, Descartes, Locke, Hume, Vico, Condorcet, Kant, Fichte, Hegel, Marx, Spencer, Comte, Bergson, Dewey, Cassirer, Wittgenstein, Brunschvicg, Husserl, Popper, Kuhn, Lakatos, Toulmin and a wealth of contemporary philosophers. But aside from the work of some non-philosophers, there has been no systematic attempt to outline the major features of this theory of knowledge and to define its distinctive nature.

All epistemologies are concerned with how knowledge changes over time. But no one yet has adequately distinguished the characteristics marking off the differences between genetic epistemology, EVOLUTIONARY EPISTEMOLOGY, developmental epistemology and historical epistemology. Further-more, it remains unclear how current philos-ophy of science (*see* NATURAL SCIENCE), which is largely committed to an historically-based approach (and hence concerned with the growth of scientific knowledge) is related to the traditional epistemology of the indi-vidual subject whose knowledge changes over time. In addition, it remains unclear how both of these branches of the theory of knowledge are related to the psychology of knowledge, the SOCIOLOGY OF KNOWLEDGE and the history of knowledge. In short, as a distinct and well-defined discipline, genetic epistemology remains inchoate.

## THE FOUNDERS OF GENETIC EPISTEMOLOGY

The first explicit concern with the creation of a field called genetic epistemology can be ascribed to the philosopher-psychologist James Mark Baldwin (1861–1934). In addition to writing several works on the psychological growth of knowledge in the individual, his genetic epistemology is con-tained in his four-volume *magnum opus*: *Thought and Things: a Study of the Development and Meaning of Thought, or Genetic Logic* (1906–15), especially vol. 1 (*Genetic Theory of Knowledge*) and vol. 3 (*Genetic Epistemology*).

Although Baldwin was perhaps the origi-nator of 'genetic epistemology', it was surely the views of Jean Piaget (1896–1980) that have been most closely identified with this field. In fact, during his long career he wrote several major treatises explicitly devoted to characterizing the nature of genetic epistem-ology and its relation to philosophy and psy-chology; his most notable philosophical works include his 3-volume *Introduction à L'Epistémologie génétique* (1950), *Etudes Socio-logiques* (1967), his articles in *Logique et Con-naissance Scientifique* (1967) and *Insight and Illusions of Philosophy* (1971). Not surprisingly, many of the views of Baldwin can also be found in Piaget; unlike Baldwin, however, Piaget has been much more explicitly con-cerned with the philosophical basis of genetic epistemology (Kitchener, 1986).

## CONTEMPORARY GENETIC EPISTEMOLOGY

Although contemporary epistemologists and philosophers of science would not use the term genetic epistemology to characterize their views, many of them can be said to be engaged in constructing a theory of genetic epistemology. This applies to the work of individuals doing more traditional post-Gettier epistemology, to those concerned with BAYESIAN 'belief kinematics', to those working in EVOLUTIONARY EPISTE-MOLOGY, and to those philosophers of science concerned with constructing a theory of 'the growth of knowledge'. All of these contemporary philosophers are concerned, in one way or another, with describing and explaining how epistemic states (beliefs, theories, conceptual schemes, etc.) change over time. In so doing, they are tacitly con-cerned with constructing a genetic epistemol-ogy.

## NATURE AND SCOPE OF GENETIC EPISTEMOLOGY

Serious conceptual issues surround the defi-nition, nature, and scope of genetic epistem-ology. Perhaps no one would take issue over genetic epistemology, taken as the study of the growth of knowledge, but serious dis-agreements would arise over the philosophi-cal analysis of various details of this definition and over the connection between philosophy and psychology and the relation between ontogenesis and the history of science. Thus construed, the scope of genetic epistemology is so broad as to encompass all examples of the development of knowledge. This would include: *Ontogenesis* (the growth of knowlege in the individual person from birth to maturity), *History of Science* (the growth of [scientific] knowledge in historical cultures), *The anthropology (anthropogenesis) of knowl-edge* (the growth of knowledge in pre-literate ['primitive']) cultures, and *The biology (phylo-genesis) of knowledge* (the growth of knowl-edge during phylogenesis [from amoeba to humans]). It goes without saying that no one has constructed an adequate genetic epistem-ology to cover all these fields.

EPISTEMIC KINEMATICS AND DYNAMICS

By and large, the history of epistemology has been committed to the thesis that a complete description of the nature of knowledge consists of a set of logical relations between a belief (or set of beliefs) and an evidential statement (or set of evidential statements). This kind of logicism is still prevalent in twentieth-century epistemology (e.g. the traditional analysis of 'S knows that *p*'; *see* TRIPARTITE DEFINITION OF KNOWLEDGE), and philosophy of science (e.g. CARNAP'S theory of confirmation, and HEMPEL'S theory of EXPLANATION).

Genetic epistemology is fundamentally opposed to a logicist epistemology and, in place of it, advances a historical, historicist or dynamic theory of knowledge. Adopting the distinction in physics between 'kinematics' and 'dynamics', we can say that genetic epistemology includes, first, an *epistemic kinematics* and, secondly, an *epistemic dynamics*.

Any historically-oriented epistemology is concerned with how knowledge changes over time. Epistemic kinematics is concerned with *describing* the succession of these epistemic states over time: $S_1(t_1)$, $S_2(t_2)$, . . . $S_n(t_n)$. Each state can be construed as a stage in a larger sequence, characterized as a *stage law* of epistemic development: knowledge proceeds via stages of epistemic development, each stage possessing an underlying logical structure related to the preceding and succeeding stages in logically structured ways such that the entire sequence manifests progress in knowledge.

It is a fundamental assumption of genetic epistemology that changing epistemic states abide by certain rational (morphological) constraints, limiting the logical form any such trajectory may take. These constraints are both internal (constraints limiting its logical form) and external (constraints due to a changing evidential or informational basis).

Epistemic dynamics is concerned with explaining epistemic stage laws by reference to rational, epistemic factors – what are called (in the history of science) internalist explanations. (Psychological dynamics, by contrast, would explain such epistemic change by mentioning purely psychological facts and hence would be providing externalist explanations.)

Virtually all individuals concerned with the dynamics of epistemic change have offered (basically) the same explanation, whether it is called equilibrium, lack of dissonance, consistency or coherence (*see* COHERENTISM). Most frequently it has been called 'equilibrium'. Most generally we can say:

An epistemic state is in *equilibrium* if (1) there are actual or potential internal or external disturbances and (2) there are epistemic operatory transformations, such that these disturbances are compensated for and there is a return to the initial epistemic state (or goal-tending state) or such that these disturbances are averted.

(Clearly, there are degrees of equilibrium corresponding to the degree of adequacy of compensatory mechanisms.)

Equilibration can be used to explain epistemic change in the following sense: epistemic state $S_1$ at time $t_1$ changes into epistemic state $S_2$ at time $t_2$ because $S_2$ has more equilibrium than $S_1$ has. The same notion can be used to characterize the concept of rationality:

an epistemic state is *rational* if it is in equilibrium under all epistemic disturbances. (An epistemic state is rational to a degree corresponding to its degree of equilibrium.)

And

an epistemic stage law is *rational* if there is a progressive increase in its degree of equilibration.

Genetic epistemology is committed to providing epistemic explanations of belief revision; as such it offers internalist explanations, not externalist ones. Such explanations appear to be inescapably normative in nature. At the same time, however, genetic epistemology is thoroughly committed to a some version of NATURALISTIC EPISTEMOLOGY. How to reconcile these positions is one central issue facing contemporary genetic epistemologists and other naturalistic epistemologists. A closely related issue concerns the connection between PSYCHOLOGY AND EPISTEMOLOGY. Genetic epistemologists are committed to the thesis that empirical psychology is *relevant* to normative epistemology although precisely how remains controversial since it involves bridging the FACT/VALUE distinction in some way or reducing value to fact. All of these issues are clearly related.

## CRITICAL EVALUATION

Finally, something must be said of the current status of the programme of genetic epistemology. Most epistemologists have paid scant attention to it largely because they have mistakenly thought Piaget was merely doing child psychology, because they were unfamiliar with his major epistemological works in French, and because they held on to a strict separation of psychology and epistemology. Much of this is now changing, with the result that the programme of a genetic epistemology now seems more plausible. As mentioned earlier, this programme is very sketchy and needs further discussion, criticism and development.

Current issues that seem especially important in clarifying and developing this programme include:

1. The problematic nature of epistemic stages.
2. The tacit commitment to some kind of teleological notion of progress and to a cumulativity condition for the growth of knowledge.
3. The relevance of empirical psychology to normative epistemology.
4. The question of the social dimensions of knowledge and the reliance on a biological theory of knowledge.
5. The conceptual adequacy of key genetic epistemological concepts such as equilibrium.
6. The empirical adequacy of the psychological theory underlying genetic epistem-

ology and the question of whether another psychological theory, e.g., contemporary AI-based cognitive psychology, is not more adequate.

Although several individuals have raised serious objections to genetic epistemology on a variety of conceptual and empirical grounds, these objections do not seem insurmountable. Although still in its germinal stage, genetic epistemology appears to be an epistemological programme with considerable philosophical promise.

*See also* EVOLUTIONARY EPISTEMOLOGY.

### BIBLIOGRAPHY

Broughton, J.M. and Freeman-Moir, D.J. eds: *The Cognitive-Developmental Psychology of James Mark Baldwin* (Norwood: Ablex, 1981).
Hamlyn, D.: *Experience and the Growth of Understanding* (London: Routledge and Kegan Paul, 1978).
Haroutunian, S.: *Equilibrium in the Balance: A Study of Psychological Explanation* (New York: Springer-Verlag, 1983).
Jean Piaget Archives ed.: *Bibliographie Jean Piaget* (Geneva: Fondation Archives Jean Piaget, 1989); a complete bibliography of Piaget's works.
Kitchener, R.F.: 'Bibliography of philosophical work on Piaget', *Synthese* 65 (1985), 139–52.
Kitchener, R.F.: *Piaget's Theory of Knowledge: Genetic Epistemology and Scientific Reason* (New Haven: Yale University Press, 1986).
Mischel, T. ed.: *Cognitive Development and Epistemology* (New York: Academic, 1971).
Rotman, B.: *Jean Piaget: Psychologist of the Real* (Ithaca, NY: Cornell University Press, 1977).
Russell, J.: *The Acquisition of Knowledge* (New York: St. Martin's, 1978).
Seltman, M. and Seltman, P.: *Piaget's Logic: a Critique of Genetic Epistemology* (London: Allen and Unwin, 1985).

RICHARD F. KITCHENER

**genetic fallacy** The tactic of attacking the origin or original context of some practice, concept or argument that is instrumental to an opponent's point of view, in an attempt to discredit that point of view unfairly. For example: 'The wedding ring originated from the ankle chain used by men to confine their wives; therefore, wearing a wedding ring is a sexist (bad) practice.' Arguments based on origins are not always fallacious, but this kind of argument can be used as a sophistical tactic to try to transfer negative connotations in lieu of going into the real merits of an argument or practice.

*See Argumentum ad Hominem* in INFORMAL FALLACIES.

BIBLIOGRAPHY

Damer, T.E.: *Attacking Faulty Reasoning* (Belmont: Wadsworth, 1980).
Pirie, M.: *The Book of the Fallacy* (London: Routledge, 1985).

DOUGLAS N. WALTON

**geometry**  At the hands of the early Greeks, especially Euclid (*c.*300 BC), geometry achieved a degree of perfection unmatched by any other science prior to the modern period. Ancient and medieval astronomy, although extensively pursued, was little more than applied geometry, for it lacked an adequate dynamical explanation of the phenomena it studied. Indeed, not until Newton's *Principia* (1687) did any scientific body of knowledge equal Euclid's *Elements* in fertility, scope, rigour, or systematic development. For almost exactly two millennia, Euclidean geometry constituted *the* paradigm of systematic scientific knowledge. The import of this fact for the history of philosophy would be hard to overrate.

Geometry did not originate with Euclid; as every school-child knows, the ancient Egyptians used geometry as a practical art in building pyramids and surveying land. At some time – perhaps about 600 BC – the Greeks began to transform this art into a rigorous deductive science. Certainly by PLATO'S time (*c.*429–347 BC) it had reached a high level of sophistication, and Plato was duly impressed. According to legend, a sign at the entrance to his ACADEMY read, 'Let no one enter here who does not know geometry.'

Plato realized that, strictly speaking, geometry is not *about* physical things; its subject matter consists of such abstract entities as perfect straight lines, perfect circles, and perfect triangles. In relation to his famous metaphor of the divided line, the objects of geometry belong, not to the material world of Becoming, but to the ideal world of Being. Geometry thus provides the entrance to Plato's ideal realm of the forms. Knowledge of the forms comes, not from sense experience, but from human thought. However, since physical things 'participate' in the forms, geometry provides information that is useful for practical affairs. Thus, Plato offered an early version of the doctrine, later formulated by Kant, that there is such a thing as synthetic a priori knowledge (*see* KANT).

Euclid apparently originated the idea that all of the truths of geometry could be deduced from a small number of basic assumptions; in so doing, he invented the axiomatic method, which still pervades mathematics and logic. We do not know how Euclid regarded his postulates (whether they are called 'postulates' or 'axioms' is unimportant); it is clear that many of his successors through the ages took them to be self-evident truths. The picture of scientific knowledge that emerges is a body of propositions all of which are rigorously deduced from premises that are evident to reason (*see* AXIOMATICS, RATIONALISM).

It is often said that DESCARTES is the first modern philosopher; with the invention of analytic geometry, he also furnished an epoch-making contribution to mathematics. The affinity of his philosophical thought to geometry is manifest. In his work on method, the procedure he recommends is just what would be appropriate for discovering and proving geometrical propositions, but it bears hardly any resemblance to the methods of the empirical sciences. In the *Meditations*, where he builds his philosophical system from scratch, he seeks and finds an *indubitable* proposition, the COGITO ('I think, therefore, I exist'), on which to found it. He appeals to principles *evident to the natural light of reason* in his a priori 'proofs' of the existence of God. He emphasizes the certainty of clear and distinct ideas. All of this strongly suggests the kind of self-evident certainty that was often accorded to the axioms of geometry. His metaphysical view that *extension* is the essence of matter also reveals the deep influence of geometry upon his philosophy.

When KANT took up the question of synthetic a priori knowledge, he did not have to linger over the question of whether synthetic A PRIORI knowledge exists. Euclidean geometry obviously filled the bill. Its propositions can be established by pure reason, and they inform us about the structure of the physical space of our universe and of the spatial relationships among the entities within it. The serious question was how such knowledge is possible. He saw Euclidean geometry as a necessary form of spatial intuition – that is, a framework for the visualization of things and events in the physical world. If scientific knowledge is to be possible at all, this framework is indispensable.

Euclid's geometry was based on five postulates:

P1 A straight line can be drawn between any two points.

P2 A finite straight line can be extended continuously in a straight line.

P3 A circle can be drawn with any centre and any radius.

P4 All right angles are equal to one another.

P5 Given a straight line and a point not on that line, there is one and only one line through that point parallel to the given line. (This form, known as Playfair's axiom, is not Euclid's fifth postulate but is equivalent to it; it has the advantage of focusing directly on the question of parallelism.)

Throughout the centuries, from antiquity to the beginning of the nineteenth century, there had been numerous attempts to prove the fifth postulate – perhaps it was not considered quite as self-evident as the other four. At about the time of Kant's death, in the early years of the nineteenth century, various mathematicians began to realize that the parallel postulate is not a necessary truth, and the development of non-Euclidean geometry began. In all probability, Carl Friedrich Gauss was the first to take this step, but he did not publish this work. His excuse was that he did not want to listen to the braying of the asses – i.e. the cries of outrage that would result were he to make public his denial of the parallel postulate. About twenty years later, Johann Bolyai and Nikolai Ivanovich Lobachevski developed and published systems of geometry in which Playfair's axiom was replaced by the postulate that through the given point there is more than one parallel. Although Euclid's first four postulates are sufficient to prove that there is at least one parallel, Georg F.B. Riemann, about the middle of the nineteenth century, showed how to construct a non-Euclidean geometry without parallels by making minor modifications of the first four postulates.

By the mid-nineteenth century, then, there existed three types of geometry: (1) no parallels, (2) one parallel, and (3) more than one parallel. The question of the logical consistency of the non-Euclidean geometries naturally arises, and it was answered by a proof of relative consistency. Although it is impossible to demonstrate the absolute consistency of any of these geometries it was shown that all three types stand or fall together. If either type of non-Euclidean geometry contains a contradiction so does Euclidean geometry.

The discovery of non-Euclidean geometries that are on a par with Euclidean geometry with respect to logical consistency constituted an intellectual revolution perhaps as profound as the Copernican Revolution. No longer could one point to a unique geometry as the only possible representation of physical space. It should be emphasized, however, that Kant's doctrine of the synthetic a priori was *not* thereby refuted. If Euclidean geometry were the only logically consistent geometry, then it would seem to be *analytic a priori* rather than *synthetic a priori*. Kant's view was not that Euclidean geometry is logically privileged, but rather, that it is epistemologically privileged (as a *necessary* form of visualization).

Various philosophers addressed the epistemological status of geometry. Around the turn of the twentieth century, Henri Poincaré argued that the choice of a geometry to describe physical space has a large component of convention; he believed, however, that we will always choose Euclidean geometry to describe our world because it is simpler than the non-Euclidean ones. Later in this century, when Einstein employed non-Euclidean geometry in formulating his general theory of relativity, he advocated the rejection of Euclidean geometry on the ground that the total system including both geometry and physics is simpler, even though Euclidean geometry by itself is simpler than non-Euclidean geometry. The classic philosophical work on this topic is by Hans REICHENBACH.

Another result of the emergence of non-Euclidean geometry was a careful study of the nature of axiomatic systems. Although Euclid's work was truly remarkable it did not meet modern standards of logical rigour. David Hilbert, for example, formalized both Euclidean and non-Euclidean geometries according to much more exacting standards. Hilbert's work led to the position known as *formalism* in the philosophy of mathematics.

In the light of developments since the discovery of non-Euclidean geometries, we must distinguish between *pure* geometry and *applied* geometry. A pure geometry is simply an uninterpreted axiomatic system that, in and of itself, has no bearing on the nature of physical space. It is, however, a priori. An applied geometry is a discription of some aspect of physical reality, but it is not a priori. It is, however, synthetic. There is no geometry that is both synthetic and a priori.

*See also* ANALYTICITY; MATHEMATICAL KNOWLEDGE.

BIBLIOGRAPHY

Cajori, F.: *Sir Isaac Newton's Mathematical Principles of Natural Philosophy and his System of the World* (Berkeley: University of California Press, 1947).

Friedman, M.: *Foundations of Space–Time Theories* (Princeton: Princeton University Press, 1983).

Grünbaum, A.: *Philosophic Problems of Space and Time* 2nd edn (Dordrecht: Reidel, 1974).

Heath, Sir Thomas L.: *The Thirteen Books of Euclid's Elements* (New York: Dover Publications, 1956).

Hilbert, D.: *Foundations of Geometry* 2nd edn (LaSalle: Open Court, 1971).

Poincaré, H.: *Science and Hypothesis* (New York: Dover, 1952).

Reichenbach, H.: *The Philosophy of Space and Time* (New York: Dover, 1958).

Salmon, W.C.: *Space, Time, and Motion: A Philosophical Introduction* (Encino: Dickenson, 1975).

WESLEY C. SALMON

**Gettier problem** The so-called 'standard analysis' of propositional knowledge, suggested by Plato and Kant among others, implies that if one has a justified true belief that *p*, then one knows that *p*. (*see* TRIPARTITE DEFINITION OF KNOWLEDGE). In 1963 Edmund Gettier published two counterexamples to this implication of the standard analysis. In essence, they are:

(1) Smith and Jones have applied for the same job. Smith is justified in believing that (a) Jones will get the job, and that (b) Jones has ten coins in his pocket. On the basis of (a) and (b) Smith infers, and thus is justified in believing, that (c) the person who will get the job has ten coins in his pocket. At it turns out, Smith himself will get the job, and he also happens to have ten coins in his pocket. So, although Smith is justified in believing the true proposition (c), Smith does not know (c).

(2) Smith is justified in believing the false proposition that (a) Jones owns a Ford. On the basis of (a) Smith infers, and thus is justified in believing, that (b) either Jones owns a Ford or Brown is in Barcelona. As it turns out, Brown is in Barcelona, and so (b) is true. So although Smith is justified in believing the true proposition (b), Smith does not know (b).

Gettier's counterexamples are thus cases where one has justified true belief that *p*, but lacks knowledge that *p*. The *Gettier problem* is the problem of finding a modification of, or an alternative to, the standard justified-true-belief analysis of knowledge that avoids counterexamples like Gettier's. Some philosophers have suggested that Gettier-style counterexamples are defective owing to their reliance on the false principle that false propositions can justify one's belief in other propositions. But there are examples much like Gettier's that do not depend on this allegedly false principle. Here is one example inspired by Keith Lehrer and Richard Feldman:

(3) Suppose Smith knows the following proposition, *m*: Jones, whom Smith has always found to be reliable and whom Smith has no reason to distrust now, has told Smith, his office-mate, that *p*: He, Jones, owns a Ford. Suppose also that Jones has told Smith that *p* only because of a state of hypnosis Jones is in, and that *p* is true only because, unknown to himself, Jones has won a Ford in a lottery since entering the state of hypnosis. And suppose further that Smith deduces from *m* its existential generalization, *q*: There is someone, whom Smith has always found to be reliable and whom Smith has no reason to distrust now, who has told Smith, his office-mate, that he owns a Ford. Smith, then, knows that *q*, since he has correctly deduced *q* from *m*, which he also knows. But suppose also that on the basis of his knowledge that *q*, Smith believes that *r*: Someone in the office owns a Ford. Under these conditions, Smith has justified true belief that *r*, knows his evidence for *r*, but does not know that *r*.

Gettier-style examples of this sort have proven especially difficult for attempts to analyse the concept of PROPOSITIONAL KNOWLEDGE.

The history of attempted solutions to the Gettier problem is complex and open-ended; it has not produced consensus on any solution. Many philosophers hold, in light of Gettier-style examples, that propositional knowledge requires a fourth condition, beyond the justification, truth and belief conditions. Although no particular fourth condition enjoys widespread endorsement, there are some prominent general proposals in circulation. One sort of proposed modification, the so-called *defeasibility analysis*, requires that the justification appropriate to knowledge be 'undefeated' in the general sense that some appropriate subjunctive conditional

concerning genuine defeaters of justification be true of that justification. One straightforward defeasibility fourth condition, for instance, requires of Smith's knowing that *p* that there be no true proposition *q*, such that if *q* became justified for Smith, *p* would no longer be justified for Smith (*see* the articles by Lehrer and Paxson, and by Swain, in Pappas and Swain, 1978). A different prominent modification requires that the actual justification for a true belief qualifying as knowledge not depend in a specified way on any falsehood (*see* Armstrong, 1973). The details proposed to elaborate such approaches have met with considerable controversy.

My own proposed solution to the Gettier problem relies on a fourth condition of evidential truth-sustenance. More specifically, for a person, S, to have knowledge that *p* on justifying evidence *e*, *e* must be truth-sustained in this sense: for every true proposition *t* that, when conjoined with *e*, undermines S's justification for *p* on *e*, there is a true proposition, *t'*, that, when conjoined with *e* & *t*, restores the justification of *p* for S in a way that S is actually justified in believing that *p*. The gist of my solution, put roughly, is that propositional knowledge requires justified true belief that is sustained by the collective totality of truths. I have argued in *Knowledge and Evidence* that this approach handles not only such Gettier-style examples as (1)–(3), but various others as well.

Three features of my proposed solution merit emphasis. First, it avoids a subjunctive conditional in its fourth condition, and so escapes some difficult problems facing the use of such a conditional in an analysis of knowledge. Second, it allows for non-deductive justifying evidence as a component of propositional knowledge. An adequacy condition on an analysis of knowledge is that it not restrict justifying evidence to relations of deductive support. Third, my proposed solution is sufficiently flexible to handle cases describable as follows:

(4) Smith has a justified true belief that *p*, but there is a true proposition, *t*, which undermines Smith's justification for *p* when conjoined with it, and which is such that it is

either physically or humanly impossible for Smith to be justified in believing that *t*.

Examples represented by (4) suggest that we should countenance varying strengths in notions of propositional knowledge. These strengths are determined by accessibility qualifications on the set of relevant knowledge-precluding underminers. A very demanding concept of knowledge assumes that it need only be logically possible for a knower to believe a knowledge-precluding underminer. Less demanding concepts assume that it must be physically or humanly possible for a knower to believe knowledge-precluding underminers. But even such less demanding concepts of knowledge need to rely on a notion of truth-sustained evidence if they are to survive a threatening range of Gettier-style examples. Given my solution, the needed fourth condition for a notion of knowledge is not a function simply of the evidence a knower actually possesses.

The highly controversial aftermath of Gettier's original counterexamples has left some philosophers doubtful of the real philosophical significance of the Gettier problem. Such doubt, however, seems misplaced. One fundamental branch of epistemology seeks understanding of the nature of propositional knowledge. And our understanding exactly what propositional knowledge is essentially involves our having a Gettier-resistant analysis of such knowledge. If our analysis is not Gettier-resistant, we will lack an exact understanding of what propositional knowledge is. It is epistemologically important, therefore, to have a defensible solution to the Gettier problem, however demanding such a solution is.

*See also* CAUSAL THEORIES; COHERENTISM; PROPOSITIONAL KNOWLEDGE; RELIABILISM.

BIBLIOGRAPHY

Armstrong, D.M.: *Belief, Truth, and Knowledge* (Cambridge: Cambridge University Press, 1973).
Chisholm, R.M.: *Theory of Knowledge* 3rd edn (Englewood Cliffs: Prentice-Hall, 1989).
Conee, E.: 'Why solve the Gettier problem?', in *Philosophical Analysis* ed. D. Austin (Dordrecht: Kluwer, 1988), 55–8.
Feldman, R.: 'An alleged defect in Gettier counter-examples', *Australasian Journal of Philosophy* 52 (1974), 68–9.
Gettier, E.L.: 'Is justified true belief knowledge?', *Analysis* 23 (1963), 121–3.
Lehrer, K.: *Theory of Knowledge* (Boulder: Westview Press, 1990).
Moser, P.K.: *Knowledge and Evidence* (Cambridge: Cambridge University Press, 1989).
Moser, P.K. and van der Nat, A. eds: *Human Knowledge: Classical and Contemporary Approaches* (New York: Oxford University Press, 1987).
Pappas, G.S. and Swain, M. eds: *Essays on Knowledge and Justification* (Ithaca, NY: Cornell University Press, 1978).
Roth, M.D. and Galis, L. eds: *Knowing: Essays in the Analysis of Knowledge* (New York: Random House, 1970).
Shope, R.K.: *The Analysis of Knowing* (Princeton: Princeton University Press, 1983).

PAUL K. MOSER

**given, the** The concept of the given refers to the immediate apprehension of the contents of sense experience, expressed in first person, present tense reports of appearances. Apprehension of the given is seen as immediate both in a causal sense, since it lacks the usual causal chain involved in perceiving real qualities of physical objects, and in an epistemic sense, since judgements expressing it are justified independently of all other beliefs and evidence. Some proponents of the idea of the given maintain that its apprehension is absolutely CERTAIN: INFALLIBLE, INCORRIGIBLE and INDUBITABLE. It has been claimed also that a subject is omniscient with regard to the given: if a property appears, then the subject knows this.

The doctrine dates back at least to DESCARTES, who argued in *Meditation II* that it was beyond all possible doubt and error that he seemed to see light, hear noise, and so on. The empiricists added the claim that the mind is passive in receiving sense impressions, so that there is no subjective contamination or distortion here (even though the states apprehended are mental). The idea was taken up in

159

twentieth-century epistemology by C.I. LEWIS and A.J. AYER, among others, who appealed to the given as the foundation for all empirical knowledge (see EMPIRICISM). Since beliefs expressing only the given were held to be certain and justified in themselves, they could serve as solid foundations.

There are two main arguments to the conclusion that foundations for knowledge are required, and one argument that such foundations must be certain. The first argument for foundations is THE INFINITE REGRESS ARGUMENT. It points out that beliefs justified only in relation to others are justified only if those others are also. This fact is held to create a regress that can be terminated only by beliefs justified independently of all others. The argument ignores the possibility of mutually supportive beliefs, however, and so it is not sound.

The second argument for the need for foundations is sound. It appeals to the possibility of incompatible but fully coherent systems of belief, only one of which could be completely true. In light of this possibility, coherence cannot suffice for complete justification (see COHERENTISM). Without some independent indication that some of the beliefs within a coherent system are true, coherence in itself is no indication of truth. Fairy stories can cohere. But our criteria for justification must indicate to us the probable truth of our beliefs. Hence, within any system of beliefs there must be some privileged class with which others must cohere to be justified. In the case of empirical knowledge, such privileged beliefs must represent the point of contact between subject and world: they must originate in perception. When challenged, however, we justify our ordinary perceptual beliefs about physical properties by appeal to beliefs about appearances. The latter seem more suitable as foundations, since there is no class of more certain perceptual beliefs to which we appeal for their justification.

The argument that foundations must be certain was offered by LEWIS (1946). He held that no propositions can be probable unless some are certain. If the probability of all propositions or beliefs were relative to

evidence expressed in others, and if these relations were linear, then any regress would apparently have to terminate in propositions or beliefs that are certain. But Lewis shows neither that such relations must be linear nor that regresses cannot terminate in beliefs that are merely probable or justified in themselves without being certain or infallible.

Arguments against the idea of the given originate with KANT, who argues in Book I of the *Transcendental Analytic* that percepts without concepts do not yet constitute any form of knowing. Being non-epistemic, they presumably cannot serve as epistemic foundations. Once we recognize that we must apply concepts of properties to appearances and formulate beliefs utilizing those concepts before the appearances can play any epistemic role, it becomes more plausible that such beliefs are fallible. The argument was developed in this century by Wilfrid SELLARS (1963). According to him, the idea of the given involves a confusion between sensing particulars (having sense impressions), which is non-epistemic, and having non-inferential knowledge of propositions referring to appearances. The former may be necessary for acquiring perceptual knowledge, but it is not itself a primitive kind of knowing. Its being non-epistemic renders it immune from error, but also unsuitable for epistemological foundations. The latter, non-inferential perceptual knowledge, is fallible, requiring concepts acquired through trained responses to public physical objects.

The contention that even reports of appearances are fallible can be supported from several directions. First, it seems doubtful that we can look beyond our beliefs to compare them with an unconceptualized reality, whether mental or physical. Second, to judge that anything, including an appearance, is F, we must remember which property F is, and memory is admitted by all to be fallible. Our ascribing F is normally not explicitly comparative, but its correctness requires memory nevertheless, at least if we intend to ascribe a reinstantiable property. We must apply the concept of F consistently, and it seems always at least logically possible to apply it inconsistently. If the latter is not possible, if, for example, I intend in referring to an appearance merely to pick out demonstratively whatever property appears, then I seem not to be expressing a genuine belief. My apprehension of the appearance will not justify any other beliefs. Once more it will be unsuitable as an epistemological foundation.

AYER (1950) sought to distinguish propositions expressing the given not by their infallibility, but by the alleged fact that grasping their meanings suffices for knowing their truth. But this will be so only if the terms of such propositions have the sort of purely demonstrative meaning just discussed, and so only if the propositions fail to express beliefs that could ground others. If one uses genuine predicates, for example C# as applied to tones, then one may grasp their meaning and yet be unsure in their application, even if one limits that application to appearances. Limiting claims to appearances eliminates one major source of error in claims about physical objects – appearances cannot appear other than they are. Ayer's requirement of grasping meaning eliminates a second source of error, conceptual confusion. But a third major source, misclassification, is genuine and can obtain in this limited domain, even when Ayer's requirement is satisfied.

Any proponent of the given faces the following dilemma. If the terms used in statements expressing its apprehension are purely demonstrative, then such statements (assuming they are statements) are certain, but fail to express beliefs that could serve as foundations for knowledge. If what is expressed is not awareness of genuine properties, then the awareness does not justify its subject in believing anything else. But if statements about what appears use genuine predicates that apply to reinstantiable properties, then beliefs expressed cannot be infallible and understanding will not suffice for truth or knowledge. COHERENTISTS would add that such genuine beliefs stand in need of justification themselves and so cannot be foundations.

Contemporary FOUNDATIONALISTS deny the coherentists' claim while eschewing the claim that foundations, in the form of reports about appearances, are infallible. They seek alternatives to the given as foundations. Although arguments against infallibility are sound, other objections to the idea of foundations are not. That concepts of objective properties are learned prior to concepts of appearances, for example, implies neither that claims about appearances are less certain than claims about objective properties, nor that the latter are prior in chains of justification. That there can be no knowledge prior to the acquisition and consistent application of concepts allows for propositions whose truth requires only consistent application of concepts, and this may be so for some claims about appearances.

Coherentists will claim that a subject requires evidence that he applies concepts consistently, that he is able, for example, consistently to distinguish red from other colours that appear. Beliefs about red appearances could not then be justified independently of other beliefs expressing that evidence. To save that part of the doctrine of the given that holds beliefs about appearances to be self-justified, we require an account of how such justification is possible, how some beliefs about appearances can be justified without appeal to evidence. Some foundationalists simply assert such warrant as derived from experience; but, unlike appeals to certainty by proponents of the given, this assertion seem *ad hoc*.

A better strategy is to tie an account of self-justification to a broader exposition of epistemic warrant. One such account sees justification as a kind of inference to the best explanation. A belief is shown to be justified if its truth is shown to be part of the best explanation for why it is held. A belief is self-justified if the best explanation for it is its truth alone (Goldman, 1988). The best explanation for my belief that I am appeared to redly may be that I am. Such accounts seek to ground knowledge in perceptual experience without appealing to an infallible given, now universally dismissed.

*See also* ARGUMENT FROM ILLUSION; CERTAINTY; EXPERIENCE; HEIDEGGER; HERMENEUTICS; KNOWLEDGE BY ACQUAINTANCE/

BY DESCRIPTION; NIETZSCHE; PROTOCOL SENTEN-
CES; SENSATION/COGNITION.

BIBLIOGRAPHY

Aune, B.: *Knowledge, Mind, and Nature* (New
York: Random House, 1967), ch. 2.
Ayer, A.J.: 'Basic propositions', in *Philosophical
Analysis* ed. M. Black (Englewood Cliffs: Pren-
tice-Hall, 1950), 60–74.
BonJour, L.: *The Structure of Empirical Knowledge*
(Cambridge, MA: Harvard University Press,
1985), ch. 4.
Firth, R.: 'The anatomy of certainty', *Philosophi-
cal Review* 76 (1967), 3–27.
Goldman, A.: *Empirical Knowledge* (Berkeley:
University of California Press, 1988), Part II.
Goodman, N.: 'Sense and certainty', in his
*Problems and Projects* (Indianapolis: Hackett,
1972), 60–8.
Kant, I.: *Critique of Pure Reason* trans. N. Kemp
Smith (London: Macmillan, 1964).
Lewis, C.I.: *An Analysis of Knowledge and Valu-
ation* (La Salle: Open Court, 1946), ch. 7.
Sellars, W.: 'Empiricism and the philosophy of
mind', in his *Science, Perception, and Reality*
(London: Routledge and Kegan Paul, 1963).

ALAN H. GOLDMAN

**Goodman, Nelson (1906–)** American
philosopher. Goodman maintains that epistemology comprehends understanding or
cognition in all its modes. It does not restrict
itself to the theory of knowledge.

SYSTEMS

Goodman repudiates analyticity, necessity
and certainties grounded in immediate
experience. But even though any conviction
can be abandoned, some are initially credible
(Goodman, 1972, pp. 60–8). We construct
systems of thought around these, revising or
relinquishing them only as required to
maximize overall credibility. Typically, any of
several modifications yields a maximally
credible system. Each such system is acceptable. Pluralism results, for maximally
credible systems need neither reduce to nor
supervene on a single base. In particular, the
tenability of PHENOMENALISM does not

turn on its being reducible to or the basis for
physicalism (Goodman, 1951).

In (1988), Goodman and Elgin suggest
that something even more modest than
initial credibility may suffice – current
adoption. In theorizing, we order, emend,
elaborate and extend considerations currently
under adoption, whether credible or not. And
we judge their enduring epistemic worth by
the cognitive efficacy of the systems that
emerge.

Initially credible statements and current
adoptions typically underdetermine individuation and classification. For example,
our initially credible statements about stars
do not settle whether black holes are stars.
Systems answering to the same initially
credible statements may decide such matters
differently. One might consider black holes
stars; another, the residue of extinguished
stars. Both systems may be maximally
credible. Then both answers are right.

Obviously, we cannot countenance contradiction. So, Goodman concludes, rightness
is relative to acceptable system or world-
version. Relative to one such version, black
holes are stars. Relative to another, they are
not. Still, it does not follow that anything
goes. Relative to no acceptable system are
black holes both stars and not stars
(Goodman, 1978).

Cognitive rightness, Goodman suggests,
consists in fitting and working. Right considerations intertwine to form a system that
fits our initially credible statements and
works to further our cognitive objectives.
Truth is neither necessary nor sufficient for
rightness. Truths are often wrong because
irrelevant, trivial, convoluted or uninform-
ative; falsehoods often right because relevant,
illuminating, fruitful and/or elegant. Boyle's
Law, although literally false, enhances
understanding of gases as no true description
of the phenomena can (Goodman and Elgin,
1988, pp. 153–66).

PROJECTION

The *grue paradox* demonstrates the importance of rightness of categorization (*see* PRO-
JECTION, PROJECTIBILITY). Something is

grue if examined before future time $t$ and green, or not so examined and blue. Even though all emeralds in our evidence class are grue, we ought not infer that all emeralds are grue. For 'grue' is unprojectible. It cannot transmit credibility from known to unknown cases. Only projectible predicates are right for induction.

Goodman considers entrenchment the key to projectibility. Having a long history of successful projections, 'green' is entrenched; lacking such a history, 'grue' is not. A hypothesis is projectible, Goodman suggests, only if its predicates (or suitably related ones) are much better entrenched than its rivals'.

Past successes do not assure future ones. Induction remains a risky business. The rationale for favouring entrenched predicates is pragmatic. Of the possible projections from our evidence class, the one that fits with past practice enables us to best utilize our cognitive resources. Its prospects of being true are no worse than its competitors' and its cognitive utility is greater.

Respect for entrenchment does not preclude conceptual innovation. A term like 'quark' may be introduced where no entrenched predicate serves. Having no history of projection, it lacks earned entrenchment. Its projectibility derives from entrenchment inherited from related terms, e.g. 'electron'. When competing hypotheses are equal in earned entrenchment, marked differences in inherited entrenchment determine projectibility.

Despite their entrenchment, predicates whose projection leads regularly from true premises to false conclusions are unprojectible. The history of failed Newtonian projections drained classical physical categories of their projectibility, making way for relativistic categories. Novel predicates thus become projectible by fitting into working inductive systems or into replacements for ineffective ones (see INDUCTION; PROBLEMS OF INDUCTION).

## ART

According to Goodman, aesthetics is a branch of epistemology. The arts enhance understanding and aesthetics explains how they do so (Goodman, 1964).

Works of art, he maintains, belong to symbol systems. To understand a work is not to 'appreciate' or enjoy it or find it beautiful, but to interpret it correctly – to recognize what and how it symbolizes and how what it symbolizes bears on other aspects of our worlds. An encounter with art can engender new modes of apprehension, provoking novel classifications that cut across stale categories to reveal hitherto unrecognized patterns and discrepancies. Not all are literal. Metaphor, allusion and more complex forms of reference often make connections that available literal terminology cannot capture (Goodman, 1984, pp. 55–77).

One prominent mode of symbolization in the arts is exemplification, whereby a symbol refers to some of its own properties. An early Picasso might literally exemplify blue and metaphorically exemplify melancholy. But exemplification is not peculiar to art. Being the relation of samples to what they sample, it is a staple of science and commerce as well.

A sample affords epistemic access to the stuff it samples. From a fabric swatch, one can infer the character of the corresponding fabric. Likewise, when works of art exemplify, they supply epistemic access to some of their features and to things that share those features. Largely through literal and metaphorical exemplification, *Guernica* enables us to understand something of the horror of war (Goodman, 1964, pp. 45–95). With samples, as with other symbols, rightness of interpretation is crucial.

Goodman does not deny the emotional impact of art, but relocates its importance. In the arts, he maintains, emotions function cognitively. We use our reactions to a work as tools for exploring it. And the more refined our sensibilities, the more insight emotion provides (ibid., pp. 248–52).

Merit too functions as means. Rather than attending to a work to determine its worth, Goodman believes, we should use evaluation to focus attention. That seemingly similar sculptures differ in value provokes a search for differences. It may lead to discovery of features we could not previously discern, thereby extending our perceptual capacities (Goodman, 1972, pp. 120–1).

Goodman's epistemology is thus a wide-ranging inquiry into cognitive excellences and the conditions that foster them. It comprehends the arts as well as the sciences. And it considers the contributions to the advancement of understanding made by perception, emotion, theory, practice, and symbolizing.

WRITINGS

*Fact, Fiction, and Forecast* 4th edn (Cambridge, MA: Harvard University Press, 1983).
*Languages of Art* 2nd edn (Indianapolis: Hackett, 1976).
*Of Mind and Other Matters* (Cambridge, MA: Harvard University Press, 1984).
*Problems and Projects* (Indianapolis: Hackett, 1972).
*The Structure of Appearance* 3rd edn (Dordrecht: Reidel, 1977).
*Ways of Worldmaking* (Indianapolis: Hackett, 1978).
with Elgin, C.Z.: *Reconceptions* (Indianapolis: Hackett, 1988).

BIBLIOGRAPHY

Elgin, C.Z.: *With Reference to Reference* (Indianapolis: Hackett, 1983).
Mitchell, W.J.T.: *Iconology* (Chicago: University of Chicago Press, 1986), ch. 2.
Scheffler, I.: *The Anatomy of Inquiry* (Indianapolis: Hackett, 1981), chs 8–10.
Schwartz, R.: 'The power of pictures', *Journal of Philosophy* 82 (1985), 711–20.

CATHERINE Z. ELGIN

**Grice, H. Paul (1913–88)** British philosopher. Grice, who worked first at Oxford and then at the University of California at Berkeley, is best known for his work on philosophy of language and mind, but in later years he worked extensively in ethics and metaphysics. Most of this work remained unpublished at his death.

Grice's contributions to epistemology are two – one direct and one indirect. The direct contribution is his attempt to provide a new twist on causal theories of perception; such theories can be found at least as early as OCKHAM and more recently in Price, but they were out of favour at the time Grice wrote. Grice's defence of the theory utilizes an important methodological distinction between the domain of philosophy and that of the specialized sciences. It is thus antithetical to current naturalized approaches to epistemology (*see* NATURALIZED EPISTEMOLOGY), even though it shares with such approaches an emphasis on causal connections. He argued that philosophical analyses of knowledge should leave one or more blanks to be filled in by psychology or neuropsychology, and that the philosophical aspect of the account should be sufficiently neutral to allow particular causal accounts to fit in. His very tentative account was in terms of an appropriate causal relation (details to be specified by the specialist) between a state of affairs and a true present tense sense-datum report.

His indirect contribution is his theory of conversational implicature. The conversational implications of a statement are (roughly) those propositions that cannot be inferred from the explicit literal statement, but that can be inferred from the fact that it was made at all, or from the way the statement was made (choice of words, tone, etc.). One specific philosophical point which Grice wished to counter with the distinction was the claim that, for example, we do not know that we have two hands under normal circumstances because it would be odd to assert in those circumstances that we know that we have two hands. Grice's distinction enables us to say why it is odd, namely because the statement is obviously true and there is a general conversational injunction not to waste everyone's time by stating obvious truths. A second epistemological use he envisaged for the theory, related to the first point above, was to define sense-data theories against the argument that it is odd to say that one 'seems to see a dog' under normal circumstances. Grice continued to believe that sense-data theories were defensible after most sense-data theorists had abandoned the approach. His suggestion was that sense-data theories be reformulated in linguistic terms that would enable them to be ontologically neutral, but he never developed this approach in detail.

*See also* CAUSAL THEORIES IN EPISTEMOLOGY; PSYCHOLOGY AND EPISTEMOLOGY; REPRESENTATIVE REALISM; SENSE-DATA.

BIBLIOGRAPHY

'The causal theory of perception', *Proceedings of the Aristotelian Society* supp. vol. (1961), 121–52.
*Studies in the Ways of Words* (Harvard, MA: Harvard University Press, 1989).

RICHARD E. GRANDY

# H

---

Habermas, Jürgen (1929–) German philosopher and sociologist, the leading contemporary representative of critical theory, a tradition of Marxist social philosophy initiated by the Frankfurt School in the 1930s. The aim of Critical Theory is to explain the development of modern capitalist society, but also to indicate ways in which it may be released from relations of domination and exploitation. Unlike other forms of MARXISM, Critical Theory has been acutely aware of the need to examine its own cognitive status and has therefore given great weight to epistemological questions. Defining itself in contrast both to 'metaphysics' and to 'scientism', it has repudiated the search for timeless philosophical foundations, while insisting that there are legitimate theoretical and moral pursuits beyond those of the natural sciences. In particular, it deplores the modern tendency of confining RATIONALITY to 'instrumental reason', the efficient marshalling of means in the services of ends which are left unjustified.

Habermas has tried to provide Critical Theory with a new and systematic epistemological basis by developing, first, a broad conception of reason with ethical implications, and second, a non-positivist methodology of the SOCIAL SCIENCES. His main theme is a switch from the 'subject–object scheme' of post-Cartesian epistemology (the 'philosophy of consciousness') to a theory of intersubjective communication.

*Knowledge and Human Interests* (1968) contains what Habermas calls a 'critical self-reflection' on the foundations of knowledge which results in a kind of transcendental pragmatism. Habermas distinguishes three types of inquiry – the 'empirical analytical sciences', i.e. those that provide nomological causal knowledge, the 'historical-hermeneutic sciences', and the 'critically-oriented sciences' (psychoanalysis, critical social theory). He claims that each is guided by its own 'cognitive interest', respectively, the 'technical' interest in the prediction and control of nature, the 'practical' interest in understanding other human beings, and the 'emancipatory' interest in freedom and the overcoming of unconscious compulsion. These cognitive interests are 'general orientations' or 'cognitive strategies' with a 'quasi-transcendental' status. On the one hand, they have their basis in the productive labour and communication, and hence ultimately in the 'natural history of the human species'. On the other hand, they are not merely permanent features of human history, but are virtually transcendental preconditions of human knowledge. For example, empirical science does not investigate an antecedently given domain of objects: empirical reality is 'constituted' in the course of our pursuit of the technical interest.

In spite of the IDEALIST terminology, this need not mean that we create nature, but only that there are no true empirical statements independent of our pursuit of the technical interest. However, the nature of this dependency remains obscure: as part of our natural history cognitive interests might *de facto* be invariant, but they remain contingent, and hence cannot be transcendental in Kant's sense. Moreover, it remains unclear how a Kantian 'critique', an examination of the preconditions of knowledge, can underpin a Marxist critique of social structures.

In response to the objection that his assimilation of knowledge and human interests reduces epistemology in a NATURALISTIC or instrumentalist way, Habermas has distinguished between 'action', which is guided by pragmatic interests, and 'discourse', an intersubjective search for knowledge which is guided solely by the aim of reaching a rational consensus. He has also distinguished between 'critical sciences', which investigate the possibilities of emancipation, and 'reconstructive sciences', the name he has given to sciences like linguistics, which aim to make explicit in a theoretical form the various capacities needed for human interaction. Among the latter, pride of place goes to 'universal pragmatics', a theory that is modelled on Chomsky's reconstruction of linguistic competence, but aims to accommodate the pragmatic and intersubjective aspects of language highlighted by speech-act theories. Universal pragmatics examines the universal conditions of communication and interaction. Habermas argues that it provides a basis for critical theory, since the universal preconditions of linguistic communication include normative commitments with ethical implications. When we engage in a discourse, we 'counterfactually anticipate' an 'ideal speech situation' characterized by 'equality' and 'reciprocity of participipation'. Perhaps these sibylline pronouncements can be taken to mean that in an argumentative discourse we are entitled to assume that all participants seek an agreement not on the basis of coercion or deceit, but only through reasoning.

Habermas's theory of communication includes a 'consensus theory of truth', according to which a statement is true if and only if it would be accepted by all in an ideal speech situation. Several reformulations notwithstanding, this approach commits a genetic fallacy: that a statement is accepted as true by any number of speakers, however free they may be from coercion or prejudice, does not entail that it is true.

Habermas's methodology of the social sciences is fully presented in *The Theory of Communicative Action* (1981). Against positivism he insists that the social sciences cannot adopt the 'objectivizing' attitude of causal explanation, but must seek to understand human practices from the perspective of potential participants, by focusing on the explanations the participants themselves would give for their actions. But against the relativistic tendencies of hermeneutical and Wittgensteinian sociologists he insists that social science can nevertheless criticize these practices on theoretical and ethical grounds. Perhaps the most interesting contribution of Habermas's theory of discourse is a kind of TRANSCENDENTAL ARGUMENT against RELATIVISM. In order to contribute to a discourse with their opponents, the arguments relativists advance on behalf of 'primitive' cultures have to abide by standards of argumentation that are absent from the cultures they defend.

Habermas's work is eclectic and often obscure. But his untiring endeavours to provide an account of rationality that avoids both OBJECTIVISM and relativism (*see* SOCIOLOGY OF KNOWLEDGE) are impressive.

*See also* CONTINENTAL EPISTEMOLOGY; SOCIAL SCIENCE.

WRITINGS

*Knowledge and Human Interests* (London: Heinemann, 1971).
*Communication and the Evolution of Society* (London: Heinemann, 1979), ch. 1.
*The Theory of Communicative Action* 2 vols (Cambridge: Polity, 1984, 1987).
*Moral Consciousness and Communicative Action* (Cambridge: Polity, 1990), ch. 1.

BIBLIOGRAPHY

McCarthy, T.: *The Critical Theory of Jürgen Habermas* (Cambridge: Polity, 1984).
Thompson, J.B. and Held, D. eds: *Habermas, Critical Debates* (London: Macmillan, 1982).

HANS-JOHANN GLOCK

**Hegel, Georg Wilhelm Friedrich** (1770–1831) Though widely misunderstood, Hegel's theory of knowledge is rich and often insightful. The standard view of Hegel is that he sought to overcome the sceptical character of Kant's distinction between appearances and things in themselves by rejecting epistemology and 'purifying' Kant's transcendental idealism to dispense with things in themselves. Instead, Hegel criticized Kant's arguments for idealism, and his epistemology has great contemporary relevance. Hegel was the first epistemologist to realise that a socially and historically-based epistemology is consistent with REALISM. His epistemology is anti-FOUNDATIONALIST; he rejects non-conceptual knowledge and the ideal of CERTAINTY, especially for alleged 'elementary' beliefs or experiences. He holds a correspondence analysis of truth, though not a correspondence criterion of truth, and he defends a fallibilist account of justification.

Hegel's theory of justification contains both EXTERNALIST and COHERENTIST elements. He recognizes that some *prima facie* justification is provided by percepts and beliefs being generated reliably by our interaction with the environment. Hegel contends that full justification additionally requires a self-conscious, reflective comprehension of one's beliefs and experiences which integrates them into a systematic conceptual scheme (outlined in his *Logic*) which provides an account for them which is both coherent and reflexively self-consistent.

RATIONALIST elements appear in Hegel's epistemology in his theses that knowledge of particulars requires applying conceptions to them, that observation terms and formal logic are insufficient for empirical knowledge, and that statements of laws of nature are conceptual constructs which express actual structures of nature. He also holds the rationalist ideal that everything worth knowing is rationally comprehensible, which he calls 'absolute knowledge'.

NATURALIST elements appear in Hegel's epistemology in his theses that biological needs (one root of consciousness) involve elementary classification of objects, that the contents of consciousness are derived from a public world, and that classificatory thought presupposes natural structures in the world. Hegel insists that philosophy is grounded in the empirical sciences: 'Not only must philosophy accord with the experience nature gives rise to; in its *formation* and in its *development*, philosophic science presupposes and is conditioned by empirical physics' (*Encyclopedia* § 246 Remark). He holds similar views about grounding social philosophy in both the nascent cultural sciences of his day and in political economy.

Hegel contends that the corrigibility of conceptual categories is a social phenomenon. Our partial ignorance about the world can be revealed and corrected because one and the same claim or principle can be applied, asserted and assessed by different people in the same context or by the same person in different contexts. Hegel's theory of justification requires that an account be shown to be adequate to its domain and to be superior to its alternatives. In this regard, Hegel is a FALLIBILIST according to whom justification is provisional and ineluctably historical, since it occurs against the background of less adequate alternative views.

REALISM in epistemology requires two things: that there be things whose characteristics do not depend upon our thoughts or language, and that those things be knowable; it requires that there be no metaphysical distinction between appearance and reality which blocks knowledge of reality. Hegel's 'idealism' is in fact such a realism; it is a kind of ontological holism, and not the view typically associated with 'absolute idealism' (*see* IDEALISM). According to Hegel, the causal characteristics of things are essential to their identity conditions, and the individual properties of things obtain only as members of contrastive sets of properties. Hence the causal interdependence of particulars, along with the constitutive similarities and differences among their properties, establish the mutual dependence of their identity conditions. The result is two-fold. On the one hand, particulars have their ground in the whole world-system, because their characteristics obtain only in and through contrast with opposed characteristics of other things and because they are generated and corrupted through their causal interaction with other things. On the other hand, Hegel analyses 'the concept' (*der Begriff*) as an ontological structure. Hegel's 'concept' is a principle of the constitution of characteristics through contrast; it exists only in and as the interconnection of things and their properties in the world. Hegel's 'idea' is the instantiation of this conceptual structure by worldly things and phenomena. Hegel describes particular things as 'ideal' because they are not individually self-sufficient, and thus not ultimately real. He characterizes the world-system as 'spirit' because he believes it has a normative *telos* towards which it develops historically. Part of this *telos* is self-knowledge, which the world-system gains through human knowledge of the world.

The sceptical view that things are the unsensed causes of sensory experience has been popular from Protagoras to PUTNAM; it appears in Locke's 'thing I know not what' and Kant's unknowable 'thing in itself'. Hegel's analysis of forces and scientific laws responds to this view and provides support for his holistic ontology. Hegel objects to the hypothetico-deductive model of explanation in ways which have only recently become commonplace. He defends a 'phenomenological' account of laws of nature. (This account is distinct from Hegel's 'phenomenological' method.) According to such an account, laws of nature are relations among manifest phenomena. This view was prominent throughout the nineteenth century in German and British physics. Hegel purports to show that nothing more can be attributed to any force or set of forces than precisely the array of manifest phenomena which they are postulated to explain, so that ultimately there is nothing more to 'forces' than the conceptual interrelation of manifest phenomena. These interrelations are, on Hegel's view, objective features of those phenomena, and the aim of conceiving those phenomena is to formulate those interrelations accurately. Because the interrelations among and within natural phenomena are not strictly speaking perceptible, but none the less are objective features of those phenomena, those interrelations are conceptual and concepts are structures of nature.

Hegel develops various aspects of his epistemology in different parts of his philosophical system. The *Phenomenology of Spirit* presents a sophisticated meta-epistemology which responds to Sextus Empiricus' PROBLEM OF THE CRITERION (the problem of establishing standards of assess-

ment without circularity or dogmatism) and defends an outline of a substantive epistemology against a wide range of SCEPTICAL, RELATIVIST and SUBJECTIVIST views. Hegel defends his views by criticizing opposed views internally, on the basis of the principles and examples cited in those views. Accordingly, a core element in his meta-epistemology is a subtle account of self-criticism, used to explain his method of internal criticism and to avoid problems of question-begging.

Hegel's 'System of Philosophical Science', comprising his *Logic*, *Philosophy of Nature* and *Philosophy of Spirit*, takes up a wide range of substantive epistemological issues. The *Logic* examines the ontological and cognitive roles of ontological categories (e.g. being, existence, quantity, essence, appearance, relation, thing, cause) and principles of logic (e.g. identity, excluded middle, non-contradiction). His *Logic* also analyses syllogism, judgement and principles of scientific explanation (mechanical, chemical and organic or teleological functions) in accordance with which we are able to know the world. The *Philosophy of Nature* treats these principles of explanation in connection with a wide range of examples drawn from the sciences of his day, about which he was quite informed.

Hegel's philosophical psychology is deeply naturalist and draws heavily from Aristotle. The first part of his *Philosophy of Spirit*, the 'Philosophy of Subjective Spirit', treats psychological topics pertinent to epistemology, including sensibility, feeling and habit under the heading 'anthropology'; the conscious phenomena of sense-perception, intellect, and desire under the heading of 'phenomenology'; and theoretical intelligence, including intuition, representation, memory, imagination and thought under the heading 'psychology'.

*See also* CONTINENTAL EPISTEMOLOGY; DIALECTIC (HEGEL); IDEALISM; IN ITSELF/FOR ITSELF; RATIONALISM.

WRITINGS

*Die Phänomenologie des Geistes* (Bamberg and

Würtzburg: 1807); trans. A.V. Miller *The Phenomenology of Spirit* (Oxford: Clarendon Press, 1977).

*Wissenschaft der Logik* 2 vols (Nürnberg: 1812–16, Berlin: 1831); trans. A.V. Miller *Hegel's Science of Logic* (London: Allen and Unwin, 1969).

*Enzyklopädie der philosophischen Wissenschaften im Grundrisse* 3 vols (Heidelberg: 1817, 1827, 1830); vol. I trans. T.F. Geraets, H.S. Harris and W.A. Suchting *The Encyclopedia Logic* (Indianopolis: Hackett, 1991); vol. II ed. and trans. M.J. Petry *Hegel's Philosophy of Nature* (London: Allen and Unwin, 1970); vol. III ed. and trans. M.J. Petry, *Hegel's Philosophy of Subjective Spirit* (Dordrecht: Reidel, 1978).

BIBLIOGRAPHY

Beaumont, B.: 'Hegel and the seven planets', *Mind* 62 (1954), 246–8.

Beiser, F. ed.: *The Cambridge Companion to Hegel* (Cambridge: Cambridge University Press, 1992).

Buchdahl, G.: 'Hegel's philosophy of nature and the structure of science', in *Hegel* ed. M. Inwood (Oxford: Oxford University Press, 1985), 110–36.

deVries, W.: *Hegel's Theory of Mental Activity* (Ithaca, NY: Cornell University Press, 1988).

Fulda, H.F.: *Das Problem einer Einleitung in Hegels Wissenschaft der Logik* 2nd edn (Frankfurt: Kostermann, 1975).

Westphal, K.R.: *Hegel's Epistemological Realism: A Study of the Aim and Method of Hegel's Phenomenology of Spirit* (Dordrecht: Kluwer, 1989).

Will, F.L.: *Beyond Deduction: Ampliative Aspects of Philosophical Reflection* (London: Routledge, 1988).

KENNETH R. WESTPHAL

**Heidegger, Martin (1889–1976)** German philosopher. From the start of his career Heidegger defined his project as answering the question: What is the meaning of being? This metaphysical concern was motivated by the conviction that the dominant movements at the turn of the century – NATURALISM and KANTIAN theories of science – are loaded down with uncritical assumptions about reality and our place in it. Traditional epistemology assumes: (1) a picture of the self as essentially a mind or subject trying to correctly represent objects in the external world (the subject/object model), and (2) a conception of our everyday beliefs as needing a philosophical account to show how they are possible (foundationalism).

Heidegger's PHENOMENOLOGY of average everydayness – the description of everyday agency prior to reflection and theorizing – aims at dissolving the assumptions built into epistemology. According to this description, Dasein (or human existence) is 'being-in-the-world', a unified totality consisting of practical 'dealings' with things and the meaningful equipmental contexts of the familiar life-world. This 'unified phenomenon' is revealed in Heidegger's description of hammering in a workshop. When everything is running smoothly in such activities, what initially shows up for us is not a brute hammer-thing invested with a use, but rather 'hammering' which is for realizing a project. The hammer is 'ontologically defined' by its relations of 'in-order-to', 'for-which', 'by-means-of' and 'for-the-sake-of-which' as these are woven together by our practices. This totality of the 'ready-to-hand' makes up the 'world' as the tacit 'dwelling' for our involvements. At the same time, Dasein's own identity as an agent of a particular type is defined by the specific worlds in which it finds itself. Given this reciprocal interdependence of self and context, there is no way to distinguish a subject from the brute objects it supposedly seeks to represent.

The world of everydayness is always a public world. Its intelligibility is constituted by the linguistic articulations of a historical community (the 'they'). As the context of standardized interpretations, the public predefines possible ways of understanding humans and equipment. Because we are 'outside ourselves', dealing with things along the guidelines of a communally attuned 'pre-understanding of being', we are caught in a HERMENEUTIC circle with no access to an uninterpreted GIVEN. But the fact that the world and our involvements are already intelligible suggests that there is no need for a philosophical account of our beliefs and practices. The concern with foundations, like the subject/object model, arises only when there is a 'breakdown' in our everyday dealings with things. Only when entities obtrude as brute, meaningless 'present-at-hand' objects can we come to regard ourselves as mere spectators collecting data about items independent of us. Yet, since this specialized stance of theoretical reflection is derivative from being-in-the-world, it can have no broader implications for grasping our everyday epistemic predicament.

The later Heidegger discards the vestiges of humanism in *Being and Time* and describes both Dasein and worldly entities as emerging through manifestations of being itself. Epistemology is treated as part of technology, the Western tendency to treat reality as a 'worldview' on hand for our inspection and use. The antidote to technology is described as a special sort of thoughtful 'letting-be' which no longer tries to achieve mastery over things.

WRITINGS

*Sein und Zeit* (Tübingen, 1927); trans. J. Macquarrie and E. Robinson *Being and Time* (New York: Harper and Row, 1962).
'Die Zeit des Weltbildes', *Vorträge und Aufsätze* (Pfullingen: 1954); trans. W. Lovitt 'The age of the world picture', in *The Question Concerning Technology and Other Essays* (New York: Harper Colophon, 1977), 115–54.

BIBLIOGRAPHY

Guignon, C.: *Heidegger and the Problem of Knowledge* (Indianapolis: Hackett, 1983).
Okrent, M.: *Heidegger's Pragmatism: Understanding, Being, and the Critique of Metaphysics* (Ithaca, NY: Cornell University Press, 1988).
Olafson, F.A.: *Heidegger and the Philosophy of Mind* (New Haven: Yale University Press, 1987).

CHARLES GUIGNON

**Hempel, Carl Gustav (1905––)** Born in Oranienburg, Germany, Hempel studied mathematics and physics as well as philosophy, at the universities of Göttingen, Heidelberg and Berlin. After a brief period of research in Europe, Hempel migrated to the United States in 1937 and taught at Yale, Princeton and Pittsburgh.

Hempel was strongly influenced by the positivist philosophers of the early twentieth century, notably Reichenbach, Schlick and Carnap, and became a prominent representative of the LOGICAL POSITIVIST perspective on knowledge, language and science. Although he stayed largely within the empiricist and scientific framework of positivism, he was also a highly effective internal critic of the positivist excesses, and his many writings, well known for their lucidity and judicious argumentation, contributed greatly to the process of transforming the positivist movement and integrating it with the mainstream philosophy of the English-speaking world.

Hempel's early critical work on the positivist criterion of meaning (*see* VERIFICATIONISM) helped to liberalize the restrictive positivist doctrine on what is 'cognitively significant' and what is 'cognitively meaningless'. His mature views on meaning came to incorporate an important holistic element: whole scientific theories must be taken as the ultimate units of cognitive significance, and it is only when a theory is taken together with its 'interpretative system' (i.e. a set of statements in which both 'theoretical' and 'observational' terms occur) that one can meaningfully speak of its empirical content.

Hempel was among the first to develop precise definitions of 'evidence *e* confirms hypothesis *h*' and related concepts. His approach was largely formal and syntactical. His celebrated 'Raven Paradox' concerning confirmation of generalizations by 'positive instances' inspired an active debate in confirmation theory for a number of years (*see* HEMPEL'S PARADOX).

Hempel's most influential work by far was on the nature of scientific explanation. According to his 'covering-law' conception of explanation, the occurrence of an event is explained by subsuming, or 'covering', that event under a general law. When the covering laws are deterministic, the explanation takes the form of a deductive argument with laws and statements of antecedent conditions as premises and an appropriate statement describing the event to be explained as its conclusion. Explanations conforming to this deductive model are called 'deductive-nomological explanations'. Hempel applied the model to explanations in history, explanations of human actions and functional explanations in biology and the social sciences.

Hempel's covering-law approach also allowed 'statistical explanations', explanations in which statistical or probabilistic laws are used to show that the event to be explained is made highly probable, rather than deductively necessitated, by the explanatory premises. The nature of the precise constraints to be placed on this 'statistical model' has become a topic of much productive discussion in philosophy of science during the last three decades, spawning numerous alternative models.

Underlying Hempel's work on explanation are the following two central ideas: first, explanation, or scientific understanding, is not merely a matter of 'intellectual satisfaction' but must have an objective, testable basis; second, this testability condition is to be implemented by the requirement that an acceptable explanation must show that the occurrence of the phenomenon to be explained can be rationally expected on the basis of the information contained in the explanatory premisses.

*See also* BAYESIANISM; EXPLANATION.

WRITINGS

*Fundamentals of Concept Formation in Empirical Science* (Chicago: Chicago University Press, 1952).

*Aspects of Scientific Explanation* (New York: Free Press, 1965). This volume includes most of Hempel's important philosophical papers.

*Philosophy of Natural Science* (Englewood Cliffs: Prentice-Hall, 1966).

JAEGWON KIM

**Hempel's paradox of the ravens** In a pioneering study of confirmation, Carl G. Hempel (1945) introduced a paradox that raises fundamental questions about what counts as confirming evidence for a universal hypothesis. To generate the paradox three intuitive principles are invoked:

1. *Nicod's Principle* (after Jean Nicod, 1930): Instances of As that are Bs provide confirming evidence for the universal hypothesis that all As are Bs; while instances of As that are non-Bs provide disconfirming evidence. For example, instances of ravens that are black constitute confirming evidence for the hypothesis 'All ravens are black', while instances of non-black ravens are disconfirming.

2. *Equivalence Principle*: If *e* is confirming evidence for hypothesis *h1*, and if *h1* is logically equivalent to hypothesis *h2*, then *e* is confirming evidence for *h2*. For example, if instances of ravens that are black are confirming evidence that all ravens are black, they are also confirming evidence that all non-black things are non-ravens, since the latter hypothesis is logically equivalent to the former.

3. *A Principle of Deductive Logic*: A sentence of the form 'All As are Bs' is logically equivalent to one of the form 'All non-Bs are non-As'.

Using these principles, the paradox is generated by supposing that all the non-black things so far observed have been non-ravens. These might include white shoes, green leaves and red apples. By Nicod's principle, this is confirming evidence for the hypothesis 'All non-black things are non-ravens'. (In the schematic version of Nicod's principle, let As be non-black things and Bs be non-ravens.) But by principle (3) of deductive logic, the hypothesis 'All non-black things are non-ravens' is logically equivalent to 'All ravens are black'. Therefore by the equivalence principle (2), the fact that all the non-black things so far observed have been non-ravens is confirming evidence for the hypothesis that all ravens are black. That is, instances of white shoes, green leaves and red apples count as evidence for this hypothesis, which seems absurd. This is Hempel's ravens paradox.

Various solutions have been proposed, of which three will be noted. The first is due to Hempel himself, who accepts all three generating principles and the conclusion that follows from them. Hempel's solution or resolution consists in an attempt to show that the conclusion is not in fact paradoxical, although it may seem so. One reason the conclusion may seem paradoxical is that the hypothesis 'All ravens are black' appears to be about ravens, and not about shoes, leaves or apples. Therefore, information about the latter may appear to be irrelevant. But, says Hempel, the hypothesis that all ravens are black is in fact about *everything*, including shoes, leaves and apples. It claims that everything is such that if it is a raven then it is black. It is what logicians call a universal quantification of the form 'for all $x$, if $x$ is a raven then $x$ is black'. A second reason the conclusion may seem paradoxical is that if we know in advance that a certain item, which is white, is a shoe, then we know in advance that it is not a raven. So this would not be a genuine test, since information is presupposed that could not falsify the hypothesis. But, Hempel notes, if this additional information is unavailable beforehand – if we know only that is is white, and then determine by observation whether or not it is a raven – we have a genuine test. In short, one can test the hypothesis that all ravens are black by finding a raven and determining whether it is black, or by finding a non-black thing and determining whether it is a non-raven.

Many commentators have felt, however, that testing the hypothesis by examining ravens is better than doing so by examining non-black things. Solutions of this sort usually appeal to the idea of class size. It is provable that if the class of ravens is smaller than the class of non-black things, then finding a raven that is black increases the probability of the hypothesis that all ravens are black more than does finding a non-black non-raven. (For a proof, and a general defence of this approach, *see* Hosiasson-Lindenbaum, 1940; somewhat similar

proposals were made by Pears, 1950; von Wright, 1957; Alexander, 1958; and Good 1960.) This solution is closely associated with the idea that information is confirming evidence for a hypothesis if and only if it increases the probability of the hypothesis. So assuming the class of ravens is smaller than the class of non-black things, information that examined ravens are black is better confirming evidence for the hypothesis that all ravens are black than is information that examined non-black things are non-ravens.

Some writers on evidence, however, reject the principle that information is evidence for a hypothesis if and only if it increases its probability (*see* Achinstein, 1983; Glymour, 1980). One approach (adopted by Achinstein) is to assume that a necessary but not a sufficient condition for information $e$ to be evidence for hypothesis $h$ is that $h$'s probability on $e$ be 'high', say, greater than $1/2$. (Nicod's principle thus requires modification to satisfy this necessary condition.) The solution to the ravens paradox then proceeds by showing that, in normal circumstances, the probability that all ravens are black, given that all observed ravens are black, will be high; whereas the probability that all non-black things are non-ravens, given that all observed non-black things are non-ravens, will not be high. The reason is that in the latter case the selection procedure for choosing non-black things to observe will usually be strongly biased in favour of non-ravens, whereas this will not normally happen when choosing ravens to observe. A selection procedure (or rule) $S$ for choosing $A$s to observe is strongly biased in favour of $B$s if and only if the probability that all observed $A$s are $B$s, given that $A$s are selected for observation in accordance with $S$, is close to $1$; whereas the probability that all observed $A$s are $B$s (without this assumption) is not close to $1$. In choosing non-black things to observe, say white shoes, one may well be following the procedure to select non-black things from inside one's house, or within one's immediate visual field, or that are inanimate, or that are known in advance to be non-ravens. All these selection procedures are strongly biased in favour of non-ravens.

Now a probability theorem is provable to the effect that if the selection procedure S for choosing As to observe is strongly biased in favour of Bs, then – given certain conditions that will normally be satisfied – the probability that all As are Bs, given that all observed As have been Bs, will not be high. Accordingly the high probability condition for confirming evidence mentioned earlier will be violated. In brief, if in choosing non-black things to observe (which turn out to be shoes, leaves or apples) one is following a selection procedure such as one of those mentioned above that is strongly biased in favour of non-ravens, then the fact that all the non-black things observed have been non-ravens would not be confirming evidence that all non-black things are non-ravens, i.e. that all ravens are black.

To be sure, there are selection procedures for non-black things that are not strongly biased in favour of non-ravens. But unlike the biased ones, they are difficult to follow and to know that we have followed. By contrast, there are simple, straightforward selection procedures for ravens that are not strongly biased in favour of blackness (e.g. 'Select ravens from different locales, at different times of year'). Since they are unbiased, the probability of the general hypothesis 'All ravens are black' can become high with the observation of more and more black ravens, thus satisfying the necessary condition for confirming evidence. This is why in testing the ravens hypothesis we should prefer to select ravens rather than non-black things.

BIBLIOGRAPHY

Achinstein, P.: *The Nature of Explanation* (New York: Oxford University Press, 1983).
Alexander, H.G.: 'The paradoxes of confirmation', *British Journal for the Philosophy of Science* 9 (1958), 227–33.
Glymour, C.: *Theory and Evidence* (Princeton: Princeton University Press, 1980).
Good, I.J.: 'The paradox of confirmation', Parts I & II, *British Journal for the Philosophy of Science* 11 (1960), 145–8; 12 (1961), 63–4.

Hempel, C.G.: 'Studies in the logic of confirmation', Parts I & II, *Mind* 54 (1945), 1–26, 97–121. Reprinted, with additions, in Hempel, *Aspects of Scientific Explanation* (New York: Free Press, 1965), 3–51.
Hosiasson-Lindenbaum, J.: 'On confirmation', *The Journal of Symbolic Logic* 5 (1940), 133–48.
Nicod, J.: *Foundations of Geometry and Induction* (London: K. Paul, Trench, Trubner, 1930).
Pears, D.F.: 'Hypotheticals', *Analysis* 10 (1950), 49–63.
von Wright, G.H.: *The Logical Problem of Induction* (Oxford: Blackwell, 1957).

PETER ACHINSTEIN

**hermeneutics** The theory of interpretation, originating in older concerns with textual exegesis, today deals less with issues of the correctness of interpretations and more with the ontological question, What is the being of the entity which has an understanding of itself and its world? According to ontological hermeneutics, humans are self-constituting beings. We are what we make of ourselves in the course of our activities. Moreover, because we are already dealing with things in our practical affairs, we always have some 'pre-understanding' of how things count in the familiar life-world. This tacit 'know-how', embodied in our practices and made accessible in language, is prior to explicit propositional knowledge. There can be no exit from this all-pervasive shared background of understanding to gain access to brute facts or neutral data which might ground our interpretations. We are caught in a 'hermeneutic circle': we grasp the world in terms of its components, but we can grasp things within the world only in terms of our prior mastery of the web of significance of the world as a whole. Nevertheless, as 'insiders' initiated into the practices of a historical culture, the world is already intelligible to us. As a result, the questions of traditional epistemology are topics for specialized 'regional' inquiries which have no wider consequences for making sense of our ordinary beliefs and practices.

*See also* SOCIAL SCIENCE.

BIBLIOGRAPHY

Gadamer, H.-G.: *Truth and Method* (1960) trans. J. Weinsheimer and D.G. Marshall (New York: Crossroad, 1989).

Heidegger, M.: *Being and Time* (1927) trans. J. Macquarrie and E. Robinson (New York: Harper and Row, 1962).

Hiley, D., Bohman, J. and Schusterman, R., eds: *The Interpretive Turn* (Ithaca, NY: Cornell University Press, 1991).

CHARLES GUIGNON

**Hintikka, Jaakko (1929–)** Finnish philosopher. Hintikka has made important contributions to many areas of philosophical research, including logic, epistemology, philosophy of language, philosophy of science and the history of philosophy.

In his early works *Distributive Normal Forms* (1953) and 'Form and Content in Quantification Theory' (in *Two Papers on Symbolic Logic*, 1955), Hintikka developed two logical theories which he has later applied to many different areas: the theory of distributive normal forms for quantification theory, and the theory of model sets which yields semantically motivated proof procedures for quantification theory and modal logics.

In his 1957 paper, 'Modality as Referential Multiplicity', Hintikka argued that intensional contexts involve a multiplicity of possible scenarios or worlds in which the referents of linguistic expressions can vary. This paper is one of the earliest formulations of the so-called possible worlds semantics. In his 1962 book *Knowledge and Belief* Hintikka developed an explicit modal logic for the concepts of knowledge and belief, employing the method of model sets, and applied it to various conceptual problems in epistemology, including the problem of knowing that one knows and MOORE'S PARADOX of saying and disbelieving. This work opened a virtually new area of logical research, epistemic logic. This logic is the foundation of Hintikka's theory of questions and answers, in which questions are construed as epistemic imperatives (or requests). He has applied this theory to the methodology of knowledge acquisition,

especially the scientific method; the resulting question-theoretic model of inquiry illuminates the role of inference, observation, experiment and strategy in inquiry (*see* KNOWLEDGE-SEEKING BY QUESTIONING; KK-THESIS).

By means of distributive normal forms Hintikka has defined new probability-measures for first-order languages which overcome some traditional difficulties in inductive logic. These measures can assign positive probabilities to non-trivial general hypotheses even in infinite universes and thus enable us to study inductive generalization within probabilistic confirmation theory. Likewise Hintikka has defined interesting new measures of information. He has shown that certain forms of deductive inference yield new information (in his perfectly objective sense of 'information'), establishing thus an interesting distinction between 'analytic' and 'synthetic' deductive reasoning. In this way Hintikka has illuminated and partly vindicated KANT'S conception of the synthetic character of mathematical reasoning (*see* MATHEMATICAL KNOWLEDGE).

Much of Hintikka's work in the semantics of natural language is based on the general theoretical framework called game-theoretical semantics. The philosophical precedent of this semantics is WITTGENSTEIN'S idea of language-game, but Hintikka conceives semantical games as games in the precise sense of the mathematical theory of games and as games of verification, not as games played by performing linguistic acts. Game-theoretical semantics has proved an immensely fruitful theoretical tool for the study of natural language, both as a general account of meaning and as a means of solving particular problems (for example, problems concerning coreference).

Although Hintikka has worked in a wide area, his work shows a great deal of conceptual and theoretical unity. This is partly due to the logical and semantical methods he uses, partly to the transcendental character (in the Kantian sense) of his philosophy. Hintikka has emphasized the role of rule-governed human activities in knowledge acquisition and in cognitive representation;

his game-theoretical approach to meaning is a case in point. The structures of such activities can be taken to provide the synthetic a priori features of our knowledge. In this respect Hintikka's philosophy is Kantian in spirit.

See also DIFFERENT CONSTRUCTIONS IN TERMS OF 'KNOWS'; KNOWLEDGE-SEEKING BY QUESTIONING.

WRITINGS

Distributive Normal Forms in the Calculus of Predicates (Acta Philosophica Fennica 6, 1953).
Two Papers on Symbolic Logic (Acta Philosophica Fennica 8, 1955).
Knowledge and Belief: An Introduction to the Logic of the Two Notions (Ithaca, NY: Cornell University Press, 1962).
Models for Modalities (Dordrecht: Reidel, 1969).
Logic, Language-Games, and Information (Oxford: Oxford University Press, 1973).
Knowledge and the Known: Historical Perspectives in Epistemology (Dordrecht: Reidel, 1974).
The Intentions of Intentionality and Other New Models for Modalities (Dordrecht: Reidel, 1975).
The Semantics of Questions and the Questions of Semantics (Acta Philosophica Fennica, 28: 4, 1976).
with J. Kulas: The Game of Language: Studies in Game-Theoretical Semantics and Its Applications (Dordrecht: Reidel, 1983).


BIBLIOGRAPHY

Bodgan, R.J. ed.: Jaakko Hintikka (Dordrecht: Reidel, 1987).
Philosophia 11: 1–2 (1982).

RISTO HILPINEN

**historical knowledge** Knowledge acquired by the use of present evidence from which the knower draws conclusions about the past is called historical knowledge. This tripartite conception of historical knowledge – knower, evidence and known – gives rise to a great many problems.

THE REALITY OF THE PAST

In historical knowledge, the object of knowledge is *transcendental*. That is, we never have experience with past events *as past*. This makes it impossible to verify directly the conclusions that we reach about the past on the basis of evidence. Bertrand Russell has put the problem in a particularly trenchant way by pointing out that it is possible that there is no past for historical knowledge to be about: 'There is no logical impossibility in the hypothesis that the world sprang into being five minutes ago, exactly as it then was, with a population that "remembered" a wholly unreal past' (Russell, 1921). One might think that this difficulty about knowing an unexperiencable past could be avoided by the use of induction in the following way: we use evidence to gain knowledge about past events which now-living people participated in and remember; once we find that our methods and types of evidence give us reliable knowledge, as certified by living memory, about these recent events, we are justified in extending these methods and types of evidence to the more distant past; we thus infer from this reliability in the case of one class of past events to reliability for all past events. But this will surely not work. This test for reliability makes essential use of memories which are themselves often unreliable and in critical need of independent verification. But we can never achieve the needed verification, even in the case of very recent memories, by directly comparing our memories to the past events remembered. Some thinkers have suggested that we regard historical knowledge as a construct – a way of making sense of *present* experience – rather than as knowledge about an unexperiencable object (Oakeshott, 1933; Croce, 1960; Meiland, 1965; Goldstein, 1976). Other thinkers believe that the hypothesis that there is a real past is the best explanation of present evidence being as it is; and they accordingly take historical statements to be true or false about that real past. (This dispute is structurally the exact equivalent of the dispute between scientific realism and constructive empiricism in the philosophy of science. *See* van Fraassen, 1980.)

## SUBJECTIVITY, INTERPRETATION AND KNOWLEDGE

Let us suppose that there is a real past about which statements can be true or false. The evidence used by the historian often consists of texts created by participants in the events being studied or created by non-participant earlier historians after the events occurred. (Other types of evidence include works of art, rolls, records, speeches, letters, diaries, architectural remains, and monuments.) As in the case of all texts, the authors of these sources made *decisions*. They decided what was important to mention and what should be left out. This necessary process of selection is thought to introduce an inevitable element of *subjectivity* into these primary and secondary sources. Each source will, because of the necessity of selection, give a different account of the facts – of what the facts are, let alone what they mean – and consequently, each text will present an interpretation. For example, some sources may state that the prince was at the front of his troops throughout the battle, while other sources may state that he stayed in the rear. The historian's sources will thus disagree about what the facts are. On top of this, the historian must then make his or her own selection from the sources to construct a narrative or interpretation of what happened, thus telling us what the facts *mean*. This additional layer of selection introduces still more subjectivity into the historical work.

What guides this selectivity? The Scottish historian A.J. Youngson (1985) gives two accounts of the unsuccessful Jacobite rebellion of 1745–6 led by Charles Edward (Bonnie Prince Charlie), one from the Hanoverian point of view and the other from the Jacobite point of view. Each account includes all of the agreed-upon facts of the case. Each is an honest account, sticking strictly to the canons of historical inquiry and avoiding any element of propaganda. And yet the two accounts are very different from one another. Youngson says this about what guides the selection and interpretation represented in these accounts: 'In the meantime it is clear only that many historians, whether they recognize the fact or not, base their work on some prior set of principles or beliefs, and that what they write is an elaboration or illustration or defence of these principles or beliefs; and that all the others, however impartial they may try to be, have their personal preferences and their natural sympathies and therefore inevitably, although perhaps quite unconsciously, design their version of events to be consonant with their ideas about life in general' (Youngson, 1985, p. 14).

Of course, if we take this line, we will find ourselves committed to a general scepticism about events – that is, a scepticism that includes complex present events too, since the same problems of selectivity and interpretation will apply to the present too. This is not specifically a problem about knowledge of the past.

## EXPLANATION AND UNDERSTANDING

Historical knowledge is often compared to scientific knowledge. Scientific knowledge is regarded as knowledge of the laws and regularities of nature which operate throughout past, present, and future. Some thinkers (e.g. the German historian Ranke) have argued that historical knowledge should be 'scientific' in the sense of being based on research, on scrupulous verification of facts as far as possible, with an objective account being the principal aim. Others have gone further, asserting that historical inquiry and scientific inquiry have the same goal, namely providing explanations of particular events by discovering general laws from which (together with initial conditions) the particular events can be inferred (Hempel, 1942). This is often called 'The Covering Law Theory' of historical explanation. Proponents of this view usually admit a difference in direction of interest between the two types of inquiry: historians are more interested in explaining particular events, while scientists are more interested in discovering general laws. But the logic of explanation is said to be the same for both (*see* EXPLANATION; HEMPEL).

Yet a cursory glance at the articles and books that historians produce does not support this view. Those books and articles focus overwhelmingly on the particular – e.g. the particular social structure of Tudor England, the rise to power of a particular political party, the social, cultural and economic interactions between two particular peoples. Nor is some standard body of theory or set of explanatory principles cited in the footnotes of history texts as providing the fundamental materials of historical explanation. In view of this, other thinkers have proposed that narrative itself, apart from general laws, can produce understanding, and that this is the characteristic form of historical explanation (Dray, 1957). If we wonder why things are the way they are – and, analogously, why they were the way they were – we are often satisfied by being told a story about how they got that way.

What we seek in historical inquiry is an understanding that respects the agreed-upon facts. A chronicle can present a factually correct account of a historical event without making that event intelligible to us – for example, without showing us why that event occurred and how the various phases and aspects of the event are related to one another. Historical narrative aims to provide intelligibility by showing how one thing led to another even when there is no relation of causal determination between them. In this way, narrative provides a form of understanding especially suited to a temporal course of events and alternative to scientific, or lawlike, explanation.

Another approach is understanding through knowledge of the purposes, intentions and points of view of historical agents. If we know how Julius Caesar or Leon Trotsky saw and understood their times and know what they meant to accomplish, then we can better understand why they did what they did. Purposes, intentions, and points of view are varieties of thought and can be ascertained through acts of empathy by the historian. R.G. Collingwood (1946) goes further and argues that those very same past thoughts can be re-enacted (and thereby made present) by the historian. Historical

explanations of this type cannot be reduced to the covering law model (Dray, 1957; Atkinson, 1978) and allow historical inquiry to achieve a different type of intelligibility.

See also EXPLANATION; MEMORY; SOCIAL SCIENCE; VICO.

BIBLIOGRAPHY

Atkinson, R.F.: Knowledge and Explanation in History (London: Macmillan, 1978).

Collingwood, R.G.: The Idea of History (Oxford: Clarendon Press, 1946).

Croce, B.: History: Its Theory and Practice (New York: Russell and Russell, 1960).

Dray, W.: Laws and Explanation in History (Oxford: Oxford University Press, 1957).

van Fraassen, B.C.: The Scientific Image (Oxford: Clarendon Press, 1980).

Goldstein, L.J.: Historical Knowledge (Austin: University of Texas Press, 1976).

Hempel, C.G.: 'The function of general laws in history', Journal of Philosophy 29 (1942), 35–48.

Hobart, M.E.: 'The paradox of historical constructionism', History and Theory 28 (1989), 43–58.

Hurst, B.C.: 'The myth of historical evidence', History and Theory 20 (1981), 278–90.

Kempt, P.: 'History as narrative and practice', Philosophy Today 29 (1985), 213–22.

Meiland, J.W.: Scepticism and Historical Knowledge (New York: Random House, 1965).

Mink, L.O.: Historical Understanding (Ithaca, NY: Cornell University Press, 1987).

Oakeshott, M.: Experience and its Modes (Cambridge: Cambridge University Press, 1933).

Russell, B.: The Analysis of Mind (London: Allen and Unsin, 1921).

Veyne, P.: Writing History, Essay in Epistemology (Middletown: Wesleyan University Press, 1984).

Youngson, A.J.: The Prince and the Pretender (London: Croom Helm, 1985).

White, H.: 'Historical pluralism', Critical Inquiry 12 (1986), 480–93.

JACK W. MEILAND

**historicism** The view that the nature and value of some phenomenon can be understood only in the context of its historical development. Since our concepts and theories are themselves developing phenomena, historicists usually deny that there is a trans-historical perspective from which to write history. Our theories must be evaluated in a process of immanent critique, and the history of that process is our final resource to understand the character of our present conceptions and their attraction for us. Historicists are therefore divided between those who deny that there are objective standards by which one historical stage may be assessed from the standpoint of another (Mannheim, RORTY), and those who argue that history itself ultimately yields the perspective from which objective standards of criticism emerge. The latter view is clearest in HEGEL, who held that the end of history yields a state of 'absolute knowledge' where the historical subject, the world spirit, attains an authentic understanding of the character of its own development. Historicist perspectives are usually contrasted with the methodology of natural science, which seeks to understand phenomena by reference to universal physical laws (the term initially gained currency in German debates about the relation between the *Geistes-* and *Naturwissenschaften*). It is thus odd that POPPER denounced historicism as the view that history is governed by principles analogous to scientific laws, though his critics may find a pleasing irony in his manifestly ahistorical use of the term.

DAVID BAKHURST

**Hobbes, Thomas** (1588–1679) English philosopher and political thinker. Hobbes's epistemology is not only an account of the nature and sources of knowledge; it is also a theory of the relative values of different types of knowledge, and especially of the surpassing value of scientific knowledge. The two principal types of knowledge that he recognizes are differently labelled in his various writings. Sometimes, as in the relatively early *Elements of Law* (1640), he speaks of 'knowledge original' on the one hand and science on the other (Tonnies, 1889, p. 24); at other times, as in *Leviathan* (1651), he distin-

guishes between knowledge of fact and knowledge of consequence (Molesworth, 1839–45, vol. 3. p. 71). It is essentially the same distinction in both places. Original knowledge or knowledge of fact is the registration by the senses of some accident or property of an object at a time; it is easily acquired knowledge, but it is also piecemeal, touching only this or that local object, and fleeting, lasting only as long as there are traces of it in the imagination. It can also be idiosyncratic, reflecting the peculiarities of one person's experience or vantage point. Original knowledge is not necessarily miscellaneous or inchoate: over time it enables people to recognize one accident or property as a sign of another, and thereby to register regularities in experience. But original knowledge does not alert us to any causal or necessary connections between properties or facts, and the range of regularities that it discloses is likely to be very narrow.

Scientific knowledge overcomes some of these limitations. It does hit on necessary connections. It is also general, synoptic, uncontroversial, well adapted to communication at a time and suitable for preservation over time. The key to its superiority over original knowledge is its linguistic medium. Whereas the medium of original knowledge is sense, scientific knowledge presupposes the existence of names, ways of combining names into propositions, and ways of combining true propositions into demonstrations (Molesworth, vol. 3, p. 35). It is only with the availability of names that we have a means of preserving sensory information beyond its half-life in one person's head. Names are vital aids to memory and help to make possible the communication of original knowledge. They also enable people to represent whole classes of things on the basis of similitudes between a few observed members of a class.

Propositions that link general names allow us to reason about things we could not even have thoughts about in the absence of language, namely relations between classes. Thanks to these 'universal propositions', we are able to conceive truths about relations between classes, e.g. all triangles and all

179

figures whose interior angles add up to two right angles: thanks to demonstrations made out of universal propositions we are also able to register relations of dependence between such truths, which is what constitutes scientific knowledge. Science, as Hobbes puts it in *Leviathan*, is the knowledge of the consequence of one affirmation to another (Molesworth, vol. 3, p. 71). It is knowledge of what follows from what or what is caused or necessitated by what (cf. Molesworth, vol. 1, p. 3). Hobbes's model of a work of science was Euclid's *Elements*, in which informative and even surprising conclusions are shown to be remote consequences of undeniable and obvious axioms and postulates (*see* GEOMETRY). He also admired writings in physics, such as Galileo's, which presented scientific demonstrations as exercises in applied geometry. Mere tabulations or registers of scientific results, such as were insisted upon by Bacon's method, Hobbes regarded as works of natural history only, and a cut below natural science or philosophy. The reason was that they only listed, and did not find principles or axioms from which to derive, the facts that were registered. The experimentalists who were responsible for the contents of the registers were in their turn not really scientists, for they lacked the demonstrative understanding that science required (Molesworth, vol. 4, pp. 436–7). The same went for the craftsmen, engineers and artificers who were skilled in such applied sciences as fortification-making: though they received the credit for their products, it was really mathematics that gave birth to them (Molesworth, vol. 3, p. 75).

Scientific knowledge could overcome more than limitations of original knowledge; it could act against some of the distorted valuations suggested by the passions. In other words, it could improve upon the pre-scientific practice of distinguishing good from bad or good from evil according to what gives pleasure or pain. That the practice was unreliable Hobbes thought needed little demonstration. He points out that something pleasant is good only in relation to an occasion and the constitution of the one who experiences the pleasure (cf. Molesworth, vol.

3, pp. 40–1). A person may find a thing pleasant on one occasion and call it 'good' then, only to change his mind later (Molesworth, vol. 2, p. 196; vol. 3, p. 146). And the very thing that one person calls 'good' on an occasion, another person may call 'bad' on the same occasion. Experiences of pleasure and pain, then, cannot be expected to generate consistent valuations over time or between people. Worse, such experiences can suggest defeasible valuations. Something that seems to be worth avoiding because it is unpleasant may turn out to be worth suffering all things considered, and something that seems to be worth pursuing because it is gratifying may not really be worth pursuing when all relevant considerations, including calculable consequences, are allowed to weigh. To give some illustrations drawn from politics, the felt unpleasantness of losing one's liberty under government does not by itself show that the loss of liberty is evil and to be avoided (Tonnies, pp. 138–40; Molesworth, vol. 2, pp. 126–9). Maybe the loss of liberty is acceptably unpleasant when one considers the unpleasant consequences of everyone's holding on to their liberty. Symmetrically, the fact that it is exhilarating to people to compete with one another, and highly gratifying to win, does not mean that competing and winning are good without qualification: on the contrary, a knowledge of the consequences of competing and winning may show that, on balance, they are not good after all. What Hobbes calls civil science or the science of politics is in large part a doctrine for correcting naive valuations in the light of a knowledge of the consequences.

One of the more striking features of Hobbes's account of scientific knowledge is his extravagant praise of its benefits. If it were not for natural philosophy and geometry, he claims repeatedly in his writings, human existence would largely be devoid of well-being. The fruits of navigation, architecture and agriculture – the main ingredients of 'commodious living' as he and his contemporaries knew it – would have been enjoyed far less widely, if at all, and life would have been reduced to 'the rude simpleness of antiquity' (Molesworth, vol. 2, p. iv). Not that natural philosophy and geometry on their own were able to supply the best life people were capable of: they did not provide for security. A distinct branch of science – a science of bodies politic or civil science – was required to ensure that material prosperity and life itself were not lost through war – through reversion to a life that was 'solitary, poor, nasty, brutish and short' (Molesworth, vol. 3, p. 113). Hobbes did not hold, then, that all of the good things in life were due to natural philosophy or geometry, but he did look to science of one kind or another to make human beings flourish or at least to keep human life from deteriorating.

Though Hobbes thinks that human beings need science in order to live well, he denies that science comes naturally to human beings. All of the abilities that science requires – from a knack for the apt imposition of names to an ability to develop or follow a long train of reasoning – can only be acquired with great effort, and probably only by a few. Perhaps surprisingly for a philosopher who thinks that human beings are not cut out by nature to discover natural causes or to live according to clear conceptions of the good and the just, Hobbes never confronts the sceptical arguments that suggest that human intellectual limitations forever put a true natural science or a true civil or moral science beyond our reach.

He was certainly aware of such arguments and of attempts in the 1600s to refute them. He was a close friend of Marin Mersenne and Pierre Gassendi, both of whom had published treatises concerned with scepticism as early as the 1620s, and he was one of the first readers of DESCARTES' *Meditations*, being among the few handpicked to supply Objections (his was the Third Set) to the work in advance of its publication. However, his extremely terse comments on Meditation I show that he was unmoved by the sceptical hypotheses unfolded there, and probably that he did not appreciate their novelty. In his own published writings there is scarcely any mention of philosophical scepticism, let alone any investigation or refutation of it. Perhaps he did not need to vindicate his belief in the possibility of science against scepticism: he believed in a pretty modest sort of natural science and an unpresumptuous civil science. In common with many writers of the 1600s Hobbes held that the hypotheses proposed by a modern physics could not be conclusively demonstrated to be true, because there was no natural effect an omnipotent God could not have produced in more than one way. A physics that attempted to show that a given effect couldn't but have been produced in a certain way was thus out of the question. Yet this was the sort of physics that sceptical arguments were primarily directed against. Hobbes did believe that a demonstrative geometry and pure mechanics was possible, because the effects dealt with in those sciences were human artefacts rather than divine ones. But physics was less certain than these sciences. By aiming only to show what could have caused natural phenomena, it was suitably modest by sceptical standards. It had no pretensions to conclusiveness. Hobbesian civil philosophy did have such pretensions, but justifiably so in Hobbes's opinion, since in telling us how to make and keep the peace it did not trace a natural phenomenon independent of our will to an equally independent cause; it traced something that depends on our will – namely peace – to precepts that can govern the will, and it motivated the will to accept the precepts. It thus did not attempt to transcend the order of things that were accessible to demonstrative science.

*See also* SCEPTICISM, MODERN.

WRITINGS

*English Works of Thomas Hobbes* ed. Sir W. Molesworth, 11 vols (London; J. Bohn, 1839–45).

*Thomas Hobbes Malmesburiensis Opera Philosophica quae Latine scripsit omnia* ed. Sir W. Molesworth, 5 vols (London: J. Bohn, 1839–45).

*The Elements of Law* ed. F. Tonnies (London: Marshall and Simpkin, 1889).

New editions are being published by the Clarendon Press under the direction of N. Malcolm, and, in French, by Vrin, under the direction of Y.-C. Zarka.

BIBLIOGRAPHY

Jessop, T.E.: *Thomas Hobbes* (London: Longmans, 1960).
Laird, J.: *Hobbes* (London: Ernest Benn, 1934).
Peters, R.: *Hobbes* (Harmondsworth: Penguin, 1956).
Reik, M.: *The Golden Lands of Thomas Hobbes* (Detroit: Wayne State University Press, 1977).
Robertson, G.C.: *Hobbes* (Edinburgh: Blackwood, 1886).
Sorell, T.: *Hobbes* (London: Routledge, 1986).
Spragens, T.: *The Politics of Motion: The World of Thomas Hobbes* (Lexington: University Press of Kentucky, 1973).
Taylor, A.E.: *Hobbes* (London: Constable, 1908).
Tuck, R.: *Hobbes* (Oxford: Oxford University Press, 1989).

TOM SORELL

**holism** Epistemological holism is the view that whole theories are the units of confirmation. Single hypotheses yield observational predictions only with the aid of a body of background theory. This means that a failed prediction does not conclusively refute the hypothesis from which it is derived: it is always possible to save the hypothesis by revising some of the background beliefs. Such holism has been defended by many twentieth-century philosophers, including Pierre Duhem, Rudolf Carnap and W.V. Quine. It is a consequence of epistemological holism that whether a belief is justified depends upon the support of the whole structure of beliefs to which it belongs. For empiricist philosophers who wish to explain meaning in terms of verification, epistemological holism may lead to a controversial semantic holism which asserts that more inclusive bodies of theory serve as the units of meaning.

BIBLIOGRAPHY

Carnap, R.: *The Logical Syntax of Language* (London: Routledge and Kegan Paul, 1937).
Duhem, P.: *The Aim and Structure of Physical Theory* (New York: Atheneum, 1962).
Quine, W.V.: *Pursuit of Truth* (Cambridge, MA: Harvard University Press, 1990), ch. 1.

CHRISTOPHER HOOKWAY

**Hume, David (1711–76)** Scottish philosopher, born in Edinburgh. Hume's theory of knowledge starts from the distinction between perception and thought. When we see, hear, feel, etc. (in general, perceive) something we are aware of something immediately present to the mind through the senses. But we can also think and believe and reason about things which are not present to our senses at the time: e.g. objects and events in the past, the future or the present beyond our current perceptual experience. Such beliefs make it possible for us to deliberate and so to act on the basis of information we have acquired about the world.

For Hume all mental activity involves the presence before the mind of some mental entity. Perception is said to differ from thought only in that the kinds of things that are present to the mind in each case are different. In the case of perception it is an 'impression'; in the case of thought, although what is thought about is absent, what is present to the mind is an 'idea' of whatever is thought about. The only difference between an impression and its corresponding idea is the greater 'force and liveliness' with which it 'strikes upon the mind'.

All the things that we can think or believe or reason about are either 'relations of ideas' or 'matters of fact'. Each of the former (e.g. that three times five equals half of thirty) holds necessarily; its negation implies a contradiction. Such truths are 'discoverable by the operation of pure thought, without dependence on what is anywhere existent in the universe'. Hume has no systematic theory of this kind of knowledge; what is or is not included in a given idea, and how we know whether it is, is taken as largely unproblematic.

Each 'matter of fact' is contingent; its negation is distinctly conceivable and represents a possibility. That the sun will not rise tomorrow is no less intelligible and no more implies a contradiction than the proposition that it will rise. Thought alone is therefore never sufficient to assure us of the truth of any matter of fact. Sense experience is needed. Only what is directly present to the senses at a given moment is known by perception alone. A belief in a matter of fact which is not present at the time must therefore be arrived at by a transition of some kind from present impressions to a belief in the matter of fact in question. Hume's theory of knowledge is primarily an explanation of how that transition is in fact made. It takes the form of an empirical 'science of human nature' which is to be based on careful observation of what human beings do and what happens to them.

Hume finds that all reasonings from a current impression to an absent matter of fact are founded on the relation of cause and effect. He therefore seeks the source of the idea of causality. That one thing is the cause of another cannot be discovered by thought alone. It must be derived from experience. It cannot be derived from any single observed instance; the most we can observe is that two things are contiguous and one happens before the other. But that is not sufficient for causation; 'there is a *necessary connexion* to be taken into consideration'.

We get that idea only after the repeated experience of things of one kind being followed by things of another kind. That sets up a connection in thought between things of the two kinds; the thought of one of them naturally leads the mind to a thought of the other. Then whenever we actually perceive (i.e. get an impression of) a thing of the first kind, we come, not just to think about, but to believe that a thing of the second kind will occur. What turns the mere thought of something into the belief that it is so is the presence of an impression, not just an idea, of something associated with that thing in the past. A belief, for Hume, is therefore 'a lively idea related to or associated with a present impression'. It is in following out connections established in our minds by past experience that we are led by a present impression to believe in an absent matter of fact.

In explaining in detail how this works, Hume first rejects the traditional idea that the 'faculty of reason' or 'the understanding', either when operating on its own or in combination with the results of sense experience, is the source of the inference to an absent matter of fact. Reason alone cannot be the source of the inference, since one matter of fact never by itself implies any other distinct matter of fact. We need the help of experience. But reason, even in combination with past experience, cannot be what leads us from an observed correlation between things of two kinds to the belief that that correlation will continue in the future. If it did, it would have to 'proceed upon the supposition' that future instances will resemble past instances, or that 'the course of nature continues always uniformly the same'.

All inferences from past or present experience to an unobserved matter of fact 'proceed upon' that principle. But no assurance can be given to that principle from reason alone; it is not impossible, in the sense of implying a contradiction, for the future to be different from the past. Whether the future will resemble the past is a contingent matter of fact. Experience is therefore needed to assure us of that principle. It cannot do so alone, since the principle partly concerns the future, and past experience alone can tell us only how things have been in the past. Something more than past experience is needed.

But reason, even when combined with past experience, cannot be what leads us to believe that the future will resemble the past. If it did, it would be by means of an inference from past experience to the principle that the future will resemble the past. And, as before, any such inference would have to 'proceed on the supposition' that the future will resemble the past. But that would 'be evidently going in a circle, and taking that for granted which is the very point in question'.

Reason, or the understanding, is therefore not in play. 'There is nothing in any object, consider'd in itself, which can afford us a reason for drawing a conclusion beyond it; and, . . . even after the observation of the frequent or constant conjunction of objects, we have no reason to draw any inference concerning any object beyond those of which we have had experience.'

It is not reason but 'the imagination' that is found to be responsible for our making the empirical inferences that we do. There are certain general 'principles of the imagination' according to which ideas naturally come and go in the mind under certain conditions. It is the task of the 'science of human nature' to discover such principles, but without itself going beyond experience. For example, an observed correlation between things of two kinds can be seen to produce in everyone a propensity to expect a thing of the second sort given an experience of a thing of the first sort. We get a feeling, or an 'impression', when the mind makes such a transition, and that is what leads us to attribute *necessity* to the relation between things of the two kinds. There is no necessity in the relations between things that happen in the world, but, given our experience and the way our minds naturally work, we cannot help thinking that there is.

A similar appeal to certain 'principles of the imagination' is what explains our belief in a world of enduring objects. Experience alone cannot produce that belief; everything we directly perceive is 'momentary and fleeting'. And whatever our experience is like, no reasoning could assure us of the existence of something independent of our impressions which continues to exist when they cease. The series of our constantly changing sense impressions presents us with observable features which Hume calls 'constancy' and 'coherence', and these naturally operate on the mind in such a way as eventually to produce 'the opinion of a continu'd and distinct existence'. The explanation is complicated, but it is meant to appeal only to psychological mechanisms which can be discovered by 'careful and exact experiments, and the observation of those particular effects, which result from [the mind's] different circumstances and situations'.

We believe not only in bodies, but also in persons, or selves, which continue to exist through time, and this belief too can be explained only by the operation of certain 'principles of the imagination'. We never directly perceive anything we can call ourselves; the most we can be aware of in ourselves are our constantly changing, momentary perceptions, not the mind or self which has them. For Hume, there is nothing that really binds the different perceptions together; we are led into the 'fiction' that they

form a unity only because of the way in which the thought of such series of perceptions works upon our minds. 'The mind is a kind of theatre, where several perceptions successively make their appearance; . . . there is properly no *simplicity* in it at one time, nor *identity* in different; whatever natural propensity we may have to imagine that simplicity and identity. The comparison of the theatre must not mislead us. They are the successive perceptions only, that constitute the mind' (*see* APPERCEPTION; KANT).

Hume is often described as a SCEPTIC in epistemology, largely because of his rejection of the role of reason, as traditionally understood, in the genesis of our fundamental beliefs. That rejection, although allied to the scepticism of antiquity, is only one part of an otherwise positive general theory of human nature which would explain how and why we think and believe and do all the things we do.

*See also* KANT; PROBLEMS OF INDUCTION; RATIONALISM; SCEPTICISM, MODERN; SELF-KNOWLEDGE AND SELF-IDENTITY.

WRITINGS

A Treatise of Human Nature (London: 1739–40); ed. L.A. Selby-Bigge, revised P.H. Nidditch (Oxford: Oxford University Press, 1978).

Enquiry Concerning the Human Understanding (London: 1748); in *Enquiries Concerning Human Understanding and Concerning the Principles of Morals* ed. L.A. Selby-Bigge, revised P.H. Nidditch (Oxford: Oxford University Press, 1975).

BIBLIOGRAPHY

Fogelin, R.: *Hume's Scepticism in the Treatise of Human Nature* (London: Routledge and Kegan Paul, 1985).

Kemp Smith, N.: *The Philosophy of David Hume* (London: Macmillan, 1941).

Pears, D.: *Hume's System: An Examination of the First Book of His Treatise* (Oxford: Oxford University Press, 1991).

Penelhum, T.: *Hume* (New York: St. Martin's Press, 1975).

Stove, D.C.: *Probability and Hume's Inductive Scepticism* (Oxford: Oxford University Press, 1973).

Stroud, B.: *Hume* (London: Routledge and Kegan Paul, 1977).

BARRY STROUD

**Husserl, Edmund (1859–1938)** German philosopher. Husserl was the creator of PHENOMENOLOGY, in his *Logical Investigations* (1900–1), *Ideas* (1913) and later works. He was born in Moravia, received a PhD in mathematics, working with Weierstrass, and then turned to philosophy under the influence of Franz BRENTANO. He took over the latter's concern with intentionality and developed it further into what was to become phenomenology. After an attempt to found mathematics in psychology, in *Philosophie der Arithmetik* (vol. 1, 1891: vol. 2 never appeared), he gave up PSYCHOLOGISM and started, around 1895, the work on *Logical Investigations*, his first phenomenological work. The first volume is a critique of psychologism; the second consists of six studies of basic logical notions.

In 1906 Husserl got the idea of the transcendental reduction, or EPOCHE, and he developed phenomenology in an 'idealist' direction. His *Ideas* is the first work which gives a full and systematic presentation of phenomenology. Husserl here distinguishes between the natural attitude and the transcendental, or phenomenological, attitude. The natural attitude we have when we are dealing with the objects in the world around us: physical things, events, actions, persons and the various features of these things (their shape, colour, etc.). These latter features, which can be shared by several objects, Husserl calls ESSENCES or *eidos*. Essences are studied in the eidetic sciences, of which mathematics is the most highly developed. Phenomenology is for Husserl a study of a different realm of objects, the *noemata*, the features that make one's consciousness be consciousness of objects. We arrive at these features through a special kind of reflection upon our own consciousness, the EPOCHE.

The notion of a noema is a key to the understanding of Husserl's phenomenology. Brentano had characterized intentionality as 'directedness upon an object'. This characterization may work well when the act has an object, but leads to problems in the case of acts that fail to have an object, like hallucinations or people who are thinking about Pegasus. Instead of characterizing intentionality by appeal to an object towards which our consciousness is directed, Husserl concentrated on the features of our consciousness which make our acts be *as if of* an object. The *noema* is the collection of all these 'as if of' features. The *noemata* are akin to FREGE's 'third world' objects, that is, the meanings of linguistic expressions. According to Husserl, 'the *noema* is nothing but a generalization of the notion of meaning (*Bedeutung*) to the field of all acts' (*Ideas* III, 89, 2–4). Just as by distinguishing between an expression's meaning and its reference one can account for the meaningful use of expressions that fail to refer, so, according to Husserl, can the distinction between an act's *noema* and its object help us to overcome Brentano's problem of acts without an object.

The *noema* has two components: first, the 'object meaning' that integrates the various components of our experience into experiences of the various features of *one* object, and, second, the 'thetic' component that differentiates acts of different kinds, e.g. the act of perceiving an object from the act of remembering it or thinking about it. In acts of perception the *noema* that we can have is restricted by what goes on at our sensory surfaces, but the restriction does not narrow our possibilities down to just one. Thus in a given situation I may perceive a man, but later come to see that it was a doll, with a corresponding shift of *noema*. Such a shift of *noema* is always possible, corresponding to the fact that perception is always fallible. These boundary conditions, which constrain the *noema* that we can have, Husserl calls *hyle*. The *hyle* are not objects experienced by us, but are experiences of a kind which we typically have when our sensory organs are affected, but also can have in other cases, for example, under the influence of fever or drugs.

Unlike the meaning of linguistic expressions, as usually conceived, the *noemata* are rich objects, with an inexhaustible pattern of components. These are largely sedimentations of past experience and are to a high degree culture-dependent. They are influenced by our living together with other subjects where we mutually adapt to one another and come to conceive the world as a common world in which we all live, but which we experience from different perspectives. This adaptation (*Einfühlung*) was extensively studied by many of Husserl's students, notably Edith Stein. The common world, as experienced by us, Husserl calls our *lifeworld*. It was the main theme of his last big work *The Crisis of the European Sciences*, of which a part was published in 1930. Husserl's conception of the lifeworld has become important for the methodology of the humanities and the social sciences, largely because it provides a framework for discussing the subjective perspective and the many features of our way of structuring the world of which we are unaware, e.g. the many features of the culture we have grown up in.

From 1917 on, Husserl became increasingly interested in the role of the body and of human activities in the way we structure the world. These ideas recur in different versions in HEIDEGGER's existentialism and in MERLEAU-PONTY's phenomenology. Sartre too was strongly influenced by Husserl, particularly by the idea that our material surroundings do not uniquely determine our *noema*. Sartre developed this idea into a philosophy of freedom.

Husserl died in Freiburg just in time to avoid being sent to a concentration camp (he was a Jew). His family, his library and all his 40,000 pages of manuscripts were rescued from Germany by the Franciscan Van Breda, who established the Husserl archive in Louvain where the material is now accessible to researchers.

WRITINGS

*Logische Untersuchungen* I–II, in *Husserliana* (the standard edition of Husserl's works; The Hague: Martinus Nijhoff vols 18–19; trans. J.N. Findlay *Logical Investigations*, 2 vols (London: Routledge and Kegan Paul, 1970).
*Ideen* I–III, in *Husserliana* vols 3–5; Book 1 trans. F. Kersten as *Ideas* (The Hague: Martinus Nijhoff, 1982).
*Formale und transzendentale Logik*, in *Husserliana* vol. 17; trans. D. Cairns *Formal and Transcendental Logic* (The Hague: Martinus Nijhoff, 1969).
*Kartesianische Meditationen*, in *Husserliana* vol. 1; trans. D. Cairns *Cartesian Meditations* (The Hague: Martinus Nijhoff, 1960).
*Krisis der europäischen Wissenschaften und die transzendentale Phänomenologie*, in *Husserliana* vol. 6; trans. D. Carr *The Crisis of European Sciences and Transcendental Phenomenology* (Evanston Ill: Northwestern University Press, 1970).

BIBLIOGRAPHY

Bell, D.: *Husserl* (London: Routledge, 1990).
Dreyfus, H. ed.: *Husserl, Intentionality and Cognitive Science* (Cambridge, MA: MIT Press, 1982).
Miller, I.: *Husserl, Perception and Temporal Awareness* (Cambridge, MA: MIT Press, 1984).
Mohanty, J.: *The Possibility of Transcendental Philosophy* (Dordrecht: Martinus Nijhoff, 1985).
Smith, D. and McIntyre, R.: *Husserl and Intentionality: a Study of Mind, Meaning and Language* (Dordrecht: Reidel, 1982).

DAGFINN FØLLESDAL

# I

idea 'Ideas' began with Plato, as eternal, mind-independent forms or archetypes of the things in the material world. NEOPLATON-ISM made them thoughts in the mind of God who created the world. The much criticized 'new way of ideas', so much a part of seventeenth- and eighteenth-century philosophy, began with DESCARTES' conscious extension of 'idea' to cover whatever is in human minds too, an extension of which LOCKE made much use. But are they like mental images, of things outside the mind; or non-representational, like sensations? If representational, are they mental objects, standing between the mind and what they represent; or are they acts and modifications of a mind perceiving the world directly? Finally, are they neither objects nor acts, but dispositions? Malebranche and Arnauld (and then Leibniz) famously disagreed about how 'ideas' should be understood, and recent scholars disagree about how Arnauld, Descartes, Locke and Malebranche in fact understood them.

BIBLIOGRAPHY

Ashworth, F.J.: 'Descartes' theory of clear and distinct ideas', in *Cartesian Studies* ed. R.J. Butler (Oxford: Blackwell, 1972), 89–105.
Gibson, J.: *Locke's Theory of Knowledge, and its Historical Relations* (Cambridge: Cambridge University Press, 1960), pp. 13–28.
Jolley, N.: *The Light of the Soul: Theories of Ideas in Leibniz, Malebranche, and Descartes* (Oxford: Clarendon Press, 1990).
McRae, R.: ' "Idea" as a philosophical term in the seventeenth century', *Journal of the History of Ideas* 26 (1965), 175–90.
Yolton, J.W.: 'Ideas and knowledge in seventeenth-century philosophy', *Journal of the History of Philosophy* 13 (1975), 145–65.

R.S. WOOLHOUSE

idealism The philosophical doctrine that reality is somehow mind-correlative or mind-co-ordinated – that the real objects comprising the 'external world' are not independent of cognizing minds, but only exist as in some way correlative to the mental operations. The doctrine centres on the conception that reality as we understand it reflects the workings of mind. And it construes this as meaning that the inquiring mind itself makes a formative contribution not merely to our understanding of the nature of the real but even to the resulting character we attribute to it.

For a long time, a dispute raged within the idealist camp over whether 'the mind' at issue in such idealistic formulas was a mind emplaced outside of or behind nature (*absolute* idealism), or a nature-pervasive power of rationality of some sort (*cosmic* idealism), or the collective impersonal social mind of people-in-general (*social* idealism), or simply the distributive collection of individual minds (*personal* idealism). Over the years, the less grandiose versions of the theory came increasingly to the fore, and in recent times virtually all idealists have construed 'the minds' at issue in their theory as a matter of separate individual minds equipped with socially engendered resources.

As the accompanying table shows, idealist doctrine takes many forms. Perhaps the most radical of these is the ancient Oriental spiritualistic or panpsychistic idea – renewed in Christian Science – that minds and their thoughts are all there is; that reality is simply

## Table I  Versions of Idealism

I. ONTOLOGICAL VERSIONS

(1) *Causal idealism*
Everything there is, apart from minds themselves, arises causally from the operations of minds.

(2) *Supervenience idealism*
Everything there is, apart from minds themselves, is SUPERVENIENT upon the operations of minds (i.e. somehow inheres in them in ways that are not necessarily causal but involve some other mode of existential dependency).

II. EPISTEMIC VERSIONS

(1) *Fact idealism*
To be as a fact, is to be a language-formulable fact – that is, a truth. Every fact can be semantically captured in a language-formulated truth.

(2) *Cognitive idealism*
To be as a truth is to be knowable. Every truth can – potentially – be cognitively captured as an item of knowledge. Truth stands co-ordinate with the cognitive potential of mind.

(3) *Strong substantival idealism*
To be as a thing or entity is to be actually discerned (discriminated, identified, perceived) by some knower. (This is simply a restatement of Berkeley's idealistic thesis that 'To be is to be perceived.')

(4) *Weak substantival idealism*
To be as a thing or entity is to be discernible (discriminable, identifiable, perceivable). Any real thing (entity, object) can, in principle, be discerned by some knower; it must, in principle, be of a nature that admits cognitive access.

(5) *Explanatory idealism*
An adequate explanation of the nature of physical ('material') reality requires some recourse to mental characteristics or operations within the substantive content of the explanation.

(6) *Conceptual idealism*
Reality is to be understood in terms of the category of mind: Our knowledge of the real is grasped not merely in mind-supplied but indeed to some extent even in mind-patterned terms of reference. Our knowledge of fact always reflects the circumstances of its being a human artifact. It is always formed through the use of mind-made and indeed mind-invoking conceptions and its contents inevitably bear the traces of its man-made origins. Whatever we have any knowledge of we know in terms of mind-construed terms of reference *in whose conceptual content* there is some reflection of its origin in operations characteristic of mind.

the sum-total of the visions (or dreams?) of one or more minds.

It is quite unjust to charge idealism with an antipathy to reality, with *ontophobia*, as Ortega y Gasset called it. For it is not the *existence* but the *nature* of reality that the idealist puts in question. It is not reality but materialism that classical idealism rejects – and even here the idealists speak with divided voice. Berkeley's 'immaterialism' does not so much reject the existence of material objects as their unperceivedness.

There are certainly versions of idealism short of the spiritualistic position of an ontological idealism that holds that (as Kant puts it at *Prolegomena*, s. 13, n. 2) 'there are none but thinking beings'. Idealism need certainly not go so far as to affirm that mind *makes or constitutes* matter; it is quite enough to maintain (for example) that all of the characterizing properties of physical existents resemble phenomenal sensory properties in representing dispositions to affect mind-endowed creatures in a certain sort of way, so that these properties have no standing at all without reference to minds. Weaker still is an explanatory idealism which merely holds that an adequate *explanation* of the real always requires some recourse to the operations of mind.

Historically, positions of the generally idealistic type have been espoused by numerous thinkers. For example, BERKELEY maintained that 'to be (real) is to be perceived' (*esse est percipi*). This does not seem particularly plausible because of its inherent commitment to omniscience; it seems more sensible to claim 'to be is to be perceivable' (*esse est percipi posse*). For Berkeley, of course, this was a distinction without a difference: if something is perceivable at all, then God perceives it. But if we forgo philosophical reliance on God, the issue looks different, and now comes to pivot on the question of what is perceivable for perceivers who are *physically realizable* in 'the real world', so that *physical* existence could be seen – not so implausibly – as tantamount to observability-in-principle.

The three positions to the effect that real things just exactly are things as *philosophy* or as *science* or as '*commonsense*' takes them to be – positions generally designated as *scholastic*, *scientific* and *naïve* realism, respectively – are in fact versions of epistemic idealism exactly because they see reals as inherently knowable and do not contemplate mind-transcendence for the real. Thus, for example, the thesis of naïve ('commonsense') realism that 'External things exist exactly as we know them' sounds realistic or idealistic

according as one stresses the first three words of the dictum or the last four.

There is also another sort of idealism at work in philosophical discussion, an *axiological* idealism that maintains both that values play an objective causal or constitutive role in nature and that value is not wholly reducible to something that lies in the minds of its beholders. Its exponents join the Socrates of Plato's *Phaedo* in seeing value as objective and as productively operative in the world.

Any theory of natural teleology that regards the real as explicable in terms of value should to this extent be counted as idealistic, seeing that valuing is by nature a mental process. To be sure, the good of a creature or species of creatures (e.g. their well-being or survival, for example) need not be actually mind-represented. But nevertheless, goods count as such precisely because if the creatures at issue *could* think about it, they *would* adopt them as purposes. It is this circumstance that renders any sort of teleological explanation at least conceptually idealistic in nature. Doctrines of this sort have been the stock in trade of philosophy from the days of Plato to those of LEIBNIZ, with his insistence that the real world must be the best possible. And this line of thought has recently surfaced once more in the controversial 'anthropic principle' espoused by some theoretical physicists.

Then too, it is possible to contemplate a position along the lines envisioned in Fichte's *Wissenschaftslehre*, which sees the ideal as providing the determining factor for the real. On such a view, the real is not characterized by the science we actually have but by the ideal science that is the *telos* of our scientific efforts. On this approach, which Wilhelm Wundt characterized as 'ideal-realism' (*Idealrealismus*; see his *Logik*, vol. I 2nd edn, 1895, pp. 86ff), the knowledge that achieves adequation to the real (*adaequatio ad rem*) by adequately characterizing the true facts in scientific matters is not the knowledge actually afforded by present-day science as we have it, but only that of an *ideal* or *perfected* science. On such an approach – which has seen a lively revival in recent philosophy – a tenable version of 'scientific realism' requires the step to idealization, and realism becomes predicated on assuming a fundamentally idealistic point of view.

Over the years, many objections to idealism have been advanced. Samuel Johnson thought to refute Berkeley's phenomenalism by kicking a stone. He conveniently forgot that Berkeley's theory goes to great lengths to provide for stones – even to the point of invoking the aid of God on their behalf. G.E. MOORE pointed to the human hand as an undeniably mind-external material object. He overlooked that, gesticulate as he would, he would do no more than *induce people to accept* the presence of a hand on the basis of the hand-orientation of their *experience*. C.S. PEIRCE's 'Harvard experiment' of letting go of a stone held aloft was supposed to establish scholastic realism because his audience could not control their expectation of the stone's falling to earth. But an uncontrollable expectation is still an expectation, and the realism at issue is no more than a realistic thought-posture.

Immanuel KANT's famous 'Refutation of idealism' argues that our conception of ourselves as mind-endowed beings presupposes material objects because we view our mind-endowed selves as existing in an objective temporal order, and such an order requires the existence of periodic physical processes (clocks, pendula, planetary regularities) for its establishment. At most, however, this argumentation succeeds in showing that such physical processes *have to be assumed by minds*, the issue of their actual mind-independent existence remaining unaddressed. (Kantian realism is an intra-experiential 'empirical' realism.)

It is sometimes said that idealism is predicated on a confusion of objects with our knowledge of them and conflates the real with our thought about it. But this charge misses the point. The only reality with which we inquirers can have any cognitive commerce is reality as we conceive it to be. Our only information about reality is via the operations of mind – our only cognitive access to reality is through the mediation of mind-devised models of it.

Perhaps the most common objection to idealism turns on the supposed mind-independence of the real. 'Surely', so runs the objection, 'things in nature would remain substantially unchanged if there were no minds.' This is perfectly plausible in one sense, namely the *causal* one – which is why causal idealism has its problems. But it is certainly not true *conceptually*. The objection's exponent has to face the question of specifying *just exactly what* it is that would remain the same. 'Surely roses would smell just as sweet in a mind-denuded world!' Well . . . yes and no. Agreed; the absence of minds would not *change* roses. But roses and rose-fragrance and sweetness – and even the *size* of roses – are all factors whose determination hinges on such mental operations as smelling, scanning, measuring, and the like. Mind-requiring processes are required for something in the world to be discriminated as being a rose and determined as being the bearer of certain features. Identification, classification, property attribution are all required and by their very nature are all mental operations. To be sure, the role of mind is here *hypothetical*. ('*If* certain interactions with duly constituted observers took place, *then* certain outcomes would be noted.') But the fact remains that nothing could be discriminated or characterized as a rose in context where the prospect of performing suitable mental operations (measuring, smelling, etc.) is not presupposed.

The preceding inventory of versions of idealism at once suggests the variety of corresponding rivals or contraries to idealism. On the *ontological* side, there is *materialism*, which takes two major forms: (1) a *causal* materialism which asserts that mind arises from the causal operations of matter, and (2) a *supervenience* materialism which sees mind as an epiphenomenon to the machinations of matter (albeit not a *causal* product thereof – presumably because it is somewhere between difficult and impossible to explain how physical processes could engender psychological results). On the *epistemic* side, the inventory of idealism-opposed positions includes: (1) A factual realism that maintains linguistically inaccessible facts, holding that the complexity and diversity of fact outruns the limits of the reach of the mind's actual or possible linguistic (or, generally, symbolic) resources; (2) A cognitive realism that maintains that there are unknowable truths – that the domain of *truth* runs beyond the limits of the mind's cognitive access; (3) A substantival realism that maintains that there exist entities in the world which cannot possibly be known or identified: incognizables lying in principle beyond our cognitive reach; (4) A conceptual realism which holds that the real can be characterized and explained by us without the use of any such specifically mind-invoking conceptions as dispositions to affect minds in particular ways. This variety of different versions of idealism/realism means that some versions of the one will be unproblematically combinable with some versions of the other. In particular, a conceptual idealism maintaining that we standardly understand the real in somehow mind-invoking terms of reference is perfectly compatible with a materialism which holds that the human mind and its operations ultimately root (be it causally or superveniently) in the machinations of physical process.

Perhaps the strongest argument favouring idealism is that any characterization of the real that we can devise is bound to be a mind-constructed one: *our* only access to information about what the real is through the mediation of mind. What seems right about idealism is inherent in the fact that in investigating the real we are clearly constrained to use our own concepts to address our own issues; we can only learn about the real in our own terms of reference. But what seems right about realism is that the answers to the questions we put to the real are provided by reality itself – whatever the answers may be, they are substantially what they are because it is reality itself that determines them to be that way. Mind proposes but reality disposes. But, of course, in so far as one can learn about this reality, it has to be done in terms accessible to minds. Accordingly, while philosophical idealism has a long and varied past and a lively present, it undoubtedly has a promising future as well.

See also BERKELEY; KANT; OBJECTIVITY; REALISM.

BIBLIOGRAPHY

For the history of idealism: Otto Willmann, *Geschichte des Idealismus* 3 vols (Braunschweig: Vieweg, 1894–7).

For the German tradition: M. Krönenberg, *Geschichte des deutschen Idealismus* 2 vols (Munich: Beck, 1909 and 1912), and Nicolai Hartmann, *Die Philosophie des deutschen Idealismus* 2 vols (Berlin: De Gruyter, 1923 and 1929).

For British idealism: J. Pucelle, *L'Idéalisme en Angleterre de Coleridge à Bradley* (Paris: Presses Universitaires de France, 1955), and A.C. Ewing, *Idealism: A Critical Survey* (London: Macmillan, 1934), as well as his collection of texts, *The Idealist Tradition* (Glencoe: Free Press, 1957).

Contemporary defences of idealist doctrines are presented in N. Rescher, *Conceptual Idealism* (Oxford: Blackwell, 1973); J. Foster, *The Case for Idealism* (London: Routledge and Kegan Paul, 1982); and T. Sprigge, *The Vindication of Absolute Idealism* (Edinburgh: Edinburgh University Press, 1983).

NICHOLAS RESCHER

**ideology**    The term 'ideology' was coined by Destutt de Tracy in 1796 to refer to the 'science of ideas'. This discipline, inspired by the EMPIRICISM of BACON, LOCKE and Condillac, was to give a NATURALISTIC explanation of the processes by which the mind forms thoughts. The aims of *idéologie* were ultimately pedagogical and political. A 'natural history of ideas' was to provide valuable knowledge of human nature and, by revealing the sources of erroneous belief, aid the perfection of scientific method. In turn, this knowledge was to facilitate the creation of a harmonious social order answering to the permanent needs of human beings.

After a brief period of eminence in the *Institut National*, the *idéologistes* were dismissed by Napoleon in 1803, and ridiculed as utopian visionaries under the name *idéologues*. In the 1840s, Marx and Engels appropriated the term 'ideology' in their critique of the Young Hegelians, and perpetuated its pejorative use, employing it to mean, not a discipline devoted to the persecution of error, but a distorted system of beliefs or 'false consciousness'. For Marx and Engels, an ideology is a set of ideas pertaining to social life (philosophical, religious, historical, economic, political ideas, etc.) that systematically misrepresents or 'inverts' reality. Ideologies are born and sustained by certain socio-economic conditions and, in turn, serve to bolster and legitimize those very conditions. For instance, it is characteristic of ideological inversion to 'objectify' products of human activity (e.g. religious phenomena and economic relations), representing them as autonomous forces and entities. As a result, contingent social relations appear as immutable parts of the 'natural order'. The capitalist market, for example, is seen as the sole mode of economic organization corresponding to 'human nature', political constitutions are represented as expressions of 'natural law', etc. At the same time, human behaviour rendered economically necessary by the prevailing social order is portrayed, and legitimized, as an outcome of 'free choice' (e.g. the worker's 'decision' to sell his or her labour). Ideologies also typically contain self-fulfilling beliefs that are not recognized as such (e.g. the belief that members of some racial group are intellectually inferior causes them to be denied educational resources which, in turn, causes their poor academic performance).

On a classical Marxist position, ideological misconceptions cannot be dispelled simply by presenting those in their grip with 'the truth', since ideologies contain features (e.g. standards of evidence and argumentation) that inhibit recognition of reality as it is. Consequently, many Marxists have argued that ideologies can be defeated only through the transformation of those socio-economic relations that generate them. Moreover, human beings will be trapped in ideological delusion until history produces a class, the proletariat, the true interests of which coincide with the necessity of conceiving things as they are.

However, some thinkers inspired by Marx, such as members of the Frankfurt School,

have been sceptical of this vision of the proletariat as the vehicle of Reason in history, and have argued that effective critique of dominant ideologies can occur without a wholesale transformation of social relations. Victims of an ideology may appreciate the falsehood of their conceptions if they can be brought to see the true source of their beliefs and the political function they fulfil. Developing parallels between Marx and Freud, the Frankfurt School present *ideologiekritik* as akin to psychoanalysis: the victim's emancipation depends on an exercise of self-understanding, in which the real nature and origin of his or her fundamental beliefs is gradually unmasked. On this view, an adequate conception of society must be fundamentally reflexive or self-aware; hence 'critical theories', in contrast to ideologies, understand their own origin and function.

In twentieth-century discussions of ideology, the term has often been employed in a purely descriptive and non-pejorative sense, being used simply to refer to the set of beliefs, attitudes, standards of rationality, etc. that embody the basic values of some social group and that group's conception of the political order appropriate to those values. Thus, in this sense, we may speak of 'liberal', 'conservative' or 'socialist' ideologies. This change of meaning was motivated principally by two developments, the first being the growth of the SOCIOLOGY OF KNOWLEDGE, pioneered by the work of Karl Mannheim. While, like Marx, sociologists of knowledge have been concerned with the way in which ideas and theories are created and mediated by economic relations, social institutions, class interests etc., they have frequently rejected the idea that ideologies are forms of 'false' consciousness, either because there is no possible non-ideological perspective on the world, or because the normative content of ideologies renders it inappropriate to describe them as true or false, or because ideologies, as symbolic systems with which individuals interpret social life, are functionally indispensable.

The second move towards a non-pejorative use of 'ideology' occurred within the MARXIST tradition itself. Lenin, Lukács and Gramsci each in different ways use the term to refer to forms of 'class consciousness', including the progressive vision of the proletariat. And in orthodox Marxism-Leninism, 'ideology' refers to any form of social consciousness, including 'scientific' accounts of the world supposedly free of mystification. Hence, many twentieth-century Marxists write of 'proletarian', 'Marxist' and 'scientific' ideologies in a way that Marx himself would have found nonsensical.

Another common twentieth-century use of the term 'ideology' is found in American social science of the 1960s, especially in the work of Daniel Bell and the 'end of ideology' theorists. For these thinkers, an ideology is a programme for the radical transformation of social life based on an explicit theory of society and embodying certain clearly articulated values. Ideologies function as forms of 'secular religion'; their proponents are obsessed with doctrinal purity, fidelity to the pronouncements of canonized authorities, and unquestioning obedience to charismatic leaders. After the defeat of Nazism, and with the apparent 'thaw' in post-Stalinist Russia, Bell and others suggested that the pre-eminence of such 'total ideologies' on the world political stage was finally over, to be replaced by the politics of liberal compromise. (Bell's critics were quick to point out the ideological role his own theories played as a contribution to the American liberalism of the Cold War.)

Whatever the merits of the original 'end of ideology' thesis, the recent demise of Marxism-Leninism in Eastern Europe indeed represents the passing of one of the most powerful of this century's ideologies (in Bell's sense). However, while the age of the 'total ideology' may indeed be waning, the significance of the concept of ideology has not diminished in the social sciences. Indeed, recent years have seen a renewed interest, particularly in the areas of feminism, postmodernism and cultural studies, in the project of unmasking relations of power and domination implicit in culturally dominant forms of theoretical and social discourse. While much of this work does not explicitly invoke the notion of ideology as such, there is no question of its debt to the critical project Marx began.

*See also* SOCIAL SCIENCE.

BIBLIOGRAPHY

Bell, D.: *The End of Ideology* 2nd edn (New York: Collier, 1962).

Geuss, R.: *The Idea of a Critical Theory* (Cambridge: Cambridge University Press, 1981), esp. ch. 1.

Gramsci, A.: *Selections from the Prison Notebooks* eds Q. Hoare and G. Nowell Smith (London: Lawrence and Wishart, 1971).

Habermas, J.: *Legitimation Crisis* (London: Heinemann, 1976).

Kolakowksi, L.: *Main Currents of Marxism* (Oxford: Oxford University Press, 1978), vol. I, ch. 8.

Lenin, V.I.: 'What is to be done?' in his *Collected Works* (Moscow: Foreign Language Publishing House, 1960–3; Progress, 1964–70), vol. 5.

Lichtheim, G.: 'The concept of ideology', in his *The Concept of Ideology and Other Essays* (New York: Random House, 1967).

Lukács, G.: *History and Class Consciousness* (London: Merlin, 1971).

Mannheim, K.: *Ideology and Utopia* (New York: Harcourt, Brace, and World, 1936).

Marx, K. and Engels, F.: *The German Ideology* in K. Marx and F. Engels, Collected Works (London: Lawrence and Wishart, 1976), vol. 5.

Shils, E.: 'The concept and function of ideology', in *International Encyclopedia of the Social and Sciences* ed. D.L. Sills (London: Macmillan and the Free Press, 1968), pp. 66–76.

DAVID BAKHURST

**illusion** see ARGUMENT FROM ILLUSION.

**immediacy, presence** The concepts of immediacy and presence refer to an alleged contrast between our knowledge of our own mental states on the one hand, and, on the other hand, our knowledge of physical objects and the mental states of others. Knowledge of the mental states of others is inferred from their behavior. Knowledge of physical objects may not be inferred, but it is acquired via complex causal chains involving spatially intermediate causes, and if challenged, it is justified by appeal to appearances. Knowledge of our own mental states is said to be known without such causal chains, and beliefs about these states are not justified by appeal to properties of a different sort. As Alston (1971) points out, the claim about causal immediacy is problematic, since we are ignorant of the causal antecedents involved in knowing our own mental states. However, the justification of beliefs about certain of our mental states does seem to appeal only to those states themselves.

*See also* BRENTANO; EXPERIENCE; THE GIVEN; KNOWLEDGE BY ACQUAINTANCE/ BY DESCRIPTION.

BIBLIOGRAPHY

Alston, W.: 'Varieties of privileged access', *American Philosophical Quarterly* 8 (1971), 223–41.
Brentano, F.: *Psychology from an Empirical Standpoint* trans. A.C. Rancurello, D.B. Terrell and L.L. McAlister (New York: Humanities Press, 1973), Bk 2, ch. 1.
Lewis, C.I.: 'Some logical considerations concerning the mental', in *Body and Mind* ed. G. Vesey (London: Allen and Unwin, 1964), 330–7.

ALAN H. GOLDMAN

**in itself/for itself** The distinction between the 'in itself' and the 'for itself' originated in the Kantian logical and epistemological distinction between a thing as it is in itself, and that thing as an appearance, or as it is *for us*. For KANT, the thing in itself is the thing as it is intrinsically, that is, the character of the thing apart from any relations in which it happens to stand. The thing for us, or as an appearance, on the other hand, is the thing in so far as it stands in relation to our cognitive faculties and other objects. 'Now a thing in itself cannot be known through mere relations; and we may therefore conclude that since outer sense gives us nothing but mere relations, this sense can contain in its representation only the relation of an object to the subject, and not the inner properties of the object in itself' (CPR, B. 67). Kant applies this same distinction to the subject's cognition of itself. Since the subject can know itself only in so far as it can intuit itself, and it can intuit itself only in terms of temporal relations, and thus as it is related to its' own self, it represents itself 'as it appears to itself, not as it is' (CPR, B. 69). Thus, the distinction between what the *subject* is in itself and what it is for itself arises in Kant in so far as the distinction between what an object is in itself and what it is for a knower is applied to the subject's own knowledge of itself.

HEGEL begins the transition of the epistemological distinction between what the subject is in itself and what it is for itself into an ontological distinction. Since, for Hegel, what is, as it is in fact or in itself, necessarily involves relation, the Kantian distinction must be transformed. Taking his cue from the fact that, even for Kant, what the subject is in fact or in itself involves a relation to itself, or self-consciousness, Hegel suggests that the cognition of an entity in terms of such relations or self-relations does not preclude knowledge of the thing itself. Rather, what an entity is intrinsically, or in itself, is best understood in terms of the potentiality of that thing to enter into specific explicit relations with itself. And, just as for consciousness to be explicitly itself is for it to be for itself by being in relation to itself (i.e. to be explicitly self-conscious), the for itself of any entity is that entity in so far as it is actually related to itself. The distinction between the entity in itself and the entity for itself is thus taken to apply to every entity, and not only to the subject. For example, the seed of a plant is that plant in itself or implicitly, while the mature plant which involves actual relations among the plant's various organs is the plant 'for itself'. In Hegel, then, the in itself/for itself distinction becomes universalized, in that it is applied to all entities, and not merely to conscious entities. In addition, the distinction takes on an ontological dimension. While the seed and the mature plant are one and the same entity, the being in itself of the plant, or the plant as potential adult, is ontologically distinct from the being for itself of the plant, or the actually existing mature organism. At the same time, the distinction retains an epistemological dimension in Hegel, although its import is quite different from that of the Kantian distinction. To know a thing it is necessary to know both the actual, explicit self-relations which mark the thing (the being for itself of the thing) and the inherent simple principle of these relations, or the being in itself of the thing. Real knowledge, for Hegel, thus consists in a knowledge of the thing as it is in and for itself.

SARTRE's distinction between being in itself and being for itself, which is an entirely ontological distinction with minimal epistemological import, is descended from the Hegelian distinction. Sartre distinguishes between what it is for consciousness to be, (i.e. being for itself), and the being of the transcendent being which is intended by consciousness (i.e. being in itself). Being in itself is marked by the total absence of relation, either with itself or with another. On the other hand, what it is for consciousness to be, being for itself, is marked by self relation. Sartre posits a 'pre-reflective Cogito', such that every consciousness of $x$ necessarily involves a 'non-positional' (in Husserlian terms, 'horizonal') consciousness of the consciousness of $x$. While in Kant every subject is both in itself, i.e. as it is apart from its relations, and for itself in so far as it is related to itself by appearing to itself, and in Hegel every entity can be considered as it is both in itself and for itself, in Sartre, to be self related or for itself is the distinctive ontological mark of consciousness, while to lack relations or to be in itself is the distinctive ontological mark of non-conscious entities.

*See also* NOUMENAL/PHENOMENAL.

BIBLIOGRAPHY

Hegel, G.W.F.: *The Phenomenology of Spirit* (1807) trans. A.V. Miller (Oxford: Clarendon Press, 1977).
Hegel, G.W.F.: *Hegel's Science of Logic* (1812–16,

1831) trans. A.V. Miller (London: Allen and Unwin, 1969).
Kant, I.: *Critique of Pure Reason* (1781) trans. N. Kemp Smith (London: Macmillan, 1964).
Sartre, J.P.: *Being and Nothingness* trans. H. Barnes (New York: Philosophical Library, 1956).
Taylor, C.: *Hegel* (Cambridge: Cambridge University Press, 1975).

M. OKRENT

**incorrigibility** Etymologically, 'incorrigibility' is most aptly used for the impossibility of one's being refuted, 'corrected', shown to be mistaken, in a belief, though there is a persistent misuse of the term for the impossibility of being mistaken (*see* INFALLIBILITY). As with infallibility, incorrigibility is most often asserted of one's beliefs about one's own current states of consciousness. It is plausible to think that a person is the final authority on what s/he is thinking, feeling, or sensing at the moment, and that his/her sincere report will always prevail against any counterevidence (Ayer, 1963, ch. 3). On the other hand, it seems plausible to suppose that physiological psychology could develop to the point that we would be justified in preferring neural readings to the subject's report where they conflicted (Armstrong, 1963).

BIBLIOGRAPHY

Armstrong, D.M.: 'Is introspective knowledge incorrigible?', *Philosophical Review* 72 (1963), 417–32.
Ayer, A.J.: *The Concept of a Person* (New York: St. Martin's Press, 1963).

*See also* bibliography of INFALLIBILITY.

WILLIAM P. ALSTON

**indeterminacy of reference** The 'inscrutability' or 'indeterminacy' of reference (Quine, 1990, p. 50) is a thesis of QUINE's related to the INDETERMINACY OF TRANSLATION: there is no fact of the matter what kinds of objects the terms of a language refer to. By making compensating adjustments in the translations of other words in a sentence, a predicate might be interpreted as applying to rabbits, to stages in the history of rabbits, to volumes of space one mile north of rabbits, and so on. Such indeterminacy is compatible with determinacy in the translation of sentences as a whole (Quine, 1990, p. 50).

*See also* ONTOLOGICAL RELATIVITY.

BIBLIOGRAPHY

Davidson, D.: *Inquiries into Truth and Interpretation* (Oxford: Oxford University Press, 1984), ch. 16.
Quine, W.V.: *Word and Object* (Cambridge, MA: MIT Press, 1960), ch. 2.
Quine, W.V.: *Pursuit of Truth* (Cambridge, MA: Harvard University Press, 1990), chs 2–3.

CHRISTOPHER HOOKWAY

**indeterminacy of translation** Radical translation is the attempt to understand a hitherto unencountered language without the aid of dictionaries or knowledge of related tongues. QUINE argues that such translation must exploit information about the stimulus conditions under which utterances are accepted, and he holds that alternative incompatible translations will be compatible with all such evidence. He concludes that there is no fact of the matter what any expression of the alien language means, and thus that a naturalistic philosophy cannot make sense of objective semantic facts. This reinforces his opposition to the analytic/synthetic distinction and to philosophical use of intensional notions. If effective, the argument also challenges the objectivity of intentional notions, propositional attitudes like belief and desire. Critics have claimed that he ignores much of the evidence relevant to translation although a version of the doctrine has been defended by some, like Davidson, who dispute Quine's empiricism and naturalism.

*See also* DAVIDSON.

BIBLIOGRAPHY

Quine, W.V.: *Word and Object* (Cambridge, MA: MIT Press), ch. 2.

Quine, W.V.: *Pursuit of Truth* (Cambridge, MA: Harvard University Press, 1990), ch. 3.

CHRISTOPHER HOOKWAY

**Indian epistemology** The Sanskrit synonym for 'cognition' is '*jñāna*', and for 'knowledge' is '*pramā*'. As is then to be expected '*jñāna*' applies to all cognitive states including true and false cognitions as well as doubt (*saṃśaya*) and mere conceptual thinking (*kalpanā*). *Pramā* is restricted to true cognition. Theories of knowledge, in the Indian tradition, are concerned, first, with (1) cognitions in general, (2) specifically, with true cognitions, and also (3) with false cognitions. The abstract noun 'truth' translates into '*pramatva*', also into '*prāmāṇya*'. The instrumental cause of a true cognition is called '*pramāṇa*'. A *pramāṇa* theory is one which theorizes about the (causal) modes by which true cognitions are acquired and their truth claims validated.

In India, the *pramāṇa* theories seem to have come into being in order to answer burgeoning sceptical tendencies. Sanjaya (pre-Buddhist) raised sceptical questions about religious, ethical and eschatological beliefs. Nāgārjuna (second century AD) questioned the very foundations of the distinction between means of true cognition and objects of such cognition. These sceptical arguments were later – by which time, the *pramana* theories had been considerably developed – strengthened and made more pointed by Jayarasi (eighth century AD) and Śri Harṣa (eleventh century AD). In order to show that definitions of knowledge in terms of correspondence or in terms of appropriate causal chains won't do, Śri Harṣa cites cases like a lucky guess of a gambler, a true conclusion derived from false premises (mistaking a column of dust for smoke, one infers the presence of fire which happens to be there), or inferring rightly that the animal over there is a bull from observing his horns where the real horns of the animal had been sawed off and replaced by imitation ones.

The Indian epistemologists asked certain standard questions. These questions may be divided into two groups: A: questions concerning any cognitive state or episode, and B: questions concerning those cognitions which have a truth value.

A. With regard to any cognitive state or episode (irrespective of its truth-value), two major questions were asked, leaving out of consideration ontological questions regarding the mode of being of cognitions (e.g. are they substances, qualities or actions?): (1) do cognitions have a form ('ākāra') intrinsic to them or are they intrinsically formless, deriving their seeming form ('blue', 'yellow', etc.) from their objects? and (2) are cognitions themselves known at the very moment of their occurrence, or are they only subsequently known by another cognition? As regards (1), the Buddhists defended the thesis that the cognition 'This is blue' really has 'blue' as its form (or content), while the Nyāya philosophers argued that the cognition 'This is blue' is itself formless, it is only *of* a blue thing which is out there in the world. However, according to the Nyāya, although the cognition of blue is not itself blue and does not have 'blue' as a *real* form, its logical analysis requires bringing out its intentional contents, called its qualifiers (*prakāratā*) which indeed constitute its total logical content. Thus the cognition expressed in the sentence 'This is blue' has a qualificandum-content 'this', which is determined by a qualifier-content 'thisness', another qualificandum-content 'blue' which again is determined by a qualifier-content 'blueness'. In general, on the Nyāya view, a cognition must have a content that is not linguistically expressed (in the above example, 'thisness' and 'blueness' are not), and it must have a content which is only a qualificandum and not also a qualifier (in the above example, 'this' is such a content).

Over issue (2), likewise, the Buddhists, the Prābhākara Mīmāmsakas and the Vedāntins insisted – overlooking the differences between them – that a cognition is always self-revealing (*svaprakāsa*); it is known by its mere presence, so that it is never the case that I know something but do not know that I know (*see* KK-THESIS). The Nyāya defended the opposite thesis according to which if $K_I$ is knowledge of the object o at

time $t_I$, $K_I$ itself is not known at $t_I$. $K_I$ can be known, and is usually known, by another cognition $K_2$ occurring at the succeeding moment $t_2$.

B. Keeping these two issues in mind, let us focus upon the concepts 'true cognition', 'means of true cognition' and 'truth'. The specific questions to be discussed are: (1) What are the different, not further reducible, types of true cognition? and, what are the instrumental causes of each? (2) How is 'truth' to be defined? (3) How is truth known?

(1) The list of irreducible types of true cognition ranged, in the history of Indian thought on these matters, from perception alone (the Cārvākas), to the most liberal Vedānta list which includes perception, inference, word, comparison, postulation and non-perception. In between these are the Vaiśeṣikas who admitted only perception and inference, and the Nyāya which would have the first four alone from the Vedānta list. The uniqueness of a type of cognition (and so its admissibility onto the list) required that it had a unique set of causal conditions, and that it be not reducible to any other. In this essay we shall consider only perception, inference and what is called 'word' (*śabda*).

(a) Perception (*pratyakṣa*) is defined (*Nyāyasûtra* 1.1.4) as the cognition which is caused by contact of the (appropriate) sense-organs with (their) objects. There were two extreme views about what perceptual cognition is like. At the one end, there was the Buddhist view that if it is caused by the object, the perceptual cognition must be non-linguistic and non-conceptual, it can only be an instantaneous and ineffable awareness of the mere *this*. At the other extreme, is the view of the Grammarians (chiefly, Bhartṛhari, fifth century AD) that all cognition, perception included, is linguistic. The Nyāya prefers an intermediate position: perceptual cognition is initially non-linguistic and non-conceptual, but this initial phase is soon replaced by a linguistic and conceptual cognition which is still perceptual, though now a perceptual judgement. A distinctive feature of the Nyāya view is that we perceive not only physical objects and their sensuous qualities, but also universals, relations and even absences. Looking at my blue pencil, I perceive the *thing* (*dravya*) pencil, the blue-particular inhering in that pencil, the universal blueness inhering in the blue-particular, (under certain conditions) the absence of red colour in the pencil, and the relation of inherence obtaining between the pencil and its colour – in each case, the visual sense-organ is in contact with the object in an appropriate relation (the Nyāya has here a ramified theory of relations at its disposal). I have also a perceptual cognition of my own self, which is expressed in judgements such as 'I am happy'. Some other schools of philosophy do not accept the Nyāya account of perception. The Jainas define perception by its 'clarity and distinctness' (*vaiśadya*). The Advaita Vedāntins regard perception as being of the nature of consciousness, meaning that the only thing that is directly evident is one's consciousness, everything else is given only as its content. The Nyāya view, however, was widely accepted and was most developed in detail.

(b) Inferential cognition (*anumiti*) is introspectively recognized by the cognizer as such, i.e. she says 'I am inferring'. It is caused by a succession of cognitive episodes: first, I see a column of smoke rising from the top of the yonder mountain. On seeing it, I remember the law-like relation (*vyāpti*) 'wherever there is smoke, there is fire' which I had previously learnt, and which is instantiated in the familiar and uncontroversial case of the stove in the kitchen. This remembrance makes me now see the smoke on the mountain top *as* a mark of fire. This last perceptual cognition (called by the Nyāya ('*parāmarśa*') gives rise to the inferential cognition 'Therefore, there is fire on the mountain'. Let us for the present purpose overlook the large discussions in the literature regarding the precise number and nature of these cognitive episodes which culminate in inferential cognition. What is noteworthy is that here we have a psychology of inference which is made to serve the purposes of a logic of inference. It is interesting and important to ask if this does not entail the sort of PSYCHOLOGISM which FREGE and HUSSERL wanted to overcome: brief

remarks will be made about this question at the end of this essay.

(c) *Śabda*: What is most distinctive of Indian epistemologies is the recognition of a type of cognition which the auditor (or reader) acquires upon hearing (or reading) the sentence or sentences uttered (or written) by a speaker (or writer) who is intellectually competent (i.e. knows what he is talking about) and morally honest (i.e. is not lying, does not want to mislead, etc.). Those who did not want to recognize such an irreducible class of knowledge generally sought to reduce the cases of such cognition to cases of inference, but it was easy to show that the accepted theories of inference stipulated requirements which the alleged inference (to which the word-generated cognition was to be reduced) could not satisfy. Examples of word-generated cognition are our knowledge of the past derived from reading history books, of contemporary events from reading newspapers, of moral rules and supersensible truths from reading the scriptures. This sort of cognition presupposes that the auditor/reader knows the meaning of the words that make up the sentence. Over and above that, each of the words needs to arouse a semantic expectancy (*ākāṅkṣā*) pointing to what follows; the words must have semantic fitness (*yogyatā*) (which rules out 'virtue is green' from producing a cognition); the words must succeed each other contiguously (in space and/or in time); and there must be an understanding of what the speaker/writer intends to convey. Granted that one understands a sentence *p* uttered by a competent speaker who is also known to be competent – so the theory goes – this *understanding* of the meaning of *p* itself amounts to *knowing* that *p*. The theory then rules out the possibility of understanding a false sentence, and has to deny any theory of 'sense' as distinguished from 'reference'.

(2) '*Truth*' (*prāmāṇya*): There are three *kinds* of definition of 'truth' in Indian theories of knowledge. One group of definitions define 'truth' in terms entirely of epistemic concepts, of features intrinsic to a cognition. For example, according to one such definition, a cognition is true if it has a qualifier which is

possessed by its qualificandum. Since 'qualifier' and 'qualificandum' are epistemic features, on this and kindred definitions (advanced by the Prābhākara School of *Mīmāṃsā*) every cognition is true, there is no (unitary) false cognition, the seemingly false cognition being a complex of cognitions each of which is true, but which are not distinguished from each other. Another group of definitions take a cognition to be true as long as it is not known to be false, or is not contradicted: on this view then 'truth' cannot be 'established', 'falsity' however can, and a cognition is *eo ipso* taken to be true as long as it is not determined to be false. In this sense again, truth is intrinsic to knowledge. Neither of these two sets of definitions can make room for the possibility of determining the truth *or* the falsity of a cognition. For a more satisfactory account, then, we turn to the Nyāya theory which unlike the first group makes truth consist of both epistemic and ontological features (so that merely inspecting the internal epistemic structure of a cognition leaves it undecided if the cognition is true or false), and unlike the second group, makes it possible to *ascertain* if a cognition is true or if it is false by advancing, beside the definition of 'truth', also a set of marks or tests of truth. First the definition:

Let the cognition under consideration be 'S is F'. This cognition has among others two qualifiers, 'S-ness' and 'F-ness'. The cognition is true if these qualifiers belong to the *thing* (not merely the epistemic object) that is allegedly known by that cognition. This celebrated definition of 'prāmāṇya' as *tadvati tatprakārakatva*, was first advanced by Gaṅgeśa (fourteenth century) and refined and elaborated by a whole series of illustrious commentators (*see* Mohanty, 1967).

The Nyāya distinguishes the definition of 'truth' from the test of truth. Truth is ascertained either through the ability of a cognition to lead to successful practice or through consensus. Most Indian philosophers, except the Vedāntins, have accepted some notion of pragmatic workability as a *test* of truth. The Vedāntins who reject this test – for, on their view, there is no test of truth, one can only test falsity – contend that

within the context of a dream dream-water may satisfy dream-thirst, and so may indeed work.

With regard to the last of the issues stated at the beginning, we have two major positions:

On the Nyāya view, a cognition is intrinsically neither true nor false. Both truth and falsity are 'extrinsic' possibilities, depending upon (1) how it relates to the ontological reality that is allegedly being cognized, and (2) if in addition to the generic causal factors for the sort of cognition, there is a special excellence (*guṇa*) or a special defect (*doṣa*). On the Vedāntin's view, a cognition is intrinsically true (= taken to be true), unless and until it is proved to be otherwise, thus only falsity is extrinsic. Gaṅgeśa argues that if this latter view were correct, immediately after I have a cognition, I could not have the *doubt* 'Is my cognition true or false?' The Vedāntins argue that if a cognition were not taken to be true, it could not stimulate appropriate practical response, to which Gaṅgeśa replies that in most cases what is needed for such response is not truth-determination but absence of doubt about falsity.

*General features*: The Indian epistemological theories are characterised by the following general features:

1. The analysis of a cognition is made under the 'guidance' of both its linguistic expression and one's phenomenological experience: the two constraints supplement and correct each other.
2. A cognition is construed as an episode in the inner life of the cognizer. Thus it is individuated by an ego and a temporal location. However, a cognition has a logical structure which allows for being exemplified in another numerically distinct episode belonging to another ego and/or another temporal location. This avoids the ruinous consequences of psychologism.
3. The theories are predominantly CAUSAL. The *pramāṇas* are construed both as (specific) causes of (specific sorts of) true cognitions and also as providing evidence and justificatory ground for them.

4. There is an overall FALLIBILISM. There is no cognition for which error is ruled out on logical grounds (unless, it is by definition, as with the Mīmāṃsā theories referred to in B (2)).

5. The distinction between ANALYTIC and synthetic truths either is not to be found, or at most, remains on the distant horizon.

6. The opposition between RATIONALISM and EMPIRICISM never made its appearance. The question whether perception is the only *pramāna* or inference and *śabda* are also to be counted amongst *pramānas* is not to be construed as the question whether experience is the only source of knowledge or not. Neither is perception (*pratyaksa*) the same as 'experience' (one also perceives, according to Nyāya, universals) nor is 'inference' (*anumana*) the same as 'reason'. Strictly speaking no concept of a priori knowledge is available.

BIBLIOGRAPHY

Chatterjee, S.C.: *Nyaya Theory of Knowledge* (Calcutta: Calcutta University Press, 1978).
Datta, D.M.: *Six Ways of Knowing* (Calcutta: Calcutta University Press, 1972).
Hattori Masaaki, D.: *On Perception* (Cambridge, MA: Harvard University Press, 1968).
Jayatilleke, K.N.: *Early Buddhist Theory of Knowledge* (London: Allen and Unwin, 1963).
Matilal, B.K.: *Perception: An Essay on Classical Indian Theories of Knowledge* (Oxford: Clarendon Press, 1986).
Mohanty, J.N.: *Gangesa's Theory of Truth* 2nd edn revised (Delhi: Motilal Banarasidass, 1989).
Potter, K.H. ed.: *Encyclopedia of Indian Philosophies* vol. II: *Indian Metaphysics and Epistemology. The Tradition of Nyaya-Vaisesika up to Gangesa* (Princeton: Princeton University Press, 1977).

J.N. MOHANTY

**indubitability** 'Indubitability' means, of course, not being subject to doubt, or, modally expressed, the impossibility of doubt.

Think of the term as applied to a particular bit of knowledge or a particular belief, for example, my knowledge that the wind is blowing hard here and now. We may distinguish at least three importantly different understandings of indubitability: (1) a psychological impossibility of entertaining a doubt; (2) a logical impossibility of entertaining a doubt (it is sometimes held that no sense can be attached to a person's being in doubt as to whether s/he is having a certain sensation); (3) the impossibility of there being any (real) grounds for doubt (Alston, 1989, ch. 10). Each of these has been supposed by various philosophers to attach to knowledge of self-evident truths or of one's current conscious states, though it is (3) that is of the most obvious and indubitable epistemological significance. DESCARTES is a philosopher who notoriously put great stock in indubitability (of the third sort) as necessary for knowledge.

BIBLIOGRAPHY

Alston, W.P.: *Epistemic Justification* (Ithaca, NY: Cornell University Press, 1989).

WILLIAM P. ALSTON

**induction, problem of** see PROBLEMS OF INDUCTION.

## induction: enumerative and hypothetical

### KINDS OF INDUCTION

In *enumerative induction*, a generalization is inferred from evidence about instances of the generalization. Suppose, for example, that Sam has examined several peaches and found pits in them and has not found any peaches without pits. Making an enumerative induction, Sam concludes that all peaches have pits.

Sam's inference is non-demonstrative; its conclusion does not follow necessarily from his evidence. In contrast, a valid deductive argument is demonstrative. The conclusion of a valid deductive argument is guaranteed to be true if the premises are true. The premises, (P1) 'All peaches have pits', and (P2) 'X is a peach', logically entail the conclusion, (C) 'X has a pit'. (C) cannot be false if both (P1) and (P2) are true. But Sam's evidence, consisting of instances of peaches with pits, does not guarantee the truth of his conclusion that all peaches have pits. Other peaches, not yet examined, could conceivably fail to have pits.

This familiar contrast between non-demonstrative induction and demonstrative deduction is useful here, but it can also be misleading, as we shall see.

In *hypothetical induction*, a hypothesis is inferred as the best explanation of the evidence. Seeing the tips of a man's shoes peeping out from under the curtain, Sam concludes that a man is hiding behind the curtain. Again Sam's inference is non-demonstrative. The shoes might be empty shoes that just happen to have ended up pointing out from under the curtains (*see* INFERENCE TO THE BEST EXPLANATION).

Induction in the widest sense includes any non-demonstrative inference, including non-demonstrative predictive inferences and default assumptions. Given that Albert now plans to be in Pittsburgh tomorrow, Sam infers that Albert will be in Pittsburgh tomorrow; this is a non-demonstrative predictive inference because Sam realizes that his evidence concerning Albert's present plan does not guarantee that Albert will carry out his plan.

This is not enumerative induction, since Sam's conclusion is not a generalization of his evidence. It is not hypothetical induction, because Sam's conclusion is not a hypothesis that might explain his evidence – Sam does not suppose that Albert's being in Pittsburgh tomorrow explains Albert's current plan to be there tomorrow. Instead he makes the converse supposition, namely, that Albert's having this plan explains why Albert will be in Pittsburgh tomorrow.

Given that Albert is a person, Sam assumes that Albert can walk up some stairs, so Sam invites Albert to visit his third-floor apartment; here Sam relies on a default assumption that could be incorrect, since it is possible that Albert cannot walk up stairs even though he is a person. Induction in the widest sense includes such default assumptions (Ginsberg, 1987).

Induction in this sense is, of course, to be sharply distinguished from so-called mathematical induction, which is a form of demonstrative proof. (Mathematical induction is the following principle. Suppose you can show that a claim about natural numbers (0, 1, 2, ...) holds for zero, and you can show that, for any natural number $n$, if the claim holds for all natural numbers less than or equal to $n$ the claim also holds for $n$. Then you can conclude that the claim holds for all natural numbers.)

In all cases of non-demonstrative induction, the evidence is compatible with several hypotheses. We can only draw a conclusion if it is more reasonable to accept one of these hypotheses rather than another.

Consider Sam's evidence that several peaches have been found to have pits and no peaches have been found not to have pits. That evidence is compatible with Sam's hypothesis that all peaches have pits and also with the hypothesis that only some peaches have pits but Albert has been removing all the peaches without pits before Sam sees them.

## THE BASIC RIDDLE

An important question about induction is how people are to decide among the hypotheses that are compatible with the evidence. Perhaps there are two questions here: (1) How do people decide among such hypotheses? and (2) How should people decide among such hypotheses? A sceptical answer to (2) is that people should not decide; people can have no reason to believe that one rather than another hypothesis is true, if both hypotheses are compatible with the evidence. A non-sceptical answer to (2) is that people are justified in deciding among hypotheses in whatever way it is they do decide, at least until they are presented with special reasons not to decide among hypotheses in that particular way. Further pursuit of this non-sceptical approach requires trying to answer the first question about how people actually do decide among those hypotheses that are compatible with the evidence.

After examining a few peaches, Sam concludes that all peaches have pits. When asked why he prefers that conclusion to the hypothesis that, although there are peaches without pits, Albert has been removing those peaches before Sam sees them, Sam responds that he hasn't even considered the other hypothesis and has no reason to consider it since there is no reason to suspect Albert of removing peaches without pits.

Consider the reply that there is reason to suspect Albert of removing such peaches, namely, the very evidence that Sam is relying on! Given that the evidence is compatible with both possibilities, is there any more reason for Sam to take the evidence to support his conclusion, that all peaches have pits, than there is for him to take the evidence to support the hypothesis that Albert has been removing the peaches that have no pits?

Sam might answer that there is more reason to accept his conclusion than to accept the suggested competitor: namely, his conclusion is simpler than the suggested alternative, and it leaves him with fewer questions to answer. Although his conclusion leaves him with the question why all peaches have pits, the alternative hypothesis not only leaves him with a similar question, namely, why some peaches do and some peaches do not have pits, but also raises additional questions such as why Albert should be removing the peaches without pits and how Albert would be able to tell when peaches don't have pits so that he could screen them out.

People prefer simpler hypotheses that raise fewer questions to more complex hypotheses that raise more questions. But it is not easy to say what makes one hypothesis simpler than another and what it is for a hypothesis to raise further questions.

So far, we have been considering competition between an enumerative induction and a hypothetical induction – an enumerative induction to the generalization, 'All peaches have pits', and a hypothetical induction to the conclusion, 'Albert is removing peaches with pits before Sam can see them'.

Goodman (1965) has stressed that there are also competing enumerative inductions. Let $t$ be the present time and consider the following generalization, 'All peaches either have been examined by Sam at or before $t$ and have pits or have not been examined by Sam at or before $t$ and do not have pits'. Let us abbreviate this generalization as 'All peaches are pitst', where by definition something is pitst if and only if, either Sam examines it at or before $t$ and it has a pit or Sam does not examine it at or before $t$ and it does not have a pit. The evidence for this generalization parallels the evidence for Sam's generalization. Just has Sam has found several peaches to have pits and has not found any to be without pits, Sam has found several peaches to be pitst and has not found any not to be pitst. In a case like this, what distinguishes a reasonable generalization, like 'All peaches have pits', from an unreasonable generalization, like 'All peaches are pitst'?

Goodman calls this the 'new riddle' of induction. The problem is not to justify our practice of preferring the first sort of generalization to the second. The problem is to characterize our practice by specifying those features of these generalizations that can lead us to infer one conclusion rather than any of its competitors (see GOODMAN; PROBLEMS OF INDUCTION; PROJECTION).

Goodman's own answer is that, other things being equal, we prefer generalizations using 'entrenched' predicates to generalizations using less entrenched predicates, where a predicate is more entrenched the more we have used it as a principal predicate in previous inductions. Sam has used 'has a pit' in previous inductive conclusions and has never used 'is pitst', i.e. 'is such that, either Sam examines it at or before $t$ and it has a pit or Sam does not examine it at or before $t$ and it does not have a pit'. So the former predicate is better entrenched than the second and Sam is led to accept the generalization, 'All peaches have pits', rather than its competitor 'All peaches are pitst'.

So far so good. But what if Sam is a young child who has never before made inferences about things having pits? In that case,

Goodman's answer is not available, although Sam will still be more inclined to infer that all peaches have pits rather than that all peaches are pitst. What distinguishes these hypotheses for Sam at this stage?

SIMPLICITY

SIMPLICITY may play a role, but not just the simplicity with which a hypothesis is stated, since competing hypotheses can always be expressed equally simply. Any hypothesis can be given an arbitrarily simple formulation by using a single symbol, e.g. H, to stand for that hypothesis.

It is possibly relevant that the favoured hypothesis, 'All peaches have pits', is much easier for Sam to comprehend than the other hypothesis, 'All peaches are pitst', which Sam has to understand as, 'All peaches are such that either Sam examines them at or before t and they have pits or Sam does not examine them at or before t and they do not have pits'.

More significantly, the psychological relation for Sam between Sam's first hypothesis and his evidence is much simpler than the relation between this second hypothesis and his evidence. It is easier for Sam to understand how his favoured hypothesis can account for his finding some peaches with pits and none without pits than it is for Sam to understand how the second hypothesis would account for this evidence. The argument from his favoured hypothesis to the evidence is briefer and more direct than the argument from the other hypothesis to his evidence.

This is so, at any rate, if Sam's evidence is expressed as we have just expressed it. The matter would be otherwise if the evidence were described as follows: 'Sam has found some peaches to be pitst and has not found any peaches not to be pitst.' If the evidence were described that way, then it would be simpler to account for the evidence using the hypothesis that all peaches are pitst than it would be to account for the evidence using the hypothesis that all peaches have pits. But Sam is not interested in describing his evidence in this second way. He is interested in the fact that he has found peaches with

pits and has not found peaches without pits. That is what he wants to account for. He is not directly interested in accounting for the fact that he has found peaches to be pitst, etc. (If Sam were unusually precocious, he might be interested in accounting for the fact that all peaches are pitst to the extent that such an account would help to explain why he has found peaches to have pits.)

So one thing that may lead Sam to distinguish these hypotheses in the way that he does is a concern to have the simplest account for aspects of evidence in which he is interested.

Notice that, in this view, the simplest, most inferable hypothesis is not to be identified with the hypothesis with the simplest natural formulation. It is the simplicity of the connection between that hypothesis and the evidence that is important, not just the simplicity of the hypothesis taken by itself (if that even makes sense).

A contrary view would hold that the only relevant question about the connection between evidence and hypothesis is whether the hypothesis is compatible with the evidence. In this contrary view, Sam should be concerned to find the simplest hypothesis compatible with the evidence. But that could not be right. The evidence might be completely irrelevant to the simplest hypothesis compatible with it. An ideally simple true hypothesis, such as 'Everything exists', would on this view pre-empt and prevent any other inductive inference, since it would always be the simplest hypothesis compatible with the evidence!

We would need at the very least to restrict attention to competing hypotheses: find the simplest of competing hypotheses compatible with the evidence. But that would still be unacceptable. Given several competing hypotheses, there can be evidence for one that does not rule out the others.

Sam's hypothesis that all peaches have pits competes with the hypothesis that Albert is removing the peaches with pits before Sam sees them and there may come to be evidence for this second hypothesis that does not absolutely rule out the first hypothesis. Sam may notice that Albert always does something to the peaches before Sam gets to examine them. He may discover that Albert has recently bet Alice that Sam will never find a peach without a pit, something that gives Albert a motive to remove peaches without pits. He may learn that Sam has a pit-detecting machine that can be used to determine whether or not a given piece of fruit has a pit in it. Enough evidence of this sort may eventually lead Sam to conclude that the second hypothesis is correct – Albert is removing peaches without pits before he, Sam, sees them. Sam may reach this conclusion even though the evidence remains compatible with both hypotheses so that there is no change in which is the simpler hypothesis compatible with the evidence.

## COHERENCE

For evidence that is compatible with several competing hypotheses to support one hypothesis over the others, there has to be some further special connection between the evidence and that particular hypothesis that does not hold between the evidence and the others. The hypothesis must cohere better with that evidence than the competing hypotheses do.

A potential conclusion can relevantly cohere with evidence by helping to account for the evidence, as for example 'Albert is removing peaches without pits' would help to account for Sam's complex evidence. But there are other cases too, as in predictive induction. When Sam concludes from Albert's intention to be in Pittsburgh tomorrow that Albert will be in Pittsburgh tomorrow, Sam's conclusion does not help to account for his evidence. Things are the other way round: Sam infers that Albert's having that intention will help to account for his being in Pittsburgh.

Coherence is not an isolated relation between Sam's hypothesis and the evidence for it. Other things that Sam accepts are relevant also. Sam's conclusion that Albert will be in Pittsburgh tomorrow coheres with his evidence only given Sam's beliefs about how intentions can lead to action. What is really relevant, we might say, is how the

acceptance of this conclusion will affect the overall coherence of Sam's view.

It can be difficult to achieve total overall coherence even in science. Sometimes there are two or more large internally coherent disciplines that do not cohere with each other. For example, in nineteenth-century science, thermodynamics implied that the earth was younger than the biological theory of evolution held it to be.

A further complication is that evidence is sometimes left unaccounted for or even abandoned as 'observational error' in the interest of a larger coherence. Favoured background assumptions may be given up for similar reasons. Inference is really a process of change in view. One's initial views are modified in order to make them more coherent. This can involve adding new beliefs but it can also involve removing old beliefs.

This is why it can be (and usually is) misleading to contrast induction with deduction. Induction and deduction are of very different categories. Deduction is concerned with implication and consistency. It is not directly concerned with inference. For a conclusion to be deducible from certain premises is not for that conclusion to be inferable from those premises. If you believe those premises and then deduce that conclusion, you learn that your beliefs imply that conclusion. That by itself is not enough for you to be able to be justified in inferring that conclusion. It may instead provide a reason for you to question your belief in the premises.

Coherence is not the only factor in inductive inference. Otherwise, Sam would make his view as coherent as possible, without any other constraint, perhaps by adopting as his only belief the principle, 'All is one'. But that would be to throw away all of his evidence and all of his prior beliefs without sufficient reason.

## CONSERVATISM

Sam balances coherence against conservatism. He tries to make a minimal change in his overall view that will improve its coherence. To give up everything else in favour of the single belief that 'All is one' would be to put too much emphasis on coherence and not enough on conservatism. Never to abandon prior beliefs and evidence would be to put too much emphasis on conservatism.

The conflicting demands of conservatism versus coherence can lead to the acceptance of two largish views that are each internally coherent although they conflict with each other on certain points, as in the example of nineteenth-century thermodynamics and evolutionary theory.

Historically, some philosophers seem to have supposed that we should ignore conservatism. We should build up a secure view via self-evident steps from a self-evident foundation. In this view, anything that cannot be given such a justification is to be rejected. Other philosophers have assumed, more reasonably, that what requires justification is changing what you believe; you are justified in believing as you do in the absence of any specific challenge to that belief.

Sam's goals, desires, needs and interests also play a role in his inductive reasoning. As we have seen, his tendency to choose the simpler of two competing hypotheses is a tendency to choose the hypothesis that gives simpler answers to questions in which he is interested. Furthermore, Sam's goals limit the conclusions he is interested in drawing. When Sam is trying to answer a particular question, he will try to restrict his inferences to conclusions that might bear on that question. He will try not to waste his time on trivial conclusions that do not advance the matter at hand.

Sam may be affected by a certain amount of wishful thinking. He may end up accepting one hypothesis (all peaches have pits) rather than another (Albert is removing peaches with pits before I can test them) because he would prefer the first hypothesis to be true (Sam doesn't want to think that he is being manipulated by Albert).

## UNRESOLVED ISSUES

There are many unsolved problems about induction. One is to characterize coherence in a relatively precise way. Another is to provide a rule for balancing coherence against conservatism. There are questions about wishful thinking. When does wishful thinking occur? Is wishful thinking ever justified?

Also, there is the following unsolved, difficult and generally unrecognized problem about induction: to provide a non-circular account of what constitutes competition among hypotheses.

Although hypotheses compete if they cannot both be true, there are often competing explanations that could all be true. It is consistent with Sam's evidence to suppose both (1) that Albert is screening peaches and is not going to allow any peaches without pits to be seen by Sam and (2) that all peaches have pits (so that, in fact, Albert will never have to remove any peaches before Sam sees them). However, if Sam comes to accept hypothesis (2), he cannot continue to suppose that his evidence – that all the peaches he has examined have pits – supports (1).

On the other hand, we cannot say that all explanations of certain data are in conflict. Suppose Sam has certain evidence concerning how Max died. The hypothesis that Max was strangled might conflict with the hypothesis that Max was poisoned, but neither of these hypotheses automatically conflicts with the hypothesis that Max died because oxygen wasn't getting to his brain (Harman, 1989).

Finally, it should be observed that some writers believe that probability theory offers the key to problems like these (van Fraassen, 1980, 1989; Jeffrey, 1983). However, probability theory yields results only given a distribution of prior probabilities and the issues discussed here will reemerge as issues about how these prior probabilities are to be determined.

See also BAYESIANISM; INFERENCE TO THE BEST EXPLANATION; PROBLEMS OF INDUCTION.

BIBLIOGRAPHY

van Fraassen, B.: The Scientific Image (Oxford: Oxford University Press, 1980).

van Fraassen, B.: *Laws and Symmetry* (Oxford: Oxford University Press, 1989).

Ginsberg, M.L.: *Readings in Nonmonotonic Reasoning* (Los Altos: Morgan Kaufmann, 1987).

Glymour, C.: *Theory and Evidence* (Princeton: Princeton University Press, 1980).

Goodman, N.: *Fact, Fiction, and Forecast* 2nd edn (Indianapolis: Bobbs Merrill, 1965).

Harman, G.: *Change in View: Principles of Reasoning* (Cambridge, MA: MIT/Bradford Books, 1986).

Harman, G.: 'Competition for evidential support', in *Proceedings of the Eleventh Annual Meeting of the Cognitive Science Society* (Hillsdale: Lawrence Erlbaum, 1989), 220–6.

Hempel, C.G.: *Aspects of Scientific Explanation* (New York: Free Press, 1965).

Hempel, C.G.: 'Provisos: a problem concerning the inferential function of scientific theories', in *The Limits of Deductivism* eds A. Grunbaum and W.C. Salmon (Berkeley: University of California Press, 1988), 19–36.

Holland, J., Holyoak, K., Nisbett, R. and Thagard, P.: *Induction: Processes of Inference, Learning, and Discovery* (Cambridge, MA: MIT/Bradford Books, 1986).

Jeffrey, R.C.: *The Logic of Decision* 2nd edn (Chicago: University of Chicago Press, 1983).

Quine, W.V. and Ullian, J.S.: *The Web of Belief* (New York: Random House, 1978).

GILBERT HARMAN

**infallibility** In epistemology this term is most appropriately used for the epistemic position of a subject vis-à-vis a given subject-matter, more specifically for the impossibility of the subject's being mistaken about that subject matter. Thus it is often held, and as often denied, that a normal human being cannot be mistaken as to whether s/he is currently in a certain kind of conscious state – a thought, feeling or sensation. Those who reject infallibility here do not, of course, deny that people have a high degree of cognitive access to such matters; they only deny that it is *impossible* for mistake to occur. It is claimed, for example, that there is always the possibility of applying the wrong concept to an item. Infallibility will be differently conceived (as will INCORRIGIBILITY, INDUBITABILITY) depending on the kind of impossibility involved (Alston, 1989, ch. 10),

whether, for example, this is logical or causal impossibility.

BIBLIOGRAPHY

Alston, W.P.: *Epistemic Justification* (Ithaca, NY: Cornell University Press, 1989).

Chisholm, R.M. and Swartz, R.J. eds: *Empirical Knowledge* (Englewood Cliffs: Prentice-Hall, 1973), pt IV.

WILLIAM P. ALSTON

**inference** It is not unusual to find it said that, an inference is a (perhaps very complex) act of thought by virtue of which act (1) I pass from a set of one or more propositions or statements to a proposition or statement and (2) it appears that the latter is true if the former is or are. This psychological characterization has occurred widely in the literature under more or less inessential variations.

It is natural to desire a better characterization of inference. But attempts to do so by constructing a fuller psychological explanation fail to comprehend the grounds on which inferences will be objectively valid – a point elaborately made by Gottlob FREGE. And attempts to better understand the nature of inference through the device of the representation of inferences by formal-logical calculations or derivations (1) leaves us puzzled about the relation of formal-logical derivations to the informal inferences they are supposed to represent or reconstruct, and (2) leaves us worried about the sense of such formal derivations. Are these derivations inferences? And aren't informal inferences needed in order to apply the rules governing the constructions of formal derivations (inferring that this operation is an application of that formal rule)? These are concerns cultivated by, for example, WITTGENSTEIN.

Coming up with a good and adequate characterization of inference – and even working out what would count as a good and adequate characterization here – is a hard and by no means nearly solved philosophical problem.

*See also* INTUITION AND DEDUCTION; PROBLEM OF RULE-FOLLOWING; PROOF.

BIBLIOGRAPHY

Baldwin, J.M. ed.: *Dictionary of Philosophy and Psychology* (Gloucester: Peter Smith, 1901, 1960).

Frege, G.: *The Basic Laws of Arithmetic* trans. and ed. M. Furth (Berkeley: University of California Press, 1964).

Harman, G.: *Thought* (Princeton: Princeton University Press, 1973).

Wittgenstein, L.: *Remarks on the Foundations of Mathematics* trans. G.E.M. Anscombe (Oxford: Blackwell, 1956).

ROBERT S. TRAGESSER

**inference to the best explanation** This is claimed by many to be a legitimate form of non-deductive reasoning, which provides an important alternative to both deduction and enumerative induction. Indeed, some would claim that it is only through reasoning to the best explanation that one can justify beliefs about the external world, the past, theoretical entities in science, and even the future. Consider belief about the external world and assume that we know what we do about the external world through our knowledge of our subjective and fleeting sensations. It seems obvious that we cannot *deduce* any truths about the existence of physical objects from truths describing the character of our sensations. But neither can we *observe* a correlation between sensations and something other than sensations since by hypothesis all we ever have to rely on ultimately is knowledge of our sensations. Nevertheless, we may be able to posit physical objects as the best explanation for the character and order of our sensations. In the same way, various hypotheses about the past might best explain present memory; theoretical postulates in physics might best explain phenomena in the macro-world; and it is even possible that our access to the future is through universal laws that are formulated to explain past observations. But what exactly is the form of an inference to the best explanation?

When one presents such an inference in ordinary discourse it often seems to have the following form:

1. O is the case.

2. If E had been the case O is what we would expect.

Therefore there is a high probability that

3. E was the case.

This is the argument form that PEIRCE called hypothesis or ABDUCTION. To consider a very simple example, we might upon coming across some footprints on a beach, reason to the conclusion that a person walked along the beach recently by noting that if a person had walked along the beach one would expect to find just such footprints.

But is abduction a legitimate form of reasoning? Obviously, if the conditional in 2 above is read as a material conditional such arguments would be hopelessly bad. Since the proposition that E materially implies O is entailed by O, there would always be an infinite number of competing inferences to the best explanation and none of them would seem to lend even *prima facie* support to its conclusion. The conditionals we employ in ordinary discourse, however, are seldom, if ever, material conditionals. Indeed, the vast majority of 'if . . ., then . . .' statements do not seem to be truth-functionally complex. Rather, they seem to assert a *connection* of some sort between the states of affairs referred to in the antecedent (after the 'if') and in the consequent (after the 'then'). Perhaps the argument form has more plausibility if the conditional is read in this more natural way. But consider an alternative footprints explanation:

1. There are footprints on the beach.
2. If cows wearing boots had walked along the beach recently one would expect to find such footprints.

Therefore, there is a high probability that

3. Cows wearing boots walked along the beach recently.

This inference has precisely the same form as the earlier inference to the conclusion that people walked along the beach recently and its premises are just as true, but we would no doubt regard both the conclusion and the inference as simply silly. If we are to distinguish between legitimate and illegitimate reasoning to the best explanation it would seem that we need a more sophisticated model of the argument form. It would seem that in reasoning to an explanation we need *criteria* for choosing between alternative explanations. If reasoning to the best explanation is to constitute a genuine alternative to inductive reasoning, it is important that these criteria not be implicit premises which will convert our argument into an inductive argument. Thus, for example, if the reason we conclude that people rather than cows walked along the beach is *only* that we are implicitly relying on the premiss that footprints of this sort are usually produced by people, then it is certainly tempting to suppose that our inference to the best explanation was really a disguised inductive inference of the form:

1. Most footprints are produced by people.
2. Here are footprints.

Therefore in all probability

3. These footprints were produced by people.

If we follow the suggestion made above, we might construe the form of reasoning to the best explanation as follows:

1. O (a description of some phenomenon).
2. Of the set of available and competing explanations E1, E2, . . ., En capable of explaining O, E1 is the best according to the correct criteria for choosing among potential explanations.

Therefore in all probability,

3. E1.

Notice that there is a crucial ambiguity in the concept of the best explanation. It might be true of an explanation E1 that it has the best chance of being correct without it being probable that E1 is correct. If I have two tickets in the lottery and one hundred other people each have one ticket, I am the person who has the best chance of winning, but it would be completely irrational to conclude on that basis that I am likely to win. It is much more likely that one of the other people will win than that I will win. To conclude that a given explanation is actually likely to

be correct one must hold that it is more likely that it is true than that the disjunction of all other possible explanations is correct. And since on many models of explanation the number of potential explanations satisfying the formal requirements of adequate explanation is unlimited this will be no small feat.

The model of explanation sketched above must be filled out, of course. Specifically, we need to know what the relevant criteria are for choosing among alternative explanations. Perhaps the single most common virtue of explanation cited by philosophers is *simplicity*. Sometimes simplicity seems to be understood in terms of the number of things or events the explanation commits one to. Sometimes the crucial question concerns the number of *kinds* of things the theory commits one to.

Explanations are also sometimes taken to be more plausible the more explanatory 'power' they have. This power is usually defined in terms of the number of things or more likely, the number of kinds of things, the theory can explain. Thus Newtonian mechanics was so attractive, the argument goes, partly because of the range of phenomena the theory could explain.

The familiarity of an explanation in terms of its resemblance to already accepted kinds of explanations is also sometimes cited as a reason for preferring that explanation to less familiar kinds of explanation. So if one provides a kind of evolutionary explanation for the disappearance of one organ in a creature, one should look more favourably on a similar sort of explanation for the disappearance of another organ.

The above are just three examples of criteria one might use in choosing among alternative explanations. There are many other candidates. But in evaluating the claim that inference to the best explanation constitutes a legitimate and *independent* argument form, one must explore the question of whether it is a *contingent* fact that at least most phenomena have explanations and that explanations that satisfy a given criterion, simplicity, for example, are more likely to be correct. While it might be nice (for scientists and writers of textbooks) if the universe were structured in such a way that simple, powerful, familiar explanations were usually the correct explanation, it is difficult to avoid the conclusion that if this is true it would be an empirical fact about our universe discovered only a posteriori. If the reasoning to the explanation relies on such criteria, it seems that one cannot without circularity use reasoning to the best explanation to discover that the reliance on such criteria is safe. But if one has some independent way of discovering that simple, powerful, familiar explanations are more often correct, then why should we think that reasoning to the best explanation is an independent source of information about the world? Indeed, why should we not conclude that it would be more perspicuous to represent the reasoning this way?

1. Most phenomena have the simplest, most powerful, familiar explanations available.
2. Here is an observed phenomenon, and EI is the simplest, most powerful, familiar explanation available.

Therefore, in all probability,

3. This is to be explained by EI.

But the above is simply an instance of familiar *inductive* reasoning.

*See also* EXPLANATION; the GIVEN; INDUCTION; PROBLEM OF THE EXTERNAL WORLD.

BIBLIOGRAPHY

Harman, G.: 'The inference to the best explanation', *Philosophical Review* 74 (1965), 88–95.
Lipton, P.: *Inference to the Best Explanation* (London: Routledge, 1991).
Peirce, C.S.: *Collected Papers* eds C. Hartshorne and P. Weiss (Cambridge, MA: Harvard University Press, 1931–5).
Russell, B.: *The Problems of Philosophy* (Oxford: Oxford University Press, 1959).
Thagard, P.: 'The best explanation: criterion for theory choice', *Journal of Philosophy* 75 (1978), 76–92.

RICHARD FUMERTON

**infinite regress argument**   According to the infinite regress argument for FOUNDATION-ALISM, if every justified belief could be justified only by inferring it from some further justified belief, there would have to be an infinite regress of justifications; because there can be no such regress, there must be justified beliefs that are not justified by appeal to some further justified belief. Instead, they are non-inferentially or immediately justified; they are basic or foundational, the ground on which all our other justified beliefs are to rest.

Variants of this ancient argument have persuaded and continue to persuade many philosophers that the structure of epistemic justification must be foundational. ARISTOTLE recognized that if we are to have knowledge of the conclusion of an argument on the basis of its premises, we must know the premises. But if knowledge of a premiss always required knowledge of some further proposition, he argued, then in order to know the premise we would have to know each proposition in an infinite regress of propositions. Since this is impossible, there must be some propositions that are known, but not by demonstration from further propositions; there must be basic, non-demonstrable knowledge, which grounds the rest of our knowledge.

Foundationalist enthusiasm for regress arguments often overlooks the fact that they have also been advanced on behalf of SCEPTICISM, RELATIVISM, fideism, contextualism (Annis, 1978) and COHERENTISM. Sceptics agree with foundationalists both that there can be no infinite regress of justifications and that nevertheless there must be one if every justified belief can be justified only inferentially, by appeal to some further justified belief. But sceptics think all true justification must be inferential in this way – the foundationalist's talk of immediate justification merely obscures the lack of any rational justification properly so-called. Sceptics conclude that none of our beliefs is justified. Relativists follow essentially the same pattern of sceptical argument, concluding that our beliefs can only be justified relative to the arbitrary starting assumptions or presuppositions either of an individual or of a form of life.

Fideists also agree with foundationalists that there can be no infinite regress and that nevertheless there must be one if every justified belief can be justified only inferentially. And, again like sceptics and relativists, fideists reject foundationalist talk of rational but immediate justification. Instead, there are beliefs (the fideist's core religious beliefs) that are certified–hence justified, but non-rationally–by faith, where faith is usually construed as some divinely inspired act, state or faculty that yields warranted trust in the otherwise unjustified beliefs. What stops the fatal regress of justifications is not belief justified by some immediate foundationalist rationalist intuition, but belief certified by a non-inferential affair beyond the pale of rationality.

Sceptics and relativists see little to choose between such fideism and foundationalism. They are not alone in doing so. Contextualists and coherentists are likely to agree that whether one appeals to faith or to immediacy, the effect is the same: arbitrariness in one's starting point, which would lie beyond responsible canons of justification and criticism (Annis, 1978; BonJour, 1978).

Regress arguments are not limited to epistemology. In ethics there is Aristotle's regress argument (in *Nichomachean Ethics*) for the existence of a single final end of rational action. In metaphysics there is AQUINAS'S regress argument for an unmoved mover: if everything in motion were moved only by a mover that itself is in motion, there would have to be an infinite sequence of movers each moved by a further mover; since there can be no such sequence, there is an unmoved mover. A related argument has recently been given to show that not every state of affairs can have an explanation or cause of the sort posited by principles of sufficient reason; such principles are false, for a priori reasons having to do with their own concepts of explanation (Post, 1980; Post, 1987, pp. 84–98).

How can the same argument serve so many masters, from epistemology to ethics to metaphysics, from foundationalism to coherentism to scepticism? One reason is that the argument has the form of a reduction to absurdity of conjoined assumptions. Like all such arguments, it cannot tell us, by itself, which assumption we should reject in order to escape the absurdity. Foundationalists reject one, coherentists another, sceptics a third, and so on. Furthermore, the same argument form can be instantiated by different subject matters, of which epistemology is but one.

What exactly is the form of the argument? Black (1988) suggests the following. The first assumption or premiss has the form

$$(1) \quad (\forall x)(Ax \rightarrow (\exists y)(Ay \ \& \ xRy)).$$

That is, for every $x$ that has property A, there is a $y$ such that $y$ has A and $x$ bears relation R to $y$. Compare: for every belief $x$ that is justified, there is a belief $y$ such that $y$ is justified and $x$ is justified by $y$ (or $x$ is based on $y$, or $x$ is inferrable from $y$, or $y$ is a reason for $x$). Compare also: for everything $x$ that is in motion, there is a $y$ in motion that moves $x$. The next assumption is

$$(2) \quad (\exists x)Ax.$$

That is, there are A's – there are justified beliefs, there are things in motion. Additionally, one must assume

(3) R is irreflexive, and
(4) R is transitive.

That is, (3) nothing bears R to itself; and (4) if $x$ bears R to $y$ and $y$ bears R to $z$, $x$ bears R to $z$. For instance, if $x$ justifies $y$ and $y$ justifies $z$, $x$ justifies $z$; if $x$ moves $y$ and $y$ moves $z$, $x$ moves $z$. Finally, the argument assumes

(5) There is no infinite sequence each of whose elements both has A and bears R to its predecessor.

These five assumptions entail a contradiction. In particular, it follows from (1)–(4) that, contrary to (5),

(6) There is an infinite sequence each of whose elements both has A and bears R to its predecessor.

It can be shown rigorously not only that (1)–(4) entail (6), but that each of (1)–(4) is necessary for the entailment (Black, 1988). For example, (6) is not entailed by (1)–(3); R must also be transitive. Thus the regress argument for foundationalism works only if all inferential justification is transitive (Post, 1980).

Since (1)–(5) entail a contradiction, one or more of (1)–(5) must be rejected. Foundationalists reject (1), or rather the relevant instantiation of (l); there are beliefs that are justified but not by appeal to some further justified belief. (A few foundationalists may also reject (3), allowing some beliefs to be self-justifying.) Fideists likewise reject the relevant instantiation of (1), but disagree with foundationalists about the nature of the justification of the otherwise unjustified beliefs (faith versus rational intuition). Sceptics and relativists, on the other hand, hold to (1) but reject (2); there are no justified beliefs. Coherentists hold to (1)–(3) but reject (4); inferential justification is often a holistic affair that is non-transitive. Contextualists may also reject (4), but mainly reject (1) in favour of *contextually* justified beliefs (Annis, 1978) – those which are unchallenged by the relevant objectors in a given context of justification.

Few philosophers if any seem to have rejected the relevant instantiation of (5), thus opting for what we might call justificational infinitism (as Peirce may do in *Collected Papers* 5.259–5.263). Nevertheless, foundationalists and others have often argued at length against the infinitist option. The usual attempts to do so prove to beg the question against infinitists, typically in favour of foundationalism. For example, it is often said that a regress of justifications would at best provide only conditional justification for its elements, and that we must appeal to some affair outside the regress (hence to something non-inferentially justified, so far as the resources of the regress are concerned). This is to assume just what the infinitist denies. But it now appears that a non-question-begging argument can be given, in the form of a reduction to absurdity of infinitism (Post, 1980; 1987, p. 91: for objections *see* Sosa, 1980; Moser, 1985). Other instantiations of

(5), for example in metaphysics, have often been rejected, as when philosophers argue that there can be an infinite sequence of movers or causes each moved or caused by its predecessor.

Regress arguments evidently are not the knock-down affairs their advocates have so often supposed them to be. Only if one's favoured way out of the contradiction is the only way, or at least the best way, need such arguments persuade. But showing this has proved surprisingly difficult, requiring forms of argument and evidence that go well beyond the resources of the regress argument itself.

For example, consider a regress argument for foundationalism. Suppose we grant the foundationalist that there are justified beliefs and that justification is irreflexive; this is to grant the relevant instantiations of (2) and (3). What about (4)? Is justification transitive? Some varieties clearly are, including deductive inferential justification, according to which $x$ justifies $y$ if $x$ is justified and $y$ is deductively inferrable from $x$. Suppose further that $y$ justifies $z$ in the same sense. It follows that $z$ is justified and deducible from $x$, hence that $x$ justifies $z$; deductive inferential justification is transitive. Indeed the model or ideal of deductive justification, from Aristotle's theory of demonstration through Euclid nearly to the present, helps explain why so many have supposed that inferential justification must be transitive.

But not all justification is deductive. For example, the justified belief $b$, that Sam is a bartender, inductively justifies belief $c$, that Sam can make a whisky-sour. Now consider the justified belief $a$, that Sam is a bartender who has forgotten how to make a whisky-sour. Belief $a$ justifies $b$ which inductively justifies $c$, yet obviously $a$ does not justify $c$ and indeed defeats it; transitivity apparently fails (Klein, 1976, pp. 806–7; Post, 1980, p. 39; Black, 1988, p. 431). Related problems affect varieties of justification according to which $x$ justifies $y$ only if $x$ confers a sufficiently high degree of probability on $y$ (Lehrer, 1970, pp. 122–3; Klein, 1976, p. 806; Black, 1988, pp. 431–2).

Another variety of inferential justification

is INFERENCE TO THE BEST EXPLANA-TION, roughly what Peirce called ABDUC-TION. Here $x$ justifies $y$ if $y$ is the best explanation of (the phenomena described by) $x$; if evolutionary theory best explains the fossil record, the record justifies the theory. But explanation relations may not all be transitive (Lehrer, 1970, pp. 112-3). Furthermore, as regards inference to *the best* explanation, suppose $y$ is the best explanation of $x$ (so that $x$ justifies $y$) and $z$ is the best explanation of $y$ (so that $y$ justifies $z$). If transitivity held, $z$ would be the best explanation of $x$. Yet this contradicts the supposition that $y$ is the best explanation of $x$; presumably there can be only one *best* explanation of $x$ (Post, 1980, p. 40).

Foundationalists are not the only ones affected by these troubles with transitivity. So are those fideists, sceptics and relativists who advance regress arguments for their distinctive views. Like foundationalists, they must assume that justification is transitive; otherwise we are not forced to reject (1) or (2), as they contend we are, in order to escape vicious regress. It therefore seems that coherentists, who reject transitivity, are in the best position of all to advance a regress argument for their view – a situation of some irony, in light of long tradition to the contrary, from Aristotle on. But the regress argument is slippery footing even for coherentists. If all beliefs are to be justified by inferring them from other beliefs, as (1) requires, how do we break out of the circle of beliefs to make contact with the world beyond? There are good coherentist answers to this question, some having the possibly welcome effect of denying (1), but they all require support from kinds of argument and evidence that exceed anything to be found in the regress argument itself.

BIBLIOGRAPHY

Alston, W.P.: 'Two types of foundationalism', *Journal of Philosophy* 73 (1976), 165-85.
Annis, D.B.: 'A contextualist theory of epistemic justification', *American Philosophical Quarterly* 15 (1978), 213-19.
Black, O.: 'Infinite regresses of justification',

*International Philosophical Quarterly* 28 (1988), 421-37.
BonJour, L.: 'Can empirical knowledge have a foundation?', *American Philosophical Quarterly* 15 (1978), 1-13.
Klein, P.D.: 'Knowledge, causality, and defeasibility', *Journal of Philosophy* 73 (1976), 792-812.
Lehrer, K.: 'Justification, explanation, and induction', in *Induction, Acceptance, and Rational Belief* ed. M. Swain (Dordrecht: Reidel, 1970), 100-33.
Moser, P.K.: 'Whither infinite regresses of justification?', *Southern Journal of Philosophy* 23 (1985), 65-74.
Post, J.F.: 'Infinite regresses of justification and of explanation', *Philosophical Studies* 38 (1980), 31-52.
Post, J.F.: *The Faces of Existence: An Essay in Nonreductive Metaphysics* (Ithaca, NY: Cornell University Press, 1987).
Sosa, E.: 'The raft and the pyramid: coherence versus foundations in the theory of knowledge', *Midwest Studies in Philosophy* 5 (1980), 3-25.

JOHN F. POST

**informal fallacies**   There are two basic kinds of informal fallacy: – sophistical tactics and erroneous inferences. A sophistical tactic is a technique of argumentation used to get an unfair advantage over one's opponent. This sort of fallacy need not involve an actual intention to cheat in every case, but it does have to be the kind of tactic that would characteristically be used for this purpose. Erroneous inferences, however, can be used in contexts other than those where two people are arguing with each other; one person is enough. This type of fallacy is an inference that falls short of some standard of correct inference (deductive, inductive, or whatever). All that is required, as far as context is concerned, is an appropriate standard of correct inference.

With both kinds of fallacy, it is important to distinguish between a fallacy as an error in a particular case and a fallacy as a general type of inference or sophistical tactic that can often go wrong, or be used wrongly in argumentation, and which we need to watch out for and guard against. It is also important to distinguish between fallacies and other less serious kinds of errors in argumentation, for example, blunders and weak arguments. For these reasons, there is always a burden of proof on a critic who makes a charge of fallacy in a particular case; he must bring forward evidence to substantiate his claim. (See BURDEN OF PROOF.) All fallacies (but especially the sophistical tactic type) presuppose a 'context of dialogue' from which the relevant evidence should be drawn.

Such 'contexts of dialogue' differ according to the purpose of the argument at hand. In a critical discussion, the purpose is to resolve a conflict of opinion. In a negotiation, the purpose is to come to an agreement on how to divide goods or interests that are in short supply. In an inquiry, the purpose is to prove some proposition, based on premises that can be agreed on as established knowledge. In an eristic dialogue, the purpose is to hit out verbally at the other party, defeating and humiliating the other party, even by violating rules of polite conversation. Many instances of fallacies involve a dialectical shift from one context of dialogue to another. An argument that is correct or appropriate in one context of dialogue may be incorrect or fallacious in another context.

To call a fallacy 'informal' is to say that in deciding whether it has been committed we need to take into account both the actual discourse (as with any fallacy) and the context of dialogue for the case. An argument may have a fallacious form, but not every instance of an invalid form of inference is an invalid inference. The reason is that a given argument can have many forms, some valid, and some invalid. If an argument is an instance of an invalid form of inference, it does not follow that the argument must be invalid. Whether the argument is fallacious or not depends on whether and how that form of inference has been used in the context of dialogue. Erroneous inference fallacies are generally less sensitive to context, and are therefore sometimes classified as 'formal' fallacies. But it is best to see them as informal, because the context of dialogue can still make some difference.

Only the most prominent fallacies are mentioned below. For more extensive treatments, *see* Hamblin (1970) or Walton (1987).

ERRONEOUS INFERENCES

*Improper Contraposition.* The form of inference 'If A then B; therefore if not A then not B' is deductively invalid. An argument having this form may well be fallacious. But it may not. For example, 'If the nations disarm, there will be peace; therefore if the nations do not disarm, there will not be peace' is an instance of *improper contraposition*. But that does not necessarily mean that it is a fallacious argument in every context of dialogue. It depends on how it was used, and on what went before in the dialogue. If the premiss were to have been supported, for example, by an earlier argument that war would break out if disarmament did not take place soon enough, it could be that no fallacy was committed.

*Composition* Inference from a property of the part to a property of the whole is warranted only in some cases. An example of a case where it is an erroneous inference: 'All the players on this hockey team are good, therefore this is a good hockey team.' If the players lack team skills, even though each player is individually good, it could be a poor team.

*Division* Inference from a property of the whole to a property of the part is warranted only in some cases. An example of a case where it is an erroneous inference: 'This machine is heavy, therefore all the parts of this machine are heavy.' In this case, the property of heaviness does not necessarily transfer from the whole to the parts.

*Denying the antecedent* An example: 'If capital punishment deters offenders, it is justified, but it does not deter offenders; therefore it is not justified.' An inference of this type may seem correct, perhaps because it resembles the valid form of inference on the left. But actually its specific form is that of the invalid inference form on the right. It would be an error to take it as a valid inference.

If A then B    If A then B
Not B            Not A
———————  ———————
Not A (*valid*)  Not B (*invalid*)

The valid type of inference on the left is called *modus tollens*.

*Affirming the consequent* An example: 'If abortion is acceptable, then it is a woman's right; but abortion is a woman's right; therefore it is acceptable.' It would be an error to take this reasoning as a valid inference. It may seem correct, perhaps because it resembles the valid form of inference on the left. But its specific form is that of the invalid inference form on the right.

If A then B   If A then B
A            B
—————    —————
B (*valid*)   A (*invalid*)

The valid type of inference on the left is called *modus ponens*.

*Post hoc arguments* A *post hoc* inference starts from a premiss postulating a positive correlation between two events or states, and concludes with postulating a causal relationship between them. This kind of inference is, in general, reasonable as defeasible, presumptive reasoning, because positive correlation is one good, though not infallible sign of the existence of a causal relationship. However, this kind of inference can be erroneous or even fallacious if other factors are overlooked or suppressed. You need to ask several questions. How large is the correlation? Could the causal relationship go the other way? Could it be accounted for by a third factor, a common cause? Could there be an intervening variable, a chain of causality? The causal hypothesis gains in presumptive weight as these factors can be ruled out.

*Insufficient statistics* The error of insufficient statistics may be committed where a sample selected is so small that a statistical generalization to a larger population may be worthless or highly unreliable.

*Biased statistics* The error of biased statistics arises where the distribution of a property in a sample may not match the distribution in the population as a whole. In such a case, the sample is said to be biased. For example, a civic election poll taken in one neighbourhood may not match voter preferences in the whole city, e.g. it may be a wealthy suburb, while the majority live in poorer urban areas and have different voting preferences.

## SOPHISTICAL TACTICS

*Argumentum ad verecundiam* To support your argument in a critical discussion by citing the opinion of an expert is, in general, a reasonable and legitimate move. But it is a kind of tactic that can go wrong in many ways. The expert opinion could be misquoted, or interpreted incorrectly, for example. A secondary context of dialogue, a type of information-seeking expert consultation dialogue, is always involved. The fallacious type of *ad verecundiam* argument occurs in cases where the purported expert opinion is used too aggressively or uncritically by a proponent who, for example, tries to browbeat a respondent by making him appear to lack sufficient respect for the word of an authority.

*Argumentum ad hominem* Personal attack in argumentation occurs in two basic forms. In the *personal* or *abusive ad hominem* argument, the respondent's argument is attacked on the ground that the respondent has a bad moral character, and in particular, bad character for veracity is often emphasized. In the circumstantial *ad hominem* argument, the respondent's personal circumstances are claimed to be at variance with his own argument, e.g. 'You don't practise what you preach.' The circumstantial attack imputes a pragmatic inconsistency, whereas the abusive argument is a direct personal attack. *Ad hominem* argumentation can be reasonable in many cases, e.g. in law, it is legitimate, within limits, to question the character for veracity of a witness. But it is a kind of argumentation that can go badly wrong if pressed too hard, or used in an inappropriate context of dialogue. For example, in a scientific inquiry, attacking the character of a fellow scientist would normally have no legitimate place as a part of the inquiry.

*Arguing in a Circle* Arguing in a circle is

only fallacious where the context of dialogue contains a requirement of evidential priority, i.e. where the premises must each be better established than the conclusion in order for an argument to be successful. This requirement generally holds in a scientific inquiry, but not always in a critical discussion, where circular argumentation can sometimes be a blunder, due to confusion or inefficiency, rather than a fallacy. Thus circular arguments are not necessarily fallacious, and there is a burden of proof on a critic to show that a circular argument is fallacious in a given case, by referring to evidence from the context of dialogue. The fallacy of arguing in a circle is sometimes called *petitio principii* or begging the question. (*See* CIRCULAR REASONING.)

*Argumentum ad ignorantiam* Most arguments are based on a tacit agreement about how much evidence or support one is required to give for one's view in order to have won. This is because hard knowledge is generally insufficient to resolve conflicts of opinion on controversial issues, especially those relating to values and practical conduct. Arguments from ignorance are attempts to change the amount of support required in a given case. They come in two forms: (1) this proposition is not known to be true, therefore it is false, or (2) this proposition is not known to be false, therefore it is true. Whether a particular instance of one of these inferences is warranted or fallacious depends on how it is used in a context of dialogue. For example, 'It has not been established that Mr X is a spy, therefore he is not a spy.' could be a warranted inference to draw at the conclusion of a thorough and exhaustive inquiry, but it could be fallacious in another context, e.g. in a critical discussion which aims to establish its conclusion 'beyond doubt'.

*The fallacy of many questions* The question, 'Have you stopped beating your spouse?' could be reasonable in some contexts, e.g. if put to a confessed spouse-beater by a cross-examining barrister in a court of law. However, a complex question of this type which contains presuppositions highly detrimental to the respondent can be an unfairly aggressive tactic aimed at trapping him into making concessions that will be harmful to his side. When this occurs, the respondent should question the question (if possible), requesting that it be broken down into a series of smaller questions asked in a reasonable order, allowing for better possibilities of choice (Walton, 1989). In some cases, such questions involve unfair dichotomies, needing the reply, 'None of the above'.

*Argumentum ad baculum* Appeal to threat of force or sanctions can be quite legitimate in negotiation dialogue, especially where the threat is expressed (as an indirect speech act) in the form of a warning, e.g. 'If you don't meet these terms, our union will go out on strike.' But in the context of a critical discussion, an attempt to block or close off the discussion by using a threat is often an illicit dialectical shift. This move is a common tactic called the *ad baculum* fallacy.

*Argumentum ad misericordiam* Appeal to the emotion of pity can be quite reasonable as a guide to action in some cases, but it becomes fallacious when used to distract attention from relevant evidence that should be taken into account in arriving at a conclusion.

*Argumentum ad populum* Critical discussion is an opinion-based type of dialogue which has as its goal the resolution of a conflict of opinions, often on controversial issues of public policy. Therefore, appealing to a weight of common presumption or popular opinion is by no means out of place. However, when such an appeal is made in an uncritical manner, by suggesting that popular opinion can never be wrong, for example, the fallacy of *ad populum* is said to be committed. It should be noted that appeal to popular opinion is a kind of defeasible argumentation that is inherently open to critical questioning.

*Equivocation* One way of getting in trouble with vague or ambiguous terms in reasoning arises through a shift in context, where the same word or phrase has been used twice, making it plausible to seem that there is a correct inference, erroneously. A transparent case: 'Smith went to the bank to get some cash; the bank is receding from the river; therefore, Smith went to an area that is receding from the river to get some cash.' It could be, in such a case that each premiss is individually true, but the conclusion is false, despite the (apparent) validity of the inference. Equivocation tends to be an especially serious problem in longer sequences of reasoning, where such shifts can easily pass unnoticed (Walton, 1987, ch. 10).

*Slippery slope* A slippery slope argument is a kind of argument that warns you if you take a first step, you will find yourself involved in an irreversible sequence of consequences, speeding faster and faster towards some disastrous outcome. A good example was the argument used to support the majority opinion in the recent US Supreme Court decision not to ban burning of the American flag as a criminal act. Justice William J. Brennan, Jr argued that any ruling to ban physical desecration of the flag would lead to further cases that would 'enter territory having no discernible or defensible boundaries'. Wouldn't the court then have to consider prohibiting the burning of state flags, or the Constitution? Justice Brennan worried that in order to evaluate these choices, the court would end up imposing its own political preferences to suppress all kinds of unpopular protests. This kind of outcome is obviously dangerous in a democratic country where freedom of speech is important. In many cases, the slippery slope is a legitimate technique of practical reasoning which a proponent can use in action-directed dialogue to warn a respondent about the consequences of a path of action the respondent is embarking upon. However, in some cases, the technique can take the form of a scare tactic used fallaciously, without sufficient justification, to try to forestall action without fairly considering the consequences or alternatives.

BIBLIOGRAPHY

Fearnside, W.W. and Holther, W.B.: *Fallacy: The Counterfeit of Argument* (Englewood Cliffs: Prentice-Hall, 1959).
Hamblin, C.L.: *Fallacies* (London: Methuen, 1970).
Mackie, J.L.: 'Fallacies', in *The Encyclopedia of Philosophy* ed. P. Edwards (New York and London: Collier-Macmillan, 1967), vol. 3, 169–79.
Pirie, M.: *The Book of the Fallacy* (London: Routledge, 1985).
Sidgwick, A.: *Fallacies* (London: Kegan Paul, Trench, 1886).
Van Eemeren, F.H. and Grootendorst, R.: 'Fallacies in dialectical perspective', *Argumentation* 1 (1987), 283–302.
Van Eemeren, F.H. and Grootendorst, R.: *Argumentation, Communication and Fallacies* (Hillsdale: Lawrence Erlbaum, 1992).
Walton, D.N.: *Informal Fallacies* (Amsterdam: Benjamins, 1987).
Walton, D.N.: *Question–Reply Argumentation* (New York: Greenwood Press, 1989).
Woods J. and Walton, D.N. eds: *Fallacies: Selected Papers: 1972–1982* (Dordrecht: Foris, 1990).

DOUGLAS N. WALTON

**innate ideas** These have been variously defined by philosophers either as ideas consciously present to the mind prior to sense experience (the non-dispositional sense), or as ideas which we have an innate disposition to form (though we need not be actually aware of them at any particular time, e.g. as babies) – the dispositional sense.

Understood in either way they were invoked to account for our recognition of certain truths without recourse to experiential verification, such as those of mathematics, or to justify certain moral and religious claims which were held to be capable of being known by introspection of our innate ideas. Examples of such supposed truths might include 'murder is wrong' or 'God exists'.

One difficulty with the doctrine is that it is sometimes formulated as one about concepts or ideas which are held to be innate and at other times as one about a source of propositional knowledge. In so far as concepts are taken to be innate the doctrine relates primarily to claims about meaning: our idea of God, for example, is taken as a source for the meaning of the word God. When innate ideas are understood propositionally their supposed innateness is taken as evidence for their truth. This latter thesis clearly rests on the assumption that innate propositions have an unimpeachable source, usually taken to be God, but then any appeal to innate ideas to justify the existence of God is circular. Despite such difficulties the doctrine of innate ideas had a long and influential history until the eighteenth century and the concept has in recent decades been revitalized through its employment in Noam Chomsky's influential account of the mind's linguistic capacities.

The attraction of the theory has been felt strongly by those philosophers who have been unable to give an alternative account of our capacity to recognise that some propositions are certainly true where that recognition cannot be justified solely on the basis of an appeal to sense experience. Thus PLATO argued that, for example, recognition of mathematical truths could only be explained on the assumption of some form of recollection (*see* ANAMNESIS). Since there was no plausible post-natal source the recollection must refer back to a pre-natal acquisition of knowledge. Thus understood, the doctrine of innate ideas supported the view that there were important truths innate in human beings and it was the senses which hindered their proper apprehension.

The ascetic implications of the doctrine were important in Christian philosophy throughout the Middle Ages and the doctrine featured powerfully in scholastic teaching until its displacement by LOCKE'S philosophy in the eighteenth century. It had in the meantime acquired modern expression in the philosophy of DESCARTES who argued that we can come to know certain important truths before we have any empirical knowledge at all. Our idea of God, for example, and our coming to recognize that God must necessarily exist, are, Descartes held, logically independent of sense experience. In England the Cambridge Platonists such as Henry More and Ralph Cudworth added considerable support.

Locke's rejection of innate ideas and his alternative empiricist account was powerful enough to displace the doctrine from philosophy almost totally. LEIBNIZ, in his critique of Locke, attempted to defend it with a sophisticated dispositional version of the theory, but it attracted few followers.

The empiricist alternative to innate ideas as an explanation of the certainty of propositions was in the direction of construing all necessary truths as analytic. KANT's refinement of the classification of propositions with the fourfold distinctions ANALYTIC/synthetic and a priori/a posteriori did nothing to encourage a return to the innate ideas doctrine, which slipped from view. The doctrine may fruitfully be understood as the production of confusion between explaining the genesis of ideas or concepts and the basis for regarding some propositions as necessarily true.

Chomsky's revival of the term in connection with his account of human speech acquisition has once more made the issue topical. He claims that the principles of language and 'natural logic' are known unconsciously and are a precondition for language acquisition. But for his purposes innate ideas must be taken in a strongly dispositional sense – so strong that it is far from clear that Chomsky's claims are as in conflict with empiricists' accounts as some (including Chomsky) have supposed. Quine, for example, sees no clash with his own version of empirical behaviourism, in which old talk of ideas is eschewed in favour of dispositions to observable behaviour.

*See also* ANALYTICITY, A PRIORI KNOWLEDGE, EMPIRICISM.

BIBLIOGRAPHY

Chomsky, N.: *Cartesian Linguistics* (New York: Harper and Row, 1966).
Leibniz, G.W.: *New Essays on Human Understanding* (1704) trans. P. Remnant and J. Bennett (Cambridge: Cambridge University Press, 1981).
Locke, J.: *An Essay Concerning Human Understanding* (1690) ed. P.H. Nidditch (Oxford: Oxford University Press, 1975).
Plato: *Meno*.
Quine, W.V.: 'Linguistics and philosophy', in Stich, 1975.

Stich, S.P. ed.: *Innate Ideas* (Berkeley: University of California Press, 1975).

G.A.J. ROGERS

**introspection** Derived from the Latin *intro* (within) + *specere* (to look), introspection is the attention the mind gives to itself or to its own operations and occurrences. I can know there is a fat hairy spider in my bath by looking there and seeing it. But how do I know that I am seeing it rather than smelling it, or that my attitude to it is one of disgust rather than delight? One answer is: by a subsequent introspective act of 'looking within' and attending to the psychological state – *my seeing the spider*. Introspection, therefore, is a mental occurrence, which has as its object some other psychological state like perceiving, desiring, willing, feeling, etc. In being a distinct awareness-episode it is different from a more general 'self-consciousness' which characterizes all or some of our mental history.

The awareness generated by an introspective act can have varying degrees of complexity. It might be a simple *knowledge of (mental) things* – such as a particular perception-episode; or it might be the more complex *knowledge of truths* about one's own mind. In this latter full-blown judgemental form, introspection is usually the self-ascription of psychological properties and, when linguistically expressed, results in statements like 'I am watching the spider' or 'I am repulsed'.

In psychology this deliberate inward look becomes a *scientific method* when it is 'directed towards answering questions of theoretical importance for the advancement of our systematic knowledge of the laws and conditions of mental processes' (Stout, 1938). In philosophy, introspection (sometimes also called 'reflection') remains simply 'that notice which the Mind takes of its own Operations' (Locke, 1690, 2.1.4) and has been used to serve the following important functions:

1. *Methodological*: Thought experiments are a powerful tool in philosophical investigation. The Ontological Argument, for example, asks us to try to think of the most Perfect Being as lacking existence and Berkeley's Master Argument challenges us to conceive of an unseen tree. Conceptual results are then drawn from our failure or success. For such experiments to work, we must not only have (or fail to have) the relevant conceptions but also *know* that we have (or fail to have) them – presumably by introspection.

2. *Metaphysical*: A metaphysics of mind needs to take cognisance of introspection. One can argue for 'ghostly' mental entities, for 'qualia', for 'sense-data' by claiming introspective awareness of them. First-person psychological reports can have special consequences for the nature of persons and personal identity: HUME, for example, was content to reject the notion of a soul-substance because he failed to find such a thing by 'looking within'. Moreover, some philosophers argue for the existence of additional *perspectival facts* – the fact of 'what it is like' to be the person I am or to have an experience of such-and-such-a-kind (Nagel, 1974). Introspection as our access to such facts becomes important when we construct a complete metaphysics of the world.

3. *Epistemological*: Surprisingly, the most important use made of introspection has been in accounting for our knowledge of the *outside* world. According to a FOUNDATIONALIST theory of justification an empirical belief is either *basic* and 'self-justifying' or is justified in relation to basic beliefs. Basic beliefs therefore, constitute the rock-bottom of all justification and knowledge. Now introspective awareness is said to have a unique epistemological status: in it, we are said to achieve the best possible epistemological position and consequently, introspective beliefs become prime candidates for 'basic' beliefs and thereby constitute the foundation of all justification (*see* the GIVEN).

THE TRADITIONAL THEORY

The traditional theory of introspection, as I call it, is an explanation of this capacity of our 'looking within' constructed from a Descartes-Locke-Kant perspective. It develops as an epistemological corollary to a metaphysical dualism. The world of Matter is known through external/outer sense-perception. So cognitive access to Mind must be based on a *parallel* process of introspection which 'though . . . not Sense, as having nothing to do with external Objects; yet (it) is very like it, and might properly enough be call'd *internal Sense*' (Locke, 1690, 2.1.4). However, 'having mind as object' is not sufficient to make a way of knowing 'inner' in the relevant sense because mental facts can be grasped through sources other than introspection. The point is rather that an 'inner perception' provides a *kind* of access to the mental not obtained otherwise – it is a 'look within *from within*'. Stripped of metaphor this indicates the following epistemological features:

1. *Only I* can introspect my mind.
2. I can introspect *only my* mind.
3. Introspective awareness is *superior* to any other knowledge of contingent facts that I or others might have.

(1) and (2) are grounded in the Cartesian idea of 'privacy' of the mental. Normally, a single object can be perceptually or inferentially grasped by many subjects, just as the same subject can perceive and infer different things. The epistemic peculiarity of introspection is that is is exclusive – it gives knowledge only of the *mental history of the subject introspecting*.

Tenet (3) of the traditional theory is grounded in the Cartesian idea of 'privileged access'. The epistemic superiority of introspection lies in its being an infallible source of knowledge. First-person psychological statements which are its typical results cannot be mistaken. This claim is sometimes supported by an 'imaginability test', i.e. the impossibility of imagining that I believe that I am in pain while at the same time imagining evidence that I am *not* in pain. An apparent counter-example to this infallibility claim would be the introspective judgement 'I am perceiving a dead friend' when I am really hallucinating. This is taken care of by refor-

mulating such introspective reports as 'I *seem* to be perceiving a dead friend'. The importance of such privileged access is that introspection becomes a way of knowing immune from the pitfalls of other sources of cognition. The basic asymmetry between first and third-person psychological statements can be traced to their being generated (respectively) by introspective and non-introspective methods.

The traditional theory of introspection, therefore, can be encapsulated in the following four theses: (1) Perceptual Model Thesis, (2) Distinct Act Thesis, (3) Privacy Thesis and (4) Privileged Access Thesis.

Before looking at the criticisms of this theory, an important qualification needs to be made regarding tenets (1) and (2) stated above. Introspection, so far, has been defined as yielding the knowledge of the subject's own mind or mental history. The umbrella terms 'mental history' or 'my mind', however, tend to gloss over an important controversy centring on the actual mental *items* revealed in introspection. The debate here has greater significance than just generating a list: if we find uncontroversial psychological entities not amenable to introspection or dubiously 'mental' items that are uncontroversially introspected, then it would be clear that introspectibility is either not a necessary or not a sufficient criterion of the mental. Some of the philosophically interesting putative objects of introspection are:

1. Psychological/mental states: Even if many psychological states are introspected it is doubtful if *all* such states can be known in this manner. There are many types of mental states and it is not clear that all of them are introspectible or introspectible in the same way. A *dispositional* psychological state is a possible exception.
2. Self or I: Introspection is generally supposed to reveal not only psychological states but also the *subject* or *seat* of these states. Some (*à la* HUME) however, confess to a failure to discover a Self over and above its states by 'looking within'. The issue here hinges on whether, in

becoming aware of my experiences, I am also not aware of them as-*my*-experiences and whether the latter awareness is possible without an *introspective* awareness of the Self.

3. Bodily sensations like aches, itches, etc: Reports like 'I am dizzy', 'I have a sinking feeling in my stomach' are sometimes said to be known introspectively. To hold them to be bona fide introspections we would need either to construe bodily sensations as mental or to allow an 'introspective awareness' of some physical states.

4. Time and temporal determination: This is part of KANT's idiosyncratic theory of 'inner sense'. Our faculty of Sensibility is exercised either as 'outer sense' or as 'inner sense'. The 'intuitional aspect' or Form of outer sense is Space and that of inner sense is Time. This means that while all objects of outer sense are represented as spatial, all inner perceptions are processed as temporal. But more interestingly, even our ascription of temporal succession to events in the world is dependent on and derived from the (introspected?) successiveness of our inner perceptions.

## OBJECTIONS TO THE TRADITIONAL THEORY

These either question the *plausibility* of the four theses constituting the theory or expose their *incompatibility*.

### Against the perceptual model thesis

The motivation for construing introspection along the lines of perception is a desire for theoretical neatness. Though Mind and Matter are metaphysically different, we become aware of them in fundamentally parallel ways. But the difficulty is that we cannot find introspectional analogues to many crucial elements in ordinary perceptual processes. Many *de facto* disanalogies have been pointed out (for example, the absence of an introspective sense-organ and an absence of a distinct phenomenological character of our 'experience' of the inner) but the difficulty is really logical. Any theory of

perception must leave room for *mis*perceptions, for perception is an 'achievement' or 'success' word. Introspective awareness allegedly cannot be mistaken. Consequently, to account for it in terms of the same theoretical structure as perception is misconceived. At best, the Perceptual Model Thesis is at odds with the Privileged Access Thesis.

### Against the distinct act thesis

S's awareness of O, written as (i) S-a-O, if grasped by *another* awareness-episode (ii) S-a-(S-a-O) immediately suggests a regress – for would not we need yet another episode to know (ii)? However, this is not a problem. Mental states need only be introspect*ible* and not introspect*ed*. (i) as a conscious mental state reveals its object and this illumination (of O) is not borrowed from the subsequent act (ii); similarly, if all we want is to know (i), it is sufficient to move to (ii) which, as a conscious mental episode, can adequately reveal *its* object (S-a-O) without requiring a move higher. Of course, with nothing better to do we *could* introspect our introspections *ad infinitum* and *ad nauseam* – but this is not necessary if our purpose was to grasp an initial awareness.

RYLE (1949) has a stronger objection to the Distinct Act Thesis. Introspection is logically self-defeating because it destroys its very object. In (i) S knows O because S attends to O. In (ii) S knows (i) because S attends to (S-a-O). But S can attend to only one object at a time. Thus, while attending to (S-a-O) in (ii), S must withdraw attention from O in which case there will be *no* (S-a-O). But without its object (S-a-O), there can be no introspective awareness at all of the form (ii). Ryle's suggested way out of this in terms of 'retrospection' virtually abandons the Perceptual Model for a 'Memory (or at best a Very-Fresh-Memory) Model' of introspection.

Again, we cannot in the same breath say that introspection is a distinct mental operation *and* that it is a *logically* infallible way of knowing. If pain and the awareness of pain are 'distinct existences' then the logical possibility of awareness of pain without pain is still present (*see* Armstrong, 1968) and the doctrine of infallibility falls. There is thus a tension between the Distinct Act Thesis and Privileged Access.

### Against the privacy thesis

A broadly WITTGENSTEINIAN approach questions the idea of an inward look picking out mental phenomena not accessible from a third-person perspective. The argument has many versions. On one version, there would be a tension between our Privacy Thesis and Privileged Access. According to the latter, introspective awareness cannot be mistaken. But if such awareness is of what is 'private' then there can be no way of *checking* our experience. And without the notion of a check or test, no sense can be made of being *right*. Furthermore, even if the possibility of such an inward look is granted, what it would yield could not be *reported* in a learnable language.

### Against the privileged access thesis

We *can* think of instances of introspection yielding mistaken belief. We have been known to misidentify our mental states and we can think of cases where a physiologist says that the brain state responsible for a particular mental state has not occurred even though my introspective report is that I am in that state. And so it seems better to weaken the claim that introspective reports are infallible. But any substantial weakening of this idea that introspection is a different *kind* of knowing.

### ALTERNATIVES TO THE TRADITIONAL THEORY

These reject one or more of its constitutive tenets. By denying dualism, physicalists about the mind abolish the metaphysical foundations of the standard view; but even *dualists* can account for introspective awareness in different ways. I sketch a few features of some of these options.

1. Non-perceptual models: Self-scrutiny need not be perceptual. My awareness of an object O changes the status of O. It now acquires the property of 'being an object of awareness'. On the basis of this or the fact that the object is seen by me, I *infer* that I am aware of O. Such an 'Inferential Model' of awareness is suggested by the Bhatta Mimamsa school of INDIAN EPISTEMOLOGY. (*See* Matilal, 1986.) This view of introspection does not construe it as a *direct* awareness of mental operations but, interestingly, we will have occasion to refer to theories where the emphasis on directness itself leads to a non-perceptual or at least a non-observational account of introspection.

2. Reflexive models: Epistemic access to our minds need not involve a separate attentive act. Part of the meaning of a *conscious* state is that I *know* that I am in that state when I am in that state. Consciousness here is conceived as a 'phosphorescence' attached to some mental occurrences and in no need of a subsequent illumination to reveal itself. Of course, if introspection is defined as a distinct act then reflexive models are really accounts of first-person access that make no appeal to introspection.

3. Public-mind theories and fallibility/infallibility models: The physicalists' denial of metaphysically private mental facts naturally suggests that 'looking within' is not merely *like* perception but *is* perception. For Ryle, mental states are 'iffy' behavioural facts which, in principle, are equally accessible to everyone *in the same way*. One's *own* self-awareness therefore is, in effect, no different in type from anyone else's observations about one's minds.

A more interesting move is for the physicalist to retain the truism that I grasp that I am sad in a very different way from that in which I know *you* to be sad. This *directness* or non-inferential nature of self-knowledge can be preserved in some physicalist theories of introspection. For instance, Armstrong's identification of mental states with *causes* of bodily behaviour and of the latter with brain states, makes introspection the process of acquiring information about such inner physical causes. But since introspection is itself a *mental state*, it is a process in the brain as well; and since its grasp of the relevant causal information is *direct*, it becomes a process in which the brain scans itself.

Alternatively, a broadly 'functionalist' view of mental states suggests the following machine-analogue of the introspective situation: a machine-table with the instruction 'Print: "I am in state A" when in state A' results in the output 'I am in state A' when state A occurs. Similarly, if we define mental states and events functionally, we can say that introspection occurs when an occurrence of a mental state M directly results in an awareness of M. Note that this way of emphasizing *directness* yields a non-perceptual and *non-observational* model of introspection. The machine in printing 'I am in state A' does so (when it is not making a 'verbal mistake') just *because* it is in state A. There is no computation of information or process of *ascertaining* involved. The latter, at best, consists simply in passing through a sequence of states.

This casts new light on the discussion. The legitimate question: How do I know that I am seeing a spider? was interpreted as a demand for the *faculty* or information-processing-mechanism whereby I come to acquire this knowledge. Peculiarities of first-person psychological awareness and reports were carried over as peculiarities of this mechanism. However, the question *need* not demand the search for a *method* of knowing but rather for an *explanation* of the special epistemic features of first-person psychological statements. On this reading, the problem of introspection (as a way of knowing) dissolves but the problem of explaining 'introspective' or first-person authority remains.

*See also* APPERCEPTION; CARTESIANISM; THE GIVEN; PRIVATE LANGUAGE ARGUMENT; RYLE; SELF-CONSCIOUSNESS; SELF-KNOWLEDGE AND SELF-IDENTITY; SUBJECTIVITY.

BIBLIOGRAPHY

Armstrong, D.M.: *A Materialist Theory of Mind* (London: Routledge and Kegan Paul, 1968).
Descartes, R.: *Meditations on First Philosophy* (1641) in *Philosophical Works of Descartes* eds J. Cottingham, R. Stoothoff and D. Murdoch (Cambridge: Cambridge University Press, 1975).
Kant, I.: *Critique of Pure Reason* (1781) trans. N. Kemp Smith (London: Macmillan, 1964).
Locke, J.: *An Essay Concerning Human Understanding* (1690) ed. P.H. Nidditch (Oxford: Oxford University Press, 1975).
Matilal, B.K.: *Perception: An Essay on Classical Indian Theories of Knowledge* (Oxford: Clarendon Press, 1986).
Nagel, T.: 'What is it like to be a bat?', *Philosophical Review* 83 (1974), 435–50.
Ryle, G.: *The Concept of Mind* (Harmondsworth: Penguin, 1949).
Shoemaker, S.: 'First-person access', in *Philosophical Perspectives* 4 (1990).
Stout, G.F.: *A Manual of Psychology* 5th edn (London: University Tutorial Press, 1938).
Wittgenstein, L.: *Philosophical Investigations* trans. G.E.M. Anscombe (Oxford: Blackwell, 1953).

VRINDA DALMIYA

**intuition and deduction** Most generally, one has *intuitive* 'knowledge' that $p$ when,

1. one knows that $p$,
2. one's knowledge that $p$ is immediate, and
3. one's knowledge that $p$ is not an instance of the operation of any of the five senses (so that knowledge of the nature of one's own experience is not intuitive).

On this account neither mediated nor sensory knowledge is intuitive knowledge. Some philosophers, however, want to allow sensory knowledge to count as intuitive; to do this, omit clause (3) above.

The two principal families of examples of *mediated* (i.e. not immediate) knowledge that have interested philosophers are, knowledge via *representation* and knowledge via *inference*. Knowledge by representation occurs when the thing known is not what one appeals to as a basis for claiming to know it, as when one appeals to sensory phenomena as a basis for knowledge of the world (and the world is not taken to be a sense-phenomenal construct) or as when one appeals to words as a source of knowledge of the world (as when one claims that a proposition is true of the world solely by virtue of the meanings of the words expressing it).

(There are other idioms that are used to mark out the differences between non-intuitional and intuitional ways of knowing, such as knowing indirectly and knowing directly, or knowing in the absence of the thing known and knowing by virtue of the presence of the thing known. It is sometimes useful to speak of the object of knowledge being *intuitively given*, meaning that we can know things about it without mediation. The justification of a claim to knowledge by appeal to its object being intuitively given is surely as good as could be. What could be a better basis for a claim to knowledge than the object of knowledge itself given just as it is?)

We might say that *deductive inference* is a mode of achieving *conditional* knowledge. One *infers* a proposition $p$ from one or more propositions $p_1,..., p_n$, called *premisses* of the inference, $p$ being called the *conclusion* of the inference. Most generally, to *validly infer* $p$ from premisses $p_1, ..., p_n$ is to think or reason one's way to $p$ from those premisses in such a way that one can see that, if the premisses are known (and so true), then the conclusion is thereby known (and so true).

One of the fundamental problems of philosophy, overlapping epistemology and the philosophy of logic, is that of giving criteria for when a deductive inference is valid, criteria for when an INFERENCE does or can continue knowledge or truth. There are in fact two very different proposals for solutions to this problem, one that had slowly come into fashion during the early part of this century, and another that has been much out of fashion, but is gaining in admirers. The former, which develops out of the tradition of Aristotelian syllogistic, holds that all valid deductive inferences can be analysed and paraphrased as follows:

- The sentences occurring in the deduction are aptly paraphrased by sentences with an explicit, *interpreted* logical syntax, which in the main consists of expressions for logical operations, e.g. predication, negation, conjunction, disjunction, quan-

tification, abstraction. . .; and
- The validity of the inferences made from sentences in that syntax to sentences in that syntax is entirely a function of the meaning of the signs for logical operations expressed in the syntax.

In particular, it is principally the meaning of the signs for logical operations that justify taking considered rules of inference as valid. (For a thorough discussion of which operations are to count as logical, and of what can count as a logical constant, see Koslow, 1991.) Here, for example, is such a justification as given by FREGE, one of the great developers of this view of the nature of the proper criteria for valid deductive inference, someone who in fact, in the late nineteenth century, gave us an interpreted logical syntax (and so a formal deductive logic) far, far greater and more powerful than had been available through the tradition of Aristotelian syllogistic:

> $A \rightarrow B$ is meant to be a propostion that is false when A is true and B is false; otherwise it is true (Frege, 1964, p. 51; paraphrased; variables restricted to the True,, the False).

> The following is a valid rule of inference, From A and $A \rightarrow B$, infer B, for if B were false, since A is true, $A \rightarrow B$ would be false; but it is supposed to be true (Frege, 1964 p. 57; paraphrased).

Frege believed that the principal virtue of such formal-syntactical reconstructions of inferences – as validly moving on the basis of the meanings of the signs for the logical operations alone – was that it eliminated dependence on intuition and let one see exactly on what our inferences depended, e.g.:

> we divide all truths that require justification into two kinds, those for which the proof can be carried out purely by means of logic and those for which it must be supported by facts of experience.
> . . . Now, when I came to consider the question to which of these two kinds the judgments of arithmetic belong, I first

had to ascertain how far one could proceed in arithmetic by means of inferences alone, with the sole support of those laws of thought that transcend all particulars . . . . To prevent anything intuitive [*Anschauliches*] from penetrating here unnoticed, I had to bend every effort to keep the chain of inferences free from gaps. (Frege, 1967, p. 5)

In the literature most ready to hand, the alternative view was supported by DESCARTES and elaborated by John LOCKE, who maintained that inferences move best and most soundly when based on *intuition* (their word):

Syllogism serves our Reason [in that it shows] the connexion of the Proofs [i.e. the connexion between premisses and conclusion] in any one instance and no more; but in this, it is of no great use, since the Mind can perceive such connexion where it really is, as easily, nay, perhaps better without [Syllogism].

If we observe the Actings of our own Minds, we shall find, that we reason best and clearest, when we only observe the connexion of the [ideas], without reducing our Thoughts to any Rule of Syllogism. (Locke, 1975, p. 670)

What is it that one is intuiting? Ideas, or meanings, and relationships among them. Ideas or meaning are taken to be directly given. The difference being marked by Locke is between (a) inferring Socrates is mortal from the premisses All men are mortal and Socrates is a man by appealing to the formal-logical rule, All A are B, C is an A, therefore C is B, which is supposed to be done without any appeal to the intuitive meanings of 'All' and 'is', and (b) seeing that Socrates is mortal follows from All men are mortal and Socrates is a man by virtue of understanding (the meanings of) those informal sentences without any appeal to the formal-logical rule. Locke is also making the point that inferences made on the basis of such an understanding of meanings are better, and more fundamental, than inferences made on the basis of an appeal to a formal-logical schema. Indeed, Locke would certainly maintain that such

informal, intuitive inferences made on the basis of understanding the meanings of sentences serve better as a check on the correctness of formal inferences than formal-logical inference serve as a check on intuitive inferences.

Such distrust of formal logical inference or greater trust in intuitive inference has been promoted in recent times by Henri Poincaré and L.E.J. Brouwer (Detlefsen, 1991).

We might say that for Frege, too, logical inferences moved by virtue of intuition of meaning, the meaning of the signs for logical inference, for we have seen how Frege appealed to such meanings in order to justify formal-logical rules of inference. Of course, once the formal-logical rules are so justified, Frege is quite content to appeal to them in the construction of deductions, not returning each time to the intuited meanings of the logical signs. What is new in Frege is the conviction that inferences that proceed wholly on the basis of the logical signs, signs for logical operations, are complete with respect to logical implication – that if B logically follows from A, then we should in principle be able to deduce B from A by rules which mention only logical operations and not, e.g., the concrete meanings of predicate-expressions in the relevant propositions. There is a deep issue here which is destined to become the principal issue in the philosophy and epistemology of logical theory, viz. *To what extent, in what measure, does intuition of the non-logical content of propositions (i.e. contents other than the meanings of the signs for logical operations) rightly sustain inference?*

This is the issue that really concerned Brouwer and Poincaré (Detlefsen, 1991). But consider: Katz (1988) argued that Descartes' COGITO is a sound inference made on the basis of intuitions of meanings and *is incapable of being articulated or paraphrased as formal-syntactic reasoning* after the now ubiquitously deployed method of Frege depending – as described above – on logical operations alone (*see* ANALYTICITY). But one does not really need to reach for such examples. Virtually all inferences set out in mathematical proofs most obviously proceed on the basis of intuitively given meaning content

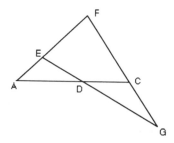

Figure 1

rather than appeal to formal-logical rules, and it is easy to find examples of such proofs that clearly do not depend on the meanings of signs for logical operators, but rather on the non-logical content of the mathematical propositions. There is a good example in Hilbert (1971, p. 6, paraphrased):

*Theorem 3.* For two points A and C there always exists at least one point D on the line AC that lies between A and C.

Proof: By virtue of the axiom which says that there exists three points not on a line, there exists a point E not on the line AC.

By virtue of the axiom which says the for any two points A, E, there is a third point F on the line AE, E between A and F, there exists on AE a point F such that E is a point of the segment AF.

By the same axiom and the axiom that says of any three points on a line there exists no more than one that lies between the other two, there exists on FC a point G, and G does not lie on the segment FC.

Given the axiom which says, if three points A, B, C do not lie on a line and if a is a line which passes through a point of the segment AB, the line a also passes through either a point of the segment AC or a point of the segment BC – it follows that the line EG must then intersect the segment AC at a point D.

The proof actually consists of four lemmas put together via the picture Figure 1 to yield the construction of the point required by the theorem. Here the picture, which is to say, something expressive of the intuitively given

content of the theorem, stands in for a formal-logical construction that would bring the four lemmas together to yield the theorem. The intuitive understanding of the pictured content of the theorem stands in for the formal-logical construction. Of course, we could in fact formalize Hilbert, and give a formal-logical proof of the formal counterpart of the above theorem from the formal-logical counterparts of the relevant ones among Hilbert's axioms. It would not of course be anything like 'the same' proof, for the formal-logical proof would trade on the signs for logical operations only, whereas the proof above trades on an understanding of what one means to be proving theorems about. And the formal-logical proof would consist of perhaps hundreds of steps. (Recall Locke's remark, more apt than he could have realized, that intuitive proofs are shorter.)

Most usually, then, instead of deductive inferences being something achieved independently of our intuition, they are by and large founded on intuition, and by no means just on the intuition of the maning of signs for logical operations. The great task before us is to understand better the nature of such intuition and to sharply distinguish its varieties.

See also ANALYTICITY; LOGICAL POSITIVISM; LOGICISM.

BIBLIOGRAPHY

Detlefsen, M.: 'Brouwer's philosophy of mathematics', in *Essays on Proof* ed. M. Detlefsen (London: Routledge, 1991).

Frege, G.: *The Basic Laws of Arithmetic* trans. and ed. M. Furth (Berkeley: University of California Press, 1964).

Frege, G.: '*Begriffsschrift*, a formula language, modelled upon that of arithmetic, for pure thought', in *From Frege to Gödel: a Source Book in Mathematical Logic* ed. J. van Heijernoort (Cambridge, MA: Harvard University Press, 1967).

Hilbert, D.: *Foundations of Geometry* 2nd English edn. trans. L. Unger (La Salle: Open Court, 1971).

Hilbert, D. and Ackermann, W.: *Principles of Mathematical Logic* trans. L.M. Hammond,

G.G. Leckie, F. Steinhardt with R.E. Luce (New York: Chelsea, 1950).

Katz, J.J.: *Cogitations* (Oxford: Oxford University Press, 1988).

Koslow, A.: *A Structuralist Account of Logic* (Cambridge: Cambridge University Press, 1991).

Locke, J.: *An Essay Concerning Human Understanding* (1690) ed. P.H. Nidditch (Oxford: Oxford University Press, 1975).

Parsons, C.: 'Intuition in constructive mathematics', in *Language, Mind and Logic* ed. J. Butterfield (Cambridge: Cambridge University Press, 1986), 211–29.

Rosen, S.: *The Limits of Analysis* (New Haven: Yale University Press, 1980).

Tragesser, R.S.: *Phenomenology and Logic* (Ithaca, NY: Cornell University Press, 1977).

Tragesser, R.S.: 'Three little noticed aspects of mathematical proof', in Detlefsen, 1991.

ROBERT S. TRAGESSER

**isostheneia**   This is a term used by ancient Greek sceptics and is usually rendered into English by 'equipollence'. It refers to the equal weight and credibility of opposing points of view discovered upon examining the evidence and arguments on both sides of a question. Greek sceptics made a practice of setting up oppositions between appearances and arguments to show that the theories of dogmatic philosophers are equally balanced and therefore equally unconvincing in their various claims to truth.

*See also* SEXTUS EMPIRICUS.

CHARLOTTE STOUGH

# J

**James, William** (1842–1910) James, whose formal education was in chemistry, comparative anatomy, physiology and medicine, taught physiology and psychology before teaching philosophy. His entire career as student and teacher was spent at Harvard University.

Although with characteristic generosity he exaggerated his debt to PEIRCE, James co-founded PRAGMATISM. His 'Remarks on Spencer's Definition of Mind as Correspondence' was published in the same month of 1878 that Peirce's 'How to Make Our Ideas Clear' appeared. Peirce introduced to the world the 'pragmatic maxim', while James outlined the interconnected set of doctrines that came to be associated with the label Peirce first used. James's epistemology is found in both his pragmatism and his 'radical empiricism'.

## PRAGMATISM

From his earliest writing James understood cognitive processes in teleological terms; thought, he held, assists us in the satisfaction of our interests. His Will to Believe doctrine, the view that we are sometimes justified in believing beyond the evidence, relies on the notion that a belief's benefits are relevant to its justification. His pragmatic method of analysing philosophical problems, which requires that we find the meaning of terms by examining their applications to objects in experimental situations, similarly reflects a teleological approach in its attention to consequences (James, 1975a, pp. 27–44).

Such an approach sets James's theory of meaning apart from verificationisms dismissive of metaphysics. Unlike the VERIFICATIONIST, who takes cognitive meaning to be a matter only of consequences in sensory experience, James took pragmatic meaning to include emotional and motor responses. Moreover, his method was a way of clarifying the meanings of metaphysical propositions, not a way of dismissing them as meaningless (James, 1975a, pp. 45–62). It should be also noted that in his more circumspect moments James did not hold that even his broad set of consequences was exhaustive of a term's meaning. 'Theism', for example, he took to have antecedent, definitional meaning in addition to its more important pragmatic meaning (Giuffrida and Madden, 1975, pp. 18–35).

James's theory of truth reflects his teleological conception of cognition by considering a true belief to be one which is compatible with our existing system of beliefs and leads us to satisfactory interaction with the world (James, 1975b, passim). Although many commentators have supposed that James was thus committed to SUBJECTIVISM, it has been persuasively argued by H.S. Thayer that James did not intend his speaking of truth in these terms to replace the concept of truth as a relation to reality (Thayer, 1981, pp. 527–56). Instead, James was insisting that objective reference was only one of three conditions of truth. Unfortunately, in both technical polemics and popular lectures James often neglected to mention objective reference.

## RADICAL EMPIRICISM

Although James always considered himself an empiricist, from his earliest writing he was intent on modifying the concept of experience traditional in empiricism. Central to this modification was the claim that we are directly acquainted with relations – temporal relations, causal relations, etc. In some of the most vivid philosophy ever written, he described how we directly experience continuities in the world (1976, pp. 21–44, 79–95). Of equal importance was his functional theory of consciousness in which the existence of mental entities was rejected in favour of functional processes (1976, pp. 3–19).

Like his theory of truth, James's radical empiricism has led many commentators to suppose that James rejected epistemological realism (i.e. the view that objects exist independently of the perceiver and can be known as they are) in favour of PHENOM-ENALISM. Regrettably, James's speaking sometimes of the objects of knowledge as 'pure experience' was misleading. Despite his insistence that pure experience was neither mental nor physical, readers have found it difficult to avoid the conclusion that he is speaking of mental entities. Fortunately, more discerning commentators have understood that James was attempting to use his radical empiricism to support the 'natural realism' he repeatedly avowed throughout his career (Madden and Chakrabarti, 1976, pp. 3–17). He wished to use a theory of experience in which relational continuities are fundamental to substitute an 'ambulatory' conception of the knower-known relation for a 'saltatory' one (James, 1975b, pp. 13–32, 78–89). In the saltatory view, it is supposed that there is a gap between knower and known requiring a self-transcending leap, while in the view James proposed, 'ambulation' mediates in a continuous process between knower and known, a process different from the messenger mediation found in REPRESENTATIVE REALISM.

Undeniably, James in his earlier work was unwilling in print to declare himself a REALIST. This reluctance is understandable if one is sensitive to James's intellectual biography (Hare and Chakrabarti, 1980, pp. 231–45). Although James throughout his life believed in natural realism, for many years he felt intensely his inability to marshall convincing arguments for such an epistemology. Only late in life, when he had fully developed both his radical empiricism and his theory of truth, did he feel that he possessed adequate justification for the realism to which he had always been committed.

See also DEWEY; KNOWLEDGE BY AC-QUAINTANCE/BY DESCRIPTION; PRAG-MATISM; PEIRCE.

WRITINGS

*Pragmatism: A New Name for Some Old Ways of Thinking* (Cambridge, MA: Harvard University Press, 1975).
*The Meaning of Truth: A Sequel to Pragmatism* (Cambridge, MA: Harvard University Press, 1975).
*Essays in Radical Empiricism* (Cambridge, MA: Harvard University Press, 1976).

BIBLIOGRAPHY

Giuffrida, R. and Madden, E.H.: 'James on meaning and significance', *Transactions of the C.S. Peirce Society* 11 (1975), 18–35.
Hare, P.H. and Chakrabarti, C.: 'The development of William James's epistemological realism', in *History, Religion and Spiritual Democracy* ed. M. Wohlgelernter (New York: Columbia University Press, 1980), 231–45.
Madden, E.H. and Chakrabarti, C.: 'James' "pure experience" versus Ayer's "weak phenomenalism"', *Transactions of the C.S. Peirce Society* 12 (1976), 3–17.
Myers, G.E.: *William James: His Life and Thought* (New Haven: Yale University Press, 1986), ch. 10.
Thayer, H.S.: *Meaning and Action: A Critical History of Pragmatism* 2nd edn (Indianapolis: Hackett, 1981), pp. 527–56.

PETER H. HARE

**judgement**   This term may refer to a faculty (of judgement), an act (of judging), or the product of an act (what is judged). My judging that this is warm might be thought to consist in my coming to be in a state with the content, 'This is warm', as a result of the operation of a particular mental faculty of judgement (distinguishable from other faculties: will, imagination, memory). Kant equates judging with the application of concepts: In judging this to be warm, I judge this to satisfy the concept *warm*.

Aristotle identified four logical forms of judgement – All S are P, Some S are P, No S are P, and Some S are not-P – noting that some combinations of these basic forms yield valid arguments, while others do not, an idea that survives in modern logic.

Whatever their source, acts of judgement may be spontaneous or result from theoretical or practical deliberation. Thus, you may judge that this is warm simply on the basis of touching it; I judge the same on the basis of evidential considerations. Practical judgement invokes values and may be partial (this is politically best) or all-out (this is best *tout court*).

BIBLIOGRAPHY

Aristotle: *Prior Analytics* trans. W.D. Ross (Oxford: Clarendon Press, 1949).
Kant, I.: *Critique of Pure Reason* (1781) trans. N. Kemp Smith (London: Macmillan, 1964).

JOHN HEIL

**justification** *see* CAUSAL THEORIES IN EPISTEMOLOGY; COHERENTISM; EVIDENCE; FOUNDATIONALISM; PRAGMATISM; RELIABILISM; RELATIVISM; SUBJECTIVISM.

# K

Kant, Immanuel (1724–1804) Kant is often regarded as the greatest of the modern philosophers. He spent his entire life in or near the East Prussian city of Königsberg (now Kaliningrad), holding the post of Professor of Philosophy at the University of Königsberg from 1770 onwards. His best-known works are his three *Critiques*: the *Critique of Pure Reason* (1781, with a second edition in 1787), which deals with epistemology and metaphysics; the *Critique of Practical Reason* (1788), which deals with ethics, and the *Critique of Judgement* (1790), which deals with aesthetics and teleology. Other important works are the *Dissertation on the Form and Principles of the Sensible and Intelligible World* (1770), *Prolegomena to Any Future Metaphysics* (1783), *Foundations of the Metaphysics of Morals* (1785), *Metaphysical Foundations of Natural Science* (1786), and *Religion Within the Limits of Reason Alone* (1793). His contributions to epistemology are contained mainly in the first of the three Critiques.

The *Critique of Pure Reason* has both positive and negative aims: its task is to 'institute a tribunal which will assure to reason its lawful claims, and dismiss all groundless pretensions' (A xi). In other words, Kant seeks to determine the scope and possibility of a priori knowledge, defending such knowledge against sceptical suspicion in areas where it is legitimate and exposing its lack of credentials in areas where it is not.

## SYNTHETIC A PRIORI JUDGEMENTS

In the Introduction to the *Critique*, Kant draws three important distinctions: a priori vs. empirical, necessary vs. contingent, and analytic vs. synthetic. Each of these has its own entry in this volume, which the reader should consult. Briefly, a proposition or judgment is knowable a priori if it is knowable without relying on experience; otherwise it is empirical. A true proposition is necessary if it is true not just in the actual world, but in any possible world; otherwise it is contingent. Kant believes these two distinctions divide up the field of truths in exactly the same way: a proposition is necessary if and only if it is knowable a priori and contingent if and only if it is knowable (if at all) only empirically.

The third distinction, between analytic and synthetic judgements, cuts across the two distinctions just mentioned. In an analytic judgement, the predicate belongs to the concept of the subject (as in 'all bodies are extended'); in a synthetic judgement, the predicate lies outside the subject concept (as in 'all bodies are heavy'). For our purposes, we can perhaps say that an analytic judgement is one in which the predicate belongs to the definition of the subject concept, or can at least be derived from the subject concept using only definitions and logical laws. That would bring Kant's analytic/synthetic distinction into alignment with more recent versions of the distinction, e.g., FREGE'S. Many philosophers (including LEIBNIZ and HUME among Kant's predecessors and the logical positivists among his successors) have held that a priori knowledge is to be had only of analytic propositions. This view, if true, would take much of the mystery out of a priori knowledge. Kant, however, was convinced that there are important classes of propositions that are both a priori and synthetic. Such propositions are to be found in abundance in arithmetic and geometry (e.g. 7 + 5 = 12, a straight line is the shortest distance between two points), and they include as well certain framework propositions of natural science (e.g. every event has a cause). In addition, most of the propositions of traditional metaphysics (e.g., the soul is a substance, the compound must be composed of the simple) are synthetic and *purportedly* a priori. Kant therefore set the following as the central question of the *Critique of Pure Reason*: how are synthetic a priori propositions possible?

GEOMETRICAL KNOWLEDGE

What assures us of the truth of propositions of GEOMETRY? We know many of them because we prove them from others, but how do we ascertain the truth of those we do not need to prove? It is not by finding that they are analytic, for 'however long [one] meditates on [the subject] concept, he will never produce anything new' (A716/B744). Nor is it by relying on observation (e.g. inspecting dozens of triangular objects and measuring their angle sums), for that would not yield 'universality, still less necessity' (A718/B746). The answer is rather that we exhibit to ourselves by 'pure intuition' (imagination or visualization) an object answering to the concept and 'read off' further properties not contained in the concept itself. For example, a cube is defined as a regular solid composed of six square faces; there is nothing said about the number of edges. Yet by visualizing a cube and counting, we can see that any cube must have twelve edges. A simple act of intuition thus convinces us that we will never encounter a cube having more than twelve edges.

How is it possible for intuition thus to 'anticipate' its objects, to give us knowledge of the properties of objects in advance of our experiential encounters with them? To answer this question, Kant instituted his 'Copernican Revolution' in philosophy:

If intuition must conform to the constitution of the objects, I do not see how we could know anything of the latter *a priori*; but if the object (as object of the senses) must conform to our faculty of intuition, I have no difficulty in conceiving such a possibility (B xvii).

Ptolemy tried to explain the apparent motion of the heavenly bodies about the earth by attributing this motion to the bodies themselves; Copernicus fared better by explaining the apparent motion by referring to the observer's own motion. Comparing his own strategy with that of Copernicus, Kant proposed to explain many of the observed features of objects by reference to traits of the observer rather than to traits of the objects themselves. In the case at hand, he sought to explain the geometrical properties of objects in terms of the structure of the human knower, or what Kant called our 'form of intuition'.

Now what manner of object must conform to our own form of intuition? It is hard indeed to see why *things in themselves* – that is, things whose existence is in no way dependent on human cognition – should so conform. Hence Kant unhesitatingly draws the conclusion that the objects of geometrical knowledge must not be things in themselves:

If the object (the triangle) were something in itself, apart from any relation to you, the subject, how could you say that what necessarily exist in you as subjective conditions for the construction [i.e. exhibition in pure intuition] of a triangle, must of necessity belong to the triangle itself? (A48/B65)

The objects of geometrical knowledge potentially include all spatial configurations – everything that exists in space. Hence, it is a corollary of Kant's Copernican strategy that spatial features cannot belong to things in themselves. This is the doctrine he calls transcendental idealism: things in space (and as he also holds, things in time) are merely appearances, not things in themselves.

By an appearance, Kant means something that exists only as the object of a representation (or perhaps as the possible object of a representation). Since appearances exist only if they are representable, and since they are representable only if they conform with the laws of Euclidean geometry, it can be known in advance that Euclid's laws hold of all appearances.

Many objections have been raised against Kant's account, more than can be discussed here. Some have cited the rise of alternative geometries as casting doubt on the alleged necessity of Euclid's geometry. Some have questioned whether intuition plays any legitimate role in geometrical knowledge. Some have denied that the laws of geometry are a priori, assimilating them rather to the laws of physics, which are known in virtue of the way they help us to systematize empirical data. Some, notably QUINE, have challenged the analytic-synthetic distinction and questioned whether anything at all is a priori.

I shall discuss here only one objection to Kant's view, a composite of objections raised by Russell and Moore. Kant sought to account for the necessity of arithmetical and geometrical truths, and for our ability to know them a priori, by appeal to the structure of our cognitive faculties. But it is contingent that our faculties are the way they are; so if Kant is right, might we not wake up tomorrow and find that cubes have thirteen edges? Or if that is *not* possible, if we can rule out a priori any such change in our constitution, what is the ground of that piece of a priori knowledge? It is evidently unaccounted for by Kant's theory.

This is a difficult dilemma, and unless Kant wants to water down the necessity he claims for mathematics (to something like 'truth in all worlds experienceable by beings constituted as we are now'), there may be no escaping it. It is worth pointing out, however, that a similar objection applies with equal force to the leading theory of a priori knowledge developed in the twentieth century as an alternative to Kant's. This is conventionalism, the theory that necessary truth and a priori knowledge are the products of convention. If the role of convention is merely to map certain sentences onto pre-existing necessarily true propositions, the objection I am about to raise does not apply. But most conventionalists have been more ambitious, seeing convention as the very source of necessity. Since it is contingent that we have the conventions we do instead of some others, these more thoroughgoing conventionalists have made the same mistake as Kant – they have tried to account for the necessary in terms of the contingent.

## INTUITION AND CONCEPT

According to Kant, our knowledge arises from two fundamentally different faculties of the mind, sensibility and understanding. He criticized his predecessors for running these faculties together, Leibniz for treating sensing as a confused mode of understanding and Locke for treating understanding as an abstracted mode of sensing. Kant held that each of the faculties operates with its own distinctive type of mental representation. Concepts, the instruments of the understanding, are mental representations that apply potentially to many things in virtue of their possession of a common feature. Intuitions, the instruments of sensibility, are representations that refer to just one thing and to that thing directly. Intuitions play the role that is played in Russell's philosophy by 'acquaintance' (*see* KNOWLEDGE BY ACQUAINTANCE/BY DESCRIPTION). Through intuitions objects are given to us, Kant said; through concepts they are thought.

It is a famous Kantian thesis that knowledge is yielded neither by intuitions nor by concepts alone, but only by the two in conjunction. 'Thoughts without content are empty,' he says in an often quoted remark, and 'intuitions without concepts are blind' (A51/B75). Exactly what Kant means by the remark is a debated question, however, answered in different ways by scholars who bring different elements of Kant's text to bear on it. A minimal reading is that it is only propositionally structured knowledge that requires the collaboration of intuition and concept; this view allows that intuitions without concepts constitute some kind of non-judgemental awareness. A stronger reading is that it is reference or intentionality that depends on intuition and concept together, so that the blindness of intuition without concept is its referring to no object. A more radical view yet is that intuitions without concepts are indeterminate, a mere blur, perhaps nothing at all. This last interpretation, though admittedly suggested by some things Kant says, is at odds with his official view about the separation of the faculties.

## A PRIORI CONCEPTS

'A priori origin is manifest in certain concepts,' Kant writes, 'no less than in judgements' (B5). Kant was thus not only a judgement RATIONALIST, i.e. a believer in synthetic a priori judgements, but also a concept rationalist, i.e. a believer in a priori concepts. He believed that there are certain concepts that are not abstracted from experience (nor compounded out of concepts so abstracted), but which are applicable to objects of experience none the less. These are his categories, of which substance and cause are perhaps the most important. He realized the puzzling nature of these concepts in a letter to his pupil Marcus Herz in 1772. How is it possible, he asked, for a concept to 'relate to an object' if the concept has not been derived from objects (as happens with empirical concepts), nor the object brought into being by the concept (as Kant believed happens with the divine understanding)? This is the problem he addressed in the 'transcendental deduction of the categories'. It is impossible to do more here than give the barest outline of the transcendental deduction. Kant's starting point is the *unity of* APPERCEPTION – the fact that all my representations have the property of being co-apprehendable in one consciousness. Kant argues that representations have such unity only because they have been synthesized according to rules encapsulated in the categories. As a result, (1) there are objects to which the representations refer, and (2) the categories apply to these objects. If successful, the transcendental deduction simultaneously demonstrates the 'objective validity' of the categories – their applicability to objects of experience – and the objectivity of our experience – its having objects corresponding to it, rather than being a mere play of representations. Kant's main concern was the validity of the categories, but the objectivity of experience has seemed a more significant result to many contemporary philosophers, such as STRAWSON, who have seen in Kant the promise of a TRANSCENDENTAL ARGUMENT against SCEPTICISM. It must be borne in mind, however, that the 'reference to objects' secured by the

transcendental deduction is to be understood in accordance with the idealist strategy of Kant's Copernican Revolution. The objects are not mind-independent things in themselves, but phenomenal objects constructed out of patterns of representations.

## THE LIMITS OF A PRIORI KNOWLEDGE

As was said at the beginning, Kant's purposes in the *Critique of Pure Reason* are both constructive and critical. He wants to give a theory that will explain and defend our legitimate claims to a priori knowledge, but at the same time to expose the pretensions of those that are spurious. It turns out that the factors making a priori knowledge possible (our forms of intuition in the case of arithmetic and geometry, our category-governed modes of synthesis in the case of natural science) can operate only on sense-given materials, so that our a priori knowledge is limited to the world of experience. The *source* of a priori knowledge is not experience, but its only legitimate *subject matter* is objects of possible experience – such is Kant's compromise between rationalism and empiricism. In the portion of the *Critique* entitled 'Transcendental Dialectic', he argues that we can have no knowledge of the properties of the soul, the outer limits and inmost nature of the cosmos, or the existence of God. As matters transcending possible experience, these can be matters of faith or speculation, but not of knowledge.

See also A PRIORI KNOWLEDGE; ANALYTICITY; IDEALISM; IN ITSELF/FOR ITSELF; MATHEMATICAL KNOWLEDGE; NOUMENAL/PHENOMENAL; REALISM; SELF-KNOWLEDGE AND SELF-IDENTITY; TRANSCENDENTAL ARGUMENTS.

WRITINGS

*Kritik der reinen Vernunft* (Riga, 1781), 2nd edn (Riga, 1787); trans. N. Kemp Smith *Critique of Pure Reason* (London: Macmillan, 1964).
*Dissertation on the Form and Principles of the Sensible and Intelligible World* trans. G.B. Kerferd and D.E. Walford, in *Kant: Selected*

*Pre-Critical Writings* (Manchester: Manchester University Press, 1968).
*Prolegomena zu einer jeden Metaphysik*; trans. L.W. Beck *Prolegomena to Any Future Metaphysics* (Indianapolis: Bobbs-Merrill, 1950).

BIBLIOGRAPHY

Allison, H.: *Kant's Transcendental Idealism* (New Haven: Yale University Press, 1973).
Ameriks, K.: 'Recent work on Kant's theoretical philosophy', *American Philosophical Quarterly* 19 (1982), 1–24.
Aquila, R.: *Representational Mind: A Study of Kant's Theory of Knowledge* (Bloomington: Indiana University Press, 1983).
Beck, L.W.: 'Did the sage of Königsberg have no dreams?', in his *Essays on Kant and Hume* (New Haven: Yale University Press, 1978), 38–60.
Bennett, J.: *Kant's Analytic* (Cambridge: Cambridge University Press, 1966).
Bird, G.: *Kant's Theory of Knowledge* (London: Routledge and Kegan Paul, 1962).
Broad, C.D.: *Kant: An Introduction* (Cambridge: Cambridge University Press, 1978).
George, R.: 'Kant's sensationism', *Synthese* 47 (1981), 229–55.
Guyer, P.: *Kant and the Claims of Knowledge* (Cambridge: Cambridge University Press, 1987).
Kemp Smith, N.: *A Commentary on Kant's Critique of Pure Reason* 2nd edn (London: Macmillan, 1923).
Paton, H.J.: *Kant's Metaphysic of Experience* (London: Allen and Unwin, 1936).
Prichard, H.A.: *Kant's Theory of Knowledge* (Oxford: Clarendon Press, 1909).
Sellars, W.: *Science and Metaphysics: Variations on Kantian Themes* (London: Routledge and Kegan Paul, 1968).
Strawson, P.F.: *The Bounds of Sense* (London: Methuen, 1966).
Wolff, R.P.: *Kant's Theory of Mental Activity* (Cambridge, MA: Harvard University Press, 1963).

JAMES VAN CLEVE

**KK-thesis** The thesis that knowing entails knowing that one knows, often symbolized in epistemic logic as '$Kp \rightarrow KKp$', where 'K' stands for the concept of knowing. According to the KK-thesis, the logic of knowledge resembles the modal system S4. The KK-thesis was introduced into the contemporary epistemological discussion by Jaakko HINTIKKA in *Knowledge and Belief* (1962), but a tacit or an explicit acceptance of the thesis has been part of many philosophers' views about knowledge since Plato and Aristotle. The validity of the thesis is sensitive to shifts in the sense of 'know'; it has often been thought to characterize a strong concept of knowledge (e.g. knowledge based on conclusive grounds), or active as opposed to implicit knowledge.

BIBLIOGRAPHY

Hintikka, J.: *Knowledge and Belief: An Introduction to the Logic of the Two Notions* (Ithaca, NY: Cornell University Press, 1962).
*Synthese* 21:2 (1970).

RISTO HILPINEN

**knower paradox** *see* PARADOX OF THE KNOWER.

**knowledge** *see* CAUSAL THEORIES IN EPISTEMOLOGY; COHERENTISM; DIFFERENT CONSTRUCTIONS IN TERMS OF 'KNOWS'; FOUNDATIONALISM; GETTIER PROBLEM; KNOWLEDGE AND BELIEF; PROPOSITIONAL KNOWLEDGE; RELIABILISM.

**knowledge and belief** According to most epistemologists, knowledge entails belief, so that I cannot know that such and such is the case unless I believe that such and such is the case. Others think this *entailment thesis* can be rendered more accurately if we substitute for belief some closely related attitude. For instance, several philosophers would prefer to say that knowledge entails psychological CERTAINTY (Prichard, 1950; Ayer, 1956) or conviction (Lehrer, 1974) or acceptance (Lehrer, 1989). None the less, there are arguments against all versions of the thesis that knowledge requires having a belief-like attitude toward the known. These arguments

KNOWLEDGE AND BELIEF

are given by philosophers who think that knowledge and belief (or a facsimile) are mutually incompatible (the *incompatibility thesis*), or by ones who say that knowledge does not entail belief, or vice versa, so that each may exist without the other, but the two may also coexist (the *separability thesis*).

The incompatibility thesis is sometimes traced to PLATO in view of his claim that knowledge is infallible while belief or opinion is fallible (*Republic* 476–9). But this claim would not support the thesis. Belief might be a component of an infallible form of knowledge in spite of the fallibility of belief. Perhaps knowledge involves some factor that compensates for the fallibility of belief.

A. Duncan-Jones (1938; cf. also Vendler, 1978) cites linguistic evidence to back up the incompatibility thesis. He notes that people often say 'I don't believe she is guilty, I *know* she is!' and the like, which suggests that belief rules out knowledge. However, as Lehrer (1974) indicates, the above exclamation is only a more emphatic way of saying, 'I don't *just* believe she is guilty, I know she is!' where 'just' makes it especially clear that the speaker is signalling that she has something more salient than mere belief, not that she has something inconsistent with belief, namely knowledge. Compare: 'You didn't hurt him, you killed him!'

H.A. Prichard (1966) offers a defense of the incompatibility thesis which hinges on the equation of knowledge with certainty (both infallibility and psychological certitude) and the assumption that when we believe in the truth of a claim we are not certain about its truth. Given that belief always involves uncertainly while knowledge never does, believing something rules out the possibility of knowing it. Unfortunately, however, Prichard gives us no good reason to grant that states of belief are never ones involving confidence. Conscious beliefs clearly involve some level of confidence; to suggest that we cease to believe things about which we are *completely* confident is bizarre.

A.D. Woozley (1953) defends a version of the separability thesis. Woozley's version, which deals with psychological certainty rather than belief *per se*, is that knowledge can exist in the absence of confidence about the item known, although knowledge might also be accompanied by confidence as well. Woozley remarks that the test of whether I know something is 'what I can do, where what I can do may include answering questions'. On the basis of this remark he suggests that even when people are unsure of the truth of a claim, they might know that the claim is true. We unhesitatingly attribute knowledge to people who give correct responses on examinations even if those people show no confidence in their answers. Woozley acknowledges, however, that it would be *odd* for those who lack confidence to claim knowledge. It would be peculiar to say, 'I am unsure whether my answer is true; still, I know it is correct.' But this tension Woozley explains using a distinction between conditions under which we are justified in making a claim (such as a claim to know something), and conditions under which the claim we make is true. While 'I know such and such' might be true even if I am unsure whether such and such holds, nonetheless it would be inappropriate for me to claim that I know that such and such unless I were sure of the truth of my claim.

Colin Radford (1966) extends Woozley's defence of the separability thesis. In Radford's view, not only is knowledge compatible with the lack of certainty, it is also compatible with a complete lack of belief. He argues by example. In one example, Jean has forgotten that he learned some English history years prior and yet he is able to give several correct responses to questions such as 'When did the Battle of Hastings occur?' Since he forgot that he took history, he considers his correct responses to be no more than guesses. Thus when he says that the Battle of Hastings took place in 1066 he would deny having the *belief* that the Battle of Hastings took place in 1066. *A fortiori* he would deny being sure (or having the right to be sure) that 1066 was the correct date. Radford would none the less insist that Jean knows when the Battle occurred, since clearly he remembers the correct date. Radford admits that it would be inappropriate for Jean to *say* that he knew when the Battle of Hastings occurred, but, like

235

Woozley, he attributes the impropriety to a fact about when it is and is not appropriate to *claim* knowledge. When we claim knowledge, we ought at least to believe that we have the knowledge we claim, or else our behavior is 'intentionally misleading'.

Those who agree with Radford's defence of the separability thesis will probably think of belief as an inner state that can be detected through introspection. That Jean lacks beliefs about English history is plausible on this Cartesian picture since Jean does not find himself with any beliefs about English history when he seeks them out. One might criticize Radford, however, by rejecting the Cartesian view of BELIEF. One could argue that some beliefs are thoroughly unconscious, for example. Or one could adopt a BEHAVIOUR-IST conception of belief, such as Alexander Bain's (1859), according to which having beliefs is a matter of the way people are disposed to behave (and hasn't Radford already adopted a behaviourist conception of knowledge?). Since Jean gives the correct response when queried, a form of verbal behaviour, a behaviourist would be tempted to credit him with the belief that the Battle of Hastings occurred in 1066.

D.M. Armstrong (1973) takes a different tack against Radford. Jean does know that the Battle of Hastings took place in 1066. Armstrong will grant Radford that point. In fact, Armstrong suggests that Jean believes that 1066 is *not* the date the Battle of Hastings occurred, for Armstrong equates the belief that such and such is just possible but no more than just possible with the belief that such and such is not the case. However, Armstrong insists, Jean also believes that the Battle *did* occur in 1066. After all, had Jean been mistaught that the Battle occurred in 1060, and had he forgotten being 'taught' this and subsequently 'guessed' that it took place in 1060, we would surely describe the situation as one in which Jean's false belief about the Battle became unconscious over time but persisted as a memory trace that was causally responsible for his guess. Out of consistency, we must describe Radford's original case as one in which Jean's *true* belief became unconscious but persisted long

enough to cause his guess. Thus while Jean consciously believes that the Battle did not occur in 1066, unconsciously he does believe it occurred in 1066. So after all Radford does not have a counterexample to the claim that knowledge entails belief.

Armstrong's response to Radford was to reject Radford's claim that the examinee lacked the relevant belief about English history. Another response is to argue that the examinee lacks the knowledge Radford attributes to him (cf. Sorensen, 1982). If Armstrong is correct in suggesting that Jean believes both that 1066 is and that it is not the date of the Battle of Hastings, one might deny Jean knowledge on the grounds that people who believe the denial of what they believe cannot be said to know the truth of their belief. Another strategy might be to liken the examinee case to examples of ignorance given in recent attacks on EXTERNAL-IST accounts of knowledge (needless to say, externalists themselves would tend not to favour this strategy). Consider the following case developed by BonJour (1985): For no apparent reason, Samantha believes that she is clairvoyant. Again for no apparent reason, she one day comes to believe that the President is in New York City, even though she has every reason to believe that the President is in Washington, DC. In fact, Samantha *is* a completely reliable clairvoyant, and she has arrived at her belief about the whereabouts of the President through the power of her clairvoyance. Yet surely Samantha's belief is completely irrational. She is not justified in thinking what she does. If so, then she does not know where the President is. But Radford's examinee is little different. Even if Jean lacks the belief which Radford denies him, Radford does not have an example of knowledge that is unattended with belief. Suppose that Jean's memory had been sufficiently powerful to produce the relevant belief. As Radford says, Jean has every reason to suppose that his response is mere guesswork, and so he has every reason to consider his belief false. His belief would be an irrational one, and hence one about whose truth Jean would be ignorant.

*See also* PROPOSITIONAL KNOWLEDGE.

BIBLIOGRAPHY

Armstrong, D.M.: *Belief, Truth and Knowledge* (Cambridge: Cambridge University Press, 1973).
Ayer, A.J.: *The Problem of Knowledge* (Harmondsworth: Penguin Books, 1956).
Bain, A.: *The Emotions and the Will* (London: Longmans, Green, 1859).
BonJour, L.: *The Structure of Empirical Knowledge* (Cambridge, MA: Harvard University Press, 1985).
Duncan-Jones, A.: 'Further questions about "know" and "think"', in *Philosophy and Analysis* ed. M. MacDonald (Oxford: Blackwell, 1966).
Lehrer, K.: *Knowledge* (Oxford: Oxford University Press, 1974).
Lehrer, K.: 'Knowledge reconsidered', in *Knowledge and Skepticism* eds M. Clay and K. Lehrer (Boulder: Westview, 1989).
Prichard, H.A.: *Knowledge and Perception* (Oxford: Clarendon Press 1950).
Radford, C.: 'Knowledge – by examples', *Analysis* 27 (1966), 1–11.
Sorensen, R.A.: 'Knowing, believing, and guessing', *Analysis* 42 (1982), 212–13.
Vendler, Z.: *Res Cogitans* (Ithaca, NY: Cornell University Press, 1978).
Woozley, A.D.: 'Knowing and not knowing', *Proceedings of the Aristotelian Society* 53 (1952–3), 151–72.

STEVEN LUPER-FOY

**knowledge by acquaintance/by description** The expressions 'knowledge by acquaintance' and 'knowledge by description', and the distinction they mark between knowing *things* and knowing *about* things, are now generally associated with Bertrand RUSSELL. However, John Grote and Hermann von Helmholtz had earlier and independently used essentially similar terminology to mark the same distinction, and William JAMES adopted Grote's terminology in his investigation of the distinction. Philosophers have perennially investigated this and related distinctions using varying terminology.

GROTE AND HELMHOLTZ

Grote introduced the distinction by noting that natural language 'distinguishes between these two applications of the notion of knowledge, the one being γνῶναι, noscere, kennen, connaître, the other being εἰδέναι, scire, wissen, savoir' (Grote, 1865, p. 60). On Grote's account, the distinction is a matter of degree, and there are three sorts of dimensions of variability: epistemic, causal and semantic.

We know things by experiencing them, and knowledge of acquaintance (Russell changed the preposition to 'by') is epistemically prior to and has a relatively higher degree of epistemic justification than knowledge about things. Indeed, sensation has 'the one great value of trueness or freedom from mistake' (1900, p. 206).

A thought (using that term broadly, to mean any mental state) constituting knowledge of acquaintance with a thing is more or less causally proximate to sensations caused by that thing, while a thought constituting knowledge about the thing is more or less distant causally, being separated from the thing and experience of it by processes of attention and inference. At the limit, if a thought is maximally of the acquaintance type, it is the first mental state occurring in a perceptual causal chain originating in the object to which the thought refers, i.e. it is a sensation. The things presented to us in sensation and of which we have knowledge of acquaintance include ordinary objects in the external world, such as the sun.

Grote contrasted the imagistic thoughts involved in knowledge of acquaintance with things, with the judgements involved in knowledge about things, suggesting that the latter but not the former are contentful mental states. Elsewhere, however, he suggested that every thought capable of constituting knowledge of or about a thing involves a form, idea, or what we might call conceptual propositional content, referring the thought to its object. Whether contentful or not, thoughts constituting knowledge of acquaintance with a thing are relatively indistinct, although this indistinctness does not imply incommunicability. On the other hand, thoughts constituting knowledge about a thing are relatively distinct, as a result of 'the application of notice or attention' to the 'confusion or chaos' of sensation (1900, pp. 206–7). Grote did not have an explicit theory of reference, the relation by which a thought is *of* or *about* a specific thing. Nor did he explain how thoughts can be more or less indistinct.

Helmholtz held unequivocally that all thoughts capable of constituting knowledge, whether 'knowledge which has to do with Notions' (*Wissen*) or 'mere familiarity with phenomena' (*Kennen*), are judgements or, we may say, have conceptual propositional contents. Where Grote saw a difference between distinct and indistinct thoughts, Helmholtz found a difference between precise judgements which are expressible in words and equally precise judgments which, in principle, are not expressible in words, and so are not communicable (Helmholtz, 1962, pp. 269–75).

## JAMES

James was influenced by Helmholtz and, especially, by Grote. (James, 1975, pp. 17–18; 1890, vol. 1, p. 221n.) Adopting the latter's terminology, James agreed with Grote that the distinction between knowledge of acquaintance with things and knowledge about things involves a difference in the degree of vagueness or distinctness of thoughts, though he, too, said little to explain how such differences are possible. At one extreme is knowledge of acquaintance with people and things, and with sensations of colour, flavour, spatial extension, temporal duration, effort and perceptible difference, unaccompanied by knowledge about these things. Such pure knowledge of acquaintance is vague and inexplicit. Movement away from this extreme, by a process of notice and analysis, yields a spectrum of less vague, more explicit thoughts constituting knowledge about things.

However, the distinction was not merely a relative one for James. He was more explicit than Grote in not imputing content to every

thought capable of constituting knowledge of or about things. At the extreme where a thought constitutes pure knowledge of acquaintance with a thing, there is a complete absence of conceptual propositional content in the thought (which is a sensation, feeling, or percept), which also renders the thought incommunicable. James's reasons for positing an absolute discontinuity between pure knowledge of acquaintance and knowledge at all about things seem to have been that any theory adequate to the facts about reference must allow that some reference is not conceptually mediated; that conceptually unmediated reference is necessary if there are to be judgements at all about things and, especially, if there are to be judgments about relations between things; and that any theory faithful to the common person's 'sense of life' must allow that some things are directly perceived.

James made a genuine advance over Grote and Helmholtz by analysing the reference relation holding between a thought and the specific thing of or about which it is knowledge. In fact, he gave two different analyses. On both analyses, a thought constituting knowledge about a thing refers to and is knowledge about 'a reality, whenever it actually or potentially terminates in' a thought constituting knowledge of acquaintance with that thing (1975, pp. 27–8). The two analyses differ in their treatments of knowledge of acquaintance. On James's first analysis, reference in both sorts of knowledge is mediated by causal chains. A thought constituting pure knowledge of acquaintance with a thing refers to and is knowledge of 'whatever reality it directly or indirectly operates on and resembles' (1975, p. 27). The concepts of a thought 'operating on' a thing or 'terminating in' another thought are causal, but where Grote found chains of efficient causation connecting thought and referent, James found teleology and final causes. On James's later analysis, the reference involved in knowledge of acquaintance with a thing is direct. A thought constituting knowledge of acquaintance with a thing either *is* that thing, or has that thing as a constituent, and the thing and the experience of it are identical (1975, ch. 2; 1976, chs 1 and 2).

James further agreed with Grote that pure knowledge of acquaintance with things (i.e. sensory experience) is epistemically prior to knowledge about things. While the epistemic justification involved in knowledge about things rests on the foundation of sensation, all thoughts about things are fallible and their justification is augmented by their mutual coherence. James was unclear about the precise epistemic status of knowledge of acquaintance. At times, thoughts constituting pure knowledge of acquaintance are said to possess 'absolute veritableness' (1890, vol. I, p. 189) and 'the maximal conceivable truth' (1975, p. 87), suggesting that such thoughts are genuinely cognitive and that they provide an infallible epistemic foundation. At other times, such thoughts are said not to bear truth-values, suggesting that 'knowledge' of acquaintance is not genuine knowledge at all, but only a non-cognitive necessary condition of genuine knowledge, viz. knowledge about things (1976, p. 102). Russell understood James to hold the latter view.

## RUSSELL

Russell agreed with Grote and James on the following points. First, knowing things involves experiencing them. Second, knowledge of things by acquaintance is epistemically basic and provides an infallible epistemic foundation for knowledge about things. (Like James, Russell vacillated about the epistemic status of knowledge by acquaintance, and it eventually was replaced at the epistemic foundation by the concept of noticing.) Third, knowledge about things is more articulate and explicit than knowledge by acquaintance with things. Fourth, knowledge about things is causally removed from knowledge of things by acquaintance, by processes of reflection, analysis and inference (1911, 1913, 1959).

But Russell also held that the term 'experience' must not be used uncritically in philosophy, on account of the 'vague, fluctuating and ambiguous' meaning of the term in its ordinary use. The precise concept found by Russell 'in the nucleus of this uncertain patch of meaning' is that of direct occurrent experience of a thing, and he used the term 'acquaintance' to express this relation, though he used that term technically, and not with all of its ordinary meaning (1913, pt I, ch. 1). Nor did he undertake to give a constitutive analysis of the relation of acquaintance, though he allowed that it may not be unanalysable, and did characterize it as a generic concept. If the use of the term 'experience' is restricted to expressing the determinate core of the concept it ordinarily expresses, then we do not experience ordinary objects in the external world, as we commonly think and as Grote and James held we do. In fact, Russell held, one can be acquainted only with one's SENSE-DATA (i.e. particular colours, sounds, etc.), one's occurrent mental states, universals, logical forms, and (perhaps) oneself.

Russell agreed with James that knowledge of things by acquaintance 'is essentially simpler than any knowledge of truths, and logically independent of knowledge of truths' (1912, p. 46; 1929, p. 115). The mental states involved when one is acquainted with things do not have propositional contents. Russell's reasons here seem to have been similar to James's. Conceptually unmediated reference to particulars is necessary for understanding any proposition mentioning a particular (e.g. 1918–19, p. 33) and, if scepticism about the external world is to be avoided, some particulars must be directly perceived (1911, p. 119). Russell vacillated about whether or not the absence of propositional content renders knowledge by acquaintance incommunicable.

Russell agreed with James that different accounts should be given of reference as it occurs in knowledge by acquaintance and in knowledge about things, and that in the former case reference is direct. But Russell objected on a number of grounds to James's causal account of the indirect reference involved in knowledge about things. Russell gave a descriptional rather than a causal analysis of that sort of reference: A thought is about a thing when the content of the thought involves a definite description uniquely satisfied by the thing referred to. Indeed, he preferred to speak of knowledge of things by description, rather than of knowledge about things.

Russell advanced beyond Grote and James by explaining how thoughts can be more or less articulate and explicit. If one is acquainted with a complex thing without being aware of or acquainted with its complexity, the knowledge one has by acquaintance with that thing is vague and inexplicit. Reflection and analysis can lead one to distinguish constituent parts of the object of acquaintance and to obtain progressively more distinct, explicit, and complete knowledge about it (1913, 1918–19, 1950, 1959).

## SUMMARY CONSIDERATIONS

Apparent facts to be explained about the distinction between knowing things and knowing about things are these. Knowledge about things is essentially propositional knowledge, where the mental states involved refer to specific things. This propositional knowledge can be more or less complete, can be justified inferentially and on the basis of experience, and can be communicated. Knowing things, on the other hand, involves experience of things. This experiential knowledge provides an epistemic basis for knowledge about things, and in some sense is difficult or impossible to communicate, perhaps because it is more or less vague.

If one is unconvinced by James's and Russell's reasons for holding that experience of and reference to things are at least sometimes direct, it may seem preferable to join Helmholtz in asserting that knowing things and knowing about things both involve propositional attitudes. To do so would at least allow one the advantages of unified accounts of the nature of knowledge (propositional knowledge would be fundamental) and of the nature of reference (indirect reference would be the only kind). The two kinds of knowledge might yet be importantly different if the mental states involved have different sorts of causal origins in the thinker's cognitive faculties, involve different sorts of propositional attitudes, and differ in other constitutive respects relevant to the relative vagueness and communicability of the mental states.

*See also* EXPERIENCE; FOUNDATIONALISM; the GIVEN; INTROSPECTION.

BIBLIOGRAPHY

Grote, J.: *Exploratio Philosophica* Part I (Cambridge: Cambridge University Press, 1865); Part II, ed. J.B. Mayor (Cambridge: Cambridge University Press, 1900).

Helmholtz, H. von: 'The recent progress of the theory of vision', trans. P.H. Pye-Smith, in *Popular Scientific Lectures* ed. M. Kline (New York: Dover, 1962), 93–115.

James, W.: *The Principles of Psychology* 2 vols (New York: Henry Holt, 1890).

James, W.: *The Meaning of Truth: A Sequel to Pragmatism* (Cambridge, MA: Harvard University Press, 1975).

James, W.: *Essays in Radical Empiricism* (Cambridge, MA: Harvard University Press, 1976).

Russell, B.: 'Knowledge by acquaintance and knowledge by description', *Proceedings of the Aristotelian Society* 11 (1910–11), 108–28. Reprinted as ch. 10 in his *Mysticism and Logic and Other Essays* (New York: Longmans, Green, 1918); adapted as ch. 5 in his *The Problems of Philosophy* (1912).

Russell, B.: *Theory of Knowledge: The 1913 Manuscript* eds E.R. Eames and K. Blackwell (London: Allen and Unwin, 1984). Chs 1–3 of part 1 published as 'On the nature of acquaintance', *The Monist* 24 (1914), 1–16, 161–87, 435–53; reprinted in *Logic and Knowledge: Essays 1901–1950* ed. R.C. Marsh (London: Allen and Unwin, 1956).

Russell, B.: *Our Knowledge of the External World* revised edn (London: Allen and Unwin, 1929).

Russell, B.: 'The philosophy of logical atomism', *The Monist* (1918–19); reprinted in *Logic and Knowledge*.

Russell, B.: *An Inquiry into Meaning and Truth* (London: Allen and Unwin, 1950).

Russell, B.: *My Philosophical Development* (London: Allen and Unwin, 1959).

DAVID B. MARTENS

**knowledge how, who, why etc.** *see* DIF-

FERENT CONSTRUCTIONS IN TERMS OF 'KNOWS'

**knowledge-seeking by questioning** Much of traditional epistemology is devoted to the study of the justification or, more generally, the evaluation of the beliefs we have on the basis of some given body of evidence. Recently, belief revision has claimed its place as a further chapter of epistemology. In contrast, relatively little attention has been devoted to the epistemology of knowledge acquisition. One (usually tacit) reason for this neglect is the belief that the most important types of knowledge acquisition, e.g. the discovery of a new scientific theory, are not subject to rules, and hence cannot be studied logically or epistemologically.

In direct opposition to such traditional views, theories of knowledge-seeking by questioning seek to develop explicit logical models of knowledge acquisition. The natural range of application of such theories is, in fact, wider than the title suggests. For consider a knowledge-seeking argument, conceptualized as a sequence of propositions. Take any proposition in the sequence: where does it come from? In some cases, it is a logical consequence of the earlier stages of the argument, and hence does not introduce any new information into the argument; in others, it is not. In such cases some new information enters into the argument. In order to evaluate the argument, we have to know what the source of the new information is and why the arguer resorted to this particular oracle (i.e. source of information). But if we know both of these two things, we might as well think of the new information as an answer to a question addressed by the inquirer to that oracle. Thus a theory of information acquisition by questioning can serve as a framework for argumentation theory in general.

The most explicit form of a theory of knowledge-seeking by questioning is Jaakko Hintikka's interrogative model of inquiry. In spite of the name, it is really a model schema which can be varied in different ways and which leaves open certain parameters needed to specify a model fully.

The interrogative model of inquiry can be thought of as an explicit modern version of the Socratic *elenchus* or method of questioning. Like the Socratic method, it can be cast into the form of a game, with the important proviso that in the interrogative model the answerer need not be a human interlocutor. In its simplest form, interrogative inquiry is accordingly represented as a two-person game, where the players are the *inquirer* (who need not be an individual investigator but can be a research team or even the scientific community) and a single source of information called *the oracle*. The inquirer is trying to prove a given conclusion C starting from a given initial premise T. The inquirer has two sorts of moves available to him or her. The inquirer can either draw a logical conclusion from T and from the results so far established (a *logical inference move*), or she or he can put a question to the oracle (an *interrogative move*). For the purpose, the inquirer must have previously established (or assumed) the *presupposition* of the question. For instance, if the disjunction $(S_1 \vee S_2)$ has been established, the inquirer can use it as a presupposition for the question, "Is $S_1$ or $S_2$ true?" If the oracle answers, the inquirer has made progress: now he or she knows not only that the disjunction is true (or can be treated as being true for the purposes of the argument), but which disjunct makes it true.

Formally, the course of an interrogative game can be recorded in a semantical *tableau* in the sense of E.W. Beth. The initial situation involves an initial premise T and a fixed ultimate conclusion C. At each stage the inquirer can choose to make either a *logical inference* move or an *interrogative* move. The rules for logical inference moves are Beth's *tableau* rules modified so as not to allow any traffic from the right column to the left one. (Subformula property is preserved.) If the presupposition of a question occurs in the left column, the inquirer may make an interrogative move and address the corresponding question to the oracle. If the oracle gives a (conclusive) answer, the answer is added as an extra premise to the left column. The game is played with respect to a given model M of the underlying first-order language, and in the simplest version all of the oracle's answers are assumed to be true in M, provided only that a true answer is possible in the first place. The inquirer wins the game iff (if and only if) he or she closes the *tableau*, and the closure rules are *mutatis mutandis* the same as in the deductive case. Iff the inquirer can win the game no matter what the oracle does, C is said to be an interrogative consequence of T in M, in short

(1) $$M: T \vdash C$$

For the logical theory of questions relied on here, see Hintikka (1976) and (1984).

Several variations are possible here:

1. The aim of the inquiry may be to answer a question rather than to prove a fixed conclusion.

   It is easy to see how one can try to answer a propositional question by means of interrogative inquiry: one constructs a separate *tableau* for each (propositional) answer. It is far from obvious how a wh-question can be answered interrogatively; see (e) below.

2. The range of answers the oracle will give is usually assumed to be fixed throughout the inquiry, but it can initially be chosen in different ways.

3. The oracle may be chosen differently in different applications. It can be an actual person, for instance, a witness in a court of law or a patient in a diagnostic interview, but it can also be nature as a target of observations and experiments, computer memory or one's own tacit knowledge. There may also be several different oracles.

4. Instead of assuming that the oracle's answers are always true (whenever they can be), we can assume that they can be false. Then the inquirer must be given the option at each stage to reject (at least temporarily) an earlier answer (or initial premise), together with those steps that depend on it. By the same token, the inquirer is allowed to restore a previously rejected answer or premise (together with its rejected dependents).

What insights are suggested or given rise to by the theory of knowledge-seeking by questioning? The following are some partial answers:

(a) In so far as even a simple form of the interrogative model leads to an interesting theory, one of the main dogmas of recent epistemology and philosophy of science will be refuted, viz. that there cannot be a rational (logical) theory of discovery, only a theory of justification or evaluation.

What can be shown, however, is that there normally are no mechanical (recursive) rules of discovery. Hence this new 'logic of discovery' does not contradict the impossibility of subjecting discovery to (mechanical) rules; on the contrary, it enables us to prove that impossibility.

(b) In interrogative games with uncertain answers, the interrogative process itself can be used to evaluate oracles and their answers for reliability, assuming of course some amount of suitable prior information of their credibility. Hence the interrogative model of inquiry can serve as a framework for discussing the self-correcting character of knowledge-seeking methods.

(c) The relation (1) of interrogative provability can be compared with the relation of logical consequence:

(2) $$T \vdash C$$

and with the notion of truth in a model:

(3) $$M \vDash C$$

In a certain sense, (1) is between (2) and (3). If no answers are available, (1) reduces to (2). If all questions and answers are available (in a sense that can be made precise), (3) is the case iff

(4) $$M: \varnothing \vDash C$$

i.e. iff C can be proved interrogatively without any premises ($\varnothing$ is the empty set).

Thus the interrogative model can serve as a framework for examining the idea of truth as the ideal limit of inquiry.

(d) Heuristically, (1) can be studied by

trying to prove for it analogues to well-known metatheorems of deductive logic. This strategy has already proved to be fruitful. For instance, a form of Craig's interpolation theorem has been shown to hold for (1) (*see* Hintikka, 1991a).

(e) The interrogative counterpart to the logical notion of definability (on the basis of a given theory) turns out to be a generalization of a notion well known from the methodology of several particular disciplines, viz. the notion of identifiability (*see* Hintikka, 1991a).

Here the strategy mentioned in (d) serves us especially well. In ordinary logic, the interpolation theorem has as its corollary Beth's theorem which serves as a cornerstone of a theory of definability. Likewise, the interrogative extension of the interpolation theorem has as its corollary an extension of Beth's theorem which can serve as a starting-point of a general logical theory of identifiability. This theory shows among other things how one can try to answer wh-questions by means of interrogative inquiry (*see* DIFFERENT CONSTRUCTIONS IN TERMS OF 'KNOWS').

(f) The most interesting kind of restriction on the answers the oracle will give is in terms of their maximal allowed quantificational complexity. The different allowed maximal complexity can range from quantifier-free answers (the atomistic case) to A-answers (a prefix of universal quantifiers only) to AE-answers all the way to quantificationally unrestricted answers.

These different restrictions characterize different types of inquiry. For instance, purely observational inquiry is atomistic whereas clinical inquiry can be thought of as being unrestricted in this dimension.

(g) This line of thought can be pushed further. It is generally but mistakenly assumed in effect that empirical scientific inquiry is atomistic. If that were the case, general conclusions, e.g. scientific theories, could not be derived interrogatively without strong (general) antecedent premises. This fact has in effect prompted some of the characteristic models of scientific theorizing, including the inductivistic and the hypothetico-deductive one.

Both become redundant if the result of a controlled experiment (establishing the dependence between the controlled variable and the observed one) is construed *à la* Kant as nature's answer to an inquirer's question. For such an answer is at least of the AE-complexity, and hence can logically imply general truths. In general, experimental inquiry is characterized by at least the AE-complexity of its answers (*see* Hintikka, 1988).

This analysis of the logic of experimental inquiry throws light on the actual methodology of scientists, e.g. Isaac Newton's actual methodology and on his methodological views.

(h) Unlike ordinary first-order logic, interrogative inquiry does not allow cut-elimination or the elimination of *modus ponens*. In other words, tautological extra premises $(S \vee \sim S)$ can strengthen interrogative inquiry, essentially by serving as presuppositions of yes-or-no questions. The introduction of such a premise can be interpreted as extending the inquirer's range of attention, for the main function of a new tautological premise $(S \vee \sim S)$ is to enable the inquirer to ask the yes-or-no question 'Is it the case that S or not?

(i) The interrogative model facilitates the study of strategies of knowledge-seeking in contrast to the evaluation of beliefs on the basis of already acquired data. One important result in this direction is that strategies of questioning are largely parallel, especially when the oracle's answers are forthcoming and true, to strategies of deduction. (Cf. here Hintikka, 1989a.) This brings out an element of truth in the old conception of logic as the gist of all good reasoning.

In another direction, the question can be raised as to whether many of the rules of inductive and statistical reasoning should be construed as strategic rules rather than rules definitory of the 'game' of inquiry.

(j) The interrogative model can be used to distinguish kinds of knowledge from each other, such as active, tacit, virtual, potential, etc., knowledge. It also yields a framework for studying suggestions like Ramsey's according to which knowledge equals true belief obtained by an appropriate method (*see* Hintikka, 1989b).

(k) When the aim of the game is to answer a question and not to prove a predetermined conclusion, we have to distinguish the *principal question* to be answered through the entire interrogative inquiry from the *operative questions* whose answers (when available) are used for that purpose. This makes it possible to construe interrogative knowledge-seeking as a multi-level process where the operative question of a higher-level inquiry are principal questions for a series of lower-level interrogative inquiries.

The mistake of trying to ask the principal question rather than an operative one is precisely what the so-called fallacy of *petitio principii* meant (*see* Robinson, 1971). In general, the interrogative model helps to put the entire traditional theory of fallacies in a new light (*see* Hintikka 1987).

An early popular exposition of the interrogative approach to inquiry is Hintikka and Hintikka (1982). A textbook treatment of the interrogative model and its applications is Hintikka and Bachman (1990). An alternative treatment of some of the same matters is found in Rescher (1977).

BIBLIOGRAPHY

Hintikka, J.: *The Semantics of Questions and the Questions of Semantics*, Acta Philosophica Fennica 28, no. 4 (1976).
Hintikka, J.: 'Questioning as a philosophical method', in *Principles of Philosophical Reasoning* ed. J.H. Fetzer (Totowa: Rowman and Allanheld, 1984), 25–43.
Hintikka, J.: 'The fallacy of fallacies', *Argumentation* 1 (1987), 211–38.
Hintikka, J.: 'What is the logic of experimental inquiry?', *Synthese* 74 (1988), 173–90.
Hintikka, J.: 'The role of logic in argumentation', *The Monist* 72 (1989[a]), 3–24.
Hintikka, J.: 'Knowledge representation and the interrogative model of inquiry', in *Knowledge and Skepticism* eds M. Clay and K. Lehrer (Boulder: Westview Press, 1989[b]), 155–83.
Hintikka, J.: 'Toward a general theory of identification', in *Definitions and Definability: Philosophical Perspectives* eds J. Fetzer, D. Shatz and G. Schlesinger (Dordrecht: Kluwer, 1991[a], forthcoming).
Hintikka, J.: 'Overcoming metaphysics through logical analysis of language', *Dialectica* 1991[b], forthcoming.
Hintikka, J. and Bachman, J.: *What If . . .? Toward Excellence in Reasoning* (Mountain-View: Mayfield, 1990).
Hintikka, J. and Hintikka, M.B.: 'Sherlock Holmes confronts modern logic: toward a theory of information-seeking through questioning', in *Argumentation: Approaches to Theory Formation* eds E.M. Barth and J.L. Martens (Amsterdam: John Benjamins, 1982), 55–70.
Rescher, N.: *Dialectics: A Controversy-Oriented Approach to the Theory of Knowledge* (Albany: SUNY Press, 1977).
Robinson, R.: 'Begging the question', *Analysis* 31 (1971), 113–17.

JAAKKO HINTIKKA

# L

---

**Leibniz, Gottfried Wilhelm (1646–1716)**
German philosopher and mathematician.
Leibniz's fundamental philosophical interests
were in metaphysics, natural theology, logic
and the philosophy of science. Leibniz did not
produce a work that constitutes his theory of
knowledge, nor did he consider in detail the
basic epistemological issues that so moved
Descartes and Locke. Commenting on Descartes' alleged proof of the existence of
material objects in article one of the second
part of *The Principles of Philosophy*, Leibniz
affirmed that Descartes' argument is weak,
and added: 'It would be better not to try'
(Loemker, p. 391). Note also that there is no
section in Leibniz's *New Essays on Human
Understanding* – essentially a commentary on
Locke's *An Essay Concerning Human Understanding* – corresponding to Chapter 1 of Book
I of Locke's *Essay*, in which Locke outlined
the epistemological purposes of the *Essay*.
None the less, Leibniz made important contributions to epistemology, some of which make
plausible the usual listing of Leibniz under the
rubric RATIONALIST.

Leibniz's account of truth has the following
striking consequence: a proposition is true
just in case it is conceptually true, i.e. true in
virtue of a relation of containment holding
among its concepts. Leibniz was acutely
aware that his characterization of truth
appears to imply that all truth is necessary
truth. (*See*, for example, Parkinson and
Morris, 1973, p. 97.) In his mature work he
set out to avoid this unacceptable conclusion
by defending the following claims: (1) in a
proposition that is necessarily true there is a
containment relation among its concepts
such that there are definitional analyses of
those concepts in virtue of which the original
proposition is reducible to an identity, i.e.
something of the form AB is A, in a finite

number of steps; and (2) in a proposition that
is contingently true there is no such analysis,
although there are definitional analyses in
virtue of which the original proposition converges on an identity. Leibniz took this distinction between finite and infinite analysis to
allow him to hold the following doctrines, all
of which he thought to be worthy of support:

1. Truth is fundamentally a matter of the
   containment of the concept of the predicate of a proposition in the concept of its
   subject.
2. The distinction between necessary truth
   and contingent truth is absolute, and in
   no way relative to a corresponding distinction between divine and human
   sources of knowledge.
3. A proposition is known a priori by a finite
   mind only if that proposition is a necessary truth. (*See*, for example, Parkinson
   and Morris, 1973, p. 98.)

Hence, although Leibniz commenced with an
account of truth that one might expect to
lead to the conclusion that all knowledge is
ultimately A PRIORI KNOWLEDGE, he set out to
avoid that conclusion.

Leibniz's account of our knowledge of contingent truths is remarkably similar to what
we would expect to find in an empiricist's
epistemology. Leibniz claimed that our knowledge of particular contingent truths has its
basis in sense perception. He argued that our
knowledge of universal contingent truths can
not be based entirely on simple enumerative
inductions, but must be supplemented by
what he called 'the conjectural method a
priori', which he described as follows:

The conjectural method a priori
proceeds by hypotheses, assuming
certain causes, perhaps, without proof,

and showing that the things that happen would follow from those assumptions. A hypothesis of this kind is like the key to a cryptograph, and the simpler it is, and the greater the number of events that can be explained by it, the more probable it is. (Loemker, 1969, p. 283)

Leibniz's conception of the conjectural method a priori is a precursor of the hypothetico-deductive method. He placed emphasis on the need for a formal theory of probability, in order to formulate an adequate theory of our knowledge of contingent truths.

Leibniz sided with his rationalist colleagues, e.g. Descartes, in maintaining, contrary to the empiricists, that, since thought is an essential property of the mind, there is no time at which a mind exists without a thought, a perception. But Leibniz insisted on a distinction between having a perception and being aware of it. He argued forcefully on both empirical grounds and conceptual grounds that finite minds have numerous perceptions of which they are not aware at the time at which they have them. (*See*, for example, Remnant and Bennett, 1981, pp. 53–5.)

Leibniz's rationalism in epistemology is most evident in his account of our a priori knowledge, that is, according to (3), our knowledge of NECESSARY TRUTHS. One of Leibniz's persistent criticisms of LOCKE's EMPIRICISM is the thesis that Locke's theory of knowledge provides no explanation of how we know of certain propositions that they are not only true, but necessarily true. Leibniz argued that Locke offered no adequate account of how we know propositions to be true whose justification does not depend upon experience; hence, that Locke had no acceptable account of our a priori knowledge. Leibniz's diagnosis of Locke's failing was straightforward: Locke lacked an adequate account of our a priori knowledge because, on Locke's theory, all the material for the justification of beliefs must come from experience, thus overlooking what Leibniz took to be the source of our a priori knowledge,

namely, what is innate to the mind. Leibniz summarized his dispute with Locke thus:

Our differences are on matters of some importance. It is a matter of knowing if the soul in itself is entirely empty like a writing tablet on which nothing has as yet been written (tabula rasa) . . . and if everything inscribed there comes solely from the senses and experience, or if the soul contains originally the sources of various concepts and doctrines that external objects merely reveal on occasion . . . (Remnant and Bennett, 1981, p. 48).

Leibniz argued for the second alternative, the theory of innate doctrines and concepts. (*See*, for example ibid., pp. 69–108.)

The thesis that some concepts are innate to the mind is crucial to Leibniz's philosophy. He held that the most basic metaphysical concepts, e.g. the concepts of substance and causation, are innate. Hence, he was unmoved by the inability of empiricists to reconstruct full-blown versions of those concepts from the materials of sense experience.

*See also* INNATE IDEAS.

WRITINGS

Loemker, L.E. ed. and trans.: *Gottfried Wilhelm Leibniz – Philosophical Papers and Letters* (Dordrecht, 1969).
Parkinson, G.H.R. and Morris, M. ed. and trans.: *Leibniz – Philosophical Writings* (London, 1973).
Remnant, P. and Bennett, J. ed. and trans.: *Leibniz – New Essays on Human Understanding* (Cambridge, 1981).

BIBLIOGRAPHY

Broad, C.D.: *Leibniz – An Introduction*, ed. C. Lewy, chapter 5, 'Psychology and theory of knowledge' (Cambridge, 1975).
Jolley, N.: *Leibniz and Locke – A Study of the New Essays on Human Understanding* (Oxford, 1984).
McRae, R.: *Leibniz – Perception, Apperception, and Thought* (Toronto, 1976).

Rescher, N.: *Leibniz – An Introduction to His Philosophy*, chapter 2, 'Human knowledge' (Totowa, NJ, 1979).

R.C. SLEIGH, JR

**Lewis, Clarence Irving (1883–1964)** Lewis was educated at Harvard and taught there from 1920 until his retirement in 1953. His first work was in logic, and his investigation of what he called 'strict implication' is still of interest. Lewis also wrote extensively on ethics, but is best known for his work in epistemology.

Lewis defended a strong form of FOUND-ATIONALISM; he held that beliefs about the external world are at most highly probable, and that their probability derives from beliefs about sense-experience which are not just probable but certain. Lewis frequently claims that his position is the only alternative to COHERENTISM, and should be adopted because no beliefs can be probable unless some are certain. Unfortunately, Lewis found these claims so obvious that his support for them is cursory and rests heavily on metaphor. His most explicit argument for the claim that probability requires certainty runs as follows: if the probability of $h$, given $e$, is $n$, and the probability of $e$ is $m$ $(m < 1)$, we should reassess the probability of $h$ as $n \times m$ (Lewis, 1952, p. 172). If this reasoning is correct, and every $h$ rests on evidence which is itself less than certain, then the probability of $h$ will indeed be 'whittled down to nothing' (ibid.). But this argument rests on dubious assumptions and, like similar arguments in HUME and RUSSELL, leads to the conclusion that the probability of *every h* approaches 0, which violates the principle that the probabilities of $h$ and not -$h$ must sum to 1. The argument also conflicts with Lewis's views on MEMORY. The reliability of memory is crucial to inductive inference, but no beliefs of the form 'I remember eating breakfast' are certain, and attempts to ground them on the CERTAINTY of judgements of the form 'I seem to remember eating breakfast' are doomed to circularity. Lewis meets this problem by assigning memory beliefs an initial probability less than 1 but greater than 0.5, and noting that sets of 'congruent' memory beliefs can make a remembered event more probable than any of the memory beliefs taken by itself. This is an ingenious proposal, but it conflicts with the claim that probability must ultimately derive from certainty.

Another of Lewis's central claims is that the meaning of every empirical judgment is equivalent to some (very large) set of judgements of the form 'If such-and-such sense-experiences occurred, and such-and-such volitions followed, then in all probability such-and-such sense-experiences would ensue'. Lewis calls these conditionals 'terminating judgements', and holds that they can be conclusively verified and thus confirm our judgements about the external world. The claim that empirical judgements entail terminating judgements has been challenged by CHISHOLM (1948), and Lewis's rebuttal (1948) raises doubts about the consistency of his claims that: (1) non-terminating judgements *entail* terminating judgments, and (2) terminating judgements can be *conclusively* verified.

Despite these problems, and others, Lewis's writings provide an exceptionally rich and cogent version of classical EMPIRICISM as revised by a very fine philosopher well aware of its strengths and weaknesses.

*See also* the GIVEN; INFINITE REGRESS ARGUMENT; PHENOMENALISM.

WRITINGS

with Langford, C.H.: *Symbolic Logic* (New York: Appleton-Century, 1932).

*Mind and the World Order* (New York: Scribner's, 1929).

*An Analysis of Knowledge and Valuation* (La Salle, Illinois: Open Court, 1946).

'Professor Chisholm and Empiricism', *Journal of Philosophy* 45 (1948), 517–124.

'The given element in empirical knowledge', *Philosophical Review* 61 (1952), 168–75.

BIBLIOGRAPHY

Chisholm, R.M.: 'The problem of empiricism', *Journal of Philosophy* 45 (1948), 512–7.

Schilpp, P.A. ed.: *The Philosophy of C.I. Lewis* (La Salle: Open Court, 1968).

JOHN TROYER

**limits of human knowledge**   The issue of the extent and limits of human knowledge is a perplexing one. We can reliably estimate the amount of gold or oil yet to be discovered because we know the earth's extent as a priori given, and can thus establish a proportion between what has been explored and what has not. But we cannot comparably estimate the amount of knowledge yet to be discovered (both because there is no *measure* of what is known and because we have no reliable information regarding new knowledge yet to come). There is thus no way of establishing a proportion between what we know and what we do not.

The idea of the question-oriented completeness of the body of knowledge prevailing at a particular historical juncture can be construed in four alternative ways: (1) *Perceived Q-completeness*: every then-asked question has a then-given answer. (2) *Weak Q-completeness:* every then-asked question has a then-available answer. (3) *Strong Q-Completeness: Completeness in Principle*: every then-askable question has a then-available answer. (4) *An Unrealistic Case*: Every then-askable question has a then-given answer. The concept of strong Q-completeness points directly to the idea of an *equilibrium* between questions and answers. Such an *erotetic equilibrium* subsists when the questions that can be raised on the basis of the concepts and theses of a body of accepted knowledge can be answered with recourse to this same body of knowledge, as per the situation of figure 1.

But it is sobering to realize that even the strong Q-completeness of a state of knowledge *K* does not necessarily betoken its comprehensiveness or sufficiency, but might simply reflect the paucity of the range of questions we are in a position to contemplate on its basis. When the range of our knowledge is sufficiently restricted, then its Q-completeness will merely reflect this restrictedness rather than its intrinsic adequacy. For even as its capacity to resolve our questions counts as a merit of a body of knowledge, so also does its capacity to raise new questions of significance and 'depth'. Completeness is a hallmark of pseudoscience, which is generally so contrived that the questions that are allowed to be raised are the questions the projected machinery is in a position to resolve.

The idea of incompletable scientific progress is wholly compatible with the view that *every* question that can be asked at each and every particular state is going to be answered – or dissolved – at some future state: it does not commit one to the idea that there are any unanswerable questions placed altogether beyond the limits of possible resolution. It thus suffices for the prospect of endless cognitive progress to rely on Kant's idea that old problems when solved or dissolved give birth to others whose inherent significance is of no lesser magnitude than that of their predecessors. No recourse to *insolubilia* need be made to maintain the incompletability of our scientific knowledge.

Someone may ask: 'But will it still be appropriate to persist in maintaining the incompleteness of scientific knowledge when science can predict *everything?*' The reply is simply that science will *never* be able to predict literally everything: the very idea of predicting *everything* is simply unworkable since future scientific discoveries always lie beyond the reach of present science. We can only make predictions about matters that lie, at least broadly speaking, within our cognitive horizons; Newton could not have predicted findings in quantum theory any more than he could have predicted the outcome of American presidential elections. The only viable limits to knowability are those which root in knowledge – that is, in a model of nature which entails that certain sorts of things – the outcome of stochastic processes, for example – are in principle unknowable.

On the supposition that we are not discussing God, but dealing with finite, imperfect knowers, one must *reject* the contention that all truths are known. But this plausible concession has problematic consequences. Consider the thesis that all truths are known, $(\forall p)\,(p \to Kp)$. If this is false, that is, if $-(\forall p)$

EROTETIC COMPLETENESS EQUILIBRIUM

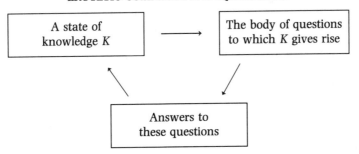

Figure 1

$(p \rightarrow Kp)$, then obviously $(\exists p)$ $(p \ \& \ -Kp)$ is true. Accordingly, let it now be supposed that there is a particular value of '$p$', say $p_o$, for which this holds, so that: $p_o \ \& \ -Kp_o$. But we have it in general that $(\exists p) -\Diamond K (p \ \& \ -Kp)$ or, equivalently, $-(\forall p) \ \Diamond K (p \ \& \ -Kp)$. This emerges from the following reasoning:

(1) $(\exists p) \ \Diamond K (p \ \& \ -Kp)$ by assumption

(2) $(\exists p) \ \Diamond \ (Kp \ \& \ K (-Kp))$ from (1) by the principle: $K (p \ \& \ q) \rightarrow (Kp \ \& \ Kq)$

(3) $(\exists p) \ \Diamond \ (Kp \ \& \ -Kp)$ from (2) by the principle: $Kp \rightarrow p$.

Since (3) is self contradictory its negation is established and that of (1) follows in its wake – as claimed at the start. And now, combining the two preceding findings we have:

$$(p_o \ \& \ -Kp_o) \ \& \ -\Diamond K (p_o \ \& \ -Kp_o)$$

And this at once yields $(\exists p) (p \ \& \ -\Diamond Kp)$ since the proposition $p_o \ \& \ -Kp_o$ itself represents a specific value of '$p$' for which this thesis obtains. Accordingly, $(\exists p) (p \ \& \ -Kp)$ entails $(\exists p) (p \ \& \ -\Diamond Kp)$.

What does this rather striking finding mean? It means that if we want to reject (for finite knowers) the clearly untenable thesis $p \rightarrow Kp$, then we must accept not just $(\exists p)$ $(p \ \& \ -Kp)$ but even $(\exists p) (p \ \& \ -\Diamond Kp)$. For finite knowers there are not just unknown but even unknowable facts. For if there indeed is an item of fact that is unknown – that is, if $p_o$ $\& \ -Kp_o$ – then this particular fact is one that cannot possibly be known in its full specificity, seeing that $K (p_o \ \& \ -Kp_o)$ leads ad absurdum by way of the above demonstration. Certain facts about the nature of their own ignorance must necessarily be outside the cognitive

range of finite knowers. (However, the incapacity reflected in this unknowability means that, as regards finite knowers, $(\forall x)$ $(\exists p)$ $(p \ \& \ -\Diamond Kp)$; it does not entail $(\exists p)$ $(\forall x)$ $(p \ \& \ -\Diamond Kp)$, that is, establish the existence of particular unknowable facts.)

To identify concretely an insoluble question in natural science, we would have to show that a certain scientifically appropriate question $Q$ is such that its resolution lies 'in principle' beyond the reach of science. But how could we possibly establish that a question $Q$ will continue to be both raisable and unanswerable in every future state of science, seeing that we cannot now circumscribe the changes that science might undergo in the future? The best we can do here and now is put $Q$'s resolvability beyond the power of any future state of science that looks to be a real possibility from where we stand. But the ground we stand on here is always to some extent shifting. If a question belongs to science at all – if it reflects the sort of issue that science might possibly resolve in principle and in theory – then we shall never be in a position to put it beyond the reach of possible future states of science as such. The course of wisdom accordingly lies with the stance that there are no particular scientific questions – and certainly no presently identifiable ones – that science cannot resolve as a matter of principle.

The inherent unpredictability of its internal changes is an ineradicable feature of science. It sets real science apart from the closed structures of pseudoscience, whose deficiencies are reflected precisely in the 'elegance' with which everything falls much too neatly into place. As regards the question-resolving potential of real science, we can set no a priori restrictions, but have to be flexible. Nobody can say what natural science will and will not be able to do, simply because the science of today is unable to speak decisively for that of tomorrow.

BIBLIOGRAPHY

du Bois-Reymond, E.: *über die Grenzen des Naturekennens* (Leipzig, 1916).

Kant, I.: *Critique of Pure Reason* trans N. Kemp Smith (London: Macmillan, 1964).

McMullin, E: 'Limits of scientific inquiry', in *Science and the Modern World* ed. J.C. Steinhardt (New York, 1966).

Rescher, N.: *The Limits of Science* (Berkeley and Los Angeles, 1984).

Wigner, E.P.: 'The limits of science', *Proceedings of the American Philosophical Society* 94 (1950), 422–7.

NICHOLAS RESCHER

**linguistic understanding**  The most influential idea in the theory of meaning in the past hundred years is the thesis that the meaning of an indicative sentence is given by its truth-conditions. On this conception, to understand a sentence is to know its truth-conditions. The conception was first clearly formulated by FREGE, was developed in a distinctive way by the early WITTGENSTEIN, and is a leading idea of DAVIDSON. The conception has remained so central that those who offer opposing theories characteristically define their position by reference to it.

The conception of meaning as truth-conditions need not and should not be advanced as being in itself a complete account of meaning. For instance, one who understands a language must have some idea of the range of speech acts conventionally performed by the various types of sentence in the language, and must have some idea of the significance of various kinds of speech act. The claim of the theorist of truth-conditions should rather be targeted on the notion of content: if two indicative sentences differ in what they strictly and literally say, then this difference is fully accounted for by the difference in their truth-conditions. It is this claim, and its attendant problems, which will be the concern of this article.

The meaning of a complex expression is a function of the meaning of its constituents. This is indeed just a statement of what it is for an expression to be semantically complex. It is one of the initial attractions of the conception of meaning as truth-conditions that it permits a smooth and satisfying account of the way in which the meaning of a complex expression is a function of the meaning of its constituents. On the truth-conditional conception, to give the meaning of an expression is to state the contribution it makes to the truth-conditions of sentences in which it occurs. For singular terms – proper names, indexicals, and certain pronouns – this is done by stating the reference of the term in question. For predicates, it is done either by stating the conditions under which the predicate is true of arbitrary objects, or by stating the conditions under which arbitrary atomic sentences containing it are true. The meaning of a sentence-forming operator is given by stating its contribution to the truth-conditions of a complete sentence, as a function of the semantic values of the sentences on which it operates. For an extremely simple, but nevertheless structured, language, we can state the contributions various expressions make to truth conditions as follows:

A1: The referent of 'London' is London.

A2: The referent of 'Paris' is Paris.

A3: Any sentence of the form '*a* is beautiful' is true if and only if the referent of *a* is beautiful.

A4: Any sentence of the form '*a* is larger than *b*' is true if and only if the referent of *a* is larger than the referent of *b*.

A5: Any sentence of the form 'It's not the case that *A*' is true if and only if it is not the case that *A* is true.

A6: Any sentence of the form '*A* and *B*' is true if and only if *A* is true and *B* is true.

The principles A1–A6 form a simple theory of truth for a fragment of English. In this theory, it is possible to derive these consequences: that 'Paris is beautiful' is true if and only if Paris is beautiful (from A2 and A3); that 'London is larger than Paris and it is not the case that London is beautiful' is true if and only if London is larger than Paris and it is not the case that London is beautiful (from A1–A5); and in general, for any sentence A of this simple language, we can derive something of the form ' "A" is true if and only if A'.

The theorist of truth conditions should insist that not every true statement about the reference of an expression is fit to be an axiom in a meaning-giving theory of truth for a language. The axiom

'London' refers to the city in which there was a huge fire in 1666

is a true statement about the reference of 'London'. It is a consequence of a theory which substitutes this axiom for A1 in our simple truth theory that 'London is beautiful' is true if and only if the city in which there was a huge fire in 1666 is beautiful. Since a subject can understand the name 'London' without knowing that last-mentioned truth condition, this replacement axiom is not fit to be an axiom in a meaning-specifying truth theory. It is, of course, incumbent on a theorist of meaning as truth conditions to state the constraints on the acceptability of axioms in a way which does not presuppose any prior, non-truth conditional conception of meaning. We will return to this crux later.

Among the many challenges facing the theorist of truth conditions, two are particularly salient and fundamental. First, the theorist has to answer the charge of triviality or vacuity. Second, the theorist must offer an account of what it is for a person's language to be truly describable by a semantic theory containing a given semantic axiom.

We can take the charge of triviality first. In more detail, it would run thus: since the content of a claim that the sentence 'Paris is beautiful' is true amounts to no more than the claim that Paris is beautiful, we can trivially describe understanding a sentence, if we wish, as knowing its truth-conditions, but this gives us no substantive account of

understanding whatsoever. Something other than grasp of truth conditions must provide the substantive account. The charge rests upon what has been called the redundancy theory of truth, the theory which, somewhat more discriminatingly, Horwich calls the minimal theory of truth (see TRUTH) The minimal theory states that the concept of truth is exhausted by the fact that it conforms to the equivalence principle, the principle that for any proposition $p$, it is true that $p$ if and only if $p$. Many different philosophical theories of truth will, with suitable qualifications, accept that equivalence principle. The distinguishing feature of the minimal theory is its claim that the equivalence principle exhausts the notion of truth. It is indeed now widely accepted, both by opponents and supporters of truth conditional theories of meaning, that it is inconsistent to accept both the minimal theory of truth and a truth conditional account of meaning (see Davidson, 1990; Dummett, 1959; Horwich, 1990). If the claim that the sentence 'Paris is beautiful' is true is exhausted by its equivalence to the claim that Paris is beautiful, it is circular to try to explain the sentence's meaning in terms of its truth conditions. The minimal theory of truth has been endorsed by Ramsey, Ayer, the later Wittgenstein, Quine, Strawson, Horwich and – confusingly and inconsistently if this article is correct – Frege himself. But is the minimal theory correct?

The minimal theory treats instances of the equivalence principle as definitional of truth for a given sentence. But in fact it seems that each instance of the equivalence principle can itself be explained. The truths from which such an instance as

'London is beautiful' is true if and only if London is beautiful

can be explained are precisely A1 and A3 above. This would be a pseudo-explanation if the fact that 'London' refers to London consists in part in the fact that 'London is beautiful' has the truth-condition it does. But that is very implausible: it is, after all, possible to understand the name 'London' without understanding the predicate 'is beautiful'.

The idea that facts about the reference of particular words can be explanatory of facts about the truth conditions of sentences containing them in no way requires any naturalistic or any other kind of reduction of the notion of reference. Nor is the idea incompatible with the plausible point that singular reference can be attributed at all only to something which is capable of combining with other expressions to form complete sentences. That still leaves room for facts about an expression's having the particular reference it does to be partially explanatory of the particular truth condition possessed by a given sentence containing it. The minimal theory thus treats as definitional or stipulative something which is in fact open to explanation. What makes this explanation possible is that there is a general notion of truth which has, among the many links which hold it in place, systematic connections with the semantic values of subsentential expressions.

A second problem with the minimal theory is that it seems impossible to formulate it without at some point relying implicitly on features and principles involving truth which go beyond anything countenanced by the minimal theory. If the minimal theory treats truth as a predicate of anything linguistic, be it utterances, types-in-a-language, or whatever, then the equivalence schema will not cover all cases, but only those in the theorist's own language. Some account has to be given of truth for sentences of other languages. Speaking of the truth of language-independent propositions or thoughts will only postpone, not avoid, this issue, since at some point principles have to be stated associating these language-independent entities with sentences of particular languages. The defender of the minimalist theory is likely to say that if a sentence S of a foreign language is best translated by our sentence p, then the foreign sentence S is true if and only if p. Now the best translation of a sentence must preserve the concepts expressed in the sentence. Constraints involving a general notion of truth are pervasive in a plausible philosophical theory of concepts. It is, for example, a condition of adequacy on an individuating account of any concept that there exist what I have called a 'Determination Theory' for that account – that is, a specification of how the account contributes to fixing the semantic value of that concept. The notion of a concept's semantic value is the notion of something which makes a certain contribution to the truth conditions of thoughts in which the concept occurs. But this is to presuppose, rather than to elucidate, a general notion of truth.

It is also plausible that there are general constraints on the form of such Determination Theories, constraints which involve truth and which are not derivable from the minimalist's conception. Suppose that concepts are individuated by their possession conditions (see CONCEPTS). One such plausible general constraint is then the requirement that when a thinker forms beliefs involving a concept in accordance with its possession condition, a semantic value is assigned to the concept in such a way that the belief is true. Some general principles involving truth can indeed, as Horwich has emphasized, be derived from the equivalence schema using minimal logical apparatus. Consider, for instance, the principle that 'Paris is beautiful and London is beautiful' is true if and only if 'Paris is beautiful' is true and 'London is beautiful' is true. This follows logically from the three instances of the equivalence principle: 'Paris is beautiful and London is beautiful' is true if and only if Paris is beautiful and London is beautiful; 'Paris is beautiful' is true if and only if Paris is beautiful; and 'London is beautiful' is true if and only if London is beautiful. But no logical manipulations of the equivalence schema will allow the derivation of that general constraint governing possession conditions, truth and the assignment of semantic values. That constraint can of course be regarded as a further elaboration of the idea that truth is one of the aims of judgement.

We now turn to the other question, 'What is it for a person's language to be correctly describable by a semantic theory containing a particular axiom, such as the axiom A6 above for conjunction?' This question may be addressed at two depths of generality. At the shallower level, the question may take for granted the person's possession of the concept of conjunction, and be concerned with what has to be true for the axiom to correctly describe his language. At a deeper level, an answer should not duck the issue of what it is to possess the concept. The answers to both questions are of great interest; we will take the lesser level of generality first.

When a person means conjunction by 'and', he is not necessarily capable of formulating the axiom A6 explicitly. Even if he can formulate it, his ability to formulate it is not the causal basis of his capacity to hear sentences containing the word 'and' as meaning something involving conjunction. Nor is it the causal basis of his capacity to mean something involving conjunction by sentences he utters containing the word 'and'. Is it then right to regard a truth theory as part of an unconscious psychological computation, and to regard understanding a sentence as involving a particular way of deriving a theorem from a truth theory at some level of unconscious processing? One problem with this is that it is quite implausible that everyone who speaks exactly the same language has to use exactly the same algorithms for computing the meaning of a sentence. In the past thirteen years, thanks particularly to the work of Davies and Evans, a conception has evolved according to which an axiom like A6 is true of a person's language only if there is a common component in the explanation of his understanding of each sentence containing the word 'and', a common component which explains why each such sentence is understood as meaning something involving conjunction (Davies, 1987). This conception can also be elaborated in computational terms: I suggested that for an axiom like A6 to be true of a person's language is for the unconscious mechanisms which produce understanding to draw on the information that a sentence of the form 'A and B' is true if and only if A is true and B is true (Peacocke, 1986). Many different algorithms may equally draw on this information. The psychological reality of a semantic theory thus involves, in Marr's (1982) famous classification, something

intermediate between his level one, the function computed, and his level two, the algorithm by which it is computed. This conception of the psychological reality of a semantic theory can also be applied to syntactic and phonological theories. Theories in semantics, syntax and phonology are not themselves required to specify the particular algorithms which the language user employs. The identification of the particular computational methods employed is a task for psychology. But semantic, syntactic and phonological theories are answerable to psychological data, and are potentially refutable by them – for these linguistic theories do make commitments to the information drawn upon by mechanisms in the language user.

This answer to the question of what it is for an axiom to be true of a person's language clearly takes for granted the person's possession of the concept expressed by the word treated by the axiom. In the example of the axiom A6, the information drawn upon is that sentences of the form 'A and B' are true if and only if A is true and B is true. This informational content employs, as it has to if it is to be adequate, the concept of conjunction used in stating the meaning of sentences containing 'and'. So the computational answer we have returned needs further elaboration if we are to address the deeper question, which does not want to take for granted possession of the concepts expressed in the language. It is at this point that the theory of linguistic understanding has to draw upon a theory of concepts. I would argue that it has to draw upon a theory of the conditions for possessing a given concept (see CONCEPTS). Let us continue to fix on the example of conjunction. It is plausible that the concept of conjunction is individuated by the following condition for a thinker to possess it:

the concept *and* is that concept C to possess which a thinker must meet the following condition: he finds inferences of the following forms compelling, does not find them compelling as a result of any reasoning, and finds them compelling because they are of these forms:

$$\frac{pCq}{p} \quad \frac{pCq}{q} \quad \frac{pq}{pCq}$$

Here $p$ and $q$ range over complete propositional thoughts, not sentences. When axiom A6 is true of a person's language, there is a global dovetailing between this possession condition for the concept of conjunction and certain of his practices involving the word 'and'. For the case of conjunction, the dovetailing involves at least this:

> If the possession condition for conjunction entails that the thinker who possesses the concept of conjunction must be willing to make certain transitions involving the thought $p\&q$, and if the thinker's sentence A means that $p$ and his sentence 'B' means that $q$, then: the thinker must be willing to make the corresponding linguistic transitions involving the sentence 'A and B'.

This is only part of what is involved in the required dovetailing. Given what we have already said about the uniform explanation of the understanding of the various occurrences of a given word, we should also add that there is a uniform (unconscious, computational) explanation of the language user's willingness to make the corresponding transitions involving the sentence 'A and B'.

This dovetailing account returns an answer to the deeper question, because neither the possession condition for conjunction, nor the dovetailing condition which builds upon that possession condition, takes for granted the thinker's possession of the concept expressed by 'and'. The dovetailing account for conjunction is an instance of a more general schema, which can be applied to any concept. The case of conjunction is of course exceptionally simple in several respects. Possession conditions for other concepts will speak not just of inferential transitions, but of certain conditions in which beliefs involving the concept in question are accepted or rejected; and the corresponding dovetailing condition will inherit these features. This dovetailing

account has also to be underpinned by a general rationale linking contributions to truth conditions with the particular possession conditions proposed for concepts. It is part of the task of the theory of concepts to supply this in developing Determination Theories for particular concepts.

In some cases, a relatively clear account is possible of how a concept can feature in thoughts which may be true though unverifiable. The possession condition for the quantificational concept *all natural numbers* can in outline run thus: this quantifier is that concept $Cx \ldots x \ldots$ to possess which the thinker has to find any inference of the form

$$\frac{CxFx}{Fn}$$

compelling, where $n$ is a concept of a natural number, and does not have to find anything else essentially containing $Cx \ldots x \ldots$ compelling. The straightforward Determination Theory for this possession condition is one on which the truth of such a thought $CxFx$ ensures that the displayed inference is always truth-preserving. This requires that $CxFx$ is true only if all natural numbers are F. That all natural numbers are F is a condition which can hold without our being able to establish that it holds. So an axiom of a truth theory which dovetails with this possession condition for universal quantification over the natural numbers will be a component of a realistic, non-verificationist theory of truth conditions (*see* REALISM).

Finally, this response to the deeper question allows us to answer two challenges to the conception of meaning as truth-conditions. First, there was the question left hanging earlier, of how the theorist of truth-conditions is to say what makes one axiom of a semantic theory correct rather than another, when the two axioms assign the same semantic values, but do so by means of different concepts. Since the different concepts will have different possession conditions, the dovetailing accounts, at the deeper level, of what it is for each axiom to be correct for a person's language will be different accounts. Second, there is a challenge repeatedly made by the minimalist theorist of truth, to the effect that the theorist of meaning as truth-conditions should give some non-circular account of what it is to understand a sentence, or to be capable of understanding all sentences containing a given constituent. For each expression in a sentence, the corresponding dovetailing account, together with the possession condition, supplies a non-circular account of what it is to understand any sentence containing that expression. The combined accounts for each of the expressions which comprise a given sentence together constitute a non-circular account of what it is to understand the complete sentence. Taken together, they allow the theorist of meaning as truth-conditions fully to meet the challenge.

*See also* CONCEPTS; OSTENSIVE DEFINITION; TRUTH.

BIBLIOGRAPHY

Davidson, D.: 'The structure and content of truth', *Journal of Philosophy* 87 (1990), 279–328.

Davies, M.: 'Tacit knowledge and semantic theory: Can a five per cent difference matter?', *Mind* 96 (1987), 441–62.

Dummett, M.: 'Truth' (1959): reprinted in his *Truth and Other Enigmas* (Duckworth: London, 1978).

Horwich, P.: *Truth* (Oxford: Blackwell, 1990).

Marr, D.: *Vision: A Computational Investigation into the Human Representation and Processing of Visual Information* (San Francisco: Freeman, 1982).

Peacocke, C.: 'Explanation in computational psychology: language, perception and level 1.5', *Mind and Language* 1 (1986), 101–23.

Peacocke, C.: *A Study of Concepts* (Cambridge, MA: MIT Press, 1992).

Wittgenstein, L.: *Philosophical Investigations* (Oxford: Blackwell, 1953), esp. §136.

CHRISTOPHER PEACOCKE

**literature and knowledge** In the traditional approach to the question of the relation between these two multifarious notions, literary works of art are assessed as possible means to knowledge defined along 'classical' lines (propositional knowledge or 'knowledge that', typically construed as true and justified belief). Three major stances may be identified: (1) condemnations of literature as a source of irrationality for author and audience alike (e.g. Platonic attacks on poetic *mimesis*); (2) defences of literary autonomy based on the idea that knowledge is neither hindered nor advanced by literature because the two move on separate tracks (e.g. Ingarden, 1950, 1973); and (3) various contentions that literary works do in fact contribute to knowledge. A weak version of the latter position holds that some literary works can be used to provide valuable illustrations of knowledge that has been already been formulated outside literature (Simon, 1983, pp. 32–3). Another sort of claim is that theoretically-oriented readings of literary works can contribute to the formation of new hypotheses in the human sciences, hypotheses that may then be empirically evaluated through non-literary means (Beardsley, 1958, pp. 429–31; Livingston, 1988, 1991). For example, reading an Icelandic saga's insightful depictions of revenge could help someone improve a theoretical model of the actions and motives typical of blood feuds, in which case the literary work's implicit heuristic value would be revealed. A stronger thesis is that some literary works convey significant and even systematic knowledge discovered by their authors, an example being Girard's (1965) contention that a number of novelists have expressed genuine insights into the imitative nature of desire.

In the stances just evoked, literature is taken to be one among several effective means to a single kind of epistemic end. It is often contended, however, that 'properly literary' features of a work (e.g. its fictional status, narrative form, use of dialogue, pseudonyms, allegory, tropes, etc.) are somehow necessary or essential to literature's contributions to knowledge. A typical claim along these lines is that Nietzsche required the fictional persona of Zarathustra, a quasi-biblical style, parables and mythological imagery to formulate aspects of his thought.

Yet if the knowledge in question is propositional and can be paraphrased faithfully, it is not clear why literary devices are necessary or essential to its discovery or formulation. One way of responding to this objection is to contend that literature's cognitive value should not in any case be evaluated in terms of paraphrasable contributions to propositional knowledge. Instead, literature is prized as an indispensable means of realizing various other epistemically valuable results. Literature's distinct and valuable mode of cognition has been identified, for example, as 'knowing by vicarious living through', a sort of knowledge by acquaintance that amounts to 'knowing what an experience is like' (Walsh, 1969, p. 129). Several variations on this theme have been proposed, but all such theories have the problem of making convincing claims about epistemic states that cannot by definition be restated in the non-literary language in which the theories themselves are couched. As a result, literature's putative unique cognitive value is in danger of becoming an epistemic *je ne sais quoi* towards which a non-literary discourse can only point, this pointing being neither a literary nor a propositional form of knowledge. On the other hand, a clear and detailed argumentative essay that purports to unpack the philosophical content of *Zarathustra* can hardly convince us that the parables and imagery are indispensable.

Another major approach to the topic finds its point of departure in a rejection of the 'classical' conception of knowledge in terms of which literary cognition has typically been assessed. In a moderate version, this rejection is not taken to entail a generalized deflation of epistemic values. Instead, the credit formerly reserved to what is deemed a narrow and unrealistic model of knowledge is generously transferred across a broad range of symbolic activities, sheltered beneath the liberal rubric of 'understanding'. Once the goals of truth, certainty and rational justification have been abandoned, literature can be granted its place alongside the other arts and sciences as a worthwhile mode of cognition, characterized by non-denotative forms of reference (Goodman and Elgin, 1988). Many literary

rejections of 'classical' epistemology are more extreme, swerves away from reason, rationality and science having been common in literary culture since the beginning of romanticism. Literature is said to free us from the shackles of a pedestrian reason chained to facts, consistency, evidence, justification and other dull strictures. In some versions, literature's radical 'displacements' of so-called knowledge are fancied to involve a privileged access to special domains, including various dimensions of subjectivity – emotions, 'qualia', primary processes, the properties of an essential feminine 'difference' manifested only in a particular form of *écriture* – or such metaphysical items as *die Erde*, the body and the 'non-oppositional difference', a post-structuralist grail. Sometimes literature is said to have the special merit of actively manifesting the impossibility of the kind of knowledge to which other discourses, such as philosophy and the sciences, blindly lay claim. The fragments of textuality embody a kind of epistemic virtue, be it a matter of a radical irony, a generalized negativity (Blanchot, 1968), or a sceptical *arrhepsia* or EPOCHE. In more extreme tendencies, literary theorists proclaim all epistemological demarcations and criteria to be always already overdetermined by social, pragmatic, psychodynamic and/or discursive conditions: literature and knowledge alike are phantasms; they are simply tokens in a struggle for distinction and power; or they are dissolved within a sea of chaotic textuality, subject to a generalized 'illogic' of dispersion and indeterminacy.

The conjunction of the terms 'literature' and 'knowledge' also raises the issue of the kinds of knowledge produced by literary scholars. The literary disciplines rightly figure among what Miller (1987) calls the 'self-questioning' fields (those lacking solid realist foundations, where the latter are a matter of reliable descriptions of relevant domain-specific causal processes). Critical practice is indeed quite diverse, and it is not obvious, to say the least, that its results are typically true, justified, systematic or progressive. In such a context, critical theory's reflexion on the basic assumptions, methods and aims of literary enquiry is a crucial part of the discipline. The central debate in critical theory has concerned what critics call the question of the 'validity' (i.e. veracity) of interpretation, which amounts to asking whether and how a critic can assign the right meaning, or a range of correct meanings, to a text or work. Some designate the author's intended meanings as the sole target of valid elucidations, while others have labelled this a fallacy. Yet this debate itself rests on assumptions that may be challenged. One such assumption is that critics advance literary knowledge whenever they perform a new correct reading of a literary text or work, and this independent of the correctness of the doctrine thereby elucidated. Showing that literary item $x$ meant $y$ is deemed a genuine finding, even if the message drawn from the bottle is irrational or is flatly contradicted by the best contemporary theories relevant to the topic. An important assumption supporting such megaphone criticism seems to be that writing and publishing elaborate interpretations is a good, and perhaps even the best manner of appreciating literature, an additional assumption being that engaging in such appreciations is the primary goal of literary research. Two relevant counter-claims are that elaborate interpretive raids do not always contribute to genuine aesthetic experiences, and that scholarly explanations of literary phenomena are not in any case reducible to the performance of aesthetical appreciations and/or interpretations of works. Literary phenomena also have psycho-social conditions and consequences that would not be adequately captured by even the most successful appreciations and interpretations. Participating in critical appreciations is one kind of task, but describing and explaining the actions constitutive of literary facts and institutions – including the practice of appreciation – is another (Schmidt, 1980–2). Often the two are conflated. We may also speak of a prevalent 'poetic fallacy', the attitude that scholarly research on literary topics should somehow reproduce and exemplify the qualities of the artefacts and practices to which they refer, instead of being guided by norms and aims typical of rational-empirical enquiry.

The prevalent tendency to look at literature as a collection of autonomous works of art requiring elaborate interpretation is relatively recent, and its conceptual foundations are anything but unproblematic (Todorov, 1973, 1982). Critics who remain committed to the tasks of appreciation and interpretation (as opposed to enquiry into the social and psychological history of literary practices and institutions) should pay more attention to the practical conditions that are necessary not only to the production, but to the critical individuation of literary works of art (Currie, 1989; Davies, 1991). It is far from obvious that works can be adequately individuated as objectively identifiable types of token texts or inscriptions, as is often supposed. No semantic function – not even a partial function – maps all types of textual inscriptions onto works of art: some types of inscriptions are not correlated with works at all, and some types of inscriptions may be correlated with more than one work (as in Borges's Pierre Menard). Nor is there even a partial function mapping works onto types of inscriptions: some works may be correlated with more than one type of inscription (e.g. cases where there are different versions of the same work). Particular correlations between text types and works are in practice guided by pragmatic factors involving aspects of the attitudes (beliefs, motives, plans, etc.) of the agent(s) responsible for the creation of the artefacts in a given context. The latter point entails some non-trivial constraints on literary appreciation in so far as the identification of important types of aesthetic qualities is linked to knowledge of these pragmatic factors. For example, reference to such factors may be needed to determine the assignment of an inscription to a particular genre, as in cases where a text may be read as fantastic fiction, as a hoax, or as earnest supernaturalism. Reference to the author's context can determine the nature of a work's stylistic properties: features recognized as highly innovative and unconventional in one context could be viewed as archaic and imitative in another, e.g. should it be learned that

257

the inscription was a twentieth-century work and not a faithful reprinting of an eighteenth-century original. The upshot is that even an aesthetic orientation towards literary phenomena cannot be sundered from action descriptions and the related assumptions about agency. Bringing these assumptions into the foreground reveals the shortcomings of prevalent romantic notions of the 'autonomous', 'organic' and 'self-organizing' nature of literary works.

Pragmatic factors should also be stressed in a discussion of the cognitive value of literary works and of critics' interpretations of them. Texts or symbolic artefacts are not the sorts of items that can literally embody or contain the kinds of intentional attitudes that are plausible candidates for the title of knowledge, and this on a wide range of understandings of the latter. If it is dubious that texts and works can know or fail to know anything at all, attention should be shifted to relations between the artefacts and their users, those authors and readers whose relevant actions and attitudes may literally be said to manifest epistemic states and values. Writing was for Proust a genuine form of research, and moreover, one that led to greater self-knowledge, even if the resultant artefacts are not always (and certainly not only) reliable reports of the author's actual experiences. Moreover, there is no good reason to believe that every reader's experience of Proust's writings deserves to be called knowledge or even understanding, although in some hands these works may very well result in some valuable epistemic results.

See also HISTORICAL KNOWLEDGE; SOCIAL SCIENCE.

BIBLIOGRAPHY

Beardsley, M.C.: Aesthetics: Problems in the Philosophy of Criticism (New York: Harcourt, Brace, 1958).
Blanchot, M.: L'Espace littéraire (Paris: Gallimard, 1968).
Currie, G.: An Ontology of Art (New York: St. Martin's, 1989).
Davies, D.: 'Works, texts and contexts: Goodman on the literary artwork', Canadian Journal of Philosophy 21 (1991), 331–45.
Girard, R.: Deceit, Desire, and the Novel: Self and Other in Literary Structure trans. Y. Freccero (Baltimore: Johns Hopkins University Press, 1965).
Goodman, N. and Elgin, C.Z.: Reconceptions in Philosophy and Other Arts and Sciences (Indianapolis: Hackett, 1988).
Ingarden, R.: 'Des différentes conceptions de vérité dans l'oeuvre d'art', Revue d'esthétique, 2 (1950), 162–80.
Ingarden, R.: The Cognition of the Literary Work of Art trans. R.A. Crowley and K.R. Olson (Evanston: Northwestern University Press, 1973).
Livingston, P.: Literary Knowledge: Humanistic Inquiry and the Philosophy of Science (Ithaca, NY: Cornell University Press, 1988).
Livingston, P.: Literature and Rationality: Conceptions of Agency in Theory and Fiction (Cambridge: Cambridge University Press, 1991).
Miller, R.W.: Fact and Method: Explanation, Confirmation and Reality in the Natural and the Social Sciences (Princeton: Princeton University Press, 1987).
Schmidt, S.J.: Grundriss der empirischen Literaturwissenschaft, 2 vols (Braunschweig: Vieweg, 1980–2); vol. 1 trans. R. de Beaugrande, Foundation for the Empirical Study of Literature (Hamburg: Helmut Buske, 1982).
Simon, H.A.: Reason in Human Affairs (Stanford: Stanford University Press, 1983).
Todorov, T.: 'The notion of literature', New Literary History 5 (1973), pp. 5–16.
Todorov, T.: Theories of the Symbol trans. C. Porter (Ithaca, NY: Cornell University Press, 1982).
Walsh, D.: Literature and Knowledge (Middletown: Wesleyan University Press, 1969).

PAISLEY LIVINGSTON

**Locke, John (1632–1704)** English philosopher. Aside from his *Two Treatises of Government* (1690) and *The Reasonableness of Christianity* (1695), Locke is known for his epistemological masterpiece, *An Essay concerning Human Understanding* (1690). Implicitly believing that we have been put here by God in this world with some expectation of an after-life in another, Locke's aim in this work is to discover what kind of thing

God has fitted us to know, and so how we should direct and use our intellect and understandings. 'My purpose', he tells us, is 'to enquire into the original, certainty, and extent of human knowledge; together, with the grounds and degrees of belief, opinion, and assent' (1.1.2).

In opposition to some at the time Locke vigorously denies, throughout Book 1 of the *Essay*, that any of our knowledge – whether theoretical or ethical – is innate and there in our minds from the very outset (*see* INNATE IDEAS). The mind at birth, he says, is like 'white paper' (2.1.2) (*see* TABULA RASA); and as a consequence he is often described as an EMPIRICIST. He certainly thinks that all our IDEAS are derived from experience; but they are only what he calls 'the materials of knowledge' (2.1.2). Unlike ideas, knowledge itself is *not* 'made out to us by our senses' (Locke, 1671, p. 157). Somewhat after the style of DESCARTES, knowledge is very much a product of reason and understanding for Locke. In line with what a RATIONALIST might say, without reason all we have is belief, not knowledge. 'Reason must be our last judge and guide in everything' (4.19.14).

In Book 2 Locke substantiates the claim that all our ideas, all the materials of knowledge, come from experience – in either of its two forms, of sensory perception of the material world and of reflection on the operations of our own minds. His argument is facilitated by a distinction between simple and complex ideas – the former being unanalysable and indefinable, the latter being mentally constructible out of simples. Complex ideas are of various sorts – substances (e.g. gold, lead, horses) which represent things in the material world, modes (e.g. triangle, gratitude) which are 'dependences on, or affections of substances' (2.12.4), and relations (e.g. parent of, whiter than). In the course of showing how any idea has its source in experience Locke gives us analyses of various philosophically important notions: perception, solidity, memory, space, time, number, infinity, volition, substance, cause and effect, personal identity. He also makes a distinction between PRIMARY AND SECONDARY QUALITIES. There is considerable implicit criticism in these chapters of various views of DESCARTES: the identification of extension as the whole essence of material substance, and the denial of the vacuum; the belief that thought and personal identity necessarily require an immaterial substance; the view that the mind is always thinking. Nevertheless it was his reading of Descartes which first led Locke away from the verbal trivialities and mystifications (as they seemed) of the then-prevailing Aristotelian scholasticism to which he had been exposed as a student in Oxford. It was Descartes too from whom Locke takes the term 'idea', whose frequent use (for which he begs pardon (1.1.8)) is such a feature of the Essay.

Many of the 'vague and insignificant forms of speech, and abuse of language' of the Scholastics to which Locke refers in his preface come in for criticism in Book 3, 'On Words'. Here he rejects the view that the general and classificatory words which form such a large part of our language stand for 'real essences' or 'substantial forms' which, by being embodied in things, make them to be of one sort of another. According to this view, the world, prior to any intellectual activity of ours, is already divided up into various sorts of thing. In opposition to this, Locke argues that 'all things, that exist, . . . [are] particulars' (3.3.1), that classification is a matter of human interests and convenience, and that general words stand for 'nominal essences', mental abstract ideas which we ourselves construct. Generality and universality, he says, 'belong not to the real existence of things; but are the inventions and creatures of the understanding, made by it for its own use' (3.3.11).

In Book 4, knowledge is defined as the intellectual 'perception' of connections, or agreements and disagreements, between ideas. Such connections may be immediate and intuitively perceived, or mediated by other ideas and so a matter of demonstration. Where we can perceive such connections we have certain and universal knowledge; where we cannot, we lack 'knowledge', and, at best, have 'belief' or 'opinion'. This account fits well with our knowledge in a priori subjects such as mathematics and geometry (*see* A PRIORI KNOWLEDGE). These, because of their systematic development, were standard seventeenth-century examples of 'science'. But, like others of the 'new philosophers' of the time, Locke did not accept the details of the Scholastic account of *scientia*, according to which scientific knowledge involved a rigidly defined structure, and is arranged and developed according to strict canons of syllogistic reasoning which has as its premises abstract maxims and definitions of the real essences of things (*see* AQUINAS). Science for Locke is, as in mathematics and geometry, a matter of deduction, but he places no particular value on syllogistic techniques, and the associated apparatus of Scholastic logic.

Yet though he rejects much of what the Scholastics say about real essences and of their associated account of science Locke does not reject completely any idea of real essence. He retains the general idea that there is something about a mode, such as a triangle, or a substance, such as gold, which accounts for and explains the characteristic properties of those things. Indeed, it is because we know the real essences of geometrical figures that we can discern necessary connections in geometry – as between our complex idea of the real essence of a triangle ('three lines, including a space') (2.31.6) and its various properties.

On the other hand we can, in general, discern no necessary connections between our ideas of substances and their properties. 'Beliefs' about the properties of, for example, gold depend on observation and experiment, and not on the a priori contemplation of our own abstract ideas. The reason for this lack of knowledge, with its consequence that 'natural philosophy', the study of the properties of the things of the material world, 'is not capable of being made a science' (4.12.10) is that we are ignorant of the relevant substantial real essences. Locke's conception of the real essences of substances differs from that of the scholastics, according to which they are 'real definitions'; rather, he sees them in terms of the classical Greek atomic theory of

matter of Leucippus, Democritus and Epicurus which was revived in the seventeenth century. If we knew the real essences of substances then chemistry would be as a priori as mathematics. In the absence of detailed ideas of these things, however, our beliefs about the properties of substances are to be based on careful and systematic observation and experiments. In advocating this 'historical, plain method' (1.1.2) for natural philosophy and in his belief in the corpuscular theory of matter Locke aligns with natural philosophers of the time such as Robert Boyle, people to whom in his preface to the *Essay*, Locke refers as 'master-builders' of 'the commonwealth of learning'. He, like them, was a Fellow of the anti-scholastic Royal Society of London for the Improving of Natural Knowledge.

In response to sceptical arguments about the existence of the EXTERNAL WORLD and the possibility of our living a perpetual dream, Locke reacts in his practical way. 'No body can, in earnest, be so sceptical, as to be uncertain of the existence of those things which he sees and feels' (4.11.3) (*see* SCEPTICISM, MODERN). His account of this 'sensitive knowledge' (4.2.14) does not fit his definition of knowledge as the perception of connections between ideas. However, though its certainty is not so great as that from INTUITION and demonstration it still, he says, deserves the name of knowledge. Traditionally, Locke's theory of perception has been taken to be a REPRESENTATIONAL REALISM – according to which, since the mind 'perceives nothing but its own ideas' (4.4.3), our perception of the external world is indirect. In recent years, however, it has been argued that he is a DIRECT REALIST.

GEOMETRY is not the only case where real knowledge can be had. Morality is another, since there too the relevant ideas are modes whose real essences we do or could know. According to Locke, moral principles express the will of God, and so a science of morality would be based partly on a proof of the existence of God and partly on the idea that as His dependants we should obey his will, as children should obey that of their parents. Despite the urgings of friends Locke said he had neither the time nor the ability to produce a systematic moral science himself. Nevertheless, some individual moral truths have been worked out by reason, though many people, 'perplexed in the necessary affairs of life' (1.3.25), have no time for this. It is fortunate, then, that such people can get morality from the revelations of the Bible; though of course what they acquire in that way is not moral knowledge but only belief.

There are other ways in which the beliefs based on the Bible are inferior and secondary to reasoned knowledge. Revelation is actually answerable to reason in that reason is needed to decide what is a genuine revelation. If something *is* the message of God then undoubtedly it is true; but *is* it the message of God? Furthermore, any religious or moral knowledge that is necessary for salvation can be acquired by our natural faculties alone and without the assistance of revelation. This is a claim which gives Locke a place in the history of the development of a deistic natural religion.

The upshot of his enquiry is that there are things that we do not know, things about which we can only form beliefs and things about which we must remain in ignorance. Natural philosophy as a whole will never be a science; and Locke is more agnostic than Descartes about the possibility of ever knowing how the mind acts on the body or the body on the mind, or of whether thought necessarily needs an immaterial soul. But some things we do know – and our beliefs are often not foundationless.

Locke's general picture is that what we do know, and the things we justifiably believe, answer to our true needs and real interests. We are not in ignorance of our duties and obligations to each other and to God; and we have beliefs enough for everyday practicalities. 'Men have reason to be well satisfied with what God hath thought fit for them, since he has given them . . . whatsoever is necessary for the conveniences of life, and information of virtue; and has put within the reach of their discovery the comfortable provision for this life and the way that leads to a better' (1.1.5). Not only should we thank God for what we have, but we should also be less

greedy and 'more cautious in meddling with things exceeding our comprehension' (1.1.4).

Much of what is in the Essay, such as its stress on the descriptive 'historical, plain method' (11.2) in natural philosophy, its advocacy of the corpuscular theory of matter, its attacks on the Scholastics, its stress on working things out for oneself and its dislike of authority, its giving reason a central place in religion, and its criticisms of various teachings of Descartes on the twin substances of thought and extension, belong to his time as well as to him. But though much of what he says can thus be found in lesser contemporaries, he brings together much of the thought of the seventeenth century in a fresh and coherent way.

*See also* ANALYTICITY; INTUITION AND DEDUCTION; REPRESENTATIVE REALISM.

WRITINGS

*Draft A of Locke's Essay concerning Human Understanding* (1671), transcribed by P.H. Nidditch (Sheffield: Dept. of Philosophy, University of Sheffield, 1980).

*An Essay concerning Human Understanding* (1690) ed. P.H. Nidditch (Oxford: Clarendon Press, 1975).

BIBLIOGRAPHY

Aaron, R.I.: *John Locke* 3rd edn (Oxford: Clarendon Press, 1971).

Alexander, P.: *Ideas, Qualities and Corpuscles: Locke and Boyle on the External World* (Cambridge: Cambridge University Press, 1985).

Gibson, J.: *Locke's Theory of Knowledge and its Historical Relations* (Cambridge: Cambridge University Press, 1960).

Hall, R. and Woolhouse, R.: *Eighty Years of Locke Scholarship: A Bibliographical Guide* (Edinburgh: Edinburgh University Press, 1983).

Schapiro, B.J.: *Probability and Certainty in Seventeenth-Century England* (Princeton: Princeton University Press, 1983).

Tipton, I. ed.: *Locke and Human Understanding* (Oxford: Oxford University Press, 1977).

Woolhouse, R.S.: *Locke* (Brighton: Harvester Press, 1983).

Yolton, J.W.: *Locke and the Compass of the Human Understanding* (Cambridge: Cambridge University Press, 1970).

R.S. WOOLHOUSE

**logical construction**   The phrase was coined by RUSSELL: 'Wherever possible, logical constructions are to be substituted for inferred entities' (Russell, 1914, p. 115). Instead of thinking of our world as containing 'metaphysical monsters' like material, mind-independent continuants, we should think of these as logical constructions out of SENSE-DATA. For Russell, thinking of material things as logical constructions amounted to a revision, rather than merely a description, of ordinary views (which incorporate the 'savage superstitions of cannibals' (Russell, 1925, p. 143)). Russell's constructions were sets. For CARNAP, who also used the notion, constructions were sums (to be consistent with his nominalism). A recent exponent of logical construction is Quine, who holds up as a model the definition ('construction') of an ordered pair $<x,y>$ as the set $\{x,\{x,y\}\}$ (*see* his 1960, §53). An important feature of constuctions is that, although one can 'paraphrase' everything one wanted to say about the original entity in terms of the construction, substituting an expression for the one by an expression for the other does not always preserve intuitive truth, let alone meaning. Thus 'each of $<x,y>$'s members is an individual' is intuitively true, whereas 'each of $\{x,\{x,y\}\}$'s members is an individual' is false. To accept the construction is to forgo the intuition.

*See also* PHENOMENALISM.

BIBLIOGRAPHY

Carnap, R.: *The Logical Structure of the World: Pseudo-problems in Philosophy* trans. R.A. George (London: Routledge and Kegan Paul, 1967).

Russell, B.: 'The relation of sense-data to physics', *Scientia* 4 (1914); reprinted in his *Mysticism and Logic* (New York: Longmans, 1918; London: Allen and Unwin, 1963).

Russell, B.: 'Mind and matter', *Nation and Athenaeum* 37 (1925); reprinted in his *Portraits from Memory* (London: Readers Union, 1958).

Quine, W.V.: *Word and Object* (Cambridge, MA: MIT Press, 1960).

R.M. SAINSBURY

**logical empiricism**   see LOGICAL POSITIVISM; REICHENBACH.

**logical positivism**   A loosely defined movement or set of ideas (sometimes also called 'logical empiricism') which coalesced in Vienna in the 1920s and early 1930s and found many followers and sympathizers elsewhere and at other times. It was a dominant force in philosophy, at least in English-speaking countries, into the 1960s, and its influence, if not specific theses, remains present in the views and attitudes of many philosophers. It was 'positivism' in its adherence to the doctrine that science is the only form of knowledge and that there is nothing in the universe beyond what can in principle be scientifically known. It was 'logical' in its dependence on developments in logic and mathematics in the early years of this century which were taken to reveal how a priori knowledge of necessary truths is compatible with a thorough-going empiricism.

The exclusiveness of a scientific world-view was to be secured by showing that everything beyond the reach of science is strictly or 'cognitively' meaningless, in the sense of being incapable of truth or falsity, and so not a possible object of cognition. This required a criterion of meaningfulness, and it was found in the idea of empirical verification. A sentence is said to be cognitively meaningful if and only if it can be verified or falsified in experience. This is not meant to require that the sentence be conclusively verified or falsified, since universal scientific laws or hypotheses (which are supposed to pass the test) are not logically deducible from any amount of actually observed evidence. The criterion is accordingly to be understood to require only verifiability or falsifiability, in the sense of empirical evidence which would count either for or against the truth of the sentence in question, without having to logically imply it. Verification or confirmation is not necessarily something that can be carried out by the person who entertains the sentence or hypothesis in question, or even by anyone at all at the stage of intellectual and technological development achieved at the time it is entertained. A sentence is cognitively meaningful if and only if it is in principle empirically verifiable or falsifiable.

Anything which does not fulfil this criterion is declared literally meaningless. There is no significant 'cognitive' question as to its truth or falsity; it is not an appropriate object of enquiry. Moral and aesthetic and other 'evaluative' sentences are held to be neither confirmable nor disconfirmable on empirical grounds, and so are cognitively meaningless. They are at best expressions of feeling or preference which are neither true nor false. Whatever is cognitively meaningful and therefore factual is value-free. The positivists claimed that many of the sentences of traditional philosophy, especially those in what they called 'metaphysics', also lack cognitive meaning and say nothing that could be true or false. But they did not spend much time trying to show this in detail about the philosophy of the past. They were more concerned with developing a theory of meaning and of knowledge adequate to the understanding and perhaps even the improvement of science.

The logical positivist conception of knowledge in its original and purest form sees human knowledge as a complex intellectual structure employed for the successful anticipation of future experience. It requires, on the one hand, a linguistic or conceptual framework in which to express what is to be categorized and predicted and, on the other, a factual element which provides that abstract form with content. This comes, ultimately, from sense experience. No matter of fact that anyone can understand or intelligibly think to be so could go beyond the possibility of human experience, and the only reasons anyone could ever have for believing anything must come, ultimately, from actual experience.

The general project of the positivistic theory of knowledge is to exhibit the structure, content, and basis of human knowledge in accordance with these empiricist principles. Since science is regarded as the repository of all genuine human knowledge, this becomes the task of exhibiting the structure, or as it was called, the 'logic' of science. The theory of knowledge thus becomes the philosophy of science. It has three major tasks: (1) to analyse the meanings of the statements of science exclusively in terms of observations or experiences in principle available to human beings; (2) to show how certain observations or experiences serve to confirm a given statement in the sense of making it more warranted or reasonable; (3) to show how non-empirical or a priori knowledge of the necessary truths of logic and mathematics is possible even though every matter of fact which can be intelligibly thought or known is empirically verifiable or falsifiable.

1. The slogan 'the meaning of a statement is its method of verification' expresses the empirical *verification theory of meaning*. It is more than the general criterion of meaningfulness according to which a sentence is cognitively meaningful if and only if it is empirically verifiable. It says in addition what the meaning of each sentence is: it is all those observations which would confirm or disconfirm the sentence. Sentences which would be verified or falsified by all the same observations are empirically equivalent or have the same meaning.

A sentence recording the result of a single observation is an observation or 'protocol' sentence. It can be conclusively verified or falsified on a single occasion. Every other meaningful statement is a 'hypothesis' which implies an indefinitely large number of observation sentences which together exhaust its meaning, but at no time will all of them have been verified or falsified. To give an 'analysis' of the statements of science is to show how the content of each scientific statement can be reduced in this way to nothing more than a complex combination of directly verifiable 'protocol' sentences (*see* VERIFICATIONISM).

2. The observations recorded in particular 'protocol' sentences are said to confirm those 'hypotheses' of which they are instances. The task of confirmation theory is therefore to define the notion of a confirming instance of a hypothesis and to show how the occurrence of more and more such instances adds credibility or warrant to the hypothesis in question. A complete answer would involve a solution to the PROBLEM OF INDUCTION: to explain how any past or present experience makes it reasonable to believe in something that has not yet been experienced (*see* HUME).

3. Logical and mathematical propositions, and other necessary truths, do not predict the course of future sense experience. They cannot be empirically confirmed or disconfirmed. But they are essential to science, and so must be accounted for. They are one and all 'analytic' in something like KANT's sense: true solely in virtue of the meanings of their constituent terms. They serve only to make explicit the contents of and the logical relations among the terms or concepts which make up the conceptual framework through which we interpret and predict experience. Our knowledge of such truths is simply knowledge of what is and what is not contained in the concepts we use (*see* ANALYTICITY).

Experience can perhaps show that a given concept has no instances, or that it is not a useful concept for us to employ. But that would not show that what we understand to be included in that concept is not really included in it, or that it is not the concept we take it to be. Our knowledge of the constituents of and the relations among our concepts is therefore not dependent on experience; it is a priori. It is knowledge of what holds necessarily, and all necessary truths are 'analytic'. There is no synthetic a priori knowledge (*see* A PRIORI KNOWLEDGE).

The anti-metaphysical EMPIRICISM of logical positivism requires that there be no access to any facts beyond sense experience.

The appeal to analyticity succeeds in accounting for knowledge of necessary truths only if analytic truths state no facts, and our knowledge of them does not require non-sensory awareness of matters of fact. The reduction of all the concepts of arithmetic, for example, to those of logic alone, as was taken to have been achieved in Whitehead and Russell's *Principia Mathematica*, showed that the truths of arithmetic were derivable from nothing more than definitions of their constituent terms and general logical laws. Frege would have called them 'analytic' for that reason alone. But for a complete account positivism would have also to show that general logical laws state no facts.

Under the influence of their reading of WITTGENSTEIN's *Tractatus Logico-Philosophicus*, the positivists regarded all necessary and therefore all analytic truths as 'tautologies'. They do not state relations holding independently of us within an objective domain of concepts. Their truth is 'purely formal'; they are completely 'empty' and 'devoid of factual content'. They are to be understood as made true solely by our decisions to think and speak in one way rather than another, as somehow true 'by convention'. A priori knowledge of them is in this way held to be compatible with there being no non-sensory access to a world of things beyond sense experience.

The full criterion of meaningfulness therefore says that a sentence is cognitively meaningful if and only if either it is analytic or it is in principle empirically verifiable or falsifiable.

*See also* A PRIORI KNOWLEDGE; ANALYTICITY; CARNAP, EMPIRICISM; NEURATH; PHILOSOPHICAL KNOWLEDGE; SCHLICK; VIENNA CIRCLE.

BIBLIOGRAPHY

Ayer, A.J.: *Language, Truth and Logic* (London: Gollancz, 1946).

Ayer, A.J. ed.: *Logical Positivism* (Glencoe: Free Press, 1959).

Carnap, R.: *The Logical Structure of the World:*

*Pseudoproblems in Philosophy* trans. R. George (London: Routledge and Kegan Paul, 1967).

Carnap, R.: *The Logical Syntax of Language* trans. A. Smeaton (Paterson: Littlefield, Adams, 1959).

Carnap, R.: *Logical Foundations of Probability* (Chicago: University of Chicago Press, 1950).

Feigl, H. and Sellars, W. eds: *Readings in Philosophical Analysis* (New York: Appleton-Century-Crofts, 1949).

Hempel, C.: *Aspects of Scientific Explanation* (New York: The Free Press, 1965).

Wittgenstein, L.: *Tractatus Logico-Philosophicus* trans. C.K. Ogden (London: Routledge and Kegan Paul, 1922).

BARRY STROUD

**logicism** First formulated by Gottlob FREGE and Bertrand RUSSELL, logicism is the view that number theory is reducible in its entirety to pure, deductive logic. It involves the claim that arithmetical concepts are logical concepts; that arithmetical truths are truths of logic; and that proofs in arithmetic are valid to the extent that they are logically, deductively valid. If this view could be substantiated it would show that arithmetical knowledge has the same origin, content, and justification as our knowledge of logical truths.

*See also* A PRIORI KNOWLEDGE; INTUITION AND DEDUCTION; MATHEMATICAL KNOWLEDGE.

BIBLIOGRAPHY

Frege, G.: *The Foundations of Arithmetic* trans. J.L. Austin (Oxford: Blackwell, 1974).

Frege, G.: *The Basic Laws of Arithmetic* trans. M. Furth (Berkeley: University of California Press, 1964).

Russell, B.: *The Principles of Mathematics* (London: Allen and Unwin, 1903).

Whitehead, A.N. and Russell, B.: *Principia Mathematica* (Cambridge: Cambridge University Press, 1910).

DAVID BELL

**lottery paradox** Due originally to Henry Kyburg (Kyburg, 1961 and 1970), the lottery paradox is a demonstration that certain appealing principles about rational acceptance (or perhaps justified belief or knowledge) turn out to be logically inconsistent. The key assumptions are:

1. If it is very likely that a conclusion is true, then it is rational to accept that conclusion.

2. If it is rational to accept that $p$ is the case and it is rational to accept that $q$ is the case, then it is rational to accept that both $p$ and $q$ are the case.

3. It is never rational to accept propositions you realize to be logically inconsistent.

How do these assumptions lead to paradox? Suppose there is a fair lottery with a thousand tickets. It is determined that one ticket will be drawn as the winner; however, the probability that each particular ticket will lose is very high (i.e., .999). Let us imagine that the tickets are numbered from 1 to 1000. Since it is overwhelmingly probable that Ticket 1 will lose, by Assumption (A) you should conclude that it will, indeed, lose. Now, the same thing can be said about each of the other tickets in turn, hence you should accept that Ticket 1 will lose, and you should accept that Ticket 2 will lose, and so on. But according to Assumption (B), this means that you should accept that Ticket 1 will lose and that Ticket 2 will lose . . . *and* that Ticket 1000 will lose. That is, it is rational for you to believe that *all* the tickets will lose, which is to say that no ticket will win. The trouble is that you have already accepted that some ticket or other will be chosen as the winner, and it seems, then, that it is now rational for you to accept something logically inconsistent: namely, that no ticket will win and that some ticket will win. However, such an outcome conflicts with Assumption (C). It is worth noting that, in arriving at this point, nothing essential turned on the choice of .999 as a sufficient degree of likelihood to warrant rational belief. The required odds can be set as high as we like; so long as they are less than one, we can generate the paradox just by increasing the number of tickets in the imagined lottery.

This general result has elicited a wide range of responses. An extreme position has been taken by Richard Jeffrey (Jeffrey, 1970). Jeffrey holds that it is misguided from the start to try to frame a notion of rational acceptance in probabilistic terms. For Jeffrey, probabilities (understood as degrees of confidence) are, in effect, all there is to rational belief formation. We do not simply believe or reject a proposition, we just become inclined to risk more or less on its truth (*see* THEORIES OF PROBABILITY).

Other philosophers, who remain committed to providing an account of rational acceptance, have taken the Lottery Paradox to show that one or more of the assumptions (A)–(C) is faulty or incorrect. Kyburg himself has urged that we deny Assumption (B) (Kyburg, 1970). That is, you may well rationally accept separately that Ticket 1 will lose and that Ticket 2 will lose, and so on; however, you may not accept the conjunction that Ticket 1 will lose *and* Ticket 2 will lose *and* . . . (at least for sufficiently long conjunctions). This restriction has a plausible motivation in the facts about probability. For it is a theorem that the probability of a conjunction is less than or equal to that of its conjuncts. And if high probability is the basis for rational acceptance, we should expect that a conjunction, when significantly less probable than its conjuncts, will be unacceptable even though the conjuncts themselves are acceptable.

Still, one can marshal considerations in favour of Assumption (B). Mark Kaplan (1981) has suggested that, without it, we could not account for the recognized force of arguments by *reductio ad absurdum*. That a contradiction can be derived from the conjunction of things I believe gives me reason to change one or more of those beliefs, and I could not evade the critical force of such a demonstration simply by forswearing acceptance of the conjunction (while retaining belief in the conjuncts). Another difficulty is that to distinguish between believing a conjunction and believing its conjuncts seems to commit one to the view that the objects of belief have a particular syntactic structure or other (here, that of conjunction). Such a view

is controversial, and it would be desirable to find a solution to the Lottery Paradox that did not depend upon a particular theory about the character of intentional mental states (Stalnaker, 1984).

A case has also been made for abandoning Assumption (C). To be sure, an out-and-out contradiction is not rationally acceptable. But it has been claimed that the conflict between accepting that each ticket individually will lose and accepting that some ticket will win is of a different, less objectionable sort. This tension is seen as an unavoidable aspect of cognitive life (which figures in the PREFACE PARADOX as well) (Klein, 1985).

The alternative to denying Assumptions (B) and (C) is to reject (A). There are several possibilities here. One might draw the lesson from the Lottery Paradox that rational acceptance (or at least the kind of rational belief necessary for knowledge) requires absolute certainty rather than mere likelihood. That is, you should not believe anything for which there is a chance, however small, that you might be wrong. In particular, given that there is some (perhaps tiny) probability that 'Ticket 1 (or 2, or 3, etc.) will lose' is false, you should not accept any of these propositions (*see* Heidelberger, 1963; Dretske, 1981). The threat of paradox is obviated, but still, it would seem, at a very high cost. Almost every belief we hold is such that there is some chance of being wrong about it; we can be perfectly certain about very little. Thus, if the Lottery Paradox shows that rational acceptance requires absolute certainty, then, by extension, the Paradox seems to demonstrate that we may rationally accept almost nothing.

A more moderate response would be to maintain that high probability may license rational acceptance given certain additional constraints or qualifications. Thus, it has been proposed (Lehrer, 1980; Pollock, 1983; and others) that we may rationally accept a likely conclusion so long as it is part of some overall coherent scheme of beliefs; in the Lottery Paradox, accepting claims that individual tickets will lose would violate this condition, and so is barred. A different approach, due to Isaac Levi, relativizes the notion of acceptance to a context of inquiry. Levi holds that we may accept that Ticket 1 will lose, if the question asked concerns the outcome with respect to Ticket 1 in particular; however, whether *all* tickets (Ticket 1 and Ticket 2, etc.) will lose is another matter, and must be dealt with independently of the former (Levi, 1967).

In this brief survey, I have only hinted at the wealth of issues and ideas associated with the Lottery Paradox. There are various psychological and technical aspects of the Paradox that are of great interest, and there are important complexities that arise when one considers lottery situations in which the chances of winning vary from entrant to entrant. The interested reader may consult the sources listed below for further details.

*See also* BAYESIANISM; EVIDENCE; LEWIS; PARADOX; RATIONALITY; SURPRISE EXAMINATION PARADOX.

BIBLIOGRAPHY

Dretske, F.I.: *Knowledge and the Flow of Information* (Cambridge, MA: MIT Press, 1981).
Eells, E.: 'On a recent theory of rational acceptance', *Philosophical Studies* 44 (1983), 331–43.
Heidelberger, H.: 'Knowledge, certainty, and probability', *Inquiry* 6 (1963), 242–50.
Jeffrey, R.C.: 'Dracula meets Wolfman: acceptance vs. partial belief', in *Induction, Acceptance, and Rational Belief* ed. M. Swain (Dordrecht: Reidel, 1970), 157–85.
Kaplan, M.: 'A Bayesian theory of rational acceptance', *Journal of Philosophy* 78 (1981), 305–30.
Klein, P.: 'The virtues of inconsistency', *The Monist* 68 (1985), 105–35.
Kyburg, Jr, H.E.: *Probability and the Logic of Rational Belief* (Middletown: Wesleyan University Press, 1961).
Kyburg, Jr, H.E.: 'Conjunctivitis', in *Induction, Acceptance, and Rational Belief* ed. M. Swain (Dordrecht: Reidel, 1970), 55–82.
Lehrer, K.: 'Coherence and the racehorse paradox', *Midwest Studies in Philosophy* 5 (1980), 183–91.
Levi, I.: *Gambling with Truth* (Cambridge, MA: MIT Press, 1967).
Pollock, J.: 'Epistemology and probability', *Synthese* 55 (1983), 231–52.
Sanford, D.H.: 'Lotteries, horseraces, probability, and projection' (abstract), *Nous* 17 (1983), 70–1.
Stalnaker, R.: *Inquiry* (Cambridge, MA: MIT Press, 1984).

JONATHAN VOGEL

# M

**Marxism** Marx had no patience for the traditional projects of epistemology: the attempt to refute scepticism by establishing a foundation of certainty for human knowledge, and the search for philosophical criteria by which to adjudicate knowledge claims. He rejected the methodological SOL-IPSISM of the epistemologist's customary point of departure: the Cartesian picture of a disembodied mind, reflecting on its own self-awareness, and seeking grounds to believe that its ideas accurately represent an 'external world'. For Marx, this approach unintelligibly supposes that the subject can attain a form of self-awareness prior to and independent of a relation to nature and society. Marx shared Hegel's contempt for the idea that the philosopher may occupy a privileged position, somehow outside our evolving conceptual scheme, from which to assess the relation our concepts bear to reality itself. At the centre of his alternative vision, Marx places the concept of *activity* or *practice*. He urges that we replace the abstract contemplating self of classical epistemology with a historically situated subject, engaged in an active relation to the natural and social environment, and intelligible only in light of that relation. Marx thus dismisses philosophical disputes over the possibility of knowledge as 'purely *scholastic*'. Whether objective truth may be attributed to human thought is, he maintains, ultimately 'a *practical* question' ('Theses on Feuerbach').

Marx's position forms part of a general critique of speculative philosophy, developed in the *Economic and Philosophical Manuscripts of 1844*, the 'Theses on Feuerbach' (1845), the *German Ideology* (with Engels) (1845–6), and other writings. Philosophy, at its most progressive, seeks to characterize the human essence so as to determine the circumstances in which human flourishing is possible. Human misery, however, has its cause, not in intellectual confusions about the nature of man, but in the alienated character of existing economic and social life. Indeed, the philosopher's characteristic questions, and his inevitably empty answers, are symptoms of this alienation rather than a potential cure. Philosophy is thus at best impotent, and at worst a source of ideological mystification that serves to perpetuate the status quo.

Almost all of Marx's diverse followers have endorsed both his hostility to epistemology and his emphasis on 'practice'. This does not mean, however, that they have neglected issues of the nature and origin of knowledge. On the contrary, Marx's legacy has prompted intense theoretical discussions of scientific method, of OBJECTIVITY, of the relation between natural and social scientific modes of EXPLANATION, of necessity and prediction, of the nature of 'false consciousness', and many other issues which are 'epistemological' in a broad sense. There is little consensus on these questions; indeed, political disagreements between Marxist factions have often been accompanied by differences in their stances on such theoretical concerns. The various interpretations of Marx's vision of the relation of 'subject' and 'object', individual and world, form a spectrum with, at one end, austere varieties of *scientific realism* that accentuate Marx's confidence in the power of science to render objective reality transparent, and at the other, forms of *anthropocentrism*, which represent human practice as in some sense constituting the reality we come to know.

Scientific realist interpretations, which have their precedent in Engels, Plekhanov and Lenin, begin from the assertion that an 'external', material world exists as an objective reality prior to, and independently of, human beings. In virtue of its independent existence, this world may be described as a reality of 'things-in-themselves'. *Contra* Kant, however, 'things-in-themselves' are knowable, and as we acquire knowledge of the world, so it is transformed from a 'thing-in-itself' into a 'thing-for-us' (*see* IN ITSELF/FOR ITSELF). Our primary access to reality is through sense-perception. Some Marxists of this persuasion subscribe to REPRESENTATIVE REALISM, on which we are directly acquainted only with sensations caused in us by objects, and others to DIRECT REALISM, where the senses yield direct access to material objects themselves (Lenin's position is intriguingly ambiguous between the two). All agree, however, that on the basis of our senses we construct theories that are able to reflect the world accurately: objective truth is possible. At any point in history, our theories are only 'relatively' true, since they capture the truth only partially. However, as history progresses, so our theories tend towards 'absolute' truth. Marx's emphasis on activity finds its reflection in the claim that 'practice is the criterion of truth': through action and experimentation we verify our conceptions. Accordingly, sceptical objections are also dismissed by appeal to 'practice', either on the grounds that the sceptic's doubts are empty because they have no impact upon action, or because once we have established, by all the usual practices, that *p* is true, there is no longer room for genuine doubt that *p*. Finally, this approach holds that it is science, and not philosophy, that determines the nature of reality. Philosophy's role is to generalize the results of the sciences (thus Engels makes his controversial claim that the development of nature is governed by dialectical laws, not as a metaphysical conclusion, but as a generalization from instances of scientific explanation).

At the opposite end of the spectrum, *anthropocentric* readings emphasize Marx's claim that not only is the human subject an active being, but the object world itself must also be conceived as 'human sensuous activity, practice' ('Theses on Feuerbach'). Marx takes human praxis to have a world-transforming

character. By acting upon reality, human beings change its very nature: the world they confront is no longer brutely physical in kind; it is a 'humanized' environment. The strongest version of this view (attributed to Marx by Habermas, and by the Soviet philosopher E.V. Ilyenkov) takes Marx to be addressing a Kantian question: What are the necessary conditions for the possibility of experience and thought? Marx's answer invokes activity, the material transformation of the natural world, as the essential precondition of objectivity. Everything Kant treats as a priori forms of thought must in fact be construed as 'forms of the self-consciousness of social beings', embodied in the material, linguistic and intellectual activities of the community (Ilyenkov). On this 'transcendental pragmatism', human individuals become thinking beings as they appropriate these forms of activity in socialization (a claim developed in the Soviet psychological tradition, especially by Vygotsky and Leontiev). This is the sense in which the human essence is 'the ensemble of social relations', and human agents socially-constituted beings.

What sense can such a position make of the world as it is 'in itself' independent of human activity? Since the world is said to be given to us only through incorporation into our activities, there can be no transcendent perspective from which we may determine how the world is prior to that incorporation. Some Marxists have concluded that 'no "reality" exists in and for itself, but only in historical relation to human beings who modify it' (Gramsci). Nevertheless, the Marxist can argue that the distinction between features of the world that depend on our activity and those which do not is an empirical distinction drawn within the framework of our activities, and that the criteria by which we determine these features are just those of our everyday and scientific practices. Most Marxists, however, have pursued a less quietist line, either by proposing to analyse empirical truth in terms of activity (i.e. a set of 'activity conditions' may be given for each sentence setting out the constraints its acceptance would have on possible activity), or by offering a functional account of truth where, as Kolakowski puts it, 'knowledge has no epistemological value distinct from its value as an organ of human self-affirmation'. Kolakowski attributes to Marx a 'generic subjectivism' on which 'truth' is ultimately a property of beliefs which promote human liberation, and 'false-hood' a property of forms of ideological mystification which serve to perpetuate human alienation. (Similar interpretations have provoked a range of contrasting views, from the crudest identification of truth with class interest, to the sophisticated *ideologiekritik* of the Frankfurt School.) It remains controversial, however, whether such anthropocentric readings can make real sense of a world independent of human agency, and they are often accused of collapsing into an idealism incompatible with Marx's avowed NATURALISM and materialism.

Although not all of Marx's followers may be represented as subscribing to pure scientific realism or anthropocentrism, it is often fruitful to read those who cannot (e.g. Althusser, Lukács, Marcuse) as seeking an intermediate position that would reconcile the insights of both stances. However, whether it is possible to give substantive theoretical content to the concept of activity within the terms of a realist epistemology remains a live issue in the Marxist tradition.

*See also* CONTINENTAL EPISTEMOLOGY.

BIBLIOGRAPHY

Engels, F.: *Anti-Dühring* trans. E. Burns (Moscow: Progress, 1947).
Engels, F.: *Dialectics of Nature* trans. C. Dutt (Moscow: Progress, 1934).
Gramsci, A.: *Il materialismo storico e la filosofia di Benedetto Croce* (Turin, 1949).
Habermas, J.: *Knowledge and Human Interests* trans. J. Shapiro (London: Heinemann, 1971).
Ilyenkov, E.: 'The concept of the ideal', in *Philosophy in the USSR: Problems of Dialectical Materialism* trans. R. Daglish (Moscow: Progress, 1977).
Kolakowski, L.: *Main Currents of Marxism* 3 vols (Oxford: Oxford University Press, 1978).
Lektorsky, V.A.: *Subject, Object, Cognition* (Moscow: Progress, 1984).
Lenin, V.I.: *Materialism and Empirio-criticism*, in his *Collected Works* (London: Lawrence and Wishart, 1960–72), vol. 14.
Marx, K.: *Economic and Philosophical Manuscripts of 1844*, in K. Marx and F. Engels, *Collected Works* (*CW*) (London: Lawrence and Wishart), vol. 3.
Marx, K.: 'Theses on Feuerbach' in *CW* vol. 5.
Marx, K. and Engels, F.: *German Ideology* in *CW*, vol. 5.

DAVID BAKHURST

**mathematical knowledge** The following paradox is presented by mathematical knowledge:

Mathematics is, historically, perhaps the earliest science. For many thinkers mathematical knowledge, by virtue of its seeming absolute certainty, has served as an ideal or paradigm for all the sciences. For example, the mathematical method was extended by rationalistic scientists like Galileo and Descartes to the realm of what we today call physics. Even if we do not go so far as to regard physics as the 'mathematics of motion', mathematical knowledge seems to be indispensable for modern scientific knowledge – the mathematically illiterate cannot read the papers of Dirac, Einstein, or Feynman. We can say, therefore, that mathematics is at least continuous with scientific knowledge.

Yet mathematics seems continuous also with metaphysics. Indeed, mathematics seems not to deal with nature – its subject matter could be variously described as 'ideal, or 'abstract'. Figures like triangles and spheres, etc. are ideal – they are perfectly shaped, and have no breadth. They seem to be the limit of some infinite process unattainable in the actual world. Numbers, on the other hand, are abstract: they are not, apparently, the idealization of any actual objects. Furthermore, the very certainty of mathematical knowledge seems to set it apart from empirical knowledge. Kant put the matter polemically in his 'good company' argument: one cannot reject metaphysics without rejecting mathematics. This argument, of course, was intended as an *ad hominem* argument against the EMPIRICISTS (like David Hume) who, being pro-science, would never reject mathematics.

Latter-day 'naturalists' are also subject to Kant's 'good company' argument. As formulated by Paul Benacerraf, the argument goes: for the NATURALIST, who takes seriously the findings of modern science, knowledge is a causal interaction between knower and environment. (The causal interaction involved may be seen as an energy transfer between an individual knower and his environment, or – as in 'evolutionary epistemology' – a process of natural selection that shapes an entire species.) But mathematical objects do not participate in causal interactions. Hence mathematical knowledge is impossible, unless we drop naturalism. (It is interesting that something like this argument already occurs in Plato's *Sophist* at §248: 'If knowing is to be acting on something, it follows that what is known must be acted upon by it, and, so on this showing, reality when it is being known by the act of knowledge must, in so far as it is known, be changed owing to being so acted upon – and that, we say, cannot happen to the changeless'.)

We can, therefore, sum up the paradox of mathematical knowledge as follows: without mathematical knowledge, there is no scientific knowledge – yet the epistemology ('naturalism') suggested by scientific knowledge seems to make mathematical knowledge impossible!

In what follows, I shall outline the various strategies to deal with the paradox of mathematical knowledge that have been suggested by philosophers throughout the ages.

## REALIST STRATEGIES

There is a non-causal relationship between the soul, or mind, of humanity, and the world of mathematics. The naturalist epistemology is inadequate. (This need not involve rejection of 'naturalism' *in toto*, however.) Of course, this idea is the basis of PLATO's entire metaphysics, but many mathematicians have felt the same way. G.H. Hardy (1929) and Roger Penrose (1989), for example, speak of 'seeing' that a mathematical proposition is true, proof being necessary only to persuade others. In our century, the great logician Gödel (1948) endorsed the view that there is some other connection between ourselves and reality than sense perception, and that this 'mathematical intuition' can account for mathematical knowledge. In fact Gödel's discoveries in logic have been used to support the realist position: Gödel's theorem has been interpreted as showing that, for any serious system of mathematical axioms, the mathematician can know a mathematical truth that does not follow from those axioms; realists argue that the only way this could be true is by mathematical intuition. This argument can be resisted, however, since it presupposes what is doubtful: that we *know* that the axioms of mathematics are jointly consistent. (The unprovable truth, call it G, says, roughly, 'I am not provable' – but if the axioms are inconsistent, then everything is a provable, so G is false.) Granted, one could argue that we know that the axioms of mathematics are consistent because we intuit their truth – true axioms are perforce consistent. But the appeal to Gödel's theorem then becomes superfluous and circular.

Though 'Platonist' realism in a sense accounts for mathematical knowledge, it postulates such a gulf between both the ontology and the epistemology of science and that of mathematics that realism is often said to make the applicability of mathematics in natural science into an inexplicable mystery.

Recently, therefore, some writers have attempted a broadly realist position based on 'structuralism': mathematics is about structures, not objects. Benacerraf (1965) already suggested such a position in 'What Numbers Could Not Be', but such writers as Michael Resnik (1982) and Penelope Maddy (1980) have developed the position, which can be seen as an 'Aristotelian' attempt to reconcile the naturalist epistemology with an attenuated mathematical realism. There is a mathematical intuition, but it is not a separate faculty from empirical sense perception. This idea is supported also by the work of the influential American philosopher of mathematics, Charles Parsons (1979–80), and by that of the present author (Steiner, 1975). Its proponents claim to make the applicability of mathematics to the empirical world intelligible.

## KANTIAN STRATEGIES

These argue that mathematical knowledge is a necessary condition of empirical knowledge. KANT himself argued that the laws of mathematics are actually constraints on our perception of space and time. In knowing mathematics, then, we know only the laws of our own perception. Physical space in itself, for all we know, may not obey the laws of Euclidean geometry and arithmetic, but the world as perceived by us must. Mathematics is objective – or 'intersubjective' – in the sense that it holds good of all perceptions of the whole human race, past, present, and future. For this reason, also, there is no problem with the applicability of mathematics in empirical science – or so the Kantians claim.

Kant's view of mathematical knowledge is often regarded as having been refuted by the discovery of non-Euclidean geometry, and curved spaces, but these geometries are 'locally Euclidean' (i.e. a curved region looks flatter and flatter the smaller it gets), and Kant could have made the more modest claim that any single field of vision is, a priori, a locally Euclidean space.

At any rate, the modern branch of mathematics known as topology, developed by the famous mathematician Henri Poincaré, can be regarded as that part of geometry for which the Kantian thesis remains a viable option.

Poincaré (1907) was a Kantian in arithmetic as well. For him the law of 'mathematical induction' was the essence of arithmetic: any property P of zero which is 'hereditary' (i.e. it holds of $n + 1$ whenever it holds for $n$) holds of every natural number. This principle is justified by noting that if P holds of zero then it holds of 1, so by *modus ponens*, it actually holds of 1. By continual use of *modus ponens* and hereditariness we know that we can eventually 'arrive at' any number $n$ and

show that P holds of $n$. This is the kind of self-knowledge of which Kant spoke; Poincaré held, inspired by Kant, that it cannot be reduced to 'logic'; on the contrary, mathematical induction is a principle about what logic can do. Poincaré knew of FREGE's and RUSSELL's efforts (as part of their 'LOGICISM') to convert the principle of mathematical induction to a logical definition: (roughly) $n$ is a natural number just if it is subject to the law of induction. But he regarded this definition as circular.

In the 1920s, of the present century, two outstanding logicians – Hilbert and Brouwer – argued for competing versions of Kantianism: 'formalism' and 'intuitionism'. Both men accepted that the ultimate content of mathematics is intuition, and that classical mathematics goes beyond the merely intuitive (for example, in its acquiescence in infinite totalities), and therefore does not give knowledge. But where Brouwer (1913) advocated replacing classical mathematics by a new kind of mathematics (which he and his followers proceeded to develop), Hilbert (1926) took the conservative approach of justifying the so-called 'ideal' proofs of classical mechanics as instruments of discovery.

## EMPIRICIST STRATEGIES

John Stuart MILL (1843) is the most outstanding EMPIRICIST to adopt the radical stance that mathematics is a branch, not of logic, but of physics. The relative certainty – and applicability – that attaches to mathematics results from the great range of empirical confirmation that mathematics enjoys. For geometry, of course, the position is widely accepted today, but it is more difficult to see how one could regard arithmetic as empirical. For example, what would be empirical evidence for $1234 \times 1234 = 1,522,756$? Certainly nothing that would justify our actual conviction concerning this product. Recently some authors, most notably Philip Kitcher (1983), have attempted to refurbish this position by arguing that the axioms of arithmetic can be given an empirical interpretation and supported by evidence.

## LOGICIST STRATEGIES

The logicist argues that mathematics is just a branch of logic, or, more generally, and more traditionally, 'analytic truth'. Though this is not an empiricist interpretation *of mathematics*, it is congenial to empiricism, since it appears to give a non-metaphysical account of mathematical knowledge. Empiricists have assumed that once it is proved that 'mathematics is logic' the problem of mathematical knowledge no longer arises, since there is no philosophical problem about logical knowledge. Nevertheless, it should be remembered that it was Leibniz who first conjectured, and tried to prove, mathematics is logic – but he had a metaphysical picture of logical knowledge, as being 'true in all possible worlds'. Nor was Frege, who invented modern logic, in part, to prove that mathematics is nothing but logic (and thus founded the modern logicist school), an empiricist. Conversely, the common belief that Hume's view of mathematics as the study of 'relations among ideas' prefigures modern logism is actually due to Kant's influence. For Kant (in the *Prolegomena*) characterized Hume's theory as 'amounting to' the claim that mathematics is 'analytic', a quite doubtful characterization, in the light of Hume's explicit declaration (*Treatise* I, ii, 4) that such propositions as 'The shortest distance between two points is a straight line' are not true by 'definition'. (Perhaps a better translation of Hume's doctrine into Kantian language would be: mathematics is synthetic a priori. This does not mean that Kant and Hume had the same philosophy of mathematics, though, because their theories of the a priori, i.e. their theories of necessary truth, were quite different.)

Nevertheless, twentieth-century empiricists like the later Russell, CARNAP, AYER and HEMPEL saw logicism as an appropriate doctrine. They, unlike Leibniz, saw logical validity as a matter of linguistic rules, the rules governing words like 'all', 'and' and 'not'; knowledge of these was considered free of metaphysics (*see* LOGICAL POSITIVISM). The problem with this 'logicism', as it has come to be called, was a technical one: no logician was ever able to reduce mathematics to a system of 'logic' which could plausibly be called 'analytic'. (E.g. classical mathematics can be reduced to set theory, but set theory does not qualify as an 'analytic' science.)

A neglected virtue of logicism, in my opinion, is that it solves – or dissolves – some of the problems of mathematical applicability. Logicism shows that all mathematical science can be represented in set theory. Thus the only relation between physical objects and mathematical objects we need recognize is that physical object can be members of sets (sets being mathematical objects). Presumably, if we believe in sets at all, we have no further problem of seeing how physical objects can be members of sets, so some (but not all – *see* Steiner, 1989) of the problems concerning mathematical applicability disappear. This virtue of logicism does not depend upon our recognizing set theory as 'logic'.

## PRAGMATISM

In PRAGMATIST theories of mathematical knowledge, the indispensability of mathematics in all other knowledge, especially in physical sciences, is converted into a justification of mathematical 'commitment'. The only justification of mathematical assertions is that we can't help ourselves, if we want to achieve the goals of science and everyday life. While this might be regarded as weak confirmation indeed (and certainly no explanation of the 'obviousness' of mathematics, as Parsons has pointed out), pragmatists argue that mathematics is in the same boat as every scientific theory. In this sense, their argument is similar to the 'good company' argument of Kant.

QUINE (e.g. 1960, 1970, and many other writings), who has made this pragmatist-'Kantian' argument famous (though Quine's predecessor at Harvard, C.I. Lewis, already preached a synthesis of Kantianism and pragmatism in *Mind and the World Order*), adds a Deweyite 'naturalistic' element: ultimately what justifies mathematics and every justified theory is its usefulness in predicting 'surface irritations'. What is striking about Quine's philosophy of mathematics, however, is that it is explicitly Platonist in its ontology (though not, of course, in its epistemology). Quine agrees with Frege that modern mathematics is heavily 'committed' to abstract objects – and disagrees with Wittgenstein and the British 'ordinary language' school, who regard the 'commitment' as a manner of speaking, similar, if you will, to the commitments of a politician which nobody takes seriously.

For Quine, again, commitment to abstract objects is justified on pragmatic grounds: we have no choice if we want to do science. However, by combining Platonism, pragmatism and naturalism, Quine seems to make it impossible to give a theory of mathematical discovery. His reasoning can give, at best, a *post facto* pragmatist justification for mathematics once it has been discovered. For Quine has no place, in his philosophy, for 'mathematical intuition' either in the Kantian sense or the Platonic sense. Thus, Quine's picture of mathematical discovery is that of a senseless procedure that accidentally gets *post facto* justification.

I will now present approaches that 'solve' the paradox by denying the very existence of mathematical knowledge! According to these approaches, mathematical theorems do not express 'truths'. hence there is nothing to 'know.' Mathematics can play its role in science and daily life without being 'true'.

## INSTRUMENTALISM

According to this view, mathematics is a tool for making inferences in other fields, but is not itself a science. Perhaps the simplest and most radical form of this view is 'fictionalism'. The fictionalist is not interested in intervening in mathematical discourse, but in interpreting it as fiction. The fictionalist argues that, in principle, one could do without mathematics – even in science. But mathematics allows the scientist the use of compact, elegant proofs, of what otherwise would be cumbersome deductions. A recent defence of this position is by Hartry Field (1980). Field argues that one can rewrite physical theories without any reference to 'mathematical objects', and then prove that adding mathematical axioms does not

increase the deductive power of the rewritten theory. He actually shows how one might get 'rid of' mathematical objects in a particular theory, namely classical gravitation, and how, by what amounts to a consistency proof, one shows that adding mathematics produces a 'conservative extension' of this 'nominalistic' theory of gravitation. Field claims explicitly, as a virtue of his fictionalism, that it eliminates the puzzles concerning mathematical applicability, since we have no longer to worry about the alleged gulf between the subject matter of mathematics and that of the natural sciences.

However, Field's thesis is controversial. Instead of 'mathematical objects', Field's version of gravitation takes points in space–time as real entities, and some argue that this is out of the frying pan and into the fire. Others protest that there are physical theories that are not space–time theories at all, like quantum mechanics. Some argue that the consistency proof will itself raise the ghosts of the departed mathematical entities up in the 'metalanguage'. And there are technical objections based on the use by Field of 'higher-order' logic in his version of gravity.

## CONVENTIONALISM

Conventionalism is the view that mathematical theorems are 'true by convention' (*see* CONVENTION). Poincaré argued, for example, that the difference between Euclidean and non-Euclidean geometry is not a factual, but only a conventional, difference. That is, we can adopt either Euclidean or non-Euclidean geometry according to convenience, since geometry is the study of measurements, and measuring instruments are subject to the forces of nature. For example, we can explain the failure of angles of triangles to sum to 180 degrees either by postulating 'deforming' forces, or by invoking non-Euclidean geometry. This is another way of saying that there is no such thing as 'knowledge' in geometry, unless 'knowledge' that such-and-such are the consequences of our conventions is meant. Note that Poincaré does not extend his conventionalism to mathematics in general: his general point of view in topology (and arithmetic, as we have seen) is not conventionalist, but Kantian.

Thus, for example, Poincaré's position implies that whether a surface is flat or parabolic is a matter of convention; but that the surface is of two dimensions is not conventional at all. No conceivable force could alter our 'rulers' in such a way as to cause a two-dimensional surface to appear three-dimensional. Though this position is Kantian, it should be noted that Poincaré gives a biological explanation for our perception of dimension, particularly why we perceive the world in three dimensions and not more.

The later WITTGENSTEIN (1956, 1976) is often regarded as a conventionalist, though a much more thoroughgoing one than Poincaré, since Wittgenstein makes no distinction between geometry and other branches of mathematics, including arithmetic. And it is true that Wittgenstein often refers to mathematical theorems as conventions; for this reason, he is discussed here.

Yet I have grave reservations about calling Wittgenstein a 'conventionalist' (aside from the general problem that he rejected all philosophical 'positions' or theories):

1. Wittgenstein does not say that mathematical theories 'follow from' conventions. On the contrary, for Wittgenstein, each step in a mathematical proof is a new convention, not just the axioms (as for Poincaré). Conventions, for Wittgenstein, do not 'bind' anybody.

2. This apparent anarchical element in Wittgenstein's position, however, can mislead. When Wittgenstein speaks of a theorem as a convention, he does not mean that there is a genuine option to ignore the proof and accept the negation of the theorem. All mathematical conventions, for Wittgenstein, presuppose empirical regularities which, in his words, are then 'hardened' into rules. That is, what happens most of the time is regarded as the norm, and deviations are to be explained as mistakes, perturbations, etc. Empirical regularities connected with measuring are 'hardened' into theorems of geometry, while regularities in counting are 'hardened' into theorems of arithmetic and number theory.

3. Wittgenstein does side with the conventionalist in one sense, however, in that he regards it as very misleading to speak of mathematical knowledge. To say that someone knows the Pythagorean Theorem is, for Wittgenstein, like saying that someone knows that 12 inches = 1 foot. But there is a tendency for us to regard mathematical knowledge, rather, as like empirical knowledge, a tendency which leads either to empiricist or Platonist theories of mathematics, both of which Wittgenstein rejected.

*See also* A PRIORI KNOWLEDGE; GEOMETRY.

BIBLIOGRAPHY

Benacerraf, P. and Putnam, H. eds: *Philosophy of Mathematics: Selected Readings* (Cambridge: Cambridge University Press, 1984).

Benacerraf, P.: 'What numbers could not be', *Philosophical Review* 74 (1965), 7–73.

Brouwer, L.E.J.: 'Intuitionism and formalism' (1913); reprinted in Benacerraf and Putnam, 1984.

Field, H.: *Science Without Numbers: A Defense of Nominalism* (Princeton: Princeton University Press, 1980).

Gödel, K.: 'What is Cantor's continuum problem?' (1964); reprinted in Benacerraf and Putnam, 1984.

Hardy G.H.: 'Mathematical proof', *Mind* 38 (1929), 1–25.

Hilbert, D.: 'On the Infinite' (1926); reprinted in Benacerraf and Putnam, 1984.

Kitcher, P.: *The Nature of Mathematical Knowledge* (Oxford: Oxford University Press, 1983).

Maddy, P.: 'Perception and mathematical intuition', *Philosophical Review* 89 (1980), 163–96.

Mill, J.S.: *A System of Logic* (London: Longmans, 1843).

Parsons, C.: 'Mathematical intuition', *Proceedings of the Aristotelian Society* 80 (1979–80), 142–68.

Penrose, R.: *The Emperor's New Mind* (Oxford: Oxford University Press, 1989).

Poincaré, H.: 'Science and Hypothesis' (1907); excerpt reprinted in Benacerraf and Putnam, 1984.

Quine, W.V.: *Word and Object* (Cambridge, MA: MIT Press, 1960).

Quine, W.V.: *Philosophy of Logic* (Englewood Cliffs: Prentice-Hall, 1970).

Resnik, M.D.: 'Mathematics as a science of patterns: epistemology', *Nous* 16 (1982), 95–105.

Steiner, M.: *Mathematical Knowledge* (Ithaca, NY: Cornell University Press, 1975).

Steiner, M.: 'The application of mathematics to natural science', *Journal of Philosophy* 86 (1989), 449–80.

Wittgenstein, L.: *Remarks on the Foundations of Mathematics* (Oxford: Blackwell, 1956).

Wittgenstein, L.: *Wittgenstein's Lectures on the Foundation of Mathematics* ed. C. Diamond (Ithaca, NY: Cornell University Press, 1976).

MARK STEINER

**memory**  The capacity to remember: to (1) recall past experiences and (2) retain knowledge that was acquired in the past. It would be a mistake to omit (1), for not any instance of remembering something is an instance of *retaining* knowledge. Suppose that as a young child you saw the Colosseum in Rome, but you did not know at the time which building it was. Later you learn what the Colosseum is, and you remember having seen it when you were a child. This is an example of obtaining knowledge of a past fact – your seeing the Colosseum during your childhood – by recalling a past experience, but not an example of retaining knowledge because at the time you were seeing it you did not *know* you were since you did not know what the Colosseum was. Furthermore, it would be a mistake to omit (2), for not any instance of remembering something is an instance of recalling the *past*, let alone a past experience. For example, by remembering my telephone number, I retain knowledge of a present fact, and by remembering the date of the next elections, of a future fact.

According to Aristotle (*De Memoria* 450a 13), memory cannot exist without imagery; we remember past experiences by recalling images that represent them. This theory – the representative theory of memory – was also held by David HUME (*Treatise* 1, 1, 3) and Bertrand RUSSELL (1921, p. 162). It is subject to three objections, the first of which was recognized by Aristotle himself (*De Memoria* 450a 13). If what I remember is an image present to me *now*, how can it be that what I remember belongs to the *past*? And if what I remember belongs to the *past*, how can it be that it is an image *now* present to my mind? According to the second objection, we cannot tell the difference between images that represent actual memories and those that are mere figments of the imagination. Hume suggested two criteria to distinguish between these two kinds of images, vivacity and orderliness, and Russell a third, an accompanying feeling of familiarity. Critics of the representative theory would argue that these criteria are not good enough, that they do not allow us to distinguish reliably between true memories and mere imagination. This objection is not decisive; it only calls for a refinement of the proposed criteria. Nevertheless, the representative theory succumbs to the third objection, which is fatal: remembering something does not require an image. In remembering their dates of birth, or telephone numbers, people do not, at least not normally, have an image of anything. In developing an account of memory, we must, therefore, proceed without making images an essential ingredient. One way of accomplishing this is to take the thing that is remembered to be a proposition, the content of which may be about the past, present, or future. Doing so would provide us with an answer to the problem pointed out by Aristotle. If the proposition we remember is a truth about the *past*, then we remember the past by virtue of having a cognition of something *present*: the proposition that is remembered.

What, then, are the necessary and sufficient conditions of remembering a proposition, of remembering that *p*? To begin with, *believing* that *p* is not a necessary condition, for at a given moment *t* I may not be aware of the fact that I still remember that *p* and thus do not believe that *p* at *t*. Indeed, it is possible that I remember that *p* but, perhaps because I gullibly trust another person's judgement, unreasonably disbelieve that *p*. It will, however, be helpful to focus on the narrower question: Under which conditions is S's *belief* that *p* an instance of *remembering* that *p*? It is such an instance only if S either (1) previously came to know that *p*, or (2) had an experience that put S in a position subsequently to come to know that *p*. Call this the *original input* condition. (The necessity of distinguishing between (1) and (2) was explained in the first paragraph; not every case of remembering something is one of recalling a piece of knowledge that was acquired in the past.) The original input condition is not sufficient. Suppose, having learned in the past that $12 \times 12 = 144$ but subsequently having forgotten it, I now come to know again that $12 \times 12 = 144$ by using a pocket calculator. Here the original input condition is fulfilled, but obviously this is not an example of remembering that $12 \times 12 = 144$. Thus a further condition is necessary: For S's belief that *p* to be a case of remembering that *p*, the belief must be connected in the right way with the original input. Call this the *connection* condition. According to Carl Ginet (1988, p. 166), the connection must be *epistemic*; at any time since the original input at which S acquires evidence sufficient for knowing that *p*, S already knew that *p*. Critics would dispute that a purely epistemic account of the connection condition will suffice. They would insist that the connection be *causal*: For S to remember that *p*, there must be an uninterrupted causal chain connecting the original input with the present belief. (For a causal account, see Martin and Deutscher, 1960.)

Not every case of remembering that *p* is one of *knowing* that *p*. As pointed out already, although I remember that *p* I might not believe that *p*. Second, although I remember and believe that *p*, I might not be *justified* in believing that *p*, for I might have information that undermines or casts doubt on *p*. When, however, *do* we know something by remembering it? What are the necessary and sufficient conditions of knowing that *p* on the basis of memory? Applying the traditional conception of knowledge, we may say that S

knows that *p* on the basis of memory just in case (1) S clearly and distinctly remembers that *p*; (2) S believes that *p* and (3) S is justified in believing that *p*. (Since (1) entails that *p* is true, adding a condition requiring *p*'s truth is not necessary.) Whether this account of memory knowledge is correct, and how it is to be fleshed out in detail, are questions which concern the nature of knowledge and epistemic justification in general, and thus will give rise to much controversy.

Memory knowledge is possible only if memory is a source of justification. Commonsense assumes it is. We naturally believe that, unless there are specific reasons for doubt, we may trust our memory. In other words, we believe that we do remember what we seem to remember, unless it is undermined or even contradicted by our background beliefs. Thus we trust that we have knowledge of the past because we remember the past. Sceptics, however, would argue that this trust is ill-founded. According to a famous argument by Bertrand Russell (1927, p. 6), it is logically possible that the world sprang into existence five minutes ago, complete with our memories and evidence, such as fossils and petrified trees, suggesting a past of millions of years. If it is, then there is no logical *guarantee* that we actually do remember what we seem to remember. Consequently, so the sceptics would argue, there is no reason to trust memory. Some philosophers have replied to this line of reasoning by trying to establish that memory is necessarily reliable, that it is logically impossible for the majority of our memory beliefs to be false. (Cf. Malcolm, 1963, pp. 195ff; Shoemaker, 1963, pp. 229ff.) Alternatively, our commonsense view may be defended by pointing out that the conclusion of the sceptical argument – it is unreasonable to trust memory – does not follow from its premise: memory fails to provide us with a guarantee that what we seem to remember is true. For the argument to be valid, it would have to be supplemented with a further premise: For a belief to be justified, its justifying reason must guarantee its truth. Many contemporary epistemologists would dismiss this premise as unreasonably strict. One of the chief reasons for resist-

ing it is that accepting it is hardly more reasonable than our trust in particular, clear
and vivid deliverances of memory. To the
contrary, accepting these as true would
actually appear less error prone than accepting an abstract philosophical principle which
implies that our acceptance of such deliverances is unjustified.

See also CAUSAL THEORIES IN EPISTE-
MOLOGY; COMMONSENSISM AND CRITICAL
COGNITIVISM; CRITERIA AND KNOWLEDGE;
HISTORICAL KNOWLEDGE; PROBLEM OF THE
CRITERION; TESTIMONY.

BIBLIOGRAPHY

Dancy, J.: An Introduction to Contemporary
  Epistemology (Oxford: Blackwell, 1985), ch.
  12.
Ginet, C.: 'Memory', in The Handbook of Western
  Philosophy ed. G.H.R. Parkinson (New York:
  Macmillan, 1988), 159–78.
Ginet, C.: Knowledge, Perception, and Memory
  (Dordrecht: Reidel, 1975).
Locke, D.: Memory (London: Macmillan, 1971).
Malcolm, N.: 'Memory and the past', in
  Malcolm (1963).
Malcolm, N.: Knowledge and Certainty (Engle-
  wood Cliffs: Prentice Hall, 1963).
Martin, C.B. and Deutscher, M.: 'Remembering',
  Philosophical Review 75 (1966), 161–96.
O'Connor, D.J. and Carr, B.: Introduction to the
  Theory of Knowledge (Minneapolis: University
  of Minnesota Press, 1982), ch. 5.
Russell, B.: An Outline of Philosophy (London:
  Allen and Unwin, 1927).
Russell, B.: The Analysis of Mind (London: Mac-
  millan, 1921).
Shoemaker, S.: Self-Knowledge and Self-Identity
  (Ithaca, NY: Cornell University Press, 1963).

MATTHIAS STEUP

**Merleau-Ponty, Maurice (1908–61)** Merleau-Ponty, French philosopher of the period
immediately following World War II, is best
known in epistemology for his analyses of
perceptual experience and of the interplay
between perception and action, between perception of self and the perception of others,
and between perceptual life, taken as a
whole, and its various expressions and transformations in language, reflective thought,
art, science, and philosophy.

Merleau-Ponty's theory of knowledge
begins with a rejection of 'the problem of
knowledge' in what he takes to be the Cartesian sense. We do not have to respond to
radical scepticism; we do not have to seek
conclusive reasons to justify an inference
beyond perception to knowledge of an
'external' world. To think that we do is to
demand an inappropriate sort of certainty in
perception and to assume an unwarranted
dichotomy between perception and world.
Merleau-Ponty contends that perception is,
in its own way, intrinsically cognitive. 'We
must not, therefore, wonder whether we
really perceive a world, we must instead say:
the world is what we perceive' (1962, p. xvi).
Not, of course, if 'perceive' is understood as
the reception of sensory data or some form of
explicit judgement based on sense-data;
instead, we must understand perception to be
the way in which humans are already, in
Heidegger's phrase, 'in the world'. Perception
is precisely our 'access' to the world. The task
for a theory of knowledge, as Merleau-Ponty
sees it, is to explicate the meaning and implications of taking perception in this sense.

In his major work, The Phenomenology of
Perception, Merleau-Ponty's strategy is to try
to refute EMPIRICIST and IDEALIST (what
he calls 'intellectualist') views of perception
by evoking essential features of perceptual
experience through the use of exemplary
cases from ordinary life, from experimental
psychology (centrally from the Gestaltists)
and from studies of aphasia and agnosia in
brain-injured patients. In this way, he falls
broadly within the phenomenological tradition (see CONTINENTAL EPISTEMOLOGY
and HUSSERL), but gives it a distinctive
methodological direction (See his 'Phenomenology and the Sciences of Man' in Edie,
1964). Substantively, his rejection of psychophysical dualism and his insistence equally
on a sort of 'realism' and on the centrality of
the active, bodily and historical subject in all
perceptual (and other cognitive) life, give his
thought an existential character and a great
affinity to PRAGMATISM. (see also JAMES)

His epistemology forms part of a total philosophical anthropology and ontology, a philosophy of society and of history.

Among Merleau-Ponty's distinctive theses are the following: (1) Perception is a developed skill, a 'knowing how', not a matter of forming explicit beliefs, in which we, as impersonal, species-specific, living organisms explore, through our sense-organs, an already significant environment; (2) Perceived things are disclosed as unities through perspectival variations – this is their 'lived' and always contingent objectivity; (3) Spatial features of things, including depth and distance, are perceived directly (that is, non-inferentially) in reciprocity with bodily motility, and we see the possibilities which things afford for movement and manipulation; (4) Perceived things are 'intersensory unities' too – that is, we see their tactile, auditory and other properties; (5) Our awareness of ourselves as individual selves develops after, and upon the basis of a primordial awareness of the presence of others; (6) We are able directly to perceive the gestural and affective significance of the behavior of other persons; (7) Language and other cultural practices, although constructive and creative, are parasitic upon perceptual practice – they express features of the perceived world while they transform them; (8) Specifically, the sciences, as forms of knowing, constitute their understandings of the world by exercising and transforming the bodily (and instrumental) way in which we ordinarily explore it in perception; (9) Thus the objectivity of science is parasitic upon the objectivity of ordinary perception; and (10) the realities disclosed by well tested scientific theories can be no more real than, although they inform us in distinctive ways about, the things of ordinary perception.

See also EXPERIENCE; PERCEPTUAL KNOWLEDGE; SENSATION/COGNITION.

WRITINGS

*Phénoménologie de la Perception* (Paris: Gallimard, 1945); trans. C. Smith, *The*
*Phenomenology of Perception* (New York: Humanities Press, 1962).
*The Primacy of Perception* ed. J.M. Edie (Evanston: Northwestern University Press, 1964).
*Le Visible et l'Invisible* (Paris: Gallimard, 1964); trans. A. Lingis *The Visible and the Invisible* (Evanston: Northwestern University Press, 1968).

BIBLIOGRAPHY

Madison, G.: *The Phenomenology of Merleau-Ponty* (Athens: Ohio University Press, 1981).
Pietersma, H.: 'Merleau-Ponty's theory of knowledge', in *Merleau-Ponty: Critical Essays* ed. H. Pietersma (Washington, DC: Center for Advanced Research in Phenomenology and University Press of America, 1989).

JOHN J. COMPTON

**methodology** A term occurring frequently in philosophy of science, but without any precisely established usage. It suggests considerations closer to the actual practice of science (e.g. issues associated with statistical testing) than are some of the more general problems in philosophy of science (e.g. the instrumentalism/realism debate). Often it refers to features that differ from one field of science to another, as in the methodology of physics as compared to the methodology of sociology. In contrast to the logic of science, methodology may include heuristic considerations or other aspects of the context of discovery.

WESLEY C. SALMON

**Mill, John Stuart** (1806–73) British philosopher and economist. Mill's epistemology is thoroughgoingly NATURALISTIC. Human beings are entirely a part of the natural causal order studied by science. Like Kant, Mill thought this had consequences for knowledge: if minds are a part of nature then no knowledge of the world can be a priori. Grounds for any assertion which has real content must be empirical grounds. Mill thought knowledge remained possible on such a basis; Kant did not.

Kant's distinction between 'analytic' and 'synthetic' judgements (*see* ANALYTICITY) is paralleled in Mill's *System of Logic* (1843) by a distinction between 'verbal' and 'real propositions' and, correspondingly, between 'merely apparent' and 'real inferences'. Verbal propositions have no genuine content; in a merely apparent inference no real inferential move has been made. The conclusion has literally been asserted in the premises.

Unlike Kant, Mill takes this strictly. He does not assume that a proposition derivable from logic by definitional substitutions alone is verbal. He develops an 'analysis of language' – of the 'import of propositions' – distinguishing between the 'connotation' and 'denotation' of terms ('names') and applying that distinction to the syntactic forms recognised by syllogistic logic. On this basis he demonstrates that mathematics, and pure logic itself, consist mainly of real propositions and inferences. He points out that logic and mathematics yield new knowledge. They could not do so if they consisted exclusively of strictly verbal propositions; the syllogism would then be a *petitio principii*. Logical and mathematical knowledge is real, so it must be a posteriori, vindicated ultimately by induction; he takes this view even of the logical laws of contradiction and excluded middle.

This is the first thoroughly naturalistic analysis of deductive reasoning. Mill distinguishes it from 'Conceptualism', which confuses logic and psychology by assimilating propositions to judgements and attributes of objects to ideas, 'Realism', which holds that general terms signify abstract universals, and 'Nominalism', which fails to distinguish connotation from denotation and considers all logic and mathematics to be verbal. (In the contemporary sense however Mill himself is a nominalist: he does not countenance abstract entities, holding that number terms denote aggregates – natural entities – and connote their attributes.)

To accuse Mill of PSYCHOLOGISM is an error; what is true however is that he wanted to explain the facts which lend colour to claims to a priori knowledge. They concern the limits to what we are able to cognise or imagine. Mill seeks to explain them in ASSOCIATIONIST terms – not very convincingly. But that does not affect his essential point, which is that when the facts are conceived naturalistically, the step from our inability to represent to ourselves the negation of a proposition to acceptance of its truth calls for justification. Moreover, the justification itself must be a priori if it is to show that the proposition is known a priori; and that is what, on a naturalistic assumption, it cannot be. Mill is prepared to concede the *reliability* of, for example, geometrical 'intuition': but he stresses that its reliability is an empirical fact.

He recognizes only one basic form of inference – both epistemologically and genetically: enumerative induction, simple generalization from experience. But if enumerative inferences are real, must they not also be a posteriori? Mill agrees. 'Principles of Evidence and Theories of Method are not to be constructed a priori. The laws of our rational faculty, like those of every other natural agency, are only learnt by seeing the agent at work.' Like 'Happiness is desirable', 'Enumerative induction is rational' is neither verbal nor an a priori intuition. All that Mill will say is that people agree in practice and theory in accepting it.

Logic is 'the science of science'. It must accept, contrary to the 'well-meant but impracticable precept' of Descartes, that any truly spontaneous form of reasoning has a *prima facie* claim to acceptance. Its task is to describe, codify and systematize. So Mill gives a natural history of the 'inductive process' which shows how it starts by establishing local regularities, how induction on these established regularities leads to the conclusion that all events are subject to regularity, and how that conclusion in turn sustains his eliminative 'Methods of Experimental Inquiry' – whose success stabilizes the whole structure. The problem of induction is to exhibit this cumulative and interactive process perspicuously and to explain why some inductions have greater weight than do other, formally similar, ones. 'We have no ulterior test to which we subject experience in general, but we make experience its own test' – the COHERENTIST element in this is often explicit. The sceptical problem, as posed by HUME, he totally ignores. It is a feature of his philosophy that he takes neither Cartesian nor Humean formulations of scepticism at all seriously (see PROBLEMS OF INDUCTION).

Unlike Whewell or PEIRCE, Mill rejects hypothetical reasoning as a means, in its own right, of achieving attested knowledge; though he affirms its heuristic value. He reasons that there can always be more than one hypothesis consistent with the data. The point is powerful, but this rejection substantially weakens his empiricist account of logic, arithmetic and geometry. It is also in tension, if not in contradiction, with his principle of accepting as *prima facie* sound what is spontaneously accepted in theory and practice. For hypotheses are central to commonsense and scientific reasoning, as Whewell (with whom Mill had a famous controversy on the subject) was to show.

The rejection of hypotheses produces a further tension in Mill's naturalism when combined, as Mill combined it, with the thesis that our immediate consciousness is of our own experience alone. For while enumerative induction can establish correlations within subjective experience (granting the epistemic credentials of memory – a point which troubled Mill) it cannot justify inferences beyond it. Thus Mill arrived at the conclusion that physical objects are knowable only as 'Permanent [i.e. 'certified' or 'guaranteed'] Possibilities of Sensation'. The reconcilability of this view with his overall naturalism is moot – though Mill saw no tension, arguing that any finding of natural science could be expressed in PHENOMENALIST terms. A conception of meaning and inference which might have removed the tension, by legitimizing hypotheses as proper methods of arriving at truth, is latent in Mill's functional treatment of reasoning with general propositions, but it is not developed. Nevertheless, in this respect, and in others (such as its FALLIBILISM), the *System of Logic* represents a vital step on the road from an eighteenth-century to a PRAGMATIST naturalism.

See also A PRIORI KNOWLEDGE; INDUCTION, ENUMERATIVE AND HYPOTHETICAL; INTUITION AND DEDUCTION; MATHEMATICAL KNOWLEDGE; PRAGMATISM.

WRITINGS

*An Examination of Sir William Hamilton's Philosophy* (1865) in *Collected Works of J. S. Mill* ed. J.M. Robson (London: Routledge, 1965–), vol. 9.
*System of Logic* (1843) in his *Collected Works* vols 7–8.

BIBLIOGRAPHY

Gillies, D.: *Frege, Dedekind and Peano on the Foundations of Arithmetic.*
Kessler, G.: 'Frege, Mill, and the foundations of arithmetic', *Journal of Philosophy* 76 (1980), 65–74.
Kitcher, P.S.: 'Arithmetic for the Millian', *Philosophical Studies* 37 (1980), 215–36.
Mackie, J.L.: *The Cement of the Universe* (Oxford: Clarendon Press, 1973), appendix.
Skorupski, J.: *J. S. Mill* (London: Routledge, 1979).

JOHN SKORUPSKI

**Molyneux's problem** William Molyneux (1656–98) raised the following query in a letter to Locke: 'Suppose a Man born blind, and now adult, and taught by his touch to distinguish between a Cube, and a Sphere of the same metal, and nighly of the same bigness, so as to tell, when he felt one and t'other, which is the Cube, which the Sphere. Suppose then the Cube and Sphere placed on a Table, and the Blind Man to be made to see. *Quære*, Whether by his sight, before he touch'd them, he could now distinguish, and tell, which is the Globe, which the Cube' (quoted in Locke, *Essay* 2.9.8). Locke agrees with Molyneux that the man would not be able to do this, since 'he has not yet attained the Experience, that what affects his touch so or so, must affect his sight so or so; Or that a protuberant angle in the Cube, that pressed his hand unequally, shall appear to his eye, as it does in the Cube.'

At face value, the problem concerns the correspondence between the perceptual modalities. Among the questions raised are whether primary qualities (such as shape, size, weight, and motion) are perceived by more than one sense, and whether the visual and tactile perceptions 'resemble' each other. But, as Molyneux expressed it, the main issue is whether we have or could have any *innate* visual capacity for distinguishing form, or whether perception presupposes an acquired (unconscious) interpretative skill on the part of the subject.

A different version of the problem (due to Diderot (*Lettre sur les aveugles*, 1749; as translated in Morgan, 1977, p. 108; and recently revived by Evans, 1985)) asks whether or not the blind man, upon acquiring vision, would be able to distinguish two-dimensional shapes, such as a *square* and *circle* (rather than three-dimensional shapes, such as *sphere* and *cube*). By modifying the terms in which the problem was originally posed, the issue whether previous experience would be sufficient to trigger in Molyneux's man an innate visual capacity to appreciate the depth cues available in perception (including Necker cubes and similar line drawings) appears somewhat immaterial, since the disputants need not disagree about this.

Despite the different versions, the main question concerns the epistemological relation between perceptual modalities – in particular, the connection between a tangible perceptual representation of a primary quality and a visual perceptual representation of a primary quality. The problem is not whether the newly sighted man would be able to recognize visual shapes as distinct features of objects, but whether he would be able to extend the sortal or primary quality concepts previously acquired in order to identify tactually particular shapes, such as a square or a circle, to an application based on visual evidence alone; or, conversely, whether Molyneux's man would be able to extend the sortal or primary quality concepts acquired in the visual identification of particular shapes, to an application grounded exclusively in tactual experience. The crux of the dispute, then, is whether sortal or primary quality concepts have their 'home' in any single one of the five sensory modalities, or association thereof; in effect, whether sortal or primary quality concepts are particular to the bearers of properties presented in any single sensory modality, or whether those concepts are used to discriminate objects which can be the bearers of properties presented in all or in some combination of the five sensory modalities.

There is a question whether, and to what degree, Molyneux's problem can be discussed independently of experimental evidence; and whether it can properly be said to admit of a philosophical solution. Although there is some experimental evidence in favour of Locke's negative reply (*see* Morgan, 1977; Gregory, 1974), the results are inconclusive, and may not bear unequivocally upon the issue.

*See also* BERKELEY; CONCEPT, EMPIRICISM; LOCKE; PERCEPTUAL KNOWLEDGE; PRIMARY/SECONDARY QUALITIES.

BIBLIOGRAPHY

Berkeley, G.: *An Essay towards a New Theory of Vision* (1709): in *Berkeley: Philosophical Works* ed. M.R. Ayers (London: Dent, 1975), esp. §§132–6.

Evans, G.: 'Molyneux's question', *Collected Papers* (Oxford: Oxford University Press, 1985), 364–99.

Gregory, R.L. and Wallace, J.C.: 'Recovery from early blindness – a case study', in R.L. Gregory *Concepts and Mechanisms of Perception* (London: Duckworth, 1974), 65–129.

Leibniz, G.W.: *New Essays on Human Understanding* (1704) trans. P. Remnant and J. Bennett (Cambridge: Cambridge University Press, 1981), esp. 2.10.

Locke, J.: *An Essay concerning Human Understanding* (1690) ed. P.H. Nidditch (Oxford: Clarendon Press, 1975), esp. 2.9.8.

Mackie, J.L.: *Problems from Locke* (Oxford: Clarendon Press, 1976), esp. 29–32, 210–11.

Mérian, J.-B.: *Sur le problème de Molyneux* ed. F. Markovits (Paris: Flammarion, 1984).

Morgan, M.J.: *Molyneux's Question* (Cambridge: Cambridge University Press, 1977).

STEVE SMITH

**Montaigne, Michel de (1533–92)** French essayist. Montaigne was born near Bordeaux to a Catholic father and Spanish Jewish mother, who became a Calvinist. He studied at the College de Guyenne, and perhaps at the University of Toulouse. He held some political positions, including being Mayor of Bordeaux. He was a friend of Reformation and the Counter-Reformation leaders, including Henri of Navarre who became King Henri IV.

Montaigne translated the rationalist theological treatise by Raimond Sebond. His 'Apology for Raimond Sebond' (1576) is the most extended statement of his philosophy. It was composed after he had read the Greek sceptic, SEXTUS EMPIRICUS, and while he was undergoing a personal sceptical crisis, in which he found everything in doubt. In the 'Apology' Montaigne presented and modernized the ancient sceptical arguments about the unreliability of information gained by the senses or by reason, about the inability of human beings to find a satisfactory criterion of knowledge, and about the relativity of moral opinions. He suggested people should suspend judgement on all matters, and wait until God reveals principles to them. One should follow customs, traditions and social rules undogmatically, and should be tolerant of other views. Religious beliefs should be based on faith rather than doubtful evidence. Montaigne's rambling presentation of PYRRHONIAN scepticism quickly became the best-known statement of this view. Bacon, Descartes and Pascal, among others, were greatly influenced by Montaigne's scepticism. His advocacy of accepting customary views because there was no adequate reason to change them became a defence of Catholicism against the Reformation.

WRITINGS

'Apology for Raimond Sebond', in *The Complete Works of Montaigne* trans. D.M. Frame (Stanford: Stanford University Press, 1958).

BIBLIOGRAPHY

Frame, D.M.: *Montaigne. A Biography* (New York: Harcourt Brace, 1965)
Frame, D.M.: *Montaigne's Discovery of Man: The Humanization of a Humanist* (New York: Columbia University Press, 1955).

RICHARD H. POPKIN

**Moore, G(eorge) E(dward) (1873–1958)** Moore was one of the most influential British philosophers of the first half of this century. His reputation in epistemology rests on his defence of commonsense and his point of view, as standardly expounded (cf. Stroud, 1984), is that of the plain man who insists that the validity of our everyday claims to knowledge is not open to serious question, so that philosophers who maintain the contrary can be confidently dismissed.

In truth, Moore's position was rather more complex. Where the standard account suggests that he simply affirmed the existence of the types of knowledge denied by sceptics, Moore actually developed an intricate anti-sceptical dialectic. One strand of this is his argument from differential certainty (1953, VI, VII). Moore argues that we are entitled to be more certain of the falsity of the conclusions of sceptical arguments than we are of the truth of their premises. For the premises will always include general claims about the nature and limits of human knowledge, and the acceptability of such general claims is answerable to their implications concerning particular cases of knowledge; so the conclusions of sceptical arguments undermine our reasons for accepting their premises. In presenting this argument Moore oversimplifies by suggesting that it just rests on a point about empirical induction; none the less, the argument can be reformulated in the context of an attempt to attain a reflective equilibrium concerning the limits of knowledge, and it brings out a real difficulty sceptics face in arguing for their own position. In my opinion the difficulty is not as decisive as Moore maintains, for sceptical arguments often combine apparently uncontentious theses concerning knowledge with theses from metaphysics and the philosophy of mind that we do not find it easy to abandon. None the less, even though Moore's argument only establishes a defeasible presumption against scepticism, it is not just the question-begging contraposition that the standard account of his position represents him as propounding.

Another strand in Moore's anti-sceptical dialectic is the charge that the sceptic's presentation of his position is incoherent since the sceptic cannot argue for his conclusion without representing himself as having knowledge of his premises and of their implications. Moore's charge rests on the thesis that assertion essentially involves a claim to knowledge (1959, p. 248), which is the epistemic analogue of the principle underlying MOORE'S PARADOX and is suggested by the problematic nature of statements of the form 'p but I do not know whether p'. In my view, however, the possibility of making hedged assertions, of the form 'p I think', which manifestly do not involve a claim to knowledge, undermines this argument. For this possibility strongly suggests that the claims to knowledge implied by normal assertions are just conversational implicatures, in GRICE'S sense, which can be cancelled by hedging when the situation requires. Furthermore, even if Moore's thesis about assertion is accepted, the sceptic can just present his argument as a series of hedged assertions and thereby avoid the incoherence Moore imputes to him.

The writings in which Moore seems to live up to the standard account of him are his 1925 paper 'A Defence of Common Sense' and his 1939 lecture 'Proof of an External World' (both in Moore, 1959). For in the first paper he sets out, without any apparent argument, a list of commonsense truisms of which he maintains that he has certain knowledge; and in the second he famously maintains that it would be absurd to question his knowledge of such things as that his hands are before him. Yet I think that in both cases the standard account misunderstands Moore's purport. The 'Defence' was originally written in response to an invitation to provide a 'personal statement' of his philosophical position; so Moore's initial affirmations of common sense knowledge are just

statements of his position, not attempts to establish its validity, though Moore does also attempt here to refute sceptical theses, which he attacks as incoherent. In the 'Proof' Moore aimed to prove only the existence of an external world, not the existence of *knowledge* of such a world – i.e. to refute IDEALISM, not scepticism. This distinction may seem tenuous: if Moore's proof succeeds, then, in giving it, does he not also prove the existence of his own knowledge of an external world? Yet that was not what Moore felt; in his view, a proof of knowledge that p requires the refutation of sceptical arguments, but such a refutation is neither required for, nor accomplished by, a proof that p itself. Admittedly this latter proof requires premises that are in fact known, but Moore does not think he needs to prove the existence of this knowledge – it will suffice to remind his audience of the kinds of thing we all take it for granted that we know (cf. Moore, 1942, pp. 668–9 for an unequivocal repudiation of the thought that sceptical arguments can be refuted by the dialectical strategy employed in the 'Proof').

What, then, is Moore's contribution to epistemology? If he was not the philosopher's idealized plain man but just another plain philosopher unsuccessfully defending commonsense against sceptical arguments (cf. 'Certainty' in Moore, 1959), wherein lies the value of his writings? In my view it does lie in his attempted defence of common sense, but that defence needs to be set in the context of a NATURALISTIC EPISTEMOLOGY which Moore himself never adumbrated. In this context Moore's affirmations of certainty concerning particular matters of fact ('Here is one hand', etc.) signal that involuntary commitment to the existence of our perceptible environment on which a naturalistic epistemology relies in order to get itself started. And Moore's remarks about the 'strangeness' of our epistemological situation vis-à-vis his commonsense truisms (1959, p. 44) reflect the fact that a naturalistic epistemology just incorporates our general presumptions about the structure of the world and our relationship to it rather than providing us with an independent method for verifying them. This last line of thought was famously developed by WITTGENSTEIN in *On Certainty*, particularly in his remarks concerning 'Moorean propositions' (which correspond to Moore's truisms). So my judgement is that it was Wittgenstein who brought to fruition the potential of Moore's epistemology.

See also COMMONSENSISM AND CRITICAL COGNITIVISM; SCEPTICISM, CONTEMPORARY.

WRITINGS

*Philosophical Studies* (London: Routledge, 1922).
'A reply to my critics', in *The Philosophy of G.E. Moore* ed. P.A., Schilpp, 3rd edn (La Salle: Open Court, 1968) pp. 533–687.
*Some Main Problems of Philosophy* (London: Allen and Unwin, 1953).
*Philosophical Papers* (London: Allen and Unwin, 1959).

BIBLIOGRAPHY

Stroud, B.: *The Significance of Philosophical Scepticism* (Oxford: Clarendon, 1984).
Wittgenstein, L.: *On Certainty* (Oxford: Blackwell, 1969).

THOMAS BALDWIN

**Moore's paradox** Moore's problem is that of explaining the oddity of sentences such as

(1) Uranus spins sideways but it is not the case that I believe it.
(2) The Mediterranean Sea once dried up but I believe it did not.

Although (2) describes a commissive error and (1) only an error of omission, they both seem self-contradictory. Sensitivity to this aura of irrationality dates back to SPINOZA:

> If anyone says, then, that he has a clear and distinct, that is, a true idea of substance and nevertheless doubts whether such substance exists, he is like one who says he has a true idea and yet doubts whether it may not be false. (*Ethics* 1p8s2)

Aesthetic appreciation of the tension is reflected in Samuel Beckett's *Waiting for Godot*. For it depicts two tramps as waiting for a man who they believe will never show.

Only within the last fifty years has the characterization of this tension come to be regarded a philosophical problem. Moore thought the absurdity of sentences such as (1) could be explained as a clash between what the speaker asserts and what he implies. The speaker *implies* that he believes Uranus spins sideways because speakers almost always believe what they assert. Yet contrary to the expectation based on this regularity, the speaker *asserts* that he does not believe Uranus spins sideways. So we are pulled in one direction by the statistical syllogism and in another by the speaker's authority.

Moore's explanation fails to show why (1) is more paradoxical than other sentences that send mixed signals. When the village atheist sneers 'Prayer works!', we readily resolve the conflict between what is said and how it was said; there is no paradox here. It is also doubtful whether one can *assert* (1). Of course, one can merely utter the words. But to perform the speech act of assertion, one must give the appearance of believing what one has said.

Some philosophers have tried to amplify this objection into a solution. They say that (1) is queer because it is a consistent but unassertible sentence. This invites a generalization to other speech acts. For example, 'Never follow advice' is paradoxical because it cannot be used to advise people. Although this analysis picks out an interesting class of sentences, there are counter examples to the claim that Moorean sentences are unassertible. A Christian might assert.

(3) The atheism of my mother's nieceless brother's only nephew angers God

because his favourite authority said so. Since this implies 'God exists but I believe God does not exist', it is a hidden Moorean sentence.

This example also causes trouble for those who characterise Moorean sentences as consistent but *unbelievable*. For it forces them into a normative rather than a descriptive analysis of credibility. Jaakko HINTIKKA developed the normative approach by working out a 'doxastic logic' that holds for ideal thinkers. Unlike ordinary people, they are perfectly consistent and believe all the logical consequences of what they believe. (More precisely, they believe in accordance with a doxastic interpretation of the modal system deontic S4.)

Critics have complained that Hintikka's system fails even as a normative model. For in addition to being impossible to satisfy, it cannot even be rationally approximated. A person who works out the trivial consequences of his beliefs is squandering intellectual resources. Further, a certain amount of inconsistency seems mandatory. For any reasonable person believes:

(4) I have at least one false belief.

My belief in (4) makes it impossible for all of my beliefs to be true, hence it ensures that my beliefs are indirectly inconsistent.

Our survey suggests that an adequate solution to Moore's problem must satisfy two main conditions. The first is a sorting task. All Moorean sentences must be counted as such even if they do not look absurd at first glance. (Surprisingly many proposals only manage to include the commissive variation of the paradox or only the omissive.) Conversely, phony Moorean sentences must be systematically excluded. Thus, (4) and the following must be ruled out.

(5) Michael Jackson owns a chimp but I did not believe it.
(6) I believe octopuses attack people and I believe they don't.

The next requirement is a diagnosis of the air of personal inconsistency. Why is the self-ascription of a specific current error absurd? After all, it is all right to ascribe errors to others or even to a past or future self.

The explanation would gain extra merit if it also accounted for the resemblance between Moorean sentences and close look-alikes such as:

(7) Nero wore a concave emerald in one eye but I do not know it.

(8) G.E. Moore was born in 1873 but I guess he was born in 1874.
(9) Pentagonal crystals are impossible but we intend to grow one.

Commentators have connected Moore's problem with the LOTTERY PARADOX, the PREFACE PARADOX, the SURPRISE EXAMINATION PARADOX, offshoots of Newcomb's problem, certain issues of freewill, and epistemic semantics. So it is likely that progress on Moore's problem will lead to advances on other puzzles.

See also EPISTEMIC VIRTUES; PARADOX OF THE KNOWER; PRINCIPLE OF CHARITY.

BIBLIOGRAPHY

Hintikka, J.: Knowledge and Belief (Ithaca: Cornell University Press, 1962).
Linsky, L.: 'On interpreting doxastic logic', Journal of Philosophy 65 (1968), 500–2.
Martinich, A.P.: 'Conversational maxims', Philosophical Quarterly 30 (1980), 215–28.
Sorensen, R.: Blindspots (Oxford: Clarendon Press, 1988).
Williams, J.: 'Moore's problem: one or two?', Analysis 39 (1979), 141–2.

ROY A. SORENSEN

**moral epistemology** This neglected area involves the discussion of two main topics:

1. How do we find out what is right and what is wrong?
2. Which of our moral views are justified? Do any count as knowledge?

I start with the first of these. The first point to make is that in any area one's epistemology will depend heavily on one's favoured analysis of the nature of the 'facts' that are to be known or believed. The more disputed the latter, the more contentious the former. In ethics there is, of course, the view that there are no moral facts to be known or believed at all. This is commonly called moral scepticism, but it should not be, for if there are no relevant facts there is nothing to be ignorant of; we do better to call it non-cognitivism. Like scepticism, it seems to require of its proponents that they avoid all talk of moral knowledge; if there are no facts, how can there be knowledge? But this would be a mistake, for there are non-cognitive theories of knowledge as well as of ethics. A non-cognitive theory of knowledge like that of J.L. AUSTIN concentrates on what it is to *say* that one knows; Austin held that to say that one knows is to give a sort of personal guarantee, or to put one's reputation more on the line in this case. We can easily conceive of an extension of this approach to claims of moral knowledge. But it would be fair to say that most approaches to knowledge are not like this, but suppose that knowledge requires the possibility of truth and facts. If we are to take it that there is such a thing as moral knowledge, then we are going to have to take it that there are moral truths to be known.

Within the cognitivist tradition, there are two main styles of approach to our first question. A *particularist* epistemology takes it that our first awareness is of facts which are restricted to the particular case before us; we may hope to move on from these later and come to grasp more general truths, but we have to start with the particular case. Philosophies of science are commonly particularist in this sense, for good reason. A *generalist* epistemology holds that we first become aware of general truths which we are then able to apply to particular cases as they come along. This approach is unconvincing in most areas, but it has gained many adherents in moral epistemology. Many theorists find themselves holding that we learn moral principles first, and that there is nothing in a particular case that one could extract a principle from; one has to learn it in other ways, directly.

This contrast between generalist and particularist epistemologies is only a contrast in direction. As stated, both admit that we are able to know both general principles and particular moral truths about what to do here; the only question is what comes first and what must come second. There are, however, more trenchant versions of both approaches. There is a form of particularism which holds that general moral truths

cannot be known (because there are none to know) and there are many types of view which hold that our ability to find out what is right in a particular case is never reliable enough to count as knowledge. An example here is Moore's form of utilitarianism. Moore (1903) held that an action's rightness was a function of the goodness of its consequences, but that since even a simple action's consequences reverberate to the end of time we could never know enough about them to know that the balance will be of the right sort. That this inference is unsound is not to the point here.

RATIONALIST moral theories of a traditional sort are generalist; they attempt to establish certain highly general moral rules as deliverances of reason. The classic example is that of Kant (1785). Kant's view is that a moral law is one that we can consistently conceive that all rational beings should use as a principle of action. More recently, Gewirth (1978) tries to show that the denial of a single central Principle of Generic Consistency is contradictory, and to derive other principles from that. Kant's rules are much more specific than Gewirth's. They are still general, but since they are more specific it is easier to use them to derive answers to the question what to do in a particular situation. Gert (1966) suggests that the moral rules he propounds can only be rejected at the cost of a sort of practical irrationality which cannot be reduced to a formal contradiction.

There are other, non-rationalist, ways of being a generalist in ethics. It would be a mistake to cite R.M. Hare's universal prescriptivism here, since his is a non-cognitive theory. But Sidgwick held that basic moral laws are discovered not by reason (e.g. by deriving contradictions from their falsehood) but by intuition (*see* INTUITION AND DEDUCTION). This view is not uncommon among utilitarians. It must be admitted, however, that any appeal to intuition has traditionally been viewed with the deepest suspicion. We are driven to announce that basic principles are the products of intuition because we take it that (1) we know them to be true and (2) no other account of how this knowledge might have been gained is at all plausible. So intuition is definitely a last resort. The rationalist programme has been far more attractive to philosophers, partly because it promises to put ethical knowledge on a really secure and independent footing, and partly because if it can be achieved it will produce moral principles which cannot be denied except on pain of irrationality. This would enable us to find an answer to the mythical person (who, like the sceptic, worries philosophers without actually existing) who wants to know what reason there is to be moral at all – the amoralist.

I turn now to particularist approaches to moral epistemology. I start with the views of W.D. Ross. Ross held that what we learn first is that a feature makes a difference to how we should act *here*. We learn by experience how important tact can be, in the sense that we simply see that someone else's sensitivity goes to make it right to tread carefully here. Given this entirely particular knowledge, however, we can immediately move to something general. For we recognize by a process called *intuitive induction* that what makes a difference here must make the same difference wherever it occurs. So we can learn the truth of a moral principle from what we can see in the particular case; the principle is self-evident to us, given what the present case has taught us, since nothing more is necessary to reveal it to us than what the present case contains.

Intuitive induction is perhaps an unfamiliar process (*but see* Johnson, 1922). Its use is not however confined to ethics. An example Ross gives is that of discovering the truth of a principle of inference (*modus ponens*, say) by seeing it in the soundness of one instance. The soundness of the inference 'If he is here he'll kill her: he is here: so he will kill her' is one which reveals to those that can see it the soundness of its general principle 'If $p$ then $q$: $p$: so $q$'.

How then do we come to decide what we ought to do in the case before us? All we have noticed so far is that one feature goes to make a certain course of action right (and hence goes to make any action that has it right). But there will be other features pulling in other directions. How are we to judge how to

act all things considered? Ross's answer here is just that we should consider all things and come to the best view we can. He sees our choosing here as a sort of balancing of things that count for and against, and he holds that the result of this process is never knowledge, since the whole thing is far too insecure ever to deserve that title.

Two things are worth stressing here. The first is that we do not use the moral principles we have learnt in coming to an overall decision about what to do; the principles play no epistemological role at all, for Ross. The second is that moral knowledge is available, but it is all about the way in which individual features go to make their bearers right or wrong, and never about what we ought to do here. We can know that the deceitfulness of this action goes to make it wrong, and so by intuitive induction that all deceitful actions are wrong, so far as that goes. But we can never know that overall we should not do this deceitful action; our decision will never be more than 'probable opinion'.

For Ross, therefore, the crucial point is our original knowledge that some feature goes to make this action wrong. How do we know this? The only answer he can give is 'by intuition', and critics not unfairly suggested that this was just a confession of ignorance got up to look like an answer. An apparently more promising answer is given by the 'moral sense' theorists (*see* Hutcheson, 1725; and Broad, 1971). This tradition, which is equally particularist, claims as Broad puts it (1971, p. 195) that 'singular moral judgements are analogous in certain important respects to judgements of sense perception, such as "That thing is yellow"'. The analogy depends upon taking a dispositional view of colour, so that the yellowness of this banana is a disposition it has to cause certain experiences in suitably placed observers. Similarly, it is held that the wrongness of an action is a disposition the action has to cause feelings or emotions of a distinctive sort in a suitable observer. In both cases, this analysis is supposed to be compatible with the view that the relevant property can be directly observed. We can effectively *see* these dispositions instantiated in the particular case.

This moral sense theory seems initially more promising than Ross's position, but it does of course have some disadvantages. First, one has to accept a dispositional analysis both of colour and of moral qualities. Second, something has to be said about how general moral truths can be discovered by this method, it being admitted in this tradition that there are such things to be discovered at all. It appears to be inevitable that the model will still be that of our knowledge of colour. We know that bananas are yellow by ordinary enumerative induction (see INDUCTION, ENUMERATIVE AND HYPOTHETICAL), not by intuitive induction à la Ross, and presumably we are to find out that deceitful actions are wrong in the same sort of way. This one is wrong, that one is wrong, and so with increasing probability we conclude that all are wrong. This is a possible view, but it seems to me mistaken. Knowing the truth of the general principle that deceitfulness is wrong, we know not just that all (or most) deceitful acts are wrong, but also that they are wrong partly because of being deceitful. Ordinary enumerative induction will not be able to reveal facts of that sort to us unless it has facts of that sort as input, namely that this action is wrong partly because of its deceitfulness, so is that one, so is yet another, and so (probably) all deceitful acts are wrong, and wrong because of their deceitfulness.

The question now is whether the moral sense theory will be able to give a good sense to an initial awareness that this action is wrong partly because of its deceitfulness. There appears to be no analogy between the moral case and the colour case on this point, and this is a definite advantage for Ross. He is able to give a strong sense to the idea that moral properties such as rightness and wrongness stem from others. They exist in virtue of others, and very commonly (to say the least) our awareness of them is mediated by our awareness of other features as those which ground them here. However, an analogy may be significant without being perfect; all analogies give out at some point. And we can surely give a good sense to the idea that our moral perception is tied to the properties that ground the rightness/wrongness here. The dispositional story will just be that we experience this action as disposed to cause suitable observers to respond to its deceitfulness (or to it in the light of its deceitfulness) in a certain characteristic way.

These are the two main forms of particularist epistemology in ethics. They both suffer from the same defect, which is that the things they allow us to know are not clearly things whose presence should motivate us. It seems, for all that is said, that one might notice them and be entirely unmoved by them. The moral sense theory is particularly weak here. Surely one might notice that a suitably placed observer would respond in a certain way to this action in respect of this property without taking this as relevant to how one should behave oneself. And if so, this leaves moral distinctions as peculiarly inert, as not essentially relevant to action. It is natural to think that one cannot notice that an action is wrong in a certain respect or overall without this influencing one's decisions, and the theory has failed to capture this element of our thought.

I now turn to the second question, which of our moral views are justified. One approach here is to debate the rival merits of FOUNDATIONALISM and COHERENTISM in their application to justification in ethics. (I don't think that RELIABILISM recommends itself in this area.) The first thing to say is that what, e.g., a foundationalist position will amount to will vary radically according to the substantive moral epistemology we adopt. Both rationalist and intuitionist forms of generalism will suppose that there are basic, highly general truths from which particular moral prescriptions can be derived. This position is unlike standard forms of foundationalism in the theory of empirical knowledge, since it makes no pretence to ground moral knowledge on particular facts of moral experience. But it is none the worse for that; it still retains the distinctions between basis and superstructure and between two forms of justification, so characteristic of foundationalism, and its insistence that justification is all one-way. The difficulty I see for these views is that it is going to be impossible to derive from what is allowed at the basis any detailed and specific suggestion about our moral duties in a particular case. This is a complaint often made against Kant, but it seems to infect all forms of generalist foundationalism.

Much more promising is some form of coherentism, which refuses to draw the standard foundationalist distinctions. It allows that moral justification grows as we achieve a good fit between different aspects of our moral views, those more general and those more specific. Coherentism of this sort is hardly distinct from the view associated with Rawls, that what we seek on the epistemological front is a form of rational equilibrium, in which we have achieved maximal resolution of the tensions between different views with independent appeal to us. To the extent that coherentists accept this aim, however, they also hope to offer an explanation of why it is a reasonable aim.

Particularist approaches, however, appear to lend themselves much more easily to foundationalist structuring, if only because they take the view that some of our moral knowledge is empirical. This may give us hope that we are able to acquire some knowledge in the particular case which is solid enough to support the rest. My own view, however, is again that at the end of the day this will show itself to be an empty dream. The status of moral intuition is too weak to support anything recognizable as a distinction between foundations and superstructure, in Ross's case. Even if we were to admit that we have absolutely certain knowledge that it is wrong to torture innocent children, there will not be enough of such knowledge to support the rest. And there is little prospect of treating as foundational anything as theoretically loaded as the view that the present action has a disposition to elicit certain responses in suitably placed observers. (*See* Brink, 1989, ch. 5.)

A different approach to the nature of moral justification would be to use the ideas of WITTGENSTEIN. We could see certain moral beliefs as 'frame' beliefs which play in ethics the role played in ordinary perceptual justification by such beliefs as 'I have two hands' and 'The sun is a very long way away'. These 'frame' beliefs are not justified but stand in no need of justification; they are the things we appeal to in the justification of other beliefs. Candidates would be 'All have equal rights' and 'One should not torture innocent children'. This would give us something of the structure of foundationalism but from a completely different perspective.

Even if we succeed in giving an adequate account of justification in ethics, this will not in itself yield an account of moral knowledge (unless the TRIPARTITE DEFINITION is correct). For that we would have to go further afield. There is a strong tradition to the effect that we cannot *know* that something is wrong. Various reasons have been suggested: the differences between different moral cultures, the complexity of moral judgement, the unobservability of moral properties. RELATIVISM and SCEPTICISM aside, however, the driving thought is that moral matters are too complex and subtle for us to claim knowledge. Unless the possibility of justification requires the availability of knowledge, this need not disturb the moral epistemologist.

*See also* COMMONSENSISM AND CRITICAL COGNITIVISM; PROBLEM OF THE CRITERION.

BIBLIOGRAPHY

Austin, J.L.: 'Other minds', in his *Philosophical Papers* (Oxford: Oxford University Press, 1970).
Brink, D.O.: *Moral Realism and the Foundations of Ethics* (Cambridge: Cambridge University Press, 1989).
Broad, C.D.: 'Some reflections on moral-sense theories in ethics', in *Broad's Critical Essays in Moral Philosophy* ed. D. Cheney (London: Allen and Unwin, 1971).
Gert, B.: *The Moral Rules* (New York: Harper and Row, 1966).
Gewirth, A.: *Reason and Morality* (Chicago: Chicago University Press, 1978)
Hutcheson, F.: *An Inquiry Concerning the Original of our Ideas of Virtue or Moral Good* (1725), in *British Moralists* ed. L.A. Selby-Bigge (Indianapolis: Bobbs-Merrill, 1964).

Johnson, W.E.: *Logic* (Cambridge: Cambridge University Press, 1922) pt. 2, ch. 7.

Kant, I.: *Groundwork of the Metaphysic of Morals* (1785); trans. J. Paton *The Moral Law* (London: Hutchinson, 1972).

Moore, G.E.: *Principia Ethica* (Cambridge: Cambridge University Press, 1903).

Ross, W.D.: *The Right and The Good* (Oxford: Clarendon Press, 1930).

Sidgwick, H.: *The Methods of Ethics* (London: Macmillan, 1874).

Wittgenstein, L.: *On Certainty* (Oxford: Blackwell, 1969).

JONATHAN DANCY

**myth of the given**  *see* FOUNDATIONALISM; the GIVEN; SELLARS.

# N

naïve realism *see* ARGUMENT FROM ILLUSION; DIRECT REALISM; PROBLEM OF THE EXTERNAL WORLD.

**natural science, epistemology of** The natural sciences (physics, chemistry, astronomy, geology, biology) are of special importance to epistemology because collectively they contain the most extensive, systematic, reliable knowledge that we have. Prior to Newton, Euclidean geometry played that role, and its influence on the history of epistemology was vast (*see* GEOMETRY).

Before the middle of the twentieth century, many philosophers and scientists (e.g. Ernst Mach, Bertrand RUSSELL) sought a secure foundation for scientific knowledge in SENSE-DATA; the more recent fashion is to take perceptions of middle sized physical objects as fundamental data for natural science. Although it had been argued that sense-data furnish a basis in CERTAINTY, whereas perceptions of a material objects may not be veridical, most philosophers despair of logically constructing material objects from sense-data (*see* LOGICAL CONSTRUCTION, PHENOMENALISM). Following Karl Popper (1959) and Hans Reichenbach (1938), they accept a physicalistic basis and acknowledge its corrigibility. The quest for certainty that had motivated phenomenalism has been largely abandoned. Errors of perception are considered, on the whole, detectable and correctable.

Granting the physicalistic basis, several epistemological problems concerning natural science arise. The first of these is David HUME'S notorious problem of the justification of induction (*see* PROBLEMS OF INDUCTION). Natural science provides knowledge of events that have not yet occurred (e.g. a future solar eclipse), events that happened in the remote past (e.g. the extinction of dinosaurs), and events that are happening elsewhere, unexperienced by any human observer (e.g. occurrences on the surface of Venus). This raises the problem of inferences from the observed to the unobserved, or more generally, the problem of ampliative inferences – arguments whose conclusions have factual content not present in their premises. Hume argued persuasively that, without some assumption regarding the uniformity of nature, we have no rational basis for concluding that any of our predictive inferences, even though based on true premises, will ever again have true conclusions. Moreover, he argued, it is impossible to establish the uniformity of nature by arguments a priori or a posteriori. His conclusion was not merely that knowledge of the unobserved is fallible – a point that had been recognized in antiquity by the sceptics – but that it cannot be considered even probable. Although Hume seemed to direct his attack chiefly at induction by simple enumeration, his argument is cogent with respect to any form of ampliative inference.

A wide variety of responses have been made to Hume's inductive scepticism. Immanuel KANT, who claimed to have been awakened from his dogmatic slumbers by Hume's work, offered a transcendental deduction of a principle of universal causation. P.F. STRAWSON (1952) offered an ordinary language dissolution, arguing that Hume's problem of induction is a pseudo-problem. Russell (1948) offered a set of 'postulates of scientific inference'. Rudolf Carnap (1963) appealed to 'inductive intuition' as the ultimate source of justification. In an approach rather similar to Carnap's, Nelson GOODMAN (1955) attempted to replace Hume's old problem of induction with his 'new problem of induction' (*see* PROBLEMS OF INDUCTION). POPPER (1935) sought to evade the problem by advocating deductivism, the view that science does not employ induction at all. REICHENBACH (1938, 1949) offered a pragmatic justification. All of these approaches seem beset by fundamental difficulties (Salmon, 1967).

Natural science, in addition to making inferences regarding particular events and facts, is also concerned to establish general laws of nature (e.g. conservation of momentum) that are presumed to hold at all times and places in the entire history of the universe. Clearly, Hume's problem of induction applies to this enterprise; there is no way to establish such laws a priori, and any a posteriori method will involve ampliative inferences. This difficulty notwithstanding, various philosophers have addressed the problem of knowledge of laws. A traditional approach is the hypothetico-deductive (H-D) method. Given a hypothesis H that is to be tested, one deduces from H (in conjunction with suitable initial conditions) an observational prediction O. If O turns out to be true, the hypothesis H is said to be confirmed to some extent. One of many major problems with the H-D method is that if H is thus confirmed, so is H&X, where X is any arbitrary statement (*see also* HEMPEL'S PARADOX).

If, in the foregoing H-D schema, O turns out to be false, one can immediately conclude by *modus tollens* that at least one of the premises is false. If one has sufficient confidence in the truth of the initial conditions, one can conclude that H is refuted. Rejecting the positive form of the H-D method, Popper advocates the method of 'conjectures and refutations'. The method of science, he claims, is to advance bold explanatory hypotheses (conjectures) and to subject them to the most severe experiential tests in a sincere effort to refute them. Hypotheses that survive such severe tests are said to be 'corroborated'. It is important to emphasize that 'corroboration' is not just another word for 'confirmation'. Confirmation enhances the probability of the hypothesis in question; hypotheses that

are highly confirmed have high probability. Hypotheses that are highly corroborated are very improbable according to Popper. The fundamental problem with Popper's approach is that, in banishing induction from science, he also bans all predictive power. From the content of our observations alone we cannot deduce anything about future occurrences (Salmon, 1981).

Pierre Duhem (1954) pointed out that, in addition to the hypothesis being tested and statements of initial conditions under which the test is conducted, we also need auxiliary hypotheses to carry out the deduction of observational consequences in the H-D schema. When the observational prediction turns out to be false, we are not entitled to conclude that the test hypothesis is false; at best, we can assert that the conjunction of the test hypothesis and the auxiliaries has been refuted. These and other considerations have led some philosophers, most notably QUINE (1951), to maintain the HOLISTIC thesis that individual scientific hypotheses are not subject to separate tests, but rather, the entire fabric of scientific knowledge confronts empirical evidence as a whole.

Many philosophers have turned to the theory of PROBABILITY as a way of understanding the confirmation of scientific hypotheses. The most extensive and systematic example is CARNAP's inductive logic, the major features of which are given in Carnap (1950, 1952). Ironically, in this system, universal generalizations that range over infinite domains always have degree of confirmation zero on any finite body of evidence. One has to be satisfied with 'qualified instance confirmation', the non-zero confirmation of the statement that the generalization will hold in the next instance encountered. This is, however, a technical difficulty that can be overcome (Hintikka, 1966). A far more serious difficulty – one of principle – is the fact that a priori measures of prior probabilities, which appear to be altogether arbitrary, are required (Salmon, 1967).

As many philosophers view the situation, Bayes's theorem holds the key to the confirmation of scientific hypotheses. It may be written

$$Pr(H/E\&B)$$

$$= \frac{Pr(H/B)\ Pr(E/H\&B)}{Pr(H/B)\ Pr(E/H\&B)\ +\ Pr(\text{-}H/B)\ Pr(E/\text{-}H\&B)}$$

where H is the hypothesis, B our background knowledge (including initial conditions and auxiliary hypotheses, if any), E is the specific evidence being brought to bear on H and $Pr(H/E\&B)$ is the probability of H on evidence E given background B. If a hypothetico-deductive test yielding a positive outcome has been conducted, $Pr(E/H\&B) = 1$. $Pr(H/B)$ and $Pr(\text{-}H/B)$ are known as prior probabilities; their status has been the subject of much controversy. Personalists, who are often referred to as 'Bayesians', take them to be subjective degrees of belief. Their critics object to such an infusion of subjectivity into the logic of science. Carnap's above-mentioned inductive logic also rests on Bayes's theorem; in that system the prior probabilities are established a priori. Holders of frequency or propensity interpretations of probability are hard put to provide a reasonable interpretation of prior probabilities (Salmon, 1967).

Up to this point, we have considered problems associated with knowledge of unobserved matters of fact, but natural science also poses problems regarding knowledge of unobservable entities. At the turn of the twentieth century, many philosophers and scientists (e.g. Mach, Karl Pearson, and some early LOGICAL POSITIVISTS) denied the existence of such objects as molecules and atoms. Taking an instrumentalist position, they held, for example, that the molecular-kinetic theory of gases, which seems to make reference to molecules, is merely a useful tool for the organization of experience, but does not establish the existence of such things. They are nothing more than useful fictions. In recent years, Bas van Fraassen (1980) has advocated a position he calls 'constructive empiricism', which is not a form of instrumentalism, but takes an agnostic attitude toward unobservable entities.

A good deal of the philosophical discussion of this issue has focused on the meaning of theoretical terms and statements. Operation-ists have maintained that all meaningful scientific concepts are operationally definable in terms of physical operations that can be carried out in the laboratory or in the field and 'pencil and paper' operations (calculations or mathematical derivations), while logical positivists have identified the meaning of a statement with the means of its conclusive verification. Operationists and logical positivists thus deny that we can have knowledge of unobservable entities, for discourse putatively about them is strictly meaningless. Carnap (1956) makes a distinction between internal and external questions of EXISTENCE. If one has adopted the standard language of physics and chemistry, one can establish the internal existence of atoms and molecules by appeal to the standard theories. The question of whether to adopt a linguistic framework that incorporates terms that refer to atoms and molecules is an external question; it should be answered with regard to the utility of the theory, not by appeal to metaphysical arguments about the 'real existence' of these entities. An excellent survey of the issues regarding the meaning of scientific theories can be found in Carl G. Hempel (1958).

The emphasis on meaning of theoretical terms seems, however, somewhat misplaced. The basic epistemological question is whether we can have knowledge of unobservable entities. We can, after all, make statements about unobservable entities without invoking a special theoretical vocabulary. In his work on Brownian movement, Jean Perrin created large numbers of tiny spheres of gamboge (a yellow resinous substance). He suspended them in water, observed their motions with a microscope, and inferred that many smaller particles were colliding with them. Without using any non-observational terms, I have just described the essentials of an epoch-making experiment on the reality of molecules, namely, the ascertainment of Avogadro's number (the number of molecules in a mole of any substance).

The foregoing example suggests that we can make at least a rough and ready tripartite division among objects that are directly perceivable by normal human senses, those that are indirectly perceivable through the use of such instrumental extensions of our senses as microscopes and telescopes, and those whose existence and properties can be inferred on the basis of direct and indirect observation. To avoid begging the epistemological questions, we must allow for the possibility that either the second or the third, or both categories, are empty. In adopting a physicalist approach from the outset, we assured the nonemptiness of the first category.

Ian Hacking (1981) has addressed the question of microscopic observations with unprecedented sophistication, and has offered powerful arguments for their veridicality. The veridicality of telescopic observation can be supported by considerations at least as strong. It would seem that the category of indirectly observable entities is not empty. The problem of the third category still remains. It would be unwarranted, at this stage in the history of science at least, to claim that we see the quarks within a proton by means of accelerator experiments or the interior of the sun by means of neutrino detectors.

The problem of the existence of entities not even indirectly observable was essentially settled for natural science as a result of the work of Perrin and others in roughly the first decade of the twentieth century. It is well recounted in Perrin's semi-popular (1923) and Mary Jo Nye elaborates the development in fine historical detail in her (1972). The crux of the argument is this. From a series of physical experiments that are superficially extremely diverse, it is possible to infer the value of Avogadro's number, and the values obtained in all of these types of experiment agree with one another remarkably well. If matter were not actually composed of such micro-entities as molecules, atoms, ions, electrons, etc., this agreement would be an unbelievably improbable coincidence. My analysis of this argument is in terms of common causes (Salmon, 1985), but even if it is analysed in other ways, the argument is exceedingly robust.

Recent thought about the epistemology of natural science has been strongly influenced by the work of Thomas S. Kuhn (1962), who has emphasized the importance of historical considerations for purposes of philosophical analysis. Instead of viewing the development of the natural sciences as a process of gradual accumulation of objective knowledge of the physical world, he sees it as a series of episodes of normal science alternating with periods of scientific revolution. Each episode of normal science is characterized by a paradigm, consisting of a problem domain, a standard set of problem-solving techniques, general principles, and theories. When a problem in that domain is recalcitrant with respect to the available techniques it constitutes an anomaly. Too many anomalies constitute a crisis for that paradigm, and a revolution may occur, in which a new paradigm replaces the older one. When this replacement has taken place, a new period of normal science ensues. The new paradigm, according to Kuhn, does not incorporate the old, but rather, is incommensurable with it. For example, instead of solving the problems that were anomalies for the old paradigm, the new paradigm may simply dismiss them as inconsequential. To change from one paradigm to another requires something like a Gestalt-shift.

According to Kuhn, the choice between theories represented by the old and new paradigms is not determined solely by observed facts and logic; instead, it involves persuasion and judgment as well. The transition from one to another is a social fact accomplished by a community of scientists. There is no single point in the transition at which it is irrational to hold onto the old theory rather than switching to the new. When, on the basis of such comments, various philosophers interpreted Kuhn as denying the objectivity of science, he vehemently denied the charge. On his view, mature physical science is the best example of objective knowledge we have. To understand what objective knowledge consists in we should not lay down formal criteria a priori, but rather, we should examine the methodology of physical science. When we do, he says, we see that theories are evaluated on the basis of such criteria as simplicity, consistency, scope, accuracy and fertility. This list is neither exclusive nor exhaustive, and there cannot be precise rules for application of its members.

I am inclined to think that Kuhn's view that theory choice goes beyond empirical data and logic is based on an overly narrow conception of the logic of science. If we think of scientific confirmation in terms of Bayes's theorem, we recognize that it not only allows for, but actually demands, prior probabilities of the theories under consideration. Such prior probabilities are plausibility judgements. At least some of the criteria Kuhn mentions seem clearly to be qualitative evaluations of prior probabilities. A Bayesian treatment of scientific confirmation appears to bridge the gap, at least to a significant extent, between historically oriented analyses of knowledge in the natural sciences and more traditional approaches (Salmon, 1990).

See also BAYESIANISM; EXPLANATION; PROBABILITY; PROBLEMS OF INDUCTION; SOCIAL SCIENCE; SOCIOLOGY OF KNOWLEDGE.

BIBLIOGRAPHY

Carnap, R.: *Logical Foundations of Probability* (Chicago: University of Chicago Press, 1950).
Carnap, R.: 'Empiricism, semantics, and ontology', in his *Meaning and Necessity* 2nd edn (Chicago: University of Chicago Press, 1956), 205–21.
Carnap, R.: *The Continuum of Inductive Methods* (Chicago: University of Chicago Press, 1952).
Carnap, R.: 'Replies and systematic expositions', in *The Philosophy of Rudolf Carnap* ed. P.A. Schilpp (La Salle: Open Court, 1963), 859–1016.
Duhem, P.: *The Aim and Structure of Physical Theory* trans. P. Wiener (Princeton: Princeton University Press, 1954).
van Fraassen, B.C.: *The Scientific Image* (Oxford: Clarendon Press, 1980).
Goodman, N.: *Fact, Fiction, and Forecast* (Cambridge, MA: Harvard University Press, 1955).
Hacking, I.: 'Do we see through a microscope?', *Pacific Philosophical Quarterly* 62 (1981), 305–22.

Hempel, C.G.: 'The theoretician's dilemma', *Minnesota Studies in the Philosophy of Science* vol. II, eds H. Feigl, M. Scriven and G. Maxwell (Minneapolis: University of Minnesota Press, 1958), 37–98.
Hintikka, J.: 'A two-dimensional continuum of inductive methods', in *Aspects of Inductive Logic* eds J. Hintikka and P. Suppes (Amsterdam: North-Holland, 1966), 113–32.
Kuhn, T.S.: *The Structure of Scientific Revolutions* (Chicago: University of Chicago Press, 1962).
Nye, M.J.: *Molecular Reality* (London: Macdonald, 1972).
Perrin, J.: *Les Atomes* (Paris: 1913); trans. D. L. Hammick, *Atoms* (New York: Van Nostrand, 1923).
Popper, K.R.: *Logik der Forschung* (Vienna: 1935); trans. the author, *The Logic of Scientific Discovery* (New York: Basic Books, 1959).
Quine, W.V.: 'Two dogmas of empiricism', *Philosophical Review* 60 (1951), 20–43.
Reichenbach, H.: *Experience and Prediction* (Chicago: University of Chicago Press, 1938).
Reichenbach, H.: *The Theory of Probability* (Berkeley: University of California Press, 1949).
Russell, B.: *Human Knowledge, Its Scope and Limits* (New York: Simon & Schuster, 1948).
Salmon, W.C.: *The Foundations of Scientific Inference* (Pittsburgh: University of Pittsburgh Press, 1967).
Salmon, W.C.: 'Rational prediction', *British Journal for the Philosophy of Science* 32 (1981), 115–25.
Salmon, W.C.: 'Empiricism: The key question', in *The Heritage of Logical Positivism* ed. N. Rescher (Lanham: University Press of America, 1985), 1–21.
Salmon, W.C: 'Rationality and objectivity in science, *or* Tom Kuhn meets Tom Bayes', *Minnesota Studies in the Philosophy of Science* vol. XIV, ed. C. Wade Savage (Minneapolis: University of Minnesota Press, 1990), 175–204.
Strawson, P.F.: *Introduction to Logical Theory* (New York: John Wiley & Sons, 1952).

WESLEY C. SALMON

**naturalism** This is the doctrine that there are only natural things: only natural particulars and only natural properties. It is a close relative of the doctrine of materialism or physicalism according to which there are only material or physical things. If there is a difference between materialism and physicalism, it is that the materialist takes the category of the material to be given intuitively, the physicalist takes it to be given by an idealization from contemporary physics. A similar difference affects naturalists. Some take the category of the natural to be given intuitively whereas others – in particular, most contemporary proponents – take it to be given by an idealisation from the natural sciences.

As with physicalism, the science-based version of naturalism is beset with two ambiguities. First, an ontological ambiguity. In holding that there are only natural things, it may take natural things to be, or to be definable in terms of, just the sorts of particulars and properties countenanced in the (idealized) natural sciences; this doctrine is often described as reductionism. Alternatively, it may take natural things to be a broader class: say, to be the things that SUPERVENE appropriately on what is countenanced in the natural sciences. Second, a methodological ambiguity. In holding that there are only natural things, naturalism may suggest that the natural sciences offer the unique model for discovering what there is – this view is sometimes described as scientism – or it may be open to the possibility that other approaches – say, those of commonsense or those of the humanities – may also tell us about what there is.

Reductionism and scientism often go together. A reductionist, scientistic naturalism will tend to deny reality to many commonsense posits: say, to colours and secondary properties, to free will and related psychological capacities, or to moral and other values. It will constitute a hard or strict naturalism. A non-reductionist, non-scientistic view will tend on the other hand to be much more liberal in what it can countenance. It will constitute a soft or tolerant naturalism.

*See also* SUPERVENIENCE.

PHILIP PETTIT

**naturalized epistemology** This term denotes a family of views which closely tie epistemological theorizing to theorizing in the sciences. The *locus classicus* here is Quine (1969). QUINE argued that the classical FOUNDATIONALIST project was a failure, both in its details and in its conception. On the classical view, an epistemological theory would tell us how we ought to arrive at our beliefs; only by developing such a theory and then applying it could we reasonably come to believe anything about the world around us. Thus, on this classical view, an epistemological theory must be developed independently of, and prior to, any scientific theorizing; proper scientific theorizing could only occur after such a theory was developed and deployed. This was Descartes' view of how an epistemological theory ought to proceed; it was what he called FIRST PHILOSOPHY. Moreover, it is this approach to epistemological issues which motivated not only foundationalism, but virtually all epistemological theorizing for the next 300 years.

Quine urged a rejection of this approach to epistemological questions. Epistemology, on Quine's view, is a branch of natural science. It studies the relationship between human beings and their environment; in particular, it asks how it is that human beings can arrive at beliefs about the world around them on the basis of sensory stimulation, the only source of belief there is. Thus Quine commented, 'The relation between the meager input [sensory stimulation] and the torrential output [our total science] is a relation we are prompted to study for somewhat the same reasons that always prompted epistemology; namely, in order to see how evidence relates to theory, and in what ways one's theory of nature transcends any available evidence' (Quine, 1969, p. 83). Quine spoke of this projected study as 'epistemology naturalized'.

SCEPTICISM

One important difference between this approach and more traditional ones becomes plain when the two are applied to sceptical questions. On the classical view, if we are to explain how knowledge is possible, it is illegitimate to make use of the resources of science; this would simply beg the question against the sceptic by making use of the very knowledge which he calls into question. Thus, DESCARTES' attempt to answer the sceptic begins by rejecting all those beliefs about which any doubt is possible. Descartes must respond to the sceptic from a starting place which includes no beliefs at all. Naturalistic epistemologists, however, understand the demand to explain the possibility of knowledge differently. As Quine argues, sceptical questions arise from within science. It is precisely our success in understanding the world, and thus in seeing that appearance and reality may differ, that raises the sceptical question in the first place. We may thus legitimately use the resources of science to answer the question which science itself has raised. The question about how knowledge is possible should thus be construed as an empirical question: it is a question about how creatures such as we (given what our best current scientific theories tell us we are like) may come to have accurate beliefs about the world (given what our best current scientific theories tell us the world is like). Quine suggests that the Darwinian account of the origin of species gives a very general explanation of why it is that we should be well adapted to getting true beliefs about our environment (see Stich, 1990, ch. 3 for a useful discussion of this suggestion), while an examination of human psychology will fill in the details of such an account. Although Quine himself does not suggest it, investigations in the SOCIOLOGY OF KNOWLEDGE are obviously relevant here as well.

This approach to sceptical questions clearly makes them quite tractable, and its proponents see this, understandably, as an important advantage of the naturalistic approach. It is in part for this reason that current work in psychology and sociology is under such close scrutiny by many epistemologists. By the same token, the detractors of the naturalistic approach argue that this way of dealing with sceptical questions simply bypasses the very questions which philosophers have long dealt with. Far from

answering the traditional sceptical question, it is argued, the naturalistic approach merely changes the topic (see, e.g., Stroud, 1981). Debates between naturalistic epistemologists and their critics thus frequently focus on whether this new way of doing epistemology adequately answers, transforms, or simply ignores the questions which others see as central to epistemological inquiry. Some see the naturalistic approach as an attempt to abandon the philosophical study of knowledge entirely (see DEATH OF EPISTEMOLOGY).

NORMATIVITY

Precisely what the Quinean project amounts to is also a subject of some controversy. Both those who see themselves as opponents of naturalized epistemology and those who are eager to sign onto the project frequently disagree about what the project is. The essay of Quine's which prompted this controversy (Quine, 1969) leaves a great deal of room for interpretation.

At the centre of this controversy is the issue of the normative dimension of epistemological inquiry (see FACT/VALUE). Perhaps the central role which epistemological theories have traditionally played is normative. Such theories were meant not merely to describe the various processes of belief acquisition and retention, but rather to tell us which of these processes we ought to be using. By describing his preferred epistemological approach as 'a chapter of psychology and hence of natural science' (Quine, 1969, p. 82), Quine has encouraged many to interpret his view as a rejection of the normative dimension of epistemological theorizing. (See e.g. Goldman 1986, p. 2; Kim, 1988.) Quine has, however, since repudiated this reading: 'Naturalization of epistemology does not jettison the normative and settle for the indiscriminate description of ongoing procedures' (Quine, 1986, p. 664; see also Quine, 1990, pp. 19–21).

Unfortunately, matters are not quite as simple as this quotation makes things seem. Quine goes on to say, 'For me normative epistemology is a branch of engineering. It is the technology of truth-seeking. . . . There is no question here of ultimate value, as in morals; it is a matter of efficacy for an ulterior end, truth or prediction. The normative here, as elsewhere in engineering, becomes descriptive when the terminal parameter is expressed' (Quine, 1986, pp. 664–5). But this suggestion, brief as it is, is compatible with a number of different approaches.

On one approach, championed by Alvin Goldman (Goldman, 1986), knowledge is just true belief which is produced by a reliable process, that is, a process which tends to produce true beliefs (see RELIABILISM). Here the 'technological' question arises in asking which processes tend to produce true belief. Questions of this sort are clearly part of natural science. But there is also the account of knowledge itself. On Goldman's view, the claim that knowledge is reliably produced true belief is arrived at independent of, and prior to, scientific investigation; it is a product of conceptual analysis. Given Quine's rejection of appeals to meaning, the analytic/synthetic distinction, and thus the very enterprise of conceptual analysis, this position is not open to him. Nevertheless, it is for many an attractive way of allowing scientific theorizing to play a larger role in epistemology than it traditionally has, and thus one important approach which might reasonably be thought of as a naturalistic epistemology.

Those who eschew conceptual analysis will need another way of explaining how the normative dimension of epistemology arises within the context of empirical inquiry. Quine says that this normativity is not mysterious once we recognize that it 'becomes descriptive when the terminal parameter is expressed'. But why is it conduciveness to truth, rather than something else, such as survival, which is at issue here? Why is it that truth counts as the goal for which we should aim? Is this merely a sociological point, that people do seem to have this goal? Or is conduciveness to truth itself instrumental to our other goals in some way that makes it of special pragmatic importance? It is not that Quine has no way to answer these questions within the confines of the nat-

uralistic position he defines, but rather that there seem to be many different options open here, all of which need further exploration and elaboration.

A number of attempts to fill in the naturalistic account draw a close connection between how people actually reason and how they ought to reason, thereby attempting to illuminate the relation between the normative and the descriptive. One view has it that these two are identical. (For discussion of this view, see the introduction to Kornblith, 1985; Sober, 1978; see also PSYCHOLOGISM, RATIONALITY.) Some have argued that these two are, at least, far harder to distinguish than is commonly thought (Harman, 1986). Others hold that while the two are distinct, any attempt to understand how we ought to reason must proceed in part by an examination of how we do reason (Introduction to Kornblith, 1985). Finally, there are thoroughgoing pragmatic accounts, which prescribe processes of belief acquisition solely on the basis of their conduciveness to whatever we might value. (Stich, 1990). In each of these views, the alliance between epistemological theorizing and empirical considerations, especially by way of psychology, is far closer than it is on more traditional views, and it is in virtue of this that these theories are rightly spoken of as naturalistic epistemologies.

See also FIRST PHILOSOPHY; PSYCHOLOGY AND EPISTEMOLOGY; QUINE; SCEPTICISM, CONTEMPORARY.

BIBLIOGRAPHY

Cherniak, C.: *Minimal Rationality* (Cambridge, MA: Bradford Books/MIT Press, 1986).
Goldman, A.: *Epistemology and Cognition* (Cambridge, MA: Harvard University Press, 1986).
Harman, G.: *Change in View: Principles of Reasoning* (Cambridge, MA: Bradford Books/MIT Press, 1986).
Kim, J.: 'What is "naturalized epistemology"?', *Philosophical Perspectives* 2 (1988), 381–405.
Kornblith, H. ed.: *Naturalizing Epistemology* (Cambridge, MA: Bradford Books/MIT Press, 1985).
Quine, W.V.: 'Epistemology naturalized', in his

*Ontological Relativity and Other Essays* (New York: Columbia University Press, 1969), 69–90; reprinted in Kornblith, 1985.

Quine, W.V.: 'Reply to Morton White', in *The Philosophy of W. V. Quine* eds L.E. Hahn and P.A. Schilpp (La Salle: Open Court, 1986), 663–5.

Quine, W.V.: *Pursuit of Truth* (Cambridge, MA: Harvard University Press, 1990).

Sober, E.: 'Psychologism', *Journal for the Theory of Social Behavior* 8 (1978), 165–91.

Stich, S.: *The Fragmentation of Reason* (Cambridge, MA: Bradford Books/MIT Press, 1990).

Stroud, B.: 'The significance of naturalized epistemology', *Midwest Studies in Philosophy* 6 (1981), 455–71; reprinted in Kornblith, 1985.

White, M.: 'Normative ethics, normative epistemology, and Quine's holism', in *The Philosophy of W.V. Quine* eds L.E. Hahn and P.A. Schilpp (La Salle : Open Court, 1986), 649–62.

HILARY KORNBLITH

**necessary/contingent**  Necessary truths are ones which *must* be true, or whose opposite is impossible. Contingent truths are those that are not necessary and whose opposite is therefore possible. 1–3 below are necessary, 4–6, contingent.

1. It is not the case that it is raining and not raining.
2. $2 + 2 = 4$.
3. All bachelors are unmarried.
4. It seldom rains in the Sahara.
5. There are more than four states in the USA.
6. Some bachelors drive Maseratis.

Plantinga (1974, p. 2) characterizes the sense of necessity illustrated in 1–3 as 'broadly logical'. For it includes not only truths of logic, but those of mathematics, set theory, and other quasi-logical ones. Yet it is not so broad as to include matters of causal or natural necessity, such as

7. Nothing travels faster than the speed of light.

One would like an account of the basis of our

distinction and a criterion by which to apply it. Some suppose that necessary truths are those we know a priori. But we lack a criterion for a priori truths, and there are necessary truths we don't know at all (e.g. undiscovered mathematical ones). It won't help to say that necessary truths are ones it is *possible*, in the broadly logical sense, to know a priori, for this is circular. Finally, Kripke (1972, p. 253) and Plantinga (1974, p. 8) argue that some contingent truths are knowable a priori (*see* A PRIORI KNOWLEDGE). Similar problems face the suggestion that necessary truths are the ones we know with CERTAINTY: we lack a criterion for certainty; there are necessary truths we don't know; and (barring dubious arguments for scepticism) it is reasonable to suppose that we know some contingent truths with certainty.

LEIBNIZ defined a necessary truth as one whose opposite implies a contradiction. Every such proposition, he held, is either an explicit identity (i.e. of the form 'A is A', 'AB is B', etc.) or is reducible to an identity by successively substituting equivalent terms. (Thus, 3 above might be so reduced by substituting 'unmarried man' for 'bachelor'.) This has several advantages over the ideas of the previous paragraph. First, it *explicates* the notions of necessity and possibility and seems to provide a criterion we can apply. Second, because explicit identities are self-evident a priori propositions, the theory implies that all necessary truths are knowable a priori, but it does not entail that we actually know all of them, nor does it define 'knowable' in a circular way. Third, it implies that necessary truths are knowable with certainty, but does not preclude our having certain knowledge of contingent truths by means other than a reduction.

Nevertheless, this view is also problematic. Leibniz's examples of reductions are too sparse to prove a claim about *all* necessary truths. Some of his reductions, moreover, are deficient: Frege has pointed out, for example, that his proof of '$2 + 2 = 4$' presupposes the principle of association and so does not depend only on the principle of identity. More generally, it has been shown that arithmetic cannot be reduced to logic, but requires the resources of set theory as well. Finally, there are other necessary propositions (e.g. 'Nothing can be red and green all over') which do not *seem* to be reducible to identities and which Leibniz does not show how to reduce.

Leibniz and others have thought of truth as a property of propositions, where the latter are conceived as things which may be expressed by, but are distinct from, linguistic items like statements. On another approach, truth is a property of linguistic entities, and the basis of necessary truth is convention. Thus A.J. AYER, for example, argued that the only necessary truths are analytic statements and that the latter rest entirely on our commitment to use words in certain ways (*see* LOGICAL POSITIVISM). But while there have been many attempts to define analyticity, QUINE has criticized the most powerful ones and rendered it uncertain whether a criterion for this notion can be given.

When one predicates necessary truth of a proposition one speaks of modality *de dicto*. For one ascribes the modal property, *necessary truth*, to a *dictum*, namely, whatever proposition is taken as necessary. A venerable tradition, however, distinguishes this from necessity *de re*, wherein one predicates *necessary* or *essential possession* of some property to an *object*. For example, the statement '4 is necessarily greater than 2' might be used to predicate of the object, 4, the property, *being necessarily greater than 2*. That objects have some of their properties necessarily, or essentially, and others only contingently, or accidentally, is a main part of the doctrine called 'essentialism'. Thus, an essentialist might say that Socrates had the property of *being bald* accidentally, but that of *being self-identical*, or perhaps of *being human*, essentially. Although essentialism has been vigorously attacked in recent years, most particularly by Quine, it also has able contemporary proponents, such as Plantinga.

*See also* A PRIORI/A POSTERIORI; A PRIORI KNOWLEDGE; ANALYTICITY; LOGICAL POSTIVISM; MODAL KNOWLEDGE; TRUTHS OF REASON/OF FACT.

BIBLIOGRAPHY

Hamlyn, D.W.: 'Necessary and contingent statements', in *The Encyclopedia of Philosophy* ed. P. Edwards (New York: Macmillan and the Free Press, 1967), vol. 2, 198–205.

Kripke, S.: 'Naming and necessity', in *Semantics of Natural Language* ed. D. Davidson and G. Harman (Dordrecht: Reidel, 1972), 253–355.

Plantinga, A.: *The Nature of Necessity* (Oxford: Oxford University Press, 1974).

Quine, W.V.: *Word and Object* (Cambridge, MA: MIT Press, 1960).

Wilson, M.D.: *Leibniz' Doctrine of Necessary Truth* (New York: Garland, 1990).

DAVID BLUMENFELD

**necessity, modal knowledge** Philosophers have traditionally held that every proposition has a *modal status* as well as a *truth value*. Every proposition is either necessary or contingent as well as either true or false (*see* NECESSARY/CONTINGENT). The issue of knowledge of the modal status of propositions has received much attention because of its intimate relationship to the issue of a priori knowledge. For example, many proponents of the a priori contend that all knowledge of necessary propositions is a priori (*see* A PRIORI KNOWLEDGE). Others reject this claim by citing Kripke's (1980) alleged cases of necessary a posteriori propositions (*see* A PRIORI/A POSTERIORI). Such contentions are often inconclusive, for they fail to take into account the following tripartite distinction: S knows the *general modal status* of p just in case S knows that p is a necessary proposition or S knows that p is a contingent proposition. S knows the *truth value* of p just in case S knows that p is true or S knows that p is false. S knows the *specific modal status* of p just in case S knows that p is necessarily true or S knows that p is necessarily false or S knows that p is contingently true or S knows that p is contingently false. It does not follow from the fact that knowledge of the general modal status of a proposition is a priori that knowledge of its specific modal status is also a priori. Nor does it follow from the fact that knowledge of the specific modal status of a proposition is a posteriori that knowledge of its general modal status is also a posteriori.

BIBLIOGRAPHY

Casullo, A.: 'Kripke on the *a priori* and the necessary', *Analysis* 37 (1977), 152–9; reprinted in Moser, 1987.
Kitcher, P.: 'Apriority and necessity', *Australasian Journal of Philosophy* 58 (1980), 89–101; reprinted in Moser, 1987.
Kripke, S.: *Naming and Necessity* (Cambridge, MA: Harvard University Press, 1980); excerpted in Moser, 1987.
Moser, P. ed.: *A Priori Knowledge* (Oxford: Oxford University Press, 1987).
Swinburne, R.G.: 'Analyticity, necessity, and apriority', *Mind* 84 (1975), 225–43; reprinted in Moser, 1987.

ALBERT CASULLO

**Neoplatonism** This is the conventional designation for the revived form of Platonism inspired by Plotinus (205–70 AD) and popularised by Porphyry (233–c.305) and Iamblichus (c.245–c.326). Its most important later figures were the Athenian philosophers Syrianus (d. c.437), Proclus (412–85) and Damascius (c.462–after 538), as well as the Aristotelian commentators Ammonius (late fifth–early sixth century), and Simplicius and Philoponus (younger contemporaries of Damascius). The last major figure in Greek Neoplatonism was Olympiodorus of Alexandria (late sixth century), but Neoplatonism continued to exercise a major influence on Arabic and Latin medieval philosophy.

Neoplatonists were largely unconcerned with questions about knowledge of the sensible world and with the debates over justification of knowledge – claims that had been prominent earlier in Greek philosophy. Nevertheless they did have views about the nature and origin of knowledge. They were less interested in the nature of empirical knowledge than in theoretical knowledge: Plotinus' only references to sceptical

arguments come in discussions of Intellect's relation to the Ideas (*Enn.* V.5.1; V.3.5). Their most explicit texts on the nature of empirical knowledge are found in Plotinus (V.5.2–3; V.3.4–5: cf. also I.6.3, I.3.5 and IV.4.22–3) and Porphyry (*Commentary on Ptolemy* pp. 13–14, Düring), both of whom are following earlier tradition. There are also important discussions of cognition in Proclus' commentary on the *Timaeus*, and we would know considerably more about Neoplatonist epistemology if anything of Proclus' commentary on Plato's *Theaetetus* had survived. Plotinus' account of empirical knowledge, which is presumably typical, is based on Plato's theory of recollection (*see* ANAMNESIS), and has important connections with the view of recollection found in earlier Platonist texts (Cicero, *Tusculan Disputations* I.57–8; Albinus, *Didaskalikos* §4 and §25; Plutarch *apud* Olympiodorus, *Commentary on the Gorgias* p. 156).

According to Plotinus one judges a sensible thing to have a certain attribute by comparing it, i.e. its abstracted sensible form (here following ARISTOTLE's theory of perception, except that the soul does not actually receive the form) with an apparently innate standard in the soul (V.3.3), which is conceived as a trace or reflection of the corresponding Idea. Mistaken judgements can be accounted for, as in the Wax Tablet analogy of the *Theaetetus*, as mismatches due to the trace or standard's initially being confused or obscure. These traces in the soul are identified with the so-called common or natural conceptions, concepts or beliefs about the natures of things that are innate or develop naturally and hence are shared by all or nearly all human beings (e.g. *Enn.* VI.5.1 *init*; cf. Sallustius, *De diis et mundo* §1).

Theoretical knowledge or understanding, identified with the grasp of Platonic Ideas, is attained by a reflective process of clarifying or 'articulating' these initially confused innate traces or conceptions (*Enn.* I.2.4, 18ff.; cf. Porphyry *On Abstinence* I.31.2 and *To Marcella* §10). One who has reached such understanding has come to participate directly in Intellect, an eternal mental act whose content is the Ideas. False theoretical beliefs on such a view are mere opinions, belonging to a lower cognitive level: Intellect by definition is always correct (*Enn.* I.1.9,12). Indeed, Plotinus asserts that Intellect's thinking, which is the Ideas, is identical with Truth itself (V.5.1–2). Correct theoretical judgements are therefore not true *of* independently existing entities, but rather true thoughts *are* those entities. This is inspired by Aristotle's theory of the nature of Intellect (*De Anima* III.4, 430a 3–4), though Plotinus does not go so far as to identify Intellect as opposed to its acts of thought with their objects. Plotinus thus holds a non-correspondence, direct realist view of theoretical truth. Truth is in turn identified with real Being, conceived as the system of interrelated ideas, which may be investigated by Platonic dialectic (*Enn.* I.3.4; VI.2.19–22). Other Neoplatonists did not disagree with this basic picture; they also agreed with Plotinus that what is prior to Intellect, which Plotinus called the One or the Good, is ineffable and unknowable though like him they persisted in efforts to indicate something of its nature. Such issues, with which they were deeply concerned, involve something higher than mere rational knowledge, though they have implications for its status. It must be said that the Neoplatonists were no more successful than was Plato in explaining how theoretical knowledge, conceived as having special, separate objects, could apply to the sensible world. Indeed apart from Plotinus (VI.7.1–14) they did not much occupy themselves with this problem.

BIBLIOGRAPHY

*Texts*

Alcinous: *Enseignement des Doctrines de Platon* [*Didaskalikos*], ed. J. Whittaker and P. Louis (Paris: 1990).

Olympiodorus: *In Platonis Gorgiam Commentaria* ed. W. Norvin (Leipzig: 1936).

Plotinus: *Enneads* 7 vols trans. A.H. Armstrong (Cambridge, MA: Loeb Classical Library, 1966–88).

Porphyry: *De l'Abstinence* Book 1, ed. J. Bouffartigue and M. Patillon (Paris: 1977).

Porphyry: *Lettre à Marcella*, ed. E. des Places (Paris: 1982).

Porphyry: *Kommentar zur Harmonielehre des Ptolemaios* ed. I. Düring (Göteborg: 1932); (reprinted New York: 1979).

Proclus: *Commentaire sur le Timée* 5 vols, trans. A.J. Festugière (Paris: 1966–8).

Sallustius: *Concerning the Gods and the Universe* ed. A.D. Nock (Cambridge: 1936).

*Secondary sources*

Blumenthal, H.J.: 'Plotin and Proclus on the criterion of truth', in *The Criterion of Truth: Essays Written in Honour of George Kerferd*, eds P. Huby and G. Neal (Liverpool: 1989).

Lloyd, A.C.: *The Anatomy of Neoplatonism* (Oxford: 1990), ch. 6.

Wallis, R.T.: *Neoplatonism* (London: 1972).

S. STRANGE

**Neurath, Otto (1882–1945)** Austrian philosopher. Neurath was one of the leading LOGICAL POSITIVISTS, whose major work was in sociology, economics and scientific method. He wanted to accord sociology an empirical scientific status, and hoped for the development of a unified, physicalist, scientific language which excluded all imprecision and unverifiable metaphysics. This aspiration led him in the 1930s to plan the *International Encyclopedia of Unified Science*, but only the first two introductory volumes ever appeared. As Passmore (1968) says, 'his philosophical position was never worked out in detail: agitation was his *forte*.'

There was a tension in logical positivism between EMPIRICISM on the one hand, and physicalism and the goal of the 'unity of science' on the other. Neurath was never attracted to the empiricist, FOUNDATIONALIST strand; from the start, he insisted on the possibility of intersubjective confirmation afforded by a physicalist as opposed to a PHENOMENALIST language. This advocacy of a robust physicalism led him, in 'Protocol Sentences' (1932–3), to reject the 'methodological' approach to competing metaphysical standpoints advocated in CARNAP's *Der logische Aufbau der Welt* (1928).

Neurath's most important contribution to epistemology, however, lies in his advocacy of COHERENTISM and HOLISM, which seemed to follow from his physicalist rejection of foundationalism. In his (1931–2), he argued (albeit laconically) that *'statements are compared with statements*, not with "experiences", "the world", or anything else', And in 'Sociology and Physicalism' (1932–3) he argued further that 'no sentence enjoys the *noli me tangere* which Carnap ordains for PROTOCOL SENTENCES'. In a celebrated metaphor, he compared science to a boat: 'There is no way of taking conclusively established pure protocol sentences as the starting point of the sciences. . . . We are like sailors who must rebuild their ship on the open sea, never able to dismantle it in dry-dock and to reconstruct it there out of the best materials.' These views were criticized by SCHLICK (1934), who called the 'coherence theory of truth' an 'astounding error', and vigorously affirmed the foundational role of an obscure class of unrevisable *Konstatierungen* or quasi-judgements of immediate experience.

This debate between the 'right' and 'left' wings of the Vienna Circle probably generated more heat than light. Neurath and his supporters ended up by abandoning the distinction between basic and non-basic classes of knowledge-claims; Schlick (1935) issued the 'gentle warning of a true empiricist', criticizing this move as 'rationalistic'. Carnap, who always liked to think that everyone was in agreement really, urged a compromise in 'Truth and Conformation' (1935). Rejecting the idea of certain knowledge of basic sentences, Carnap maintained that 'the confrontation of statements with observations' was central to logical empiricism. At least partly because of his social science background, Neurath, unlike the other logical positivists, was ready to endorse a naturalistic picture of philosophy as a branch of empirical (perhaps social) science rather than seeing it as the 'logic of science'. His views look forward to the NATURALIZED EPISTEMOLOGY of QUINE, who extended Neurath's holism to cover logical, mathematical and ANALYTIC truths in general.

*See also* PROTOCOL SENTENCES.

WRITINGS

'Sociology and physicalism', *Erkenntnis* 2 (1931–2); in A.J. Ayer (ed.) *Logical Positivism* (New York: Free Press, 1959).
'Protokollsatze', *Erkenntnis* 3 (1932–3); trans. as 'Protocol Sentences' in A.J. Ayer (ed.) *Logical Positivism* (New York: Free Press, 1959).
*Otto Neurath, Empiricism and Sociology* ed. M. Neurath and R. Cohen (Dordrecht: Reidel, 1973).

BIBLIOGRAPHY

Carnap, R.: *Der logische Aufbau der Welt* (1928); trans. as *The Logical Structure of the World* (Berkeley: University of California Press, 1967).
Carnap, R.: 'Truth and confirmation' (1935), trans. and adapted in H. Feigl and W. Sellars (eds.) *Readings in Philosophical Analysis* (New York: Appleton-Century-Crofts, 1949).
Jacob, P.: 'The Neurath–Schlick controversy', *Fundamenta Scientiae* 5 (1984), 351–66.
For articles by Schlick, *see* the bibliography to SCHLICK.

ANDY HAMILTON

**Nietzsche, Friedrich (1844–1900)** German philosopher and writer. Nietzsche is openly pessimistic about the possibility of knowledge: 'We simply lack any organ for knowledge, for "truth": we "know" (or believe or imagine) just as much as may be *useful* in the interests of the human herd, the species: and even what is here called "utility" is ultimately also a mere belief, something imaginary and perhaps precisely that most calamitous stupidity of which we shall perish some day' (*The Gay Science*, 354).

This position is very radical. Nietzsche does not simply deny that knowledge, construed as the adequate representation of the world by the intellect, exists. He also refuses the PRAGMATIST identification of knowledge and truth with usefulness: he writes that we think we know what we think is useful, and that we can be quite wrong about the latter.

Nietzsche's view, his 'perspectivism', depends on his claim that there is no sensible conception of a world independent of human interpretation and to which interpretations would correspond if they were to constitute knowledge. He sums up this highly controversial position in *The Will to Power*: 'Facts are precisely what there is not, only interpretations' (481).

It is often claimed that perspectivism is self-undermining. If the thesis that all views are interpretations is true then, it is argued, there is at least one view that is not an interpretation. If, on the other hand, the thesis is itself an interpretation, then there is no reason to believe that it is true, and it follows again that not every view is an interpretation.

But this refutation assumes that if a view (in this case, perspectivism itself) is an interpretation it is *ipso facto* wrong. This is not the case. To call any view, including perspectivism, an interpretation is to say that it can be wrong, which is true of all views, and that is not a sufficient refutation. To show the perspectivism is actually false it is necessary to produce another view superior to it on specific epistemological grounds.

Perspectivism does not deny that particular views can be true. Like some versions of contemporary anti-realism, it attributes to specific approaches truth in relation to facts specified internally by those approaches themselves. But it refuses to envisage a single independent set of facts, to be accounted for by all theories. Thus Nietzsche grants the truth of specific scientific theories; he does, however, deny that a scientific interpretation can possibly be 'the only justifiable interpretation of the world' (*The Gay Science*, 354): neither the facts science addresses nor the methods it employs are privileged. Scientific theories serve the purposes for which they have been devised: but these have no priority over the many other purposes of human life.

The existence of many purposes and needs relative to which the value of theories is established–another crucial element of perspectivism–is sometimes thought to imply a rampant RELATIVISM, according to which no standards for evaluating purposes and theories can be devised. This is correct only in that Nietzsche denies the existence of a single set of standards for determining epistemic value once and for all. But he holds that *specific* views can be compared with and evaluated in relation to one another. The ability to use criteria acceptable in particular circumstances does not presuppose the existence of criteria applicable in all. Agreement is therefore not always possible, since individuals may sometimes differ over the most fundamental issues dividing them.

But Nietzsche would not be troubled by this fact, which his opponents too also have to confront only, as he would argue, to suppress it by insisting on the hope that all disagreements are in principle eliminable even if our practice falls woefully short of the ideal. Nietzsche abandons that ideal. He considers irresoluble disagreement an essential part of human life.

*See also* CONTINENTAL EPISTEMOLOGY.

WRITINGS

*Jenseits von Gut und Böse* (Leipzig, 1886); trans. W. Kaufmann *Beyond Good and Evil* (New York: Random House, 1966).

*Die fröliche Wissenschaft* (Leipzig, 1887); trans. W. Kaufmann *The Gay Science* (New York: Random House, 1974).

*Zur Genealogie der Moral* (Leipzig, 1887); trans. W. Kaufmann and R.J. Hollingdale *On the Genealogy of Morals* (New York: Random House, 1969).

*Der Wille zur Macht* ed. E. Förster-Nietzsche (Leipzig, 1906); trans. W. Kaufmann and R.J. Hollingdale *The Will to Power* (New York: Random House, 1968).

BIBLIOGRAPHY

Clark, M.: *Nietzsche on Truth and Philosophy* (Cambridge: Cambridge University Press, 1990).

Danto, A.C.: *Nietzsche as Philosopher* (New York: Macmillan, 1965).

Kaufmann, W.: *Nietzsche: Philosopher, Psychologist, Antichrist* (Princeton: Princeton University Press, 1974).

Nehamas, A.: *Nietzsche: Life as Literature* (Cambridge, MA: Harvard University Press, 1985).

ALEXANDER NEHAMAS

**nihilism**  *see* DEATH OF EPISTEMOLOGY.

**noumenal/phenomenal**  In the philosophy of KANT, the terms 'noumena' and 'phenomena' are coextensive (though not exactly synonymous) with the terms 'things in themselves' and 'appearances'. Things in themselves are things as they exist independently of human cognition; appearances are things that exist only as contents or objects of sensible representations. (*See* A491/B519–A494/B522. Numbers preceded by 'A' and 'B' are references to pages in the first and second editions respectively of Kant's *Critique of Pure Reason*.) The adjectives 'noumenal' and 'phenomenal' have therefore come to mark the distinction between those entities or aspects of reality that exist independently of human cognition and those that exist only in relation to it. How much of the world is noumenal, how much phenomenal, and the extent to which the noumenal portion can be known are, of course, central questions of philosophy.

Some of Kant's major views about noumena and phenomena may be listed as follows. (1) There certainly is a noumenal element in the world; otherwise 'we should be landed in the absurd conclusion that there can be appearance without anything that appears' (Bxxvii). (2) The noumenal element in some way affects us, giving rise to the representations through which phenomena are presented and constituted. (*See* e.g. A190/B235 and *Prolegomena* pp. 61–2.) (3) More of the world's features fall on the phenomenal side of the line than either Descartes or Locke believed. In particular, space and time (and thus nearly all of Locke's PRIMARY QUALITIES) are merely phenomenal, space and time being 'forms of intuition' rather than features of things in themselves. Kant called this view 'transcendental idealism'. (A26/B42–A28/B44; *Prolegomena* pp. 36–7.) (4) Things in themselves are unknowable by human beings (A30/B45, A44/B62). We can have knowledge only concerning what is given in intuition (roughly, perception or introspection), and things in themselves are not thus given. So for human beings, things in themselves are

not noumena in the positive (and etymological) sense of entities knowable by *nous*, or pure intelligence; they are noumena only in the negative sense of entities not knowable by sensible means. (For the distinction between the positive and the negative senses of 'noumenon', *see* B307–9.)

Kant's combination of views has struck many of his readers as highly problematic. Two notorious problems are the following: (1) If things in themselves are unknowable, how can Kant be in a position to affirm that they are outside of space and time, or indeed, that they exist at all? (2) If things in themselves are non-spatial and non-temporal, what sense can we make of the supposition that they cause our representations? To answer (1), Kant would have to qualify the claim that there can be no knowledge concerning things in themselves. He did certainly think that the non-spatiality and non-temporality of things in themselves could be proved, by the following considerations among others: if noumena were spatial and temporal, there would be no accounting for our a priori knowledge of arithmetical and geometrical truths (A46/B64–A49/B66); nor would there be any way of avoiding certain antinomies, e.g. that the world both does and does not have a beginning in time. (*See* the chapter of the *Critique of Pure Reason* entitled 'The Antinomy of Pure Reason'.) As for (2), Kant himself insisted that things in themselves cannot *cause* appearances, causation being a concept applicable only to phenomena in time, but he maintained none the less that things in themselves are in some mysterious sense the *ground* of appearances (A380).

Not satisfied with these answers, Post-Kantian German philosophers tended to jettison the thing in itself, moving closer to pure IDEALISM. Others, including the British realists beginning with MOORE, reinvested the thing in itself with the features that Kant had stripped away.

What has been said so far suggests that noumena and phenomena are for Kant two distinct realms of objects. This is the traditional interpretation of Kant, but it is a view now in disfavour among many Kant scholars. The main opposing view, sometimes called the 'one world' or 'double aspect' view, holds instead that there is only one set of objects, but two ways of considering them or talking about them (Allison, 1983). To talk of appearances is to talk of objects as we know them; to talk of things in themselves is to talk of these same objects as they are independently of our knowledge. Kant's transcendental idealism then comes to this: things have certain features (e.g. spatial form) *qua* appearances that they lack *in themselves*.

But how can the same things be both spatial and non-spatial? If we omit the qualifying phrases '*qua* appearances' and 'in themselves', we get a contradiction; how does retaining the qualifiers avoid the contradiction? This is a question that proponents of the one-world view have not adequately addressed (Van Cleve, 1992). Another problem for the view is that Kant believes that there are certain principles, for example, Leibniz's principle of the identity of indiscernibles, that hold for noumena but not for phenomena (A264/B320; A272/B328). For a one-worlder, this apparently has the following implication: A and B, if indiscernible, will be identical *qua* noumena, but distinct *qua* phenomena. How can that be?

The traditional two-worlds interpretation (which treats appearances as existents distinct from mental representings, though dependent on them) also gives rise to problems. For one thing, some real existents, namely appearances, would be in space and time, a result apparently ruled out by Kant's argument in the antinomies (Moore, 1953, ch. 9). For another, if appearances are entities genuinely distinct from the acts that apprehend them, it becomes difficult to see why they should have to 'conform to our knowledge' in the manner required by the Copernican Revolution (for which, *see* KANT).

There is a third interpretation that seeks to avoid the problems besetting the first two. According to it, phenomena are not the same objects as noumena, considered from a specially human viewpoint; nor are they a second class of objects existing alongside noumena. Instead, they are what we might call *virtual objects*. A virtual object is similar to what BRENTANO called an 'intentional object', except that it is not to be conceived as having its own special kind of being. Instead, to say that a virtual object of a certain sort (e.g. a patch of red) exists is shorthand for saying that a certain kind of representation occurs; in the case of a more complex virtual object (e.g. a house or a ship), it is to say that an entire rule-governed sequence of representations occurs or is in the offing. According to this suggestion, Kant's transcendental idealism is a form of PHENOMENALISM. Unlike some phenomenalists, however, Kant was also a noumenalist: he believed there are some objects, the things in themselves, that resist phenomenalist reduction. (If nothing else, there are the cognitive acts and agents to which phenomena are reduced, for these can hardly be supposed to exist only as the virtual objects of further acts.)

The third view gets between the alternatives of one world versus two. In a sense there are two worlds, because noumena and phenomena constitute separate domains of discourse rather than two ways of discoursing about the same entities; but in a sense there is only one, since phenomena are logical constructions out of noumenal beings and their states rather than things existing in their own right.

Interesting comparisons of Kant's views about noumena and phenomena with recent developments in anti-realist philosophy may be found in Putnam (1981, ch. 3) and Posy (1983).

*See also* IN ITSELF/FOR ITSELF ; PRIMARY AND SECONDARY QUALITIES.

BIBLIOGRAPHY

Kant, I.: *Critique of Pure Reason* (1781) trans. N. Kemp Smith (London: Macmillan, 1964).
Kant, I.: *Prolegomena to Any Future Metaphysics* (1783) trans. L.W. Beck (Indianapolis: Bobbs-Merrill, 1950).
Allison, H.: *Kant's Transcendental Idealism* (New Haven: Yale University Press, 1973).
Ameriks, K.: 'Recent work on Kant's theoretical

philosophy', *American Philosophical Quarterly* 19 (1982), 1–24.

Aquila, R.: 'Things in themselves and appearances: intentionality and reality in Kant', *Archiv für Geschichte der Philosophie* 61 (1979), 293–307.

Kemp Smith, N.: *A Commentary on Kant's Critique of Pure Reason* 2nd edn (London: Macmillan, 1923).

Moore, G.E.: *Some Main Problems of Philosophy* (London: Macmillan, 1953).

Posy, C.: 'Dancing to the antinomy', *American Philosophical Quarterly* 20 (1983), 81–94.

Prauss, G.: *Kant und das Problem der Dinge an sich* (Bonn: Bouvier, 1974).

Putnam, H.: *Reason, Truth, and History* (Cambridge: Cambridge University Press, 1981).

Strawson, P.F.: *The Bounds of Sense* (London: Methuen, 1966).

Van Cleve, J.: 'Geometry, Transcendental Idealism, and Kant's Two Worlds', forthcoming in the North American Kant Society Studies in Philosophy Series.

JAMES VAN CLEVE

**Nyāya** The Nyāya system of philosophy (traceable to Gotama's *Nyāyasūtras* (*c.*150 AD) and Vatsyāyana's commentary (fourth century AD) on them, developed by a host of brilliant authors such as Uddyotakara (sixth century AD), Vacaspati (ninth century AD) and Udayana (eleventh century AD) developed a theory of *pramāṇas*, i.e. means of true cognition. The Neo-Nyāya school founded by Gaṅgeśa (fourteenth century AD) developed a technical language for analysing the structure of propositional cognitions whose objects are relational complexes of the form *aRb*. Here *a* is the qualificandum, and *b* is the qualifier; *aRb* is a complex term, not a proposition. For the mode of cognition, the system introduced the idea of 'limitor' (*avacchedaka*). The cognition expressed in the term 'a brown jar' has as its qualificandum the thing jar and as its qualifier the brown colour. In this case, the qualifierness (*prakāratā*) is limited by brownness and the relation of inherence (*samavāya*), and as so limited it determines the qualificandumness limited by jarness. This pattern of analysis is employed to elaborate/analyse and develop the structures of various kinds of cognitions.

*See also* INDIAN EPISTEMOLOGY.

BIBLIOGRAPHY

Annambhatta: *Tarkasamgraha*, trans. with notes by G. Bhattacharya (Calcutta: Progressive Publishers, 1976).

Bhattacharya, S.: 'Some features of the technical language of Navya-Nyaya', *Philosophy East & West* 40, (1990), 129–40.

Chattopadhyaya, D. and Gangopadhyaya, M.: *Nyaya Philosophy with Vatsyayana Bhasya* (Calcutta, 1975).

Visvanatha: *Bhasaparichheda* with *Karikavali*, trans. S. Madhavananda (Calcutta, 1951).

J.N. MOHANTY

# O

objective/subjective  The contrast between the subjective and the objective is made in both the epistemic and the ontological domains. In the former it is often identified with the distinction between the *intra*personal and the *inter*personal, or with that between matters whose resolution depends on the psychology of the person in question and those not thus dependent, or, sometimes, with the distinction between the biased and the impartial. Thus, an objective question might be one answerable by a method usable by any competent investigator, while a subjective question would be answerable only from the questioner's point of view. In the ontological domain, the subjective–objective contrast is often between what is and what is not mind-dependent; secondary qualities, e.g. colours, have been thought subjective owing to their apparent variability with observation conditions. The truth of a proposition, for instance (apart from certain propositions about oneself), would be objective if it is independent of the perspective, especially the beliefs, of those judging it. Truth would be subjective if it lacks such independence, say because it is a construct from justified beliefs, e.g. those well-confirmed by observations.

One notion of objectivity might be basic and the other derivative. If the epistemic notion is basic, then the criteria for objectivity in the ontological sense derive from considerations of justification: an objective question is one answerable by a procedure that yields (adequate) *justification* for one's answer; and mind-independence is a matter of amenability to such a method. If, on the other hand, the ontological notion is basic, the criteria for an interpersonal method and its objective use are a matter of its mind-independence and tendency to lead to objective truth, say its applying to external objects and yielding predictive success. Since the use of these criteria requires employing the methods which, on the epistemic conception, define objectivity – most notably scientific methods – but no similar dependence obtains in the other direction, the epistemic notion is often taken as basic.

In epistemology, the subjective–objective contrast arises above all for the concept of justification and its relatives. EXTERNALISM, particularly RELIABILISM, construes justification objectivistically, since, for reliabilism, truth-conduciveness (non-subjectively conceived) is central for justified belief. Internalism may or may not construe justification subjectivistically, depending on whether the proposed epistemic standards are interpersonally grounded (say, a priori). There are also various kinds of subjectivity; justification may, e.g., be grounded in one's considered standards or simply in what one believes to be sound. On the former view, my justified beliefs accord with my considered standards whether or not I think them justified; on the latter, my thinking them justified makes it so.

Any conception of objectivity may treat one domain as fundamental and the others derivatively. Thus, objectivity for methods (including sensory observation) might be thought basic. Let an objective method be one that is (1) interpersonally usable and tends to yield justification regarding the questions to which it applies (an epistemic conception), or (2) tends to yield truth when properly applied (an ontological conception), or (3) both. Then an objective person is one who appropriately uses objective methods; an objective statement is one appraisable by an objective method; an objective discipline is one whose methods are objective; and so on. Typically, those who conceive objectivity epistemically tend to take methods as fundamental; those who conceive it ontologically tend to take statements as basic.

See also IN ITSELF/FOR ITSELF; NOUMENAL/PHENOMENAL; OBJECTIVITY; PRIMARY AND SECONDARY QUALITIES; SUBJECTIVITY.

BIBLIOGRAPHY

Audi, R.: 'Scientific objectivity and the evaluation of hypotheses', in The Philosophy of Logical Mechanism ed. M.H. Salmon (Dordrecht: Kluwer, 1990).
Chisholm, R.M.: The Foundations of Knowing (Minneapolis: University of Minnesota Press, 1982).
Foley, R.: The Theory of Epistemic Rationality (Cambridge, MA: Harvard University Press, 1987).
Nagel, E.: The Structure of Science (New York: Harcourt, Brace, and World, 1961).
Weber, M.: The Methodology of the Social Sciences (Glencoe: Free Press, 1949).

ROBERT AUDI

**objectivity** Among the various notions of objectivity that philosophers have investigated and employed, two can claim to be fundamental.

On the one hand, there is a straightforwardly ontological concept: something is objective if it exists, and is the way it is, independently of any knowledge, perception, conception or consciousness there may be of it. Obvious candidates here include plants, rocks, atoms, galaxies and other material denizens of the external world. Less obvious candidates include such things as numbers, sets, propositions, primary qualities, facts, time and space. Subjective entities, conversely, will be those which could not exist or be the way they are if they were not known, perceived or at least conceived by one or more conscious beings. Such things as sensations, dreams, memories, secondary qualities, aesthetic properties, and moral values have been construed as subjective in this sense. (I shall call this ontological notion O-objectivity.)

There is, on the other hand, a notion of objectivity that belongs primarily within epistemology. According to this conception, the objective/subjective distinction is not intended to mark a split in reality between autonomous and dependent entities, but serves rather to distinguish two grades of cognitive achievement. In this sense only such things as judgements, beliefs, theories, concepts and perceptions can significantly be said to be objective or subjective. Here objectivity can be construed as a property of the contents of mental acts and states. We might say, for example, that a belief that the speed of light is 187,000 miles per second, or that Leeds is to the north of Sheffield, has an objective content; a judgement that rice pudding is disgusting, on the other hand, or that Beethoven is a greater artist than Mozart, will be merely subjective. (I shall call this epistemological concept E-objectivity.)

If E-objectivity is to be a property of contents of mental acts and states, then at this point we clearly need to specify which property it is to be. This is a delicate matter; for what we require here is a minimal concept of objectivity, one that will be neutral with respect to the competing and sometimes contentious philosophical theories which attempt to specify what objectivity is. In principle this neutral concept will then be capable of comprising the pre-theoretical datum to which the various competing theories of objectivity are themselves addressed, as attempts to supply an analysis and explanation. Perhaps the best notion is one that exploits Kant's insight that E-objectivity entails what he calls 'presumptive universality': for a judgement to be objective it must at least possess a content that 'may be presupposed to be valid for all men.' (See Kant, 1953, §19).

It is worth noting that an entity that is O-subjective can be the subject of E-objective judgements and beliefs. For example, on most accounts colours are O-subjective: in the analysis of the property of being red, say, there will occur ineliminable appeal to the perceptions and judgements of normal observers under normal conditions. And yet the judgement that a given object is red is an entirely objective one. Rather more bizarrely,

Kant argued that space was nothing more than the form of inner sense, and so was O-subjective. And yet the propositions of geometry, the science of space, are for Kant the very paradigms of E-objectivity; for they are necessarily, universally and objectively true. One of the liveliest debates in recent years (in logic, set theory, the foundations of mathematics, the philosophy of science, semantics and the philosophy of language) concerns precisely this issue: does the E-objectivity of a given class of assertions require the O-objectivity of the entities those assertions apparently invoke or range over? By and large, theories that answer this question in the affirmative can be called *realist*; those that defend a negative answer, *anti-realist*.

One intuition that lies at the heart of the REALIST's account of objectivity is that, in the last analysis, the objectivity of a belief is to be explained by appeal to the independent existence of the entities it concerns: E-objectivity, that is, is to be analysed in terms of O-objectivity. A judgement or belief is E-objective if and only if it stands in some specified relation to an independently existing, determinate reality. FREGE, for example, believed that arithmetic could comprise objective knowledge only if the numbers it refers to, the propositions it consists of, the functions it employs, and the truth-values it aims at, are all mind-independent entities. And conversely, within a realist framework, to show that the members of a given class of judgements are merely subjective, it is sufficient to show that there exists no independent reality that those judgements characterize or refer to. Thus J.L. Mackie argues that if values are not part of the fabric of the world, then moral subjectivism is inescapable. For the realist, then, E-objectivity is to be elucidated by appeal to the existence of determinate facts, objects, properties, events, and the like, which exist or obtain independently of any cognitive access we may have to them. And one of the strongest impulses towards platonic realism – the theoretical commitment to the existence of abstract objects like sets, numbers, and propositions – stems from the widespread belief that only if

such things exist in their own right can we allow that logic, arithmetic, and science are indeed objective (*see* MATHEMATICAL KNOWLEDGE).

This picture is rejected by anti-realists. The possibility that our beliefs and theories are objectively true is not, according to them, capable of being rendered intelligible by invoking the nature and existence of reality as it is in and of itself. If our conception of E-objectivity is minimal, requiring only 'presumptive universality', then alternative, non-realist analyses of it can seem possible – and even attractive. Such analyses have construed the objectivity of an arbitrary judgement as a function of its coherence with other judgements, of its possession of grounds that warrant it, of its acceptance within a given community, of its conformity to the a priori rules that constitute understanding, of its verifiability (or falsifiability), or of its permanent presence in the mind of God. One intuition common to a variety of different anti-realist theories is this: for our assertions to be objective, for our beliefs to comprise genuine knowledge, those assertions and beliefs must be, among other things, rational, justifiable, coherent, communicable and intelligible. But it is hard, the anti-realist claims, to see how such properties as these can be explained by appeal to entities 'as they are in and of themselves'; for it is not on the basis of their relation to any such things as these that our assertions become intelligible, say, or justifiable. On the contrary, according to most forms of anti-realism, it is only on the basis of O-subjective notions like 'the way reality seems to us', 'the evidence that is available to us', 'the criteria we apply', 'the experiences we undergo' or 'the concepts we have acquired' that the E-objectivity of our beliefs can possibly be explained.

In addition to marking the ontological and epistemic contrasts mentioned already, the objective/subjective distinction has also been put to a third use, namely to differentiate intrinsically perspectival from non-perspectival points of view. An objective, non-perspectival view of the world finds its clearest expression in sentences that are devoid of demonstrative, personal, tensed or other token reflexive elements. Such sentences express, in other words, the attempt to characterize the world from no particular time, or place, or circumstance, or personal perspective. Nagel calls this 'the view from nowhere'. (Anyone might say: 'At 15.30 G.M.T., on Tuesday, 6 May 1991, Mr J. Smith gives Mr R. Brown the sum of £5.00. Mr Brown's immediate emotion is one of delight'.) A subjective point of view, by contrast, is one that possesses characteristics determined by the identity or circumstances of the person whose point of view it is. (In the envisaged situation, only Brown can say: 'It is now 15.30, and that man over there just gave me £5.00. I'm delighted!') The philosophical problems here centre on the question whether there is anything that an exclusively objective description would necessarily fail to reveal about oneself or the world. Can there, for instance, be a language with the same expressive power as our own, but which lacks all token reflexive elements? (Perry, 1979). Or, more metaphysically, are there genuinely and irreducibly subjective aspects to my existence – aspects which belong only to my unique perspective on the world and which must therefore resist capture by any purely objective conception of that world? (Nagel, 1986, passim; Wittgenstein, 1922, 5.6–5.641, 6.4–7; Wittgenstein, 1953, §§241–420).

HISTORICAL NOTE

The terms 'objective', 'subjective' are used, above, in their contemporary sense. This usage is relatively recent, however, appearing in English for the first time in the nineteenth century as the translation of the Kantian terms *objektiv* and *subjektiv*. Kant was in fact the first major philosopher to use these terms in what is recognizably their modern sense. (*See* Kant, 1781, B.44.) For four centuries before Kant – in the writings of the scholastics, Descartes, Spinoza, Berkeley and others – the contrast between objectivity and subjectivity had a quite different sense: one that is, confusingly, more or less the converse of the modern one. In the pre-Kantian sense, for something to be objective,

or for it to exist objectively, was for it to comprise an idea, a mental representation, a content of consciousness. Conversely, the adjective 'subjective' was reserved, in Descartes's words, for 'the reality that philosophers call actual or formal' (Descartes, 1641, III, §11). According to this usage for something to exist actually, formally or subjectively was for it to exist independently of any mental representation there might be of it. Anachronistically, Franz Brentano's notion of objectivity (*Gegenständlichkeit*) conforms to the older usage. He takes objectivity to be an intrinsic property of mental acts – the property, namely, of possessing an intentional content. His pupils Edmund Husserl and Alexius Meinong followed him in employing a notion of objectivity which owes more to mediaeval scholasticism than to Kant's critical philosophy.

*See also* IN ITSELF/FOR ITSELF; NOUMENAL/PHENOMENAL; OBJECTIVE/SUBJECTIVE; REALISM; SUBJECTIVITY.

BIBLIOGRAPHY

Descartes, R.: *Meditations* (1641), in *The Philosophical Writings of Descartes* eds J. Cottingham, R. Stoothoff and D. Murdoch (Cambridge: Cambridge University Press, 1975).

Frege, G.: 'Thoughts', in *Collected Papers on Mathematics, Logic and Philosophy* ed. B. McGuinness (Oxford: Blackwell, 1984), 351–72.

Kant, I.: *Critique of Pure Reason* (1781) trans. N. Kemp Smith (London: Macmillan, 1964).

Kant, I.: *Prolegomena to any Future Metaphysics* (1783) trans. L.W. Beck (Indianapolis: Bobbs-Merrill, 1950).

Kripke, S.: 'Wittgenstein on rules and private language: an elementary exposition', in *Perspectives on the Philosophy of Wittgenstein* ed. I. Block (Oxford: Blackwell, 1981), 238–312.

Mackie, J.L.: *Ethics. Inventing Right and Wrong* (Harmondsworth: Penguin Books, 1977).

McGinn, C.: *The Subjective View* (Oxford: Clarendon Press, 1983).

Nagel, T.: *The View From Nowhere* (New York: Oxford University Press, 1986).

Perry, J.: 'The problem of the essential indexical', *Nous* 13 (1979), 3–21.

Schlick, M.: 'Meaning and verification', in *Readings in Philosophical Analysis* eds H. Feigl and W. Sellars (New York: Appleton-Century-Crofts, 1949), 146–70.

Wittgenstein, L.: *Tractatus Logico-Philosophicus* (1922) trans. D.F. Pears and B. McGuinness (London: Routledge and Kegan Paul, 1974).

Wittgenstein, L.: *Philosophical Investigations* trans. G.E.M. Anscombe (Oxford: Blackwell, 1953).

DAVID BELL

**Ockham, William of** (*c.* 1285–1347) English philosopher. While Ockham intended to follow Aristotle in philosophy of mind, cognitive psychology, and epistemology, he in fact dismantled traditional interpretations in the first two areas. With Scotus against AQUINAS, Ockham affirms a plurality of substantial forms for living substances; in humans, the forms of corporeity, sensory soul and intellectual soul, all really distinct from one another (where Scotus had regarded the latter two as only formally distinct) (*Rep* II, q.7; OTh v 137; *cf. Rep* III, q.3; OTh vi 118). Further, he insists, the cognitive and appetitive powers of the sensory and intellectual forms are neither really distinct inherent accidents (as Aquinas claimed; *Rep* II, q.20; OTh v 425–9; *Rep* III, q.4; OTh vi 131–4) nor formally distinct from one another and the soul (as Scotus said; *Rep* II, 1.20; OTh v 433–5), but in every way really the same. Thus, 'intellect' is a connotative term signifying the substance of the soul able to understand, while 'will' signifies the same substance able to will (*Rep* II, q.20; OTh v 435). If 'sensory power' means 'that in the soul which elicits the act as its partial cause', the sensory powers are really the same as the sensory soul: the part that inheres in the eye is the visual power, that in the ear, the auditory power; etc. While all these parts are alike, their different functions are the result of different accidental dispositions in the various sense organs (*Rep* III, q.4; OTh vi 138–9).

Likewise, Ockham scraps traditional Aristotelian cognitive psychology. Aquinas had endorsed the tag 'like is known by like', and insisted that every knower must have a *species* – a mental representation distinct from both the cognitive act and its object – by means of which s/he is assimilated to the object known. In human beings, all knowledge begins with sensation, which involves the reception of sensible species, which in turn gives rise to phantasms, which in turn require to be 'illumined' by the agent intellect to produce the intelligible species received into the possible intellect. Ockham replaces this whole scheme with his theory of intuitive and abstractive cognition and his psychology of habit. If knowledge must still be 'by assimilation', it is enough that the act of apprehending itself resemble its object in some relevant way. For both angels and humans, intuitive cognitions are caused by the object and the intellect, together with the general concurrence of God (*Rep* II, qq.12–13; OTh v 268–9, 274); no causal role remains for species to play (ibid.; OTh v 305). For abstractive cognitions (e.g. of memory or imagination), something more is needed – a habit which actively inclines the power to produce acts of apprehending the same objects under the same aspects (ibid.; OTh v 269–71). If human knowledge begins with sensation, and there are no *ante-mortem* intellectual intuitive cognitions of material things apart from a corresponding sensory cognition, the latter is related to the former only as a partial efficient cause (*Rep* II, qq.12–13; OTh v 302–3; *cf. Prologue*, q.1; OTh i, 27, 64). Created intellects further act to produce abstract general concepts, to formulate necessary and contingent propositions, and to reason discursively. Because for Ockham particulars are fully intelligible (so that the first intellectual intuitive cognitions are of the same object under the same aspect as sensory ones), there is no need to posit any 'agency' to 'illumine' enmattered, particularized mental representations, to abstract intelligible content from them. Hence, the traditional distinction between agent and possible intellect loses much of its point: alike connotative, 'agent intellect' signifies the intellect *qua* partial efficient cause of its actions, while 'possible intellect' signifies the intellect *qua* subject that receives those actions (*Rep* II, qq. 12–13; OTh v 304–5). Ockham finds his opponents' case for species stronger where after-images and sensory imagination are concerned, but still prefers to fill explanatory gaps in other ways (*Rep* III, 1.3; OTh vi 105–21).

Despite an undeserved reputation as father of scepticism, Ockham is a fully conventional Aristotelian RELIABILIST in epistemology. Taking for granted the general reliability of our cognitive faculties, Ockham assumes that we have certain knowledge of mind-independent material things (*Quodl* 1, q.15; OTh ix 83; *Prologue*, q.1; OTh i 23) as well as of our own present mental acts (*Prologue*, q.1; OTh i 40, 43), and proceeds to trace such evident judgements to a distinctive species of acts of awareness – intuitive cognitions (*Prologue*, q.1; OTh i 31–2; *Rep* II, qq.12–13; OTh v 256–8) – which (by contrast with abstractive cognitions of the same things) are the power to produce evident judgements concerning their objects. Similarly, where our sensory faculties are concerned, Ockham appeals to the Aristotelian maxim that where the sensory faculty is well-disposed and close enough to its object, and where conditions in the medium are suitable, sense does not err with respect to its proper object (*Rep* III, q.2; OTh vi 57).

Like other Aristotelian reliabilists, Ockham admits that the operation of such cognitive powers can be *naturally obstructed*. He accepts in a matter of fact way that while we have evident knowledge of sensible things (e.g. that S is white) through intuitive cognitions, sometimes the flow of information gets blocked through imperfections in the object or in intuitive cognition or through obstacles in the medium. Ockham also allows that demons and God can deceive us in various ways. This admission is no daring Cartesian innovation, however, but rather accommodation to his colleagues' interpretation of Divine omnipotence in the wake of the Condemnation of 1277. Indeed, like Aristotle and Scotus, Ockham does not understand CERTAINTY to involve freedom from the natural or metaphysical or logical possibility of error, but absence of actual doubt and error. For him, the arguments of the Academic sceptics no longer merit serious attention, having been sufficiently refuted by Scotus before him.

WRITINGS

*Guillelmi de Ockham: Opera Philosophica et Theologica* (St Bonaventure: The Franciscan Institute), vols I–VI & IX–X.

BIBLIOGRAPHY

Adams, M. McCord: *William Ockham* (Notre Dame: University of Notre Dame Press, 1987), chs 13–14.
Day, S.: *Intuitive Cognition: A Key to the Significance of the Later Scholastics* (St Bonaventure: The Franciscan Institute, 1947).
Fuchs, O.: *The Psychology of Habit according to William Ockham* (St Bonaventure: The Franciscan Institute, 1952).
Tachau, K.H.: *Vision and Certitude in the Age of Ockham: Optics, Epistemology, and the Foundations of Semantics 1250–1345* (Leiden: E.J. Brill, 1988).

MARILYN McCORD ADAMS

**ontological commitment** A criterion of ontological commitment is a rule determinlng which things or sorts of things there must be if a given theory is true; these are the things to whose existence the theory is committed. It cannot settle whether there really are such things as numbers or sense data, but only whether such things are part of the ontological baggage of some theory or theorist. Since we understand names which fail to refer, and acknowledge many objects which lack names, we cannot rely upon the use of names for this purpose, but must find a locution which always signals an ontological commitment. The most famous criterion is QUINE's. If we formulate our views in a canonical notation based upon first order logic, we are ontologically committed to an object if and only if it must be among the values of the variables if all of the statements we accept are true. This rests upon Quine's controversial view that the existential quantifier captures the notion of existence.

*See also* EXISTENCE; ONTOLOGICAL RELATIVITY.

BIBLIOGRAPHY

Alston, W.: 'Ontological commitment', *Philosophical Studies* 6 (1958), 8–17.
Church, A.: 'Ontological commitment', *Journal of Philosophy* 55 (1958), 1008–14.
Quine, W.V.: *From a Logical Point of View* (Cambridge, MA: Harvard University Press, 1961), ch. 1.
Quine, W.V.: *Ontological Relativity and Other Essays* (New York: Columbia University Press, 1969), ch. 4.

CHRISTOPHER HOOKWAY

## ontological relativity

If QUINE's thesis of the INDETERMINACY OF REFERENCE were true, then there would be no fact of the matter what the ontological commitments of a given theory were. Depending upon the background language in which we try to state a theory's ontological commitments and, most important, the choice of a translation manual from the language of the theory into this background language, Quine's criterion of ontological commitment would yield different results. The thesis of ontological relativity, which Quine admits is not really distinct from the indeterminacy of reference, holds that claims about ontological commitment are thus doubly relative to background language and to the interpretation of the theory in the background language. In reflecting on our own ontological commitments, such indeterminacy and relativity are disguised since we use the 'identity transformation' as our translation manual, translating 'rabbit' as 'rabbit', and so on.

*See also* INDETERMINACY OF REFERENCE; ONTOLOGICAL COMMITMENT; PRINCIPLE OF CHARITY; RELATIVISM; SOCIAL SCIENCE.

BIBLIOGRAPHY

Quine, W.V.: *Ontological Relativity and Other Essays* (New York: Columbia University Press, 1969), ch. 2.
Quine, W.V.: *Pursuit of Truth* (Cambridge, MA: Harvard University Press, 1990), ch. 2.

CHRISTOPHER HOOKWAY

## ostensive definition

An ostensive definition is an explanation of the meaning of a word typically involving three elements: (1) an ostensive gesture, (2) an object pointed at which functions as a sample, (3) the utterance 'This is (a) W'. Like other forms of explanation of word-meaning, an ostensive definition functions as a rule or standard of correctness for the application of a word. The utterance 'This is W' when employed in giving an ostensive definition does not describe an object (i.e. the thing pointed at) as having the property W, but defines a word. It is most illuminatingly viewed as providing a kind of substitution-rule in accord with which one symbol, e.g. 'red', is replaceable by a complex symbol consisting of utterance ('This' or 'This colour'), gesture, and sample. Hence instead of 'The curtains are red' one can say 'The curtains are *this* ↗ colour', while pointing at a red sample. The ostensive definition specifies that anything which is *this* ↗ is correctly characterized as being W.

Like all definitions, ostensive definitions are misinterpretable. One way of warding off misunderstanding is to specify the 'grammatical signpost' by which the definiendum is stationed, i.e. to give the logico-grammatical category to which it belongs, viz. 'This C is W', where 'C' is a place-holder for, e.g. 'colour', 'length', 'shape', 'weight'. Like all rules, an ostensive definition does not provide its own method of application. Understanding an ostensive definition involves grasping the 'method of projection' from the sample to what it represents or from the ostensive gesture accompanying the definition to the application of the word. Thus in the case of defining a length by reference to a measuring rod, one must grasp the method of laying the measuring rod alongside objects to determine their length before one can be said to grasp the use of the definiendum. Ostensive definitions fulfil a crucial role both in explaining word meaning and in justifying or criticizing the application of that word (e.g. 'Those curtains are not ultramarine – *this* ↗ colour is ultramarine [pointing at a colour chart] and the curtains are not *this* colour'). An ostensive definition does not give evidential grounds for the application of a word 'W', but rather specifies what counts as being W.

The boundaries of the notion of ostensive definition are vague. A definition of a smell, taste or sound by reference to a sample typically involves no deictic gesture but a presentation of a sample (by striking a keyboard, for example). Conversely, defining directions (for example, 'north') by a deictic gesture involves no sample. Nor is the form of words 'This is (a) W' essential. 'This is called "W"' or 'W is this C' can fulfil the same role.

Whether something functions as a sample (or paradigm) for the correct application of a word is not a matter of its essential nature, but of human choice and convention. Being a sample is a role conferred upon an object momentarily, temporarily or relatively permanently by us – it is a use to which we put the object. Thus we can use the curtains here and now to explain what 'ultramarine' means – but perhaps never again, although we may often characterize (describe) them as being ultramarine. Or we can use a standard colour chart to explain what 'ultramarine' means, although if it is left in the sun and fades, it will no longer be so used. Or we may establish relatively permanent canonical samples, as *was* the case with the Standard Metre bar. A sample *represents* that of which it is a sample, and hence must be typical of its kind. It can characteristically be copied or reproduced and has associated with it a method of comparison. It is noteworthy that one and the same object may function now as a sample in an explanation of meaning or evaluation of correct application and now as an item described as having the defined property. But these roles are exclusive in as much as what functions as a norm for description cannot simultaneously be described as falling under that norm. *Qua* sample the object belongs to the means of representation and is properly conceived as belonging to grammar in an extended sense of the term. Hence the Standard Metre bar cannot be said to be (or not to be) one metre long. Furthermore, one and the same object may be used as a defining sample for more than one expression. Thus a black patch on a colour chart may serve both to explain what 'black'

means and as part of an explanation of what 'darker than' means.

Although the expression 'ostensive definition' is modern philosophical jargon (W.E. Johnson, *Logic* 1921) the idea of ostensive definition is venerable. It is a fundamental constituent of what WITTGENSTEIN called 'Augustine's picture of language' in which it is conceived as the fundamental mechanism whereby language is 'connected with reality'. The mainstream philosophical tradition has represented language as having a hierarchical structure, its expressions being either 'definables' or 'indefinables', the former constituting a network of lexically definable terms, the latter of simple, unanalysable expressions that link language with reality and that inject 'content' into the network. Ostensive definitions thus constitute the 'foundations' of language and the terminal point of philosophical analysis, correlating primitive terms with entities which are their meanings. On this conception, ostensive definition is privileged: it is final and unambiguous, settling all aspects of word use – the grammar of the definiendum being conceived to flow from the nature of the entity with which the indefinable expression is associated. In classical EMPIRICISM definables stand for complex ideas, indefinables for simple ideas that are 'given' in experience. Accordingly the 'given' is mental in nature, the linking mechanism is private 'mental' ostensive definition, and the basic samples, stored in the mind, are ideas which are essentially epistemically private and unshareable (cf. Locke, *Essay* II, XI, 9).

Wittgenstein, who wrote more extensively on ostensive definition than any other philosopher, held this picture of language to be profoundly misleading. Far from samples being 'entities in reality' to which indefinables are linked by ostensive definition, they themselves belong to the means of representation. In that sense, there is no 'link between language and reality', for explanations of meaning, including ostensive definitions, remain within language. Ostensive definitions are not privileged but are as misinterpretable as any other form of explanation. The objects pointed at are not 'simples' that constitute the ultimate metaphysical constituents of reality, but samples with a distinctive use in our language-games. They are not the meanings of words, but instruments of our means of representation. The grammar of a word ostensively defined does not flow from the essential nature of the object pointed at, but is constituted by *all* the rules for the use of the word, of which ostensive definition is but one. It is a confusion to suppose that expressions *must* be explained exclusively either by analytic definition (definables) or by ostension (indefinables), for many expressions can be explained in both ways, and there are many other licit forms of explanation of meaning. The idea of 'private' or 'mental' ostensive definition is wholly misconceived, for there can be no such thing as a rule for the use of a word which cannot logically be understood or followed by more than one person, there can be no such thing as a logically private sample nor any such thing as a mental sample (*see* PRIVATE LANGUAGE ARGUMENT).

Apart from these negative lessons, a correct conception of ostensive definition by reference to samples resolves the venerable puzzles of the alleged synthetic *apriority* of colour exclusion (e.g. that nothing can be simultaneously red and green all over) and of the nature of the necessity of such apparently metaphysical propositions as 'black is darker than white'. Such 'necessary truths' are indeed not derivable from explicit definitions and the laws of logic alone (i.e. are not ANALYTIC) but nor are they descriptions of the essential natures of objects in reality. They are rules for the use of colour words, exhibited in our practices of explaining and applying words defined by reference to samples. What we employ as a sample of red we do not also employ as a sample of green; and a sample of black can, in conjunction with a sample of white, also be used to explain what 'darker than' means. What appear to be metaphysical propositions about essential natures are but the shadows cast by grammar.

*See also* DEFINITION; LINGUISTIC UNDER-STANDING; PRIVATE LANGUAGE ARGUMENT.

BIBLIOGRAPHY

Arrington, R.L.: '"Mechanism" and "Calculus": Wittgenstein on Augustine's theory of ostension', in *Wittgenstein. Sources and Perspectives* ed. C.G. Luckhardt (Ithaca, NY: Cornell University Press, 1979), 303–38.

Baker, G.P. and Hacker, P.M.S.: 'Wittgenstein and the Vienna Circle: the exaltation and deposition of ostensive definition', in *Ludwig Wittgenstein: Critical Assessments* ed. S. Shanker, 4 vols (London: Croom Helm, 1986), vol. 1, 241–62.

Baker, G.P. and Hacker, P.M.S.: *Wittgenstein: Understanding and Meaning* (Oxford: Blackwell, 1980), pp. 168–205, 284–96.

Locke, J.: *An Essay Concerning Human Understanding* (1690) ed. P.H. Nidditch (Oxford: Clarendon Press, 1975).

Wittgenstein, L.: *Philosophical Grammar* trans. A. Kenny (Oxford: Blackwell, 1974).

Wittgenstein, L.: *Philosophical Investigations* trans. G.E.M. Anscombe (Oxford: Blackwell, 1953).

P.M.S. HACKER

**other minds** The interest in the traditional philosophical problem about other minds lies in the question whether, given what would seem a natural way we have of thinking about the meaning of mental terms, we can even make sense of the sentences we use to attribute mental states to others. This distinguishes the problem from a less interesting sceptical problem about other minds, in which it is a purely epistemological question of how we know about other minds, on a par with the question of how we know about the external world.

The distinctive problem arises because there is a natural tendency to assume that our mental terms ('pain', 'belief', etc.) get their meaning from our relating them to our own experiences (call this 'The Assumption'). If we understand what it is to have a pain or a belief from our own case, a question arises as to whether such a perspective on them will even allow our talk of others having pains and beliefs to make sense. This perspective is a strictly first person perspective. The idea that these terms get their meaning from our own case is meant to emphasize that we have an irreducibly subjective conception of pain, belief and so on. DESCARTES proposed such a conception of mentality in his 'Second Meditation', though he did compromise it somewhat in other places by talking of the mental as a substance and, therefore, as an objective thing. HUSSERL (1960) later embraced a more uncompromising version of the Cartesian first person point of view. As WITTGENSTEIN'S (1953) discussion of these issues brought out, all such positions are subjectivist in the strong sense that they rest on the claim that terms get their meaning from logically private states or episodes. The stricter versions of PHENOMENALISM, where all things in the empirical domain which are not themselves SENSE-DATA are LOGICAL CONSTRUCTS out of (and not just entities inferred from) sense-data, also give rise to the distinctive problem of other minds. This doctrine allows one to retain the intelligibility of our concept of material objects by reducing them to one's own sense-data, but it is not clear that it allows one to find intelligible the idea of another *mind* since all we have to work with are our own sense-data and logical constructs out of them. Such sense-data theories are no longer current, but Thomas Nagel (1986) has done much to revive the uncompromising Cartesian and Husserlian version of the problem by stressing the irreducibility of the first person point of view.

There are, as one might expect, two strategies of response to such a problem. One is to reject The Assumption, which underlies it; the other is to accept The Assumption and then struggle to solve the problem.

The latter course is most famously pursued in the ARGUMENT FROM ANALOGY, which was first formulated by MILL (1867). When faced with the problem of other minds, it is tempting to say first: The very same thing that I describe when I say 'John is in pain' is what John describes when he says 'I am in pain'. But it is not clear what gives us the right to say this if words like 'pain' are defined in terms of

The Assumption. The argument from analogy is intended to help provide that right. It proceeds from the observation of a causal connection between one's own mental states and one's bodily behaviour, and the observation of similar forms of behaviour in other bodies, to a conclusion about mental states of others similarly causing their behaviour.

The deepest criticism of this argument is due to Wittgenstein (1953) who, in effect, notices that if one takes The Assumption seriously, then the sense of 'mind' or 'mental states' that is being delivered up for others by the argument is not going to be the same as has been defined in one's own case. Whatever it is in one's own case that confers meaning on them is, *ex hypothesi*, not available when one is applying those terms to others. The argument, thus, does not even as much as address the problem raised by The Assumption; and it is not clear that anything can, for if the states which confer meaning are logically private then nothing could bridge the gap which gives rise to the problem. There are other less interesting criticisms of the argument from analogy (such as that it is an induction on the basis of just one case), but they seem to proceed without recognizing the fact that the *distinctive* problem of other minds is not even addressed by the argument.

Wittgenstein extends his critique to The Assumption itself, and in doing so, takes up the second strategy of response to the problem. In his well-known attack on the idea of a private language (*see* PRIVATE LANGUAGE ARGUMENT), he denies the plausibility of the suggestion that we can define mental terms by relating them to our own thoughts and experiences, since that procedure allows for no possibility of one's ever being able to make a mistake in the application of the terms. Whatever seems to us to be a right application would be a right application. Unless there is a more publicly available source of the meaning of mental terms, one would not have any standard for their incorrect (and therefore also for their correct) use; and without that, it would be quite wrong to say that we have a mastery of the use of these terms.

Strawson (1959) also raises an interesting objection to The Assumption. He denies that anyone possesses a concept or has a mastery of terms unless he or she can apply the term to more than one thing. Gareth Evans has called this the 'generality constraint' which demands that 'any thought which . . . has the content "a is F" involves the exercise of an ability which can be exercised in indefinitely many distinct thoughts, and would be exercised in, for instance, the thought that "b is F" ' (Evans, 1982, p. 101). Strawson specifically explores the effect of imposing this constraint on the concept of pain. The constraint forbids attributing to someone the thought expressed by 'I am in pain' unless he or she is also possessed of the idea of someone being in pain, where that someone need not be himself or herself. This does not allow the distinctive problem of other minds to arise since it rejects the coherence of The Assumption (that we can define mental terms on the basis of just our own experiences).

These arguments have not convinced everyone. But, whether one has an effective argument against The Assumption, the fact still remains that it raises an insuperable problem of other minds, a problem which can only be removed if one at least provides some cogent alternative to it.

Wittgenstein's proposed alternative to the rejected Assumption is that mental terms get their meaning due to a special connection that holds between them and the publicly observable behaviour of agents who possess mental states. He therefore shifts the emphasis to a third person conception. This shift has been favoured by a number of philosophers since Wittgenstein. Though there are very important differences between them, when the direction is described as generally as I have, it is fair to say that philosophers as diverse as Ryle (1948), Quine (1960), Davidson (1948a), and a substantial infantry marching under the influence of the doctrine of functionalism have all been following it (e.g. Putnam, 1975).

However problematic the first person perspective on mentality might be, the fact that it has some intuitive appeal should make us expect that simply reversing The Assumption

to a third person mode of defining mental terms would raise various difficult problems of its own.

The two problems which have received the most attention in recent philosophy are first, how knowledge of others is related to self-knowledge, and second, how exactly the special connection between behaviour and mentality must be conceived in this third person characterization of the mind.

The first problem arises because with the shift in direction it would now seem that when we know our own mental states we do so on the basis of our behaviour – which is highly implausible and counterintuitive. A basic dilemma thus emerges: if one accepts The Assumption, one has a seemingly insuperable problem of other minds, and if one rejects it and adopts a more third person perspective, that leads to unintuitive consequences about knowledge of our own minds.

Gilbert RYLE was so fearful of the first person perspective, and of the Cartesian idea that one knows one's mental states by an inner observation or INTROSPECTION of items in one's consciousness, that he accepted this highly implausible and unintuitive consequence of the alternative view. But Wittgenstein himself did not. He avoided it by denying that reports made in the first person of states such as pain were genuinely reports, and by denying that assertions such as 'I know that I am in pain' were well-formed knowledge claims. My assertion 'I am in pain' is rather to be thought of as an expression of my pain, albeit a rather more schooled expression than a cry or a grimace (see AVOWALS).

The dilemma, as we saw, emerged as a result of a thorough-going asymmetry that afflicts the epistemology of mind: we seem to know *other* minds on the basis of behaviour but not – usually – *our own* minds. Strawson saw this asymmetry as an essential feature of the very idea of creatures with minds, of 'persons'. But what is needed is not simply an acknowledgement of the feature but some effort to explain it or to illuminate it by situating it in a wider context. And, moreover, to do so, without relinquishing the third person account of mentality so that we are not landed again with the problem of other minds. Ryle's response, as we saw, is to deny the feature, Wittgenstein's to explain it by claiming that self-knowledge unlike knowledge of others is not a cognitive achievement. But there may be less drastic ways of dealing with the asymmetry within a basically third person point of view of mental terms.

A response due to David Armstrong (1968) is that agents possess a special mechanism of iterated belief-acquisition such that whenever the agent acquires a mental state he or she also acquires a belief that it has that mental state. This is an empirical thesis about how mental states cause one to have beliefs about them. It does not submit to the Rylean idea that we know our own mental states by inferring them from our behaviour, thereby capturing something special about self-knowledge missing in one's knowledge of others.

Some remarks of Gareth Evans's (1982, ch. 7) suggest another explanation of the asymmetry for a more restricted class of mental states, i.e. beliefs. He points out that when one is asked what one believes – as opposed to what another believes – about some subject matter, one does not survey one's own mind for the answer but rather one thinks about the subject matter itself. This seems to describe things accurately for the most part and it shows that the asymmetry need not take the form of making self-knowledge introspective and thereby spoil the basically third person perspective on mental terms. Evans' point also suggests the following further context in which the asymmetry emerges. If we find that someone's answer about another's belief does not square with that person's behaviour, we find ourselves saying that the answer was wrong. On the other hand, if it turns out that someone's answer about himself did not square with his behaviour, we would be just as inclined to say that the person was divided and irrational than that he had given the wrong answer – since his answer was a response to the subject matter rather than derived from an inner survey of his mind. This establishes a satisfying asymmetry between knowledge of others' beliefs and knowledge of one's own.

The second problem created by the shift in direction to the third person is about how the connection between behaviour and mental states ought to be conceived.

Wittgenstein himself introduces the term 'criterion' to convey that the connection is not merely that one or other kind of behaviour is caused by one or other kind of mental state. Rather there is (also) a *conceptual* connection. Behavioural circumstances are the 'criteria' rather than merely the effects or 'symptoms' of mentality. If it were just a contingent connection, the sceptical worry would persist that, for all one knows, the behaviour we observe in others might be a sustained deceit, reflecting nothing mental at all – in much the same way that one might by a comprehensive sensory illusion come to believe falsely that there is an external world.

This idea of a 'criterial' connection has been much discussed in the philosophical literature. The most interesting recent discussions may be found in McDowell (1983) and Wright (1984). Wright takes the notion of criterion to support an 'anti-realist' view of the meanings of sentences attributing mental states to others. The view replaces the 'realist' idea that the meanings of such sentences are given by the conditions in which they are true (*see* LINGUISTIC UNDERSTANDING) with the idea that they are given by conditions which warrant their assertion, i.e. given by their criteria. The truth-conditions for these sentences are undetectable by the person making the attributions, since the mental states being attributed (pain, say) are not themselves directly available to his experience in a way that they are to the subject of the attribution. Thus it cannot be knowledge of the truth-conditions which underlies his linguistic competence with these sentences, as the realist claims. What underlies his competence rather is knowledge of the criteria since the subject's behaviour *is* within the purview of the attributor's experience. Wright, following Wittgenstein, claims that there is a conceptual rather than a contingent link between the behaviour of the subject and the mental state because it is not on the basis of an inference (based on an empirical theory) that one goes from an observation of the behaviour to an attribution of the mental state. But Wright, following a widely-held interpretation of Wittgenstein, also claims that the criteria are DEFEASIBLE. That is, it is possible that the criteria should be fulfilled but that the attribution of the relevant mental state turn out to be false.

McDowell raises two objections against this. He first points out that defeasibility spoils the non-inferentiality of criteria since the idea that an attribution based on the fulfilment of criteria could turn out to be false suggests that there is a logical gap between the behaviour and the mental state, just what the conceptual connection is supposed to be disallowing. It looks as if the gap suggests that it is an empirical theoretical connection between them, at best. The second objection has to do with certain modal notions that surround the concept of knowledge, in this case knowledge of another's mental states. When one claims to *know* that James, say, is angry, one cannot accept that, for all one knows, he is not angry. For a claim to know that *p* is incompatible with an admission that for all one knows, *p* is false. But if the criteria for *p* are defeasible, and all we know is whether the criteria are satisfied, it will always be true that, for all we know, not-*p*. And so, if the relevant criteria are defeasible, we never know anything beyond them.

McDowell proposes instead to take criteria to be non-defeasible and to give up on an idea that seems to be shared by the anti-realist and the realist in Wright's exposition. This is the idea that a subject's mental state (and therefore the truth-condition of an attribution of it to him) is necessarily unavailable to the experience of another who is attributing the state to him. He thinks we may rightly say that one can directly perceive another person's pain (say) in his facial expressions and visible bodily states and behaviour. There is no need to see the behaviour, then, as a 'proxy' for the real thing which is undetectable by direct experience. This means that the special connection between behaviour and mental states which defines the notion of a 'criterion' is not to be expounded by saying that behaviour is a privileged kind of evidence. It is not evidence at all. 'Evidence' suggests that it is better known than what it is evidence for, and that brings in the invidious idea of a 'proxy'. What makes the connection special is simply that there is no gap between the two, and therefore there is no theoretical inference to be made from an observation of behaviour to an attribution of mental state. There is no gap because the mental state is taken in in the experience of the behaviour itself. It is not that one can never be wrong in making mental attributions to others, but that when one is wrong the criteria – despite appearances – have not been fulfilled.

McDowell takes this not only to be the right view of our knowledge of other minds but also to have been Wittgenstein's view. He says that Wittgenstein never thought that the behaviour of others was better known than their mental states. Instead he always viewed 'human beings' as basic, which is to say that he saw their behaviour and their mentality as more integrated than the traditional interpretation of his view of 'criteria' has taken them to be.

There is an obvious and immediate response to McDowell's second objection to the more traditional interpretation of the notion of 'criterion': criteria are only intended to provide the basis for claims to know something, not to knowing it. Such claims may be allowed later as being false. A full analysis of knowledge of a proposition merely requires that the knower has a criterial basis for claiming knowledge and that the proposition be true; it does not require that the knower have a guarantee of its truth. So the claim to knowledge can be withdrawn if it turns out that the proposition is not true.

The trouble with this response is that it seems to have surrendered to the sceptic, who can now claim that if criteria can only get us as far as claims to knowledge of other minds rather than to knowledge, then there is the always the sceptical possibility that a claim to know that a person is in a certain mental state is false.

But is it really a surrender? Notice, first,

that this sceptical position is no longer the distinctive position that we sketched at the outset. This is merely the less interesting epistemological scepticism. But putting that aside, even this less interesting scepticism (whether about other minds or the external world) is not correctly describable as insisting that any given knowledge claim could turn out to be false. It claims, much more dramatically, that it is always a conceptual possibility that all our claims in a certain region (the external world, other minds) should turn out to be false. This shows that all that one has to do to oppose the sceptic is not to argue that particular claims to being knowledge should be guaranteed correct, but rather that there should be a way of preventing the slide from admitting that any given belief could be false to allowing that all beliefs in a certain region could be false. One may or may not be able to produce an argument that prevents the slide, but the point for now is that once the sceptic's position has been properly described, the modalities surrounding the concept of knowledge show that even if we conceive of criteria as defeasible we can still find some defence against the sceptic.

In any case, McDowell's own positive alternative view of criteria does not help against the sceptic either. It just pushes the sceptical issue to another place. McDowell does after all have to allow for error in mental attributions to others. The only difference is that he accounts for error not in terms of the defeasibility of criterial evidence but by saying that the criteria have not been fulfilled, even though they appear to have been fulfilled. But then it is always open to the sceptic to say that, *for all we know*, the criteria are never fulfilled, they only appear to be fulfilled.

McDowell's first objection is on stronger ground since it shows a serious tension between the twin insistence on non-inferentiality and defeasibility. But even here the response to the second objection suggests a way out. If the only reason to insist on the non-inferentiality is that allowing an inference would be to allow that any given attribution of a mental state could be false, then one may cease to insist on it since, as we just

saw, allowing this need not amount to a surrender to the sceptic.

If, however, the defeasibility of criteria is purchased at the cost of allowing the inferentiality of the connection between criteria and ascription of mental states to others, then what is special about the connection between behaviour and mentality, which the notion of criteria is supposed to convey? Is it not now, like all inference, something based on empirical theory? An answer – one which captures much of the spirit of Wittgenstein's conception of the mental – might be that what is special is that the theory upon which the inferences are based is necessarily a commonsense theory and not a scientific theory. The idea of an inferential but nevertheless *criterial* connection points to a mediating theory, which, like our theory of the middle-sized objects around us, is highly internalized in our ordinary, unscientific thinking about others' minds.

*See also* ARGUMENT FROM ANALOGY; CRITERIA AND KNOWLEDGE; INTROSPECTION; PRIVATE LANGUAGE ARGUMENT; SELF-KNOWLEDGE AND SELF-IDENTITY; SOLIPSISM; TRANSCENDENTAL ARGUMENTS; WITTGENSTEIN.

BIBLIOGRAPHY

Armstrong, D.M.: *A Materialist Theory of Mind* (London: Routledge and Kegan Paul, 1968).
Davidson, D.: *Inquiries into Truth and Interpretation* (Oxford: Clarendon Press, 1984).
Descartes, R.: *Meditations on First Philosophy* (1641) in *The Philosophical Works of Descartes* eds J. Cottingham, R. Stoothoff and D. Murdoch (Cambridge: Cambridge University Press, 1975).
Evans, G.: *Varieties of Reference* (Oxford: Oxford University Press, (1982).
Husserl, E.: *Cartesian Meditations* trans. D. Cairns (The Hague: Martinus Nijhoff, 1960).
McDowell, J.: 'Criteria, defeasibility and knowledge', *Proceedings of the British Academy* 68 (1982), 455–79.
Mill, J.S.: *An Examination of Sir William Hamilton's Philosophy* (London: Longmans, 1867).
Nagel, T.: 'Subjective and objective', in his

*Mortal Questions* (New York: Oxford University Press, 1979).

Quine, W.V.: *Word and Object* (Cambridge, MA: MIT Press, 1960).

Ryle, G.: *The Concept of Mind* (London: Hutchinsons, 1949).

Strawson, P.F.: *Individuals* (London: Methuen, 1959).

Wittgenstein, L.: *Philosophical Investigations* trans. G.E.M. Anscombe (Oxford: Blackwell, 1953).

Wright, C. : 'Second thoughts about criteria', *Synthese* 58 (1984), 383–405.

AKEEL BILGRAMI

# P

paradox Somewhat loosely, a paradox is a compelling argument from unexceptionable premisses to an unacceptable conclusion; more strictly speaking, a paradox is specified to be a sentence that is true if and only if it is false. An example of the latter would be:

The displayed sentence is false.

It is easy to see that this sentence is false if true, and true if false. A paradox, in either of the senses distinguished, presents an important philosophical challenge. Epistemologists are especially concerned with various paradoxes having to do with knowledge and belief.

*See also* ANTINOMY; LOTTERY PARADOX; MOORE'S PARADOX; PARADOXES OF ANALYSIS; PREFACE PARADOX; PARADOX OF THE KNOWER.

BIBLIOGRAPHY

Quine, W.V.: 'The ways of paradox', in his *The Ways of Paradox and other Essays* (Cambridge, MA: Harvard University Press, 1966).
Sainsbury, R.M.: *Paradoxes* (Cambridge: Cambridge University Press, 1988).

JONATHAN VOGEL

paradox of the knower The knower paradox is an argument which begins with apparently impeccable premisses about the concepts of knowledge and inference and derives an explicit contradiction. The origin of the reasoning is the SURPRISE EXAMINATION PARADOX. Suppose your teacher announces that an examination will be given next week but that it will not be possible for you to predict the day upon which it will occur. Apparently one can prove that it won't be on Friday: it wouldn't then be a surprise. Having ruled out Friday, one can infer that it won't be on Thursday, else again, no surprise. In a similar manner every day of the week can be eliminated, but when the exam is given on Wednesday you are surprised! By analysing this puzzle and focusing on a single day, Kaplan and Montague (1960) distilled the following 'self-referential' paradox, the Knower. Consider the sentence:

(S) The negation of this sentence is known (to be true).

Suppose that S is true. Then its negation is known and hence true. But if its negation is true, then S must be false. So we may conclude that if S is true, then S is false. Therefore *S is false*. Or, what is the same, the negation of S is true.

This conclusion does not depend on our initial assumption that S is true – that hypothesis has been discharged. So we have here a proof that the negation of S is true. And having thus given a rigorous proof it appears that we know that the negation of S is true. But now consider again what S says. Isn't this what we have just concluded? So S is true after all! It looks as if we have proved a contradiction: S is false and S is true.

This paradox and its accompanying reasoning are strongly reminiscent of the Liar Paradox which (in one version) begins by considering a sentence 'This sentence is false' and derives a contradiction. Versions of both arguments using axiomatic formulations of arithmetic and Gödel-numbers to achieve the effect of self-reference yield important metatheorems about what can be expressed in such systems. (*See* Montague,

1963, for rigorous and detailed formulations.) Roughly these are to the effect that no predicates definable in the formalized arithmetics can have the properties we demand of truth (Tarski's Theorem) or of knowledge (Montague, 1963).

These metatheorems still leave us with the following problem. Suppose we *add* to these formalized languages predicates intended to express the concepts of knowledge (or truth) and inference – as one might do if a logic of these concepts is desired. Then the sentences expressing the leading principles of the Knower Paradox will apparently be true. Explicitly, the assumptions about knowledge and inference are:

(K1) If sentence A is known, then A.

(K2) (K1) is known.

(K3) If B is correctly inferred from A, and A is known, then B is known.

To give an absolutely explicit derivation of the paradox by applying these principles to S, we must add (contingent) assumptions to the effect that certain inferences have been performed (*see* Anderson, 1983). But as we go through the argument of the Knower, these inferences *are* performed. And even if we can somehow restrict such principles and construct a consistent formal logic of knowledge and inference, the paradoxical argument as expressed in the natural language still demands some explanation.

The usual proposals for dealing with the Liar often have their analogues for the Knower, e.g. that there is something wrong with self-reference or that knowledge (or truth) is properly a predicate of propositions and not of sentences. And the replies which show that some of these are not adequate are often parallel to those for the Liar paradox (*see* Kripke, 1975; Mates, 1981; Anderson, 1983). In addition one can try here what seems to be an adequate solution for the Surprise Examination Paradox, namely the observation that 'new knowledge can drive out old knowledge' (*see* Ayer, 1973). But this doesn't seem to work on the Knower (Anderson, 1983).

The two approaches which have some hope of adequately dealing with this paradox are 'hierarchy' solutions and 'truth-value gap' solutions. According to the first, knowledge is structured into 'levels'. It is urged that there is no one coherent notion expressed by the verb 'knows', but rather a whole series of notions: $knows_0$, $knows_1$, . . ., and so on (perhaps into the transfinite). Stated in terms of predicates expressing such 'ramified' concepts and properly restricted, (K1)–(K3) lead to no contradictions. (*See* Burge (1979) for a version of the idea as applied to truth, Anderson (1983) for an analogous approach to knowledge.) The main objections to this procedure are that the meaning of these levels has not been adequately explained and that the idea of such subscripts, even implicit, in a natural language is highly counter-intuitive. The 'truth-value gap' solution takes sentences such as S to lack truth-value, they are neither true nor false – they do not express propositions. This defeats a crucial step in the reasoning used in the derivation of the paradox. Kripke (1975) has developed this approach in connection with the Liar and Asher and Kamp (1986) have worked out some details of a parallel solution to the Knower. The principal objection is that 'strengthened' or 'super' versions of the paradoxes tend to reappear when the solution itself is stated.

Since the paradoxical deduction uses only the properties (K1)–(K3) and since the argument is formally valid, any notions which satisfy these conditions will lead to paradox. Thus Grim (1988) notes that 'K' may be read as 'is known by an omniscient God' and concludes that there is no coherent single notion of omniscience. And Thomason (1980) observes that with some slightly different conditions, analogous reasoning about belief can lead to paradoxical consequences.

All things considered it looks as if we should conclude that knowledge and truth are ultimately intrinsically 'stratified' concepts. And it would seem that we must simply accept the fact that these (and similar) concepts cannot be assigned any one fixed level, finite or infinite. But the meaning of this idea certainly needs further clarification.

BIBLIOGRAPHY

Anderson, C.A.: 'The paradox of the knower', *Journal of Philosophy* 80 (1983), 338–55.

Asher, N. and Kamp, J.A.W.: 'The knower's paradox and representational theories of attitudes', *Proceedings of the IBM Conference on Theoretical Aspects of Reasoning about Knowledge* ed. J. Halpern (Morgan Kaufman, 1986), 131–48.

Ayer, A.J.: 'On a supposed antinomy', *Mind* 83 (1973), 125–6.

Burge, T.: 'Semantical paradox', *Journal of Philosophy* 76 (1979), 169–98.

Grim, P.: 'Truth, omniscience, and the knower', *Philosophical Studies* 54 (1988), 9–41.

Kaplan, D. and Montague, R.: 'A paradox regained', *Notre Dame Journal of Formal Logic* (1960), 79–90.

Kripke, S.: 'Outline of a theory of truth', *Journal of Philosophy* 72 (1975), 690–716.

Mates, B.: *Sceptical Essays* (Chicago and London: University of Chicago Press, 1981).

Montague, R.: 'Syntactical treatments of modality, with corollaries on reflexion principles and finite axiomatizability', *Acta Philosophica Fennica* 16 (1963), 153–67.

Thomason, R.: 'A note on syntactical treatments of modality', *Synthese* 44 (1980), 391–5.

C. ANTHONY ANDERSON

**paradoxes of analysis** How can analysis be informative? This is the question that gives rise to what philosophers have traditionally called 'the' paradox of analysis. Thus, consider the following proposition.

(1) To be an instance of knowledge is to be an instance of justified true belief not essentially grounded in any falsehood.

(1), if true, illustrates an important type of philosophical analysis. For convenience of exposition, I will assume (1) is a *correct* analysis. The paradox arises from the fact that if the concept of justified true belief not essentially grounded in any falsehood is the *analysans* of the concept of knowledge, it would seem that they are the same concept and hence that

(2) To be an instance of knowledge is to be an instance of knowledge

would have to be the same proposition as (1). But then how can (1) be informative when (2) is not? This is what I call the first paradox of analysis.

Classical writings on analysis suggest a second paradox of analysis (Moore, 1942). Consider this proposition:

(3) An analysis of the concept of being a brother is that to be a brother is to be a male sibling.

If (3) is true, it would seem that the concept of being a brother would have to be the same concept as the concept of being a male sibling and that

(4) An analysis of the concept of being a brother is that to be a brother is to be a brother

would also have to be true and in fact would have to be the same proposition as (3). Yet (3) is true and (4) is false.

Both these paradoxes rest upon the assumptions that analysis is a relation between concepts, rather than one involving entities of other sorts, such as linguistic expressions, and that in a true analysis, *analysans* and *analysandum* are the same concept. Both these assumptions are explicit in Moore. But some of Moore's remarks hint at a solution – that a statement of an analysis is a statement partly about the concept involved and partly about the verbal expressions used to express it. He says he thinks a solution of this sort is bound to be right, but fails to suggest one because he cannot see a way in which the analysis can be even partly about the expressions (Moore, 1942).

Elsewhere, I have suggested such a way as a solution to the second paradox, which is to explicate (3) as

(5) An analysis is given by saying that the verbal expression 'x is a brother' expresses the same concept as is expressed by the conjunction of the verbal expressions

'x is male' when used to express the concept of being male and 'x is a sibling' when used to express the concept of being a sibling. (Ackerman, 1990).

An important point about (5) is as follows. Stripped of its philosophical jargon ('analysis', 'concept', 'x is a. . .'), (5) seems to state the sort of information generally stated in a definition of the verbal expression 'brother' in terms of the verbal expressions 'male' and 'sibling', *where this definition is designed to draw upon listeners' antecedent understanding of the verbal expressions 'male' and 'sibling'*, and thus to tell listeners what the verbal expression 'brother' really means, instead of merely providing the information that two verbal expressions are synonymous without specifying the meaning of either one. Thus, my solution to the second paradox seems to make the sort of analysis that gives rise to this paradox a matter of specifying the meaning of a verbal expression in terms of separate verbal expressions already understood and saying how the meanings of these separate, already-understood verbal expressions are combined. (This corresponds to Moore's intuitive requirement that an analysis should both specify the constituent concepts of the *analysandum* and tell how they are combined; *see* Moore, 1942.) But is this all there is to philosophical analysis?

To answer this question, we must note that, in addition to there being two paradoxes of analysis, there are two types of analysis that are relevant here. (There are also other types of analysis, such as reformatory analysis, where the *analysans* is intended to improve on and replace the *analysandum*. But since reformatory analysis involves no commitment to conceptual identity between *analysans* and *analysandum*, reformatory analysis does not generate a paradox of analysis and so will not concern us here.) One way to recognize the difference between the two types of analysis concerning us here is to focus on the difference between the two paradoxes. This can be done by means of the Frege-inspired sense-individuation condition, which is the condition that two expressions have the same sense if and only if they can be interchanged *salva veritate* whenever used in propositional attitude contexts. If the expressions for the *analysans* and the *analysandum* in (1) met this condition, (1) and (2) would not raise the first paradox, but the second paradox arises regardless of whether the expressions for the *analysans* and the *analysandum* meet this condition. The second paradox is a matter of the failure of such expressions to be interchangeable *salva veritate* in sentences involving such contexts as 'an analysis is given by'. Thus, a solution (such as the one I have offered) that is aimed only at such contexts can solve the second paradox. This is clearly false for the first paradox, however, which will apply to all pairs of propositions expressed by sentences in which expressions for pairs of *analysanda* and *analysantia* raising the first paradox are interchanged. For example, consider the following proposition:

(6) Mary knows that some cats lack tails.

It is possible for John to believe (6) without believing

(7) Mary has justified true belief, not essentially grounded in any falsehood, that some cats lack tails.

Yet this possibility clearly does not mean that the proposition that Mary knows that some cats lack tails is partly about language.

One approach to the first paradox is to argue that, despite the apparent epistemic inequivalence of (1) and (2), the concept of justified true belief not essentially grounded in any falsehood is still identical with the concept of knowledge (*see* Sosa, 1983). Another approach is to argue that in the sort of analysis raising the first paradox, the *analysans* and *analysandum* are concepts that are different but that bear a special epistemic relation to each other. Elsewhere I have developed such an approach and suggested that this *analysans–analysandum* relation has the following facets (Ackerman, forthcoming).

(a) The *analysans* and *analysandum* are necessarily coextensive; i.e. necessarily

every instance of one is an instance of the other.
(b) The *analysans* and *analysandum* are knowable a priori to be coextensive.
(c) The *analysandum* is simpler than the *analysans* (a condition whose necessity is recognized in classical writings on analysis, such as Langford, 1942).
(d) The *analysans* does not have the *analysandum* as a constituent.

Condition (d) rules out circularity. But since many valuable quasi-analyses are partly circular (e.g. knowledge is justified true belief supported by *known* reasons not essentially grounded in any falsehood), it seems best to distinguish between full analysis, for which (d) is a necessary condition, and partial analysis, for which it is not.

These conditions, while necessary, are clearly insufficient. The basic problem is that they apply to many pairs of concepts that do not seem closely enough related epistemically to count as *analysans* and *analysandum*, such as the concept of being 6 and the concept of being the fourth root of 1296. Accordingly, my solution finds the fifth condition by drawing upon what actually seems epistemically distinctive about analyses of the sort under consideration, which is a certain way they can be justified. This is by the philosophical example-and-counterexample method, which in general terms goes as follows. J investigates the analysis of K's concept Q (where K can but need not be identical to J) by setting K a series of armchair thought experiments, i.e. presenting K with a series of simple described hypothetical test cases and asking K questions of the form 'If such-and-such were the case, would this count as a case of Q?' J then contrasts the descriptions of the cases to which K answers affirmatively with the descriptions of the cases to which K does not, and J generalizes upon these descriptions to arrive at the concepts (if possible not including the *analysandum*) and their mode of combination that constitute the *analysans* of K's concept Q. Since J need not be identical with K, there is no requirement that K himself be able to perform this generalization, to recognize its

result as correct, or even to understand the *analysans* that is its result. This is reminiscent of Walton's observation that one can simply recognize a bird as a swallow without realizing just what features of the bird (beak, wing configuration, etc.) form the basis of this recognition. (The philosophical significance of this way of recognizing is discussed in Walton, 1972.) K answers the questions based solely on whether the described hypothetical cases just strike him as cases of Q. J observes certain strictures in formulating the cases and questions. He makes the cases as simple as possible, to minimize the possibility of confusion and also to minimize the likelihood that K will draw upon his philosophical theories (or quasi-philosophical, rudimentary notions if he is unsophisticated philosophically) in answering the questions. For this reason, if two hypothetical test cases yield conflicting results, the conflict should *ceteris paribus* be resolved in favour of the simpler case. J makes the series of described cases wide-ranging and varied, with the aim of having it be a *complete* series, where I say a series is complete if and only if no case that is omitted is such that, if included, it would change the analysis arrived at. J does not, of course, use as a test-case description anything complicated and general enough to express the *analysans*. There is no requirement that the described hypothetical test cases be formulated only in terms of what can be observed. Moreover, using described hypothetical situations as test cases enables J to frame the questions in such a way as to rule out extraneous background assumptions to a degree. Thus, even if K correctly believes that all and only P's are R's, the question of whether the concepts of P, R, or both enter into the *analysans* of his concept Q can be investigated by asking him such questions as 'Suppose (even if it seems preposterous to you) that you were to find out that there was a P that was not an R. Would you still consider it a case of Q?'

Taking all this into account, the fifth necessary condition for this sort of *analysans–analysandum* relation is as follows

(e) If S is the *analysans* of Q, the proposition

that necessarily all and only instances of S are instances of Q can be justified by generalizing from intuitions about the correct answers to questions of the sort indicated about a varied and wide-ranging series of simple described hypothetical situations.

Are these five necessary conditions jointly sufficient? For a discussion of qualifications and additional conditions that some objections may be necessitate, *see* Ackerman, forthcoming.

*See also* PARADOX.

BIBLIOGRAPHY

Ackerman, D.F.: 'The informativeness of philosophical analysis', *Midwest Studies in Philosophy* 6 (1981), 313–20.
Ackerman, F.: 'Analysis, language, and concepts: the second paradox of analysis', *Philosophical Perspectives* 4 (1990), 535–43.
Ackerman, F.: 'Analysis and its paradoxes', *The Scientific Enterprise: The Israel Colloquium Studies in History, Philosophy, and Sociology of Science* 4, ed. E. Ullman-Margalit (Norwell: Kluwer, forthcoming).
Langford, C.H.: 'The notion of analysis in Moore's philosophy', in *The Philosophy of G.E. Moore* ed. P.A. Schilpp (Evanston: Northwestern University Press, 1942), 319–43.
Moore, G.E.: 'A reply to my critics', in *The Philosophy of G.E. Moore*, ed. P.A. Schilpp (Evanston: Northwestern University Press, 1942), 660–7.
Pap, A.: *Semantics and Necessary Truth: An Inquiry into the Foundations of Analytic Philosophy* (New Haven: Yale University Press, 1958).
Sosa, E.: 'Classical analysis', *Journal of Philosophy* 53 (1983), 695–710.
Walton, K.L.: 'Linguistic relativity', in *Conceptual Change* ed. G. Pearce and P. Maynard (Dordrecht: Reidel, 1972), 1–29.

FELICIA ACKERMAN

**paranormal knowledge** Among claimed forms of paranormal knowledge are clairvoyance, telepathy and precognition, sometimes grouped together as 'ESP' or as 'psi-gamma'. Intriguing philosophical questions arise regarding both basic conceptions at issue and the character of the parapsychological data.

PROBLEMS IN DEFINING 'PARANORMAL'

What does it mean to claim that something is 'paranormal'? A tempting beginning, perhaps, is something like (1):

(1) P is paranormal $=_{df}$ P violates the laws of nature

If 'the laws of nature' are taken to be the ideal principles which science attempts to discover, however – an assumed set of true and complete generalizations regarding the universe – a definition such as (1) would seem to guarantee that no paranormal phenomena could possibly occur. Were paranormal phenomena by definition those which no complete true description of the universe would include, there *could* be no genuinely paranormal phenomena.

For that reason most philosophers who have addressed the question have preferred a definition more along these lines:

(2) P is paranormal $=_{df}$ P violates the laws of nature *as currently understood*

As an account of common usage, definition (2) may still face objections. So defined, 'paranormal' carries an indexical reference to laws of nature as understood at a particular time. In the year 1500, on such a definition, it would thus have been *true* to say that the northern lights or schizophrenia were paranormal, though they are not paranormal now. Such a definition may also be too broad. Because incorrect and incomplete, our science is constantly faced with anomalies. But not even those anomalies that have occasioned the most profound changes in scientific theory have been regarded as *paranormal* (see Braude, 1979).

In what has become a very influential piece, C.D. Broad (1949) defined the (ostensibly) paranormal as that which (*prima facie*) violates one or more of a list of fundamental assumptions or 'basic limiting principles'. Among these he included:

(a) general principles of causation, including the principle that a cause must precede its effect, and

(b) limitations on ways of acquiring knowledge, including the principle that all knowledge is the end product of a causal chain that at some point involves the sense organs of the knower.

Broad's list can be accused of building too much into our fundamental assumptions, however – in particular, an explicit Cartesian dualism and fairly radical empiricism.

There are also questions of definition regarding other terms at issue. Despite the familiarity of the term 'ESP' or 'extra-sensory perception', for example, it seems to be widely agreed that phenomena at issue – even if genuine – may not properly be characterized on the model of perception (see Mundle, 1964). Phenomena of 'precognition', despite the term, may not properly be conceived of as phenomena of cognition. Despite the fact that the gamma of 'psi-gamma' is taken from the Greek word for knowledge, whether the phenomena at issue can be characterized in terms of knowledge remains an open question.

The notion of precognition faces particularly pointed conceptual questions, since as standardly characterized it would seem to demand that a later 'precognized' event at $t_2$ was in some way causally responsible for an earlier event of precognition at $t_1$. In accord with Broad's basic limiting principle (a), it has been argued that the backwards causation so demanded is logically impossible in virtue of the meaning of 'cause', and thus that precognition must itself be logically impossible (see esp. Flew, 1980). Others have argued, often using the example of tachyons in physics – hypothetical particles moving backward in time – that what such an argument establishes is merely that a new and non-temporal notion of 'cause' is required. It is not clear that tachyons don't face their own philosophical problems, however (see Craig, 1988) nor that any mere revision of the meaning of 'cause' would genuinely address the central difficulty at issue (see esp. Flew, 1987).

Attempts have also been made to argue that clairvoyance and telepathy must be impossible on the grounds that they violate Broad's basic limiting principles (see esp. Duran, 1990). Here the argument turns on principles that prohibit action at a distance or knowledge by means of other than the standard senses. It's not clear that clairvoyance and telepathy would necessarily violate these, however, nor that the principles at issue should command our allegiance without exception.

Defined as in (2) above or in terms of Broad's 'basic limiting principles', paranormal phenomena will at least not be ruled out as impossible by definition. On the basis of such definitions it can still be argued, however, that it would be irrational to believe any evidence offered for a case of the paranormal. Here the basic argument, which appears in one form or another throughout the literature, is essentially Hume's against miracles. A miracle, as Hume characterizes it, is a violation of the laws of nature as we understand them. But

> . . .as a firm and unalterable experience has established these laws, the proof against a miracle. . .is as entire as any argument from experience can possibly be imagined. (Enquiry, X)

THE CHARACTER OF THE DATA

Here we have concentrated on conceptual questions, but any serious consideration of claims regarding paranormal knowledge must confront the wealth of existing parapsychological data. Questions of basic statistical technique in parapsychological experiment seem to have been settled, though questions may remain regarding selective publication of positive results and experimental repeatability. A particularly sensitive issue is that of fraud, which does unfortunately have a history in parapsychology; at least some of the work of S.G. Soal and W.J. Levy has been shown to be fraudulent, for example. Critics often discount particular experiments on the basis that fraud could have occurred; defenders often object that the mere possibility of fraud should no more discredit results in parapsychology than in other fields. J.B. Rhine attempts to give a summary of fraud-proof evidence in Rhine (1975).

Even if entirely genuine, a question remains as to whether the data would support a claim of paranormal *knowledge*. Necessary conditions for knowledge (even if not sufficient) have standardly been taken to include justified true belief. In cases at issue, truth is granted. But do purported cases of precognition, telepathy and clairvoyance as they appear in the literature support a claim of justified belief?

It can be argued that such cases don't even characteristically involve *belief*. In standard statistical tests, for example, it does not appear that the subject has any feeling of conviction which distinguishes 'hits' from 'misses' (*see* Mundle, 1964). Even in a large percentage of spontaneous cases, it appears, there is no feeling of conviction which distinguishes the true experiences from the false (*see* Ducasse, 1954).

The argument that such cases would not at any rate involve *justified* belief is similarly factual: the success rates simply don't seem good enough to justify belief in any particular instance. In Flew's words,

> . . . it is easy to see how preposterous it is to describe even star performers on their best days as knowing the values of the targets . . . they will, if it is a very good day, be averaging 7 or 8 out of 25 where mean chance expectation is 5. . . . (Flew, 1987, p. 91)

For spontaneous cases we would have to make similar estimates of success rates, and here too the data seem none too strong. It should also be emphasized that among the strongest parapsychological evidence we find data involving temporal displacement (a pattern of 'hits' systematically displaced from the subject's intended targets) and psi-missing (a statistically significant pattern of 'misses'). Neither of these would seem to fit a pattern of either justified belief or knowledge.

By this stage we are considering not so much whether there *could* be such things as precognition, telepathy, etc., but whether the evidence in their favour is in fact strong enough. Were evidence produced which showed a particularly reliable record of 'hits' with a corresponding pattern of conviction these particular objections would seem to be overridden.

BIBLIOGRAPHY

The *Journal of Parapsychology* is a primary source regarding the parapsychological data.

Braude, S.E.: *ESP and Psychokinesis* (Philadelphia: Temple University Press, 1979).

Broad, C.D.: 'The relevance of psychical research to philosophy', *Philosophy* 24 (1949), 291–309; reprinted in Flew (1987), 37–52.

Craig, W.L.: 'Tachyons, time travel and divine omniscience', *Journal of Philosophy* 85 (1988), 135–50.

Ducasse, C.J.: 'The philosophical importance of "psychic phenomena"', *Journal of Philosophy* 51 (1954), 810–23.

Duran, J.: 'Philosophical difficulties with paranormal knowledge claims', in Grim (1990), pp. 232–42.

Flew, A. ed.: *Readings in the Philosophical Problems of Parapsychology* (Buffalo: Prometheus Books, 1987).

Flew, A.: 'Analysing the concepts of parapsychology', in Flew (1987), pp. 87–106.

Flew, A.: 'Parapsychology: science or pseudoscience?', in *Science, Pseudoscience, and Society* eds M. Hanen, M.J. Osler and R.G. Weyant (Waterloo, Ontario: Calgary Institute for the Humanities and Wilfrid Laurier University Press, 1980); reprinted in Grim (1990), pp. 214–31.

Grim, P. ed.: *Philosophy of Science and the Occult* 2nd edn (Albany: State University of New York Press, 1990).

Ludwig, J. ed.: *Philosophy and Parapsychology* (Buffalo: Prometheus Books, 1978).

Mundle, C.W.K.: 'Is "paranormal precognition" a coherent concept?', *Journal of Parapsychology* 6 (1964) 179–94.

Rhine, J.B.: 'Second report on a case of experimenter fraud', *Journal of Parapsychology* 39 (1975), 306–25; excerpted in Grim (1990), pp. 253–63.

PATRICK GRIM

**Peirce, Charles S. (1839–1914)** Peirce was

an American philosopher and logician best known as the founder of PRAGMATISM (he called his own version of the doctrine 'Pragmaticism'). A systematic philosopher influenced by Kant, he attempted to provide a vindication of the scientific method exploiting a sophisticated general theory of representation and a system of categories which, he claimed, improved on Kant's. Throughout he sought to bring 'mathematical exactitude' to philosophy, and was an innovator in logic and mathematics.

From his earliest writings Peirce was critical of CARTESIAN approaches to epistemology. He charged that the method of doubt encouraged people to pretend to doubt what they did not doubt in their hearts, and criticized its individualist insistence that 'the ultimate test of certainty is to be found in the individual consciousness'. We should rather begin from what we cannot in fact doubt, progressing towards the truth as part of a community of inquirers trusting to the multitude and variety of our reasonings rather than to the strength of any one. He claimed to be a contrite FALLIBILIST and urged that our reasonings 'should not form a chain that is no stronger than its weakest link, but a cable whose fibres may be ever so slender, provided they are sufficiently numerous and intimately connected'. In later writings his anti-Cartesianism took the form of 'critical COMMONSENSISM': our inquiries are guided by a slowly evolving body of vague commonsense certainties which are, in principle, fallible; rational self-control requires that we try to doubt these in order to establish that they genuinely form part of commonsense.

Peirce insisted that something can serve as a sign, can represent an object, only if it is interpreted in subsequent thought as standing for that object, and he argued that all thoughts were signs. His extensive writings in 'semiotic', the general theory of signs, provide a sophisticated model of mind and language which was intended to serve as the foundations of his logical doctrines. He held that we investigate the world as members of a scientific community of sign interpretation engaged in co-operative investigation, criticizing and challenging opinions, attempting to eliminate error and thus progress towards truth.

In 'The fixation of belief' (published 1877) Peirce argued that the aim of inquiry must be characterized as fixation or settlement of belief: once doubt is removed we cannot but be satisfied with what we then believe. He compared different methods for fixing belief, concluding that the only method which can be sustained, the only one which is consistent with the presuppositions of inquiry, is the method of science. Its 'fundamental principle' is that there are real things entirely independent of our opinions about them which affect our senses in regular ways; any inquirers with sufficient experience who reason hard enough on the matter will be fated to participate in a consensus about how these realities are. Much of his work was concerned with describing the method of science in more detail and with attempting to prove that it will take us to the truth.

For Peirce, the method of science has three components, ABDUCTION (or retroduction), DEDUCTION and INDUCTION. His vindication of induction rests upon the claims that all induction resembles statistical sampling and that such reasoning has a self-correcting character. Although there is no logical basis for relying on induction in the short run, we can be confident that repeated use of induction will lead the community of inquirers eventually to eliminate error and reach the truth (see PROBLEMS OF INDUCTION). The logic of abduction is the logic of discovery: it is concerned with which hypotheses are worth taking seriously; and Peirce made many contributions to our understanding of these issues.

Peirce's famous pragmatist principle is a rule of logic to be employed in clarifying our concepts and ideas. Consider the claim that the liquid in a flask is an acid. If we believe this, we expect that if we were to place blue litmus paper in the flask, it would turn red: we expect an action of ours to have certain experiential results. The pragmatist principle holds that listing the conditional expectations of this kind that we associate with applications of a concept provides a *complete* clarification of the concept. This is relevant to the logic of abduction: clarification using the pragmatist principle provides all the information about the content of an hypothesis that is relevant to deciding whether it is worth testing.

The most famous application of the pragmatist principle is Peirce's account of reality: when we take something to be really the case, we think it is 'fated to be agreed upon by all who investigate' the matter; in other words, if I believe that it is really the case that *p*, then I expect that if anyone were to inquire well enough and for long enough into whether *p*, they would arrive at the belief that *p*. It is not part of the theory that the experiential consequences of our actions should be specified in a narrowly empiricist vocabulary – Peirce insisted that perception was theory laden. Nor is it his view that the conditionals listed when we clarify a concept are all analytic. Moreover, in later writings, he urged that the pragmatist principle could only be plausible to someone who accepted metaphysical REALISM: it requires that 'would-be's' are objective and real. Indeed much of Peirce's later work is concerned with developing a 'scientific metaphysics' which vindicates his metaphysical realism. His use of the term 'pragmaticism' to describe his own position was designed to distinguish it from the views of avowed 'pragmatists' like William JAMES who, Peirce thought, had failed to see the necessity of defending realism.

*See also* JAMES; PRAGMATISM.

WRITINGS

*Collected Papers of Charles S. Peirce* 8 vols (Cambridge, MA: Harvard University Press, 1931–58).
*Charles S. Peirce: Selected Writings* ed. P.P. Weiner (New York: Dover Publications, 1966).
*Reasoning and the Logic of Things* ed. K. Ketner with introductions by Ketner and H. Putnam (Cambridge, MA: Harvard University Press, 1991).
*The Writings of Charles S. Peirce: a Chronological*
*Edition* (Indianapolis: Indiana University Press, 1982- ).

BIBLIOGRAPHY

Hookway, C.J.: *Peirce* (London: Routledge and Kegan Paul, 1985).
Scheffler, I.: *Four Pragmatists* (London: Routledge and Kegan Paul, 1974), pt 1.
Skagestad, P.: *The Road of Inquiry* (New York: Columbia University Press, 1981).

CHRISTOPHER HOOKWAY

**perceptual knowledge** Perceptual knowledge is knowledge acquired by or through the senses. This includes most of what we know. Some would say it includes *everything* we know. We cross intersections when we see the light turn green, head for the kitchen when we smell the roast burning, squeeze the fruit to determine its ripeness, and climb out of bed when we hear the alarm ring. In each case we come to know something – that the light has turned green, that the roast is burning, that the melon is overripe, and that it is time to get up – by some sensory means. Seeing that the light has turned green is learning something – that the light has turned green – by use of the eyes. Feeling that the melon is overripe is coming to know a fact – that the melon is overripe – by one's sense of touch. In each case the resulting knowledge is somehow *based on, derived from* or *grounded in* the sort of experience that characterizes the sense modality in question.

Seeing a rotten kumquat is not at all like the experience of smelling, tasting or feeling a rotten kumquat. Yet all these experiences can result in the same knowledge – knowledge that the kumquat is rotten. Although the experiences are much different, they must, if they are to yield knowledge, embody information about the kumquat: the information that it is rotten. Seeing that the fruit is rotten differs from smelling that it is rotten, not in *what* is known, but *how* it is known. In each case, the information has the same source – the rotten kumquat – but it is, so to speak, delivered via different channels and coded in different experiences.

It is important to avoid confusing perceptual knowledge of facts (e.g. that the kumquat is rotten) with the perception of objects (e.g. rotten kumquats). It is one thing to see (taste, smell, feel) a rotten kumquat, quite another to *know* (by seeing or tasting) that it is a rotten kumquat. Some people, after all, don't know what kumquats look like. They see a kumquat but do not realize (do not *see that*) it is a kumquat. Some people don't know what kumquats smell like. They smell a rotten kumquat and – thinking, perhaps, that this is the way this strange fruit is supposed to smell – do not realize from the smell (i.e. do not *smell that*) it is rotten. In such cases people see and smell rotten kumquats – and in this sense *perceive* rotten kumquats – and never know that they are kumquats – let alone rotten kumquats. They cannot, not at least by seeing and smelling, and not until they have learned something about (rotten) kumquats, come to *know* that what they are seeing or smelling is a (rotten) kumquat. Since the topic of this essay is perceptual *knowledge* – knowing, by sensory means, that something is F – we will be primarily concerned with the question of what *more*, *beyond* the perception of Fs, is needed to see that (and thereby know that) they are F. The question is, not how we *see* kumquats (for even the ignorant can do this), but, how we know (if, indeed, we do) that that is what we see.

Much of our perceptual knowledge is indirect, dependent or derived. By this I mean that the facts we describe ourselves as learning, as coming to know, by perceptual means are pieces of knowledge that depend on our coming to know something else, some other fact, in a more direct way. We see, *by the gauge*, that we need gas; see, *by the newspapers*, that our team has lost again; see, *by her expression*, that she is nervous. This derived or dependent sort of knowledge is particulary prevalent in the case of vision, but it occurs, to a lesser degree, in every sense modality. We install bells and other noise-makers so that we can, for example, *hear* (by the bell) that someone is at the door and (by the alarm) that its time to get up. When we obtain knowledge in this way, it is clear that

unless one sees – hence, comes to know – something about the gauge (that it reads 'empty'), the newspaper (what it says) and the person's expression, one would not see (hence, know) what one is described as coming to know by perceptual means. If one can't hear that the bell is ringing, one cannot – not at least in *this* way – hear that one's visitors have arrived. In such cases one sees (hears, smells, etc.) that *a* is F, coming to know thereby that *a* is F, *by* seeing (hearing, etc.) that some *other* condition, *b*'s being G, obtains. When this occurs, the knowledge (that *a* is F) is derived from, or dependent on, the more basic perceptual knowledge that *b* is G.

Though perceptual knowledge about objects is often, in this way, dependent on knowledge of facts about *different* objects, the derived knowledge is sometimes about the *same* object. That is, we see that *a* is F by seeing, not that some other object is G, but that *a* itself is G. We see, by *her* expression, that *she* is nervous. She tells that the fabric is silk (not polyester) by the characteristic 'greasy' feel of the fabric itself (not, as I do, by what is printed on the label). We tell whether its an oak tree, a Porsche, a geranium, an igneous rock or a misprint by its shape, colour, texture, size, behaviour and distinctive markings. Perceptual knowledge of this sort is also *derived* – derived *from* the more basic facts (about *a*) we use to make the identification. In this case the perceptual knowledge is still indirect because, although the same object is involved, the facts we come to know about it are different than the facts that enable us to know it.

Derived knowledge is sometimes described as *inferential*, but this is misleading. At the conscious level there is no passage of the mind from premise to conclusion, no reasoning, no problem-solving. The observer, the one who sees that *a* is F by seeing that *b* (or *a* itself) is G, needn't be (and typically isn't) aware of any process of inference, any passage of the mind from one belief to another. The resulting knowledge, though logically derivative, is psychologically immediate. I could *see* that she was getting angry; so I moved my hand. I did not – at least not at any conscious level – *infer* (from her expression and behaviour) that she was getting angry. I could (or so it seems to me) *see* that she was getting angry. It is this psychological immediacy that makes indirect perceptual knowledge a species of *perceptual* knowledge.

The psychological immediacy that characterizes so much of our perceptual knowledge – even (sometimes) the most indirect and derived forms of it – does not mean that *learning* is not required to know in this way. One isn't born with (may, in fact, never develop) the ability to recognize daffodils, muskrats and angry companions. It is only after a long experience that one is able visually to identify such things. Beginners may do something corresponding to inference: they recognize relevant features of trees, birds and flowers, features they already know how to perceptually identify, and *then* infer (conclude), on the basis of what they see, and under the guidance of more expert observers, that its an oak, a finch or a geranium. But the experts (and we are all experts on many aspects of our familiar surroundings) do not typically go through such a process. The expert just *sees* that its an oak, a finch or a geranium. The perceptual knowledge of the expert is still dependent, of course, since even an expert can't see what kind of flower it is if she can't first see its colour and shape, but it is to say that the expert has developed identificatory skills that no longer require the sort of conscious inferential processes that characterize a beginner's efforts.

Coming to know that *a* is F by seeing that *b* is G obviously requires some background assumption on the part of the observer, an assumption to the effect that *a* is F (or perhaps only probably F) when *b* is G. If one doesn't assume (take it for granted) that the gauge is *properly connected*, doesn't (thereby) assume that it would not register 'Empty' unless the tank was nearly empty, then even if one could see that it registered 'Empty', one wouldn't learn (hence, wouldn't see) that one needed gas. At least one wouldn't see it *by* consulting the gauge. Likewise, in trying to identify birds, it's no use being able to see

their markings if one doesn't know something about which birds have which marks – something of the form: a bird with these markings is (probably) a finch.

It would seem, moreover, that these background assumptions, if they are to yield *knowledge* that *a* is F, as they must if the observer is to *see* (by *b*'s being G) that *a* is F, must themselves qualify as knowledge. For if this background fact isn't known, if it isn't known whether *a* is F *when b* is G, then the knowledge of *b*'s being G is, taken by itself, powerless to generate the knowledge that *a* is F. If the conclusion is to be *known* to be true, *both* the premises used to reach that conclusion must be known to be true. Or so it would seem.

Externalists (*see* EXTERNALISM/INTERNALISM), however, argue that the indirect knowledge that *a* is F, though it may depend on the knowledge that *b* is G, does not require *knowledge* of the connecting fact, the fact that *a* is F *when b* is G. Simple belief (or, perhaps, justified belief; there are stronger and weaker versions of externalism) in the connecting fact is sufficient to confer a knowledge of the connected fact. Even if, strictly speaking, I don't *know* she is nervous whenever she fidgets like that, I can none the less *see* (hence, know) that she is nervous (by the way she fidgets) if I (correctly) assume that this behaviour is a reliable expression of nervousness. One needn't *know* the gauge is working well to make observations (acquire observational knowledge) with it. All that is required, besides the observer *believing* that the gauge is reliable, is that the gauge, in fact, be reliable (i.e. that the observer's background beliefs be *true*). Critics of externalism have been quick to point out that this theory has the unpalatable consequence that knowledge can be made possible by – and, in this sense, be made to rest on – lucky hunches (that turn out true) and unsupported (even irrational) beliefs. Surely, internalists argue, if one is going to know that *a* is F on the basis of *b*'s being G, one should have (as a bare minimum) some justification for thinking that *a* is F, or is probably F, when *b* is G.

Whatever view one takes about these matters (with the possible exception of extreme externalism), indirect perception obviously requires some understanding (knowledge? justification? belief?) of the general relationship between the fact one comes to know (that $a$ is F) and the facts (that $b$ is G) that enable one to know it. And it is this requirement on background knowledge or understanding that leads to questions about the possibility of indirect perceptual knowledge. Is it really knowledge? Even if it is, is it really *perceptual* knowledge? The first question is inspired by sceptical doubts about whether we can ever know the connecting facts in question. How is it possible to learn, to acquire knowledge of, the connecting facts knowledge of which is necessary to see (by $b$'s being G) that $a$ is F? These connecting facts do not appear to be *perceptually* knowable. Quite the contrary; they appear to be general truths knowable (if knowable at all) by inductive inference from past observations. And if one is sceptical about obtaining knowledge in this indirect, inductive, way, one is, perforce, sceptical about the existence of the kind of indirect knowledge, including indirect perceptual knowledge of the sort described above, that depends on it.

Even if one puts aside such sceptical questions, however, there remains a legitimate concern about the *perceptual* character of this kind of knowledge. If one sees that $a$ is F *by* seeing that $b$ is G, is one really *seeing* that $a$ is F? Isn't perception merely a part – and, indeed, from an epistemological standpoint, the less significant part – of the process whereby one comes to know that $a$ is F. One must, it is true, see that $b$ is G, but this is only one of the premises needed to reach the conclusion (knowledge) that $a$ is F. There is also the background knowledge that is essential to the process. If we think of a *theory* as any factual proposition, or set of factual propositions, that cannot itself be known in some direct observational way, we can express this worry by saying that indirect perception is always theory-loaded: seeing (indirectly) that $a$ is F is only possible if the observer *already* has knowledge of (justification for, belief in) some theory, the theory 'connecting' the fact one comes to know (that $a$ is F) with the fact (that $b$ is G) that enables one to know it.

This, of course, reverses the standard (FOUNDATIONALIST) picture of human knowledge. Instead of theoretical knowledge depending on, and being derived from, perception, perception (of the indirect sort) presupposes a prior knowledge of theories.

Foundationalists are quick to point out that this apparent reversal in the structure of human knowledge is *only* apparent. Our indirect perception of facts depends on theory, yes, but this merely shows that indirect perceptual knowledge is not part of the foundation. To reach the kind of perceptual knowledge that lies at the foundation, we need to look at a form of perception that is purified of all theoretical elements. This, then, will be perceptual knowledge *pure* and *direct*. No background knowledge or assumptions about connecting regularities are needed in direct perception because the known facts are presented directly and immediately and not (as in indirect perception) on the basis of some *other* facts. In direct perception *all* the justification (needed for knowledge) is right there in the experience itself.

What, then, about the possibility of perceptual knowledge pure and direct, the possibility of coming to know, on the basis of sensory experience, that $a$ is F where this does *not* require, and in no way presupposes, background assumptions or knowledge that has a source outside the experience itself? Where is this epistemological 'pure gold' to be found?

There are, basically, two views about the nature of direct perceptual knowledge (COHERENTISTS would deny that any of our knowledge is basic in this sense). These views (following traditional nomenclature) can be called DIRECT REALISM and representationalism (or REPRESENTATIVE REALISM). A representationalist restricts direct perceptual knowledge to objects of a very special sort: ideas, impressions, or sensations (sometimes called sense-data) – entities in the mind of the observer. One *directly* perceives a fact (e.g. that $b$ is G) only when $b$ is a mental entity of some sort – a subjective appearance or sense-datum – and G is a property of this datum. Knowledge of these sensory states is supposed to be certain and infallible. These sensory facts are, so to speak, right up against the mind's eye. One cannot be mistaken about these facts for these facts are, in reality, facts about the way things appear to be, and one can't be mistaken about the way things appear to be. Normal perception of external conditions, then, turns out to be (always!) a type of *indirect* perception. One 'sees' that there is a tomato in front of one *by* seeing that the appearances (of the tomato) have a certain quality (reddish and bulgy) and inferring (this is typically said to be automatic and unconscious), on the basis of certain background assumptions (e.g. that there typically *is* a tomato in front of one when one has experiences of this sort) that there is a tomato in front of one. All knowledge of objective reality, then, even what commonsense regards as the most direct perceptual knowledge, is based on an even more direct knowledge of the appearances.

For the representationalist, then, perceptual knowledge of our physical surroundings is always theory-loaded and indirect. Such perception is 'loaded' with the theory that there is some regular, some uniform, correlation between the way things appear (known in a perceptually direct way) and the way things actually are (known, if known at all, in a perceptually indirect way).

The second view, *direct* realism, refuses to restrict direct perceptual knowledge to an inner world of subjective experience. Though the direct realist is willing to concede that much of our knowledge of the physical world is indirect (however direct and immediate it may sometimes *feel*), *some* perceptual knowledge of physical reality is direct. What makes it direct is that such knowledge is not based on, nor in any way dependent on, other knowledge and belief. The justification needed for the knowledge is right there in the experience itself.

To understand the way this is supposed to work, consider an ordinary example. S identifies a banana (learns that it is a banana) *by* noting its shape and colour – perhaps even tasting and smelling it (to make sure its not wax). In this case the perceptual knowledge that it is a banana is (the direct realist admits) indirect, dependent on S's perceptual knowledge of its shape, colour, smell and taste. S learns that it is a banana by seeing that it is yellow, banana-shaped, etc. None the less, S's perception of the banana's colour and shape is not indirect. S does not see that the object is yellow, for example, by seeing (knowing, believing) anything more basic – either about the banana or anything else (e.g. his own sensations of the banana). S has *learned* to identify such features, of course, but what S learned to do is not make an inference, even a unconscious inference, from other things he believes. What S acquired was a cognitive skill, a disposition to believe of yellow objects he saw that they were yellow. The exercise of this skill does not require, and in no way depends on, the having of any *other* beliefs. S's identificatory successes will depend on his operating in certain special conditions, of course. S will not, perhaps, be able to visually identify yellow objects in drastically reduced lighting, at funny viewing angles, or when afflicted with certain nervous disorders. But these facts about *when* S can see that something is yellow does not show that his perceptual knowledge (that *a* is yellow) in any way depends on a *belief* (let alone *knowledge*) that he is in such special conditions. It merely shows that direct perceptual knowledge is the result of exercising a skill, an identificatory skill, that like any skill, requires certain conditions for its successful exercise. An expert basketball player can't shoot accurately in a hurricane. He needs normal conditions to do what he has learned to do. So also with individuals who have developed perceptual (cognitive) skills. They need normal conditions to do what they have learned to do. They need normal conditions to see, for example, that something is yellow. But they don't, any more than the basketball player, have to know they are in these conditions to do what being in these conditions enables them to do.

This means, of course, that for the direct realist direct perceptual knowledge is fallible and corrigible. Whether S sees that *a* is F depends on his being caused to believe that *a* is F in conditions that are appropriate for an exercise of that cognitive skill. If conditions *are* right, then S sees (hence, knows) that *a* is

F. If they aren't, he doesn't. Whether or not S knows depends, then, not on what else (if anything) S believes, but on the circumstances in *which* S comes to believe. This being so, this type of direct realism is a form of externalism (*see* the discussion above and EXTERNALISM/INTERNALISM). Direct perception of objective facts, pure perceptual knowledge of external events, is made possible because what is needed (by way of justification) for such knowledge has been reduced. Background knowledge – and, in particular, the knowledge that the experience does, indeed, suffice for knowing – isn't needed.

This means that the foundations of knowledge are fallible. None the less, though fallible, they are in no way derived. That is what makes them foundations. Even if they are brittle, as foundations sometimes are, everything else rests upon them.

*See also* DIRECT REALISM; EXPERIENCE; REPRESENTATIVE REALISM; SENSATION/COGNITION.

BIBLIOGRAPHY

BonJour, L.: *The Structure of Empirical Knowledge* (Cambridge: Cambridge University Press, 1985).
Chisholm, R.: *Perceiving: A Philosophical Study* (Ithaca, NY: Cornell University Press, 1957).
Dretske, F.: *Seeing and Knowing* (Chicago: University of Chicago Press, 1969).
Dretske, F.: *Knowledge and the Flow of Information* (Cambridge, MA; MIT Press, 1981).
Goldman, A.: 'Discrimination and perceptual knowledge', *Journal of Philosophy* 73 (1976), 771–91.
Jackson, F.: *Perception* (Cambridge: Cambridge University Press, 1977).
Lehrer, K.: *Knowledge* (Oxford: Clarendon Press, 1974).
Pitcher, G.A. : *Theory of Perception* (Princeton: Princeton University Press, 1971).
Price, H.H.: *Perception* (Oxford: Methuen, 1932).
Swartz, R. ed.: *Perceiving, Sensing and Knowing* (Berkeley: University of California Press, 1965).

FRED DRETSKE

**perspectivism**    *see* NIETZSCHE

**phenomenalism**    Classical phenomenalism is the view that propositions asserting the existence of physical objects are analytically equivalent to propositions asserting that subjects would have certain sequences of sensations were they to have certain others. Although it is primarily a metaphysical view, phenomenalism is a theory with important epistemological implications and, indeed, it is often accepted by philosophers for its alleged epistemological advantages.

The basic idea behind phenomenalism is compatible with a number of different analyses of the self or conscious subject. Thus a phenomenalist might understand the self as a mind of the sort that BERKELEY was committed to, or as a Humean construct of actual and possible experience (*see* HUME). Also, as I use the term, a phenomenalist might adopt any number of different analyses of the visual, tactile, auditory, olfactory, gustatory and kinesthetic sensations described in the antecedents and consequents of the subjunctive conditionals that, according to the phenomenalist, analyse physical object propositions. Probably the most common analysis of sensations adopted by the phenomenalist is a SENSE-DATUM theory with the sense-data construed as mind-dependent entities (*see* ACT/OBJECT ANALYSIS). But there is nothing to prevent a phenomenalist from accepting an ADVERBIAL THEORY instead.

HISTORICAL ORIGINS

The historical origins of classical phenomenalism are difficult to trace, in part because, as one would expect, early statements of the view were usually not very careful. In his *Dialogues*, Berkeley hinted at classical phenomenalism when he had Philonous explain how he could reconcile an ontology containing only minds and ideas with the story of a creation that took place before the existence of humans:

Why, I imagine that if I had been present at the Creation, I should have seen things produced into being; that is, become perceptible, in the order described by the sacred historian. (Berkeley, 1713, p. 251)

More often, however, Berkeley seemed to rely on actual ideas in the mind of God to secure the existence of a physical world that is independent of the existence of any finite being.

John Stuart MILL (1867) may have been the first philosopher to put forth a phenomenalistic analysis. In that work he says that matter is a 'permanent possibility of sensation' and in explaining what permanent possibilities of sensation are Mill often seems to suggest that they could be understood in terms of the sensations one would have under certain conditions.

The attraction of classical phenomenalism grew with the rise of LOGICAL POSITIVISM and increasing acceptance of VERIFIC-ATIONISM. Phenomenalism, the argument went, is the only view that can accommodate both the ordinary conception of physical objects as mind-independent, enduring entities and the commonsense view that it is possible to confirm through experience the existence of physical objects. To understand the argument in support of this claim it is necessary to understand the epistemological framework presupposed by most phenomenalists. Classical phenomenalists were invariably FOUNDATIONALISTS, who further endorsed the radical empiricist's claim that the only contingent propositions we know directly are propositions describing the contents of our minds. If any belief about the physical world is to be justified at all it must be *inferentially* justified from what we know about the contents of our minds.

Classical phenomenalists were also usually implicitly *internalists* in epistemology (*see* EXTERNALISM/INTERNALISM) – at least they were implicitly committed to the view one might call *inferential* internalism. According to the inferential internalist one can be justified in believing one proposition *p* on the basis of another *e* only if one is justified in believing that *e* makes it likely that *p*. But how can one establish the occurrence of certain sensations as evidence for the exist-

ence of physical objects when all one knows directly is that certain sensations occur? If one's paradigm for establishing one thing as the sign of something else is inductive reasoning, there is obviously a fundamental and apparently insuperable problem (*see* PROBLEM OF THE EXTERNAL WORLD). To establish inductively that sensations are signs of physical objects one would have to *observe* a correlation between the occurrence of certain sensations and the existence of certain physical objects. But to observe such a correlation in order to establish a connection, one would need independent access to physical objects and, by hypothesis, this one cannot have. If one further adopts the verificationist's stance that the ability to comprehend is parasitic on the ability to confirm, one can easily be driven to HUME's conclusion:

Let us chace our imagination to the heavens, or to the utmost limits of the universe; we never really advance a step beyond ourselves, nor can conceive any kind of existence, but those perceptions, which have appear'd in that narrow compass. This is the universe of the imagination, nor have we have any idea but what is there produc'd. (Hume, 1739–40, pp. 67–8)

If one reaches such a conclusion but wants to maintain the intelligibility and verifiability of assertions about the physical world, one can go either the idealistic or the phenomenalistic route. The idealist (Berkeley, for example) tries to identify physical objects with bundles of sensations. The obvious difficulty (of which Berkeley was certainly aware) is how to preserve the mind-independent status of physical objects. The ordinary conception of a physical object just is the concept of something that could exist even in the absence of any minds (and their sensations). As an alternative to idealism, the phenomenalist proposes that we invoke the conceptual machinery of subjunctive conditionals. To say that a given physical object exists is not to say that there exists some entity of an ontologically different sort from that with which we are directly acquainted in sensation; nor, of course, is it to say that someone is actually having some sensation. Rather, we should view such propositions as equivalent in meaning to assertions about what sensations or sequences of sensation a subject would have were he to have certain others. The truth or falsity of such propositions is mind-independent and so with this analysis we could secure the mind-independent status of the physical world. What is more, to the empiricist's great relief, it looks as if such propositions could be established inductively. Subjunctives that assert connections holding between sensations can presumably be justified without having to correlate anything but sensations.

## OBJECTIONS TO PHENOMENALISM

Many philosophers today would reject the epistemological, ontological and meta-philosophical presuppositions with which phenomenalists approached the problem of perception. Foundationalism is hardly the received view in contemporary epistemology, and even those sympathetic to a kind of foundationalism are more likely to embrace an externalist version of the view, a version that circumvents the sceptical problems the phenomenalist was trying to solve with a phenomenalistic analysis. Other philosophers reject the conception of philosophical analysis as an attempt to specify necessary and sufficient conditions for the truth of propositions (*see* PARADOXES OF ANALYSIS). Some of these embrace an externalist or causal theory of meaning which makes the meaning of expressions in our language largely an empirical question inaccessible to an a priori method of analysis.

Still, the idea behind phenomenalism was, in the abstract, enormously attractive for many philosophers sympathetic to the presuppositions of radical empiricism and to suggest that it is rejected for the above reasons is probably to put the cart before the horse. In fact, it may have been the widespread conclusion that phenomenalism is false that led to rejection of some of the philosophical presuppositions on which it rested. Many of the objections which led to a general abandonment of phenomenalism surfaced with the attempt to spell out in detail how the theory is supposed to work.

One preliminary difficulty concerns the analysis of contingent subjunctive conditionals. The concepts of a law of nature, causation and the relation expressed by contingent subjunctive conditionals are all closely intertwined, and the problem has been to find an analysis of one of these concepts that does not presuppose an understanding of the others. The relationship between laws of nature and contingent subjunctive conditionals is also the source of at least two objections to phenomenalism. Some philosophers would argue that the subjunctive conditionals employed in the phenomenalist's analysis presuppose the existence of lawful regularities between patterns of sensations. But it is problematic to suppose that there are any genuine laws whose antecedents and consequents refer only to the occurrence of sensations. Unless the antecedents of such generalizations are protected by qualifications referring to the *physical* conditions under which certain sensations have occurred, it is implausible, the argument goes, to suppose that there are any lawful consequences concerning subsequent sensations. But if the assertion of such conditionals carries with it implicit reference to physical conditions, the phenomenalist programme of fully reducing talk about the physical world to talk about sensation fails. Furthermore, if anything like a regularity theory of law were correct, the existence of lawful connections between patterns of sensations might presuppose once again the existence of minds and sensations and thus make both the truth of the phenomenalist's subjunctives and the propositions about the physical world they are supposed to analyse parasitic upon the existence of minds – just what the phenomenalist is trying to avoid with an alternative to idealism. The phenomenalist, you will recall, is trying to accommodate the commonsense conception of the physical world as something that could have existed even in the absence of any conscious beings.

The above are certainly concerns, but the

argument against phenomenalism that was so widely viewed as decisive is the argument from perceptual relativity, most clearly and concisely presented by Roderick CHISHOLM (1948). Chisholm offers, in effect, a strategy for attacking any phenomenalistic analysis. The first move in the strategy is to force the phenomenalist into giving at least one example of an alleged analytic consequence (expressed in purely phenomenal language) of a proposition asserting the existence of some physical object. When one gets the example, one simply describes a hypothetical situation in which, though the physical object proposition is true, its alleged analytic consequence would obviously be false. If the physical object proposition really did entail the experiential proposition, then there could be no hypothetical situation in which the one is true and the other false, and so we would have constructed a reductio of the proposed analysis. C.I. LEWIS (1948, p. 240), for example, claimed that the proposition that there is a doorknob in front of me and to the left (p) entails the proposition that if I should seem to see such a doorknob in front of me and to the left and should seem to be initiating a certain grasping motion, then in all probability the feeling of contacting a doorknob would follow (r). (Lewis used the 'seems to perceive' terminology to report the occurrence of mind-dependent sensations.) Chisholm argues that p does not entail r, for there is another proposition q (the proposition that I am unable to move my limbs and my hands but am subject to delusions such that I think I am moving them; I often seem to myself to be initiating a certain grasping motion, but when I do I never have the feeling of contacting anything), which is obviously consistent with p and which when conjoined with p entails not-r.

RESPONSES

To escape the argument from perceptual relativity the phenomenalist might try to 'protect' the conditionals he employs in his analysis with a 'normal or standard conditions' clause added to the antecedents. It is crucial, however, that the phenomenalist not refer to the external or internal *physical* conditions of the subject for to do so would be to violate the conditions for a successful phenomenalistic analysis. A primary goal of phenomenalism was to reduce (completely) talk about the physical world to talk about sensations so as to make physical object propositions epistemically accessible. Can one protect the antecedents of the conditionals without resorting to physical description? One option would be to embed conditionals within conditionals but since we know that such conditionals are really designed to eliminate the existence of various physical conditions that might distort the normal sequence of sensations, we also know that any subjunctives designed to guarantee the absence of such distorting conditions will fail to do so because they will themselves be subject to distorting physical conditions.

There is one other avenue open to the phenomenalist, though this involves a subtle move away from classical versions of the view. One can attempt to introduce a normal or standard conditions clause in the antecedents of the phenomenalist's subjunctive whose purpose is to *denote* those conditions *whatever they are* that normally (defined statistically) accompany certain sequences of sensations. The conditions denoted by such a clause might include other facts about what sensations would follow others, facts about Kantian things-in-themselves, or facts about the intentions of a Berkeleian God. The claim might be made that even though a normal conditions clause of this sort involves denoting things in ontological categories other than sensations, such denotation is epistemically harmless, for one is always justified in believing, *ceteris paribus*, that things are as they usually are.

Once one modifies phenomenalism enough to allow into the phenomenalistic analysis expressions that might denote things other than sensations, however, one can argue that we might as well embrace a version of a causal theory of objects that is much more closely related to classical phenomenalism than the more familiar REPRESENTATIVE REALISM replete with its primary/secondary quality distinction and a conception of objects that *resemble* in important respects the contents of our minds. On this 'phenomenalistic' causal theory, to assert the existence of a physical object is to assert the existence of a thing (whatever it is – its intrinsic character might be in principle unknowable) that has the potential to produce certain sensations and that would produce certain sequences of sensations were it to produce certain others *under normal conditions*. This version of a causal theory contains no ontological commitments that extend beyond our modified phenomenalism and it seems that it allows one a much more natural way of analyzing bare existential statements, e.g. there exists a table (somewhere, some time). Such statements are a nightmare for classical phenomenalism for they provide no 'setting' that makes even *prima facie* plausible the entailment of any conditional about what any particular subject would experience. Because the causal theorist's analysis of such statements begins with the bare existential claim about the existence of a potential cause of sensations, we eliminate that problem. Indeed, when Mill identified objects with the permanent possibilities of sensations he may well have been pointing not to classical phenomenalism but to the causal theory that is closely related to it. Notice that this causal theory faces precisely the same problem of perceptual relativity as pure versions of phenomenalism. One still needs a way of specifying subjunctively the 'powers' that define the cause as a physical object of a given kind, and to avoid a regress one must define such powers without presupposing an understanding of physical object propositions. If so, two views long considered radically different may have a vested interest in finding common solutions to common problems.

*See also* FIRTH; LOGICAL POSITIVISM; PROBLEM OF THE EXTERNAL WORLD.

BIBLIOGRAPHY

Ayer, A.J.: *Language, Truth and Logic* 2nd edn (New York: Dover, 1946).
Berkeley, G.: *Three Dialogues between Hylas and Philonous* (1713) in *Berkeley: Philosophical Works* ed. M.R. Ayers (London: Dent, 1975).
Chisholm, R.: 'The problem of empiricism', *Journal of Philosophy* 45 (1948), 512–17.
Hume, D.: *A Treatise of Human Nature* (1739–40); ed. L.A. Selby-Bigge, revised P.H. Nidditch (Oxford: Oxford University Press, 1978).
Lewis, C.I.: *An Analysis of Knowledge and Valuation* (La Salle: Open Court, 1946).
Mackie, J.L.: 'What's really wrong with phenomenalism', *Proceedings of the British Academy* 55 (1969), 113–27.
Mill, J.S.: *An Examination of Sir William Hamilton's Philosophy* (London: Longmans Green, 1867).

RICHARD FUMERTON

**phenomenology** As summed up in HUSSERL's slogan, 'To the things themselves!', the aim of phenomenology is to bypass the presuppositions built into traditional theories (including psychology, physiology and epistemology) in order to describe what shows up in the flow of lived experience prior to reflection. The focus is solely on the essential structures of experience itself. The key discovery is that all forms of consciousness are characterized by 'intentionality', a directedness toward things such that consciousness is always *of* or *about* something. Husserl distinguished the intentional act (*noesis*), which is occasional and transient, from the act's content (*noema*), the timeless, intersubjective object-as-meant. Later phenomenologists like HEIDEGGER and MERLEAU-PONTY rejected the distinctions of consciousness vs. object or act vs. content, and tried to describe the 'natural conception of the world' prior to the EPOCHE.

CHARLES GUIGNON

**philosophical knowledge** A traditional view of philosophical knowledge can be sketched by comparing and contrasting philosophical and scientific investigation, as follows. The two types of investigations differ both in their methods (the former is a priori, and the latter a posteriori) and in the metaphysical status of their results (the former yields facts that are metaphysically necessary and the latter yields facts that are metaphysically contingent). Yet the two types of investigations resemble each other in that both, if successful, uncover new facts, and these facts, although *expressed* in language, are generally not *about* language (except for investigations in such specialized areas as philosophy of language and empirical linguistics).

This view of philosophical knowledge has considerable appeal. But it faces problems. First, the conclusions of some common philosophical arguments seem preposterous. Such positions as that it is no more reasonable to eat bread than arsenic (because it is only in the past that arsenic poisoned people), or that one can never know he is not dreaming, may seem to go so far against commonsense as to be for that reason unacceptable. Second, philosophical investigation does not lead to consensus among philosophers. Philosophy, unlike the sciences, lacks an established body of generally-agreed-upon truths. Moreover, philosophy lacks an unequivocally applicable method of settling disagreements. (The qualifier 'unequivocally applicable' is to forestall the objection that philosophical disagreements are settled by the method of a priori argumentation; there is often unresolvable disagreement about which side has won a philosophical argument.)

In the face of these and other considerations, various philosophical movements have repudiated the above traditional view of philosophical knowledge. Thus, VERIFICA-TIONISM responds to the unresolvability of traditional philosophical disagreements by putting forth a criterion of literal meaningfulness that renders such questions literally meaningless: 'A statement is held to be literally meaningful if and only if it is either analytic or empirically verifiable' (Ayer, 1952, p. 9), where a statement is analytic iff it is just a matter of definition, and traditional controversial philosophical views, such as that it is metaphysically impossible to have knowledge of the world outside one's own mind, would count as neither analytic nor empirically verifiable (*see* LOGICAL POS-ITIVISM).

Various objections have been raised to this verification principle. The most important is that the principle is self-refuting, i.e. that when one attempts to apply the verification principle to itself, the result is that the principle comes out as literally meaningless (hence not true) because it is neither empirically verifiable nor analytic. This move may seem like a trick. But it reveals a deep methodological problem with the verificationist approach. The verification principle is intended to delegitimize all controversy that is not resolvable either empirically or by recourse to definitions. The principle itself, however, cannot be established either empirically or by recourse to definitions. The principle is an attempt to rule out synthetic a priori controversy; yet the principle itself is both synthetic a priori and controversial. It is ironic that the self-refutingness of the verification principle is one of the very few points on which philosophers nowadays approach consensus.

Ordinary language philosophy, another twentieth-century attempt to delegitimize traditional philosophical problems, faces a parallel but unrecognized problem of self-refutingness. Just as verificationism can be characterized as reacting against unresolvable a priori controversy, ordinary language philosophy can be characterized as reacting against a priori counterintuitiveness. The ordinary language philosopher rejects counterintuitive philosophical positions (such as the view that time is unreal or that one can never know anything about other minds) by saying that these views '*go against ordinary language*' (Malcolm, in Rorty, 1970, p.113); i.e. that these views go against the way the ordinary person uses such terms as 'know' and 'unreal', since the ordinary person would reject the above counterintuitive statements about knowledge and time. On the ordinary language view, it follows that the sceptic does not mean the same thing by 'know' as does the non-philosopher, since they use the terms differently and meaning is use. Thus, on this view, sceptics and anti-sceptics no more have a non-linguistic disagreement about knowledge than someone who says 'Banks are financial institutions' and someone who says

'Banks are the shores of rivers' have a non-linguistic disagreement about banks.

An obvious objection here is that many factors besides meaning help to determine use. For example, two people who disagree about whether the world is round use the word 'round' differently in that one applies it to the world while the other does not; yet they do not thereby mean different things by 'world' or 'round'. Ordinary language philosophy allows that this aspect of use is not part of the meaning, since it rests on a disagreement about empirical facts. But in relegating all non-empirical disagreements to differences in linguistic meaning, the ordinary language philosopher denies the possibility of substantive, non-linguistic disagreement over a priori facts and thus, like the verificationist, disallows the synthetic a priori. Malcolm claims that 'if a child who was learning the language were to say, in a situation where we were sitting in a room with chairs about, that it was "highly probable" that there were chairs there, we should smile *and correct his language* 1970, (p. 116). Malcolm may be right about this particular case, since it is so unlikely that a child would have independently developed a sceptical philosophy. But a parallel response seems obviously inappropriate as a reply to a philosopher who says 'One can never know that one is not dreaming', or, for that matter, as a reply to an inept arithmetic student who says '$33 = 12 + 19$'. If it were true that a philosopher uttering the first of these sentences were not using 'know' in the usual sense, he could not convey his philosophical views to a French speaker by uttering that sentence's French translation ( 'On ne peut jamais savoir qu'on ne rêve pas'), any more than one can convey his eight-year-old cousin Mary's opinion that her teacher is vicious by saying 'Mary's teacher is viscous' if Mary wrongly thinks 'viscous' means vicious and is using it that way. But it seems obvious that failure to translate 'know' or its cognates into their French synonyms would prevent an English-speaking sceptic from accurately representing his views in French at all. The ordinary language view that all non-empirical disagreements are linguistic disagreements

entails that if someone believes the sentence 'a is F' when this sentence expresses the a priori proposition that a is F, then having the property he takes 'F' to express is part of what he means by 'a'. But this obviously goes against the Malcolmian 'ordinary use' of the term 'meaning', i.e. what ordinary people, once they understand the term 'meaning', believe on a priori grounds about the extension of the term 'meaning'. For example, the ordinary man would deny that the inept student mentioned above cannot be using his words with our usual meaning when he says '$33 = 12 + 19$'. Like the earlier objection of self-refutingness to verificationism, this objection reveals a deep methodological problem. Just as synthetic a priori controversy cannot be ruled out by a principle that is both synthetic a priori and controversial, a priori counterintuitiveness cannot be ruled out by a principle that is both a priori and counterintuitive.

Although verificationism and ordinary language philosophy thus are both self-refuting, the problems that helped motivate these positions need to be addressed. What are we to say about the fact that (a) many philosophical conclusions seem wildly counterintuitive and (b) philosophical investigations do not lead to philosophical consensus?

To put the first problem in perspective, it is important to see that even highly counter-intuitive philosophical views generally have arguments behind them – arguments that 'start with something so simple as not to seem worth stating', and proceed by steps so obvious as not to seem worth taking, before '[ending] with something so paradoxical that no one will believe it' (Russell, 1956, p.193). But since repeated applications of common-sense can thus lead to philosophical conclusions that conflict with commonsense, commonsense is a problematic criterion for assessing philosophical views. It is true that, once we have weighed the relevant arguments, we must ultimately rely on our judgement about whether, in the light of these arguments, it just seems reasonable to accept a given philosophical view. But this truism should not be confused with the problematic position that our considered philosophical judgment in the light of philosophical arguments must not conflict with our commonsense *pre*-philosophical views.

As for philosophers' inability to reach consensus, it is important to see that this does not entail that there is no fact of the matter as to who is right. There are other possible explanations for this inability (*see* Rescher, 1978). Moreover, supposing that the existence of unresolvable a priori disagreement over the truth of *p* shows that *p* lacks a truth-value would make the matter of whether *p* has a truth-value too dependent on which people happen to exist and what they can be persuaded to believe.

Both verificationism and ordinary language philosophy deny the synthetic a priori. QUINE goes further; he denies the analytic a priori as well; he denies both the analytic–synthetic distinction and the a priori – a posteriori distinction. In 'Two Dogmas of Empiricism' Quine considers several reductive definitions of analyticity synonymy, argues that all are inadequate, and concludes that there is no analytic and synthetic distinction. But clearly there is a substantial gap in this argument. One would not conclude from the absence of adequate reductive definitions of 'red' and 'blue' that there is no red–blue distinction, or no such thing as redness. Instead, one would hold that such terms as 'red' and 'blue' are defined by example. But this also seems plausible for such terms as 'synonymous' and 'analytic' (Grice and Strawson, 1956).

On Quine's view, the distinction between philosophical and scientific inquiry is a matter of degree. His later writings indicate that the sort of account he would require to make analyticity, necessity, or a priority acceptable is one that explicates these notions in terms of 'people's dispositions to overt behavior' in response to socially observable stimuli (Quine, 1969, p. 29). A discussion of this BEHAVIOURISM, however, lies beyond the scope of this essay.

*See also* ANALYTICITY; NATURALIZED EPISTEMOLOGY; PSYCHOLOGY AND EPISTEMOLOGY; RYLE.

BIBLIOGRAPHY

Ayer, A.J.: *Language, Truth and Logic* (New York: Dover, 1952).

Grice, H.P. and Strawson, P.F.: 'In defense of a dogma', *Philosophical Review* 65 (1956), 141–68.

Quine, W.V.: 'Two dogmas of empiricism', in his *From a Logical Point of View* (Cambridge, MA: Harvard University Press, 1953), ch. 2.

Quine, W.V.: *The Ways of Paradox and Other Essays* (New York: Random House, 1966), chs 18 and 20.

Quine, W.V.: *Ontological Relativity and Other Essays* (New York: Columbia University Press, 1969).

Rescher, N.: 'Philosophical disagreement,' *Review of Metaphysics* 22 (1978), 217–51.

Rorty, R. ed.: *The Linguistic Turn* (Chicago: University of Chicago Press, 1970).

Russell, B.: 'The philosophy of logical atomism', in his *Logic and Knowledge* ed. R. C. Marsh (London: Allen and Unwin, 1956), 177–281.

Wittgenstein, L.: *Philosophical Investigations* (Oxford: Blackwell, 1953).

FELICIA ACKERMAN

**Plato** (*c*.429–347 BC) Greek philospher, founder of the Academy at Athens. Plato's thinking about epistemology has two aspects. One concerns questions about what statements a person is justified in making and what he can justifiably claim to know. Here there is discussion of the grounds on which a statement might be established or refuted, and of the kinds of arguments that can be given for or against something. This part of Plato's view is quite close to modern epistemology. The second aspect of his thinking is much closer to what is nowadays thought of as metaphysics. This part grows mainly out of the question, What must we and the world be like if it is to be the case that we know something? Here the issues have to do, not so much with ways of refuting and establishing statements, but rather with what appropriate conditions on knowledge are and with what the world and we ourselves must be like if we are to be able to fulfil them. It seems to Plato crucial that knowledge be thought of as concerning objective facts that hold non-relatively to a particular observer or circumstance of observation.

The first aspect of Plato's epistemology was strongly influenced by Socrates, particularly that part of his activity that suggests a sceptical stance. Socrates is said to have claimed that he knew either nothing or very little (e.g. *Meno* 80, 86). In Plato's works this claim is loosely associated with the portrayal of Socrates as practising a procedure of *elenchus*, 'scrutiny' (often also translated 'refutation'). Arguably this procedure is capable only of refuting a statement, never of establishing one (except perhaps the negation of the statement refuted, though the state of logic in Plato does not allow this issue to be fruitfully raised). At any rate Socrates gained a reputation for skill at refuting things that others said, and he apparently practised the skill on himself, thereby becoming disinclined to make claims to knowledge.

This aspect of Plato's thinking appears mostly in earlier works, such as the *Laches*, the *Euthyphro* and parts of the *Meno*, as well as *Republic* I, which is probably not early but mimics his earlier works. (The classification of Plato's works as early, middle and late involves some controversy and conjecture, but is widely enough agreed upon to be presupposed here.)

The first aspect of Plato's epistemology shares important preoccupations with epistemology since Descartes. First, as indicated, Socrates is portrayed as finding reason to reject most claims to knowledge. Next, Plato's early investigations are launched mainly from a first-person standpoint: one must ask whether one's own judgements are justified, and try to find justifications that will seem compelling to oneself. In this way they adopt a standpoint similar to that of what are now called 'internalist' epistemological views (*see* EXTERNALISM/INTERNALISM). Third, it is often said to be important to make statements on the basis only of what oneself believes, and not to rely on hearsay or other's beliefs. In addition, although Plato does not explicitly introduce the notion of 'doubt', he

emphasizes the instability of most beliefs, i.e. the fact that they can often be easily dislodged by argument or other kinds of persuasion.

The second aspect of Plato's epistemology is prominent in his middle period, when he is usually taken to have moved beyond Socrates' influence and to have developed a positive doctrine of his own. This phase begins in the *Meno*, continues in the *Phaedo*, the *Symposium* and the *Republic*, and shows itself also in the *Timaeus* (usually regarded as one of Plato's last works).

This part of Plato's thinking is given over to developing a metaphysical theory about how we and the world must be if we are to have knowledge (*episteme*). It is either assumed or perhaps argued (*see Phdo.* 74, *Rep*, 475–80, *Tim.* 51) that we do have knowledge, and taken as obvious that knowledge is distinct from certain other cognitive states, in particular 'belief' or 'opinion', *doxa*. Plato then tries to show what the world must contain, and what we ourselves must be like, if these two things are to hold. In this phase virtually no attempt is made at dogged socratic scrutiny of Plato's own theory, at least until the *Theaetetus* and the *Parmenides*. In those enigmatic works Plato raises various questions about what state of affairs must obtain if knowledge is to be possible, including (it seems) questions about whether his own theory really accounts for that possibility. In the end it remains unclear what his answers to these questions are.

Before further examining this second phase of Plato's thinking, which produces his most influential ideas in epistemology, it will be helpful to consider how it arose from the first phase.

Virtually without exception, each of Plato's early works is dominated by an attempt to define some notion, usually an evaluative notion like moderation, courage, holiness, virtue, and so on. Most of the refutations appearing on those works are directed at the definitions that are offered, and these do always end up refuted. As Plato presents things, Socrates' view was that before a person can know certain facts about virtue (for example, how it is acquired), one has to know a definition of it, or, as Plato also says, to know 'what it is' (*Protagoras* 360–1, *Rep.* 354). In early dialogues a definition is often refuted by citing something that fits the definiendum but not the definiens, or vice versa. Sometimes, though, a definiens will be attacked for being not sufficiently clearer than the definiendum is (*Meno* 75–7), or for introducing some kind of circularity (e.g. *Meno* 79).

Plato's middle works, however, are not organized wholly around searches for definitions. Rather, they expound a metaphysical theory that is designed to show how knowledge is possible. It seems natural to suppose that the failure of earlier searches for definitions somehow led him to construct this theory. The way in which this happened, however, is not easy to reconstruct. One possibility is that the theory is supposed to provide a way of discovering definitions which does not rely on the use of *elenchus*. Another possibility is that Plato decided that finding definitions is not, after all, the first step of the epistemological enterprise, and hoped that his theory would show a different way to gain knowledge, and eventually also definitions, of the things that he had earlier taken to need defining at the first stage of any discussion involving them. Thus, for example, the *Republic* is able to say quite a lot about justice before it finally (at 443) arrives at an account (and even then not a formally stated one) of what justice is.

Plato's theory is built around the idea that there are objects, often called 'Forms' (*eide*), that we do not sense but can have knowledge about. The idea of knowledge here is closely intertwined, in a way not easy to disentangle, with a notion of the understanding of terms. Some of this knowledge-*cum*-understanding is expressed in the form of propositions, for example the proposition that the Good is not pleasure (*Rep.* 505), and sometimes it is described as a kind of intellectual 'viewing' (500, 511) – which shares something with (and led historically to) Frege's notion of 'grasping' a sense and Russell's notion of 'acquaintance' with a universal.

Much of Plato's metaphysics of Forms arises from his reasons for thinking that

knowledge in the proper sense cannot consist simply in the use of the senses and cannot concern sensible objects. On the other hand, this view leads him into severe problems, many of which are investigated in his later works.

In particular it strikes him as important that a sensible object that has a certain predicate true of it can both present the simultaneous appearance of having the contrary predicate true of it (*Phdo.* 74, *Rep.* 479), and also can have had, or come to have, that contrary predicate true of it at some other time (*Tim.* 49–50). For this reason he tries to construct his theory about Forms so that unlike a sensible, a Form will be depicted as incapable, at least under favourable circumstances, of presenting to the mind any appearance that is, so to speak, contrary to that of being the particular Form that it is. Thus, for example, the Form of equality is said to be incapable of appearing to be inequality (*Phdo.* 74), and Forms are in general said to be incapable of change whereas sensible objects are said to be constantly changing (*Phdo.* 78–9, *Rep.* 484–5, *Tim.* 51). However, at certain points in his later works Plato may suggest that nothing at all can satisfy this stringent condition (*Soph.* 248–9), and that therefore his view about Forms may need either more careful formulation, qualification, or rethinking.

This same line of thought seemingly makes Plato suggest that it is possible to have knowledge only about Forms, and that knowledge about sensible objects is impossible (*Rep.* 477–80, *Tim.* 51). Moreover he also seems to hold sometimes that we cannot have about Forms that kind of cognition, belief or opinion, that we do have of sensibles (ibid.). On the other hand, he allows that it is possible to make mistakes about Forms, and also to be in a cognitive state vis-à-vis a Form that seems indistinguishable from what he seems obliged to call false belief or opinion. This idea, too, requires some kind of further explanation of the distinction between Forms and sensibles – a requirement that Plato seems to see some difficulty in satisfying (e.g. *Tht.* 187–200).

Although in this phase of his work Plato

PLATO

concentrates, as indicated, on constructing a metaphysics that will make room for the possibility of knowledge, he does at the same time pay some attention to the problems that are characteristic of the first phase of his epistemology. In the *Meno*, the *Phaedo* and the *Republic*, he develops what has been called the 'method of hypothesis', which seems to be a method by which things can ultimately be demonstrated unconditionally. In the *Meno* (87–9) and the *Phaedo* (99–101) he indicates that hypotheses are to be accepted only provisionally and not regarded as certain or unrevisable. In the *Republic*, however, he seems to maintain that one can somehow reach an 'unhypothesized' principle (511) which will somehow serve as the basis for demonstrating everything hitherto accepted merely hypothetically. He apparently implies that what is demonstrated thereby will have to do only with Forms (ibid.). He also makes a suggestion, not clearly explained, that this 'principle' (*arche*) has something to do with the Form of the Good (533–4). There is no generally accepted interpretation of what Plato says here, but it seems to indicate that he accepted or was seriously considering some kind of *foundationalist* epistemological position, which would start from some unshakable principle and derive from it the rest of what there is to be known about Forms. (As often, however, Plato here seems to waver between thinking of the principle and what is to be derived as possessing propositional structure and treating them as non-propositionally structured objects.)

This method of hypothesis is earlier offered as something that is used by 'dialectic', the style of philosophizing that takes place through conversational questions and answers (*see* DIALECTIC). In later works, however, such as the *Phaedrus* and the *Sophist*, Plato says that dialectic makes use of the 'method of collection and division', which is a method for constructing taxonomies and definitions. Nothing in his description of this method, however, indicates that it could be used to demonstrate or justify definitions. (In *Posterior Analytics* II. 5 Aristotle attacks the contention, presumably due to someone other than Plato, that division could be used

to demonstrate the correctness of a definition.) Interestingly, Plato here never tries to show clearly how such definitions might be subjected to, or could stand up against, the sort of scrutiny that is practised in the early dialogues.

Plato's most concerted effort to explain what knowledge is appears in the *Theaetetus*. This work has not yet been given a satisfactory interpretation. It represents itself as a failed attempt, in the manner of earlier dialogues, to find a definition, this time, of knowledge. Among other points of obscurity, it is disputed whether the *Theaetetus* accepts, is neutral on or rejects the metaphysical views that dominate the *Phaedo*, *Republic*, *Symposium* and *Timaeus*. In addition, the work is divided into sections whose relation to each other, as well as to Plato's views as expressed elsewhere, is not fully clear. The first part (to 186) is a refutation of the thesis that knowledge is perception (*aisthesis*, a word that may also be translated 'sensation'). The next part (187–200) is a failed attempt to defend the possibility of false belief and particularly false identity-beliefs) against some objections. The last part (200–10) is a failed attempt to define knowledge as 'true belief with an account (*logos*)'.

The first part of the work plainly has something to do with Plato's claim in his middle period that knowledge has to do not with sensible objects but with Forms. But although this part of the dialogue definitely denies that to know is to perceive, it does not explicitly deny that there is knowledge concerning sensible objects, and some interpreters take the dialogue as a whole, on the contrary, to imply or even to assert that there is.

The latter two parts of the dialogue do not explicitly mention Forms, but many interpreters have thought that they tacitly deal with them. It seems more likely that they are intended to be neutral on the question whether Forms are the only objects of knowledge, and to deal with problems that arise for any kind of objects that it might reasonably be taken to be possible to have knowledge about, whether these be Forms or something else. Indeed, the problems discussed here are more abstract than the ones that Plato deals with when he is expounding his metaphysics of knowledge, as in the *Republic*, and even when he is scrutinizing it and raising problems for it, as in the *Parmenides*. Indeed, some of the issues raised in the *Theaetetus*, and also in the *Sophist*, involve questions about the conditions under which a person can be said to have designated, or be thinking about, a particular object or concept. As such, they would nowadays be associated less with epistemology than with the philosophy of language. On the other hand, *Theaetetus* 187–200 seems to presuppose, against what seems to be suggested in the *Phaedo* and the *Republic* (*see supra*), that an object of knowledge can in some sense present to the mind an appearance somehow conflicting with its being the thing that it is.

Although like early works the *Theaetetus* aims unsuccessfully at a definition, its main concern is with the metaphysics of thought and knowledge, and it is not centred on questions about justification of belief or knowledge. It thus shows Plato to have moved farther away than ever from concerns that were characteristic of the first phase of his epistemological thinking.

WRITINGS

*Platonis Opera* ed. J. Burnet, 5 vols (Oxford: Clarendon Press, 1900–7).
*The Collected Dialogues of Plato* eds E. Hamilton and H. Cairns (Princeton: Princeton University Press, 1961).

BIBLIOGRAPHY

Bostock, D.: *Plato's Theaetetus* (Oxford: Clarendon Press, 1988).
Burnyeat, M.: *The Theaetetus of Plato* (Indianapolis: Hackett, 1990).
Cooper, J.H.: 'Plato on sense perception and knowledge', *Phronesis* 15 (1970), 123–46.
Fine, G.: 'Knowledge and belief in *Republic V*', *Archiv für Geschichte der Philosophie* 58 (1978), 121–39.
Matthews, G.B. and Blackson, T.A.: 'Causes in the *Phaedo*', *Synthesis* 79 (1989), 581–91.
McDowell, J.: *Plato, Theaetetus* (Oxford: Clarendon Press, 1973).

Penner, T.: *The Ascent from Nominalism* (Dordrecht: Reidel, 1987).
Robinson, R.: *Plato's Earlier Dialectic* 2nd edn (Oxford: Clarendon Press, 1953).
Vlastos, G.: 'Degrees of reality in Plato', in *New Essays on Plato and Aristotle* ed. R. Bambrough (New York: Routledge, 1965), 1–18.
White, N.P.: *Plato on Knowledge and Reality* (Indianapolis: Hackett, 1976).
White, N.P.: 'Plato's epistemological metaphysics', in *Cambridge Companion to Plato* ed. R. Kraut (Cambridge: Cambridge University Press, 1991).

NICHOLAS WHITE

**Popper, Karl (1902–)** Austrian-born philosopher who now lives in Britain. Although widely regarded as primarily a philosopher of science and then a political philosopher, Popper might equally be regarded as first and foremost an epistemologist in that his conclusions in these other areas derive from his epistemological stance. Indeed, in his early *Logic of Scientific Discovery* he writes that 'the main problem of philosophy is the critical analysis of the appeal to the authority of experience' (pp. 51–2). In the Preface to the same work, Popper writes that the central problem of epistemology is the problem of the growth of knowledge, and that this is best studied by studying the growth of scientific knowledge. His philosophy of science may then be seen as part of his epistemology, rather than vice versa. And both his attitude to politics and society and his later work in the philosophy of biology derive from his epistemology.

Popper's epistemology itself rests on a deep scepticism about the validity of inductive inference, a scepticism which, in the opinion of many critics, undermines his own attempt to establish a non-inductive account of knowledge (*see* PROBLEMS OF INDUCTION). On induction, Popper is basically Humean, but instead of following normal practice and attempting to rebut Hume directly, Popper develops an epistemology which supposedly does without induction altogether. The fundamental insight here is to exploit the asymmetry in empirical matters between proof and disproof. While no universal empirical theory can be proved, owing to our ignorance of the totality of phenomena, a universal theory can be disproved by only one counter-instance to it. Popper believes that not only the grand theories of mature science should be regarded as universal theories in the relevant sense. Even the statement 'Here is a glass of water' involves universal terms ('glass', 'water') and cannot be verified by observational experience, as it implies law-like behaviour on the part of the object in question, behaviour which is beyond our powers to verify fully. Nevertheless, just as one planet moving once in an elliptical orbit would be enough to refute the theory that all planets move in circles, so one unglass-like bit of behaviour would convince us that what we had before us was no glass.

How then are we to proceed epistemologically? Popper's view is that we should consciously seek theories which are falsifiable by counter-evidence, that we should seek to falsify them and those which survive testing should then be tentatively accepted and regarded as corroborated or closer to the truth than the ones which have been falsified. How this method – of conjecture and refutation, Popper calls it – differs from standard types of induction in which we also rely on severely tested theories is something which has escaped most critics of Popper. Others have questioned his right to base anything as substantial as the falsification of a theory on singular observations, given his belief that they too are theory-laden, a problem Popper wrestles with somewhat inconclusively in *The Logic of Scientific Discovery*.

If Popper's specific attempt to solve the problem of induction through a non-inductive epistemology has convinced few of his readers, his approach to science and knowledge generally has won many followers. The idea that we cannot know but only guess, and that we should avoid DOGMATISM in science and human affairs more generally is attractive on a number of levels.

First, it sets human knowledge in a Darwinian context, something to which Popper has increasingly turned his attention in recent years. Our perceptual faculties and our theories are seen *modo biologico*, as natural or human attempts to anticipate the environment, attempts which will be weeded out if the environment does not match them sufficiently well or if the environment itself changes (*see* EVOLUTIONARY EPISTEMOLOGY, EPISTEMOLOGY NATURALIZED).

Secondly, Popper's FALLIBILISM leads him to see science itself as a construction of the human imagination, rather than something simply read passively and mechanically off the facts of nature. This aspect of his thinking has been found liberating by many scientists. Connected to his fallibilism concerning science, though more controversial, are Popper's famous attempts to demarcate true science from pseudo-science in terms of empirical falsifiability and also his anti-essentialism (*see* NECESSARY/CONTINGENT). The former view would have true scientists not just proposing bold theories, but crucially, then seeking to reject them (in contrast, according to Popper, to proponents of such influential systems as Marxism and psychoanalysis). Unfortunately for the demarcation criterion, though, it seems that even the physical sciences need a higher degree of dogmatism than Popper's criterion can allow. His anti-essentialism amounts to little more than the view that as any current theory of science is likely to turn out to be false, we should not regard it as giving us the essence of the world. But it does not follow from this that science and scientists should not be seeking natural kinds or essences.

Finally, Popper's attitude to politics, adumbrated passionately and memorably in *The Open Society and its Enemies*, is that any social policy, like any other proposal, is bound to have unsuspected and unintended consequences. Society should, therefore, be organized so that criticisms can be heard from those affected by policies and governments should be changed peacefully in response to the wishes of the governed. From our point of view, what is significant here is not so much the analysis Popper gives of the open society as the way his social philosophy follows directly from his epistemological fallibilism.

See also HISTORICISM; NATURAL SCIENCE.

WRITINGS

*The Logic of Scientific Discovery* (London: Hutchinson, 1959): his translation of *Logik der Forschung* (Vienna, 1935).
*The Open Society and Its Enemies* 2 vols (London: Routledge and Kegan Paul, 1945).
*Conjectures and Refutations* (London: Routledge and Kegan Paul, 1963).
*Objective Knowledge* (Oxford: Clarendon Press, 1972).
*Realism and the Aim of Science* (London: Hutchinson, 1983).
'Intellectual Autobiography' and 'Replies to Critics', in *The Philosophy of Karl Popper* ed. P.A. Schillp (La Salle: Open Court, 1974), 1–181 and 959–1197.

BIBLIOGRAPHY

Lakatos, I. and Musgrave, A. eds: *Criticism and the Growth of Knowledge* (Cambridge: Cambridge University Press, 1970).
O'Hear, A.: *Karl Popper* (London: Routledge and Kegan Paul, 1980).
Stove, D.C.: *Popper and After: Four Modern Irrationalists* (Oxford: Pergamon Press, 1982).
Watkins, J.W.N.: *Science and Scepticism* (London: Hutchinson, 1984).

ANTHONY O'HEAR

**positivism** see LOGICAL POSITIVISM.

**pragmatism** A (primarily American) school of philosophy initiated by PEIRCE and JAMES; characterized by the 'pragmatic maxim', according to which the meaning of a concept is to be sought in the experiential or practical consequences of its application. The epistemology of pragmatism is typically anti-Cartesian, fallibilistic, naturalistic; in some versions it is also realistic, in others not.

'It has probably never happened', Peirce wrote in 1905, 'that a philosopher has attempted to give a general name to his own doctrine without that name's soon acquiring in common philosophical usage, a significa-tion much broader than was originally intended'. His 'pragmatism', he continued, had by then acquired a signification so much broader than, and indeed so much at odds with, his original intention, that it was 'time to kiss his child good-bye' and 'to announce the birth of the word "pragmaticism", which is ugly enough to be safe from kidnappers' (*Collected Papers* 5.414).

As this suggests, the problem of giving an accurate brief characterization of the philosophical tendencies known as 'pragmatism' is far from trivial. It is hard enough to specify what important philosophical ideas were shared by Peirce and James, the founders of pragmatism; harder yet to find a characterization that would also comfortably accommodate Dewey, Schiller and Mead; nearly impossible to extend it to include more recent neo-pragmatists and sympathizers, overt and covert, as diverse as Ramsey, Lewis, Quine, Sellars, Putnam, Apel, Rorty, Rescher, etc. There is a large element of truth in Schiller's observation, that there are as many pragmatisms as pragmatists.

With respect specifically to the theory of knowledge, however, it is possible, not indeed to identify a set of shared doctrines, but instead to discern two broad styles of pragmatism, sharing the conviction that a CARTESIAN approach is fundamentally flawed, but responding very differently to that failure. Repudiating the requirement of absolute certainty in knowledge, insisting on the connection of knowledge with action, pragmatism of a reformist stripe still acknowledges the legitimacy of traditional questions about the truth-conduciveness of our cognitive practices, and sustains a conception of truth objective enough to give those questions bite. Pragmatism of a revolutionary stripe, by contrast, relinquishing the objectivity of truth, acknowledges no legitimate epistemological questions over and above those internal to our current cognitive conventions.

This distinction between reformists and revolutionaries (adapted from one in Migotti, 1988) will not map perfectly on to my list of pragmatists, neo-pragmatists and sympathizers. Peirce would count as a reformist, as would Lewis, Ramsey, Sellars and Rescher; Schiller would count as a revolutionary, as would Rorty. But in James, to a degree, and more markedly in Dewey – arguably also in Quine and Putnam – elements of both tendencies are to be found. But this does not detract from the usefulness of the distinction as a diagnostic tool, either historically or philosophically; it will provide both a framework for understanding something of the shifts within pragmatism from Peirce through James and Dewey to Schiller, and the backdrop to an assessment of what is of most permanent value in the pragmatists' contributions to the theory of knowledge.

At the heart of PEIRCE's pragmatism lies the pragmatic maxim: 'if one can define accurately all the conceivable experimental phenomena which the affirmation or denial of a concept could imply, one will have therein a complete definition of the concept, and *there is absolutely nothing more in it*' (ibid. 5.412). Meaning is a matter of the conceivable experimental, experiential consequences of a concept's applying: *pragmatisch*, in the Kantian sense. Pragmatism is thus, Peirce acknowledges, a kind of 'prope-Positivism'; one role of the pragmatic maxim is to reveal that 'almost every proposition of ontological metaphysics . . . is gibberish' (5.423). But the maxim is not intended to rule out metaphysics altogether, but rather to discriminate the illegitimate, the pragmatically meaningless, from *scientific* metaphysics, which uses the method of the sciences, observation and reasoning. Philosophy, where it is legitimate, is an observational science, differing from other sciences not in its method, but in its reliance on the most familiar kinds of experience, the least sophisticated kinds of observation.

Peirce's thorough-going critique of Cartesian epistemology, and his own engagingly naturalistic theory of inquiry, are of a piece with this conception of a reformed, scientific philosophy.

With Descartes, philosophy 'put off childish things, and began to be a conceited young man' (4.71). Descartes' method (*see* DESCARTES) is a sham, a matter of feigned doubt which inevitably leads to the eventual reinstatement of all the beliefs supposedly doubted. There is no such faculty as the intuition on which Descartes' criterion of clearness and distinctness relies, and no such intuitive self-consciousness as Descartes' reliance on the COGITO as the indubitable starting point for the reconstruction of knowledge requires. Descartes' aspiration to certainty is misplaced, his subjective stance viciously individualistic.

Unlike Descartes, and in strikingly Darwinian spirit, Peirce sees human belief as continuous with animal expectation, human inquiry as continuous with animals' exploration of their environment. He agrees that inquiry begins with doubt, but insists that it must be *real* doubt. Peirce conceives of belief as a habit of action, a disposition to behave, and of doubt as the result of some belief-habit's being interrupted by recalcitrance on the part of experience. Real doubt is thus involuntary, and unpleasant; inquiry is a homeostatic process by which the organism strives to return to equilibrium, a new habit, a revised belief. Since what prompts inquiry is is the urge to eliminate the irritation of doubt, the end of inquiry is stable, permanently doubt-proof belief.

Among possible methods for the 'fixation of belief' the scientific method, Peirce holds, is distinguished by its appropriateness to the end of inquiry. Unlike, e.g., the a priori method favoured by traditional metaphysics, the scientific method, if it were sufficiently persisted in, would enable inquiry eventually to come to rest with beliefs which are stable because permanently safe from recalcitrance. Scientific method, according to Peirce, accommodates the perceptual judgements forced upon one by brute experience in an explanatory framework arrived at by reasoning of three types: ABDUCTION, the postulation of a hypothesis to explain some puzzling phenomenon; DEDUCTION of consequences from such abductive hypotheses; and INDUCTIVE testing of those hypotheses. Though mathematical truths are necessary, even mathematical inquiry, according to Peirce, is in a sense experiential – though in mathematics what is relevant is not outer but inner experience, the construction and observation of imagined diagrams (*see* MATHE-MATICAL KNOWLEDGE). Peirce's disinclination to accept the Cartesian requirement that any knowledge worthy of the name must be certain or indubitable moves into sharper focus in the context of his insistence that the scientific inquirer is distinguished by his 'contrite fallibilism', his readiness to 'dump the whole cartload of his beliefs, the moment experience is against them' (1.14, 1.55). And his distaste for the individualism of Cartesian epistemology moves into sharper focus in the context of his conception of the individual scientific inquirer as just one contributor to a vast co-operative enterprise, extending both within and across generations.

Fallible and imperfect as scientific inquiry is, however, if this vast co-operative enterprise were to continue long enough – Peirce is aware there is no guarantee that it will – eventually a final, stable opinion would be reached. The idea that evolutionary adaptation has given human beings an instinct for guessing right which enables them to make successful abductions, and the thesis that induction is in a sense self-corrective, play an obvious role here. Less obvious, but no less important, is the role of the thesis Peirce calls 'scholastic realism'. This is the thesis that there are natural kinds and laws, 'generals' as Peirce calls them, which are real, i.e. independent of how we think about or characterize the world. There is a pattern of generals, natural kinds and laws, underlying the particular facts and events we observe, which is 'independent of what you, or I, or any number of men think'. And so the 'arbitrary, accidental element' (8.13) in inquiry introduced by the peculiar circumstances and idiosyncrasies of individual inquirers can be expected gradually to be discarded as co-operative scientific inquiry proceeds, and the real pattern eventually to emerge.

Peirce contrasts his scholastic realism with 'nominalism', by which he means the idea that generals are 'figments', i.e. dependent on how we think about or describe things. But he is equally opposed to what one might call 'noumenism', the idea that the really real is

in principle inaccessible to human cognition. This is a characteristically pragmatist attitude, for the pragmatic maxim disqualifies as bogus any question which would resist settlement however long scientific inquiry were to continue.

Peirce does not think it false to say that truth is correspondence with reality, but shallow – at best a nominal definition, giving no insight into the pragmatic meaning of the concept. His pragmatic definition identifies the truth with the hypothetical final upshot of scientific inquiry, and the real with the object of that opinion. 'Truth is that concordance of [a] . . . statement with the ideal limit towards which endless investigation would tend to bring scientific beliefs'; '. . . any truth more perfect than this destined conclusion, any reality more absolute than what is thought in it, is a fiction of metaphysics' (5.564, 8.13). Peirce's is a pragmatic realism, between nominalism and noumenism, neither IDEALIST nor transcendentalist; his definition of truth aims at a delicate compromise between the twin desiderata of objectivity and accessibility.

'There can *be* no difference anywhere that doesn't *make* a difference elsewhere' (James, 1907, p. 30): his version of the pragmatic maxim lies at the heart of James's pragmatism too. Unlike Peirce, however, James thought philosophy would do well to go round Kant, rather than through him; and his interpretation of the maxim, stressing *praxis*, the practical, not simply the experiential, consequences of a concept's applying, reflects this. Related, no doubt, is his willingness to include emotions among experiential consequences, and to include the practical consequences of *a subject's believing a proposition*, as well as the practical consequences of *the belief's being true* – which connect, in turn, with his doctrine of the 'will to believe', the thesis that religious beliefs which cannot by their nature be verified or falsified may nevertheless be legitimated by their salutory effects on the believer's conduct of life. Another difference is less often stressed but no less significant. James is, in Peirce's sense, a nominalist; when he writes of a belief's practical effects he is concerned with its *particular* practical effects; and he takes it that all classifications are human constructs to be judged rather by their convenience and utility than by their coincidence with real kinds.

Like Peirce, James thinks it not false but inadequate to say that truth is correspondence with reality. Again much like Peirce, he characterizes 'truth absolute' as 'an ideal set of formulations towards which all opinions may in the long run of experience be expected to converge' (1909, p. 147). The difference between true beliefs and false ones is that true beliefs are 'verifiable', i.e. they would be confirmed by experience. The true, James sometimes says, is the satisfactory, the useful in the way of belief; true beliefs *work*. Critics like Moore and Russell were scandalized by what they took to be a crass identification of truth and utility: a criticism James describes as a 'slander' (1909, p. 147), for, though indeed he had written that '*the true . . . is only the expedient in the way of belief*', he had gone on to explain, '. . . expedient in the long run and on the whole of course; for what meets expediently all the experience in sight won't necessarily meet all further experience equally satisfactorily. Experience . . . has ways of *boiling over*, and making us correct our present formulas' (1907, p. 106).

But unlike Peirce James cannot appeal to the real constitution of the world to explain why, in the long run of experience, opinions can be expected to converge; and he is preoccupied more with truth in the concrete than with truth in the abstract, manifesting discomfort with the notion of verifi*ability* and preferring to talk of particular truths actually verifi*ed*. These nominalist predilections lead to apparent inconsistencies, as James seems sometimes to allow that beliefs which are verified are thereby shown to have been true all along, sometimes to suggest that beliefs become true when they are verified. Consistency may be restored by means of a distinction James sometimes makes between 'abstract' or 'absolute', and 'concrete' or 'relative' truth, identifying abstract truth with the verifiable and concrete truth with the verified. But what James calls concrete truth isn't really *truth* at all; his distinction is really between a belief's being true and its

being shown to be true – or more accurately, since James allows that what is at one time 'verified' may later turn out to be false, between a belief's being true and its being confirmed. James's stress on the particular, the concrete, amounts in effect to a tendency to downplay the concept of truth, as such, and to emphasize what is confirmed as inquiry proceeds.

In DEWEY, though he describes one of Peirce's best-known characterizations – '[t]he opinion which is fated to be agreed by all who investigate' – as 'the best definition of truth' (Peirce, 5.414; Dewey, 1938, p. 345n.), this shift of emphasis is even more marked. Dewey, like James, is drawn to the idea of the mutability of truth; though he admits that what is verified is thereby shown to have been true all along, he interprets this as meaning only that it was going to be verified. Not surprisingly (given that concrete, mutable 'truth' isn't really truth at all) he is also drawn to the idea that it might be as well to stop talking of truth, and to work, instead, with the concept of warranted assertibility.

The attraction, for Dewey, of the doctrine of the mutability of truth no doubt relates to its consonance with his theory of inquiry, which shows some markedly revolutionary tendencies. Like Peirce and James, Dewey repudiates the 'quest for certainty'. Unlike them, he goes on to suggest a psycho-sociological diagnosis of the desire for certainty: it arose, he conjectures, from the sharp dichotomy of theory versus practice, and the distaste for the practical, the changeable, the uncertain, embodied in the slave-owning culture of ancient Greece. The most Hegelian of the pragmatists, Dewey is suspicious of traditional philosophical dualisms; and this is reflected in his epistemological writings, which are critical of the whole tradition from Plato through Descartes to his own contemporaries, because of its dependence on the dichotomies of subject/object, fact/value, theory/practice. 'Special theories of knowledge differ enormously from one another. Their quarrels . . . fill the air. The din thus created makes us deaf to the way in which they all say one thing in common. . . .

They all hold that the operation of inquiry excludes any element of practical activity that enters into the construction of the object known' (Dewey, 1929, p. 22). Dewey, by contrast, insists that knowing is not isolated from, but is itself a kind of, practice – to be judged, like other practices, by its purposive success rather than by some supposed standards of accuracy of its reflection of its objects; for the object of knowledge is not an immutable, independent reality, but is changed and even in part constituted by our cognitive interactions with it. Inquiry transforms an indeterminate situation into a determinate one.

Peirce's theory of inquiry is behaviouristic, naturalistic, fallibilistic; thoroughly anti-Cartesian, but essentially reformist. James's is predominantly reformist too, though his nominalistic preference for concrete 'truths' introduces a potentially revolutionary element. In Dewey's theory revolutionary themes, especially the denial of an independent reality to which our theories may or may not conform, are unmistakable. But reformist elements are also discernible. Laws are 'intellectual instrumentalities', he says, and there is no question of their literally conforming to what exists; but this doesn't mean that they are merely mental, or that they need not 'take account' of what exists (1929, pp. 205, 207). Important reformist themes in Dewey include: a distinction between the state and the content senses of 'belief'; a conception of EXPERIENCE much richer, thicker, than the old 'sensationalist' idea; the aspiration to transcend the old dichotomy of RATIONALISM versus EMPIRICISM and allow a more realistic interplay of experience with reason.

Schiller is uncompromisingly revolutionary. While in both James and Dewey one finds a shift between the identification of truth with verifiability and the identification of truth with verification, and a more (James) or less (Dewey) equivocal commitment to the mutability of truth, in Schiller one finds a straightforward identification of truth with verification, and an unequivocal commitment to the mutability of truth. James acknowledges that his account of concrete truths could not stand alone: 'to admit, as we pragmatists do, that we are liable to correction . . . involves the use on our part of an ideal standard' (1909, p. 142). But Schiller offers a theory of concrete truths as *a complete theory of truth*. He denies outright the idea that truth is correspondence with reality, an idea which he describes as not only worthless as a criterion but absurd in itself. Truth is practical working. 'True', he says, means 'valued by us'; a proposition is true if it 'forwards our ends'. Truth is mutable, since propositions become true only when successfully applied; a 'truth which will not . . . submit to verification, is not yet a truth at all' (Schiller, 1907, p. 8). Reality is also mutable, growing as truth grows. Truth is dependent on us, relative to our purposes. And so is reality; facts are not simply discovered, but selected, even made, by us. In a spirit, no doubt, of deliberate provocation, Schiller likens his views to those of Protagoras; and, indeed, his revolutionary, relativistic humanism seems very far from Peirce's realistic pragmaticism. As Peirce himself was well aware: 'It seems to me a pity', he wrote in 1908, 'that [Mr Schiller and the pragmatists of today] should allow a philosophy so instinct with life to become infected with the seeds of death in such notions as . . . the mutability of truth' (Peirce, 6.485).

A poignant, and prophetic, observation: RORTY, most radical of contemporary self-styled pragmatists, and the closest to Schiller, uses 'pragmatism' as the contrast to 'realism'; takes the pragmatist view to be that truth is not the kind of thing there can be an interesting theory about; holds that there is nothing to be said about the criteria of rational belief, about what counts as good or flimsy evidence, over and above the conventions of our cognitive practices; conceives of pragmatism, in short, as a revolutionary repudiation of the questions, as well as the answers, of the epistemological tradition.

Other contemporaries, Bernstein and Margolis for example, have more or less self-consciously sought habitable middle ground between the revolutionary and the reformist wings of the pragmatist tradition; an enterprise which seems, however, rather to trade on than to resolve the relevant ambiguities.

It is rather, to my mind, within the tradition of reformist pragmatism that the most enduringly interesting epistemological contributions are to be found: for example, Mead's theory of the social construction of the self, inspired by Peirce's critique of the intuitive self-consciousness assumed by Descartes; LEWIS's – somewhat nominalistic – 'pragmatic a priori', itself an inspiration for QUINE's call for 'a more thorough-going pragmatism' (Quine, 1953, p. 46); Ramsey's behaviouristic approach to belief, and Quine's, also, to meaning (Quine cites Dewey: 'meaning is . . . primarily a property of behavior' (Quine, 1969, p. 27; Dewey, 1925, p. 179)); Quine's association of natural kinds, induction and EVOLUTIONARY EPISTEMOLOGY; REICHENBACH's pragmatic vindication of induction; Hanson's defence of the idea of an abductive logic of scientific discovery, SELLARS' appeal to the notion of explanatory coherence, Harman's to INFERENCE TO THE BEST EXPLANATION; PUTNAM's explorations of conceptions of truth intermediate between metaphysical realism and relativism, Apel's of consensual theories and their relation to the social dimensions of inquiry; RESCHER's investigations of criteria of success and improvement of cognitive methods, Jardine's of scientific progress; and many more. In my own work, such key ideas as explanatory integration, central to the articulated quasi-holism of my account of evidential support, and the distinction of belief-states and belief-contents, central to my account of the role of experience, were mined, as I can testify, from the same vein.

Unifying this rich but, it must be admitted, formidably diverse profusion of philosophical ideas is what one might call the ongoing project of reformist pragmatism: the aspiration to find a middle ground between dogmatism and SCEPTICISM; a conception of truth accessible enough to be realistically aspired to, yet objective enough to be worthy of the name; an articulation of the interplay between the world's contribution to knowledge, and ours. This is the essential spirit of reformist pragmatism, succinctly summed up by James: '. . . please observe . . . that when . . . we give up the doctrine of objective certitude, we do not thereby give up the quest or hope of truth itself' (1897, p. 17). So conceived, the tradition of reformist pragmatism still flourishes; and, though very far as yet from the 'catholic consent' Peirce saw (8.13) as the end of inquiry, it is, indeed, 'instinct with life'.

*See also* EMPIRICISM; EVOLUTIONARY EPISTEMOLOGY; EXPERIENCE; GENETIC EPISTEMOLOGY; NATURALIZED EPISTEMOLOGY; NIHILISM; REALISM.

PRAGMATIST WRITINGS

Dewey, J., *Logic, the Theory of Inquiry* (New York: Henry Holt, 1938).

Dewey, J.: *Experience and Nature* (1925) (La Salle: Open Court, 1958).

Dewey, J.: *The Quest for Certainty* (1929) (New York: Capricorn Books, 1960).

James, W.: *The Will to Believe and Other Essays in Popular Philosophy* (1897), (New York: Dover, 1956).

James, W.: *Pragmatism* (1907), eds F. Burkhardt and F. Bowers (Cambridge, MA: Harvard University Press, 1975).

James, W.: *The Meaning of Truth* (1909), eds F. Burkhardt and F. Bowers (Cambridge, MA: Harvard University Press, 1975).

Peirce, C.S.: *Collected Papers* eds C. Hartshorne, P. Weiss and A. Burks (Cambridge, MA: Harvard University Press, 1931–58). References to Peirce are by volume and paragraph number in this edition.

Schiller, F.C.S.: *Studies in Humanism* (London: MacMillan, 1907).

Thayer, H.S. ed.: *Pragmatism: The Classic Writings* (New York: New American Library, 1970).

BIBLIOGRAPHY

Dewey, J.: 'The Development of American pragmatism', in his *Philosophy and Civilization* (New York: Minton, Balch, 1931).

Haack, S.: ' "Extreme scholastic realism": its relevance to philosophy of science today', *Transactions of the Charles S. Peirce Society* XXVIII, No. 1 (1992), 19–50.

Migotti, M.: 'Recent work in pragmatism: revolution or reform in the theory of knowledge?', *Philosophical Books* 29, (1988), 65–73.

Quine, W.V.: 'Two dogmas of empiricism', in his *From a Logical Point of View* (Cambridge, MA: Harper Torchbooks, 1953), 20–46.

Quine, W.V.: *Ontological Relativity and Other Essays* (New York: Columbia University Press, 1969).

Rorty, R.: *The Consequences of Pragmatism* (Hassocks: Harvester, 1982).

SUSAN HAACK

**preface paradox**  The paradox of the preface poses a problem that concerns the nature of rational belief. The paradox was introduced by D.C. Makinson (1965). The following example illustrates how the problem arises.

In his latest work an author asserts some of his rationally held beliefs: b1, b2, . . . , b*n*. Since the author realizes that his previous works have all turned out to contain false assertions in spite of his best efforts, he modestly and reasonably acknowledges in the preface of his new book that it too contains some false assertion somewhere. This acknowledgement serves to convey the author's belief in a proposition which has the logical form: -(b1 & b2 & . . . & b*n*), a proposition that we can call 'the prefatory belief'.

It is logically impossible for all of the beliefs that have just been attributed to the author to be true. We should suppose that the author knows this. None the less, there seems to be no good reason to deny that the beliefs could all be rational under such circumstances. Is this situation really possible? If so, what is the relevant difference between such a case and cases of known logical conflict among beliefs that exemplify irrational belief? If the situation is not really possible, why not? Answering these questions constitutes the problem.

This is a serious problem. There is no easy way to show that the situation is either impossible or unproblematic. It is instructive to observe that a common approach to solving the LOTTERY PARADOX cannot work here. The lottery paradox involves certain predictive propositions for each of which someone has a high level of purely statistical support. These propositions seem to be rationally believed by the person on the basis of that evidence, even though the person knows that there is a falsehood somewhere among them. A common approach to solving the lottery paradox rests on denying that purely statistical evidence is ever sufficient for the rational justification of a belief. However well that approach works for the lottery problem, it does not solve the general problem posed by the paradox of the preface. Statistical evidence is not essential to the latter. The author's beliefs that are expressed in the body of his work can be made rational by any sort of evidence that can be rationally believed to allow mistakes. This includes diverse familiar forms of evidence, e.g. perception, memory, testimony, formal reasoning and introspection, as well as statistical evidence. In order to follow closely Makinson's original exposition of the paradox, the case described above provides support for the prefatory belief from essentially statistical considerations. But in equally plausible examples the prefatory belief is supported in other ways. For instance, the author may be given reliable testimonial evidence to the effect that his new manuscript contains some false assertion, or the author may seem to recall having previously discovered some error in the work without being able any longer to recall what it is, or the work may be a formal effort in which b1, b2 . . . b*n* purport to be proven, while the prefatory belief is based on the author's last minute discovery of a proof that b1, b2, . . . , b*n* together imply a contradiction. Thus, the inconsistent beliefs can be supported by virtually any sort of evidence. It is noteworthy that the above sorts of evidence for the prefatory belief give the author no indication of any particular flaw in his rational support for each of b1, b2, . . . b*n*. The general problem posed by the preface paradox cannot be solved on the basis of a denial that statistical evidence suffices for the rational justification of belief.

In light of the diversity of plausible cases of the phenomenon, it may seem most reasonable to accept that inconsistent rational beliefs are possible. Makinson reports in opposition to this view that we feel compelled to hold on general grounds that inconsistent rational beliefs are not possible (1965, p. 206). Makinson does not identify any of these general grounds, but John Pollock suggests one. Pollock contends that denying a need for consistency among rational beliefs would reduce to insignificance the role of deductive inference in rational belief acquisition (1986, p. 249). One problem with inconsistent rational beliefs that involves deduction is brought out by the following argument.

The argument begins with the assumption that every proposition is a deductive consequence of logically inconsistent premises. The second assumption is that valid deductive inference from rationally held beliefs is a sufficient basis for rational belief in the deduced conclusion. Given the hypothesis that there are logically inconsistent rational beliefs, these assumptions imply that any proposition whatever is rationally accepted as long as it is accepted on the basis of its deduction from inconsistent rational beliefs. Yet it is clear that the author in our example does not gain rational belief in wild, arbitrary propositions simply by accepting them on the basis of deductions from b1, b2, . . . , bn together with the prefatory belief. The argument concludes that the correct way to avoid this result is to deny that inconsistency among rational beliefs is possible.

This argument helps to draw attention to a problem involving deduction, but it does not show that inconsistent rational beliefs are impossible. The argument employs a premiss asserting that it is always rational to believe a proposition on the basis of a valid deduction from rational beliefs. This premiss can be refuted on entirely independent grounds. In certain cases, a *modus ponens* argument's premisses are not merely rationally believed but known, and yet it is not rational to accept the conclusion of the argument by deducing it from the premisses (Conee, 1987). The rationality of believing a proposition sometimes depends on what the believing is foreseen to bring about. In some cases not involving inconsistent beliefs, believing a given proposition is foreseen to bring with it the falsehood of that proposition. (One way this can happen

is for the proposition in effect to say of itself that it is not believed.) When this is foreseen and nothing else is at stake, it is not rational to believe the proposition. This is true even if the proposition is known to be a logical implication of rationally believed or even known premises. Hence, even propositions known to follow from rational beliefs are not always rational to believe, whether or not there can be inconsistent rational beliefs. The argument under consideration against the possibility of inconsistent rational beliefs thus fails.

A difficult task remains, however. Deduction from rational beliefs does very often yield new rational beliefs, and the new beliefs seem to be rational primarily because they are so inferred. Mathematics provides numerous illustrations of this. More poignant examples are provided by the cases that constitute the preface paradox. Virtually any valid deduction that the author could make from b1, b2, . . . , bn, or from the prefatory belief, would afford an adequate basis for rational belief in the inferred proposition. Any tenable theory of rational belief must allow deduction from rational beliefs to play some important role in rendering belief rational. Those who accept the possibility of inconsistent rational beliefs face the delicate task of reconciling this important role of deduction with the manifest failure of deduction to yield rational belief in many (though not all) of the deductive consequences of the inconsistent beliefs which they count as rational. Those who reject the possibility of inconsistent rational beliefs face the formidable challenge of explaining why the myriad apparent cases all turn out to be spurious or impossible.

*See also* PARADOX.

BIBLIOGRAPHY

Conee, E.B.: 'Evident, but rationally unacceptable', *Australasian Journal of Philosophy* 65 (1987), 316–26.
Hoffman, R.: 'Mr Makinson's paradox', *Mind* 77 (1968), 122–3.
Hoffman, R.: 'The paradox of the preface again', *Mind* 82 (1973), 441.

Klein, P.: 'The virtues of inconsistency', *The Monist* 68 (1985), 105–35.

Lacey, A.R.: 'The paradox of the preface', *Mind* 79 (1970), 614–15.

Makinson, D.C.: 'The paradox of the preface', *Analysis* 25 (1965), 205–7.

Pollock, J.L.: 'Epistemology and probability', *Synthese* 55 (1983), 231–52.

Pollock, J.L.: 'The paradox of the preface', *Philosophy of Science* 53 (1986), 246–58.

EARL CONEE

**presence**  see IMMEDIACY.

**presocratic epistemology** The beginning of philosophical interest in knowledge has been dated by some to the critical challenge to knowledge raised by fifth-century Sophists (Hamlyn, 1961), but the inability of human intelligence to comprehend the larger scheme of events was a commonplace of the earliest Greek poetry (cf. *Iliad* II, 484ff; *Odyssey* XVIII, 137ff.; Archilochus Fr. 70; etc.). Snell (1953) traced the poet's pessimism to an identification of knowledge with eye-witness experience (cf. the Greek *oida*, 'I know', lit. 'I have seen'): what can be known is only what can be seen or otherwise perceived within the narrow limits of a human lifetime. Presocratic reflection on knowledge begins from this assumption of the joint inadequacy and indispensability of sense experience for knowledge.

Xenophanes of Colophon (*c*.565–*c*.470 BC) claimed that no man ever saw 'the clear and certain truth' (*to saphes*), opinion (*dokos*) being 'allotted to all' (Fr. 34.1, 4). The character of his scepticism and its supporting rationale have been the subject of debate since antiquity. Since the topic mentioned at 34.2 is 'the gods and such as I say about all things' (i.e. divine attributes and the basic principles of the physical cosmos that Xenophanes has so far identified; cf. his comments on 'all things' in Frr. 27 and 29), Fr. 34 falls well short of the universal scepticism characteristic of a later period. While Fränkel's thesis (1974) that Xenophanes' word for 'know' just meant 'know by means of sight' has not gained acceptance (*see* Barnes,

1979), it is clear that Xenophanes' near-contemporary Herodotus held that knowledge, i.e. *clear and certain* awareness of truth, required confirmation on the basis of first-hand observation (cf. *History* II, 44). Xenophanes probably assumed, then, that our knowledge could extend no further than our direct experience, and drew the appropriate conclusion for the (inaccessible) realm of the divine and the (universal) principles of nature he had identified.

Whether Xenophanes countenanced a priori knowledge (e.g. about the divine, as proposed by Barnes and Hussey) is less clear. Fr. 34 would lead one to expect only 'opinion' in this area; his explicit remarks on the 'one greatest god' (Frr. 23–6) are all flat assertion; and the complex set of logical deductions credited to him in the pseudo-Aristotelian treatise *de Melisso Gorgia Xenophane* are almost certainly constructions of a later period. Xenophanes encouraged inquiry into the wonders of nature (Frr. 18, 27–33) and reflection about general principles based on knowledge of new-found facts (cf. A 33 – his theory of alternating periods of flood and drought based on the discovery far inland of remains of ancient sea creatures), even if clear and certain knowledge of basic principles lay beyond mortal capacities.

Heraclitus of Ephesus (early fifth century) also spoke of inquiry as essential to knowledge (Frr. 35, 55), but listed Xenophanes among those who proved that 'much-learning does not teach *noos*' (Fr. 40, roughly translated: 'one can fail to see the forest for the trees'). It has been argued (Hamlyn, 1961; Kahn, 1979) that Heraclitus was less interested in knowledge than in the unity of the cosmos, but Frr.1, 17, 34, 45, 72 appear designed to provoke reflection on the nature of knowledge by simultaneously identifying and contrasting sense experience with genuine understanding (Lesher, 1983). Other fragments highlight the roles played by the concepts one, many, same, different, motion, and rest (Mackenzie, 1988) as well as the importance of thinking, reflection, and interpretation (Frr. 19, 93, 107, 113, 116).

Pythagoras of Samos (late sixth century BC) was famous for claiming knowledge (Xenophanes Fr. 7; Heraclitus Fr. 129) rather than for explaining it, but two fifth-century(?) followers, Alcmaeon and Philolaus, discussed human cognitive capacities in relation to those of other animals (Frr. 1a and 13 respectively) and the divine (Frr. 1 and 6). The empiricist account of knowledge stated in Plato's *Phaedo* (96b) may go back to Alcmaeon (Barnes, 1979), but it sits uncomfortably with Alcmaeon's view of human awareness as mere 'conjecture from signs' (Fr. 1). Philolaus' thesis that number was a condition for thought and knowledge (Frr. 3, 4, 6, 11) has been challenged as too explicit an epistemological opinion for so early a period (Kirk and Raven, 1957), but a connection between knowledge, measures and the limits of things appeared in Fr. 16 of Solon (c.640–c.561) and ran through Heraclitus' Frr. 30, 31b, 45, 94 and 120. Recent accounts credit Philolaus with an epistemology along Pythagorean (mathematical) lines developed either in response to attacks on pluralism launched by followers of Parmenides (Huffman, 1988) or by extension from Parmenides' own principles (Hussey, 1990).

Parmenides of Elea (late sixth–early fifth century) set out an account of 'the existent' or 'what is' (*to eon*) and of what can be thought and known about it, evidently in order to correct the confused way of thinking displayed in earlier cosmologies. After presenting a serial 'critique' (*elenchos*) of the possible ways of thinking ('it is', 'it is not', it is and it is not', and 'it is or it is not' – arguably the world's first Boolean analysis), he concluded only 'it is' can be said and thought, a verdict based partly on the claim that all thought, knowledge, and meaningful speech about 'the non-existent' are impossible (for interpretations of this thesis *see* Furth, 1968; Mourelatos, 1970; Owen, 1960).

The goddess of Parmenides' poem promised 'the unshaking heart of well rounded – or well persuasive – truth' (Fr. 1.29; cf. 'trustworthy account' at Fr. 8.50). Her preference for 'tied down', fixed, or invariably true ways of speaking ('that the existent exists', 'either it exists or it does not exist', 'what does not exist cannot possibly

exist', etc.) can be restated in more contemporary terms as a restriction of the class of knowable propositions to necessarily true ones. Parmenides' serial critique of mortal opinion and repudiation of sense perception in pursuit of 'well-persuasive' truth has invited comparison with Plato's preference for a priori knowledge (at *Phaedo*, 100dff and *Rep.* 511bff) and with Descartes' meditative review of his opinions in pursuit of those (clear and distinct) ideas that have the power to convince him completely (Owen, Kirk et al.).

The impact of Parmenides' teaching is evident from Empedocles Fr. 11, Melissus Fr. 2, Zeno Frr. 1–4, and Anaxagoras Fr. 17 (for Leucippus and Democritus, cf. Aristotle, *de gen. et corr.*, 325a2ff). His successors did, however, offer materialistic explanations of thought of just the sort he appears to have repudiated in the *doxa* section of his poem (cf. Alcmaeon A 5; Empedocles Frr. 2, 109; Anaxagoras A 92; Democritus A 135; for this reading of the *doxa*, see Long, 1963; for a contrasting view of the Parmenidean character of the *doxa* section, *see* Coxon, 1986).

The essential but inadequate contribution to knowledge made by sense perception also led Anaxagoras and Democritus to flirt with scepticism (Frr. 21 and 7, 9, 11, 125 respectively). Democritus tied his scepticism to a distinction between the real properties of things and the qualities (e.g. sweetness) perceived 'by custom' (*nomôi*, Fr. 9 - a distinction anticipated by Xenophanes' comment (Fr. 38) that men would think figs were far sweeter if they had never tasted honey). Empedocles held that ordinary men lacked 'knowledge of the whole' (Fr. 2) but (perhaps invoking the idea of multiple paths to understanding – Fr. 3) assigned a vast knowledge to himself (Frr. 17, 23).

Neither Plato nor Aristotle gave entirely accurate summaries of presocratic ideas about knowledge, but both spoke of the physical causes of sensation and the relation of sense experience to knowledge as questions raised by their predecessors (cf. Plato, *Phaedo*, 96b; *Theaetetus*, 152ff; Aristotle, *de anima* I, 2; III, 4; *Meta.* I, 5). Later sceptics appropriately traced their philosophical pedigree back to views expressed by the presocratics (cf. Cicero, *Academica* I.43ff: 'Democritus, Anaxagoras, Empedocles, and almost all the ancients who said that nothing could be grasped or cognized or known, saying that the senses are restricted, the mind weak, the course of life short and that . . . truth has been submerged in an abyss . . .'; cf. also D. Laertius, 9.66; Timon Frr. 59, 60, 818–20, etc.).

*See also* ARISTOTLE; PLATO.

BIBLIOGRAPHY

Barnes, J.: *The Presocratics* (London: Routledge and Kegan Paul, 1979).

Coxon, A.: *The Fragments of Parmenides* vol. III in the *Phronesis* Supplemental Series (Assen/Maastricht, 1986).

Diels, K. and Kranz, W.: *Die Fragmente der Vorsokratiker* 6th edn (Berlin, 1951); references to fragments and *testimonia* are to the B-fragment and A-*testimonia* sections.

Fränkel, H.: 'Xenophanes' empiricism and his critique of knowledge', in *The Pre-Socratics* ed. A.P.D. Mourelatos (Garden City: Anchor Press/Doubleday, 1974), 118–31.

Furth, M.: 'Elements of Eleatic ontology', *Journal of the History of Philosophy* 6 (1968), 111–32.

Hamlyn, D.W.: *Sensation and Perception* (London: Routledge and Kegan Paul, 1961).

Huffman, C.: 'The role of number in Philolaus' philosophy', *Phronesis* 33 (1988), 1–29.

Hussey, E.: 'The beginnings of epistemology: from Homer to Philolaus', in *Epistemology* ed. S. Everson (Cambridge: Cambridge University Press, 1990), 11–38.

Kahn, C.: *The Art and Thought of Heraclitus* (Cambridge: Cambridge University Press, 1979).

Kirk, G.S., Raven, J.E. and Schofield, M.: *The Presocratic Philosophers* (Cambridge: Cambridge University Press, 1st edn 1957; 2nd edn 1983).

Lesher, J.H.: 'Heraclitus' epistemological vocabulary', *Hermes* 111 (1983), 155–70.

Long, A.A.: 'The principles of Parmenides' cosmology', *Phronesis* 8 (1963), 90–107.

Mackenzie, M.M.: 'Heraclitus and the art of paradox', *Oxford Studies in Ancient Philosophy*, 6 (1988), 1–37.

Mourelatos, A.P.D.: *The Route of Parmenides*

(Yale University Press: New Haven and London, 1970).

Nussbaum, M.: 'Eleatic conventionalism and Philolaus on the conditions of thought', *Harvard Studies in Classical Philology* 83 (1979), 63–108.

Owen, G.E.L.: 'Eleatic questions', *Classical Quarterly* 10 (1960), 84–102.

Snell, B.: *The Discovery of the Mind* trans. T. G. Rosenmeyer (Oxford: Oxford University Press, 1953).

J. H. LESHER

**prima facie reasons**   There are two notions of the *prima facie* used in epistemology. The first is familiar from the law. For someone to be committed to stand trial, a *prima facie* case has to be made against them. A case of this sort is one which is strong enough to need an answer. It is called a *prima facie* case because of the Latin meaning of the terms: a *prima facie* case is one which *at first sight* looks impressive enough to need an answer. Such a case may collapse completely under further scrutiny.

The second notion of the *prima facie* is a technical use that derives from the moral philosophy of W.D. Ross. He introduced a notion of a *prima facie* duty in the following way: we have a *prima facie* duty to keep our promises if every action of promise-keeping is to that extent right – if all actions of promise-keeping are the better for it. An action may be a *prima facie* duty (in virtue of some property it has) in this sense even though it is wrong overall, and so not a 'duty proper', in Ross's terms.

Those who speak of *prima facie* reasons may do so in either of the above senses, but they should be clear which they intend since the two senses are so different. The main difference is that reasons of the first sort may collapse completely under scrutiny, so that something that seemed to be a reason (was a *prima facie* reason) ceases to be so on further enquiry; those of the second sort always remain as reasons, though they may be overridden by stronger *prima facie* reasons on the other side.

BIBLIOGRAPHY

Dancy, J.: 'Intuitionism in meta-epistemology', *Philosophical Studies* 42 (1982), 395–408.
Ross, W.D.: *The Right and the Good* (Oxford: Clarendon Press, 1930), ch. 2.

JONATHAN DANCY

**primary and secondary qualities** A metaphysical distinction was drawn in antiquity between qualities which really belong to objects in the world and qualities which only appear to belong to them, or which human beings only believe to belong to them, because of the effects those objects produce in human beings, typically through the sense organs. Thus Democritus: 'by convention (*nomoi*) colour, by convention the sweet, by convention bitter; but in truth (*eteei*) atoms and the void'. Colour, sweetness, bitterness are here said to exist only 'by convention': as something that does not hold everywhere by nature, but is produced in or contributed by human beings in their interaction with a world which really contains only atoms of certain kinds in a void. To think that some objects in the world are coloured, or sweet, or bitter is to attribute to objects qualities which on this view they do not actually possess.

Objects must possess some qualities or other in order to produce their effects, so the view is not that there are no qualities at all in the objects which cause perceivers to impute certain qualities to them. Rather, it is only that some of the qualities which are imputed to objects (e.g. colour, sweetness, bitterness) are not possessed by those objects. Knowledge of nature is knowledge of what qualities objects actually have, and of how they bring about their effects. For Democritus, atoms really possess those qualities (e.g. shape, size, motion) which are responsible for their having all the effects they have. To claim such knowledge is to impute certain qualities to objects; the richer one's knowledge, the more such qualities will be imputed. But when the imputation is true, or amounts to knowledge, the qualities are not *merely* imputed; they are also in fact present in the objects. The metaphysical view holds that

those are the only qualities which objects really have. The rest of our conception of the world has a human source.

Galileo drew a similar distinction in explaining the wide gap between the way the world normally appears to perceiving beings on earth and the truth revealed about it by the 'new science'. If the sense organs of animals were taken away, he said, the figure, the number, and the motions of bodies would remain, but all colours, odours, sounds, etc., would be 'abolished and annihilated'. For him, all such qualities, 'without the living animal', are 'nothing but names'. Although we have words for such things, we do not succeed in speaking of anything that really belongs to objects in the world. Objects possess only those qualities referred to in a perfected mathematical science which would explain why everything in the world happens as it does.

This is so far not a distinction between two kinds of qualities ('primary' and 'secondary') which objects possess, or between qualities which are imputed to objects and qualities which are not, but rather between qualities which objects really have and qualities which are merely imputed to them but which they do not in fact possess. It is a claim about what is really so.

DESCARTES found nothing but confusion in the attempt even to impute to objects those very effects which they bring about through the senses. The 'sensations' caused in people's minds by the qualities of bodies which affect them could not themselves be in the external objects. Nor does it make sense to suppose that bodies could in some way 'resemble' those sensory effects. For Descartes the essence of body is extension, so no quality that is not a mode of extension could possibly belong to body at all. Colours, odours, sounds, etc., are on his view nothing but sensations. 'When we say that we perceive colours in objects, this is really just the same as saying that we perceive something in the objects whose nature we do not know, but which produces in us a certain very clear and vivid sensation which we call the sensation of colour.' If we try to think of colours as something real outside our minds 'there is no way of understanding what sort of things they are'.

This again is not a distinction between two kinds of qualities which belong to bodies; it is a distinction between qualities which belong to bodies (all of which are modes of extension such as shape, position, motion, etc.) and what we unreflectively and confusedly come to think are qualities of bodies.

The term 'secondary quality' appears to have been coined by Robert Boyle (1627–91) whose 'corpuscular philosophy' was shared by Locke. But it is not easy to say what either he or Locke meant by the term. They were not consistent in their use of it. LOCKE, like Boyle, distinguished an object's qualities from the powers it has to produce effects. It has such powers only in virtue of possessing some 'primary' or 'real' qualities. The effects it is capable of producing occur either in other bodies or in minds. If in minds, the effects are 'ideas' (e.g. of colour or sweetness or bitterness, or of roundness or squareness or motion). These ideas in turn are employed in thoughts to the effect that the object in question is, e.g., coloured or sweet or bitter, or round or square or moving. We have such thoughts, according to Locke, by thinking that the object in question 'resembles' the idea we have in the mind.

Boyle and Locke sometimes call colour, sweetness, bitterness, etc., 'secondary' qualities. In the view of Democritus, Galileo and Descartes, colour, sweetness, bitterness, etc. are only mistakenly or confusedly believed to belong to objects. That would imply that objects do not really have such 'secondary' qualities. But Locke also identifies 'secondary qualities' as 'such qualities which in truth are nothing in the objects themselves but powers to produce various sensations in us by their primary qualities' (Essay, 2.8.9). This can be taken in at least two ways. It could mean that, in addition to its 'primary' qualities, all there really is in an object we call coloured, sweet, or bitter, etc. is its power to produce ideas of colour, sweetness, or bitterness, etc. in us by virtue of the operation of those 'primary' or 'real' qualities. That is compatible with the earlier view that colour, sweetness, bitterness, etc. are not really in

objects. Or it could (and does seem to) mean that 'secondary qualities' such as colour, sweetness, bitterness, etc. are themselves nothing more than certain powers which objects have to affect us in certain ways. But such powers, on Locke's view, really do belong to objects endowed with the appropriate 'primary' or 'real' properties. To identify 'secondary qualities' with such powers in this way would imply that such 'secondary qualities' as colour, sweetness, bitterness, etc., since they are nothing but powers, really do belong to or exist in objects after all. Imputations of colour, sweetness, etc. to objects would then be true, not false or confused, as on those earlier views.

A distinction drawn in this way between 'primary' and 'secondary' qualities would not be a distinction between qualities which objects really possess and qualities which we only mistakenly or confusedly think they possess. Nor would it even be a distinction between two kinds of qualities, strictly speaking. Rather it would be a distinction between qualities and (certain kinds of) powers, both of which really belong to objects. But Locke confusingly sometimes calls both of them 'qualities'.

He also held that our ideas of 'primary' qualities such as bulk, figure, motion, etc. 'resemble' qualities in bodies, but our ideas of 'secondary qualities' such as colour, sweetness, bitterness, etc. do not. In the latter case, but not the former, 'there is nothing like our ideas, existing in the bodies themselves' (Essay, 2.8.15). This is Locke's way of saying what really belongs to the objects around us: only what the 'corpuscular philosophy' says about them is so. We only mistakenly impute 'secondary' qualities to objects; but in the case of the 'primary' qualities the imputations are true. But that is inconsistent with the idea that the 'secondary' qualities which we impute are nothing but powers, since the imputations would then be imputations of certain powers, and so would be true of all objects with the appropriate 'primary' or 'real' qualities.

BERKELEY objected to Locke that it is nonsense to speak of a 'resemblance' between an idea and an object, just as Descartes had ridiculed the idea that a sensation could resemble the object that causes it. 'An idea can be like nothing but an idea,' Berkeley says (*Principles* §8). This is a general rejection of Locke's account of how we are able to think of things existing independently of the mind. It it is correct, it works as much against what Locke says of our ideas of 'primary' qualities as it does against what he says of our ideas of 'secondary' qualities.

Boyle speaks of the 'texture' of a body whose minute corpuscles are arranged in a certain way. It is in virtue of possessing that 'texture' that the body is 'disposed' or has the power to produce ideas of certain kinds in perceivers, even if no one is perceiving it at the moment. For Locke, objects have the powers they have only because their minute parts are arranged in the ways they are (and the laws of nature are what they are). In each case there is acknowledged to be a categorical 'base' of the power; the object *can* do such-and-such only because it *is* so-and-so, even if the relevant way it *is* happens to remain unknown to us. This has tempted some philosophers in recent years to identify 'secondary' qualities, not with the powers which objects have to affect us in certain ways, but with the qualitative 'bases' of those causal powers. The colour or sweetness or bitterness, etc. of an object would then be some real (but possibly unknown) quality of the object which is responsible for the specific effects it has on us. This again would imply that 'secondary' qualities, so understood, are really in objects. And it would have the consequence that 'secondary' qualities are true qualities, not just powers. But it would seem to leave no room for a distinction between 'secondary' and 'primary' or 'real' qualities of bodies. The 'bases' of all the causal powers of objects are to be understood in terms of their 'primary' or 'real' qualities.

Defence of a distinction between those qualities which really belong to objects and qualities which are only mistakenly thought to belong to them faces the epistemic problem of how we can know, of any particular kind of quality, whether it belongs to the first group or the second. Scientific knowledge of nature purports to tell us what objects there

are and what sorts of qualities they have. Democritus, Galileo, Descartes, Locke and most other philosophers who have invoked the distinction thought they possessed some such knowledge. They relied on it to identify the first group of qualities. But atomistic or corpuscular or nuclear or any other specific physical science at best says only what is so; it does not also say what qualities objects do *not* have. So the metaphysical theory must establish in addition the further claim that the kinds of qualities mentioned in the preferred science are the *only* kinds of qualities which objects have.

Some have apparently thought that the wide variability among humans' perceptions of the colours, sweetness or bitterness, etc. of objects, as contrasted with the uniformity in their perceptions of their shape, size, or position, etc., is enough to show that the former qualities do not belong to objects, while the latter do. But such appeals to 'the relativity of perception' alone are at best inconclusive. It is not clear that there is in fact greater variability among our perceptions of the one kind of qualities than there is among those of the other. But even if there were, the most it would show is that we cannot tell by a single perception alone that an object is coloured, or sweet, or bitter, etc., not that it has no such qualities at all. Berkeley argued in this way against 'modern philosophers' who tried to prove on 'relativity' grounds that certain 'sensible qualities' do not exist outside the mind.

Two main strategies remain for accounting for such 'secondary' qualities as colour, sweetness, bitterness, etc. in a world containing only objects with nothing but the 'primary' or 'real' qualities mentioned in a comprehensive physical science. One, in the spirit of Democritus, Galileo and Descartes, is to grant that we do have perceptions of and beliefs about such qualities, and to argue that all of them can none the less be explained without having to assume that any object anywhere actually has any colour, sweetness or bitterness, etc. The explanations would proceed solely in terms of the 'primary' or 'real' qualities mentioned in the preferred comprehensive physical science. They would thereby expose the perceptions as illusory and the beliefs as false or confused. This raises large issues about the relation between the mental and physical, and about the possibility of explaining psychological phenomena in exclusively physical terms.

Another strategy is to show that the qualities said to be perceived or thought about in such cases are really qualities that do belong to objects after all. This can take the form of arguing that, e.g., the word 'coloured' just means the same as 'has the power to produce perceptions of colour in human beings', or means the same as 'has that quality which produces perceptions of colour in human beings', or means the same as that physical term, whatever it is, which denotes that quality which in fact produces perceptions of colour in human beings. These are all theses about the *meanings* of terms for allegedly 'secondary' qualities. Or it might be held only that a so-called 'secondary' quality term in fact denotes the very same quality as is denoted by some purely physical term. This would simply identify the very quality in question with some physical quality or power (not two different qualities, but only one), without holding that the terms that denote it must have the same meaning. In either case it would have the consequence that when we see colour, or believe that an object is coloured, what we see, or what we believe to belong to the object, is that very physical quality or power which colour is said to be. This again would leave no distinction between qualities which really belong to objects and qualities which are only mistakenly or confusedly imputed to them.

*See also* MOLYNEUX'S PROBLEM; NATURA-LISM; NOUMENAL/PHENOMENAL; OBJECTIVE/SUBJECTIVE; OBJECTIVITY; SUBJECTIVITY.

BIBLIOGRAPHY

Bennett, J.: *Locke, Berkeley, Hume: Central Themes* (Oxford: Oxford University Press, 1971).
Berkeley, G.: *Principles of Human Knowledge* (1710) in *Berkeley: Philosophical Writings* ed. M.R. Ayers (London: Dent, 1975).
Boyle, R.: 'Experiments and observations upon colours' and 'The origins and forms of qualities', in his *Works* vols 1, 3 (London: Birch, 1772).
Descartes, R.: 'Optics' and 'Principles of Philosophy', in *The Philosophical Writings of Descartes* vol. 1, eds J. Cottingham, R. Stoothoff and D. Murdoch (Cambridge: Cambridge University Press, 1985).
Galileo, G.: 'The Assayer', in *Discoveries and Opinions of Galileo* ed. S. Drake (New York: Doubleday, 1957).
Locke, J.: *An Essay concerning Human Understanding* (1690) ed. P.H. Nidditch (Oxford: Clarendon Press, 1975).
Mackie, J.: *Problems from Locke* (Oxford: Oxford University Press, 1976).
Williams, B.: *Descartes: The Project of Pure Enquiry* (Harmondsworth: Penguin, 1978).

BARRY STROUD

**principle of charity** Davidson thinks – and this is one of his most characteristic doctrines – that *ceteris paribus* a sentence of the form 'L-speakers hold S true in circumstance C' licenses the corresponding T-sentence 'S is true (in L) iff C', but only if a 'constitutive principle' of intentional ascription is presupposed; namely, that truth-conditions must be assigned to formulas of L under the constraint that most of the sentences held true by a speaker of L are true (by the interpreter's own lights). This is the principle of charity. It is supposed to be HOLISTIC on the intended interpretation, which is that 'most of the sentences' means a lot of them. It is primarily on the grounds that the principle of charity is constitutive of intentional ascription, but not of the ascription of physicalistic properties, that Davidson denies the possiblity of psychophysical laws. And it also has striking consequences for epistemology; if it is right, then the refutation of scepticism requires only the weak premise of belief coherence.

*See also* DAVIDSON; SOCIAL SCIENCE.

BIBLIOGRAPHY

Davidson, D.: 'Radical interpretation', in his *Inquiries into Truth and Interpretation* (Oxford: Oxford University Press, 1984).

Davidson, D.: 'Belief and the basis of meaning', ibid.

ERNEST LEPORE

**principle of contradiction** This is a law of truth. Roughly speaking, a contradictory of a proposition $p$ is one that can be expressed in the form $not\text{-}p$, or, if $p$ can be expressed in the form $not\text{-}q$, then a contradictory is one that can be expressed in the form $q$. Thus, e.g., if $p$ is $2 + 1 = 4$, then $2 + 1 \neq 4$ is the contradictory of $p$, for $2 + 1 \neq 4$ can be expressed in the form not-$(2 + 1 = 4)$. If $p$ is $2 + 1 \neq 4$, then $2 + 1 = 4$ is a contradictory of $p$, since $2 + 1 \neq 4$ can be expressed in the form not-$(2 + 1 = 4)$. Thus, mutually contradictory propositions can be expressed in the form, $r$, $not\text{-}r$. The Principle of Contradiction says that mutually contradictory propositions cannot both be true and cannot both be false. Thus, by this principle, since if $p$ is true, $not\text{-}p$ is false, no proposition $p$ can be at once true and false (otherwise both $p$ and its contradictory would be false). In particular, for any predicate $p$ and object $x$, it cannot be that $p$ is at once true of $x$ and also false of $x$. This is the classical formulation of the Principle of Contradiction. There are some senses in which the Principle of Contradiction is not above controversy (see Priest, 1985).

BIBLIOGRAPHY

Kneale, W. and Kneale, M.: *The Development of Logic* (Oxford: Clarendon Press, 1962).
Priest, G., Routley, R. and Norman, J. eds: *Paraconsistent Logics* (Munich: Philosophia Verlag, 1985).

ROBERT S. TRAGESSER

**principle of credulity** This is a term given by Thomas REID, in *An Inquiry Into the Human Mind*, Pt VI, sec. 24 (1846, pp. 196–7), to an 'original principle' of human nature that involves a 'disposition to confide in the veracity of others, and to believe what they tell us' (p. 196). This is an 'original principle' in that it operates independently of learning or reasoning. We are so constituted that we naturally, unreflectively, tend to give credence to the testimony of our fellows. This 'tendency is unlimited in children, until they meet with instances of deceit and falsehood; and it retains a very considerable degree of strength throughout life' (ibid.). As Reid points out, if 'no proposition that is uttered in discourse would be believed, until it was examined and tried by reason . . . most men would be unable to find reasons for believing the thousandth part of what is told them. Such distrust and incredulity would deprive us of the greatest benefits of society. . .' (p. 197). Without such an original tendency children would be incapable of learning by instruction. It is only later that the person 'sets bounds to that authority to which she was at first entirely subject' (ibid.) (see TESTIMONY). Reid pairs this principle with the 'principle of veracity', which is 'a propensity to tell the truth, and to use the signs of language, so as to convey our real sentiments' (p. 196). And he analogizes the principle of credulity with the 'inductive principle', which is an original tendency to suppose that two things that have been constantly conjoined in the past will continue to be so in the future (p. 197). Here too, Reid argues that if there were no original tendency to such suppositions we could never acquire any by reasoning (see PROBLEMS OF INDUCTION).

Richard Swinburne (1979) uses the term for a quite different principle according to which perceptual beliefs – beliefs based on perceptual experience about what a person seems to be perceiving – are likely to be correct, and hence are rationally acceptable, in the absence of specific reasons against this. 'I suggest that it is a principle of rationality that (in the absence of special considerations) if it seems (epistemically) to a subject that $x$ is present, then probably $x$ is present; what one seems to perceive is probably so. How things seem to be is good grounds for a belief about how things are' (p. 254). Swinburne enunciates this principle in the course of defending an argument for the existence of God from religious experience (from putative experience of God), but it has much wider application, as he points out. (Reid enunciates a similar principle in his *Essays on the Intellectual Powers of Man*, Essay VI. ch. 5 (1846, p. 445).) Many philosophers are willing to apply it to sense perception, though many of those same philosophers balk at its application to alleged experience (perception) of God. Swinburne, along with other advocates, points out that unless perceptual beliefs are accorded a PRIMA FACIE credibility, just by virtue of being based on perception, it is difficult, if not impossible, to avoid a thoroughgoing scepticism about perception. (*See* e.g. Reid, (ibid.), Essay II; Moore, 1953, p. 125; Price, 1932, ch. VII.) Many attempts have been made in recent centuries to give a non-circular justification of the reliability of sense perception, but none of them have been generally accepted, and all are subject to severe criticism. (*See* Alston, 1991, ch. 3 for a critical survey of such attempts.)

We have seen that Swinburne claims only a DEFEASIBLE justification for all perceptual beliefs, and it is evident that no stronger claim would be warranted. Since perceptual beliefs are not infrequently mutually contradictory, they cannot all be true. And we are familiar with many cases in which one can be shown to be mistaken in one's suppositions about what one saw. Thus such a principle is only as good as the account of defeasibility that accompany it. Swinburne lists four kinds of defeaters:

1. '. . .the apparent perception was made under conditions or by a subject found in the past to be unreliable'. (p. 260)
2. '. . .the perceptual claim was to have perceived an object of a certain kind in circumstances where similar perceptual claims have proved false'. (p. 261)
3. '. . .one can challenge a perceptual claim to have perceived *x* either by showing that probably *x* was not present. . .
4. . . . 'or by showing that even if *x* was present, it probably did not cause the experience of its seeming that *x* was present.' (p. 261)

Though these are are relevant considerations, I believe we can do better than this by way of a systematic list. For one thing, Swinburne adulterates the classification by mixing grounds for the defeater (inductive or not) with types of defeaters. Thus both (2) and (3) have to do with reasons for thinking the perceptual belief to be false (though in (3) this is somewhat masked by the restriction to what is perceived, in contrast to what is believed about it), and they differ primarily in the kinds of grounds adduced for this. For another, this orientation results in worthy candidates being omitted. Thus we can have reasons for thinking that the experience in question is not a sufficient indication of the truth of the belief. Some cases of this will fall under (1), (2) or (4), but others will not. I would suggest a much simpler classification into *rebutters* (reasons for thinking the belief to be false) and *underminers* (reasons for thinking that in this case the experience is not a sufficient ground for the belief in question). We can then proceed to distinguish various kinds of rebutters and underminers.

Swinburne argues that many religious experiences are not eliminated by the kinds of defeaters he lists. However many thinkers have argued that claims to have experienced God are of doubtful credibility because of more general considerations, such as the spotty distribution of such experiences and the lack of the kinds of intersubjective checks we have with sense perception. For a response to such aguments, *see* Alston (1991), chs. 5 and 6.

BIBLIOGRAPHY

Alston, W.P.: *Perceiving God* (Ithaca, NY: Cornell University Press, 1991).
Moore, G.E.: *Some Main Problems of Philosophy* (London: Allen and Unwin, 1953).
Price, H.H.: *Perception* (London: Methuen, 1932).
Reid, T.: *Works* ed. Sir W. Hamilton, 2 vols (London: Longmans, Green, 1846).
Swinburne, R.: *The Existence of God* (Oxford: Clarendon Press, 1979).

WILLIAM P. ALSTON

**principle of identity** Since the same thing

may look different at different times, or different things might look the same, or the same thing may be presented in different ways (as $2 + 3$ and $4 + 1$ present the same thing, 5, in different ways), we might well raise the question of which of many things (however presented) are the very same things. We would hope that we could answer this question as a matter of principle: given a thing $x$, and things of the same kind $y$, $z$. . . ., we might ask for a principle $P_x$ that determines which of those things $y$, $z$, . . ., if any, $= x$. For any considered $x$ there might be no such principle, or there might be a principle for $x$ and other things of that kind, or there might be one principle for all things.

It does seem that, outside of mathematics, we do not have any successful, logically impeccable, principles of identity. In mathematics, or some major parts of mathematics, there is LEIBNIZ's Principle of the Identity of Indiscernibles – that $x$ is the very same thing as $y$ if, and only if, $y$ has any property that $x$ has, and conversely. One of Leibniz's main uses of the principle was to deny that there is any more to things than their properties (to deny, against, e.g., Locke, that there are property-bearing substances). But it is clear that this principle is much too strong for, say, trees and persons, at least with respect to properties we might ordinarily attribute to them, for such of their properties are constantly changing. And yet, in some strong sense, despite persons and trees changing, they remain the same. But in exactly what sense? Or is there an exact sense? Are there logically exact principles legislating or articulating that sameness we sense in changing things?

Both the quest for principles of identity (e.g. principles of personal identity), and broodings over what might count as adequate principles of identity, form flourishing fields of philosophical research.

BIBLIOGRAPHY

Chisholm, R.M.: *Person and Object: A Metaphysical Study* (La Salle: Open Court, 1976).
Leibniz, G.W.: *New Essays on Human Understanding* ed. & trans. P. Remnant and J.
Bennett (Cambridge: Cambridge University Press, 1981).
Locke, J.: *An Essay Concerning Human Understanding* ed. P.H. Nidditch (Oxford: Oxford University Press, 1975).
Salmon, N.: *Frege's Puzzle* (Cambridge, MA: MIT Press, 1986).
Wiggins, D.: *Identity and Spatio-Temporal Continuity* (Oxford: Blackwell, 1971).

ROBERT A. TRAGESSER

**private language argument**  The expression 'the private language argument' is sometimes used broadly to refer to a battery of arguments in Wittgenstein's *Philosophical Investigations* §§ 243–315 which are concerned with the concepts of, and relations between, the mental and its behavioural manifestations (the inner and the outer), self-knowledge and knowledge of others' mental states, AVOWALS of experiences and descriptions of experiences. It is sometimes used narrowly to refer to a single chain of argument in which Wittgenstein demonstrates the incoherence of the idea that sensation-names and names of experiences are given meaning by association with a mental 'object' (e.g. the word 'pain' by association with the sensation of pain) or by mental (private) OSTENSIVE DEFINITION in which a mental 'entity' supposedly functions as a sample (e.g. a mental image, stored in memory, is conceived as providing a paradigm for the application of the name).

A 'private language' is not a private code, which could be cracked by another person, nor a language spoken by only one person, which could be taught to others, but rather a putative language, the individual words of which refer to what can (apparently) be known only by the speaker, i.e. to his immediate private sensations or, to use empiricist jargon, to the 'IDEAS' in his mind. It has been a presupposition of the mainstream of modern philosophy, EMPIRICIST, RATIONALIST and Kantian alike, of representational IDEALISM no less than of pure idealism, and of contemporary cognitive REPRESENTATIONALISM that the languages we all speak are such private languages, that the foundations of language no less than the foundations of knowledge lie in private experience. To undermine this picture with all its complex ramifications is the purpose of Wittgenstein's private language arguments (*see also* FOUNDATIONALISM, THE GIVEN).

The idea that the language each of us speaks is essentially private, that learning a language is a matter of associating words with, or ostensively defining words by reference to, subjective experiences (the 'given'), and that communication is a matter of stimulating a pattern of associations in the mind of the hearer qualitatively identical with that in the mind of the speaker is linked with multiple mutually supporting misconceptions about language, experiences and their identity, the mental and its relation to behaviour, self-knowledge and knowledge of the states of mind of others.

1. The idea that there can be such a thing as a private language is one manifestation of a tacit commitment to what Wittgenstein called 'Augustine's picture of language' – a pre-theoretical picture according to which the essential function of words is to name items in reality, that the link between word and world is effected by OSTENSIVE DEFINITION, and that the essential function of sentences is to describe a state of affairs. Applied to the mental, this preconception yields the following picture: one knows what a psychological predicate such as 'pain' means if one knows, is acquainted with, what it stands for – a sensation one has. The word 'pain' is linked to the sensation it names by way of private ostensive definition, which is effected by *concentrating* (the subjective analogue of pointing) on the sensation and undertaking to use the word of *that* sensation. First-person present tense psychological utterances, such as 'I have a pain' are conceived to be descriptions which the speaker, as it were, reads off the facts which are privately accessible to him.

2. Experiences are conceived to be privately owned and inalienable – no one else can have my pain, but at best only a pain that is qualitatively, but not numerically, identical with mine. They are also thought to be epistemically private – only I *really* know that

what I have is a pain, others can at best only believe or surmise that I am in pain.

3. Avowals of experience are expressions of self-knowledge. When I have an experience (e.g. a pain) I am conscious or aware of what I have by INTROSPECTION (conceived as a faculty of inner sense). Consequently, I have direct or immediate knowledge of my subjective experience. Since no one else can have what I have, or peer into my mind, my access is privileged. I *know*, and am *certain*, that I have a certain experience whenever I have it, for I cannot doubt that *this*, which I now have, is a pain.

4. One cannot gain introspective access to the experiences of others, so one can obtain only indirect knowledge or belief about them. They are hidden behind the observable behaviour, inaccessible to direct observation, and inferred either analogically (*see* ARGUMENT FROM ANALOGY) or as cause from effect (*see* INFERENCE TO THE BEST EXPLANATION).

5. The observable behaviour from which we thus infer consists of bare bodily movements caused by inner mental events. The outer (behaviour) is not logically connected with the inner (the mental). Hence the mental is essentially private, known *strictu sensu* only to its owner, and the private and subjective is better known than the public.

The resultant picture leads first to scepticism then, ineluctably, to SOLIPSISM. Since pretence and deceit are always logically possible, one can never be sure whether another person is really having the experience he behaviourally appears to be having. But worse, if a given psychological predicate means *THIS* (which I have, and no one else *could* logically have – since experience is inalienable), then it is unintelligible that there should be any other subjects of experience. Similar scepticism about communication is unavoidable: if the defining samples of the primitive terms of a language are private, then I cannot be sure that what you mean by 'red' or 'pain' is not qualitatively identical with what I mean by 'green' or 'pleasure'. And nothing can stop us from concluding that all languages are private and strictly mutually unintelligible.

Philosophers had always been aware of the problematic nature of knowledge of OTHER MINDS and of mutual intelligibility of speech on their favoured picture. It is a manifestation of Wittgenstein's genius to have launched his attack at the point which seemed incontestable – namely, not whether I can know of the experiences of others, but whether I can know of my own, not whether I can understand the 'private language' of another in attempted communication, but whether I can understand my own allegedly private language.

## THE UNINTELLIGIBILITY OF PRIVATE OSTENSIVE DEFINITION

Whether private ostensive definition is an intelligible notion depends on whether there are private (mental) analogues of the constitutive elements of public ostensive definition (*see* OSTENSIVE DEFINITION): (1) 'stage-setting', which determines the grammatical category of the definiendum – the ostensive definition being only one rule among others, (2) an ostensive gesture, (3) a sample, (4) a method of projection.

(1) Public ostensive definition gives a rule for the use of a word. Pointing at a tomato and saying 'This is red' *by itself* no more determines the use of 'red' than pointing at the moon and howling determines a use for a howl. 'Red' is a colour word, and the grammatical category of *colour* fixes a whole host of rules. The grammar of the definiendum does not flow from the object pointed at. Concentrating on one's toothache and saying 'This is pain' does not determine what *this* is. It would have to presuppose the grammar of 'sensation', but that is a word in our public language and is not defined by private ostension.

(2) The private analogue of pointing is supposedly concentrating one's attention on one's pain (which one can do). But concentrating one's attention on a sensation is not a kind of pointing for oneself alone (although one can point, publicly, at one's sensation). It does not determine a criterion of identity for subsequent uses of 'pain', and emphatically saying 'This' does not either, for what is the 'this' one concentrates on? (One cannot reply 'a pain', since that presupposes the very concept one is trying to determine. Nor can one reply 'a certain sensation', or even 'a something', for these are words in our public language with a determinate grammar of their own.)

(3) A sample functions as a standard of correctness for indefinitely many applications. It must be preservable or reproducible, and the identity of the sample must be fixed (there must be a distinction between a correct and an incorrect selection of a sample in explaining the use of a word). But one cannot preserve a sensation, sense-impression or experience for future use as a defining sample. Remembering that pain is *THIS* (conjuring up a mental image) is no substitute, for on such presuppositions there can be no criterion for reproducing the *right* sample or mental surrogate. Here there would be no distinction between remembering correctly the connection between 'S' and the paradigm that defines it and merely thinking one remembers, and there is no independent court of appeal to fix that distinction. But 'S', a sensation-name, does not mean: 'whatever occurs to one when one says "S"'.

(4) It must be possible to lay a sample alongside reality for match and mismatch. A method of projection is associated with each category of samples (the methods of projection for samples of colours, lengths, sounds or weights are altogether different). A mental image or representation cannot satisfy this requirement. One cannot *perceive* it (one *has* it). Nor can one lay it alongside reality for match or mismatch. One can say that the curtains are the colour one imagined, but not by *comparing* one's mental image (which one cannot *see*) with the visible curtains. One may have the same pain in one's left foot as in one's right foot, but one cannot justify asserting that one has a pain in one's left foot by saying 'Pain is *THIS*' (and concentrating on one's pain in the right foot) and adding 'and what is in my left foot *is THIS*'. For nothing determines what *THIS* is, and there is here no technique of application for the definiendum, no method of laying the sample alongside reality and nothing that deter-

mines identity or difference between sample and the described item.

In short, a 'private ostensive definition' cannot determine a rule for the use of a word, can provide neither a private explanation of meaning nor a norm of correctness for the application of a word. It cannot function in a practice with a determinate technique of application. What then replaces the private language account? Truly, 'pain' is the name of a sensation, as 'red' is the name of a colour. But the moot question is: What is it for a word 'S' to name a sensation? It is, *inter alia*, for the utterance 'I have an S' to be the expression or manifestation of a sensation, and to constitute a *criterion* for others to assert 'He has an S'.

## CONFUSIONS ABOUT THE PRIVACY OF EXPERIENCE

It is easy to construe 'You can't have my pain' to mean that two people cannot have the same pain (i.e. the numerically identical pain) but only similar (qualitatively identical) pains. From this it seems to follow that no one else can really know whether I am in pain or what I really mean by 'pain'. This is mistaken. The distinction between numerical and qualitative identity which applies to substances has no application to sensations or experiences. One is inclined to think that since, e.g., your headache is in your head and mine is in my head, difference in location, by Leibniz's law, implies numerical difference. This is confused, since for two people to have the same pain in the same place just is for them to have a pain of such-and-such phenomenal characteristics in corresponding parts of their bodies. But one might waive this, and point out that Siamese twins might each suffer pain at the point of juncture; now it might be argued that for all that A's pain is his pain, and B's pain is distinct – for it belongs to him. This is muddled, for the subject of a pain is not a distinguishing mark of the pain, any more than an object is a distinguishing characteristic of its colour. The criteria of identity of a pain include phenomenal characteristics, intensity and location. If these tally between two people, then they do have the same pain.

## CONFUSIONS ABOUT EPISTEMIC PRIVACY

The doctrines of epistemic privacy, privileged access and immediacy ('direct' knowledge of one's own states of mind) are distortions of various grammatical propositions, viz., that there is no such thing as my *not* knowing, my doubting or wondering, my not being certain whether I am, e.g., in pain, and no such thing as my having behavioural grounds or evidence for being in pain, as there is no such thing as my misrecognizing and misidentifying my pains. But the grammatical exclusion of doubt does not make room for certainty – rather, it excludes it likewise, as the exclusion of ignorance precludes the intelligibility of knowledge. The grammatical exclusion of behavioural grounds for 'self-ascription of experience' does not imply that there are directly observable (introspectible) inner grounds, which are akin to perception. It implies that avowals of experience are not self-ascriptions parallel to other-ascriptions, but groundless *expressions* of the inner – as a groan is a groundless expression of pain. The exclusion of error, misrecognition and mis-identification does not ensure infallible knowledge, recognition and identification – rather it precludes any such thing. Hence, Wittgenstein insisted, 'I know I am in pain' is either just an emphatic assertion that I am in pain (or a joke) or it is philosophers' nonsense. It is erroneous to think that we know how things are with us inwardly by the faculty of 'introspection'. Rather we *can* say what we feel, as we can say how things strike us perceptually, or what we intend, imagine or think. The avowal 'I have a pain' is typically an *expression* of pain – a learnt extension and partial replacement of a groan (*see* AVOWALS). It is a criterion for others to ascribe pain to the speaker in a description 'He has a pain', but it is not itself a description (though it may be a report). Description typically goes with observing, scrutinizing, examining and investigating; it characteristically involves perceptual competence exercised in various observational conditions, recognition and identification, skill and accuracy of representation (and ways of improving these by closer scrutiny, improved observational conditions, consulting others), the possibility of error (and ways of correcting it), and grounds of judgement. But in the case of expressive uses of first-person present tense psychological utterances (manifestations or avowals of the inner) no perception or perceptual skill is involved, there are no *observational* conditions, there is neither recognition nor misrecognition, identification or misidentification, no checking by closer scrutiny, no consulting others or discovering from evidence how things are with oneself. One does not 'read off' from the 'inner facts' how things are with one and render a *description* of them in words for the benefit of others. And much the same goes for one's sense-impressions, desires, thoughts and intentions – although there are also great differences here. The articulate expression of the inner is not as such a manifestation of self-knowledge, but it is true that a rich inner life is the prerogative of language-users. A dog may expect its master now, but it cannot now expect its master to return next week, for its behavioural repertoire is too impoverished. Nothing it can now *do* will count as a criterion for now expecting or wanting something to happen next week, or for feeling remorse over what it did last week. Such feelings and desires presuppose the mastery of linguistic skills and their manifestation in articulate expressive behaviour.

## ASCRIPTION OF EXPERIENCE TO OTHERS

The classical picture of our knowledge of 'other minds' similarly rests on a wide range of misconceptions. It presupposes that psychological predicates are given meaning by private ostensive definition, and hence that other-ascription of experience involves attributing to others *THIS* (which one now has), on the basis of analogy or 'inference to the best explanation'. But private ostensive definition is a *contradictio in adjectio*, and to say that since I know what it is for me to be in pain, therefore I must know what it is for another to be in pain is akin to thinking that

since I know what it is to be 5 o'clock here I must know what it is to be 5 o'clock on the sun. This is incoherent. It must first be determined what *counts* as being in pain, i.e. what justifies the employment of this expression. The first-person present tense use is typically a manifestation of the inner, parallel to and in the simplest case a partial substitute for prelinguistic expressive behaviour. The utterance and the non-linguistic behaviour alike constitute *logical criteria* for third-person ascriptions. More generally, third-person psychological propositions are justifiably asserted on the basis of appropriate behavioural criteria, e.g. typical forms of pain-behaviour (including avowals), in appropriate circumstances. These are not inductive evidence discovered by non-inductive identification of the relata and observation of regular correlation, but are logical (grammatical) grounds: *this* is what is called 'a cry of pain', 'a scream of agony', etc. An avowal of experience and an avowal of the identity of a current experience with an antecedent one rest on no criteria, but such avowals together with other forms of expressive behaviour in appropriate circumstances constitute criteria, and criteria of sameness and difference, for the experiences of other people. But it is important to correct misconceptions of human behaviour, for what we call 'behaviour', what we observe when we observe our fellow men, is not 'bare bodily movements', but – laughing with joy, wincing in pain, smiling in amusement, etc. The joy, pain, or amusement are not *accompaniments* of 'bare bodily movements' – as it were *hidden* behind the behaviour (i.e. in the mind). They are not hidden, but manifest; they do not accompany the behaviour (as thunder accompanies lightening) but infuse it; they are not behind the behaviour (as the movement of a clock is behind the dial) but visible in it.

To be sure, contrary to BEHAVIOURISM pain is not the same as pain-behaviour and joy is distinct from joyful behaviour. For one can be in pain and not show it, and feel joyful without manifesting it. But to feel pain or joy and not show it is not to *hide* anything. One hides one's feelings when one deliberately *suppresses* them (as one hides one's thoughts by keeping one's diary under lock and key, not merely by thinking and not expressing one's thoughts). When one avows a headache, expresses one's pleasure or says one thinks it cannot be said that the utterances are mere words and that the inner is still hidden. Talk of the inner is a *metaphor*, and one must beware of looking for an inside *behind* that which in this metaphor *is* the inside.

We do often know when others are, e.g., in pain, and can be as certain of it as of '2 + 2 = 4'. One cannot say of someone screaming in agony after an accident 'Maybe he is not really in pain'. One sees the pain on his face, sees that he is suffering. Such knowledge is not *indirect*, for there is no more direct way of knowing that a person is in pain. *He* does not know 'directly', since he cannot be said to *know* that he is in pain. Rather, he is in pain and says so! (*See* PERCEPTUAL KNOWLEDGE).

It can be misleading to say that one *infers* that someone is in pain from his behaviour, although one might infer from the fact that someone has arthritis that he has pains in his joints. Of course, I may justify saying that I knew he was in pain on the grounds that I saw him writhing in agony (and here I describe the outer in terms of the inner), but it would be misleading to represent this as inferring that he was in pain from his mere behaviour and absurd to say 'I saw only his behaviour and inferred that he was in pain'.

It is true that pretence is possible and that our judgements here are fallible and defeasible. But it is not *always* possible. It is unintelligible to suppose that a neonate pretends, for pretence has to be *learnt*. Nor is it possible in all circumstances, e.g. when someone falls into flames. Rather, there are circumstance-dependent criteria for pretence no less than for that which is pretended. Hence the possibility of pretence is no more a ground for scepticism about other minds than the possibility of illusion is a ground for scepticism about the existence of objects (*see* ARGUMENT FROM ILLUSION).

Wittgenstein's private language arguments are not a form of behaviourism.

On the contrary, he insists upon the distinction between pain and pain-behaviour and does not claim that the inner is a fiction, but rather that a certain philosophical picture of the inner is a *grammatical* fiction. His arguments do not rely upon a form of verificationism to rebut the supposition of the intelligibility of private ostensive definition, they merely remind us that if we are to talk of a rule for the use of a word, then there must be an operative distinction between the correct and the incorrect application of the rule. He did not argue that the only refuge against scepticism with regard to language lies in community (public) consensus (and hence that language is essentially social), but rather that the idea of a rule (e.g. of grammar) that can in principle be understood by only one person is unintelligible. The private language arguments overturn the whole tradition of philosophical thought about the nature of the mind and about the relation between the inner and the outer. Their implications ramify widely through philosophy of language (undercutting the idea that the foundations of language lie in private experience), epistemology (undermining the thought that knowledge has private foundations) and philosophical psychology (demolishing the presuppositions of mentalism and behaviourism alike).

*See also* AVOWALS; FOUNDATIONALISM; INTROSPECTION; OSTENSIVE DEFINITION; OTHER MINDS; SELF-KNOWLEDGE AND SELF-IDENTITY; WITTGENSTEIN.

BIBLIOGRAPHY

Wittgenstein, L.: *Philosophical Investigations* (Oxford: Blackwell, 1953), §§243–315.
Wittgenstein, L.: 'Notes for lectures on "private experience" and "sense data"', ed. R. Rhees, *Philosophical Review* 77 (1968), 275–320.

Cooke, J.W.: 'Human beings', in *Studies in the Philosophy of Wittgenstein* ed. P. Winch (London, Routledge and Kegan Paul, 1969), 117–51.
Hacker, P.M.S.: *Wittgenstein: Meaning and Mind*, vol. 3 of *An Analytical Commentary on the*

*Philosophical Investigations* (Oxford: Blackwell, 1990), 1–286.

Hacker, P.M.S.: *Insight and Illusion. Themes in the Philosophy of Wittgenstein* rev. edn (Oxford: Oxford University Press, 1986), 245–336.

Hanfling, O.: *Wittgenstein's Later Philosophy* (London: Macmillan, 1989), 88–126.

Kenny, A.J.P.: *Wittgenstein* (London: Allen Lane, 1973), 178–202.

Malcolm, N.: 'Consciousness and causality', in D.M. Armstrong and N. Malcolm *Consciousness and Causality: a Debate on the Nature of Mind* (Oxford: Blackwell, 1984), 3–102.

Malcolm, N.: *Thought and Knowledge* (Ithaca, NY: Cornell University Press, 1977), 85–169.

P. M. S. HACKER

**probability, theories of** Philosophical theories of the meaning of 'probability' have dealt with a variety of concepts which may be loosely grouped into three families: *degree of belief, relative frequency* and *chance*. The mathematics of probability has been less controversial than its interpretation, largely because all theories treat probability as some kind of proportion. Frequentists treat probability as the proportion of actual cases displaying an attribute. Degree of belief and chance theories treat probability as a proportion of possible cases, with the measure on which the proportions are based reflecting respectively intensities of belief that one has or ought to have or intensities of causal tendency. Proportions add. If I have one half of the pie and you have one quarter of it (and we aren't sharing any) then together we have three quarters of the pie. Proportions are normalized. All of the pie is 100 per cent. Proportions can't be negative.

## PROBABILITY CALCULUS

Formally, we can think of a probability as a function mapping elements of a Boolean algebra B (possible pie slices including the null slice and the whole pie) to real numbers in the interval [0,1] which satisfies:

1. If b, c are disjoint then pr(b ∪ c) = pr(b) + pr(c)
2. pr (universal element) = 1
3. For no b, is pr(b) < 0.

(It is often assumed that there is an underlying space (the set of pie atoms) such that the Boolean algebra in the foregoing is an algebra of subsets of that space, but this is not essential.) The probability of *b* conditional on *a* is then defined for elements, *a*, with non-zero probability as pr(a ∩ b)/pr(a). Taking probability conditional on *a* is just taking the proportion of *a* rather than the proportion of the universal element.

It is often mathematically convenient to strengthen the foregoing framework by requiring the operative Boolean algebra to be closed under countably infinite Boolean operations and to strengthen the principle of additivity to that of countable additivity: If the elements of a countable set, $\{b_j\}$, are pairwise disjoint, then:

$$pr \cup_i (b_j) \;=\; \sum_I pr(b_j)$$

For example, we idealize to say that a countable infinity of disjoint pie slices of 1/4, 1/8, 1/16 . . . of the pie taken together account for half of the pie. This is essentially the standard mathematical formulation of probability as set forth by Kolmogorov in 1933. It allows probability theory to be taken as a branch of measure theory, but on some interpretations of probability the additional requirements are problematic.

(Variations of the foregoing framework are possible. The requirement that the probability function be real-valued can be relaxed to allow infinitesimal probabilities. Interval-valued rather than point-valued probabilities can be considered. Conditional probabilities can be taken as primitive. Domains for the probability function which do not have the full Boolean structure can be considered.)

## DEGREE OF BELIEF

It is evident that belief need not be an all or nothing affair; belief comes in degrees. How actual degrees of belief work is a question for psychology, and our best evidence indicates that they systematically fail to satisfy the rules of the probability calculus. It was argued, however, by Frank Ramsey (1926) and by Bruno de Finetti (1937) that consistent or coherent degrees of belief should satisfy the rules of the probability calculus. From this point of view probability theory should be thought of as logic rather than psychology – that is, as the logic of partial belief.

There are different levels on which the argument can be carried out. At the level where complications involving the concept of utility are assumed away, we have the dutch book arguments. At a deeper level there are representation theorems which show that a rich, consistent preference ordering must be representable as generated by expected utility computed from underlying probability and utility assignments.

Suppose that a very rich and reliable bookie posts odds on a horse race. He values a contract which pays a pound of gold if Stewball wins at one ounce of gold. He values a contract which pays a pound of gold if Molly wins at one ounce of gold. He will buy or sell these contracts in any quantity at what he considers a fair price or better. Suppose that he also deals in contracts which pay a pound of gold if either Stewball or Molly win, and that he values these at four ounces of gold. You can buy separate contracts for Stewball and for Molly to win at a net outlay of two ounces of gold and sell back a disjunctive contract for either Stewball or Molly to win for four ounces of gold – for a net profit of two ounces of gold. You are able to make a *dutch book* against the bookie – a finite number of bets whose net gain is positive no matter what the outcome of the race – because his evaluation of the disjunctive contract does not cohere with his evaluation of the separate contracts on the disjuncts.

The bookie is said to be *coherent* if no dutch book can be made against him. Coherence requires that if the bookie values the separate contracts at one ounce of gold each, he values the disjunctive contract which pays off exactly as holding both separate contracts together would, at two ounces of gold. Coherence also requires that a contract that pays off a pound of gold no matter what, is worth a pound of gold and that a contract that pays off a pound of gold in some circumstances and requires no payment otherwise has non-negative value (i.e. the bookie

will not pay someone to take it off his hands.) Now let us take the value to a person (in pounds of gold) of a contract which pays a pound of gold if $p$ and nothing otherwise as that person's personal probability of $p$. Then it follows immediately from the foregoing that coherence requires that one's personal probabilities satisfy principles 1–3 of the probability calculus. Coherence, as defined, does not require that personal probabilities be countably additive. Strengthening the definition of coherence by allowing a countable number of bets gets countable additivity, but the epistemological status of such a strengthened notion of coherence is controversial.

Along similar lines, dynamic coherence arguments can be made for updating by Bayes' rule of conditioning – to take one's new probabilities equal to one's old conditional on the evidence – and for more general rules in updating situations in which Bayes' rule is not directly applicable. If we allow the bookie a 'spread' between buying and selling prices, we have a natural way of getting interval-valued degrees of belief. C.A.B. Smith (1961) shows that in such a setting coherence requires behaving as if one had a convex set of point probability measures and accepted a transaction just in case it had positive expected value according to all members of that set.

The dutch book arguments idealize away complications arising from the value of goods, such as the declining marginal utility of gold. Ramsey gave a deeper analysis. Consistency requirements are put directly on a decision-maker's preference order, and a probability-utility representation is gotten from the preferences with the probabilities obeying principles 1–3, and preferences agreeing with expected utility. This general sort of representation theorem can be implemented in a variety of ways. The most well-known probability-utility representation – that of L.J. Savage – does not get countable additivity, but imposition of an additional continuity requirement on preferences will guarantee a countably additivity probability.

Some degree-of-belief theorists, for example de Finetti, hold that rational degrees of belief have to satisfy only the constraints imposed by the probability calculus. Others hold that prior to having any evidence everyone should have the same probability assignment – one determined by symmetry of ignorance or 'insufficient reason' or, more recently, computational complexity. The origin of this sort of approach goes back to Bayes and Laplace. In modern times, Jeffreys, Carnap, Jaynes and Solomonoff are – in different ways – exponents of logical determination of the appropriate prior probabilities.

## RELATIVE FREQUENCY

Suppose a six-sided die is roughly chiselled from stone, rolled one hundred times, and then smashed. We take as our events the boolean algebra generated by the possible outcomes on a trial. If we define the probability of an event as the number of trials which exhibit it divided by one hundred, we have a definition which clearly satisfies 1–3. However, such a finite frequency interpretation cannot capture what usually mean when we talk of the probability of an event, for we usually allow that an unlikely sequence of outcomes can occur and we do not want to canonize the frequencies in such a sequence as the true probabilities.

For this reason, frequentists have moved to limiting relative frequency interpretations. Limiting relative frequencies are defined relative to an infinite *sequence* of trials. Here, unlike in the finite case, the order of the sequence can make a difference – so that talk of a reference *class* is highly misleading. There are possible infinite sequences in which the relevant limits do not exist, so the definition must be restricted to those sequences in which they do. Even in this case it should be noted that limiting relative frequencies need not be countably additive. Consider the sequence of the integers, and the properties of being $=1, =2, =3, \ldots$ Each of these properties has limiting relative frequency of zero, but their countable disjunction has limiting relative frequency of one.

Some frequentists – for example, Reichnbach – are content to deal with reference sequences where the relevant limiting relative frequencies exist, but others –

notably von Mises – wished to restrict the theory to sequences which are objectively *random*. This notion of objective randomness is somewhat problematic in von Mises, but has subsequently been substantially clarified.

A version of the strong law of large numbers can be invoked for whatever it is worth. *An infinite sequence of independent and identically distributed trials will with probability I produce a random sequence with limiting relative frequencies of outcomes such that the relative frequency of an outcome is equal to its probability.* But this justification must already refer to a different notion of probability according to which the probability of a single event – of an outcome on a given trial – makes sense. The probability calculus then guarantees agreement with the limiting relative frequencies with probability 1, where that probability 1 is in the antecedent non-frequentist sense of probability.

There are further difficulties with the limiting relative frequency interpretation. Why should the special case of independent identically distributed trials be used to model all probability? In a world in which causation operates many processes do not give independent trials. And if our stone die is to be rolled an infinite number of times, it will presumably become worn so that the trials may not preserve the probabilities. Finally, we may not have infinite sequences at all. Is there no probability is the universe is finite?

To deal with these difficulties a kind of counterfactual limiting relative frequency view has been proposed. The probability of a outcome is taken as the relative frequency that it would have if the experiment were repeated independently an infinite number of times without altering the relevant causal factors in the experimental set-up. This quite sophisticated version of the limiting relative frequency view is already to be found in John Venn's *The Logic of Chance* (1866). It, of course, raises its own set of philosophical questions: specifying the relevant causal factors which individuate the chance set-up, giving the relevant sense of independence in a way that is not circular and interpreting the key counterfactual conditionals.

CHANCE

Instead of trying to tell a story in which fictional relative frequencies agree with chances, one might take the course of directly postulating chances as theoretical entities. The chances for outcomes on a single throw of the die are conceived of as elements of physical reality which represent *probabilistic tendencies* or *propensities* to produce those outcomes. The connection between chances and frequencies is then specified by the strong law of large numbers, the ergodic theorem and other limit theorems of the probability calculus itself.

Why should the chances have the mathematical structure of the probability calculus? This is simply postulated as part of the statistical model under consideration. So the use of countably additive probabilities in classical theories does not – on this view – pose any foundational problem. On the other hand, a propensity theorist might find it plausible to consider modifications of the classical probability calculus in physical theories where such a modified structure would be a useful theoretical tool. This flexibility is just a reflection of the lack of content of the propensity theory as stated. Some advocates of this general approach attempt to say more: for instance, that the chances are determined by the chance set-up, or even that propensities correspond to hypothetical limiting relative frequencies. Evidently, there is no sharp line between relative frequency and propensity conceptions of probability and hybrid philosophical theories are possible.

If chances are to be taken as theoretical entities, then it is important to ask how statements of chance are confirmed or disconfirmed. This is to bring the discussion full circle since it raises the question of rational degrees of belief about the chances. For example, consider our rough stone die. When it is created the true chances are unknown, although we may have some degrees of belief about where the true chances may be. After the die is tossed one hundred times we have some frequency evidence which should enable us to modify our degrees of belief about the true chances.

If, for each chance hypothesis, we have the degree-of-belief probability of the observed outcome sequence conditional on that chance hypothesis, then we can use Bayes' theorem to update our degrees of belief about chance. The natural thing to do – and what everyone does do – is to take the (degree of belief) probability of an outcome sequence conditional on a chance hypothesis to be equal to what the chance hypothesis says it is. That is, we use the following principle, or some close relation to it:

$$pr[outcome|Chance(outcome) = a]$$
$$= a \qquad (M)$$

*Example: A coin with unknown bias is to be flipped. My degree of belief that the coin will come up heads conditional on the hypothesis that it is really biased 2 to 1 in favour of heads, is 2/3.*

The foregoing gives a brief indication of how the three conceptions of chance, frequency and degree-of-belief can interact within a parametric Bayesian framework. It raises another philosophical question: that of the status of (M).

Subjective Bayesians want to do without the metaphysics of chance, and deal with only degrees of belief (which, of course, include degrees of belief about relative frequencies). However, subjective Bayesians do not have to forgo the language of chance and the mathematics of parametric Bayesian statistics. Rather, they regard such talk as a manner of speaking that can be mathematically justified in the presence of symmetries in your degrees of belief. A case in point is de Finetti's famous representation theorem. If one's degrees of belief about a sequence of trials is exchangeable (invariant under finite permutations of trials) then one's degrees of belief are a mixture of probabilities which make the trials independent and identically distributed. Thus one's degrees of belief are *just as if* one had a parametric model with unknown chances. Generalizations of de Finetti's representation theorem handle other important cases. In this subjective setting one can reconstruct the random variable, *chance*, as probability conditional on an appropriate partition or sigma-algebra. One consequence of such a construction is that (M) becomes a theorem.

*See also* BAYESIANISM.

BIBLIOGRAPHY

Bayes, T.: 'An essay towards solving a problem in the doctrine of chances', *Philosophical Transactions of the Royal Society* 53 (1763), 370–418; 54: 296–325: reprinted in *Biometrika* 45 (1958), 293–315.

Carnap, R.: *Logical Foundations of Probability* (Chicago: University of Chicago Press, 1950).

Diaconis, P. and Freedman, D.: 'Partial exchangeability and sufficiency', in *Statistics: Applications and New Directions* (Calcutta: Indian Statistical Institute, 1981), 205–36.

Diaconis, P. and Zabell, S.: 'Updating subjective probability', *Journal of the American Statistical Association* 77 (1982), 822–30.

de Finetti, B.: 'La Prévision: ses lois logiques, ses sources subjectives', in *Annales de l'Institut Henri Poincaré* 7 (1937), 1–68; trans. as 'Foresight: its logical laws, its subjective sources', in *Studies in Subjective Probability* eds H.E. Kyburg, Jr and H. Smokler (Huntington: Kreiger, 1980).

Fine, T.: *Theories of Probability* (New York: Academic Press, 1973).

Jeffrey, R.: *The Logic of Decision* 2nd edn (Chicago: University of Chicago Press, 1983).

Jeffreys, H.: *The Theory of Probability* (Oxford: Oxford University Press, 1939).

Kolmogorov, A.N.: *Foundations of the Theory of Probability* (New York: Chelsea, 1959).

Kyburg, H.: 'Propensities and probabilities', *British Journal for the Philosophy of Science* 25, (1974), 358–75.

Lane, D.A. and Sudderth, W.D.: 'Coherent predictive inference', *Sankhya*, ser A, 46 (1984), 166–85.

von Mises, R. and Geiringer, H.: *The Mathematical Theory of Probability and Statistics* (New York: Academic Press, 1964).

Ramsey, F.P.: 'Truth and probability', in his *The Foundations of Mathematics and Other Essays* ed. R.B. Braithwaite (New York: Harcourt Brace, 1931).

Reichenbach, H.: *The Theory of Probability* (Berkeley: University of California Press, 1949).

Savage, L.J.: *The Foundations of Statistics* (New York: Wiley, 1954).

Skyrms, B.: *Pragmatics and Empiricism* (New Haven: Yale University Press, 1984).

Skyrms, B.: 'Stability and chance' with an Appendix by P. Vanderschraaf in *Existence and Explanation* eds W. Spohn et al. (Dordrecht: Kluwer 1991).

Venn, J.: *The Logic of Chance* (1886); 4th edn (New York: Chelsea, 1962).

BRIAN SKYRMS

**problem of the criterion**  This is the problem of how both to formulate the *criteria*, and to determine the *extent*, of knowledge and justified belief. The following account will focus on justification. The problem arises from the seeming plausibility of the following two propositions:

(1) I can identify instances (and thus determine the extent) of justified belief only if I already know the criteria of it.

(2) I can know the criteria of justified belief only if I can already identify the instances of it.

If both (1) and (2) were true, I would be caught in a circle: I could know neither the criteria nor the extent of justified belief. In order to show that both can be known after all, a way out of the circle must be found. The nature of this task is best illustrated by considering the four positions that may be taken concerning the truth values of (1) and (2):

(a) Scepticism as to the possibility of constructing a theory of justification: Both (1) and (2) are true; consequently, I can know neither the criteria nor the extent of justified belief. (This kind of scepticism is restricted in its scope to epistemic propositions. While it allows for the possibility of justified beliefs, it denies that we can *know* which beliefs are justified and which are not.)

(b) (2) is true but (1) is false: I can identify instances of justification without applying a criterion.

(c) (1) is true but (2) is false: I can identify the criteria of justified belief without prior knowledge of its instances.

(d) Both (1) and (2) are false; I can know the extent of justified belief without applying criteria, and vice versa.

The problem of the criterion may be seen as the problem of providing a rationale for a non-sceptical response, that is, for either (b), (c), or (d).

Roderick CHISHOLM, who has devoted particular attention to this problem, calls the second response *particularism*, and the third *methodism*. HUME, who draws a sceptical conclusion as to the extent of empirical knowledge using 'deducibility from sense-experience' as the criterion of justification, was a methodist. Thomas REID and G.E. MOORE were particularists; they rejected Hume's criterion on the ground that it turns obvious cases of knowledge into cases of ignorance. Chisholm advocates particularism as the correct response. His view, which has also become known as CRITICAL COGNITIVISM, may be summarized as follows. Criteria for the application of epistemic concepts are expressed by EPISTEMIC PRINCIPLES. The antecedent of such a principle states the non-normative ground on which the epistemic status ascribed by the consequent SUPERVENES. (Cf. Chisholm, 1957, pp. 30–9, 1982, p. 12.) An example is the following:

If S is appeared to F-ly, then S is justified in believing that there is an F in front of S.

According to this principle, a criterion for justifiably believing that there is something red in front of me is 'being appeared to redly'. In constructing his theory of knowledge, Chisholm considers various principles of this kind, accepting or rejecting them depending on whether or not they fit what he identifies, without using any criterion, as the instances of justified belief. As the result of using this method, he rejects the principle above as too broad, and Hume's empiricist criterion (which, unlike the criteria Chisholm tries to formulate, states a necessary condition),

If S is justified in believing that there is an F in front of S, then S's belief is deducible from S's sense-experience

as too narrow. (Cf. Chisholm, 1982, ch. 5; 1977, chs 4 and 7.)

Regarding the viability of particularism, this approach raises the question of how it is possible to identify instances of justified belief without applying any criteria. Chisholm's answer rests on the premise that, in order to know, no criterion of knowledge or justification is needed (1982, p. 53). He claims that this holds also for knowledge of epistemic facts. Supposing I am justified in believing that $p$, what justifies me in believing that I am justified in believing that $p$ is the same body of evidence that justifies me in believing that $p$. Put differently, both $JJp$ and $Jp$ supervene on the same non-epistemic ground. (Cf. Chisholm 1982, ch. 4. For a dissenting view, *see* Alston, 1989, p. 24; cf. van Cleve, 1979, p. 86.) Thus in order to become justified in believing myself to be justified in believing that $p$, I need not apply any criterion of justified belief; I need only *consider* the evidence supporting $p$. The key assumption of particularism, then, is that in order to acquire knowledge of an epistemic fact, one need not *apply*, but only *satisfy* the antecedent condition of, the epistemic principle that governs the fact in question. Hence it is possible to have knowledge of epistemic facts such as 'I am justified in believing that there is an F in front of me' without applying epistemic principles, and to use this knowledge in order to reject those principles that are either too broad or too narrow.

According to methodism, the correct solution to the problem proceeds the opposite way: epistemic principles are to be formulated without using knowledge of epistemic facts. But how could methodists distinguish between correct and incorrect principles, given that an appeal to instances of epistemic knowledge is illegitimate? Against what could they check the correctness of a putative principle? Unless the correct criteria are immediately obvious, which is doubtful, it remains unclear how methodists could rationally prefer one principle over another. Thus Chisholm rejects Hume's criterion not only because of its sceptical implications but also on the ground of its arbitrariness: Hume 'leaves us completely in the dark so far as concerns what *reason* he may have for adopting this particular criterion rather than some other' (1982, p. 67). Particularists, then, accept proposition (2), and thus reject responses (c) and (d), both of which affirm that (2) is false.

One problem for particularism is that it appears to beg the question against scepticism. (cf. BonJour, 1985, p. 13). In order to evaluate this criticism, it must be kept in mind that particularists reject criteria with sceptical consequences on the basis of instances, whereas sceptics reject instances of justification on the basis of criteria. This difference in methodology is illustrated by the following two arguments:

*An Anti-Sceptical Argument*
(A) If the 'deducibility from sense-experience' criterion is correct, then I am not justified in believing that these are my hands.
(B) I am justified in believing that these are my hands.
Therefore:
(-C) The 'deducibility from sense-experience' criterion is not correct.

*A Sceptical Argument*
(A) If the 'deducibility from sense-experience' criterion is correct, then I am not justified in believing that these are my hands.
(C) The 'deducibility from sense-experience' criterion is correct.
Therefore:
(-B) I am not justified in believing that these are my hands.

The problematic premises are (B) and (C). Particularists reject (C) on the basis of (B), and sceptics (B) on the basis of (C). Regarding question-begging, then, the situation is symmetrical: both beg the question against each other. Who, though, has the better argument? Particularists would say that accepting (B) is more reasonable than accepting (C) because the risk of making an error in accepting a general criterion is greater than in taking a specific belief to be justified.

The problem of the criterion is not restricted to epistemic justification and knowledge but is posed by any attempt to formulate general principles of philosophy or logic. In response to the problem of induction, Nelson GOODMAN has proposed bringing the principles of inductive inference into agreement with the instances of inductive inference we accept. John Rawls has attempted to formulate principles of justice with the objective of bringing the principles and what we count as examples of justice into a state of reflective equilibrium (cf. Goodman. 1966, pp. 66–7; Rawls, 1971, pp. 19–21, 48–51). Goodman and Rawls believe that in order to identify the principles they seek their instances must be known to begin with. But they believe also that in the process of bringing principles and instances into agreement, principles may be saved by sacrificing instances. They may, therefore, be considered advocates of a view analogous to response (iv), a hybrid of particularism and methodism. (For a critical discussion of Goodman's approach, *see* Stich, 1988; cf. Sosa, 1989.)

*See also* CHISHOLM; COMMONSENSISM AND CRITICAL COGNITIVISM; CRITERIA AND KNOWLEDGE; SEXTUS EMPIRICUS.

BIBLIOGRAPHY

Alston, W.P.: *Epistemic Justification* (Ithaca, NY: Cornell University Press, 1989).
BonJour, L.: *The Structure of Empirical Knowledge* (Cambridge, MA: Harvard University Press, 1985).
Chisholm, R.: *Perceiving* (Ithaca, NY: Cornell University Press, 1957).
Chisholm, R.: *The Foundations of Knowing* (Minneapolis: University of Minnesota Press, 1982).
Chisholm, R.: *Theory of Knowledge* 2nd edn (Englewood Cliffs: Prentice-Hall, 1977).
van Cleve, J.: 'Foundationalism, epistemic principles, and the Cartesian circle', *Philosophical Review* 88 (1979), 55–91.

Goodman, N.: *Fact, Fiction, and Forecast* (Indianapolis: Bobbs-Merrill, 1965).

Rawls, J.: *A Theory of Justice* (Cambridge, MA: Harvard University Press, 1971).

Sosa, E.: 'Equilibrium in coherence', in *The Current State of the Coherence Theory*, ed. J.W. Bender (Dordrecht: Kluwer, 1989), 242–50.

Sosa, E.: 'The foundations of foundationalism', *Nous* 14 (1980), 547–64.

Stich, S.: 'Reflective equilibrium, analytic epistemology and the problem of cognitive diversity', *Synthese* 74 (1988), 391–413.

MATTHIAS STEUP

**problem of the external world**  An external world, as philosophers have used the term, is not some distant planet external to earth. Nor is the external world, strictly speaking, a *world*. Rather, the external world consists of all those objects and events which exist external to perceivers. So the table across the room is part of the external world, and so is its brown colour and roughly rectangular shape. Similarly, if the table falls apart when a heavy object is placed on it, the event of its disintegration is a part of the external world.

One object external to and distinct from any given perceiver is any other perceiver. So, relative to one perceiver, every other perceiver is a part of the external world. However, another way of understanding the external world results if we think of the objects and events external to and distinct from every perceiver. So conceived the set of all perceivers makes up a vast community, with all of the objects and events external to that community making up the external world. In this essay we will understand the notion of an external world in the former way. We will thus suppose that perceivers are entities which occupy physical space, if only because they are partly composed of items which take up physical space.

What, then, is the problem of the external world (hereafter the PEW)? Certainly it is not whether there is an external world; this much is taken for granted. Instead, the problem is an epistemological one which, in rough approximation, can be formulated by asking whether and if so how a person gains knowledge of the external world. So under-

stood, the problem seems to admit of an easy solution. There is knowledge of the external world which persons acquire primarily by perceiving objects and events which make up the external world.

However, many philosphers have found this easy solution problematic. Indeed, the very statement of the PEW itself will be altered once we consider the main arguments against the easy solution.

AN EPISTEMIC ARGUMENT

One way in which the easy solution, mentioned above, has been further articulated is in terms of epistemological DIRECT REALISM (hereafter, EDR). This theory is realist in so far as it claims that objects and events in the external world, along with many of their various features, exist independently of and are generally unaffected by perceivers and acts of perception in which they engage. And this theory is epistemologically direct since it also claims that in perception people often, indeed typically, acquire immediate non-inferential knowledge of objects and events in the external world. It is on this latter point that it is thought to face serious problems.

The main reason for this is that knowledge of objects in the external world seems to be dependent on some other knowledge, and so would not qualify as immediate and non-inferential. It is claimed that I do not gain immediate non-inferential perceptual knowledge that there is a brown and rectangular table before me, because I would not know such a proposition unless I knew that something then appeared brown and rectangular. Hence, knowledge of the table is dependent upon knowledge of how it appears. Alternately expressed, if there is knowledge of the table at all, it is indirect knowledge, secured only if the proposition about the table may be inferred from propositions about appearances. If so, EDR is false (*see* Chisholm, 1957, pp. 55ff).

This argument suggests a new way to formulate the PEW:

> PEW1 Can one have knowledge of propositions about objects and events in the

external world based upon propositions which describe how the external world appears, i.e. upon appearances?

Unlike our original formulation of the PEW, this formulation does not admit of an easy solution. Indeed, it has seemed to many philosophers that it admits of no solution at all, so that scepticism regarding the external world is the only remaining alternative.

## PERCEPTUAL ARGUMENTS

If we think back to the easy solution to the first version of PEW, we note that it says that a person gains knowledge of objects and events in the external world primarily by perceiving them. If we concentrate on perception, a slightly different version of the easy solution emerges, one which incorporates perceptual direct realism (PDR). This theory is realist in just the way described earlier, but it adds, secondly, that objects and events in the external world are typically directly perceived, as are many of their features such as their colours, shapes and textures.

Often, PDR is developed further by simply adding EDR to it. Such an addition is supported by claiming that direct perception of objects in the external world provides us with immediate non-inferential knowledge of such objects. Seen in this way, PDR is supposed to support EDR, though strictly speaking they are independent doctrines. One might consistently, perhaps even plausibly, hold one without also accepting the other. (I think BERKELEY did so; see Pappas, 1991.)

Direct perception is that perception which is not dependent on some other perception. The main opposition to the claim that we directly perceive external objects comes from indirect or REPRESENTATIVE REALISM. That theory holds that whenever an object in the external world is perceived, some other object is also perceived, namely a sensum – a phenomenal entity of some sort. Further, one would not perceive the external object if one were to fail to perceive the sensum. In this sense the sensum is a perceived intermediary, and the perception of the external object is dependent on the perception of the sensum. For such a theory, perception of the sensum

is direct, since it is not dependent on some other perception, while perception of the external object is indirect. More generally, for the indirect realist, all directly perceived entities are sensa. On the other hand, those who accept PDR claim that perception of objects in the external world is typically direct, since that perception is not dependent on some perceived intermediaries such as sensa.

It has often been supposed, however, that the ARGUMENT FROM ILLUSION suffices to refute all forms of PDR. The argument from illusion is actually a family of different arguments rather than one argument (see Pitcher 1970; Cornman, 1971). Perhaps the most familiar argument in this family begins by noting that objects appear differently to different observers, and even to the same observer on different occasions or in different circumstances. For example, a round dish may appear round to a person viewing it from directly above and elliptical to another viewing it from one side. As one changes position the dish will appear to have still different shapes, more and more elliptical in some cases, closer and closer to round in others. In each such case, it is argued, the observer directly sees an entity with that apparent shape. Thus, when the dish appears elliptical, the observer is said to see directly something which is elliptical. Certainly this elliptical entity is not the dish nor the top surface of the dish, since that is round. This elliptical entity, a sensum, is thought to be wholly distinct from the dish.

In seeing the dish from straight above it appears round, and it might be thought that then one directly sees the dish rather than a sensum. But here too relativity sets in; the dish will appear different in size as one is placed at different distances from the dish. So even if in all of these cases the dish appears round, it will also appear to have many different diameters. Hence, in these cases as well, the observer is said to directly see some sensum, and not the dish.

This argument concerning the dish can be generalized in two ways. First, more or less the same argument can be mounted for all other cases of seeing and across the full range of sensible qualities – textures and colours in addition to shapes and sizes. Second, one can utilize related relativity arguments for other sense modalities. With the argument thus completed, one will have reached the conclusion that in all cases of non-hallucinatory perception, the observer directly perceives a sensum, and not an external physical object. Presumably in cases of hallucination a related result holds, so that one reaches the fully general result that in all cases of perceptual experience, what is directly perceived is a sensum or group of sensa, and not an external physical object. PDR, therefore, is deemed false.

Yet even if PDR is refuted, this by itself does not generate a problem of the external world. We need to add that if no person ever directly perceives an external physical object, then no person ever gains immediate non-inferential knowledge of such objects. Armed with this additional premise, we could conclude that if there is knowledge of external objects, it is indirect and based upon immediate knowledge of sensa. We can then formulate the problem of the external world in another way:

PEW2 Can one have knowledge of propositions about objects and events in the external world based upon propositions about directly perceived sensa?

It is worth noting the differences between PEW1 and PEW2. The arguments which lead to these problems are quite different, with those directing us to PEW2 concerned with perception in a way not mentioned in arguments leading to PEW1. Also, attempts to solve PEW2 require accounts of perception alternative to PDR, while this is not so for PEW1.

PROPOSED SOLUTIONS TO PEW1

If the argument leading to PEW1 is satisfactory, then we have knowledge of the external world only if propositions about objects and events in the external world (hereafter E-propositions) are inferrable from propositions about appearances (A-propositions). They will be so inferrable only if they are either deducible from E-propositions, or are inferrable by some cogent inductive inference. It is clear, however, that E-propositions are not deducible from any finite group of A-propositions. We can see this by noting that the A-propositions might all be true in a case of a hallucination, when the E-proposition in question is plainly false. Thus, A-propositions such as those expressed by 'I seem to see something round, and red and spherical' and 'I seem to be tasting something sweet and slightly tart' do not entail that one is seeing or tasting an apple.

Some philosophers have thought that if analytical PHENOMENALISM were true, the situation would be different. Analytical phenomenalism is the doctrine that every E-proposition is fully analysable into, and thus is equivalent in meaning to, a group of A-propositions (see Ayer, 1940; Lewis, 1946). The numbers of A-propositions making up the analysis of any single E-proposition would likely be enormous, perhaps indefinitely many. Nevertheless, analytical phenomenalism might be of help in solving PEW1 because the required deductions of E-propositions from A-propositions could be readily made. An E-proposition equivalent in meaning to some A-propositions can certainly be deduced from those A-propositions.

However, matters are not as simple as these remarks make it seem. Even if analytical phenomenalism is true, no reasonably sized set of A-propositions will *entail* an E-proposition. For, given analytical phenomenalism there are indefinitely many A-propositions in the analysis of each E-proposition. Hence, the inference from any set of A-propositions to an E-proposition is apt to be inductive, even granting the truth of analytical phenomenalism. Moreover, most of the A-propositions into which we might hope to analyse an E-proposition would be complex subjunctive conditionals such as that expressed by 'If I were to seem to see something red, round and spherical, and if I were to seem to try to taste what I seem to see, then most likely I would seem to taste something sweet and slightly tart.' But A-propositions of this complex sort will not typically be immediately known, and thus knowledge of E-propositions will not generally be based upon immediate knowledge of such A-propositions.

Moreover, there is good reason to think that analytical phenomenalism is false. For each proposed translation of an E-proposition into A-propositions has been shown to be defective, and there is no reason to suppose that any new attempt at a translation of this sort will succeed where all others have failed (*see* Chisholm, in Swartz, 1965).

But neither are E-propositions *inductively* derivable from A-propositions. Plainly enumerative induction is of no help in this regard, for that is an inference from premises about observed objects in a certain class having some properties F and G, to unobserved objects in the same class having properties F and G. A-propositions, however, concern appearances while E-propositions concern external objects and events. So, the most likely inductive inference to consider is a causal one: we infer from certain effects, described by A-propositions, to their likely causes, described by P-propositions. But here, too, the inference is apt to prove problematic.

Consider the A-propositions expressed by 'I seem to see something red, round and spherical' and 'I seem to taste something sweet and slightly tart.' To infer cogently from these propositions to that expressed by 'There is an apple before me' we need additional information, such as that expressed by 'Apples generally cause visual appearances of redness, roundness and spherical shape, and gustatory appearances of sweetness and tartness.' With this additional information, the inference is a good one, and it is likely to be true that there is an apple there relative to those premises. The cogency of the inference, however, depends squarely on this additional premise; relative only to the stated A-propositions, it is not highly probable that there is an apple there.

Defenders of indirect realism have sometimes appealed to an INFERENCE TO THE BEST EXPLANATION to help justify E-propositions. We might say that the best explanation of the appearances is that they are caused by external objects. However, even if

this is true, as no doubt it is, it is unclear how establishing this *general* hypothesis helps to justify *specific* E-propositions such as that these particular appearances are caused by that red apple.

The point here is a general one: cogent inductive inferences from A-propositions to E-propositions are available only with some added premiss expressing the requisite causal relation, or perhaps some other premiss describing some other sort of correlation between appearances and external objects. So there is no reason to think that PEW1 can be solved by exhibiting inductive inferences from A-propositions to E-propositions (*see* Chisholm, 1957, pp. 73–4). And since deductive and inductive inferences from A-propositions to E-propositions seem to exhaust the options, no solution to PEW1 is at hand. So, unless there is some solution to PEW2, it would appear that scepticism concerning knowledge of the external world would be the most reasonable position to take.

## PROPOSED SOLUTIONS TO PEW2

PEW2 is generated by the supposed refutation of PDR, conjoined with the principle that one has immediate perceptual knowledge of something only if one directly perceives that object. Broadly speaking, there are two alternatives to PDR: (perceptual) indirect realism and (perceptual) phenomenalism. In contrast to indirect realism, described above, perceptual phenomenalism rejects realism outright, and holds instead that: (1) physical objects are collections of sensa; (2) in all cases of perception, at least one sensum is directly perceived; and (3) to perceive a physical object one directly perceives some of the sensa which are constituents of the collection making up that object.

Proponents of each of these positions try to solve PEW2 in different ways. But are they in fact any better able to solve PEW2 than related doctrines we discussed earlier were able to solve PEW1? The answer has seemed to most philosophers to be NO, for in general indirect realists and phenomenalists have used strategies we have already considered and rejected.

To see this, let us use the term 'S-proposition' for propositions which describe presently directly perceived sensa. Indirect realists typically claim that the inference from S-propositions to E-propositions would be an inductive one, specifically a causal inference from effects to causes. Inferences of such a sort will be perfectly cogent provided we can use a premiss which specifies that physical objects of a certain type are causally correlated with sensa of the sort currently directly perceived. Such a premiss will itself be justified, if at all, solely on the basis of S-propositions. Certainly for the indirect realist one never directly perceives the causes of sensa. So, if one knows that, say, apples typically cause such-and-such visual sensa, one knows this only indirectly on the basis of knowledge of sensa. But no group of S-propositions by itself supports any inferences to causal correlations of this sort. Consequently, indirect realists are in no position to solve PEW2 by showing that E-propositions are inductively derivable from S-propositions.

Phenomenalists have often supported their position, in part, by noting the difficulties facing indirect realism. But phenomenalism is no better off with respect to PEW2. Phenomenalists construe physical objects as collections of sensa. So, to infer an E-proposition from some S-propositions is to infer a proposition about a collection from propositions about constituent members of the collection. This inference, too, will be an inductive one, albeit not a causal one. None the less, a related problem faces the phenomenalist, namely the inferences in question will require a premiss that such-and-such directly perceived sensa are constituents of some collection C, where C is some physical object such as an apple. The problem comes with trying to justify such a premiss. To do this, one will need some plausible account of what is meant by claiming that physical objects are collections of sensa. To explicate this idea, however, phenomenalists have typically turned to analytical phenomenalism: physical objects are collections of sensa in the sense that propositions about physical objects are analysable into propositions about sensa.

And analytical phenomenalism, we have seen, has been discredited.

If neither PEW1 nor PEW2 can be easily solved, then scepticism about the external world is a doctrine we would be forced to adopt. One might even say that it is here that we locate the real problem of the external world: how can we avoid being forced into accepting scepticism.

AVOIDING SCEPTICISM

The best answer, I think, is to question the arguments which lead to PEW1 and PEW2. Beginning with the latter, the crucial question is whether any part of the argument from illusion really forces us to abandon PDR. To help see that the answer is NO we may note that a key premise in the relativity argument considered earlier links how something appears with direct perception: the fact that the dish appears elliptical is supposed to entail that one directly perceives something which is elliptical (*see* Moore, 1965). But is there an entailment here? Certainly we do not think that the proposition expressed by 'The book appears worn and dusty and more than two hundred years old' entails that the observer directly perceives something which is worn and dusty and more than two hundred years old (Chisholm, 1964, p. 95). And there are countless other examples like this one, where we will resist the inference from a property F appearing to someone to the claim that F is instantiated in some entity.

Proponents of the argument from illusion might complain that the inference they favour works only for certain adjectives, specifically for adjectives referring to non-relational sensible qualities such as colour, taste, shape, and the like. Such a move, however, requires an argument which shows why the inference works in these restricted cases and fails in all others. No such argument has ever been provided, and it is difficult to see what it might be.

If the argument from illusion is defused, the major threat facing PDR will have been removed. Hence, there will no longer be any real motivation for PEW2. Of course, even if PDR is reinstated, this does not solve PEW1.

That problem might arise even for one who accepts PDR. But here, as well, there is reason to be suspicious. In keeping with the argument used to generate PEW1, let us grant that one would not know that one is seeing something blue if one failed to know that something looked blue. In this sense there is a dependence of the former on the latter, as noted in the argument. What is not clear is whether the dependence is *epistemic* or *semantic*. It is the latter if, in order to understand what it is to see something blue, one must also understand what it is for something to look blue. This may be true, even when the belief that one is seeing something blue is not epistemically dependent on (based upon) the belief that something looks blue. Merely claiming, as in the first argument, that there is a dependence relation does not discriminate between epistemic and semantic dependence. Moreover, there is reason to think it is not an epistemic dependence. For in general, observers rarely have beliefs about how objects appear, but this fact does not impugn their knowledge that they are seeing, e.g. blue objects (*see* Pollock, 1986, p. 61).

This criticism of the argument used for PEW1 is narrow, in the sense that it focuses only on individual elements within the argument but does not question the background assumptions on which the argument seems to be based. Those assumptions, broadly speaking, are foundationalist in character: knowledge and justified belief are divided into the basic, immediate and non-inferential cases, and the non-basic, inferential knowledge and justified belief which is supported by the basic. However, though FOUNDATIONALISM was widely assumed when the problem of the external world was given currency in DESCARTES and the classical EMPIRICISTS, it has been repeatedly challenged and there are in place well-worked alternative accounts of knowledge and justified belief, some of which seem to be as plausible as the most tenable version of foundationalism. So we have some good reason to suspect, quite as one might have initially thought, that the problem of the external world just does not arise, at least not in the forms in which it has usually been presented.

*See also* ARGUMENT FROM ILLUSION; DIRECT REALISM; EXPERIENCE; INFERENCE TO THE BEST EXPLANATION; PHENOMENALISM; REPRESENTATIVE REALISM; SCEPTICISM, CONTEMPORARY; TRANSCENDENTAL ARGUMENTS.

BIBLIOGRAPHY

Ayer, A.J.: *Foundations of Empirical Knowledge* (London: Macmillan, 1940).
Chisholm, R.: 'The problem of empiricism', in Swartz, 1965.
Chisholm, R.: *Perceiving* (Ithaca, NY: Cornell University Press, 1957).
Chisholm, R.: *Theory of Knowledge* 1st edn (Englewood Cliffs: Prentice-Hall, 1964).
Cornman, J.: *Materialism and Sensations* (New Haven: Yale University Press, 1971).
Lewis, C.I.: *An Analysis of Knowledge and Valuation* (La Salle: Open Court, 1946).
Moore, G.E.: 'Visual sense-data', in Swartz, 1965.
Pappas, G.: 'Berkeley and common sense realism', *History of Philosophy Quarterly* 8 (1991), 27–42.
Pitcher, G.: *A Theory of Perception* (Princeton: Princeton University Press, 1970).
Pollock, J.: *Contemporary Theories of Knowledge* (Totowa: Rowman and Littlefield, 1986).
Swartz, R. ed.: *Perceiving, Sensing and Knowing*, (New York: Doubleday, 1965).

GEORGE PAPPAS

**problem of induction** *see* PROBLEMS OF INDUCTION.

**problem of other minds** *see* OTHER MINDS.

**problem of rule-following** Rule-following is an intentional activity of the sort that may be involved in using words, moving chess-pieces, adopting local custom and thinking straight. It is the activity of intentionally conforming or trying to conform to the rules relevant in such areas. The problem of rule-following is that of explaining how such activity is possible. Rule-following requires the agent to identify something – a rule – that prescribes what to do in an indefinitely large and varied range of situations and then to try to remain faithful to the prescriptions of that rule. It is difficult to see what sort of thing, among the items that a human mind can access, could serve this indefinitely prescriptive function. The problem of rule-following is to resolve that difficulty.

The problem derives from the later work of Ludwig WITTGENSTEIN. (*See especially* Wittgenstein, 1953, 1956.) Although it had attracted considerable attention in the first phase of Wittgenstein's influence, it tended to be eclipsed by issues associated with the PRIVATE LANGUAGE ARGUMENT. It was only in the 1970s and 1980s that it came to the fore as a problem in its own right. This was due in particular to the work of Robert Fogelin (1987), Saul Kripke (1982) and Crispin Wright (1980). (*See also* Holtzman and Leich, 1981; Wright, 1984.)

There has been a variety of approaches canvassed to the solution of the rule-following problem. The possible solutions would include ones that take rules as platonic entities and that ascribe to us an ability to get in tune with those entities: to main-line them, as it were. But most approaches attempt to solve the problem within a NATURALISTIC framework that precludes the positing of such non-natural entities and the ascription of such non-routine abilities. They try to show that naturalists are not forced to the iconoclastic position described in Kripke (1982) – the so-called sceptical solution – according to which rule-following is an illusion; there is simply nothing of the kind going on. But the concern here is not with the different possible solutions to the problem. (For a survey of solutions, *see* Boghossian, 1989; *see also* Pettit, 1990a and b.) The concern is rather with the characterization of the problem of rule-following. I will pursue that concern by dealing in turn with three distinct questions. What are rules? What is it to follow rules? And what is the problem with the notion of following rules?

## WHAT ARE RULES?

As I invoke the notion, and as it is commonly invoked, rules are normative constraints in types of decision or, more generally, judgement; decisions can be taken to be judgements as to what is best. That something is a normative constraint in a type of judgement means that it identifies one or more options among the alternatives to be adjudicated as more appropriate in some way than others. The option may be the most polite, as with a rule of etiquette; the most becoming, as with a rule of fashion; the just option, as with a rule of fairness; the proper verdict, as with a rule of evidence; the right thing to say, as with a rule of truth-telling; or whatever.

The rules with which the tradition has been concerned are relevant in an indefinitely large variety of situations and it will be useful if we build the assumption of such open-ended relevance into our conception of rules. Thus we take rules as normative constraints that are relevant in an indefinitely large number of judgement-types. Most of the rules with which we are familiar involve normative constraints that are relevant in an indefinite variety of situations. There is usually no mechanical way of specifying even the different situations where a rule of etiquette applies; such rules, as it is often put, are open-textured.

What sort of an entity is going to represent a normative constraint over an indefinite variety of situations? One type of entity that could serve in that role would be an indefinitely large set of pairs, one for every judgement-type to which the rule is relevant: the first member in the pair would be the type of situation involved, the other the appropriate type of option. We might refer to such an indefinitely extended object as the rule-in-extension. Another sort of entity that could serve in the role required would be the abstract object which is conceived as having the property of identifying the appropriate option for every relevant situation to which it is applied; the entity would be an abstract function which, given a situation-type as input, delivers the appropriate type of option as output. We might call this the rule-in-intension.

## WHAT IS IT TO FOLLOW A RULE?

Here the important distinction to draw is between conforming to a rule and following it. To conform to a rule is to form judgements or make decisions which satisfy the normative constraint in question: to behave in the manner that is appropriate according to that rule. Conforming to a rule in this sense does not require a knowledge of what the rule is, or a knowledge that conformity has been achieved. All the more obviously it does not require a desire on the agent's part to conform, or an attempt to satisfy that desire. That a subject conforms to a certain rule is a relational fact about its behaviour that tells us nothing, in itself, about the agent's state of mind.

To follow a rule however, as distinct from just conforming to it, is to exhibit a certain state of mind; it is not just to satisfy a behavioural specification. To follow a rule is to conform to the rule intentionally, to conform to the rule through trying to conform to it, to conform to the rule because of acting on the basis of a desire to achieve conformity. An agent follows a rule in the judgements it forms just in case its making judgements in accordance with that rule is intentional: just in case a rationalizing set of beliefs and desires suitably explains its making such judgements.

(There may seem to be a problem with the notion of an agent intentionally making judgements that conform to a rule. We know that it cannot be intentional on an agent's part that it judges that $p$ or that $q$. So how can it be intentional that it judges in accordance with a certain rule? No problem. An agent may not judge intentionally that $p$, though it does judge intentionally in accordance with a certain rule, where so judging is just judging that $p$. That it judges that $p$ is not due, even in part, to any desire that it has; that it judges in conformity to a rule is due, at least in part, to such a desire. In the context of its other beliefs the desire to conform to the rule explains the subject's judging in conformity to the rule but the desire does not in the same way explain the subject's judging that $p$; the desire would tend to promote a judgement that $q$, did the rule require that $q$.)

## THE PROBLEM OF RULE-FOLLOWING

There are two conditions that must be fulfilled by any rule, if the rule is to be capable of being followed. It must meet the objective condition of being or fixing a normative constraint that applies in an indefinite variety of cases. And it must meet the subjective condition of engaging appropriately with our intentional projects: of being something to which a creature like one of us can try to conform. The problem of rule-following is how anything can meet both sorts of conditions at once.

The subjective condition breaks down into at least three distinct sub-conditions and it will be useful to distinguish these, if we are to get the measure of the problem on hand. The first sub-condition is that the rule must be determinable or identifiable by a finite subject, in particular that it must be determinable or identifiable independently of any particular application. If the subject is to try to conform, then there must be something presented to it to which it can address its efforts. And if the subject is to be in a position to try to conform in any instance, then the rule to which it is to try and conform must be presented independently of how the rule applies in that instance. Allow that the rule is partly identified as requiring such and such an option in this situation, and it makes no sense to think of the subject trying to be faithful to it in that situation.

The second sub-condition that a rule must satisfy if it is to engage with the intentional projects of a creature like one of us is that it should not only be identifiable as a target of conformity for a finite subject, it should also be capable of instructing the subject, so to speak, on what it requires in the different instances where the subject tries to conform. This means that the rule must be directly readable, in the sense that the finite subject can tell straight off what it seems to require – this is the case with basic rules – or can tell what it requires by the application of rules whose apparent requirements it can ultimately tell straight off: this is the case with non-basic rules. Unless a finite subject can read off the requirements of a rule in this way, then it is not in a position to try to conform.

The third sub-condition complements the second. Where the second says that a rule must be readable by a finite subject, the third says that it can only be fallibly readable. No matter how directly the rule speaks to the subject, no matter how quickly the subject can tell what the rule seems to require, that fact alone cannot provide an epistemic guarantee that it has got the requirement of the rule right. The subject must not be an infallible authority, in at least one sense of that phrase. It may be in a position to know what a rule requires in a given situation. It may even be in a position to know that it will get the rule right in that situation. Whether these claims are allowed will depend on how precisely the limits of knowledge are drawn. But no matter how knowledge is understood, the subject cannot be in a position to rule out altogether the possibility that it might get a rule wrong; the subject cannot know it for a fact that error is impossible in its reading of a rule. Otherwise it would make no sense for us to think of the subject as trying to get the rule right.

To return then to the problem of rule-following, the challenge is to identify something that can simultaneously satisfy the objective condition of being a normative constraint that is relevant in an indefinite variety of situations and the subjective conditions of being independently identifiable, directly readable and fallibly readable. There are two ways in which we might think of meeting this challenge: by taking something which we know to satisfy the objective condition and then showing how it can also satisfy the subjective constraints; or by taking something which certainly satisfies the subjective constraints and then showing how it can also satisfy the objective condition. But both paths look to be blocked and that is the essence of the rule-following problem. In setting out the problem I follow Saul Kripke (1982),

adopting roughly the same presentation as in Pettit (1990a).

Take the sorts of entities which we know to satisfy the objective condition: the rule-in-extension and the rule-in-intension. The rule-in-extension is not capable of satisfying the subjective conditions, because it is liable to be an infinitely large set. There is no way that I could get in touch appropriately with such an infinite object. There is no way that I could get in touch with the infinite extension of a property across actual and possible worlds – say, the extension associated with boxes or triangles or games–as I try to be faithful to the appropriate rule in descriptive classification. And, to take the sort of rule discussed by Kripke, there is no way I could get in touch with the rule-in-extension associated with the plus-function: the rule determining what number is the referent of '$x + y$', for any two numbers $x$ and $y$. 'The infinitely many cases of the table are not in my mind for my future self to consult' (Kripke, 1982, p. 22).

What of the rule-in-intension? What, for example, of the addition function, as Frege would conceive of it, which determines the correct option in any judgement about the sum of two numbers? What is there against the idea that this abstract object might be able to satisfy the subjective conditions, engaging a finite mind appropriately? Here the problem is to explain how a creature like one of us is able to get in contact with such an abstract object. It does not affect our senses like a physical object and so we are not causally connected with it in the ordinary way. So how then does it become present to such a creature?

Moving from the entities which can clearly satisfy the objective condition on a rule to entities that look more likely to be able to satisfy the subjective conditions, the question here is whether such entities can be objectively satisfactory: whether they can serve as normative constraints over an indefinite variety of cases. Kripke mentions two main candidates for entities of this kind: first, actual or possible examples of the application of the rule in question, such as examples of a property or examples of addition; and

389

secondly, introspectible states of consciousness, as for instance a suitable idea or feeling. But there is an objection that applies to all such candidates, so Kripke argues, and indeed to any finite object that is proposed for the role in question. The objection, and this is clearly derived from Wittgensteinian materials, is that no finite object can unambiguously identify a constraint that is normative over an indefinite variety of cases. Consider a series of examples of addition: $1 + 1 = 2$, $1 + 2 = 3$, $2 + 2 = 4$, and the like. Or consider any set of examples of boxes or triangles or games. For all that any such finite object can determine, the right way to go with a novel case remains open. 'Plus', as we understand it, forces us to say that $68 + 57 = 125$ but the examples given do nothing to identify the plus-rule as distinct from, say, the *quus*-rule, where this says that the answer in the case of 68 and 57 is 5. 'Is a triangle', as we understand it, forces us to say that a square page, diagonally folded, is a triangle but the examples given, if they do not include this case, will be consistent with the folded page's not being a triangle; perhaps the rule illustrated outlaws paper triangles or perhaps it outlaws triangles made by folding. The fact is that any finite set of examples, mathematical or otherwise, can be extrapolated in an infinite number of ways; equivalently, any finite set of examples instantiates an infinite number of rules.

The upshot of these considerations is that rules do not appear to be the sorts of things that our finite minds can identify as items to follow; or, looking at the matter from the other way around, that among the items that our finite minds can suitably identify there appears to be nothing that could put us in touch with rules. Rule-following is a mysterious activity. It is central to human life and thought but its very possibility is philosophically problematic.

The rule-following problem is an important challenge for philosophers, in particular for philosophers of a naturalistic bent. What in the world – what in the natural world – does rule-following involve? Perhaps the only widely agreed point is that it certainly involves the development of an extrapolative disposition, a disposition generated by some examples to apply the rule after a certain pattern in new cases. But such a disposition is not enough on its own to constitute rule-following. While it provides a mechanism for prompting responses, it does not provide something which might tell us how to go on in new instances, something from which we might intentionally take our guidance (Kripke, 1982, p. 24).

Perhaps the best hope of a naturalistic solution is not to try to reduce rule-following to the operation of such a disposition but to give an account, using the disposition, of how a subject can identify a rule to follow. Under the account favoured by the present author, for example, the extrapolative disposition serves a second role over and beyond that of prompting responses in new cases: it enables certain applications to exemplify the rule and to present it as something that the subject can try to follow; although the applications given as examples will instantiate an indefinite number of rules, as we noted above, the extrapolative disposition may ensure that they exemplify only one. (Pettit, 1990a and b, 1992). Future discussions will probably centre on such attempts to make naturalistic sense of the rule-following phenomenon.

*See also* OSTENSIVE DEFINITION; PRIVATE LANGUAGE ARGUMENT; WITTGENSTEIN.

BIBLIOGRAPHY

Boghossian, P.: 'The rule-following considerations', *Mind* 98 (1989), 504–50.
Fogelin, R.: *Wittgenstein* (London: Routledge, 1987).
Holtzman, S.H. and Leich, C.M. eds: *Wittgenstein: to Follow a Rule* (London: Routledge and Kegan Paul, 1981).
Kripke, S.A.: *Wittgenstein on Rules and Private Language* (Oxford: Blackwell, 1982).
Pettit, P.: 'The reality of rule-following', *Mind* 99 (1990[a]), 1–21.
Pettit, P.: 'Affirming the reality of rule-following', *Mind* 99 (1990[b]), 433–9.
Pettit, P: *The Common Mind* (New York: Oxford University Press, 1992).
Wittgenstein, L.: *Philosophical Investigations*

trans. G.E.M. Anscombe (Oxford: Blackwell, 1953).

Wittgenstein, L.: *Remarks on the Foundations of Mathematics* (Oxford: Blackwell, 1956).

Wright, C.: *Wittgenstein on the Foundations of Mathematics* (Cambridge, MA: Harvard University Press, 1980).

Wright, C. ed.: *Synthese: Special Issue on Rule-following* vol. 58 (1984).

PHILIP PETTIT

## problems of induction

### THE HUMEAN PROBLEM OF INDUCTION

Suppose that there is some property A pertaining to an observational or experimental situation, and that out of a large number of observed instances of A, some fraction $m/n$ (possibly equal to 1) have also been instances of some logically independent property B. Suppose further that the background circumstances not specified in these descriptions have been varied to a substantial degree and also that there is no collateral information available concerning the frequency of B's among A's or concerning causal or nomological connections between instances of A and instances of B.

In this situation, an *enumerative* or *instantial* inductive inference would move from the premise that $m/n$ of observed A's are B's to the conclusion that approximately $m/n$ of all A's are B's. (The usual probability qualification will be assumed to apply to the inference, rather than being part of the conclusion.) Here the class of A's should be taken to include not only unobserved A's and future A's, but also possible or hypothetical A's. (An alternative conclusion would concern the probability or likelihood of the very next observed A being a B.)

The traditional or Humean problem of induction, often referred to simply as *the* problem of induction, is the problem of whether and why inferences that fit this schema should be considered rationally acceptable or justified from an epistemic or cognitive standpoint, i.e. whether and why reasoning in this way is likely to lead to true claims about the world. Is there any sort of argument or rationale that can be offered for thinking that conclusions reached in this way are likely to be true if the corresponding premiss is true – or even that their chances of truth are significantly enhanced?

HUME's discussion of this issue deals explicitly only with cases where *all* observed A's are B's and where A is claimed to be the cause of B, but his argument applies just as well to the more general case. His conclusion is entirely negative and sceptical: inductive inferences are not rationally justified, but are instead the result of an essentially a-rational process, custom or habit. Hume challenges the proponent of induction to supply a cogent line of reasoning that leads from an inductive premise to the corresponding conclusion and offers an extremely influential argument in the form of a dilemma (sometimes referred to as 'Hume's fork') to show that there can be no such reasoning. Such reasoning would, he argues, have to be either a priori demonstrative reasoning concerning relations of ideas or 'experimental' (i.e. empirical) reasoning concerning matters of fact or existence. It cannot be the former, because all demonstrative reasoning relies on the avoidance of contradiction, and it is not a contradiction to suppose that 'the course of nature may change', that an order that was observed in the past will not continue in the future; but it also cannot be the latter, since any empirical argument would appeal to the success of such reasoning in previous experience, and the justifiability of generalizing from previous experience is precisely what is at issue – so that any such appeal would be question-begging. Hence, Hume concludes, there can be no such reasoning (1748, pp. 35–6).

An alternative version of the problem may be obtained by formulating it with reference to the so-called *Principle of Induction*, which says roughly that the future will resemble the past or, somewhat better, that unobserved cases will resemble observed cases. An inductive argument may be viewed as enthymematic, with this principle serving as a suppressed premiss, in which case the issue is obviously how such a premiss can be justified. Hume's argument is then that no such justification is possible: the principle cannot

391

be justified a priori because it is not contradictory to deny it; and it cannot be justified by appeal to its having been true in previous experience without obviously begging the question.

The predominant recent responses to the problem of induction, at least in the analytic tradition, in effect accept the main conclusion of Hume's argument, viz. that inductive inferences cannot be justified in the sense of showing that the conclusion of such an inference is likely to be true if the premise is true, and thus attempt to find some other sort of justification for induction. Such responses fall into two main categories: (1) pragmatic justifications or 'vindications' of induction, mainly developed by REICHENBACH; and (2) ordinary language justifications of induction, whose most important proponent is STRAWSON. In contrast, some philosophers still attempt to reject Hume's dilemma by arguing either (3) that, contrary to appearances, induction can be inductively justified without vicious circularity, or (4) that an a priori justification of induction is possible after all. We will look briefly at all four of these responses.

(1) REICHENBACH's view is that induction is best regarded, not as a form of inference, but rather as a *method* for arriving at *posits* regarding, e.g., the proportion of A's that are also B's. Such a posit is not a claim asserted to be true, but is instead an intellectual wager analogous to a bet made by a gambler. Understood in this way, the inductive method says that one should posit that the observed proportion is, within some measure of approximation, the true proportion and then continually correct that initial posit as new information comes in.

The gambler's bet is normally an 'appraised posit', i.e. he knows the chances or odds that the outcome on which he bets will actually occur. In contrast, the inductive bet is a 'blind posit': we do not know the chances that it will succeed or even that success is possible. What we are gambling on when we make such a bet is the value of a certain proportion in the independent world, which Reichenbach construes as the limit of the observed proportion as the number of cases increases to infinity. But we have no way of knowing that there even is such a limit, no way of knowing that the proportion of A's that are also B's converges in the long run on some stable value rather than varying at random. And if we cannot know that this limit exists, then we obviously cannot know that we have any definite chance of finding it.

What we can know, according to Reichenbach, is that *if* there is a truth of this sort to be found, the inductive method will eventually find it. That this is so is an analytic consequence of Reichenbach's account of what it is for such a limit to exist. The only way that the inductive method of making an initial posit and then refining it in light of new observations can fail to eventually arrive at the true proportion is if the series of observed proportions never converges on any stable value, which means that there is no truth to be found concerning the proportion of A's that are B's. Thus induction is justified, not by showing that it will succeed or indeed that it has any definite likelihood of success, but only by showing that it will succeed if success is possible. Reichenbach's claim is that no more than this can be established for any method, and hence that induction gives us our best chance for success, our best gamble in a situation where there is no alternative to gambling.

This pragmatic response to the problem of induction faces several serious problems. First, there are indefinitely many other 'methods' for arriving at posits for which the same sort of defence can be given – methods which yield the same result as the inductive method in the long run but differ arbitrarily in the short run. Despite the efforts of Salmon and others, it is unclear that there is any satisfactory way to exclude such alternatives, in order to avoid the result that any arbitrarily chosen short-term posit is just as reasonable as the inductive posit. Second, even if there is a truth of the requisite sort to be found, the inductive method is only guaranteed to find it or even to come within any specifiable distance of it in the indefinitely long run. But any actual application of inductive results always takes place in the short run, making the relevance of the pragmatic justification to actual practice uncertain. Third, and most importantly, it needs to be emphasized that Reichenbach's response to the problem simply accepts the claim of the Humean sceptic that an inductive premiss never provides the slightest reason for thinking that the corresponding inductive conclusion is true. Reichenbach himself is quite candid on this point, but this does not alleviate the intuitive implausibility of saying that we have no more reason for thinking that our scientific and commonsense conclusions that result from induction are true than, to use Reichenbach's own analogy (1949, p. 482), a blind man wandering in the mountains who feels an apparent trail with his stick has for thinking that following it will lead him to safety.

An approach to induction that resembles Reichenbach's in claiming that particular inductive conclusions are posits or conjectures, rather than the conclusions of cogent inferences, is offered by POPPER. But Popper's view is even more overtly sceptical: it amounts to saying that all that can ever be said in favour of the truth of an inductive claim is that the claim has been tested and has not yet been shown to be false.

(2) The ordinary language response to the problem of induction has been advocated by many philosophers, but the discussion here will be restricted to STRAWSON's paradigmatic version. Strawson claims that the question whether induction is justified or reasonable makes sense only if it tacitly involves the demand that inductive reasoning meet the standards appropriate to deductive reasoning, i.e. that the inductive conclusion be shown to follow deductively from the inductive premiss. Such a demand cannot of course be met, but only because it is illegitimate: inductive and deductive reasoning are simply fundamentally different kinds of reasoning, each possessing its own autonomous standards, and there is no reason to demand or expect that one of these kinds meet the standards of the other. Whereas if induction is assessed by inductive standards,

the only ones that are appropriate, then it is obviously justified.

The problem here is to understand what this allegedly obvious justification of induction amounts to. In his main discussion of the point (1952, pp. 256–7), Strawson claims that it is an analytic truth that it is reasonable to believe a conclusion for which there is strong evidence and also an analytic truth that inductive evidence of the sort captured by the schema presented earlier constitutes strong evidence for the corresponding inductive conclusion, thus apparently yielding the *analytic* conclusion that it is reasonable to believe a conclusion for which there is inductive evidence. But he also admits, indeed insists, that the claim that inductive conclusions will be true in the future is contingent, empirical, and may turn out to be false (1952, p. 261). Thus the notion of reasonable belief and the correlative notion of strong evidence must apparently be understood in ways that have nothing to do with likelihood of truth, presumably by appeal to the standards of reasonableness and strength of evidence that are accepted by the community and are embodied in ordinary usage.

Understood in this way, Strawson's response to the problem of induction does not speak to the central issue raised by Humean scepticism: the issue of whether the conclusions of inductive arguments are likely to be true when the corresponding premises are true. It amounts to saying merely that if we reason in this way, we can correctly call ourselves 'reasonable' and our evidence 'strong', according to our accepted community standards. But to the underlying issue of whether following these standards is a good way to find the truth, the ordinary language response appears to have nothing to say.

(3) The main attempts to show that induction can be justified inductively have concentrated on showing how such a defense can avoid circularity. Skyrms (1975, pp. 30–6) formulates perhaps the clearest version of this general strategy. The basic idea is to distinguish different levels of inductive argument: a first level in which induction is

applied to things other than arguments; a second level in which it is applied to arguments at the first level, arguing that they have been observed to succeed so far and hence are likely to succeed in general; a third level in which it is applied in the same way to arguments at the second level; and so on. Circularity is allegedly avoided by treating each of these levels as autonomous and justifying the arguments at each level by appeal to an argument at the next higher level.

One problem with this sort of move is that even if circularity is avoided, it seems clear that the movement to higher and higher levels will eventually fail simply for lack of evidence: a level will reached at which there have not been enough successful inductive arguments to provide a basis for an inductive justification at the next higher level. And if this is so, then the whole series of justifications collapses. A more fundamental difficulty is that the epistemological significance of the distinction between levels is obscure. If the issue is whether reasoning in accord with the original schema offered above ever provides a good reason for thinking that the conclusion is likely to be true, then it still seems question-begging, even if not flatly circular, to answer this question by appeal to another argument of the same form.

(4) The idea that induction can be justified on a purely a priori basis is in one way the most natural response of all: it alone treats an inductive argument as an independently cogent piece of reasoning whose conclusion can be seen rationally to follow, albeit perhaps only with probability, from its premise. Such an approach has, however, only rarely been advocated (see Russell, 1912; BonJour, 1986), and is widely thought to be clearly and demonstrably hopeless.

Many of the reasons for this pessimistic view depend on general epistemological theses about the possibility or nature of A PRIORI KNOWLEDGE. Thus if, as QUINE alleges, there is no a priori justification of any kind, then obviously an a priori justification for induction is ruled out. Or if, as more moderate empiricists have claimed, a priori knowledge must be analytic, then again an a

priori justification for induction seems to be precluded, since the claim that if an inductive premise is true, then the conclusion is likely to be true does not fit the standard conceptions of ANALYTICITY. A consideration of these matters is beyond the scope of the present article.

There are, however, two more specific and quite influential reasons for thinking that an a priori approach is impossible that can be briefly considered here. First, there is the assumption, originating in Hume but since adopted by very many others, that an a priori defence of induction would have to involve 'turning induction into deduction,' i.e. showing, per impossibile, that the inductive conclusion follows deductively from the premise, so that it is a formal contradiction to accept the latter and deny the former. But it is unclear why an a priori approach need be committed to anything this strong. It would be enough if it could be argued that it is a priori unlikely that such a premiss is true and the corresponding conclusion false.

Second, Reichenbach defends his view that the pragmatic justification is the best that is possible by pointing out that a completely chaotic world in which there simply is no true conclusion to be found as to the proportion of A's that are B's is neither impossible nor unlikely from a purely a priori standpoint, the suggestion being that therefore there can be no a priori reason for thinking that such a conclusion is true. But there is a subtle confusion lurking here: that a chaotic world is a priori neither impossible nor unlikely in the absence of any further evidence does not show that such a world is not a priori unlikely and a world containing a certain regularity a priori likely in relation to the occurrence of a long-run pattern of evidence in which a certain stable proportion of observed A's are B's – an occurrence, it might be claimed, that would be highly unlikely in a chaotic world (see BonJour, 1986).

## GOODMAN'S 'NEW RIDDLE OF INDUCTION'

Suppose that prior to some specified time t

(perhaps the year 2000) we observe a large number of emeralds (property A) and find them all to be green (property B). We proceed to reason inductively and conclude that all emeralds are green. GOODMAN points out, however, that we could have drawn a quite different conclusion from the same evidence. If we define the term 'grue' to mean 'green if examined before $t$ and blue if examined after $t$', then all of our observed emeralds will also be grue, and a parallel inductive argument will yield the conclusion that all emeralds are grue, and hence that all those examined after the year 2000 will be blue. Presumably the first of these conclusions is genuinely supported by our observations and the second is not, but the problem is to say *why* this is so and to impose some further restriction upon inductive reasoning that will permit the first argument and exclude the second.

Goodman himself formulates the problem in terms of the notion of PROJECTIBILITY: a generalization that receives genuine inductive support from observed instances is *projectible* onto unobserved cases. His suggestion is that projectibility is a matter of the history of the terms involved: a projectible generalization is one whose terms are well *entrenched*, where this means that they have been used frequently in past generalizations of this sort. Thus it is because (and only because) the term 'green' is better entrenched than the term 'grue' that the first inductive argument in the preceding paragraph is to be preferred to the second.

The obvious alternative suggestion is that 'grue' and similar predicates do not correspond to genuine, purely qualitative properties in the way that 'green' and 'blue' do, and that this is why inductive arguments involving them are unacceptable. Goodman, however, claims to be unable to make clear sense of this suggestion, pointing out that the relations of formal definability are perfectly symmetrical: 'grue' may be defined in terms of 'green' and 'blue', but 'green' can equally well be defined in terms of 'grue' and 'bleen' (blue if examined before $t$, and green if examined after $t$).

*See also* GOODMAN; HUME.

BIBLIOGRAPHY

BonJour, L.: 'A reconsideration of the problem of induction', *Philosophical Topics* 14 (1986), 93–124.

Goodman, N.: *Fact, Fiction, and Forecast* (Cambridge, MA: Harvard University Press, 1955).

Hume, D.: *An Enquiry concerning Human Understanding* (1748) ed. L.A. Selby-Bigge, revised P.H. Nidditch (Oxford: Oxford University Press, 1975).

Popper, K.: 'Conjectural knowledge: my solution to the problem of induction', reprinted in his *Objective Knowledge* (Oxford: Clarendon Press, 1972).

Reichenbach, H.: *Experience and Prediction* (Chicago: University of Chicago Press, 1938), 339–63.

Reichenbach, H.: *Theory of Probability* (Berkeley: University of California Press, 1949), 469–82.

Russell, B.: *The Problems of Philosophy* (Oxford: Oxford University Press, 1912), ch. 6.

Salmon, W.: *The Foundations of Scientific Inference* (Pittsburgh: Pittsburgh University Press, 1967).

Skyrms, B.: *Choice and Chance: An Introduction to Inductive Logic* 2nd edn (Encino: Dickenson, 1975).

Strawson, P.F.: *Introduction to Logical Theory* (London: Methuen, 1952), 248–63.

LAURENCE BONJOUR

**projection, projectibility** Projection from present to absent cases occurs in inductive, hypothetical and counterfactual reasoning. Goodman's grue paradox reveals that valid projection depends not only on the constitution of the evidence class, but also on its characterization (*see* GOODMAN). If all known emeralds are green, we may infer:

H1: All emeralds are green

but not

H2: All emeralds are grue,

where something is grue if examined before some future time $t$ and found to be green, or not so examined and blue. H1 is valid, for 'green' is projectible. But even though all members of our evidence class are grue as well as green, $H_2$ is invalid since 'grue' is unprojectible. A valid ampliative inference must be supported by evidence, unviolated by counterevidence, unexhausted (else it would not be ampliative), and must be framed in terms of projectible predicates. For only if a predicate is projectible can it convey credibility from known to unknown cases. How to distinguish between projectible and unprojectible predicates is a critical question for epistemology.

*See also* PROBLEMS OF INDUCTION.

CATHERINE Z. ELGIN

**proof** A proof is a collection of considerations and reasonings that instill and sustain the conviction that some proposed theorem – the theorem proved – is not only true, but could not possibly be false. A perceptual observation may instill the conviction that the water is cold, but not that the water could not but be cold. But a proof that $2 + 3 = 5$ must not only instill the conviction that it is true that $2 + 3 = 5$, but also that $2 + 3$ could not be anything but $5$.

No one has succeeded in replacing this largely psychological characterization of proofs by a more objective characterization. The representations or reconstructions of proofs as mechanical and semiotical derivations in formal-logical systems all but completely fail to capture 'proofs' as mathematicians are quite content to give them. For example, formal-logical derivations depend solely on the logical form of the considered propositions, whereas usually proofs depend in large measure on contents of propositions other than their logical form.

*See also* INTUITION AND DEDUCTION.

BIBLIOGRAPHY

Detlefsen, M. ed.: *Essays on Proof* (London, Routledge, 1991).
Tragesser, R.S.: 'Three little noticed aspects of mathematical proof', in Detlefsen, 1991.

ROBERT S. TRAGESSER

**propositional knowledge** Propositional knowledge (PK) is the type of knowing whose instances are labelled by means of a phrase expressing some proposition, e.g. in English a phrase of the form 'that $h$', where some complete declarative sentence is instantiable for '$h$'.

Theories of PK differ over whether the proposition that $h$ is involved in a more intimate fashion, such as serving as a way of picking out a propositional attitude required for knowing (e.g. believing that $h$, accepting that $h$ or being sure that $h$) (*see also* BELIEF; CERTAINTY; KNOWLEDGE AND BELIEF). For instance, the tripartite analysis of PK, sometimes called the traditional or standard analysis, treats PK as consisting in having a justified, true belief that $h$ (*see* TRIPARTITE DEFINITION OF KNOWLEDGE). In contrast, we shall later consider theories that treat PK as the possession of specific abilities, capacities, or powers, and that view the proposition that $h$ as needing to be expressed only in order to label a specific instance of PK.

Although most theories of PK purport to analyse it, philosophers disagree about the goal of a philosophical analysis. Theories of PK may differ over whether they aim to cover all species of PK and, if they do not have this goal, over whether they aim to reveal any unifying link between the species that they investigate, e.g. empirical knowledge, and other species of knowing.

Very many accounts of PK have been inspired by the quest to add a fourth condition to the tripartite analysis so as to avoid Gettier-type counterexamples to it (*see* GETTIER PROBLEM), and by the resulting need to deal with more counterexamples provoked by these new analyses (*see* Shope, 1983, for a survey). Keith Lehrer (1965) originated a Gettier-type example that has been a fertile source of important variants. It is the case of Mr Nogot, who is in one's office and has provided some evidence, $e$, in response to all of which one forms a justified belief that Mr Nogot is in the office and owns a Ford, thanks to which one arrives at the justified belief that $h_1$: 'Someone in the office owns a Ford.' In the example, $e$ consists of such things as Mr Nogot's presently showing one a certificate of Ford ownership while claiming to own a Ford and having been reliable in the past. Yet Mr Nogot has just now been shamming, and the only reason that it is true that $h_1$ is because, unbeknown to oneself, a different person in the office owns a Ford.

Variants on this example continue to challenge efforts to analyse species of PK. For instance, Alan Goldman (1988) has proposed that when one has empirical knowledge that $h$, then the state of affairs (call it $h^*$) expressed by the proposition that $h$ figures prominently in an explanation of the occurrence of one's believing that $h$, where explanation is taken to involve one of a variety of probability relations concerning $h^*$ and the belief state. But this account runs foul of a variant on the Nogot case akin to one that Lehrer (1979) has described. In Lehrer's variant, Mr Nogot has manifested a compulsion to trick people into justifiedly believing truths yet falling short of knowledge by means of concocting Gettierized evidence for those truths. It we make the trickster's neurosis highly specific to the type of information contained in the proposition that $h$, we obtain a variant satisfying Goldman's requirement that the occurrence of $h^*$ significantly raises the probability of one's believing that $h$. (Lehrer himself (1990, pp. 103–4) has criticized Goldman by questioning whether, when one has ordinary perceptual knowledge that an object is present, the presence of the object is what explains one's believing it to be present.)

In grappling with Gettier-type examples, some analyses proscribe specific relations between falsehoods and the evidence or grounds that justify one's believing. A simple restriction of this type requires that one's reasoning to the belief that $h$ does not crucially depend upon any false lemma (such as the false proposition that Mr Nogot is in the office and owns a Ford). However, Gettier-type examples have been constructed where one does not reason through any false belief (e.g. a variant of the Nogot case where one arrives at belief that $h_1$ by basing it upon a true existential generalization of one's

evidence: 'There is someone in the office who has provided evidence $e$'). In response to similar cases, Sosa (1991) has proposed that for PK the 'basis' for the justification of one's belief that $h$ must not involve one's being justified in believing or in 'presupposing' any falsehood, even if one's reasoning to the belief does not employ that falsehood as a lemma. Alternatively, Roderick CHISHOLM (1989) requires that if there is something that makes the proposition that $h$ 'evident' for one and yet makes something else that is false evident for one, then the proposition that $h$ is implied by a conjunction of propositions, each of which is evident for one and is such that something that makes it evident for one makes no falsehood evident for one. (See Shope, 1983, for discussion of earlier, related analyses by Sosa and Chisholm.) Other types of analyses are concerned with the role of falsehoods within the justification of the proposition that $h$ (versus the justification of one's believing that $h$). Such a theory may require that one's evidence bearing on this justification not already contain falsehoods. Or it may require that no falsehoods are involved at specified places in a special explanatory structure relating to the justification of the proposition that $h$. (See Shope, 1983, and forthcoming, for details.)

A frequently pursued line of research concerning a fourth condition of knowing seeks what is called a DEFEASIBILITY analysis of PK. Early versions characterized defeasibility by means of subjunctive conditionals of the form, 'If A were the case then B would be the case.' But more recently the label has been applied to conditions about evidential or justificational relations that are not themselves characterized in terms of conditionals. Early versions of defeasibility theories advanced conditionals where A is a hypothetical situation concerning one's acquisition of a specified sort of epistemic status for specified propositions (e.g. one's acquiring justified belief in some further evidence or truths) and B concerns, for instance, the continued justified status of the proposition that $h$ or of one's believing that $h$.

A unifying thread connecting the conditional and non-conditional approaches to defeasibility may lie in the following facts: (1) What is a reason for being in a propositional attitude is in part a consideration, instances of the thought of which have the power to affect relevant processes of propositional attitude formation; (2) Philosophers have often hoped to analyse power ascriptions by means of conditional statements; and (3) Arguments portraying evidential or justificational relations are abstractions from those processes of propositional attitude maintenance and formation that manifest rationality. So even when some circumstance, $R$, is a reason for believing or accepting that $h$, some other circumstance, $K$, may prevent an occasion from being present for a rational manifestation of the relevant power of the thought of $R$, and it will not be a good argument to base a conclusion that $h$ on the premiss that $R$ and $K$ obtain. Whether $K$ does play this interfering, 'defeating', role will depend upon the total relevant situation.

Accordingly, one of the most sophisticated defeasibility accounts, which has been proposed by John Pollock (1986), requires that in order to know that $h$, one must believe that $h$ on the basis of an argument whose force is not defeated in the above way, given the total set of circumstances described by all truths. More specifically, Pollock defines defeat as a situation where (1) one believes that $p$ and it is logically possible for one to become justified in believing that $h$ by believing that $p$, and (2) one actually has a further set of beliefs, $S$, logically consistent with the proposition that $h$, such that it is not logically possible for one to become justified in believing that $h$ by believing it on the basis of holding the set of beliefs which is the union of $S$ with the belief that $p$ (cf. Pollock, 1986, pp. 36, 38). Furthermore, Pollock requires for PK that the rational presumption in favour of one's believing that $h$ created by one's believing that $p$ is undefeated by the set of all truths, including considerations that one does not actually believe. Pollock offers no definition of what this requirement means. But he may intend roughly the following, where $T$ is the set of all true propositions: (I) one believes that $p$ and it is logically possible for one to become justified in believing that $h$

by believing that $p$, and (II) there are logically possible situations in which one becomes justified in believing that $h$ on the basis of having the belief that $p$ and the beliefs in $T$. Thus, in the Nogot examples, since $T$ includes the proposition that Mr Nogot does not own a Ford, one lacks knowledge because condition (II) is not satisifed.

But given such an interpretation, Pollock's account illustrates the fact that defeasibility theories typically have difficulty dealing with introspective knowledge of one's own beliefs. Suppose that some proposition, say, that $f$, is false, but one does not realize this and holds the belief that $f$. Condition (II) has no coherent application to one's introspective knowledge that $h_2$: 'I believe that $f$.' At least, this is so if one's reason for believing that $h_2$ includes the presence of the very condition of which one is aware, i.e. one's believing that $f$. It is incoherent to suppose that one retains the latter reason yet also believes the truth that $not$-$f$. This objection can be avoided, but at the cost of adopting what is a controversial view about introspective knowledge that $h$, namely, the view that one's belief that $h$ is in such cases mediated by some mental state intervening between the mental state of which there is introspective knowledge and the belief that $h$, so that it is the mediating state rather than the introspected state that is included in one's reason for believing that $h$. In order to avoid adopting this controversial view, Paul Moser (1989) has proposed a disjunctive analysis of PK, which requires that either one satisfies a defeasibility condition rather like Pollock's or else one believes that $h$ by introspection. However, Moser leaves obscure exactly why beliefs arrived at by introspection count as knowledge (see GETTIER PROBLEM).

Early versions of defeasibility theories had difficulty allowing for the existence of evidence that is 'merely misleading', as in the case where one does know that $h_3$: 'Tom Grabit stole a book from the library', thanks to having seen him steal it, yet where, unbeknown to oneself, 'Tom's mother out of dementia has testified that Tom was far away from the library at the time of the theft. One's justifiably believing that she gave the testimony would destroy one's justification for believing that $h_3$ if added by itself to one's present evidence.

At least some defeasibility theories cannot deal with the knowledge one has while dying that $h_4$: 'In this life there is no time at which I believe that $d$', where the proposition that $d$ expresses the details regarding some erudite matter, e.g. the maximum number of blades of grass ever simultaneously growing on the earth. When it just so happens that it is true that $d$, defeasibility analyses typically consider the addition to one's dying thoughts of a belief that $d$ in such a way as to improperly rule out actual knowledge that $h_4$. (See Shope, forthcoming, for further discussion.)

A quite different approach to knowledge, and one able to deal with some Gettier-type cases, involves developing some type of causal theory of PK (see CAUSAL THEORIES IN EPISTEMOLOGY). Such theories require that one or another specified relation holds that can be characterized by mention of some aspect of causation concerning one's belief that $h$ (or one's acceptance of the proposition that $h$) and its relation to state of affairs $h^*$, e.g. $h^*$ causes the belief; $h^*$ is causally sufficient for the belief; $h^*$ and the belief have a common cause. Such simple versions of a causal theory are able to deal with the original Nogot case, since it involves no such causal relationship, but cannot explain why there is ignorance in the variants where Nogot is a neurotic trickster. Moreover, Fred Dretske and Berent Enç (1984) have pointed out that sometimes one knows of $x$ that it is $\phi$ thanks to recognizing a feature merely correlated with the presence of $\phi$ness. Without endorsing a causal theory themselves, they suggest that it would need to be elaborated so as to allow that one's belief that $x$ has $\phi$ has been caused by a factor whose correlation with the presence of $\phi$ness has caused in oneself (e.g. by evolutionary adaption in one's ancestors) the disposition that one manifests in acquiring the belief in response to the correlated factor. Not only does this strain the unity of a causal theory by complicating it, but no causal theory without other shortcomings has been able to cover instances of a priori knowledge.

Causal theories of PK differ over whether they deviate from the tripartite analysis by dropping the requirement that one's believing (accepting) that $h$ be justified. The same variation occurs regarding reliability theories (see RELIABILISM), which present the knower as reliable concerning the issue of whether or not $h$, in the sense that some of one's cognitive or epistemic states, $\theta$, are such that, given further characteristics of oneself – possibly including relations to factors external to one and of which one may not be aware (see EXTERNALISM/INTERNALISM) – it is nomologically necessary (or at least probable) that $h$. In some versions, the reliability is required to be 'global' in so far as it must concern a nomological (probabilistic) relationship of states of type $\theta$ to the acquisition of true beliefs about a wider range of issues than merely whether or not $h$. There is also controversy about how to delineate the limits of what constitutes a type of relevant personal state or characteristic. (For instance, in a case where Mr Nogot has not been shamming and one does know thereby that someone in the office owns a Ford, does $\theta$ concern a way of forming beliefs about Ford owners in offices, or something broader, such as a way of forming beliefs about the properties of persons spatially close to one, or instead something narrower, such as a way of forming beliefs about Ford owners in offices partly upon the basis of their relevant testimony?)

One important variety of reliability theory is a conclusive reasons account, which includes a requirement that one's reasons for believing that $h$ be such that in one's circumstances, if $h^*$ were not to occur then, e.g., one would not have the reasons one does for believing that $h$; or, e.g., one would not believe that $h$. Roughly, the latter is demanded by theories that treat a knower as 'tracking the truth', theories which include the further demand that, roughly, if it were the case that $h$, then one would believe that $h$. A version of the tracking theory has been defended by Robert Nozick (1981), who adds that if what he calls a 'method' has been used to arrive at the belief that $h$, then the antecedent clauses of the two conditionals that characterize tracking will need to include the hypothesis that one would employ the very same method.

But unless more conditions are added to Nozick's analysis, it will be too weak to explain why one lacks knowledge in a version of the last variant of the tricky Mr Nogot case described above, where we add the following details: (a) Mr Nogot's compulsion is not easily changed; (b) while in the office, Mr Nogot has no other easy trick of the relevant type to play on one; and (c) one arrives at one's belief that $h_1$ not by reasoning through a false belief but by basing the belief that $h_1$ upon a true existential generalization of one's evidence.

Nozick's analysis is also too strong to permit anyone ever to know that $h_5$; 'Some of my beliefs about beliefs might be otherwise, e.g., I might have rejected one of them.' If I know that $h_5$ then satisfaction of the antecedent of one of Nozick's conditionals would involve its being false that $h_5$, thereby thwarting satisfaction of the consequent's requirement that I not then believe that $h_5$. For the belief that $h_5$ is itself one of my beliefs about beliefs (see Shope (1984) for further discussion).

Some philosophers think that the category of knowing for which true, justified believing (accepting) is a requirement constitutes only a species of PK construed as an even broader category. They have proposed various examples of PK that do not satisfy the belief and/or justification conditions of the tripartite analysis. Such cases are often recognized by analyses of PK in terms of powers, capacities, or abilities. For instance, Alan R. White (1982) treats PK as merely the ability to provide a correct answer to a possible question. However, White may be equating 'producing' knowledge in the sense of producing 'the correct answer to a possible question' with 'displaying' knowledge in the sense of manifesting knowledge (cf. White, 1982, pp. 119–20). The latter can be done even by very young children and some non-human animals independently of their being asked questions, understanding questions, or recognizing answers to questions. Indeed, an example that has been proposed as an

instance of knowing that $h$ without believing or accepting that $h$ can be modified so as to illustrate this point. The example concerns an imaginary person who has no special training or information about horses or racing, but who in an experiment persistently and correctly picks the winner of upcoming horseraces. If the example is modified so that the hypothetical 'seer' never picks winners but only muses over whether those horses might win, or only reports picturing their winning, this behaviour should be as much of a candidate for the person's manifesting knowledge that the horse in question will win as would the behaviour of picking it as a winner.

These considerations expose limitations in Edward Craig's analysis (1990) of the concept of knowing as the concept of a person's being a satisfactory informant in relation to an inquirer who wants to find out whether or not $h$. Craig realizes that counter-examples to his analysis appear to be constituted by knowers who are too recalcitrant to inform the inquirer, or too incapacitated to inform, or too discredited to be worth considering (as with the boy who cried 'Wolf!'). Craig admits that this might make preferable some alternative view of knowledge as a different state that helps to explain the presence of the state of being a suitable informant when the latter does obtain. I have proposed (Shope, forthcoming) such an alternative, which offers a recursive definition that concerns one's having the power to proceed in a way representing the state of affairs $h^*$ and the capacity to have the thought of $h^*$ be causally involved in one's proceeding in this way. When combined with a suitable analysis of representing, this theory of PK can be unified with a structurally similar analysis of knowing how to do something.

See also EVIDENCE; GETTIER PROBLEM; KNOWLEDGE AND BELIEF.

BIBLIOGRAPHY

Chisholm, R.M.: *Theory of Knowledge* (Englewood Cliffs: Prentice-Hall, 1966; 3rd edn (Englewood Cliffs: Prentice-Hall, 1989).

Craig, E.: *Knowledge and the State of Nature: An Essay in Conceptual Synthesis* (Oxford: Clarendon Press, 1990).

Dretske, F. and Enç, B.: 'Causal theories of knowledge', *Midwest Studies in Philosophy, vol. IX. Causation and Causal Theories*, ed. P.A. French, T.E. Uehling, Jr and H.K. Wettstein (Minneapolis: University of Minnesota Press, 1984), pp. 517–28.

Goldman, A.: *Empirical Knowledge* (Berkeley and Los Angeles: University of California Press, 1988).

Goldman, A.: *Epistemology and Cognition* (Cambridge, MA: Harvard University Press, 1986).

Lehrer, K.: 'Knowledge, truth, and evidence', *Analysis*, 25 (1965), 168–75; reprinted in *Knowing: Essays in the Analysis of Knowledge*, eds M.D. Roth and L. Galis (New York: Random House, 1970), 55–66.

Lehrer, K.: 'The Gettier problem and the analysis of knowledge', *Justification and Knowledge* ed. G. Pappas (Dordrecht, Boston and London: D. Reidel, 1979), 65–78.

Lehrer, K.: *Theory of Knowledge* (Boulder and San Francisco: Westview, 1990).

Moser, P.: *Knowledge and Evidence* (Cambridge: Cambridge University Press, 1989).

Nozick, R.: *Philosophical Explanation* (Cambridge, MA: Harvard University Press, 1981).

Pollock, J.L.: *Contemporary Theories of Knowledge* (Totowa: Rowman and Littlefield, 1986).

Shope, R.K.: *The Analysis of Knowing* (Princeton: Princeton University Press, 1983).

Shope, R.K.: 'Cognitive abilities, conditionals, and knowledge: a response to Nozick', *The Journal of Philosophy*, 81 (1984), 29–48.

Shope, R.K.: *Knowledge as Power: An Essay in Epistemological Metaphysics with an Application to Ethical Theory* (forthcoming).

Sosa, E.: *Knowledge in Perspective: Selected Essays in Epistemology* (Cambridge: Cambridge University Press, 1991).

White, A.R.: *The Nature of Knowledge* (Totowa: Rowman and Littlefield, 1982).

ROBERT K. SHOPE

**protocol sentences** 'Protocol sentences' or 'protocol statements' were defined by CARNAP in *The Unity of Science* (1932) as belonging to the 'direct record of a scientist's . . . experience'. 'A "primitive" protocol . . . exclude[s] all statements obtained indirectly by induction or otherwise and postulates therefore a sharp (theoretical) distinction between the raw material of scientific investigation and its organisation.' The problem for the LOGICAL POSITIVISTS was how such records of 'private experience' could serve as FOUNDATIONAL for the public language of a unified science; in effect, how their EMPIRICISM and their physicalism could be reconciled. Carnap himself was undecided whether protocol sentences should take the form of PHENOMENALISTIC SENSE-DATUM statements (e.g. most crudely 'Joy now', 'Here now blue'), or whether they should be more like ordinary reports of observation (e.g. 'A red cube is on the table'); he hoped to escape metaphysical commitment by his use of the distinction between 'formal' and 'material' modes of speech (*see* CARNAP). Neurath insisted that protocol sentences should make explicit the identity and location of the speaker, and the time of utterance; but later recognized that there is no reason to regard such sentences as foundational (*see* NEURATH, SCHLICK). Carnap later argued that which statements should serve as protocols was 'a matter of decision' (i.e. convention); one may choose one's own observation-statements, but that is only because 'intersubjective testing of statements about observations (brain-processes) is relatively inconvenient . . .'

ANDY HAMILTON

**psychologism** With respect to a given subject-matter psychologism is the theory that the subject-matter in question can be reduced to, or explained in terms of, psychological phenomena: mental acts, events, states, dispositions and the like. Psychologism was widespread in both Britain and Germany during the latter half of the nineteenth century. It fell into disrepute at the beginning of the present century, however, largely as a result of the objections raised against it by two philosophers, Edmund HUSSERL and Gottlob FREGE (*see* Husserl, 1970, *passim*; Frege, 1974, pp. i–xi). They attacked psychologism in logic and the foundations of mathematics by showing that a psychologistic theory could never account for the objectivity, the necessity, or the universality of the truths belonging to these disciplines. Ludwig WITTGENSTEIN continued this anti-psychologistic tradition by arguing that even meaning and understanding should not be construed as species of mental act (*see* Wittgenstein, 1953, §§329, 541 and pp. 175–6).

BIBLIOGRAPHY

Frege, G.: *The Foundations of Arithmetic* trans. J.L. Austin (Oxford: Blackwell, 1974).
Husserl, E.: *Logical Investigations* trans. J.N. Findlay, vol. 1: *Prolegomena to Pure Logic* (London: Routledge & Kegan Paul, 1970).
Wittgenstein, L.: *Philosophical Investigations* trans. G.E.M. Anscombe (Oxford: Blackwell, 1953).

DAVID BELL

**psychology and epistemology** There has been a steady stream of two-way traffic between epistemology and psychology. Philosophers and psychologists have relied on novel epistemological doctrines and arguments to support psychological views; more recently, epistemologists have been drawn to psychology in an attempt to solve their own problems.

Many epistemological disagreements within psychology pertain in some way or other to disputes about BEHAVIOURISM. Beginning in 1908, John Watson argued forcefully that the science of psychology had not advanced very far. His proposed remedy was to transform the discipline into a natural science by changing the subject matter: behaviour, rather than consciousness or the mind, was to be the proper object of study by psychologists. In fact, all reference to the mental, he argued, should be excluded from psychology. Sometimes, he supported this recommendation by arguing that the mental does not exist, or, more weakly, that there is no evidence of its existence. At other times, he appealed to what was later called 'methodological behaviourism', the view that all mentalistic explanations be rejected for methodological reasons. In defending this latter

view, he and his behaviourist successors developed a series of distinctive epistemological arguments.

One of these arguments, used by B.F. Skinner, runs like this: We can avoid reference to mentalistic causes by going directly to the prior physical causes while bypassing intermediate feelings or other mental events. If all linkages are lawful, Skinner argues, nothing is lost by neglecting a mentalistic link. In saying that nothing is lost, Skinner presumably means nothing that would hamper our predicting or controlling behaviour. Suppose, however, that one of our goals is to *explain* someone's behaviour. Something significant, then, would be lost if a mental event caused, or partially caused, the behaviour in question. By neglecting that cause, we would be guaranteeing that our proposed explanation of the person's behaviour is incorrect. Some behaviourists are not convinced by this reply because they deny that explaining phenomena is a legitimate goal of science. This denial may be buttressed by saying that explanation is valuable only as a guide to understanding, but understanding is something mentalistic and hence should not be sought in a scientific psychology. To resort to this defence, however, is to assume what is at issue: that the behaviourist view of what constitutes a scientific psychology is correct. A behaviourist may have other reasons for denying that scientists should try to explain psychological phenomena, but if they are also unsatisfactory, then Skinner's argument is likely to fail.

A second argument used by Skinner concerns the failure to explain cognitive or other mentalistic causes. A disturbance in behaviour, he contends, is not explained by relating it to anxiety until the anxiety in turn is explained. The postulation of mentalistic events, however, discourages the tracing of the causal sequence; investigators, Skinner claims, simply stop with the anxiety and fail to ask what caused *it*. One problem with this argument is the assumption that non-behaviourists generally end inquiry with the postulation of a mentalistic cause. Some do and some do not. For example, a Freudian psychologist who explains a client's behaviour in terms of anxiety might well go on and try to explain the anxiety in terms of a repressed wish. A more serious problem, however, lies with Skinner's initial assumption that even if anxiety causes a certain behaviour, citing it is not explanatory unless it is in turn explained. It is not generally true that postulating B as the cause of A explains A's occurrence only if, and when, B's occurrence is also explained. If B had to be explained in terms of C, and C in terms of D, and so on *ad infinitum*, then all causal explanation would be impossible. It could be replied that we have a satisfactory explanation once B's occurrence is explained; there is no need to go any further. However, stopping at precisely that point seems arbitrary. Why does explanation require citing the cause of the cause of a phenomenon but not the next link in the chain of causes? Perhaps what is not generally true of explanation is true only of mentalistic explanation; only in giving the latter type are we obligated to give the cause of a cause. However, this too seems arbitrary. What is the difference between mentalistic and non-mentalistic explanation that would justify imposing more stringent restrictions on the former?

The epistemological argument most widely used by behaviourists turns on the alleged unobservability of mental events or states. If cognitions are unobservable in principle, the argument runs, we have no warrant for believing that they exist and, hence, no warrant for accepting cognitive explanations. The same argument applies to non–cognitive mental states, such as sensations or emotions. Opponents of behaviourism sometimes reply that mental states can be observed: Each of us, through INTROSPECTION, can observe at least some mental states, namely our own (at least those of which we are conscious). To this point, behaviourists have made several replies. Some (e.g. Zuriff, 1985) argue that introspection is too unreliable for introspective reports to qualify as firm scientific evidence. Others have replied that, even if introspective reports were reliable, what we introspect is private and that this fact alone renders introspective data unsuitable as evidence in a science of behaviour. A more radical reply, advanced by certain philosophers, is that introspection is not a form of observation, but rather a kind of theorizing. More precisely, when we report on the basis of introspection that we have a painful sensation, a thought, a mental image, etc., we are theorizing about what is present. The resulting theory may or may not be correct, but, on this view, the fact that we introspect does not show that any mental states are observable (*see* PERCEPTUAL KNOWLEDGE, PRIVATE LANGUAGE ARGUMENT).

Whether or not introspection is reliable or is a form of observation, there remains the problem of determining the content of, or even the existence of, other people's minds. The traditional solution to this problem, the ARGUMENT FROM ANALOGY, is now generally thought to be a failure. An INFERENCE TO THE BEST EXPLANATION might serve instead, but some philosophers (e.g. van Fraassen, 1980) have challenged the validity of this mode of inference. If that challenge can be sustained, then behaviourists may be able to defend at least one of the central planks in their programme: the rejection of all mentalistic explanations.

Many cognitivists and behaviourists agree about the desirability of making psychology a rigorous, natural science; what they often disagree about is what that requires. Some philosophers and psychologists, however, have serious reservations about rendering psychology 'scientific', at least if that means employing the same sort of epistemological standards as are used in biology, chemistry and physics. These latter sciences, some in the Hermeneutic tradition argue, are primarily *causal* sciences, i.e. they involve both the search for causal laws and the widespread use of causal explanations. In psychology, however, we should be explaining human actions, some argue, in non-causal terms, perhaps in terms of meaning or motives (*see* REASONS/CAUSES). Karl Jaspers, the German philosopher-psychiatrist, appears to be an early exponent of this view. In the 1922 edition of his *General Psychopathology* (1963, p. 539), he criticizes Freud as follows: 'The falseness of the Freudian claim lies in the mistaking of meaningful connections for causal connections.' Earlier in the same work, he discusses the sort of psychology that would replace the Freudian sort: a science of meaningful connections.

Some contemporary Hermeneuticians (e.g. Ricoeur, 1981) agree with Jaspers about meaning connections, but unlike him they defend Freudian theory. They take the view that the theory really is about meanings rather than causes, but that Freud sometimes misinterpreted his own theory. Properly interpreted, at least some central parts of the theory, they argue, are true. Freud was right, moreover, in denying the need for experimental confirmation of his various hypotheses. Meeting such a requirement, some Hermeneuticians argue, is reasonable only if we use the same evidential standards as physics or chemistry, but doing that is inappropriate. Other Hermeneuticians (e.g. Taylor, 1971) would not restrict their epistemological point about standards to Freudian theory; more generally, any psychological theory that purports to explain human actions, they argue, is to be evaluated by criteria not applicable to theories in the natural sciences (See HERMENEUTICS).

Some who reject the hermeneutical viewpoint argue that meanings, in so far as they are explanatory, are causes. For example, suppose that I vote for a certain candidate and the meaning of my vote is that I am taking a stand against abortion. That is, I see myself as objecting to the views of the rival candidate who favors abortion. Did my seeing what I am doing in this way make any difference to how I voted? If it did, it is argued, then the meaning of my action was a contributing cause; if it did not, then talking about the meaning of my action does not explain why it occurred. The same sort of point is often made about motives (Grunbaum, 1984). I may have been motivated not to promote Tom because I do not trust him, but that may have made no difference to my promoting someone else instead. If it did make a difference, citing my motive helps explain my action; but, in that case, the motive is also a cause. The general suggestion, then, is this: where meanings and motives make no difference to what a human being does, then citing them is not explanatory; where they do make a difference, they are causes. A problem, then, for some Hermeneutical views is to explain how psychologists can explain human actions while simultaneously rejecting all causal explanations of such actions.

The idea that psychology requires different evidential standards from the natural sciences (and hence is not itself a natural science) need not be tied to the view that its explanations should be non-causal. Some who promote the first idea reject the second; they agree that motives and meanings can be causes, but still argue for the use of standards other than those of natural science. Those who argue for this thesis, however, must face the following question: What are these different, and presumably lower, evidential standards that are to be employed in psychology? Karl Jaspers gave an answer to this question (1963, p. 303). In assessing claims of meaning connections, he argued, we must be willing to accept what is, on his view, self-evident. As an example of self-evidence, he cites Nietzsche's claim of a general connection between awareness of one's wretchedness and the development of a slave morality. Many later Hermeneuticians have also appealed to the idea of self-evidence or, what is very similar, the idea of what is intuitively obvious. It is difficult to see, however, how either can be an acceptable standard for any area in psychology in which rival hypotheses are relatively equal in plausibility given our current evidence. In fact, even where we can think of only one hypothesis that appears self-evident we may still have no rational grounds for believing it. At one time, it seemed self-evident to most observers that some people acted strangely because they were possessed by the devil; yet, that hypothesis may have had no evidential support at all. Of course, one can draw a distinction between hypotheses that only appear to be self-evident and those that truly are, but does this help if we are not given any way to tell the difference?

In the cases discussed so far, philosophers and psychologists have employed novel and controversial epistemological arguments to support their psychological views. In a related development, some philosophers have engaged in what might be termed 'applied epistemology'. That is, they have relied on epistemological assumptions *plus* empirical data to criticize or defend such items as Freudian theory (Grunbaum, 1984), the foundations of behaviour therapy (Erwin, 1978), behaviourism and various theories in cognitive psychology. What is mainly new in these applied studies is the greater attention paid to the empirical details of psychology compared to earlier attempts to rest psychological views primarily on abstract epistemological doctrines.

The appeal to empirical data is also evident in the movement to 'naturalize' epistemology (*see* NATURALIZED EPISTEMOLOGY). Here the direction is reversed: psychology is used to support epistemology instead of the other way around. In one respect, this development is not new; earlier philosophers, such as David HUME and Immanuel KANT, often tried to buttress their epistemologies by appeal to what they believed to be facts about the human mind. In the immediate post-World War II period, however, many epistemologists in English speaking countries placed great emphasis on conceptual analysis. The result was that epistemology was often practiced as if it were primarily, or solely, an a priori discipline. Relatively few attempts were made by epistemologists to make use of empirical studies in psychology (or, for that matter, in any other science).

One reason for naturalizing epistemology is that the traditional quest for a foundation of knowledge is said to have ended in failure. This appears to be the main reason given by QUINE in his classic paper 'Epistemology Naturalized'.

To this point, traditional epistemologists have made several replies. First, it is argued that there are new variants of 'FOUNDA-TIONALISM' and that one of these might turn out to be right. Second, COHERENT-ISTS argue that they can explain how knowledge claims can be ultimately justified without invoking foundationalism of any sort. Third, it is argued that there is more to traditional epistemology than providing a foundation for knowledge. For example,

epistemologists have been interested in analysing the concept of knowledge, developing theories of evidence and justification, and justifying non-demonstrative rules of inference. The pursuit of these projects might be warranted even if the traditional foundational problem cannot be solved. The alleged failure to solve that problem, however, is not the only reason cited by naturalists. Both in epistemology and in its sister discipline, the philosophy of science, there have been complaints about the lack of interesting, positive results. A related reason is that traditional epistemology has relied too heavily, it is argued, on a priori claims. Some naturalists argue that either there is no A PRIORI KNOWLEDGE at all or that there is no such knowledge of non-trivial propositions. To get firm, interesting positive results, as opposed merely to finding more and more counter-examples to false theories or generating more triviality, an epistemologist must, it is argued, appeal to empirical results of psychology and other sciences. Naturalists disagree among themselves, however, about the nature of this appeal.

One naturalist view, associated with Quine (1985), is that we should replace traditional epistemological questions with questions answerable by empirical studies in psychology. For example, he suggests that the traditional question about the foundations of knowledge be replaced by one about how sensory stimulations result in the storing of information. Some philosophers are likely to reply, however, that by substituting psychological questions for epistemological ones, we are not naturalizing epistemology; we are simply changing the subject.

A second view is that we should abandon a priori arguments altogether and restrict ourselves to appeals to empirical evidence in answering epistemological questions. The key issue here, itself partly empirical, is whether any interesting results will (could?) emerge from this approach. A more modest view is that epistemologists should continue to use a priori arguments as before but, where possible, to appeal to empirical results as well. A possible example concerns the dispute between some experimental psychologists and their opponents about the epistemological value of clinical case studies. Some argue that the data from case studies generally have only heuristic rather than evidential value, although they may occasionally refute some psychological theory. To confirm causal hypotheses, it is argued, we generally need experimental evidence rather than evidence from case studies.

Other psychologists, however, contend that case studies can often confirm as well as disconfirm causal hypotheses. An epistemologist, in commenting on this dispute, might appeal partly to abstract, a priori considerations about the nature of evidence and confirmation, but might also have to appeal to empirical data about the presence or absence of competing, plausible alternatives to the hypothesis being tested. For example, it might turn out that in certain areas in psychology, case studies can be confirmatory because the hypotheses being tested often have no plausible competitors; in other areas, experimentation may generally be needed to adjudicate between plausible rivals.

The above example concerns an epistemological dispute within psychology. Whether empirical data from psychology are likely to be helpful in resolving issues within epistemology itself is still controversial. Nevertheless, recent work in epistemology does indicate a greater willingness among epistemologists, even among those not describing themselves as 'naturalists,' to at least consider empirical data from psychology to be relevant to their concerns.

See also NATURAL SCIENCE; REASONS/ CAUSES; SOCIAL SCIENCE.

BIBLIOGRAPHY

Erwin, E.: *Behavior Therapy: Scientific Philosophical and Moral Foundations* (New York: Cambridge University Press, 1978).
van Fraassen, B.: *The Scientific Image* (Oxford: Oxford University Press, 1980).
Goldman, A.: *Epistemology and Cognition* (Cambridge, MA: Harvard University Press, 1984).
Grünbaum, A.: *The Foundations of Psychoanalysis: A Philosophical Critique* (Berkeley: University of California Press, 1984).
Jaspers, K.: *General Psychopathology* (Chicago: University of Chicago Press, 1963).
Quine, W.V.: 'Epistemology naturalized', in his *Ontological Relativity and Other Essays* (New York: Columbia University Press, 1969).
Ricoeur, P.: *Hermeneutics and the Human Sciences* trans. J.B. Thompson (New York: Cambridge University Press, 1981).
Taylor, C., 'Interpretation and the sciences of man', *The Review of Metaphysics* 25 (1971), 1–51.
Zuriff, G.E.: *Behaviorism: A Conceptual Reconstruction* (New York: Columbia University Press, 1985).

EDWARD ERWIN

**Putnam, Hilary (1926–)** One of the most influential philosophers of the latter half of the twentieth century, Putnam (Professor of Mathematical Logic at Harvard University) has discussed epistemology only late in his career. But he has recently made some major contributions to this field: his arguments that truth is ultimately an epistemic concept, i.e. that truth and 'ideal rational acceptability' (or ideal justification) are *interdependent* concepts and his criticisms of radical or evidence-transcendent scepticism. The two themes are tied together by Putnam's defence of what he calls 'internal realism'.

In the early 1970s Putnam was a staunch realist with respect to science and language. In both the philosophies of language and science, he argued for REALISM against VERIFICATIONISM (e.g. 1978, parts 1 and 3), and for the priority of reference over meaning (i.e. that most terms refer directly without mediating ideas, senses, or properties; cf. e.g. Putnam, 1975). Against antirealism, Putnam argued truth couldn't be warranted assertibility since we can recognize the possibility that a proposition might be warrantedly assertible but false (1978, part 3). However, about 1976, Putnam's philosophy took a dramatic turn. He abandoned his view that truth was essentially non-epistemic and instead argued that truth was *idealized* warranted assertibility (1978, part 4; 1981).

A key step in his development was Putnam's realization that, on his own view, evidence-transcendent scepticism was self-refuting. One naïvely assumes that if we were all brains in a vat (assuming we're not now), then the sentence 'we are brains in a vat' would continue to *mean* just what it does now and so would be true in the vat case. But this is to assume meanings 'are in the head', an assumption repudiated by Putnam's causal or direct theory of reference. In fact, in a world in which we were all brains in a vat, there would be a 'referential shift' and the sentence 'we are brains in a vat' would mean something very different. While 'brains' now refers directly to certain organs, in the vat world 'brains' would refer directly to aspects of the computer program, perhaps, controlling the subjects' brain-images; similarly for 'vats'. But then in that case, the brains' assertion 'we are brains in a vat' would be *false*, since they are not aspects of a computer program. Consequently, the *utterance* 'we are brains in a vat' is always false, regardless of who says it and so radical scepticism is refuted (Putnam, 1981). It is useful to compare Putnam's analysis to Skolem's paradox where, because of a similar referential shift, the sentence 'the real numbers are uncountable' is true not only for us in an uncountable world but even *true in a countable model of set theory*! (Tymoczko, 1990).

The residual feeling that we could somehow step outside the world (or model) and discover that we really were brains in a vat is an expression of what Putnam calls 'metaphysical realism' (Putnam, 1978, part 4; 1981). He points out that this view is, strictly speaking, false or incoherent. It is false if expressed in our language (since 'we are brains in a vat' is false). Moreover, to the response 'Yes, but if we could adopt a God's-eye point of view we'd see we really *are* brains in a vat', Putnam could reply that this requires using a language *other* than the language we now use – in order to say 'we really are brains in a vat' and make it come out true. In that case, the quoted sentence is meaningless. (In analogous fashion, the sentence 'the reals are countable' is either trivially false by Cantor's Theorem, or else a sentence of a language that by hypothesis, we don't understand.)

For Putnam, 'metaphysical realism' is the view that even an epistemically ideal theory could be false (in other words, that truth is non-epistemic). His recent argument purports to show this view has no content. Nevertheless, if we abandon metaphysical realism, we should still hold to the internal or pragmatic realism suggested by PEIRCE, according to Putnam. Internal realism is realism about science and language, but only as an empirical theory internal to science. It is stronger than verificationism (because true beliefs are not justified beliefs but only *ideally* justified beliefs) and it still maintains the priority of reference over meaning, and in this sense is realist. On the other hand, reference is seen as dependent on use and on what can be ideally verified, and since truth is tied to reference, truth too is an epistemic concept. Crudely: the only criterion for what is a fact is what it is (ideally) rational to accept (and so bivalence might not be preserved since, for certain *p*, it might not be ideally rational either to accept *p* or to reject it). Thus, truth and justification are two separate, but interdependent notions. (Putnam 1981, 1989).

(Putnam's argument can be formulated more abstractly in model theoretic terms, as in Putnam, 1983, 1981. For a concise summary of internal realism, *see* Putnam, 1989.)

*See also* ANALYTICITY; PRAGMATISM; REALISM; SCEPTICISM, CONTEMPORARY; TRUTH.

WRITINGS

'The meaning of "meaning"', reprinted in his *Mind, Language and Reality: Philosophical Papers*, vol. 2 (Cambridge: Cambridge University Press, 1975).

*Meaning and the Moral Sciences* (London: Routledge and Kegan Paul, 1978), esp. part 3, 'Reference and Understanding', and part 4, 'Realism and Reason'.

*Reason, Truth and History* (Cambridge: Cambridge University Press, 1981).

*Realism and Reason* (Cambridge: Cambridge University Press, 1983), esp. Introduction and ch. 1.

*The Many Faces of Realism* (La Salle: Open Court, 1987).
*Representation and Reality* (Cambridge, MA: MIT Press, 1989), ch. 7.

BIBLIOGRAPHY

Tymoczko, T.: 'Brains don't lie', in *Doubting: Contemporary Perspectives on Scepticism*, eds M. Roth and G. Ross (Dordrecht: Kluwer, 1990)

THOMAS TYMOCZKO

**Pyrrhonism** A sceptical school in ancient Greek philosophy, which traced its origins to Pyrrho of Elis (*c*.365–270 BC). Pyrrhonists together with Academic sceptics account for a strong tradition of scepticism in the Hellenistic period of Greek philosophy. Pyrrho himself wrote nothing, but through the satirical poetry of his pupil Timon of Phlius he became legendary for his disdainful attitude toward speculative philosophy and for the detachment and simplicity of his way of life. This anti-theoretical orientation, and the practical view of philosophy as a way of life leading to ATARAXIA, became two important characteristics of Pyrrhonian scepticism. After the death of Timon, Pyrrho's sceptical ideas seem not to have been revived until the first century BC, when they were adopted by a radical sceptic from the Academy under Philo of Larissa. Aenesidemus, dissatisfied with the scepticism of the Fourth Academy, which had become increasingly dogmatic and influenced by STOIC views, broke away from it to form his own school of scepticism, claiming Pyrrho as its founder. Aenesidemus built upon the anti-speculative foundation of Pyrrhonian scepticism by formulating arguments against all dogmatic philosophies, while giving particular attention to refuting the Stoics. He also compiled all the sceptical arguments known to Greek philosophers and grouped them into 'modes', patterns of argument leading to suspense of judgment. The sceptical arguments produce oppositions of appearances equal in weight and credibility (*see* ISOSTHENEIA). The Pyrrhonian sceptic finds no good reason to prefer this appearance over that, so he suspends judgement. He is able to say how things appear to him but not how things really are. It was no doubt due to the influence of Aenesidemus that Pyrrhonian scepticism evolved to produce a sophisticated philosophical methodology. Agrippa, a Pyrrhonist probably from the first century AD, also formulated a set of 'modes' classifying different argument forms. Sextus Empiricus, who lived in the late second century AD, is the last major representative of Pyrrhonian scepticism in Greek philosophy. Besides being a sceptic himself Sextus is the most important source of our knowledge of ancient Pyrrhonism. After the time of Sextus, Pyrrhonian scepticism diminished in importance and finally died out in later antiquity. The writings of Sextus were rediscovered in the sixteenth century and were influential in shaping modern philosophical scepticism (Popkin, 1979).

*See also* SEXTUS EMPIRICUS; SCEPTICISM.

BIBLIOGRAPHY

Annas, J. and Barnes, J.: *The Modes of Scepticism* (Cambridge: Cambridge University Press, 1985).
Burnyeat, M.: 'Can the sceptic live his scepticism?', in *Doubt and Dogmatism* eds M. Schofield, M. Burnyeat and J. Barnes (Oxford: Clarendon Press, 1980), 20–53.
Flintoff, E.: 'Pyrrho and India', *Phronesis* 25 (1980), 88–108.
Popkin, R.: *The History of Skepticism from Erasmus to Spinoza* (Berkeley: University of California Press, 1979).
Sedley, D: 'The protagonists', in *Doubt and Dogmatism* eds M. Schofield, M. Burnyeat and J. Barnes (Oxford: Clarendon Press, 1980), 1–19.
Sedley, D.: 'The motivation of Greek scepticism', in *The Sceptical Tradition* ed. M. Burnyeat (Berkeley: University of California Press, 1983), 9–29.
Stough, C.: *Greek Scepticism* (Berkeley: University of California Press, 1969).

CHARLOTTE STOUGH

# Q

Quine, Willard Van Orman (1908- ) Born in Akron, Ohio, Quine's professional career was spent in the philosophy department at Harvard University. A visit to the Vienna Circle during the 1930s, when he encountered LOGICAL EMPIRICISTS such as Rudolf Carnap, shaped his work: although he challenged some of their most fundamental doctrines, he shares their commitment to empiricism and their view that philosophy should be pursued as part of science. His earliest work was in mathematical logic and the foundations of set theory. But several of the papers in *From a Logical Point of View* (1953) have had a major influence upon epistemology, and his major work, *Word and Object* (1960), together with many subsequent writings, have been instrumental in the development of NATURALIZED EPISTEMOLOGY.

'Two dogmas of empiricism', contained in the former book, identified and rejected two assumptions of traditional empiricism. The first of these was the distinction between analytic statements such as 'All bachelors are male' which are true by virtue of meaning, and other synthetic truths which are grounded in 'fact' (p. 20). The second was 'radical reductionism': 'every meaningful statement is held to be translatable into a statement (true or false) about immediate experience' (p. 38). Quine held that the analytic/synthetic distinction could be sustained only if radical reductionism was true. The latter doctrine gains support from a verificationist theory of meaning: by translating each statement into a statement about immediate experience, we show its true meaning by showing what experiences would be required to verify it. And the analytic statements are those which are 'vacuously confirmed. . . come what may' (p. 41) (*see* ANALYTICITY)

As well as explaining the distinctive epistemological and modal status of disciplines like mathematics and logic, these 'dogmas' provided a theory of rationality: analytic truths, linking other statements to ones about immediate experience, determine how we should revise our beliefs in the face of surprising observations. Quine rejected reductionism and the epistemological picture that went with it. He did this primarily by presenting an alternative picture of how our beliefs relate to experience, likening the whole of our knowledge to 'a man-made fabric which impinges on experience only along the edges' (p. 42). Although experiential surprise requires us to revise our beliefs, 'there is much latitude of choice as to what statements to reevaluate in the light of any single contrary experience' (pp. 2–3): 'any statement can be held true come what may, if we make drastic enough adjustments elsewhere in the system'; and 'no statement is immune from revision' (p. 43). The resulting HOLISTIC picture allows that we may make revisions in logic or mathematics in order to restore harmony between our beliefs and our experience. It is a psychological matter, a 'natural tendency to disturb the total system as little as possible' which explains our treating some beliefs as answerable to experience while other, more embedded ones seem secure from empirical falsification (*see* UNDERDETERMINATION OF THEORY).

In these relatively early writings, Quine espoused a 'thorough pragmatism' (p. 46): our scientific knowledge is a 'tool' for effective prediction; physical objects are introduced as 'convenient intermediaries', or as 'cultural posits' (p. 44). He says that the epistemological superiority of the 'myth' of physical objects means only that it is 'more efficacious than other myths as a device for working a manageable structure into the flux of experience'. This suggests an anti-realist or instrumentalist view of physical object talk and scientific theories – although even in these papers Quine admitted to *believing in* physical objects but not in the gods of Homer. In later writings, his holism is expressed much more moderately and this PRAGMATISM is in eclipse. His focus is on the naturalistic idea that epistemology, like all philosophy, is continuous with, or part of, natural science; and science is interpreted realistically. These later writings convert the metaphors and suggestions of 'Two dogmas of empiricism' into a scientific account of how experience and theory are related.

In a 1968 lecture, 'Epistemology naturalized', Quine stated his mature view of epistemology, a discipline he takes to be concerned with 'the foundations of science' (1969, ch. 3). He holds that the stimulation of sensory receptors is all a scientist has to go on in constructing and defending theories. Arguing, once again, that radical reductionism fails, he proposes that we study how this construction actually proceeds: epistemology 'falls into place as a chapter of psychology and hence of natural science'. This study answers to the traditional concern of epistemology: 'to see how evidence relates to theory, and in what ways one's theory of nature transcends any available evidence' (pp. 82–3).

Some have objected that Quine has changed the subject: for the tradition, it would have been circular to use science in order to ground the legitimacy of science, or to defeat scepticism. Quine's response is to challenge the aspiration to ground science as a whole. Turning his back on the Cartesian search for certainty, he insists that the desire to understand science has always been something that arose within science itself. Unless we are given good scientific reasons for doubting the legitimacy of science, we are warranted in standing firm on our scientific view of the world in order to understand its undoubted legitimacy (*see* FIRST PHILOSOPHY). Others accuse Quine of a naturalistic fallacy: epistemology is concerned with understanding the normative standards that guide our inquiries, but psychology can only tell us how we actually do defend our beliefs. His response is that once we abandon the Cartesian desire to ground science as a whole, normative epistemology becomes applied science: we can use our scientific understanding of ourselves and our surroundings to debate the best ways of answering particular questions.

*See also* EMPIRICISM; INDETERMINACY OF TRANSLATION; NATURALIZED EPISTEMOLOGY; ONTOLOGICAL COMMITMENT; ONTOLOGICAL RELATIVITY; PHILOSOPHICAL KNOWLEDGE; PRAGMATISM; PSYCHOLOGY AND PHILOSOPHY.

WRITINGS

*From a Logical Point of View* (Cambridge, MA: Harvard University Press, 1953).

*Word and Object* (Cambridge, MA: MIT Press, 1960).

*Ontological Relativity and Other Essays* (New York: Columbia University Press, 1969).

*The Roots of Reference* (La Salle: Open Court, 1973).

'The nature of natural knowledge', in *Mind and Language* ed. S. Guttenplan (Oxford: Oxford University Press, 1975), 57–81.

*Theories and Things* (Cambridge, MA: Harvard University Press, 1981).

*Pursuit of Truth* (Cambridge, MA: Harvard University Press, 1990).

CHRISTOPHER HOOKWAY

# R

---

**rationalism** 'rationalism' is a multiply ambiguous term whose meaning varies greatly according to the context. The common thread running through its various uses seems to be that the philosopher classified as a rationalist gives undue weight to reason at the expense of something else: in religion, that may be revelation or faith; in politics, tradition; in morals, feeling or sentiment; in epistemology, experience, etc. This apparent commonality is deceptive, however, since 'reason' tends to bear different meanings in the different contexts, referring to a faculty of a priori knowledge in epistemology, but being construed much more broadly in religion, morals or politics. The term does generally seem to carry a negative connotation; it is one philosophers typically apply to those with whom they disagree, not to themselves.

The most significant use of the concept of epistemological rationalism is to organize the textual data of the period from Descartes to Kant so that they tell a coherent story with an edifying moral. Modern philosophy, it is often said, begins with a rationalist reaction against scholastic Aristotelianism, a reaction that privileges mathematics as a model of human knowledge. Ideally our knowledge of ourselves, of God and of the world ought to be organized into a deductive system, in which all truths are derived from a relatively small number of axioms and definitions, whose truth is guaranteed by their self-evidence (*see* AXIOMATIZATION). Only if our starting points are absolutely certain, and we proceed by careful, certainty-preserving, deductive steps from them, can we achieve knowledge, for genuine knowledge requires certainty. On this picture of knowledge, experience is essentially irrelevant; it is not needed and cannot provide the certainty we require. This is the textbook rationalist programme in epistemology, to which DESCARTES, SPINOZA and LEIBNIZ are all supposed to subscribe.

So understood, rationalism is an exercise in extravagant optimism, as might be argued either by considering the mutually inconsistent (and often bizarre) metaphysical systems the rationalists advocated, or by noting the crucial role arguments from experience play in the development of the sciences. It was only natural, the story then goes, that there should develop in opposition to rationalism a school of philosophy which would (over-) emphasize the importance of experience, not only in verifying claims to knowledge, but also in acquiring the concepts those claims employ. All real knowledge depends ultimately on experience. That is the textbook empiricist programme in epistemology, to which LOCKE, BERKELEY and HUME are supposed, with varying degrees of ideological purity, to subscribe. But strict empiricism leads inevitably to radical scepticism and cannot account adequately for the a priori knowledge we do possess. What is required is a theory of knowledge which synthesizes these two opposed tendencies, rescuing what is true in each, but avoiding their exaggerations. We can then see the Kantian system as reconciling the competing claims of reason and experience, giving each its due.

This way of telling the story of philosophy in the seventeenth and eighteenth centuries is aesthetically pleasing, and gratifies our desire to think of philosophy as a progressive discipline, whose later practitioners have a better grasp of its problems than their predecessors had. Those are two reasons for its influence on the construction of university curricula, anthologies and general histories of philosophy (e.g. Copleston, 1958, ch. 1). It probably represents fairly enough KANT's view of his relation to his predecessors (cf. Kant, 1781, A854/B882). It also has the advantage that it is not entirely false. With judicious attention to the right evidence, it can even be made to seem a fairly accurate picture of the way philosophy developed in this period. To some extent it may represent the way Kant's predecessors thought of themselves (cf. Leibniz, 1765, Preface). Still, many historians specializing in the early modern period now regard this story as a gross distortion of what happened. The remainder of this article will sketch the reasons why the picture is appealing to some people and sharply rejected by others.

Descartes did much to encourage reading him as a rationalist when he wrote in the *Discourse* (1637, VI/19) of his admiration for 'those long chains composed of very simple and easy reasonings', which geometers use to demonstrate their most difficult propositions. This led him to suppose that 'all the things which can fall under human knowledge are interconnected in the same way.' All we need to do, it seems, is withhold our assent from anything we do not see clearly and distinctly to be true, and then proceed in a careful and orderly fashion from our initial certainties. The method the *Discourse* advocates would seem from this description to be wholly A PRIORI.

The reader might then be surprised by the scientific essays which accompany the *Discourse*, and illustrate what Descartes has accomplished with his method. Descriptions of what can only be characterized as experiments seem to be crucial to its application (there are particularly striking examples in the Fifth Discourse of the *Optics*, or the Eigth of the *Meteorology*). Surprise is unwarranted, however, since an appeal to experience is an acknowledged part of the method in the *Discourse* itself. In the end it appears that what can be demonstrated a priori are only the fundamental principles of physics. Presumably these include the basic laws of motion deduced in the unpublished *Le monde* from God's immutability; what else they might include is obscure (but see Curley 1978, ch. 8). 'The further we advance in our knowledge, the more necessary observations become' (VI/63). The first principles are so simple and general that effects can be deduced from them in a variety of ways. To learn which way an effect really depends on first principles, we must conduct experiments whose outcomes will vary depending on which hypothesis is correct (VI/65).

If Descartes' scientific theory and practice are less a priori than the rationalist paradigm would lead us to expect, the paradigm also has deficiencies in explaining his approach to metaphysical issues. Descartes claimed to have written his *Meditations* in geometrical order (VII/155), but his work does not have the external trappings of a mathematical treatise. Unlike Spinoza's *Ethics*, it does not begin with definitions and axioms, and proceed from them by formal deductions of theorems. Descartes distinguished between the geometric *order* and geometric *manner* of writing. The essence of the geometric order was that no proposition should be advanced which could not be known solely by consideration of what had preceded it in the argument, without the aid of anything later. Descartes tried to adhere to that order, but regarded the geometric manner of writing as inappropriate in metaphysics, since it presupposes that its first principles are already clear and distinct. This presupposition holds in mathematics, but not in metaphysics, where the main problem is to get a clear and distinct perception of the primary notions (VII/157). Achieving that kind of perception requires use of the analytic method; to judge from the *Meditations* themselves, which exemplify it, the analytic method involves a systematic reflection on our past beliefs and suspense of judgment whenever one belief suggests ground for doubting another (Curley, 1986a). Though Descartes' earliest work on method (the unpublished and unfinished *Rules for the Direction of the Mind*) seemed to assume uncritically that we possess an infallible faculty of intuiting first principles, the Descartes of the *Meditations* is more ambitious and more interesting; he is prepared to doubt (provisionally, at least) even the simplest propositions of mathematics, and undertakes a dialectical defence of his first principles and the reliability of the faculty by which we know them (Curley, 1978, chs 2–5).

If Descartes does not fit the rationalist profile, it may be thought, Spinoza must. After all, he does organize the definitive exposition of his philosophy in the geometric manner. Doesn't this imply that he regards the axioms and definitions of his *Ethics* as self-evident truths, which neither require nor admit of argument, but are necessarily seen to be true as soon as we understand the terms in which they are framed? Doesn't it imply that the propositions of the *Ethics* derive their certainty from that of the axioms and definitions, and not conversely?

Oldenburg put the first question to Spinoza when they corresponded about an early draft of the *Ethics* (1677, IV/10–11). Spinoza's reply was that he did not care whether Oldenburg regarded these principles as self-evident, so long as he would allow that they were true (IV/13). Significantly, in the final version of the *Ethics* Spinoza treats most of the principles Oldenburg questioned, not as axioms, but as propositions. What does Spinoza think the status of his axioms is? No doubt he thought some were self-evident. Others seem to be propositions whose warrant is empirical, e.g., 'We feel that a certain body is affected in many ways' (II/86). The view seems to be that there are some empirical propositions so fundamental to our thought about the world that we cannot rationally doubt them. And the system does not make its claim on our belief solely because its axioms are absolutely certain and its deductions valid. When Spinoza reaches conclusions he knows his readers will find hard to accept, he asks them 'to continue on with me slowly, step by step, and to make no judgement on these matters until they have read through them all' (II/95). We are to judge the system as a whole, partly on the basis of the coherence of its conclusions with our experience (on this *see* Bennett, 1984, pp. 16–25; and Curley, 1986b). The contrast we find in Spinoza between reason and experience may be misleading, since it seems that 'experience' often refers only to a casual, uncritical use of experience, as opposed to a systematic, critical use of it (cf. II/10–11 with II/36–7),

and since reason does not appear to be conceived as a wholly a priori faculty (cf. Curley, 1973). Researchers have not sufficiently noted the absence of a theory of INNATE IDEAS in Spinoza, or his account of our knowledge of the common notions which are the basis of reason (II/118–22).

Turning from metaphysics to the sciences, we encounter similar difficulties in making Spinoza fit preconceived notions of rationalism. Some regard his correspondence with Boyle as a classic confrontation between a rationalist and an empiricist (Hall and Hall, 1964). But this seems a very unsympathetic reading of the correspondence. Spinoza's principal complaints about Boyle are that some of his experiments were unnecessary, because the conclusions drawn from them had already been established adequately by the simpler experiments of BACON and Descartes (IV/25), and that other conclusions required further experiment to justify the conclusion drawn (IV/16–17). Some invoke Spinoza's (supposed) rationalism to explain his (supposed) failure to make any substantial contribution to the sciences (Maull, 1986). But if biblical hermeneutics is a science, the *explanandum* should not be granted. Spinoza played an important role in the development of that discipline; his success resulted from his extending to textual interpretation a model of scientific procedure which emphasizes the importance of the careful, systematic collection of relevant data and rejects any attempt to determine the meaning of the text by applying principles known by the light of reason (Savan, 1986, commenting on Spinoza, 1670).

If neither Descartes nor Spinoza fits the rationalist profile, perhaps there is hope for Leibniz. Doesn't he maintain that every true proposition is either an identity or reducible to an identity by the analysis of concepts, thereby making possible an a priori proof of every truth (Leibniz, 1903, p. 267)? Doesn't he claim to deduce from that theory of truth factual propositions which could only be known by experience, e.g. that in nature there cannot be two individuals which differ only numerically (1903, p. 268)? Doesn't he defend innate ideas and principles against the Lockean attack (1765, Book I)?

The answer to all the above questions is yes. Yet Leibniz can be quite Baconian about the need to compile 'histories of nature', cataloguing, classifying and verifying the experiments already performed; he also advocates setting up laboratories at public expense to perform new experiments (Leibniz, 1956, pp. 281–2). When Locke expresses pessimism about the possibility of attaining scientific knowledge however far 'human industry may advance . . . experimental philosophy in physical things', Leibniz replies that 'considerable progress will eventually be made in explaining various phenomena . . . because the great number of experiments which are within our reach can supply us with more than sufficient data' (1765, p. 389). The distinction between TRUTHS OF REASON AND TRUTHS OF FACT is as fundamental in Leibniz's philosophy as that between relations of ideas and matters of fact in Hume's. If even truths of fact are ultimately ANALYTIC in Leibniz's system, still, only God can perceive the a priori demonstration of truths about individuals (1857, p. 264). Human use of the a priori method in science is 'not entirely impossible', so long as we don't descend to particular things, but even at the level of general truths only superior geniuses can hope for anything from it in this life. Most of us must rely on what Leibniz calls 'the conjectural a priori method', which we might nowadays call 'the hypothetico-deductive method' (1956, p. 283, cf. Descartes, 1644, VIII-1/327–8, Spinoza, 1663, I/226–9). Even in mathematics, where we deal with truths of reason, Leibniz is reluctant to rely on the supposed self-evidence of the axioms, urging that mathematicians demonstrate 'the secondary axioms we ordinarily use' by reducing them to identities (1765, p. 408).

None of the three great philosophers commonly counted as paradigms of epistemological rationalism was as dismissive of experience or as trusting of a priori intuition as traditional accounts of rationalism imply. Such difficulties have made specialists increasingly reluctant to accept that classification.

(For further elaboration, beyond the works already cited, see Clarke, 1982; Rescher, 1986. For an attempt to rescue something of the traditional picture in the face of acknowledged difficulties, see Cottingham, 1988.) Determining the exact relation between reason and experience in the three paradigm 'rationalists' is difficult; an accurate account would be too complicated to make for a readable general history, and would probably not conclude that they had any significant epistemological programme in common, or that they constituted a school of thought to which empiricism could usefully be opposed.

Nevertheless, the traditional way of structuring that history will continue to be influential so long as historians do not provide a more attractive alternative paradigm. Loeb 1981 is a lively attempt to do just that, arguing that the figures should be classified according to their metaphysical, not their epistemological, doctrines, and grouping Malebranche and Berkeley with Descartes, Spinoza and Leibniz, because of their common willingness to deny generally accepted causal relations. Another alternative, possibly more fruitful, would be to group the figures by their approach to the conflict between religion and science, depending on whether they thought (1) that we can reconcile traditional religion with the new science (Descartes, Malebranche, Leibniz, Locke); or (2) that we should abandon or radically revise traditional religion because of its inconsistency with a scientific worldview (HOBBES, Spinoza, Hume); or (3) that we should revise the worldview presupposed by the new science to make it compatible with traditional religion (Berkeley). Accepting this principle of classification would require delicate judgements about how free philosophers felt they were to openly advocate views radically opposed to those of their culture, and what they might have said had they felt completely free. How historians of early modern philosophy sort out these matters of interpretation and classification will do much to determine whether the next generation of reference works such as this will still count rationalism as a major 'movement' in the history of philosophy.

*See also* A PRIORI KNOWLEDGE; EMPIRICISM; GEOMETRY.

BIBLIOGRAPHY

Dates used in the text are those of the first publication; pagination is that of the standard modern edition, when that is given in the margins of the standard translation, in which case 'II/86' means 'volume II, p. 86' otherwise the pagination is that of the translation cited.

Bennett, Jonathan: *A Study of Spinoza's Ethics* (Hackett, 1984).

Clarke, Desmond: *Descartes' Philosophy of Science* (Manchester: Manchester University Press, 1982).

Copleston, F.: *A History of Philosophy* (Westminster, MD: Newman Press, 1958), vol. IV.

Cottingham, John: *The Rationalists* (Oxford: Oxford University Press, 1988).

Curley, Edwin: 'Experience in Spinoza's theory of knowledge', in Marjorie Grene, *Spinoza* (New York: Anchor, 1973).

Curley, Edwin: *Descartes Against the Skeptics* (Cambridge, MA: Harvard University Press, 1978).

Curley, Edwin: 'Analysis in the *Meditations*: the quest for clear and distinct ideas', in A. Rorty, *Essays on Descartes' Meditations* (University of California Press, 1986[a]).

Curley Edwin: 'Spinoza's Geometric Method', *Studia Spinozana* 2 (1986[b]), 151–68.

Descartes, René: *Discours de la méthode et les essais* (Leiden, 1637); *Meditationes de prima philosophia* (Paris, 1641); *Principia philosophiae* (Amsterdam, 1644); trans J. Cottingham, R. Stoothoff and D. Murdoch, *Philosophical Writings of Descartes*, 2 vols (Cambridge: Cambridge University Press, 1984).

Hall, A. R. and Hall, M. B.: 'Philosophy and Natural Philosophy: Boyle and Spinoza', in *Mélanges Alexandre Koyré* (Paris: Hermann, 1964), vol. II, pp. 241–6.

Kant, Immanuel: *Kritik der reinen Vernunft* (Riga, 1781); trans. N. K. Smith, *Critique of Pure Reason* (New York: St. Martin's, 1965).

Leibniz, G. W.: 'On freedom' (Paris, 1857), 'First truths' (Paris, 1903), 'An introduction on the value and method of natural science' (Chicago, 1956), trans. in L. Loemker, *Philosophical Papers and Letters of G. W. Leibniz* (first edition, Chicago, 1956; page references to the second edition, Dordrecht: Reidel, 1969).

Leibniz, G. W.: *Nouveaux essais sur l'entendement humain* (Berlin, 1765), trans. P. Remnant and J. Bennett, *New Essays on Human Understanding* (Cambridge: Cambridge University Press, 1981).

Loeb, Louis: *From Descartes to Hume* (Ithaca, NY: Cornell University Press, 1981).

Maull, Nancy: 'Spinoza in the century of science', *Spinoza and the Sciences*, ed. Marjorie Grene and Debra Nails (Dordrecht: D. Reidel, 1986).

Rescher, Nicholas: *Leibniz, an Introduction to his Philosophy* (Lanham, MD: University Press of America, 1986), ch. 12.

Savan, David: 'Spinoza: Scientist and theorist of scientific method', *Spinoza and the Sciences*, 95–123.

Spinoza, Benedict: *Renati Descartes Principiorum philosophiae pars I & II* (Amsterdam, 1663); *Opera posthuma* (*Ethics* and correspondence, Amsterdam, 1677); texts cited in this article from these works are translated in E. Curley, *The Collected Works of Spinoza* (Princeton: Princeton University Press, 1985), vol. I. The translation of the *Tractatus theologicophilosophicus* (Hamburg, 1670) is to appear in vol. II, forthcoming.

EDWIN CURLEY

**rationality**   To be rational is to be guided by legitimate reasoning. But different criteria of legitimacy are normally considered appropriate for different types of reasoning and so at least nine types of rationality, or roles for the faculty of reason, seem to be commonly recognized in Western culture.

First, there is the rationality that consists in conformity with the laws of deductive logic. Thus it would be termed rational (as an instance of the law termed '*modus ponens*') to infer 'The streets are wet' from the two premisses 'It is raining' and 'If it is raining, the streets are wet', whereas it would be irrational to infer 'The streets are not wet' from those premisses. The exact extent of such laws is, however, controversial. For example, deductive logic may or may not be conceived to include laws not only about inferences depending on propositional connectives like 'if' and 'or', or on quantifiers like 'some' and 'all', but also about those depending on modalities such as 'possibly' and 'necessarily'.

A second form of rationality is exhibited by correct mathematical calculations. Thus it is rational to infer '$x > 12$' from the premises '$x$ is a prime number' and '$x > 11$'. Of course, this has nothing to do with the technical sense in which numbers, like the square root of $2$, that are not equivalent to the ratio of one integer to another, are termed 'irrational' and others 'rational'.

A third form of rationality is exhibited by reasoning that depends for its correctness solely on the meanings of words that belong neither to our logical nor to our mathematical vocabulary. Thus it would be rational to infer that, if two people are first cousins of one another, they share at least one grandparent.

A fourth form of rationality is exhibited by ampliative inductions that conform to appropriate criteria, as in an inference from experimental data to a general theory that explains them. For example, a hypothesis about the cause of a phenomenon needs to be tested in a relevant variety of controlled conditions in order to eliminate other possible explanations of the phenomenon, and it would be irrational to judge the hypothesis to be well-supported unless it had survived a suitable set of such tests. Similarly, it would be irrational to suppose a rule of common law to be well-supported if it had not been implicit in a suitable range of judicial decisions.

A fifth form of rationality is exhibited by correct assessments of mathematical probability. For example, it would be irrational to infer that a particular person, John Smith, has a $2/5$ probability of dying before the age of 70 just because he is a lorry-driver and $2/5$ of all lorry-drivers die before the age of 70: he might have many other attributes relevant to his prospects of survival. Of course, the rationality of a probability judgement may also be affected by its mathematical relationship to other judgements of probability. For example, if the mathematical probability of a particular outcome is at issue it would be irrational to assess both the occurrence and the non-occurrence of the outcome at values greater than $.5$.

A sixth form of rationality is exhibited by inferences that are licensed by an accepted factual generalization. For example, if the pavement is wet, it would normally be rational to infer that it has recently rained and irrational to infer that it has not.

A seventh form of rationality, unlike the previous six, is concerned with practice rather than cognition. It is exhibited by actions that further the purposes or interests of the agent. Thus, if a model of economic behaviour is said to assume the rationality of those operating a free market, what is implied is that each agent conducts his transactions in the way that will maximize his own profits. And, where the agent cannot be certain about what will promote his purposes or interests, rationality is often assumed to require him to prefer that course of action which will maximize the arithmetical product of the probability and utility.

An eighth form of rationality that is sometimes supposed to exist is also concerned with practice but with the choice of ends rather than of means to ends. Thus it might be considered rational to treat other human beings as ends in themselves rather than as means to your own ends. The ascription of such rationality would constitute a fundamental moral judgement.

A ninth form of rationality is also concerned with practice but with linguistic communication rather than with action and decision. Successful communication is a co-operative endeavour that has to engage the participants' reasoning powers over and above the comprehension of literal meanings. In particular there is a presumption, at least within Western culture, that persons conversing with one another will conform to certain tacit maxims prescribing relevance, informativeness, brevity, orderliness, etc. Consequently, as GRICE (1975) argued, it is rational to draw certain inferences from what they say over and above whatever inferences are licensed by standard principles of deductive or inductive reasoning. For example, it may be rational to suppose, in an appropriate context, that a professor who is described just as being a good bicyclist is thereby implied to possess no other skills or accomplishments.

Philosophical theories about rationality may be classified as either affirmative or negative. Affirmative theories endorse one or more culturally accepted roles for rationality, or propose some further role, while negative theories are sceptical about the validity of one or more such roles.

Thus the tripartite analysis of the soul that PLATO propounds in his *Republic* guarantees a dominant role for the faculty of reason both in the cognitive task of discovering the explanation of how things are and the justification of how they ought to be and also in the practical task of correctly managing a person's life. Reason, according to Plato, is like an eye of the soul and, after a due process of education and study, it can discern ultimate reality. Knowledge and virtue are therefore so bound up together in Plato's conception of rationality that no-one who knows the right way to act can act wrongly. ARISTOTLE, however, insisted on the independence of cognitive and practical rationality, and thus allowed for the possibility of a person's doing what he knows to be wrong. Both Plato and Aristotle may be said to have held affirmative theories of rationality. But, while Aristotle's theory endorses culturally accepted norms in allowing room for an agent to feel remorse, Plato's theory attributes greater potential to the faculty of reason than ordinary norms of rationality assume.

The rise of modern science gave new impetus to affirmative theorising about rationality. It was probably at least in part because of the important part played by mathematics in the new mechanics of Kepler, Galileo and Newton, that some philosophers thought it plausible to suppose that rationality was just as much the touchstone of scientific truth as of mathematical truth. At any rate that supposition seems to underlie the epistemologies of Descartes and Spinoza, for example, in which observation and experiment are assigned relatively little importance compared with the role of reason. Correspondingly it was widely held that knowledge of right and wrong is knowledge of necessary truths that are to be discovered by rational intuition in much the same way as it was believed that the fundamental principles of arithmetic and geometry are discovered. For example, Richard Price argued that 'a rational agent void of all moral judgment . . . is not possible to be imagined' (1787, p. 72).

In contrast with this thoroughgoing rationalism, KANT's critical philosophy may be seen as attempting a more restrictively affirmative account. On his view reason supplies the human mind with regulative ideals, not constitutive ideas. Such principles guide us in the systematization of knowledge but generate irresoluble antinomies if interpreted as representations of features of reality. In ethics, too, on Kant's view, reason guides our choice of maxims on which to act, but does not actually supply those maxims itself.

Negative theorizing about rationality generates a sceptical challenge to one or more culturally accepted principles. Even the fundamental laws of deductive logic have been exposed to such challenges. For example, the principle that every proposition is either true or false but not both was called into question in the Fourth century BC by the paradox of Eubulides. (Suppose only one sentence is written on a piece of paper, viz. 'The sentence on this piece of paper is false': then that sentence is arguably both false if it is true and true if it is false.)

But in modern philosophy the most influential sceptical challenge to everyday beliefs about rationality was originated by HUME. Hume argued the impossibility of reasoning from the past to the future or from knowledge about some instances of a particular kind of situation to knowledge about all instances of that kind. There would be nothing contradictory, he claimed, in supposing both that the sun had always risen in the past and that it would not rise tomorrow. In effect therefore Hume assumed the only valid standards of cognitive rationality were those of the first three kinds listed above – viz. deductive, mathematical or semantical. Induction was not a rational procedure, on his view, because it could not be reduced to the exercise of reason in one or another of these

three roles (*see* PROBLEMS OF INDUC-
TION).

Hume's argument here is often criticized
for begging the question on the ground that
induction should be held to be a valid process
in its own right and with its own criteria of
good and bad reasoning. But this response to
Hume seems just to beg the question in the
opposite direction. What is needed instead,
perhaps, is to demonstrate a continuity
between inductive and deductive reasoning,
with the latter exhibited as a limiting case of
the former (Cohen, 1989, pp. 186-7). Even
so, Hume's is not the only challenge that
defenders of inductive rationality need to
rebuff. POPPER has also denied the possibility of inductive reasoning, and much-discussed
paradoxes about inductive reasoning have
been proposed by GOODMAN and HEMPEL
(*see* HEMPEL'S PARADOX).

Hume also argued, as against philosophers
like Richard Price (1787), that it was impossible for any reasoning to demonstrate the
moral rightness or wrongness of a particular
action. There would be nothing self-contradictory in preferring the destruction of the
whole world to the scratching of one's little
finger. The only role for reason in decision-
making was to determine the means to
desired ends. Nevertheless Price's kind of
ethical rationalism has been revived in more
recent times by W.D. Ross (1930) and others.
Perhaps Hume's argument here was again
based on question-begging assumptions, and
it may be more cogent to point out that
ethical rationalism implies a unity of moral
standards that is not found to exist in the real
world.

Probabilistic reasoning is another area in
which the possibility of attaining fully
rational results has sometimes been queried,
as in the LOTTERY PARADOX. And serious
doubts have also been raised (Sen, 1982)
about the concept of a rational agent that is
required by classical models of economic behaviour. No doubt a successful piece of embezzle-
ment may in certain circumstances further
the purposes or interests of an accountant,
and need not be an irrational action. But is it
entitled to the accolade of rationality? And
how should its immorality be weighed against

its utility in the scales of practical reasoning?
Or is honesty always the rationally preferable
policy?

These philosophical challenges to rationality have been directed against the very possibility of there existing valid standards of
reasoning in this or that area of enquiry.
They have thus been concerned with the
integrity of the concept of rationality rather
than with the extent to which that concept is
in fact instantiated by the actual thoughts,
procedures and actions of human beings.
Indeed the latter issue seems at first sight to
be a matter for psychological, rather than
philosophical, research. Some of this research
will no doubt be concerned with the circumstances under which people fail to perform in
accordance with valid principles that they
have nevertheless developed or adopted, as
when they make occasional mistakes in their
arithmetical calculations. But there also
seems to be room for research into the
content of the principles that particular categories of the population have developed or
adopted. Some of this would be research into
the success with which the relevant principles have been taught, as when students are
educated in formal logic or statistical theory.
Some would be research into the extent to
which those who have not had any relevant
education are, or are not, prone to any systematic patterns of error in their reasoning.
And it is this last type of research that has
claimed results with 'bleak implications for
human rationality' (Nisbett and Borgida,
1975).

One robust result here is when (Wason,
1966) logically untutored subjects are
presented with four cards showing, respectively, 'A', 'D', '4' and '7' and they know that
every card has a letter on one side and a
number on the other. They are then given
the rule 'If a card has a vowel on one side, it
has an even number on the other', and told
that their task is to say which of the cards
they need to turn over in order to find out
whether the rule is true or false. The most
frequent answers are 'A and 4' and 'Only A'
which are both wrong, while the right answer
'A and 7' is given spontaneously by very few
subjects. Wason interpreted this result as

demonstrating that most subjects have a systematic bias towards seeking verification rather than falsification in testing the rule, and he regarded this bias as a fallacy of the same kind as Popper claimed to have discerned in the belief that induction could be a valid form of human reasoning.

Some of these results concern probabilistic reasoning. For example, in an experiment (Kahneman and Tversky, 1972) on statistically untutored students the subjects are told that in a certain town blue and green cabs operate in a ratio of 85 to 15 respectively. A witness identifies the cab in an accident as green and the court is told that in the relevant circumstances he says that a cab is blue when it is blue, or that a cab is green when it is green, in 80 per cent of cases. When asked the probability that the cab involved in the accident was blue subjects tend to say 20 per cent. The experimenters have claimed that this robust result shows the prevalence of a systematic fallacy in ordinary people's probabilistic reasoning, viz. a failure to pay proper attention to prior probabilities. And it has been argued (Saks and Kidd, 1980–1, p. 134) that the existence of several such results demonstrates the inherent unsoundness of mandating lay juries to decide issues of fact in law courts.

However, it is by no means clear that these psychological experimenters have interpreted their data correctly or that the implications for human rationality are as bleak as they suppose (Cohen, 1981, 1982). For example, it might be argued that Wason's experiment merely shows the difficulty that people have in applying the familiar rule of contraposition to artificial conditional relationships that lack any basis in causality or in any other explanatory system. And as for the cabs, it might well be disputed whether the size of the fleet to which a cab belongs should be accepted as determining a prior probability that can count against a posterior probability founded on the causal relation between a witness's mental powers and his courtroom testimony. To count against such a posterior probability one would need a prior one that was also rooted in causality, such as the ratio in which cabs from the blue fleet and cabs from the

green fleet (which may have different policies about vehicle maintenance and driver training) are involved in accidents of the kind in question. In other words the subjects may interpret the question to concern probabilities conceived as causal propensities, not probabilities conceived as relative frequencies that may be accidental. Indeed it is always necessary to consider whether the dominant responses given by subjects in such experiments should be taken, on the assumption that they are correct, as indicating how the task is generally understood – instead of as indicating, on the assumption that the task is understood exactly in the way intended, what errors are being made.

Finally, there is an obvious paradox in supposing that untutored human intuitions may be systematically erroneous over a wide range of issues in human reasoning. On what non-circular basis other than such intuitions can philosophers ultimately found their theories about the correct norms of deductive or probabilistic reasoning? No doubt an occasional intuition may have to be sacrificed in order to construct an adequately comprehensive system of norms. But empirical data seem in principle incapable of showing that the untutored human mind is deficient in rationality, since we need to assume the existence of this rationality – in most situations – in order to provide a basis for those normative theories in terms of which we feel confident in criticizing occasional errors of performance in arithmetical calculations, etc.

*See also* PSYCHOLOGY AND EPISTEMOLOGY.

BIBLIOGRAPHY

Cohen, L.J.: 'Can human irrationality be experimentally demonstrated?', *The Behavioral and Brain Sciences* 4 (1981), 317–31 and 359–67.
Cohen, L.J.: 'Are people programmed to commit fallacies? Further thoughts about the interpretation of experimental data on probability judgment', *Journal for the Theory of Social Behaviour* 12 (1982), 251–74.
Cohen, L.J.: *An Introduction to the Philosophy of*

*Induction and Probability* (Oxford: Clarendon Press, 1989).

Grice, H.P.: 'Logic and conversation', in *The Logic of Grammar* eds D. Davidson and G. Harman (Encino: Dickinson, 1975), 64–75.

Kahneman, D. and Tversky, A.: 'On the psychology of prediction', *Oregon Research Institute Bulletin* 12 (1972), no. 4

Nisbett, R.E. and Borgida, E.: 'Attribution and the psychology of prediction', *Journal of Personal and Social Psychology* 32 (1975), 932–43.

Price, R.: *A Review of the Principal Questions in Morals* (London: T. Cadell, 1787).

Ross, W.D.: *The Right and the Good* (Oxford: Clarendon Press, 1930).

Saks, M.J. and Kidd, R.F.: 'Human information-processing and adjudication: trial by heuristics', *Law and Society Review* 15 (1980–1), 123–60.

Sen, A.: *Choice, Welfare and Measurement* (Oxford: Blackwell, 1982), 84–106.

Wason, P.C.: 'Reasoning', in *New Horizons in Psychology* ed. B. Foss (Harmondsworth: Penguin, 1966), vol. I.

L. JONATHAN COHEN

**realism**  Realism in any area of thought is the doctrine that certain entities allegedly associated with that area are indeed real. Common sense realism – sometimes called 'realism', without qualification – says that ordinary things like chairs and trees and people are real. Scientific realism says that theoretical posits like electrons and fields of force and quarks are equally real. And psychological realism says mental states like pains and beliefs are real. Realism can be upheld – and opposed – in all such areas, as it can with differently or more finely drawn provinces of discourse: for example, with discourse about colours, about the past, about possibility and necessity, or about matters of moral right and wrong. The realist in any such area insists on the reality of the entities in question in the discourse.

If realism itself can be given a fairly quick characterization, it is more difficult to chart the various forms of opposition, for they are legion. Some opponents deny that there are any distinctive posits associated with the area of discourse under dispute; a good example is the emotivist doctrine that moral discourse does not posit values but serves only, like applause and exclamation, to express feelings. Other opponents deny that the entities posited by the relevant discourse exist or at least exist independently of our thinking about them; here the standard example is IDEALISM. And others again insist that the entities associated with the discourse in question are tailored to our human capacities and interests and, to that extent, are as much a product of invention as a matter of discovery.

The variety of the opposition shows that realism about any area of discourse, though apparently simple, actually involves a number of distinct claims. I distinguish three, which I call respectively descriptivism, objectivism and cosmocentrism.

THE DESCRIPTIVIST THESIS

Participants in the discourse necessarily posit the existence of distinctive items, believing and asserting things about them: the utterances fail to come off, as an understanding of them reveals, if there are no such entities. The entities posited are distinctive in the sense that, for all that participants are in a position to know, the entities need not be identifiable with, or otherwise replaceable by, entities independently posited. Although realists about any discourse agree that it posits such entities, they may differ about what sorts of things are involved. BERKELEY differs from the rest of us about what common sense posits and, less dramatically, colour realists differ about the nature of colours, mental realists about the status of psychological states, modal realists about the locus of possibility, and moral realists about the place of value.

THE OBJECTIVIST THESIS

The objects posited exist and have their character fixed independently of the dispositions of participants in the discourse to assert and believe things about them. Thus the epistemic states of the participants have no causal influence on the existence or character of those objects, nor are the objects SUPERVENIENT in any way – that is, non-causally dependent – on such epistemic states. In short, the entities posited in the discourse enjoy a substantial kind of objectivity.

## THE COSMOCENTRIC THESIS

In order to avoid error and ignorance with regard to substantive propositions of the discourse – in order to get at the truth – participants have to make suitable contact with the objects of the discourse and there is no guarantee that they will succeed in doing so. The human search for truth is a matter of discovery, not invention, and discovery is a matter of contingent success. Ignorance is possible, because normally it is possible that human subjects lack contact with certain regions of the independent reality in question. Error is possible, because normally it is possible that human subjects are only imperfectly attuned to the regions with which they do make contact.

The realist's first thesis puts him in conflict with at least three sorts of opponent: the reductivist, the instrumentalist and theorists who explore sophisticated variations on instrumentalism. The reductivist says of the area of discourse in question, that it can be reduced to some other area and does not therefore introduce any distinctive posits. Thus she may say that commonsense discourse about physical objects or scientific discourse about unobservable entities reduces to talk about the purely phenomenal level, that moral discourse reduces to talk about the attitudinal or that mental discourse reduces to talk about the purely behavioural level. The instrumentalist says of the discourse that it does not involve talk about anything at all, let alone novel existential posits, because it is not assertoric: it does not involve assertions, only utterances with the force of imperatives, exclamations, or whatever. Thus she says that theoretical discourse in science is really just a way of generating appropriate laboratory dispositions – 'That's fragile' has the imperative force of 'Be careful!' – and that moral discourse is just a way of expressing emotions, a way of making exclamations of approval or disapproval: emotivism, on this account, is a variety of

moral instrumentalism. There are two currently influential variants on instrumentalism, projectivism and constructive empiricism. The projectivist holds that the discourse in question serves the sort of role ascribed to it by the instrumentalist, and does not involve distinctive posits, but that it still has the marks of assertoric talk that impress – and mislead – the realist. (Blackburn, 1984) The constructive empiricist – a sort of fictionalist – holds that while the discourse represents assertoric talk about the relevant sorts of objects, accepting what is said – participating in the discourse – does not mean positing those objects; it may only mean treating the propositions involved as empirically adequate, treating them as adequate for the practical purposes on which instrumentalists focus (van Fraassen, 1980).

The realist's second thesis puts him in conflict with two main sorts of opponent: the error theorist and the idealist. The error theorist denies that there are any objects of the kind that the discourse in question posits (Mackie, 1977). While admitting that modal discourse posits the existence of possibilities, and moral discourse posits that of values, she denies that there are any such things; thus she says that assertions and beliefs within the area of discourse inevitably fail to be true. Unlike the error theorist, the idealist admits that the objects posited do exist, as Berkeley admits the existence of the items he takes common sense to posit. What she denies is that the objects are independent of people's dispositions to believe and assert things about them. Such objects are held to depend in some way on people's dispositions; the dispositions invoked may be individual or shared, depending on whether the idealism involved is of the subjective or objective variety (see IDEALISM). Berkeley is a subjective idealist, whereas someone like HEGEL is usually counted as an idealist of an objective – better, an intersubjective – kind.

The realist's first two theses in any area of discourse can be run together into a straightforward claim, made within the discourse itself, that there are such and such entities and they are independent of our epistemic influence. On this representation, the realist about commonsense says that there are independent chairs and tables and other such objects, the realist about science says that there are independent protons and electrons and things of that ordinarily unobservable kind (Devitt, 1984). This is a perfectly accurate way of expressing the realist's first two claims, though it fails to make clear that there are very different ways of rejecting his position: the ways that correspond with the denial of the descriptivist and objectivist theses, respectively.

The third, cosmocentric thesis is made central to realism by some writers (Smart, 1982; Papineau, 1987) but not by all (Devitt, 1984). It puts the realist in conflict with an opponent that we can describe as the anthropocentric. The anthropocentric says that with certain substantive propositions within the discourse in question – with a certain number or with certain specific cases – there is no possibility that specified individuals or groups could be in ignorance or error. The anthropocentric may deny the possibility of a certain error or ignorance by taking the interpretationist line that the objects posited by a discourse are whatever objects participants are mostly right about; this will put limits on error (Davidson, 1984; Rorty, 1980). She may do it by going the verificationist or anti-realist way of refusing to acknowledge that propositions for which we lack adjudication procedures have a determinate truth-value; this will put limits on ignorance (Tennant, 1987, ch. 2). She may do it through becoming a relativist and increasing a group's chances of hitting the truth by moving the target nearer: by defining truth, in the relevant sense, as truth relative to that group. Or she may take any of a variety of other approaches (Goodman, 1978; Putnam, 1981; Price, 1988; Pettit, 1990). Whatever form the anthropocentric claim takes, however, the realist will deny it. He says of any discourse he judges favourably that error and ignorance are always possible with regard to the substantive propositions of the discourse. It is possible that participants are wrong about all and every substantive claim in the discourse.

It may at first seem that there is going to be an inconsistency involved in agreeing to the first two realist theses and then, in the anthropocentric style, denying the third. If there were, that would mean that anthropocentrism was not really an independent way of rejecting realism. But there is no inconsistency involved and anthropocentrism does represent an independent mode of opposition to realism. It may be entailed by certain ways of denying the first two theses but it does not require the denial of either. Consistently with thinking that a discourse introduces distinctive posits, and that the posited objects are suitably independent of people's epistemic states, a philosopher might hold that the posited objects are tailored to human interests and capacities. Consider the popular view of colour according to which it is *a priori* true that something is red if and only if it looks red to normal observers under normal conditions. This view allows that the redness property is posited in colour discourse and it may identify that property with a certain physical feature: say, a certain surface reflectance. Thus it may be compatible with descriptivism and objectivism about colour. But under the view in question, cosmocentrism fails, for there are limits on human error: normal observers in normal conditions cannot be wrong about the colour of something. Objective though it is on this approach, colour is nevertheless an anthropocentric property, a property that reflects an element of invention as well as discovery.

There are three things that need to be said in further commentary on the realist's cosmocentric thesis. The first is that while it invokes the notion of truth, the notion involved is just that which is given by the disquotational schema, ' "$p$" is true if and only if $p$'. I assume that the notion of assertion is given, so that we understand what is involved in asserting that $p$, for any arbitrary '$p$'; for example, we understand that it is inconsistent with asserting that not-$p$, that it is equivalent to denying that not-$p$, and that it combines with the assertion that if $p$, then $q$ to license the assertion that $q$. Given an understanding of assertion, the disquotational schema is sufficient to communicate an understanding of truth in the sense in which the realist's third thesis – or the anthropocentric's counter-thesis – invokes the notion.

The second thing that needs to be said about the realist's third thesis bears on the question of what truths are sufficiently substantive to be relevant to the thesis. The realist says that error and ignorance are possible with regard to the substantive propositions in any area of discourse. So which propositions, if any, are non-substantive? My answer is brief: if a proposition is such that just to count as a proper participant in the discourse in question, just to count as someone who understands what is going on, you must accept the proposition or you must reject it, then it is non-substantive; otherwise it is substantive. By many accounts, there are truths in every area of discourse whose acceptance or whose rejection is criterial for counting as a proper participant there: you must accept them – they are so obviously true – or you must reject them – they are so obviously false – if you are going to be held as someone who genuinely asserts and believes things in the discourse, as someone who understands enough not to be seen as a mere mouther of words. If a realist accepts such an account, then he will naturally deny that error and ignorance are possible for proper participants in the discourse with such propositions. But that denial will not come of any faltering in his realist commitments; it will merely give expression to his view of what proper participation in the discourse presupposes. The realist will have to regard it as a non-substantive proposition of a discourse that there are the entities associated with the discourse since, by the descriptivist thesis, participants necessarily posit such items and by the objectivist thesis they cannot be wrong to do so. Otherwise he can be uncommitted: he may or may not acknowledge further non-substantive propositions. If further non-substantive propositions are countenanced, they will presumably be the platitudes and the howlers whose acceptance and rejection, respectively, are generally taken to reveal little more than an understanding of an area of discourse; these will overlap with the traditional analytic truths

and falsehoods but the two categories may not be co-terminous.

The third thing I need to say about the realist's cosmocentric thesis is that it may come in any of a variety of strengths, depending on whether it is maintained *vis-à-vis* individuals or groups – at the limit, the community as a whole – and depending on how the circumstances of those individuals and groups are specified. It is one thing to say that an individual may fall into error or ignorance, it is something much stronger to say that the community as a whole may do so. It is one thing to say that individual or community may, in their actual circumstances, fall into error or ignorance; it is something much stronger to say that they may do so in normal or even in ideal circumstances. Normal circumstances will be ones in which certain obstacles are lacking, ideal circumstances will be ones in which certain desirable facilities are present: say, all the relevant evidence is available. The strongest version of the realist thesis says that ignorance and error are possible for any of the epistemic combinations represented in these six boxes.

|  | Individual judgement | Community concensus |
|---|---|---|
| in actual | 1 | 4 |
| or normal | 2 | 5 |
| or ideal circumstances | 3 | 6 |

In conclusion, a summary. The realist about any area of discourse asserts three theses, setting himself against three differents kinds of opponent. Marking his opposition to reductivists, instrumentalists and the like, he asserts that the discourse introduces distinctive posits; this is the descriptivist thesis. Marking his opposition to error theorists and idealists, he holds that the objects posited exist and are independent of people's dispositions to assert and believe things about them; this is the objectivist thesis. Finally, taking his stand against the many varieties of anthropocentric, he maintains the cosmocentric thesis that participants may be in error or ignorance with regard to any or all substantive propositions in the discourse.

*See also* IDEALISM; NOUMENAL/ PHENOMENAL; OBJECTIVITY; PRIMARY AND SECONDARY QUALITIES; TRUTH.

BIBLIOGRAPHY

Blackburn, S.: *Spreading the Word* (Oxford: Oxford University Press, 1984).
Davidson, D.: *Inquiries into Truth and Interpretation* (Oxford: Clarendon Press, 1984).
Devitt, M.: *Realism and Truth* (Oxford: Blackwell, 1984).
van Fraassen, B.: *The Scientific Image* (Oxford: Oxford University Press, 1980).
Goodman, N.: *Ways of Worldmaking* (Brighton: Harvester, 1978).
Mackie, J.L.: *Ethics: Inventing Right and Wrong* (Harmondsworth: Penguin, 1977).
Papineau, D.: *Reality and Representation* (Oxford: Blackwell, 1987).
Pettit, P.: 'The reality of rule-following', *Mind* 99 (1990), 1–21.
Price, H.: *Facts and the Function of Truth* (Oxford: Blackwell, 1988).
Putman, H.: *Reason, Truth and History* (Cambridge: Cambridge University Press, 1981).
Rorty, R.: *Philosophy and the Mirror of Nature* (Oxford: Blackwell, 1980).
Smart, J.J.C.: 'Metaphysical realism', *Analysis* 42 (1982), 1–3.
Tennant, N.: *Anti-Realism and Logic* (Oxford: Oxford University Press, 1987).

PHILIP PETTIT

**reasons/causes** The distinction between reasons and causes is motivated in good part by a desire to separate the rational from the natural order. Historically, it probably traces back at least to Aristotle's similar (but not identical) distinction between final and efficient cause. Recently, the contrast has been drawn primarily in the domain of actions and, secondarily, elsewhere.

Many who have insisted on distinguishing reasons from causes have failed to distinguish two kinds of reason. Consider my reason for sending a letter by express mail. Asked why I did so, I might say I wanted to get it there

in a day, or simply: to get it there in a day. Strictly, the *reason* is expressed by 'to get it there in a day'. But what this expresses is *my* reason only because I am suitably motivated; I am in a *reason state*: wanting to get the letter there in a day. It is reason states – especially wants, beliefs and intentions – and not reasons strictly so called, that are candidates for causes. The latter are abstract contents of propositional attitudes; the former are psychological elements that play motivational roles.

If reason states can motivate, however, why (apart from confusing them with reasons proper) deny that they are causes? For one thing, they are not events, at least in the usual sense entailing change; they are dispositional states (this contrasts them with occurrences, but does not imply that they admit of dispositional *analysis*). It has also seemed to those who deny that reasons are causes that the former *justify* as well as explain the actions for which they are reasons, whereas the role of causes is at most to explain. Another claim is that the relation between reasons (and here reason states are often cited explicitly) and the actions they explain is non-contingent, whereas the relation of causes to their effects is contingent. The 'logical connection argument' proceeds from this claim to the conclusion that reasons are not causes.

These arguments are inconclusive. First, even if causes are events, *sustaining causation* may explain, as where the (state of) standing of a broken table is explained by the (condition of) support of stacked boards replacing its missing legs. Second, the 'because' in 'I sent it by express because I wanted to get it there in a day' is in *some* sense causal – indeed, where it is not so taken, this purported explanation would at best be construed as only rationalizing, rather than justifying, my action. And third, *if* any non-contingent connection can be established between, say, my wanting something and the action it explains, there are close causal analogues, such as the connection between bringing a magnet to iron filings and their gravitating to it: this is, after all, a 'definitive' connection, expressing part of what it *is* to be magnetic, yet the magnet *causes* the filings to move.

There is, then, a clear distinction between reasons proper and causes, and even between reason states and *event* causes; but the distinction cannot be used to show that the relation between reasons and the actions they justify is in no way causal. Precisely parallel points hold in the epistemic domain (and indeed for all the propositional attitudes, since they all similarly admit of justification, and explanation, by reasons). Suppose my reason for believing that you received my letter today is that I sent it by express yesterday. My reason, strictly speaking, is *that* I sent it by express yesterday; my reason *state* is my *believing* this. Arguably, my reason justifies the further *proposition* I believe for which it *is* my reason, and my reason state – my evidence belief – both explains and justifies my *belief* that you received the letter today. I can *say* that what justifies that belief is (the fact) that I sent the letter by express yesterday; but this statement *expresses* my believing that evidence proposition, and indeed if I do not believe it then my belief that you received the letter is not justified: it is not justified by the mere truth of the proposition (and can be justified even if that proposition is false).

Similarly, there are, for belief as for action, at least five main kinds of reason: (1) *normative reasons*, reasons (objective grounds) there are to believe (say, to believe that there is a greenhouse effect); (2) *person-relative normative reasons*, reasons for (say) me to believe; (3) *subjective reasons*, reasons I have to believe; (4) *explanatory reasons*, reasons *why* I believe; and (5) *motivating reasons*, reasons *for which* I believe. (1) and (2) are propositions and thus not serious candidates to be causal factors. The *states* corresponding to (3) may or may not be causal elements. Reasons why, case (4), are always (sustaining) explainers, though not necessarily even *prima facie* justifiers, since a belief can be causally sustained by factors with no evidential value. Motivating reasons are both explanatory and possess whatever minimal PRIMA FACIE justificatory power (if any) a reason must have to be a basis of belief.

Current discussion of the reasons-causes issue has shifted from the question whether reason states can causally explain to the perhaps deeper questions whether they can justify *without* so explaining, and what *kind* of causal chain non-waywardly connects reason states with actions and beliefs they do explain. RELIABILISTS tend to take a belief as justified *by* a reason only if it is held at least in part *for* that reason, in a sense implying, but not entailed by, being causally based on that reason. INTERNALISTS often deny this, perhaps thinking we lack internal access to the relevant causal connections (*see* EXTERNALISM/INTERNALISM). But internalists need not deny it, particularly if they require only internal access to *what* justifies – say, the reason state – and not to the (perhaps quite complex) relations it bears to the belief it justifies, by virtue of which it does so. Many questions also remain concerning the very nature of causation, reasonhood, explanation and justification.

*See also* NATURAL SCIENCE; SOCIAL SCIENCE.

BIBLIOGRAPHY

Alston, W.P.: 'Wants, actions, and causal explanations', in *Intentionality, Minds, and Perception* ed. H.-N. Castaneda (Detroit: Wayne State University Press, 1967).
Aristotle: *Nicomachean Ethics*.
Audi, R.: 'Acting for reasons', *Philosophical Review* 95 (1986), 511–46.
Audi, R.: *Practical Reasoning* (London: Routledge, 1989).
Brandt, R.B. and Kim, J.: 'Wants as explanations of actions', *Journal of Philosophy* 60 (1963), 425–35.
Bratman, M.E.: *Intention, Plans, and Practical Reason* (Cambridge, MA: Harvard University Press, 1987).
Castaneda, H.-N.: *Thinking and Doing* (Dordrecht: Reidel, 1975).
Davidson, D.: 'Actions, reasons, and causes', in his *Essays on Actions and Events* (Oxford: Clarendon Press, 1980).
Goldman, A.I.: *A Theory of Human Action* (Englewood Cliffs: Prentice-Hall, 1970).

Melden, A.I.: *Free Action* (London: Routledge and Kegan Paul, 1961).

ROBERT AUDI

**Reichenbach, Hans (1891–1953)** Reichenbach was born in Hamburg, Germany, and died in Los Angeles, California. He was a leading figure in the movement known as LOGICAL EMPIRICISM.

Reichenbach began his career as a Kantian, but soon rejected that position. In a series of works, the most important being (1920, 1928, 1956), he argued that KANT's doctrine of the synthetic a priori character of space, time and causality is incompatible with modern science, especially the theory of relativity. His principal argument was that it is possible to cling to Euclidean geometry, but only at the cost of relinquishing normal causality, or to retain normal causality, but only at the cost of relinquishing Euclidean geometry. General relativity precludes the retention of both on any a priori grounds (*see* GEOMETRY).

Having abandoned Kantianism, Reichenbach remained a steadfast empiricist for the rest of his life. He adopted a verifiability criterion of cognitive meaningfulness, but unlike the LOGICAL POSITIVISTS of the Vienna Circle, he held that probabilistic (as opposed to conclusive) verifiability is sufficient.

Reichenbach's views differed from those of the positivists in other ways as well. He rejected PHENOMENALISM, maintaining instead that our knowledge of the world is based on perceptions of physical things, even though such experiences cannot be certified as always veridical. Moreover, he was a REALIST with regard to unobservable entities, maintaining that it is possible to have probabilistic knowledge of them. These views were stated in his (1938), a work he regarded as a refutation of logical positivism.

A great deal of Reichenbach's work was devoted to probability and induction. In his major work on the subject (1935, revised in 1949), he presented a mathematical calculus of probability and advocated a limiting frequency interpretation, showing that the axioms of the calculus become arithmetical truisms if that interpretation is adopted. He advanced his 'rule of induction' (essentially induction by enumeration) as a method of positing values of limiting frequencies.

Reichenbach took seriously HUME's challenge to induction (*see* PROBLEMS OF INDUCTION) and, in answer thereto, offered a pragmatic justification of his rule. Roughly stated, his justification maintained that, although we cannot know whether nature will continue to be uniform, we have everything to gain and nothing to lose by using induction, for if any method works, induction will. More precisely, he argued that, if sequences of events have limiting frequencies, his rule of induction is bound, sooner or later, to lead to posits that become and remain accurate to any desired degree of accuracy. That result follows immediately from the definition of a limit and the character of his rule. He realized, however, that an infinite class of 'asymptotic rules' have the same convergence property, but he never successfully showed how to justify the selection of his rule in preference to any other asymptotic rule.

Reichenbach's epistemology was totally EMPIRICIST and FALLIBILIST. Our factual knowledge is based entirely on experience, and experience does not provide any certain knowledge of the world.

WRITINGS

*Relativitätstheorie und Erkenntnis Apriori* (Berlin: 1920); trans. M. Reichenbach, *The Theory of Relativity and A Priori Knowledge* (Berkeley: University of California Press, 1965).

*Philosophie der Raum-Zeit-Lehre* (Berlin and Leipzig: 1928); trans. M. Reichenbach and J. Freund, *The Philosophy of Space and Time* (New York: Dover, 1958).

*Wahrscheinlichkeitslehre* (Leiden: 1935); trans. E.H. Hutten and M. Reichenbach, *The Theory of Probability* 2nd edn revised (Berkeley: University of California Press, 1949).

*Experience and Prediction* (Chicago: University of Chicago Press, 1938).

*The Direction of Time* (Berkeley: University of California Press, 1956).

BIBLIOGRAPHY

Salmon, W.C.: *Hans Reichenbach: Logical Empiricist* (Dordrecht: Reidel, 1979).

WESLEY C. SALMON

**Reid, Thomas (1710–96)** Thomas Reid was born, worked and died in Scotland. Beginning in 1751, he was a regent and lecturer at King's College in Old Aberdeen where he founded the Aberdeen Philosophical Society with John Gregory, until, in 1764, he succeeded Adam Smith in the Chair of Moral Philosophy in the Old College at Glasgow. In the same year, 1764, his first book, *Inquiry into the Human Mind on the Principles of Common Sense*, which emerged from his lectures to the Aberdeen Philosophical Society, was published. His other two works, his *Essays on the Intellectual Powers*, 1785, and his *Essays on the Active Powers*, 1788, which resulted from his Glasgow lectures, were published after his retirement.

Thomas Reid is most famous as a defender of commonsense against the scepticism of David HUME. Reid's defence of commonsense is based on a sophisticated theory of conception and justification which combines naturalistic nativism and normative epistemology. It is this positive theory rather than his criticism of Hume that constitutes his major contribution. Reid claimed that our most basic conceptions of qualities, for example, movement, figure and colour, result from original faculties of the mind. Faculties are innate powers of the mind. These faculties give rise to conceptions of external objects in immediate response to sensory stimulation and the sensations that accompany such stimulation. Sensations give rise to our conceptions of the qualities of objects of our commonsense world.

Reid denied that such qualities of objects were reducible to sensations, or, for that matter, to the impressions of Hume. A conception is necessarily a conception of something, of some immanent or intentional object. We can conceive of things that do not exist, centaurs, for example, but conception is always about something, even if a non-existent thing. Sensations are only modifications of the mind that have no object.

Conviction as well as conception arises from original principles and irreducible operations of the faculties of the mind. For example, a sensation acts as input to our innate faculty of perception, which gives rise according to the first principles of the faculty to the conception of a moving object and to the immediate and irresistible conviction of the existence of such an object as output. This nativist theory of conception and belief is joined to Reid's epistemology by a simple connecting premise, namely, that beliefs resulting from first principles are justified beliefs supported by evidence. The justification and evidence of such beliefs is immediate, which is his reply to Hume. Evidence, Reid says, is the ground of belief, and beliefs arising immediately from first principles receive their evidence as a birthright.

This conception of evidence is a form of naturalized FOUNDATIONALISM, but there is also a COHERENTIST component to Reid. Suppose we ask why we should trust this evidence arising from the first principles of our faculties. Reid has two answers. The first is that if we do not trust our faculties our situation is desperate and without remedy. We shall be led to total scepticism. Reason, for example, is a faculty, and if we do not trust reason, then it cannot provide us relief from scepticism, and of course the same is true of perception, consciousness and all the rest of our faculties. If, on the other hand, we do trust our faculties, it appears that we should treat them equally, at least initially, and trust them all.

However, it is not just desperation that leads us to trust our faculties. We trust our faculties as a result of a first principle of our faculties, a sort of metaprinciple, to the effect that our faculties are not fallacious but are, instead, trustworthy. Other first principles tell us that the things we distinctly perceive really do exist, that the events we clearly remember did really happen, but the metaprinciple, which is also a first principle, tells us that all the first principles of our faculties, which includes the metaprinciple itself, are trustworthy. The metaprinciple is a source of evidence for the other principles and for itself. Though all first principles yield convictions that are immediately evident, that is, evident without reasoning, the metaprinciple supports the others, and, when the convictions they yield turn out to be true and not fallacious, the metaprinciple is also supported.

Reid's system thus provides us with an epistemology featuring elements of coherence, foundationalism and a natural connection with truth. Nature bestows faculties containing first principles of conception and belief upon us which are, contrary to Hume, also principles of evidence. We must trust the evidence of our faculties in our practical and scientific concerns or fall defeated into the coalpit of scepticism.

This epistemology is applied to diverse areas by Reid, and one interesting application is to MORAL EPISTEMOLOGY. Reid holds that there is a moral faculty. Reid contends that children have moral convictions, such as that of being treated unjustly, before they are taught any moral conceptions. So there is an innate capacity to form moral judgements and, contrary to Hume, judgements of justice and injustice. The faculty responds to our conceptions of actions with judgements as to whether those actions are just or unjust. Differences in moral judgement, Reid contends, are the result of differences in the way in which we conceive of the action. These in turn result from differences in moral education. For any two people, given exactly the same conception of an action as input, the same judgement will result as output.

Reid has important contributions to the theory of human action and liberty as well as to perception, epistemology and morals. His system is based on his fundamental premise of the trustworthiness of the innate faculties of the human mind. A detailed account of his system is contained in Lehrer (1989).

See also COMMONSENSISM AND CRITICAL COGNITIVISM; PRINCIPLE OF CREDULITY; TESTIMONY.

WRITINGS

Essays on the Intellectual Powers of Man (1785)

ed. B. Brody (Cambridge, MA: MIT Press, 1969).
Thomas Reid's Inquiry and Essays eds K. Lehrer and R.E. Beanblossom (Indianapolis: Bobbs-Merrill, 1975).

BIBLIOGRAPHY

Lehrer, K.: Thomas Reid (London: Routledge, 1989).

KEITH LEHRER

**reification, hypostatization** We interpret our world as composed of things or objects. As well as everyday external things and the posits of scientific theory, there are more controversial objects like universals, sense-data, classes and numbers. When we *reify* objects we accept their existence as distinct things in the world, and this requires us to be able to count them and quantify over them; it also requires us to understand identity statements involving objects of the appropriate kinds. Claims about the existence of particular kinds of objects can be challenged by arguing that we lack criteria for counting them or for evaluating identity statements, and by denying that they contribute to our understanding of our surroundings.

*See also* EXISTENCE.

BIBLIOGRAPHY

Quine, W.V.: *From a Logical Point of View* (Cambridge, MA: Harvard University Press, 1953), ch. 4.
Quine, W.V.: *Ontological Relativity and Other Essays* (New York: Columbia University Press, 1969), ch. 1.
Quine, W.V.: *Theories and Things* (Cambridge, MA: Harvard University Press, 1981), ch. 1.
Quine, W.V.: *Pursuit of Truth* (Cambridge, MA: Harvard University Press, 1990), ch. 2.

CHRISTOPHER HOOKWAY

**relativism** Epistemological relativism may be defined as the view that knowledge (and/ or truth) is relative – to time, to place, to society, to culture, to historical epoch, to conceptual scheme or framework, or to personal training or conviction – so that what counts as knowledge depends upon the value of one or more of these variables. If knowledge and truth are relative in this way, this will be because different cultures, societies, etc. accept different sets of background principles and standards of evaluation for knowledge-claims, and there is no neutral way of choosing between these alternative sets of standards. So the relativist's basic claim is that the truth and rational justifiability of knowledge-claims are relative to the standards used in evaluating such claims. (For a more technical definition, *see* Siegel, 1987, p. 6.)

The doctrine of relativism is usually traced to Protagoras, who is portrayed in Plato's *Theaetetus* as holding that 'man is the measure of all things' ('homo mensura'), and that any given thing 'is to me such as it appears to me, and is to you such as it appears to you' (152a). Plato's Socrates characterizes Protagorean relativism as consisting in the view that 'what seems true to anyone is true for him to whom it seems so' (*Theaetetus* 170a). This view is a form of relativism in our sense, since for Protagoras there is no standard higher than the individual with reference to which claims to truth and knowledge can be adjudicated. But relativism as defined above is more general than Protagorean relativism, for it places the source of relativism at the level of standards rather than at the level of personal opinion or perception, and as such aptly characterizes more recent versions of relativism.

Opponents of relativism have made many criticisms of the doctrine; by far the most fundamental is the charge that relativism is *self-referentially incoherent*, in that defending the doctrine requires one to give it up. There are several versions of the incoherence charge. The most powerful (for others, *see* Siegel, 1987) is that relativism precludes the possibility of determining the truth, warrant or epistemic merit of contentious claims and doctrines – including itself – since according to relativism no claim or doctrine can fail any test of epistemic

adequacy or be judged unjustified, false or unwarranted. Take Protagorean relativism as an example. If 'what seems true [or warranted] to anyone *is* true [or warranted] for him to whom it seems so', then no sincere claim can fail any test of epistemic adequacy or be judged unjustified or false. But if there is no possibility that a claim or doctrine can fail a test of epistemic adequacy or rightness, then the distinction between adequacy and inadequacy, rightness and wrongness is given up. If so, then the very notions of rightness, truth and warrantedness are undermined. But if this is so, then relativism itself cannot be right. In short: relativism is incoherent because, if it is right, the very notion of rightness is undermined, in which case relativism itself cannot be right. The assertion *and defence* of relativism requires one to presuppose neutral standards in accordance with which contentious claims and doctrines can be assessed; but relativism denies the possibility of evaluation in accordance with such neutral standards. Thus the doctrine of relativism cannot be coherently defended – it can be defended only by being given up. Relativism is thus impotent to defend itself, and falls to this fundamental reflexive difficulty. (Siegel, 1987, ch. 1.)

A further difficulty worth noting is that concerning the notion of *relative truth*. Many versions of relativism rely on such a notion, but it is very difficult to make sense of it. An assertion that a proposition is 'true for me' (or 'true for members of my culture') is more readily understood as a claim about what I (or members of my culture) *believe* than it is as a claim ascribing to that proposition some peculiar form of truth. Moreover, even if this notion could be made sense of, it would still fall to the incoherence argument above (Siegel, 1987, ch. 1).

Despite these ancient and powerful responses to relativism, the last several decades have witnessed a resurgence of the doctrine. This is at least in part due to the difficulty of formulating a defensible conception of non-relativism. Many relativists argue for relativism on the grounds that any non-relativistic alternative will require repugnant epistemological commitments, e.g. to CERTAINTY, privileged frameworks, or DOGMATISM. The challenge to opponents of relativism is to develop a non-relativistic epistemology ('absolutism') which includes an acceptable account of RATIONALITY and rational justification, which is fallibilistic and non-dogmatic, which rejects any notion of a privileged framework in which knowledge-claims must be couched, and which is self-referentially coherent (see Siegel 1987, ch. 8; also TRANSCENDENTAL ARGUMENTS and PROBLEM OF THE CRITERION).

Contemporary versions of relativism occur in a wide variety of philosophical contexts and enjoy an equally wide variety of philosophical pedigrees. Chief among them are versions of relativism spawned by Wittgensteinian considerations concerning language use, conceptual schemes or frameworks, and 'forms of life' (see here the essays in Wilson, 1970, and WITTGENSTEIN); proponents of the STRONG PROGRAMME in the sociology of knowledge (see here the paper by Barnes and Bloor, in Hollis and Lukes, 1982, and SOCIOLOGY OF KNOWLEDGE); a variety of quite different positions which might be grouped together under the heading of 'contemporary neo-Pragmatism' (e.g. Rorty, 1979, 1982; see DEATH OF EPISTEMOLOGY; Goodman, 1978; Putnam, 1981); and, perhaps most surprisingly, recent work in philosophy of science (Kuhn, 1970; Feyerabend, 1975). These and other contemporary versions of relativism make clear that the doctrine is alive and well, and is the subject of intense philosophical debate, as philosophers sympathetic to relativism attempt to develop versions of the doctrine which are immune to the standard criticisms. Of course, philosophers who are unsympathetic to the doctrine continue to press traditional and more recently developed objections to it. The current scene is then one in which interest in relativism remains high.

See also ONTOLOGICAL RELATIVITY; SUBJECTIVISM.

BIBLIOGRAPHY

Feyerabend, P.: *Against Method: Outline of an Anarchist Theory of Knowledge* (London: Verso, 1975).
Goodman, N.: *Ways of Worldmaking* (Indianapolis: Hackett, 1978).
Hollis, M. and Lukes, S. eds: *Rationality and Relativism* (Cambridge, MA: MIT Press, 1982).
Krausz, M. ed.: *Relativism: Interpretation and Confrontation* (Notre Dame: University of Notre Dame Press, 1989).
Kuhn, T.S.: *The Structure of Scientific Revolutions* 2nd edn (Chicago: University of Chicago Press, 1970).
Meiland, J.W. and Krausz, M. eds: *Relativism: Cognitive and Moral* (Notre Dame: University of Notre Dame Press, 1982).
Plato: *Theaetetus* trans. F.M. Cornford, in *The Collected Dialogues of Plato* eds E. Hamilton and H. Cairns (Bollingen Series, Pantheon Books, 1961), 845–919.
Putnam, H.: *Reason, Truth and History* (Cambridge: Cambridge University Press, 1981).
Rorty, R.: *Philosophy and the Mirror of Nature* (Princeton: Princeton University Press, 1979).
Rorty, R.: *Consequences of Pragmatism* (Minneapolis: University of Minnesota Press, 1982).
Siegel, H.: *Relativism Refuted: A Critique of Contemporary Epistemological Relativism* (Dordrecht: Reidel, 1987).
Wilson, B.R. ed.: *Rationality* (London: Blackwell, 1970).

HARVEY SIEGEL

**relevant alternatives** The theory of relevant alternatives is best viewed as an attempt to accommodate two opposing strands in our thinking about knowledge. The first is that knowledge is an *absolute* concept. On one interpretation, this means that the justification or evidence one must have in order to know a proposition *p* must be sufficient to eliminate all the alternatives to *p* (where an alternative to a proposition *p* is a proposition incompatible with *p*). That is, one's justification or evidence for *p* must be sufficient for one to know that every alternative to *p* is false. This element of our thinking about knowledge is exploited by sceptical arguments. These arguments call our attention to alternatives that our evidence can not eliminate. For example (Dretske, 1970), when we are at the zoo, we might claim to know that we see a zebra on the basis of certain visual evidence, viz. a zebra-like appearance. The sceptic inquires how we know that we are not seeing a cleverly disguised mule. While we do have some evidence against the likelihood of such a deception, intuitively it is not strong enough for us to *know* that we are not so deceived. By pointing out alternatives of this nature that we cannot eliminate, as well as others with more general application (dreams, hallucinations, etc.), the sceptic appears to show that this requirement that our evidence eliminate every alternative is seldom, if ever, satisfied (*see* SCEPTICISM).

This conclusion conflicts with another strand in our thinking about knowledge, viz. that we know many things. Thus there is a tension in our ordinary thinking about knowledge – we believe that knowledge is, in the sense indicated, an absolute concept and yet we also believe that there are many instances of that concept.

There would seem to be two options for removing this tension, each involving the denial of one of the components on the basis of the other. If one finds absoluteness to be too central a component of our concept of knowledge to be relinquished, one could argue from the absolute character of knowledge to a sceptical conclusion (Unger, 1975). Most philosophers, however, have taken the other course, choosing to respond to the conflict by giving up, perhaps reluctantly, the absoluteness criterion. This latter response holds as sacrosanct our commonsense belief that we know many things (Pollock, 1979; Chisholm, 1977). Each approach is subject to the criticism that it preserves one aspect of our ordinary thinking about knowledge at the expense of denying another (*see* CHISHOLM; COMMONSENSISM AND CRITICAL COGNITIVISM).

The theory of relevant alternatives can be viewed as an attempt to provide a more satisfactory response to this tension in our thinking about knowledge. It attempts to characterize knowledge in a way that preserves both our belief that knowledge is an absolute concept and our belief that we have knowledge.

According to the theory, we need to qualify rather than deny the absolute character of knowledge. We should view knowledge as absolute, relative to a certain standard (Dretske, 1981; Cohen, 1988). That is to say, in order to know a proposition, our evidence need not eliminate all the alternatives to that proposition. Rather we can know when our evidence eliminates all the *relevant* alternatives, where the set of relevant alternatives (a proper subset of the set of all alternatives) is determined by some standard. Moreover, according to the relevant alternatives view, the standards determine that the alternatives raised by the sceptic are not relevant. If this is correct, then the fact that our evidence can not eliminate the sceptic's alternatives does not lead to a sceptical result. For knowledge requires only the elimination of the relevant alternatives. So the relevant alternatives view preserves both strands in our thinking about knowledge. Knowledge is an absolute concept, but because the absoluteness is relative to a standard, we can know many things.

The relevant alternatives account of knowledge can be motivated by noting that other concepts exhibit the same logical structure. Two examples of this are the concept *flat* and the concept *empty* (Dretske, 1981). Both appear to be absolute concepts – a space is empty only if it does not contain anything and a surface is flat only if it does not have any bumps. However, the absolute character of these concepts is relative to a standard. In the case of *flat*, there is a standard for what counts as a bump and in the case of *empty*, there is a standard for what counts as a thing. We would not deny that a table is flat because a microscope reveals irregularities in its surface. Nor would we deny that a warehouse is empty because it contains particles of dust. To be flat is to be free of any relevant bumps. To be empty is to be devoid of all relevant things. Analogously, the relevant alternatives theory says that to know a proposition is (*inter alia*) to have evidence that eliminates all relevant alternatives.

Some philosophers (Dretske, 1970) have argued that the relevant alternatives theory of knowledge entails the falsity of the principle that the set of known (by S) propositions is closed under known (by S) entailment; although others have disputed this (Stine, 1976; Cohen, 1988). This principle affirms the following conditional (the *closure principle*):

If S knows *p* and S knows that *p* entails *q*, then S knows *q*.

According to the theory of relevant alternatives, we can know a proposition *p*, without knowing that some (non-relevant) alternative to *p* is false. But since an alternative *h* to *p* is incompatible with *p*, then *p* will trivially entail not-*h*. So it will be possible to know some proposition without knowing another proposition trivially entailed by it. For example, we can know that we see a zebra without knowing that it is not the case that we see a cleverly disguised mule (on the assumption that 'we see a cleverly disguised mule' is not a relevant alternative). This will involve a violation of the closure principle. This is an interesting consequence of the theory because the closure principle seems to many to be quite intuitive. In fact, we can view sceptical arguments as employing the closure principle as a premiss, along with the premiss that we do not know that the alternatives raised by the sceptic are false. From these two premisses, it follows (on the assumption that we see that the propositions we believe entail the falsity of sceptical alternatives) that we do not know the propositions we believe. For example, it follows from the closure principle and the fact that we do not know that we do not see a cleverly disguised mule, that we do not know that we see a zebra. We can view the relevant alternatives theory as replying to the sceptical arguments by denying the closure principle.

What makes an alternative relevant? What standard do the alternatives raised by the sceptic fail to meet? These questions have been notoriously difficult to answer with any degree of precision or generality. This dif-

ficulty has led critics to view the theory as *ad hoc* or obscure (Sosa, 1988). The problem can be illustrated through an example (Goldman, 1976). Suppose Smith sees a barn and believes that he does, on the basis of very good perceptual evidence. When is the alternative that Smith sees a papier-mâché replica relevant? If there are many such replicas in the immediate area, then this alternative can be relevant. In these circumstances, Smith fails to know that he sees a barn unless he knows that it is not the case that he sees a barn replica. Where no such replicas exist, this alternative will not be relevant (*ceteris paribus*). Smith can know that he sees a barn without knowing that he does not see a barn replica.

This suggests that a criterion of relevance is something like probability conditional on Smith's evidence and certain features of the circumstances. But which circumstances in particular do we count? Consider a case where we want the result that the barn replica alternative is clearly relevant, e.g. a case where the circumstances are such that there are numerous barn replicas in the area. Does the suggested criterion give us the result we wanted? The probability that Smith sees a barn replica given his evidence and his location in an area where there are many barn replicas is high. However, that same probability conditional on his evidence and his particular visual orientation toward a real barn is quite low. We want the probability to be conditional on features of the circumstances like the former but not on features of the circumstances like the latter. But how do we capture the difference in a general formulation?

How significant a problem is this for the theory of relevant alternatives? This depends on how we construe the theory. If the theory is supposed to provide us with an analysis of knowledge, then the lack of precise criteria of relevance surely constitutes a serious problem. However, if the theory is viewed instead as providing a response to sceptical arguments, then it can be argued that the difficulty has little significance for the overall success of the theory (Cohen, 1988; forthcoming).

See also CAUSAL THEORIES IN EPISTEM-
OLOGY; GETTIER PROBLEM; RELIABILISM.

BIBLIOGRAPHY

Chisholm, R.M.: *Theory of Knowledge* 2nd edn
(Englewood Cliffs: Prentice-Hall, 1977).
Cohen, S.: 'How to be a fallibilist', *Philosophical
Perspectives* 2 (1988), 91–123.
Cohen, S.: 'Scepticism, relevance, and relativ-
ity', in *Critical Essays on the Philosophy of Fred
Dretske* ed. B. McGlaughlin (Oxford: forth-
coming).
Dretske, F.: 'Epistemic operators', *Journal of
Philosophy* 69 (1970), 1007–23.
Dretske, F.: 'The pragmatic dimension of knowl-
edge', *Philosophical Studies* 40 (1981), 363–
78.
Goldman, A.: 'Discrimination and perceptual
knowledge', *Journal of Philosophy* 73 (1976),
771–91.
Pollock, J.: *Knowledge and Justification* (Princeton: Princeton University Press, 1974).
Sosa, E.: 'Knowledge in context, scepticism in
doubt', *Philosophical Perspectives* 2 (1988),
139–56.
Stine, G.C.: 'Scepticism, relevant alternatives,
and deductive closure', *Philosophical Studies*
29 (1976), 249–61.
Unger, P.: *Ignorance* (Oxford: Clarendon Press,
1975).

STEWART COHEN

**reliabilism** The view that a belief acquires
favourable epistemic status by having some
kind of reliable linkage to the truth. Variations of this view have been advanced for
both knowledge and justified belief. The first
formulation of a reliability account of
knowing appeared in a note by F.P. Ramsey
(1931), who said that a belief is knowledge if
it is true, certain and obtained by a reliable
process. P. Unger (1968) suggested that S
knows that *p* just in case it is not at all
accidental that S is right about its being the
case that *p*. D.M. Armstrong (1973) drew an
analogy between a thermometer that reliably
indicates the temperature and a belief that
reliably indicates the truth. Armstrong said
that a non-inferential belief qualifies as
knowledge if the belief has properties that are
nomically sufficient for its truth, i.e. guarantee its truth via laws of nature.

Closely allied to the nomic sufficiency
account is the counterfactual or subjunctive
account of knowledge, primarily due to F.I.
Dretske (1971, 1981), A.I. Goldman (1976,
1986) and R. Nozick (1981). The core of this
approach is that S's belief that *p* qualifies as
knowledge just in case S believes *p* because of
reasons that would not obtain unless *p* were
true, or because of a process or method that
would not yield belief in *p* if *p* were not true.
For example, S would not have his current
reasons for believing there is a telephone
before him, or would not come to believe this
in the way he does, unless there *were* a telephone before him. Thus, there is a counterfactually reliable guarantor of the belief's
being true. A variant of the counterfactual
approach says that S knows that *p* only if
there is no 'relevant alternative' situation in
which *p* is false but S would still believe that
*p* (*see* RELEVANT ALTERNATIVES).

Reliabilism is standardly classified as an
'externalist' theory because it invokes some
truth-linked factor, and truth is 'external' to
the believer (*see* EXTERNALISM/INTER-
NALISM). Virtually all theories of knowledge, of course, share an externalist component in requiring truth as a condition for
knowing. Reliabilism goes further, however,
in trying to capture additional conditions for
knowledge by means of a nomic, counterfactual or other such 'external' relation between
belief and truth.

Among reliabilist theories of justification
(as opposed to knowledge) there are two
main varieties: reliable indicator theories and
reliable process theories. In their simplest
forms, the reliable indicator theory says that
a belief is justified in case it is based on
reasons that are reliable indicators of the
truth (Swain, 1981), and the reliable process
theory says that a belief is justified in case it
is produced by cognitive processes that are
generally reliable (Goldman, 1979; Talbott,
1990). The latter approach has been more
influential, and will be examined here in
some detail.

The reliable process theory is grounded on
two main points. First, the justificational

433

status of a belief depends on the psychological processes that cause (or causally sustain) it, not simply on the logical status of the proposition, or its evidential relation to other propositions. Even a tautology can be believed unjustifiably if one arrives at that belief through inappropriate psychological processes. Similarly, a detective might have a body of evidence supporting the hypothesis that Jones is guilty. But if the detective fails to put the pieces of evidence together, and instead believes in Jones's guilt only because of his unsavoury appearance, the detective's belief is unjustified. The critical determinants of justificational status, then, are psychological processes, i.e. belief-forming or belief-preserving processes such as perception, memory, reasoning, guessing, or introspecting. Process reliabilism is a species of causal theory (see CAUSAL THEORIES IN EPISTEMOLOGY). The causation in question, however, is 'beneath the skin'. In this respect process reliabilism is not externalist, since it focuses on 'inner' processes.

Clearly not all psychological processes are justification-conferring. What distinguishes justificational processes from the rest, according to reliabilism, is their truth ratio. 'Good' processes are ones whose belief outputs have a high ratio of truths; 'bad' processes are those with a low truth ratio. A belief's justificational status is a function of the truth-ratio of the type of process, or series of processes, that are causally responsible for it. Since a belief may result from an extended history of mental processes, this form of reliabilism is sometimes called 'historical reliabilism'.

One might wonder whether de facto ancestry and reliability are sufficient to confer justification. Doesn't the agent have to know the history, and know that those processes are reliable? Or doesn't he have to be 'in a position' to know these things (or at least believe them reliably)? The reliabilist replies that an added requirement of this sort is inappropriate. People do not generally keep a mental diary of their beliefs' ancestries, nor are they always in a position to reconstruct such ancestries. This does not prevent these beliefs from being justified. Of course, an agent who lacks such a reconstruction does not have second-level knowledge or justification: he does not know, or justifiably believe, that his belief is justified. But it does not follow that the original belief is unjustified. That conclusion would involve a 'level confusion', a confusion between a belief's being justified (first-level justification) and a person's being justified in believing that it is justified (second-level justification).

None the less, reliabilists often agree that some kind of strengthening of the simple reliability requirement is needed. Suppose that a given process is reliable, but the agent has decisive (though misleading) evidence for its unreliability. For example, he might have evidence that his vision has been tampered with by a brain surgeon. If he still relies on vision, is the resulting belief justified? Intuitively no; but the simple reliability theory implies otherwise. This leads some reliabilists, e.g. Goldman (1986), to strengthen the theory with a 'non-undermining' condition. This condition requires that the agent not believe that the generating process is unreliable, and not be in any mental state (such as the possession of relevant evidence) from which reliable processes would lead him to conclude that the generating process is unreliable.

Even so modified, reliabilism faces at least four main problems: two concerning points of clarification and two involving counterexamples. The issues of clarification concern (A) the 'generality problem' and (B) the range of reliability. A particular belief is produced by a process token, but that token may be an instance of many process types. Different types, moreover, have different truth ratios. Which type fixes a belief's justifiedness (see Feldman, 1985)? If the types are chosen too broadly (e.g. 'perceiving' or 'inferring'), an unjustified belief may be deemed justified. If types are chosen too narrowly, they may have only one actual instance, viz. the process token in question. In this 'single case' situation, the process type has a truth ratio of either 1 or 0, depending on whether the belief is true or false. This implies that the belief is justified if and only if it is true, which seems wrong. The single case problem is also related to problem (B), the range question. Is a process's reliability the truth ratio it exhibits in the actual world, or should we consider how it would fare in other possible worlds as well?

The most influential counterexamples to reliabilism are the demon-world and the clairvoyance examples. The demon-world example challenges the necessity of the reliability requirement. In a possible world in which an evil demon creates deceptive visual experience, the process of vision is not reliable. Still, the visually formed beliefs in this world are intuitively justified. The clairvoyance example challenges the sufficiency of reliability. Suppose a cognitive agent possesses a reliable clairvoyance power, but has no evidence for or against his possessing such a power. Intuitively, his clairvoyantly formed beliefs are unjustified, but reliabilism declares them justified.

Returning to the generality problem, one proposal is that the relevant process type is the narrowest that is causally operative in producing the belief in question. It is not clear, however, whether this yields intuitively correct classifications. Concerning the 'range' problem, the prospects seem brighter with a propensity construal of the truth ratio rather than a strict frequency construal, letting the process's performance in nearby possible worlds as well as the actual world be relevant. Among other things, this would avert the problem of the 'single case'.

Another form of reliabilism, 'normal worlds' reliabilism (Goldman, 1986), answers the range problem differently, and treats the demon-world problem in the same stroke. Let a 'normal world' be one that is consistent with our general beliefs about the actual world. Normal-worlds reliabilism says that a belief (in any possible world) is justified just in case its generating processes have high truth ratios in normal worlds. This resolves the demon-world problem because the relevant truth ratio of the visual process is not its truth ratio in the demon world itself, but its ratio in normal worlds. Since this ratio is presumably high, visually formed beliefs in the demon world turn out to be justified.

Yet a different version of reliabilism attempts to meet the demon-world and clairvoyance problems without recourse to the questionable notion of 'normal worlds'. Consider Sosa's (1992) suggestion that justified belief is belief acquired through 'intellectual virtues' (and not through intellectual 'vices'), where virtues are reliable cognitive faculties or processes. The task is to explain how the notion of intellectual virtues (and vices) is used by epistemic evaluators to arrive at their judgements, especially in the problematic cases. Goldman (1992) proposes a two-stage reconstruction of an evaluator's activity. The first stage is a reliability-based acquisition of a 'list' of virtues and vices. The second stage is application of this list to queried cases. The second stage is executed by determining whether processes in the queried cases resemble virtues or vices. Visual beliefs in the demon world are classified as justified because visual belief formation is one of the virtues. Clairvoyantly formed beliefs are classified as unjustified because clairvoyance resembles scientifically suspect processes that the evaluator represents as vices (e.g. mental telepathy, ESP, and so forth).

Clearly, there are many forms of reliabilism, just as there are many forms of FOUNDATIONALISM and COHERENTISM. How is reliabilism related to these other two theories of justification? It is usually regarded as a rival, and this is apt in so far as foundationalism and coherentism traditionally focused on purely evidential relations rather than psychological processes. But reliabilism might also be offered as a deeper-level theory, subsuming some of the precepts of either foundationalism or coherentism. Foundationalism says that there are 'basic' beliefs, which acquire justification without dependence on inference. Reliabilism might rationalize this by indicating that the basic beliefs are formed by reliable non-inferential processes. Coherentism stresses the primacy of systematicity in all doxastic decision-making. Reliabilism might rationalize this by pointing to increases in reliability that accrue from systematicity. Thus, reliabilism could complement foundationalism and coherentism rather than compete with them.

*See also* CAUSAL THEORIES IN EPISTEMOLOGY; EPISTEMOLOGY NATURALIZED; EXTERNALISM/INTERNALISM.

BIBLIOGRAPHY

Armstrong, D.M.: *Belief, Truth and Knowledge* (Cambridge: Cambridge University Press, 1973).

Dretske, F.: 'Conclusive reasons', *Australasian Journal of Philosophy* 49 (1971), 1–22.

Dretske, F.: *Knowledge and the Flow of Information* (Cambridge, MA: MIT Press, 1981).

Feldman, R.: 'Reliability and justification', *The Monist* 68 (1985), 159–74.

Goldman, A.I.: 'Discrimination and perceptual knowledge', *Journal of Philosophy* 73 (1976), 771–91.

Goldman, A. I.: 'What is justified belief?', in *Justification and Knowledge* ed. G. Pappas (Dordrecht: Reidel, 1979).

Goldman, A.I.: *Epistemology and Cognition* (Cambridge, MA: Harvard University Press, 1986).

Goldman, A.I.: 'Epistemic folkways and scientific epistemology', in *Liaisons: Philosophy Meets the Cognitive and Social Sciences* (Cambridge, MA: MIT Press, 1992).

Nozick, R.: *Philosophical Explanations* (Cambridge, MA: Harvard University Press, 1981).

Ramsey, F.P.: 'Knowledge', in his *The Foundations of Mathematics and Other Essays* ed. R.B. Braithwaite (New York: Harcourt Brace, 1931).

Sosa, E.: *Knowledge in Perspective* (Cambridge: Cambridge University Press, 1991).

Swain, M.: *Reasons and Knowledge* (Ithaca, NY: Cornell University Press, 1981).

Talbott, W.J.: *The Reliability of the Cognitive Mechanism* (New York: Garland Publishing, 1990).

Unger, P.: 'An analysis of factual knowledge', *Journal of Philosophy* 65 (1968), 157–70.

ALVIN I. GOLDMAN

**religious belief, epistemology of**  At least two large sets of questions are properly treated under this heading. First, there is a set of broadly theological questions about the relationship between faith and reason, between what one knows by way of reason, broadly construed, and what one knows by way of faith. I call these questions *theological*, because, of course, one will find them of interest only if one thinks that in fact there *is* such a thing as faith, and that we do know something by way of it. Secondly, there is a whole set of questions having to do with whether and to what degree religious beliefs have *warrant*, or *justification*, or *positive epistemic status*. I shall concentrate upon the second of these two sets of questions.

Epistemology, so we are told, is *theory of knowledge*; its aim is to discern and explain that quality or quantity enough of which distinguishes knowledge from mere true belief. We need a name for this quality or quantity, whatever precisely it is: call it 'warrant'. From this point of view, the epistemology of religious belief should centre on the question whether religious belief has warrant, and if it does, how much it has and how it gets it. As a matter of fact, however, epistemological discussion of religious belief, at least since the Enlightenment (and in the Western world, especially the English-speaking Western world) has tended to focus, not on the question whether religious belief has *warrant*, but whether it is *justified*. More precisely, it has tended to focus on the question whether those properties are enjoyed by *theistic belief* – the belief that there exists a person like the God of traditional Christianity, Judaism and Islam: an almighty, all-knowing, wholly benevolent and loving spiritual person who has created the world. The chief question, therefore, has been whether theistic belief is justified; the same question is often put by asking whether theistic belief is *rational* or rationally acceptable. Still further, the typical way of addressing this question has been by way of discussing *arguments* for and against the existence of God. On the pro side, there are the traditional theistic proofs or arguments: the ontological, cosmological and teleological arguments, to use Kant's terms for them. On the other side, the antitheistic side, the principal argument is the argument from evil, the argument that it is not possible or at least not probable that there be such a person as God, given all the pain, suffering and evil the world displays. This argument is flanked by subsidiary arguments, such as the claim that the very concept of God is incoherent (because, for example, it is impossible that there be a person without a body), and Freudian and Marxist claims that religious belief arises out of a sort of magnification and projection into the heavens of human attributes we think important.

But why has discussion centred on *justification* rather than warrant? And precisely what is justification? And why has the discussion of the justification of theistic belief focused so heavily on arguments for and against the existence of God?

As to the first question, we can see why once we see that the dominant epistemological tradition in modern Western philosophy has tended to *identify* warrant with justification. On this way of looking at the matter, warrant, that which distinguishes knowledge from mere true belief, just *is* justification. Indeed, until recently the 'Justified True Belief' theory of knowledge – the theory according to which knowledge is justified true belief – has enjoyed the status of orthodoxy. According to this view, knowledge is justified true belief; therefore any of your beliefs has warrant for you if and only if you are justified in holding it.

But what *is* justification? What is it to be justified in holding a belief? To get a proper sense of the answer, we must turn to those twin towers of western epistemology, René DESCARTES and (especially) John LOCKE. The first thing to see is that according to Descartes and Locke, there are *epistemic* or intellectual *duties*, or obligations, or requirements. Thus Locke:

Faith is nothing but a firm assent of the mind: which if it be regulated, as is our duty, cannot be afforded to anything, but upon good reason; and so cannot be opposite to it. He that believes, without having any reason for believing, may be in love with his own fancies; but neither seeks truth as he ought, nor pays the obedience due his maker, who would have him use those discerning faculties he has given him, to keep him out of mistake and error. He that does not this to the best of his power, however he

sometimes lights on truth, is in the right but by chance; and I know not whether the luckiness of the accident will excuse the irregularity of his proceeding. This at least is certain, that he must be accountable for whatever mistakes he runs into: whereas he that makes use of the light and faculties God has given him, and seeks sincerely to discover truth, by those helps and abilities he has, may have this satisfaction in doing his duty as a rational creature, that though he should miss truth, he will not miss the reward of it. For he governs his assent right, and places it as he should, who in any case or matter whatsoever, believes or disbelieves, according as reason directs him. He that does otherwise, transgresses against his own light, and misuses those faculties, which were given him . . . (*Essay* 4.17.24)

Rational creatures, creatures with reason, creatures capable of *believing* propositions (and of disbelieving and being agnostic with respect to them), says Locke, have duties and obligations with respect to the regulation of their belief or assent. Now the central core of the notion of justification (as the etymology of the term indicates) is this: one is justified in doing something or in behaving a certain way, if in so doing one is innocent of wrongdoing and hence not properly subject to blame or censure. You are justified, therefore, if you have violated no duties or obligations, if you have conformed to the relevant requirements, if you are within your rights. To be justified in *believing* something, then, is to be within your rights in so believing, to be doing no wrong in believing in this way, to be flouting no duty, to be satisfying your epistemic duties and obligations. This way of thinking of justification has been the dominant way of thinking about justification; and this way of thinking has many important contemporary representatives. Roderick CHISHOLM, for example (as distinguished an epistemologist as the twentieth century can boast), in his earlier work explicitly explains justification in terms of epistemic duty (Chisholm, 1977, p. 14; 1982, p. 7).

437

The (or a) main epistemological question about religious belief, therefore, has been the question whether or not religious belief in general and theistic belief in particular is justified. And the traditional way to answer that question has been to inquire into the *arguments* for and against theism. Why this emphasis upon these arguments? An argument is a way of marshalling your *propositional evidence* – the evidence from other propositions you believe – for or against a given proposition. And the reason for the emphasis upon argument is the assumption that theistic belief is justified if and only if there is sufficient propositional evidence for it. If there isn't much by way of propositional evidence for theism, then you are not justified in accepting it. More exactly, if you accept theistic belief without having propositional evidence for it, then you are going contrary to epistemic duty and are therefore unjustified in accepting it. Thus W.K. Clifford (that 'delicious *enfant terrible*', as William James calls him) trumpets that 'it is wrong, always, everywhere, and for anyone to believe anything upon insufficient evidence'; his is only the most strident in a vast chorus of voices insisting that there is an intellectual duty not to believe in God unless you have propositional evidence for that belief. (A few others in the choir: Sigmund Freud, Brand Blanshard, H.H. Price, Bertrand Russell and Michael Scriven.)

Now how is it that the *justification* of theistic belief gets identified with there being *propositional evidence* for it? Justification is a matter of being blameless, of having done one's duty (in this context, one's epistemic duty); what, precisely, has this to do with having propositional evidence?

The answer, again, is to be found in Descartes and especially Locke. Justification is the property your beliefs have when, in forming and holding them, you conform to your epistemic duties and obligations. But according to Locke, a central epistemic duty is this: *to believe a proposition only to the degree that it is probable with respect to what is certain for you.* What propositions are certain for you? First (according to Descartes and Locke), propositions about your own imme-

diate experience: that you have a mild headache, or that it seems to you that you see something red; and second, propositions that are self-evident for you: necessarily true propositions so obvious that you can't so much as entertain them without seeing that they must be true. (Examples would be simple arithmetical and logical propositions, together with such propositions as that the whole is at least as large as the part, that red is a colour, and that whatever exists has properties.) Propositions of these two sorts are certain for you; as for other propositions, you are justified in believing one of them only to the degree to which it is probable with respect to what is certain for you. According to Locke, therefore, and according to the whole modern FOUNDATIONALIST tradition initiated by Locke and Descartes (a tradition that until recently has dominated Western thinking about these topics) there is a duty not to accept a proposition unless it is certain or probable with respect to what is certain.

In the present context, therefore, the central Lockean assumption is that there is an epistemic duty not to accept theistic belief unless it is probable with respect to what is certain for you; as a consequence, theistic belief is justified only if the existence of God is probable with respect to what is certain. Locke doesn't *argue* for this proposition; he simply *announces* it; and epistemological discussion of theistic belief has for the most part followed him in making this assumption. This enables us to see why epistemological discussion of theistic belief has tended to focus on the arguments for and against theism: on the view in question, theistic belief is justified only if it is probable with respect to what is certain; and the way to show that it is probable with respect to what is certain is to give arguments for it from premises that are certain (or are sufficiently probable with respect to what is certain).

There are at least three important problems with this approach to the epistemology of theistic belief. First, the standards for theistic arguments have traditionally been set absurdly high (and perhaps part of the responsibility for this must be laid at the door of some who have offered these arguments and claimed that they constitute wholly demonstrative proofs). The idea seems to be that a good theistic argument must start from what is self-evident and proceed majestically by way of self-evidently valid argument forms to its conclusion. It is no wonder that few if any theistic arguments meet *that* lofty standard – particularly in view of the fact that almost no philosophical arguments of *any* sort meet it. (Think of your favourite philosophical argument; does it really start from premises that are self-evident and move by way of self-evident argument forms to its conclusion?)

Secondly, attention has been mostly confined to three theistic arguments: the traditional ontological, cosmological and teleological arguments, to use Kant's classification. But in fact there are many more good arguments: arguments from the nature of proper function, and from the nature of propositions, numbers and sets. There are arguments from intentionality, from counterfactuals, from the confluence of epistemic reliability with epistemic justification, from reference, simplicity, intuition and love. There are arguments from colours and flavours, from miracles, play and enjoyment, morality, from beauty, and from the meaning of life. There is even a theistic argument from the existence of evil.

But there is a third and deeper problem here. The basic assumption is that theistic belief is justified only if it is or can be shown to be probable with respect to some body of evidence or propositions – perhaps those that are self-evident or about one's own mental life, as Locke thought. But is this assumption true? The idea is that theistic belief is very much like a *scientific hypothesis*: it is acceptable if and only if there is an appropriate balance of propositional evidence in favour of it. But why believe a thing like that? Perhaps the theory of relativity or the theory of evolution is like that: such a theory has been devised to explain the phenomena and gets all its warrant from its success in so doing. But other beliefs – e.g. MEMORY beliefs, belief in OTHER MINDS – are not like that; they aren't hypotheses at all, and are not

accepted because of their explanatory powers. They are instead the propositions from which one starts in attempting to give evidence for a hypothesis. Now why assume that theistic belief, belief in God, is in this regard more like a scientific hypothesis than like, say, a memory belief? Why think that the justification of theistic belief depends upon the evidential relation of theistic belief to other things one believes? According to Locke and the beginning of this tradition, it is because there is a duty not to assent to a proposition unless it is probable with respect to what is certain to you; but is there really any such duty? No one has succeeded in showing that, say, belief in other minds or the belief that there has been a past, is probable with respect to what is certain for us. Suppose it isn't: does it follow that you are living in epistemic sin if you believe that there are other minds? Or a past?

There are urgent questions about any view according to which one has duties of the sort *don't believe p unless it is probable with respect to what is certain for you.* First, if this is a duty, is it one to which I can conform? My beliefs are for the most part not within my control: certainly they are not within my direct control. I believe that there has been a past and that there are other people; even if these beliefs are not probable with respect to what is certain for me (and even if I came to know this) I couldn't give them up. Whether or not I accept such beliefs isn't really up to me at all; I can no more refrain from believing these things than I can refrain from conforming to the law of gravity. Second, is there really any reason for thinking I *have* such a duty? Nearly everyone recognizes such duties as that of not engaging in gratuitous cruelty, taking care of one's children and one's aged parents, and the like; but do we also find ourselves recognizing that there is a duty not to believe what isn't probable (or what we can't see to be probable) with respect to what is certain for us? It hardly seems so. But if so, it is hard to see why being justified in believing in God requires that the existence of God be probable with respect to some such body of evidence as the set of propositions certain for you. Perhaps theistic belief is *properly basic*, i.e.

such that one is perfectly justified in accepting it without accepting it on the evidential basis of other propositions one believes.

Taking *justification* in that original etymological fashion, therefore, there is every reason to doubt that one is justified in holding theistic belief only if one has evidence for it. Of course, the term 'justification' has undergone various analogical extensions in the work of various philosophers; it has been used to name various properties that are different from justification etymologically so-called, but analogically related to it. Thus the term is sometimes used just to mean propositional EVIDENCE: to say that a belief is justified for someone is to say that he has propositional evidence (or sufficient propositional evidence) for it. So taken, however, the question whether theistic belief is justified loses some of its interest; for it isn't clear (given this use) that there is anything amiss with holding beliefs that are unjustified in *that* sense. Perhaps one also doesn't have propositional evidence for one's memory beliefs; if so, that would not be a mark against them and would not suggest that there is something wrong with holding them.

Another analogically connected way to think about justification (a way endorsed by the later Chisholm) is to think of it as simply a *relation of fittingness* between a given proposition and one's epistemic base – which includes the other things one believes, as well as one's experience. Perhaps that is the way justification is to be thought of; but then it is no longer at all obvious that theistic belief has this property of justification only if it is probable with respect to some body of evidence. Perhaps, again, it is like memory beliefs in this regard.

To recapitulate: the dominant Western tradition has been inclined to identify warrant with justification; it has been inclined to take the latter in terms of duty and the fulfillment of obligation, and hence to suppose that there is an epistemic duty not to believe in God unless you have good propositional evidence for the existence of God. Epistemological discussion of theistic belief, as a consequence, has concentrated upon the propositional evidence for and against theistic belief – i.e. on arguments for and against theistic belief. But there is excellent reason to doubt that there are epistemic duties of the sort the tradition appeals to here.

And perhaps it was a mistake to identify warrant with justification in the first place. The beliefs of a madman who thinks he is Napoleon have little warrant for him; his problem, however, need not be dereliction of epistemic duty. He is in difficulty, but it is not or not necessarily that of failing to fulfill epistemic duty. He may be doing his epistemic best; he may be doing his epistemic duty *in excelsis*; but his madness prevents his beliefs from having much by way of warrant. His lack of warrant is not a matter of being unjustified, i.e., failing to fulfill epistemic duty. So warrant and *being epistemically justified* are by no means the same thing. Another example: suppose (to use the favourite twentieth-century variant of Descartes' evil demon example) I have been captured by Alpha-Centaurian super-scientists; running a cognitive experiment, they remove my brain, keep it alive in a vat of artificial nutrients, and by virtue of their advanced technology induce in me the beliefs I might otherwise have if I were going about my usual business. Then my beliefs would not have much by way of warrant; but would it be because I was failing to do my epistemic duty? Hardly.

As a result of these and other problems, another, *externalist* way of thinking about knowledge has appeared in recent epistemology (*see* EXTERNALISM/INTERNALISM). Or perhaps the thing to say is that it has reappeared; for the dominant strains in epistemology prior to the Enlightenment were really externalist. According to this externalist way of thinking, warrant does not depend upon satisfaction of duty, or upon anything else to which the knower has special cognitive access (as he does to what is about his own experience and to whether he is trying his best to do his epistemic duty); it depends instead upon factors 'external' to the epistemic agent – such factors as whether his beliefs are produced by a reliable cognitive mechanism, or whether they are produced by epistemic faculties functioning properly in an appropriate epistemic environment.

How shall we think about the epistemology of theistic belief in this more externalist way (which is at once both satisfyingly traditional and agreeably up to date)? The chief thing to see here, I think, is that the *ontological* question whether there is such a person as God is in a way prior to the *epistemological* question about the warrant of theistic belief. It is natural to think that if in fact we *have* been created by God, then the cognitive processes that issue in belief in God are indeed reliable belief-producing processes; if in fact God has created us, then no doubt the cognitive faculties that produce belief in God are functioning properly in an epistemically congenial environment. On the other hand, if there isn't any such person as God, if theistic belief is an illusion of some sort, then things are much less clear. Then belief in God in the basic way will no doubt be produced by wishful thinking or some other cognitive process not aimed at truth; thus it will have little or no warrant. And belief in God on the basis of argument would be like belief in false philosophical theories on the basis of argument: do such beliefs have warrant? More exactly, would they have warrant if the externalist views of warrant I mentioned above are true? It isn't easy to say.

In any event, the usual custom of discussing the epistemological questions about theistic belief as if they could be profitably discussed independently of the ontological issue as to whether or not theism is true, is misguided. These two issues are intimately intertwined.

*See also* BELIEF IN AND BELIEF THAT; EPISTEMIC VIRTUES; ETHICS AND EPISTEMOLOGY; VIRTUE EPISTEMOLOGY.

BIBLIOGRAPHY

Alston, William P.: *Perceiving God* (Ithaca, NY: Cornell University Press, 1992).
Blanshard, Brand: *Reason and Belief* (London: Allen and Unwin, 1974).
Chisholm, Roderick: *Theory of Knowledge* (New York: Prentice-Hall, 1st edn 1966 2nd edn 1977).
Chisholm, Roderick: *The Foundations of Knowing* (Minneapolis: University of Minnesota Press, 1982).
Clifford, William K.: 'The ethics of belief', in *Lectures and Essays* (London: Macmillan, 1879).
Freud, Sigmund: *The Future of an Illusion* (New York, W.W. Norton & Co. 1961; first German edn 1927).
Mackie, John: *The Miracle of Theism* (Oxford: Oxford University Press, 1982).
Mavrodes, George: *Belief in God; a Study in the Epistemology of Religion* (New York: Random House, 1970).
Plantinga, A. and N. Wolterstorff eds: *Faith and Rationality* (Notre Dame: University of Notre Dame Press, 1983).
Price, Henry H.: *Belief* (London: George Allen & Unwin, 1969).
Russell, Bertrand: *A History of Western Philosophy* (New York: Simon & Schuster, 1945).
Scriven, Michael: *Primary Philosophy* (New York: McGraw-Hill, 1966).

ALVIN PLANTINGA

## representation

### TERMINOLOGY

*Representation*   Contemporary philosophy of mind, following cognitive science, uses the term 'representation' to mean just about anything that can be semantically evaluated. Thus, representations may be said to be true, to refer, to be true-of something, to be about something, to be accurate, etc. Representation thus conceived comes in many varieties. The most familiar are pictures, three-dimensional models (e.g. statues, scale models), linguistic text (including mathematical formulas) and various hybrids of these such as diagrams, maps, graphs and tables. It is an open question in cognitive science whether mental representation, which is our real topic here, falls within any of these familiar sorts.

*Content*   'Content' has become a technical term in philosophy for whatever it is a representation has that makes it semantically evaluable. Thus, a statement is sometimes said to have a proposition or truth condition as its content; a term is sometimes said to have a concept as its content. Much less is known about how to characterize the contents of non-linguistic representations than is known about characterizing linguistic representations. 'Content' is a useful term precisely because it allows one to abstract away from questions about what semantic properties representations have; a representation's content is just whatever it is that underwrites its semantic evaluation.

## REPRESENTATION AND THOUGHT

*The representational theory of cognition* It is uncontroversial in contemporary cognitive science that cognitive processes are processes that manipulate representations. This idea seems nearly inevitable. What makes the difference between processes that are cognitive – solving a problem, say – and those that are not – a patellar reflex, for example – is just that cognitive processes are epistemically assessable. A solution procedure can be justified or correct; a reflex cannot. Since only things with content can be epistemically assessed, processes appear to count as cognitive only in so far as they implicate representations.

It is tempting to think that thoughts are the mind's representations: Aren't thoughts just those mental states that have (semantic) content? This is, no doubt, harmless enough provided we keep in mind that cognitive science may attribute to thoughts properties and contents that are foreign to common-sense. First, most of the representations hypothesized by cognitive science do not correspond to anything common sense would recognize as thoughts. Standard psycholinguistic theory, for instance, hypothesizes the construction of representations of the syntactic structures of the utterances one hears and understands. Yet we are not aware of, and non-specialists do not even understand, the structures represented. Thus, cognitive science may attribute thoughts where common sense would not. Second, cognitive science may find it useful to individuate thoughts in ways foreign to common sense. (*See* the discussion of 'internalistic' theories of content below.)

*The representational theory of intentionality* The representational theory of cognition gives rise to a natural theory of intentional states such as believing, desiring and intending. According to this theory, intentional states factor into two aspects: a *functional* aspect that distinguishes believing from desiring and so on, and a *content* aspect that distinguishes beliefs from each other, desires from each other, and so on. A belief that $p$ might be realized as a representation with the content that $p$ and the function of serving as a premise in inference. A desire that $p$ might be realized as a representation with the content that $p$ and the function of initiating processing designed to bring it about that $p$ and terminating such processing when a belief that $p$ is formed.

## REPRESENTATION AND THE THEORY OF CONTENT

A great deal of philosophical effort has been lavished on the attempt to *naturalize content*, i.e. to explain in non-semantic, non-intentional terms what it is for something to be a representation (have content), and what it is for something to have some particular content rather than some other. There appear to be only four types of theory that have been proposed: theories that ground representation in (1) similarity, (2) covariance, (3) functional role, (4) teleology.

*Similarity theories* hold that r represents $x$ in virtue of being similar to $x$. This has seemed hopeless to most as a theory of mental representation because it appears to require that things in the brain must share properties with the things they represent: To represent a cat as furry appears to require something furry in the brain. Perhaps a notion of similarity that is naturalistic and does not involve property sharing can be worked out, but it is not obvious how.

*Covariance theories* hold that $r$'s representing $x$ is grounded in the fact that $r$'s occurrence covaries with that of $x$. This is most compelling when one thinks about detection systems: the firing a neural structure in the visual system is said to represent vertical orientations if its firing covaries with the occurrence of vertical lines in the visual field. Dretske (1981) and Fodor (1987) have, in different ways, attempted to promote this idea into a general theory of content.

*Functional role theories* hold that *r*'s representing *x* is grounded in the functional role *r* has in the representing system, i.e. on the relations imposed by specified cognitive processes between *r* and other representations in the system's repertoire. Functional role theories take their cue from such common-sense ideas as that people cannot believe that cats are furry if they do not know that cats are animals or that fur is like hair. For a defence of the functional role approach, *see* Block (1986), Loar (1982), and Harman (1982).

*Teleological theories* hold that *r* represents *x* if it is *r*'s function to indicate (i.e. covary with) *x*. Teleological theories differ depending on the theory of functions they import. Perhaps the most important distinction is that between historical theories of functions (Millikan, 1984; Papineau, 1988), and a-historical theories (Stampe, 1977; Fodor, 1987, 1990; Cummins, 1989). Historical theories individuate functional states (hence contents) in a way that is sensitive to the historical development of the state, i.e. to factors such as the way the state was 'learned', or the way it evolved. An historical theory might hold that the function of *r* is to indicate *x* only if the capacity to token *r* was developed (selected, learned) because it indicates *x*. Thus a state physically indistinguishable from *r* (physical states being a-historical) but lacking *r*'s historical origins would not represent *x* according to historical theories.

Theories of representational content may be classified according to whether they are atomistic or holistic and according to whether they are externalistic or internalistic. (*see* EXTERNALISM/INTERNALISM; HOLISM). Atomistic theories take a representation's content to be something that can be specified independently of that representation's relations to other representations. What Fodor (1987) calls the crude causal theory, for example, takes a representation to be a |cow| – a mental representation with the same content as the word 'cow' – if its tokens

are caused by instantiations of the property of being-a-cow, and this is a condition that places no explicit constraints on how |cow|'s must or might relate to other representations. Holistic theories contrast with atomistic theories in taking the relations a representation bears to others to be essential to its content. According to functional role theories, a representation is a |cow| if it behaves like a |cow| should behave in inference.

Internalist theories take the content of a representation to be a matter determined by factors internal to the system that uses it. Thus, what Block (1986) calls 'short-armed' functional role theories are internalist. Externalist theories take the content of a representation to be determined, in part at least, by factors external to the system that uses it. Covariance theories, as well as teleological theories that invoke an historical theory of functions, take content to be determined by 'external' factors. Crossing the atomist–holist distinction with the internalist–externalist distinction gives us the table below.

Externalist theories (sometimes called non-individualistic theories, following Burge, 1979) have the consequence that molecule for molecule identical cognitive systems might yet harbor representations with different contents (Putnam, 1975; Burge, 1979; Millikan, 1984). This has given rise to a controversy concerning 'narrow' content. If we assume some form of externalist theory is correct, then content is, in the first instance 'wide' content, i.e. determined in part by factors external to the representing system. On the other hand, it seems clear that, on plausible assumptions about how to individuate psychological capacities, internally equivalent systems must have the same psychological capacities. Hence, it would appear that wide content cannot be relevant to characterizing psychological equivalence. Since cognitive science generally assumes that content is relevant to characterizing psychological equivalence, philosophers attracted to externalist theories of content have sometimes attempted to introduce 'narrow' content, i.e. an aspect or kind of content that is equivalent in internally equi-

|  | *Atomist* | *Holist* |
|---|---|---|
| *Externalist* | Covariance<br>Historical–teleological | 'Long-armed' functional role |
| *Internalist* | Ahistorical–teleological<br>Similarity | 'Short-armed' Functional role |

valent systems. The simplest such theory is Fodor's idea (1987) that narrow content is a function from contexts (i.e. from whatever the external factors are) to wide contents.

MISREPRESENTATION

Perhaps the most serious single problem facing the theory of representation is to give a satisfactory account of misrepresentation. Consider covariance theories. A paradigm case of misrepresentation is a case in which a |cow| is tokened in response to a horse. But if r is tokened in response to a horse, then it's tokenings don't covary with the occurrence of cows, hence it cannot be a |cow|. Perhaps it represents something common to cows and horses, e.g. the property of being a cow-or-horse. (This is why Fodor (1987) has dubbed the problem the disjunction problem.) But then it is not a |cow|, and not a misrepresentation.

Functional role theories face an analogous problem. A case of error is a case in which Σ tokens a representation m that it uses as a |mouse|, in a situation in which it should have tokened something else, say s, something Σ uses as a |shrew|. So m was tokened by a process C that is designed to work only if the slot that Σ fills with m is something that represents shrews. But if C uses m, then m isn't used (exclusively) as a |mouse| in Σ, contrary to hypothesis. It appears that, at a minimum, Σ uses m as a |mouse or shrew|. Hence, m represents being-a-mouse-or-shrew, and there was no error after all.

Teleological theories appear to have the right form to deal with misrepresentation, for they distinguish between what r indicates (what it covaries with) and what it is r's function to indicate, thus making room for error as a mismatch between the two. A representation r misrepresents x, according to this approach, when it is r's function to indicate x but r does not indicate x.

A problem with this approach is that many representations do not have indication as their function – the antecedents of hypothetical thoughts, for example. Teleological theories are therefore forced to hold that representations that do not have indication as their function are complex, the idea being that non-indicating representations derive their content from their structure together with their indicating constituents. Teleological theories are therefore committed to a kind of VERIFICATIONIST reductionism: the content of every representation must reduce to the contents of those whose function is to indicate. Aside from general worries about semantic reductionism, this commits the teleological theory to the view that every serious scheme of mental representation must have a componential semantics.

Covariationist theories seem to have the same implication, since many non-erroneous representations do not covary with what they represent (almost every case of non-perceptual thought). While it might be true that every serious scheme of mental representation must have a componential semantics. (for an argument, *see* Fodor and Pylyshyn, 1988), it appears to be an empirical hypothesis about the mind, and therefore should not be an analytic consequence of the theory of content.

*See also* CONCEPT, EXTERNALISM/INTERNALISM.

BIBLIOGRAPHY

Block, N.: 'Advertisement for a semantics for psychology', *Midwest Studies in Philosophy* 10 (1986), 615–78.
Burge, T.: 'Individualism and the mental', *Philosophical Review* 95 (1979), 3–45.

Cummins, R.: *Meaning and Mental Representation* (Cambridge, MA: MIT Press, a Bradford Book, 1987).

Dretske, F.: *Knowledge and the Flow of Information* (Cambridge, MA: MIT Press, a Bradford Book, 1981).

Dretske, F.: 'Misrepresentation', in *Belief* ed. R. Bogdan (Oxford: Oxford University Press, 1986).

Fodor, J. and Pylyshyn, Z.: 'Connectionism and cognitive architecture', *Cognition* 28 (1988), 3–71.

Fodor, J.: *Psychosemantics: the Problem of Meaning in the Philosophy of Mind* (Cambridge, MA: MIT Press, a Bradford Book, 1987).

Fodor, J.: *A Theory of Content and Other Essays* (Cambridge, MA.: MIT Press, a Bradford Book, 1990).

Harman, G.: 'Conceptual role semantics', *Notre Dame Journal of Formal Logic* 23 (1982), 242–56.

Loar, B.: *Mind and Meaning* (Cambridge: Cambridge University Press, 1981).

Millikan, R.: *Language, Thought and other Biological Categories* (Cambridge, MA: MIT Press, a Bradford Book, 1984).

Papineau, D.: *Reality and Representation* (Oxford: Blackwell, 1988).

Putnam, H.: 'The meaning of meaning', in *Language, Mind and Knowledge* ed. K. Gunderson, (Minneapolis: University of Minnesota Press, 1975).

Stampe, D.: 'Towards a causal theory of linguistic representation', *Midwest Studies in Philosophy* 2 (1977), 42–63.

ROBERT CUMMINS

**representative realism** This theory holds that (1) there is a world whose existence and nature is independent of us and of our perceptual experience of it, (2) perceiving an object located in that external world necessarily involves causally interacting with that object, and (3) the information acquired in perceiving an object is indirect; it is information most immediately about the perceptual experience caused in us by the object, and only derivatively about the object itself. Clause (1) makes representative realism a species of REALISM , clause (2) makes it a species of CAUSAL THEORY OF PERCEP-TION, and clause (3) makes it a species of representative as opposed to DIRECT REALISM.

Traditionally, representative realism has been allied with an ACT/OBJECT ANALYSIS of sensory experience. (*See*, for instance, Locke, 1690, representative realism's most famous advocate.) Indeed, this act/object analysis is traditionally a major plank in arguments for representative realism.

One use of terms such as 'looks', 'seems' and 'feels' is to express opinion. 'It looks as if the Labour Party will win the next election' expresses an opinion about the party's chances, and does not describe a particular kind of perceptual experience. We can, however, use such terms to describe perceptual experience divorced from any opinion to which the experience may incline us. A straight stick half in water looks bent, and does so to people completely familiar with this illusion who have, therefore, no inclination to hold that the stick is in fact bent. Such uses of 'looks', 'seems', 'tastes', etc. are commonly called phenomenological.

The act/object theory holds that the sensory experiences recorded by sentences employing these terms in their phenomenological sense are a matter of being directly acquainted with something which actually bears the apparent property. When something looks red to me, I am acquainted with a red expanse (in my visual field); when something looks bent to me, I am acquainted with a bent shape (in my visual field); when something tastes bitter to me I am directly acquainted with a sensation with the property of being bitter; and so on and so forth. (If you do not understand the term 'directly acquainted', stick a pin into your finger. The relation you will then bear to your pain, as opposed to the relation of concern you might bear to another's pain when told about it, is an instance of direct acquaintance in the intended sense.)

The act/object account of sensory experience combines with various considerations traditionally grouped under the head of the argument from illusion to provide arguments for representative realism, or more precisely for the clause in it that contends that our sensorily derived information about the world comes indirectly, that what we are most directly acquainted with is not an aspect of the world but an aspect of our mental, sensory response to it. Consider, for instance, the familiar refractive illusion mentioned already, that of a straight stick in water looking bent. The act/object account holds that in this case we are directly acquainted with a bent shape. This shape, so the argument runs, cannot be the stick as it is straight, and thus must be a mental item, commonly called a sense-datum. And, in general, sense-data – visual, tactual, etc – are held to be the objects of direct acquaintance. Perhaps the most striking use of the act/object analysis to bolster representative realism turns on what modern science tells us about the fundamental nature of the physical world. Modern science tells us that the objects of the physical world around us are literally made up of enormously many, widely separated, tiny particles whose nature can be given in terms of a small number of properties like mass, charge, spin and so on.(These properties are commonly called the primary qualities; see PRIMARY AND SECONDARY QUALITIES.) But of course, that is not how the objects look to us, not how they present to our senses. They look continuous and coloured. What then can these coloured expanses with which we are directly acquainted be other than mental sense-data?

Two objections dominate the literature on representative realism: one goes back to BERKELEY and is that representative realism leads straight to scepticism about the external world; the other is that the act/object account of sensory awareness is to be rejected in favour of an adverbial account.

Traditional representative realism is a 'veil of perception' doctrine, in Bennett's (1971) phrase. LOCKE's idea was that the physical world was revealed by science to be in essence colourless, odourless, tasteless and silent, and that we perceive it by, to put it metaphorically, throwing a veil over it by means of our senses. It is the veil we see, in the strictest sense of 'see'. This does not mean that we do not really see the objects around

us. It means that we see an object in virtue of seeing the veil, the sense-data, causally related in the right way to that object. An obvious question to ask, therefore, is what justifies us in believing that there is anything behind the veil; and if we are somehow justified in believing that there is something behind the veil, how can we be confident of what it is like? (See PROBLEM OF THE EXTERNAL WORLD.)

There seems, however, to be a good answer to this fair question. The hypothesis of the external world is the best explanation of the course of our sensory experience. The tracks in a Wilson cloud chamber justify believing in electrons because electrons are the best explanation of those tracks. On a vastly more massive scale, the history of our sense-data justify believing in an external world because the external world is the best explanation of the sensory history (see INFERENCE TO THE BEST EXPLANATION).

It might well be observed that this reply to scepticism fares better as a justification for believing in the existence of external objects, than as a justification of the views we have about their nature. It *is* incredible that nothing independent of us is responsible for the manifest patterns displayed by our sense-data, but granting this leaves open many possibilities about the nature of the hypothesized external reality. Direct realists often make much of the apparent advantage that their view has on the question of the nature of the external world. The fact of the matter is, though, that it *is* much harder to arrive at tenable views about the nature of external reality than it is to defend the view that there is an external reality of some kind or other. The history of human thought about the nature of the external world is littered with what are now seen (with the benefit of hindsight) to be egregious errors – the four element theory, phlogiston, the crystal spheres, vitalism, and so on. It can hardly be an objection to a theory that it makes the question of the nature of external reality much harder than the question of its existence.

The way we talk about sensory experience certainly suggests an act/object view. When something looks thus and so in the phenomenological sense, we naturally describe the nature of our sensory experience by saying that we are acquainted with a thus and so 'given'. But suppose that this is a misleading grammatical appearance, engendered by the linguistic propriety of forming complex, putatively referring expressions like 'the bent shape in my visual field', and that there is no more a bent shape in existence for the representative realist to contend to be a mental sense-datum, than there is a bad limp in existence when someone has, as we say, a bad limp. When someone has a bad limp, they limp badly. Similarly, according to adverbial theorists, when, as we naturally put it, I am aware of a bent shape, we would better express the way things are by saying that I sense bent shape-ly. What the act/object theorist analyses as a feature of the object which gives the nature of the sensory experience, the adverbial theorist analyses as a mode of sensing which gives the nature of the sensory experience. (The decision between the act/object and adverbial theories is a hard one, addressed in detail in e.g. Jackson, 1977; Chisholm, 1957; and Cornman, 1975. Jackson defends the act/object view, Chisholm and Cornman defend the adverbial view. *See* ACT/OBJECT ANALYSIS and ADVERBIAL THEORY).

As we noted above, traditionally representative realism is allied with the act/object theory. But we can approach the debate between representative realism and direct realism via the notion of information processing. (Indeed, Mackie (1976, ch. 2) argues that Locke can be read as approaching the debate in this way.) I am watching a football game on television. My senses, in particular my eyes and ears, 'tell' me that Carlton is winning. What makes this possible is the existence of a long and complex causal chain of electro-magnetic radiation running from the game through the television cameras, various cables, my television set and a region of space between my eyes and the television screen. Each stage of this process carries information about preceding stages in the sense that the the way things are at a given stage depends on the way things are at preceding stages. Otherwise the information

would not be transferred from the game to my brain. There needs to be a systematic covariance between the state of my brain and the state of the match, and that will not obtain unless it obtains between intermediate members of the long causal chain. For instance, if the state of my retina did not systematically covary with the state of the television screen before me, my optic nerve would have, so to speak, nothing to go on to tell my brain about the screen, and so in turn would have nothing to go on to tell my brain about the game. There is no 'information at a distance'.

A few of the stages in this transmission of information between game and brain are special in the sense that I am in some sense perceptually aware of them. Much of what happens between brain and match I am quite ignorant about, some of what happens I know about from books, but some of what happens I am *perceptually* aware of. For instance, I am perceptually aware of the images on the screen. I am also perceptually aware of the game. Otherwise I could not be said to *watch* the game on television. Now my perceptual awareness of the match depends on my perceptual awareness of the screen. The former goes via the latter. In saying this I am not saying that I go through some sort of internal monologue like 'Such and such images on the screen are moving thus and so, therefore, Carlton is attacking the goal'. Indeed, if you suddenly covered the screen with a cloth and asked me (1) to report on the images, and (2) to report on the game, I might well find it easier to report on the game than on the images. But that does not mean that my awareness of the game does not go via my awareness of the images on the screen. It shows that I am more interested in the game than in the screen, and so am storing beliefs about it in preference to beliefs about the screen.

We can now see how to elucidate representative realism independently of the debate between act/object and adverbial theorists about sensory experience. Our initial statement of representative realism talked of the information acquired in perceiving an object being most immediately about the perceptual

447

experience caused in us by the object, and only derivatively about the object itself. In the act/object, sense-datum approach, what is held to make that true is that the fact that what we are immediately aware of is a mental sense-datum. But instead, representative realists can put their view this way: just as awareness of the match goes via awareness of the screen, so awareness of the screen goes via awareness of experience, and in general when subjects perceive objects, their perceptual awareness always goes via awareness of experience.

Why believe such a view? Because of the point we referred to earlier: the picture of the world provided by our senses is so very different from the picture provided by modern science. It is so different in fact that it is hard to grasp what might be meant by insisting that we are in epistemologically *direct* contact with that world.

*See also* ACT/OBJECT ANALYSIS; ADVERBIAL THEORY; DIRECT REALISM; EXPERIENCE; THE GIVEN; PERCEPTUAL KNOWLEDGE.

BIBLIOGRAPHY

Bennett, J.: *Locke, Berkeley, Hume: Central Themes* (Oxford: Oxford University Press, 1971).

Berkeley, G.: *The Principles of Human Knowledge* (1710) in *Berkeley: Philosophical Works* ed. M.R. Ayers (London: Dent, 1975).

Chisholm, R.M. *Perceiving* (Ithaca, NY: Cornell University Press, 1957).

Cornman, J.: *Perception, Commonsense and Science* (New Haven, CT: Yale University Press, 1975).

Jackson, F.: *Perception* (Cambridge: Cambridge University Press, 1977).

Locke, J.: *Essay Concerning Human Understanding* (1690) ed. P.H. Nidditch (Oxford: Oxford University Press, 1975).

Mackie, J.L.: *Problems from Locke* (Oxford: Oxford University Press, 1976).

FRANK JACKSON

**Rescher, Nicholas (1928– )** In various publications Rescher offers a detailed and systematic view of human knowledge and its limits along with core implications for value theory and ethics broadly conceived. In epistemology and philosophy of science, Rescher is best described as an analytic PRAGMATIST placing epistemic priority on the methods of the natural sciences as a source of both understanding the empirical world and directing our actions within it. Rescher regards science as seeking the best fit between the data of experience and the conjectures we make in our attempts to resolve questions. He sees scientific methods as the product of an evolutionary process of *rational* selection which leaves us with only those methods that have proved to work.

With regard to *foundational beliefs* or *basic knowledge*, Rescher asserts that basic beliefs, like all factual beliefs, are fallible and hence subject to revision in the light of ongoing evidence. Such beliefs begin as working presumptions and are accepted as true until experience requires rejection; but until experience forces such rejection they qualify for acceptance as items of human knowledge.

On the question of *non-basic knowledge* or *scientific knowledge*, he has argued in *Methodological Pragmatism* that while particular scientific theses established by the inductive methods of science may be false (although we must presume them to be true) *rationality* requires us to use such methods because they generally tend to produce more effectively supplementable beliefs about the physical world than any other methods available to us.

*Truth* Rescher construes in terms of correspondence and argues that the criterion for it is fully warrantedly assertible belief. The satisfaction of the criterion does not entail logically that the proposition is true as construed, but it would be irrational to ask for anything more in the pursuit of truth.

*Human knowledge* should not be construed in terms of an impossibly idealized requirement assuring logical certainty. Such a requirement can only guarantee a global scepticism having no plausible justification.

Though Rescher ascribes a certain primacy to induction and the methods of the natural sciences because they are the product of the evolutionary process, he has not argued that the *only* answerable questions are those that admit of answer by appeal to the methods of the natural sciences; he has argued against that thesis. On the question of *scientific progress*, he has argued that unto eternity science is progressive and revolutionary, meaning thereby that there will never be a time when we would be justified in believing that we had answered all answerable questions about the world; but owing to an inevitable exponential decay in our economic capacity to fund scientific technology, scientific progress will accordingly slow, without stopping, to increasingly infrequent theoretical and factual advances.

On the question of *scientific realism*, Rescher has argued for a particular form of instrumentalism in science without endorsing instrumentalism as a whole on the issue of factual knowledge. For Rescher, common-sense beliefs (those beliefs so obviously true that we cannot even imagine factual conditions under which they would be false) do succeed in correctly describing the physical world because such beliefs are not in any way likely to suffer truth value revision. Scientific beliefs, however, have no such property and must, for that reason, be regarded as instrumentally reliable beliefs which we can plausibly presume to be true.

Finally, the characteristic feature of Rescher's epistemology is its systematic integration of matters of value (i.e. norms – be they cognitive or affective) and matters of experientially determined fact. For Rescher morality is basically a matter of safeguarding the real or best interests of people, and while the identification of such interests involves an irreducibly normative element, the processes of their effective cultivation are something we can only learn about empirically. Morality thus weaves issues of fact and value into a seamless whole.

*See also* IDEALISM; PRAGMATISM.

WRITINGS

*The Coherence Theory of Truth* (Oxford: Clarendon Press, 1973).

*Empirical Inquiry* (Totowa: Rowman and Littlefield, 1981).
*Methodological Pragmatism* (Oxford: Blackwell, 1977).
*Scepticism* (Oxford: Blackwell, 1980).
*Scientific Progress* (Oxford: Blackwell, 1978).
*Scientific Realism* (Dordrecht: Reidel, 1987).

ROBERT ALMEDER

**Rorty, Richard (1931–)** American philosopher who has taught at Wellesley, Princeton and the University of Virginia.

Much of Rorty's early writing was in the philosophy of mind, where he became an influential defender of eliminative materialism. But beginning with *Philosophy and the Mirror of Nature* (1979), his work has taken an increasingly radical turn. Rorty is a critic of the very idea of a 'theory of knowledge' and hence of philosophy itself, conceived as a distinct, professionalized research activity with epistemological questions at its core. It is Rorty's work that has done most to fuel speculation about the DEATH OF EPISTEMOLOGY.

Rorty presents a complex historical-explanatory argument in support of the thesis that epistemology and its problems are not a perennial concern, arising as soon as one reflects, but rather the products of a distinctive, historically contingent constellation of ideas. Developments that led to the emergence of epistemology include DESCARTES' redefinition of the 'mind' as that to which each of use has privileged access; LOCKE's suggestion that by investigating the Cartesian mind we can determine the scope and limits of human knowledge; and KANT's thought that since all empirically knowable objects, 'outer' as well as 'inner', are subject to conditions inherent in our cognitive constitution, we can have A PRIORI KNOWLEDGE of features necessarily characteristic of the world as we know it. The culmination of these developments is the idea of a nonempirical discipline that determines the cognitive status of all other forms of discourse – science, morality, art or religion – according to how well they represent reality, if indeed they represent it at all.

What human beings have put together,

they can take apart. This, Rorty argues, should and indeed has begun to happen with the discipline we think of as the theory of knowledge. One idea that is absolutely crucial to this essentially neo-Kantian project is that there are two cleanly distinguishable components in knowledge: the factual element 'given' to consciousness and the constructive or interpretative element contributed by the mind, or latterly language. But taken together, SELLARS's attack on the 'myth of the given' and QUINE's scepticism about the language–fact distinction constitute a decisive rejection of these indispensable ideas. Another idea, equally indispensable, is that the aim of thought or language is correspondence to reality, accuracy of representation. But in the light of Wittgenstein's later philosophy, which approaches language through the notion of 'use' rather than that of 'picturing', this idea too has come to seem increasingly dubious. This rejection of the 'representationalist' model of mind and language becomes increasingly prominent in Rorty's later writings and reflects his growing identification with the tradition of American PRAGMATISM. It should be noted, however, that Rorty does not endorse a pragmatist definition of truth, holding with Donald Davidson that, with a primitive concept like truth, the real mistake is not to offer this or that particular analysis but to try to provide any kind of informative analysis at all.

WRITINGS

*Philosophy and the Mirror of Nature* (Princeton: Princeton University Press, 1979).
*Consequences of Pragmatism* (Minneapolis: University of Minnesota Press, 1982).
*Contingency, Irony and Solidarity* (Cambridge: Cambridge University Press, 1989).
*Essays on Reality and Representation* (Cambridge: Cambridge University Press, 1991).

MICHAEL WILLIAMS

**rule-following** *see* PROBLEM OF RULE-FOLLOWING.

**Russell, Bertrand Arthur William** (1872–1970) British philosopher, mathematician and social campaigner. Russell himself used the phrase 'theory of knowledge' to include a wide variety of topics: REALISM and IDEALISM, neutral monism, the nature of experience, the epistemology of language, the nature of truth and falsehood, induction and causation, and the nature of judgement and thought. Part of the explanation for this broad taxonomy is that, like many of his empiricist predecessors, his theory of knowledge constrained his metaphysics. The question of the nature of such-and-such would turn into a question which can reasonably be classified as epistemological: what would such-and-such have to be like in order for us to know it? Moreover, he included under theory of knowledge issues which are now often classified under philosophy of mind or of language, those which concern the nature of the vehicles and sources of knowledge: mental states with content and perceptual experiences. For Russell, an account of experience was, for most of his philosophical career, inseparable from the question whether there is a genuine subject of experience, which is why even neutral monism, an apparently purely metaphysical doctrine, gets classified under theory of knowledge.

These close connections are one of the exciting features of Russell's philosophy. However, I will concentrate on his epistemology in the narrower sense current today; in particular, I will describe some of his views concerning our knowledge of the external world. (It is noteworthy that, despite the importance he attached to logicism in his early work, he has almost nothing to say about the nature of a priori knowledge.)

We can roughly divide Russell's working life into three periods: that belonging to the nineteenth century, when he had still not found the voice for which he is now famous; the middle period, occupying the first two decades of this century, in which most of his best-known views were formulated; and the late period, in which, although his output was still considerable, he was rather detached from the mainstream of academic philosophy. In the middle period, the problem of 'knowledge of the external world' presented itself to him in an entirely traditional way: 'I think on the whole the sort of method adopted by Descartes is right: that you should set to work to doubt things and retain only what you cannot doubt because of its clearness and distinctness' (Russell, 1918, p. 182). Our own experiences or sense-data resist doubt, and the problem is to give an account of how we in addition have knowledge of mind-independent continuants. He adopts three kinds of strategy. One aims to narrow the gap between experience and material continuants by construing the latter as close in nature to the former; the other proceeds in the reverse direction, by enlarging the cognitive capacities available to the mind; the third allows a measure of scepticism, but tries to identify a kind of knowledge of physical continuants (merely structural) which is available without taking too narrow a view of their nature, or too generous a view of our capacities.

As an example of the first strategy, Russell (1914) suggests that material continuants are LOGICAL CONSTRUCTIONS out of sense-data, so they are at least of a kind with things which we can unproblematically know. Although AYER has found some merit in this approach, it seems to me not to touch the problem as stated. A material continuant is construed as a very large set of sense-data, actual and merely possible, and no one subject's experience contains them all. Thus no subject can know any proposition of the form 'This (material continuant) is thus-and-so' merely by knowing what sense-data he has. New principles of knowledge are involved, and these principles are no more plausible when they involve extrapolation to the existence of sense-data with which one will never be acquainted than when they involve extrapolation to material continuants which will never themselves be directly accessible to experience.

In his (1948) Russell deploys the second strategy, claiming that unless we have a priori knowledge of certain substantive contingent facts, then 'science is moonshine' (1948, p. 524). These facts he called 'postulates of scientific inference'. An example is:

'Given any event A, it happens very frequently that, at any neighbouring time, there is at some neighbouring place an event very similar to A' (p. 506). Russell implies that we do indeed have a priori knowledge of such facts, the knowledge being of a kind which he explains in terms of 'animal expectation'. This kind of knowledge is available to non-language users and is arguably non-propositional. This is a cognitive faculty often ignored in attempts to show how scepticism can be avoided.

The third strategy is hinted at in his (1912) and developed in more detail in his (1927). Russell lays down as a basic postulate that experiences are caused by something other than experiences – call the causes material events. Implicitly assuming some principle of like cause, like effect, he says that one can infer that properties of or relations among experiences mirror properties of or relations among material events. Material continuants are constructed out of material events. The upshot is that we know the structure of matter, but not its intrinsic nature. The strategy leaves room for scepticism about the real nature of material continuants, but is supposed to capture enough for an interpretation of science upon which most scientific beliefs are true.

Russell's views, different as they were among themselves, no doubt all deserve to be called FOUNDATIONALIST. However, his (1948) is very explicit that a datum is to be defined merely as a proposition having some intrinsic credibility. A datum does not have to be certain, and does not have to be incapable of having its credibility raised by other propositions. Some standard objections to foundationalism will not touch this position.

In this same work, there is also a quite radical streak, suggesting that Russell came close to breaking out of his formulation of the problem. He stresses the importance of 'animal expectation' as a model for the kind of knowledge we possess of the postulates of scientific inference. This is non-propositional, and a matter of the animal's causal relations with its environment. Here we see Russell operating in a different mode: NATURALIZING EPISTEMOLOGY, rather than keeping within the confines of the Cartesian problematic.

See also KNOWLEDGE BY ACQUAINTANCE/ BY DESCRIPTION; PHENOMENALISM; PROBLEM OF THE EXTERNAL WORLD; SANTAYANA.

WRITINGS

The Problems of Philosophy (London: Williams and Norgate, 1912).

'The relation of sense-data to physics', Scientia 16 (1914), 1–27; reprinted in his Mysticism and Logic (New York: Longmans, 1918; London: Allen and Unwin, 1963).

Theory of Knowledge: The 1913 Manuscript (London: Allen and Unwin, 1984).

The Analysis of Matter (London: Allen and Unwin, 1927).

Human Knowledge: Its Scope and Limits (London: Allen and Unwin, 1948).

BIBLIOGRAPHY

Ayer, A.J.: Russell (London: Fontana, 1972).

Chisholm, R.M.: 'On the nature of acquaintance: a discussion of Russell's theory of knowledge', in Bertrand Russell's Philosophy ed. G. Nakhnikian (London: Duckworth, 1974), 47–56.

Eames, E.R.: Bertrand Russell's Theory of Knowledge (London: Allen and Unwin, 1969).

R.M. SAINSBURY

**Ryle, Gilbert (1900–76)** British philosopher, who spent most of his working life at Oxford. Ryle rejected many of the ideas and issues of traditional epistemology. Just as his work in the philosophy of mind rejected the whole traditional framework of Cartesian dualism, so his detailed accounts of knowledge, belief and perception sought to move beyond that tradition.

Like many analytic philosophers during the 1950s and 1960s Ryle took the central role of philosophy to be that of 'conceptual geography'. In such early papers as 'Systematically Misleading Expressions' and 'Categories' he constructed a framework for philosophy which was later the foundation for his pioneering work The Concept of Mind. He claimed that philosophical clarification has to do with the categorization of concepts, and is carried out for the sake of philosophers only and not for the benefit of the ordinary users of those concepts. In 'Categories' he expresses a preference for the idea that philosophy has to do with the formulation of type liaisons, or type disciplines, rather than with the usual analysis associated with formal logic. Though he recognized a link between his category disciplines and Russell's theory of types, Ryle insisted in the final chapter of Dilemmas that his own methods belonged to 'informal' rather than to formal logic.

In those early papers the central thought is that the grammatical form of some expression may be 'improper to the states of affairs it records' (1931–2, p. 142). When grammatical and logical form diverge in this way the expressions will be 'systematically misleading' and will produce paralogisms and antinomies. These will then typically form the basis for traditional rivalries where the opposed theories are both wrong, since their disagreements rest on underlying confusions which an appropriate category discipline will resolve.

Ryle gives many examples of such simple category mistakes. The statement 'Jones hates the thought of going to hospital' is not of the same logical type as 'Jones hates Smith'. 'Jones is popular' has a tacitly relational, rather than subject–predicate, form. The phrase 'alleged murderer' does not ascribe a further property to one already classified as a murderer, just as the phrase 'fictional country' does not identify a real country and characterize it with a further property. Though these may not be philosophically significant, or even contentious cases, Ryle believed that comparable errors were committed in traditional philosophy. In many such cases the error is that of treating a noun phrase as if it were a straightforward name for some identifiable object. He claims, for example, that the phrase 'the meaning of . . .' is not referential and does not pick out any object as a meaning.

The most celebrated use of this apparatus

The most celebrated use of this apparatus came in Ryle's attempt to demolish Cartesian dualism in *The Concept of Mind*. There Ryle offers the opposition between dualism and materialism as the erroneous consequence of a basic category mistake about mind. In *On Thinking* it is the opposition between dualism and behaviourism which is cited as the mistaken consequence. In both cases the category mistake is that of supposing that the phrase 'the mind' and similar expressions for specific mental features name some specific object. With that mistaken assumption it seems inevitable that we should identify minds either with physical objects (materialism) or with occult spiritual objects (dualism). Both such opposed theories, on Ryle's view, failed to grasp the logical complexities and status of our mental language. This view is famously illustrated with Ryle's account of the difference in logical status between expressions such as 'the Oxford colleges' and 'the university'. He thought that while specific colleges could be identified there was no comparable object for which the expression 'the university' stood.

Though Ryle argued that there was one central category mistake at the heart of these traditional theories he examines in detail a wide variety of mental features, ranging from knowledge and belief to moods, emotions, sensations, memory and imagination. In that exploration he further deploys an ingenious array of informal devices, contrasting dispositions and occurrences, mongrel categoricals and hypotheticals, single-track and multi-track dispositions, task words and achievement words, in order to throw light on the logical complexities of our mental language. If there is one central point which his discussion seeks to make it is that while we do not believe that physical movements alone constitute mentality, or even evidence of mentality, nevertheless any additional feature required cannot be located within the occult framework of a Cartesian conception of mental substance.

At some points Ryle's discussion impinges directly on issues of traditional epistemology. In *Dilemmas*, for example, he rejects a set of arguments for scepticism by insisting that descriptions such as 'illusory', or 'fake', make sense only where their contrasts, such as 'veridical', or 'genuine', make sense. In that argument he also sometimes seems to canvass the stronger, and fallacious, consequence that this establishes the existence and certainty of some veridical perception. In *The Concept of Mind*, too, his discussion of sensation and observation, about the success of which he expresses some doubt, criticises traditional theories of perception such as phenomenalism.

But perhaps the closest link with traditional epistemology is his discussion of 'knowing how' and 'knowing that'. There he not only extends the traditional interest in knowledge, but also argues strongly against the traditional priority accorded to 'knowing that'. He thought that this put too great a weight on intellectual theorizing, and wished instead to acknowledge the existence of other kinds of knowledge, particularly the practical skills of 'knowing how'. He argued further that the traditional priority ought to be reversed, since even intellectual theorising presupposed some practical skill. His argument for this deployed characteristically a device of 'informal logic' in claiming that to give priority to 'knowing that' led to an infinite regress. For if intellectual knowledge required us to exercise practical mastery over the elements of some theory, and if that practical skill required another underlying theory to support it, then an endless regress would be bound to arise.

Ryle's rejection of an extreme Cartesian dualism was successful, but critics objected that it had led him into an unacceptable BEHAVIOURISM. His own text seemed to some ambiguous between two distinct theses: (A) the rejection of Cartesian dualism, and (B) the behaviourist rejection of *any* coherent notion of inner mental experience. Although Ryle's official view treated behaviourism as an error on a par with its Cartesian rival, nevertheless his own discussion seemed to some to canvass thesis (B).

*See also* BELIEF; DISPOSITION; INTROSPECTION; OTHER MINDS.

WRITINGS

'Systematically misleading expressions', *Proceedings of the Aristotelian Society* 22 (1931–2), 139–70.

'Categories', *Proceedings of the Aristotelian Society* 38 (1937–8), 189–206.

'Knowing how and knowing that', *Proceedings of the Aristotelian Society* 46 (1945–6), 1–16.

*The Concept of Mind* (London: Hutchinson, 1949).

*Dilemmas* (Cambridge: Cambridge University Press, 1954).

*On Thinking* ed. K. Kolenda (Oxford: Blackwell, 1979).

'Ordinary language', *Philosophical Review* 62 (1963), 167–86.

BIBLIOGRAPHY

Lyons, W.: *Gilbert Ryle: An Introduction to his Philosophy* (Hassocks: Harvester, 1980).

Wood, O.P. and Pitcher, G. eds: *Ryle* (London: Macmillan, 1970).

GRAHAM BIRD

# S

Santayana, George (1863–1952)   American philosopher and writer, born in Spain. Santayana may well be the most resolute and most extreme REALIST in the history of thought. He maintained that both the immediate objects of consciousness (which he thought were universals) and the objects of knowledge (which he believed were entities in the material world) enjoy a reality independent of the mind. Universals have for him a timeless, self-identical being free from reliance on their embodiment in matter and envisagement by mind. They are infinite in number and constitute a realm of essence which includes every quality, every relation, and every form of definiteness.

In *Scepticism and Animal Faith* (1923), Santayana undertook to complete DESCARTES' project of universal doubt. He found that the resolute sceptic can doubt the existence of everything and is reduced to the unmeaning and non-existent vista of universals (essences) in present consciousness. Only this is certain but, since it is all transparent immediacy, it yields no knowledge of anything. Scepticism is, in this way, undefeatable, but it stands revealed as a self-stultifying mental exercise unfit to ground philosophy.

Santayana insists on the importance of honesty in philosophy, arguing that we should incorporate nothing into theory that we cannot act on in practice. Universal doubt fails to meet this criterion: the sceptic happily eats the food in whose existence he refuses to believe. Philosophy should consist of those beliefs that, in our actions, we constantly affirm.

This leads Santayana to a new, and hitherto inadequately appreciated, philosophical method. The procedure he adopts consists of the critical reconstruction of the tenets of animal faith. Our actions reveal, and in a sense justify, certain commitments concerning the world; properly clarified and systematized, these constitute the philosophy of animal faith or the enduring commonsense of mankind.

To the animal in action, knowledge is belief or confidence mediated by the essences before the mind. In perception, we harness the immediate objects of consciousness and use them as symbols of surrounding material realities. The sign-significate relation between the contents of consciousness and the objects of knowledge enables Santayana to sidestep many of the problems of the correspondence theory of truth. The identity of the universal in mind with the one embodied in nature remains, for him, the ideal, but it is neither necessary for knowledge nor, given the discrepancy between subatomic reality and the scale of our senses, likely to be achieved.

Consciousness, for Santayana, is an irreducible by-product of material processes. It consists of a sequence of intentional acts directed upon essences. It lacks causal power and has as its sole function the grasp or intuition of non-existent forms. Although tethered to the organism, it provides escape from the cares of daily life by aesthetic immediacy or the disinterested contemplation of pure forms that Santayana calls 'the spiritual life'.

Santayana can be credited with three significant achievements. He pushed the sceptical enterprise farther than any other philosopher. He developed the promising new method of the philosophy of animal faith. Remarkably, he managed to combine in a single system a naturalistic view of human beings, a platonic theory of universals and an account of spirituality without theological trappings.

*See also* RUSSELL.

WRITINGS

*The Life of Reason; Or, The Phases of Human
Progress: I. Introduction and Reason in Common
Sense* and *V. Reason in Science* (New York:
Charles Scribner's Sons, 1905, 1906)
*Obiter Scripta* (New York: Charles Scribner's
Sons, 1936)
*Physical Order and Moral Liberty* eds J. and S.
Lachs (Nashville: Vanderbilt University Press,
1969)
*Realms of Being* (New York: Charles Scribner's
Sons, 1942).
*Scepticism and Animal Faith* (New York: Dover,
1955)
*Winds of Doctrine* (New York: Charles Scribner's
Sons, 1926)

JOHN LACHS

**Sartre, Jean-Paul (1905–80)** Sartre lived
and worked for the most part in Paris, and
wrote novels and plays, as well as philosophy, on the main themes of EXISTENTIAL-
ISM, which borrow from and criticized
elements of HUSSERL'S PHENOMENOLOGY. After
the Second World War he became increasingly involved in political issues and in the
debates about Marxism.

In his main philosophical work, *Being and
Nothingness*, Sartre examines the relationships between Being For-itself (consciousness), and Being In-itself (the non-conscious
world). He rejects central tenets of the RA-
TIONALIST and EMPIRICIST traditions, calling
the view that the mind or self is a thing or
substance 'Descartes's substantialist illusion'
(1958, p. 84), and claiming also that consciousness does not contain IDEAS or representations of the material world ('representations . . . are idols invented by the psychologists'; 1958, p. 125). Sartre also attacks
IDEALISM in the forms associated with
BERKELEY and KANT, and concludes that his
account of the relationship between consciousness and the world is neither REALIST
nor idealist (1958, Introduction).

Sartre also discusses Being For-others,
which comprises the aspects of experience
pertaining to interactions with OTHER MINDS.

His views here are subtle: roughly, he holds
that one's awareness of others is constituted
by feelings of shame, pride, and so on.

Sartre's rejection of ideas, and the denial of
idealism, appear to commit him to DIRECT
REALISM in the theory of perception. This is
not inconsistent with his claim to be neither
realist nor idealist, since by 'realist' he means
views which allow for the mutual independence or in-principle separability of mind and
world. Against this Sartre emphasizes, after
HEIDEGGER, that perceptual experience has an
active dimension, in that it is a way of interacting and dealing with the world, rather
than a way of merely contemplating it
('activity, as spontaneous, unreflecting consciousness, constitutes a certain existential
stratum in the world'; 1962, p. 61). Consequently, he holds that experience is richer,
and open to more aspects of the world, than
empiricist writers customarily claim:

> When I run after a streetcar . . . there is
> consciousness of-the-streetcar-having-
> to-be-overtaken, etc. . . . I am then
> plunged into the world of objects; it is
> they which constitute the unity of my
> consciousness; it is they which present
> themselves with values, with attractive
> and repellent qualities . . . (1957, p. 49)

Relatedly, he insists that I experience
material things as having certain potentiali-
ties-for-me ('nothingnesses'). I see doors and
bottles as openable, bicycles as ridable (these
matters he links ultimately to the doctrine of
extreme existentialist freedom). Similarly, if
my friend is not where I expect to meet her,
then I experience her absence 'as a real event'
(1958, p. 10).

These phenomenological claims are
striking and compelling. But Sartre pays insufficient attention to such things as illusions
and hallucinations, which are normally cited
as problems for direct realists. In his discussion of mental imagery (1972), however, he
describes the act of imaging as a 'transformation' of 'psychic material'. This connects with
his view that even a physical image such as
a photograph of a tree does not figure as an
object of consciousness when it is experienced as a tree-representation (rather than as

a piece of coloured card). But even so, the fact remains that the photograph continues to contribute to the character of the experience. Given this, it is hard to see how Sartre avoids positing a mental analogue of a photograph for episodes of mental imaging, and harder still to reconcile this with his rejection of visual representations. It may be that the regards imaging as debased and derivative perceptual knowledge (1972, ch. 2), but this merely raises once more the issue of perceptual illusion and hallucination, and the problem of reconciling them with direct realism.

WRITINGS

*La Transcendance de l'Ego* (Paris: Vrin, 1936); trans. F. Williams and R. Kirkpatrick, *The Transcendence of the Ego* (New York: Hill and Wang, 1957).

*Esquisse d'une théorie des émotions* (Paris: Hermann, 1939); trans. P. Mairet, *Sketch for a Theory of the Emotions* (London: Methuen, 1962).

*L'Imaginaire* (Paris: Gallimard, 1940); trans. anon., *The Psychology of Imagination* (London: Methuen, 1972).

*L'Être et le Néant* (Paris: Gallimard, 1943); trans. H. Barnes, *Being and Nothingness* (London: Methuen, 1958).

GREGORY McCULLOCH

**scepticism** Scepticism is the view that we lack knowledge. It can be rather 'local' (Pappas, 1978). For example, the view could be that we lack all knowledge of the future because we do not know that the future will resemble the past; or we could be sceptical about the existence of 'other minds'. But there is another view – the absolute global view that we do not have any knowledge whatsoever.

It is doubtful that any philosopher seriously entertained absolute global scepticism. Even the PYRRHONIST sceptics who held that we should refrain from assenting to any non-evident proposition had no such hesitancy about assenting to 'the evident'. The non-evident is any belief that requires evidence in order to be epistemically acceptable, i.e. acceptable because it is warranted.

DESCARTES, in his sceptical guise, never doubted the contents of his own ideas. The issue for him was whether they 'corresponded' to anything beyond ideas.

But Pyrrhonist and Cartesian forms of *virtual* global scepticism have been held and defended. Assuming that knowledge is some form of true, sufficiently warranted belief, it is the warrant condition, as opposed to the truth or belief condition, that provides the grist for the sceptic's mill. The Pyrrhonists will suggest that no non-evident, empirical proposition is sufficiently warranted because its denial will be equally warranted. A Cartesian sceptic will argue that no empirical proposition about anything other than one's own mind and its contents is sufficiently warranted because there are always legitimate grounds for doubting it. Thus, an essential difference between the two views concerns the stringency of the requirements for a belief's being sufficiently warranted to count as knowledge. A Cartesian requires certainty. A Pyrrhonist merely requires that the proposition be more warranted than its negation.

The Pyrrhonists do not *assert* that no non-evident proposition can be known, because that assertion itself is such a knowledge claim. Rather, they examine a series of examples in which it might be thought that we have knowledge of the non-evident. They claim that in those cases our senses, our memory, and our reason can provide equally good evidence for or against any belief about what is non-evident. Better, they would say, to withhold belief than to assent. They can be considered the sceptical 'agnostics'.

Cartesian scepticism, more impressed with Descartes' argument for scepticism than his own reply, holds that we do not have any knowledge of any empirical proposition about anything beyond the contents of our own minds. The reason, roughly put, is that there is a legitimate doubt about all such propositions because there is no way to justifiably deny that our senses are being stimulated by some cause (an evil spirit, for example) which is radically different from the objects which we normally think affect our senses. Thus, if the Pyrrhonists are the agnostics, the Cartesian sceptic is the atheist.

Because the Pyrrhonist requires much less of a belief in order for it to be certified as knowledge than does the Cartesian, the arguments for Pyrrhonism are much more difficult to construct. A Pyrrhonist must show that there is no better set of reasons for believing any proposition than for denying it. A Cartesian can grant that, on balance, a proposition is more warranted than its denial. The Cartesian need only show that there remains some legitimate doubt about the truth of the proposition.

Thus, in assessing scepticism, the issues to consider are these: Are there ever better reasons for believing a non-evident proposition than there are for believing its negation? Does knowledge, at least in some of its forms, require certainty? And, if so, is any non-evident proposition certain?

*See also* CERTAINTY; DESCARTES; PYRRHONISM; SCEPTICISM, CONTEMPORARY.

BIBLIOGRAPHY

Burnyeat, M. ed.: *The Sceptical Tradition* (Berkeley: University of California Press, 1983).
Descartes, R.: *Meditations on First Philosophy* (1641) in *The Philosophical Writings of Descartes* eds J. Cottingham, R. Stoothoff and D. Murdoch (Cambridge: Cambridge University Press, 1975), esp. Meditation 1.
Klein, P.: *Certainty: A Refutation of Scepticism* (Minneapolis: University of Minnesota Press, 1981).
Moore, G.E.: 'Four forms of scepticism', in his *Philosophical Papers* (New York: Macmillan, 1959).
Pappas, G.S.: 'Some forms of epistemological scepticism', in *Essays on Knowledge and Justification* eds G.S. Pappas and M. Swain (Ithaca, NY: Cornell University Press, 1978), 309–16.
Popkin, R.: *The History of Skepticism* (Berkeley: University of California Press, 1979).
Sextus Empiricus: *Outlines of Pyrrhonism* trans. R.G. Bury (Cambridge, MA: Harvard University Press, 1976).
Unger, P.: *Ignorance: A Case for Scepticism* (Oxford: Oxford University Press, 1975).
Wittgenstein, L.: *On Certainty* (Oxford: Blackwell, 1969).

PETER D. KLEIN

**scepticism, contemporary** As with many things in contemporary philosophy, the current discussions about scepticism originate with DESCARTES' discussion of the issue, in particular, with his discussion of the so-called 'evil spirit hypothesis'. Roughly put, that hypothesis is that instead of there being a world filled with familiar objects, there is just me and my beliefs and an evil genius who causes me to have just those beliefs that I would have were there to be the world which one normally supposes to exist. The sceptical hypothesis can be 'up-dated' by replacing me and my beliefs with a brain-in-a-vat and brain-states and replacing the evil genius with a computer connected to my brain stimulating it to be in just those states it would be in were its states caused by objects in the world.

The hypothesis is designed to impugn our knowledge of empirical propositions by showing that our experience is not a reliable source of beliefs. Thus, one form of traditional scepticism developed by the Pyrrhonists, namely that reason is incapable of producing knowledge, is ignored by contemporary scepticism (*see* SCEPTICISM). Apparently, the sceptical hypothesis can be employed in two distinct ways. It can be used to show that our beliefs fall short of being certain and it can be used to show that they are not even justified. In fact, as we will see, the first use depends upon the second.

Letting '*p*' stand for any ordinary belief (e.g. there is a table before me) the first type of argument employing the sceptical hypothesis can be stated as follows:

1. If S knows that *p*, then *p* is certain.
2. The sceptical hypothesis shows that *p* is not certain.

Therefore, S does not know that *p*.

No argument for the first premiss is needed because this first form of the argument employing the sceptical hypothesis is only concerned with cases in which certainty is thought to be a necessary condition of knowledge (*see* CERTAINTY). Nevertheless, it could be pointed out that we often do say that we know something, although we would not claim that it is certain. In fact, Wittgenstein (1972) claims, roughly, that propositions which are known are always subject to challenge, whereas, when we say that *p* is certain, we are foreclosing challenges to *p*. As he puts it, ' "Knowledge" and "certainty" belong to different categories' (Wittgenstein, 1969, §308).

Both of these replies miss the basic point at issue – namely, whether ordinary empirical propositions are certain. A Cartesian sceptic could grant that there is a use of 'know' – perhaps a paradigmatic use – such that we can legitimately claim to know something and yet not be certain of it. But it is precisely whether such a claim as 'here's one hand' is certain that is at issue. For if such propositions are not certain, then so much the worse for those propositions that we claim to know in virtue of being of being certain of our observations. The sceptical challenge is that, in spite of what is ordinarily believed, no empirical proposition is immune to doubt.

Implicit in the second premiss of the argument is a Cartesian notion of doubt which is roughly that a proposition, *p*, is doubtful for S if there is a proposition that (1) S is not justified in denying and (2) if added to S's beliefs, would lower the warrant of *p* (*see* CERTAINTY). The sceptical hypothesis would lower the warrant of *p* if added to S's beliefs. So it becomes clear that this first argument for scepticism will succeed just in case there is a good argument for the claim that S is not justified in denying the sceptical hypothesis.

That leads directly to a consideration of the second, more common, way in which the sceptical hypothesis has played a role in the contemporary debate over scepticism:

1. If S is justified in believing that *p*, then, since *p* entails the denial of the sceptical hypothesis, S is justified in believing the denial of the sceptical hypothesis.
2. S is not justified in denying the sceptical hypothesis.

Therefore, S is not justified in believing that *p*.

There are several things to note about this argument. First, if justification is a necessary condition of knowledge, this argument would succeed in showing that S does not know that *p*. Second, it explicitly employs the premiss needed by the first argument, discussed above, namely that S is not justified in denying the sceptical hypothesis. Third, the first premiss employs a version of the so-called transmissibility principle which probably first occurred in Edmund Gettier's famous article (1963) (*see* GETTIER PROBLEM). Fourth, it is clear that *p* does, in fact, entail the denial of the most natural construction of the sceptical hypothesis since that hypothesis includes the statement that *p* is false. Fifth, the first premiss can be reformulated using some epistemic notion other than justification; in particular, with the appropriate revisions, 'knows' could be substituted for 'is justified in believing'. As such, the principle will fail for *uninteresting* reasons. For example, if belief is a necessary condition of knowledge, since we can believe a proposition without believing all of the propositions entailed by it, it is clear that the principle is false. Similarly, the principle fails for other *uninteresting* reasons. For example, if the entailment is a very complex one, S may not be justified in believing what is entailed because S does not recognize the entailment. In addition, S may recognize the entailment but believe the entailed proposition for silly reasons. But the *interesting* question is this: If S is justified in believing (or knows) that *p*, and *p* obviously (to S) entails *q*, and S believes *q* on the basis of believing *p*, then is S justified in believing (or in a position to know) that *q*?

The contemporary literature contains two general responses to the argument for scepticism employing an interesting version of the transmissibility principle. The most common is to challenge the principle. The second claims that the argument will, of necessity, beg the question against the anti-sceptic.

Nozick (1981), Goldman (1986), Thalberg (1974), Dretske (1970) and Audi (1988) have objected to various forms of the transmissibility principle. Some of the arguments are designed to show that the first premiss with 'knowledge' substituted for 'justification' is interestingly false. But it is crucial to note that even if the principle, so understood, were false, as long as knowledge requires justification, the argument given above could still be used to show that $p$ is beyond our ken because the belief that $p$ would not be justified. Equally important, even if there is some legitimate conception of knowledge in which it did not entail justification, the sceptical challenge could simply be reformulated in terms of justification. For not being justified in believing that there is a table before me seems as disturbing as not knowing it.

The arguments against the first premiss take two forms: Some are based on supposedly clear-cut counterexamples to the principle; some are based on general theories of justification or knowledge which entail that the transmissibility principle is false.

Audi (1988) presents a plausible counterexample: Consider a person who adds a column of numbers enough times to be justified in believing that the sum is 1066. Now, *if the transmissibility principle is correct*, S is justified in believing that an expert arithmetician is wrong who has added the column and believes that column sums to 1067. But, so the objection continues, S is not justified in believing that the expert arithmetician is wrong. Dretske (1970) and Thalberg (1974) present similar counterexamples.

Nozick (1981) and Goldman (1986) develop general theories of knowledge which have the consequence that the transmissibility principle fails in an interesting way when 'knowledge' is substituted for 'is justified in believing'. There are many important differences in their accounts, but very roughly put, the claim is that in order for a belief to count as knowledge, the mechanisms which produce our beliefs must be reliable. That is, those mechanisms must produce true beliefs in the actual as well as in a defined subset of the possible circumstances. Thus, we know that $p$ but we are not in a position to know the denial of the sceptical hypothesis because there are reliable processes which produces the belief that $p$ but none which reliably produce the belief that the sceptical hypothesis is false.

Both the counterexamples to the principle

and the general theory of knowledge which has the consequence that the principle fails for interesting reasons seem to me to ignore what makes the principle intuitively plausible. It is plausible precisely because deduction is the very best way of expanding the corpus of what is justified or known. One is justified in believing some consequence of $p$ or one is in a position to know some consequence of $p$ because $p$, itself, is justified or known. Thus, if S is justified in believing that $p$, and $p$ entails the denial of the sceptical hypothesis, then S is justified in denying that hypothesis because S has an adequate reason available, namely, $p$.

To return to the purported counterexample, if S is justified in believing that the sum is 1066, then S is justified in believing that anyone who says that it is 1067 is wrong because S has an adequate reason for that belief – namely that the sum is 1066. Of course, upon recognizing the entailment, S might re-evaluate the epistemic status of the original proposition that the sum is 1066. But that is a vindication of the principle. For S's re-evaluation is based upon recognizing that if the original proposition is justified, so is the entailed proposition. But, as S now reasons, the latter is not justified. So, there is no time when S is both justified in believing that the sum is 1066 and not justified in believing that the expert is wrong.

Thus there is a plausible defence of the transmissibility principle that depends upon an internalist account of justification (*see* EXTERNALISM/INTERNALISM). But that very defence shows that the argument employing the transmissibility principle will beg the question. For if the transmissibility principle is true, then some form of the internalist account of justification must be correct and what justifies S in denying the sceptical hypothesis is $p$ itself. But, then, an argument for the second premiss, i.e. that S is not justified in denying the sceptical hypothesis, must be sufficient to show that S does not have adequate 'internal' reasons to deny the sceptical hypothesis. But since $p$ would be such an adequate reason, the argument for the second premiss would, of necessity, have to show that S is not justified in believing $p$.

That, of course, is just the conclusion of the argument. Thus, there is an adequate response to the argument for scepticism which employs the transmissibility principle (*see* Klein, 1981).

A discussion of contemporary scepticism would not be complete without mentioning the views of PUTNAM (1981) and DAVIDSON (1986) concerning the sceptical hypothesis. They do not focus on the epistemic notions of certainty or justification. Rather, they have argued that the hypothesis, itself, must be false.

Their arguments differ in many important respects, but there is one central feature common to them both. Subtleties aside, it is this: the beliefs which we have depend upon the objects in our surroundings. Beliefs have a causal history such that it is not possible that most of them are false. Putnam argues that it is not possible, for example, for us to have the belief that water is $H_2O$ if, in fact, no one has ever experienced water. Roughly, if humans had always been on a planet which contained no water, our beliefs could not be about *water*. Again, subtleties aside, Davidson's view is that our beliefs must be true in the main because 'what stands in the way of global scepticism of the senses . . . is the fact that we must, in the plainest and methodologically most basic cases, take the objects of belief to be the causes of those beliefs' (Davidson, 1986, pp. 317–18).

There are at least four plausible responses to this way of regarding the sceptical hypothesis. First, even if some subset of my beliefs could not be false at some point in time because of the way in which they arise, a very strong form of scepticism remains possible. I could have acquired my beliefs just as the causal accounts dictate and then, later, I could be placed in the scenario described in the sceptical hypothesis and, from then on, my beliefs about my immediate environment would be in the main false. Second, one could argue that Davidson and Putnam are not entitled to employ claims about the causal order of things in presenting an argument against scepticism, because it is exactly knowledge about the causal order which the sceptic is questioning. Third, if beliefs (as

opposed to wishes, for example) are just those (mental) states of humans which have their intentional objects as their typical causes, then we cannot presuppose the existence of beliefs in an argument against scepticism. The Cartesian can do so because he/she thinks that types of mental states can be differentiated through 'introspection'. Thus, the sphere of the doubtful has increased because, now, one may have doubts that there are beliefs. Finally, one could hold that if an account of meaning is such that it makes global scepticism a priori impossible, then that view of meaning is *ipso facto* false. I have argued for the first three objections to this approach to scepticism (Klein, 1986). The final objection is due to McGinn (1986).

*See also* GETTIER PROBLEM; KNOWLEDGE AND BELIEF; PROPOSITIONAL KNOWLEDGE; RELIABILISM; SCEPTICISM; SEXTUS EMPIRICUS; TRANSCENDENTAL ARGUMENTS.

BIBLIOGRAPHY

Audi, R.: *Belief, Justification, and Knowledge* (Belmont: Wadsworth, 1988).

Davidson, D.: 'A coherence theory of truth and knowledge', in *Truth and Interpretation* ed. E. LePore (New York: Blackwell, 1986), 307–19.

Dretske, F.: 'Epistemic operators', *Journal of Philosophy* 67 (1970), 1003–13.

Gettier, E.: 'Is justified true belief knowledge?', *Analysis* 23 (1963), 121–3.

Goldman, A.I.: *Epistemology and Cognition* (Cambridge, MA: Harvard University Press, 1986).

Klein, P.: *Certainty: A Refutation of Skepticism* (Minneapolis: University of Minnesota Press, 1981).

Klein, P.: 'Radical interpretation and global scepticism', in *Truth and Interpretation* ed. E. LePore (New York: Blackwell, 1986), 369–86.

Lehrer, K.: *Knowledge* (Oxford: Oxford University Press, 1974).

McGinn, C.: 'Radical interpretation and epistemology', in *Truth and Interpretation* ed. E. LePore (New York: Blackwell, 1986), 356–68.

Nozick, R.: *Philosophical Explanations* (Cambridge, MA: Harvard University Press, 1981).

Putnam, H.: *Reason, Truth and History* (Cambridge: Cambridge University Press, 1981).

Thalberg, I.: 'Is justification transmissible through deduction?', *Philosophical Studies* 25 (1974), 357–64.

Unger, P.: *Ignorance: A Case for Scepticism* (Oxford: Oxford University Press, 1975).

Wittgenstein, L.: *On Certainty* (Oxford: Blackwell, 1969).

PETER D. KLEIN

**scepticism, modern** Modern scepticism began in the sixteenth century with the revival of knowledge of and interest in ancient Greek Pyrrhonian scepticism, as posed in the writings of SEXTUS EMPIRICUS, and Academic scepticism as presented in Cicero's *De Academica*. The term 'sceptic' was not used in the Middle Ages, and was first just transliterated from the Greek. Sextus's writings were published in Latin in 1562 and 1569, and in Greek in 1621. Editions of Cicero's text appeared during the sixteenth century. The revival of these writings took place at a time when a fundamental issue concerning religious knowledge had been raised by the Reformation and Counter-Reformation – how does one distinguish true religious knowledge from false or dubious views? Erasmus denied that this could be done, and advised following the sceptics in suspending judgement, *and* accepting the views of the Catholic Church on questions in dispute. The translator of Sextus, Gentian Hervet, a Catholic priest, said that the views of the Pyrrhonists constituted the perfect and complete answer to Calvinism. If nothing can be known, then Calvinism cannot be known. Counter-Reformers used the sceptical arguments to constitute a 'machine of war' against their Protestant opponents, and Protestants sought to show that the Catholics would undermine their own views because of the same sceptical challenges.

The most important presentation of scepticism at the time was that of MONTAIGNE, as presented in his 'Apology for Raimond Sebond'. Montaigne had studied and been overwhelmed by the arguments in Sextus and Cicero. He put them together in his long, rambling essay, and modernized them to fit sixteenth-century intellectual concerns. He also stated them in a vernacular language (French), which provided the vocabulary for modern discussions of the problem of knowledge.

Montaigne's questioning of the evidence for any knowledge claims, the adequacy of any purported criterion of knowledge, and the possibility of any universal ethical standards posed challenges to all views then being presented. Montaigne's work became a bestseller in France, and in English translation. With rising doubts about the prevailing intellectual tradition, Montaigne's effort set forth a general scepticism, not just against scholasticism or Renaissance naturalism, but against the possibility of there being any system of ideas that could not be cast in doubt. Montaigne's disciple, Father Pierre Charron, presented scepticism in a didactic form that was very widely read.

Early seventeenth-century philosophers tried to formulate answers to the new scepticism as a way of grounding modern philosophical theories that could justify the new science. BACON, Mersenne, Gassendi, DESCARTES, Pascal, among others, tried to deal with the sceptical menace that was overwhelming the intellectual world.

Mersenne and Gassendi in different ways formulated a mitigated or constructive scepticism, conceding a major part of the sceptic's case, while still contending that some kind of limited knowledge was possible and useful. Mersenne, in a dialogue with a sceptic, who set forth arguments from Sextus, said that although one could not answer the basic challenges of the sceptics, it did not matter because one did in fact have ways of dealing with the questions. One could predict from one experiential situation what would follow although one did not know the *real* causes of events. One could doubt whether any metaphysical knowledge is possible, while still developing a science relating appearances to appearances.

Gassendi carried this further in what he called a *via media* between scepticism and dogmatism. He developed a hypothetical Epicurean atomic theory relating appearances together. This would provide a shadow of truth, rather than Truth itself.

DESCARTES was unwilling to settle for this limited certitude. He sought truths that no sceptics could challenge. To find these, he first adopted a sceptical method of doubt, rejecting any beliefs that might, under any conceivable conditions, be false or dubious. He quickly rejected sensory beliefs, because our senses sometimes deceive us. He rejected beliefs about physical reality, because what we take to be such a reality may only be part of dream. He rejected beliefs based on reasoning, because we may be systematically deceived by some demonic force.

At this point, Descartes appeared to have created a greater scepticism than that of Montaigne. But Descartes went on to ask whether one can doubt or reject one's belief in one's own existence. Here we find that any attempt to do so is immediately overriden by our awareness that we, ourselves, are doing the doubting. So, the first truth Descartes claimed that could not be doubted was 'I think, Therefore I am' (the COGITO). From this truth one could elicit the criterion that whatever we clearly and distinctly conceive is true. Using the criterion, we establish that God exists, that He is all-powerful, the creator of everything that exists, *and* that because He is perfect, He cannot deceive us. Therefore, whatever God makes us believe clearly and distinctly must be true. In this way Descartes' new philosophy is intended to rebut the new scepticism.

Descartes' system became the main target of the modern sceptics. It was criticized by Gassendi, HOBBES and Mersenne, as based on unjustified and unjustifiable dogmas. Why could an all-powerful God not deceive? How do we know that there is not a truth for God or angels that is different from what we are forced to accept as true? Why must what we clearly and distinctly conceive be true in reality, and be not just in our minds? How do we know that our entire subjective picture of the world, no matter how certain, is not just our illusion? Descartes retorted that to take such questions seriously was to shut the door on reason. But this argument from cata-

strophe did not really answer the sceptical challenges.

In the next generation, highly detailed sceptical analyses of the questionable portions of Descartes' philosophy appeared. Pierre-Daniel Huet sought to show that all of Descartes' views, including the *cogito*, were open to doubt. Simon Foucher directed a similar attack against Malebranche as soon as the latter's philosophy was published. Foucher also fought with Leibniz's attempt to found a dogmatic system. The culmination of seventeenth-century scepticism appeared in the writings of Pierre Bayle, especially in his *Historical and Critical Dictionary* (1697–1702). Bayle put together all kinds of doubts to undermine both ancient and modern philosophy. He raised devastating sceptical challenges against Cartesianism, against Leibniz's new rationalism, against any and all contenders. The arguments in Bayle's *Dictionary*, especially in his articles on the Greek sceptic, PYRRHO of Elis, and on Zeno of Elea, posed central problems for the next generation of philosophers.

LOCKE offered a way of evading scepticism by admitting that one could have no *real* knowledge beyond intuition and demonstration, but that nobody was so mad as to doubt that fire is hot, that rocks are solid, etc. Experience would defeat scepticism. Locke's critic, Bishop Stillingfleet, tried to show that his empiricism would end up in scepticism. BERKELEY, raised on Bayle's arguments, saw that they could be turned against Locke's philosophy. Bayle had already shown that the distinction between primary and secondary qualities was indefensible. If the latter were subjective, and just in the mind, so were the former. Berkeley pressed this point to drive Locke's view into total scepticism. Berkeley claimed to have found an answer to scepticism in insisting that appearance is reality, whatever is perceived is real.

HUME, a devoted Bayle reader, developed a more encompassing scepticism. We could know nothing beyond impressions and ideas. Our causal knowledge, all that takes us beyond our immediate experience, is based on no rational or defensible principle, but just on a natural and unalterable psychological tendency to expect future experiences to resemble those we have had in the past. Any attempt to defend our unavoidable beliefs in causes, in the external world, or in a constitutive real self within us, end in absurdity and contradiction. So we are driven by any investigation of our beliefs in to total scepticism, but nature will not let us rest in this; we cannot help believing. So, Hume concludes, it is by animal faith that we get on in life, and calm our irresistible sceptical doubts.

Hume's scepticism was met by two sorts of answers that have played important roles in contemporary theories of knowledge, the Commonsense realist response of Thomas REID and the critical theory of Immanuel KANT. Reid, a contemporary of Hume, insisted that though one could not answer the sceptical problems raised, no one really had doubts about the existence of causes, the external or internal world. Our commonsense leads us to positive views on these scores, and when commonsense conflicts with philosophy, one has to reject the philosophical conclusions. Hume indicated he agreed with Reid, but did not find this an answer to scepticism. In Hume's view this forced belief is a psychological fact of life, but not an anti-sceptical argument.

Kant said that Hume awoke him from his dogmatic slumbers, and made him see how parlous our knowledge claims are. But he insisted Hume had asked the wrong question. We do have unquestionable knowledge that tells us something about all possible experience, such as that all experience will be temporal and spatial. How is such knowledge possible, if we cannot get beyond our world of experience? Kant insisted that experience is the combination of how we project it and its content. There are forms of all possible perceptions, and there are categories through which we make judgements about all possible experiences. Whether these correspond to a world beyond experience, we can not know, but we can analyse what we can be sure of about possible experience. Hence, we can have some kind of knowledge, but not knowledge of things-in-themselves.

Kant proposed his critical philosophy as a way of resolving the sceptical problems

imbedded in modern philosophy. He was quickly attacked as being himself just a very high-brow sceptic, since he too ended up denying our ability to have necessary knowledge about the world. German philosophy of the next half century consisted of attempts to avoid or overcome the scepticism implicit in Kant's analysis of the knowledge situation.

*See also* COMMONSENSISM AND CRITICAL COGNITIVISM; IN ITSELF/FOR ITSELF; NOUMENAL/PHENOMENAL; SEXTUS EMPIRICUS.

BIBLIOGRAPHY

Bayle, P.: *Historical and Critical Dictionary, Selections* trans. R.H. Popkin (Indianapolis: Hackett, 1991).
Charron, P.: *Toutes les Oeuvres de Pierre Charron*, dernière édition (Paris: J. Villery, 1635).
Descartes, R.: *The Philosophical Writings of Descartes* eds J. Cottingham, R. Stoothoff and D. Murdoch, 2 vols (Cambridge: Cambridge University Press, 1975).
Gassendi, P.: *The Selected Works of Pierre Gassendi*, trans. and ed. C. Brush (New York: Johnson Reprint, 1972).
Huet, P.-D.: *Traité Philosophique de la Faiblesse de l'Esprit Humain* (Amsterdam, 1723).
Hume, D.: *A Treatise of Human Nature* (1739–40) ed. L.A. Selby-Bigge, revised P.H. Nidditch (Oxford: Oxford University Press, 1978).
Hume, D.: *Dialogues Concerning Natural Religion* (1779) ed. R.H. Popkin (Indianapolis: Hackett, 1988).
Mersenne, M.: *La Verité des Sciences Contre les Sceptiques ou Pyrrhoniens* (Paris: T. Du Bray, 1625).
Montaigne, M. de: 'Apology for Raimond Sebond', in *The Complete Works of Montaigne* trans. D. Frame (Stanford: Stanford University Press, 1958).
Pascal, B.: *Selections* trans. R.H. Popkin (New York: MacMillan, 1989).
Sextus Empiricus: *Adversus Mathematicos . . . graece nunquam latine . . .* ed. G. Hervet (Paris: Martin Juvenem, 1569).
Sextus Empiricus: *Outlines of Pyrrhonism* and *Adversus Mathematicos* 4 vols (Cambridge, MA: Harvard University Press, 1917–55).

RICHARD POPKIN

**Schlick, Moritz (1882–1936)** Schlick was the founder of what became known as the VIENNA CIRCLE and, with Rudolf Carnap and later Otto Neurath, its leading spirit. He had trained under Max Planck as a theoretical physicist, and was one of the first philosophers to understand and write on Einstein's theories of relativity. He was thus ideally qualified to lead the LOGICAL POSITIVISTS.

Schlick's most substantial contribution to epistemology is his early work, *General Theory of Knowledge*. At this time Schlick was not a strict positivist at all, though not a Kantian either. (In 1919, after the volume appeared, Einstein observed that Schlick would find it hard to obtain a professorship as 'he does not belong to the philosophical established church of the Kantians'.) The *General Theory* is EMPIRICIST in that it rejects the possibility of Kantian synthetic A PRIORI KNOWLEDGE (*see* KANT), but defends a version of what might be called 'structural realism', which Schlick termed 'physicalism'. Science deals with real, unobservable entities, which Schlick even calls 'things-in-themselves', and which are not mere logical constructions from sense-data. His account of knowledge and judgement is explicitly 'holistic', and knowledge or cognition ('*Erkennen*') is sharply separated from acquaintance ('*Kennen*') or experience ('*Erleben*') of the 'given'; so Russell's notion of KNOWLEDGE BY ACQUAINTANCE becomes incoherent. Knowledge must be propositional in nature, requiring concepts and judgements; mere acquaintance with the GIVEN is irredeemably subjective. On self-knowledge, Schlick finds an additional fact, the 'unity of consciousness', to be 'directly given'; but though expressly anti-Humean, the account is also non-Kantian in that this 'fact' seems to be empirical. Machian positivism – which tends to equate what is real with what is given in experience – receives a sympathetic diagnosis, but is firmly rejected.

Under the influence of Hilbert, the *General Theory* argued for an account of necessary propositions in GEOMETRY, arithmetic, logic and metaphysics as 'conventions of symbolism' rather than synthetic a priori truths.

However, it was WITTGENSTEIN's *Tractatus* rather than the work of Schlick which to the Vienna Circle provided the basis for a 'consistent empiricism' (one which could give a plausible account of logical necessity). (*See* LOGICAL POSITIVISM, MATHEMATICAL KNOWLEDGE.)

The standpoint of the *General Theory* illustrates (as Friedman (1983) has argued) how the doctrines of the Vienna Circle were not simply a linear development from classical empiricism, but incorporated elements of the Kantian tradition. However, under the influence of his understanding of Relativity Theory, and later of Wittgenstein, Schlick's writings after the *General Theory* take on a more VERIFICATIONIST and positivist tone. In the 1930s, he advocated a linguistic version of Mach's equation of the given and the real with his Verification Principle, which received varied definitions in the Vienna Circle; Schlick's tended to be liberal. In 'Positivism and Realism' (1932), 'On the Foundation of Knowledge' (1934) and 'Facts and Propositions' (1935) he argued, against the COHERENTIST objections of NEURATH, for the existence of an incorrigible FOUNDATIONAL class of *Konstatierungen* or 'affirmations'. What Schlick wanted to claim was that sentences *could* be compared with something distinct from other sentences; that statements may be warranted by experiences. Confusingly, though, the 'affirmations' occupied an ambiguous position mid-way in character between judgements and sensations. The change in Schlick's epistemology should not be overstated; there was an enduring and unresolved tension in his philosophy between a naturalist realism and an empiricist, positivist foundationalism (*see* Gower, forthcoming).

Under the influence of Wittgenstein and CARNAP, Schlick came to regard metaphysics as consisting of 'pseudo-problems', and, for instance, treated the dichotomy of idealism and realism as a pseudo-inconsistency between sentences devoid of cognitive significance. But he never acepted Carnap's conception of philosophy as merely the 'logic of science'.

WRITINGS

*General Theory of Knowledge* (1918), trans. A. Blumberg (La Salle: Open Court, 1974).
*Collected Philosophical Papers: Volume I (1909–22)*, ed. H.L. Mulder and B.F. van de Velde-Schlick (Dordrecht: Reidel, 1978).
'Positivism and Realism' (1932), 'On the Foundation of Knowledge' (1934) and 'Facts and Propositions' (1935), in *Collected Philosophical Papers: Volume I (1925–36)*, ed. H.L. Mulder and B.F. van de Velde-Schlick (Dordrecht: Reidel, 1979), and in *Essential Readings in Logical Positivism*, ed. O. Hanfling (Oxford: Blackwell, 1981).

BIBLIOGRAPHY

Friedman, M.: 'Critical notice: Moritz Schlick, Philosophical Papers', *Philosophy of Science* 50 (1983), 498–514.
Gower, B.: 'Realism and empiricism in Schlick's philosophy', in *Science and Subjectivity* ed. D. Bell and W. Vossenkuhl (Berlin: Akademie Verlag, forthcoming, 1993).

ANDY HAMILTON

**scientia media**   *see* SUÁREZ.

**self-consciousness**   The expression 'self-consciousness' can mean different things. In the sense (1) 'consciousness of self' it refers to the awareness a subject (of experience) has of itself i.e. of the typical referent of the pronoun 'I'. It is not merely a grasp of the entity that happens to be myself, but an awareness of myself known as myself. The philosophical issues here revolve around how such awareness is generated and what its logical structure is. Alternatively, self-consciousness can be (2) 'experience of the items *in one's consciousness* or the contents of consciousness' like sensations, thoughts, feelings etc. This leaves open the possibility of such awareness being a result of the special faculty of introspection. However, there is a use of self-consciousness that refers to the 'self-intimation' of every conscious state and in this sense it means (3) the 'ability of a conscious state to become an object to itself'. The philosophical problem here is to cash out in epistemic and metaphysical terms the metaphor of 'phosphorescence' that is generally used to capture this reflexivity of consciousness.

*See also* INTROSPECTION; SELF-KNOWLEDGE AND SELF-IDENTITY.

BIBLIOGRAPHY

Anscombe, G.E.M.: 'The first-person', in *Mind and Language* ed. S. Guttenplan (Oxford: Clarendon Press, 1975).
Kant, I.: *Critique of Pure Reason* trans. N. Kemp Smith (London: Macmillan, 1964).
Locke, D.: *Myself and Others* (Oxford: Clarendon Press, 1968), esp. ch. 2.
Ryle, G.: *The Concept of Mind* (London: Hutchinson, 1949).

VRINDA DALMIYA

**self-evidence**   Self-evident propositions are those evident in themselves or known independently of all other propositions and evidence. To comprehend such a proposition is to be fully justified in believing it, or to know it. Such propositions might include first, some necessary truths of logic, for example laws of noncontradiction and identity; second, analytically true propositions, such as 'bachelors are unmarried'; and third, some contingent propositions, such as 'I exist' or 'I am appeared to redly'. The latter two classes are more controversial: the second because the analytic/synthetic distinction may not be clear-cut, and the third because such propositions may be justified in relation to experience, if not to other propositions.

*See also* ANALYTICITY; THE GIVEN; KNOWLEDGE BY ACQUAINTANCE/KNOWLEDGE BY DESCRIPTION.

BIBLIOGRAPHY

Audi, R.: *Belief, Justification, and Knowledge* (Belmont: Wadsworth, 1988), ch. 4.
Butchvarov, P.: *The Concept of Knowledge* (Evanston: Northwestern University Press, 1970), pp. 61–75.

Chisholm R.M.: *Theory of Knowledge* 3rd edn (Englewood Cliffs: Prentice-Hall, 1989), chs 3, 4.

ALAN H. GOLDMAN

**self-knowledge and self-identity** Normally the way one knows something about oneself is significantly different from the way one knows the same sort of thing about someone else. Knowledge of one's own current mental states is ordinarily not grounded on information about behaviour and physical circumstances. Knowledge of one's actions, and of such facts as that one is sitting or standing, is usually 'without observation' or, at any rate, not based on the sorts of observations that ground one's knowledge of the actions and posture of others. One's perceptual knowledge of one's situation in the world, e.g. that one is facing a tree, differs markedly from the perceptual knowledge others have of the same facts, since it usually doesn't involve perceiving *oneself*. And one's memory knowledge of one's own past is normally very different from one's memory knowledge of the pasts of others; one remembers one's thoughts, feelings, perceptions and actions 'from the inside', in a way that does not depend on the use of any criterion of personal identity to identify a remembered self as oneself.

Although in all these cases one could speak of a 'special' first-person access, it is the access people have to their own mental states that has attracted the most attention. Some philosophers, e.g. RYLE (1949), have denied that there is a fundamental difference between first-person and third-person knowledge of mental states. Others, most notably WITTGENSTEIN (1953), have maintained that where the difference seems most pronounced, e.g. in the case of pain ascriptions, the first-person 'avowals' are not really expressions of *knowledge* at all (*see* AVOWALS). Such views are manifestations of the twentieth-century reaction against CARTESIAN views about self-knowledge that are often associated with the claim that there are radical first-person/third-person asymmetries. These include the views that the mind is transparent to itself, that mental

states are 'self-intimating', that first-person ascriptions of mental states are infallible, and that self-knowledge of mental states serves as the foundation for the rest of our empirical knowledge (*see* FOUNDATIONALISM). Such views have been undermined by the work of FREUD, with its postulation of a realm of unconscious wishes, intentions, etc., by work in cognitive psychology which shows most of the 'information processing' in the mind to be unconscious and which shows many sorts of introspective reports to be unreliable (*see*, e.g., Nisbett and Wilson, 1977), and by philosophical criticisms of foundationalist accounts of knowledge. But most recent theorists who reject these Cartesian claims would agree that the reasons for their rejection are not reasons for denying that there is first-person knowledge of mental states that differs importantly from third-person knowledge of the same phenomena.

One question about such knowledge is whether it is appropriately thought of as observational, i.e. as grounded in a kind of perception that could be called 'inner sense'. Modern defenders of the view that such knowledge is observational (e.g. D.M. Armstrong, 1968) take perceiving something to be a matter of being so related to it that its having certain properties is apt to give rise to the non-inferential belief that there is something that has them. On this conception, it seems plausible to say that one perceives mental states and events occurring in one's own mind, in virtue of an internal mechanism by which mental states give rise to true beliefs about themselves, but cannot perceive those occurring in the minds of others. and that it is in this that one's 'special access' to one's mind consists.

Some who agree with such a 'reliable internal mechanism' view of introspective awareness would object to describing such knowledge as perceptual. In paradigm cases of perception, e.g. vision, the causal connection between the object perceived and the perceiver's beliefs about it is mediated by a state of the perceiver, a 'sense-experience', which in some sense represents the object, and which the subject can be aware of (in being aware of the look or feel of a thing).

There seem to be no such intermediaries between our sensations, thoughts, beliefs, etc. and our beliefs about them, and this seems a reason for denying that our awareness of them is perceptual.

A different objection questions the idea, implicit in the perceptual model, that there is only a contingent connection between having mental states and being aware of them (just as there is only a contingent connection between there being trees and mountains and there being perceptual awareness of them). It makes doubtful sense to suppose that there are creatures that have pain without having any capacity whatever to be aware of their pains. And a consideration of the explanatory role of self-knowledge suggests that for many kinds of mental states the very capacity to have and conceive of such states involves immediate 'first person access' to the existence of these states in oneself. To mention just one instance, if being a subject of beliefs and desires involves being at least minimally rational, and if rational revision of one's belief-desire system in the light of new experience requires some knowledge of what one's current beliefs and desires are, then being a subject of such states requires the capacity to be aware of them. While we should reject any self-intimation thesis strong enough to rule out the possibility of self-deception, or to deny mental states to animals and infants, it is far from obvious that the nature of mental states is distinct from their introspective accessibility in the way the observational model implies (see Shoemaker, 1988).

Lichtenberg denied that Descartes had a right to say 'I think', claiming that he was only entitled to 'It thinks'. And HUME (1739) famously denied that when one introspects one finds any item, over and above one's individual perceptions, that could be the self or subject that 'has' them. Such denials have led some (including Hume) to deny that there is any such self or subject, and have led others to wonder how we can have knowledge of such a thing or refer to it with 'I'. Arguably, such denials lose their force if we abandon the observational model of self-knowledge; what is disturbing is the idea that we do perceive 'by inner sense' perceptions, thoughts, etc., but do not perceive anything that could be their subject. Of course, if perceiving something is construed merely as being so related to it as to acquire, in a reliable way, true beliefs about it, then our capacity for self-knowledge involves our being able to perceive both individual mental events or states and the self (person) who has them (see Shoemaker, 1986).

The peculiarities of self-knowledge are, in any case, closely tied to the peculiarities of self-reference. If the amnesiac Joe Jones discovers that Joe Jones is the culprit, without realizing that he himself is Joe Jones, this will not be a case of self-knowledge in the sense that concerns us, even though it is a case in which the person known about is the knower himself. We are concerned with cases in which someone knows that *he himself*, or *she herself*, is so and so, where this is knowledge the knower would express by saying 'I am so and so' (see Castaneda, 1968). One feature of first-person reference is that it in no way depends on the availability of individuating descriptions; one can refer to oneself with 'I' without knowing of any descriptions that could be used to fix its reference. A related feature of 'I'-judgements is their 'immunity to error through misidentification' (see Shoemaker, 1968; Evans, 1982). In central cases of the use of 'I' (what Wittgenstein (1958) called its use 'as subject'), making the judgement 'I am F' does not involve identifying as oneself the thing that is judged to be F; such a judgement may be mistaken (if the judger is not F), but one sort of mistake is ruled out: it cannot be that one is right in thinking someone to be F, but wrong in thinking that person to be oneself. This immunity to error through misidentification differs from that which characterizes judgements having demonstratives such as 'this' as subject; where both 'I am F' and 'This is F' are immune to such error, the memory judgement 'I was F' preserves the immunity while the memory judgement 'This was F' does not (for a qualification of this, see Shoemaker, 1986). This is related to the fact, already mentioned, that first-person memory judgements typically do not need to be grounded on any criterion of identity.

It is precisely where 'I'-judgements are known in distinctively first-personal ways that they have this immunity to error through misidentification. And 'I'-judgements that do not have this immunity (e.g. 'I am bleeding', if inferred from the blood on the floor) always have among their grounds some that do (e.g. '*I* see blood' or 'There is blood near *me*'). It is arguable that part of what gives first-person content to beliefs and other mental states is their relation to distinctively first-person ways of knowing, and that without such 'special access' there could be no first-person reference at all (*see* Evans, 1982). (But another important feature of 'I'-judgements is their intimate relation to action: the amnesiac Joe Jones will not be moved to action by learning that Joe Jones is in danger, but will be if he learns in addition that he is Joe Jones and so that *he himself* is in danger; *see* Perry, 1979.)

A stronger and more controversial claim is that the special access persons have to themselves enters into the very identity conditions for the sorts of things persons are. Many have argued, following Locke, that memory access is part of what determines the temporal boundaries of persons. A major determinant of the spatial boundaries of persons, i.e. of what counts as part of a person's body, is the extent of direct voluntary control, and this is intimately tied to the special epistemic access persons have to their own voluntary actions. And a familiar Kantian idea is that unity of consciousness – different states belonging to the same conscious subject – in some way involves consciousness, or the possibility of consciousness, of this unity.

*See also* APPERCEPTION; INTROSPECTION; KANT.

BIBLIOGRAPHY

Armstrong, D.A.: *A Materialist Theory of the Mind* (London: Routledge and Kegan Paul, 1968).
Evans, G.: 'Self-identification', ch. 7 of his *The Varieties of Reference* (Oxford: Clarendon Press, 1982).
Hume, D.: *Treatise of Human Nature* (1739–40) ed. L.A. Selby-Bigge, revised P.H. Nidditch (Oxford: Oxford University Press, 1978).
Nisbett, R. and Wilson, T. De C.: 'Telling more than we know: verbal reports on mental processes', *Psychological Review* 84 (1977), 231–59.
Perry, J.: 'The essential indexical', *Nous* 13 (1989), 3–21.
Ryle, G.: *The Concept of Mind* (London: Hutchinson, 1949).
Shoemaker, S.: 'Self-reference and self-awareness', *Journal of Philosophy* 65 (1968), 555–67.
Shoemaker, S.: 'Introspection and the Self', *Midwest Studies in Philosophy* 11 (1986).
Shoemaker, S.: 'On knowing one's own mind', *Philosophical Perspectives* 2 (1988), 183–209.
Wittgenstein, L.: *Philosophical Investigations* trans. G.E.M. Anscombe (Oxford: Blackwell, 1953).
Wittgenstein, L.: *The Blue and Brown Books* (Oxford: Blackwell, 1958).

SYDNEY SHOEMAKER

**self-presenting** This term refers to an alleged property of certain first-person mental states. One is supposed to be justified in believing that one is in such a state simply in virtue of being in such a state, independently of all other evidence. Alternatively, to be in such a state is to be aware that one is in such a state. These states include intentional states, such as thinking, believing and hoping, as well as perceptual states, such as being appeared to redly. Critics of the notion argue that one can be justified in ascribing properties to one's own mental states only if one is justified in believing oneself reliable in ascribing such properties generally.

*See also* EXPERIENCE; THE GIVEN; SENSATION/COGNITION.

BIBLIOGRAPHY

Brentano, F.: *Psychology from an Empirical Standpoint* trans. A.C. Rancurello, D.B. Terrell and L.L. McAlister (New York: Humanities Press, 1973), Book 2, ch. 2.

Chisholm, R.M.: *Theory of Knowledge* 3rd edn (Englewood Cliffs: Prentice-Hall, 1989), ch. 3.

Sellars, W.: 'Empiricism and the philosophy of mind', in his *Science, Perception and Reality* (London: Routledge and Kegan Paul, 1963), 127–96.

ALAN H. GOLDMAN

**Sellars, Wilfrid (1912–89)** American philosopher. The epistemological view most closely associated with Wilfrid Sellars is surely his thoroughgoing critique of what he called 'the Myth of the Given'. The philosophical framework of givenness has historically taken on many guises, of which classical sense-datum theory is but one. But Sellars considered the very idea that empirical knowledge rests on a foundation at all, of *whatever* kind, to be a manifestation of the Myth of the Given, as was the assumption that one's 'privileged access' to one's own mental states is a primitive feature of experience, logically and epistemologically prior to all intersubjective concepts pertaining to inner episodes. At the heart of Sellars' critique of 'the entire framework of givenness' is his articulate recognition of the irreducibly normative character of epistemic discourse.

> The essential point is that in characterizing an episode or a state as that of *knowing*, we are not giving an empirical description of that episode or state; we are placing it in the logical space of reasons, of justifying and being able to justify what one says. (1956, p. 169)

The mere occurrence of 'experiences', however *causally* systematic, consequently does not yet constitute perception in the epistemic sense that allows for a meaningful contrast of 'veridical perception' and 'misperception'. Perception in this sense is always of something *as* something, and so requires more than mere exercise of differential response propensities. In so far as an instance of perceiving something *as* such-and-so is a candidate for epistemic appraisal, it necessarily encompasses the judgement that something *is* such-and-so, and *a fortiori* a classification of its content *under concepts*. It follows that the senses *per se* grasp no facts, and so it becomes clear that

> instead of coming to have a concept of something because we have noticed that sort of thing, to have the ability to notice a sort of thing is already to have the concept of that sort of thing, and cannot account for it. (1956, p. 176)

Consonant with his rejection of the Myth of the Given, Sellars proceeded to interpret an individual's first-person epistemic authority with respect to aspects of his or her own experience as built on and presupposing an intersubjective status for sensory concepts. Correlatively, sensory consciousness cannot provide a form of knowledge of empirical facts that is 'foundational' in being immediate (non-inferential), presupposing no knowledge of other matters of fact (particular or general), and constituting the ultimate court of appeals for all other factual claims. Although a person can indeed *directly know* an empirical fact in a sense which implies that he has not inferred what he justifiably believes from other propositions, Sellars insisted that the belief constituting such direct knowledge was not on that account somehow *self*-justifying, *self*-warranting, or *self*-authenticating. Rather

> to say that someone directly knows that-p is to say that his right to the conviction that-p essentially involves the fact that the idea [belief] that-p occurred to the knower in a specific way. I shall call this kind of credibility 'trans-level credibility', and [speak of] the inference scheme . . . to which it refers, as trans-level inference. (Sellars, 1963a; p. 88)

So, for example, when someone sees there to be a red apple in front of him – a perceptual taking that Sellars models by a candid, spontaneous thinking-out-loud of the form: 'Lo! Here is a red apple' – then,

> given that he has learned how to use the relevant words in perceptual situations, he is justified in reasoning as follows:

> I just thought-out-loud 'Lo! Here is a red

apple' (no countervailing conditions obtain); so there is good reason to believe that there is a red apple in front of me'. (1975a, pp. 341–2)

This reasoning does not have the original perceptual judgement as its conclusion, but is rather an inference from the character and context of the original non-inferential experience to the existence of a good reason for accepting it as veridical. The 'trans-level' character of such a justificatory argument derives from the fact that its main premise asserts the occurrence (in a certain manner and context) of precisely the belief that is warranted by the reasoning as a whole, and it is this fact, too, that creates the impression that the belief in question is somehow *self-warranting*.

Sellars' thoroughgoingly HOLISTIC view of cognition and justification implies that the reasonableness of accepting even *first* principles is a matter of the availability of good arguments warranting their acceptance (Sellars, 1988). What is definitive of *first* principles, FP, is the unavailability of sound reasonings in which they are derived from still more basic premises:

(A1) . . . . . . . . . . .
        . . . . . . . . . . .
        Therefore, FP

The unavailability of sound reasonings of the form (A1), however, is entirely compatible with the existence of good 'trans-level' arguments of the form:

(A2) . . . . . . . . . .
        . . . . . . . . . .
        Therefore, *it is reasonable to accept* FP,

in whose conclusion the principle FP is, in essence, mentioned.

Since accepting principles is something persons *do*, Sellars interpreted the conclusion of (A2) as the claim that a particular course of epistemic conduct could be supported by adequate reasons, i.e. that there is a sound *practical* argument whose conclusion expresses the intention to engage in such conduct:

(A3) I shall achieve desirable epistemic end E
        Achieving E implies accepting principles of kind K.
        The principle FP is of kind K
        
        Therefore, I shall accept FP.

On Sellars' view the forms of justificatory reasoning governing the acceptance of individual lawlike generalizations (both universal and statistical) and whole theoretical systems mobilize just such patterns of practical inference. Adopting a systematic theoretical framework is ultimately justified by an appeal to the epistemic end of 'being able to give non-trivial explanatory accounts of established laws' (1964, p. 384); and adopting statistical nomologicals which project the observed frequency of a property in a class (including the case in which this frequency = 1) to unobserved finite samples of the class, by the epistemic end of

being able to draw inferences concerning the composition with respect to a given property Y of unexamined finite samples . . . of a kind, X, in a way which also provides an explanatory account of the composition with respect to Y of the total examined sample, K, of X. (1964, p. 392)

Crucially, these epistemic ends are concerned with 'the realizing of a logically necessary condition of being in the framework of explanation and prediction' at all (1964, p. 397). Since, on Sellars' view, inductive reasoning does not need to *vindicated*, i.e. shown to be truth-preserving, but rather is itself a form of *vindication*, i.e. (deductive) practical justificatory reasoning, the ends-in-view to which it appeals must be capable of being *known* to obtain or be realized. The end of being in possession of laws and principles that enable one to draw predictive inferences and produce explanatory accounts satisfies this practical constraint; such Reichenbachian ends as being in possession of (approximately) true limit-frequency statements, where such limits exist, do not.

*See also* the GIVEN.

471

WRITINGS

'Empiricism and the philosophy of mind', in Sellars 1963, pp. 127–96.

*Science, Perception and Reality* (London: Routledge & Kegan Paul, 1963).

'Phenomenalism', in Sellars 1963, pp. 60–105; cited as (1963a).

'Induction as vindication', in Sellars 1975, pp. 367–416.

*Philosophical Perspectives* (Springfield: Thomas, 1967); reprinted in two volumes, *Philosophical Perspectives: History of Philosophy* and *Philosophical Perspectives: Metaphysics and Epistemology* (Reseda: Ridgeview, 1977).

*Essays in Philosophy and Its History* (Dordrecht: Reidel, 1975).

'The structure of knowledge', in *Action, Knowledge, and Reality* ed. H.-N. Castaneda (Indianapolis: Bobbs-Merrill, 1975[a]).

The Carus Lectures for 1977–78, *The Monist* 64 (1981).

'On Accepting First Principles', *Philosophical Perspectives* 2 (1989). (Contains a complete bibliography of Sellars' published work through 1989.)

JAY ROSENBERG

**sensation/cognition** There are various ways of classifying mental activities and states. One useful distinction is that between the propositional attitudes and everything else. A propositional attitude is one whose description takes a sentence as complement of the verb. Belief is a propositional attitude: one believes (truly or falsely as the case may be) that there are cookies in the jar. That there are cookies in the jar is the proposition expressed by the sentence following the verb. Knowing, judging, inferring, concluding and doubting are also propositional attitudes: one knows, judges, infers, concludes or doubts that a certain proposition (the one expressed by the sentential complement) is true.

Though the propositions are not always explicit, hope, fear, expectation, intention and a great many other terms are also (usually) taken to describe propositional attitudes: one hopes that (is afraid that, etc.) there are cookies in the jar. Wanting a cookie is, or can be construed as, a propositional attitude: wanting that one have (or eat or

whatever) a cookie. Intending to eat a cookie is intending that one will eat a cookie.

Propositional attitudes involve the possession and use of *concepts* and are, in this sense, representational. One must have some knowledge or understanding of what Xs are in order to *think, believe* or *hope* that something is X. In order to *want* a cookie, *intend* to eat one, or be *disappointed* that they are all gone, one must, in some way, know or understand what a cookie is. One must have this concept. (There is a sense in which one can want to eat a cookie without knowing what a cookie is – if, for example, one mistakenly thinks there are muffins in the jar and, as a result, wants to eat what is in the jar (= cookies). But this sense is hardly relevant; for in this sense one can want to eat the cookies in the jar without wanting to eat any cookies.) For this reason (and in this sense) the propositional attitudes are *cognitive*: they require (or presuppose) a level of understanding and knowledge, the kind of understanding and knowledge required to *possess* the concepts involved in occupying the propositional state.

Though there is sometimes disagreement about their proper analysis, non-propositional mental states, on the other hand, do not (at least not on the surface) take propositions as their object. Being in pain, being thirsty, smelling the flowers and feeling sad are introspectively prominent mental states that do not, like the propositional attitudes, require the application or use of concepts. One doesn't have to understand what pain or thirst is to experience pain or thirst. Assuming that pain and thirst are *conscious* phenomena, one must, of course, be conscious or aware of the pain or thirst to experience them, but awareness *of* must be carefully distinguished from awareness *that*. One can be aware of X – thirst or a toothache – without being aware that that (i.e. thirst or a toothache) is what, in fact, one is aware of. Awareness *that* (like belief that and knowledge that) is a propositional attitude; awareness *of* is not.

As the examples (pain, thirst, tickles, itches, hunger) are meant to suggest, the non-propositional states have a felt or experienced ('phenomenal') quality to them that is absent in the case of the propositional attitudes. Aside from who it is we believe to be playing the tuba, believing that John is playing the tuba is much the same as believing that Joan is playing the tuba. These are different propositional states, different beliefs, yes, but they are distinguished entirely in terms of their propositional content – in terms of what they are beliefs about. Contrast this with the difference between *hearing* John play the tuba and *seeing* him play the tuba. Hearing John play the tuba and seeing John play the tuba differ, not just (as do beliefs) in what they are *of* or *about* (for these experiences are, in fact, of the same thing: John playing the tuba), but in their qualitative character: the one involves a visual, the other an auditory, experience. The difference between seeing John play the tuba and hearing John play the tuba, then, is a *sensory*, not a cognitive, difference.

Some mental states are a combination of sensory and cognitive elements. Fear and terror, sadness and anger, joy and depression, are ordinarily thought of in the way sensations are: not in terms of what proposition (if any) they are directed at, not in what (if anything) they represent, but (like visual and auditory experiences) in their intrinsic character, in how they feel to the person experiencing them. But when we describe a person as being afraid that, sad that, upset that (as opposed to merely thinking or knowing that) so-and-so happened, we typically mean to be describing the kind of sensory (feeling or emotional) quality accompanying the cognitive state. Being afraid that the dog is going to bite me is both to think (that he might bite me) – a cognitive state – and feel fear or apprehension (sensory) at the prospect.

The perceptual verbs exhibit this kind of mixture, this duality between the sensory and the cognitive. Verbs like 'to hear', 'to see', and 'to feel' are (often) used to describe propositional (cognitive) states, but they describe these states in terms of the *way* (sensory) one comes to be in them. Seeing that there are two cookies left is coming to know that there are two cookies left *by seeing*. Feeling that there are two cookies left is coming to know

this in a different way, by having tactile experiences (sensations).

On this model of the sensory-cognitive distinction (at least as it is realized in perceptual phenomena), sensations are a pre-conceptual, a pre-cognitive, vehicle of sensory information. The terms 'sensation' and 'sense-data' (or simply 'experience') were (and, in some circles, still are) used to describe this early phase of perceptual processing. It is currently more fashionable to speak of this sensory component in perception as the percept, the sensory information store, the icon (for these, *see* Neisser, 1967) or (from computer science) the $2\frac{1}{2}$-D sketch (Marr, 1982). But the result is generally the same: an acknowledgement of a stage in perceptual processing in which the incoming information is embodied in 'raw' sensory (pre-categorical, pre-recognitional) form (Crowder and Morton, 1969). This early phase of the process is comparatively modular – relatively immune to, and insulated from, cognitive influences (Fodor, 1983). The emergence of a propositional (cognitive) state – seeing *that* an object is red – depends, then, on the earlier occurrence of a conscious, but none the less non-propositional condition: seeing (under the right conditions, of course) the red object. The sensory phase of this process constitutes the delivery of information (about the red object) in a particular form (visual); cognitive mechanisms are then responsible for extracting and using this information – for generating the belief (knowledge) that the object is red. (The existence of Blindsight suggests that this information can be delivered, perhaps in degraded form, at a non-conscious level.)

To speak of sensations *of* red objects, tubas, and so forth is to say that these sensations carry information about objects, information (in the case of vision) about an object's colour, its shape, orientation and position; and (in the case of audition) information about acoustic qualities (pitch, timbre, volume). It is not to say that the sensations share the properties of the objects they are sensations of or that they *have* the properties they carry information about. Auditory sensations are not loud and visual sensations are not coloured. Sensations are bearers of (unconceptualized) information, and the bearer of the information that something is red need not itself *be* red. It need not even be the sort of thing that could be red; it might be a certain pattern of neuronal events in the brain. None the less, the sensation, though not itself red, will (being the normal bearer of this information) typically produce in the subject who undergoes the experience a belief, or tendency to believe, that something red is being experienced. Hence the existence of hallucinations.

Just as there are theories of the mind (e.g. certain forms of functionalism) that would deny the existence of any state of mind whose essence was purely qualitative (i.e. did not consist of the state's extrinsic, causal, properties), there are theories of perception and knowledge – *cognitivist theories* – that deny a sensory component to ordinary sense perception (e.g. Gibson, 1950; Armstrong, 1961; Pitcher, 1971). The sensory dimension (the look, feel, smell, taste of things) is (if it isn't altogether denied) identified with some cognitive condition (knowledge or belief) of the experiencer. All seeing (not to mention hearing, smelling, and feeling) becomes a form of believing or knowing. As a result, organisms that cannot know (believe, etc.) cannot have experiences. Often, to avoid these strikingly counterintuitive results, cognitive theorists resort to unconscious, implicit, or otherwise unobtrusive (and, typically, undetectable) forms of believing (or knowing).

Aside, though, from introspective evidence (closing and opening one's eyes, if it changes beliefs at all, doesn't *just* change beliefs; it eliminates and restores a distinctive kind of conscious experience), there is a variety of empirical evidence for the existence of a stage in perceptual processing that is conscious without being cognitive (in any recognizable sense). For example, experiments with brief visual displays (Sperling, 1960; Averbach and Coriell, 1961) reveal that when subjects are exposed for very brief (e.g. 50 msec) intervals to information-rich stimuli (e.g. a $3 \times 3$ array of numbers), there is persistence (at the conscious level) of what is called (by psychologists) an image or visual icon that embodies *more* information about the (now absent) stimulus than the subject can cognitively process or report on. Subjects can (depending on later prompts) exploit the information in this persisting icon by reporting on *any* part of the absent array of numbers (they can, for instance, report the top three numbers; the middle three; or the bottom three). They cannot, however, identify *all* nine numbers. They report *seeing* all nine, and they can identify any one of the nine (actually, any three), but they cannot identify all nine. Knowledge and belief, recognition and identification – these cognitive states, though present (on any given trial) for any two or three numbers in the array, are absent for all nine numbers in the array. Yet, the image carries information (sufficient unto recognition and identification) about *all nine* numbers (how else account for subjects' ability to identify *any* number in the absent array?). Obviously, then, information is there, in the experience itself, *whether or not it is (or even can be) used*. As psychologists (e.g., Lindsay and Norman, 1972, p. 329) conclude, there is a limit on the information processing capabilities of the later (cognitive) mechanisms that is not shared by the sensory stages themselves.

*See also* CONCEPT; EXPERIENCE; THE GIVEN; LINGUISTIC UNDERSTANDING; SENSE-DATA.

BIBLIOGRAPHY

Armstrong, D.: *Perception and the Physical World* (London: Penguin, 1961).

Averbach, E. and Coriell, A.S.: 'Short-term storage of information in vision', *Information Theory: Proceedings of the Fourth London Symposium* ed. C. Cherry (London: 1961).

Dretske, F.: *Knowledge and the Flow of Information* (Cambridge, MA: MIT Press, 1981).

Fodor, J.: *The Modularity of Mind* (Cambridge, MA: MIT Press, 1983).

Gibson, J.: *The Perception of the Visual World* (Boston: Houghton Mifflin, 1950)

Lindsay, P.H. and Norman, D.A.: *Human Information Processing* (New York: Academic Press, 1972).

Marr, D.: *Vision: A Computational Investigation*

*into the Human Representation and Processing of Visual Information* (San Francisco: Freeman, 1982).

Neisser, U.: *Cognitive Psychology* (New York: Appleton-Century-Crofts, 1967).

Pitcher, G.: *A Theory of Perception* (Princeton: Princeton University Press, 1971).

Sperling, G.: 'The information available in brief visual presentations', *Psychological Monographs* 74, no. 11 (1960).

FRED DRETSKE

**sense-data**  Sense data are the twentieth-century successors to the EMPIRICISTS' concepts of IDEAS of sense. The term 'sense-data', introduced by Moore and Russell, refers to the immediate objects of perceptual awareness, such as colour patches and shapes, usually supposed distinct from surfaces of physical objects. Qualities of sense-data are supposed to be distinct from physical qualities because their perception is more relative to conditions, more certain, and more immediate, and because sense data are private and cannot appear other than they are. They are objects that change in our perceptual fields when conditions of perception change and physical objects remain constant.

Critics of the notion question whether, just because physical objects can appear other than they are, there must be private, mental objects that have all the qualities the physical objects appear to have. There are also problems regarding the individuation and duration of sense-data and their relations to physical surfaces of objects we perceive. Contemporary proponents counter that speaking only of how things appear cannot capture the full structure within perceptual experience captured by talk of apparent objects and their qualities.

*See also* ACT/OBJECT ANALYSIS; ARGUMENT FROM ILLUSION; CERTAINTY; EXPERIENCE; FOUNDATIONALISM; THE GIVEN; INFALLIBILITY; REPRESENTATIVE REALISM.

BIBLIOGRAPHY

Barnes, W.H.F.: 'The myth of sense data', in *Perceiving, Sensing, and Knowing* ed. R. Swartz (Garden City: Anchor, 1965), 138–67.

Jackson, F.: *Perception* (Cambridge: Cambridge University Press, 1977).

Moore, G.E.: 'Sense-data', in his *Some Main Problems of Philosophy* (London: Allen and Unwin, 1953), 28–51.

Price, H.H.: *Perception* (New York: McBride, 1933).

Russell, B.: 'On our knowledge of the external world', in his *Our Knowledge of the External World* (New York: Norton, 1929), 67–103.

ALAN H. GOLDMAN

**Sextus Empiricus**  A Greek sceptic of the Pyrrhonist school, and a practicing physician, who flourished probably during the late second century AD. His exact dates are controversial and the details of his life virtually unknown to us, yet he is the most important source of our knowledge of ancient Greek sceptical philosophies. The works that have come down to us are the *Outlines of Pyrrhonism* in three books, which provides us with Sextus' own positive account of Pyrrhonian scepticism, and a larger work in eleven books, commonly referred to collectively as *Against the Mathematicians*. The latter contains much of the same material as found in the Outlines, but it also provides additional sceptical arguments against dogmatic philosophers as well as valuable information about the major philosophical schools of the Hellenistic period. It appears that little of the philosophical material in Sextus' writings is original with him. We know, for example, that he drew freely on the thought of earlier Pyrrhonian sceptics, especially Aenesidemus in the first century BC (*see* PYRRHONISM).

Sextus describes scepticism as a 'philosophy' and a 'way of life', identifying both a theoretical and an anti-theoretical practical component in Pyrrhonian scepticism. The appearance of paradox is genuine, for the sceptic engages in theoretical reasoning in order finally to do away with it. The sceptic is an 'inquirer' into truth, but unlike other philosophers whom Sextus classifies as either dogmatists or Academics, he neither claims

SEXTUS EMPIRICUS

to have discovered the truth nor does he say that it cannot be discovered (*Outlines*, I 3–4). The Pyrrhonian sceptic, *qua* philosopher, just continues to inquire. Sextus himself goes beyond the role of inquirer in presenting a positive and highly sophisticated theoretical account of scepticism as a way of life in which the practical dimension of Pyrrhonian scepticism remains one of its most important and distinctive features (Stough, 1984). Sceptical argumentation always has a practical aim. Sextus likens the sceptic's arguments to a drug designed to cure a peculiarly philosophical ailment characteristic of dogmatists, who boldly and uncritically put forth theories about how things really are (*Outlines*, III 280–1). The sceptic's strategy is intended to cure this pathological inclination and indeed, when properly understood, his own arguments refute themselves along with all the rest. Sextus' writings contain elaborate and extensive arguments which were deployed against all dogmatic philosophers, but most notably STOICS who strenuously defended a criterion of truth as the foundation of their philosophical system.

The sceptic himself, Sextus says, initially set out to determine the truth or falsity of his impressions of things in an effort to attain ATARAXIA, the tranquil and untroubled state of mind put forth as the end (*telos*) of scepticism. But instead he found himself confronted with contradictory appearances and arguments of equal weight and credibility (*see* ISOSTHENEIA). Unable to decide between them, he adopted a neutral attitude, suspending judgement about their truth or falsity (*epoche*), and found 'as if by chance' that *ataraxia* followed 'as a shadow follows its object' (*Outlines*, I 26). Sextus' narrative provides us with a model for the sceptical method. Scepticism is defined as the ability to produce oppositions between appearances and judgements 'in any manner whatsoever' as a means of facilitating the noncommittal attitude of neither affirming nor denying anything (*Outlines* I, 8). Sceptics make a practice of balancing the opposing claims of the dogmatists against each other. In doing so they find 'no more' reason to prefer one position than another. The arguments in

support of competing theories are equally strong, hence equally persuasive. Pyrrhonists therefore suspend judgement, taking no position at all about what is true or false.

Characteristic of the sceptical method are the 'modes' (*tropoi*) of Pyrrhonian scepticism preserved in Sextus' writings. The sceptical modes are patterns of argument designed to induce suspense of judgement. The best-known of several different groups of modes are the Ten Modes of *Epoche* attributed to Aenesidemus, which are elaborated at length in the first book of Sextus' *Outlines of Pyrrhonism*. Each mode makes distinctive use of the fact that things 'appear' different to us in different situations. How something looks (tastes, smells, feels, and the like) is determined by ten factors delineated by the modes, such as conditions affecting subject and object and the circumstances in which the object appears. These variations are invoked to produce 'oppositions', which are expressed in propositions typically assigning incompatible appearances (properties) to an object. The sceptic then claims *isostheneia* of appearances and ends by suspending judgement about how things really are. Schematically the argument looks like this (modification of Annas and Barnes, 1985):

1. X appears F in situation Sl.
2. x appears F' in situation S2.
3. We have no criterion (or proof) independent of Sl and S2 to judge between F and F'.
4. We can neither affirm nor deny that x is really F or F'.

F and F' represent oppositions of appearances, predicates which in the sceptic's view cannot be jointly true of a subject. In one mode Sl and S2 vary in the positions occupied by the perceiver. The same boat looks small and stationary when viewed from a distance, but large and in motion from close at hand. Another mode notes the effects of the various circumstances or conditions a subject may be in when an object is perceived. Air that feels cold to an older person feels mild to someone in his prime. Further modes appeal to differences among the senses, differences in the quantity and composition of an object, the effect of admixtures, the effect of relativity, and numerous other factors influencing the way things appear to us. Since the oppositions are equally balanced, the appearances are equally credible. The sceptic therefore withholds assent and neither affirms nor denies that x is really F or F'.

As a consequence of suspending judgement about how things really are (all such matters being 'non-evident' (*adela*) according to Sextus), the sceptic holds no true or false beliefs. Sextus insists, however, in response to criticism, that the sceptic is not reduced to inactivity, nor is he forced into inconsistency, by his neutrality in regard to belief (Frede, 1979; Burnyeat, 1980). The Pyrrhonian sceptic assents to his impressions of things and follows appearances as a criterion for acting in everyday life. Although he holds no beliefs, and makes no assertions, about what is or is not so, he never questions the fact that things appear this way or that. His speech, which merely records how things appear to him, has expressive and regulative functions pertaining solely to action (Stough, 1984). Sextus maintains that the sceptic can follow appearances as a practical criterion for everyday affairs without committing himself to any beliefs or statements about what really is the case.

*See also* MONTAIGNE; PYRRHONISM; SCEPTICISM, MODERN; STOICISM.

WRITINGS

*Opera*. 3 vols (Leipzig: Teubner, 1912–54). Vols 1, 2, ed. H. Mutschmann (1912–14); vol. 3, ed. J. Mau (Indices, K. Janacek) (1954).
*Works* 4 vols trans. R.G. Bury, Loeb Classical Library (London: William Heinemann, 1933–49): vol. 1, *Outlines of Pyrrhonism* (1933); vol. 2, *Against the Mathematicians* (1935); vol 3, *Against the Physicists*; *Against the Ethicists* (1936); vol. 4, *Against the Professors* (1949).

BIBLIOGRAPHY

Annas, J. and Barnes, J.: *The Modes of Scepticism* (Cambridge: Cambridge University Press, 1985).

Barnes, J.: 'The beliefs of a Pyrrhonist', *Proceedings of the Cambridge Philological Society* 29 (1982), 1–29 and *Elenchos* 4 (1983), 5–43.
Brochard, V.: *Les Sceptiques grecs* (Paris: F. Alcan, 1887); 2nd edn reprinted (Paris: Librairie Philosophique J. Vrin, 1959).
Burnyeat, M.: 'Can the sceptic live his scepticism?', in *Doubt and Dogmatism* eds M. Schofield, M. Burnyeat and J. Barnes (Oxford: Clarendon Press, 1980), 20–53.
Frede, M.: 'Des sceptikers Meinungen', *Neue Hefte für Philosophie* 15/16 (1979), 102–29.
Long, A.: 'Sextus Empiricus on the criterion of truth', *Bulletin of the Institute of Classical Studies* 25 (1978), 35–49.
Stough, C.: *Greek Scepticism* (Berkeley: University of California Press, 1969).
Stough, C.: 'Sextus Empiricus on non-assertion', *Phronesis* 29 (1984), 137–64.
Stough, C.: 'Knowledge and belief', *Oxford Studies in Ancient Philosophy* 5 (1987), 217–34.
Striker, G.: 'The ten tropes of Aenesidemus', in *The Sceptical Tradition* ed. M. Burnyeat (Berkeley: University of California Press, 1983), 95–115.

CHARLOTTE STOUGH

**simplicity** Philosophers and scientists have often held that the simplicity or parsimony of a theory is one reason, all else being equal, to view it as true. This goes beyond the unproblematic idea that simpler theories are easier to work with and have greater aesthetic appeal.

One theory is more parsimonious than another when it postulates fewer entities, processes, changes or explanatory principles; the simplicity of a theory depends on more or less the same considerations, though it is not obvious that parsimony and simplicity come to the same thing. It is plausible to demand clarification of what makes one theory simpler or more parsimonious than another before the justification of these methodological maxims can be addressed.

If we set this descriptive problem to one side, the major normative problem is as follows: What reason is there to think that simplicity is a sign of truth? Why should we accept a simpler theory instead of its more complex rivals? Newton and Leibniz thought that the answer was to be found in a substantive fact about nature. In *Principia*, Newton laid down as his first Rule of Reasoning in Philosophy that 'nature does nothing in vain, . . . for Nature is pleased with simplicity and affects not the pomp of superfluous causes'. Leibniz hypothesized that the actual world obeys simple laws because God's taste for simplicity influenced his decision about which world to actualize.

Epistemology since Hume and Kant has drawn back from this theological underpinning. Indeed, the very idea that nature is simple (or uniform) has come in for critique. The view has taken hold that a preference for simple and parsimonious hypotheses is *purely methodological*; it is constitutive of the attitude we call 'scientific' and makes no substantive assumption about the way the world is.

A variety of otherwise diverse twentieth-century philosophers of science have attempted, in different ways, to flesh out this position. Two examples must suffice here; see Hesse (1969) for summaries of other proposals. POPPER (1959) holds that scientists should prefer highly falsifiable (improbable) theories; he tries to show that simpler theories are more falsifiable. QUINE (1966), in contrast, sees a virtue in theories that are highly probable; he argues for a general connection between simplicity and high probability.

Both these proposals are *global*. They attempt to explain why simplicity should be part of the scientific method in a way that spans all scientific subject matters. No assumption about the details of any particular scientific problem serves as a premiss in Popper's or Quine's arguments.

Newton and Leibniz thought that the justification of parsimony and simplicity flows from the hand of God; Popper and Quine try to justify these methodological maxims without assuming anything substantive about the way the world is. In spite of these differences in approach, they have something in common. They assume that all uses of parsimony and simplicity in the separate sciences can be encompassed in a single justifying argument.

Recent developments in confirmation theory suggest that this assumption should be scrutinized. Good (1983) and Rosenkrantz (1977) have emphasized the role of auxiliary assumptions in mediating the connection between hypotheses and observations. Whether an hypothesis is well supported by some observations, or whether one hypothesis is better supported than another by those observations, crucially depends on empirical background assumptions about the inference problem at hand. The same view applies to the idea of prior PROBABILITY (or prior plausibility). If one hypothesis is preferred over another even though they are equally supported by current observations, this must be due to an empirical background assumption.

Principles of parsimony and simplicity mediate the epistemic connection between hypotheses and observations. Perhaps these principles are able to do this because they are surrogates for an empirical background theory. It isn't that there is one background theory presupposed by every appeal to parsimony; this has the quantifier order backwards. Rather, the suggestion is that each parsimony argument is justified only to the degree that it reflects an empirical background theory about the subject matter at hand. Once this theory is brought out into the open, the principle of parsimony is entirely dispensable (Sober, 1988).

This *local* approach to the principles of parsimony and simplicity resurrects the idea that they make sense only if the world is one way rather than another. It rejects the idea that these maxims are purely methodological. How defensible this point of view is will depend on detailed case studies of scientific hypothesis evaluation and on further developments in the theory of scientific inference.

*See also* NATURAL SCIENCE.

BIBLIOGRAPHY

Good, I.: *Good Thinking: the Foundations of Probability and Its Applications* (Minneapolis: University of Minnesota Press, 1983).
Hesse, M.: 'Simplicity', in *The Encyclopedia of*

*Philosophy* ed. P. Edwards (New York: Mac-Millan, 1969), 445–8.

Popper, K.R.: *The Logic of Scientific Discovery* (London: Hutchinson, 1959).

Quine, W.V.: 'Simple theories of a complex world', in his *The Ways of Paradox and Other Essays* (New York: Random House, 1966), 242–6.

Rosenkrantz, R.: *Inference Method, and Decision* (Dordrecht: Reidel, 1977).

Sober, E.: *Reconstructing the Past: Parsimony. Evolution and Inference* (Cambridge, MA: MIT Press, 1988).

ELLIOTT SOBER

**social sciences, epistemology of** Do the social sciences require any special treatment or can the results of general epistemology, which have in modern times usually been formulated with an eye to the natural sciences, be applied directly to them? This question has exercised philosophers and social scientists more or less from the beginnings of self-consciously 'scientific' investigations of social phenomena. Among the founders of modern social science, MILL, Weber and Durkheim, to name a few, all commented on it. In the contemporary context, this issue is often addressed under the heading *naturalism*, i.e. the doctrine that the methods of the natural sciences can be used in the study of society. Self-proclaimed anti-naturalists nowadays abound, but, ironically, frequently situate themselves with respect to characterisations of the natural scientific enterprise that are themselves now dated. For, after Kuhn (1970), it will certainly no longer suffice to place oneself in opposition to naturalism, to rail against the restrictive tenets of VERIFICATIONISM, a position which no longer commands great respect even in relation to epistemology of the natural sciences.

There are at least three *prima facie* reasons for wondering whether naturalism can be sustained or whether it is necessary, instead, to articulate for the social sciences an epistemology which doesn't simply ape the preoccupations and conclusions of 'mainstream' natural-scientifically-oriented epistemology.

First, there is the *reflexivity* of the social sciences in relation to the objects of their scrutiny. By this I refer, in particular, to the fact that human beings, the objects of study, come to take up points of view towards their own activities which are influenced, however indirectly, by the results of social scientific investigations, and which therefore in some sense retrospectively invalidate these investigations (which made no provision for the 'appropriation' of their results by their subjects). (Alfred Schutz (1971, p. 495) was already aware of a cognate phenomenon – the 'pre-interpreted' character of 'social reality', which implies, he thought, that social scientists are, at least in the first instance, dependent for their understanding of social reality on the understandings of their subjects.) Although this phenomenon was perhaps most poignantly identified in relation to so-called 'reflexive predictions' (self-fulfilling or self-defeating 'prophecies'), it is of much more general significance. When social actors acquire familiarity with social scientific ideas, their behaviour and attitudes are no longer 'naive' with respect to them and the ideas themselves no longer apply as straightforwardly. And this, it is sometimes said, is a distinguishing mark of the social sciences; there is nothing in the domain of natural scientific concern that corresponds to the mutual interplay that seems unavoidable between social scientists and the subjects of their research. (The influence of the observer on what is observed of quantum mechanical phenomena is, surely, only vaguely analogous.)

Secondly, there is the *complexity* of social phenomena, or perhaps, more correctly, their relative imperviousness to controlled (and thought-) experimental manipulation in the 'Galilean style' which involves abstraction, idealization and the identification of underlying mechanisms – *prima facie* complexity then being interpreted as a product of the interaction of these, themselves simple mechanisms. Mill had already identified the impediments, for the development of a genuinely predictive social science, thrown up by the complexity of social phenomena, and the difficulties seem to remain. To some, such as F.A. Hayek (1973–8, vol. 2, ch. 10), this feature of social scientific research suggests that students of social phenomena confine their interest to the elucidation of patterns and other structures of order, abandoning as futile the aspiration to develop a genuinely predictive science of human behaviour and social interaction. Since it is widely believed that such complexity as is manifested in relation to 'purely natural' phenomena *is* susceptible to manipulation using broadly 'Galilean' techniques and that the products of such manipulation *are* genuinely predictive theories, this feature is also held to mark a difference between natural and social scientific domains.

Thirdly, there is the (essential) *contestability* of many of the theoretical concepts of the social sciences (*see* Gallie, 1955–6). By this I refer, of course, to the fact that we are required to make what could reasonably be called 'value judgements' in order to apply or refuse the application of many of the most important social scientific concepts. This is so, according to Gallie and his followers, because the concepts themselves are at least partially, and ineradicably, *evaluative* rather than strictly 'descriptive' (*see* FACT/ VALUE), but, perhaps more importantly, because the criteria for their application are many and because judgements, which themselves have an evaluative dimension, need to be made in order to determine whether these criteria have been adequately satisfied in any particular case. (The evaluative character of many social scientific concepts may be a legacy of the dependence, stressed by Schutz, of social scientific concepts on the concepts of ordinary social agents, which are certainly themselves evaluative. It seems to mark a limit of neo-Weberian aspirations for a 'value-free' social science and to explain the strenuous, but apparently pointless attempts to 'operationalize' the concepts in terms of which theories are framed – or otherwise purge them of connotations unacceptable to the POSITIVIST tradition.) Since such fundamental social theoretical concepts as power and RATIONALITY are, *prima facie*, essentially contestable in this sense, while all the key concepts of the natural sciences appear not to be, this feature too is held to

mark a distinction between natural and social scientific investigations, and therefore, along with reflexivity and complexity, to herald the need for a distinctive epistemology for the social sciences.

Many are those who have been persuaded by these and similar considerations to accept that there is a difference in kind between the techniques appropriate to the social sciences and those appropriate to the natural sciences and, what is more, between the epistemological orientations of these two great branches of learning. If the fundamental orientation of the natural sciences is a *technical* one, aiming at prediction and control of natural phenomena, then, according to HABERMAS among many others, that of the social sciences is or ought to be either *practical*, aiming at understanding or *critical*, aiming at liberation. In either case, we encounter the idea that the social sciences do not or ought not to aim at the development of abstract general theories which provide a basis for fine-grained predictions of concrete social phenomena, but that they ought, instead, to aim at understanding or to interpret.

One way of capturing what's at issue on this account is by reference to a distinction between 'thin' and 'thick' descriptions of an agent's action or of some social-structure feature (cf. Geertz, in Gibbons, 1987). We give a thin description of some action, for instance, when we describe it in a more or less 'behaviouristic' vocabulary of bodily movements. We give a thick description of this same action when we describe it in the vocabulary of native members of the community in which it occurs, i.e. according to their understanding of its significance and character. So an action is thinly described as sticking pieces of flesh in the fire and thickly described as cooking or sacrificing to the gods, as the case may be. Clearly, thick descriptions are interpretations, 'from the native's point of view' according to Geertz, and the provision of them represents an important contribution to our understanding of human affairs. Furthermore, the provision of such descriptions is unthreatened by the phenomena of reflexivity, complexity, and contestability. Of course, we may have to provide different interpretations when interpretees become aware of the interpretations we have already provided – reflexivity is catered for, not eliminated. But we are not incapacitated, in the provision of interpretations, by either complexity or contestability: in the latter case, the contestability of native concepts is simply 'reflected' in the contestability of our thick descriptions or interpretations of native behaviour and structures.

(For earlier generations, the idea of *verstehen* embodied this understanding of the distinctive interpretive orientation of the social sciences. For some of our contemporaries this understanding is embodied in the project of HERMENEUTICS especially associated, perhaps, with the work of Hans-Georg GADAMER; for others in the project of genealogy especially associated perhaps with the work of Michel FOUCAULT; *see* Rabinow, 1984.)

The notion of *interpretation*, then, is central to anti-naturalist conceptions of social science. But, as has often been noted, it contains an ambiguity of crucial political importance. There is a hermeneutics of *recovery*, on the one hand, and a hermeneutics of *suspicion*, on the other hand. In the one case, we aim to recover the socially-constitutive self-understandings of ordinary social agents; in the other (Gibbons, 1987, p. 4) we aim to penetrate IDEOLOGY, self-delusion and other mystificatory aspects of agents' self-understandings to 'uncover the real or true meaning of social and political practice'. In the one case, we aim to reconstitute self-consciously and explicitly what agents have themselves already constituted as a basis for their social lives. This aim is especially important in relation to ways of life initially quite 'alien' to us and so is commonly, and rightly, associated with the anthropological enterprise. In the other case, our aim is informed by the fundamental insights of NIETZSCHE, MARX and FREUD. They have taught us that social actors do not always adequately comprehend the character of their motives or of the institutional framework in which they perform, and that any genuine understanding of these matters will require treating with suspicion agents' self-understandings, which

are, on this account, themselves to be understood rather than, as on the more 'naïve' account, treated as sources of understanding. (Also of some relevance, ironically, are the insights of 'mainstream' politico-economic theorists from the time of Adam Smith and including POPPER who have identified 'unintended consequences' as an additional source of self-misunderstanding, or, at least, of the inadequacy, for an understanding of social life, of an understanding of agents' self-understanding of their actions (*see* e.g. Hayek, 1973–8, vol. I).)

How firm is this contrast between the hermeneutics of recovery and the hermeneutics of suspicion? For the hermeneutics of recovery we need to assume a broad basis of agreement in beliefs, desires and other propositional attitudes between social scientists and the subjects of their research. This assumption is embodied in what Donald DAVIDSON (1984) calls the PRINCIPLE OF CHARITY and unless we make and can legitimately make this assumption about the subjects of our research, their activities must remain mysterious to us. Of course, it is not implied, simply because we assume a broad basis of agreement, that we will never be able to discover disagreement, should it exist. Although we may be reluctant to attribute 'odd' attitudes to the subjects of our interpretive investigations (*see* Quine, 1960) we may sometimes be right to do so – e.g. where we have a good explanation of the 'oddity' of these attitudes.

There are nevertheless many obscurities and much controversy about criteria of interpretive adequacy precisely in relation to this issue. Many interpreters have been notably reluctant to 'take literally' the religious or 'philosophical' attitudes of interpretees (at least where these diverge too much from 'mainstream' attitudes) and have claimed, in defence of this reluctance, that good reasons can be offered to treating the utterances apparently expressive of such attitudes as metaphorical, or more broadly, symbolic in character (*see* Skorupski, 1976). But these kinds of cases, as difficult as they are to resolve, point, more deeply, to the fundamentally HOLISTIC character of the interpretive project and to the potential for an apparently irreducible multiplicity of interpretations – a manifestation, in this domain, of the INDETERMINACY OF TRANSLATION.

As QUINE has emphasized, how a particular object of interpretation is to be understood is determined, where it can be, only against a very broad background of considerations. It is possible, by making adjustments at relevant loci in a complex system of attitudes, to interpret any given object in a number of different ways, each of which is 'correct' relative to the (suitably adjusted) system in which it is incorporated (see ONTOLOGICAL RELATIVITY).

Other important contributions to our understanding of the hermeneutics of recovery are John Rawls' idea (1973) of 'reflective equilibrium', which seems to capture Quinean ideas about adjusting some parts of a larger system in order to accommodate other potential elements, and Ronald Dworkin's idea (1986) of the 'interpretive attitude', which draws special attention to the requirement that we strive, in interpretation, 'to make an object the best it can be, as an instance of some assumed enterprise'.

All these ideas seem to suggest that a kind of RELATIVISM is not easily to be avoided in the realm of interpretation. They also suggest that the distinction between the hermeneutics of recovery and the hermeneutics of suspicion is somewhat overdrawn. If some attitudes of interpretees may have to be treated 'symbolically' interpretation sometimes involves *correction* of agents' naïve self-understandings, with the possibility, at least, of concomitant liberation from them. And if there are always going to be several different and incompatible ways of making 'best sense' of one's interpretes, this undermines the thought that in the hermeneutics of suspicion we look down upon our interpreters from a position whose nature gives our results a claim to objective validity.

Still, what holds the distinction in place is the idea that while a hermeneutics of recovery rests on the principle of charity and the assumption that many attitudes are shared by interpreter and interpretee, a her-

meneutics of suspicion seems to presuppose that the interpreter occupies a vantage-point which is privileged in relation to that of the interpretee (in Marxism, this is the point of view of the vanguard party, or perhaps the proletariat; in Freudianism, it is the point of view of the analyst) – or perhaps that both take up a point of view which provides a basis for some kind of superior insight. In the work of HABERMAS (1981) this appears as the notion of communicative action which may involve the testing, in discourse, of the validity claims which are implicit in the various acts of interpretation. Claims which can pass such tests provide points of leverage against our pre-reflective beliefs. (There is resonance here with the idea, in moral-political theory, of an Archimedean point – *see* Rawls, 1973, p. 41.)

The idea that the interpreter is in a privileged position, and the idea that there is a privileged position which lies at some remove from those of interpreter and interpretee, can be contrasted with the concept of geneology associated with the work of Michel Foucault (*see* Rabinow, 1984). This seems, on the one hand, to deny that there is *any* privileged perspective from which hidden realities can be perceived, while, on the other hand, claiming to provide an account of those institutional, ideological and historical contingencies (masquerading as necessities) which form our ideas and practices.

If the idea of interpretation is central to the anti-naturalistic conception of social scientific activity, it is by no means clear, as many anti-naturalists have tended to assume, that this sets their activities apart from those of natural scientist engaged in the study of non-human phenomena. Certainly, many of the themes of anti-naturalists and interpretivists are to be found in (and, perhaps ironically, are derived from) the work of Thomas Kuhn and his predecessors and successors (*see* Bernstein, 1983). Just as social scientists seek to interpret the attitudes, actions and works of human beings, so too, it might be said, do natural scientists search for an interpretation of natural phenomena, a way of making sense of them to ourselves. And they too are likely to find, as Quine has emphasized, that their efforts are only holistically constrained, rather than tied to some incorrigible funda-ment, as previously sought in both RATIONALISM and EMPIRICISM alike. And so too are they likely to find, as Richard RORTY (1986) has recently much empha-sized, that there is no absolutely secure van-tage-point which, could we take it up, would provide us with what Hilary PUTNAM has called a 'God's-eye view' of the natural world. There is, then, a kind of double irony about the epistemology of the social sciences. In articulating a distinctive account of the activities and aspirations of social scientists, philosophers have contributed to a re-orien-tation of thinking about general epistemol-ogy which somewhat effaces the distinction with which they started – between a nat-uralistically-oriented epistemology of the 'hard' sciences and an interpretivist episte-mology of the 'soft' sciences.

*See also* HISTORICAL KNOWLEDGE; IDEOLOGY; NATURAL SCIENCE.

BIBLIOGRAPHY

Bernstein, R.J.: *Beyond Objectivism and Relativ-ism* (Oxford: Blackwell, 1983).
Davidson, D.: *Inquiries Into Truth and Interpreta-tion* (Oxford: Oxford University Press, 1984).
Dworkin, R.: *Law's Empire* (London: Fontana, 1986).
Gallie, W.B.: 'Essentially contested concepts', *Proceedings of the Aristotelian Society* 56 (1955–6), 167–98.
Gibbons, M.T. ed.: *Interpreting Politics* (Oxford: Blackwell, 1987).
Habermas, J.: *The Theory of Communicative Action* trans. T. McCarthy (Boston: Beacon Press, 1981).
Hayek, F.A.: *Law, Legislation and Liberty* 3 vols (Chicago: University of Chicago Press, 1973–8).
Kuhn, T.S.: *The Structure of Scientific Revolutions* rev. edn (Chicago: University of Chicago Press, 1970).
Quine, W.V.: *Word and Object* (Cambridge, MA: MIT Press, 1960).
Rabinow, P. ed.: *The Foucault Reader* (Harmond-sworth: Penguin, 1984).
Rawls, J.: *A Theory of Justice* (Oxford: Oxford University Press, 1973).
Rorty, R.: *Philosophy and the Mirror of Nature* (Princeton: Princeton University Press, 1979).
Schutz, A.: 'Concept and theory formation in the social sciences', reprinted in *Sociological Perspectives* eds K. Thompson and J. Tunstall (Harmondsworth: Penguin, 1971).
Skorupski, J.: *Symbol and Theory* (Cambridge: Cambridge University Press, 1976).

FRED D'AGOSTINO

**sociology of knowledge** The aim of the sociology of knowledge is to locate whatever body of belief a group accepts as a true account of reality, and then try to illuminate it by reference to social variables. In the first instance the questions are:

1. What exactly is believed?
2. How is that belief distributed, e.g. who believes and who doesn't?
3. What are the sources of its credibility?
4. How is it defended against doubt and anomaly?

The explanatory resources available to socio-logists that can shed light on these issues are:

(a) a concern for the processes of socializa-tion by which a group tries to transmit its culture to new members;
(b) identifying the goals and interests of members of the group;
(c) studying the processes of negotiation by which a degree of consensus may be achieved;
(d) attending to the rhetorical devices that are used in the course of disputes; and
(e) revealing the way the classifications, meanings and judgements that structure a body of knowledge are held as conven-tions.

Thus, studying the precise *use* to which a belief is put, whether implicitly or explicitly, can prove a valuable exercise. This can show a body of knowledge in an unexpected light, revealing the operation of interests that more traditional, 'internalist' accounts may have passed over. An example would be the studies which show us the social use given to the

Corpuscular and Newtonian philosophies (cf. Jacob, 1976; Shapin and Schaffer, 1985).

The typical conception of the sociology of knowledge presents it as a limited exercise which is confined to studying the general conditions that might encourage or inhibit the growth of knowledge. Genuine knowledge, especially scientific knowledge, is assumed to be the result solely of our rational commerce with nature. The most that sociologists could hope to explain would be how we come to be in a position to conduct such enquiries and why, on occasion, our perception of their results is clouded or distorted; e.g. 'ideology' might suppress 'free enquiry', and bias the handling of evidence. Sociologists might therefore explain why, say, the Edinburgh middle classes in the mid-nineteenth century were widely attracted to phrenology, but they are unlikely to help us understand why the university anatomists and philosophers of the city dismissed it as error. Error and falsehood might need to be propped up by tradition, convention, authority and interest, but the real core of knowledge, when properly identified, will stand on its own two feet (i.e. observation and reason).

This limited conception, in which we have primarily a sociology of error, might be called the 'weak programme' in the sociology of knowledge. Over the past two decades cogent reasons have emerged for throwing aside these restrictions and pursuing a stronger programme, i.e. one which sees all knowledge claims as social phenomena that are equally problematic. On the STRONG PROGRAMME the aim is to avoid limiting our curiosity by treating what we take for granted as if it were unproblematic or self-explanatory. Consequently all bodies of institutionalized belief, whether we evaluate them as true or false, rational or irrational, are to be analysed in the same general way. For example, the practices of members of a culture where witchcraft is accepted should be no more problematic than those of a culture where it is rejected. A deviant member of the former, e.g. an individual who did not believe in witchcraft, should be no less a source of explanatory interest than deviant members of ours, i.e. individuals who *do*

believe in it. Of course, the sociologist must make various assumptions about the social agents under study, e.g. about their experience and material circumstances, but this can be done in ways that highlight the problematic character of their beliefs, whatever they are. How the world is doesn't fix how it will be described or understood by the people whose beliefs are to be explained. It is to be noted, though, that all bodies of institutionalized belief, however bizarre they may seem to us, must be compatible with ordinary human reasoning propensities, i.e. with 'natural rationality'.

Confidence in the viability of the stronger rather than the weaker programme in the sociology of knowledge has two sources: one empirical, the other theoretical. First, historians have given us impressively detailed studies of episodes from the history of science that have implicitly supported the stronger claim. Although historians do not necessarily see themselves as supporting any particular vision of knowledge, their enquiries have eroded the false distinction between socially sustained error and rationally sustained truth. This is because in practice they have uncovered ever more of the social contingencies in the development of knowledge, such as the operation of particular interests. They have done so regardless of the evaluative distinction between true or false theories, and correct or incorrect conclusions. Significantly, most of this work has not dealt with the genesis of theories (that remains locked in the enigmatic thought processes of individuals), but with their evaluation, i.e. with the context of justification, *not* the context of discovery. The scope of the historical work is very wide, ranging from studies of the way broad political concerns impinged on early conceptions of force, to the impact of narrowly professional interests on specific techniques and practices in botanical classification. Some of the work deals with episodes in the history of modern science, such as the disputes over Boyle's air pump experiments, while other work deals with early evolutionary debates, conflicts in modern statistics, and even the structure of elementary particle physics. It is far too extensive and detailed to survey here, but a bibliographical guide, including a most valuable survey, is given at the end. This work provides the real substance of current thinking in the sociology of knowledge. It is detailed and empirical, not broad or programmatic; it exemplifies the concrete virtues of Anglo-Saxon historiography rather than the more speculative standpoint of continental philosophy. The persuasive power of the discipline cannot be appreciated without it.

Such work will not, however, convince a determined sceptic. It is always possible to gloss it in ways that minimize its significance. Just as it is always possible to read, say, the record of moral diversity as a catalogue of error and evil (and hence miss its full relativizing potential), we can do the same with the social history of science. It can be read as a record of mistaken ideas plus a study of the more or less accidental circumstances surrounding certain discoveries. At most it will then reveal the contingencies that happened to place people in a position to receive the indications of reason and observation. To offset this minimizing tendency it is necessary to furnish and defend the theoretical perspective that brings out the full significance of the historical work. It is the increasing awareness of this perspective that provides the second of the reasons for appreciating the true scope of the sociology of knowledge.

Philosophers themselves, especially philosophers of science, have done most of the groundwork. In particular they have exhibited the systematic UNDERDETERMINATION OF THEORY by evidence in science. Philosophers have then gone on to ask what is the *best* way to close the evidential gap. Sociologists and historians, by contrast, have enquired into the *actual* way it is closed. Clearly, underdetermination calls for the involvement of further factors in the construction of a rounded conception of the world. These will be partly psychological – our natural tendencies to draw certain kinds of conclusion – and partly sociological, e.g. our inherited assumptions, our local purposes and interests. To study this in more detail, assume we are scientists trying to test a theory. This is the point at which we

interact most directly with reality. We begin with a body of background assumptions (A) and an hypothesis (H). From these we draw a prediction (O) about an observation to be expected under certain precise conditions. Thus we have $(A \& H) \rightarrow O$. We then compare the predicted O with the report that sums up the results of our investigations, i.e. what we actually observed (call this o'). The effect of the comparison will be some rational state of belief regarding H. Precisely what that belief should be is described differently by different philosophers depending on whether they are realists, instrumentalists, or whatever. It may be probable belief of a certain degree, pragmatic acceptance or rejection, or some other appropriate rational attitude. For our purposes these different accounts of the correct stance that ought to be taken are not important, because they are normative rather than descriptive. What does matter, however, is the underlying logical structure that we have just described that these different accounts have in common. It can serve as a general description of the structure of our thinking. It emerges – and this is the vital point – that at each stage and facet of the process we are dealing with a social phenomenon. The claim is not that the processes are 'purely' social, or 'merely' social; we must never forget the psychological component of 'natural rationality' running through them, but they each have a social aspect which is central to them and which cannot be removed without altering their character. Let us therefore go step by step through the standard structure, at each point locating its social character.

First, the background assumptions (A). These will mostly be inherited elements of an accepted culture, though they will be a special purpose selection from them, a selection sustained by the experience, traditions and purposes of some group of practitioners. Although many of these assumptions will be articulated and framed as propositions, some of them are best thought of as built into the habits and behaviour patterns of the group. They will be shared 'practices'; and even the explicitly formulated assumptions will only have a determinate meaning because of their

485

being integrated into these practices. This is the sociological significance of the work of WITTGENSTEIN and its application to the philosophy of science in Kuhn's idea of a 'paradigm' – a concrete scientific achievement that acts as a model for subsequent work.

Second, take the hypothesis under test (H). This will have no unique, privileged formulation. Any given articulation of it might be modified or improved or altered in order to bring out what it had 'all along' been meant to express. A theory, even if it is identified with a specific set of sentences, is a fluid thing whose substance is, in principle, constantly negotiable, and which at any one time will have the status of a convention. The extent to which it is modified in the face of inevitable anomaly and trouble depends on a trade-off between the theory and the background assumptions. As Duhem made clear, we have a choice here. Nature, observation and the indications of reason do not point to a unique response. Once again the judgement involved, if it becomes accepted into the scientific culture, will have the form of a convention.

Third, the process by which the implications of the theory, the prediction, are extracted from it is not simply a matter of logically drawing out meaning which is unproblematically contained within the theory. There is no such unproblematic meaning. Every avenue by which a theory may be related to a particular and concrete episode of observation is fraught with difficulty, and can be rationally contested. At every point assumptions have to be made, e.g. about the purity of chemicals, the integrity and closure of the apparatus, etc. These assumptions might be otherwise, and their acceptability and determination again depend on the conventional practices of the group.

Fourth, the process of comparison between a prediction and the results of investigation is likewise underdetermined by reason and observation alone. As Kuhn pointed out, the tables of figures in text books which set predictions and observations side by side actually serve to define what counts, in the

circumstances, as a 'good fit', i.e. what counts as good enough for the practitioners. Naïvely, it may seem simple to decide if the predicted O and the observed O' are, or are not the 'same', but of course criteria of 'sameness' pose us with a classificatory problem, and the conventional and interested character of classification is widely acknowledged. The excellent fit between Gay-Lussac's work on gases and Dalton's atomic theory didn't impress Dalton. What may pass as a negligible difference from one point of view may look like a significant divergence from another. What is mere anomaly for one scientist could be a decisive refutation for another.

Little wonder, then, that a careful scrutiny of the details of a scientific episode reveals that it is shot through with contingencies whose matter-of-fact resolution depends on the ways that practitioners organise their interactions with one another. The sociology of knowledge isn't a subject whose attractions and plausibility depend on taking a distant and vaguely focussed look at science in the attempt to trace broad patterns and trends. Quite the contrary; it makes better sense the more closely we look, because the higher the resolution of our microscope, the more obvious are the holes in the threadbare fabric of more traditional philosophical accounts.

*See also* GENETIC EPISTEMOLOGY; NATURAL SCIENCE; RELATIVISM.

BIBLIOGRAPHY

A most valuable survey of the relevant historical literature up to 1982 is S. Shapin, 'History of science and its sociological reconstructions', *History of Science* 20 (1982), 157–210. Other important works, which mostly appeared after the above, include:

Collins, H.: *Changing Order* (Beverly Hills: Sage, 1985).
Desmond, A.: *The Politics of Evolution: Morphology, Medicine and Reform in Radical London* (Chicago: Chicago University Press, 1989).
Jacob, M.C.: *The Newtonians and the English Re-*

volution, *1689–1720* (Hassocks: Harvester, 1976).

MacKenzie, D.: *Statistics in Britain, 1865–1930: The Social Construction of Scientific Knowledge* (Edinburgh: Edinburgh University Press, 1981).

Pickering, A.: *Constructing Quarks: A Sociological History of Particle Physics* (Edinburgh: Edinburgh University Press, 1984).

Pinch, T.: *Confronting Nature: The Sociology of Solar-Neutrino Detection* (Dordrecht: Reidel, 1986).

Rudwick, M.J.S.: *The Great Devonian Controversy: The Shaping of Scientific Knowledge Among Gentlemanly Specialists* (Chicago: Chicago University Press, 1985).

Shapin, S. and Schaffer, S.: *Leviathan and the Air-Pump: Hobbes, Boyle, and the Experimental Life* (Princeton: Princeton University Press, 1985).

DAVID BLOOR

**Socrates** *see* PLATO.

**solipsism** Doctrines and threats of solipsism are much older than the introduction of the term 'solipsism' to mark them. The term derives from the Latin 'solus ipse'. This means literally 'self alone', and less literally either 'I alone exist' or else 'I alone am conscious', yielding in the first case a more idealist form of solipsism querying the existence of an independent material world, and in the second case a more materialist form allowing for the (possible) existence of a material world but again not countenancing the existence of other minds or centres of consciousness.

It is common to distinguish between *metaphysical* (or ontological) *solipsism, epistemological solipsism* and *methodological solipsism*. The metaphysical solipsist contends that he alone *is* (exists, or is real); the epistemological solipsist contends that only he *certainly is* (exists, or is real); the methodological solipsist typically holds to solipsism as some sort of methodological strategy (either a method of inquiry or else a constructional programme). DESCARTES, in seeking to reconstruct his knowledge and base science on 'a foundation wholly my own', can be seen as following a policy of Methodological Solips-

ism: this involved passing through a brief phase of Epistemological Solipsism from which he escaped by (supposedly) proving the existence of a non-deceiving God, while still retaining the first-personal basis.

RUSSELL, who described solipsism as 'hard to refute, but still harder to believe', drew a distinction between what he called *dogmatic solipsism* and what he called *sceptical solipsism* (1948, pp. 191–8). The first corresponds more or less closely to Metaphysical Solipsism and the second to Epistemological Solipsism. His distinction parallels that between the atheist who denies outright and the agnostic who merely doubts. But whichever of these forms is in question Russell held that ordinary solipsism is a pusillanimous half-measure; a consistent or honest solipsist should adhere to the more radical *solipsism of the present moment*. The crux for Russell was that to go beyond the data provided by present experience required principles of inference that could not themselves be empirically justified: the cost of abandoning this radical form of solipsism was to accept that empiricism has (clearly pretty drastic!) limits. SANTAYANA saw the escape route in 'animal faith', while recognizing merit in an attitude which confines attention to the passing moment. Wittgenstein confessed a temptation to assert, 'All that is real is the experience of the present moment.'

It is notable that both Russell and WITTGENSTEIN took solipsism to be a serious philosophical issue. (The same applies to some important continental philosophers like HUSSERL.) What comes into focus with Wittgenstein's treatment is what can be called *conceptual solipsism*. Whereas the more familiar variety of solipsist denies or doubts whether there are in fact any other minds, the conceptual solipsist contends that it is inconceivable that there are any. Although the distinction between conceptual solipsism and factual versions of solipsism cuts across the distinction between dogmatic and sceptical solipsism, it remains true that a dogmatic solipsist had better be a conceptual solipsist and that a conceptual solipsist had better not be a sceptical solipsist. For the position that there are no other minds but in fact there might have been has nothing whatsoever going for it; and the conceptual solipsist cannot allow any probability at all to the proposition that other minds exist (see OTHER MINDS).

Wittgenstein famously remarked that 'If one has to imagine someone else's pain on the model of one's own, this is none too easy a thing to do: for I have to imagine pain I *do not feel* on the model of the pain which I *do feel*' (1953, §302). Somewhat similarly it might be contended that one cannot conceive of a mind of which one is not conscious on the model of one's own conscious mind: hence that other conscious minds are inconceivable to one. In order, however, not to fall too easy prey to conceptual solipsism it is worth noting that even if it is conceded that I cannot conceive of another mind it by no means follows that it is inconceivable that there are other minds. This can be seen from considering Thomas Nagel's claim that he does not know what it is like to be a bat: he implies that there exists something (the bat's mind or experiences) of which he cannot conceive. (That said, the inability to conceive some other mind does result in some sort of quasi-solipsistic isolation from it.)

A problem for the solipsist is that he or she may be well aware that others can argue exactly the same way. AYER pointed out (1986, p. 29) that philosophers are tempted by a sort of generalized solipsism for which he coined the paradoxical term *multiple solipsism*. (For example, 'pain' in A's mouth means real pain when applied to his own but pain-behaviour when applied to B's, and the same goes for 'pain' in B's mouth.) He accused the early Wittgenstein, Carnap and his own earlier self of this type of view which he came to think was incoherent (1986, p. 38). Wittgenstein overcame his early predilection for this and other forms of solipsism by means of his private language argument, but whether Carnap ever came to see the error of his ways - if such it be - is less clear.

The project to which CARNAP (1967, p. 102) applied the term 'methodological solipsism' was that of each person constructing the whole language including that about physical objects, cultural objects, other minds

and even their own mind on an 'autopsychological' basis, where that took the form of an initially subjectless given. This basis he held was a matter of choice but it possessed the (alleged) advantage of following the epistemological order (1967, p. 101). Bennett, however, has used the term for the acknowledgement of what he takes to be an inevitable feature of the human epistemic situation: each of us can utilize and assess evidence only according to how things seem to *us* (1974, pp. 66–9). The term 'methodological solipsism' has been given fresh currency from an influential article which Putnam published in 1975. He used it for the assumption that 'no psychological state, properly so called, presupposes the existence of any individual other than the subject to whom that state is ascribed' (p. 220). Putnam's usage is followed by Fodor (1987, ch. 2) in proposing methodological solipsism as a research strategy in cognitive psychology. How far that project is removed from orthodox solipsism is shown in the fact that it is to be used by psychologists in studying other minds.

*See also* ARGUMENT FROM ANALOGY; OTHER MINDS; WITTGENSTEIN.

BIBLIOGRAPHY

Ayer, A.J.: *Ludwig Wittgenstein* (Harmondsworth: Penguin, 1986).
Bennett, J.: *Kant's Dialectic* (Cambridge: Cambridge University Press, 1974).
Carnap, R.: *The Logical Structure of the World* (London: Routledge, 1967).
Fodor, J.: *Psychosemantics* (Cambridge, MA: MIT Press, 1987).
Putnam, H.: *Philosophical Papers* vol. 2 (Cambridge: Cambridge University Press, 1975).
Russell, B.: *Human Knowledge* (London: Allen and Unwin, 1948).
Wittgenstein, L.: *Philosophical Investigations* (Oxford: Blackwell, 1953).

CLIVE BORST

**Spinoza, Benedict (*also* Baruch) (1632–77)** Dutch philosopher. Spinoza's epistemology is both a response to his seventeenth-century context (*see* RATIONALISM) and an integral part of his philosophy. His 1663 *Descartes's 'Principles of Philosophy'*, which is a reformulation of the first two parts of DESCARTES' famous work into the axiomatized 'geometrical order' of presentation modelled on Euclid, manifests a deep understanding of Cartesian epistemology. Spinoza's own epistemology is presented primarily, though not exclusively, in Part II of his *Ethics* and in an earlier unfinished work, *Treatise on the Emendation of the Intellect*, both of which were first published in the *Opera postuma* of 1677. Although he follows Descartes in emphasizing the distinction between intellect and imagination as representational faculties, his epistemology nevertheless differs from that of Descartes in a number of fundamental respects.

One such difference – and one on which Spinoza particularly insists – lies in his rejection of Descartes' account of error, according to which error is the result of the will's freely affirming ideas from which it has the power to withhold assent. On Spinoza's deterministic alternative, every idea naturally involves affirmation of its own content; an idea can and will be denied or doubted only when the mind also has another idea which contradicts the first or calls it into question (*Ethics* 2 p. 49).

An equally fundamental difference lies in Spinoza's doctrine that truth 'requires no sign' (*TEI* 34–6) and is instead 'its own standard' (*Ethics* 2 p. 43s). Descartes treats 'clarity and distinctness' as an introspectible characteristic of ideas, a characteristic that can and must – after an appropriate process of vindication – be used as a criterion for the quite separate characteristic of truth. Spinoza rejects the need for any such separate criterion, and hence also for any such process of vindication. Indeed, since the truth of true ideas can be discerned directly for Spinoza – 'the true thought is distinguished from a false one not only by an extrinsic, but chiefly by an intrinsic denomination' (*TEI* 69) – Cartesian methodological scepticism becomes unnecessary. Doubt, he holds, arises only when the mind has two related ideas, at least one of which is obscure (*TEI* 78). Its proper remedy

is to proceed in the correct order, deducing effects from causes, so that the mind will never have ideas whose bearing on one another is uncertain (*TEI* 80). Thus, to begin as Descartes does, by searching out grounds for doubt, is from Spinoza's point of view simply to guarantee that one will proceed in the wrong order, and thereby to put as many obstacles as possible in the way of one's ultimate success.

Partly because of his claim that truth is 'chiefly an internal denomination', some commentators have maintained that Spinoza held a 'coherence' theory of truth; others, citing his axiom that 'a true idea must agree with its object' (*Ethics* 1a7), have maintained that he held a 'correspondence' theory of truth (*see* TRUTH). In fact, however, his well-known doctrine that modes of thought are identical with their objects (*Ethics* 2p7s) arguably allows him to hold that truth consists *both* in what he calls the internal 'adequacy' of an idea, *and* in what he calls its 'agreement' with its object, on the grounds that these two characteristics of ideas are really the same characteristic considered in two different ways. His monism requires that there be only one thinking substance, God, of which human minds are modes. He asserts that all ideas are true as they exist in God; however, they may be mutilated and confused, and hence false, as they exist in individual human minds (*Ethics* 2 pp.32–5).

Spinoza distinguishes three kinds of knowledge (*Ethics* 2 p.40s2). The first and lowest is opinion (*opinio*), consisting of 'random' sensory experience (i.e. experience not determined by the intellect) and external reports; this kind of knowledge is imaginative and inadequate. The second is reason (*ratio*), which involves adequate intellectual knowledge of things through their properties, as opposed to their essences. This knowledge includes and is largely based on the 'common notions,' which are ideas of characteristics that are 'common to all things' and are 'equally in the part and in the whole'. He gives few examples of such characteristics, but he does cite, as giving rise to common notions, the fact that all bodies involve the concept of the same attribute (i.e. extension), the fact that all bodies are susceptible to motion and rest, and the fact that all bodies are susceptible to degrees of motion (Lemma 2 after *Ethics* 2 p.13). Thus it appears that, for Spinoza, at least some knowledge of physics can be of the second kind, based on the knowledge of universal properties of bodies. (Knowledge of the second kind is, however, by no means restricted to physics; it is also possible in psychology at least.) The third and highest kind of knowledge is intuition (*scientia intuitiva*), which 'proceeds from an adequate idea of the formal essence of certain attributes of God to the adequate knowledge of the essence (as opposed to the mere properties) of things'. Knowledge of both the second and third kinds is thus 'adequate' and intellectual. In Spinoza's ethical theory, adequate knowledge, and especially knowledge of the third kind, constitutes the greatest good of life.

## WRITINGS

*Spinoza Opera* ed. C. Gebhardt, 4 vols (Heidelberg: Carl Winter, 1923).

*The Collected Works of Spinoza* ed. E.M. Curley, 2 vols, vol. 1 (Princeton: Princeton University Press, 1985).

## BIBLIOGRAPHY

Curley, E.M.: 'Experience in Spinoza's theory of knowledge', in *Spinoza: A Collection of Critical Essays* ed. M. Grene (Garden City, NY: Anchor, 1973), 25–59.

Gueroult, M.: *Spinoza* 2 vols: vol. 2, *L'Âme* (Paris: Aubier, 1974).

Matheron, A.: 'Spinoza and Euclidean arithmetic: the example of the fourth proportional', in *Spinoza and the Sciences* eds M. Grene and D. Nails (Dordrecht: Reidel, 1986), 125–50.

Parkinson, G.H.R.: *Spinoza's Theory of Knowledge* (Oxford: Clarendon Press, 1954).

*Studia Spinozana* 2 (1986): issue devoted to 'Spinoza's Epistemology'.

DON GARRETT

**Stoic epistemology**   The Stoic school was founded in Athens around the end of the fourth century BC by Zeno of Citium (335–263 BC). The school takes its name from the Stoa *poikile*, or painted colonnade, where its members met to discuss and expound their views. Following Zeno, orthodox Stoics divided philosophy into three parts: logic, physics and ethics. Epistemological issues were a concern of logic, which studied *logos*, reason and speech, in all of its aspects, not, as we might expect, only the principles of valid reasoning – these were the concern of another division of logic, dialectic. The epistemological part, that concerned with canons and criteria, belongs to logic conceived in this broader way because it aims to explain how our cognitive capacities make possible the full realization of reason in the form of wisdom, which the Stoics, in agreement with Socrates, equated with virtue and made the sole sufficient condition for human happiness. Indeed, they went so far as to identify virtue and its exercise as the sole good, and their opposites, vice and vicious action, as the sole evil. At the same time, they held that items popularly supposed to be good or evil – fame, wealth and pleasure or ill repute, poverty and pain – are strictly speaking indifferent. The attitude of superiority required by this view towards the indifferents, especially to the so-called evils, is behind our use of the expressions 'stoic' and 'stoical'. This attitude is not, however, as we would expect, an affective, but a cognitive condition; and much of the emphasis in the Stoics' position on knowledge satisfying the most exacting standards is due to the overriding moral importance they attach to wisdom.

But if the Stoics' motivations are in some ways unfamiliar, their epistemological position, in its broad outlines at any rate, is much less so; it is in many ways similar to positions familiar to us from modern philosophy, far more so than the views of PLATO or Aristotle. This is not surprising, as the ancient authors who preserve most of what we know about Stoic epistemology, Cicero, Diogenes Laertius and SEXTUS EMPIRICUS, exerted considerable influence, directly and indirectly, on the philosophers of the early modern period. Hume's acknowledged debt to Cicero is only the most conspicuous example.

The Stoics are FOUNDATIONALISTS; according to them, we must start with a stock of secure, directly given impressions which, without standing in need of any support themselves, in one way or another somehow support everything else we know. And their position is an EMPIRICIST one; for the ground-level impressions of which it makes use are furnished by the senses. But before going on to consider how these impressions do what is required of them, we should take note of an element of complexity in the Stoic account. According to it, the impressions of adult human beings, unlike those of children and animals, are rational. This does not mean their judgements, which arise according to the Stoa when assent is given to an impression, cannot be criticized as irrational. Rather, what is meant is that these impressions have a rational structure; i.e. they have propositional content; they are impressions that something is the case, which represent the world as being a certain way by means of a stock of general concepts (see SELLARS; SENSATION/COGNITION). And the Stoics' empiricism first makes its presence felt in their account of how these concepts are acquired. Indeed Zeno seems to deserve credit for being the first to have compared the mind at birth to a blank slate (see TABULA RASA). Into this slate, he maintains, experience gradually inscribes the so called common notions, which will eventually make possible rational thought by means of rational impressions. The process begins with impressions of simple perceptual features, repeated experience of which results in memories; these in turn furnish the basis for the common notions – a developmental process not unlike that described by Aristotle. The process is completed at age seven or fourteen – our sources disagree – and thought is conducted thereafter by means of rational impressions.

As we noted, this is not to say that human beings who have reached this stage cannot have false beliefs, reason invalidly or form irrational attachments. Indeed, according to the Stoa, such is the corrupt condition of mankind that all human beings are thoroughly and viciously irrational in this sense. But they are now in principle capable of realizing fully the potential for reason which nature has given them.

Reason is fully realized as knowledge, which the Stoics define as secure and firm cognition unshakeable by argument. According to them, no one except the wise man can lay claim to this condition. He is armed by his mastery of dialectic against fallacious reasoning, which might lead him to draw a false conclusion from sound evidence, and thus possibly force him to relinquish the assent he has already properly conferred on a true impression. Hence, as long as he does not assent to any false ground-level impressions, he will be secure against error, and his cognitions will have the security and firmness required of knowledge. Everything depends, then, on his ability to avoid error in his ground-level perceptual judgements. To be sure, the Stoics do not claim that the wise man can distinguish true from false perceptual impressions; that is beyond even his powers. But they do maintain that there is a kind of true perceptual impression, the so-called cognitive impression, by confining his assent to which the wise man can avoid giving error a foothold.

An impression is cognitive when it is (a) from what is (the case), (b) stamped and impressed in accordance with what is, and (c) such that could not arise from what is not. And because all of our knowledge depends directly or indirectly on it, the Stoics make the cognitive impression the criterion of truth. It makes possible a secure grasp of the truth not only by guaranteeing the truth of its own propositional content, which in turn supports the conclusions that can be drawn from it; even before we become capable of rational impressions, nature must have arranged for us to discriminate in favour of cognitive impressions so that the common notions we end up with will be sound. And it is by means of these concepts that we are able to extend our grasp of the truth through inferences beyond what is immediately given; for this reason, the Stoics sometimes also speak of two criteria: cognitive impressions and common notions.

These Stoic claims about the cognitive impression elicited a strong sceptical response from Plato's successors in the ACADEMY, who produced a mass of arguments intended to suggest that, contrary to the Stoic view, it is always possible in the case of any true impression, however clear and forceful, that another impression indistinguishable from the first could have arisen in circumstances that make it false. If so, there are no true impressions such that they could not be false as far as an intrinsic, discriminable feature of theirs is concerned, thus no guarantee in any given case that assent has not been conferred on a false impression. These arguments – including those based on the power of the gods to induce true-seeming false impressions and the inability of dreamers and madmen to distinguish true from false impressions – were to exert a tremendous influence on the later history of epistemology. We should not suppose because of our greater familiarity with the sceptics' case, however, that the Stoics were not able to mount a powerful defence of their position.

The details of that defence are beyond our present scope, but there are two features of the Stoic position which must not be overlooked if we are to avoid giving a seriously misleading picture of it. First, the emphasis placed upon the security and certainty of the wise man's judgements by the Stoa does not exclude judgement under conditions of uncertainty. The wise man will sometimes, e.g., choose actions on the basis of expectations about the future which will not be fulfilled. To be sure, he does not assent to impressions which later developments will show to have been false, but he does sometimes judge that certain expectations are reasonable. And this judgement will not be falsified by later developments. Second, the Stoics are empiricists not only regarding concept formation. Though on their view every event is the necessary outcome of antecedent causal conditions, a grasp of whose nature should in principle support a rational, conceptually sanctioned inference predicting that event, even the wise are very

rarely in a position to achieve such a grasp or draw such an inference. Instead, they must rely on observed relations of conjunction and sequence between events the underlying causal connections between which remain unknown. A large part of the knowledge on which the Stoic wise man must rely will also be empirical in this sense.

WRITINGS

Fragments of the Stoics can be found in two places:

Arnim, H. von ed.: *Stoicorum Vetera Fragmenta*, 3 vols (Leipzig: Teubner, 1903–5); vol. 4, indices by M. Adler (Leipzig: Teubner, 1924).

Long, A.A. and Sedley, D.N. ed. and trans.: *The Hellenistic Philosophers* 2 vols (Cambridge: Cambridge University Press, 1987).

There are texts with English translation of the major ancient sources in the Loeb library series:

Bury, R.G. ed. and trans.: *Sextus Empiricus: Outlines of Pyrrhonism and Against the Mathematicians*, 4 vols (London: Heinemann, 1933–49).

Hicks, R.D. ed. and trans.: *Diogenes Laertius: Lives of Eminent Philosophers*, 2 vols, vol. 2, Bk VII (London: Heinemann, 1925).

Rackham, H. ed. and trans.: *Cicero: De Natura Deorum and Academica* (London: Heinemann, 1933).

BIBLIOGRAPHY

Annas, J.: 'Stoic epistemology', in *Epistemology* ed. S. Everson (Cambridge: Cambridge University Press, 1990), 184–203.

Frede, M.: 'Stoics and sceptics on clear and distinct ideas', in *The Sceptical Tradition* ed. M.F. Burnyeat (Berkeley: University of California Press, 1983), 65–93.

Sandbach, F.H.: 'Phantasia kataleptike' and 'Ennoia and prolepsis', in *Problems in Stoicism* ed. A.A. Long (London: Athlone, 1971), 9–21, 22–37.

Striker, G.: Kriterion tes aletheias', *Nachrichten der Akademie der Wissenchaften in Göttingen* Phil-hist. klasse, Nr 2 (1974), 47–110.

J.V. ALLEN

**Strawson, Peter Frederick (1919–)** P.F.

Strawson has spent most of his career at the University of Oxford, becoming Waynflete Professor of Metaphysical Philosophy in 1968. He has published extensively, principally in metaphysics and philosophical logic. Though he has not offered a general theory of knowledge, a dominant aim has been that of devising a response to scepticism. Strawson has offered different reasons for rejecting scepticism, but he also thinks that it is wrong to provide 'justifications' for our opinions resting on a supposedly privileged foundation. In 1952 he argued that inductive scepticism has its source in confusion, and no justification of our practices is required (*see* the PROBLEM OF INDUCTION). His basic reason, though, is that our fundamental objective categories cannot be abandoned at any stage in our thinking, nor can we even describe our experiences without them (*See* Strawson, 1979). Strawson's chief preoccupation as an epistemologist has been to substantiate and explore the consequences of this.

In *Individuals* and *The Bounds of Sense*, he tried to show that scepticism is involved in a deep incoherence, because the intelligibility of the concepts which the sceptic himself employs requires acceptance of things the sceptic is doubtful of. Arguments to show this are called TRANSCENDENTAL ARGUMENTS.

In *Individuals*, Strawson argued that for us space-occupying bodies are the basic objects of thought. We also think about possessors of consciousness, persons, and they must, at least characteristically, have both psychological and material attributes. The chief epistemological thesis is that it is a condition for having such a conceptual scheme that the basis we standardly regard as sufficient for certain judgements must in fact be sufficient. Thus, our normal ways of telling that another is in a given psychological state must be 'logically adequate kinds of criteria' (Strawson, 1959, p. 105).

In *The Bounds of Sense* Strawson further developed such arguments by defending many of KANT's central views after detaching them from transcendental idealism. In particular, Strawson supported a version of Kant's thesis that for a sequence of experiences to belong to a self-conscious subject they must constitute experience of an objective world. The central idea is that a substantive concept of an experiencing subject has employment only where we can apply the distinction between how in those experiences things seem to be and how they really are. This distinction can apply only if the experience is thought of as being of an objective world.

Debate about these arguments has centred on whether the conceptual dependencies are strongly enough established, and also on what the requirement of objective experience amounts to.

In *Scepticism and Naturalism* Strawson presented a new response, with its roots in HUME and WITTGENSTEIN. The thesis is that sceptical arguments should be dismissed as idle, since they cannot persuade us. Counter-arguments, even of a transcendental type, are not needed, though they may reveal conceptual connections. The reason for this is that we cannot help believing in (say) bodies and other minds.

While the psychological claim seems indisputable, criticisms of Strawson's naturalism have focussed on whether the psychological facts justify a dismissal of sceptical arguments. It is widely felt that a rejection of scepticism is unsatisfactory unless, at the very least, some mistake can be located in such arguments.

*See also* OTHER MINDS; PROBLEMS OF INDUCTION; TRANSCENDENTAL ARGUMENTS.

WRITINGS

*Introduction to Logical Theory* (London: Methuen, 1952).

*Individuals* (London: Methuen, 1959).

*The Bounds of Sense* (London: Methuen, 1967).

*Scepticism and Naturalism* (London: Methuen, 1985).

'Perception and its objects', in *Perception and Identity* ed. G.F. Macdonald (London: Macmillan, 1979).

BIBLIOGRAPHY

Ayer, A.J.: 'The concept of a person', in his *The Concept of a Person and Other Essays* (London: Macmillan, 1963).

Evans, G.: 'Things without the mind – a commentary upon chapter two of Strawson's *Individuals*', in his *Collected Papers* (Oxford: Clarendon Press, 1985).

Stroud, B.: 'Transcendental arguments', *Journal of Philosophy* 65 (1968), 241–56.

P. F. SNOWDON

**strong programme**   In the sociology of knowledge the 'strong programme' embodies the aim of sociologically explaining not just inadequately grounded or biassed beliefs, but also true and rationally held beliefs. The hope is to provide not just a sociology of error, but a sociology of genuine knowledge. The 'weak programme' represents the more limited aim under which the sociologist studies *either* the generalized preconditions for the growth of knowledge, *or* the specific sources of distortion, but treats the rational acts of apprehending inferences and evidence as falling outside the scope of the discipline. Adopting the strong programme does not mean denying the role either of sense experience or of our natural reasoning propensities, but it does mean seeing them as inadequate by themselves to account for the phenomenon called 'knowledge'. In particular it means appreciating the way inputs from these sources must be organised and interpreted in the course of constructing a shared representation of reality that is held as a convention. One formulation of the strong programme declares its explanatory aims to be:

1. *Causal*: it would be concerned with the conditions that bring about belief – though, of course, sociological causes will always cooperate with others, e.g. psychological processes.

2. *Impartial*: both true and false, rational and irrational beliefs would require explanation.

3. *Symmetrical*: both sides of the above dichotomies would call for causal explanations of the same type, e.g. in terms of socialization, responsiveness to interests,

the pursuit of a multitude of practical goals, the need to construct conventions and sustain consensus, to integrate new knowledge in existing culture, etc.

4. *Reflexive*: in principle its patterns of explanation would have to be applicable to itself. (If they were not, it would be a standing refutation of its own theories.)

Naturally this programme has proven controversial.

*See also* SOCIOLOGY OF KNOWLEDGE.

BIBLIOGRAPHY

Barnes, B.: *Scientific Knowledge and Sociological Theory* (London: Routledge and Kegan Paul, 1974).

Barnes, B.: *T.S. Kuhn and Social Science* (London: Macmillan, 1982).

Bloor, D.: *Knowledge and Social Imagery*, 2nd edn (Chicago: Chicago University Press, 1991).

Brown, J.R. ed.: *Scientific Rationality: The Sociological Turn* (Dordrecht: Reidel, 1984).

Brown, J.R.: *The Rational and the Social* (London: Routledge, 1989).

Collins, H.: *Sociology of Scientific Knowledge: A Source Book* (Bath: Bath University Press, 1982).

DAVID BLOOR

**Suárez, Francisco (1548–1617)**   Spanish philosopher and theologian known as Doctor Eximius. Born in Granada, he joined the Society of Jesus in 1564, studied at Salamanca, and taught law, theology and philosophy there and also at Rome, Coimbra and other leading universities. Apart from his many theological works, he wrote four important philosophical treatises. *De legibus* (1612) deals with traditional legal problems and with issues arising from the discovery of America, *De Deo uno et trino* (1606) is concerned with the nature of the Trinity but has implications for philosophical theology, and *De anima* (1621) concentrates on psychology and epistemology. His most important work, however, is the *Disputationes metaphysicae* (1597), which is the first systematic and comprehensive work of metaphysics written in the West that is not a commentary on Aristotle's *Metaphysics*. It is divided into fifty-four disputations that cover every metaphysical topic known at the time. Its influence was immediate and lasting. Within a few years of its publication, it had become the standard text in the field in continental Europe. Its impact can be seen in the thought of Descartes, Leibniz, Wolff, Schopenhauer and others.

Suárez's sources are vast, ranging from antiquity to his contemporaries, but it is in ARISTOTLE and Thomas AQUINAS that he finds most frequent inspiration. His main contributions to philosophy occur in metaphysics and law, although his thought is also relevant in many other areas, including epistemology. Suárez followed the scholastic procedure of raising epistemological issues in the context of metaphysics; thus preestablished metaphysical categories determined to a great extent the type of epistemological questions he raised. Three Suárecian doctrines are of particular interest for epistemology. They concern the object of metaphysics, knowledge of the singular, and middle knowledge. The first two serve as a bridge between scholastic and modern philosophy.

According to Suárez, the proper object of metaphysics is the objective concept of being (*DM* II, 1). An objective concept is a thing as conceived in the mind rather than the thing itself (*res ipsa*) or the act of understanding (*conceptus formalis*) whereby the mind understands. This doctrine has been interpreted as a step toward the progressive mentalization of metaphysics characteristic of modern philosophy, in which the object of the discipline is not reality (*res*), but a mental representation of it.

Suárez's understanding of the knowledge of the singular is another example of how he may be considered a bridge between scholastic and modern philosophy. He holds that our intellect knows the singular through a proper and separate concept (*DA* IV, 3, 3) without having to resort to reflection (IV, 3, 7). This thesis lends support to an EMPIRICIST point of view and undermines the position, accepted by Thomists among others, that knowledge of singulars is only indirect, through universals. Moreover, it contributes

to the erosion of any kind of realistic epistemology where real natures are the object of science.

Middle knowledge (*scientia media*) is the knowledge that God has of what every free creature would freely do in every situation where the creature could possibly be. It is a 'middle' knowledge because it stands somewhere in between the knowledge God has of the merely possible and the knowledge he has of the actual. Suárez used this notion to explain how God can control human action without violating free will (*De gratia*, prol. 2, 7, 1).

*See also* AQUINAS; CONCEPT; OCKHAM.

WRITINGS

*Opera omnia* 28 vols; ed. C. Berton (Paris: Vivès, 1856–61).

BIBLIOGRAPHY

Adams, R.M.: 'Middle knowledge and the problem of evil', *American Philosophical Quarterly* 14 (1977), 109–17.
Cronin, T.J.: *Objective Being in Descartes and Suárez* (New York: Garland, 1987).
Gracia, J.J.E. and Davis, D.: *The Metaphysics of Good and Evil according to Suárez* (Munich and Vienna: Philosophia Verlag, 1989).
Peccorini, F.L.: 'Knowledge of the singular: Aquinas, Suárez and recent interpreters', *The Thomist* 38 (1974), 606–55.

JORGE J. E. GRACIA

**subjectivism**  What is a subjective account of epistemic rationality? This is none too easy to state precisely (it is no easier to say what subjectivism in ethics is), but as a rough working definition it will do to say that an account is subjective just in case it implies that the standards of rational belief are those that the individual believer or the individual's community or the human community at large would either approve of or take for granted in so far as their ends are intellectual. Subjectivism, so understood, can take an individualistic or intersubjective form, but either way a subjective account will imply that the standards of rational belief are somehow the products of our beliefs, our dispositions, or our practices.

For example, if the standards that my beliefs must meet in order to be rational, according to an account, are those that I myself would regard as intellectually sound were I to be suitably reflective, then the account is a subjective one. Similarly, if an account implies that the relevant standards are those that would be approved of by most members of my community or those that are presupposed by the intellectual practices of my community, then once again the account can be classified as a subjective one, albeit one with a social rather than an individualistic cast to it. Finally, if an account implies that the standards of rational belief are those that would be endorsed or presupposed by the human community at large, then the account yet again can be plausibly regarded as a subjective one, provided that there is nothing else in the account to guarantee that adhering to these standards is a reliable way to acquire true beliefs. Indeed, this last qualification provides a good negative test of subjectivity. If an account of epistemic rationality implies that by being rational, individuals are assured of being reliable (or at least more reliable than they would be if they were irrational), then the account is not a subjective one.

Thus RELIABILIST accounts of rational belief are paradigmatically objective. Classical FOUNDATIONALIST accounts are also objective. What about COHERENTIST accounts? It can be tempting to think they are best classified as subjective, since what it is rational for us to believe, according to coherentists, is in large part a function of what we happen to believe. But any account of rational belief will allow for subjective inputs of some sort, whether they be in the form of experiences or beliefs or whatever. The crucial question is whether the standards that relate these inputs to rational belief are objective or subjective, and in the case of coherentism the standards are typically explicated in a thoroughly objective manner. Coherentists ordinarily insist that if my beliefs are to be coherent and hence rational, they must at a minimum be consistent. It does not matter whether I think that inconsistency is always and everywhere to be avoided, and it does not matter whether I would think this were I to be reflective. Likewise, it does not matter whether the members of my community or the human community at large think this or whether their intellectual practices presuppose this. According to coherentists, inconsistency implies incoherence, and it is always irrational for us to be incoherent, regardless of our own subjective standards. (Similar things can be said about BAYESIAN approaches to epistemology.)

One simple consideration in favour of subjectivism is that many of our judgements of rationality cannot be plausibly understood in an objective manner. For example, when we are assessing the beliefs of individuals from a different culture, perhaps far removed from us in both time and place, it often seems appropriate to do so in terms of their own standards or at least in terms of some standard that is relative to their community. This will seem particularly attractive when the individuals belong to a culture that we judge to be less advanced than our own. The intellectual methods and practices used in this culture may be at odds with those that we now think are best, but we may think it is unfair to evaluate their beliefs in terms of our more sophisticated methods. However, it is not unfair, we think, to evaluate their beliefs in terms of the methods that were standard in their community.

Indeed, if we were not prepared to evaluate these individuals in terms of their own standards and to give expression to our evaluations using the language of rationality, we would find ourselves in a dilemma. Either we would have to find some way of insisting that their methods really are our methods, the ones that we take to be reliable, or we would be forced to say that there is no interesting sense in which they are rational. In short, we would be forced either to make them into us or to dismiss them as irrational.

Another consideration in favour of subjectivism appeals to first-person rather than third-person considerations. Suppose that we are under the control of an evil demon who widely deceives us without our being aware of it. The demon deprives us of an opportunity of being reliable and in so doing deprives us of knowledge, but it does not seem as if the demon thereby also deprives us of any chance of being rational. In particular, if there is nothing that indicates to us that we are under the control of this demon, it is rational for us to believe what our senses naturally incline us to believe. And yet, in this demon world, doing so is unreliable. Thus, there is at least one sense of rational belief that is not tied intimately to truth or even to likely truth. But then, the question is, what is this sense of rational belief? One natural suggestion is that it is a subjective sense. In the demon world, it is rational for us to trust our senses because, complications aside, doing so conforms to our own deep epistemic standards: even if we were deeply reflective, we would tend to think that this is part of a reliable intellectual strategy for us.

Why, then, have subjective accounts of epistemic rationality so often been considered non-starters? Part of the answer is that many epistemologists have been primarily concerned with the explication of knowledge, and they have assumed that knowledge is something like rational true belief (absent GETTIER PROBLEMS). Thus, they have thought that whatever else we may want to say about rational belief, it had better be the sort of thing that turns true belief into a good candidate for knowledge. But if rational belief is contrued subjectively, this need not be the case.

Subjectivists, for their part, will deny this assumption. They will deny that the conditions of rational belief always turn true belief into a good candidate for knowledge (see RELIGIOUS BELIEF). Of course, if it suits our philosophical purposes, we can stipulate that this is so for at least one sense of rational belief, but then subjectivists will insist that there is at least one other sense of rational belief, important for our everyday evaluations of each others' beliefs and important also given the history of epistemology, that is essentially a matter of living up to our own standards. This is a sense that equates rationality with success in meeting a certain kind of criticism, either self-criticism or criticism by one's community. And in this sense, a rational true belief need not always be a good candidate for knowledge.

Another motivation for not taking subjectivism seriously in epistemology is the fear that it commits us to some unacceptable form of RELATIVISM. But since one can be a subjectivist about questions of rational belief without being committed to any relativistic notion of truth, it is not clear that this fear has any real basis. Yet another fear has to do with irresolvable disagreements. Given subjectivism, it cannot be assumed that all theoretical disputes can in principle be settled if the disputants are equally well informed and fully rational. This is an implication of subjectivism, but it is hard to see why it is an objection to it. In the practical realm we no longer find it puzzling that two people can be in conflict despite being equally well informed and fully rational. There is no good reason for thinking that this should strike us as any more puzzling in the theoretical realm.

*See also* ETHICS AND EPISTEMOLOGY; EXTERNALISM/INTERNALISM; OBJECTIVE/SUBJECTIVE; OBJECTIVITY; SOCIAL SCIENCE.

BIBLIOGRAPHY

Foley, R.: *The Theory of Epistemic Rationality* (Cambridge, MA: Harvard University Press, 1987).

Goldman, A.I.: 'Strong and weak justification', *Philosophical Perspectives* 2 (1988), 51–71.

Kvanvig, J.: 'Subjective justification', *Mind* 93 (1984), 71–84.

MacIntyre, A.: *Whose Justice? Which Rationality?* (Notre Dame: University of Notre Dame Press, 1989).

Rorty, R.: *Philosophy and the Mirror of Nature* (Princeton: Princeton University Press, 1979).

Wilson, B. ed.: *Rationality* (New York: Harper and Row, 1970).

RICHARD FOLEY

**subjectivity** Subjectivity has been attributed

variously to certain concepts; to certain properties of objects; and to certain modes of understanding. The overarching idea of these attributions is that the nature of the concepts, properties or modes of understanding in question is dependent upon the properties and relations of the subjects who employ those concepts, possess the properties or exercise those modes of understanding. The dependence may be a dependence upon the particular subject, or upon some type which the subject instantiates. What is not so dependent is objective. In fact, there is virtually nothing which has not been declared subjective by some thinker or other, including such unlikely candidates as space and time (KANT) and the natural numbers (Brouwer). In recent years there has been a lively debate about the more plausible candidates.

There are several sorts of subjectivity to be distinguished, if subjectivity is attributed to a concept, considered as a way of thinking of some object or property. It would be much too undiscriminating to say that a concept is subjective if particular mental states are mentioned in the correct account of mastery of the concept. For instance, if the later Wittgenstein is right, the mental state of finding it natural to go on one way rather than another has to be mentioned in the account of mastery of any concept. All concepts would then be counted as subjective. We can distinguish several more discriminating criteria. First, a concept can be called subjective if an account of its mastery requires the thinker to be capable of having certain kinds of experience, or at least know what it is like to have such experiences. Variants on this criterion can be obtained by substituting other specific psychological states in place of experience. If we confine ourselves to the criterion which does mention experience, then concepts of experiences themselves plausibly meet the condition. What have traditionally been classified as concepts of secondary qualities – such as *red, tastes bitter, warm* – have also been argued to meet this criterion. The criterion does, though, also include some relatively observational shape concepts. The relatively observational

shape concepts *square* and *regular diamond* pick out exactly the same shape properties, but differ in which perceptual experiences are mentioned in accounts of their mastery – different symmetries are perceived when something is seen as a diamond from when it is seen as a square. This example shows that from the fact that a concept is subjective in this sense, nothing follows about the subjectivity of the property it picks out. Few philosophers would now count shape properties, as opposed to concepts thereof, as subjective.

Concepts with a second type of subjectivity could more specifically be called 'first-personal'. A concept is first-personal if, in an account of its mastery, the application of the concept to objects other than the thinker is related to the conditions under which the thinker is willing to apply the concept to himself. Though there is considerable disagreement on how the account should be formulated, many theories of the concept of belief treat it as first-personal in this sense. For example, this is true of any account which says that a thinker understands a third-personal attribution 'He believes that so-and-so' by understanding that it holds, very roughly indeed, if the third person in question is in circumstances in which the thinker would himself (first-person) judge that so-and-so. It is equally true of accounts which in one way or another say that the third-person attribution is understood as meaning that the other person is in some state which stands in some specified sameness relation to the state which causes the thinker to be willing to judge '*I* believe that so-and-so' (*see* OTHER MINDS).

The subjectivity of indexical concepts, such as *I, here, now*, and *that* (perceptually presented) *man*, has been widely noted. The last of these is subjective in the sense of the first criterion above; but they are all subjective in that the possibility of a subject's using any one of them to think about an object at a given time depends upon his relations to that particular object then. Indexicals are thus particularly well suited to expressing a particular point of view on the world of objects, a point of view available only to those who stand in the right relations to the objects in question.

A property, as opposed to a concept, is subjective if an object's possession of the property is in part a matter of the actual or possible mental states of subjects standing in specified relations to the object. Colour properties, secondary qualities in general, moral properties, the property of propositions of being necessary or contingent, and the property of actions and mental states of being intelligible, have all been discussed as serious contenders for subjectivity in this sense. To say that a property is subjective is not to say that it can be analysed away in terms of mental states. The mental states in terms of which subjectivists have aimed to elucidate, say, the property of being red or the property of being kind have included the mental states of experiencing something as red, and judging something to be kind, respectively. These attitudes embed reference to the original properties themselves – or at least to concepts thereof – in a way which makes eliminative analysis problematic. The same plausibly applies to a subjectivist treatment of intelligibility: here the mental state would have to be that of finding something intelligible. Even without any commitment to eliminative analysis, though, the subjectivist's claim remains substantial. The subjectivist's claim needs extensive consideration for each of the diverse areas mentioned. In the case of colour, part of the task of the subjectivist who makes his claim at the level of properties rather than concepts is to argue against those who would identify the property of being red with a physical reflectance property, or with some more complex vector of physical properties.

Suppose that for an object to have a certain property is for subjects standing in a certain relation to it to be in a certain mental state. If subjects standing in that relation to it, and in that mental state, judge the object to have the property, their judgement will be true. Some subjectivists have been tempted to work this point into a criterion of a property's being subjective. There is, though, an issue here which is not definitional. Prima facie, it seems that we can make sense of this possibility: that though in certain circumstances, a subject's judgement about whether an object has a property are guaranteed to be correct, it is not his judgement (in those circumstances) or anything else about his or others' mental states which makes the judgement correct. To many philosophers, this will seem to be the actual situation for easily decided arithmetical propositions such as $3 + 3 = 6$. If this is correct, the subjectivist will have to make essential use of some such asymmetrical notion as 'what makes a proposition true', or 'that in virtue of which a proposition is true'. Conditionals or equivalences alone, not even a priori ones, will not capture the subjectivist character of the position.

Finally, subjectivity has been attributed to modes of understanding. Elaborating a mode of understanding can in large part be seen as elaboration of the conditions of mastery of mental concepts. For instance, those who believe that some form of imagination is involved in understanding third-person ascriptions of experiences will want to write this into the account of mastery of those attributions. However, some of those who attribute subjectivity to modes of understanding include in their conception the claim that some or all mental states are themselves subjective. This can be a claim about the mental properties themselves, rather than concepts thereof; but it is not charitable to interpret it as the assertion that mental properties involve mental properties. Rather, using the distinctions we already have, it can be read as the conjunction of these two propositions: that concepts of mental states are subjective in one of the sense given above, and that mental states can only be thought about by concepts which are thus subjective. Such a position need not be opposed to philosophical materialism, since it can allow for some version of this materialism for mental states. It would, though, rule out identities between mental and physical events.

See also CONCEPT; LINGUISTIC UNDER-STANDING; OBJECTIVE/SUBJECTIVE; OBJECTIVITY.

BIBLIOGRAPHY

McDowell, J.: 'Non-cognitivism and rule-Following', in *Wittgenstein: To Follow a Rule* eds S. Holtzman and C. Leich (London: Routledge, 1981), 141–62.

McDowell, J.: 'Values and secondary qualities', in *Morality and Objectivity: A Tribute to J.L. Mackie* ed. T. Honderich (London: Routledge and Kegan Paul, 1985), 110–29.

McGinn, C.: *The Subjective View* (Oxford: Clarendon Press, 1983).

Nagel, T.: *The View From Nowhere* (New York: Oxford University Press, 1986).

Smith, M., Lewis, D. Johnston, M.: Respective contributions to the symposium 'Dispositional Theories of Value', *Proceedings of the Aristotelian Society*, supp. vol. 63 (1989), 89–111, 113–37, 139–74.

Wiggins, D.: *Needs, Values, Truth* (Oxford: Blackwell, 1987).

Williams, B.: *Descartes: The Project of Pure Enquiry* (London: Penguin, 1978); *see especially* sections on 'the absolute conception'.

Wright, C.: 'Moral values, projection and secondary qualities', *Proceedings of the Aristotelian Society*, supp. vol. 62 (1988), 1–26.

CHRISTOPHER PEACOCKE

**supervenience** A property P supervenes on a class of properties Q if and only if (1) if one thing A has P, any other thing which exactly resembles A in respect of all members of Q must have P, and (2) A cannot change in respect of P, cease to be P or become more P or less P, without changing in respect of some member of Q.

In moral philosophy this notion is often used to claim that value and rightness supervene on natural properties. This true claim should not be confused with the equally true claim that the value of an object (or the rightness of an action) exists in virtue of (some of) those members of the class of natural properties enjoyed by the object or action. The latter is a relation between value/rightness and *some* members of the class of natural properties, which is not a matter of supervenience at all. It is better expressed by saying that saying that the object's value *results* from (some of) its natural properties. (*But see* Kim, 1984.)

In epistemology normative properties such as those of justification and reasonableness are often held to be supervenient on the class of natural properties in a similar way.

The interest of supervenience is that it promises a way of tying normative properties closely to natural ones without exactly *reducing* them to natural ones; it can be the basis of a sort of weak NATURALISM. This was the motivation behind Davidson's attempt to say that mental properties supervene on physical ones – an attempt which ran into severe difficulties.

BIBLIOGRAPHY

Davidson, D.: 'Mental events', in his *Essays on Actions and Events* (Oxford: Clarendon Press, 1980), 207–27.

Kim, J.: 'Supervenience and nomological incommensurables', *American Philosophical Quarterly* 20 (1978), 149–56.

Kim, J.: 'Concepts of supervenience', *Philosophy and Phenomenological Research* 65 (1984), 257–70.

JONATHAN DANCY

**surprise examination paradox** A teacher announces that there will be a surprise examination next week. A clever student argues that this is impossible. 'The test cannot be on Friday, the last day of the week, because it wouldn't be a surprise. We would know the day of the test on Thursday evening. This means we can also rule out Thursday. For after we learn that no test has been given by Wednesday, we would know the test is on Thursday or Friday – and would already know that it is not on Friday by the previous reasoning. The remaining days can be eliminated in the same manner.'

This puzzle has over a dozen variants. The first was probably invented by the Swedish mathematician Lennart Ekbom in 1943. Although the first few commentators regarded the reverse elimination argument as cogent, every writer on the subject since 1950 agrees that the argument is unsound. The controversy has been over the proper diagnosis of the flaw.

Initial analyses of the student's argument tried to lay the blame on a simple equivocation. Their failure led to more sophisticated diagnoses. The general format has been an assimilation to better known paradoxes. One tradition casts the surprise examination paradox as a self-referential problem, as fundamentally akin to the Liar, the PARADOX OF THE KNOWER, or Gödel's incompleteness theorem. The original talk of a surprise is read as a reflexive claim about unprovability. That is, the teacher's announcement is paraphrased as:

(A) There will be an examination next week but its date cannot be deduced from the conjunction of this announcement and the record of eliminated days.

If only one day remains, the announcement implies 'The test is on Friday but its date cannot be deduced from this statement'. This consequence does bear a provocative resemblance to the liar sentence 'This statement is not true'. Critics concede that this self-referential interpretation yields a liar-type paradox but complain that the interpretation strays too far from the meaning of the original announcement.

The second main tradition places the surprise examination paradox among epistemological puzzles such as MOORE'S PARADOX and the LOTTERY PARADOX. The connection with the epistemological puzzles is made by analysing the announcement as a prediction of student ignorance. This connection can be illustrated with the two-day version of the puzzle:

(B) Either (the test is on Thursday and the students do not believe it beforehand) or (the test is on Friday and the students do not believe it beforehand).

Notice the resemblance between each disjunct and the sentence that fascinated G. E. Moore: 'I went to the pictures last Tuesday, but I don't believe I did.' Although Moore's sentence is consistent, the speaker

cannot justifiably believe it. However, others can believe the proposition it expresses since it merely ascribes an error to the speaker. Indeed, the speaker is free to attribute past mistakes to himself or future ones: 'On June 21, 1990, Nelson Mandela wore a Yankee baseball cap but by 2010 I will no longer believe so.' Also note that the speaker can justifiably believe a disjunction of Moorean sentences: 'Either Chaucer was right-handed and I do not believe it, or he was left-handed and I do not believe it.' So the students can believe (B) on the teacher's authority. But after they learn that the test is not on Thursday, the announcement implies the Moorean sentence 'The test is on Friday but the students do not believe it.' Since the students cannot believe this consequence, they can no longer believe (B). So if the teacher gives the test on the last day, the students will not justifiably expect it.

One might object that the students would expect the test because they know the teacher prefers to give an anticipated test rather than no test at all. This objection smuggles a new condition into the scenario. The original puzzle does not credit the students with this psychological insight into the teacher's desires. But let's consider the variant where they do know his preference. Here the students could indeed predict a last day examination. But the victory is hollow because the ability spoils the first step of the clever student's elimination argument. For the effect of the extra psychological premiss is to make the teacher more of an authority on whether there will be a test than on whether an event will be a surprise. So the students cannot appeal to the teacher's authority to rule out a last day examination.

A second objection starts with the observation that the students' parents could predict a last day examination. For the parents are not the surprisees. (The Moorean consequence is about the students' beliefs, not the parents'.) So if the parents can know, why can't they inform the students? No doubt, the parents could know and could tell the students that the second disjunct of (B) is true. But

Moorean sentences cannot be made credible by increasing the authority of the source. God Himself cannot make you know 'The test is on Friday but you do not believe it'. A good memory or careful record-keeping will be equally impotent.

Other objections to the Moorean analysis turn on its completeness; can it handle all the variants of the paradox? If it can, then the surprise examination paradox teaches an important lesson: when we traffic in Moorean sentences, normal mechanisms of knowledge transfer breakdown.

*See also* LOTTERY PARADOX; MOORE'S PARADOX.

BIBLIOGRAPHY

Binkley, R.: 'The surprise examination in modal logic', *Journal of Philosophy* 65 (1968), 127–36.

Kaplan, D. and Montague, R.: 'A paradox regained', *Notre Dame Journal of Formal Logic* I (1960), 79–90.

Olin, D.: 'The prediction paradox resolved', *Philosophical Studies* 44 (1983), 225–33.

Quine, W.V.: 'On a so-called paradox', *Mind* 62 (1953), 65–7.

Sorensen, R.: *Blindspots* (Oxford: Clarendon Press, 1988).

Wright, C. and Sudbury, A.: 'The paradox of the unexpected examination', *Australasian Journal of Philosophy* II (1977), 41–58.

ROY A. SORENSEN

# T

**tabula rasa** The theory that the mind at birth is a tabula rasa (blank writing tablet) awaiting ideas from experience is usually associated with LOCKE's Essay – as by Leibniz (*Nouveaux essais*, 1704), who preferred to think of the mind as a block of veined marble, not wholly indifferent to what it receives. The phrase (from Latin translations of Aristotle's *De Anima*, 430a) is not there – except in Coste's French translation (1700) of Locke's 'white paper' (*Essay*, 2.1.2); but the theory is. Taking from the Scholastics the associated thought that 'there is nothing in the intellect which was not first in the senses', Gassendi and Locke made it a cornerstone of their EMPIRICISM.

*See also* STOIC EPISTEMOLOGY.

BIBLIOGRAPHY

Aaron, R.I.: *John Locke* (Oxford: Clarendon Press, 1971), pp. 34–5, 114.

R.S. WOOLHOUSE

**testimony** Both practically and intellectually, the testimony of others is important. We rely on it for our grasp of history, geography, science, and more. Which plane to board, what to eat or drink, the instrument readings to accept – all are decided through testimony. 'Rhetoricians', writes Leibniz in his *New Essays* (Bk IV, ch. xv, sec. 4), 'distinguish two kinds of arguments: "artful" ones which are developed from things by means of reasoning, and "artless" ones which simply rest on the explicit testimony either of some man or even, perhaps, of the thing itself. But there are also "mixed" ones, *since testimony can itself provide a fact which serves in the construction of an 'artful' argument.'* Here is an example:

(E) T testifies that someone testifies, S perceives that T testifies that someone testifies, and S knows thereby that someone testifies.

In this case S can come to know that *q* through essential reliance on T's testimony that *q*, but T need not know that *q*, or be completely justified in believing that *q*, or even so much as be at all reliable on questions such as the question whether *q*.

If we are largely justified in accepting 'artless' testimony, how so? Are we presupposing a principle like this?:

(T) From the sort of people I have dealt with in the sort of circumstances now present, testimony is normally correct.

What could possibly serve as our basis for believing a general claim such as T? Call the sort of testimony referred to in T 'preferred testimony'. How could we justify our acceptance of preferred testimony? Might we rely on an appeal to induction through perception and memory? Perhaps we have noted through perception many instances of the accuracy of preferred testimony and have retained through memory a running record of such success, all of which now serves as an inductive basis for our continuing acceptance of preferred testimony, which is thereby justified.

It may help to step back and compare testimony with more easily and widely recognized faculties, such as perception, introspection, memory and reason. MEMORY, for example, turns out to resemble testimony rather closely.

Retentive memory is a psychological mechanism that conveys beliefs across stages of a life. Testimony is a social mechanism that conveys beliefs across lives at a time. In a well-ordered mind memory will tend to be selective, and a function of attention and interest. If we remembered every detail, our minds would be swamped with clutter. In a well-ordered society testimony must be selective. If everyone reported everything to their neighbours, the lines of communication would be clogged, and our heads full of a useless jumble.

Memory is, of course, not the only psychological mechanism relevant to epistemology. Perception and reason are often cited as well, with two varieties of perception – the inner and the outer; and two varieties of reason – the intuitive and the inferential. These three broad categories – memory, perception and reason – are said to be fundamental, and none reducible to the others in epistemic value. Even the COHERENTIST will need to appeal to all three in explaining the full variety of what we take ourselves to know, and perception won't be fully justifiable except by circular reasoning going back to perception again. If we wipe our *tabula* clean of all perceptual inscriptions we shall never be able to legitimate their reinscription on the basis of any linear appeal to memory and reason alone. And similar reasoning would apply to each of these in turn. All three seem needed and none certifiable by unaided appeal to the others. What about testimony?

Let's say that one 'testifies' that $p$ if and only if one states one's belief that $p$. This is a broad sense of testimony that counts posthumous publications as examples of (delayed) testimony. More commonly testimony requires an object to whom it is directed, as in a court of law. But here we opt for a broader notion of testimony which requires only that it be a statement of someone's thoughts or beliefs, which they might direct to the world at large and to no-one in particular. Thus we reach two difficult questions in the epistemology of testimony:

Q1: Does one normally through perception and memory gather a large and diverse enough basis for an inductive inference to the conclusion that preferred testimony is generally correct?

Q2: What sort of correlation would one need between preferred testimony and correctness for that correlation to serve as a good basis for the inductive inference of Q1 above? Would one need to postulate some sort of causal connection between the testimony and its correctness?

Hume offers a response to our questions as follows:

> [T]here is no species of reasoning more common, more useful, and even necessary to human life, than that which is derived from the testimony of men and the reports of eye-witnesses and spectators. . .This species of reasoning, perhaps, one may deny to be founded on the relation of cause and effect. I shall not dispute about a word. It will be sufficient to observe that our assurance in any argument of this kind is derived from no other principle than our observation of the veracity of human testimony, and of the usual conformity of facts to the reports of witnesses. It being a general maxim, that no objects have any discoverable connexion together, and that all the inferences which we can draw from one to another, are founded merely on our experience of their constant and regular conjunction; it is evident that we ought not to make an exception to this maxim in favour of human testimony, whose connexion with any event seems, in itself, as little necessary as any other. (1748, p. 111)

And shortly thereafter he adds:

> The reason why we place any credit in witnesses and historians, is not derived from any *connexion*, which we perceive *a priori*, between testimony and reality, but because we are accustomed to find a conformity between them. (1748, p. 113)

We are 'accustomed', says Hume, 'to find a conformity' between testimony and reality.

And just how do we manage that? Can we have tested a large and varied enough sample of testimony? And are the deliverances of testimony regularly enough the sorts of things that we can and do check by means other than testimony? Of course, much testimony we can and do check perceptually in a normal day. 'Coffee' reads the can. We open it, and smell the coffee. We drive to work and know the intentions of fellow motorists by their signals, verified perceptually. And so for the rest of the day. But most testimony is uncheckable by perceptual means, if only through lack of time and resources. Most of what I take myself to know about history, geography and science, for example, is in one way or another perceptually inaccessible to me.

Hume seems insensitive to the true nature of our predicament. On this question at least, Thomas Reid is more perceptive:

The wise and beneficent Author of Nature, who intended that we should be social creatures, and that we should receive the greatest and most important part of our knowledge by the information of others, hath, for these purposes, implanted in our natures two principles that tally with each other.

The first of these principles is, a propensity to speak truth, and to use the signs of language so as to convey our real sentiments. . . Another original principle implanted in us by the Supreme Being, is a disposition to confide in the veracity of others, and to believe what they tell us. This is the counterpart to the former; and, as that may be called the *principle of veracity*, we shall, for want of a more proper name, call this the *principle of credulity*. . .

It is evident that, in the matter of testimony, the balance of human judgment is by nature inclined to the side of belief; and turns to that side of itself, when there is nothing put into the opposite scale. If it was not so, no proposition that is uttered in discourse would be believed, until it was examined and tried by reason; and most men would be unable to find reasons for believing the thousandth part of what is told them. (1764, pp. 93–5)

If Reid is right, testimony is strikingly similar to memory. In each case causal mechanisms operate in us to convey beliefs from source to recipient: from one's own past to one's present, or from one's neighbour to oneself. Through experience one gradually learns to override these mechanisms in special circumstances, but normally they operate without impediment.

However, Reid does not in that passage address the question of how to justify acquiescing in the operation of his divine (and natural) principles of testimony. Have we any rational defence against a sceptical challenge to them? Clearly much testimony can be tested only by appeal to other testimony. But is this not to test one copy of a newspaper by appeal to other copies? That caricature has a point, since our whole question is how to justify accepting any testimony. Is it not therefore a vicious circle to invoke any testimony at all in pursuit of that objective?

We are told that our knowledge can derive from memory, perception and testimony. Each of these might be justified by appeal to the others, but none can be justified fully without such appeal. One thing seems clear. To support reflective knowledge, one's raft of beliefs needs central planks detailing one's ways of knowing (as is argued in Sosa, 1991; e.g. in ch. 11). The requirement of an epistemic perspective seems an indispensable prerequisite for an apt system of beliefs. This epistemic perspective would be constituted by beliefs about one's basic sources of knowledge, none of which can be accepted justifiably as a source, except by appeal to other sources unquestioned for the sake of support in favour of the one. In this sense testimony seems as basic a source of knowledge as the traditional perception, memory, introspection, and inference.

*See also* MEMORY; PRINCIPLE OF CREDULITY; PROBLEM OF THE CRITERION; REID.

BIBLIOGRAPHY

Hume, D.: *An Inquiry Concerning Human Understanding* (1748) ed. L.A. Selby-Bigge, revised P.H. Nidditch (Oxford: Oxford University Press, 1975).

Lehrer, K.: 'Personal and social knowledge', *Synthese* 73 (1987), 87–107.

Price, H.H.: *Belief* (New York: Humanities Press, 1969).

Reid, T.: *An Inquiry into the Human Mind* (1764) in his *Inquiry and Essays* ed. R.E. Beanblossom and K. Lehrer (Indianapolis: Hackett, 1983).

Ross, J.: 'Testimonial evidence', in *Analysis and Metaphysics: Essays in Honor of R.M. Chisholm* ed. K. Lehrer (Dordrecht: Reidel, 1975).

Sosa, E.: *Knowledge in Perspective: Selected Essays in Epistemology* (Cambridge: Cambridge University Press. 1991).

ERNEST SOSA

**theory**  In philosophy of science, a generalization or set of generalizations purportedly making reference to unobservable entities, e.g. atoms, genes, quarks, unconscious wishes. The ideal gas *law*, for example, refers only to such observables as pressure, temperature, and volume; the molecular-kinetic *theory* refers to molecules and their properties. Although an older usage suggests lack of adequate evidence in support thereof ('merely a theory'), current philosophical usage does *not* carry that connotation. Einstein's special theory of relativity, for example, is considered extremely well founded.

There are two main views on the nature of theories. According to the 'received view' theories are partially interpreted axiomatic systems; according to the semantic view, a theory is a collection of models (Suppe, 1974).

*See also* AXIOMATICS.

BIBLIOGRAPHY

Colodny, R.G. ed.: *The Nature and Function of Scientific Theories* (Pittsburgh: University of Pittsburgh Press, 1970).

Suppe, F. ed.: *The Structure of Scientific Theories* (Urbana: University of Illinois Press, 1974).

WESLEY C. SALMON

**transcendental arguments**  These were brought into philosophical prominence by the work of KANT, who used them to establish the role of certain fundamental a priori concepts in our knowledge of the external world. The role which transcendental arguments show these concepts to play is, Kant claims, that they make experience possible, and that therefore sceptical doubts about our possession of them are empty. It is the scepticism-refuting promise of transcendental arguments that has provoked most interest among subsequent philosophers.

Kant's central question concerns the possibility of synthetic a priori knowledge. An answer to it presupposes an answer to the more general question, what are the necessarily presupposed grounds of experience in general? In arguing for the categories, and for space and time as pure forms of sensibility, Kant is arguing that there can be experience only under certain conditions, and this strategy displays the characteristic form of a transcendental argument. Simply in respect of its form, the argument is that there must be something Y if there is something X of which Y is a necessary condition. In crude outline, therefore, the transcendental strategy consists in the search for key necessary conditions of some given region of discourse or experience.

Reasoning of this character is not unique to Kant, nor do all the varieties of it found in the philosophical literature model themselves exactly on Kant's procedure. WITTGENSTEIN in the *Philosophical Investigations* and *On Certainty* argues transcendentally about the impossibility of private language and the possibility of knowledge, respectively. J.L. AUSTIN argues transcendentally in formulating a theory of truth by distinguishing between demonstrative and descriptive conventions in language, his point being that some such distinction is required for a certain other concept – that of truth as correspondence – to have application. A different example is supplied by Gilbert RYLE in his use of 'polar concept' arguments. The sceptical suggestion that we might undetectably be in error on any given occasion is refuted, Ryle claims, by the fact that just as we cannot have counterfeit coins unless there are genuine ones, so we cannot have a concept of error unless we have the concept of being right, and therefore we must sometimes know we are right. Once again, the strategy is to argue that X cannot be the case unless Y is the case; and since X is indeed the case, Y must be the case also.

These examples show that transcendental-style arguments are commonplace in philosophy. But there is a marked difference between reasonings of these familiar sorts and the weightier, more ambitious transcendental arguments found in Kant and others. One way to mark the distinction is to say that the familiar kinds of argument just sketched share their methodology with transcendental arguments proper, but not their scope; for the latter are not concerned merely with local conceptual polarities like 'illusory-veridical', but with the conditions under which highly general concepts – the concept of other minds, or the concept of an independently existing reality – have application, given that such concepts play a key role in entire discourses and are central to our experience as a whole. So put, the aim of transcendental arguments is to establish the conditions necessary for experience, or experience of a certain kind, in general; and, at their most controversial, to establish conclusions about the nature and existence of an external world, or other minds, derived from paying attention to what has to be the case for there to be experience, or for experience to be as it is.

Classic contemporary examples of transcendental arguments are to be found in P.F. STRAWSON's *Individuals*. One of them is aimed at establishing the vacuity of sceptical doubt about the existence of other minds, and proceeds as follows. One can ascribe states of consciousness to oneself only if one is able to ascribe them to others, Strawson argues, because to doubt the existence of other minds one must employ the concept of other minds itself, and this can only be done if one can distinguish between 'my states of consciousness' and 'others' states of consciousness'. But this can only be done, in turn, if others exist, because the identification of conscious states can only be effected by reference to particulars of a certain kind, namely, persons; the concept of which – in turn again – demands that there be criteria for distinguishing one person from another, for otherwise the identification of states of consciousness would be impossible. So one can talk of 'my experiences' only if one can talk of 'others' experiences'; this is possible only if there are criteria for distinguishing between persons; and since one can indeed talk significantly of one's own experiences, such criteria must exist. But if they exist they constitute logically adequate grounds for ascription of states of consciousness to others. Hence sceptical doubts about the existence of other minds are vacuous, because the sceptic cannot so much as formulate them without employing the discourse whose very conditions of employment legitimize what he wishes to question.

Another transcendental argument in Strawson's *Individuals* concerns the perception-independent existence of material particulars, and it has been much discussed as a result of Barry Stroud's criticisms of it. The subsequent debate can be said to turn on the following points.

One of the crucial questions about transcendental arguments concerns what they might hope to establish. The options, simply put, are that either they establish the existence of something (an external world, other minds), or they establish that certain concepts are necessary to our conceptual scheme. Clearly these are quite different results, and the latter involves the further problem of whether our conceptual scheme is the only possible one, for if not the terminus of a transcendental argument is strictly relative.

To grasp the difference between these options it is useful to consider them as responses to sceptical challenges over our belief in the existence of an external world. On the first option, call it option A, the aim is to establish the existence of the external world. On the second, call it option B, the aim is to show that we must believe in the existence of an external world as a condition of the coherence of experience. To settle the sceptic's doubts outright under B one might have further to show that our conceptual scheme is the only conceivable one.

The chief difficulty faced by option A is that even if one could show that it is a necessary condition of our having coherent experience that we possess and apply a concept of an independently existing world, it still needs to be shown that something 'out there' answers to that concept; in other words, that it is a necessary condition of our having the concept of an external world that an external world exists. It is one thing to argue that we must have and employ concepts of space, time, causality and particulars conditioned by them, and another to show that there exist things corresponding to these concepts and existentially prior to their use.

The difficulty here is that it does not look possible to argue from the fact that there is experience, or from some richer premise characterising that experience, to talk about the way things are independently of experience, without either supplementing the argument with additional factual premises, or arguing that it is somehow constitutive of the concept-introducing terms employed that they have empirical conditions of application under which, and only under which, they can be known to be truly applied.

Neither move looks promising. Additional factual premises will be unacceptable from the sceptic's point of view because precisely the same doubts about entitlement to them will arise as with the belief in the existence of the external world itself. And a VERIFICA-TION principle, if it were not anyway highly debatable in itself, would make the apparatus of transcendental arguments unnecessary, because one could rely on the verification principle alone to overcome scepticism. Even in one were to weaken a verification principle to a general 'principle of significance' stating that there can only be legitimate or meaningful employment of concepts if they are governed by experiential

conditions of application, it would still be a question whether the satisfaction of such conditions guaranteed that a concept succeeded in applying to something existing independently of its use, the reason being that a verification principle can be satisfied even in an ideal universe in which systematic criteria exist for distinguishing between what counts as 'objective' and 'subjective' among a mind's experiences – perhaps, on HUME'S lines, by counting as objective all those ideas which are 'forceful' and 'vivid', and as subjective all those which are otherwise.

Option B transcendental arguments look, by comparison, relatively mundane affairs. There is no special difficulty in exploring the necessary conditions of the experience we enjoy; we are, at very least, entitled to claim attention for investigations into the role of our concepts of objects, space, time and causality, given that it at least seems to us that ours is a world of causally-interactive spatio-temporal things. If we have a concept of objects, we must have a concept of the continued unperceived existence of objects, because this is necessary to the concept of a single spatio-temporal world; and it is precisely a belief in the continued unperceived existence of objects that the sceptic asks us to justify. Showing that we must have such a belief as a condition of experience is not the same as proving that such objects exist. One is stating what we must believe, not how things are; but since the sceptic wishes us to justify the belief, doing so – the argument goes – is enough to put an end to scepticism.

The sceptic, however, can in response shift his attack to a more general level, by arguing that there might be a certain parochial interest in pointing out what a given form of experience requires as its fundamental concepts, but that this does not settle doubts about the general validity of those concepts. What if there are forms of experience which are non-spatial, or non-causal, or in which there is no need to distinguish experience from its objects? To counter scepticism at this more general level B-type transcendental arguments require supplementation by anti-relativist arguments, themselves a form of transcendental argument designed to show that the concepts required for our experience are the concepts required for any experience. That, clearly, is in its different way as ambitious a project as option A transcendental arguments themselves.

The primary importance of transcendental arguments resides in the fact that we have to reflect on our concepts and beliefs from the internal perspective of having to use them even as we investigate them. There is no external point from which we can view our conceptual scheme; like Neurath's sailors we have to rebuild our ship at sea. Transcendental arguments offer ways of reflecting on our concepts which at least promise to tell us much about their nature and interrelations, and about the degree of strength possessed by sceptical challenges to our use of them.

*See also* SCEPTICISM, CONTEMPORARY; VERIFICATIONISM.

BIBLIOGRAPHY

Davidson, D.: 'On the very idea of a conceptual scheme', in his *Inquiries into Truth and Interpretation* (Oxford: Oxford University Press, 1984), 183–98.
Grayling, A.C.: *The Refutation of Scepticism* (London: Duckworth, 1985).
Harrison, R.: *On What There Must Be* (Oxford: Clarendon Press, 1974).
Kant, I.: *Critique of Pure Reason* (1781) trans. N. Kemp Smith (London: Macmillan, 1964).
Phillips Griffiths, A. and Macintosh, J.J.: 'Transcendental arguments', *Proceedings of the Aristotelian Society* supp. vol. 43 (1969), 165–80.
Rosenberg, T.: 'Transcendental arguments revisited', *Journal of Philosophy* 25 (1975), 611–24.
Schaper, E.: 'Arguing transcendentally', *Kant-Studien* 63 (1972), 101–16.
Strawson, P.F.: *Individuals* (London: Methuen, 1959).
Strawson, P.F.: *The Bounds of Sense* (London: Methuen, 1965).
Stroud, B.: 'Transcendental arguments', *Journal of Philosophy* 65 (1968), 241–56.
Walker, R.C.S.: *Kant* (London: Routledge and Kegan Paul, 1978).

Wilkerson, T.E.: 'Transcendental arguments', *Philosophical Quarterly* 20 (1970), 200–12.

A.C. GRAYLING

**tripartite definition of knowledge** The tripartite definition of knowledge states that PROPOSITIONAL KNOWLEDGE, i.e. knowledge that *p*, has three individually necessary and jointly sufficient conditions: justification, truth and belief. In short, propositional knowledge is justified true belief. The belief condition requires that anyone who knows that *p* believe that *p*. The truth condition requires that any known proposition be true. And the justification condition requires that any known proposition be adequately justified, warranted or evidentially supported. PLATO appears to be considering the tripartite definition in the *Theaetetus* (201c–202d), and to be endorsing its jointly sufficient conditions for knowledge in the *Meno* (97e–98a). This definition has come to be called 'the standard analysis' of knowledge, and has received a serious challenge from Edmund Gettier's counterexamples in 1963.

*See* GETTIER PROBLEM; KNOWLEDGE AND BELIEF; PROPOSITIONAL KNOWLEDGE.

BIBLIOGRAPHY

Gettier, E.L.: 'Is justified true belief knowledge?', *Analysis* 23 (1963), 121–3.
Moser, P.K.: *Knowledge and Evidence* (Cambridge: Cambridge University Press, 1989).
Moser, P.K. and vander Nat, A. eds: *Human Knowledge: Classical and Contemporary Approaches* (New York: Oxford University Press, 1987).
Pappas, G.S. and Swain, M. eds: *Essays on Knowledge and Justification* (Ithaca, NY: Cornell University Press, 1978).
Shope, R.K.: *The Analysis of Knowing* (Princeton: Princeton University Press, 1983).

PAUL K. MOSER

**truth, theories of** The notion of truth occurs with remarkable frequency in our reflections on language, thought and action. We are inclined to suppose, for example, that *truth* is

509

the proper aim of scientific inquiry, that *true* beliefs help us to achieve our goals, that to understand a sentence is to know which circumstances would make it *true*, that reliable preservation of *truth* as one argues from premises to a conclusion is the mark of valid reasoning, that moral pronouncements should not be regarded as objectively true, and so on. In order to assess the plausibility of such theses, and in order to refine them and to explain why they hold (if they do), we require some view of what truth is – a theory that would account for its properties and its relations to other matters. Thus there can be little prospect of understanding our most important faculties in the absence of a good theory of truth.

Such a thing, however, has been notoriously elusive. The ancient idea that truth is some sort of 'correspondence with reality' has still never been articulated satisfactorily: the nature of the alleged 'correspondence' and the alleged 'reality' remain objectionably obscure. Yet the familiar alternative suggestions – that true beliefs are those that are 'mutually coherent', or 'pragmatically useful', or 'verifiable in suitable conditions' – have each been confronted with persuasive counterexamples. A twentieth-century departure from these traditional analyses is the view that truth is not a *property* at all – that the syntactic form of the predicate, 'is true', distorts its real semantic character, which is not to *describe* propositions but to *endorse* them. But this radical approach is also faced with difficulties and suggests, somewhat counterintuitively, that truth cannot have the vital theoretical role in semantics, epistemology and elsewhere that we are naturally inclined to give it. Thus truth threatens to remain one of the most enigmatic of notions: an explicit account of it can appear to be essential yet beyond our reach. However, recent work provides some grounds for optimism.

## TRADITIONAL THEORIES

The belief that snow is white owes its truth to a certain feature of the external world: namely, to the fact that snow is white. Simi-larly, the belief that dogs bark is true because of the fact that dogs bark. This sort of trivial observation leads to what is perhaps the most natural and popular account of truth, the *correspondence theory*, according to which a belief (statement, sentence, proposition, etc.) is true just in case there exists a fact corresponding to it (Wittgenstein, 1922; Austin, 1950). This thesis is unexceptionable in itself. However if it is to provide a rigorous, substantial and complete theory of truth – if it is to be more than merely a picturesque way of asserting all equivalences of the form:

The belief *that p* is true $\leftrightarrow$ p

then it must be supplemented with accounts of what *facts* are, and what it is for a belief to *correspond* to a fact; and these are the problems on which the correspondence theory of truth has foundered. For one thing, it is far from clear that any significant gain in understanding is achieved by reducing 'the belief that snow is white is true' to 'the fact that snow is white exists'; for these expressions seem equally resistant to analysis and too close in meaning for one to provide an illuminating account of the other. In addition, the general relationship that holds in particular between the belief that snow is white and the fact that snow is white, between the belief that dogs bark and the fact that dogs bark, and so on, is very hard to identify. The best attempt to date is WITTGENSTEIN's (1922) so-called 'picture theory', whereby an elementary proposition is a configuration of terms, an atomic fact is a configuration of simple objects, an atomic fact *corresponds* to an elementary proposition (and makes it true) when their configurations are identical and when the terms in the proposition refer to the similarly-placed objects in the fact, and the truth value of each complex proposition is entailed by the truth values of the elementary ones. However, even if this account is correct as far as it goes, it would need to be completed with plausible theories of 'logical configuration', 'elementary proposition', 'reference' and 'entailment', none of which is easy to come by.

A central characteristic of truth – one that

any adequate theory must explain – is that when a proposition satisfies its 'conditions of proof (or verification)' then it is regarded as true. To the extent that the property of *corresponding with reality* is mysterious, we are going to find it impossible to see why what we take to verify a proposition should indicate the possession of that property. Therefore a tempting alternative to the correspondence theory – an alternative which eschews obscure, metaphysical concepts and which explains quite straightforwardly why verifiability implies truth – is simply to *identify* truth with verifiability (Peirce, 1932). This idea can take on various forms. One version involves the further assumption that verification is HOLISTIC – i.e. that a belief is justified (i.e. verified) when it is part of an entire system of beliefs that is consistent and 'harmonious' (Bradley, 1914; Hempel, 1935). This is known as the *coherence theory* of truth. Another version involves the assumption that there is, associated with each proposition, some specific procedure for finding out whether one should believe it or not. On this account, to say that a proposition is true is to say that it would be verified by the appropriate procedure (Dummett, 1978; Putnam, 1981). In the context of mathematics this amounts to the identification of truth with provability.

The attractions of the VERIFICATIONIST account of truth are that it is refreshingly clear compared with the correspondence theory, and that it succeeds in connecting truth with verification. The trouble is that the bond it postulates between these notions is implausibly strong. We do indeed take verification to indicate truth. But also we recognize the possibility that a proposition may be false in spite of there being impeccable reasons to believe it, and that a proposition may be true even though we aren't able to discover that it is. Verifiability and truth are no doubt highly correlated; but surely not the same thing.

A third well-known account of truth is known as PRAGMATISM (James, 1909; Papineau, 1987). As we have just seen, the verificationist selects a prominent property of truth and considers it to be the essence of truth. Similarly the pragmatist focuses on another important characteristic – namely, that true beliefs are a good basis for action – and takes this to be the very nature of truth. True assumptions are said to be, by definition, those which provoke actions with desirable results. Again we have an account with a single attractive explanatory feature. But again the central objection is that the relationship it postulates between truth and its alleged analysans – in this case, utility – is implausibly close. Granted, true beliefs tends to foster success. But it happens regularly that actions based on true beliefs lead to disaster, while false assumptions, by pure chance, produce wonderful results.

DEFLATIONARY THEORIES

One of the few uncontroversial facts about truth is that the proposition that snow is white is true if and only if snow is white, the proposition that lying is wrong is true if and only if lying is wrong, and so on. Traditional theories acknowledge this fact but regard it as insufficient and, as we have seen, inflate it with some further principle of the form, 'X is true if and only if X has property P' (such as corresponding to reality, verifiability, or being suitable as a basis for action), which is supposed to specify what truth is. Some radical alternatives to the traditional theories result from denying the need for any such further specification (Ramsey, 1927; Strawson, 1950; Quine, 1990). For example, one might suppose that the basic theory of truth contains nothing more than equivalences of the form, 'The proposition *that p* is true if and only if *p*' (Horwich, 1990).

This sort of proposal is best presented in conjunction with an account of the *raison d'être* of our notion of truth: namely, that it enables us to express attitudes towards those propositions we can designate but not explicitly formulate. Suppose, for example, you are told that Einstein's last words expressed a claim about physics, an area in which you think he was very reliable. Suppose that, unknown to you, his claim was the proposition that quantum mechanics is wrong. What conclusion can you draw? Exactly which proposition becomes the appropriate object of your belief? Surely not that quantum mechanics is wrong; because you are not aware that that is what he said. What is needed is something equivalent to the infinite conjunction:

If what Einstein said was that E = mc, then E = mc, and if what he said was that quantum mechanics is wrong, then quantum mechanics is wrong, . . . and so on

that is, a proposition, K, with the following properties: that from K and any further premise of the form, 'Einstein's claim was the proposition *that p*' you can infer '*p*', whatever it is. Now suppose, as the deflationist says, that our understanding of the truth predicate consists in the stipulative decision to accept any instance of the schema, 'The proposition *that p* is true if and only if *p*'. Then your problem is solved. For if K is the proposition, 'Einstein's claim is true', it will have precisely the inferential power that is needed. From it and 'Einstein's claim is the proposition that quantum mechanics is wrong', you can use Leibniz' law to infer 'The proposition that quantum mechanics is wrong is true', which, given the relevant axiom of the deflationary theory, allows you to derive 'Quantum mechanics is wrong'. Thus one point in favour of the deflationary theory is that it squares with a plausible story about the function of our notion of truth: its axioms explain that function without the need for any further analysis of 'what truth is'.

Not all variants of deflationism have this virtue. According to the redundancy/performative theory of truth, the pair of sentences, 'The proposition *that p* is true' and plain '*p*', have exactly the same meaning and express the same statement as one another; so it is a syntactic illusion to think that 'is true' attributes any sort of *property* to a proposition (Ramsey, 1927; Strawson, 1950). But in that case it becomes hard to explain why we are entitled to infer 'The proposition that quantum mechanics is wrong is true' from 'Einstein's claim is the proposition that quantum mechanics is wrong' and 'Einstein's claim is true'. For if truth is not a property, then we can no longer account for the inference by invoking the law that if X is identical with Y then any property of X is a property of Y, and vice versa. Thus the redundancy/performative theory, by *identifying* rather than merely *correlating* the contents of 'The proposition *that p* is true' and '*p*', precludes the prospect of a good explanation of one of truth's most significant and useful characteristics. So it is better to restrict our claim to the weak, equivalence schema: The proposition *that p* is true if and only if *p*.

Support for deflationism depends upon the possibility of showing that its axioms – instances of the equivalence schema – unsupplemented by any further analysis, will suffice to explain all the central facts about truth: for example, that the verification of a proposition indicates its truth, and that true beliefs have a practical value. The first of these facts follows trivially from the deflationary axioms. For given our a priori knowledge of the equivalence of '*p*' and 'The proposition *that p* is true', any reason to believe that p becomes an equally good reason to believe that the proposition that p is true. The second fact can also be explained in terms of the deflationary axioms, but not quite so easily. Consider, to begin with, beliefs of the form,

(B) If I perform act A, then my desires will be fulfilled.

Notice that the psychological role of such a belief is, roughly, to cause the performance of A. In other words, given that I do have belief (B), then typically:

I will perform act A

And notice also that when the belief is true then, given the deflationary axioms, the performance of A will in fact lead to the fulfillment of one's desires. i.e.

If (B) is true, then if I perform A, my desires will be fulfilled.

Therefore,

If (B) is true, then my desires will be fulfilled

So it is quite reasonable to value the truth of beliefs of that form. But such beliefs are derived by inference from other beliefs and can be expected to be true if those other beliefs are true. So it is reasonable to value the truth of any belief that might be used in such an inference.

To the extent that such deflationary accounts can be given of *all* the facts involving truth, then the explanatory demands on a theory of truth will be met by the collection of all statements like, 'The proposition that snow is white is true if and only if snow is white', and the sense that some deep analysis of truth is needed will be undermined.

However, there are several strongly felt objections to deflationism. One reason for dissatisfaction is that the theory has an infinite number of axioms, and therefore cannot be completely written down. It can be *described* (as the theory whose axioms are the propositions of the form '*p* if and only if it is true *that p*'), but not explicitly formulated. This alleged defect has led some philosophers to develop theories which show, first, how the truth of any proposition derives from the referential properties of its constituents; and, second, how the referential properties of primitive constituents are determined (Tarski, 1943; Davidson, 1969). However, it remains controversial to assume that *all* propositions – including belief attributions, laws of nature and counterfactual conditionals – depend for their truth values on what their constituents refer to. Moreover, there is no immediate prospect of a decent, finite theory of reference. So it is far from clear that the infinite, list-like character of deflationism can be avoided.

Another source of dissatisfaction with this theory is that certain instances of the equivalence schema are clearly false. Consider.

(a) THE PROPOSITION EXPRESSED BY THE SENTENCE IN CAPITAL LETTERS IS NOT TRUE.

Substituting this into the schema one gets a version of the 'liar' paradox: specifically,

(b) The proposition *that the proposition expressed by the sentence in capital letters is not true* is true if and only if the proposition expressed by the sentence in capital letters is not true,

from which a contradiction is easily derivable. (Given (b), the supposition that (a) is true implies that (a) is not true, and the supposition that it is not true implies that it is.) Consequently, not every instance of the equivalence schema can be included in the theory of truth; but it is no simple matter to specify the ones to be excluded (*see* Kripke, 1975). Of course, deflationism is far from alone in having to confront this problem.

A third objection to the version of the deflationary theory presented here concerns its reliance on *propositions* as the basic vehicles of truth. It is widely felt that the notion of proposition is defective and that it should not be employed in semantics. If this point of view is accepted then the natural deflationary reaction is to attempt a reformulation that would appeal only to *sentences*: for example,

'*p*' is true if and only if *p*.

But this so-called 'disquotational theory of truth' (Quine, 1990) comes to grief over indexicals, demonstratives and other terms whose referents vary with the context of use. It is not the case, for example, that *every* instance of 'I am hungry' is true if and only if *I* am hungry. And there is no simple way of modifying the disquotational schema to accommodate this problem. A possible way out of these difficulties is to resist the critique of propositions. Such entities may well exhibit an unwelcome degree of indeterminacy, and may well defy reduction to familiar items. However, they do offer a plausible account of belief (as relations to propositions) and, in ordinary language at least, they are indeed taken to be the primary bearers of truth (*see* BELIEF).

THE ROLE OF TRUTH IN METAPHYSICS AND EPISTEMOLOGY

It is commonly supposed that problems about the nature of truth are intimately bound up with questions as to the accessibility and autonomy of facts in various domains: questions about whether the facts can be known, and whether they can exist independently of our capacity to discover them (Dummett, 1978; Putnam, 1981). One might reason, for example, that if 'T is true' means nothing more than 'T will be verified', then certain forms of scepticism (specifically, those that doubt the correctness of our methods of verification) will be precluded, and that the facts will have been revealed as dependent on human practices. Alternatively, it might be said that if truth were an inexplicable, primitive, non-epistemic property, then the fact that T is true would be completely independent of us. Moreover, we could, in that case, have no reason to assume that the propositions we believe actually have this property; so scepticism would be unavoidable. In a similar vein, it might be thought that a special (and perhaps undesirable) feature of the deflationary approach is that truth is deprived of any such metaphysical or epistemological implications.

On closer scrutiny, however, it is far from clear that there exists *any* account of truth with consequences regarding the accessibility or autonomy of non-semantic matters. For although an account of truth may be expected to have such implications for facts of the form 'T is true', it cannot be assumed without further argument that the same conclusions will apply to the fact, T. For it cannot be assumed that T and 'T is true' are equivalent to one another given the account of 'true' that is being employed. Of course, if truth is defined in the way that the deflationist proposes, then the equivalence holds by definition. But if truth is defined by reference to some metaphysical or epistemological characteristic, then the equivalence schema is thrown into doubt pending some demonstration that the truth predicate, in the sense assumed, will satisfy it. In so far as there are thought to be epistemological problems hanging over T that do not threaten 'T is true', it will be difficult to give the needed demonstration. Similarly, if 'truth' is so defined that the fact, T, is felt to be more (or less) independent of human practices than the fact that 'T is true', then again it is

unclear that the equivalence schema will hold. It would seem, therefore, that the attempt to base epistemological or metaphysical conclusions on a theory of truth must fail because in any such attempt the equivalence schema will be simultaneously relied on and undermined.

*See also* COHERENTISM; LINGUISTIC UNDERSTANDING; VERIFICATIONISM.

BIBLIOGRAPHY

Austin, J.L.: 'Truth', *Proceedings of the Aristotelian Society* supp. vol. 24 (1950), 111–28.

Bradley, F.H.: *Essays on Truth and Reality* (Oxford: Clarendon Press, 1914).

Davidson, D.: Truth and meaning', *Synthese* 17 (1967), 304–23.

Davidson, D.: 'True to the facts', *Journal of Philosophy* 66 (1969), 748–64.

Davidson, D.: 'Truth and meaning', *Synthese* 17 (1967), 304–23

Davidson, D.: 'The structure and content of truth', *Journal of Philosophy* 87 (1990), 279–328.

Dummett, M.: *Truth and Other Enigmas* (Oxford: Clarendon Press, 1978).

Hempel, C.: 'On the logical positivist's theory of truth', *Analysis* 2 (1935), 49–59.

Horwich, P.G.: *Truth* (Oxford: Blackwell, 1990).

James, W.: *The Meaning of Truth* (New York: Longmans Green, 1909).

Kripke, S.: 'Outline of a theory of truth', *Journal of Philosophy* 72 (1975), 690–716.

Papineau, D.: *Reality and Representation* (Oxford: Blackwell, 1987).

Peirce, C.S.: *Collected Papers* vols 2–4 (Cambridge, MA: Harvard University Press, 1932).

Putnam, H.: *Reason, Truth and History* (Cambridge: Cambridge University Press, 1981).

Quine, W.V.: *Pursuit of Truth* (Cambridge, MA: Harvard University Press, 1990).

Ramsey, F.: 'Facts and propositions', *Proceedings of the Aristotelian Society* supp. vol. 7 (1927), 153–70.

Strawson, P.: 'Truth', *Proceedings of the Aristotelian Society* supp. vol. 24 (1950), 125–56.

Tarski, A.: 'The semantic conception of truth', *Philosophy and Phenomenological Research* 4 (1943), 341–75.

Wittgenstein, L.: *Tractatus Logico-Philosophicus* (London: Routledge and Kegan Paul, 1922).

PAUL HORWICH

**truths of reason/truths of fact** This distinction is associated with LEIBNIZ, who declares that there are only two kinds of truths – truths of reason and truths of fact. The former are all either explicit identities, i.e. of the form 'A is A', 'AB is B', etc., or they are reducible to this form by successively substituting equivalent terms. Leibniz dubs them 'truths of reason' because the explicit identities are self-evident a priori truths, whereas the rest can be converted to such by purely rational operations. Because their denial involves a demonstrable contradiction, Leibniz also says that truths of reason 'rest on the principle of contradiction, or identity' and that they are necessary propositions, which are true of all possible worlds. Some examples are 'All equilateral rectangles are rectangles' and 'All bachelors are unmarried': the first is already of the form 'AB is B' and the latter can be reduced to this form by substituting 'unmarried man' for 'bachelor'. Other examples, or so Leibniz believes, are 'God exists' and the truths of logic, arithmetic and geometry.

Truths of fact, on the other hand, cannot be reduced to an identity and our only way of knowing them is a posteriori, or by reference to the facts of the empirical world. Likewise, since their denial does not involve a contradiction, their truth is merely contingent: they could have been otherwise and hold of the actual world, but not of every possible one. Some examples are 'Caesar crossed the Rubicon' and 'Leibniz was born in Leipzig', as well as propositions expressing correct scientific generalizations. In Leibniz's view, truths of fact rest on the principle of sufficient reason, which states that nothing can be so unless there is a reason why it is so. This reason is that the actual world (by which he means the total collection of things past, present and future) is better than any other possible world and was therefore created by God.

In defending the principle of sufficient reason, Leibniz runs into serious problems. He believes that in every true proposition, the concept of the predicate is contained in that of the subject. (This holds even for propositions like 'Caesar crossed the Rubicon': Leibniz thinks anyone who did not cross the Rubicon, would not have been Caesar!) And this containment relationship – which is eternal and unalterable even by God – guarantees that every truth has a sufficient reason. If truth consists in concept containment, however, then it seems that all truths are analytic and hence *necessary*; and if they are all necessary, surely they are all truths of reason. Leibniz responds that not every truth can be reduced to an identity in a finite number of steps; in some instances revealing the connection between subject and predicate concepts would require an infinite analysis. But while this may entail that we cannot prove such propositions a priori, it does not appear to show that the proposition could have been false. Intuitively, it seems a better ground for supposing that it is a necessary truth of a special sort. A related question arises from the idea that truths of fact depend on God's decision to create the best world: if it is part of the concept of this world that it is best, how could its existence be other than necessary? Leibniz answers that its existence is only hypothetically necessary, i.e. it follows from God's decision to create this world, but God had the power to decide otherwise. Yet God is necessarily good, so how *could* he have decided to do anything else? Leibniz says much more about these matters, but it is not clear whether he offers any satisfactory solutions.

*See also* A PRIORI/A POSTERIORI; ANALYTICITY; LEIBNIZ; NECESSARY/CONTINGENT.

BIBLIOGRAPHY

G.W. Leibniz: *Philosophical Essays* ed. and trans. R. Ariew and D. Garber (Indianapolis, 1989).

Blumenfeld, D.: 'Leibniz on contingency and infinite analysis', *Philosophy and Phenomenological Research* 45 (1985), 483–514.

Copleston, F.: *A History of Modern Philosophy: Descartes to Leibniz* vol. 4 (Garden City: Doubleday, 1963).

Mates, B.: *The Philosophy of Leibniz: Metaphysics and Language* (Oxford: Oxford University Press, 1986).

Rescher, N.: *Leibniz: An Introduction to his Philosophy* (Totowa: Rowman and Littlefield, 1979).

Wilson, M.D.: *Leibniz' Doctrine of Necessary Truth* (New York: Garland, 1990).

DAVID BLUMENFELD

# U

**underdetermination of theory**    It is often our position that several theories are compatible with the available evidence: we then hope that more evidence will resolve the matter. The underdetermination of theory by evidence holds that logically incompatible theories may fit all possible evidence. Alternatively, there may be pairs of empirically equivalent theories which, while not contradicting each other, use radically different theoretical notions. Examples of such underdetermination have been proposed which embarrass empiricist philosophers (Quine, 1990, pp. 95–101) who must either deny that such theories are in competition or find an empirical basis for preferring one of the pair.

*See also* HOLISM.

BIBLIOGRAPHY

Quine, W.V.: *Theories and Things* (Cambridge, MA: Harvard University Press, 1981).
Quine, W.V.: *Pursuit of Truth* (Cambridge, MA: Harvard University Press, 1990).

CHRISTOPHER HOOKWAY

**use/mention**    The words 'the cat' *in mention*:

'The cat' is on the mat.

The words 'the cat' *in use*:
*The cat is on the mat.*

BIBLIOGRAPHY

Quine, W.V.: *Mathematical Logic* (New York: Harper and Row, 1962), 23–6.

ROBERT S. TRAGESSER

# V

verificationism Any view according to which the conditions of a sentence's or a thought's being meaningful or intelligible are equated with the conditions of its being verifiable or falsifiable. An explicit defence of the position would be a defence of the verifiability principle of meaningfulness (*see* LOGICAL POSITIVISM). Implicit verificationism is often present in positions or arguments which do not defend that principle in general, but which reject suggestions to the effect that a certain sort of claim is unknowable or unconfirmable on the sole ground that it would therefore be meaningless or unintelligible. Only if meaningfulness or intelligibility is indeed a guarantee of knowability or confirmability is the position sound. If it is, nothing we understand could be unknowable or unconfirmable by us.

*See also* PHILOSOPHICAL KNOWLEDGE; REALISM; TRANSCENDENTAL ARGUMENTS; TRUTH.

BARRY STROUD

Vico, Giambattista (1668–1744) Italian philosopher, historian and rhetorician. Born and educated in Naples, Vico graduated in law in 1694 and was Professor of Rhetoric at the University from 1699 to 1741. He was disappointed by his failure to gain the chair of Civil Law in 1723, after which he concentrated upon working out his theories of the historical development of nations, expressed in the various editions of *The New Science*.

His interest as an epistemologist lies in two features of his work. The first is his rejection of CARTESIANISM in favour of a purely constructivist theory of knowledge, known as the *verum-factum* theory. The second is his later attempt to modify this in order to show how historical knowledge, usually thought to be less certain than physical knowledge, could become more certain.

A Cartesian for his first forty years, Vico accepted that the only things which could be known were those which were in principle deducible a priori. A growing interest in history, however, led to dissatisfaction with this theory, according to which the past was not a possible object of knowledge. In his *On the Study Methods of Our Time* (1709) Vico first attacked it on the ground of its inadequacy with respect to mathematics and physics: the truths of mathematics can be known not, as DESCARTES claimed, because they consist in clear and distinct ideas, but because they follow solely from axioms and methods which are of human construction. The projected Cartesian extension of the geometrical method to the physical world is accordingly impossible since the latter is not of human construction. In *On the Most Ancient Wisdom of the Italians* (1710) this insight became the basis of the *verum-factum* theory, that we can know only what we have made, and was used to reject all tenets of Cartesianism which depended upon the theory of clear and distinct ideas. Even *cogito ergo sum* (*see* COGITO) was dismissed on the ground that since the mind does not create itself, it cannot know the mode of its own construction.

Although the *verum-factum* theory undermined Descartes' account of the main areas of knowledge, it did little to rehabilitate history, for Vico could not see how it could be applied to the realm of human conduct, given the presence there of chance and contingency. It was only when, after further historical study, he came to believe that underlying the histories of different societies lay a common developmental pattern, arising from the operation of laws of historical and social growth, that he found a subject matter in history stable enough to be an object of knowledge.

So the first crucial claim of Vico's later theory of knowledge, expounded in *The Principles of a New Science of the Nature of Nations* of 1725 and the more complex Second and Third Editions of 1730 and 1744, is that the historical world has been made by men and that its principles must therefore be discovered within the modifications of the human mind. To this Vico adds the idea that the histories of different nations are to be understood as exemplifications of a single pattern, the 'ideal eternal history'. Understanding of this pattern comes not from historical research but from philosophy, which demonstrates the necessity of its various features by reflection upon the growth of mind. Thus history becomes scientific because it is pursued in the light of philosophical theory, while philosophy relates to the real through its capacity to ground the principles of historical interpretation. The result is that historical events cease to be merely contingent, being manifestions of necessary aspects of the ideal eternal history.

The theory give rise to two problems. The first concerns the question whether it is sufficiently constructivist to achieve the degree of certainty which Vico claims. The initial *verum-factum* theory is plausible, in relation to the world of mathematics at least, since the conventional nature of mathematics can be shown by the fact that its content can be altered by an alteration in its axioms and assumptions. This is not true, however, of the world of history, where Vico does not deny that the historian can alter his theories without thereby altering the activities in which historical reality consists. The real past thus remains as external to the Vichian historian as do the clear and distinct ideas, against which Vico first reacted, to the Cartesian mathematician. The second related problem arises from the necessity to treat historical reality as the exemplification of laws, in order to benefit from the combination of historical research and philosophical

reflection. For even if these laws operate through human activities, they are not themselves of human making. It is difficult to see therefore how the fact that Vico's historian makes history, in the sense of making theories about the necessary conditions of the development of mind and applying them to historical evidence, can be a reason for holding that this entitles him to a knowledge of past reality which is more certain that that which, by similar methods, could be gained in any other law-governed field.

*See also* HISTORICAL KNOWLEDGE.

WRITINGS

*De antiquissima Italorum sapientia ex linguae latinae originibus eruenda* (Naples: 1710); trans. L.M. Palmer *On the Most Ancient Wisdom of the Italian* (Ithaca, NY: Cornell University Press, 1988).
*De nostri temporis studiorum ratione* (Naples, 1709); trans. E. Gianturco, *On the Study Methods of Our Time* (Indianapolis: Bobbs-Merrill, 1968).
*Princi di una Scienza Nuova Dintorno alla Natura delle Nazioni* (Naples: 1725); abridged trans. L. Pompa, *Vico: Selected Writings* (Cambridge: Cambridge University Press, 1982).
*Principi di Scienza Nuova d'Intorno alla Comune Natura delle Nazioni* (Naples: 1730, 1744); trans. T.G. Bergin and M.H. Fisch, *The New Science of Giambattista Vico* (Ithaca, NY: Cornell University Press, 1984).
*Vita di Giambattista Vico Scritta de Se Medesimo* (Naples: 1818); trans. T.G. Bergin and M.H. Fisch, *The Autobiography of Giambattista Vico* (Ithaca, NY: Cornell University Press, 1975).

BIBLIOGRAPHY

Bedani, G.: *Vico Revisited* (Oxford: Berg, 1989).
Berlin, I.: *Vico and Herder* (London: The Hogarth Press, 1976).
Croce, B.: *La Filosofia di Giambattista Vico* (Bari: 1911); trans. R.G. Collingwood, *The Philosophy of Giambattista Vico* (London: Howard Latimer, 1913).
Pompa, L.: *Vico: A Study of the 'New Science'* 2nd edn (Cambridge: Cambridge University Press, 1990).

Verene, D.P.: *Vico's Science of Imagination* (Ithaca, NY: Cornell University Press, 1981).

LEON POMPA

**Vienna Circle** A group of philosophers, scientists and mathematicians, often known collectively as the LOGICAL POSITIVISTS, who met in Vienna under the leadership of Moritz SCHLICK in the late 1920s and 1930s. The general philosophical stance of the Circle was anti-metaphysical and 'scientific', and it was noted for its advocacy of the so-called 'VERIFICATION Principle'. Members included CARNAP, NEURATH, Herbert Feigl, Kurt Gödel and Friedrich Waismann. POPPER and REICHENBACH were associated with the Circle, and AYER and QUINE also attended meetings. The Circle were heavily influenced by their understanding (or misunderstanding) of WITTGENSTEIN's early philosophy. Schlick was assassinated by a deranged student in 1936, Popper (on his own account) 'murdered' the verification principle, and Hitler's annexation of Austria in 1938 brought the meetings to an end. By the time of the Second World War most members had emigrated to Britain or the United States.

ANDY HAMILTON

**virtue epistemology** The central idea of virtue epistemology is that justification and knowledge arise from the proper functioning of our intellectual virtues or faculties in an appropriate environment. This idea is captured in the following criterion for justified belief:

(J) S is justified in believing that *p* if an only if S's believing that *p* is the result of S's intellectual virtues or faculties functioning in an appropriate environment.

EXPLICATION

What is an intellectual virtue or faculty? A virtue or faculty in general is a power or ability or competence to achieve some result.

An intellectual virtue or faculty, in the sense intended above, is a power or ability or competence to arrive at truths in a particular field, and to avoid believing falsehoods in that field. Examples of human intellectual virtues are sight, hearing, introspection, memory, deduction and induction. More exactly,

(V) A mechanism M for generating and/or maintaining beliefs is an intellectual virtue if and only if M is a competence to believe true propositions and avoid believing false propostions within a field of propositions F, when one is in a set of circumstances C.

It is required that we specify a particular field of propositions for M, since a given cognitive mechanism will be a competence for believing some kinds of truths but not others. The faculty of sight, for example, allows us to determine the colours of objects, but not the sounds which they make. It is also required that we specify a set of circumstances for M, since a given cognitive mechanism will be a competence in some circumstances but not others. For example, the faculty of sight allows us to determine colours in a well lighted room, but not in a dark cave.

According to the above formulation, what makes a cognitive mechanism an intellectual virtue is that it is reliable in generating true beliefs rather than false beliefs in the relevant field and in the relevant circumstnaces. It is correct to say, therefore, that virtue epistemology is a kind of RELIABILISM. Whereas generic reliabilism maintains that justified belief is belief which results from a reliable cognitive process, virtue epistemology makes a restriction on the kind of process which is allowed. Namely, the cognitive processes which are important for justification and knowledge are those which have their basis in an intellectual virtue.

Finally, the above remarks concerning faculty reliability point to the importance of an appropriate environment. The idea is that a cognitive mechanism might be reliable in some environments but not in others.

Consider an example from Alvin Plantinga. On a planet revolving around Alfa Centauri, cats are invisible to human beings. Moreover, Alfa Centaurian cats emit a type of radiation which causes humans to form the belief that there is a dog barking nearby. Suppose now that you are transported to this Alfa Centaurian planet, a cat walks by, and you form the belief that there is a dog barking nearby. Surely you are not justified in believing this. However, the problem here is not with your intellectual faculties, but with your environment. Although your faculties of perception are reliable on earth, they are unreliable on the Alfa Centurian planet, which is an inappropriate environment for those faculties.

The central idea of virtue epistemology, as expressed in (J) above, has a high degree of initial plausibility. By making the idea of faculty reliability central, virtue epistemology explains nicely why beliefs caused by perception and memory are often justified, while beliefs caused by wishful thinking and superstition are not. Secondly, the theory gives us a basis for answering certain kinds of scepticism. Specifically, we may agree that *if* we were brains in a vat, or victims of a Cartesian demon, then we would not have knowledge even in those rare cases where our beliefs turned out true. But virtue epistemology explains that what is important for knowledge is that our faculties are *in fact* reliable in the environment we are in. And so we do have knowledge so long as we are in fact *not* victims of a cartesian demon, or brains in a vat. Finally, Plantinga argues that virtue epistemology deals well with GETTIER PROBLEMS. The idea is that Gettier problems give us cases of justified belief which are 'true by accident'. Virtue epistemology, Plantinga argues, helps us to understand what it means for a belief to be true by accident, and also provides a basis for saying why such cases are not knowledge. Beliefs are true by accident when they are caused by otherwise reliable faculties functioning in an inappropriate environment. Plantinga develops this line of reasoning in Plantinga (1988).

OBJECTIONS

But although virtue epistemology has good initial plausibility, it faces some substantial objections. Below I will review two of these objections, and point to places where virtue epistemologists have tried to address them. The first objection which virtue epistemology faces is a version of the generality problem. We may understand the problem more clearly if we consider the following criterion for justified belief, which results from our explication of (J).

(J') S is justified in believing that p if and only if
  (1) S believes that *p*; and
  (2) There is a field F and a set of circumstances C such that
    (a) the proposition that *p* is in F,
    (b) S is in C with respect to the proposition that *p*, and
    (c) If S were in C with respect to a proposition in F, then S would very likely believe correctly with regard to that proposition.

The problem arises in how we are to select an appropriate F and C. For given any true belief that *p*, we can *always* come up with a field F and a set of circumstances C, such that S is *perfectly* reliable in F in C (*see* RELIABILISM). For any true belief that *p*, let F be the field including only the propositions *p* and *not-p*. Let C include whatever circumstances there are which cause *p* to be true, together with the circumstances which cause S to believe that *p*. Clearly, S is perfectly reliable with respect to propositions in this field in these circumstances. But we do not want to say that all of S's true beliefs are justified for S. And of course there is an analogous problem in the other direction of generality. For given any belief that *p*, we can always specify a field of propositions F and a set of circumstances C, such that *p* is in F, S is in C, and S is not reliable with respect to propositions in F in C.

The above considerations show that virtue

epistemology must say more about the selection of relevant fields and sets of circumstances. Plantinga addresses the generality problem by introducing the concept of a design plan for our intellectual faculties. Relevant specifications for fields and sets of circumstances are determined by this plan. One might object that this approach requires the problematic assumption of a Designer of the design plan. But Plantinga disagrees on two counts; he does not think that the assumption is needed, or that it would be problematic. Plantinga discusses relevant material in Plantinga (1986, 1987 and 1988). Ernest Sosa addresses the generality problem by introducing the concept of an epistemic perspective. In order to have reflective knowledge, S must have a true grasp of the reliability of her faculties, this grasp being itself provided by a 'faculty of faculties'. Relevant specifications of an F and C are determined by this perspective. Alternatively, Sosa has suggested that relevant specifications are determined by the purposes of the epistemic community. The idea is that fields and sets of circumstances are determined by their place in useful generalizations about epistemic agents and their abilities to act as reliable information-sharers. (These strategies are developed by Sosa, in Sosa, 1988a, 1988b and 1991.)

The second objection which virtue epistemology faces is that (J) and (J') are too strong. It is possible for S to be justified in believing that p, even when S's intellectual faculties are largely unreliable. Suppose, for example, that Jane is the victim of a Cartesian deceiver. Despite her best efforts, therefore, almost none of Jane's beliefs about the world around her are true. It is clear that in this case Jane's faculties of perception are almost wholly unreliable. But we would not want to say that none of Jane's perceptual beliefs are justified. If Jane believes that there is a tree in her yard, and she bases this belief on the usual tree-like experience, then it seems that she is as justified as we would be regarding a similar belief.

Sosa addresses the current problem by arguing that justification is relative to an environment E. Accordingly, S is justified in believing that p relative to E, if and only if S's faculties would be reliable in E. Note that on this account, S need not actually be in E in order for S to be justified in believing some proposition relative to E. This allows Sosa to conclude that Jane has justified belief in the above case. For Jane is justified in her perceptual beliefs relative to our environment, although she is not justified in those beliefs relative to the environment she is actually in. Sosa develops this proposal in Sosa (1991).

*See also* CAUSAL THEORIES IN EPISTEMOLOGY; EPISTEMIC VIRTUES; RELIABILISM.

BIBLIOGRAPHY

Plantinga, A.: 'Epistemic justification', *Nous* 20 (1986), 3–18.
Plantinga, A.: 'Justification and theism', *Faith and Philosophy* 4 (1987), 403–26.
Plantinga, A.: 'Positive epistemic status and proper function', *Philosophical Persectives* 2 (1988), 1–50.
Plantinga, A.: *Warrant* (forthcoming).
Sosa, E.: 'Knowledge and intellectual virtue', *Monist* 60 (1985), 226–45.
Sosa, E.: 'Beyond scepticism, to the best of our knowledge', *Mind* 90 (1988[a]), 153–88.
Sosa, E.: 'Knowledge in context, scepticism in doubt. The virtue of our faculties', *Philosophical Perspectives* 2 (1988[b]), 139–55.
Sosa, E.: 'Methodology and apt belief', *Synthese* 74 (1988), 415–26.
Sosa, E.: 'Reliabilism and intellectual virtue', in Sosa, 1991.
Sosa, E.: *Knowledge in Perspective: Collected Essays in Epistemology* (Cambridge: Cambridge University Press, 1991).

JOHN GRECO

# W

Whitehead, Alfred North (1861–1947) Mathematician (*A Treatise on Universal Algebra*, 1898), logician (*Principia Mathematica*, with Bernard Russell, 1910–13), philosopher of science (*An Enquiry Concerning the Principles of Natural Knowledge*, 1919; *The Concept of Nature*, 1920; *The Principle of Relativity*, 1922), educator (*The Aims of Education and Other Essays*, 1929), and metaphysician (*Science and the Modern World*, 1925; *Process and Reality*, 1929; *Adventures of Ideas*, 1933), Whitehead begins the Preface to his *magnum opus*, *Process and Reality*, as follows: 'These lectures are based upon a recurrence to that phase of philosophic thought which began with Descartes and ended with Hume.' This piece of stage-setting reflects Whitehead's conviction that epistemology has been the dominant dimension of philosophy in recent centuries because of Descartes' exclusion of mind from nature, focusing subsequent attention on the issue of how mind can then know anything about the nature from which it has been divorced. The work of HUME and SANTAYANA exhibits for Whitehead the insuperable character of the epistemological problems which the Cartesian ontological commitment entails. Whitehead's response is that 'all difficulties as to first principles are only camouflaged metaphysical difficulties. Thus also the epistemological difficulty is only solvable by an appeal to ontology' (*Process and Reality*, p. 189).

His thinking enriched by the twentieth-century revolutions in science as well as by the Theory of Evolution, Whitehead replaces the Cartesian dualistic ontology with a monistic version of a philosophy of organism, which is now popularly known as process philosophy. The new ontology, bringing together what Descartes cast asunder, includes a novel theory of propositions according to which 'there is a "correspondence" theory of the truth and falsehood of propositions, and a "coherence" theory of the correctness, incorrectness and suspension of judgments' (ibid., p. 191). Whitehead's conviction is that 'At the end, in so far as the [ontological] enterprise has been successful, there should be no problem of space-time, or of epistemology, or of causality, left over for discussion. The scheme should have developed all those generic notions adequate for the expression of any possible interconnection of things' (ibid., p. xii).

WRITINGS

*Process and Reality*, corrected edition, eds D.R. Griffin and D.W. Sherburne (New York: The Free Press, 1978)

DONALD W. SHERBURNE

Wittgenstein, Ludwig (1889–1951) Austrian-born philosopher who spent much of his working life at Cambridge.

The self-criticism of thought lacks the appeal of speculation, and critical philosophy has sometimes struck people as an evasion with no right to the title 'philosophy'. The impression of irrelevance became much stronger in this century when the direct critique of thought was replaced by a critique of the language expressing the thought. Wittgenstein, the greatest philosopher in this school, once said that the subject on which he worked might be called 'one of the heirs of the subject which used to be called "philosophy"' (1958, p. 28). However, his writings have seldom been dismissed as irrelevant. He draws the line between the meaningful and the meaningless, but he draws it imaginatively and without the flat repressiveness of Positivism (see LOGICAL POSITIVISM), and he never conveys the feeling that the horizon has contracted. His work has even achieved an unusual popularity among people with no training in philosophy who find that it has something to say to them in spite of the difficulty of its interpretation.

His philosophy falls into two periods separated by an interval during which he turned to other things. Born in Vienna, he studied engineering in Berlin and Manchester, became interested in the foundations of mathematics and from 1911, when he went to Cambridge to work with Russell, until the end of the First World War, in which he served in the Austrian army and was taken prisoner, he developed the theory of language and logic which he published in his first book, *Tractatus Logico-Philosophicus* (1922). After that he abandoned philosophy and did not return to it until the end of the 1920s, when he discussed his book with some of the philosophers of the Vienna Circle, became for a short time Professor of Philosophy at Cambridge, and continued to elaborate a largely new set of ideas until his death. The first result of his later work was his posthumous *Philosophical Investigations* (1953), which has been followed by the publication of many volumes of his notes.

His aim in both periods of his philosophy was to determine what language can and cannot do. This is a more radical enterprise than fixing the scope and limits of human knowledge, because knowledge is expressed in sentences, which have to achieve sense before they can achieve truth. He develops his critique of language in two quite different ways in the two periods of his philosophy. In the *Tractatus* a general theory of language is used to fix the bounds of sense, while in *Philosophical Investigations* no such theory is offered, and the line between sense and senselessness is drawn not on any general principle but with an eye on the special features of each case that is reviewed. If his first book is like a map with a superimposed grid, his second book is like the diary of a journey recording all the deviations which looked so tempting but would have ended in the morass of senselessness. He himself drew

attention to the analogy between this later work and psychotherapy (*PI*, pp. 47, 91).

The theory that fixes the bounds of sense in the *Tractatus* assimilates sentences to pictures. A sentence can achieve sense only in one of two ways; either it will picture a fact, or else it will be analysable into further, more basic sentences which picture facts. The sense-giving relation between language and the world is called 'picturing' because the words in a basic (elementary) sentence are supposed to stand for objects in the same way that points on the surface of a picture stand for points in physical space. Everything that we can say, and equally everything that we can think, must be a projection of a possible arrangement of objects.

The Picture Theory draws the boundary of sense very tightly around factual sentences, excluding moral, aesthetic and religious discourse. The *Tractatus* was, therefore, naturally adopted by the philosophers of the Vienna Circle as a model for Logical Positivism. However, it is a work which presents many facets to the world and there is another, more sympathetic way of reading it: the excluded types of discourse are not eliminated, because they are preserved by the very different roles that they play in our lives. The assimilation of their roles to the role of factual discourse is a misunderstanding, whether it is intended to preserve them (as in H. Spencer's scientific ethics) or to destroy them (as in the writings of Positivists). The *Tractatus* gives factual language (ordinary and scientific) the central place but resists Scientism.

Consistently with their general interpretation of the *Tractatus*, the Vienna Circle construed the Picture Theory as an EMPIRICIST theory of meaning and identified Wittgenstein's 'objects' with SENSE-DATA. But he himself had avoided any such identification. His 'objects' were, by definition, simple (i.e. they had no internal structure) and he deduced from the Picture Theory that they must exist at some level of analysis in order to give factual sentences their senses. However, he never claimed to have discovered them or even to know their category, and he never shared RUSSELL'S view, that when we acquire factual language, we find that there are words whose meanings we can learn only through acquaintance with the things designated by them and that those things are simple objects (*see* Russell, 1956, pp. 193–5; and KNOWLEDGE BY ACQUAINTANCE/BY DESCRIPTION). That was an empirical argument for an empiricist account of the foundations of language, and he neither followed that route nor arrived at that destination.

The *Tractatus* is a work or rare originality and the history of philosophy shows that such books often produce effects which do not square with their authors' intentions. Fortunately, in this case we have the journal (Wittgenstein, 1961) which allows us to follow the development of the ideas that went into it, his own, Russell's and FREGE'S. This is a much better guide to its interpretation than the reactions of its early readers. It should be taken as an abstract treatise on language and, though its results affect other disciplines and even the nature of philosophy itself, it is not based on the doctrines of any particular school of philosophy.

Its main achievement is a uniform theory of language which yields an explanation of logical truth. A factual sentence achieves sense by dividing the possibilities exhaustively into two groups, those that would make it true and those that would make it false. A truth of logic does not divide the possibilities but comes out true in all of them. It, therefore, lacks sense and says nothing, but it is not nonsense. It is a self-cancellation of sense, necessarily true because it is a tautology, the limiting case of factual discourse, like the figure o in mathematics.

It was precisely the uniformity of this theory of language that Wittgenstein found unacceptable when he took up philosophy in the late 1920s for the second time. Language takes many forms and even factual discourse does not consist entirely of sentences like 'The fork is to the left of the knife'. However, the first thing that he gave up was the idea that this sentence itself needed further analysis into basic sentences mentioning simple objects with no internal structure (*see* Wittgenstein, 1929; 1975, pp. 105–14, 317). He now conceded that a descriptive word will

often get its meaning partly from its place in a system, and he applied this idea to colour-words, arguing that the essential relations between different colours do not indicate that each colour has an internal structure which needs to be taken apart. On the contrary, analysis of our colour-words would only reveal the same pattern – ranges of incompatible properties – recurring at every level, because that is how we carve up the world.

This may look like a small change, a footnote to the *Tractatus*, but in fact it was the first sign of a revolution in his philosophy. He ceased to believe that the actual structure of our discourse can only be explained as the confused manifestation of a deeper structure, which will be revealed by an analysis yet to be successfully completed. 'We make our moves in the realm of the grammar of our ordinary language, and this grammar is already there. Thus we already have everything and need not wait for the future' (1979, p. 183).

Indeed, it may even be the case that the grammar of our ordinary language is created by moves which we ourselves make. If so, the philosophy of language will lead into the philosophy of action. Certainly there is a close connection between the meaning of a word and the applications of it which its users intend to make. There is also an obvious need for people to understand each other's meanings and that requires agreement in the applications of their words. There are many links between the philosophy of language and the philosophy of mind and it is not surprising that the impersonal examination of language in the *Tractatus* was replaced by a very different, anthropocentric treatment in *Philosophical Investigations*.

If the logic of our language is created by moves which we ourselves make, various kinds of REALISM are threatened. First, the way in which our descriptive language carves up the world will not be forced on us by the natures of things, and the rules for the application of our words, which feel like external constraints, will really come from within us (*PI*, §§130–242). That is a concession to nominalism which is, perhaps, readily made. The idea that logical and mathematical necessity are also generated by what we ourselves do is more paradoxical. Yet that is the conclusion of Wittgenstein (1956) and (1976), and here his anthropocentrism has carried less conviction. However, paradox is not a sure sign of error and it is possible that what is needed here is a more sophisticated concept of OBJECTIVITY than Platonism provides.

In his later work Wittgenstein brings the great problems of philosophy down to earth and traces them to very ordinary origins. His examination of the concept of *following a rule* takes him back to a fundamental question about counting things and sorting them into types: 'What qualifies as doing the same again?' Of course, an expert would regard this question as extraneous rather than fundamental, and would suggest that we forget it and get on with the subject. But Wittgenstein's question is not so easily dismissed. It has the naive profundity of questions that children ask when they are first taught a new subject. Such questions remain unanswered without detriment to their learning, but they point the only way to a complete understanding of what is learned (*see* Wittgenstein, 1974, pp. 381–2).

The philosophy of mind, recessive in the *Tractatus*, dominates his later work, both because of its connections with meaning and necessity and in its own right. SOLIPSISM, for example, is important, not, of course, because many philosophers have adopted it but because it may well be the unavoidable consequence of more moderate and, therefore, more popular theories of mind, and it is discussed briefly in the *Tractatus* and at length in his later writings. His critique of solipsism should be contrasted with Russell's. Russell argued that the solipsist has overwhelming inductive reasons for believing in the existence of things outside his own mind and of other people like himself observing them (Russell, 1956, pp. 125–74). Wittgenstein's criticism was the more radical one, that when the solipsist cuts himself off from the external world, he deprives himself of any way of giving sense to his thoughts about his private world (*see Tract.*, 5.6–5.641; *PI* §§243ff; and Wittgenstein, 1968).

This is his famous PRIVATE LANGUAGE ARGUMENT, which in exegeses of his ideas is often presented as an isolated, self-sufficient refutation of any philosophy with a purely mentalistic basis. In fact, it is part of a more general critique of the kind of intellectualism which assumes that a philosopher can stand in the position of the solipsist and still bring all the resources of his mind to bear on his restricted set of data. But if he really turns his mental back on the physical world, how will he ever have acquired and maintained the concept of himself as a person? Any sentence beginning 'I . . .' will pose an insoluble problem for his understanding. If the sentence continues '. . . am in pain', the understanding of those words is not a purely intellectual achievement for us, because they replace our natural pain-behaviour, but he will not have that resource (*see PI*, §§244–5). Similarly, our vocabulary for identifying points in local space was not correlated with the facts directly by the intellect working alone, but based on a picture of the world which ante-dated the advent of language and in which we could already find our way around. Has the philosopher who experimentally adopts the standpoint of the solipsist and so deprives himself of all such resources any right to assume that he can keep meaning safe?

Wittgenstein does not confine himself to showing that the solipsist's position is untenable, but also offers a diagnosis of the mistakes that led him into it. The first, perhaps the most important, mistake was uncritical scepticism about the physical world. This is dismissed with characteristic brevity in the *Tractatus*: 'Scepticism is *not* irrefutable, but obviously nonsensical, when it tries to raise doubts where no questions can be asked.' Towards the end of his life he returned to this topic and developed a more detailed and satisfying critique of the sceptic's voracious doubts. The leading idea of this later treatment was holistic: some statements about the world achieve immunity from doubt not because they are more thoroughly confirmed, but because they provide the framework within which alone other statements can be questioned and confirmed or rejected (*see* Wittgenstein, 1969).

*See also* OTHER MINDS; PRIVATE LANGUAGE ARGUMENT; PROBLEM OF RULE-FOLLOWING; SOLIPSISM.

## WRITINGS

*Tractatus Logico-Philosophicus* trans. C.K. Ogden (London: Routledge and Kegan Paul, 1922); trans. D.F. Pears and B.F. McGuinness (London: Routledge and Kegan Paul, 1961; 2nd edn 1974).

'Some remarks on logical form', *Proceedings of the Aristotelian Society* supp. vol. 9 (1929), 162–71; reprinted in *Essays on Wittgenstein's Tractatus* eds R. Beard and I. Copi (London: Routledge and Kegan Paul, 1966).

*Philosophical Investigations* trans. G.E.M. Anscombe (Oxford: Blackwell, 1953).

*Remarks on the Foundations of Mathematics* trans. G.E.M. Anscombe (Oxford: Blackwell, 1956).

*The Blue and Brown Books* (Oxford: Blackwell, 1958).

*Notebooks 1914–1916* trans. G.E.M. Anscombe (Oxford: Blackwell, 1961).

Notes for Lectures on 'Private Experience' and 'Sense Data', *Philosophical Review* 77 (1968), 275–320.

*On Certainty* (Oxford: Blackwell, 1969).

*Philosophical Grammar* trans. A. Kenny (Oxford: Blackwell, 1974).

*Philosophical Remarks* trans. R. Hargreaves and R. White (Oxford: Blackwell, 1975).

*Lectures on the Foundations of Mathematics* ed. C. Diamond (Hassocks: Harvester, 1976).

*Ludwig Wittgenstein and the Vienna Circle*, *Conversations recorded by Friedrich Waismann* trans. J. Schulte and B. McGuinness (Oxford: Blackwell, 1979).

## BIBLIOGRAPHY

Kenny, A.: *Wittgenstein* (London: Penguin, 1973).

McGuinness, B.: *Wittgenstein: A Life. Young Ludwig 1889–1921* (London: Duckworth, 1988).

Monk, R.: *Ludwig Wittgenstein: The Duty of Genius* (London: Cape, 1990).

Pears, D.F.: *The False Prison* 2 vols (Oxford: Oxford University Press, 1987, 1988).

Russell, B.: *Logic and Knowledge, Essays 1901–1950* ed. R.C. Marsh (London: Allen and Unwin, 1956).

DAVID PEARS

# Index

COMPILED BY MEG DAVIES

*Note:* Page references in **bold** type indicate chief discussion of major topics. References in *italics* indicate tables or figures. Where names of contributors to the *Companion* are indexed, the references are to citations in articles other than their own.

INDEX

inferential internalism 339
and justification 10–11, 65, 69,
 115, 119, 132–5, 168, 346,
 425, 460
and knowledge 135–6, 236,
 335–6, 338, 346, 399
and phenomenalism 340
and religious belief 440–1
and representation 443
*see also* reliabilism

fact/value 119, **137–8**, 154, 298,
 449, 480
faculties, human 427–8
faith, *see* animal faith; reason, and
 faith
fallacies, *see* genetic fallacy; many
 questions fallacy
fallacies, informal **212–16**
 arguing in a circle 11, 66, 85,
 96, 215, 244
 erroneous inference 212,
 213–14
 sophistical tactics 212–13,
 214–16, 244
fallibilism 38–9, **138**, 168, 200,
 281, 332, 350, 353
Feigl, Herbert 520
Feldman, Richard 119, 158
feminist epistemology 80, 119,
 **138–42**
feminist standpoint theory 138,
 139–40
Fichte, J.G. 151, 189
fictionalism 274, 421
fideism, and infinite regress
 argument 210, 211, 212
Field, Hartry 274
first philosophy **142**, 297, 410
Firth, Roderick **142–3**
Flew, A. 331
Fodor, Jerry 45–6, 48, 442,
 443–4, 488
Fogelin, Robert 387
formalism 157, 272
forms
 distributive normal 175
 knowledge of 17, 155
Foucault, Michel 79, **143–4**, 481,
 482
Foucher, Simon 463
foundationalism **144–7**
 in Aquinas 19–20
 in Aristotle 27, 28–31
 in Chisholm 65
 classical 146
 critiques 147, 167, 297, 303
 and death of epistemology
 89–90
 denial of 38–9, 170–1
 in Firth 142

and the given 159–60, 161
and internalism 133
and introspection 218, 401,
 405, 467
and justified belief 10, 144–6,
 209, 289, 438, 448
and knowledge 144, 145, 146
in Lewis 247
and moral epistemology
 289–90
as objective 496
and perceptual knowledge 336,
 386
and phenomenalism 339, 340
in Plato 348
in Reid 427
in Russell 451
in Schlick 465
simple/iterative 146
in Stoicism 491
strong/moderate 146
*see also* coherentism; Descartes,
 René; infinite regress
 argument; reliabilism
Frankfurt School 78, 166, 192,
 270
Frassen, Bas van 294
freedom, and knowledge 78–9,
 80, 186
Frege, Gottlob **147–9**, 198, 265,
 347, 402
 on abstract objects 148, 185
 and analyticity 11, 12–16, 230,
 264
 on inference 206, 223–4
 on mathematical knowledge 5,
 12, 147, 272, 273, 274,
 311, 389
 on meaning and truth 250,
 251, 300, 525
Freud, Sigmund **149–50**, 192,
 404, 438, 467, 481, 482
Friedman, Michael 131, 465
functional role theories of
 representation 442–3, 444
functionalism 48, 319 222

Gadamer, Hans-Georg 78, **151**,
 481
Galilei, Galileo 93, 94, 180, 270,
 362–3, 364, 417
Gallie, W.B. 480
Gangesá 199, 308
Gassendi, Pierre 115, 181, 462–3,
 503
Gauss, Carl Friedrich 156
Geertz, C. 481
genetic epistemology **151–4**
genetic fallacy **154–5**, 167
geometry **155–7**, 230, 231–2,
 260, 412, 465

Euclidian 155–7, 180–1,
 231–2, 274, 292, 426, 489
 non-Euclidian 156–7, 232,
 272, 274
 pure/applied 157
Gert, B. 287
Gettier, Edmund 157, 459
Gettier problem 38, 84, 89,
 **157–9**, 396–9, 497, 509,
 521
Gewirth, A. 287
Ginet, Carl 277
Girard, R. 255
given, the 147, **159–61**, 170,
 218, 316, 369, 465
 and Sellars 160, 450, 470,
 472
God
 belief in, *see* religious belief
 existence of 55, 95, 155, 260,
 366–7, 436–40
Gödel, Kurt 37, 271, 501, 520
Goldman, A.I. 299, 397, 433–5,
 459–60
 and reliabilism 58–61, 121–2,
 134
Good, I. 478
Goodman, Nelson **162–4**
 and art 163
 'grue problem' 43, 162–3,
 395–6
 and induction 202–3, 292–3,
 380, 395, 418
 and projection 162–3
 and systems 162
Gramsci, Antonio 193, 269
Grice, H. **164–5**, 284, 416
Grim, P. 325
Grote, John 237–9, 240

Habermas, Jürgen 78–9, **166–7**,
 269, 480, 482
Hacking, Ian 295
hallucination, argument from
 **24–7**, 36, 185, 383
Hansen, N.R. 8, 356
Hardy, G.H. 271
Hare, R.M. 287
Harman, G. 356, 443
Hayek, F.A. 480
Hegel, G.W.F. 92, 151, **167–70**
 and absolute knowledge 76, 77,
 168
 dialectic 77, **98–9**
 and empiricism 168
 and historical nature of reason
 76–7, 179
 and idealism 167–9, 268, 421
 and realism 168–9
 and thing in itself/for itself
 194–5